THE ACTS OF THE APOSTLES

VOLUME 31

THE ANCHOR BIBLE is a fresh approach to the world's greatest classic. Its object is to make the Bible accessible to the modern reader; its method is to arrive at the meaning of biblical literature through exact translation and extended exposition, and to reconstruct the ancient setting of the biblical story, as well as the circumstances of its transcription and the characteristics of its transcribers.

THE ANCHOR BIBLE is a project of international and interfaith scope: Protestant, Catholic, and Jewish scholars from many countries contribute individual volumes. The project is not sponsored by any ecclesiastical organization and is not intended to reflect any particular theological doctrine. Prepared under our joint supervision, THE ANCHOR BIBLE is an effort to make available all the significant historical and linguistic knowledge which bears on the interpretation of the biblical record.

THE ANCHOR BIBLE is aimed at the general reader with no special formal training in biblical studies; yet it is written with the most exacting standards of scholarship, reflecting the highest technical accomplishment.

This project marks the beginning of a new era of cooperation among scholars in biblical research, thus forming a common body of knowledge to be shared by all.

William Foxwell Albright
David Noel Freedman
GENERAL EDITORS

THE ANCHOR BIBLE

THE ACTS OF THE APOSTLES

◆

A New Translation
with Introduction and Commentary

JOSEPH A. FITZMYER, S.J.

THE ANCHOR BIBLE
Doubleday
New York London Toronto Sydney Auckland

The Anchor Bible
Published by Doubleday
a division of Bantam Doubleday Dell Publishing Group, Inc.
1745 Broadway, New York, New York 10019

IMPRIMI POTEST
Reverend James R. Stormes, S.J., *Praepositus Provinciae Marylandiae*

NIHIL OBSTAT
Reverend Isidore Dixon, *Censor Deputatus*

IMPRIMATUR on 9 July 1997
Most Reverend William E. Lori, S.T.D., *Vicar General for the Archdiocese of Washington*

The *nihil obstat* and *imprimatur* are official declarations that a book is free of doctrinal or moral error. No implication is contained therein that those who have granted the *nihil obstat* or the *imprimatur* agree with the content, opinions, or statements expressed.

Library of Congress Cataloging-in-Publication Data

Bible. N.T. Acts. English. Fitzmyer. 1998.
The Acts of the Apostles / a new translation with introduction and commentary by Joseph A. Fitzmyer.

p. cm.—(The Anchor Bible ; v. 31)
Includes bibliographical references and indexes.
1. Bible. N.T. Acts.—Commentaries. I. Fitzmyer, Joseph A. II. Title. III. Series: Bible. English. Anchor Bible. 1964 ; v. 31.
BS2620.F58 1998
226.6'077—dc21 97-31604
CIP

ISBN 0-385-51679-7

BVG 01

This book is respectfully dedicated to
Raymond E. Brown, S.S.
and
Roland E. Murphy, O. Carm.
Devoted Interpreters of the Written Word of God
D.D.D. Auctor

CONTENTS

◆

PREFACE

◆

When the two volumes of my commentary on *The Gospel according to Luke* for the Anchor Bible series (AB 28, 28A [1981, 1985]) were finally published, the editor of the series, David Noel Freedman, asked me to write one on the Acts of the Apostles, traditionally ascribed to the same author, Luke the evangelist. I had, however, already started a commentary on Paul's Epistle to the Romans and was reluctant to be distracted from that. Once *Romans* also appeared (AB 33 [1993]), the editor renewed his request, and I acceded to it. This explains the origin of the present work.

In the course of work on this commentary, I began to realize that it too might eventually grow into a two-volume work, as did the commentary on the Lucan Gospel. So I asked the editor, whether I might proceed with a two-volume commentary on Acts. He instructed me to contact the editor at Doubleday about the matter. When I did, I received the answer that the commentary on Acts had to be restricted to one volume. That consequently meant that I had to curtail my discussion and especially the bibliographical coverage of problems in this NT book. The result is that the reader will find very few references to works prior to 1900, save in the list of commentaries. This decision was my own in light of the imposed restriction. Fortunately, there exist good bibliographies that cover older discussions, which I have listed in the general bibliography for easy consultation. The best of them is A. J. Mattill, Jr., and M. B. Mattill, *A Classified Bibliography of Literature on the Acts of the Apostles* (NTTS 7; Leiden: Brill, 1966). Most of the relevant data of older discussions have long since entered the more recent common interpretation of Acts; so little will be lost, save my reaction to some older issues that may still be alive. I have tried to make this commentary on Acts what it should be, given that restriction. If my reaction to more recent problems is curtailed, for that I beg the reader's indulgence.

In producing a fresh translation of Acts, I have used as the basic Greek text that found in the twenty-seventh edition of Nestle-Aland, *Novum Testamentum Graece* (ed. B. Aland and K. Aland; Stuttgart: Deutsche Bibelgesellschaft, 1993 [hereafter *NTG*]). It is very close to the fourth edition of *The Greek New Testament* (New York: United Bible Societies; Stuttgart: Deutsche Bibelgesellschaft, 1993 [hereafter *GNT*]), but not always identical (especially in the OT passages cited or alluded to; they are not always italicized in *NTG*). The problematic Greek text of Acts will be discussed in the Introduction, and reasons will be given there for the decision to follow the form of the Greek text in *NTG*. My translation of Acts, then, seeks to render that text as accurately as possible into modern English. Square brackets are used around words when the corresponding Greek words are so bracketed as problematic in *NTG*. The reader will have to consult that edition and its *apparatus criticus* or my note on the reading so marked. My only deviations from the Greek text in *NTG* are found at Acts 11:20, where I read "Greeks" instead of "Hellenists"; and 16:12, where I prefer "a leading city of the district" (the best attested reading) to the conjecture used by the editorial committee, "a city of the first district." I have not always followed the paragraphing of the *NTG* or *GNT* text, preferring rather to divide up the text according to the outline of Acts given in the Introduction, which at times yields better units for discussion. Old Testament quotations set in italics are those that the UBS fourth edition of *GNT* has printed in boldface and that the *NTG* has sometimes printed in italics; they are more restricted in number in the latter than in the former. Earlier editions of Nestle-Aland often set more words and phrases in boldface than do these recent editions. All of this has to do with the degree of certainty one has about a Lucan phrase as a quotation or an allusion to an OT passage.

I have used parentheses in the translation in two ways: sometimes to enclose a parenthetic remark in the text of Acts, as at times in the *RSV*, and sometimes to mark a word or phrase that I have added to make the English translation clear. In the latter case, there is nothing in the Greek text to which it corresponds.

The Introduction will state the reasons for thinking that Acts has been written by the same author as the Third Gospel. This means that references will be made in this commentary on Acts to my commentary on the Lucan Gospel (AB 28, 28A). Some terms or phrases have already been explained there in detail. I have normally supplied enough information to make the passage in Acts intelligible to the reader, but I have been reluctant to repeat all the details that have already been given. References to the commentary on the Lucan Gospel will be given as *Luke*, followed by page numbers.

Part of the Introduction to the Lucan Gospel was "A Sketch of Lucan Theology" (*Luke*, 143–270). That sketch was written with an eye on the Lucan second volume, and many references to Acts are already given under the various topics discussed. So the reader will find there a rather comprehensive treatment of Lucan theology. In writing this commentary on Acts, I have now at times expanded a note to cover more adequately some aspect of that theology beyond what is found in *Luke*. I have resisted the temptation to rewrite that sketch in this commentary. Notes in this commentary will refer the reader at times to that sketch in *Luke*.

This work purports, then, to be a modern commentary on the Acts of the Apostles in the classic style. It has been written from the standpoint of the historical-critical method, seeking to expound not only the literal meaning of the Lucan text with a view to setting forth the religious and theological message that the author sought to convey, but also that message in an actualized form. For the hermeneutics involved in my approach to the interpretation of Acts, the reader may consult two other of my books, *Scripture, the Soul of Theology* (New York/Mahwah, NJ: Paulist, 1994) 5–38; and *The Biblical Commission's Document "The*

Interpretation of the Bible in the Church": Text and Commentary (Subsidia biblica 18; Rome: Biblical Institute, 1995) 15–50, 170–76.

At the end of the Introduction there is a bibliography which includes commentaries and monographs, the latter not only on Acts, but also on Luke-Acts. Titles listed in this general bibliography will be referred to in the commentary or special bibliographies only by short titles. When readers come upon a commentator's name cited in a COMMENT or NOTE, they should look first at the select bibliography at the end of the appropriate section of the Introduction or the NOTES on a given pericope. If the name does not occur there, then the general bibliography should be consulted.

At the beginning of each pericope the translation of the Greek text in *NTG* is given. Immediately after it there is a small paragraph headed WT (= Western Text), in which its principal variants will be found for verses that have them. These variants may at times be more numerous than those mentioned in the NOTES; they have been derived from the parallel Greek texts in M.-E. Boismard and A. Lamouille, *Texte occidental des Actes des Apôtres: Reconstitution et réhabilitation* (2 vols.; Paris: Éditions Recherche sur les Civilisations, 1984) 1. 123–226. This work of Boismard and Lamouille represents the latest thorough study of the problematic WT of Acts. I have chosen to list the main variants that they present in their first volume (pp. 123–226) so that readers of this commentary will get an idea of how the WT differs from the Alexandrian. Boismard and Lamouille's form of the Alexandrian Text does not always conform exactly with that of *NTG* or UBS *GNT*; nor does their WT depend solely on the readings in MS D (Codex Bezae). Thus, I have tried to be careful to compare their form of the WT with the Alexandrian text of *NTG*. In many cases variants listed in the WT paragraph will be discussed in the NOTES on the proper verses, but some of the variants occur so regularly—and, in fact, are so insignificant—that there is no reason to list all the specific manuscripts for them. In many cases the WT omits phrases or words of the Alexandrian Text; these are usually noted. What is recorded in the WT paragraph is not a continuous translation of that text, but only those words or phrases that differ from the translation of the Alexandrian Text that precedes. The reader will have to learn to use that WT information accordingly, i.e., to read it as a modification of the preceding translation.

The reader should note that references to the OT are given according to the chapter and verse numbers of the Hebrew Bible, the MT. This is being done because of the confusing numbering in some widely used English Bibles. The *New Jewish Version* (1972) and the *New American Bible* use the MT numbering system, and English-speaking readers can always check references in those Bibles, which no longer follow the confusing system of the *King James Version* or the *Revised Standard Version*. This has to be noted particularly when reference is made to the Psalter: references even to the Greek form of a Psalm (in the LXX) will mean *the psalm as numbered in the MT*.

Finally, it is my duty to express my thanks to the editor of the Anchor Bible series, David Noel Freedman, for the many important suggestions he has made to improve this commentary; to the in-house editor at Doubleday, Mark Fretz; his assistant, Andrew Corbin; and the copy editor, Barbara Firoozye, for their help in bringing this commentary to completion; and to many librarians to whom I am indebted.

Joseph A. Fitzmyer, S.J.
Professor Emeritus, Biblical Studies
The Catholic University of America
Resident at:
Jesuit Community, Georgetown University
P.O. Box 571200
Washington, DC 20057-1200

ABBREVIATIONS

◆

PRINCIPAL ABBREVIATIONS

AB	Anchor Bible
ABD	D. N. Freedman et al., (eds.), *The Anchor Bible Dictionary* (6 vols.; New York: Doubleday, 1992)
AbhKGW	Abhandlungen der königlichen Gesellschaft der Wissenschaften
ABRL	Anchor Bible Reference Library
ACR	*Australasian Catholic Record*
AGJU	Arbeiten zur Geschichte des antiken Judentums und des Urchristentums
AGSU	Arbeiten zur Geschichte des Spätjudentums und Urchristentums
AJA	*American Journal of Archaeology*
AJBI	*Annual of the Japanese Biblical Institute*
AJBS	*African Journal of Biblical Studies*
AJP	*American Journal of Philology*
AJT	*American Journal of Theology*
AnBib	Analecta biblica
Ang	*Angelicum*
ANL	*Accademia Nazionale dei Lincei*
ANRW	H. Temporini and W. Haase (eds.), *Aufstieg und Niedergang der römischen Welt* (93 vols.; Berlin/New York: de Gruyter, 1972–)
ANTF	Arbeiten zur neutestamentlichen Textforschung
Anton	*Antonianum*
APF	*Archiv für Papyrusforschung und verwandte Gebiete*
Apg.	*Apostelgeschichte* (used especially in titles of German commentaries)
ArchAnz	*Archäologischer Anzeiger*
ASNU	Acta seminarii neotestamenti upsaliensis
AsSeign	*Assemblées du Seigneur*
ASTI	*Annual of the Swedish Theological Institute*
ATAbh	Alttestamentliche Abhandlungen
ATANT	Abhandlungen zur Theologie des Alten und Neuen Testaments

ATR	*Anglican Theological Review*
Aug	*Augustinianum*
AUSS	*Andrews University Seminary Studies*
AVTRW	*Aufsätze und Vorträge zur Theologie und Religionswissenschaft*
BA	*Biblical Archaeologist*
B-A[6]	W. Bauer, *Griechisch-deutsches Wörterbuch zu den Schriften des Neuen Testaments und der frühchristlichen Literatur* (6th ed., rev. by K. Aland and B. Aland; Berlin/New York: de Gruyter, 1988)
BAC	Biblioteca de autores cristianos
BAFCS	The Book of Acts in Its First Century Setting (ed. B. W. Winter; 5 vols.; Carlisle, UK: Paternoster; Grand Rapids, MI: Eerdmans, 1993–96)
BAGD	W. Bauer, *A Greek-English Lexicon of the New Testament and Other Christian Literature* (tr. W. F. Arndt and F. W. Gingrich; 2d ed., rev. F. W. Danker; Chicago: University of Chicago Press, 1979)
BARev	*Biblical Archaeology Review*
BASP	*Bulletin of the American Society of Papyrologists*
BBB	Bonner biblische Beiträge
BBR	*Bulletin for Bible Research*
BCH	*Bulletin de correspondance hellénique*
BCPE	*Bulletin du centre protestant d'études*
BDF	F. Blass and A. Debrunner, *A Greek Grammar of the New Testament and Other Early Christian Literature* (tr. R. W. Funk; Chicago: University of Chicago Press, 1961)
BECNT	Baker Exegetical Commentary on the New Testament
Beginnings	F. J. Foakes-Jackson and K. Lake (eds.), *The Beginnings of Christianity: Part I, The Acts of the Apostles* (5 vols.; London: Macmillan, 1920–33; repr., Grand Rapids, MI: Baker, 1979).
BeO	*Bibbia e Oriente*
BETL	Bibliotheca ephemeridum theologicarum lovaniensium
BETS	*Bulletin of the Evangelical Theological Society* (later *JETS*)
BEvT	Beihefte zur *EvT*
BFCT	Beiträge zur Förderung christlicher Theologie
BGBE	Beiträge zur Geschichte der biblischen Exegese
BI	*Biblical Interpretation*
Bib	*Biblica*
BibLeb	*Bibel und Leben*
BJRL	*Bulletin of the John Rylands (University) Library (of Manchester)*

BK	*Bibel und Kirche*
BLE	*Bulletin de littérature ecclésiastique*
BLit	*Bibel und Liturgie*
BNTC	Black's New Testament Commentary
BR	*Biblical Research*
BRev	*Bible Review*
BSac	*Bibliotheca sacra*
BT	*The Bible Translator*
BTAVO	Beihefte zum Tübinger Atlas des Vorderen Orients
BTB	*Biblical Theology Bulletin*
BTS	*Bible et terre sainte*
BullSNTS	*Bulletin of Studiorum Novi Testamenti Societas*
BVC	*Bible et vie chrétienne*
BW	*Biblical World*
BWANT	Beiträge zur Wissenschaft vom Alten und Neuen Testaments
BZ	*Biblische Zeitschrift*
BZAW	Beihefte zur ZAW
BZNW	Beihefte zur ZNW
CAGIBM	C. T. Newton (ed.), *The Collection of Ancient Greek Inscriptions in the British Museum* (4 vols.; Oxford: Clarendon, 1874–1916; repr. Milan: Goliardica, 1977–79)
CB	*Cultura Bíblica*
CBQ	*Catholic Biblical Quarterly*
CCLat	Corpus Christianorum, Latin Series
ChrT	*Christianity Today*
CIG	*Corpus inscriptionum graecarum* (ed. A. Boeckh; Berlin, 1828–77)
CIJ	J.-B. Frey, *Corpus inscriptionum judaicarum* (2 vols.; Vatican City: Istituto di Archeologia Cristiana, 1936, 1952)
CIL	*Corpus inscriptionum latinarum*
CIS	*Corpus inscriptionum semiticarum*
CJRT	*Canadian Journal of Religious Thought*
ClassBull	*Classical Bulletin*
ClassQ	*Classical Quarterly*
ClerM	*Clergy Monthly*
ClR	*Clergy Review*
CNEB	Commentary on the New English Bible
CollBrug	*Collationes brugenses*
CollDiocTor	*Collationes diocesis tornacensis*
CollGand	*Collationes gandavenses*
ConcJ	*Concordia Journal*
ConNT	Coniectanea neotestamentica

CQ	*Church Quarterly*
CQR	*Church Quarterly Review*
CR	*Classical Review*
CRINT	Compendia rerum iudaicarum ad Novum Testamentum
CrisTR	*Criswell Theological Review*
CSCO	Corpus scriptorum christianorum orientalium
CSEL	Corpus scriptorum ecclesiasticorum latinorum
CSS	Cursus sacrae Scripturae
CTM	*Concordia Theological Monthly*
CUOS	Columbia University Oriental Studies
DBSup	*Dictionnaire de la Bible, Supplément*
DH	H. Denzinger and P. Hünermann, *Enchiridion symbolorum definitionum et declarationum de rebus fidei et morum* (ed. 37; Freiburg im B.: Herder, 1991)
DKP	K. Ziegler and W. Sontheimer, *Der kleine Pauly: Lexikon der Antike* (5 vols.; Stuttgart: Druckenmüller, 1964–75)
DMOA	Documenta et monumenta orientis antiqui
DownRev	*Downside Review*
EA	*Erbe und Auftrag*
EBib	Études bibliques
EDNT	H. Balz and G. Schneider, *Exegetical Dictionary of the New Testament* (3 vols.; Grand Rapids, MI: Eerdmans, 1900–93)
EfMex	*Efemérides Mexicana*
EgT	*Eglise et théologie*
EHPR	Études d'histoire et de philosophie religieuses
EJ	*Encyclopedia Judaica* (16 vols.; ed. C. Roth; New York: Macmillan; Jerusalem: Keter, 1971–72)
EKKNT	Evangelisch-Katholischer Kommentar zum Neuen Testament
ELS	D. Baldi, *Enchiridion locorum sanctorum* (2d ed.; Jerusalem: Franciscan Press, 1955)
EnchBib	*Enchiridion biblicum: Documenti della chiesa sulla sacra Scrittura: Edizione bilingue* (Bologna: Edizioni Dehoniane, 1993)
EPRO	Études préliminaires aux religions orientales dans l'empire romain (Leiden: Brill)
ErThS	Erfurter theologische Studien/Schriften
ESBNT	J. A. Fitzmyer, *Essays on the Semitic Background of the New Testament* (London: Chapman, 1970; repr. Missoula, MT: Scholars, 1974)
EspVie	*Esprit et vie*
EstBíb	*Estudios bíblicos*
EstEcl	*Estudios eclesiásticos*
EtClass	*Études classiques*

ETL	*Ephemerides theologicae lovanienses*
ETR	*Études théologiques et religieuses*
Études	J. Dupont, *Études sur les Actes des Apôtres* (LD 45; Paris: Cerf, 1967)
EvJ	*Evangelical Journal*
EvQ	*Evangelical Quarterly*
EvT	*Evangelische Theologie*
Expos	*Expositor*
ExpTim	*Expository Times*
FilNeot	*Filología neotestamentaria*
FF	*Forschungen und Fortschritte*
FGNK	Forschungen zur Geschichte des neutestamentlichen Kanons
FKDG	Forschungen zur Kirchen- und Dogmengeschichte
FRLANT	Forschungen zur Religion und Literatur des Alten und Neuen Testaments
FV	*Foi et vie*
FzB	Forschung zur Bibel
GCS	Griechische christliche Schriftsteller
GJPA	G. Dalman, *Grammatik des jüdisch-palästinischen Aramäisch* and *Aramäische Dialektproben* (Darmstadt: Wissenschaftliche Buchgesellschaft, 1960; repr. 1981)
GNS	Good News Studies
GNT	*Greek New Testament* (4th ed.; ed. K. Aland et al.; New York: United Bible Societies; Stuttgart: Deutsche Bibelgesellschaft, 1993)
GR	*Greece and Rome*
GRBS	*Greek, Roman, and Byzantine Studies*
GTA	Göttinger theologische Arbeiten
GTJ	*Grace Theological Journal*
GTT	*Gereformeerd theologisch tijdschrift*
GuL	*Geist und Leben*
HE	Eusebius, *Historia ecclesiastica*
HeyJ	*Heythrop Journal*
HHS	Harvard Historical Studies
HJPAJC	E. Schürer, *The History of the Jewish People in the Age of Jesus Christ* (3 vols. in 4; rev. G. Vermes and F. Millar; Edinburgh: Clark, 1973–87)
HNT	Handbuch zum Neuen Testament
HPG	C. Kopp, *The Holy Places of the Gospels* (New York: Herder and Herder, 1963)
HTKNT	Herders theologischer Kommentar zum Neuen Testament

HTKNTSup	Supplements to HTKNT
HTR	*Harvard Theological Review*
HTS	Harvard Theological Studies
IB	G. A. Buttrick (ed.), *Interpreter's Bible* (12 vols.; New York: Abingdon-Cokesbury, 1951–57)
IBS	*Irish Biblical Studies*
ICC	International Critical Commentary
IBNTG	C. F. D. Moule, *An Idiom Book of New Testament Greek* (Cambridge: Cambridge University Press, 1953)
IG	*Inscriptiones graecae* (14 vols.; Berlin: Prussian Academy, 1873–)
IGRR	R. Cagnat, *Inscriptiones graecae ad res romanas pertinentes* (4 vols.; Paris: Leroux, 1911, 1906, 1927; repr. 4 vols. in 3; Chicago: Ares, 1975)
IJT	*Indian Journal of Theology*
IKZ	*Internationale kirchliche Zeitschrift*
ILN	*Illustrated London News*
ILS	H. Dessau, *Inscriptiones latinae selectae* (3 vols.; Berlin: Weidmann, 1892–1916; repr. 3 vols. in 5, 1954–55)
INJ	*Israel Numismatic Journal*
Int	*Interpretation*
ITQ	*Irish Theological Quarterly*
ITS	*Indian Theological Studies*
JAC	*Jahrbuch für Antike und Christentum*
JBC	R. E. Brown et al. (eds.), *The Jerome Biblical Commentary* (Englewood Cliffs, NJ: Prentice Hall, 1968)
JBL	*Journal of Biblical Literature*
JBR	*Journal of Bible and Religion*
JECS	*Journal of Early Christian Studies*
JEH	*Journal of Ecclesiastical History*
JerusPersp	*Jerusalem Perspective*
JETS	*Journal of the Evangelical Theological Society*
JGES	*Journal of the Grace Evangelical Society*
JITC	*Journal of the Interdenominational Theological Center*
JJS	*Journal of Jewish Studies*
JNSL	*Journal of Northwest Semitic Languages*
JOTT	*Journal of Translation and Textlinguistics*
JPT	*Journal of Pentecostal Theology*
JQR	*Jewish Quarterly Review*
JR	*Journal of Religion*
JRS	*Journal of Roman Studies*
JSJ	*Journal for the Study of Judaism*
JSNT	*Journal for the Study of the New Testament*
JSNTSup	Supplements to the *JSNT*

JSOT	*Journal for the Study of the Old Testament*
JSS	*Journal of Semitic Studies*
JTC	Journal for Theology and the Church
JTS	*Journal of Theological Studies*
JTSA	*Journal of Theology for Southern Africa*
KNT	Kommentar zum Neuen Testament
KZ	*Kirchliche Zeitschrift*
LAE	A. Deissmann, *Light from the Ancient East* (rev. ed.; London: Hodder and Stoughton, 1927)
LC	*La liberté chrétienne*
LCM	*Liverpool Classical Monthly*
LCQ	*Lutheran Church Quarterly*
LCR	*Lutheran Church Review*
LD	Lectio Divina
LS	*Louvain Studies*
LSJ	H. G. Liddell, R. Scott, and H. S. Jones, A *Greek-English Lexicon* (9th ed.; Oxford: Clarendon, 1940)
LTAHT	J. A. Fitzmyer, *Luke the Theologian: Aspects of His Teaching* (New York/Mahwah, NJ: Paulist, 1989)
LTH	G. Schneider, *Lukas, Theologe der Heilsgeschichte: Aufsätze zum lukanischen Doppelwerk* (BBB 59; Bonn: Hanstein, 1985)
LTJ	*Lutheran Theological Journal*
LTP	*Laval théologique et philosophique*
LumVie	*Lumière et vie*
LumVitae	*Lumen Vitae*
MarTS	Marburger theologische Studien
MD	*La Maison Dieu*
MDAI	*Mitteilungen des deutschen archäologischen Instituts*
MeyerK	H.A.W. Meyer, Kritisch-exegetischer Kommentar über das Neue Testament
MM	J. H. Moulton and G. Milligan, *The Vocabulary of the Greek Testament Illustrated from the Papyri and Other Non-Literary Sources* (London: Hodder and Stoughton, 1930)
MPAT	J. A. Fitzmyer and D. J. Harrington, A *Manual of Palestinian Aramaic Texts (Second Century B.C.–Second Century A.D.)* (BibOr 34; Rome: Biblical Institute, 1978)
MTS	Münchener theologische Studien
NA^{27}	E. Nestle and K. Aland, *Novum Testamentum graece* (27th ed.; Stuttgart: Deutsche Bibelgesellschaft, 1993)
NCB	New Century Bible
NClarB	New Clarendon Bible
NDIEC	G.R.H. Horsley et al., *New Documents Illustrating Early*

	Christianity (7 vols.; North Ryde, N.S.W.: Ancient History Documentary Research Centre, Macquarie University, 1976–94)
NedTT	*Nederlands theologisch tijdschrift*
NICNT	New International Commentary on the New Testament
NIDNTT	C. Brown (ed.), *The New International Dictionary of New Testament Theology* (3 vols.; Grand Rapids, MI: Zondervan, 1975–78)
NJBC	R. E. Brown et al. (eds.), *The New Jerome Biblical Commentary* (Englewood Cliffs, NJ: Prentice Hall, 1990)
NKZ	*Neue kirchliche Zeitschrift*
NorTT	*Norsk teologisk Tidsskrift*
Nouvelles études	J. Dupont, *Nouvelles études sur les Actes des Apôtres* (LD 118; Paris: Cerf, 1984)
NovT	*Novum Testamentum*
NovTSup	Supplements to *NovT*
NRT	*Nouvelle revue théologique*
NTAbh	Neutestamentliche Abhandlungen
NTB	C. K. Barrett, *New Testament Background: Selected Documents: Revised Edition* (San Francisco: Harper & Row, 1989)
NTD	Das Neue Testament deutsch
NTG	*Novum Testamentum graece* (see NA[27] above)
NThSt	*Nieuwe theologische studiën*
NThT	*Nieuw theologisch tijdschrift*
NTM	New Testament Message
NTRG	New Testament Reading Guide
NTSR	New Testament for Spiritual Reading
NTTS	New Testament Tools and Studies
OBL	Orientalia et biblica lovaniensia
OBO	Orbis biblicus et orientalis
OCD	N.G.L. Hammond and H. H. Scullard, *The Oxford Classical Dictionary* (2d ed.; Oxford: Clarendon, 1970)
OCP	*Orientalia christiana periodica*
OGIS	W. Dittenberger, *Orientis graeci inscriptiones selectae* (Leipzig: Hinrichs, 1903, 1905; repr. Hildesheim: Olms, 1960)
OLZ	*Orientalische Literaturzeitung*
OrChr	*Oriens christianus*
OrChrAn	Orientalia christiana analecta
OTL	Old Testament Library
OTP	J. H. Charlesworth (ed.), *The Old Testament Pseudepigrapha* (2 vols.; New York: Doubleday, 1983, 1985)
OTS	*Oudtestamentische Studiën*

PAHT	J. A. Fitzmyer, *Paul and His Theology: A Brief Sketch, Second Edition* (Englewood Cliffs, NJ: Prentice Hall, 1989)
PC	*Palestra del Clero*
PCB	M. Black and H. H. Rowley (eds.), *Peake's Commentary on the Bible* (London: Nelson, 1963)
PEFQS	*Palestine Exploration Fund Quarterly Statement*
PEQ	*Palestine Exploration Quarterly*
PerspTeol	*Perspectiva teológica*
PG	J.-P. Migne (ed.), Patrologia graeca
PGM	*Papyri graecae magicae* (2 vols.; ed. K. Preisendanz; Leipzig: Teubner, 1928–31)
PJ	*Palästina-Jahrbuch*
PL	J.-P. Migne (ed.), Patrologia latina
PLips.	L. Mitteis, *Griechische Urkunden der Papyrussammlung zu Leipzig* (Leipzig: Teubner, 1906)
POxy	B. P. Grenfell and A. S. Hunt, *Oxyrhynchus Papyri* (60 vols.; London: Egypt Exploration Fund, 1898–1994)
PRS	*Perspectives in Religious Studies*
PSB	*Princeton Seminary Bulletin*
PSTJ	*Perkins School of Theology Journal*
PSV	*Parola, Spirito e vita*
PTMS	Pittsburgh Theological Monograph Series
PW	G. Wissowa (ed.), *Paulys Real-Encyclopädie der classischen Altertumswissenschaft* (49 vols.; Stuttgart: Metzler/ Druckenmüller, 1893–1978)
PWSup	Supplements to PW
PzB	*Protokolle zur Bibel*
Qad	*Qadmoniot*
QD	Quaestiones disputatae
QDAP	*The Quarterly of the Department of Antiquities in Palestine*
RAC	*Reallexikon für Antike und Christentum*
RArch	*Revue archéologique*
RAT	*Revue africaine de théologie*
RB	*Revue biblique*
RBPH	*Revue belge de philosophie et d'histoire*
RCT	*Revista catalana de teología*
REAug	*Revue des études augustiniennes*
REG	*Revue des études grecques*
REJ	*Revue des études juives*
REL	*Revue des études latines*
RelSR	*Religious Studies Review*
RES	*Répertoire d'épigraphie sémitique*

ResQ	*Restoration Quarterly*
RevBíb	*Revista bíblica*
RevEcclLiége	*Revue ecclésiastique de Liége*
RevExp	*Review and Expositor*
RevScRel	*Revue des sciences religieuses*
RevThom	*Revue thomiste*
RGG	*Die Religion in Geschichte und Gegenwart* (3d ed.; 7 vols.; ed. K. Galling et al.; Tübingen: Mohr [Siebeck], 1957–65)
RhMP	*Rheinisches Museum für Philologie*
RHPR	*Revue d'histoire et de philosophie religieuses*
RHR	*Revue de l'histoire des religions*
RicRel	*Ricerche religiose*
RivB	*Rivista biblica*
RNT	Regensburger Neues Testament
RSR	*Recherches de science religieuse*
RSPT	*Revue des sciences philosophiques et théologiques*
RTL	*Revue théologique de Louvain*
RTP	*Revue de théologie et de philosophie*
RTR	*Reformed Theological Review*
SacDoc	*Sacra doctrina*
SANT	Studien zum Alten und Neuen Testament
SBA	Studies in Biblical Archaeology
SBFLA	*Studii biblici franciscani liber annuus*
SBLBSNA	Society of Biblical Literature: Biblical Scholarship in North America
SBLDS	Society of Biblical Literature: Dissertation Series
SBLMS	Society of Biblical Literature: Monograph Series
SBLSCS	Society of Biblical Literature: Septuagint and Cognate Studies
SBLSP	*Society of Biblical Literature: Seminar Papers*
SBS	Stuttgarter biblische Studien
SBT	Studies in Biblical Theology
SBU	Symbolae biblicae upsalienses
SC	Sources chrétiennes
ScCatt	*Scuola cattolica*
ScEccl	*Sciences ecclésiastiques*
ScEsp	*Science et Esprit*
Scr	*Scripture*
SE I, II etc.	*Studia evangelica I, II, III, VI* (= TU 73 [1959]; 87 [1964]; 88 [1964]; 112 [1973])
SEA	*Svensk Exegetisk Årsbok*
SecCent	*Second Century*
SEG	*Supplementum epigraphicum graecum*
SHR	Studies in the History of Religions

SIG	W. Dittenberger, *Sylloge inscriptionum graecarum* (4 vols.; 4th ed.; Hildesheim: Olms, 1960)
SJLA	Studies in Judaism in Late Antiquity
SJT	*Scottish Journal of Theology*
SMR	*Studia Montis Regii*
SNT	Studien zum Neuen Testament
SNTSMS	Studiorum Novi Testamenti Societas Monograph Series
SNTU	Studien zum Neuen Testament und seiner Umwelt
SO	*Symbolae osloenses*
SPB	Studia post-biblica
SQE	K. Aland, *Synopsis quattuor evangeliorum* (10th ed.; Stuttgart: Deutsche Bibelstiftung, 1978)
SR	*Studies in Religion/Sciences religieuses*
ST	*Studia theologica*
StLA	*Studies in Luke-Acts: Essays Presented in Honor of Paul Schubert* . . . (ed. L. E. Keck and J. L. Martyn; Nashville: Abingdon, 1966; repr. Philadelphia: Fortress, 1980)
Str-B	(H. L. Strack and) P. Billerbeck, *Kommentar zum Neuen Testament aus Talmud und Midrasch* (6 vols.; Munich: Beck, 1922–61; partly repr. 1963, 1965)
StudCath	*Studia catholica*
StudPat	*Studia patavina*
Studies	M. Dibelius, *Studies in the Acts of the Apostles* (ed. H. Greeven; London: SCM, 1956)
SwJT	*Southwestern Journal of Theology*
TBei	*Theologische Beiträge*
TBT	*The Bible Today*
TCGNT	B. M. Metzger, A *Textual Commentary on the Greek New Testament: Second Edition* (Stuttgart: Deutsche Bibelgesellschaft/United Bible Societies, 1994)
TDNT	G. Kittel (and G. Friedrich), *Theological Dictionary of the New Testament* (10 vols.; Grand Rapids, MI: Eerdmans, 1964–76)
TGl	*Theologie und Glaube*
TheolEduc	*Theological Education*
THKNT	Theologischer Hand-Kommentar zum Neuen Testament
ThSt	*Theologische Studiën*
ThV	*Theologia viatorum*
TJb	*Theologisches Jahrbuch*
TLZ	*Theologische Literaturzeitung*
TM	*Theological Monthly* (= later *CTM*)
TNT	R. Bultmann, *Theology of the New Testament* (2 vols.; New York: Scribner, 1951, 1955)

TP	*Theologie und Philosophie*
TPAPA	*Transactions and Proceedings of the American Philological Association*
TPQ	*Theologisch-Praktische Quartalschrift*
TQ	*Theologische Quartalschrift*
TRE	*Theologische Realenzyklopädie* (22 + vols.; ed. G. Krause and G. Müller; Berlin/New York: de Gruyter, 1976–)
TRev	*Theologische Revue*
TrinJ	*Trinity Journal*
TRu	*Theologische Rundschau*
TSK	*Theologische Studien und Kritiken*
TT	*Theologisch tijdschrift*
TTZ	*Trierer theologische Zeitschrift*
TU	Texte und Untersuchungen
TynBull	*Tyndale Bulletin*
TynNTC	Tyndale New Testament Commentary
TZ	*Theologische Zeitschrift*
UBS	United Bible Societies
UNT	Untersuchungen zum Neuen Testament
USQR	*Union Seminary Quarterly Review* (New York)
USR	*Union Seminary Review* (Richmond, VA)
VC	*Vigiliae christianae*
VD	*Verbum domini*
VS	Verbum salutis
VSpir	*Vie spirituelle*
VT	*Vox theologica*
WA	J. A. Fitzmyer, A *Wandering Aramean: Collected Aramaic Essays* (SBLMS 25; Missoula: Scholars, 1979)
WD	*Wort und Dienst*
WMANT	Wissenschaftliche Monographien zum Alten und Neuen Testament
WoAnt	*Wort und Antwort*
WordW	*Word and World*
WT	Western Text (see Introduction §50)
WTJ	*Westminster Theological Journal*
WUNT	Wissenschaftliche Untersuchungen zum Neuen Testament
WZ	*Wissenschaftliche Zeitschrift*
ZAW	*Zeitschrift für die alttestamentliche Wissenschaft*
ZBG	M. Zerwick, *Biblical Greek Illustrated by Examples* (Rome: Biblical Institute, 1963)
ZBKNT	Zürcher Bibel-Kommentar zum Neuen Testament

ZDPV	*Zeitschrift des deutschen Palästina-Vereins*
ZKG	*Zeitschrift für Kirchengeschichte*
ZKT	*Zeitschrift für katholische Theologie*
ZNW	*Zeitschrift für die neutestamentliche Wissenschaft*
ZPE	*Zeitschrift für Papyrologie und Epigraphik*
ZST	*Zeitschrift für systematische Theologie*
ZTK	*Zeitschrift für Theologie und Kirche*
ZVS	*Zeitschrift für vergleichende Sprachforschung*
ZWT	*Zeitschrift für wissenschaftliche Theologie*

GRAMMATICAL ABBREVIATIONS

absol.	absolute
acc.	accusative
act.	active
adj.	adjective, adjectival
adv.	adverb(ial)
aor.	aorist
art.	article
cl.	clause
conj.	conjunction
dat.	dative
def.	definite
dem.	demonstrative
fem.	feminine
fut.	future
gen.	genitive
imperf.	imperfect
impv.	imperative
indef.	indefinite
indic.	indicative
indir.	indirect
infin.	infinitive
intrans.	intransitive
masc.	masculine
mid.	middle (voice)
neut.	neuter
nom.	nominative
obj.	object
opt.	optative
pass.	passive
perf.	perfect
pers.	personal
pl.	plural
prep.	preposition(al)

pres.	present
pron.	pronoun
ptc.	participle
rel.	relative
sg.	singular
subj.	subject
subjunct.	subjunctive
vb.	verb
voc.	vocative

OTHER ABBREVIATIONS

Ag.Ap.	Josephus, *Against Apion*
Ant.	Josephus, *Antiquities of the Jews*
b.	*Babylonian Talmud* (+ tractate name)
bis	two occurrences
Boh	Bohairic (Coptic) version
cod.	codex
comm.	commentary, *commentarius*
E	English (added to biblical reference = English Bible numbering)
ep.	epistle, *epistula*
fl.	floruit
frg.	fragment
hom. in	homily on, *homilia in*
J.W.	Josephus, *Jewish War*
lit.	literally
LXX	Septuagint (the OT in Greek)
m.	*Mishnah* (+ tractate name)
MS(S)	Manuscript(s)
MT	Masoretic Text
NAB	*New American Bible*
ns	new series (in any language)
NT	New Testament
or.	*oratio*, oration
OT	Old Testament
pap.	papyrus
pl.	plate
Ps. Sol.	*Psalms of Solomon*
RSV	*Revised Standard Version* (of the Bible)
SBJ	La Sainte Bible (de Jérusalem)
Syr	Syriac (version of Bible)
T.	*Testament (of)*
tg.	targum
viz.	*videlicet*, namely

v.l.	*varia lectio,* variant reading
Vg	*Vulgata Latina* (Vulgate version of the Bible)
VL	*Vetus Latina* (Old Latin)

Dead Sea Scrolls and Related Texts

CD	Cairo (Genizah text of the) Damascus (Document)
Mur	Wadi Murabbaʿat (texts)
p	Pesher (commentary)
Q	Qumran
QL	Qumran Literature
1Q, 2Q, etc.	Numbered caves of Qumran, yielding written materials; followed by abbreviation of biblical or nonbiblical work
1QapGen	*Genesis Apocryphon* from Cave 1
1QH	*Hôdāyôt* (*Thanksgiving Psalms*) from Cave 1
1QIsa[a]	Copy a of Isaiah from Cave 1
1QM	*Milḥāmāh* (*War Scroll*) from Cave 1
1QpHab	*Pesher on Habakkuk* from Cave 1
1QS	*Serek hayyaḥad* (*Rule of the Community, Manual of Discipline*) from Cave 1
1QSa	Appendix A (*Rule of the Congregation*) to 1QS
4QEn	Enoch texts from Cave 4
11QtgJob	Targum of Job from Cave 11

The numbering of chapters and verses of the OT follows that of the Hebrew MT, especially when reference is made to the Psalter. Even if the discussion concerns the Greek form of a psalm in the LXX, the numbering still follows the Hebrew text. In case of doubt, one can always consult the *NAB,* which uses the numbering of the Hebrew OT.

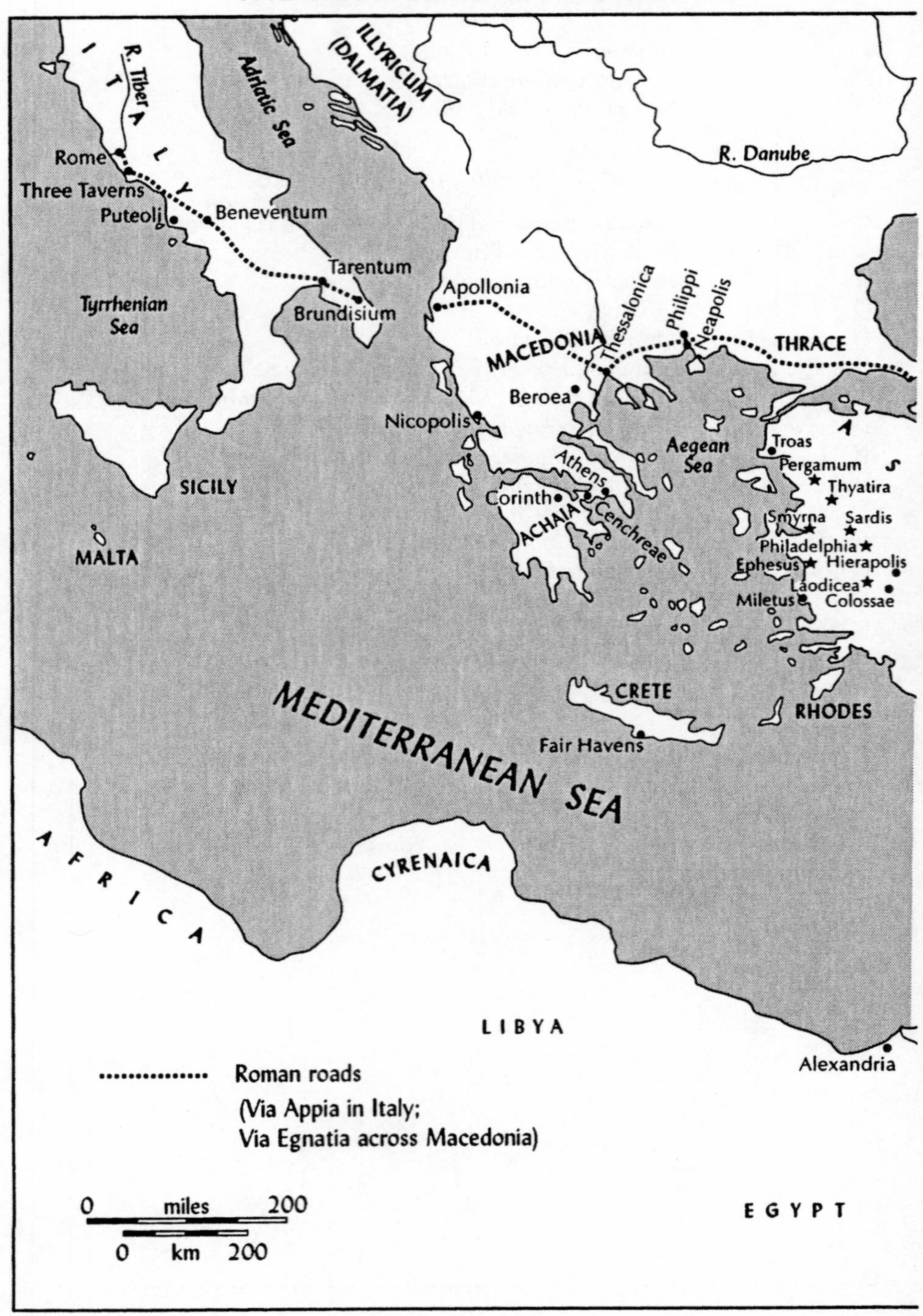

Map 1. The Mediterranean World

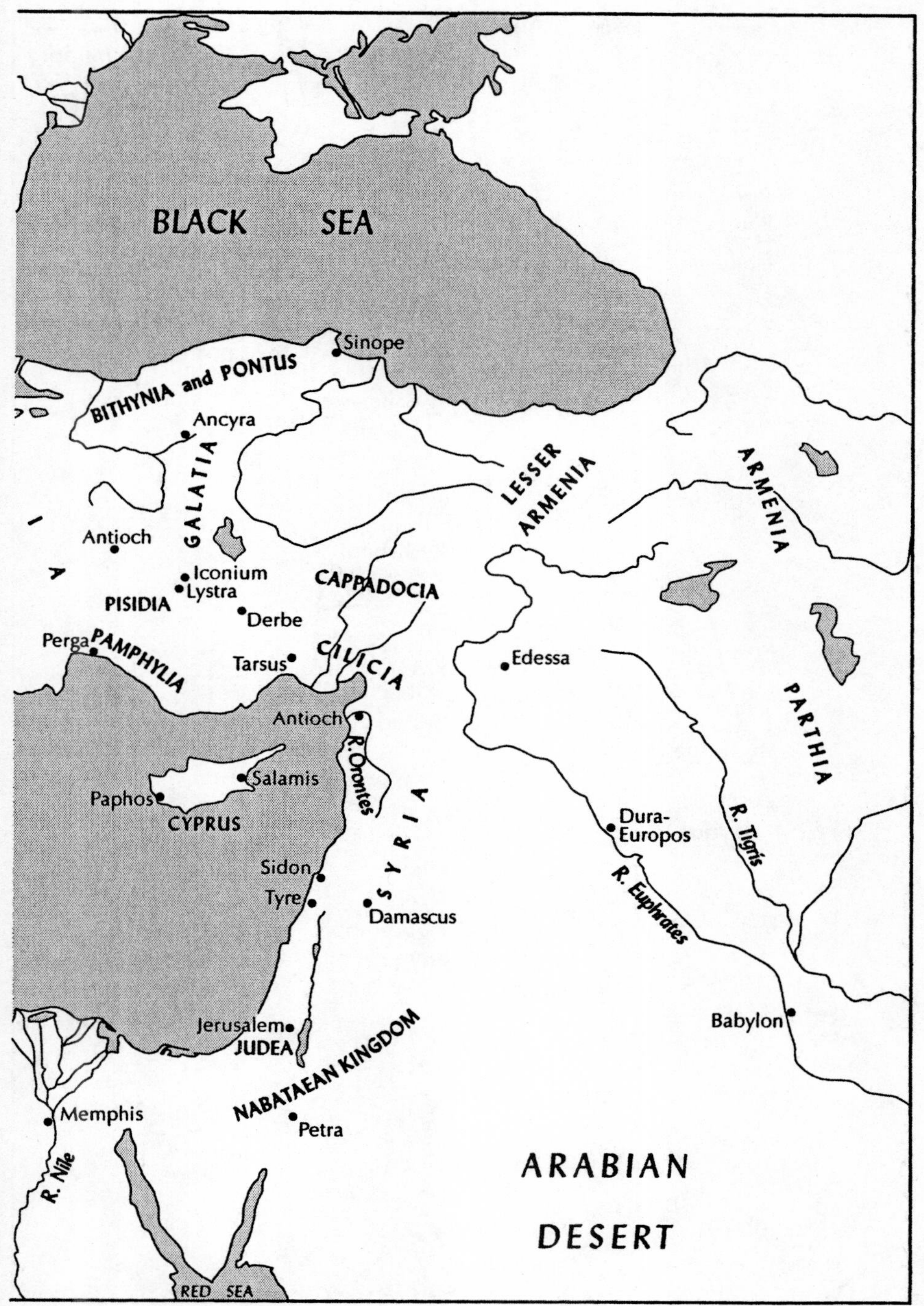

Map 1, Continued.

SYRIA AND JUDEA

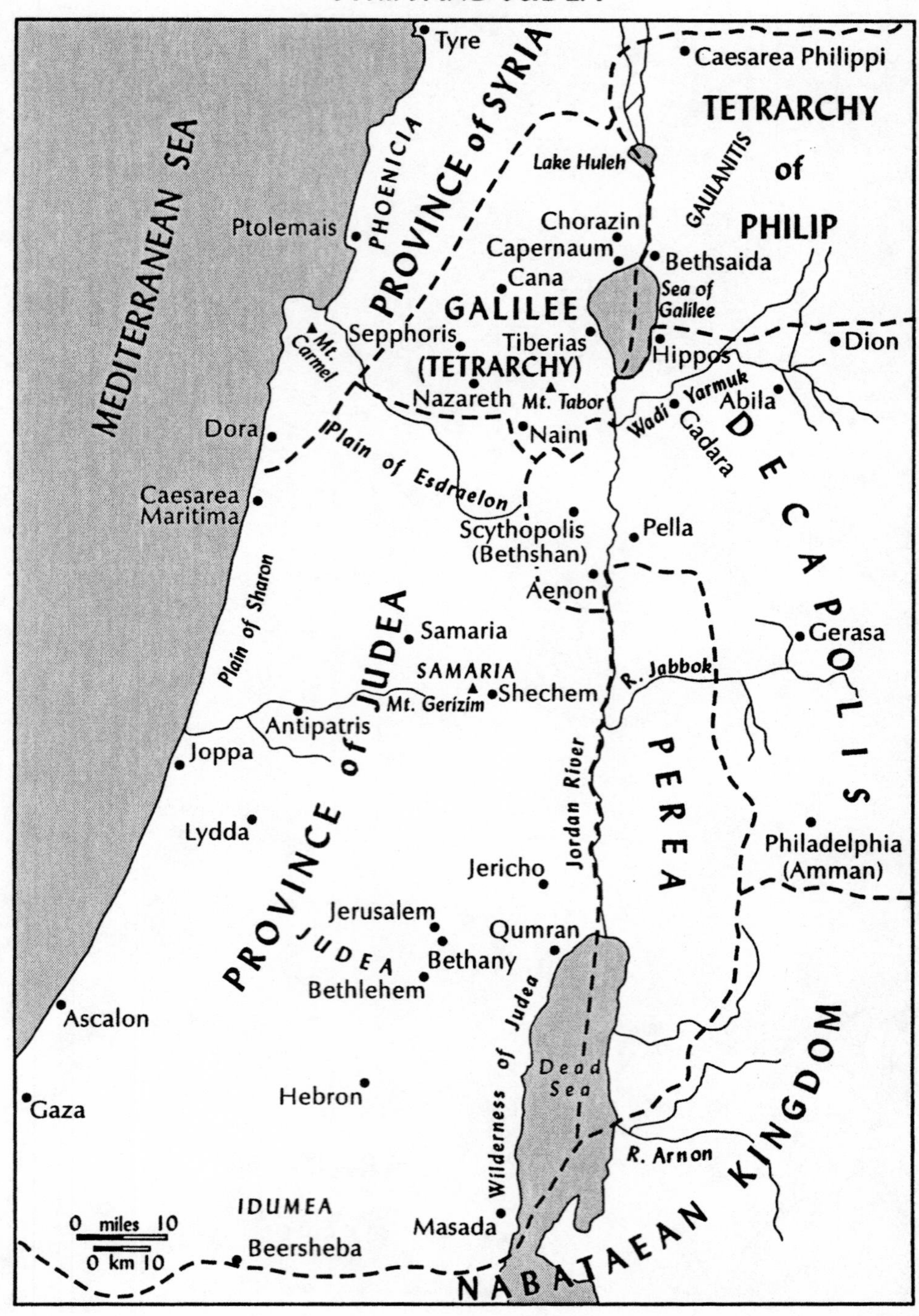

Map 2. Syria and Judea

ACTS OF THE APOSTLES: TRANSLATION

◆

1 1 In my first account, Theophilus, I dealt with all that Jesus did and taught
from the beginning, 2 until the day that he was taken up, after he had instructed
through the Holy Spirit the apostles whom he had chosen.

3 After he had suffered, he presented himself alive to them in many convincing
ways, appearing to them throughout forty days and speaking about the kingdom
of God. 4 Once when he met with them, he bade them not to depart from Jerusalem, but to await the promise of my Father, about which you have already heard
from me. 5 For John baptized with water, but in a few days you will be baptized
with the Holy Spirit. 6 When they gathered together, they used to ask him, "Lord,
is this the time when you will restore the kingship to Israel?" 7 He said to them,
"It is not for you to know the times or seasons that the Father has determined by
his own authority. 8 You will receive power, when the Holy Spirit comes upon
you, and you will be witnesses to me in Jerusalem, [in] all Judea and Samaria,
even to the end of the earth."

9 When he had said this, as they were looking on, he was lifted up before their
very eyes, and a cloud took him out of their sight. 10 While they were still staring
at the heavens, as he was going, two men dressed in white robes suddenly stood
beside them and said, 11 "Men of Galilee, why do you stand here looking at the
heavens? This Jesus, who has been taken up from you into the heavens, will
come in the same way you saw him go into the heavens."

12 Then they returned to Jerusalem from the hill called Olivet, which is near
Jerusalem, a sabbath day's journey away. 13 Entering the city, they went to the
upper room where they were staying, Peter, John and James, Andrew, Philip and
Thomas, Bartholomew, Matthew and James son of Alphaeus, Simon the Zealot,
and Judas son of James. 14 They were all devoting themselves with one accord to
prayer, together with some women and Mary, the mother of Jesus, as well as
his brothers.

15 During those days Peter stood up in the midst of the brothers (there must
have been about a hundred and twenty of them gathered together) and said,
16 "Brothers, that Scripture, which the Holy Spirit uttered long ago through David, had to be fulfilled concerning Judas, who became the leader of those who
arrested Jesus. 17 He had been numbered among us and was apportioned a share
in this ministry of ours. 18 But the wretch bought a plot of ground with ill-gotten
money and fell down on it head first so that his body burst open, and all his
entrails spilled out. 19 This became known to all the inhabitants of Jerusalem, so
that that plot came to be called in their own language Akeldama, that is, Field of
Blood. 20 For it stands written in the book of Psalms,

Let his estate become desolate,
let there be no one to dwell on it.[a]

And,

Let another take his office.[b]

---

[a] Ps 69:26

[b] Ps 109:8

21 So one of the men who have been part of our company all the while the Lord Jesus moved in and out among us, 22 from the beginning when he was baptized by John until the day when he was taken up from us, must become with us a witness to his resurrection." 23 Then they nominated two, Joseph called Barsabbas, also known as Justus, and Matthias. 24 So they prayed, "Lord, you know the hearts of all; make known to us which one of these two you choose 25 to take over this apostolic ministry, which Judas deserted to go to his own place." 26 They cast lots for them, and the lot fell on Matthias; and he was numbered with the eleven apostles.

2 1 When the day of Pentecost came round, they all happened to be gathered together in one place. 2 Suddenly there was a noise from the heavens like a strong wind sweeping along, and it filled the whole house where they were sitting. 3 There appeared to them tongues like flames of fire that parted and rested on each one of them. 4 They were all filled with the Holy Spirit and began to speak in other tongues, as the Spirit gave them to utter. 5 Now there were sojourning in Jerusalem devout men, Jews of every nation under the heavens. 6 When that sound was heard, they gathered in a large crowd and were confounded, because each one heard them speaking in his own language. 7 Bewildered, they asked in amazement, "Are not all these who speak Galileans? 8 How is it, then, that each of us hears them speaking in the language in which we were brought up? 9 We are Parthians, Medes, and Elamites, inhabitants of Mesopotamia, Judea, and Cappadocia, of Pontus and Asia, 10 Phrygia and Pamphylia, of Egypt and the regions of Libya about Cyrene; even visitors from Rome 11 (both Jews and proselytes), Cretans and Arabs, yet we hear them speaking in our own languages about the mighty deeds of God." 12 They were all bewildered and could make nothing of it, saying to one another, "What does this mean?" 13 But others scoffed and said, "They have just had too much new wine."

14 Peter stood up with the Eleven, raised his voice, and addressed them: "Fellow Jews, and all who are sojourning here in Jerusalem! Let this be known to you and listen, please, to what I have to say. 15 These people are not drunk, as you suppose. After all, it is only nine o'clock in the morning! 16 No, it is rather what was meant by Joel the prophet, when he said,

17 '*It shall happen* in the last days, God declares,
that I will pour out some of my Spirit upon all flesh;
your sons and daughters shall prophesy,
your young men shall see visions,
and your old men shall dream dreams.
18 *Yes, even upon my servants and my handmaids*
will I pour out some of my Spirit in those days, and they shall speak like prophets.
19 *I will display wonders in the heavens* above
and signs *on the earth* below,
blood and fire and a cloud of smoke.

[20]*The sun shall be turned to darkness, and the moon to blood,*
before that great and resplendent day of the Lord comes.
[21]*Then everyone who calls upon the name of the Lord shall be saved.'*[c]

[22]Fellow Israelites, listen to these words. Jesus the Nazorean was a man accredited to you by God with mighty deeds, wonders, and signs, which God wrought through him in your midst, as you yourselves are well aware. [23]Though this man was delivered up according to the set plan and foreknowledge of God, you used lawless people to crucify and kill him. [24]But God raised him up, releasing him from death's throes, since it was not possible for him to be held by it. [25]For David says about him,

'I have set the Lord ever before me,
with him at my right hand I will not be perturbed;
[26]*so my heart has been gladdened and my tongue has rejoiced,*
my flesh too shall live on in hope.
[27]*For you will not abandon my soul to the nether world,*
nor will you allow your holy one to see decay.
[28]*You have made known to me the paths of life;*
you will fill me with joy in your presence.'[d]

[29]My brothers, one can speak frankly to you about the patriarch David: he died and was buried, and his tomb is here in our midst to this very day. [30]But because he was a prophet and knew that God *had sworn an oath* to him that he *would set one of his descendants upon his throne,*[e] [31]he foresaw and spoke of the resurrection of the Messiah, saying that he was *neither abandoned to the netherworld nor has* his flesh *seen decay.*[f] [32]This Jesus God has raised up; of this we are all witnesses. [33]Exalted to God's right hand, he has received from the Father the promised Holy Spirit and poured it forth. This is what you now [both] see and hear. [34]For it was not David who went up into the heavens; yet it is he who says,

[*The*] *Lord said to my Lord: 'Sit at my right hand*
[35]*until I make your enemies a stool for your feet.'*[g]

[36]Let all the house of Israel know for sure, then, that God has made him both Lord and Messiah, this Jesus whom you crucified."

[37]Now when they heard this, they were cut to the quick and asked Peter and the rest of the apostles, "What are we to do, Brothers?" [38]Peter [said] to them, "Reform your lives and be baptized, every one of you, in the name of Jesus the Messiah for the forgiveness of your sins, and you will receive the gift of the Holy Spirit. [39]For to you and your children has the promise been made, yes, even to

---

[c] Joel 3:1–5
[d] Ps 16:8–11
[e] Ps 132:11
[f] Ps 16:10
[g] Ps 110:1

all those still far off whom the Lord our God will call to himself." [40]With many
other explanations Peter bore witness and kept urging them, "Save yourselves
from this corrupt generation." [41]Those who accepted his message were baptized,
and some three thousand persons were added that day.
[42]They continued to devote themselves to the teaching of the apostles, to a
communal form of life, to the breaking of bread, and to the prayers. [43]Reverent
awe characterized each of them; and many wonders and signs were wrought
through the apostles. [44]All who believed lived together and held all things in
common. [45]They would sell their property and belongings and divide them
among all according to each one's need. [46]Each day with one accord they devoted themselves to meeting in the Temple, and, breaking bread in their homes,
they kept taking their meals with glad and simple hearts, [47]praising God and
winning the respect of all the people. Day by day the Lord added to the total
those who were being saved.

3 [1]Once when Peter and John were going up to the Temple for the three
o'clock hour of prayer, [2]a man crippled from birth was being carried in. They
would put him each day at the gate of the Temple called Beautiful, to beg alms
from the people entering the Temple. [3]When he saw Peter and John about to go
into the Temple, he asked for alms. [4]Together with John, Peter looked intently
at him and said, "Look at us." [5]He gave them his attention, expecting to receive
something from them. [6]Then Peter said, "I have neither silver nor gold, but what
I have I give you: In the name of Jesus Christ the Nazorean [get up and] walk!"
[7]Taking him by the right hand, he drew him up. Immediately his feet and ankles
grew strong. [8]He jumped up, stood for a moment, and walked about. He went
into the Temple with them, walking about, jumping, and praising God. [9]When
all the people saw him walking about and praising God, [10]they recognized him
as "that beggar who used to sit at the Beautiful Gate of the Temple." They were
fully amazed and astonished at what had happened to him. [11]As he held fast to
Peter and John, all the people in excitement rushed over to them in the colonnade called Solomon's.
[12]When Peter saw this, he turned to the people with these words: "Fellow Israelites, why are you amazed at this? Why do you stare at us, as if we had made
this man walk by some power or holiness of our own? [13]It is *the God of Abraham,*
[*the God*] *of Isaac, and* [*the God*] *of Jacob, the God of our ancestors,*[h] who has
thus honored his servant Jesus whom you handed over and disowned in Pilate's
presence, when he had judged it right to release him. [14]You disowned the Holy
and Upright One and begged that a murderer be released to you. [15]The author
of life itself you put to death, but God raised him from the dead. Of this we are
witnesses. [16]Indeed, because of faith in the name of Jesus, that name has made
this man strong whom you see and know well. The faith that comes through
Jesus has given him the perfect health that is present before all of you. [17]Now I
know, brothers, that you acted as you did out of ignorance, just as your leaders

[h] Exod 3:6, 15

did too. [18]But God has thus brought to fulfillment what he announced long ago through all the prophets, that his Messiah would suffer. [19]So reform your lives and turn (to God) that your sins may be wiped out, [20]that times of recovery may be granted you by the Lord, and that he may send you the Messiah already appointed for you, Jesus, [21]whom heaven must retain until the time of universal restoration, about which God spoke through his holy prophets from of old. [22]For Moses said,

> 'A *prophet like me the Lord your God will raise up for you from among your kinsfolk; you must listen to him in everything that he may say*[i] to you. [23]*Everyone who does not listen to that prophet shall be ruthlessly cut off from the people.*'[j]

[24]All the prophets who have spoken, from Samuel on down, have also proclaimed these days. [25]You are the children of the prophets and of the covenant that God made with your ancestors, when he said to Abraham, '*Through your offspring shall all the families of the earth be blessed.*'[k] [26]For you, first of all, God raised up his servant and sent him, blessing you as each one of you turns from your evil ways."

4 [1]While they were still addressing the people, the priests, the captain of the Temple guard, and the Sadducees confronted them, [2]annoyed that Peter and John were teaching the people and proclaiming in Jesus the resurrection of the dead. [3]They arrested them and put them in jail for the night, for it was already evening. [4]But many of those who had heard the word came to believe, and [the] number of men grew to [about] five thousand. [5]The next day their leaders, elders, and scribes happened to assemble in Jerusalem, [6]with Annas, the high priest, and Caiaphas, John, and Alexander, and all who were of high-priestly class. [7]They brought Peter and John in before them and questioned them: "By what authority or what name have such as you done this?" [8]Then Peter, filled with the Holy Spirit, said to them, "Leaders of the people and elders, [9]if we must answer today for a good deed done to a cripple (and explain) how he has been restored to health, [10]then let it be known to all of you and to all the people of Israel that it was in the name of Jesus Christ the Nazorean, whom you crucified and whom God raised from the dead. In virtue of that name this man stands before you perfectly well. [11]This Jesus is *the stone rejected by* you *builders, which has become the cornerstone.*[l] [12]There is salvation in no one else, for there is no other name in the whole world given to human beings through which we are to be saved." [13]Seeing the bold self-assurance of Peter and John and realizing that they were uneducated, ordinary men, they were amazed; they recognized that they had been with Jesus. [14]When they looked at the man who had been cured standing there with them, they had nothing to say in reply. [15]So they ordered them out of the Sanhedrin and held a consultation among themselves: [16]"What are we going

[i] Deut 18:15–16
[j] Deut 18:19; Lev 23:29
[k] Gen 22:18; 26:4
[l] Ps 118:22

to do with these people? For it is known to all who live in Jerusalem that a remarkable sign has been done through them; we cannot deny it. 17 But that it may not
spread further among the people, we must warn them never to speak again about
that name to anyone." 18 They called them back in and ordered them not to speak
or teach in the name of Jesus under any circumstances. 19 But Peter and John
said to them in reply, "Judge for yourselves whether it is right in God's sight for
us to obey you rather than God. 20 We cannot help but speak of what we have
seen and heard." 21 So when they had threatened them further, they dismissed
them, finding no way to punish them, because of the people, who were all honoring God for what had happened. 22 For it was for a man more than forty years
old that this sign of healing had been performed.

23 After their release, Peter and John went back to their friends and reported to
them all that the chief priests and elders had told them. 24 On hearing it, they
raised their voices with one accord in prayer to God: "Sovereign Lord, *who have*
made the heaven and earth, the sea and all that is in them,[m] 25 it is you who spoke
by the Holy Spirit through our ancestor David, your servant:

Why have nations raged
and peoples plotted folly?
26 *Kings of the earth have drawn up in hostile array,*
and rulers have gathered together
against the Lord and against his Anointed.[n]

27 For truly in this very city there have indeed gathered together against your holy
servant Jesus, whom you have anointed, Herod and Pontius Pilate, together with
Gentiles and peoples of Israel, 28 to do the very things that your designing hand
planned long ago. 29 But now, O Lord, look at their threats and grant your servants
the courage to preach your word with all boldness, 30 as you stretch forth [your]
hand to cure, and as signs and wonders are performed in the name of your holy
servant Jesus." 31 As they prayed, the place trembled in which they were gathered
together; all were filled with the Holy Spirit and they continued to speak about
the word of God with boldness.

32 The community of believers was of one heart and mind; none of them ever
claimed any possession as his own, but they held all things in common. 33 With
great forcefulness the apostles continued to bear witness to the resurrection of
the Lord Jesus, and much favor was accorded them all. 34 There was never a
needy person among them, for those who owned property or houses would sell
them, bring the proceeds of what was sold, 35 and lay them at the feet of the
apostles; and it was distributed to each according to one's need.

36 Thus there was Joseph, surnamed by the apostles Barnabas (which is interpreted "Son of Consolation"), a Levite, a Cypriot by birth, 37 who owned a farm
that he sold and brought the money and put it at the feet of the apostles. **5** 1 But
there was also a certain Ananias, who with his wife Sapphira sold a piece of prop-

---

[m] Ps 146:6 [n] Ps 2:1–2

erty. 2 With the knowledge of his wife, he put aside for himself some of the proceeds; he brought only a part of them and laid them at the feet of the apostles.
3 But Peter said, "Ananias, why have you let Satan so fill your heart that you would
lie to the Holy Spirit and put aside for yourself some of the proceeds of that field?
4 Was it not yours so long as it remained unsold? Even when you had sold it, was
it not still at your disposal? What gave you the idea of such a thing? You have
lied not to human beings, but to God." 5 When Ananias heard these words, he
dropped dead. Great fear came upon all those who heard about it. 6 Some of the
young men came forward, wrapped him up, and carried him out for burial.
7 About three hours later Ananias's wife came in, unaware of what had happened.
8 Peter addressed her, "Tell me, did you sell that piece of property for such and
such an amount?" She answered, "Yes, for that amount." 9 Then Peter said to her,
"What made you agree to put the Lord's Spirit to the test? Listen, the footsteps
of those who have buried your husband are at the door, and they will carry you
out too." 10 She collapsed at once at his feet and died. The young men who had
just returned, finding her dead, carried her out too and buried her next to her
husband. 11 And great fear came upon the whole church and on all those who
heard about these things.

12 Many signs and wonders were wrought among the people at the hands of
the apostles. All of them used to meet with one accord in Solomon's Colonnade.
13 No one else dared to join them, yet the people held them in high esteem.
14 More than ever, believers in the Lord were added to them, great numbers of
men and women. 15 As a result, they would even carry the sick out into the streets
and lay them on cots and mats so that, when Peter would pass by, his shadow
might fall at least on one or another of them. 16 Then too a great number of
people from towns around Jerusalem would gather, bringing the sick and those
troubled by unclean spirits, who were all cured.

17 Then the high priest reacted, he and his colleagues, the party of the Sadducees; they were filled with jealousy 18 and arrested the apostles and put them in
the public jail. 19 But during the night the angel of the Lord opened the gates of
the prison, led them out, and said, 20 "Go, take your place in the Temple, and
tell the people all about this Life." 21 Hearing this, they entered the Temple about
dawn and continued their teaching. When the high priest and his colleagues
arrived, they convened the Sanhedrin, the full senate of the Israelites, and sent
to the prison to have the apostles brought in. 22 When the officers arrived, they
did not find them in the prison; they returned and reported, 23 "We found the
prison securely locked, with sentries posted at the gates, but when we opened
them, we found no one inside." 24 Now when the captain of the Temple guard
and the chief priests heard this report, they could make nothing of it, or what it
might become. 25 Then someone arrived and reported, "Look, the men whom
you put in prison are standing in the Temple, even teaching the people."
26 Whereupon the captain went off with his officers and brought them in, but
without using force, for they feared the people, that they might be stoned.
27 When they had brought them in and made them stand before the Sanhedrin,
the high priest interrogated them, saying, 28 "We ordered you, [did we not], not

to teach in that name? Yet you have filled Jerusalem with your teaching, and you
seek to bring that man's blood upon us." 29 But Peter and the apostles said in reply,
"One must obey God rather than human beings! 30 The God of our ancestors has
raised up Jesus, whom you had killed by hanging him on a tree. 31 It is he whom
God has exalted to his right hand as leader and savior, [to] grant Israel repentance
and forgiveness of sins. 32 We are witnesses of these things, and so is the Holy
Spirit that God has given to those who obey him." 33 When they heard this, they
were infuriated and wanted to do away with them. 34 But a certain Pharisee, Gamaliel by name, a teacher of the law esteemed by all the people, stood up in the
Sanhedrin and ordered these men out of court for a short time. 35 He said to
them, "Fellow Israelites, be careful about what you are going to do to these men.
36 Not long ago there appeared Theudas, trying to pass himself off as somebody
important, and about four hundred men joined him. But he was killed, and all
those who were duped by him were disbanded, and they came to nothing. 37 After
him, at the time of the census, there appeared Judas the Galilean, and he drew
away some of the people to follow him. But he too perished, and all those who
were duped by him were dispersed. 38 So in the present case I say to you, keep
your distance from these men and let them be. For if this scheme or this undertaking is of human design, it will destroy itself. 39 But if it is of God, you will not
be able to destroy them; you may even find yourselves fighting against God."
They were won over by him. 40 After calling in the apostles and having them
flogged, they ordered them not to speak again in the name of Jesus and let them
go. 41 These then left the presence of the Sanhedrin full of joy that they had been
judged worthy of ill-treatment for the sake of that name. 42 Day after day, both in
the Temple and in house after house, they never stopped teaching and preaching
Jesus as the Messiah.

6 1 In those days, as the disciples continued to grow more numerous, there was
a complaint of the Hellenists against the Hebrews that their widows were being
neglected in the daily distribution of food. 2 So the Twelve summoned the community of the disciples and explained, "It is not right for us to neglect the word
of God to wait on tables. 3 So look about among you, brothers, for seven men of
good reputation, filled with the Spirit and with wisdom, whom we may appoint
to this task, 4 whereas we shall continue to devote ourselves to prayer and the
ministry of the word." 5 The proposal proved acceptable to the whole community,
and they selected Stephen, a man full of faith and the Holy Spirit, Philip, Prochorus, Nicanor, Timon, Parmenas, and Nicolaus, a proselyte of Antioch.
6 These men they presented to the apostles, who prayed and laid their hands on
them. 7 The word of God continued to spread, and the number of disciples in
Jerusalem greatly increased; a large number of the priests became obedient to
the faith.

8 Now Stephen, full of grace and power, was performing great wonders and
signs among the people. 9 Some members of the Synagogue of Freedmen, as it
was called, of Cyrenians and Alexandrians, and of people from Cilicia and Asia,
came forward to debate with Stephen, 10 but they were no match for the wisdom

and spirit with which he spoke. [11]So they put up some men to claim, "We have heard him uttering blasphemous words against Moses and against God." [12]They stirred up the people, the elders, and the scribes, confronted him, seized him, and led him off to the Sanhedrin. [13]They also brought in false witnesses who maintained, "This man never stops saying things against [this] sacred place and the law. [14]We have heard him claim that this Jesus the Nazorean will destroy this place and change the customs that Moses handed down to us." [15]All those who sat in the Sanhedrin kept staring at him, and they saw that his face was like that of an angel. 7 [1]Then the high priest asked, "Is this so?"

[2]Stephen replied, "Brothers and fathers, listen to me. The God of glory appeared to our father Abraham when he was still in Mesopotamia and before he settled in Haran. [3]*He said to him, 'Leave your country and your relatives and go to the land that I shall show you.'*[o] [4]So he left the land of the Chaldeans and settled in Haran. After his father died, (God) made him move from there to this land where you now dwell. [5]But he did not give him any of it as his inheritance, not even a foot of ground, yet (God) promised *to give it to him and his descendants after him as a possession,*[p] to him who was childless! [6]These were the words God used: *'His descendants will be aliens in a foreign land, where they will be enslaved and oppressed for four hundred years.* [7]*But I will pass judgment on that nation to which they will be enslaved,*[q] God said, *and after that they shall leave it and shall worship me in this* place.'[r] [8]Then (God) gave him the covenant of circumcision. So it was that he became the father of Isaac, whom he circumcised on the eighth day, as Isaac became the father of Jacob, and Jacob the father of the twelve patriarchs.

[9]Out of jealousy, the patriarchs sold Joseph into (slavery in) Egypt. Yet God was with him [10]and rescued him from all his hardships. He granted him favor and wisdom in the presence of Pharaoh, the king of Egypt, who made him governor over Egypt and [over] all his palace. [11]But when famine and great hardship came upon all Egypt and Canaan, our ancestors could find no sustenance. [12]Hearing that there was grain in Egypt, Jacob sent our ancestors there for the first time. [13]The second time, Joseph made himself known to his brothers, and Joseph's family became known to the Pharaoh. [14]Then Joseph sent and summoned his father Jacob and the whole clan, seventy-five persons in all. [15]Jacob went down to Egypt and died there, as our ancestors did too. [16]But they were brought back to Shechem and laid in the tomb, which Abraham had bought for a sum of money from the sons of Hamor in Shechem.

[17]When the time drew near for the fulfillment of the promise that God had made to Abraham, our people in Egypt spread and grew more numerous, [18]until *a different king came to power [in Egypt], who knew nothing of Joseph.*[s] [19]This one dealt treacherously with our people and forced [our] ancestors to expose their

[o] Gen 12:1
[p] Gen 17:8; 48:4
[q] Gen 15:13–14
[r] Exod 3:12
[s] Exod 1:8

infants so that they might not survive. [20]In this crisis Moses was born, a child handsome in God's sight. For the first three months he was nursed in his father's house, [21]but when he was exposed, Pharaoh's daughter adopted him and reared him as her own son. [22]Moses was educated [in] all the wisdom of the Egyptians and became mighty in words and deeds. [23]When he was forty years old, the thought came to him to visit his fellow Israelites. [24]Seeing one of them being mistreated, he went to his aid and avenged the oppressed man by striking down the Egyptian. [25]He assumed that [his] kinsfolk would understand that God was offering them deliverance through him, but they did not understand. [26]The next day he appeared to some of them who were fighting and tried to reconcile them peacefully, saying, 'Men, you are brothers! Why do you do wrong to one another?' [27]But the man who was wronging his neighbor thrust Moses aside with the jibe, *'Who has appointed you ruler and judge over us?* [28]*You do not plan to kill me as you killed the Egyptian yesterday, do you?'*[t] [29]At that remark Moses fled and settled as an alien in the land of Midian, where he became the father of two sons. [30]When forty years had passed, *an angel appeared to him in the flame of a burning bush in the desert near Mount* Sinai.[u] [31]When Moses saw it, he was amazed at the sight; as he drew near to look better (at it), the voice of the Lord was heard. [32]*'I am the God of your ancestors, the God of Abraham, Isaac, and Jacob.'*[v] Moses trembled and dared to look no more. [33]*But the Lord said to him, 'Remove the sandals from your feet, for the place where you are standing is holy ground.*[w] [34]*I have seen indeed the ill-treatment of my people in Egypt and I have heard their cry, and I have come down to rescue them.*[x] *Now come, I shall send you to Egypt.'*[y] [35]That Moses, whom they had disowned with the words, *'Who has appointed you ruler and judge?'*,[z] God then sent as [both] ruler and deliverer through the angel that appeared to him in the bush. [36]That one led them forth, performing wonders and signs in the land of Egypt, at the Red Sea, and for forty years in the desert. [37]That is the Moses who said to the Israelites, 'A *prophet like me God will raise up for you from among your kinsfolk.'*[a] [38]That is the one who was in the congregation in the desert, was with our ancestors, and with the angel who spoke to him on Mount Sinai, and who received living oracles to give to us. [39]Our ancestors were unwilling to obey him, thrust him aside, and hankered in their hearts after Egypt. [40]They said to Aaron, *'Make us gods that will go before us. As for that fellow Moses, who brought us out of the land of Egypt, we do not know what has happened to him.'*[b] [41]So they made a calf in those days, offered sacrifice to that idol, and celebrated over a product of their own hands. [42]But God turned away and handed them over to the worship of the hosts of heaven, as it stands written in the book of the prophets,

---

[t]Exod 2:14
[u]Exod 3:2
[v]Exod 3:6
[w]Exod 3:5
[x]Exod 3:7–8
[y]Exod 3:10
[z]Exod 2:14
[a]Deut 18:15
[b]Exod 32:1, 23

'Did you bring me sacrifices and offerings
for forty years in the desert, O house of Israel?
43 *No, you took along the tent of Moloch*
and the star of [*your*] *god Rephan,*
images that you made to worship.
So I shall exile you beyond Babylon.'[c]

44 In the desert our ancestors had the tent of testimony, just as the One who had
spoken to Moses had ordered him to make it, after the model that he had seen.
45 Our ancestors who inherited it brought it in with Joshua, when they took the
land from the nations that God had driven out before our ancestors. (So it was)
until the time of David, 46 who found favor with God and begged that he might
provide a habitation for the house of Jacob. 47 But it was Solomon who built the
house for it. 48 Yet the Most High dwells not in buildings made by human hands,
as the prophet says,

49 *'The heavens are my throne,*
the earth is my footstool.
What kind of a house will you build for me? asks the Lord.
Or what is to be my resting-place?
50 *Did not my hand make all these things?'*[d]

51 You stiff-necked people, uncircumcised in hearts and ears, you are always resisting the Holy Spirit; as your ancestors did, so do you. 52 Which of the prophets
did your ancestors not persecute? Why, they even put to death those who foretold
the coming of the Upright One, of whom you have now become the betrayers
and murderers — 53 you who received the law as transmitted by angels, but have
not observed it."

54 As they listened to this, they were infuriated and were grinding their teeth
at him. 55 But Stephen, filled with the Holy Spirit, stared at the heavens and
saw the glory of God and Jesus standing at God's right hand. 56 He exclaimed, "I
see the heavens open and the Son of Man standing at God's right hand."
57 But they shouted aloud, covered their ears, and together they rushed at him;
58 they dragged him out of the city and began to throw stones. Witnesses
piled their cloaks at the feet of a young man named Saul. 59 They kept stoning
Stephen, as he called out and prayed, "Lord Jesus, receive my spirit." 60 Falling
to his knees, he shouted aloud, "Lord, do not hold this sin against them." Having
said this, he passed away. 8 1 And Saul was there, giving approval to his execution.

On that day a great persecution broke out against the church in Jerusalem,
and all except the apostles were scattered throughout the countryside of Judea

---

[c] Amos 5:25–27

[d] Isa 66:1–2

and Samaria. 2 Devout men buried Stephen and mourned him greatly. 3 But Saul
continued to ravage the church, entering house after house and dragging out
both men and women, whom he handed over for imprisonment. 4 Now those
who had been scattered went about preaching the word.

5 Philip went down to [the] town of Samaria and preached about the Messiah
to the people. 6 With one accord, crowds paid attention to what was said by
Philip, as they listened and saw the signs that he performed. 7 Unclean spirits that
possessed many people came out, shrieking loudly; many others, paralyzed or
crippled, were cured. 8 So there was much joy in that town. 9 Now a man named
Simon had been practicing magic in the town and fascinated the people of Samaria, 10 pretending to be someone great. All of them, from the least to the greatest,
paid attention to him, saying, "This man is the 'Power of God' that is called
great." 11 They paid attention to him because he had fascinated them with his
magic for quite some time. 12 But when they began to believe Philip who
preached about the kingdom of God and the name of Jesus Christ, they were
baptized, men and women alike. 13 Simon too came to believe, was baptized,
and became a devoted follower of Philip. When he saw signs and great wonders
occurring, he too was fascinated. 14 When the apostles in Jerusalem heard that
Samaria had accepted the word of God, they sent Peter and John to the people
there. 15 These went down and prayed for them that they might receive the Holy
Spirit. 16 For it had not yet come upon any of them; they had only been baptized
in the name of the Lord Jesus. 17 Then Peter and John laid their hands on them,
and they received the Holy Spirit. 18 Seeing that the Spirit was conferred through
the laying on of the apostles' hands, Simon offered them money, 19 saying, "Give
me that power too, so that anyone on whom I lay my hands will receive the Holy
Spirit." 20 But Peter said to him, "May your money perish with you! You think
that you can buy God's gift with money. 21 You can have no part or share in this
matter, for your heart is not right with God. 22 Repent of that wickedness of yours,
and beg the Lord that you may possibly be pardoned for thinking as you have.
23 For you are, I see, filled with bitterness and caught in the shackles of iniquity."
24 Simon said in reply, "Pray to the Lord for me, that nothing you have said may
happen to me." 25 So when they had borne witness and proclaimed the word of
the Lord, they gradually made their way back to Jerusalem, preaching in many
of the villages of Samaria.

26 Now the angel of the Lord said to Philip, "Get up and head south on the
road that goes down from Jerusalem to Gaza, the desert route." 27 So he got up
and set out. Now there was an Ethiopian eunuch, a court official in charge of all
the treasury of Candace (that is, the queen) of the Ethiopians. He had come to
Jerusalem to worship 28 and was returning home. Seated in his carriage, he was
reading the prophet Isaiah. 29 The Spirit said to Philip, "Run and catch up with
that carriage." 30 Philip ran up and heard the man reading Isaiah the prophet. He
said to him, "Do you really understand what you are reading?" 31 He replied,
"How should I be able, unless someone guides me?" So he invited Philip to get
in and sit with him. 32 Now this was the passage of Scripture that he was reading:

He was led like a sheep to the slaughter,
and as a lamb before its shearer is silent,
so he opened not his mouth.
[33]*In [his] humiliation justice was denied him.*
Who will ever speak of his posterity?
For his life is taken away from this earth.[e]

[34]Then the eunuch said to Philip, "Please, sir, about whom does the prophet say this? About himself or about someone else?" [35]Then Philip spoke up, and beginning with that very passage of Scripture, he preached about Jesus to him. [36]As they moved along the road, they came to some water, and the eunuch asked, "Look, there is some water. What prevents me from being baptized?"[[37]] [38]He ordered the carriage to stop, and both of them, Philip and the eunuch, went down into the water, and he baptized him. [39]When they came up out of the water, the Spirit of the Lord snatched Philip away, and the eunuch saw him no more, but continued on his way quite happy. [40]Philip, however, found himself at Azotus and went about preaching in all the towns until he reached Caesarea.

9 [1]Now Saul, still breathing murderous threats against the Lord's disciples, went to the high priest [2]and asked him for letters to the synagogues in Damascus, that, if he should find any men or women belonging to the Way, he might bring them back to Jerusalem as prisoners. [3]As he traveled along, he happened to draw near to Damascus, and a light from the heavens suddenly flashed about him. [4]He fell to the ground and heard a voice saying to him, "Saul, Saul, why are you persecuting me?" [5]He asked, "Who are you, sir?" The reply was, "I am Jesus, whom you are persecuting. [6]Get up and go into the city, and you will be told what you must do." [7]The men traveling with him stood there speechless; they heard the voice but saw no one. [8]Saul got up from the ground, and though he opened his eyes, he could see nothing. Leading him by the hand, they brought him into Damascus. [9]For three days he could not see, and he neither ate nor drank. [10]There was a certain disciple in Damascus, Ananias by name, and the Lord said to him in a vision, "Ananias." "Yes, Lord," he answered. [11]The Lord continued, "Go at once to the street called Straight and look for a man of Tarsus named Saul in the house of Judas. He is there praying, [12]and [in a vision] he has seen a man named Ananias entering and laying [his] hands on him that he might recover his sight." [13]But Ananias protested, "Lord, I have heard from many people about this man and how much harm he has done to your dedicated people in Jerusalem. [14]He is here now with authority from the chief priests to arrest all those who call upon your name." [15]But the Lord said to him, "Go! This man is a chosen instrument of mine to carry my name before Gentiles and kings, and the children of Israel. [16]I myself shall show him how much he will have to endure for the sake of my name." [17]So Ananias went and entered the house. He

[e]Isa 53:7–8

laid his hands on him, saying, "Saul, my brother, the Lord Jesus, who appeared
to you on the road as you were coming here, has sent me that you might recover
your sight and be filled with the Holy Spirit." [18]Immediately, something like
scales fell from his eyes, and he recovered his sight. He got up and was baptized;
[19]when he had taken some food, he regained his strength.

Saul stayed some days with the disciples in Damascus [20]and at once began to
preach about Jesus in the synagogues, that he was the Son of God. [21]All who
heard him were bewildered and kept saying, "Is not this the one who caused such
havoc in Jerusalem among those who invoke this name? Did he not come here
purposely to bring such people back as prisoners to the chief priests?" [22]Yet Saul
grew steadily more powerful and kept confounding [the] Jews who dwelled in
Damascus with proofs that Jesus was the Messiah. [23]After considerable time had
passed, the Jews began to conspire to kill Saul, [24]but their plot became known to
him. Day and night they were keeping close watch even at the city gates in order
to kill him. [25]But some of his disciples took him one night and let him down
through an opening in the wall, lowering him in a hamper.

[26]When Saul arrived in Jerusalem, he tried to associate with the disciples, but
they were all afraid of him, not believing that he was a disciple. [27]Finally Barnabas took charge of him, brought him to the apostles, and explained to them how
on the way he had seen the Lord, how the Lord had spoken to him, and how in
Damascus he had been preaching fearlessly in the name of Jesus. [28]Saul stayed
on with them, freely moving about in and out of Jerusalem, preaching fearlessly
in the name of the Lord. [29]He also used to speak and debate with the Hellenists,
but they kept trying to kill him. [30]When the brothers learned of this, they took
him down to Caesarea and sent him off to Tarsus. [31]Meanwhile, the church was
at peace throughout all Judea, Galilee, and Samaria. It was gradually being built
up and advanced in the fear of the Lord. With the encouragement of the Holy
Spirit, it grew in numbers.

[32]Once Peter happened to be traveling about the country and came to God's
dedicated people living in Lydda. [33]There he found a man named Aeneas, bedridden for eight years because he was paralyzed. [34]Peter said to him, "Jesus Christ
heals you, Aeneas! Get up and make your bed." He got up at once. [35]All the
inhabitants of Lydda and Sharon who saw him were converted to the Lord.
[36]Now in Joppa there was a disciple named Tabitha (which translated means
Dorcas). She lived a life full of good deeds and almsgiving. [37]Just about that time
she happened to become sick and died; after washing her, they laid [her] out in
an upstairs room. [38]Since Lydda was near Joppa, the disciples, who had heard
that Peter was there, sent two men to him with the request, "Please come over to
us without delay." [39]Peter got up and went with them. On his arrival, they took
him upstairs to the room, where all the widows came up to him in tears and
showed him the tunics and robes that Dorcas had made, while she was still with
them. [40]Peter made them all go out of the room; then he knelt down and prayed.
Turning to her body, he said, "Tabitha, get up!" She opened her eyes, looked at
Peter, and sat up. [41]He gave her his hand and helped her to her feet. Then he
called in God's dedicated people and the widows and presented her to them

alive. 42 It became known all over Joppa, and many people began to believe in
the Lord. 43 Then Peter stayed on in Joppa for many days with Simon, a tanner.

10 1 There was in Caesarea a man named Cornelius, a centurion of the Cohort
called Italica, 2 a devout and God-fearing man, along with his whole household.
He used to give many alms to the (Jewish) people and pray to God constantly.
3 One afternoon about three o'clock he saw clearly in a vision an angel of God
come to him and say, "Cornelius." 4 He stared at him and said in fear, "What is
it, sir?" The angel said to him, "Your prayers and your alms have mounted before
God as a memorial offering. 5 Now send some men to Joppa and summon a certain Simon, who is called Peter. 6 He is staying with another Simon, a tanner,
whose house is by the sea." 7 When the angel who spoke to him had left, he called
two servants and a devout soldier from his staff, 8 recounted everything to them,
and sent them to Joppa.

9 The next day, while they were traveling along and drawing near to the town,
Peter went up to the roof terrace about noon to pray. 10 He happened to get hungry and wanted something to eat. While they were preparing some food, he fell
into a trance. 11 He saw the heavens open and an object resembling a big sheet
come down, being lowered to the ground by its four corners. 12 On it were all the
four-legged creatures and reptiles of the earth, and birds of the sky. 13 A voice said
to him, "Peter, get up! Slaughter these things and eat!" 14 But Peter said, "Not on
your life, sir, for I have never eaten anything common or unclean." 15 The voice
said to him again, a second time, "What God has made clean, you are not to call
common." 16 Three times this happened, and the object was suddenly snatched
up to the heavens.

17 While Peter was trying to make something out of the vision he had seen, the
men sent by Cornelius suddenly arrived at the gate, inquiring after the house of
Simon. 18 They called out, asking whether Simon, called Peter, was staying there.
19 As Peter was still pondering over the vision, the Spirit said [to him], "Look,
three men are here, looking for you. 20 Get up, go downstairs, and go along with
them without hesitation, because I have sent them." 21 Peter went down and said
to the men, "I am the one you are looking for. What is the reason for your coming?" 22 They answered, "The centurion Cornelius, an upright and God-fearing
man, well spoken of among all the Jewish people, was instructed by a holy angel
to summon you to his house and to listen to what you have to say." 23 So he invited
them in and treated them as guests.

The next day he got up and went off with them, and some of the brothers from
Joppa accompanied him. 24 The following day he arrived in Caesarea, where Cornelius was waiting for them; he had even called in his relatives and close friends.
25 As Peter was about to enter, Cornelius went to meet him, fell at his feet, and
paid him homage. 26 But Peter pulled him up and said, "Get up! After all, I too
am only a human being." 27 Peter went in, talking with him the while, and found
many people gathered there. 28 He said to them, "You are aware that it is unlawful
for a Jew to associate with or visit a Gentile, but God has shown me that no one
should call a human being common or unclean. 29 So in response to your sum-

mons, I have come without any objection. May I ask, then, why you summoned
me?" 30 Cornelius replied, "Four days ago, at this very hour, three o'clock in the
afternoon, I was praying at home, when a man robed in dazzling clothes suddenly stood before me. 31 He said, 'Cornelius, your prayer has been heard, and
your alms have been remembered before God. 32 Send someone to Joppa and
invite here Simon who is called Peter. He is staying at the house of Simon, a
tanner, by the sea.' 33 So I sent for you immediately, and you have been kind
enough to come. Now, then, we are all here in the presence of God to listen to
all the instructions that the Lord has given you." 34 Then Peter spoke up, "Now I
realize how true it is that God shows no partiality. 35 Rather, in every nation whoever reverences him and acts uprightly is acceptable to him. 36 You know the
word [that] he sent to the children of Israel, as he proclaimed peace through
Jesus Christ, who is Lord of all; 37 you know what has happened throughout Judea, starting from Galilee after the baptism that John preached— 38 how God
anointed Jesus of Nazareth with a Holy Spirit and with power; how he went about
doing good and healing all who were in the power of the devil, because God was
with him. 39 We are witnesses of all that he did in the country of the Jews and [in]
Jerusalem. They put him to death, hanging him on a tree. 40 This man God raised
up [on] the third day and made manifest, 41 not to all the people, but to us, witnesses chosen by God beforehand, who ate and drank with him after he rose
from the dead. 42 He ordered us to preach to the people and to bear witness that
he is the one appointed by God to be judge of the living and the dead. 43 To
him all the prophets bear witness, that everyone who believes in him receives
forgiveness of sins through his name." 44 While Peter was still saying these things,
the Holy Spirit came down upon all who were listening to the word, 45 and the
circumcised believers, who had come along with Peter, were bewildered because
the gift of the Holy Spirit had been poured out on Gentiles too. 46 For they heard
them speaking in tongues and extolling God. Then Peter spoke up, 47 "Can anyone withhold from these people, who have received the Holy Spirit just as we
have, the water with which they are to be baptized?" 48 He ordered them to be
baptized in the name of Jesus Christ. Then they invited him to stay for some
days.

11 1 Now the apostles and brothers who were in Judea heard that Gentiles too
had welcomed the word of God. 2 So when Peter came up to Jerusalem, circumcised believers confronted him, 3 saying, "You entered the house of uncircumcised men and ate with them." 4 Peter explained it to them step by step from the
beginning. 5 "I was at prayer in the town of Joppa, when in a trance I had a vision.
I saw an object resembling a big sheet come down, being lowered from the heavens by its four corners, and it moved up to me. 6 As I stared at it, I could see and
make out four-legged creatures of the earth, wild beasts and reptiles, and birds of
the sky. 7 I also heard a voice say to me, 'Get up, Peter! Slaughter and eat.' 8 But I
said, 'Not on your life, sir, for nothing common or unclean has ever entered my
mouth!' 9 A second time the voice from the heavens spoke out, 'What God has
made clean, you are not to call common.' 10 Three times this happened, and

everything was drawn up again to the heavens. [11]Just then three men arrived at
the house where we were, sent to me from Caesarea. [12]The Spirit told me to go
with them without hesitation. These six brothers also accompanied me, and we
entered that man's house. [13]He informed us how he had seen [the] angel standing in his house and saying, 'Send someone to Joppa and summon Simon, who
is called Peter. [14]He will tell you things by which you and all your household will
be saved.' [15]As I began to address them, the Holy Spirit came down upon them,
just as it did on us at the beginning. [16]Then I remembered the word of the Lord,
how he said, 'John baptized with water, but you will be baptized with a Holy
Spirit.' [17]So if God gave them the same gift he gave us when we came to believe
in the Lord Jesus Christ, who was I to be able to stop God?" [18]When they heard
this, they stopped objecting; instead they began to honor God, saying, "So God
has granted life-giving repentance even to Gentiles."

[19]Now those who had been scattered by the hardship that arose because of
Stephen traveled as far as Phoenicia, Cyprus, and Antioch, addressing the word
to none but Jews alone. [20]Among them, however, were some Cypriots and Cyrenians who came to Antioch and began to address the Greeks as well, preaching
to them about the Lord Jesus. [21]The hand of the Lord was with them, and a great
number believed and turned to the Lord. [22]News about this came to the ears of
the church in Jerusalem, and they sent Barnabas [to go] to Antioch. [23]When, on
his arrival, he saw the grace of God, he rejoiced and encouraged all of them to
remain steadfast in their dedication to the Lord. [24]He was a good man, full of the
Holy Spirit and of faith, and a large number of people was added to the Lord.
[25]Then Barnabas went off to Tarsus to look for Saul. [26]When he found him, he
brought him back to Antioch, and for a whole year they met with the church and
instructed a large number of people. It was in Antioch that the disciples were first
called Christians.

[27]In those days some prophets came down from Jerusalem to Antioch, [28]and
one of them named Agabus got up and through the Spirit predicted that there
was going to be a severe famine all over the world. In fact, it happened under
Claudius. [29]So the disciples, each according to one's ability, determined to send
something for the support of the brothers living in Judea. [30]This they did, sending
it to the presbyters in the care of Barnabas and Saul.

12 [1]About the same time King Herod arrested some members of the church in
order to mistreat them. [2]He had James, the brother of John, put to the sword,
[3]and when he saw that pleased the Jews, he proceeded to arrest Peter too. That
was during [the] Feast of Unleavened Bread. [4]He had him seized and put in
prison with four squads of four soldiers to guard him. Herod intended to bring
him before the people after Passover. [5]So Peter was kept in prison, while the
church prayed fervently to God on his behalf. [6]During the very night before
Herod was going to bring him forth, Peter was sleeping between two soldiers,
secured by double chains. Outside the door sentries were also guarding the
prison. [7]Suddenly the angel of the Lord stood by him, and the cell glowed with
light. He tapped Peter on the side and woke him up, saying, "Hurry, get up!" and

the chains dropped from his wrists. [8]Then the angel said to him, "Fasten your
belt and put on your sandals." This he did, and he said to him again, "Put on
your cloak and follow me." [9]He went out following the angel, not realizing what
was really happening with the angel's help; he thought he was seeing a vision.
[10]Having passed the first sentinel and then the second, they came to the iron gate
leading to the city, which opened for them of itself. They went out and moved
along a narrow alley, and suddenly the angel left him. [11]Peter then came to himself and said, "Now I know for sure that [the] Lord has sent his angel and rescued
me from Herod's clutches and from all that the Jewish people had been expecting." [12]When he realized this, he went to the house of Mary, the mother of
John, who is called Mark, where many people were gathered in prayer. [13]When
he knocked at the door of the gateway, a maid named Rhoda came to answer it.
[14]She recognized Peter's voice and was so overjoyed that she did not stop to open
the gate but ran back and reported that Peter was standing at the gate. [15]They
said to her, "You're crazy!" But she insisted that it was so, and they kept saying,
"It must be his angel." [16]Yet Peter continued to knock. When they finally opened
the gate and saw him, they were bewildered. [17]He motioned to them to be quiet
and explained [to them] how the Lord had brought him out of prison. Then he
said, "Report this to James and the brothers." Then he departed and went off to
another place. [18]When it was day, no little confusion ensued among the soldiers
over what had become of Peter. [19]Herod, after instituting a search for him and
not finding him, had the sentries tried and ordered their execution. Then he
went down from Judea to Caesarea and spent some time there. [20]Now Herod was
infuriated with the people of Tyre and Sidon, but they came to him in a body,
having won over Blastus, the royal chamberlain, and sued for peace, because
their country was usually supplied with food from the king's territory. [21]On an
appointed day, when Herod arrayed in his royal robes took his seat on the rostrum
and publicly addressed them, [22]the assembled crowd shouted back, "This is the
voice of a god, not of a human being!" [23]At once the angel of the Lord struck
him down, because he did not ascribe the honor to God. Eaten with worms, he
breathed his last.

[24]But the word of God continued to spread and increase. [25]Barnabas and Saul
returned, when their ministry to Jerusalem was complete, bringing with them
John, who was called Mark.

13 [1]In the church at Antioch there were prophets and teachers: Barnabas, Simeon called Niger, Lucius of Cyrene, Manaen, who had been raised with Herod
the tetrarch, and Saul. [2]Once while they were holding the Lord's service and
fasting, the Holy Spirit spoke to them, "Set apart for me Barnabas and Saul, for
the work to which I have called them." [3]Then, having completed their fasting
and prayer, they laid hands upon them and sent them off.

[4]Sent forth thus by the Holy Spirit, these two went down to Seleucia and set
sail from there for Cyprus. [5]On their arrival in Salamis, they proclaimed the word
of God in the synagogues of the Jews. They also had John along as an assistant.
[6]When they had traveled through the whole island, even as far as Paphos, they

met a certain magician, a Jew whose name was Bar-Jesus, who posed as a prophet. 7 He was in the service of the proconsul Sergius Paulus, a man of intelligence, who had summoned Barnabas and Saul and was anxious to hear the word of God. 8 But Elymas the magician (for that is what his name means) opposed them, seeking to turn the proconsul away from the faith. 9 However, Saul, also known as Paul, filled with the Holy Spirit, stared at him and said, 10 "You shyster and thoroughgoing fraud, son of the devil, and enemy of all that is right, will you never stop making crooked the straight ways of [the] Lord? 11 Look, even now the Lord's hand is upon you! You will be blind, unable to see even the sunlight for a time!" At once a dark mist fell upon him, and he went groping about for someone to lead him by the hand. 12 When the proconsul saw what had happened, he became a believer, astonished at the teaching of the Lord.

13 From Paphos Paul and his companions put out to sea and came to Perga in Pamphylia, but John left them and returned to Jerusalem. 14 They continued their journey from Perga and came to Pisidian Antioch. On the sabbath they entered the synagogue and sat down. 15 After the reading of the law and the prophets, the synagogue leaders sent word to them, "Brothers, if you have a word of exhortation to address to the people, please speak up." 16 So Paul got up and with a gesture began to speak.

"Fellow Israelites and you who are Godfearers, listen to me! 17 The God of this people of Israel once chose our ancestors and made the people great during its sojourn in the land of Egypt. With uplifted arm he led them forth from it. 18 For some forty years he put up with them in the desert. 19 Then he overthrew seven nations in the land of Canaan and gave them that land as a heritage 20 for about four hundred and fifty years. Later on he set up judges to rule until Samuel [the] prophet. 21 Then, when they asked for a king, God gave them Saul, son of Kish, a man of the tribe of Benjamin, for forty years. 22 Then God removed him and raised up David as their king, about whom he testified, '*I have found David*[f] son of Jesse *a man after my own heart;*[g] he will do all that I desire.' 23 From this man's descendants God has brought forth for Israel a Savior, Jesus, according to his promise. 24 John heralded his coming, preaching a baptism of repentance to all the people of Israel. 25 As John was finishing his course, he used to say, 'What do you suppose me to be? That I am not! No, someone is coming after me, the sandal of whose feet I am not worthy to unfasten.'

26 "Brothers, children of the family of Abraham, and you who are Godfearers, to us the message of this salvation has been sent. 27 Those who live in Jerusalem and their leaders failed to recognize Jesus, and, in condemning him, they have fulfilled the oracles of the prophets that are read sabbath after sabbath. 28 Though they found no charge against him worthy of death, they demanded of Pilate that he be put to death. 29 When they thus brought about all that was written about him, they took him down from the tree and laid him in a tomb. 30 But God raised him from the dead, 31 and for many days thereafter he appeared to those who had come up with him from Galilee to Jerusalem. They are [now] his witnesses be-

[f] Ps 89:21 [g] 1 Sam 13:14

fore the people. [32]We too are proclaiming to you that the promise made to our ancestors has been realized: [33]God has fulfilled this promise for us, [their] children, by raising up Jesus, even as it stands written in the second psalm,

You are my son,
this day I have begotten you.[h]

[34]As proof that he raised him from the dead, who is never again to return to decay, he thus declared, 'I will give *you the covenant benefits assured to David.*'[i]
[35]That is why he also says in another place, *'You will not allow your holy one to see decay.'*[j] [36]For David indeed, after he had served God's purpose in his own generation, fell asleep and was buried with his ancestors, and did see decay. [37]But the one whom God raised up has not seen decay. [38]So let it be known to you, Brothers, that through him forgiveness of sin is being proclaimed to you, [39][and] through him everyone who believes is justified from everything from which you could not be justified by the law of Moses. [40]Beware, then, lest what was said in the prophets becomes true of you:

[41]*'Look, you scoffers,*
be amazed, and then disappear!
For I am doing a deed in your days,
a deed *which you will not believe, even if someone tells you about it.'"*[k]

[42]As they were leaving, the people begged them to speak further on this topic again on the following sabbath. [43]After the meeting of the synagogue had finally broken up, many Jews and devout converts to Judaism followed Paul and Barnabas, who continued to speak to them and urge them to hold fast to the grace of God. [44]The next sabbath almost the whole town gathered to hear the word of the Lord. [45]When the Jews saw the crowds, they became very jealous and with violent abuse countered what was said by Paul. [46]Both Paul and Barnabas, however, spoke out fearlessly, "To you, first of all, the word of God had to be proclaimed. Since you reject it and thus judge yourselves unworthy of eternal life, we now turn to the Gentiles. [47]For so the Lord has instructed us,

'I have made you a light of the Gentiles,
that you may be a means of salvation to the end of the earth.'"[l]

[48]The Gentiles who heard this were delighted and were continually honoring the word of the Lord. All who were destined for eternal life became believers. [49]The word of the Lord continued to be carried through that whole area. [50]The

[h] Ps 2:7
[i] Isa 55:3
[j] Ps 16:10
[k] Hab 1:5
[l] Isa 49:6

Jews, however, stirred up well-to-do women worshipers and the leading men of the town and started a persecution against Paul and Barnabas, whom they expelled from their district. 51 So they shook its dust from their feet in protest against them and went on to Iconium. 52 The disciples were filled with joy and the Holy Spirit.

14 1 In Iconium Paul and Barnabas happened to enter together into the synagogue of the Jews; they spoke in such wise that a good number of Jews and Greeks became believers. 2 But Jews who remained unbelieving stirred up the Gentiles and poisoned their minds against the brothers. 3 So they stayed there for a considerable time, speaking out fearlessly about the Lord, who confirmed the word about his grace, by causing signs and wonders to be performed by them. 4 Most of the townspeople were divided: some siding with the Jews, others with the apostles. 5 But when an attempt was made by Gentiles and Jews, together with their leaders, to mistreat and even stone them, 6 Paul and Barnabas became aware of it and fled to the Lycaonian towns of Lystra and Derbe and the surrounding countryside. 7 There they continued to preach.

8 In Lystra there sat a cripple, lame from birth, who had never walked. 9 He listened to Paul as he was talking. When Paul looked intently at him and saw that he had the faith to be saved, 10 he said to him in a loud voice, "Stand up!" The man jumped up and started to walk around. 11 When the crowds saw what Paul had done, they cried out in Lycaonian, "Gods have come down to us in human form." 12 They called Barnabas Zeus, and Paul Hermes because he was the chief speaker. 13 The priest of the temple of Zeus, which stood just outside the town, brought oxen and garlands to the gates and, accompanied by the crowds, intended to offer sacrifice. 14 When the apostles Barnabas and Paul heard of this, they tore their garments and rushed out into the crowd, shouting, 15 "Friends, why do you do this? We are human beings like you, trying to preach to you to turn from such folly to the living God, who made the heavens, the earth, the sea, and all that is in them. 16 In bygone generations he allowed all nations to go their own way; 17 yet, in bestowing his benefits, he did not leave himself without a trace, for he has sent you rains from the heavens and seasons of fruitfulness; he has filled you with food and your hearts with gladness." 18 Even with such words they hardly kept the crowds from sacrificing to them. 19 Then some Jews from Antioch and Iconium came there and won over the crowds. They stoned Paul and dragged him out of the town, leaving him there for dead. 20 But his disciples formed a circle about him, and soon he got up and went back into the town. The next day he left with Barnabas for Derbe.

21 Having evangelized that town and made many disciples, they retraced their steps to Lystra, Iconium, and Antioch. 22 They strengthened the spirits of the disciples, encouraging them to remain steadfast in the faith, because "we must undergo many hardships to enter the kingdom of God." 23 In each church they installed presbyters and with prayer and fasting commended them to the Lord, in whom they had put their faith. 24 They traveled through Pisidia and came to

Pamphylia; 25 after preaching the word in Perga, they came down to Attalia. 26 From there they sailed back to Antioch, where they had first been commended to the grace of God for the task that they had now completed. 27 On their arrival, they called together the church and related all that God had accomplished with them, and how he had opened the door of faith to the Gentiles. 28 They then spent no little time there with the disciples.

15 1 Some people came down from Judea and were teaching the brothers, "Unless you have been circumcised according to Mosaic practice, you cannot be saved." 2 Because this created dissension and no small controversy between them and Paul and Barnabas, it was decided that Paul, Barnabas, and some others of their number should go up to Jerusalem to see the apostles and the presbyters about this controversial matter.

3 Those sent off by the church traveled through Phoenicia and Samaria, telling everyone about the conversion of the Gentiles, 4 and they caused great joy among all the brothers. On their arrival in Jerusalem, they were welcomed by that church, and by the apostles and presbyters, to whom they related all that God had accomplished with them. 5 Some from the party of the Pharisees, however, who had become believers, stood up and demanded, "One must circumcise them and order them to observe the law of Moses." 6 So the apostles and presbyters gathered together to look into this matter. 7 After much controversy, Peter took the floor and said to them, "Brothers, you know that some time ago God chose me from your number to be the one from whose lips the Gentiles would hear the word of the gospel and come to believe in it. 8 God who reads the heart has given testimony, granting to them the Holy Spirit, just as to us. 9 He has made no distinction between us and them, but has purified their hearts too by faith. 10 Why then should you now put God to the test, by loading on the shoulders of these disciples a yoke that neither we nor our ancestors have been able to bear? 11 Rather, through the grace of the Lord Jesus we believe that we are saved, just as they do." 12 At that the whole assembly grew silent. Then they listened to Barnabas and Paul recounting how many signs and wonders God had performed among the Gentiles through them.

13 After they stopped talking, James spoke up, "Brothers, listen to me. 14 Simeon has recounted how God first concerned himself with acquiring from among the Gentiles a people to bear his name. 15 With this the words of the prophets agree, as it stands written:

16 *I will return hereafter*
and rebuild the fallen hut of David;
from its ruins will I rebuild it
and set it up again,
17 *that the rest of humanity may seek out the Lord*
even all the nations among whom my name is invoked.

Thus says the Lord who does these things[m] —
[18] that have been known from of old.

[19] So my judgment is that we ought to stop causing trouble for Gentiles who are turning to God. [20] We should merely write, telling them to abstain from food contaminated by idols, from illicit marital unions, from meat of strangled animals, and from eating blood. [21] For in every town, for generations now, Moses has had preachers, and he has been read aloud in the synagogues every sabbath."

[22] Then it was resolved by the apostles and presbyters, in agreement with the whole church, to choose representatives from their number and send them to Antioch along with Paul and Barnabas: Judas, called Barsabbas, and Silas, leading men among the brothers. [23] They were to deliver this letter: "The apostles and presbyters, your brothers, to the brothers of Gentile origin in Antioch, Syria, and Cilicia: Greetings! [24] Since we have heard that some of our number, who [went out] without any instruction from us, have upset you with their talk and disturbed your peace of mind, [25] it has been resolved by us with one accord to choose representatives and send them to you along with our dear friends Barnabas and Paul, [26] who have dedicated their lives to the name of our Lord Jesus Christ. [27] We send you, therefore, Judas and Silas, who will also convey this message by word of mouth: [28] 'It is the decision of the Holy Spirit, and ours too, not to lay on you any burden beyond what is strictly necessary: [29] to abstain from meat sacrificed to idols, from blood, from meats of strangled animals, and from illicit marital unions.' You will do well to avoid these things. Farewell."

[30] The representatives were sent off and traveled down to Antioch, where they called a meeting of the community to deliver the letter. [31] When it was read, there was great delight at the encouragement it gave. [32] Judas and Silas, who themselves were prophets, encouraged the brothers and strengthened them with many a discourse. [33] After passing some time there, they were sent off again with a blessing of peace from the brothers to those who had sent them. [34] [35] But Paul and Barnabas spent their time in Antioch teaching and proclaiming the word of the Lord, along with many others.

[36] Some time later, Paul said to Barnabas, "Let us go back and see how the brothers are getting on in each of the towns where we proclaimed the word of the Lord." [37] Barnabas wanted to take John, who was called Mark, along with them, [38] but Paul kept insisting that, since he had deserted them at Pamphylia and had refused to go along with them, he was not fit to be taken along for this task. [39] So sharp a disagreement about it ensued that they decided to separate from each other. Barnabas took Mark and sailed for Cyprus, [40] but Paul chose Silas and set out on his journey, commended by the brothers to the grace of the Lord.

[41] Paul traveled through Syria and Cilicia, bringing strength to the churches.
16 [1] He [also] arrived at Derbe and at Lystra, where there was a disciple named Timothy, the son of a believing Jewish woman and a Greek father. [2] The brothers

[m] Amos 9:11–12

in Lystra and Iconium spoke highly of him, 3 and Paul wanted him to come along
with him on the journey. So he took him and had him circumcised because of
the Jews of those regions, for they all knew that his father was a Greek. 4 As they
made their way from town to town, they passed on to the people for observance
the decisions made by the apostles and presbyters in Jerusalem. 5 The churches
grew stronger in faith, and day by day they increased in numbers.

6 They passed through Phrygia and Galatian territory, having been prevented
by the Holy Spirit from going to preach the word in Asia. 7 When they came to
Mysia, they tried to go on into Bithynia, but again Jesus' Spirit would not allow
them. 8 So they traversed Mysia and came down to Troas. 9 There Paul had a
vision one night: a man of Macedonia stood beckoning him and saying, "Come
over to Macedonia and help us!" 10 When he had seen this vision, we immediately made efforts to get over to Macedonia, concluding that God had summoned
us to preach to them.

11 So we put out to sea from Troas and set a straight course for Samothrace and
the next day for Neapolis; 12 from there we traveled on to Philippi, which is a
leading city of the district of Macedonia and a Roman colony. We spent several
days in that city. 13 On the sabbath we went outside the city gate along the bank
of the river, where we thought a place of prayer would be. As we sat there, we
engaged in conversation with women who had also gathered there. 14 One
woman, who was listening, was named Lydia, a dealer in purple cloth from the
town of Thyatira, who already worshiped God. The Lord opened her heart to
follow what Paul was saying. 15 When she and her household were baptized, she
extended us an invitation, "If you have judged me to be one who believes in the
Lord, come and stay at my house." And she prevailed upon us. 16 Once as we
were on our way out to the place of prayer, a slave girl with a spirit of clairvoyance
happened to meet us; her fortune-telling used to bring in considerable profits for
her masters. 17 She began to follow Paul and the rest of us, shouting, "These men
are slaves of the Most High God; they are proclaiming to you a way of salvation."
18 This she did for several days, until Paul became annoyed, turned around, and
said to the spirit within her, "In the name of Jesus Christ I order you to come out
of her!" It left her then and there. 19 When the girl's masters saw that their hope
of making money was gone, they seized Paul and Silas and dragged them to the
main square before the authorities. 20 They turned them over to the magistrates
with the complaint, "These men are disturbing the peace of our city; they are
Jews 21 and are advocating practices unlawful for us Romans to adopt or observe.
22 The crowd joined in the attack against them, and the magistrates had them
stripped of their clothes and ordered them to be flogged. 23 After they had lashed
them many times, they threw them into prison and ordered the warden to guard
them securely. 24 He took this order to heart and locked them up in the inmost
cell, even securing their feet to a stake. 25 About midnight, while Paul and Silas
were praying and singing hymns to God, and their fellow prisoners were listening, 26 such a severe earthquake occurred that the prison was shaken to its
foundations. All the doors suddenly flew open, and the chains of all were loosened. 27 When the warden woke up and saw the prison gates standing open, he

drew [his] sword to kill himself in the belief that the prisoners had escaped. 28 But
Paul shouted out, "Don't do yourself any harm! We are all still here." 29 The warden asked for a light, rushed in, and fell trembling at the feet of Paul and Silas.
30 When he had led them out, he said, "Sirs, what must I do to be saved?" 31 Their
answer was, "Believe in the Lord Jesus, and you will be saved, you and your
household." 32 So they explained to him and all the members of his house the
word of the Lord. 33 At that very hour of the night he took them and bathed their
wounds. Thereupon he and his whole household were baptized. 34 He brought
them up into his house, spread a table before them, and with his whole household rejoiced at having found faith in God. 35 When it was day, the magistrates
dispatched officers with orders, "Release those men!" 36 [This] information the
warden conveyed to Paul, "The magistrates have sent orders that you are to be
released. Now then get out and go in peace." 37 Paul, however, said to the officers,
"They flogged us in public without even a trial, though we are Roman citizens,
threw us into prison, and now they want to get rid of us quietly. No, indeed! Let
them come here in person and lead us out." 38 The officers reported these words
to the magistrates, who were alarmed when they heard that they were Roman
citizens. 39 So they came, tried to placate them, and led them out with the request
that they leave the city. 40 Once outside the prison, they made their way to Lydia's
house, where they saw and encouraged the brothers, and then departed.

17 1 They took the road through Amphipolis and Apollonia and came to Thessalonica, where there was a synagogue of the Jews. 2 Following his usual custom,
Paul went to their services, and for three sabbaths conducted discussions with
them about the Scriptures, 3 explaining and demonstrating that the Messiah had
to suffer and rise from the dead: "This Jesus, whom I am proclaiming to you, is
the Messiah!" 4 Some of the Jews were convinced and threw in their lot with Paul
and Silas, as did a great number of Greeks who were worshipers, and not a few
prominent women. 5 But Jews who resented this engaged some worthless loafers
in the public square to form a mob and start a riot in the city. They marched on
the house of Jason, demanding that Paul and Silas be brought out before the
popular assembly. 6 When they did not find them there, they dragged Jason himself and some of the brothers before the city magistrates, shouting, "These men
have been causing trouble all over the world; and now they have come here,
7 and Jason has taken them in. They all act in defiance of Caesar's decrees and
claim instead that there is another king, a certain Jesus." 8 So they threw into
confusion the populace and even the city magistrates, who, on hearing this,
9 would only release Jason and the others after they had posted bond. 10 The brothers immediately sent Paul and Silas off to Beroea during the night. On their arrival they went to the Jewish synagogue. 11 These Jews were better disposed than
those in Thessalonica and welcomed the word with great enthusiasm, reading
the Scriptures each day and checking to see whether it was all so. 12 Many of
them came, then, to believe, as did many of the influential Greek women, and
not a few men. 13 But when Jews from Thessalonica learned that God's word had
been proclaimed by Paul in Beroea too, they came there to stir up trouble and

to throw the populace into confusion. [14]So the brothers immediately sent Paul on
his way to the seacoast, but Silas and Timothy stayed behind. [15]Paul's attendants
escorted him as far as Athens and then left, with instructions for Silas and Timothy that they were to join him as soon as possible.

[16]While Paul was waiting for them in Athens, he became quite annoyed at the
sight of idols everywhere in the city. [17]In the synagogue, he used to hold discussions with the Jews and their Gentile worshipers; and every day in the public
square, with ordinary passersby. Some of the Epicurean and Stoic philosophers
would confer with him; [18]and some of them would ask, "What would this chatterer be trying to say to us?" Others commented, "He seems to be lobbying for
foreign deities," because he was preaching about "Jesus" and the "Resurrection."
[19]So they took him and led him to the Areopagus with the request, "May we
know what this new teaching is that is being proposed by you? [20]You are bringing
up subjects unfamiliar to our ears, and so we want to know what this is all about."
[21]Now all Athenians, as well as the aliens residing with them, used to spend their
time in nothing else but telling about or listening to something new. [22]Then Paul
rose in the meeting of the Areopagus and said: "People of Athens, I see that you
are in every respect religiously exact. [23]For as I walked about and looked carefully
at your objects of worship, I even came upon an altar inscribed, 'To a God Unknown.' Now what you thus worship unknowingly I would proclaim to you.
[24]The God who made the world and all that is in it, this Lord of the heavens and
earth, does not live in temples made by human hands. [25]Nor is it because he
lacks something that he is served by human hands. It is rather he who gives everyone life and breath and everything else. [26]From one stock he made the whole
human race dwell on the face of the whole earth. He it is who has fixed the dates
of their epochs and the boundaries of their habitation, [27]so that people might
seek for God, perhaps even grope for him, and eventually find him, even though
he is not really far from any one of us. [28]For in him we live and move and have
our being. As some of your own poets have put it: 'For we too are his offspring.'
[29]If we are really God's offspring, we ought not to think that divinity is something
like a statue of gold, of silver, or of stone, a work of human art and conception.
[30]God may well have overlooked bygone periods of human ignorance, but now
he orders all people everywhere to repent, [31]because he has set a day on which
he is going to judge the world with justice through the man whom he has appointed and whom he has endorsed before all, by raising him from the dead."
[32]When they heard about resurrection of the dead, some of them sneered, but
others said, "We'll listen to you about this topic some other time." [33]So Paul withdrew from their meeting. [34]A few of them, however, did join him and become
believers; among these were Dionysius, a member of the Areopagus, a woman
named Damaris, and some others.

18 [1]After that Paul left Athens and went to Corinth. [2]There he found a Jew
named Aquila, a native of Pontus who had recently arrived from Italy, and his
wife Priscilla; for Claudius had ordered all Jews to leave Rome. Paul went to
them, [3]and since he was trained in the same trade as they, made his lodging with

them and worked together, for they were tent makers by trade. 4Every sabbath
Paul would lead discussions in the synagogue and tried to convince both Jews
and Greeks. 5When Silas and Timothy came down from Macedonia, Paul continued to occupy himself with preaching the word, bearing witness to Jews that
Jesus was the Messiah. 6When they would oppose him and insult him, he would
shake his cloak at them in protest and say, "Your blood be on your own heads! I
am not to blame; from now on I shall go to the Gentiles." 7So Paul withdrew
from there and went to the house of a certain man named Titius Justus, who
worshiped God and lived next door to the synagogue. 8Crispus, the leader of the
synagogue, put his faith in the Lord, together with all his household, and many
were the Corinthians who also listened (to Paul), came to believe, and were baptized. 9One night the Lord said to Paul in a vision, "Do not be afraid! Speak out
and do not become silent, 10because I am with you. No one will attack you or
harm you, for there are many of my people in this city." 11So Paul settled there
for a year and six months, teaching the word of God among them.

12While Gallio was proconsul of Achaia, the Jews rose up in a body against
Paul and brought him to court, 13charging, "This fellow is influencing people to
worship God in ways that are against the law." 14As Paul was about to speak up,
Gallio said to the Jews, "If it were a crime or some serious evil trick, I would
tolerate the complaint of you Jews, 15but since this is a dispute about words and
titles and your own law, you must see to it yourselves. I refuse to judge such
matters." 16So he dismissed the case from court. 17Then they all pounced on
Sosthenes, the leader of the synagogue, and beat him in full view of the court.
But none of this was of concern to Gallio.

18Paul stayed on in Corinth for a considerable time; eventually he took leave
of the brothers and sailed for Syria in the company of Priscilla and Aquila. At
Cenchreae he had his hair cut off because he had made a vow. 19They landed at
Ephesus, where he left Priscilla and Aquila; he himself entered the synagogue
and held discussions with the Jews. 20Although they asked him to stay longer, he
declined. 21As he said goodbye, he promised, "God willing, I shall come back to
you again." Then he set sail from Ephesus. 22On landing at Caesarea, he went
up and paid his respects to the church; then he went down to Antioch.

23After spending some time there, he set out again and traveled systematically
through the Galatian territory and Phrygia, strengthening all the disciples.
24Meanwhile there landed at Ephesus a Jew named Apollos, a native of Alexandria, an eloquent speaker, learned in the Scriptures. 25He had been instructed in
the Way of the Lord and, being ardent in spirit, he spoke and taught accurately
enough about Jesus, even though he knew only the baptism of John. 26He too
began to speak out boldly in the synagogue there, but when Priscilla and Aquila
heard him, they took him home and explained to him the Way [of God] more
accurately. 27Because he wanted to go on to Achaia, the brothers encouraged
him by writing to the disciples there to welcome him. On his arrival, he contributed much to those who through grace had become believers, 28for he vigorously
refuted the Jews in public, demonstrating from the Scriptures that Jesus was the
Messiah.

19 ¹Now while Apollos was in Corinth, Paul happened to pass through the
inland country and came [down] to Ephesus, where he found some disciples.
²He asked them, "Did you receive the Holy Spirit, when you became believers?"
They answered, "We have not so much as heard that there is a Holy Spirit."
³"Then how were you baptized?" he asked, and they replied, "With the baptism
of John." ⁴So Paul explained, "John baptized with a baptism of repentance; he
used to tell the people about the one who would come after him, in whom they
were to believe, that is, in Jesus." ⁵When they heard this, they were baptized in
the name of the Lord Jesus. ⁶Paul laid [his] hands on them, and the Holy Spirit
came upon them; then they spoke in tongues and uttered prophecies. ⁷In all,
they were about twelve men.

⁸Paul entered the synagogue and for three months continued to speak out
boldly in debate, using persuasive arguments about the kingdom of God. ⁹When
some obstinately refused to believe and began speaking ill of the Way before the
assembly, Paul left them and took the disciples with him. Day after day he would
hold his discussions in the lecture hall of Tyrannus. ¹⁰This continued for two
years, so that all the inhabitants of Asia, Jews and Greeks alike, heard about the
word of the Lord. ¹¹Meanwhile God continued to perform extraordinary miracles
through Paul: ¹²handkerchiefs or aprons that had touched his skin were applied
to the sick and their diseases would leave them, and evil spirits would depart.
¹³Some itinerant Jewish exorcists also tried to invoke the name of the Lord Jesus
over those possessed by evil spirits, saying, "I adjure you by Jesus about whom
Paul preaches." ¹⁴It was the seven sons of Sceva, a Jew, a chief priest, who were
doing this. ¹⁵Once the evil spirit answered back, "Jesus I recognize, and Paul I
know; but who are you?" ¹⁶Then the person with the evil spirit sprang at them,
overpowered them all, and treated them with such violence that they fled from
his house naked and bruised. ¹⁷This became known to all the Jews and Greeks
living in Ephesus. Great awe came over all of them, and the name of the Lord
Jesus was held in high esteem. ¹⁸Many of those who had become believers came
forward to confess and admit their former practices. ¹⁹A good number of those
who had practiced magic even gathered their books together and burned them
in public. The value of them was assessed and found to be fifty thousand pieces
of silver. ²⁰So it was with the power of the Lord that the word continued to spread
and grow. ²¹After these things happened, Paul made up his mind to travel
through Macedonia and Achaia again and then go on to Jerusalem. He said,
"After I have been there, I must visit Rome too." ²²He sent ahead two of his assistants, Timothy and Erastus, into Macedonia, but stayed on himself for a while
in Asia.

²³It was about this time that no small disturbance occurred concerning the
Way. ²⁴A silversmith named Demetrius, who made silver miniature shrines of
Artemis and created no little business for his craftsmen, ²⁵called a meeting of
them and other workers in related crafts and said to them, "Gentlemen, you
know that our well-being depends on this business. ²⁶Yet you can see and hear
for yourselves that not only here in Ephesus, but in almost all of Asia this Paul
has convinced and led astray a great number of people. He tells them that hand-

made gods are no gods at all. 27 Now there is a danger not only that our business
may be discredited, but even that the temple of the great goddess Artemis may
come to naught. Indeed, she whom all Asia and the whole world worship may
soon be robbed of the majesty that is hers." 28 When they heard this speech, they
were filled with fury and began to shout, "Great is Artemis of the Ephesians!"
29 Soon the city was in chaos; people rushed with one impulse into the theater,
dragging with them Gaius and Aristarchus, Paul's Macedonian traveling companions. 30 Paul himself wanted to appear before the popular assembly, but the
disciples would not let him. 31 Some of the Asiarchs, who were friends of Paul,
even sent word to him, urging him not to venture into the theater. 32 Meanwhile,
some people were shouting one thing, others another; for the assembly was in
chaos, and the majority of them did not even know why they had come together.
33 Some of the crowd, however, made suggestions to Alexander, as the Jews were
pushing him forward. He motioned for silence, indicating that he wanted to explain something to the assembly. 34 But when they recognized that he was a Jew,
they all roared back in unison for about two hours, shouting, "Great is Artemis
of the Ephesians!" 35 Finally, the city clerk quieted the mob and said, "People of
Ephesus, what one is there who does not know that the city of Ephesus is the
guardian of the temple of the great Artemis and of her image that fell from the
heavens? 36 Since these facts are beyond question, you must calm yourselves and
not do anything rash. 37 You have brought here these men, who are not temple
robbers and who have not insulted our goddess. 38 If Demetrius and his fellow
craftsmen have a charge to file, there are courts in session and there are proconsuls; let the parties file their claims. 39 But if you want to investigate anything
further, it will have to be done in the statutory assembly. 40 As it is, we run the
risk of being accused of rioting because of today's conduct. We have no reason
for it, and we really cannot explain this disorderly gathering." With this speech
he dismissed the gathering.

20 1 When the turmoil had ended, Paul summoned the disciples and encouraged them. Then he said goodbye to them and set out for Macedonia. 2 He traveled through those regions, encouraged the people there with many an address,
and finally came to Greece, 3 where he stayed for three months. When a plot was
made by Jews against him, as he was on the point of embarking for Syria, he
decided to return by way of Macedonia. 4 He was accompanied by Sopater, son
of Pyrrhus, from Beroea; Aristarchus and Secundus from Thessalonica; Gaius
from Derbe; Timothy; Tychicus and Trophimus from Asia. 5 These companions
went on ahead and waited for us in Troas; 6 we ourselves set sail from Philippi, as
soon as the festival of Unleavened Bread was over. Five days later we joined them
in Troas, where we spent seven days. 7 On the first day of the week, when we
gathered to break bread, Paul preached to the people. Because he was going to
leave the next day, he prolonged his talk until midnight. 8 Now there were many
lamps in the upstairs room where we were gathered. 9 A young man named Eutychus, who was sitting on a window sill, became more and more drowsy as Paul
talked on and on. Finally he went sound asleep and fell from the third storey to

the ground. They picked him up for dead. [10]But Paul hurried down to him, threw
himself upon him, and put his arms around him; he finally said, "Do not be
alarmed! There is still life in him." [11]Then he went upstairs again, broke bread,
and ate. Afterwards he chatted with them for a good while until dawn; and so he
departed. [12]They took the boy away alive to their great comfort.

[13]We, however, went on ahead to the ship and set sail for Assos, intending to
pick Paul up there. This was the arrangement he had made, because he had
planned to travel overland on foot. [14]When he met us at Assos, we took him
aboard and sailed for Mitylene. [15]The next day we put off from there and reached
a point opposite Chios; on the second day we crossed over to Samos, and the day
after that we put in at Miletus. [16]Paul had decided to sail past Ephesus, so as not
to waste any time in Asia. For he was in a hurry to get to Jerusalem, if at all
possible, by the feast of Pentecost.

[17]From Miletus Paul sent word to Ephesus and summoned the presbyters of
that church. [18]When they came to him, he addressed them, "You know how I
lived the whole time among you from the day that I first set foot in Asia, [19]how I
served the Lord with all humility in the sorrows and trials that came to me because of the plots of Jews. [20]In nothing did I shrink from telling you what was for
your own good or from teaching you in public and from house to house. [21]I bore
witness to Jews and Greeks alike about repentance before God and faith in our
Lord Jesus. [22]But now, as you see, I am on my way to Jerusalem, compelled by
the Spirit and not knowing what will happen to me there. [23]Only this I know,
that the Holy Spirit has been warning me from city to city that chains and hardships await me. [24]I set no store by my life, but aim only at finishing my course
and the ministry to which I have been assigned by the Lord Jesus: of bearing
witness to the gospel of God's grace. [25]Now then, I am fully aware that none of
you, among whom I went about preaching the kingdom, will ever see my face
again. [26]So today I solemnly assure you that I am not responsible for the blood
of anyone. [27]I never shrank from telling you all about God's will. [28]Keep watch,
then, over yourselves and over the whole flock, of which the Holy Spirit has
appointed you overseers, to shepherd the church of God, which he has acquired
with his own blood. [29]I know that when I am gone savage wolves will enter your
fold and will not spare the flock. [30]Why, even from your own number, men will
come forward to distort the truth and lead astray disciples who will follow them.
[31]Be vigilant, then! Remember that night and day for three years I never stopped
warning each of you with tears. [32]Now I commend you to God and to the word
about his grace, which can build you up and give you an inheritance among all
those dedicated to him. [33]I have never coveted anyone's gold, silver, or garments.
[34]You know yourselves that these very hands served the needs of myself and of
those who were with me. [35]In every way I have showed you that it is by such hard
work that we must help the weak and remember the words of the Lord Jesus, for
he said, 'It is more blessed to give than to receive.'" [36]When he finished speaking,
Paul knelt down and prayed with all of them. [37]They were all weeping loudly, as
they threw their arms around Paul and kissed him. [38]They were most distressed

at his saying that they would never see his face again. Then they saw him off to
the ship.

21 [1]After we had finally parted from them, we put out to sea and set a course
straight for Cos; on the following day we came to Rhodes, and from there to
Patara. [2]When we found a ship there bound directly for Phoenicia, we boarded
it and set off. [3]We caught sight of Cyprus but passed to the south of it, as we
sailed on toward Syria. Finally we put in at Tyre, where the ship had to unload
its cargo. [4]We looked up disciples there and stayed with them for seven days.
Warned by the Spirit, they tried to tell Paul that he should not go to Jerusalem.
[5]When our time was up there, we left and moved on; all of them with their wives
and children came out of the town to see us off. On the beach we knelt down
and prayed; [6]then finally we said our good-byes. After we boarded the ship, they
returned home. [7]Continuing our voyage from Tyre, we put in at Ptolemais,
where we greeted the brothers and spent one day with them. [8]The next day we
pushed on and came to Caesarea, where we entered the house of Philip the
evangelist, one of the Seven, and stayed with him. [9]This man had four unmarried daughters who had the gift of prophecy. [10]During our stay of several days
there, a prophet named Agabus came down from Judea. [11]He came to us, took
Paul's belt, and tied his own hands and feet with it. Then he said, "Thus says the
Holy Spirit, 'In this way Jews in Jerusalem will bind the owner of this belt and
will hand him over to Gentiles.'" [12]On hearing this, we and the residents of the
place tried to urge Paul not to go up to Jerusalem. [13]Then Paul replied, "Why do
you cry and break my heart like this?" I am ready not only for imprisonment, but
even for death in Jerusalem for the sake of the name of the Lord Jesus." [14]Since
Paul would not be dissuaded, we said no more, but only, "Let the Lord's will be
done!" [15]At the end of those days we got ready and started for Jerusalem. [16]Some
of the disciples from Caesarea came along with us, escorting us to the house of
Mnason, a Cypriot and one of the early disciples, with whom we were to stay
overnight.

[17]On our arrival in Jerusalem, the brothers there welcomed us warmly. [18]The
next day Paul and the rest of us paid a visit to James, in the presence of all the
presbyters. [19]After greeting them, Paul recounted in great detail all that God had
accomplished among the Gentiles through his ministry. [20]When they heard it,
they honored God, but they said to him, "You see, Brother, how many thousands
of Jews have embraced the faith, all of them staunch upholders of the law. [21]They
have been informed, however, that you teach all the Jews who live among Gentiles to abandon Moses and tell them not to circumcise their children or observe
their customary way of life. [22]What is to be done, then? They will surely hear
that you have arrived here. [23]Our suggestion is that you do what we tell you.
There are four men among us who are making a vow. [24]Take them and purify
yourself along with them; pay the expenses for them so that they may have their
heads shaved. Then all will know that there is nothing to the information that
they have been given about you, but that you too follow and observe the law. [25]As

for Gentile believers, we sent them a letter with our decision that they should
avoid meat sacrificed to idols, blood, meat of strangled animals, and illicit marital unions."

[26]Then on the following day Paul took the men and went through the rite of
purification with them. He went into the Temple to give notice of the day when
the period of purification would be completed, when the offering would be made
for each of them. [27]The seven-day period was nearly over, when some Jews from
Asia recognized Paul in the Temple and stirred up a whole crowd there. They
arrested him, [28]shouting, "Help, fellow Israelites! Here is the one who is teaching
everyone everywhere against our people, our law, and this place. Besides, he has
even brought Greeks into the Temple and has profaned this sacred place." [29]Be-
cause they had earlier seen Trophimus, an Ephesian, with him in the city, they
now assumed that Paul had brought him into the Temple. [30]The whole city was
soon in turmoil, and people came running together from all sides. They took
hold of Paul and dragged him out of the Temple, and its gates were closed at
once. [31]They were trying to kill him, when a report reached the commander in
charge of the cohort that all Jerusalem was in chaos. [32]He immediately took his
soldiers and centurions and descended on them. When they saw the commander
and the soldiers, they stopped beating Paul. [33]The commander came up to them,
arrested Paul, and ordered him bound with double chains. Then he tried to ask
who he was and what he had been doing. [34]But some people in the mob shouted
one thing at him, others another. Since the commander could not get to the
truth because of the turmoil, he ordered Paul to be led away to headquarters.
[35]When Paul got to the steps, he actually had to be carried up by the soldiers
because of the violence of the mob, [36]for the crowd of people kept following and
shouting, "Away with him!" [37]As Paul was about to be led into the headquarters,
he said to the commander, "May I say something to you?" He answered, "Can
you speak Greek? [38]Aren't you the Egyptian who caused a riot some time ago
and led four thousand assassins out into the desert?" [39]Paul replied, "I am a Jew,
a native of Tarsus, a citizen of no mean city in Cilicia. I beg you, let me speak to
these people." [40]So with his permission Paul stood on the steps and motioned to
the people for silence. A great hush fell on them, as he began to address them
in Hebrew.

22 [1]"Brothers and fathers, listen to me now, as I make my defense before you."
[2]When they heard that he was addressing them in Hebrew, they were more inclined to be quiet. [3]"I am a Jew, born in Tarsus in Cilicia. But I was brought up
in this city and educated strictly in our ancestral law at the feet of Gamaliel. I
have been zealous for God, just as all of you are today. [4]I persecuted this Way to
the point of death, arresting and imprisoning both men and women. [5]To this the
high priest and the whole council of elders can testify for me. For from them I
even obtained letters to our brother Jews in Damascus; I went there, intending
to bring back to Jerusalem for punishment the prisoners I would take. [6]As I was
on my way and was drawing near to Damascus, suddenly about noontime a great
light happened to flash from the heavens about me. [7]I fell to the ground and

heard a voice say to me, 'Saul, Saul, why are you persecuting me?' [8]I answered, 'Who are you, sir?' He said to me, 'I am Jesus the Nazorean, whom you are persecuting.' [9]Those who were with me saw the light but did not hear the voice speaking to me. [10]I asked, 'What am I to do, sir?' and the Lord replied, 'Get up; go into Damascus and there you will be told all that you are assigned to do.' [11]Since I could not see because of the glare of that light, I had to be led into Damascus by the hand of my traveling companions. [12]There a certain Ananias, a devout observer of the law and well spoken of by all the Jews who lived there, [13]came, stood by me, and said, 'My brother Saul, recover your sight.' In that instant I regained my sight and looked at him. [14]Then he said, 'The God of our ancestors has chosen you to know his will, to see the Upright One, and to hear the sound of his voice. [15]You are to be a witness for him before all people, testifying to what you have seen and heard. [16]So why delay? Get up, be baptized, and wash your sins away, by calling on his name.' [17]When I returned to Jerusalem and was praying in the Temple, I happened to fall into a trance [18]and see the Lord speaking to me: 'Hurry, leave Jerusalem as soon as possible, because they will not accept your testimony about me.' [19]I answered, 'Lord, they know indeed that from one synagogue to another I used to imprison and flog those who believed in you. [20]While the blood of your witness Stephen was being shed, I stood by, giving my approval of it. I even guarded the cloaks of those who killed him.' [21]He said to me, 'Go, for I am sending you far away to the Gentiles.'" [22]Up to this point in his speech the crowd listened to Paul, but now they raised their voices, shouting, "Rid the earth of this creature! He's not worthy to live!" [23]They were yelling, throwing off their cloaks, and tossing dirt into the air. [24]Then the commander ordered Paul to be taken inside the headquarters, having decided that he would be examined under the lash to find out why they were raising such an outcry against him. [25]After they had strapped up Paul for the whips, he said to the centurion standing by, "Is it lawful for you to flog a Roman citizen without a trial?" [26]On hearing this, the centurion ran to the commander and reported, "What are you going to do? This man is a Roman citizen." [27]The commander rushed in and asked Paul, "Tell me, are you a Roman citizen?" He answered, "Yes, I am." [28]The commander rejoined, "Why, I had to pay much money to get that citizenship!" "Ah," said Paul, "but I was born one!" [29]At that those who were going to examine him backed away from him; the commander became alarmed, realizing that Paul was a Roman citizen and that he had trussed him up.

[30]The next day the commander wanted to find out exactly about the charge being brought against Paul by the Jews. So he released him and summoned the chief priests and the whole Sanhedrin to a meeting. He brought Paul down and had him stand before them. **23** [1]Paul looked intently at the Sanhedrin and said, "Brothers, I have lived my life with a perfectly clear conscience before God up to this day." [2]At that the high priest Ananias bade his attendants strike Paul on the mouth. [3]Then Paul said to him, "It is you that God is going to strike, you whitewashed wall! Do you sit there judging me according to the law and yet violate the law itself in ordering me to be struck?" [4]Those standing by said, "Do you dare insult God's high priest?" [5]Paul said, "Brothers, I did not know that he

was the high priest. It stands written, I know, '*You shall not curse a ruler of your people.*'"[n] [6]When Paul realized that part of them were Sadducees and part Pharisees, he shouted out before the Sanhedrin, "Brothers, I am a Pharisee, the son of Pharisees; [I] now stand trial because of my hope in the resurrection of the dead." [7]When he had said this, there arose dissension between the Pharisees and Sadducees, and the whole assembly was divided. [8]For Sadducees maintain that there is no resurrection, neither as an angel nor as a spirit, whereas Pharisees acknowledge them both. [9]A loud uproar ensued. Finally, some scribes of the Pharisaic group stood up and contended, "We find this man guilty of nothing wrong. Has a spirit or an angel perhaps spoken to him?" [10]At this the dispute became heated, and the commander feared that Paul would be torn to pieces by them. So he ordered his troops to go down and snatch him from their midst and take him back to headquarters. [11]The following night the Lord stood at Paul's side and said, "Keep up your courage! As you have borne witness to me here in Jerusalem, so you must do in Rome as well."

[12]When it was day, Jews formed a conspiracy, binding themselves by oath not to eat or drink until they had killed Paul. [13]More than forty of them made this oath together. [14]Then they went to the chief priests and elders and said, "We have bound ourselves by oath to take no food until we kill Paul. [15]Now you, together with the Sanhedrin, must suggest to the commander to have Paul brought down to you, on the grounds that you want to investigate his case more carefully. We are ready to do away with him, even before he arrives here." [16]The son of Paul's sister, however, heard about the plot; he came to headquarters, entered, and told Paul about it. [17]Paul called one of the centurions and said, "Take this young man to the commander; he has something to report to him." [18]Taking him along, the centurion led him to the commander and said, "The prisoner Paul called me and asked me to bring to you this young man who has something to tell you." [19]Taking him by the hand, the commander drew him aside and asked him privately, "What do you have to report to me?" [20]He said, "Jews have agreed among themselves to ask you to have Paul brought down to the Sanhedrin tomorrow, on the grounds that they want to question him more carefully. [21]But do not be taken in by them, because more than forty men among them are plotting and have bound themselves by oath not to eat or drink until they have done away with him. They are ready now, waiting only to get a promise from you." [22]The commander sent the young man away with the charge, "Tell no one that you have reported this to me."

[23]Then the commander summoned two of his centurions and said, "Get two hundred infantrymen ready to leave for Caesarea by nine o'clock tonight, along with seventy cavalrymen and two hundred spearmen. [24]Provide horses for Paul to ride on so that they may give him safe conduct to the Governor Felix." [25]He wrote a letter to this effect: [26]"Claudius Lysias to His Excellency, Felix the Governor: Greetings! [27]Here is a man whom Jews had seized and were about to put to death. I intervened with my troops and rescued him, when I learned that he was

[n]Exod 22:27

a Roman citizen. [28]Hoping to learn the basis of their charges against him, I
brought him before their Sanhedrin. [29]Then I discovered that he was being accused in controversial matters of their own law and was in no way guilty of anything deserving death or imprisonment. [30]When I was informed about an imminent plot against this man, I decided then and there to send him to you; I have
further instructed his accusers to take up [their case] with you." [31]So the infantrymen took Paul according to their orders and escorted him during the night to
Antipatris. [32]The next day they let the cavalrymen proceed with him, while they
returned to headquarters. [33]On their arrival in Caesarea, they delivered the letter
to the governor and brought Paul before him. [34]He read it and asked Paul from
what province he was. When he found out that he came from Cilicia, he said,
[35]"I shall hear your case when your accusers get here too." Then he ordered him
to be kept under guard in Herod's praetorium.

24 [1]Five days later the high priest Ananias came down to Caesarea with some
of the elders and an attorney named Tertullus, and they laid their case against
Paul before the governor. [2]When Paul was summoned, Tertullus began his accusation: "Your Excellency, Felix, we enjoy much peace through your efforts, and
many improvements have been made in this nation through your provident care.
[3]So we must always and everywhere acknowledge this with deep gratitude. [4]But
now, not to detain you with more of this, I would urge you to listen to us briefly
with your customary courtesy. [5]We have found this man to be a pest, one who
creates dissension among all Jews all over the world; he is a ringleader of the sect
of the Nazoreans [6]and has even tried to desecrate our Temple; but we caught
him. [7][8]Now you can interrogate him about all these things and learn for yourself
why we are accusing him." [9]The Jews also supported this indictment, maintaining that these were the facts. [10]Paul began to answer, as the governor motioned to him to speak. "I know that you have been a judge in this nation for
many years; so I am encouraged to make my defense before you. [11]You are in a
position to ascertain the facts: Not more than twelve days have passed since I
went up to Jerusalem, in order to worship there. [12]Neither in the Temple did
they discover me debating with anyone or causing a crowd to gather, nor in synagogues, nor anywhere else in the city. [13]They cannot even substantiate for you
the charges they are now making against me. [14]I do admit, however, that it is
according to the Way, which they call a sect, that I worship the God of our ancestors. I believe in all that is according to the law and that is written in the prophets.
[15]I share the same hope in God as these people themselves, that there will be a
resurrection of both the upright and the wicked. [16]Because of this, I strive constantly to keep my conscience clear before God and human beings. [17]After an
absence of several years, I had come to bring alms to the people of my race and
to make my offerings. [18]While I was engaged in completing the rites of purification in the Temple, with no crowd around me and with no turmoil, [19]certain
Jews from Asia came upon me. Those are the ones who should be here before
you to make whatever charges they have against me. [20]Or at least let these who
are here state of what crime they have found me guilty, as I stood before the

Sanhedrin — 21 unless it be that one thing that I shouted in their presence, 'It is
because of the resurrection of the dead that I stand trial before you today.'"
22 Then Felix, who was rather well informed about the Way, adjourned the
trial, saying, "When the commander Lysias comes, I shall decide your case."
23 He gave orders to the centurion that Paul was to be kept under guard but allowed some freedom, and that no one was to prevent his friends from seeing to
his needs. 24 A few days later Felix came with his wife Drusilla, who was a Jewess,
and sent for Paul and listened to him speak about faith in Christ Jesus. 25 As he
talked on about uprightness, self-control, and the coming judgment, Felix became uneasy and spoke up, "That's enough for now. Go, and I shall send for you
again, when I find the time." 26 At the same time, he hoped that he would be
offered a bribe by Paul; so he rather frequently sent for him and conversed with
him. 27 After two years had passed, Felix was succeeded by Porcius Festus. Anxious
to ingratiate himself with the Jews, Felix left Paul in prison.

25 1 Three days after he arrived in the province, Festus went up from Caesarea
to Jerusalem. 2 The chief priests and leaders of the Jews brought their charges
against Paul formally before him. They kept urging him, 3 requesting it as a favor
to be done for them, that he transfer Paul to Jerusalem, for they had been plotting
to do away with him along the way. 4 But Festus answered that Paul was being
kept at Caesarea and that he himself would be going there soon. 5 "Your prominent men," he said, "can come down with me; if this man has done anything
wrong, let them prosecute him there." 6 After spending no more than eight or ten
days among them, Festus returned to Caesarea. On the following day, he took
his seat on the bench and ordered Paul to be brought in. 7 When he came in, the
Jews who had come down from Jerusalem surrounded him and leveled against
him many serious charges. But they were unable to prove any of them. 8 In his
defense, Paul said, "I have done no wrong, either against the law of the Jews, or
against the Temple, or against Caesar." 9 Festus, however, who wanted to show
favor to the Jews, said to Paul in reply, "Are you willing to go up to Jerusalem
and stand trial before me there on these charges?" 10 Paul replied, "I am standing
before the bench of Caesar; this is where I should be tried. I have done Jews no
harm, as you realize only too well. 11 If I am guilty, if I have committed a crime
worthy of death, I am not seeking to escape the death penalty. But if there is
nothing to the charges these people are bringing against me, no one has the right
to give me over to them. I appeal to Caesar." 12 Then Festus, having conferred
with his council, replied, "You have appealed to Caesar; to Caesar you shall go."
13 A few days later King Agrippa and Bernice arrived at Caesarea and paid a
courtesy call on Festus. 14 Since they were spending several days there, Festus
referred Paul's case to the king, saying, "There is a man here who was left in
prison by Felix. 15 While I was in Jerusalem, the chief priests and elders of the
Jews pressed charges against him, demanding his condemnation. 16 To them I
replied that it was not the custom for Romans to hand over an accused person
before he could confront his accusers and had the opportunity to defend himself
against their charges. 17 So when [they] came here with me, I did not delay the

matter. The very next day I took my seat on the bench and ordered the man brought in. [18]His accusers stood around him, but brought no charge against him about crimes that I had suspected. [19]Instead, they disputed with him about controversial matters in their own religion and about a certain Jesus who had died, but who Paul claimed was alive. [20]Not knowing how to settle their controversy, I asked whether he would be willing to go to Jerusalem to stand trial there on these charges. [21]But Paul appealed that he be held in custody for an imperial decision. So I issued orders that he be kept under guard until I could send him to Caesar." [22]Then Agrippa said to Festus, "You know, I too should like to listen to this man." Festus replied, "Tomorrow you will listen to him." [23]So the next day Agrippa and Bernice arrived with great pomp and entered the audience chamber along with cohort commanders and eminent men of the city. At Festus's command Paul was brought in. [24]Then Festus said, "King Agrippa and all you gentlemen here present with us, look at this man. He it is about whom the whole Jewish community has appealed to me both here and in Jerusalem, clamoring that he must not live any longer. [25]Yet I could not discover that he had done anything deserving death. So when he himself appealed to the Emperor, I decided to send him. [26]But I have nothing definite to write about him to our sovereign. So I have brought him before all of you, and especially before you, King Agrippa, that from this investigation I might get something to write. [27]For it seems foolish to me to send on a prisoner, without indicating the charges against him."

26 [1]Then Agrippa said to Paul, "You have permission to state your case." Paul stretched out his hand and made his defense. [2]"Against all the charges leveled against me by the Jews, King Agrippa, I count myself fortunate to be able to make my defense today in your presence, [3]especially because you are expert in all the customs and controversial matters among Jews. I beg you, therefore, to listen to me patiently. [4]The way I have lived since my youth, the life that I have led from the beginning among my own people and in Jerusalem, is well known to all [the] Jews. [5]They have been acquainted with me for a long time and can testify, if they were only willing, that I lived as a Pharisee, according to the strictest party of our religion. [6]But now because of my hope in the promise made by God to our ancestors I am standing trial. [7]The twelve tribes of our people ardently worship God day and night in the hope that they may see that promise fulfilled. Because of this hope, Your Majesty, I am accused by Jews. [8]But why is it considered so unbelievable among you that God should raise the dead? [9]At any rate, I once thought it my duty to oppose in many ways the name of Jesus the Nazorean. [10]This is what I did in Jerusalem. I imprisoned many of God's dedicated people under the authority that I received from the chief priests; and when they were to be put to death, I cast my vote against them. [11]Many a time, in synagogue after synagogue, I punished them to force them to blaspheme. Indeed, so excessive was my fury that I pursued them even to foreign cities. [12]On one such occasion I was on my way to Damascus, armed with the authorization and commission of the chief priests. [13]At midday, Your Majesty, as I was on the road, I saw a light flash from the heavens, brighter than the brilliant sun, shining around me and those who

traveled with me. [14]We all fell to the ground, and I heard a voice saying to me in
Hebrew, 'Saul, Saul, why are you persecuting me? It is hard for you to kick
against the goad.' [15]I asked, 'Who are you, sir?' And the Lord said, 'I am Jesus,
whom you are persecuting. [16]Get up and stand on your feet. For this reason have
I appeared to you: to appoint you as my servant and as a witness to what you have
seen [of me] and to what you will be shown. [17]For I shall rescue you from this
people and from the nations to which I am sending you, [18]in order to open their
eyes and to turn them from darkness to light and from the dominion of Satan to
God, so that they may obtain forgiveness of sins and a place among those dedicated by faith in me.' [19]Therefore, King Agrippa, I could not be disobedient to
that heavenly vision. [20]Rather, first of all, to the people in Damascus and in Jerusalem, to all the country of Judea, yes, even to Gentiles I declared that they must
repent and turn to God and do deeds that befit their repentance. [21]That is why
Jews seized me [while I was] in the Temple and tried to murder me. [22]But to this
very day I have enjoyed God's assistance, and so I am standing here to testify to
great and small alike. Nothing that I say goes beyond what the prophets and
Moses said would come about: [23]that the Messiah must suffer and that he would
be the first to rise from the dead, to proclaim light to his people and to the Gentiles."

[24]Paul had defended himself up to this point, when Festus exclaimed aloud,
"Paul, you are mad! Your great learning is driving you mad!" [25]Paul answered,
"No, Your Excellency, Festus, I am not mad. What I am saying is the sober truth.
[26]The king well understands these matters, and to him I am speaking frankly. I
am convinced that none of this escapes him; after all, it did not take place in a
dark corner! [27]Do you believe the prophets, King Agrippa? I know that you do."
[28]At this Agrippa said to Paul, "A little more, and you are sure to make me a
Christian." [29]Paul replied, "Would to God that, with a little more time or much
more, not only you, but all who are listening to me today might become what I
am, apart from these chains." [30]Then the king got up, and with him the governor
and Bernice and the rest who were sitting there. [31]After leaving the chamber,
they continued to talk to one another and admitted, "This man is doing nothing
[at all] that deserves death or imprisonment." [32]Agrippa remarked to Festus,
"This fellow could have been set free, had he not appealed to Caesar."

27 [1]When it was decided that we were to sail for Italy, Paul and some other
prisoners were entrusted to a centurion named Julius, of the Cohort Augusta.
[2]We boarded a ship from Adramyttium bound for ports in Asia and set sail. With
us was the Macedonian, Aristarchus of Thessalonica. [3]The next day we put in at
Sidon, and Julius treated Paul kindly and allowed him to visit some friends and
be cared for by them. [4]From there we put out to sea and sailed under the lee of
Cyprus because of strong head winds. [5]We crossed the open sea off the coast of
Cilicia and Pamphylia and came to Myra in Lycia. [6]There the centurion found
an Alexandrian vessel bound for Italy, and he ordered us aboard. [7]But for many
days we made little headway; only with difficulty did we arrive at Cnidus. Since
the winds would not permit us to continue our course, we sailed to the lee of

Crete, heading for Salmone. 8 Again with difficulty we moved along the coast to a place called Fair Havens, near the town of Lasea.

9 Much time had now gone by, and sailing had become hazardous, because the autumn fast had already passed. It was then that Paul warned them, 10 "Gentlemen, I can see that this voyage is going to meet with disaster and heavy loss not only of cargo and ship, but of our own lives as well." 11 The centurion, however, preferred to listen to the pilot and the captain rather than to what Paul had said. 12 Since the harbor was not suitable to pass the winter in, the majority preferred to put out to sea from there in the hope of reaching Phoenix and spending the winter there. It was a Cretan port, facing both southwest and northwest. 13 So when a gentle south wind began to blow, they thought that they had obtained what they wanted. They weighed anchor and sailed close to the coast of Crete. 14 But it was not long before a wind of hurricane force, called a Northeaster, blew up against it. 15 The ship was caught up by it and could not head into the wind; we gave ourselves over to it and let ourselves be driven on. 16 We ran on under the lee of a small island called Cauda, and only with difficulty were we able to regain control of the ship's skiff. 17 The sailors hoisted it on board and then made use of cables to brace the ship itself. As they were afraid of being driven onto the shoals of Syrtis, they lowered the drift anchor and so let the ship be carried along. 18 We were being pounded violently by the storm, and on the next day they jettisoned some of the cargo. 19 On the third day, they deliberately threw overboard the ship's gear. 20 For many days neither the sun nor the stars were to be seen, and no small storm raged on. At last all hope of survival was gradually abandoned.

21 Because many had been without food for a long time, Paul then stood up among them and said, "Gentlemen, you should have taken my advice, not to set sail from Crete and incur this disaster or loss. 22 Now I urge you to keep up your courage; there will be no loss of life among you, but only this ship. 23 Last night an angel of the God to whom [I] belong and whom I serve stood by me 24 and said, 'Do not be afraid, Paul; you are destined to stand trial before Caesar. Look, God has favored you with the safety of all those sailing with you.' 25 So keep up your courage, gentlemen. I trust in God that it will all turn out just as I have been told, 26 even though we may still have to run aground on some island." 27 When it was the fourteenth night of the storm and we were still being driven across the Adriatic, the sailors began to suspect toward midnight that land was near. 28 They took soundings and found a depth of twenty fathoms; after sailing on a short distance, they took a sounding again and found fifteen fathoms. 29 For fear that we might be dashed against some rocky coast, they dropped four anchors from the stern and prayed for daylight. 30 Then the sailors sought to abandon ship. They let down the ship's skiff into the sea, pretending that they were going to put out anchors from the ship's prow. 31 But Paul said to the centurion and the soldiers, "If these men do not stay with the ship, you have no chance of surviving." 32 At this the soldiers cut loose the ropes of the skiff and let it drift away. 33 Before day began to dawn, Paul urged all on board to take some food. "Today is the fourteenth day that you have been in suspense and all that time you have gone hungry, taking nothing to eat. 34 Now I urge you to take some food; this is for your

own survival. Yet not a hair of the head of any of you will be lost." 35When he
had said this, he took bread, gave thanks to God in front of all of them, broke it,
and began to eat. 36All of them were encouraged by this, and they too took something to eat. 37In all there were two hundred and seventy-six of us on board.
38When all had enough to eat, they further lightened the ship by throwing the
wheat overboard. 39When it was day, they did not recognize the land, but they
could make out a bay with a beach; they proposed to run the ship aground there,
if possible. 40Cutting loose the anchors, they abandoned them to the sea; at the
same time they untied the ropes of the rudders, hoisted the foresail into the wind,
and made for the beach. 41But they encountered a place of cross seas, and the
ship was grounded there. Its bow stuck fast and could not be budged, while the
stern was being broken to pieces by the force [of the waves]. 42The soldiers were
minded to kill the prisoners lest any of them would swim away and escape. 43But
the centurion, who was anxious to save Paul, kept them from carrying out their
decision. He ordered those who could swim to jump overboard first and make
for the land; 44the rest were to follow, some on planks, others on debris from the
ship. So it was that everyone got safely to land.

28 1Once safely ashore, we learned that the island was called Malta. 2The natives showed us extraordinary kindness; they lit a fire and brought us all around
it because of the rain that had set in and the cold. 3Paul had gathered a bundle
of brushwood and was putting it on the fire, when a viper crawled out of it because of the heat and fastened on his hand. 4At the sight of the snake hanging
from his hand, the natives said to each other, "This man must really be a murderer; though he has survived death in the sea, Justice has not allowed him to go
on living." 5But Paul shook the snake from his hand into the fire and suffered no
ill effects. 6They were expecting him to swell up or suddenly fall dead, but after
waiting for quite some time and seeing nothing unusual happen to him, they
changed their minds and kept saying that he was a god. 7In the vicinity of that
place there was the estate of a prominent man on the island, named Publius. He
took us in and kindly gave us hospitality for three days. 8Now Publius's father
happened to be sick in bed, laid up with chronic fever and dysentery. Paul went
in to see the man, and with prayers laid his hands on him and cured him. 9When
this happened, the rest of the sick on the island also came to him and were
healed. 10They paid us many honors, and when we were to set sail again, they
brought us the provisions we needed.

11Three months later we set sail on a ship that had passed the winter at the
island. It was from Alexandria with the Dioscuri as its figurehead. 12We put in at
Syracuse and spent three days there. 13From there we sailed around the coast
and came to Rhegium. A day later a south wind began to blow, which enabled
us to reach Puteoli in two days. 14There we found some brothers and were urged
to stay with them for seven days. And so we came to Rome. 15Some brothers from
there heard about our coming and came out as far as Appii Forum and Tres
Tabernae to meet us. On seeing them, Paul thanked God and plucked up his

courage. [16]When we entered Rome, Paul was allowed to take a lodging of his
own, with a soldier to guard him.

[17]After three days Paul happened to invite prominent men of the Jewish community to visit him. When they came, he addressed them, "Brothers, although I
have done nothing against our people or our ancestral customs, I was handed
over as a prisoner to the Romans in Jerusalem. [18]The Romans tried my case and
wanted to release me, because they found nothing against me deserving death.
[19]When some Jews objected, I was forced to appeal to Caesar, not that I had any
charge to bring against my own people. [20]This, then, is the reason why I have
requested to see you and to speak to you. Because I share the hope of Israel, I
wear this chain!" [21]In reply, they said to him, "We have not received any letters
from Judea about you; nor has any of the brothers arrived here with a report or
rumor to your discredit. [22]For our part, we are anxious to hear you present your
views, for we know full well about that sect, that it is denounced everywhere."
[23]So they arranged a day with him and came to his lodging in great numbers.
From morning to evening he laid his case before them and kept bearing witness
about the kingdom of God. He sought to convince them about Jesus, appealing
to the law of Moses and to the prophets. [24]Some of them were convinced by what
he had to say; others would not believe. [25]Without reaching any agreement
among themselves, they started to depart, when Paul added one last word, "The
Holy Spirit stated it well, when he spoke to your ancestors through the prophet
Isaiah:

> [26]*'Go to this people and say:*
> *You may listen carefully, but never understand;*
> *you may look sharply, but never see.*
> [27]*For the mind of this people has grown dull.*
> *They have hardly used their ears to listen;*
> *they have closed their eyes,*
> *lest they see with their eyes,*
> *hear with their ears,*
> *understand with their mind,*
> *and turn;*
> *and I should heal them.'*[o]

[28]So let it be known to you that this salvation of God has been sent to the Gentiles. They will listen to it!" [29] [30]For two whole years Paul stayed on in his own
rented lodging, where he welcomed all who would come to him. [31]With all boldness and without hindrance, he preached the kingdom of God and taught about
the Lord Jesus.

---

[o] Isa 6:9–10

INTRODUCTION

◆

I. Title, Authorship, Date, Purpose of Acts

◆

(1) The Acts of the Apostles is the NT book that is often said to be an account of the early history of the Christian church, but, even though some of that history is found in it, it is seen, when one reads it carefully, to involve much more. In order to appreciate what the Acts of the Apostles is all about, one has to begin by considering its traditional title, author, date of composition, and the purpose for which it was composed.

A. Title

(2) The title found in the best Greek manuscripts is *Praxeis Apostolōn*, "Acts of Apostles" (P^{74}, ℵ, B, D, Ψ, 1, 1175). One also finds at times variants such as *hai Praxeis tōn Apostolōn*, "the Acts of the Apostles" (323, 945, 1241, 1739); or *Praxeis tōn hagiōn Apostolōn*, "Acts of the holy Apostles" (614, 1505, 1704, 1884); or occasionally *Louka euangelistou praxeis tōn hagiōn Apostolōn*, "Acts of the holy Apostles of the evangelist Luke" (33, 189, 1891, 2344). Sometimes the title appears at the end of the Greek text, as in P^{74}: *Praxis [ap]ostolōn.*

(3) This title does not necessarily come from the author of the book, although a few commentators have maintained that it did (Wendland, Wikenhauser, Zahn). It was most likely introduced by someone else in the first or second century. Being an ancient title, however, it does indicate how early Christians commonly understood this writing. In some form or other the title can be traced to the end of the second century (e.g., Irenaeus, *Adversus haereses* 3.12.11; SC 211.229; Clement of Alexandria, *Paedagogus* II.1.16.1; GCS 1.165; Origen, *Contra Celsum* 3.46; GCS 1.243). In Latin one finds either *Acta* or *Actus Apostolorum* (used by Tertullian, Cyprian), an exact translation of the best attested Greek title.

(4) The ancient title *Praxeis* was a term designating a specific Greek literary form, a narrative account of the heroic deeds of famous historical or mythological figures. For instance, in the first century B.C. Diodorus of Sicily wrote about *praxeis tōn archaiōn basileōn*, "Acts of the Early Kings" (3.1.1), and about *ē poleōn ē basileōn praxeis*, "Acts either of Cities or Kings" (16.1.1). The Jewish historian Josephus knows of those who have written about *tas kata Pompēion praxeis*, "the Acts of Pompey" (*Ant.* 14.4.3 §68), and mentions writers of similar Acts as Strabo, Nicolas, and Livy. The LXX of 2 Chronicles also mentions the *praxeis* of the

kings Rehoboam (12:15), Abijah (13:22), and Ahaz (28:26). In antiquity one recounted the Acts of Hercules, Acts of Alexander, Acts of Hannibal, and Acts of Apollonius of Tyana.

(5) *Praxeis* had its counterpart in the Roman world as *res gestae*, "deeds done." The most famous of these were the *Res gestae divi Augusti*, "the Acts of the divine Augustus," the emperor who brought peace to the world at the time of the birth of Jesus of Nazareth (see Luke 2:1). In Greek those exploits of Augustus are recorded as *praxeis te kai dōreai Sebastou theou*, "Deeds and Benefactions of the divine Augustus" (see S. Riccobono, *Acta divi Augusti* [Rome: Regia Academia Italica, 1945], 20–21; *IGRR*, 3.66–67).

(6) The author of Acts uses *praxeis* in 19:18, where it does not have the literary meaning used in the title. Moreover, the author tends to ascribe the achievements or exploits of Peter and Paul to the risen Lord or his Spirit or to God rather than to the apostles themselves (1:8a; 3:12–16; 4:10, 30; 13:2; 15:4, 12; 21:19). So the account is really *Praxeis tou Theou dia tōn Apostolōn* or *Gesta Dei per Apostolos*, to borrow a phrase from A. D. Nock. Again, Acts recounts a story the thrust of which surpasses the mere narration of deeds of early apostles. For such reasons mainly, one hesitates to ascribe the title to the author himself, in spite of his general desire to clothe the story of early Christianity in Hellenistic dress.

(7) The title *praxeis*, however, is not wholly a misnomer, as E. Norden recognized, because it does relate this NT writing to a well-known Hellenistic literary genre, a "historical monograph." This is the apt translation of Hengel (*Acts*, 36), of the classicist G. A. Kennedy (*New Testament Interpretation*, 114), and of E. Plümacher, even though it may not share with other examples of that genre all its aspects or details. Moreover, the Hellenistic historical genre did incorporate certain features with which one has to reckon in assessing the kind of account that the author has written, for such Hellenistic accounts incorporated not only historical details, but also folklore and legends.

(8) Moreover, when one recalls that the Third Gospel does not use *euangelion*, either as a designation of itself or in any other way, but rather bears the designation *diēgēsis*, "(narrative) account," as it tells of the "events that have come to fulfillment among us," then one understands how appropriate *praxeis* can be as a designation of the sequel to that account (*Luke*, 287, 292). That such a historical monograph would also include a biographical concern is not excluded, even though one might hesitate to ascribe Luke-Acts simply to a biographical genre, as C. H. Talbert has done (*Literary Patterns*, 125–36).

(9) The other operative word in the ancient Greek title is *apostolōn*. Even though some ancient writers and canonical lists referred to this NT book as *Acta omnium Apostolorum*, "the Acts of all the Apostles" (*Fragmentum Muratorianum* §3), it is not devoted to the exploits of all of them. The first part of the book recounts significant acts of Peter, and the second part, those of Paul. Hence the ancient Greek title is to be understood as referring to them, Acts of Peter and Paul.

(10) This understanding of the title, however, creates a problem. The general reluctance of the author to use *apostolos* for the hero of the second part of his

book is well known. Apart from 14:4, 14, where the title occurs in the plural for Barnabas and Paul, it is never otherwise used of Paul. The NT shows how Paul had to struggle to be regarded as *apostolos* (Gal 1:1; 1 Cor 9:1–2; 15:8–9; 2 Cor 11:5–6). Part of the author's reluctance undoubtedly stemmed from the fact that Paul was not a follower of Jesus during his public ministry; part also from the way the author understood the role of the Twelve (see COMMENT on 1:20–22) and from what he had said about the Twelve in the Gospel: "whom he [Jesus] also named apostles" (Luke 6:13 [*Luke*, 613–18]). Later on, especially in light of his own use of "the apostle of the Gentiles" (Rom 11:13), Paul became known as "the Apostle" (e.g., *Diogn.* 12.5; Apollonius, quoted by Eusebius, *HE* 5.18.5). From such an early custom stemmed the eventual title of this NT book. This is yet another reason for thinking that the title itself does not come from the author.

(11) The foregoing discussion of the genre of Acts reveals that I would not agree with R. L. Pervo that Acts is an "edifying historical novel," even if he is willing to admit that the author did not concoct "it from thin air" but used source material (*Profit with Delight*, 137). Is it true that "as a historian he [Luke] leaves much to be desired" (ibid., 138)? What notion of ancient history is involved in such a judgment? One could more readily agree with P. Gibert ("L'Invention"), that it is hagiographical history, or with F. O. Fearghail *(The Introduction)*, that it is kerygmatic history. At least the last two interpreters are willing to accord Acts some form of ancient historiography, which in my opinion has to be retained. More will be said about the historical character of Acts in due course; for the moment I take *Praxeis* to mean "historical monograph."

B. AUTHORSHIP

(12) The authorship of Acts is related to that of the Third Gospel, because Acts begins, "In my first account, Theophilus, I dealt with all that Jesus did and taught from the beginning" (1:1). It is dedicated to the "Theophilus," for whom the author wrote an account of Jesus' words and deeds (Luke 1:3). The dedication to the same person implies a common authorship of both the Gospel and Acts. Though some have denied the common authorship of Luke-Acts (A. W. Argyle, A. C. Clark, J. Wenham), it is, nevertheless, widely admitted today, mostly on the basis of the work of Harnack, Hawkins, W. L. Knox, Cadbury, Price, and Beck. The vocabulary and use of the same expressions, the style and similar mode of composition, and the themes, theology, and whole thought-world are so similar from one volume to the other that they must have come from the same author. There is also a noticeable narrative unity, marked by parallelism. The development of the parallel treatment of Jesus and Peter, and then of Peter and Paul, argues somewhat for a unity of conception that dominates the two-volume work. This parallelism and unity, however, have at times been overdrawn, and one has to agree with some of the cautions that Parsons and Pervo have noted *(Rethinking)*. See further Muhlack, *Die Parallelen;* O'Toole, *The Unity of Luke's Theology;* Talbert, *Literary Patterns;* Tannehill, *The Narrative Unity.*

(13) In this regard, one has to recognize the problem that Luke-Acts encounters in the positions this double work occupies in the NT canon. The Lucan Gospel is there separated from Acts and classed with the other Gospels, whence it has come to be known as the Third Gospel. Followed by the Johannine Gospel or the Fourth Gospel, Luke is separated from Acts, and this tends to obscure the second-volume character of Acts. Indeed, people have at times asked what that separation in the canon is supposed to convey—a question that no one can answer. It certainly tells us nothing about the identity of the author of Acts.

(14) As is the Third Gospel, so the Acts of the Apostles is anonymous. Nowhere in the latter is there any indication of the identity of the author. In this respect it differs from letters in the Pauline corpus, which bear the author's name. There are passages in Acts where the narrative shifts from the third person to the first person plural and seems to suggest that the author of Acts was a companion or an associate of Paul: the so-called We-Passages or We-Sections (16:10–17; 20:5–15; 21:1–18; 27:1–28:16 [and 11:28 in Codex Bezae]). They do not, however, give us a clue as to who the author was, and their character will be discussed in due course.

(15) A long-standing church tradition has associated both the Third Gospel and Acts with Luke, who appears in Phlm 24 as Paul's "fellow worker" and is called "the beloved physician" in Deutero-Pauline Col 4:14. 2 Tim 4:11 also speaks of him as Paul's "sole companion." Sometimes he has even been identified in church tradition with the "brother" mentioned in 2 Cor 8:18 (John Chrysostom hesitates between Luke and Barnabas, *Hom. in Ep. II ad Corinthios* 18.1; PG 61.523; J. Wenham, "evidently Luke" [*Redating*, 223]). The author of the Third Gospel is so identified in the title used in the oldest manuscript of that Gospel: Papyrus Bodmer XIV or P^{75} (pl. 61), a codex dating from A.D. 200 (±25 years), a title that no one has shown to be dependent on either Irenaeus or Tertullian. Most of the texts, in which the church tradition about Luke is reflected, can be found in the original languages in Aland, *SQE*, 531–48; cf. *Beginnings*, 2.209–50; *Luke*, 37–41.

(16) Though it had become the vogue to question or reject that traditional identification of the author of Luke-Acts, I did not share that opinion when I wrote the commentary on the Lucan Gospel in this series (*Luke*, 35–53). Since the writing of that commentary, I have seen no reason to depart from the nuanced defense of the composition of Luke-Acts by the traditional author that I had proposed: the Luke who is called a "fellow-worker" of Paul in Phlm 24 and was his "sometime collaborator." In saying "sometime collaborator" of Paul, I distinguish myself from the position of Irenaeus, who called Luke an "inseparable" companion of Paul (*Adversus haereses* 3.14.1; SC 34.258). Subsequently, I did treat the We-Sections in greater detail ("The Authorship of Luke-Acts Reconsidered"). As a consequence of my studies, I still regard the Luke of the church tradition as the best candidate for the author of both the Third Gospel and Acts.

(17) To admit that, however, does not mean that I would agree with J. Wenham that Luke is "one of the Seventy, the Emmaus disciple, Lucius of Cyrene and Paul's kinsman" (*EvQ* 63 [1991]: 43), or even a physician. I continue to regard

Luke as a Gentile Christian, a non-Jewish Semite, originally an *incola* of Syria, probably of Antioch. In this I should disagree with Epiphanius (*Panarion* 51.11; GCS 31.263) that Luke was one of the 72 disciples, and with Jervell that he was a Jewish-Christian and wrote for predominantly Jewish-Christian readers *(The Unknown Paul)*.

(18) The anonymity of the author of Acts is maintained today mainly because of a reluctance to admit that he could have been a companion of Paul (see my explanation of the companionship and the discrepancies between Luke and Paul in *Luke*, 47–51). The anonymity of the author of Luke-Acts is maintained by Conzelmann, Enslin, Haenchen, Koester, Kümmel, Marxsen, Parsons, Pervo (the last two call the author "Lukas"), Pesch, Plümacher, Roloff, Schmid, Schneider, Vielhauer, and Weiser.

(19) Wikenhauser-Schmid (*Einleitung*, 376) list the following modern interpreters who recognize the Luke of church tradition as the author of Acts: Dibelius, E. Meyer, T. W. Manson, Streeter, von Campenhausen, Eltester, Trocmé, van Unnik, Klijn, McNeile, and Bauernfeind.

To these one can add Bruce, Ellis, Filson, Gärtner, Grant, Guthrie, Hanson, Harnack, Hemer, Hengel, Kistemaker, Marshall, Meinertz, Michaelis, Nock, Polhill, Reicke, J.A.T. Robinson, Stählin, Torrey, J. Wenham, Wikenhauser, C.S.C. Williams, and D. J. Williams.

C. Date of Composition

(20) The date of the composition of Acts is related to that of the Third Gospel, which Luke calls his *prōton logon*, "first account" (1:1). The obvious meaning of that phrase is that Acts comes now as a sequel to that Gospel. Some commentators, however, have tried to argue that Acts was composed before the Gospel (H. G. Russell), but most of the reasons suggested for such a view are highly speculative and unconvincing (see *Luke*, 53).

Even if one were to admit that the prologues (Luke 1:1–4; Acts 1:1–2) were the last thing that the author composed, having written first a continuous account from Luke 3:1 to 24:49 and Acts 1:3 to 28:31 and deciding only then to make two volumes out of his work by adding the prologues (see *Luke*, 290, 310–11; cf. *Beginnings*, 2.491–92), this would still allow the traditional order of Luke and Acts.

(21) The dating of Acts is controverted. The views of modern commentators fall generally into three categories: early, late, and intermediate dating.

(a) **Early Dating:** In the mid-60s, either before the end of Paul's Roman house-arrest (probably A.D. 61–63) or within a year or so thereafter (pre-70). The usual arguments for such a dating run like this: Luke must have written Acts at such an early date because

(i) he makes no mention of Paul's death, or of Paul standing trial before Caesar, or of his acquittal; if he wrote later (70s or 80s), how could he have failed to mention these?

(ii) he makes no mention of Nero's persecution of Roman Christians in A.D. 64.

(iii) the minor apologetic purpose of Acts, to show that Christianity was *religio licita* in the Roman Empire, makes no sense once it became an object of persecution under Nero or had become *religio illicita.*

(iv) the tone of Acts is basically one of joy and peace, revealing Luke's obvious affection for Paul. Do this tone and affection reflect the attitude of one who would have been aware of Paul's martyrdom and of the persecution of the church?

(v) the description of the Jerusalem church in the 30s and 40s, when Jewish Christians were still in contact with the Temple and Synagogue and with Pharisees and Sadducees is idyllic; could that have been written after the destruction of Jerusalem in A.D. 70 without some reflection of it or at least a reference to the impending rebellion of Jerusalem Jews against Roman occupation?

(vi) Luke shows no awareness of any of Paul's letters, not even of Galatians or 2 Corinthians, with which Acts differs in some details; this suggests that Acts was written well before the Pauline corpus was assembled or the letters were widely circulated.

(vii) The literary patterns and parallels between the Third Gospel and Acts lack "the obvious parallel" to the passion of Jesus in the Gospel, viz., the death of Paul, a lack that is inexplicable unless Acts was written prior to that death.

Such modern arguments were apparently first formulated by Harnack *(Date)* and Rackham at the end of the last century and have since been repeated in some form by others who favor the early dating: Blass, Bruce, Cambier, Cerfaux, Ellis, Filson, Guthrie, Hemer, Kistemaker, Mattill ("Date and Purpose"), McNeile, Méhat, Meinertz, Munck, Reicke, J.A.T. Robinson, Torrey (Gospel: 60–61; Acts: 62–64). For a long list of early dates, see Hemer, *The Book of Acts,* 367–70.

(22) The trouble with such arguments for an early date stems mainly from one consideration: no one knows why the Lucan story ends where it does, despite many attempts to explain it (well summarized in *Beginnings,* 4.349–50). Nevertheless, the conclusion drawn from such an ending, that the Lucan writings must have been completed before Paul's trial or death or before the destruction of Jerusalem, is unwarranted (see *Luke,* 54–57). The ending of Mark's Gospel is equally abrupt; yet no one suggests that it ends where it does because the author knew no more.

Obvious parallels or literary correspondences between the Third Gospel and Acts, which allegedly reveal Luke's narrative technique, are irrelevant in the question of dating. They are not an argument for pegging chronology.

(23) Luke's failure to mention the death of Paul may be owing to his delicacy in this matter. After all, he has foreshadowed it in Paul's speech to the elders of Ephesus: you "will never see my face again" (20:25; cf. 20:38); again in Paul's reaction to the prophecy of Agabus: "I am ready not only for imprisonment, but even for death in Jerusalem" (21:13). This may be all that Luke wanted to say about the passing of the hero of the second part of Acts—or had to say in light of

subsequent events that Luke knew bore out Paul's worst forebodings. The best way to account for Acts ending where it does "is that his [Luke's] readers knew the rest of Paul's story" (R.P.C. Hanson, "The Provenance," 228; cf. Crehan, "The Purpose," 361–62).

The pseudepigraphic 2 Timothy tells us nothing about Paul's death, except that it was imminent. Moreover, what is known about Paul after the end of Acts, whether he was tried, whether he was acquitted, whether he went to Spain, or how, when, and where he died comes to us only from early legends. Such patristic references as *1 Clem.* 1.5; Eusebius, *HE* 2.25.5; Tertullian, *De Praescriptione* 36.3, which pass on some details, may be little more than legendary, even though they have been used in the church tradition about the death of the Apostle.

(24) If Luke-Acts were composed about A.D. 62/63, the dependence of the Third Gospel on Mark would demand an incredibly early date for the Second Gospel. Most scholars today would not date the latter earlier than A.D. 65 (my preference), and many consider it as late as 70. The attempt of J. O'Callaghan and of C. P. Thiede (*The Earliest Gospel Manuscript? The Qumran Papyrus 7Q5 and Its Significance for New Testament Studies* [Exeter, UK: Paternoster, 1992]) to date Mark early on the basis of a Qumran fragment (7Q5) has only raised more problems than it solves.

(25) To get around this difficulty, C.S.C. Williams and P. Parker have sought to identify the "first account" as Proto-Luke, a combination of "Q" and "L," and have suggested that Acts, like Proto-Luke, is totally unaffected by the Marcan Gospel. The Third Gospel, then, would be the result of the conflation of Proto-Luke and Mark. This would mean that Acts 1:1 no longer presupposes the Lucan Gospel, as we know it, and its dependence on Mark. All of that is problematic, however, because the argument depends on the questionable Proto-Luke hypothesis; see *Luke*, 53, 72, 89–91).

(26) (b) **Late Dating:** In the second century, or between A.D. 100–130. This view has been maintained in different forms by Burkitt, G. Klein, H. Koester, J. Knox, J. C. O'Neill, Overbeck, Schmiedel, Townsend. It is espoused because of an alleged dependence of Luke on Josephus (so Burkitt, Klausner), or a relationship of Acts to the writings of Marcion (Knox) or of Justin Martyr (O'Neill). However, the relation of Acts to or its dependence on Josephus, Marcion, and Justin is far from clear. It may be just as problematic as the view of some commentators who think that Acts was used by some of the Apostolic Fathers; (see Haenchen, *Acts*, 3–8).

(27) Josephus lived from A.D. 37/38 until some time after 100; his *Jewish War* was published in Greek between A.D. 75 and 79, and his *Antiquities of the Jews* in 93/94. His last works, *Life* and *Against Apion*, appeared shortly before his death. That Luke would have read or used Josephus's writings is highly speculative and improbable; none of the evidence for it is convincing (see A. Plummer, *Luke*, xxix–xxx; Harnack, *Date*, 114–15 n. 2; *Beginnings*, 2.355–59). The relation of Luke-Acts to Justin Martyr, which O'Neill has maintained, has been thoroughly disproved by H.D.F. Sparks and G. Schneider in their reviews of O'Neill's book. Harnack dealt adequately with the earlier views of Overbeck and Schmie-

del on Acts and Justin Martyr (*Date*, 109). The relation of the Lucan writings to Marcion, which J. Knox proposed, has been handled by L. E. Wilshire ("Was Canonical Luke"); see also *Beginnings*, 2.358.

(28) (c) **Intermediate Dating:** In the 80s. The reasons for a post-70 dating are drawn mostly from the Lucan Gospel and include the following:

(i) Luke's recognition that "many" other attempts to recount the Jesus-story (Luke 1:1) had preceded his would be difficult to understand in the early sixties.

(ii) Luke 13:35a ("your house is abandoned," addressed to Jerusalem) makes sense only after the destruction of Jerusalem (A.D. 70).

(iii) Jesus' judgment about the Temple (Mark 13:2) and his announcement about the desecration of it by the "abomination of desolation" (Mark 13:14) become a saying about "Jerusalem surrounded by camps" in the Lucan account (21:20). Thus the Marcan apocalyptic prophecy, alluding to Dan 9:27 or 12:11, about the coming desolation of the Temple has given way to a description of a siege and capture of the city of Jerusalem itself.

(iv) Luke 19:43–44 alludes to Roman earthworks of the sort described by Josephus (*J.W.* 6.2.7 §150, 156). These suggest a post-70 dating for the Third Gospel, which has made use of the Marcan Gospel; after it Acts would have been written. Even if Luke, the author, were a sometime companion of Paul, that association does not affect the fact that Acts gives the impression of having been composed after the death of Paul. Again, since Luke does not seem to have read any of the Pauline letters, the likelihood is that he had composed Acts prior to the collection of the letters into a corpus toward the end of the first century.

(29) Such reasons suggest the dating of Luke-Acts in a post-Marcan period and after the destruction of Jerusalem in A.D. 70, to which the Gospel alludes. But how much later? There is no way of telling the amount of time required. Commentators have at times argued that, since there is no awareness in Acts of the persecution of Christians in the time of Domitian (81–96), Acts must antedate that emperor's reign. That, however, says little, being mostly an argument from silence.

The reasons for the intermediate dating given above have not been accepted by everyone, especially by those who espouse either the early or the late date. I have already dealt with the specific counter-arguments of Dodd and Robinson about Luke's use of OT motifs in his discussion of the fate of Jerusalem and see no reason to repeat all that here, since that issue has not changed (*Luke*, 54–57).

(30) Many NT interpreters use the date A.D. 80–85 for the composition of Luke-Acts, and there is no good reason to oppose that date, even if there is no real proof for it. Such an intermediate dating remains the most plausible and has been espoused by Dupont (about 80), Hengel (*Acts*, 66: between 80 and 90), Kümmel (between 80 and 90 or 80 and 100), Marxsen (last decade of first century), Michaelis (about 70), Perrot (between 80 and 95), Pesch (80–90), Plümacher (about 90), Polhill (between 70 and 80), Roloff (about 90), Schneider (80–90), Vielhauer (Gospel: about 80; Acts: about 90), Weiser (80–90), Wikenhauser-Schmid (in the 80s), C.S.C. Williams.

(31) As for the place of composition of Luke-Acts, no one knows, apart from a

general agreement that it was not written in Palestine or Syria. Irenaeus thought that Acts was written in Rome (*Adversus haereses* 3.1.1; 3.14.1), likewise Eusebius (*HE* 2.22.6). Ancient tradition sometimes mentioned Achaia (the *Prologues*), sometimes Caesarea; these are mostly conclusions drawn by ancient writers from the book itself (see *Luke*, 57).

In the long run, it is a matter of little concern when or where Luke-Acts was composed, since the interpretation of it, especially of Acts, depends little on its date or place of composition.

D. Purpose

(32) Much more important is the purpose for which Luke composed Acts. Since he is the sole evangelist to compose a sequel to his Gospel, this tells us something about the way he conceived his Jesus-story. Whereas Mark's Gospel originally ended with the account of the discovery of the empty tomb (16:1–8), and Matthew and John appended to their accounts of that discovery episodes recounting appearances of the risen Christ to women and other disciples (Matt 28:9–20; John 20:11–21:23), Luke's ending of the Jesus-story is different. He did, indeed, include comparable accounts of the appearance of the risen Christ (Luke 24:13–49), but only the Lucan Christ leads forth his disciples to Bethany and from there "was carried up into heaven" (24:51). Only he commissions the disciples as "witnesses," instructing them to wait until he sends upon them "what my Father has promised." "You are to remain here in the city until you are invested with power from on high" (24:48–49). At the end of the Lucan Gospel, "what my Father has promised" remains unexplained, but it provides the transition to the sequel that Luke presents at the beginning of Acts, where what has been promised is made known to be the Holy Spirit (1:4–5). The activity of the Spirit in the testimony that the witnesses so commissioned are going to bear becomes a major theme in the Lucan second volume. Barrett has rightly seen that the Third Gospel was composed as a preface to Acts and has traced in detail the hints and items in the Gospel that reveal this prefatory function. Acts, then, is the continuation of the Lucan Gospel, not in the sense that it relates what Jesus continued to do, but how his followers carried out his commission under the guidance of his Spirit. Even more has to be said about the purpose of this two-volume Jesus-story.

(33) Looking at the outline of Acts (Introduction §128), one sees that it recounts seven major developments (I–VII) and twenty subdivisions (marked A, B, etc.). The question naturally arises, Why these episodes? They are clearly not the whole story of the Gospel's sequel; they do not purport to be comprehensive or necessarily in order. Some incidents are described in detail; others are only sketched. Once Matthias is chosen to reconstitute the Twelve, we hear no more about him. What happened to the Ethiopian eunuch after his baptism? To Cornelius and his household after their conversion? Why do the Twelve disappear from the scene after 6:2–6? Or the "apostles" after 16:4? How did Christianity

spread to Rome before Paul? Nevertheless, Luke sees the episodes he narrates as spelling out the continuation of what Jesus "began" (Acts 1:1).

(34) The selection that Luke made shaped the sequel to his Gospel for a definite purpose. He shaped it with a studied parallelism, depicting the fate of Jesus and Stephen in a similar way and portraying the missions of Peter and Paul in parallel fashion. Moreover, the speeches that he put on the lips of his principal orators, Peter, Stephen, and Paul, contribute in no small way to the literary goal that he had before him; for the whole Lucan composition is a story with a message, and Acts a historical monograph with a proclamation. Through the narrative account about Jesus and early Christians Luke himself preaches and proclaims a message.

(35) Luke was interested in writing not only a Jesus-story, as others had attempted before him (Luke 1:1), but in casting that story in a further mold. He accordingly gave it a geographical and historical framework, which is found in none of the other Gospels. I have already discussed these perspectives in some detail in the sketch of Lucan theology, because they bring out facets of that theology (*Luke*, 164–87). Certain aspects of those perspectives now have to be stressed as they bear on the purpose of Acts.

(36) Unlike other evangelists, Luke begins and ends his Gospel in Jerusalem. After the Gospel's prologue, the first scene tells of Zechariah offering incense in the Jerusalem Temple (1:9); at the end of the Gospel the disciples return to Jerusalem from Bethany and spend their time in the Temple (24:53). Another aspect of that geographical perspective is Luke's preoccupation in the Gospel with moving Jesus (without distraction) from Galilee to the city of destiny, Jerusalem, where salvation was to be accomplished and whence he would make his transit to the Father. This reveals the importance of Jerusalem in Luke's geographical conception in the Gospel. Jerusalem then takes on a pivotal role in the Lucan writings, for the risen Christ declares to his disciples that in his name "repentance for the forgiveness of sins must be preached to all the nations—beginning from Jerusalem" (Luke 24:47). The pivotal role of Jerusalem is important in Luke-Acts because it is related to "the events that have come to fulfillment among us" (Luke 1:1). Those events include not only what "Jesus did and taught from the beginning" (Acts 1:1), but also the stage-by-stage spread of the Word of God from Jerusalem, the mother church, to the rest of Judea and Samaria (8:1, 5, 26), to Caesarea Maritima (8:40), to Galilee (9:31), to Damascus (9:2), to Phoenicia, Cyprus, and Syrian Antioch (11:19), to the Roman provinces of Cilicia, Galatia, Asia, Macedonia, and Achaia, and finally to Rome itself, "the end of the earth" (Acts 1:8; 23:11c; 28:14; cf. *Ps. Sol.* 8:15). Thus in the Third Gospel all is oriented toward Jerusalem, and in Acts all goes forth from Jerusalem—to the end of the earth. This geographical perspective has colored the entire Lucan account of the Jesus-story and its sequel and reveals an important theological aspect of the purpose of Luke-Acts.

(37) Similarly, the historical perspective with which Luke cloaked his story is equally important for his purpose. If one did not have the Lucan account, it

would be somewhat difficult to anchor the Christ-event. Neither Mark nor John give us much of a clue about when the life and ministry of Jesus took place, save in the reference to Pontius Pilate (Mark 15:1–44; John 18:29–19:38 [A.D. 26–36]) and to the high priest Caiaphas (John 11:49; 18:13–28 [A.D. 18–36]). Matthew differs from these evangelists only in that he informs us that Jesus "was born in the days of Herod the king" (Matt 2:1 [i.e., 37–4 B.C.]). For Luke, however, as Bultmann once rightly noted, Christianity has become an "entity of world history" (*TNT*, 2.116). Luke's story relates the life, ministry, and career of Jesus to Roman, Palestinian, and church history.

(38) (a) **Roman history.** Luke recounts the birth of Jesus not only in the days of Herod, but links it with a decree of Caesar Augustus (Luke 2:1–2 [27 B.C.–A.D. 14]) and the Roman governorship of P. Sulpicius Quirinius (2:2 [A.D. 6–7?]). He dates the beginning of the ministry of the Baptist, and consequently that of Jesus himself, to the fifteenth year of Tiberius Caesar (A.D. 28–29) and to the prefecture of Pontius Pilate in Judea (Luke 3:1 [A.D. 26–36]). Further reference to Roman history is found in the mention of the famine in the days of the emperor Claudius (Acts 11:28 [A.D. 41–54]); the expulsion of Jews from Rome by Claudius (Acts 18:2 [A.D. 49]); and Paul's being haled before the Roman governor of Achaia, Gallio, the proconsul (Acts 18:12 [summer or early fall of A.D. 52]).

(39) (b) **Palestinian history.** The coming birth of John the Baptist is announced to his father in "the days of Herod, king of Judea" (Luke 1:5 [37–4 B.C.]). Despite the synchronic conflict that this causes with the mention of Jesus' birth (only some months later) in the time of Augustus and Quirinius (Luke 2:1–6), it is clearly meant to situate Jesus' birth in Palestinian history. Similarly, God's call comes to John the Baptist "when Pontius Pilate was governor of Judea" (Luke 3:1). Moreover, Jesus appears before Pilate (Luke 23:1–5), only to be sent by him to Herod Antipas, the tetrarch of Galilee (4 B.C.–A.D. 39); this detail is found only in the Lucan Gospel. Though the connection of Caiaphas with Jesus' trial is known from the passion narrative in other Gospels, only Luke refers to Annas and Caiaphas at the beginning of John's ministry (Luke 3:2). Further reference to them is made in Acts 4:6, when Peter and John are summoned before them along with other members of the "high-priestly class." Again, Luke mentions Herod Antipas, tetrarch of Galilee, Philip, tetrarch of Iturea and Trachonitis, and Lysanias, tetrarch of Abilene, as rulers connected with the history of Palestine (Luke 3:1). King Herod Agrippa I (10 B.C.–A.D. 44) appears in Acts 12, and his death is recounted in 12:23. King Agrippa II (A.D. 27–93?) appears in Acts 25:13. Thus Luke has anchored the Jesus-story and its sequel in Palestinian history.

(40) (c) **Church history.** The sequel to the Lucan Gospel gives a view of the rapid spread of the Word of God and the apostolic testimony borne about Jesus, who is now proclaimed as Lord and Messiah, to the end of the earth. That spread involves the emergence of a community of disciples, eventually called "Christians" (11:26) and also "church" (5:11; 8:1, 3; 9:31; 20:28). Some of the primordial events in church history are recorded. Thus Luke has related in a unique way the Jesus-story to the early history of the Christian church. In his two volumes he

seeks to show that the Jesus-story has important historical connections and that it was indeed an important part of world history.

Moreover, Christianity not only became an entity of world history, but *religio licita*, a form of worship legitimate in the Roman Empire, to use a later Latin term. One of the subsidiary purposes of the Lucan infancy narrative was to depict how Jesus of Nazareth was incorporated into Palestinian Judaism from his very birth and circumcision. Only as the story develops, however, especially in the second volume, does one begin to realize that part of Luke's concern for that incorporation of Jesus in Judaism at the outset has been to foreshadow an important aspect of Christianity itself. Though it is not the main purpose of Acts or a major concern of the author, as has sometimes been argued (Easton, Cadbury, Haenchen), one cannot deny that Luke has a subordinate concern to depict Christianity as a logical outgrowth and continuation of Judaism, especially the Pharisaic form of it. This concern is not immediately obvious at the beginning of the Jesus-story, but it gradually emerges: first of all with the triple declaration of Jesus' innocence by the Roman Pilate in the passion narrative (Luke 23:4, 14, 22), then indirectly in declarations of Paul's innocence toward the end of Acts (16:37–39; 18:15–16; 23:29; 25:8, 25; 26:30–32; 28:21), including those put on the lips of both Roman officials and Jews. See further Cassidy *(Society and Politics)*, who shows that Luke is more concerned to prepare his readers for possible persecution and to instruct them to obey God rather than human officials. However, even that remains a minor goal of the Lucan writing.

(41) Thus the historical key in which Luke has played the kerygma in his writings has a theological and apologetic purpose, even if the latter may not yet be the main purpose of Acts. In 1960 W. C. van Unnik maintained that, save for the monograph of Easton, *The Purpose of Acts* (1936), the problem of the purpose of Acts had been practically neglected. That was something of an oversimplification. Schneider ("Der Zweck," 45) subsequently showed that German interpreters of the last century had often discussed the purpose of Acts. Van Unnik noted that it had been recognized that Luke wanted to depict the spread of the Word of God from Jerusalem to Rome, that he sought to describe the disciples preaching the Word to the inhabited world of their day, that he depicted Christianity as *religio licita*, and showed how the Christian message should be preached. Van Unnik himself, however, sought to explain its purpose by presenting Acts as the confirmation of the Lucan Gospel. Using Heb 2:3–4 as a striking way of summarizing Luke's two-volume work, he argued that in the Gospel the Lucan Jesus is depicted announcing salvation, whereas in Acts the disciples are portrayed confirming the Gospel by their testimony and miracles. Hence "the gospel is not the 'initium christianismi' [beginning of Christianity]," as Käsemann once regarded it (*ZTK* 51 [1954]: 137), "but the *archē sōtērias* [the beginning of salvation] and Acts confirms it as the word for the world" ("The 'Book of Acts,'" 58–59). There is little with which one would quibble in that view, but is it the whole story?

Van Unnik's description reopened the more recent discussion about the purpose of Acts. Many attempts have been made to formulate it; some of them describe aspects of the purpose or only part of it: the spread of Christianity or the victorious course of the Gospel (Wikenhauser); the missionary endeavor of early Christians; a commendation of Christianity at the expense of Judaism (Klausner); an edifying instruction of catechumens or neophytes like Theophilus (Foakes Jackson, Kümmel); a model of how the gospel should be preached (Dibelius); a pattern of what the church should be and may be (Käsemann).

(42) Recently the purpose of Acts has been subsumed more adequately under the heading of the purpose of Luke-Acts, i.e., of the double Lucan work. In this regard one has to distinguish Luke's stated purpose and the purpose that emerges when one considers the Third Gospel and Acts together. Luke's stated purpose is found in the prologue to his Gospel, which, despite the protestations of Haenchen (*Acts*, 136 n. 3), is usually regarded today as the preface to his two-volume work: "So that your Excellency may realize what assurance you have for the instruction you have received" (Luke 1:4). *Asphaleia*, "assurance," cannot be limited merely to historical "assurance" or historicity; it is also a doctrinal assurance, or better a pastoral assurance, for Luke writes from the Period of the Church under Stress (see *Luke*, 181–87) and aims to assure Theophilus and other Gentile-Christian readers like him that what the church of his day was teaching and practicing was rooted in the Period of Jesus, in the teaching of Jesus himself, in order to strengthen them in fidelity to that teaching and practice, even when that proved unacceptable to many Jews and pagans of Luke's day. See further S. Brown, "The Role of the Prologues"; R. Maddox, *Purpose*.

When Luke 1:4, however, is related to the programmatic verse of Acts 1:8, one sees that Luke-Acts purports to be indeed "a work of edification" (Haenchen, *Acts*, 103), but not simply with the nuances that Haenchen sought to associate with that phrase; for Luke "is not just an 'edifying writer', but a historian and theologian who needs to be taken seriously" (Hengel, *Acts*, 61). As an ancient Hellenistic historian, Luke in Acts recounts the apostolic origin of the Christian community and the spread of apostolic testimony about the Word of God for a set purpose: to build up that community and to win over Gentiles to it. The narrative account of Acts thus continues the Jesus-story and spreads abroad "to the end of the earth" the Word that Jesus "taught from the beginning" (1:1). It has now become the Word about the risen Christ, his salvific work, and the activity of his Spirit. Ehrhardt has called Acts the "Gospel of the Holy Spirit" ("The Construction," 89). Again, this may be an exaggeration as far as the overall character of Acts is concerned, but it does express at least an aspect of the testimony that the chosen witnesses were commissioned to bear. It is certainly not to be understood as an exclusion of historical value in Acts.

(43) Luke insisted that all this "did not take place in a dark corner!" (Acts 26:26). In other words, the Jesus-story and its sequel had indeed become "an entity of world history," and Luke depicted it as such in his historical monograph; but, in addition to the geographical and historical perspectives with which Luke clothed the Jesus-story, he also set out to record it precisely as "a continuation of biblical history" (Dahl, "The Purpose," 88). In this respect Luke-Acts is unique

in the NT, not only in insisting that "the God of Abraham, the God of Isaac, and the God of Jacob, the God of our ancestors" is the one who has "honored his servant Jesus" (3:13) and "raised him from the dead" (3:15), but also in depicting Peter and Paul as the transmitters to Jews and Gentiles of this salvation (brought about in Jesus), which had been promised to the people of Israel and actually made available, first of all, to them. Thus Luke is concerned to pass on to a postapostolic age of Christians an account of the Jesus-tradition, which is intimately related to the biblical *history* of Israel of old, and to insist that it is only within the stream of apostolic tradition, represented by Peter and by Paul, that one finds this divinely destined salvation. The story of Jesus is but the beginning of the history of the still expanding church that Luke hopes to strengthen and build up by his two-volume narrative monograph, for the risen Christ now proclaimed by Luke is "the author of life" (3:15) and the "leader and savior" of humanity (5:31).

(44) The concern of Luke to stress the connection and the continuation between Judaism and Christianity is seen clearly in his use of the OT to interpret the Christ-event. He cites many passages of the Hebrew Scriptures that, although formally lacking predictive elements, he reads not only as prophecy but even as predictions of what came to be in the ministry of Jesus and its sequel, "the events that have come to fulfillment among us" (Luke 1:1). "All the prophets who have spoken, from Samuel on down, have also proclaimed these days" (Acts 3:24 [see G. Schneider, "Der Zweck," 51]). This idea has been variously labeled as promise and fulfillment in Luke-Acts, or as the proof-from-prophecy motif. It is no small factor in the motivation of Luke as he gathered up the tradition about Jesus and the movement that began with him. It is intimately connected with the reversal-theme related to his view of salvation-history (Dahl, "The Purpose," 95–96). Other aspects of Luke's use of the OT will be developed below, but it is mentioned now because it too is an important facet of the purpose of Luke-Acts.

(45) Along with such a predominant concern to write a continuation of biblical history, there is also a minor biographical concern (Ehrhardt, Hengel). In addition to being the first "life of Christ" (Conzelmann), Luke's account also tells us something about the lives of Peter and Paul. How "historical" it was is an issue that will be discussed further below, but one has to recognize this biographical concern as an aspect of the purpose of Luke, the ancient historian, in composing his two-volume monographical account of the Jesus-story.

(46) Lastly, Luke-Acts was not composed as a "defense against what appears to be a form of early Christian Gnosticism" (Talbert, *Luke and the Gnostics*, 110). That there were gnostics around in the period when Luke was writing is the first problem with that thesis; and second, that the gnostics, when they finally emerged in mid-second century, were Christians is equally problematic. The Church Fathers, who were contemporaries of that movement and opposed it, almost certainly did not so regard them (see *Luke*, 11). Gnosticism is, indeed, a problematic factor in church history in the second and later centuries, but opposition to it is scarcely reflected in Luke-Acts.

BIBLIOGRAPHY

Title of Acts

Balch, D. L., "The Genre of Luke-Acts: Individual Biography, Adventure Novel, or Political History?" *SwJT* 33 (1990–91): 5–19.

Barr, D. L. and J. L. Wentling, "The Conventions of Classical Biography and the Genre of Luke-Acts: A Preliminary Study," *Luke-Acts: New Perspectives* (ed. C. H. Talbert), 63–88.

Barrett, C. K., "Luke/Acts," *It Is Written: Scripture Citing Scripture: Essays in Honour of Barnabas Lindars, SSF* (ed. D. A. Carson and H.G.M. Williamson; Cambridge: Cambridge University Press, 1988), 231–44.

Bovon, F., "Evangile de Luc et Actes des Apôtres," *Evangiles synoptiques et Actes des Apôtres* (Petite bibliothèque des sciences bibliques, Nouveau Testament 4; ed. J. Auneau et al.; Paris: Desclée, 1981), 195–283.

Fuller, R. H., "The Lucan Writings," *The New Testament in Current Study* (New York: Scribner, 1962), 86–100.

Gibert, P., "L'Invention d'un genre littéraire," *LumVie* 30 (1981): 19–33.

Hengel, M., *Acts and the History of Earliest Christianity*, 35–39.

Palmer, D. W., "Acts and the Historical Monograph," *TynBull* 43 (1992): 373–88.

Pervo, R. L., *Profit with Delight.*

Praeder, S. A., "Luke-Acts and the Ancient Novel," *SBL 1981 Seminar Papers* (ed. K. H. Richards; Chico, CA: Scholars, 1981), 269–92.

Talbert, C. H., *Literary Patterns, Theological Themes and the Genre of Luke-Acts*, 125–40.

Authorship and Relation to Third Gospel

Argyle, A. W., "The Greek of Luke and Acts," *NTS* 20 (1973–74): 441–45.

Barrett, C. K., "The Third Gospel as a Preface to Acts? Some Reflections," *The Four Gospels 1992: Festschrift Frans Neirynck* (3 vols.; BETL 100; ed. F. van Segbroeck et al.; Louvain: Leuven University/Peeters, 1992), 2.1451–66.

Beck, B. E., "The Common Authorship of Luke and Acts," *NTS* 23 (1976–77): 346–52.

Blaisdell, J. A., "The Authorship of the 'We' Sections of the Book of Acts," *HTR* 13 (1920): 136–58.

Bovon, F., "Luc: Portrait et projet," *LumVie* 30/153–54 (1981): 9–18.

Cadbury, H. J., *The Making of Luke-Acts*, 353–60.

Clark, A. C., *The Acts of the Apostles* (Oxford: Clarendon, 1933), 393–408.

Dawsey, J., "The Literary Unity of Luke-Acts: Questions of Style—A Task for Literary Critics," *NTS* 35 (1989): 48–66.

Enslin, M. S., "Luke, the Literary Physician," *Studies in New Testament and Early Christian Literature: Essays in Honor of Allen P. Wikgren* (NovTSup 33; ed. D. E. Aune; Leiden: Brill, 1972), 135–43.

Fitzmyer, J. A., "The Authorship of Luke-Acts Reconsidered," *LTAHT*, 1–26.
Glover, R., "'Luke the Antiochene' and Acts," *NTS* 11 (1964–65): 97–106.
Guthrie, D., *New Testament Introduction: The Gospels and Acts* (London: Tyndale, 1965), 92–109.
Harnack, A., *Luke the Physician: The Author of the Third Gospel and the Acts of the Apostles*, 149–71.
———, "Noch einmal Lukas als Verfasser des 3. Evangeliums und der Apostelgeschichte," *TLZ* 31 (1906): 466–68.
Hawkins, J. C., *Horae Synopticae* (2d ed.; Oxford: Clarendon, 1909), 174–93.
Hemer, C. J., *The Book of Acts*, 308–64, esp. 362–63.
Hengel, M., *Between Jesus and Paul: Studies in the Earliest History of Christianity* (London: SCM, 1983), 97–128.
Hiebert, D. E., *An Introduction to the New Testament: Volume 1, The Gospels and Acts* (Chicago: Moody, 1975), 245–96.
Jervell, J., *The Unknown Paul* (Minneapolis: Augsburg, 1984), 13–25.
Knox, W. L., *The Acts of the Apostles*, 1–15, 100–9.
Kümmel, W. G., *Introduction to the New Testament* (rev. ed.; Nashville: Abingdon, 1975), 151–88.
Léon-Dufour, X. and C. Perrot, *L'Annonce de l'évangile* (Introduction à la Bible 3/2; Paris: Desclée, 1976), 239–95.
McNeile, A. H., *An Introduction to the Study of the New Testament* (2d ed., rev. C.S.C. Williams; Oxford: Clarendon, 1953), 92–123.
MacRory, J., "The Authorship of the Third Gospel and the Acts," *ITQ* 2 (1907): 190–202.
Marxsen, W., *Introduction to the New Testament: An Approach to Its Problems* (Oxford: Blackwell; Philadelphia: Fortress, 1968), 167–73.
Meinertz, M., *Einleitung in das Neue Testament* (5th ed.; Paderborn: Schöningh, 1950), 237–46.
Michaelis, W., *Einleitung in das Neue Testament* (2d ed.; Bern: B. Haller, 1954), 129–43.
Muhlack, G., *Die Parallelen.*
O'Toole, R. F., *The Unity of Luke's Theology.*
Parsons, M. C., "The Unity of the Lukan Writings: Rethinking the *Opinio Communis*," *With Steadfast Purpose: Essays on Acts in Honor of Henry Jackson Flanders, Jr.* (ed. N. H. Keathley; Waco, TX: Baylor University Press, 1990), 29–53.
Parsons, M. and R. I. Pervo, *Rethinking the Unity of Luke and Acts* (Minneapolis: Fortress, 1993).
Plooy, G.P.V. du, "The Author in Luke-Acts," *Scriptura* 32 (1990): 28–35.
Plümacher, E., "Apostelgeschichte," *TRE* 3 (1978): 483–528.
———, "Die Apostelgeschichte als historische Monographie," *Les Actes des Apôtres* (ed. J. Kremer), 457–66.
Polhill, J. B., "Introduction to the Study of Acts," *RevExp* 87 (1990): 385–401.
Powell, M. A., "Luke's Second Volume: Three Basic Issues in Contemporary Studies of Acts," *Trinity Seminary Review* 13 (1991): 69–81.
Praeder, S. M., "Jesus-Paul, Peter-Paul and Jesus-Peter Parallelisms in Luke-Acts:

A History of Reader Response," *SBL 1984 Seminar Papers* (ed. K. H. Richards; Chico, CA: Scholars, 1984), 23–39.

Russell, H. G., "Which Was Written First, Luke or Acts?" *HTR* 48 (1955): 167–74.

Schulz, M., *Der Arzt Lukas und die Apostelgeschichte* (Berlin: Evangelische Verlagsanstalt, 1959).

Solbakk, J. H., "Lukas—Legen," *NorTT* 94 (1993): 219–33.

Talbert, C. H., *Literary Patterns.*

Tannehill, R. C., *The Narrative Unity of Luke-Acts.*

Wallis, E. E., "The First and Second Epistles of Luke to Theophilus," *JOTT* 5 (1992): 225–51.

Wenham, J., "The Identification of Luke," *EvQ* 63 (1991): 3–44.

Wikenhauser, A. and J. Schmid, *Einleitung in das Neue Testament* (6th ed.; Freiburg im B.: 1973), 344–79.

Date of Composition

Burkitt, F. C., *The Gospel History and Its Transmission* (3d ed.; Edinburgh: Clark, 1911), 105–10.

Cross, J. A., "Recent Opinions on the Date of the Acts of the Apostles," *ExpTim* 12 (1900–1): 334–36, 423–25; 13 (1901–2): 43–46.

Ellis, E. E., "'The End of the Earth' (Acts 1:8)," *BBR* 1 (1991): 123–32.

Goodspeed, E. J., "The Date of Acts," *Expos* 8/17 (1919): 387–91.

Harnack, A., *The Date of the Acts and of the Synoptic Gospels,* 89–116.

Hemer, C. J., *The Book of Acts,* 365–410.

Klein, H., "Zur Frage nach dem Abfassungsort der Lukasschriften," *EvT* 32 (1972): 467–77.

Knox, J., "Acts and the Pauline Letter Corpus," *StLA,* 279–87.

———, *Marcion and the New Testament: An Essay in the Early History of the Canon* (Chicago: University of Chicago Press, 1942), 114–39.

Mattill, A. J., Jr., "The Date and Purpose of Luke-Acts: Rackham Reconsidered," *CBQ* 40 (1978): 335–50.

Méhat, A., "Les écrits de Luc et les événements de 70: Problèmes de datation," *RHR* 209 (1992): 149–80.

Moberly, R. B., "When Was Acts Planned and Shaped?" *EvQ* 65 (1993): 5–26.

O'Neill, J. C., *The Theology of Acts in Its Historical Setting* (London: SPCK, 1961), 1–53 ("The Date of Acts").

Parker, P., "The 'Former Treatise' and the Date of Acts," *JBL* 84 (1965): 52–58.

Rackham, R. B., "The Acts of the Apostles: II. A Plea for an Early Date," *JTS* 1 (1899–1900): 76–87.

Reicke, B., "Synoptic Prophecies on the Destruction of Jerusalem," *Studies in New Testament and Early Christian Literature* (see Enslin above), 121–34.

Robinson, J.A.T., *Redating the New Testament* (London: SCM; Philadelphia: Westminster, 1976), 86–117.

Schneider, G., Review of J. C. O'Neill, *The Theology of Acts, BZ* 16 (1972): 126–29.

Sparks, H.F.D., Review of J. C. O'Neill, *The Theology of Acts, JTS* 14 (1963): 454–66, esp. 457–66.

Torrey, C. C., *The Composition and Date of Acts*, 65–72.

Townsend, J. T., "The Date of Luke-Acts," *Luke-Acts: New Perspectives* (ed. C. H. Talbert), 47–62.

Trompf, G. W., "On Why Luke Declined to Recount the Death of Paul: Acts 27–28 and Beyond," *Luke-Acts: New Perspectives* (ed. C. H. Talbert), 225–39.

Vielhauer, P., *Geschichte der urchristlichen Literatur* (Berlin/New York: de Gruyter, 1975), 366–409, esp. 407.

Wenham, J., *Redating Matthew, Mark and Luke: A Fresh Assault on the Synoptic Problem* (London: Hodder and Stoughton, 1991), 223–44.

Wieseler, K., *Chronologie des apostolischen Zeitalters bis zum Tode der Apostel Paulus und Petrus: Ein Versuch über die Chronologie und Abfassungszeit der Apostelgeschichte und der paulinischen Briefe* (Göttingen: Vandenhoeck & Ruprecht, 1848).

Williams, C.S.C., "The Date of Luke-Acts," *ExpTim* 64 (1952–53): 283–84.

Wilshire, L. E., "Was Canonical Luke Written in the Second Century?—A Continuing Discussion," *NTS* 20 (1973–74): 246–53.

Purpose

Aberle, M., "Über den Zweck der Apostelgeschichte," *TQ* 37 (1855): 173–236.

Brown, S., "The Prologues of Luke-Acts in Their Relation to the Purpose of the Author," *SBL Seminar Papers 1975* (2 vols.; ed. G. W. MacRae; Missoula: Scholars, 1975), 2.1–14.

———, "The Role of the Prologues in Determining the Purpose of Luke-Acts," *Perspectives on Luke-Acts* (ed. C. H. Talbert), 99–111.

Bruce, F. F., "Paul's Apologetic and the Purpose of Acts," *BJRL* 69 (1987): 379–93.

Crehan, J. H., "The Purpose of Luke in Acts," *SE II* (TU 87): 354–68.

Dahl, N. A., "The Purpose of Luke-Acts," *Jesus in the Memory of the Early Church* (Minneapolis: Augsburg, 1976), 87–98.

Easton, B. S., *The Purpose of Acts* ("Theology" Occasional Papers 6; London: SPCK, 1936); repr. in *Early Christianity: The Purpose of Acts and Other Papers* (Greenwich, CT: Seabury, 1954; London: SPCK, 1955), 33–118.

Ehrhardt, A., "The Construction and Purpose of the Acts of the Apostles," *ST* 12 (1958): 45–79; repr. in *The Framework of the New Testament Stories* (Cambridge: Harvard University Press, 1964), 64–102.

Ellis, E. E., "Situation and Purpose of Acts," *Int* 28 (1974): 94–98.

Franklin, E., *Christ the Lord: A Study in the Purpose and Theology of Luke-Acts* (London: SPCK; Philadelphia: Westminster, 1975).

Hengel, M., *Acts and the History of Earliest Christianity.*

Hückelheim, J. F., *Zweck der Apostelgeschichte: Eine biblische Studie* (Paderborn: Schoningh, 1908).

Larsson, E., "Det doble budskap," *NorTT* 91 (1990): 66–83.

Légasse, "L'Apologétique à l'égard de Rome dans le procès de Paul: Actes 21, 27–26,32," *RSR* 69 (1981): 249–55.

Maddox, R. L., *The Purpose of Luke-Acts* (FRLANT 126; Göttingen: Vandenhoeck & Ruprecht, 1982; repr. in the series, Studies of the New Testament and Its World; Edinburgh: Clark, 1982).

Mattill, A. J., Jr., "The Good Samaritan and the Purpose of Luke-Acts: Halevy Reconsidered," *Encounter* 33 (1972): 359–76.

———, "The Jesus-Paul Parallels and the Purpose of Luke-Acts: H. H. Evans Reconsidered," *NovT* 17 (1975): 15–46.

———, "*Naherwartung, Fernerwartung,* and the Purpose of Luke-Acts: Weymouth Reconsidered," *CBQ* 34 (1972): 276–93.

———, "The Purpose of Acts: Schneckenburger Reconsidered," *Apostolic History and the Gospel: Biblical and Historical Essays Presented to F. F. Bruce . . .* (ed. W. W. Gasque and R. P. Martin; Grand Rapids, MI: Eerdmans, 1970), 108–22.

Minear, P. S., "Dear Theo: The Kerygmatic Intention and Claim of the Book of Acts," *Int* 27 (1973): 131–50.

Mussner, F., "Die Erzählintention des Lukas in der Apostelgeschichte," *Der Treue Gottes trauen: Beiträge zum Werk des Lukas: Für Gerhard Schneider* (ed. C. Bussmann and W. Radl; Freiburg im B.: Herder, 1991), 29–41.

O'Toole, R. F., "Why Did Luke Write Acts (Lk-Acts)?" *BTB* 7 (1977): 66–76.

Schneider, G., "Der Zweck des lukanischen Doppelwerks," *BZ* 21 (1977): 45–66; repr. *LTH*, 9–30.

Talbert, C. H., *Luke and the Gnostics.*

Unnik, W. C. van, "Die Apostelgeschichte und die Häresien," *ZNW* 58 (1967): 240–46; repr. *Sparsa Collecta,* 1.402–9.

———, "The 'Book of Acts' the Confirmation of the Gospel," *NovT* 4 (1960–61): 26–59; repr. *Sparsa Collecta,* 1.340–73.

———, "Remarks on the Purpose of Luke's Historical Writing (Luke 1, 1–4)," *Sparsa Collecta,* 1.6–15 (from Dutch original, *NedTT* 9 [1955]: 323–31).

Walaskay, P. W., *'And So We Came to Rome.'*

Wilson, J. M., *The Origin and Aim of the Acts of the Apostles* (London: Macmillan, 1912).

Winn, A. C., "Elusive Mystery: The Purpose of Acts," *Int* 13 (1959): 144–56.

Zwaan, J. de, "Was the Book of Acts a Posthumous Edition?" *HTR* 17 (1924): 95–153.

II. Text of Acts

◆

(47) No book of the NT has such a complicated history of its transmitted Greek text as the Acts of the Apostles. The Greek text is preserved in thirteen papyrus fragments, dating from the third to the eighth centuries; in twenty-eight uncial or majuscule manuscripts, dating from the fourth to the tenth centuries; and in a host of minuscule manuscripts, dating from the ninth to the fifteenth centuries. The most important of these texts are:

(A) The Papyri

Siglum	*Century*	*Location*	*Contents*
P^{8}	IV	Berlin, SM Inv. 8683	4:31–37; 5:2–9; 6:1–6, 8–15
P^{29}	III	Oxford, Bodl. Gr. bibl. g. 4 (P); POxy 1597	26:7–8, 20
P^{33+58}	VI	Vienna, ÖNB Pap. G. 17973, 26133, 35831 (=P^{58}), 39783	7:6–10, 13–18; 15:21–24, 26–32
P^{38}	ca. 300	Ann Arbor, UM Inv. 1571; P. Mich. 138	18:27–19:6, 12–16
P^{41}	VIII	Vienna, ÖNB Pap. K. 7541–48	17:28–18:2, 24–25, 27; 19:1–4, 6–8, 13–16, 18–19; 20:9–13, 15–16, 22–24, 26–28, 35–38; 21:1–4; 22:11–14, 16–17
P^{45}	III	Dublin, P. Chester Beatty I	4:27–36; 5:10–21, 30–39; 6:7–7:2, 10–21, 32–41; 7:52–8:1, 14–25; 8:34–9:6, 16–27; 9:35–10:2, 10–23, 31–41; 11:2–14; 11:24–12:5, 13–22; 13:6–16, 25–36; 13:46–14:3, 15–23; 15:2–7, 19–27; 15:38–16:4, 15–21, 32–40; 17:9–17

P^{48}	late III	Florence, Bibl. Laurenziana, PSI 1165	23:11–17, 23–29
P^{50}	IV–V	New Haven, Yale Univ. Libr., P. 1543	8:26–32; 10:26–31
P^{53}	III	Ann Arbor, UM Inv. 6652	9:33–10:1
P^{56}	V–VI	Vienna, ÖNB Pap. G. 19918	1:1, 4–5, 7, 10–11
P^{57}	IV–V	Vienna, ÖNB Pap. G. 26020	4:36–5:2, 8–10
P^{74}	VII	Cologny, Bibl. Bodmer, P. Bodmer XVII	1:2–5, 7–11, 13–17, 18–19, 22–25; 2:2–4; 2:6–3:26; 4:2–6, 8–27; 4:29–27:25; 27:27–28:31
P^{91}	III	Milan Inv. 1224 + P. Macquarie Inv. 360	2:30–37; 2:46–3:2

(B) Uncial Manuscripts

א	IV	London, Brit. Mus., Add. 43725	All
A	V	London, Brit. Mus., Royal 1 D. VIII	All
B	IV	Vatican City, Bibl. Vaticana, Gr. 1209	All
C	V	Paris, Bibl. Nat., Gr. 9	1:3–4:2; 5:35–6:7; 6:9–10:42; 13:2–16:36; 20:11–21:30; 22:21–23:17; 24:16–26:18; 27:17–28:4
D	V	Cambridge, Univ. Libr., Nn. II 41	1:1–8:29; 10:4–21:2; 21:10–22:10; 22:20–29
E	VI	Oxford, Bodl. Libr., Laud. Gr. 35	1:1–26:28
H	IX	Modena, Bibl. Estens. G. 196	All
L	IX	Rome, Bibl. Angelica 39	8:11–28:31
P	IX	St. Petersburg, Publ. Bibl., Gr. 225	All
Ψ	VIII–IX	Athos, Lavra, B′ 52	All
048	V	Vatican City, Bibl. Vaticana, Gr. 2061	26:6–27:4; 28:3–31
049	IX	Athos, Lavra, A′ 88	All

057	IV–V	Berlin, SM, P. 9808	3:5–6, 10–12
066	VI	St. Petersburg, Publ. Bibl., Gr. 6,II	28:8–17
076	V–VI	New York, Pierpont Morgan Libr., Pap. G. 8	2:11–22
077	V	Sinai, Harris App. 5	13:28–29
093	VI	Cambridge, Univ. Libr. T-S Coll. 12, 189. 208	24:22–25:5
095+0123	VIII	St. Petersburg, Publ. Bibl., Gr. 17; 49, 1–2	2:22–28; 2:45–3:8
096	VII	St. Petersburg, Publ. Bibl., Gr. 19	2:6–17; 26:7–18
097	VII	St. Petersburg, Publ. Bibl., Gr. 18	13:39–46
0120	IX	Vatican City, Bibl. Vaticana, Gr. 2302	16:30–17:17, 27–29, 31–34; 18:8–26
0140	X	Sinai, Harris App. 41	5:34–38
0165	V	Berlin, SM, P. 13271	3:24–4:13, 17–20
0166	V	Heidelberg, Univ. Bibl. Pap. 1357	28:30–31
0175	V	Florence, Bibl. Laurenziana, PSI 125	6:7–10, 12–15
0189	II/III	Berlin, SM, P. 11765	5:3–21
0236	V	Moscow, Mus. Pushkina, Golenishchew, Copt. 55	3:12–13, 15–16
0244	V	Louvain, Bibl. de l'Univer. PAM Kh. Mird 8	11:29–12:5

(C) Minuscule Manuscripts

1	XII	Basel, Univ. Bibl. A. N. IV. 2	All
33	IX	Paris, Bibl. Nat., Gr. 14	All
81	1044	London, Brit. Mus., Add. 20003; Alexandria, Bibl. Patriarch., 59	All but 4:8–7:17; 17:28–23:9

104	1087	London, Brit. Mus., Harley 5537	All
323	XI	Geneva, Bibl. Publ. et Univ., Gr. 20	All but 1:1–8; 2:36–45
326	XII	Oxford, Lincoln College, Lat. 82	All
614	XIII	Milan, Bibl. Ambros., E 97 sup.	All
945	XI	Athos, Dionysiou, 124 (37)	All
1175	XI	Patmos, Ioannou, 16	All
1241	XII	Sinai, Gr. 260	All but 17:10–18
1739	X	Athos, Lavra, B′ 64	All but 1:1–2:6
1891	X	Jerusalem, Saba 107; St. Petersburg, Publ. Bibl., Gr. 317	All

A number of other less important minuscules could be mentioned here: e.g., 2, 4, 6, 36, 42, 51, 61, 69, 189, 424, 453, 1704, 1884, 1891, 2464.

(48) In themselves, the manuscripts are impressive, and they attest to the carefulness of scribes over the first millennium and a half before the invention of printing. They also reveal how complicated the textual transmission of Acts has been across the centuries. There are basically three kinds of text for Acts: the Alexandrian text, which Westcott and Hort called Neutral, the so-called Western text, and the Byzantine text, sometimes called the *Koinē* or Syrian text, which is attested in the vast majority of the minuscule manuscripts. Of these the first two are important because they preserve forms of the text of Acts with the least corruption and are found in older manuscripts; the last (Byzantine) represents a text-tradition that was commonly used but was the result of harmonization, conflation, and a choice of often-corrupt readings. It was mainly reproduced in the so-called *Textus Receptus*.

(49) The Alexandrian text of Acts is chiefly found in P^{45}, P^{50}, P^{74}, ℵ, A, B, C, Ψ, 33 (especially for 11:26–28:31), 81, 104, 326, and 1175. It is also found in the Sahidic version and in citations in the writings of Clement of Alexandria and Origen. Sometimes text critics distinguish two forms of the Alexandrian text: (a) Proto-Alexandrian: found mainly in P^{45}, P^{74}, ℵ, B, Sahidic version, Clement, Origen; (b) Later Alexandrian: mainly in P^{50}, A, C, Ψ, 33, 81, 104, and 326. The important minuscule MS 1739 may also belong in the last category; see T. C. Geer, Jr., "Codex 1739 in Acts." This Alexandrian text-tradition is basically what is used in the critical editions of the *NTG* or NA^{27} and of the UBS *GNT*, fourth edition, which have always scrutinized the evidence from the Western text as well.

(50) The Western text (WT) is really a misnomer, because witnesses to it have also been found in manuscripts of the East; but the name has become so conventional that it is retained. Moreover, it would be better to speak of Western texts,

since all manuscripts or fragments or patristic quotations related to this group do not pass on an identical text. What is meant by WT is "a broad stream of textual tradition" (Strange, *Problem,* 37). For Acts, this text-tradition is found mainly in the Greek and Latin MS D (Codex Bezae Cantabrigiensis) but is also represented in P^{29}, P^{38}, P^{48}, E, 383, and 614, in the Harclean Syriac version (margin with *), in MS h of the African Vetus Latina, in the Coptic G67, in citations of some early Latin patristic writers (Tertullian, Cyprian, Augustine), and in the commentary on Acts by Ephraem of Syria. For the evidence in all ancient languages, see Boismard and Lamouille, *Le texte occidental,* 1.11–95; they have established the best available form of the WT, as it is known today. The Greek text of Acts in Codex D, usually dated to the fifth century (K. Aland [ANTF 1.37]; but cf. H. J. Frede, *Altlateinische Paulus-Handschriften* [Vetus Latina 4; Freiburg im B.: Herder, 1964], 18 n. 4: 4th cent.), is almost one-ninth longer than the Alexandrian. It adds details, which fill out the picture in a given episode, substitutes wordy paraphrases, and colors the text in literary, psychological, and theological ways, but it also omits many words or items mentioned in the Alexandrian text. For specific comparisons, based on a pre-Boismard-Lamouille form of the text, see Kenyon, "The Western Text"; Epp, *Theological Tendency;* Witherington, "The Anti-Feminist Tendencies."

(51) The Byzantine text of Acts is found in MSS H, L, P, 049, 33 (for 1:1–11:25), and the bulk of the minuscule manuscripts, or what is sometimes called the Majority Text. See Sturz, *The Byzantine Text-Type.*

(52) The difference between the Alexandrian and the longer WT of Acts gives rise to the question: Which is the more original? This question is not easy to answer. In 1581 Theodore de Bèze gave Codex D to the library of Cambridge University (thus it is often called Codex Cantabrigiensis). However, its text was not published until 1793 by T. Kipling, though already known to contain a longer text of Acts than other MSS as early as the end of the seventeenth century.

At first, both the longer and the shorter texts were ascribed to Luke: the rougher long text was supposed to have been subsequently polished by Luke into the shorter text, which he presented to Theophilus. In one form or another, this explanation was used by Leclerc (1684/85), Blass (1895/96), Zahn, Eb. Nestle, and Wilson. The latest important discussion of this view has been set forth by Boismard and Lamouille. These two scholars have not only studied the Greek forms of the two texts of Acts, but also all the traces of the WT in ancient versions (Arabic, Armenian, Coptic, Ethiopic, Georgian, Latin [VL and Vg], Syriac) and in quotations of patristic writers. There has never been such a monumental work on the WT as this contribution of Boismard and Lamouille. In the matter of the Lucan authorship of the WT, they have adopted a mediating position, concluding:

> Luke would have written a first edition of Acts, of which we find an echo in the Western text; a few years later he would have thoroughly revised his earlier work, not only from the stylistic point of view, as Blass maintained, but also from the standpoint of content. These two editions would have been subse-

> quently fused into a single edition to yield the present text of Acts, or more exactly, the Alexandrian text (in a form purer than that which we now have). In this we align ourselves with the insights of Pott: the problems of textual criticism and of literary criticism are closely linked. (*Texte occidental,* 1.9)

In other words, Boismard and Lamouille adopt a view of the WT that depends not only on textual criticism but also on what they call "literary criticism," which today is known as "source criticism." Their position, however, is more complicated than what is stated above, as will be seen when the sources of Acts are discussed.

(53) Much earlier A. C. Clark, espousing a principle that *lectio longior potior* (the longer reading carries more weight), which goes against that normally used in textual criticism, argued that the shorter text was a modification of the primary long text. At first he explained this modification by accidental omissions (1914), but later by deliberate editorial shortening (1933).

(54) The opposite explanation, that Luke expanded the early short form, was proposed by G. Salmon (1897). E. Delebecque (1986) has refined that explanation by showing that the longer text has the same stylistic characteristics as in the rest of Luke's undisputed writing but is secondary. Whereas the shorter text was composed by Luke while Paul was still under Roman house arrest, the longer text would have been a revision and enlargement of that by Luke at Ephesus after Paul's death (after A.D. 67).

Most explanations, subsequent to that of Salmon, of the difference between the two text-traditions agree that the WT was produced by a process of expansion, though not by Luke himself. Strange (1992) believes that Luke left his text of Acts unfinished at his death, but with marginal and interlinear notes. This annotated text was subsequently made into two forms by second-century editors, one of whom preserved the notes (producing the longer text), whereas the other omitted the notes (the shorter text).

(55) Other explanations see the longer text as the result of interpolations or revisions made by others to the original short text of Luke: in the form either of haphazard interpolations derived from an oral tradition (Westcott-Hort, Hatch, Kenyon), or of deliberate revisions or interpolations to produce an improved or enlarged text (Ropes, Hanson).

Harris regarded Codex Bezae as an adjustment of the short Greek text to the Latin version. A form of this explanation had been used earlier by C. Middleton, J. Mill, and J. J. Wettstein.

Codex Bezae is said to have Semitic coloring, and this has at times been used to advocate its more original character. However, this issue, which is highly debated and complicated by the modern controversy over the Aramaic background of the Gospels and Acts, does not really affect the question of the difference between the longer and shorter text of Acts. Those who have been engaged in the discussion of Semitisms are Black, Chase, Torrey, Wellhausen, Wensinck, Wilcox, and Yoder. Further comments will be made on this feature of the text of Acts under Language and Style below.

The upshot of the debate about the text of Acts seems to be that one cannot simply ascribe to Luke himself the two types of text that we describe today as the Alexandrian and the Western. This, I think, has to be maintained, despite the good work that has otherwise been done by Boismard and Lamouille in reconstituting the form of the WT. Their ascription of both forms of the text of Acts to Luke is involved in their analysis of the sources used in the composition of Acts and consequently remains highly complicated and truly debatable and will always remain so. There are too many hypotheses involved in the Boismard-Lamouille source-analysis; and hypothesis built on hypothesis does not yield certitude.

(56) The individual forms that the two text-traditions take in the main manuscript-representatives make it impossible to ascribe to Luke the two different forms of Acts, even though we are able to discern two differing traditions in a large sense. The thrust of the modern debate inclines one toward regarding the differences as a development from the shorter to the longer text, whether that be by haphazard interpolations or deliberate alterations, made later than the time of Luke himself, so that eventually a definite "Western main redaction" emerged (see further B. Aland, "Entstehung"). Despite all the good work that has been done on this WT, its reconstitution still remains hypothetical and its value even more problematic.

(57) Regarding the WT, three observations of Haenchen (*Acts,* 50–60) still seem valid. He distinguished three kinds of variant readings in it, none of which can be regarded as "original": (a) many small alterations meant to clarify, explain, or smooth out the text, often in the form of added pious phrases; (b) longer or shorter substantive additions, either historical, biographical, or geographical, that reveal the hand of a reviser or revisers; and (c) variants that are specific to Codex Bezae and are not characteristic of the WT as a whole, some of which are merely scribal errors.

(58) At the end of the nineteenth century, T. E. Page, a professor of ancient classical literature, reviewed Blass's commentaries on Acts and his theory about the two texts of Acts, and commented about the WT readings: ". . . they add practically nothing to our real knowledge of the Acts, while they frequently mar and spoil what they seek to improve" (Review, 320). True as that may be, in general, the variants of all the text-traditions, Alexandrian, Byzantine, and Western, merit consideration, even if one does not subscribe to the radical eclecticism advocated in some circles of NT textual criticism.

(59) The translation in this commentary, as already indicated in the preface, is based on the critical text of NA[27], which basically follows the Alexandrian text-tradition. I do not consider the WT to be the original text-form of Acts or even an important contender representing that form, but its differences, as established by Boismard and Lamouille, will be translated and given after the main translation of each episode. Readings in the Byzantine or *Koinē* text-tradition, when considered of some importance, will be mentioned in the NOTES.

BIBLIOGRAPHY

Aland, B., "Entstehung, Charakter und Herkunft des sog. Westlichen Textes untersucht an der Apostelgeschichte," *ETL* 62 (1986): 5–65.

Aland, K., "Neue neutestamentliche Papyri II," *NTS* 9 (1962–63): 303–16.

——— (ed.), *Text und Textwert der griechischen Handschriften des Neuen Testaments: III. Die Apostelgeschichte, Band 1. Untersuchungen und Ergänzungsliste; Band 2. Hauptliste* (ANTF 20–21; Berlin/New York: de Gruyter, 1993).

———, *Die alten Übersetzungen des Neuen Testaments, die Kirchenväterzitate und Lektionare* (ANTF 5; Berlin/New York: de Gruyter, 1972).

Aland, K. and B. Aland, *The Text of the New Testament: An Introduction to the Critical Editions and to the Theory and Practice of Modern Textual Criticism* (Grand Rapids, MI: Eerdmans; Leiden: Brill, 1987), 95, 156–59.

Aune, D. E., "The Text-Tradition of Luke-Acts," *BETS* 7 (1964): 69–82.

Barrett, C. K., "Is There a Theological Tendency in Codex Bezae?" *Text and Interpretation: Studies in the New Testament Presented to Matthew Black* (Cambridge: Cambridge University Press, 1979), 15–27.

Bartsch, H.-W., *Codex Bezae versus Codex Sinaiticus im Lukasevangelium* (Hildesheim: Olms, 1984).

Bezae Codex Cantabrigiensis: Being an Exact Copy, in Ordinary Type, of the Celebrated Uncial Graeco-Latin Manuscript of the Four Gospels and Acts of the Apostles, Written Early in the Sixth Century, and Presented to the University of Cambridge by Theodore Beza, A.D. 1581 (Pittsburgh: Pickwick, 1978; see Scrivener below).

Black, M., *An Aramaic Approach to the Gospels and Acts* (3d ed.; Oxford: Clarendon, 1967), 28–34, 277–80.

———, "The Syriac Versional Tradition," in K. Aland, *Die alten Übersetzungen*, 120–59, esp. 133–35.

Blass, F., *Acta Apostolorum sive Lucae ad Theophilum liber alter* (Göttingen: Vandenhoeck & Ruprecht, 1895, also 1896).

———, "Die zweifache Textüberlieferung in der Apostelgeschichte," *TSK* 67 (1894): 86–119.

———, *Philology of the Gospels* (London: Macmillan, 1898), 96–137.

Boismard, M.-E., "The Text of Acts: A Problem of Literary Criticism?" *New Testament Textual Criticism: Its Significance for Exegesis: Essays in Honour of Bruce M. Metzger* (ed. E. J. Epp and G. Fee; Oxford: Clarendon, 1981), 147–57.

Boismard, M.-E. and A. Lamouille, *Le texte occidental des Actes des Apôtres: Reconstitution et réhabilitation* (Synthèse 17; 2 vols.; Paris: Editions Recherche sur les civilisations, 1984).

Cerfaux, L. "Citations scripturaires et tradition textuelle dans le Livre des Actes," *Aux sources de la tradition chrétienne: Mélanges offerts à M. Maurice Goguel* . . . (Bibliothèque théologique; Paris/Neuchâtel: Delachaux et Niestlé, 1950), 43–51; repr. *Recueil Cerfaux*, 2.93–103.

Chase, F. H., *The Old Syriac Element in the Text of Codex Bezae* (London: Macmillan, 1893).

Clark, A. C., *The Acts of the Apostles: A Critical Edition with Introduction and Notes on Selected Passages* (Oxford: Clarendon, 1933; repr. 1970).

———, "The Michigan Fragment of the Acts," *JTS* 29 (1927–28): 18–28.

———, *The Primitive Text of the Gospels and Acts* (Oxford: Clarendon, 1914).

Codex Bezae Cantabrigiensis quattuor evangelia et Actus Apostolorum complectens graece et latine sumptibus Academiae phototypice repraesentatus (2 vols.; Cambridge: Cambridge University Press, 1899), fol. 415b–446b, 455–502b, 504–508b, 510a–b.

Coppieters, H., *De historia textus Actorum Apostolorum dissertatio . . .* (Louvain: J. van Linthout, 1902).

Cothenet, E., "Les deux Actes des Apôtres ou les Actes des deux apôtres," *EspVie* 100 (1990): 425–30.

Delebecque, E., *Les deux Actes des Apôtres* (EBib ns 6; Paris: Gabalda, 1986).

Dibelius, M., "The Text of Acts: An Urgent Critical Task," *Studies*, 84–92.

Elliott, J. K., *A Bibliography of Greek New Testament Manuscripts* (SNTSMS 62; Cambridge: Cambridge University Press, 1989).

———, "The Text of Acts in the Light of Two Recent Studies," *NTS* 34 (1988): 250–58.

Epp, E. J., "Coptic Manuscript G67 and the Rôle of Codex Bezae as a Western Witness in Acts," *JBL* 85 (1966): 197–212.

———, "The 'Ignorance Motif' in Acts and Anti-judaic Tendencies in Codex Bezae," *HTR* 55 (1962): 51–62.

———, *The Theological Tendency of Codex Bezae Cantabrigiensis in Acts* (SNTSMS 3; Cambridge: Cambridge University Press, 1966), 1–21.

Gallazzi, C., "P. Mil. Vogl. Inv. 1224: Novum Testamentum, Act. 2,30–37 e 2,46–3,2," *BASP* 19 (1982): 39–45.

Geer, T. C., Jr., "Codex 1739 in Acts and Its Relationship to Manuscripts 945 and 1891," *Bib* 69 (1988): 27–46.

———, "The Presence and Significance of Lucanisms in the 'Western' Text of Acts," *JSNT* 39 (1990): 59–76.

———, "The Two Faces of Codex 33 in Acts," *NovT* 31 (1989): 39–47.

Glaue, P., "Einige Stellen, die die Bedeutung des Codex D charakterisieren," *NovT* 2 (1958): 310–15.

Grässer, E., "Acta-Forschung seit 1960," *TRu* 41 (1976): 140–94, esp. 163–86.

Greber, J., *The New Testament: A New Translation and Explanation Based on the Oldest Manuscripts* (New York: John Felsberg, Inc., 1937), 207–64 (based on D).

Gregory, C. R., *Textkritik des Neuen Testaments* (3 vols.; Leipzig: Hinrichs, 1900–9), 3.1086–92.

Grenfell, B. P., and A. S. Hunt (eds.), *POxy* §1597 (+ pl. I in vol. 13 [1919]).

Haenchen, E., "Schriftzitate und Textüberlieferung in der Apostelgeschichte," *ZTK* 51 (1954): 153–67; repr. *Gott und Mensch*, 157–71.

———, "Zum Text der Apostelgeschichte," *ZTK* 54 (1957): 22–55; repr. *Gott und Mensch*, 172–205.

Haenchen, E. and P. Weigandt, "The Original Text of Acts?" *NTS* 14 (1967–68): 469–81.

Hahn, H., "Ein Unzialfragment der Apostelgeschichte auf dem Sinai (0140)," *Materialien zur neutestamentlichen Handschriftenkunde I* (ANTF 3; Berlin: de Gruyter, 1969), 186–92.

Hanson, R.P.C., "The Provenance of the Interpolator in the 'Western' Text of Acts and of Acts Itself," *NTS* 12 (1965–66): 211–30.

Harris, J. R., *The Annotators of the Codex Bezae* (London: Clay and Sons, 1901).

———, *Codex Bezae: A Study of the So-Called Western Text of the New Testament* (Text and Studies 2/1; Cambridge: Cambridge University Press, 1891).

———, *Four Lectures on the Western Text of the New Testament* (London: Clay and Sons, 1894).

Head, P. M., Review of W. A. Strange, *The Problem . . .*, *EvQ* 66 (1994): 87–91.

Heimerdinger, J. and S. Levinsohn, "The Use of the Definite Article before Names of People in the Greek Text of Acts with Particular Reference to Codex Bezae," *FilNeot* 5 (1992): 15–44.

Hilgenfeld, A., *Acta Apostolorum, graece et latine, secundum antiquissimos testes . . .* (Berlin: Reimer, 1899).

Hull, R. F., Jr., "'Lucanisms' in the Western Text of Acts? A Reappraisal," *JBL* 107 (1988): 695–707.

Kasser, R. (ed.), *Papyrus Bodmer XVII: Actes des Apôtres; Epîtres de Jacques, Pierre, Jean et Jude* (Cologny-Geneva: Bibliothèque Bodmer, 1961), 23–210 (= Acts 1:1–28:31, with small lacunae and title of book at end).

Kenyon, F. G., *The Chester Beatty Biblical Papyri: Descriptions and Texts of Twelve Manuscripts on Papyrus of the Greek Bible: Fasc. II, The Gospels and Acts* (London: Emery Walker Ltd., 1933–34); II/1 (Text); II/2 (Plates).

———, "Some Notes on the Chester Beatty Gospels and Acts," *Quantulacumque: Studies Presented to Kirsopp Lake . . .* (ed. R. P. Casey et al.; London: Christophers, 1937), 145–48.

———, "The Western Text in the Gospels and Acts," *Proceedings of the British Academy* 24 (1938): 287–315.

Kilpatrick, G. D., "An Eclectic Study of the Text of Acts," *Biblical and Patristic Studies in Memory of Robert Pierce Casey* (ed. J. N. Birdsall and R. W. Thomson; Freiburg im B.: Herder, 1963), 64–77.

———, "Western Text and Original Text in the Gospels and Acts," *JTS* 44 (1943): 24–36.

Kipling, T., *Codex Theodori Bezae Cantabrigiensis evangelia et Apostolorum Acta complectens quadratis literis graeco-latinis* (2 vols.; Cambridge: Cambridge University Press, 1793).

Klijn, A.F.J., "In Search of the Original Text of Acts," *StLA*, 103–10.

———, *A Survey of the Researches into the Western Text of the Gospels and Acts*

(Utrecht: Kemink en Zoon, 1949); *Part Two, 1949–1969* (NovTSup 21; Leiden: Brill, 1969).

———, "A Survey of the Researches into the Western Text of the Gospels and Acts (1949–1959)," *NovT* 3 (1959): 1–27, 161–73.

Kraeling, C. H., "P 50.: Two Selections from Acts," *Quantulacumque* (see above), 163–72 (+ pl.).

Lagrange, M.-J., *Introduction à l'étude du Nouveau Testament, Deuxième Partie: Critique textuelle II, La critique rationnelle* (EBib; Paris: Gabalda, 1935), 387–463.

———, "Un nouveau papyrus contenant un fragment des Actes," *RB* 36 (1927): 549–60.

———, "Le papyrus Beatty des Actes des Apôtres," *RB* 43 (1934): 161–71.

Loew [*sic*], E. A., "The Codex Bezae," *JTS* 14 (1913): 385–88.

Lowe, E. A., "An Eighth-Century List of Books in a Bodleian MS. from Würzburg and Its Probable Relation to the Laudian *Acts*," *Speculum* 3 (1928): 3–15.

MacKenzie, R. S., "The Western Text of Acts: Some Lucanisms in Selected Sermons," *JBL* 104 (1985): 637–50.

Martini, C. M., "Pierre et Paul dans l'église ancienne: Considérations sur la tradition textuelle des Actes des Apôtres," *Paul de Tarse: Apôtre du* [*sic*] *notre temps* (ed. L. De Lorenzi; Rome: Abbaye de S. Paul h. l. m., 1979), 261–68.

———, "La tradition textuelle des Actes des Apôtres et les tendances de l'église ancienne," *Les Actes* (ed. J. Kremer), 21–35.

Menoud, P.-H., "Papyrus Bodmer XIV–XV et XVII," *RTP* 3/12 (1962): 107–16, esp. 112–16.

———, "The Western Text and the Theology of Acts," *BullSNTS* 2 (1951–52): 19–32.

Merk, A., "Codex Evangeliorum et Actuum ex collectione Papyrorum Chester Beatty," *Miscellanea Biblica edita a Pontificio Instituto Biblico ad celebrandum annum xxv ex quo conditum est Institutum 1909 — vii Maii — 1934* (2 vols.; Rome: Biblical Institute, 1934), 2.375–406.

Metzger, B. M., *The Early Versions of the New Testament: Their Origin, Transmission, and Limitations* (Oxford: Clarendon, 1977).

———, *The Text of the New Testament: Its Transmission, Corruption, and Restoration* (3d ed.; New York/Oxford: Oxford University Press, 1992), 37, 41, 42–52, 65, 131–34.

———, *TCGNT*, 222–445.

Montgomery, J. A., "The Ethiopic Text of Acts of the Apostles," *HTR* 27 (1934): 169–205.

Nestle, Eb., *Novi Testamenti graeci supplementum editionibus de-Gebhardt-Tischendorfianis adcommodavit* (Leipzig: Tauchnitz, 1896), 51–66.

———, "Some Observations on the Codex Bezae," *Expos* 5/2 (1895): 235–40.

New, S., "The Michigan Papyrus Fragment 1571," *Beginnings*, 5.262–68.

Osburn, C. D., "The Search for the Original Text of Acts — The International Project on the Text of Acts," *JSNT* 44 (1991): 39–55.

Page, T. E., Review of F. Blass's Commentaries, *Acta Apostolorum* (1895, 1896), *CR* 11 (1897): 317–20.

Parker, D. C., *Codex Bezae: An Early Christian Manuscript and Its Text* (Cambridge: Cambridge University Press, 1992).

Petersen, T. C., "An Early Coptic Manuscript of Acts: An Unrevised Version of the Ancient So-called Western Text," *CBQ* 26 (1964): 225–41.

Petzer, J. H., "Tertullian's Text of Acts," *SecCent* 8 (1991): 201–15.

———, "The Textual Relationships of the Vulgate in Acts," *NTS* 39 (1993): 227–45.

Pickering, S. R., "P. Macquarie Inv. 360 (+ P.Mil.Vogl.Inv. 1224): Acta Apostolorum 2.30–37, 2.46–3.2," *ZPE* 65 (1986): 76–78 (+ pls. Ib,c).

———, Description of P^{91} in *NDIEC*, 2.140.

Pott, A., *Der abendländische Text der Apostelgeschichte und die Wir-Quelle: Eine Studie* (Leipzig: Hinrichs, 1900).

Rius-Camps, J., "Las variantes de la recensión occidental de los Hechos de los Apóstoles (I): (Hch 1,1–3)," *FilNeot* 6 (1993): 59–68; "(II): (Hch 1,4–14)," ibid., 219–29; "(III): (Hch 1,15–26)," *FilNeot* 7 (1994): 53–64; "(IV): (Hch 2,1–13)," ibid., 197–207; "(V): (Hch 2,14–40)," *FilNeot* 8 (1995): 63–78; "(VI): (Hch 2,41–47), ibid., 199–208.

Ropes, J. H., "The Text of Acts," *Beginnings*, 3.

Royse, J. R., "The Ethiopic Support for Codex Vaticanus in Acts," *ZNW* 71 (1980): 258–62.

Salonius, A. H., "Die griechischen Handschriftenfragmente des Neuen Testaments in den Staatlichen Museen zu Berlin," *ZNW* 26 (1927): 97–119 (+ pls. 1, 2), esp. 109–19.

Sanders, H. A., "A Papyrus Fragment of Acts in the Michigan Collection," *HTR* 20 (1927): 1–19.

———, "A Third Century Papyrus of Matthew and Acts," *Quantulacumque* (see above), 151–61 (+ 2 pls.).

Sanz, P., *Griechische literarische Papyri christlichen Inhaltes I* (Biblica, Väterschriften und verwandtes; Mitteilungen aus der Papyrussammlung der österreichischen National Bibliothek in Wien ns 4; Baden: Rohrer, 1946), 65–68.

Schenke, H.-M., *Apostelgeschichte 1,1–15,3 im mittelägyptischen Dialekt des Koptischen (Codex Glazier)* (TU 137; Berlin: Akademie, 1991).

Schmitz, F.-J., "Neue Fragmente zum P^{41}," *Bericht der Hermann Kunst-Stiftung zur Förderung der neutestamentlichen Textforschung für die Jahre 1985 bis 1987* (Münster in W.: Kunst-Stiftung, 1988), 78–97.

Scrivener, F.H.A., *Bezae Codex Cantabrigiensis: Being an Exact Copy, in Ordinary Type, of the Celebrated Uncial Graeco-Latin Manuscript of the Four Gospels and Acts of the Apostles Written Early in the Sixth Century, and Presented to the University of Cambridge by Theodore Beza, A.D. 1581, Edited with a Critical Introduction, Annotations, and Facsimiles* (Cambridge, UK: Deighton Bell, 1864; see *Codex Bezae* above).

Stagg, F., "Establishing a Text for Luke-Acts," *SBL 1977 Seminar Papers* (ed. P. J. Achtemeier; Missoula: Scholars, 1977), 45–58.

———, "Textual Criticism for Luke-Acts," *PRS* 5 (1978): 152–65.

Strange, W. A., *The Problem of the Text of Acts* (SNTSMS 71; Cambridge: Cambridge University Press, 1992), 1–34.

Sturz, H. A., *The Byzantine Text-Type and New Testament Textual Criticism* (Nashville/New York/Camden, NJ: Nelson, 1984).

Tavardon, P., *Le texte alexandrin et le texte occidental des Actes des Apôtres* (Cahiers de la *RB* 36; Paris: Gabalda, 1997).

Thiele, W., "Ausgewählte Beispiele zur Charakterisierung des 'westlichen' Textes der Apostelgeschichte," *ZNW* 56 (1965): 51–63.

Torrey, C. C., *Documents of the Primitive Church* (New York/London: Harper & Bros., 1941), 112–48.

Treu, K., "Christliche Papyri XI," *APF* 31 (1985): 59–71, esp. 61; see *NDIEC* 4 (1977): 140.

———, "Neue neutestamentliche Fragmente der Berliner Papyrussammlung," *APF* 18 (1966): 23–38.

Uhlig, S., "Ein pseudepigraphischer Actaschluss in der äthiopischen Version," *OrChr* 73 (1989): 129–36.

Vitelli, G. et al. (eds.), *Papiri greci e latini* (Pubblicazioni della Società Italiana per la Ricerca dei Papiri Greci e Latini in Egitto 1–14; Florence: Ariani, 1912–57), 10 (1932): 112–18 (§1165).

Vööbus, A., "Die Entdeckung von Überresten der altsyrischen Apostelgeschichte," *OrChr* 64 (1980): 32–35.

Weigandt, P., "Zwei griechisch-sahidische Acta-Handschriften: P^{41} und 0236," *Materialien zur neutestamentlichen Handschriftenkunde I* (ANTF 3; Berlin: de Gruyter, 1969), 54–95.

Wensinck, A. J., "The Semitisms of Codex Bezae and Their Relation to the Non-Western Text of the Gospel of Saint Luke," *Bulletin of the Bezan Club* 12 (1937): 11–48.

Wessely, C., *Studien zur Palaeographie und Papyruskunde* 12 (Leipzig: Avenarus, 1912), 245; 15 (Leipzig: Haessel, 1914), 107–18.

Wilcox, M., "Luke and the Bezan Text of Acts," *Les Actes* (ed. J. Kremer), 447–55.

Williams, C.S.C., *Alterations to the Text of the Synoptic Gospels and Acts* (Oxford: Blackwell, 1951), 54–82.

Wilson, J. M., *The Acts of the Apostles Translated from the Codex Bezae with an Introduction on Its Lucan Origin and Importance* (London: SPCK, 1923).

Winter, J. G. et al. (eds.), *Papyri in the University of Michigan Collection: Miscellaneous Papyri* (Michigan Papyri III; Ann Arbor, MI: University of Michigan, 1936), 14–19 (= Acts 18:27–19:6,12–16 [signed H. A. S.]).

Witherington, B., "The Anti-Feminist Tendencies of the 'Western' Text in Acts," *JBL* 103 (1984): 82–84.

Yoder, J. D., *Concordance to the Distinctive Greek Text of Codex Bezae* (NTTS 2; Leiden: Brill, 1961).

———, "The Language of the Greek Variants of Codex Bezae," *NovT* 3 (1959): 241–48.

———, "Semitisms in Codex Bezae," *JBL* 78 (1959): 317–21.

Zahn, T., *Die Urausgabe der Apostelgeschichte des Lucas* (FGNK 9; Leipzig: Deichert-Scholl, 1916).

Zuntz, G., "On the Western Text of the Acts of the Apostles," *Opuscula Selecta: Classica, Hellenistica, Christiana* (Manchester, UK: Manchester University Press; Totowa, NJ: Rowman & Littlefield, 1972), 189–215.

III. Sources of Acts

◆

(60) Almost as complicated as the question of the text of Acts is that of the sources that Luke used in writing this second part of his work. In the prologue of the Third Gospel, which many regard as a preface to both Lucan volumes, the author did not class himself among "the original eyewitnesses and ministers of the word" who passed on "the events that have come to fulfillment among us" (Luke 1:1–2). That means that Luke considered himself a third-generation Christian who inherited a preexisting tradition about the Christ-event itself, but it does not necessarily exclude his having been an eyewitness for some events of its sequel. The extent to which he might have been is hard to say. For the sequel to his Jesus-story Luke had little tradition, unlike what he had had in the case of his Gospel, save possibly oral reports and an occasional document: little would have served him as did the written sources, Mark or "Q." These at least we have in some form, and to them one can appeal for comparison in the interpretation of his Gospel. Consequently, if one appeals to sources that Luke would have used for Acts, it is largely a speculative question. Nowhere in Acts does the author say or even hint at sources that he might have used, in contrast to what is said in Luke 1:2. Yet the reader easily becomes aware of the composite or compilatory character of Acts. According to many commentators there are traces in Acts of sources used: seeming doublets, the We-Sections, the three accounts of Paul's call. This is the concern that occupies us now: the indications of possible sources in Acts apart from its quotations of the OT. Those quotations also have to be considered in the source criticism of Acts, but they will be treated separately in the next section, because they constitute a different problem. We are now interested in the sources that Luke might have used for his account apart from his Greek OT.

(61) No matter what else is going to be said about the Lucan use of sources in Acts, one has to recognize at the outset that by and large Luke freely composed his accounts, whether he was present or not for episodes that he narrates or describes. The episodes or incidents must at times have been much more drawn out than the brief accounts of them that we have in Acts; hence one has to acknowledge from the start the reality of Lucan writing, telescoping, juxtaposing, and conflating. Luke remains indeed a remarkable Hellenistic writer, but his skill as such still raises questions about his sources. Over thirty years ago Dupont surveyed the question of the sources of Acts in detail and ended by saying, "Despite the most careful and detailed research, it has not been possible to define any of the sources used by the author of Acts in a way which will meet with widespread agreement among the critics" (*Sources*, 166). The reason for this situation was "the literary work of the author: he is not satisfied with transcribing his

sources, he rewrites the text by putting the imprint of his vocabulary and his style everywhere" (ibid.). More recently, Lüdemann echoed Dupont's conclusion (*Early Christianity*, 22). Nevertheless, the question about the sources of Acts has not died.

(62) When I discuss the composition of Acts, one part of it will be devoted to the We-Sections or We-Passages (16:10–17; 20:5–15; 21:1–18; 27:1–28:16 [and 11:28 in Codex Bezae]), the nature of which will have to be determined further, but those passages may now be cited as an example of a source that Luke used. They stand out in Acts by their shift from the third person to the first plural, and more than any other reason give rise to the question of sources in Acts. Even if one has to agree with Harnack that the Lucan style pervades the We-Sections as much as it does the rest of Acts and the Third Gospel *(Luke the Physician)*, one has to reckon with the possibility of those passages having had an independent existence in some form prior to the composition of Acts itself. The similarity of Lucan style in the We-Sections is such, however, that some commentators refuse to regard them as a separate source, preferring to think that they represent merely a different literary genre that Luke adopted in those passages. More will be said about the nature of them in due course. At the moment, the We-Sections are mentioned merely as a possible source, which would affect a number of passages in the second half of Acts. See *Luke*, 293–94, 296–97.

(63) In the discussion of sources, one has to distinguish the first part of Acts (1:1–15:33) from the second part (15:35–28:31), because the problems in each part are different.

(64) Apropos of the first part of Acts, early in this century Torrey maintained that Luke had translated an Aramaic source in his writing of 1:1–15:35 (*Composition and Date*, 3–41), a document that Luke had found in Rome, which had been written "in Palestine after the Council of the Apostles at Jerusalem in the year 49" (ibid., 67). This Torrey maintained, following up suggestions of earlier scholars who had toyed with the idea but never really developed it, such as Blass, Harnack, Moffatt, Eb. Nestle, and Wendt. Blass had considered this a real probability for chaps. 1–12 (*Philology of the Gospels*, 141, 193–95, 201).

In developing his thesis, Torrey noted that the first half of Acts dealt mostly with the Jerusalem church and its Judean background and maintained that its documents would have been written in Aramaic. He appealed to a Semitic coloring of the Greek of chaps. 1–15, even calling it "distinctly translation-Greek," which differed considerably from the remaining chapters. The language of many speeches in chaps. 1–15, which reflected the vernacular then used, and the many OT quotations helped to build up this Semitic coloring. He listed a full page of Semitisms, many of which he claimed were Aramaisms, others Hebraisms, and he was reluctant to explain these as mere Septuagintisms. His main proof for this Aramaic source rested on what he called "especially striking examples of mistranslation in Acts 1–15" (*Composition and Date*, 10). These he found in 2:47; 3:16; 4:24–25; 8:10; 11:28; 15:7. (My reaction to his analysis of these verses will be found in NOTES on the respective passages.) To these instances he added a long list of "other evidence," minor examples of Greek words or phrases easily explainable as translations from Aramaic. Such translation-Greek Torrey ascribed to the author of chaps. 16–28, "the translator of 1–15" (ibid., 5).

Others who advocated an Aramaic source for Acts 1–15, not always for the same reasons as Torrey, have been H. Sahlin, A. Ehrhardt, L. Gaston, W. J. Wilson.

Torrey wrote before the discovery of the Qumran scrolls, more than a hundred of which were written in the Aramaic used in Palestine in the first century B.C. and A.D. Though many of these texts are fragmentary, they are abundant enough to give us a good sampling of such Aramaic. This kind of Aramaic reveals part of the problematic character of Torrey's thesis, because he had to rely not only on earlier Biblical Aramaic, but mostly on that of the later targums and rabbinic writings. This did not deter him, since he found it "unnecessary to reconstruct the Judean Aramaic dialect of the middle of the first century" (ibid., 9). How he might have reconstructed it is a question, indeed, but it is now clear from the Qumran Aramaic texts that many of the forms and words that he used were derived from much later Aramaic, such as is found in synagogue and tombstone inscriptions from of the fourth to sixth centuries A.D. (see Fitzmyer and Harrington, *MPAT*, 251–303), not to mention the classic targums of later date, and even Syriac.

This difference of Aramaic dialect, however, is only one aspect of Torrey's problematic thesis. A greater problem is found in his claim that certain words and phrases that he had singled out are Aramaisms, or sometimes Hebraisms, and whether this sufficiently accounts for them. A good number of them are Septuagintisms and have to be recognized as such (see *Luke*, 114–25).

Moreover, the theory of a continuous Aramaic source for Acts 1–15 has to cope with the composite character of some of these chapters, which has since been recognized, and the use in them of OT quotations, the Greek wording of which is so similar to the LXX (especially in 2:17–20; 15:16–17).

Furthermore, even with the discovery of a considerable number of Aramaic texts at Qumran, there is still the problem that none of these texts comes to us from a Jewish Christian source or writer. This remains an aspect of the difficulty that Riddle raised years before Qumran texts were discovered: why have we inherited no writings of early Jewish Christians in a Semitic language? Would Jewish Christians have been writing an Aramaic history of the early phase of their expansion "before the Christian movement was conscious of itself" ("The Logic," 16)? For still other criticism of Torrey's thesis, see Burkitt, "Professor Torrey"; Cadbury, "Luke"; Goodspeed, "The Origin." The question of an Aramaic source in Acts 1–15 has been posed anew by the work of R. A. Martin ("Syntactical Evidence"); but that is more a question of language and style.

(65) Apart from the question of an Aramaic source in Acts 1–15, the modern discussion of sources of Acts has centered on content rather than on language. For the first part of Acts, such discussion dates mainly from Harnack (*Beiträge*, 134–40), who distinguished Acts 2–5 from Acts 6–15. In the first of these sections (Acts 2–5), he singled out 3:1–5:16 as a historical *Jerusalem* narrative, considering 2:1–47 and 5:17–42 as either worthless or a doublet (possibly also the Ananias

and Sapphira episode in 5:1–11). That Jerusalem narrative he thought was prolonged in 8:5–40; 9:32–11:18; 12:1–23. In the second section (Acts 6–15), he regarded 6:1–8:4; 11:19–30; and 12:25–15:35 as a homogeneous *Antiochene* narrative. To 9:1–28 he accorded a special category and related 11:27–30 to 15:1–35 as two accounts of one event. From his treatment has stemmed the distinction of the so-called Jerusalem and Antiochene sources of Acts.

(66) Harnack's treatment of Acts 2–5 elicited other discussions. Reicke regarded 2:42–4:31 and 4:32–5:42 as two primitive church narratives. Trocmé thought rather that 3:1–5:42 was a basic narrative that Luke had expanded with speeches, summaries, and the episode of Ananias and Sapphira (5:1–11). Jeremias insisted that 4:1ff. and 5:17–42 were not parallel doublets of the same historical incident, but rather descriptions of distinct judicial proceedings. From such discussions came the conviction that the so-called Summaries in these early chapters were Lucan compositions.

(67) Harnack's treatment of Acts 6–15 likewise called forth other discussions. Jeremias insisted that 8:5–40; 9:31–11:18; and 12:1–24 (what Harnack regarded as the continuation of his Jerusalem narrative) were interpolated into the otherwise cohesive (Antiochene) account of 6:1 on, to which he further assigned the story of Paul's conversion (9:1–30), but from which he separated 15:1–33. The last account he assigned to the Palestinian source. Jeremias further regarded those interpolations as part of the account that one finds in the second part of Acts (15:36–28:31).

Both of the analyses of Harnack and Jeremias were further elaborated by Bultmann and Benoit. For Bultmann the Antiochene source, written in the "We" style, is detected in 6:1–12a; 7:54–8:4; 11:19–26; and 12:25, in a travel account beginning at 11:28 and continued at 13:2 (where Luke has changed "we" to the third person), and in interpolations by the author in 15:1–35. Few have followed Bultmann's analysis.

(68) Benoit contributed in an important way to the discussion by showing that the original Antiochene narrative, which begins in 6:1, was interrupted between 11:27–30 and 15:3–35 by a Palestinian and a Pauline tradition ("La deuxième visite"). The Palestinian tradition, 12:1–23, was already part of Harnack's Jerusalem narrative, but Benoit labeled Acts 13 and 14 part of the Pauline tradition. Intervening verses such as 12:25 and 15:1–2 would have been Lucan sutures. From this Benoit concluded that Acts 11:27–30 and 15:3–33 are two accounts of the same event, derived from different sources. Even though one has to regard 11:27–29 as part of the Antiochene source, 11:30 is rather a Lucan note, related to 12:25, so that the mention of Paul's visit to Jerusalem in 11:30 may indeed be a doublet of 15:3–33.

Despite the skepticism of Kümmel about "an Antiochene source" (*Introduction*, 176), others have adopted it (Hengel, *Acts*, 65–66; Lüdemann, *Paul*, 25–29, 156). Benoit's analysis of the first half of Acts and his overall distinction of three sources in Acts (Palestinian, Antiochene, and Pauline) are the best solution to the source-problem of Acts proposed to date.

(69) In the second part of Acts one encounters the We-Sections (16:10–17;

20:5–15; 21:1–18; 27:1–28:16). (The use of "we" in 11:28 in Codex Bezae is one of the textual vagaries of that manuscript; it cannot be allowed to affect the question of sources.) As already indicated, the We-Sections may be a separate source in this part of Acts, but much depends on the analysis of them, which will be taken up later in terms of the composition of Acts. They may form merely part of what Dibelius, modifying a proposal of Norden, once called an "itinerary of stations where Paul stopped," which he thought was used in Acts 13:1–14:28 and 15:36–21:16, apart from the discourses (13:16–41; 14:15–17; 17:22–31; 20:18–35) and some minor isolated stories (Elymas, 13:8–12; Lystra healing, 14:8–18; the conversion of the prison guard in Philippi, 16:25–34; and Sceva's sons, 19:14–16) (*Studies*, 5–6, 197–98). This itinerary source would have been largely an account written by a companion of Paul's missionary journeys. Noteworthy in this regard is the correspondence that one can find in it to Paul's movements as they are recorded in his uncontested letters (an issue that will be taken up in the discussion of Acts and the story of Paul). Even though Dibelius's analysis of this part of Acts has been contested by Ehrhardt, Schille, Haenchen, and Conzelmann, many other commentators go along with it (see Plümacher, *TRu* [1984] 123–28).

With slight modifications, this itinerary more or less coincides with what Benoit has called the Pauline source, a name that I prefer to use here. By it I do not mean that Luke has derived the information in it from Paul himself, but only that it is a source of information *about Paul.*

(70) The entire question of the use of sources in Acts has been posed anew by Boismard and Lamouille, who, in addition to their textual work on the WT of Acts, have sought to explain the present-day texts of Acts by appeal to sources as well as the text-traditions (*Les Actes des deux Apôtres*). Their analysis of Acts is at least as complicated as their earlier analysis of the Gospels (*Synopse des quatre Evangiles en français: III. L'Evangile de Jean* [Paris: Cerf, 1977]) and depends somewhat on it.

At the risk of oversimplifying a complicated theory, I understand their position about Acts to be as follows:

They distinguish three levels of redaction: I, II, and III. Redaction I has to be reconstructed from II and III, whereas II is represented by the WT and III by the Alexandrian text. The reconstructed Redaction I, a text composed by a Jewish Christian author in the early 60s, was actually the continuation of Proto-Luke. The Gospel and Acts were divided by Luke himself in the 80s only at the time of Redaction II (the WT), when the prologues were added. Redaction III (the Alexandrian text) was produced by someone other than Luke in the 90s.

Two parts of Acts are further distinguished: La geste de Pierre and la geste de Paul. In the first part, which describes the activity of Peter in 1:6–12:25 (save for 9:1–30), the author of Redaction I used a Petrine document (P), written by a Palestinian Hellenist in the 50s. In using it, Redaction I reinterpreted some accounts, producing parallels (the doublets noted by Harnack in chaps. 2–5; 2:1ff./4:31; 2:14ff./3:12ff.; 2:41/4:4; 4:5ff./5:17ff.; 2:44f./4:32, 34f.), but omitted what is in chaps. 6–8. P also incorporated elements related to the apocryphal *Gospel of*

See below Fitzmeyer's sources of Acts

Peter (1:2–5c: Herod's role) and to elements common to Luke and John in the passion and resurrection narratives (in effect, "Memoirs of Peter," document C, dating from 50s, as the authors proposed earlier). Redaction I also used a Johannite document (J) in 3:19–26 and 7:2ff., a document related to the followers of John the Baptist, as well as a travel document (Journal de voyage [Jv]) for material now in Acts 11. Luke, in producing Redaction II of the first part, made some minor changes, created the doublets, and fused with Redaction I the omitted chaps. 6–8 of P. Redaction III added the death of Judas (1:18–20) and the "other" tongues (2:4).

In the second part, La geste de Paul (9:1–30; 13:1–28:31), Redaction I used P only in chap. 15 and the Johannite document in 13:16–41, but used the travel document (Jv) for the missionary journeys of Paul, his arrest, trial in Caesarea, and journey to Rome. Jv was originally an account of a single journey with multiple stages toward Jerusalem, whither Paul was bringing the collection; but it was made into several journeys by Luke, who in Redaction II again created some doublets. Their complicated explanation of the We-Sections will be treated later. Only some of them belong to the Jv source.

Thus, three sources would have been involved in Redaction I: P (with elements of C), J, and Jv. These sources would also have been used independently in the production of Redactions II and III in addition to Redaction I; so one would have to reckon with four levels of composition: the sources, and Redactions I, II, and III.

The explanation of Boismard and Lamouille has some aspects that one has to note, but in general it is too complicated to be used in commentary such as this, despite the sympathetic attempt of Taylor in his *Commentaire historique*. The major problem with it is the building of hypothesis on hypothesis, for the linking of hypotheses decreases the probability, the more one links them. Consequently, in this question of source analysis I prefer to remain with the form of source analysis once proposed by Benoit. His proposals are simple, relatively manageable, and probable; they inspire a degree of confidence. ✓

(71) Building on Benoit's proposals, I shall list my understanding of the sources here. At the outset, however, I must repeat what was said above: Luke has imposed his own style and language on all the sources that he used; in the end, Acts is a thoroughly Lucan composition.

1:1–2	Prologue: Lucan composition
1:3–8	Lucan composition, from a possible oral Palestinian tradition
1:9–11	Lucan composition, from a possible oral Palestinian tradition
1:12–14	Lucan composition, from oral Palestinian tradition
1:15–26	Lucan composition for vv 15–17, 19a, 20–22, 24–25a; Palestinian tradition for vv 18, 19b, 23, 25b–26
2:1–13	Lucan composition, from a possible oral tradition; some written source likely in vv 9–10.

2:14–36	Peter's speech: Lucan composition, using a possible oral Palestinian tradition
2:37–41	Mostly Lucan composition
2:42–47	First major summary: Lucan composition dependent on some tradition
3:1–11	Mostly Palestinian source, with some Lucan insertions
3:12–26	Lucan discourse, using some inherited details
4:1–22	Palestinian source, save for Peter's speech (4:8b–12, 19–20)
4:23–31	Lucan composition, using some Palestinian tradition
4:32–35	Second major summary: mostly Lucan composition
4:36–5:11	Lucan composition, using a Palestinian source
5:12–16	Third major summary: mostly Lucan composition
5:17–42	Palestinian source, with Lucan composition in the discourses (vv 29–32 and 35–39ab)
6:1–7	Antiochene source
6:8–7:1	Lucan composition dependent on Antiochene tradition
7:2–53	Stephen's discourse: Lucan composition, using some inherited Antiochene tradition
7:54–8:1a	Lucan composition dependent on Antiochene tradition
8:1b–4	Antiochene source
8:5–25	Palestinian source
8:26–40	Palestinian source
9:1–19a	Pauline source
9:19b–25	Pauline source
9:26–30	Pauline source, with Lucan summary in v 31
9:32–43	Palestinian source
10:1–11:18	Palestinian source, with Lucan inserts in 10:23b, 27–29 and Peter's two speeches
10:34–43	Peter's speech: Lucan composition, using some Palestinian tradition
11:5–17	Peter's speech: Lucan composition
11:19–26	Antiochene source
11:27–29	Antiochene source, with Lucan summary in v 30
12:1–23	Palestinian source
12:24–25	Lucan summary and suture, possibly using Antiochene information
13:1–3, 4–12	Pauline source
13:13–52	Pauline source, save for Paul's speech (vv 16–41), which is Lucan composition, using some Pauline tradition
14:1–7	Pauline source
14:8–20	Pauline source, save for Paul's speech (vv 15–17), Lucan composition
14:21–28	Pauline source
15:1–2	Lucan suture

15:3–12	Antiochene source, save for Peter's speech (vv 7–11)
15:13–21	Lucan composition, using an Antiochene source
15:22–33	Antiochene source, esp. the letter in vv 23b–29
15:35	Lucan suture
15:36–40	Pauline source
15:41–16:4	Pauline source, with Lucan summary in v 5
16:6–10a	Pauline source
16:10b–17	We-Section
16:18–40	Pauline source
17:1–15, 16–22a	Pauline source
17:22b–31	Paul's Areopagus speech, Lucan composition, using details from Pauline tradition (e.g., Aratus quotation)
17:32–34	Pauline source
18:1–17	Pauline source, save for Gallio's speech (vv 14–15), Lucan composition
18:18–22, 23–28	Pauline source
19:1–7, 8–22	Pauline source
19:23–41	Pauline source, save for the city clerk's speech (vv 35–40), Lucan composition
20:1–4	Pauline source
20:5–12	We-Section (vv 5–8), with inserts from Pauline source in vv 9–12
20:13–16	We-Section (vv 13–15), with addition from Pauline source (v 16)
20:17–18a	Probably Lucan composition: introduction to Paul's speech
20:18b–35	Paul's speech at Miletus: Lucan composition with Pauline echoes
20:36–38	Lucan composition
21:1–18	We-Section
21:19–20a	Pauline source
21:20b–25	Speech of James, Lucan composition
21:26–40	Pauline source
22:1–21	Paul's speech in Jerusalem, Lucan composition, with new details possibly derived from the Pauline source
22:22–23:11	Pauline source
23:12–22	Pauline source
23:23–35	Pauline source, save for the letter (Lucan composition)
24:1–2a, 9–10a	Pauline source
24:2b–8	Tertullus's speech, Lucan composition
24:10b–21	Paul's speech, Lucan composition
24:22–27	Pauline source, but vv 24–26 may be Lucan composition
25:1–12	Pauline source, save for Paul's speech (vv 8, 10–11), Lucan composition

25:13–14a, 22–23	Pauline source
25:14b–21, 24–27	Festus's speech: Lucan composition
26:1–23	Paul's discourse: Lucan composition
26:24–32	Pauline source, save for Paul's words, Lucan composition
27:1–28:16a	We-Section, with six inserts from the Pauline source (27:9–11, 21–26, 31, 33–36, 43; 28:2b–6)
28:17–20, 25c–28	Paul's speeches in Rome: Lucan composition, using Pauline tradition
28:21–25ab, 30–31	Lucan conclusion (with a summary), using Pauline tradition

Lastly, I have made no mention of Paul's letters as a source of Acts, because I do not think that Luke read any of them.

BIBLIOGRAPHY

Argyle, A. W., "The Theory of an Aramaic Source in Acts 2,14–40," *JTS* 4 (1953): 213–14.

Barton, G. A., "Professor Torrey's Theory of the Aramaic Origin of the Gospels and the First Half of the Acts of the Apostles," *JTS* 36 (1935): 357–73, esp. 371–72.

Benoit, P., "La deuxième visite de Saint Paul à Jérusalem," *Bib* 40 (1959): 778–92; repr. *Exégèse et théologie*, 3.285–99.

Blass, F., *Philology of the Gospels* (London: Macmillan, 1898), 141, 193–95, 201.

Boismard, M.-E. and A. Lamouille, *Les Actes des deux Apôtres: I. Introduction—Textes; II. Le sens des récits; III. Analyses littéraires* (Paris: Gabalda, 1990).

Brodie, T. L., "Greco-Roman Imitation of Texts as a Partial Guide to Luke's Use of Sources," *Luke-Acts: New Perspectives* (ed. C. H. Talbert), 17–46.

Bultmann, R., "Zur Frage nach den Quellen der Apostelgeschichte," *New Testament Essays: Studies in Memory of Thomas Walter Manson 1893–1958* (ed. A.J.B. Higgins; Manchester: Manchester University Press, 1959), 68–80; repr. *Exegetica*, 412–23.

Burkitt, F. C., "Professor Torrey on 'Acts,'" *JTS* 20 (1919): 320–29.

Cadbury, H. J., "Luke—Translator or Author?" *AJT* 24 (1920): 436–55.

Cerfaux, L., "La composition de la première partie du Livre des Actes," *ETL* 13 (1936): 667–91; repr. *Recueil Lucien Cerfaux*, 2.63–91.

Dibelius, M., *Studies*, 5–6, 197–201.

Donelson, L. R., "Cult Histories and the Sources of Acts," *Bib* 68 (1987): 1–21.

Dupont, J., *The Sources of Acts: The Present Position* (London: Darton, Longman & Todd; New York: Herder and Herder, 1964).

Enslin, M., "Once Again, Luke and Paul," *ZNW* 61 (1970): 253–71.

Gaston, L., *No Stone on Another: Studies in the Significance of the Fall of Jerusalem in the Synoptic Gospels* (NovTSup 23; Leiden: Brill, 1970), 254.

Goodspeed, E. J., "The Origin of Acts," *JBL* 39 (1920): 83–101.

Grässer, E., "Acta Forschung seit 1960," *TRu* 41 (1976): 141–94, 259–90, esp. 186–94.

Haenchen, E., "Tradition und Komposition in der Apostelgeschichte," *ZTK* 52 (1955): 205–25; repr. *Gott und Mensch*, 206–26.

Harnack, A., *Luke the Physician*, 119.

Hengel, M., *Acts*, 59–68.

Jeremias, J., "Untersuchungen zum Quellenproblem der Apostelgeschichte," ZNW 36 (1937): 205–21; repr. *Abba: Studien zur neutestamentlichen Theologie und Zeitgeschichte* (Göttingen: Vandenhoeck & Ruprecht, 1966), 238–55.

Kümmel, W. G., *Introduction to the New Testament: Revised Edition* (New York/Nashville: Abingdon, 1975), 174–85.

Lüdemann, G., *Early Christianity.*

Martin, R. A., "Syntactical Evidence of Aramaic Sources in Acts i–xv," *NTS* 11 (1964–65): 38–59.

———, *Syntactical Evidence of Semitic Sources in Greek Documents* (SBLSCS 3; Cambridge, MA: Society of Biblical Literature, 1974), 87–104.

Moffatt, J., *Introduction to the Literature of the New Testament* (International Theological Library; 3d ed.: Edinburgh: Clark, 1918), 286–89, 630–31.

O'Rourke, J. J., "The Construction with a Verb of Saying as an Indication of Sources in Luke," *NTS* 21 (1974–75): 421–23.

Plümacher, E., "Acta-Forschung 1974–1982," *TRu* 48 (1983): 1–56; 49 (1984): 105–69, esp. 120–38.

Reumann, J., "The 'Itinerary' as a Form in Classical Literature and the Acts of the Apostles," *To Touch the Text: Biblical and Related Studies in Honor of Joseph A. Fitzmyer, S.J.* (ed. M. P. Horgan and P. J. Kobelski; New York: Crossroad, 1989), 335–57.

Riddle, D. W., "The Logic of the Theory of Translation Greek," *JBL* 51 (1932): 13–30.

Schille, G., "Die Fragwürdigkeit eines Itinerars der Paulusreisen," *TLZ* 84 (1959): 165–74.

Schmithals, W., "Apg 20,17–38 und das Problem einer 'Paulusquelle,'" *Der Treue Gottes trauen: Beiträge zum Werk des Lukas: Für Gerhard Schneider* (ed. C. Bussmann and W. Radl; Freiburg im B.: Herder, 1991), 307–22.

Shepherd, M. H., "A Venture in the Source Analysis of Acts," *Munera Studiosa* (Festschrift W.H.P. Hatch; ed. M. H. Shepherd and S. E. Johnson; Cambridge: Episcopal Theological School, 1946), 91–105.

Taylor, J., *Les Actes des deux Apôtres: Commentaire historique.*

———, "The Making of Acts: A New Account," *RB* 97 (1990): 504–24.

Torrey, C. C., *The Composition and Date of Acts* (HTS 1; Cambridge: Harvard University Press, 1916).

IV. Use of the Old Testament in Acts

◆

(72) Related to the question of sources in Acts is the use of the OT. Luke has at times laced his account of the sequel of the Jesus-story with references to the OT in order to emphasize the continuation of biblical history that he was writing. This aspect of his account is enhanced by the recounting of episodes in the sequel as fulfillments of what he had read in the OT. There are thirty-seven places in Acts where Luke imported either whole verses or significant phrases from the OT; a few of them are composite.

(73) The quotations are as follows:

Acts	*OT Quotation*	*Acts*	*OT Quotation*
1:20	Ps 69:26; Ps 109:8	7:32	Exod 3:6
2:17–21	Joel 3:1–5	7:33	Exod 3:5
2:25–28	Ps 16:8–11	7:34	Exod 3:7–8; Exod 3:10
2:30	Ps 132:11	7:35	Exod 2:14
2:31	Ps 16:10	7:37	Deut 18:15
2:34–35	Ps 110:1	7:40	Exod 32:1, 23
3:13	Exod 3:6, 15	7:42–43	Amos 5:25–27
3:22	Deut 18:15–16	7:49–50	Isa 66:1–2
3:23	Deut 18:19; Lev 23:29	8:32–33	Isa 53:7–8
3:25	Gen 22:18; 26:4	13:22	Ps 89:21; 1 Sam 13:14
4:11	Ps 118:22	13:33	Ps 2:7
4:24	Ps 146:6	13:34	Isa 55:3
4:25–26	Ps 2:1–2	13:35	Ps 16:10
7:3	Gen 12:1	13:41	Hab 1:5
7:5	Gen 17:8; 48:4	13:47	Isa 49:6
7:6–7	Gen 15:13–14; Exod 3:12	15:16–17	Amos 9:11–12
7:18	Exod 1:8	23:5	Exod 22:27
7:27–28	Exod 2:14	28:26–27	Isa 6:9–10
7:30	Exod 3:2		

(74) In addition to the quotations listed above, there are many instances of OT phrases that Luke has used in his composition of Acts. Sometimes these phrases take the form of allusions, when they are not exact quotations. If the boldface OT quotations in the Greek text of Acts in the fourth edition of UBS *GNT*, where they are so printed in a minimal number, are compared with earlier editions of

Nestle-Aland's *NTG* (e.g., the 25th ed.), one will find many more phrases set in boldface in earlier editions of *NTG*. Appeal to the boldface verses or phrases indicates how dependent readers are on a modern editor's decision, perhaps somewhat subjective, about the character of such phrases, whether they are quotations or allusions or nothing at all. Indeed, the boldface quotations in the fourth edition of the UBS *GNT* do not agree with the italicized quotations in NA^{27}, which purports otherwise to be the same text. In one instance, 15:16–17, NA^{27} lists Isa 45:21 as the source of the concluding line of the OT quotation, which is otherwise from Amos 9:11–12, but the allusion is so vague that I have not italicized it. In all this discussion I am following the UBS boldface quotations. The additional boldface phrases in earlier editions of Nestle-Aland, however, do give some idea of at least how much Lucan phraseology is dependent on a Greek OT text.

(75) It is not surprising that the quotations of the OT have been drawn from a Greek translation, akin to the LXX, if not the LXX as we know it. The fact that they are drawn from the LXX in most instances reveals that they cannot be ascribed to a source that would have been written in Aramaic. Because they are derived from the LXX, they enhance the account in the first part of Acts with Septuagintal coloring, which some commentators have called Semitisms. Wilcox has maintained, however, that in 24 texts of Acts where the OT is cited the citations deviate from the *textus receptus* of the LXX and agree more with the MT, targums, or other forms of the OT *(Semitisms of Acts)*. That explanation, however, needs more scrutiny than it has received so far. E. Richard has examined the 24 texts discussed by Wilcox and concluded, "In not one instance is his evidence persuasive" ("Old Testament in Acts," 340). Some of the quotations are conflated or abridged, and detailed comments will be made in the NOTES on the verses of Acts where they appear.

(76) What is surprising is that the vast majority of the OT quotations appear in the first part of Acts, in chaps. 1–15. Only two (Exod 22:27 in Acts 23:5; and Isa 6:9–10 in 28:26–27) are found in the second part, where the story of Paul's missionary endeavors is recounted. The extent to which this may be due to sources that Luke has used can be debated. Most of the quotations in the first part occur also in speeches, especially those addressed to Jewish audiences, who would be expected to comprehend the quotations or allusions to the OT.

(77) In addition to explicit quotations and obvious borrowing of phrases, there are also several global references in Acts to what God has "announced long ago through all the prophets" (3:18), or to what "all the prophets . . . from Samuel on down . . . have proclaimed" (3:24), or "to him [Jesus of Nazareth] all the prophets bear witness" (10:43). Such global references to the OT can be found further in 17:3; 18:28; 24:14; 26:22. They are called "global" references, because they usually do not cite or allude to specific OT passages but summarize what God did or said in the OT and often use the Lucan hyperbolic "all." Moreover, such global references are almost exclusively Lucan in the NT and reveal a distinctively Lucan way of using the Scriptures of old.

(78) All the references to the OT show how Luke has sought in a highly dis-

tinctive way to achieve his goal of presenting the Jesus-story and its sequel as a continuation of biblical history. It is the story of a new age of human history as he narrates how the apostles and disciples carried out the commission of the risen Christ to bear witness to him and his mission, but that story is not without its OT roots.

(79) One of the reasons why Luke has made considerable use of the OT is christology, his desire to relate the Jesus-story and its sequel to the plan of God begun in the OT and precisely Jesus' role in that plan. At the end of his Gospel, Luke depicted the risen Christ explaining to the disciples on the way to Emmaus all that the OT had already said concerning him: "Then he began with Moses and all the prophets and interpreted for them what pertained to himself in every part of Scripture" (Luke 24:27). Again, when the risen Christ appeared to the Eleven and those with them, he said, "Now this is what my words meant which I addressed to you while I was still with you: All that was written about me in the Law of Moses, in the Prophets, and in the Psalms must see fulfillment" (24:44). Those statements were put on the lips of Christ at the end of the Gospel, but they govern the Lucan use of OT quotations in the second volume of his composition, for not only the Jesus-story itself, but its sequel as well is seen as the fulfillment of what the OT predicted.

(80) The motif of promise and fulfillment is found elsewhere in NT writings, but the Lucan use of it is more pronounced, even though Luke does not use anything like the formula quotations found in Matthew (at least ten times) and occasionally in John (e.g., 12:38; 13:18; 17:12); the fact that the OT is quoted so often in Acts as well as the Gospel is part of the distinctive Lucan use of that predictive motif. For this reason Jervell rightly calls Luke "the theologian of Scripture par excellence" ("The Center," 122).

(81) Another reason for the use of OT quotations and allusions in Acts is Luke's concern to stress the role of the Spirit in the inauguration of the testimony to the risen Christ that the disciples are to bear. This use of the OT is seen in the second speech of Peter on the first Christian Pentecost (2:14–36), in which the prophet Joel is quoted and the burden of the quotation is to emphasize the outpouring of the Spirit: "I will pour some of my Spirit upon all flesh" (2:17); and "even upon my servants and my handmaids will I pour out some of my Spirit in those days" (2:18). Moreover, Luke acknowledges that the Holy Spirit spoke through David (4:25), as he quotes Ps 2:1–2 in the prayer of the early Christians.

(82) The OT quotations in Acts play a prominent part in the speeches of both Peter and Paul, and also in the speech of Stephen. In the discourses delivered by Peter, which are mostly addressed to Jews, one can see the Lucan concern to link the Christ-event to their Scriptures. In the case of Paul, his use of the OT is seen in the "word of exhortation" addressed to Jews and Godfearers in the synagogue of Pisidian Antioch (13:16–41), in which he recounts first the mighty acts of God and then relates to such a recital the role of Jesus of Nazareth. When Paul is evangelizing pagans, such as the Athenians on the Areopagus (17:22–31), there is understandably no explicit OT quotation, but phrases even in that discourse echo OT usage. Again, when he addresses Christians, the presbyters of Ephesus

summoned to Miletus (20:18–35), Paul alludes to the OT, but not as abundantly as one might have expected. See further Bruce, "Paul's Use." Most important of all, Luke depicts Paul declaring, "I believe in all that is according to the law and that is written in the prophets" (24:14).

(83) Jervell argues that for Luke "David, father of the Messiah, is the prophet par excellence, the central figure in Scripture" ("The Center," 126), more important even than Moses. See 1:16; 2:25, 30, 34; 4:25. Jervell also emphasizes the central position that the OT prophets play in Acts, and the problem that 13:38 causes: "through him [Christ, the descendant of David, the 'prophet'] everyone who believes is justified from everything from which you could not be justified by the law of Moses." The contrast of David and Moses, however, is there only implicitly, and Jervell has exaggerated it. Luke also uses Scripture in Acts to legitimate the mission to the Gentiles, as Tyson has stressed ("The Gentile Mission"). This emerges in the ending of Paul's discourse in the synagogue of Pisidian Antioch (13:44–47), in the comments of James at the Jerusalem "Council" (15:13–21), and in Paul's remarks in Rome (28:23–28); but it also appears covertly in the story of the conversion of Cornelius (10:1–11:18), where no quotation of the OT occurs, save indirectly in 10:43. Tyson, however, has overplayed the tension that such Lucan use of Scripture causes in regard to biblical regulations about food.

(84) In addition to the use of OT quotations and allusions in the speeches, the narratives of Acts have been influenced at times by phraseology from the LXX; even in the second half of Acts, where the narrative outweighs the discourses, the marginal references to the OT in NA[27] are noteworthy.

(85) Finally, in citing the OT, Luke makes use of contemporary introductory formulas, such as *kathōs gegraptai,* "as it has been written" (7:42; 15:15); or *hōs . . . gegraptai,* "even as it stands written" (13:33); or *gegraptai gar,* "for it stands written" (1:20; 23:5); but also *elalēsen de houtōs ho theos,* "these were the words God used" (lit., "in this way God spoke": 7:6; cf. 7:7); or *touto estin to eirēmenon dia tou prophētou Iōēl,* "this is what was meant by the prophet Joel, when he said" (2:16). These formulas are known to be contemporary because they have almost exact Hebrew counterparts in Qumran texts (Fitzmyer, "The Use," 7–16) and differ considerably from the introductory formulas in the Mishnah of ca. A.D. 200.

BIBLIOGRAPHY

Barrett, C. K., "Luke/Acts," *It Is Written: Scripture Citing Scripture: Essays in Honour of Barnabas Lindars, SSF* (ed. D. A. Carson and H.G.M. Williamson; Cambridge: Cambridge University Press, 1988), 231–44, esp. 237–44.

Betori, G., "L'Antico Testamento negli Atti: Stato della ricerca e spunti di riflessione," *RivB* 32 (1984): 211–36.

Black, M., "The Christological Use of the Old Testament in the New Testament," *NTS* 18 (1971–72): 1–14.

Bock, D. L., *Proclamation from Prophecy and Pattern: Lucan Old Testament Christology* (JSNTSup 12; Sheffield, UK: JSOT, 1987), 155–259.

Bruce, F. F., "Paul's Use of the Old Testament in Acts," *Tradition and Interpretation in the New Testament: Essays in Honor of E. Earle Ellis for His 60th Birthday* (ed. G. F. Hawthorne with O. Betz; Grand Rapids, MI: Eerdmans; Tübingen: Mohr [Siebeck], 1987), 71–79.

Cerfaux, L., "Citations scripturaires et tradition textuelle dans le Livre des Actes," *Aux sources de la tradition chrétienne: Mélanges offerts à M. Maurice Goguel* (Bibliothèque théologique; Paris/Neuchâtel: Delachaux et Niestlé, 1950), 43–51; repr. *Recueil Lucien Cerfaux,* 2.93–103.

Dumais, M., "Le langage des discours d'évangélisation des Actes: Une forme de langage symbolique?" *Les Actes des Apôtres* (ed. J. Kremer), 467–74.

Dupont, J., "L'Interprétation des Psaumes dans les Actes des Apôtres," *Le Psautier: Ses origines, ses problèmes littéraires, son influence* (OBL 4; Louvain: Publications Universitaires, 1962), 357–88; repr. *Études,* 283–307.

———, "L'Utilisation apologétique de l'Ancien Testament dans les discours des Actes," *ETL* 29 (1953): 289–327; repr. *Études,* 245–82.

Evans, C. A. and J. A. Sanders, *Luke and Scripture: The Function of Sacred Tradition in Luke-Acts* (Minneapolis: Fortress, 1993), 171–224.

Fitzmyer, J. A., "The Use of Explicit Old Testament Quotations in Qumran Literature and in the New Testament," *ESBNT,* 3–58.

Grelot, P. and M. Dumais, *Homélies sur l'Ecriture à l'époque apostolique* (Introduction à la Bible 3/8; Paris: Desclée, 1989), 99–145.

Haenchen, E., "Schriftzitate und Textüberlieferung in der Apostelgeschichte," *ZTK* 51 (1954): 153–67; repr. *Gott und Mensch,* 157–71.

Holtz, T., *Untersuchungen über die alttestamentlichen Zitate bei Lukas* (TU 104; Berlin: Akademie-V., 1968), 5–27, 29–37, 43–56, 71–81, 85–153.

Jervell, J., "Die Mitte der Schrift: Zum lukanischen Verständnis des Alten Testamentes," *Die Mitte des Neuen Testaments: Einheit und Vielfalt neutestamentlicher Theologie: Festschrift für Eduard Schweizer . . .* (ed. U. Luz and H. Weder; Göttingen: Vandenhoeck & Ruprecht, 1983), 79–96; trans. "The Center of Scripture in Luke," *The Unknown Paul,* 122–37.

Kilpatrick, G. D., "Some Quotations in Acts," *Les Actes des Apôtres* (ed. J. Kremer), 81–97.

Koet, B. J., *Five Studies on Interpretation of Scripture in Luke-Acts* (Studiorum Novi Testamenti auxilia 14; Louvain: Leuven University/Peeters, 1989), 73–139.

Longenecker, R. N., *Biblical Exegesis in the Apostolic Period* (Grand Rapids, MI: Eerdmans, 1975), 96–103.

Lowther Clarke, W. K., "The Use of the Septuagint in Acts," *Beginnings,* 2.66–105.

Paulo, P.-A., *Le problème ecclésial des Actes à la lumière de deux prophéties d'Amos* (Recherches ns 3; Montreal: Editions Bellarmin; Paris: Cerf, 1985).

Rese, M., *Alttestamentliche Motive in der Christologie des Lukas* (SNT 1; Gütersloh: Mohn, 1969), 43–135.

———, "Die Funktion der alttestamentlichen Zitate und Anspielungen in den Reden der Apostelgeschichte," *Les Actes des Apôtres* (ed. J. Kremer), 61–79.

Richard, E., "The Creative Use of Amos by the Author of Acts," *NovT* 24 (1982): 37–53.

———, "The Old Testament in Acts: Wilcox's Semitisms in Retrospect," *CBQ* 42 (1980): 330–41.

Ringgren, H., "Luke's Use of the Old Testament," *HTR* 79 (1986): 227–35.

Rius-Camps, J., "Cuatro paradigmas del Pentateuco refundidos en los Hechos de los Apóstoles," *EstBíb* 53 (1995): 25–54.

Sanders, J. T., "The Prophetic Use of the Scriptures in Luke-Acts," *Early Jewish and Christian Exegesis: Studies in Memory of William Hugh Brownlee* (ed. C. A. Evans and W. F. Stinespring; Atlanta: Scholars, 1987), 191–98.

Schubert, P., "The Structure and Significance of Luke 24," *Neutestamentliche Studien für R. Bultmann* (BZNW 21; ed. W. Eltester; Berlin: Töpelmann, 1954), 165–86.

Seccombe, D., "Luke and Isaiah," *NTS* 27 (1980–81): 252–59.

Steyn, G. J., *Septuagint Quotations in the Context of the Petrine and Pauline Speeches of the Acta Apostolorum* (Contributions to Biblical Exegesis and Theology 12; Kampen: Kok Pharos, 1995).

Tasker, R.V.G., *The Old Testament in the New Testament* (Grand Rapids, MI: Eerdmans, 1963), 63–79.

Tyson, J. B., "The Gentile Mission and the Authority of Scripture in Acts," *NTS* 33 (1987): 619–31.

White, P. S., *Prophétie et prédication: Une étude herméneutique des citations de l'Ancien Testament dans les sermons des Actes* (Lille: Service de Reproduction, 1973).

Wilcox, M., "The Old Testament in Acts 1–15," *AusBR* 5 (1956): 1–41.

———, *The Semitisms of Acts* (Oxford: Clarendon, 1965).

V. Composition of Acts and Its Form-Critical Analysis

◆

(86) Various compositional forms can be distinguished in Acts. It is made up of narratives, summaries, We-Sections, and speeches. These four subforms have been used in various ways, and together they make up the *Praxeis apostolōn*; they lend themselves to different modes of analysis and interpretation.

A. Narratives

(87) It is not surprising that the bulk of the episodes in Acts is given over to narratives. After all, this accords with the name that Luke himself used to describe his two-volume work, *diēgēsis*, "narrative account," the meaning of which has already been discussed (*Luke*, 17, 172–73, 292). This aspect of Acts is also one of the reasons why the title "Acts" was put on it. See §§4–7 above.

The continuous narrative character of the account in Acts makes it different from the Lucan Gospel, in which besides the sayings and parables of Jesus one could class as narratives the miracle stories, the pronouncement stories, and the stories about Jesus (or John the Baptist), as well as the infancy, the passion, and the resurrection narratives. The narratives of Acts, however, recount a more extended period of the spread of the Word of God than the brief one-year account of Jesus' ministry in the Gospel, and they also have a more extended geographical sweep.

(88) The narrative episodes in Acts at times do include miracle stories, but most of the narratives are more like the stories about Jesus or John in the Gospel. Besides miracle stories, the accounts of the journeys and missionary activity of Peter and Paul are related to the narrative form in Acts. What makes the difference in the narrative episodes of Acts is that they are often interspersed with speeches or discourses. These episodes differ from pronouncement stories, because the speeches are not preserved in the tradition merely because of a pronouncement or a punchline, which is a characteristic of that subform of gospel narrative. Luke intends the speeches to be integral parts of the narrative episodes.

(89) The narrative is a story form that in select dramatic episodes recounts the spread of the Word of God from Jerusalem to "the end of the earth" (1:8) and, in a less important way, recounts the evangelization of the Gentiles without insisting on their observance of the Mosaic law. The drama in the episodes tells of the progress of that spread, but also depicts its obstacles and its failure, since at

times the Word is not accepted. The narrative is not triumphalistic or without its problems. The testimony that the disciples bear to the risen Christ is sometimes successful, but it encounters opposition, rejection, and persecution. Such is the main function of the narrative episodes, but they also paint the portraits and characters of Peter and Paul, the two main protagonists. The narratives are not to be taken merely as edifying stories told by Luke (as Haenchen would have us believe, *Acts,* 103–10), but are related to the broad tradition of Hellenistic historiography and have been transformed by Luke "into a new 'kerygmatic' form of historiography" (Hengel, *Acts,* 34).

(90) Moreover, the narrative in Acts is mainly the way Luke presents his theology, as B. R. Gaventa has well argued: "Lukan theology is intricately and irreversibly bound up with the story he tells and cannot be separated from it. An attempt to do justice to the theology of Acts must struggle to reclaim the character of Acts as a narrative" ("Toward a Theology," 150).

B. Summaries

(91) The title *Sammelbericht* was used by K. L. Schmidt for passages in the Marcan Gospel (1:39; 3:10–12) that belonged to the evangelist's redactional framework and filled in gaps, thus serving to give a certain continuity to the narrative of the Gospel (*Der Rahmen der Geschichte Jesu* [Berlin: Trowitzsch & Sohn, 1919], 7–8, 13, 66). From Schmidt's work has come the designation "summary" for such generic descriptions of Jesus' activity in the gospel tradition.

(92) Although there are summary statements of the evangelist in the Third Gospel (4:14–15; 4:31–32, 40–41; 6:17–19; 8:1–3; 19:47–49; 21:37–38), one of the noteworthy differences in Acts is the number of verses or blocks of verses with summary statements linked to the narratives. They are generalized reports on circumstances that create a chain of events punctuating the narratives and describing the growth and development of the early Christian community. They serve as signals to the readers, reminding them of the progress that the Word of God is making despite the author's preoccupation with the narration of details. They constitute, then, a separate form-critical category in Acts.

(93) The summaries are of three sorts:

(a) **Major Summaries:** 2:42–47; 4:32–35; 5:12–16. Statements of several verses in length, which are found in the early chapters of Acts and are somewhat related to each other. These summary statements depict in idyllic fashion the springtime of the Christian church in Jerusalem. They are probably composite or conflated and share or borrow details, as Benoit ("Remarques") and others (Cerfaux, Jeremias) have shown.

(b) **Minor Summaries:** 1:14; 6:7; 9:31; 12:24; 16:5; 19:20; 28:30–31. These seven summaries, which are usually only of one verse, have been used by C. H. Turner to divide Acts into six historical "panels" (see J. Hastings [ed.], *A Dictionary of the Bible* [New York: Scribner's Sons, 1900], 1.421; cf. A. H. McNeile, *An Introduction to the Study of the New Testament* [2d ed.; Oxford: Clarendon,

1953], 97–99). Whether they were so intended by Luke is another question, because 5:42 may also belong to this sort of summary statement.

(c) **Numerical Summaries:** 2:41; 4:4; 5:14; 6:1, 7; 9:31; 11:21, 24; 12:24; 14:1; 19:20. A few of these have already been listed in (a) or (b). They are characterized by the use of numbers and serve to measure the numerical growth of the church.

Though Luke, in composing these summaries, may be in part dependent on such forms found in the Marcan Gospel, it is much more likely that he uses them while depending on Hellenistic descriptions of religious or philosophical groups penned by such writers as Chaeremon of Alexandria, Philo, Josephus; similar summaries are also found in the second-century writer Philostratus and the third-century Iamblichus. In other words, summaries were part of a Hellenistic mode of narrative prose writing.

C. We-Sections

(94) The narrative in Acts is usually recounted in the third person (singular or plural), but in the second part of Acts there are four distinct passages in which the narrative changes suddenly from the third person to the first plural and thereby stand out from the rest of the Lucan story. They are 16:10–17; 20:5–15; 21:1–18; 27:1–28:16, all of them part of the Pauline or Itinerary source. The author never tells us who are meant by this "we," and one naturally supposes that he is including himself among them, but that is part of the problem that these passages cause.

Moreover, 11:28 in Codex Bezae, some VL texts, Coptic versions, and a quotation of Augustine reads: *ēn de pollē agalliasis. synestrammenōn de hēmōn ephē heis ex autōn onomati Agabos sēmainōn*, "and there was much rejoicing. When we had gathered together, one of them named Agabus said, predicting through the Spirit. . . ." This problematic reading of the WT, which introduces into the first part of Acts a We-Section, is otherwise unknown in the vast majority of MSS of Acts. Since it is not found in the Alexandrian text, I do not consider it part of the original text of Acts or even part of the original We-Sections.

(95) The character of the We-Sections has been much debated. Until recently, three different explanations were usually proposed for them.

(a) From earliest times the We-Sections have been understood as a means whereby the author expressed his personal association with part of the missionary journeys and endeavors of Paul. This explanation of the We-Sections first appears in the writings of Irenaeus (*Adversus haereses* 3.1.1; 3.14.1–3 [*SQE*, 533–37]) and has been borrowed by other patristic writers whom he influenced. Irenaeus appealed to the We-Sections in Acts to show how Luke was *akolouthos, sectator*, "a follower," of Paul. See *Luke*, 36–41, where I admitted that the evidence used by Irenaeus would tolerate the identification of Luke as a "sometime collaborator" of Paul, but not as an "inseparable" companion, as Irenaeus read it.

In modern times, this explanation has often taken the form of a travel diary or travel notes that Luke would have kept and later used in writing Acts, preserving the "we" as an indication of his association with Paul in certain episodes. This use of "we" would be like similar passages in Hellenistic literature where the shift from the third person to the first plural indicates the author's personal involvement in events so narrated, as Norden and Nock have noted. Such a "we" is absent from Acts 1–15, because Luke would not be implying such an association with the events recounted there. It is sometimes said, however, that 16:17 and 21:18 argue against this inclusion of Luke in the "we," because Paul there seems to be distinguished from the "we" (Kümmel, *Introduction*, 176). Yet, even though Paul may be so distinguished in the formula used, the sentence in each case still suggests such an association, and the distinction does not really militate against this explanation of the We-Sections. Moreover, Nock has shown that the keeping of such diaries was not confined to kings and officials and has called attention to ancient examples in *Pap. Osloensis* 2 (see S. Eitrem and L. Amundsen, *Papyri Osloenses* I–III [Oslo: Dybwad, 1925–36], 40; *Pap. Rylands* 627); see further Nock's *Essays on Religion and the Ancient World* (2 vols.; ed. Z. Stewart; Cambridge: Harvard University Press, 1972), 824–25.

Such an explanation of the We-Sections has been used by Cerfaux, Dupont, Feine-Behm, Fusco, R. M. Grant, J. Knox, McNeile, Munck, Nock, Polhill, Meinertz, Michaelis, Wikenhauser. The major objection to this explanation comes from the picture that Acts presents of Paul, on which more will be said in due course.

(96) (b) Some modern commentators, usually those who find it difficult to regard the traditional Luke as the author of Acts, have explained the We-Sections as memoirs or an itinerary record or an eyewitness report composed by someone other than the author, but which was used by the author, who allowed the first-person plural formulation to stand. For such commentators the We-Sections would be either a separate source that the author would have used along with the Pauline or Itinerary source, or possibly part of the latter. So Schwanbeck (memorandum written by Silas), Hilgenfeld and Wendt (both of whom compared the memoirs in Ezra and Nehemiah), Norden (who called them *hypomnēmata*, "memoirs"), Dibelius (who argued that "both the linguistic and the literary styles of the 'we-passages' are not essentially different from other passages [in the Itinerary source behind 13:4–21:18] which deal with similar events" [*Studies*, 5; cf. 196–97]). From such views arose the common designation of the We-Sections as an itinerary. This explanation has also been used by Borse, Dockx, Haenchen, Roloff, and Wehnert.

Such an explanation of the We-Sections is not without its problems. If it stems from someone other than the author of Acts, whose itinerary notes would they have been? Numerous candidates have been suggested: Aristarchus, Epaphroditus, Silas, Timothy, Titus. Such suggestions are all based on speculation alone, with no evidence for any of them. Again, if the We-Sections have the same literary style as the rest of the Itinerary, as Harnack insisted and Dibelius admitted, then why separate them? Further, if one is going to explain the "we" in these sections by appeal to an earlier non-Lucan written text, then one has to reckon with all the problems about such a source raised by Dupont (*Sources*, 94–112).

Moreover, Haenchen showed that the alleged list of stopping places and the use of "we" are rarely found together and that such an itinerary is, by and large, not found in the latter half of Acts.

(97) (c) The We-Sections have also been regarded as a distinct literary form used by the author (usually not Luke) for certain passages in Acts. This has been proposed in two different ways:

(98) (i) The We-Sections would be a literary means to achieve certain effects: either to make the account vivid by giving the reader the impression that the author was fully informed about some events (so Haenchen, " 'We' in Acts," 85: it "gives the reader the certainty that he is learning firsthand about these things," when the author is not focusing "all attention on Paul alone"), or else to make readers realize that in some sections they are in touch with personal recollections or eyewitness testimony (Haenchen: "it makes the reader feel himself directly connected with Paul's life"). In this sort of explanation the We-Sections may possibly be derived from a particular source; the first-person plural formulation would then have been retained in the final redaction of Acts as a literary artifice to achieve such a goal. This explanation of the We-Sections has been similarly used by Schneider (*Apg.*, 1.92) and Barrett (*Luke the Historian*, 22). This explanation is also proposed in an extreme form as a pseudepigraphic device or a deliberate fiction: the author, who was never really a companion of Paul wants to pass himself off as such (so Overbeck, Vielhauer, Conzelmann and Lindemann [*Interpreting*, 241]).

The major objection raised against this explanation of the We-Sections is its fictive character and the lack of a contemporary literary convention to illustrate it. Ancient extrabiblical parallels, in which first-person plural formulation is found, as noted by Norden, Dibelius, and Nock, are strikingly different from its alleged use in Acts in that their authors so express themselves because they were indeed eyewitnesses of the events portrayed, such as sea voyages. There is in them scarcely a suggestion that they might be a literary fiction. Moreover, the "we" is used in some episodes of Acts, where the events are hardly important or striking, to which eyewitness testimony adds little. Furthermore, why would the author have used "the 'we' in such sporadic fashion if he wanted to give his report the appearance of an eyewitness record"? (Kümmel, *Introduction*, 184). Why would he have used "we" in such an inconspicuous way? In the anonymous writing that is called Acts, the "we" scarcely serves a pseudepigraphic purpose. Presumably Theophilus, to whom the work is dedicated, and other readers like him in the last decades of the first Christian century would have understood the We-Sections as expressing the author's self-identification.

(99) (ii) The We-Sections were not derived from a particular source but represent a different literary genre used by the author, especially in episodes related to sea voyages, thus employing a "conventional generic style within Hellenistic literature." The last phrase comes from Robbins ("The We-Passages," 6), who has collected extrabiblical examples of such style that he claims explain the We-Sections as an ancient literary form that the author of Acts is imitating. The use of "we" would merely express the collective experience of those depicted as trav-

eling together on a ship, "whether or not the author was an actual participant in the voyage" (ibid., 17). The extrabiblical examples describe sea voyages with storms, shipwrecks, landings on unknown coasts, encounters with hostile or friendly natives, all recounted in the first person. This explanation of the We-sections has appealed to a number of recent commentators: Bovon ("Luc: Portrait," 17); Dillon (*NJBC*, 723); Karris (*What*, 39); H. Koester (*Introduction*, 2.50).

(100) If the We-Sections were to represent a studied literary device such as this, it creates problems of its own. (aa) Why does it appear only in four passages of Acts: from Troas to Philippi, from Philippi to Jerusalem, and from Caesarea to Rome? Sailing is otherwise mentioned in 13:4 (from Seleucia, port of Antioch on the Orontes, to Salamis in Cyprus), in 13:13 (from Cypriot Paphos to Perga in Pamphylia), and in 14:26 (from Attalia near Perga back to Antioch), all recounted in the third person. Moreover, sailing is implied in 17:14 (where Christians in Beroea send Paul off), in 18:18 (where Paul departs from Corinth for Syria), in 18:21 (where he sails from Ephesus to Caesarea Maritima), and perhaps also in 20:1–2; yet in none of these passages is the first-person plural employed.

(bb) Further difficulty is sensed in the first We-Section (16:10–17), where the "we" in vv 10–12 is related, indeed, to a crossing of the sea. However, why does the "we" continue as Paul makes his way to a place of prayer outside Philippi alongside some river, and in only the first part of the story about Paul's exorcism of the girl with the python-spirit (16:13–17)? Moreover, 16:10 is the declaration of an intention (to pass over to Macedonia); if the "we" were related to a sea voyage, it should begin in 16:11. A similar query would have to be raised about 20:7–8, which provides the setting for Paul's long-winded speech in Troas and the Eutychus incident. Eventually, vv 13–16 continue in the first plural, but v 16, which tells about Paul sailing "past Ephesus," recounts it in the third singular. This is also found in vv 9–12. Again, why does the "we" continue during the account of the overland journey from Ptolemais to Caesarea Maritima (21:7–8a), during the story about Philip the evangelist, his daughters, and Agabus (21:8b–14), and during the narrative of the further overland journey from Caesarea to Jerusalem (21:15–18)? To get around this problem, Robbins in his later article tried to attenuate it by entitling it, "By Land and Sea," while retaining "Sea Voyages" in the latter half of the title!

(cc) A more serious question has to be raised about the alleged convention in contemporary Hellenistic literature, which Robbins has invoked. He maintains that in such literature "sea voyages are often couched in the first person narration" ("The We-Passages," 5). For parallels, however, he cites *The Story of Sinuhe* (from ca. 1800 B.C.) and *The Journey of Wen-Amun to Phoenicia* (from ca. 1100 B.C.). Aside from the fact that they are not writings of Greek literature, let alone of "Hellenistic literature," they are narratives that use the first-person singular, not the first plural. *The Story of Sinuhe* is recounted almost entirely in the first singular. Not just the sea voyages or lake crossings, but also his dealings with Ammi-enshi, ruler of Upper Retenu (near Byblos), and his "many years" of married life and military service are all recounted in the first singular. This is hardly a text with which the We-Sections of Acts ought to be compared.

The same has to be said about the Wen-Amun report; the first-person singular is used for the journey from Tanis across the great Syrian Sea to Dor (northern coast of Palestine) and then to Byblos. It is also utilized for the narrative of all of Wen-Amun's dealings with the prince of Byblos (see *ANET*, 18–22 [esp. 18], 25–29). Robbins further cites the Akkadian *Epic of Gilgamesh* (hardly Hellenistic literature!), where the first-singular narrative is not confined to the journey to Mt. Nisir, but tells about the building of a ship, the pouring of a libation on a mountaintop, and the granting to Atraḫasis to see a dream. Moreover, when a voyage is mentioned, the third-person plural is used: "Gilgamesh and Urshanabi boarded the ship; [they launch]ed the ship on the way [and] sailed away" (XI. 256–57; *ANET*, 96).

Robbins's use of Homer's *Odyssey* and admittedly Hellenistic writers such as Varro and Dio Chrysostom encounters similar difficulties (see my "Authorship of Luke-Acts," 20–21). The upshot is that this "conventional" literary device is more alleged than demonstrated. The evidence reveals that sea voyages were a topic described in ancient, even Hellenistic, literature, but it does not show that there was really a literary form that demanded the use of the first-person plural. That the We-Sections in Acts are "certainly a literary subterfuge" (Bovon) still has to be shown. As Praeder has put it, "It is not the case that sea voyages in ancient literature were 'expected to contain first person narration' [quoting Robbins, 'The We-Passages,' 228]" ("Acts 27:1–28:16," 684 n. 3). See further her articles, "The Problem" and "Luke-Acts and the Ancient Novel."

(101) (d) Most recently, Boismard and Lamouille have addressed the problem of the We-Sections and proposed an entirely different solution. According to them, the narrative of 27:1–13 reveals that it is composed of two more or less parallel accounts, one in the first-person plural and the other in the third person. The latter comes from Redaction I (see §70 above), but the former from a document related to 20:5–21:17 (a list of stops made by the ship on which Paul and his companions traveled). It is a travel diary (Journal de voyage [Jv]) kept by a companion of Paul (probably Silas), which did not, however, include all the We-Sections; it did not include 16:13–15; 20:7–12, which stem rather from Redaction II. But passages such as 16:16–18 (in the first-person plural) and 16:19–40 (in the third person) would have been part of Jv (apart from vv 23b–34), as well as 19:21 and 20:2b–3 (in the third person). Moreover, in the form of Acts that we now have, the We-Sections appear in Paul's second and third missionary journeys and in his journey to Rome. This might argue against their being drawn from one diary. But when the We-Sections are read consecutively, they seem to recount stages of a single journey (to Macedonia, to Jerusalem, and to Rome; see indications of time in 20:6, 16; 27:9). Such a journey, connected with the taking of a collection up to Jerusalem, is implied in Paul's own letters. This would have been the story of Jv, which the author of Redaction I would have known, but which the author of Redaction II would have not only known but utilized in different journeys.

This explanation of the We-Sections is, of course, related to the complicated Boismard-Lamouille analysis of the sources used in Acts, and it encounters all the same problems: hypothesis built on hypothesis, but little convincing evidence. Moreover, it relates to the same passages those that are not in the first plural, in a way that makes the problem almost disappear.

(102) Consequently, the best explanation among all these proposals remains the suggestion that the "we" was already in a source used by the author and that source was a diary or travel notes that the author himself (Luke) would have kept and incorporated into Acts when he later came to compose it. Whether such a source would have been part of a larger Itinerary source or not is hard to say and matters little in reality. Luke's retention of the first-person plural formulation of his diary stands as a device by which he showed his sometime involvement in some of Paul's missionary endeavors.

Such an understanding of the We-Sections is also the one best related to the use of *en hēmin,* "among us," in the prologue of the Lucan Gospel (1:1) and *kamoi* (1:3; see *Luke,* 293–94). Moreover, it is far from certain that "there is lacking any hint of participation by the author of Lk-Acts in any of the events, and any preparation [in *en hēmin* and *kamoi*] for the 'we' in Acts 16 ff." (Kümmel, *Introduction,* 179). Kümmel has shown that Dupont's interpretation of *parēkolouthēkoti* (Luke 1:3) is wrong and that it has to mean "after tracing (everything)," but his conclusion, as stated there, is simply extreme and untenable (*any* hint of participation; *any preparation*).

As Hengel has put it (*Acts,* 66):

> From the beginning, this is the only way in which readers—and first of all Theophilus, to whom the two-volume work was dedicated and who must have known the author personally—could have understood the "we" passages. "We" therefore appears in travel accounts because Luke simply wanted to indicate that he was there. However, his personal experiences are uninteresting. Paul remains the sole focal point.

See further, in a similar vein of explanation, Fusco, "Le sezioni-noi"; Plümacher, "Wirklichkeitserfahrung."

D. Speeches

(103) The last subform used in Acts is the speech or discourse. Almost a third of Acts (about 295 verses out of 1,000) is given over to this form. It reduces the amount of indirect discourse in the narratives of Acts, and the connection of the speeches to the narratives into which they are inserted varies. Part of the problem that one immediately encounters in discussing this literary form is the definition of what a "speech" is. I understand it as an address directed to a group or an individual in a nonprivate setting, usually involving the attention of a number of people. When there is an extended discourse, there is no problem in recognizing

it, but when one encounters dialogue or conversation, how much of it should be included? Consequently, commentators are not at one as to the number of speeches in Acts; many consider them to be only 24. The issue has been well discussed by Soards *(The Speeches)*, but I do not include all the verses that he does, because I limit the discourse or speech to that given by one and the same person, and I do not include prayers or forms of dialogue.

(104) The following list shows the passages of Acts that I think should be considered as speeches or discourses:

1. 1:4–5, 7–8 — Risen Christ to Apostles and Disciples
2. 1:16–22 — Peter at the Choosing of Matthias
3. 2:14b–36, 38–39 — Peter to Jews Gathered in Jerusalem on Pentecost
4. 3:12b–26 — Peter in Temple after Cure of the Lame Man
5. 4:8b–12, 19b–20 — Peter before the Sanhedrin, I
6. 5:29b–32 — Peter before the Sanhedrin, II
7. 5:35b–39 — Gamaliel before the Sanhedrin
8. 6:2b–4 — The Twelve before the Assembled Disciples
9. 7:2–53 — Stephen before the Sanhedrin
10. 10:34b–43 — Peter at Cornelius's Conversion
11. 11:5–17 — Peter to the Apostles and Brothers in Jerusalem
12. 13:16b–41 — Paul at Antioch in Pisidia
13. 14:15–17 — Barnabas and Paul to the Crowd in Lystra
14. 15:7b–11 — Peter at the "Council" in Jerusalem
15. 15:13b–21 — James to the Assembly in Jerusalem
16. 17:22–31 — Paul to the Athenians at the Areopagus
17. 18:14b–15 — Gallio to the Jews of Corinth
18. 19:25b–27 — Demetrius to Fellow Silversmiths
19. 19:35b–40 — Town Clerk to the Ephesians
20. 20:18b–35 — Paul to Ephesian Presbyters at Miletus
21. 22:1, 3–21 — Paul to the Jerusalem Crowd at His Arrest
22. 24:2b–8 — Tertullus before Governor Felix
23. 24:10b–21 — Paul before Governor Felix
24. 25:8b, 10b–11 — Paul's Appeal to Caesar
25. 25:14c–21, 24–27 — Festus before King Agrippa
26. 26:2–23, 25–27, 29 — Paul before King Agrippa
27. 27:21–26 — Paul to Fellow Travelers aboard Ship
28. 28:17c–20, 25b–28 — Paul to Jewish Leaders of Rome

(105) In this list of 28 speeches one has to distinguish different sorts: there are ten Pauline and eight Petrine discourses, and one each of the risen Christ, Demetrius, the governor Festus, Gallio, Gamaliel, James, Stephen, Tertullus, the town clerk of Ephesus, and the Twelve. Moreover, there are six missionary speeches addressed to Jews (2:14b–36, 38–39; 3:12b–26; 4:8b–12; 5:29b–32; 10:34b–43; 13:16b–41), two evangelizing sermons addressed to Gentiles (14:15–17; 17:22–31), a prophetic indictment (Stephen's speech, 7:2–53), two

didactic speeches (15:7b–11; 15:13b–21), two *apologiai* or defense speeches (22:1, 3–21; 26:2–23, 25–27, 29), and one debate (24:2b–8; 24:10b–21). Two of the speeches of Paul (22:1, 3–21 and 26:2–3, 25–27, 29) present in oratorical form what the reader has already read about in narrative form in 9:1–31, and details do not always agree in the three forms of the story of Saul's call.

(106) Speeches are a subform found in ancient Greek historiography, used to produce a dramatic effect and often serving to aid the author's purpose in writing. The main question that speeches raise is their historicity. In the form in which we have the speeches in Acts they are clearly Lucan compositions. Years ago Dibelius (*Studies*, 138–85) compared them with the orations inserted in Thucydides' *Histories*. Thucydides himself admitted about them:

> As to the speeches that were made by different people . . . it has been difficult to call to mind with exact accuracy what was actually said, both for me about what I myself heard and for those who have reported them to me from other sources. As each one seemed to me to have spoken most likely about the topics under consideration, so it has been expressed, adhering as closely as possible to the general sense of what was actually said. (1.22.1)

That mode of recording speeches enabled Thucydides not to reproduce what a stenographer would have recorded, but to give the general sense of what had been said. His claim, however, might imply a certain amount of subjectivism, because Thucydides commented on events and their significance, providing insight into their context, historic situation, the character of the speaker and his thought-world. In Dibelius's estimation, one should not expect more of an ancient writer like Luke than of Thucydides, when one reads the speeches in Acts: "Luke tells a story, but, while doing so, he is also preaching" (*Studies*, 151). That may be so, and no one can deny the value of such a comparison with a famous Greek historian in this matter, but one cannot conclude from it that Luke's fertile imagination was wholly responsible for the speeches or that they have been created out of whole cloth. Glasson has rightly noted the difference between Thucydides and Livy. Livy, in dealing with a long period of history, might be accused of fabricating some speeches, but both Thucydides and Luke were recording events that were more or less of their own times. That would explain an important difference between likely nonverbatim speeches and fabricated discourses.

Given the same Lucan phraseology, style, and vocabulary that runs throughout the speeches as well as the narratives (and the Third Gospel) and also the literary parallelism with which one has to reckon at times (Paul depicted preaching as Peter preached), there is no easy way of assessing what is authentic in the speeches in Acts and what is of Lucan composition. In their final form, however, the speeches are clearly Lucan compositions. In this regard it is good to recall what Dionysius of Halicarnassus said about the uniformity of Thucydides' style: "He is of one form *(homoeidēs)* in everything, both in speeches and in narratives" (*Ep. ad Gnaeum Pompeium* 3.20). Nevertheless, despite such uniformity Thucydides could claim to give the general sense of what was actually said.

The Lucan speeches, however, often incorporate "older formulae of kerygmatic or liturgical nature" (Dibelius, *Studies,* 3), pre-Lucan traditional phrases, and even OT proof-texts (see Schweizer, "Concerning the Speeches"; R. H. Fuller, *The Foundations of New Testament Christology* [New York: Scribner's Sons, 1965], 20).

(107) Moreover, interpreters such as Gärtner have insisted that Luke's model was not solely secular Greek historians like Thucydides, but also Jewish Greek historians like the author of Maccabees and Josephus, who sought to recount, with speeches, a course of events in a religious setting or with a religious interpretive aim.

(108) The question about authenticity or accuracy of the speeches is also partly involved in the kind of speech recorded, distinguishing (a) missionary sermons, usually addressed to Jews; (b) evangelizing sermons, addressed to Gentiles; (c) an indictment (Stephen's speech); (d) defense speeches (Paul); (e) a farewell speech (Paul at Miletus); (f) constitutive speech (the Twelve); (g) political speech (town clerk); (h) exhortation (Paul in Rome). This difference of kind may affect the amount of the speech that has been recalled by the author or others who may have told him about them.

(109) C. H. Dodd introduced still another consideration, when he argued that some of the speeches, especially those of Peter in the early chapters, were good examples of the primitive *kērygma,* of the way apostles first proclaimed the Christ-event. He regarded "the speeches attributed to Peter" as "based upon material which proceeded from the Aramaic-speaking Church at Jerusalem," and so they were "substantially earlier than the period at which the book was written" (*The Apostolic Preaching,* 20). This Dodd contended because of a certain sameness of persistent elements or a repetition of ideas and phrases in various speeches, which had been pointed out ever since J. G. Eichhorn in the nineteenth century analyzed them. For Dibelius, Wilckens, and others, such sameness in the speeches reflected rather the way the Christian message was being proclaimed in the days of Luke himself, and not necessarily earlier. Either Dodd or Dibelius may be right, but there is really no way to be certain about the provenience of such common and persistent elements in the speeches of Acts.

In this regard the speeches are part of the question concerning the sources of Acts. Neither the narratives nor the speeches can be regarded as merely *creatio ex nihilo* on Luke's part. In the pre-Lucan tradition there were stories about the deeds and sayings of apostles and disciples that were more or less similar to those about Jesus, as Jervell has insisted *(The Unknown Paul).* The thorny question of sources has already been discussed, and even if there is uncertainty about the extent to which Luke depended on them, they are, nevertheless, involved in this matter of the speeches in Acts.

(110) Because it is impossible to ascertain the historicity of the speeches, it is more important to concentrate on the reason why Luke chose to introduce them into his narrative account. The speeches are addressed to the readers of Acts rather than to the individual audiences named in the narratives (Dibelius), but that scarcely tells us much. Soards, having noted how many earlier commenta-

tors stressed the speeches either as a literary construct, as a convention of ancient historiography, or as a theological (or ideological) device, and while admitting such views as valid characterizations of the Lucan speeches, believes rather that the speeches produce "the unification of the otherwise diverse and incoherent elements" that make up Acts. "Through the regular introduction of formally repetitive speeches, Luke has unified his narrative; and, more important, he has unified the image of an otherwise personally, ethnically, and geographically diverse early Christianity" (*The Speeches*, 12).

(111) It is not easy to set forth the common elements that earlier commentators often tried to isolate in many of the speeches in Acts, because not all focus on the same items. The following list will give at least some idea of commonly occurring elements in speeches directed to Jerusalem or diaspora Jews and to Gentiles. It is based mainly on that given by Schweizer ("Concerning the Speeches"), although modified a bit; and it shares items with the list given by Conzelmann (*Acts*, xliv). (00 for verse numbers means that the element does not occur in the given chapter.)

Uniform Elements in Missionary and Evangelizing Speeches

1. Direct Address (adapted to situation): 2:14a; 3:12a; 4:9a; 5:00; 10:00; 13:16b; 14:15a; 17:22
2. Appeal for Attention: 2:14b; 3:00; 4:10a; 5:00; 10:37a; 13:16b; 14:15c; 17:23c
3. Misunderstanding of Listeners Noted: 2:15–16; 3:12b; 4:9b; 5:29; 10:00; 13:00; 14:15a; 17:22b, 23ab
4. Quotation of OT Introducing Body of Speech: 2:17–21; 3:13a; 4:00; 5:30 (allusion only); 13:17–25 (summary of salvation history); 14:15d (God as creator); 17:24
5. Christological/Theological Kerygma: 2:22b–24; 3:13b–15; 4:10; 5:30–31a; 10:37b–42; 13:27–31; 14:16–17; 17:24–27
6. Proof from OT about Kerygma: 2:25–31, 34–35; 3:18, 22–25; 4:11; 5:00; 10:43a; 13:33–37; 14:00; 17:28 (Aratus quoted instead)
7. Reply to Problem Posed by Misunderstanding: 2:33b–36; 3:16; 4:10c; 5:00; 10:00; 13:00; 14:15b; 17:29
8. Call for Repentance; Proclamation of Salvation: 2:[37–]38; 3:19; 4:12; 5:31b–32; 10:43b; 13:38–39; 14:15c; 17:30–31
9. Focus of Message on Audience: 2:22a, 29; 3:17, 25–26; 4:12; 5:00; 10:36, 44; 13:26, 32, 38, 40–41; 14:00; 17:30 ("all people everywhere")

Such elements are not always verbally identical, but they reveal the common conception that underlies the speeches in Acts. They seem to argue for the guiding mind of a final redactor of them; hence my characterization of the speeches as ultimately Lucan compositions.

(112) The speeches in Acts are clearly part of the way that Luke has introduced his own theological and missionary aims; in recounting his story, he is preaching to his readers. At times the speeches are only loosely connected to the context in

which they appear, but they enliven Luke's recital of what happened as the apostles began to carry the Word of God from Jerusalem to "the end of the earth." In the case of the speeches of Jesus in the Third Gospel one often finds Synoptic parallels, which reveal something about the form of the tradition that Luke inherited. There is no such counterpart of that for the speeches in Acts, nevertheless the speeches make up for the lack of the author's psychological analyses or reflections on the meanings of events recorded, because Luke has inserted them at crucial points in his narrative to explain a development in the history of the early Christian community. Thus, Stephen's indictment serves to make the rejection of the Christian gospel by some Jews intelligible; Paul's speech to the Jerusalem crowd (Acts 22) explains the Christian mission to Gentiles; Peter's evangelizing sermon at Cornelius's conversion explains that God himself has ordained the mission to non-Jews; Paul's speech at the Areopagus reveals how Christianity adapts itself to Greek culture and ideas.

(113) Lastly, many of the speeches in Acts conform to known forms of Greek rhetoric. This has been well worked out by the classicist G. A. Kennedy in *New Testament Interpretation through Rhetorical Criticism,* where he has analysed each of the speeches. He remarks,

> Speeches attributed to Paul in Acts through chapter 19 do not appear to be based on a firsthand knowledge of what he actually said and have the characteristics of construction that Luke seems to have used in speeches attributed to Peter and others. The speech to the elders of Ephesus (20:18–35 . . .) is the first in Acts that seems based on direct knowledge by the narrator, and the only speech evocative of Paul's personal style, though simplified for use in an historiographic work. Subsequent speeches are not markedly Pauline in style, except perhaps the exchange with Agrippa. They seem to have been written with some knowledge of Paul's arguments, but probably not of his actual words. . . . Of the rhetorical features of Acts the most important historically is the way the apostles utilize occasions to preach the gospel. (139–40)

BIBLIOGRAPHY

Narratives

Barrett, C. K., "Sayings of Jesus in the Acts of the Apostles," *A cause de l'évangile,* 681–708.

Darr, J. A., "Narrator as Character: Mapping a Reader-Oriented Approach to Narration in Luke-Acts," *Semeia* 63 (1993): 43–60.

Gaventa, B. R., "Toward a Theology of Acts: Reading and Rereading," *Int* 42 (1988): 146–57.

Kurz, W. S., "Narrative Approaches to Luke-Acts," *Bib* 68 (1987): 195–220.

Miesner, D. R., "The Missionary Journeys Narrative: Patterns and Implications," *Perspectives on Luke-Acts* (ed. C. H. Talbert), 199–214.

Neirynck, F., "The Miracle Stories in the Acts of the Apostles: An Introduction,"

Les Actes des Apôtres (ed. J. Kremer), 169–213; repr. *Evangelica* (BETL 60, 99; 2 vols.; Louvain: Leuven University/Peeters, 1982, 1991), 1.835–80.

Tannehill, R. C., "The Functions of Peter's Mission Speeches in the Narrative of Acts," *NTS* 37 (1991): 400–14.

———, *The Narrative Unity of Luke-Acts.*

Summaries

Benoit, P., "Remarques sur les 'sommaires' de Actes 2.42 á 5," *Aux sources de la tradition chrétienne: Mélanges offerts à M. Maurice Goguel . . .* (Bibliothèque théologique; Paris/Neuchâtel: Delachaux & Niestlé, 1950), 1–10; repr. *Exégèse et théologie,* 2.181–92.

———, "Some Notes on the 'Summaries' in Acts 2, 4, and 5," *Jesus and the Gospel: Volume* 2 (London: Darton, Longman & Todd; New York: Herder and Herder — Seabury, 1974), 94–103.

Brehm, H. A., "The Significance of the Summaries for Interpreting Acts," *SwJT* 33 (1990): 29–40.

Cadbury, H. J., "The Summaries in Acts," *Beginnings,* 5.392–402.

Cerfaux, L., "La composition de la première partie du livre des Actes," *ETL* 13 (1936): 667–91; repr. *Recueil Lucien Cerfaux,* 2.63–91.

———, "La première communauté chrétienne à Jérusalem (*Act.*, II, 41–V, 42)," *ETL* 16 (1939): 5–31; repr. *Recueil Lucien Cerfaux,* 2.125–56.

Co, M. A., "The Major Summaries in Acts: Acts 2,42–47; 4,32–35; 5,12–16: Linguistic and Literary Relationship," *ETL* 68 (1992): 49–85.

Dupont, J., "La communauté des biens aux premiers jours de l'église (Actes 2, 42,44–45; 4, 32.34–35)," *Études,* 503–19.

———, "L'Union entre les premiers chrétiens dans les Actes des Apôtres," *NRT* 91 (1969): 897–915; repr. *Nouvelles études,* 296–318.

Jeremias, J., "Untersuchungen zum Quellenproblem der Apostelgeschichte," *ZNW* 36 (1937): 205–21, esp. 206–8; repr. *Abba,* 238–55, esp. 240–41.

Noorda, S. J., "Scene and Summary: A Proposal for Reading Acts 4,32–5,16," *Les Actes des Apôtres* (ed. J. Kremer), 475–83.

Sterling, G. E., "'Athletes of Virtue': An Analysis of the Summaries in Acts (2:41–47; 4:32–35; 5:12–16)," *JBL* 113 (1994): 679–96.

Zimmermann, H., "Die Sammelberichte der Apostelgeschichte," *BZ* 5 (1961): 71–82.

Zwaan, J. de, "Was the Book of Acts a Posthumous Edition?" *HTR* 17 (1924): 95–153, esp. 103–6.

We-Sections

Boismard, M.-E. and A. Lamouille, *Les Actes des deux Apôtres,* 1.3–51.

Borse, U., "Die Wir-Stellen der Apostelgeschichte und Timotheus," *SNTU* A/10 (1985): 63–92.

Cadbury, H. J., "'We' and 'I' Passages in Luke-Acts," *NTS* 3 (1956–57): 128–32.

Conzelmann, H. and A. Lindemann, *Interpreting the New Testament,* 236–44.

Dockx, S., "Luc a-t-il été le compagnon d'apostolat de Paul?" *NRT* 103 (1981): 385–400.

Dumais, M., "Les Actes des Apôtres: Bilan et orientations," *"De bien des manières": La recherche biblique aux bords du XXIe siècle* (LD 163; Paris: Cerf, 1995), 308–64, esp. 320–22.

Fitzmyer, J. A., *Luke the Theologian,* 16–22.

Fusco, V., "Le sezioni-noi degli Atti nella discussione recente," *BeO* 25 (1983): 73–86.

Gilchrist, J. M., "The Historicity of Paul's Shipwreck," *JSNT* 61 (1996): 29–51.

Haenchen, E., "The Book of Acts as Source Material for the History of Early Christianity," *StLA,* 258–78, esp. 272.

———, " 'We' in Acts and the Itinerary," *The Bultmann School of Biblical Interpretation: New Directions?* (JTC 1; Tübingen: Mohr [Siebeck]; New York: Harper & Row, 1965), 65–99.

Harnack, A., *Date,* 1–29, esp. 20–21.

Hemer, C. J., "First Person Narrative in Acts 27–28," *TynBull* 36 (1985): 79–109.

Hengel, M., *Acts,* 59–68.

Karris, R. J., *What Are They Saying about Luke and Acts? A Theology of the Faithful God* (New York: Paulist, 1979).

Kurz, W. S., "Narrative Approaches to Luke-Acts" (see "Narratives" above), 216–17.

Nock, A. D., Review of M. Dibelius, *Aufsätze zur Apostelgeschichte, Gnomon* 25 (1953): 497–506, esp. 502–3; repr. as "The Book of Acts," in *Essays on Religion and the Ancient World* (2 vols.; Cambridge: Harvard University, 1972), 2.821–32.

Norden, E., *Agnostos Theos,* 34–35, 313–31.

Plümacher, E., "Wirklichkeitserfahrung und Geschichtsschreibung bei Lukas: Erwägungen zu den Wir-Stücken der Apostelgeschichte," ZNW 68 (1977): 2–22.

Porter, S. E., "The 'We' Passages," *The Book of Acts in Its Graeco-Roman Setting* (BAFCS 2), 545–74.

Praeder, S. M., "Acts 27:1–28:16: Sea Voyages in Ancient Literature and the Theology of Luke-Acts," *CBQ* 46 (1984): 683–706.

———, "Luke-Acts and the Ancient Novel," *SBL 1981 Seminar Papers* (ed. K. H. Richards; Chico, CA: Scholars, 1981): 269–92.

———, "The Problem of First Person Narration in Acts," *NovT* 29 (1987): 193–218.

Robbins, V. K., "By Land and by Sea: The We-Passages and Ancient Sea Voyages," *Perspectives on Luke-Acts* (ed. C. H. Talbert), 215–42.

———, "The We-Passages in Acts and Ancient Sea Voyages," *BR* 20 (1975): 5–18.

Taylor, J., "The Making of Acts: A New Account," *RB* 97 (1990): 504–24, esp. 511–16.

Wehnert, J., *Die Wir-Passagen der Apostelgeschichte: Ein lukanisches Stilmittel aus jüdischer Tradition* (GTA 40; Göttingen: Vandenhoeck & Ruprecht, 1989).

Speeches

Ambroggi, P. de, "I discorsi di S. Pietro negli Atti: Realtà storica o finzione letteraria?" *ScCatt* 6/11 (1928): 81–97, 161–86, 243–64.

Asting, R., "Til spørsmålet om prekenen i urkristendommen," *NorTT* 33 (1932): 79–90.

Bowker, J. W., "Speeches in Acts: A Study in Proem and Yelammedenu Form," *NTS* 14 (1967–68): 96–111.

Bruce, F. F., "The Significance of the Speeches for Interpreting Acts," *SwJT* 33 (1990–91): 20–28.

———, "The Speeches in Acts—Thirty Years After," *Reconciliation and Hope: New Testament Essays on Atonement and Eschatology Presented to L. L. Morris* . . . (ed. R. Banks; Grand Rapids, MI: Eerdmans, 1974), 53–68.

———, *The Speeches in the Acts of the Apostles* (London: Tyndale, 1942).

Burini, C., "Gli studi dal 1950 ad oggi sul numero e sulla classificazione dei discorsi degli 'Atti degli Apostoli': Un contributo d'individuazione," *Laurentianum* 15 (1974): 349–65.

Cadbury, H. J., "The Speeches in Acts," *Beginnings,* 5.402–27.

Chrestos, P. K., "Hē proeleusis tōn en tais Praxesi tōn Apostolōn logōn," *Theologia* 24 (1953): 94–116.

Davies, P. E., "Paul's Missionary Message," *JBR* 16 (1948): 205–11.

Dibelius, M., "Literary Allusions in the Speeches in Acts," *Studies,* 186–91.

———, *From Tradition to Gospel* (New York: Scribner's Sons, n.d.), 9–36.

———, "The Speeches in Acts and Ancient Historiography," *Studies,* 138–85.

Dillon, R. J., "The Prophecy of Christ and His Witnesses according to the Discourses of Acts," *NTS* 32 (1986): 544–56.

Dodd, C. H., *The Apostolic Preaching.*

Downing, F. G., "Ethical Pagan Theism and the Speeches in Acts," *NTS* 27 (1980–81): 544–63.

Dumais, M., "Le langage des discours d'évangélisation des Actes: Une forme de langage symbolique?" *Les Actes des Apôtres* (ed. J. Kremer), 467–74.

Dupont, J., "Les discours de Pierre dans les Actes et le chapitre xxiv de l'évangile de Luc," *L'Evangile de Luc: Problèmes littéraires et théologiques: Mémorial Lucien Cerfaux* (BETL 32; ed. F. Neirynck; Gembloux: Duculot, 1973), 329–74; repr. *Nouvelles études,* 58–111.

———, "Les discours missionnaires des Actes des Apôtres d'après un ouvrage récent," *RB* 69 (1962): 37–60; repr. *Études,* 133–55.

———, "Le salut des Gentils et la signification théologique du livre des Actes," *NTS* 6 (1959–60): 132–55; repr. *Études,* 393–419.

Ellis, E. E., "Midrashic Features in the Speeches of Acts," *Mélanges bibliques en hommage au R. P. Béda Rigaux* (ed. A. Descamps et A. de Halleux; Gembloux: Duculot, 1970), 303–12.

Evans, C. F., "'Speeches' in Acts," ibid., 287–302.

Gardner, P., "The Speeches of St Paul in Acts," *Essays on Some Biblical Questions of the Day* (Cambridge Biblical Essays; ed. H. B. Swete; London: Macmillan, 1909), 379–419.

Gasque, W. W., "The Speeches of Acts: Dibelius Reconsidered," *New Dimensions in New Testament Study* (ed. R. N. Longenecker and M. C. Tenney; Grand Rapids, MI: Zondervan, 1974), 232–50.

Glasson, T. F., "The Speeches in Acts and Thucydides," *ExpTim* 76 (1964–65): 165.

Heinecken, F., "Inhalt und Form der apostolischen Predigt nach der Apostelgeschichte und was wir davon lernen können," *KZ* 33 (1909): 1–9, 49–59.

Horsley, G.H.R., "Speeches and Dialogue in Acts," *NTS* 32 (1986): 609–14.

Kennedy, G. A., *New Testament Interpretation through Rhetorical Criticism* (Chapel Hill: University of North Carolina Press, 1984), 114–40.

Kistemaker, S. J., "The Speeches in Acts," *CrisTR* 5 (1990): 31–41.

Kliesch, K., *Das heilsgeschichtliche Credo in den Reden der Apostelgeschichte* (BBB 44; Bonn: Hanstein, 1975).

Miesner, D. R., "The Circumferential Speeches of Luke-Acts: Patterns and Purpose," *SBL 1978 Seminar Papers* (2 vols.; ed. P. J. Achtemeier; Missoula: Scholars, 1978), 223–37.

Neyrey, J., "The Forensic Defense Speech and Paul's Trial Speeches in Acts 22–26: Form and Function," *Luke-Acts: New Perspectives* (ed. C. H. Talbert), 210–24.

Plümacher, E., "Die Missionsreden der Apostelgeschichte und Dionys von Halikarnass," *NTS* 39 (1993): 161–77.

Reicke, B., "A Synopsis of Early Christian Preaching," *The Root of the Vine: Essays in Biblical Theology* (ed. A. Fridrichsen et al.; New York: Philosophical Library, 1953), 128–60.

Rese, M., "Die Funktion der alttestamentlichen Zitate und Anspielungen in den Reden der Apostelgeschichte," *Les Actes des Apôtres* (ed. J. Kremer), 61–79.

Ridderbos, H. N., *The Speeches of Peter in the Acts of the Apostles* (London: Tyndale, 1962).

Rodríguez Ruiz, M., "Hacia una definición del 'discurso misionero': Los discursos misioneros de los Hechos de los Apóstoles a la luz de la retórica antigua," *EstBíb* 49 (1991): 425–50.

Schmitt, J., "Les discours missionnaires des Actes et l'histoire des traditions prépauliniennes," *RSR* 69 (1981): 165–80.

Schubert, P., "The Final Cycle of Speeches in the Book of Acts," *JBL* 87 (1968): 1–16.

Schweizer, E., "Concerning the Speeches in Acts," *StLA*, 208–16.

Soards, M. L., "The Speeches in Acts in Relation to Other Pertinent Ancient Literature," *ETL* 70 (1994): 65–90.

———, *The Speeches in Acts: Their Content, Context, and Concerns* (Louisville: Westminster/John Knox, 1994).

Standaert, B., "L'Art de composer dans l'oeuvre de Luc," *A cause de l'évangile,* 323–47, esp. 323–32.

Steyn, G. J., *Septuagint Quotations in the Context of the Petrine and Pauline Speeches of the Acta Apostolorum* (Contributions to Biblical Exegesis and Theology 12; Kampen: Kok Pharos, 1995).

Tannehill, R. C., "The Functions of Peter's Mission Speeches" (see "Narratives" above).

Townsend, J. T., "The Speeches in Acts," *ATR* 42 (1960): 150–59.

Unnik, W. C. van, "Luke's Second Book and the Rules of Hellenistic Historiography," *Les Actes des Apôtres* (ed. J. Kremer), 37–60.

Wilckens, U., *Die Missionsreden der Apostelgeschichte: Form- und traditionsgeschichtliche Untersuchungen* (WMANT 5; Neukirchen: Neukirchener-V., 1961; 3d ed., 1974).

Wilcox, M., "A Foreword to the Study of the Speeches in Acts," *Christianity, Judaism and Other Greco-Roman Cults: Studies for Morton Smith at Sixty* (SJLA 12; 4 parts; ed. J. Neusner; Leiden: Brill, 1975), 1.206–25.

Wolfe, R. F., "Rhetorical Elements in the Speeches of Acts 7 and 17," *JOTT* 6 (1993): 274–83.

VI. Language and Style of Acts

◆

(114) Lucan language and style have already been treated in the commentary on the Lucan Gospel (*Luke*, 107–27), and much of what has been said there applies to the Acts of the Apostles as well, seeing that the two books stem from the same author. I have already mentioned the views of A. W. Argyle and A. C. Clark, who have maintained that the two works are not by the same author (see §12 above). Argyle, in particular, argued mainly from the kind of Greek found in them, but his arguments have fallen on deaf scholarly ears.

(115) Certain aspects of Lucan language and style still have to be treated, since the writing of Acts was not exactly the same as that of the Third Gospel. When Luke composed his Gospel, he depended on Mark, "Q," and the private source "L." How Luke handled the first two of these sources in writing the Gospel is not unrelated to his literary style and use of the Greek language. In writing Acts, however, Luke may have used sources, but they were not of the same character as Mark or "Q." Moreover, the Marcan Gospel can easily be compared with the Lucan Gospel, and Lucan passages usually attributed to "Q" with their Matthean counterparts, thus making clear how Luke at times modified the Greek of what he inherited. There is, however, no way of making a similar comparison in the case of Acts.

(116) The following remarks will simply supplement what is already found in *Luke*, 113–25, for the most part adding references to Acts that supply further examples of what is already given there. Apropos of Jewish Greek vocabulary (*Luke*, 113), one may add the following: *angelos* ("angel," Acts 6:15; 7:35; 10:7); *angelos Kyriou* ("angel of the Lord," 5:19; 8:26; 12:7, 23); *azyma* ("unleavened bread," 12:3; 20:6); *aperitmētos* ("uncircumcised," 7:51; *grammateus* ("scribe," 4:5; 6:12; 23:9); *diabolos* ("devil," 10:38; 13:10); *ethnē* ("Gentiles," 9:15; 10:45; 11:1, 18; 28:28); *hodos* ("the Way" [= Christianity], 9:2; 19:9, 23; 22:4; 24:14, 22 [cf. 16:17; 25:25, 26]); *Kyrios* ("the Lord," 2:39; 17:24); *pascha* ("Passover," 12:4); *sabbata* ("Sabbath," 13:14; 16:13; 17:2; 20:7). Further Christian words would be *apostolos* ("apostle," 1:2, 26; 2:37, 42; 4:33, 35, 36, etc.); *baptizein* ("baptize," 2:38, 41; 8:36, 38; 9:18; 10:47, 48, etc.); *christianoi* ("Christian," 11:26; 26:28); *euangelion* ("gospel," 15:7; 20:24); *ekklēsia* ("church," 5:11; 8:1, 3; 9:31, etc.); *episkopos* ("bishop," 20:28); *pisteuein epi* ("believe in," 9:42; 11:17; 16:31; 22:19); *pisteuein eis* ("believe in," 10:43; 14:23; 19:4).

(117) To the list of Septuagintisms (*Luke*, 114–16), one may add the following:

anastas, "rising up," used inchoatively: Acts 1:15; 5:6, 17, 34; 8:27; 9:11, 18, 39, etc.

apokritheis eipen, "answering, he said": 4:19; 5:29; 8:24, 34; 9:37; 19:15; 25:9

doxazein ton theon, "glorify God": 4:21; 11:18; 21:20

ek koilias mētros, "from (his) mother's womb": 3:2; 14:8

enōpion, "before, in the sight of": 4:10, 19; 6:5, 6 [in all, 15 times]

kai idou, "and behold": 5:28; 10:30; 27:24; *kai nyn idou*: 13:11; 20:22, 25

kata prosōpon, "before the face (of)": 3:13, 20; 25:16

legōn, "saying": 1:6; 2:40; 5:23, 25, 28; 8:10, 19; 10:26; 11:18, etc.

pro prosōpou, "before the face (of)": 13:24

pros + acc. of verb of saying: 1:7; 2:7, 12, 29, 37, 38; 3:12, 22bis, 25, etc.

prostithenai + infin., lit. "he added to (do something)": 12:3

rhēma, "word, thing": 5:32; 10:37; 13:42

New Septuagintisms:

ei, introducing a direct question: 1:6; 19:2; 21:37; 22:25; 26:23bis (see Gen 17:17; 44:19; 3:3–6; 6:12bis)

epairein tēn phōnēn, "raise (one's) voice": 2:14; 14:11; 22:22 (see Judg 2:4; 9:7; 21:2; Ruth 1:9; 2 Sam 13:36)

(118) Related to Septuagintisms is the construction of *egeneto de* or *kai egeneto* with verbal forms (*Luke*, 118–19). In Acts the most frequently used form of this construction is (a) *kai egeneto* + infin. (with subject acc., *Luke*, 118): 4:5; 9:3, 32, 37, 43; (10:25); 11:26; 14:1; 16:16; 19:1; 21:1, 5; 22:6, 17; 27:44; 28:8, 17. Compare the more common classical and Hellenistic Greek construction *synebē* (with acc. + infin.): Acts 21:35. The form (b), *kai egeneto* + a finite verb without an intervening *kai* (*Luke*, 119), is not found in Acts, but form (c), *kai egeneto* + *kai* + finite verb, occurs in 5:7; 9:19.

(119) One should note the frequent use of the genitive absolute in Acts. Sometimes it is properly used, without any grammatical relation to a word in the clause that it modifies (BDF §423): Acts 7:5; 12:18; 13:24; 20:3, 7; 23:30; 24:10; 25:8, 25; 28:20. Sometimes, however, Luke uses it in connection with a word in the main clause, in violation of the rules of good syntax: 7:21; 21:17; 22:17; 25:21.

(120) Likewise noteworthy are the following constructions frequently found in Acts:

(a) the use of the historic present (most often with a verb of saying): (2:38); 8:36; 10:11, 27, 31; 12:8; 19:35; 21:37; 22:2; 23:18; 25:5, 22, 24; 26:24, 25

(b) the relative pronoun followed by *kai/te*: *hos kai* (or *te*): 1:3, 11, 19; 7:45; 10:39; 11:30; 12:4; 13:22; 17:34; 22:5; 24:6bis, 15; 26:10, 16, 22, 26; 27:23; 28:10

(c) the correlated use of *men . . . de:* 1:5; 2:42; 3:14, 24; 5:23; 9:7; 13:37; 14:4; 17:32; 18:15; 19:15, 39; 22:3, 9; 23:8; 25:4, 11; 27:41, 44; 28:6, 24
(d) the attraction of the relative pronoun to the case of the antecedent: 1:1, 22; 2:22; 3:25; 7:16; 8:27; 10:36; 13:2, 38; 17:31; 20:38; 24:21; inverse attraction is found in 10:36; 21:16; 25:7
(e) the use of the optative mood: in a wish (8:20); in indirect discourse (17:11, 27; 27:12, 39; 25:16, 20; in indirect questions: 5:24; 10:17; 17:11, 18, (WT 20); 21:33; 25:20; in conditions: 24:19; 20:16; in potential expressions: 8:31; 17:18; 24:19; 26:29
(f) the genitive of the article with an infinitive: 7:19; 26:18; 27:20; 18:10; 20:3, 20, 27, 30; 23:15, 20; 26:18bis; 21:18; 27:1, 20; cf. 19:25; 15:19, 20; 21:12; 9:15; 14:9; 20:3; 23:21; 26:17, 18
(g) the use of *en tō* + infinitive (often in a temporal sense, used with the *kai egeneto* construction): 2:1; 3:26; 4:30; 8:6; 9:3; 11:15; 19:1
(h) the dative of a cognate abstract noun used to intensify the meaning of a verb: 5:28; 23:14

(121) Also of note is the number of Latin words used in Acts: *Christianoi* (Christiani); *Kaisar* (Caesar); *kolōnia* (colonia); *praitōrion* (praetorium); *soudarion* (sudarium); and many transcribed Latin names: Agrippa, Alexandrini, Aquila, Caesarea, Claudius, Cornelius, Felix, Festus, Forum Appii, Gallio, Libertini, Lysias, Marcus, Melita, Paulus, Pilatus, Priscilla, Puteoli, Rhegium, Roma, Syracusa, Tiberias, Titus, Tres Tabernae. There are several grecized Latin expressions: *to hikanon lambanein* (= satis accipere, 17:5); *opsesthe autoi* (= vos ipsi videritis, 18:15); *agoraioi agontai* (= conventus forenses aguntur, 19:39); *ou meta pollas tautas hēmeras* (= non post multos hos dies, 1:5); *ek mesou exēlthen* (= exire de medio, 17:33).

(122) Finally, the reader will note the absence of discussion of Aramaisms in the Greek text of Acts. This is because the attempts of writers such as Torrey and Wilcox to find such expressions have not succeeded. Their critics have been many, and I find the criticism most telling. Barton once wrote, "Of Torrey's 102 evidences of translation from the Aramaic I have studied . . . I find not one of them convincing" ("Prof. Torrey's Theory," 369). Of Wilcox's data, Richard has written: "In not one single instance is his evidence persuasive" ("The Old Testament in Acts," 340). To which I say, "Amen!" Most of the instances cited as alleged Aramaisms are to be explained more correctly as Septuagintisms. In the Septuagint there may be Aramaisms or Hebraisms, but to claim that there are such in Lucan writing fails to reckon properly with the influence of the Septuagint on his Hellenistic Greek. Further remarks will be made in NOTES on various passages. Meanwhile, see *Luke*, 116–18.

BIBLIOGRAPHY

Antoniadis, S., *L'Evangile de Luc: Esquisse de grammaire et de style* (Collection de l'institut néo-hellénique de l'Université de Paris 7; Paris: Société d'Edition 'Les Belles Lettres,' 1930).

Argyle, A. W., "The Greek of Luke and Acts," *NTS* 20 (1973–74): 441–45.

Barton, G. A., "Prof. Torrey's Theory of the Aramaic Origin of the Gospels and the First Half of the Acts of the Apostles," *JTS* 36 (1935): 357–73.

Black, M., *An Aramaic Approach to the Gospels and Acts* (3d ed.; Oxford: Clarendon, 1967).

Cadbury, H. J., "Animals and Symbolism in Luke (Lexical Notes on Luke-Acts, IX)," *Studies in New Testament and Early Christian Literature: Essays in Honor of Allen P. Wikgren* (NovTSup 33; ed. D. E. Aune; Leiden: Brill, 1972), 3–15.

———, "Four Features of Lucan Style," *StLA*, 87–102.

———, "Lexical Notes on Luke-Acts. I," *JBL* 44 (1925): 214–27.

———, "Lexical Notes on Luke-Acts: II. Recent Arguments for Medical Language," *JBL* 45 (1926): 190–209.

———, "Lexical Notes on Luke-Acts: III. Luke's Interest in Lodging," *JBL* 45 (1926): 305–22.

———, "Lexical Notes on Luke-Acts: IV. On Direct Quotation, with Some Uses of *hoti* and *ei*," *JBL* 48 (1929): 412–25.

———, "Lexical Notes on Luke-Acts: V. Luke and the Horse-Doctors," *JBL* 52 (1933): 55–65.

———, "Some Lukan Expressions of Time (Lexical Notes on Luke-Acts VII)," *JBL* 82 (1963): 272–78.

———, *The Style and Literary Method of Luke* (HTS 6; Cambridge: Harvard University Press, 1920; repr. New York: Kraus Reprint Co., 1969), 1–72.

Goodspeed, E. J., "The Vocabulary of Luke and Acts," *JBL* 31 (1912): 92–94.

Grant, F. C., "A Critique of the Style and Literary Method of Luke by Cadbury," *ATR* 2 (1919–20): 318–23.

Hawkins, J. C., *Horae Synopticae: Contributions to the Study of the Synoptic Problem* (2d ed.; Oxford: Clarendon, 1909), 174–89.

Hobart, W. K., *The Medical Language of St. Luke: A Proof from Internal Evidence that 'The Gospel according to St. Luke' and 'The Acts of the Apostles' Were Written by the Same Person, and That the Writer Was a Medical Man* (Dublin: Hodges, Figgis, 1882; repr. Grand Rapids, MI: Baker Book House, 1954).

Horton, F. L., Jr., "Reflections on the Semitisms of Luke-Acts," *Perspectives on Luke-Acts* (ed. C. H. Talbert), 1–23.

Howard, W. F., "Semitisms in the New Testament," in J. H. Moulton and W. F. Howard, A *Grammar of New Testament Greek* (4 vols.; Edinburgh: Clark, 1978, 1979, 1980, 1976), 2.411–85.

Hunkin, J. W., "'Pleonastic' *archomai* in the New Testament," *JTS* 25 (1923–24): 390–402.

Jacquier, E., *Actes*, clxiv–cc.

Johannessohn, M., "Das biblische *kai egeneto* und seine Geschichte," *ZVS* 53 (1925): 161–212.

Kilpatrick, G. D., "The Historic Present in the Gospels and Acts," ZNW 68 (1977): 258–62.

Knowling, R. J., "The Medical Language of St. Luke," *BW* 20 (1902): 260–71, 370–79.

Levinsohn, S. H., *Textual Connections in Acts* (SBLMS 31; Atlanta: Scholars, 1987).

Michaelis, W., "Das unbetonte *kai autos* bei Lukas," *ST* 4 (1950): 86–93.

Moule, C.F.D., *IBNTG*, 171–91, 197.

Mussies, G., "Variation in the Book of Acts," *FilNeot* 4 (1991): 165–82; "(Part II)," *FilNeot* 8 (1995): 23–61.

Neirynck, F. and F. van Segbroeck, "Le texte des Actes des Apôtres et les caractéristiques stylistiques lucaniennes," *ETL* 61 (1985): 304–39; repr. *Evangelica II* (BETL 99; Louvain: Leuven University/Peeters, 1991), 243–78.

Norden, E., *Die antike Kunstprosa von vi. Jahrhundert v. Chr. bis in die Zeit der Renaissance* (2 vols.; Leipzig/Berlin: Teubner, 1923; 5th ed., repr. Darmstadt: Wissenschaftliche Buchgesellschaft, 1958), 2.480–92.

Payne, D. F., "Semitisms in the Book of Acts," *Apostolic History and the Gospel: Biblical and Historical Essays Presented to F. F. Bruce* . . . (eds. W. W. Gasque and R. P. Martin; Grand Rapids, MI: Eerdmans, 1970), 134–50.

Richard, E., "The Old Testament in Acts: Wilcox's Semitisms in Retrospect," *CBQ* 42 (1980): 330–41.

Riddle, D. W., "The Logic of the Theory of Translation Greek," *JBL* 51 (1932): 13–30.

Rodríguez Carmona, A., "Los semitismos de los Hechos de los Apóstoles: Estado de la cuestión," *EstEcl* 65 (1990): 385–401.

Smit Sibinga, J., "The Function of Verbal Forms in Luke-Acts," *FilNeot* 6 (1993): 31–50.

Sparks, H.F.D., "The Semitisms of the Acts," *JTS* 1 (1950): 16–28.

———, "Some Observations on the Semitic Background of the New Testament," *BullSNTS* 2 (1951): 33–42.

Stanton, V. H., "Style and Authorship in the Acts of the Apostles," *JTS* 24 (1922–23): 362–81.

Turner, N., "The Quality of the Greek of Luke-Acts," *Studies in New Testament Language and Text: Essays in Honour of George D. Kilpatrick* . . . (NovTSup 44; ed. J. K. Elliott; Leiden: Brill, 1976), 387–400.

———, "The Style of Luke-Acts," in J. H. Moulton and W. F. Howard, *A Grammar of the New Testament Greek* (see Howard above), 4.45–63.

Voelz, J. W., "The Language of the New Testament," *ANRW* 2/25.2 (1984): 893–977.

Wilcox, M., *The Semitisms of Acts* (Oxford: Clarendon, 1965).

———, "Semitisms in the New Testament," *ANRW* 2/25.2 (1984): 978–1029.

Williams, C. B., *The Participle in the Book of Acts* (Chicago: University of Chicago Press, 1909).

Yoder, J. D., "Semitisms in Codex Bezae," *JBL* 78 (1959): 317–21.

VII. Structure and Outline of Acts

◆

(123) The structure of Acts is not easy to determine, and there are almost as many suggestions for its outline as there are heads that think about it. A suggestion of its structure can be detected in the programmatic verse 1:8, where the apostles are told by the risen Christ that they are to be witnesses to him in Jerusalem, in the whole of Judea and Samaria, and even to the end of the earth. The last phrase is to be understood as a reference to Rome (see NOTE on 1:8); thus the verse sketches the spread of the Word of God from the pivotal city, Jerusalem, to the capital of the Roman empire at the time of Luke's writing. Its path leads from Jerusalem to Rome, where Paul "preached the kingdom and taught about the Lord Jesus" without hindrance (28:31). In general, one can see new starts in the Lucan account at 8:5 (testimony to Samaria and Judea); 13:1 (Paul's testimony in Mission I); 15:35 (Paul's testimony on further missionary journeys); 21:1 (Paul's testimony in Jerusalem); 27:1 (Paul's journey to Rome and testimony there).

(124) There is a certain overlapping or interweaving of details at times, what Dupont has called "entrelacement" ("La question"). In this he compares the advice of Lucian of Samosata, *How to Write History* 55:

> Then let its clarity be limpid, achieved, as I have said, both by diction and interweaving of the subject-matter. For one will make everything distinct and complete, and when one has finished the first topic one will introduce the second, joined to it and linked with it like a chain, to avoid breaks and a multiplicity of disjointed narratives; no, the first and second topics must always be not merely neighbors but must have common matter and overlap.

Using this notion, Dupont divides the account into four major stages: 2:1–8:1a; 8:1b–15:35; 15:36–19:40; 20:1–28:31. Such a division, however, leaves out the important matter in chapter 1, which is not merely what Lucian calls *prooimion*, "preface." It also divides Paul's third missionary journey almost in two.

(125) The account in Acts narrates the work mainly of two apostles, Peter and Paul, but it is not easy to divide up Acts according to their ministries, as Marxsen would have it (*Introduction*, 167): Acts 1–12, in which Peter is the main figure, and Acts 13–28, in which Paul is. In this Marxsen is following the division of many older commentators (Schneckenburger, Wellhausen, Turner, Dibelius, Renié, Cerfaux). There are, however, strange overlaps in such a division: Paul's call is narrated (chap. 9), before Peter begins his testimony to Gentiles (chap.

10). Paul's first missionary journey (chaps. 13–14) is recounted before Peter disappears from the scene. These overlaps show that Luke is much more interested in the account of the spread of the Word of God than in the activity of the two apostles, or perhaps better, the spread of testimony in the ministry of these two prominent early witnesses.

(126) A modern scholar who has wrestled in some detail with this problem is G. Betori. He has not only studied the earlier modes of outlining Acts and especially the suggestions of Dupont and Menoud, but has proposed a structure in seven parts: 1:1–14 (Introduction); 1:12–8:4 (Part 1); 8:1b–14:28 (Part 2); 14:27–16:5 (Part 3); 15:35–19:22 (Part 4); 19:20–28:31 (Part 5); 28:14b–31 (Conclusion). In his structure certain verses are regarded as transitional: 1:12–14; 8:1b–4; 14:27–28; 15:35–16:5; 19:20–22; 28:14b–16. But precisely these transitional verses complicate his proposal unduly.

(127) Neirynck has provided a table of the various ways Acts has been divided by modern scholars: Westcott-Hort, NA[26], Schneider, Weiser, Roloff, Kümmel, Dupont, and Haenchen ("Le livre des Actes," 342–44). From these Neirynck finds the principal caesuras to occur at 2:1; 6:1; 8:4; 9:32; 11:19; 13:1; 15:36; 19:21. With many of these I agree.

Following Betori, I see the structure of Acts falling into seven parts, but I use as a guide for the divisions in the following outline the programmatic verse, Acts 1:8, in which the risen Christ commissions his disciples to be witnesses to him in Jerusalem, all Judea, Samaria, and "to the end of the earth." It is not just the geographical areas mentioned, but the theme of *testimony* that is important in the articulation of the structure. So the structure of Acts is set out in seven major divisions, indicated in the following outline by capital roman numerals. These divisions gradually spell out how testimony is borne to the Word of God from Jerusalem by stages to Rome itself, the capital of the civilized world of that time.

(128) Outline of Acts

I. The Early Christian Community (1:1–26)
  A. Commission of Witnesses and Jesus' Farewell (1:1–14)
    1. The Prologue (1:1–2)
    2. Setting: Jesus' Farewell and Commission (1:3–8)
    3. Jesus' Ascension (1:9–11)
    4. The Primitive Congregation in Jerusalem (1:12–14)
  B. Reconstitution of the Twelve (1:15–26)

II. The Mission of Testimony in Jerusalem (2:1–8:4)
  A. Appeal to All Israel (2:1–3:26)
    1. The Pentecost Event: Baptism in the Spirit (2:1–13)
    2. Peter's Discourse to Assembled Israel (2:14–36)
    3. Reaction to Peter's Discourse (2:37–41)
    4. First Major Summary: Unified Community Life (2:42–47)
    5. Peter's Miracle in the Temple (3:1–11)
    6. Peter's Temple Discourse (3:12–26)

B. Life and Trials of the Primitive Jerusalem Community (4:1–8:4)
 1. Peter and John before the Sanhedrin (4:1–22)
 2. The Prayer of Jerusalem Christians (4:23–31)
 3. Second Major Summary: A Sharing Community (4:32–35)
 4. Individual Examples of Christian Conduct (4:36–5:11)
 5. Third Major Summary: A Caring Community (5:12–16)
 6. Further Persecution of the Apostles (5:17–42)
 7. Community Restructured: Commission of the Seven (6:1–7)
 8. Testimony of Stephen (6:8–7:1)
 9. Stephen's Discourse (7:2–53)
 10. Reaction to Stephen's Testimony; His Martyrdom (7:54–8:1a)
 11. Further Persecution in Jerusalem (8:1b–4)

III. The Mission of Testimony in Judea and Samaria (8:5–40)
 1. Philip in Samaria Encounters Simon (8:5–25)
 2. Philip and the Ethiopian Eunuch on the Gaza Road (8:26–40)

IV. The Word Is Carried Further: Testimony Even to Gentiles (9:1–14:28)
A. The Persecutor Becomes a Christian Witness (9:1–31)
 1. The Call of Saul (9:1–19a)
 2. Saul's Preaching and Problems in Damascus (9:19b–25)
 3. Saul's First Visit to Jerusalem (9:26–31)
B. Peter Initiates the Mission to Gentiles (9:32–11:18)
 1. Peter's Miracles in Lydda and Joppa (9:32–43)
 2. Conversion of Cornelius and His Household in Caesarea (10:1–11:18)
  a) Cornelius's Vision (10:1–8)
  b) Peter's Vision (10:9–16)
  c) Welcome for Messengers from Cornelius (10:17–23a)
  d) Peter's Testimony in Cornelius's House (10:23b–48)
  e) Peter's Self-Defense at Jerusalem (11:1–18)
C. Spread of the Word to Gentiles Elsewhere (11:19–12:25)
 1. Greeks in Antioch Evangelized by Barnabas (11:19–26)
 2. Prophet Agabus and the Collection for Jerusalem (11:27–30)
 3. Herod's Persecution of James and Peter; Herod's Death (12:1–23)
 4. Summary and Lucan Suture (12:24–25)
D. Paul's First Missionary Journey to Gentiles in Asia Minor (13:1–14:28)
 1. Mission of Barnabas and Saul (13:1–3)
 2. Evangelization of Cyprus (13:4–12)
 3. Evangelization of Pisidian Antioch; Paul's Discourse (13:13–52)
 4. Evangelization of Iconium (14:1–7)
 5. Evangelization of Lystra and Derbe (14:8–20)
 6. Paul's Return to Antioch in Syria (14:21–28)

V. The Jerusalem Decision about Gentile Christians (15:1–35)
 1. Prehistory (15:1–2)
 2. Convocation and Peter's Appeal to Precedent (15:3–12)
 3. James's Confirmation and Proposals (15:13–21)

4. The Jerusalem Letter to Local Gentile Churches (15:22–29)
5. Aftermath of the Jerusalem Decision and Letter (15:30–35)

VI. Paul's Universal Mission and Testimony (15:36–22:21)
A. Paul's Further Missionary Journeys (15:36–20:38)
1. Paul and Barnabas Differ and Separate (15:36–40)
2. Paul's Second Missionary Journey (15:41–18:22)
a) In Derbe and Lystra: Timothy as Companion (15:41–16:5)
b) Paul Crosses Asia Minor (16:6–10)
c) Evangelization of Philippi (16:11–40)
d) Paul in Thessalonica and Beroea (17:1–15)
e) Paul Evangelizes Athens; at the Areopagus (17:16–34)
f) Paul Evangelizes Corinth; Haled before Gallio (18:1–17)
g) Paul Returns to Antioch (18:18–22)
3. Paul's Third Missionary Journey (18:23–20:38)
a) Apollos in Ephesus and Achaia (18:23–28)
b) Paul in Ephesus and Disciples of the Baptist (19:1–7)
c) Paul's Evangelization of Ephesus (19:8–22)
d) Riot of the Ephesian Silversmiths (19:23–41)
e) Paul leaves for Macedonia, Achaia, and Syria (20:1–6)
f) Paul Revives Eutychus at Troas (20:7–12)
g) Paul's Journey to Miletus (20:13–16)
h) Farewell Discourse at Miletus (20:17–38)
B. Paul in Jerusalem (21:1–22:21)
1. Paul's Journey to Jerusalem (21:1–16)
2. Paul Visits James and the Jerusalem Presbyters (21:17–25)
3. Paul's Arrest in Jerusalem (21:26–40)
4. Paul's Discourse to the Jerusalem Crowd (22:1–21)

VII. Paul Imprisoned for the Sake of Testimony to the Word (22:22–28:31)
A. Prisoner in Jerusalem and Testimony There (22:22–23:22)
1. Paul Taken to Roman Headquarters; the Roman Citizen (22:22–29)
2. Paul Brought before the Jerusalem Sanhedrin (22:30–23:11)
3. Plot of Jerusalemites to Kill Paul (23:12–22)
B. Prisoner in Caesarea and Testimony There (23:23–26:32)
1. Transfer to Caesarea (23:23–35)
2. Trial before Governor Felix (24:1–21)
3. Imprisonment of Paul at Caesarea (24:22–27)
4. Before Governor Festus Paul Appeals to Caesar (25:1–12)
5. Festus Invites Agrippa to Listen to Paul (25:13–27)
6. Paul's Discourse before Agrippa and Festus (26:1–23)
7. Reactions to Paul's Discourse (26:24–32)
C. Prisoner in Rome, Testimony and Ministry There (27:1–28:31)
1. Departure for Rome (27:1–8)
2. Storm at Sea and Shipwreck (27:9–44)
3. Paul Spends the Winter on Malta (28:1–10)

4. Paul's Arrival in Rome and House Arrest (28:11–16)
5. Paul's Testimony to Prominent Jews of Rome (28:17–31)

BIBLIOGRAPHY

Betori, G., "Alla ricerca di un'articolazione per il libro degli Atti," *RivB* 37 (1989): 185–205.

———, "Strutturazione degli Atti e storiografia antica," *Cristianesimo nella storia* 12 (1991): 251–63.

———, "La strutturazione del libro degli Atti: Una proposta," *RivB* 42 (1994): 3–34.

Cook, C., "Travellers' Tales and After-Dinner Speeches: The Shape of *Acts of the Apostles*," *New Blackfriars* 74 (1993): 442–57.

Dupont, J., "La question du plan des Actes des Apôtres à la lumière d'un texte de Lucien de Samosate," *NovT* 21 (1979) 220–31; repr. *Nouvelles études*, 24–36.

Menoud, P. H., "The Plan of the Acts of the Apostles," *Jesus Christ and the Faith: A Collection of Studies* (PTMS 18; Pittsburgh: Pickwick, 1978) 121–32; original in *NTS* 1 (1954–55): 44–51.

Morton, A. Q. and G.H.C. Macgregor, *The Structure of Luke and Acts* (London: Hodder and Stoughton, 1964), 34–51.

Neirynck, F., "Le livre des Actes dans les récents commentaires," *ETL* 59 (1983): 338–49, esp. 342–44.

Rolland, P., "L'Organisation du Livre des Actes et de l'ensemble de l'oeuvre de Luc," *Bib* 65 (1984): 81–86.

VIII. Historical Character of Acts

◆

(129) The major problem that confronts any interpreter of the Acts of the Apostles today is the historicity of the Lucan account. The viewpoint adopted in this century, mainly due to the interpretations of Conzelmann, Dibelius, Haenchen, Lüdemann, Pervo, Vielhauer, and others, has been skeptical. This has led to a minimal understanding of Acts as a document of the early church and as a source for its early history. There have, however, been many others who have reacted against that interpretation as exaggerated and extreme. This reaction can be found in the writings of Bruce, Gasque, Hemer, Hengel, Marshall, Sherwin-White, and others who have taught us not to neglect the earlier contributions of interpreters such as Nock, Ramsay, and Wikenhauser.

(130) The issue of the historical character of the Lucan account in Acts has been well studied, and it is clear today that a middle ground has to be sought between the skeptical approach and a conservative reaction to it. One has to admit that at times Luke's information is faulty and that he has confused some things in his narrative, but by and large he does present us with a reliable account of much of what he recounts. From it we can indeed "profit with delight," without buying all the tendentious implications of Pervo's interpretation of Acts.

(131) In the prologue to the two-volume Lucan composition the author claims that he has done his homework in preparation for writing the story of Jesus and its sequel. He protests that the account that he has written is characterized by its thoroughness, completeness, accuracy, and order (Luke 1:3), but we recognize that that is an author's projected aim. Whether he has achieved all that is up to the historian to judge. That judgment, however, cannot be measured solely by the criteria that a historian might use in the assessment of modern works of history or literature. Luke has not written according to the canons of modern history, and so he has to be judged according to the kind of historical writing that would have been current in his day. The trouble is that we as modern readers tend to ask about the historical character of Acts with the (often hidden) modern skeptical attitude, "Well, did it really happen just that way?" In doing so, we forget that Luke's objective was not that of L. von Ranke, to tell it *wie es eigentlich gewesen!*

(132) Further remarks, however, are called for concerning some episodes in the Lucan story of Acts. In discussing the composition of Acts, I have already distinguished the literary forms of Luke's mode of writing: narratives, summaries, We-Sections, and speeches. The summaries and speeches are clearly of Lucan composition, and, though they may have utilized some historical details derived

by Luke from his various sources, they are presented in the way Luke wants his readers to understand them. No one can claim that they represent exactly what happened or what was said on a given occasion. They are at most suitable accounts enjoying some verisimilitude.

(133) Even the We-Sections, which may be derived from a Lucan diary or travel notes, may have well been used later on by Luke with some curtailment or redaction; but I should be inclined to accord them more historical value than the summaries or speeches, simply because of Luke's personal involvement. In his discussion of these sections, Haenchen finally admitted, "Luke, despite his considerable ability as a narrator, is not a novelist but a historian" ("'We' in Acts," 99). I have already explained that Robbins's understanding of the We-Sections as a Hellenistic literary device, which Luke would be employing, is a highly questionable analysis of such sections (see §§99–100 above).

(134) Similarly, in judging the historical character of the many narratives in Acts, one has to reckon with the author's possible abridgment of details and even tendentious presentation of some of the events recounted. The Lucan story line at times bears an apologetic thrust; yet to admit that is not to write off the whole episode as unhistorical. For instance, that Peter summoned the early Christians to reconstitute the Twelve (chap. 1), that he addressed Jews assembled in Jerusalem for the first feast after Jesus' death and burial (chap. 2), that he and John were apprehended by Jerusalem religious authorities and forbidden to teach in Jesus' name (chaps. 3–4), and many other such events recounted in Acts, I take to be substantially historical. Such a list of events could easily be expanded, not only for those recounted in the episodes of chaps. 1–8, 10–12, but also for the conversion of Paul (chap. 9) and his missionary journeys, not only in chaps. 16–21, but also those in chaps. 13–14 (Mission I). The same would hold true for the events associated with Paul in Jerusalem, Caesarea, and Rome (chaps. 21–26, 28). The account of Paul's sea voyage to Rome and his shipwreck in chap. 27 is mainly part of the final We-Section and would be governed by what I have said about those sections above.

(135) The main problem in this regard is chap. 15, the Lucan account of the "Council" of Jerusalem. This chapter represents the joining of details of two decisions made by the Jerusalem church on different occasions. Luke has joined them, because he has inherited the details from Antiochene sources. One decision, that of the "Council," concerns the exemption from circumcision for Gentiles who become Christians or from their observance of the Mosaic law (15:6–12). The other is that of James and other Jerusalem authorities, about dietary regulations sent to the local churches of Antioch, Syria, and Cilicia subsequent to the "Council" (15:13–29). Luke has joined the two into the one account in chap. 15 because they are both Jerusalem decisions and have come to him from Antiochene traditions. He has related them to one occasion but has given enough evidence of his telescoping of events that the reader realizes what he has done. See further the COMMENTS on 15:3–12, 13–21, 22–29.

(136) From the point of view of historicity, the most problematic narratives in Acts are those that recount a miracle. These are found in 3:1–11; 5:1–11, 12–15,

19; 8:7; 9:32–34, 40; 12:6–11; 13:10–11; 14:8–10; 16:18, 26; 19:11; 20:10; 28:3–5(?). Other problematic narratives are the accounts of other heavenly interventions, such as the outpouring of the Spirit on Pentecost (2:1–4); the visions accorded to Stephen (7:55–56), Saul (9:3–7), Ananias (9:10–16), Cornelius (10:3–6), Peter (10:10–16; 11:5–10), and Paul (18:9; 22:7–10; 26:14–18); the descent of the Spirit on Gentiles (10:44; 19:6); and communications from the Spirit (13:2; 16:6–7). Judgment about the historical character of these items is not simple, because it invariably involves a philosophical judgment as well. If one is philosophically convinced that miracles do not happen or that God does not so intervene in human history, then all such narratives immediately become unhistorical or nonhistorical. If, however, one accepts the possibility of such divine intervention, judgment is then open to their historical validation. Clearly, Luke himself reckoned with such a possibility, for he did not hesitate to include such items in his narratives in Acts. At any rate, there is no way to offer any proof of their historicity. (Needless to say, the fact that Acts forms part of the inspired New Testament does not make the Lucan account, narrated in the past tense, necessarily historical. Neither church teaching nor theologians have ever maintained that the necessary formal effect of inspiration is historicity.)

(137) There are a number of incidents that Luke has recounted that find confirmation elsewhere. For instance, Paul's escape from Damascus (9:24b–25) is confirmed by what Paul himself relates in 2 Cor 11:32, even though a minor detail differs; Paul's plan to go to Rome after a journey to Jerusalem (19:21) is confirmed by what Paul himself says in Rom 15:22–25; Luke depicts Paul earning his own livelihood (18:3; 20:34), which is confirmed in 1 Thess 2:9; 1 Cor 9:15; 2 Cor 11:7–8. The story of the sudden death of Herod Agrippa (12:21–23) is confirmed by Josephus, *Ant.* 19.8.2 §§343–46, who dates it to the third regnal year of emperor Claudius, A.D. 44. Gallio as proconsul of Achaia (18:12) is confirmed by an inscription found at Delphi (see COMMENT on 18:12–17). The procuratorships of Felix and Festus in Judea (23:24; 24:27) are confirmed by Josephus, *Ant.* 20.7.1–2 §§137–44; 20.8.9–11 §§189–94; 20.9.1 §§197, 200; *J.W.* 2.12.8 §247; 2.14.1 §§271–72; Suetonius, *Claudii vita* 28; Tacitus, *Annales* 12.54; *Historiae* 2.2. Drusilla as the wife of Felix (24:24) is confirmed by Josephus, *Ant.* 19.9.1 §§354–55; 20.7.1–2 §§138–44; *J.W.* 2.11.6 §220; Suetonius, *Claudii vita* 28. Bernice as the wife of King Agrippa II (25:13) is confirmed by Josephus, *Ant.* 20.7.3 §145; *J.W.* 2.11.5 §217; Suetonius, *Titi vita* 7.1; Juvenal, *Satires* 6.156–60; Tacitus, *Historiae* 2.2. The contemporary high priest Ananias (son of Nedebaeus), who was in office from A.D. 47 to 59, is confirmed by Josephus, *Ant.* 20.5.2 §103; 20.6.2 §131; 20.9.2–4 §§205–13.

(138) Modern interpreters have often called attention to the accuracy of minor details in the Lucan narratives. Among these I might mention the appellation of Philippi as *kolōnia*, "colony" (16:12); the city magistrates of Thessalonica as *politarchai* (17:6), a title nowhere attested in Greek literature but well known from Macedonian inscriptions; the correctness of titles such as *anthypatos*, "proconsul," for Sergius Paulus (13:7) and Gallio (18:12) or *agoraioi* for provincial

assizes (19:38); of *sebomenoi*, "worshipers," for Gentile sympathizers of Judaism (17:4,17) or *proselytoi*, "proselytes" for Gentile converts to Judaism (13:43).

(139) Consequently, we have to admit that the Lucan story in Acts is a good example of a Hellenistic historical monograph, to use the designation proposed by Hengel and others (see §§42–43 above). That designation does not guarantee, of course, the historicity of every Lucan statement or episode, but it reveals that what is recounted in Acts is substantially more trustworthy from a historical point of view than not. To admit that, however, does not absolve one of the obligation of checking the historical value of every episode.

BIBLIOGRAPHY

Blaiklock, E. M., "The Acts of the Apostles as a Document of First Century History," *Apostolic History and the Gospel: Biblical and Historical Essays Presented to F. F. Bruce* . . . (ed. W. W. Gasque and R. P. Martin; Grand Rapids, MI: Eerdmans, 1970), 41–54.

Botermann, H., "Der Heidenapostel und sein Historiker: Zur historischen Kritik der Apostelgeschichte," *TBei* 24 (1993): 62–84.

Bruce, F. F., "The Acts of the Apostles: Historical Record or Theological Reconstruction?" ANRW II/25.3 (1985): 2569–2603.

———, *New Testament History* (Garden City, NY: Doubleday, 1969).

Cadbury, H. J., *The Book of Acts in History* (London: Black, 1955).

Cairns, E. E., "Luke as a Historian," *BSac* 122 (1965): 220–26.

Conzelmann, H., "Geschichte, Geschichtsbild und Geschichtsdarstellung bei Lukas," *TLZ* 85 (1960): 241–50.

Dinkler, E., "The Idea of History in Earliest Christianity," *Signum Crucis: Aufsätze zum Neuen Testament und zur christlichen Archäologie* (Tübingen: Mohr [Siebeck], 1967), 313–50.

Gasque, W. W., "The Historical Value of Acts," *TynBull* 40 (1989): 136–57.

———, *A History of the Criticism of the Acts of the Apostles* (Grand Rapids, MI: Eerdmans, 1975), 136–63.

———, "Sir William Ramsay and the New Testament," *SE V* (TU 103, 1968): 277–85.

Green, J. B. and M. C. McKeever, *Luke-Acts and New Testament Historiography* (Grand Rapids, MI: Baker Book House, 1994).

Haenchen, E., "The Book of Acts as Source Material for the History of Early Christianity," *StLA*, 258–78.

———, "'We' in Acts and the Itinerary," *JTC* 1 (1965): 65–99.

Hemer, C. J., *The Book of Acts in the Setting of Hellenistic History.*

Hengel, M., *Acts and the History of Earliest Christianity.*

———, "Der Historiker Lukas und die Geographie Palästinas in der Apostelgeschichte," *ZDPV* 99 (1983): 147–83.

Jáuregui, J. A., "Historiografía y teología en Hechos: Estado de la investigación desde 1980," *EstBíb* 53 (1995): 97–123.

Kurz, W. S., "Luke-Acts and Historiography in the Greek Bible," *SBL 1980 Seminar Papers* (ed. P. J. Achtemeier; Chico, CA: Scholars, 1980), 283–300.

Luedemann, G., "Acts of the Apostles as a Historical Source," *The Social World of Formative Christianity and Judaism: Essays in Tribute to Howard Clark Kee* (ed. J. Neusner et al.; Philadelphia: Fortress, 1988), 109–25.

———, *Early Christianity according to the Traditions in Acts.*

Mealand, D. L., "Hellenistic Historians and the Style of Acts," *ZNW* 82 (1991): 42–66.

Ommeren, N. M. van, "Was Luke an Accurate Historian?" *BSac* 148 (1991): 57–71.

Palmer, D. W., "Acts and the Historical Monograph," *TynBull* 43 (1992): 373–88.

Pervo, R. I., *Profit with Delight.*

Plümacher, E., "Lukas als griechischer Historiker," *PWSup* 14 (1974): 235–64.

Ramsay, W. M., *The Bearing of Recent Discovery on the Trustworthiness of the New Testament* (2d ed.; London: Hodder and Stoughton, 1915).

Schneider, G., "Apostelgeschichte und Kirchengeschichte," *IKZ/Communio* 8 (1979): 481–87; repr. *LTH*, 206–12.

Sherwin-White, A. N., *Roman Society.*

Sterling, G. E., "Luke-Acts and Apologetic Historiography," *SBL 1989 Seminar Papers* (ed. D. Lull; Atlanta: Scholars, 1989), 326–42.

Taylor, J., "Acts and History," *Colloquium* 26 (1994): 105–15.

Unnik, W. C. van, "Luke's Second Book and the Rules of Hellenistic Historiography," *Les Actes des Apôtres* (ed. J. Kremer), 37–60.

Wansbrough, H., "The Book of Acts and History," *Downside Review* 113 (1995): 96–103.

Wikenhauser, A., *Die Apostelgeschichte und ihr Geschichtswert* (NTAbh 8/3–5; Münster in W.: Aschendorff, 1921).

IX. The Lucan Story of Paul

◆

(140) The hero of the second part of Acts is Paul of Tarsus, who calls himself "the apostle of the Gentiles" in Rom 11:13. We know something of Paul's apostolate among the Gentiles of the eastern Mediterranean area from his own letters. A narrative form of that apostolate is presented by Luke in Acts, and his narrative also becomes an interpretation of Paul.

At first the apostle is called "Saul," but, long after the story of his call and conversion, Luke writes, "Saul, also known as Paul" (13:9 [see Note there]), and from that point on in the Lucan story he is known as "Paul," the only name that the apostle uses of himself in his letters. This minor detail, however, serves only to show that the Lucan Paul does not correspond in all respects to the picture of Paul in his own writings, and the lack of correspondence has to be reckoned with. The difference is partly involved in the problem whether Luke was a companion of Paul during any of his ministry, an issue that has already been mentioned apropos of the authorship of Acts (see §§16, 18 above). It is also partly involved in whether Luke ever read any of Paul's letters, and, if he did, to what extent he understood the apostle's theology.

A. The Story of Paul in Acts

(141) When the Apostle first appears in the Lucan story, he is depicted as a "young man" (*neanias*, 7:58), at whose feet the witnesses stoning Stephen pile their cloaks and who gives his approval to Stephen's execution (8:1; cf. 22:20). Soon thereafter Saul's own persecuting activity is recounted, as he "ravaged the church, entering house after house and dragging out both men and women, whom he handed over for imprisonment" (8:3). Presumably, he so ravages the church in Jerusalem. Then in chap. 9 Saul, the archpersecutor, becomes the archwitness to Christ in his encounter with the risen Lord on the road to Damascus. For the significance of that encounter, see the Comment on 9:1–19a. There too we learn of his flight from Damascus and return to Jerusalem, where he is reconciled with Jerusalem Christians through the intervention of Barnabas and eventually sent back to his hometown of Tarsus by them.

(142) After Peter's official evangelization of the first Gentiles (10:1–11:18), Barnabas, who has been evangelizing Antioch, seeks out Saul in Tarsus (11:25) and brings him to Antioch, where the two labor in spreading the Word for a whole year. Barnabas and Saul are sent by the Antiochene Christians to Jerusalem to bring relief to the poor Christians there (11:30) and then return to Antioch

(12:25). At the inspiration of the Spirit, the church in Antioch sets apart Barnabas and Saul for missionary work (13:2–3).

(143) Luke has organized Saul's missionary work into three segments, or three missionary journeys. Although, as J. Knox once wrote, "If you had stopped Paul on the streets of Ephesus and said to him, 'Paul, which of your missionary journeys are you on now?' he would have looked at you blankly without the remotest idea of what was in your mind" (*Chapters*, 41–42). The division of Paul's missionary activity into three segments is the way modern interpreters of Acts read the Lucan story of Paul, because Luke himself does not distinguish Mission I from Mission II or Mission III, as we often count them today.

Mission I, which takes place in the period prior to the Jerusalem "Council" is recounted in Acts 13:3–14:28. The Lucan story is confined to essentials in an effort to suit the author's literary purpose of the spread of the testimony to the risen Christ. Paul himself has given us very little information about his missionary activity in the period prior to the "Council." In Gal 2:1 he speaks of that period as "fourteen years" since his experience on the road to Damascus. From his letters we learn only that during that time he was in "the regions of Syria and Cilicia" and was "preaching the faith" (Gal 1:21, 23), "among the Gentiles" (Gal 2:2).

(144) The Lucan story of Mission I begins with Barnabas and Saul being singled out and commissioned by the church in Antioch for missionary work under the guidance of the Holy Spirit. The two of them start out with John Mark, the cousin of Barnabas (Col 4:10), depart from Seleucia, the Mediterranean port on which Antioch depended, head for Cyprus, and pass through the island from Salamis to Paphos. In Paphos the proconsul Sergius Paulus is converted (13:7–12), and afterwards they leave Paphos and sail for Perga in Pamphylia on the southern coast of central Asia Minor. There John Mark deserts them to return to Jerusalem. Barnabas and Paul make their way to towns in southern Galatia: Pisidian Antioch, Iconium, Lystra, and Derbe. In Antioch Paul preaches first to Jews in their synagogue, and when resistance to his testimony is manifested, he announces that he is turning henceforth to Gentiles (13:46). After evangelizing the area and encountering opposition from Jews in various towns (even stoning in Iconium), Barnabas and Paul retrace their steps to Pisidian Antioch, Perga, and Attalia, whence they sail for Syrian Antioch. There Paul spends "no little time" with Christians (14:28).

One of the issues that surfaces during Mission I is the relation of Gentile Christians to older Jewish Christians: Would Gentile Christians have to be circumcised and required to observe the Mosaic law? The Lucan story recounts Paul's visit to Jerusalem for the "Council." His visit is occasioned by the arrival of Christians from Judea in Antioch, who insist on the circumcision of Gentiles as necessary for salvation (15:1–3). The ensuing perplexity in the Antiochene church leads to the sending of Paul and Barnabas to consult the apostles and elders in Jerusalem about the status of Gentile converts. Part of the Lucan account of this visit of Paul to Jerusalem corresponds to what Paul himself related in Gal 2:1–10, his visit to Jerusalem once again, fourteen years after his experience on the road to Damascus. There he told how he laid before "those of repute" in Jerusalem the gospel that he had been preaching to the Gentiles; and James, Cephas, and John "added nothing to it" (Gal 2:6). This Pauline report corresponds to what Luke recounts in the first part of Acts 15 (vv 4–12). Those whom Paul had labeled "false brethren" (Gal 2:4) now become "some from the party of the Pharisees who had become believers" (Acts 15:5), who advocate the circumcision of Gentile converts. The issue is finally settled, after Peter speaks on the matter, citing his own experience; the Jerusalem "Council" thus frees the nascent church from its Jewish roots and opens it to the world apostolate that lies before it. Paul's position is thus vindicated, even though his role in that meeting, according to the Lucan account, appears to have been minimal.

(145) Mission II begins in Antioch on the Orontes, whither Paul returned after the "Council." The Lucan story of it is recounted in Acts 15:41–18:22. Paul refuses to take John Mark along with him because of the latter's earlier desertion, and this refusal causes Barnabas to separate from Paul and take Mark with him on a separate mission. Silas instead becomes Paul's companion on Mission II. Setting out from Antioch, they make their way overland through Syria and Cilicia to the south Galatian towns of Derbe and Lystra, where Paul takes on Timothy as a coworker, having had him circumcised (16:1–3). From there they pass through Phrygia to north Galatia (Pessinus, Ancyra, Tavium) and found new churches there. Hindered from moving on to Bithynia, Paul goes from Galatia to Mysia and Troas, where he seems to have been joined by Luke—or where data from the Lucan diary begin to be incorporated into the account (16:10–17), the first of the "We-Sections."

In response to a dream, Paul passes over from Troas to Philippi, and the church he founds there becomes the first Christian church in Europe. Imprisoned in Philippi at first, he is then released and makes his way to Amphipolis, Apollonia, and Thessalonica (17:1–9). After a short period of evangelization and controversy with Jews in Thessalonica, he flees to Beroea (17:10) and eventually to Athens (17:15). There he tries to interest Athenians in the gospel, but fails: "We'll listen to you about this topic some other time" (17:32). So Paul moves on to Corinth (A.D. 51), where he at first lives with Aquila and Priscilla (18:2–3), Jewish converts recently come from Italy after their expulsion from Rome by the emperor Claudius (in A.D. 49). During his sojourn in Corinth, which lasts 18 months, Paul converts many Jews and Greeks and founds a vigorous, predominantly Gentile Christian church there. Toward the end of this stay he is haled by Corinthian Jews before the proconsul L. Junius Gallio, who dismisses the case against him as a matter of words, names, and intra-Jewish dispute (18:15). Shortly thereafter Paul departs from Corinth, sailing from its port Cenchreae for Ephesus and Caesarea Maritima. After paying a visit to the church in Jerusalem (18:22), he goes down to Antioch, where he stays well over a year.

(146) Mission III is recounted in Acts 18:23–20:38. Paul leaves Antioch on the Orontes and travels overland again through Galatia and Phrygia to Ephesus, where he is based during much of this time. Ephesus in the Roman province of Asia becomes the center of his missionary work during the next "three years" (20:31), and "for two years" he lectures in the hall of Tyrannus (19:10). (As we

learn from his letters, but not from the Lucan account, from Ephesus Paul made an excursion to Corinth to handle some of the problems that had emerged in that church.) Toward the end of his stay in Ephesus a revolt of silversmiths occurs (19:23–20:1): his preaching of the "Way" incites Demetrius, an Ephesian silversmith, to lead a tumultuous crowd into the theater in protest against Paul and the spread of Christianity. Shortly thereafter Paul leaves Ephesus to go to Macedonia and eventually comes to Corinth, where he spends the winter. When spring arrives, Paul wants to sail from Corinth for Syria, but learns of a plot against him and departs instead overland for Philippi in Macedonia. From there he sails to Troas and then takes a ship from Assos to return to Jerusalem. He stops briefly at Miletus, whither he summons the elders of the church of Ephesus, to address to them his last will and testament (20:17–35). Thence Paul makes his way to Jerusalem: he sails on to Cos, Rhodes, Patara in Lycia, Tyre in Phoenicia, Ptolemais, and Caesarea Maritima, and an overland journey eventually brings him to his destination (21:1–17). So ends Mission III.

(147) These three missions are the backbone of the Lucan story of Paul in Acts. After the account of them ends, there follows the narrative of Paul's testimony in Jerusalem and his imprisonment there, a story that is known to us only from Acts. We can trace some of the missionary work of Paul in his letters, but once Mission III is over there is no longer any correlation with the Pauline corpus, even though we may know of his plans to visit Jerusalem and Rome (en route to Spain) from Romans 15.

Paul arrives in Jerusalem in the spring and pays his respects to James and the elders of the church there (21:18). After going through a rite of purification and paying the expenses for the Nazirite vow of four Jewish Christians in Jerusalem, he is accused of having introduced a Gentile Greek into the Temple. Paul is surrounded but eventually saved by the commander of Roman troops stationed in Jerusalem from the violence of a mob attempting to kill him. After addressing the Jerusalem mob (22:1–21), Paul is placed in custody, a mode of protective arrest (22:27), and eventually interrogated by the Roman tribune, who uses the Sanhedrin in advisory capacity. Fear of the Jews, however, makes the tribune send Paul on to the procurator of Judea, Felix, residing in Caesarea Maritima (23:23–33). Felix, who expects Paul to bribe him (24:26), keeps him in prison for two years.

(148) When a new procurator, Porcius Festus, arrives (possibly A.D. 60), Paul "appeals to Caesar" (25:11), in virtue of his Roman citizenship. Festus grants that request. Escorted by a Roman centurion, Paul sets sail from Caesarea Maritima for Sidon and from there sails past Cyprus to come to Myra in Lycia. In the late autumn (27:9), he leaves Myra on an Alexandrian ship bound for Italy, expecting bad weather. Its route takes them south of Asia Minor into the Adriatic Sea, where a northeaster blows up and carries them for days to Malta, where they are finally shipwrecked (27:10–28:1). After spending the winter on Malta, Paul and his fellow travelers sail for Syracuse in Sicily, Rhegium in Italy, and Puteoli (near Naples). From there their overland journey brings them to Rome (28:15), the capital of the empire, where Paul is put under house arrest with a soldier to guard

him. That house arrest, however, does not hinder him from bearing testimony to Jewish leaders in Rome (28:17–28). With that the story of Paul in Acts ends. He has thus brought the Word of God "to the end of the earth" (1:8).

B. The Problems of the Lucan Story

(149) Recent study of Paul's life and its chronology has rightly insisted on the need to give priority to what Paul in his uncontested letters (1 Thessalonians, Galatians, Philippians, 1–2 Corinthians, Romans, and Philemon) tells us about himself. If there is any discrepancy between such Pauline information and what the Lucan story recounts, it is the latter that must yield to the former.

(150) Despite the claims of some authors (Enslin, J. Knox, Schenk), it is highly unlikely that Luke ever read any of Paul's letters; none of their arguments have really proved convincing (see *Luke*, 49). If Luke had read them, we would scarcely encounter the discrepancies that commentators often point out today. Nowhere in Acts does Luke ever depict Paul writing a letter to any of the churches that he has evangelized, and apart from 13:38–39 and a few phrases in Paul's speech to the presbyters of Ephesus at Miletus, there is hardly an echo of the teaching that one finds in his uncontested letters. What a contrast there is between Acts and the Deutero-Paulines, especially Ephesians, where echoes of the uncontested letters are abundant.

(151) At the same time, it is almost universally admitted that certain details in the Lucan story are to be accepted: the fact that Paul came from Tarsus (21:39), that he was haled before the proconsul L. Junius Gallio in Achaia (18:12)—the "one link between the Apostle's career and general history that is accepted by all scholars" (Murphy-O'Connor, *St. Paul's Corinth*, 141)—or that he was a Roman citizen (22:25–27). Such details are never mentioned by Paul and are supplied only by Luke. Moreover, there are many other things that the Lucan story does contribute to the reconstruction of Paul's life and career.

(152) There is, above all, the correlation of evidence that the two sources, the Pauline uncontested letters and Acts, contain with which one has to reckon. The main points of that correlation were pointed out years ago by T. H. Campbell, "Paul's 'Missionary Journeys' as Reflected in His Letters" (*JBL* 74 [1955], 80–87), which I subsequently modified slightly (*According to Paul*, 36–41). In the letters of Paul there is a sequence of movement from his experience on the Damascus road to his (projected) journey to Rome that more or less parallels the more detailed account of his movements in the Lucan story of Acts.

The main passages in which Paul gives us personal details about his career and movements, which can be used in such a correlation, are the following: 1 Thess 2:1–2, 17–18; 3:1–3a, 6; Gal 1:13–23; 2:1–14; 4:13; Phil 3:5–6; 4:15–16; 1 Cor 1:11; 4:17; 5:9; 7:7–8; 15:32; 16:1–10, 12, 17; 2 Cor 1:8, 15–16, 19; 2:1, 9–13; 7:5–6; 9:2–4; 11:7–9, 23–27, 32–33; 12:2–4, 14, 21; 13:1–2, 10; Rom 11:1c; 15:19b, 22–32; 16:1.

(153) The correlation itself can be seen in the following comparison:

Letters	*Acts*
Conversion/Call near Damascus (implied in Gal 1:17c)	Damascus (9:1–22)
To Arabia (Gal 1:17b)	
Return to Damascus (Gal 1:17c): 3 years	
Flight from Damascus (2 Cor 11:32–33)	Flight from Damascus (9:23–25)
To Jerusalem (Gal 1:18–20)	To Jerusalem (9:26–29)
To "the regions of Syria and Cilicia" (Gal 1:21–22)	Caesarea and Tarsus (9:30)
	Antioch (11:26a)
	(Jerusalem [11:29–30; 12:25])
	Mission I: Antioch (13:1–4a), Seleucia, Salamis, Cyprus (13:4b–12)
Churches evangelized before Macedonia (Philippi, Phil 4:15)	South Galatian towns (13:13–14:25)
	Return to Antioch (14:26–28)
"Once again during 14 years I went up to Jerusalem (for the "Council," Gal 2:1)	Jerusalem (15:1–12)
Antioch Incident (Gal 2:11–14)	Mission II: from Antioch (15:35)
	Syria and Cilicia (15:41)
	South Galatia (16:1–5)
Galatia (1 Cor 16:1) evangelized (Gal 4:13)	Phrygia and North Galatia (16:6)
	Mysia and Troas (16:7–10)
Philippi (1 Thess 2:2 [= Macedonia, 2 Cor 11:9])	Philippi (16:11–40)
Thessalonica (1 Thess 2:2; cf. 3:6; Phil 4:15–16)	Amphipolis, Apollonia, Thessalonica (17:1–9)
	Beroea (17:10–14)
Athens (1 Thess 3:1; cf. 2:17–18)	Athens (17:15–34)
Corinth evangelized (cf. 2 Cor 1:19; 11:7–9)	Corinth for 18 months (18:1–18a)
Timothy arrives in Corinth (1 Thess 3:6), probably accompanied by Silvanus (1 Thess 1:1)	Silas and Timothy come from Macedonia (18:5)
	Paul leaves from Cenchreae (18:18b)
	Leaves Priscilla and Aquila at Ephesus (18:19–21)
Apollos (in Ephesus) urged by Paul to go to Corinth (1 Cor 16:12)	Apollos dispatched to Achaia by Priscilla and Aquila (18:17)
	Paul to Caesarea Maritima (18:22a)

	Paul to Jerusalem (18:22b [implied])
	In Antioch for a certain time (18:22c)
North Galatia, second visit (Gal 4:13)	Mission III: North Galatia and Phrygia (18:23)
Ephesus (1 Cor 16:1–8)	Ephesus (for 3 yrs. or 2 yrs., 3 mos. (19:1–20:1; cf. 20:31)
Visit of Chloe, Stephanas et al. to Paul in Ephesus (1 Cor 1:11; 16:17), bringing a letter (7:1)	
Paul imprisoned (cf. 1 Cor 15:32; 2 Cor 1:8)	
Timothy sent to Corinth (1 Cor 4:17; 16:10)	
Paul's second "painful" visit to Corinth (2 Cor 13:2); return to Ephesus	
Titus sent to Corinth with letter "written in tears" (2 Cor 2:13)	
(Paul's plans to visit Macedonia, Corinth, and Jerusalem/Judea [1 Cor 16:3–8; cf. 2 Cor 1:15–16])	(Paul's plans to visit Macedonia, Achaia, Jerusalem, Rome [19:21])
Ministry in Troas (2 Cor 2:12)	
To Macedonia (2 Cor 2:13; 7:5; 9:2b–4); arrival of Titus (2 Cor 7:6)	Macedonia (20:1b)
Titus sent on ahead to Corinth (2 Cor 7:16–17), with part of 2 Cor	
Illyricum (Rom 15:19)?	
Achaia (Rom 15:26; 16:1); Paul's third visit to Corinth (2 Cor 13:1)	3 mos. in Greece (Achaia, 20:2–3)
	Paul plans to return by ship to Syria (20:3), but goes instead via Macedonia and Philippi (20:3b–6a)
	Troas (20:6b–12)
	Miletus (20:15c–38)
	Tyre, Ptolemais, Caesarea Maritima (21:7–14)
(Paul plans to visit Jerusalem, Rome, Spain [Rom 15:22–27])	Jerusalem (21:15–23:30)
	Caesarea Maritima (23:31–26:32)
	Journey to Rome (27:1–28:14)
	Rome (28:15–31)

Cf. J. M. Gilchrist, "Paul and the Corinthians—The Sequence of Letters and Visits," *JSNT* 34 (1988) 47–69.

(154) The differences between the Pauline and Lucan data in this comparison are the following five: (a) Luke says nothing about Paul's withdrawal to Arabia after the Damascus experience (Gal 1:17b); (b) Luke says nothing about the different visits of Paul to Corinth from Ephesus (2 Corinthians); (c) Luke treats Paul's missionary work in three blocks (I: 13:1–14:28; II: 15:36–18:22; III: 18:23–21:16); (d) Whereas Paul relates his departure from Damascus to the attempt of the ethnarch of Aretas to take him captive (2 Cor 11:32–33), Luke ascribes it to a plot of "the Jews" (Acts 9:23). (e) Whereas Paul speaks of having persecuted "the church of God" (Gal 1:13) or "the church" (Phil 3:6), Luke depicts Paul "consenting" to the stoning of Stephen (7:58–8:1), about which Paul says nothing in his letters, and further pursuing Christian men and women as far as Damascus, to bring them to prison (Acts 8:3). Some of these differences are more important than others, but apart from these differences, the correlation of the rest is significant.

(155) There is a further problem that needs comment, the question of Mission I in the period prior to the "Council." The Lucan story of Mission I has been summarized above in section A (see §144). Much of that story seems to have no correspondence in Paul's own letters; as a result modern interpreters are skeptical about the historicity of the Lucan account of so-called Mission I. Paul never recounts any of his movements in that period, apart from a few verses of Galatians 1–2, which actually serve a rhetorical and apologetic purpose. But they do deserve another look.

In Galatians Paul tells how he returned to Damascus after his sojourn in Arabia (1:17c), how after three years in Damascus he went to Jerusalem "to consult Cephas" (1:18), and then how "during (the course of) fourteen years I went up again to Jerusalem with Barnabas, taking Titus along with me" (2:1). The last visit is to be regarded as the equivalent of the "Council" visit (= Acts 15:1–12).

Between the two visits to Jerusalem recounted in Galatians (1:18; 2:1), Paul states that he went *eis ta klimata tēs Syrias kai tēs Kilikias*, "into the regions of Syria and Cilicia" (1:21). He was then still personally unknown "to the churches of Christ in Judea," which had only heard "that he who once persecuted us was now preaching the faith he had once tried to destroy" (1:23). Paul also indicates that during this time he had been "preaching to the Gentiles" (2:2). It may be difficult to specify what he meant by *klimata* (1:21), but it undoubtedly refers to "districts" or "subdivisions" of the Roman province of Syria-Cilicia (compare *ta klimata tēs Achaias*, 2 Cor 11:10, or *en tois klimasi toutois*, Rom 15:23). The Lucan notice, therefore, about Saul's withdrawal to Tarsus (Acts 9:30) can be correlated with his visit to the region of Cilicia (Gal 1:21). Moreover, because Mission I in the Lucan story begins in Antioch on the Orontes (Acts 13:1–4), that too can be correlated with the region of Syria (Gal 1:21). In any case, Paul insists that Christians in Judea had heard that he was "preaching the faith" (Gal 1:23), apparently "in the regions of Syria and Cilicia" (1:21). Again the year of labor spent by Barnabas and Saul in Antioch is specified as "teaching a large number of people" (Acts 11:26). That could be the Lucan way of saying what Paul meant by "preaching the faith" to Gentiles in the regions of Syria and Cilicia in the period prior to the "Council."

In writing to the Philippians, Paul moreover noted that, when he "at the beginning of the evangelization" (4:15) left Macedonia, no church entered into partnership with him in giving and receiving except the Philippian community (cf. 4:16). Now "no church" could mean no church in Macedonia, none of which Paul ever mentions. It is not out of the question, however, that Paul is thus referring to his evangelization of "the regions of Syria and Cilicia." After all, Gal 1:23 does explain how Paul began his evangelization and implies that it was there, in Syria and Cilicia, that it began. So it could correspond to those churches mentioned in Acts 13:1–14:28.

Paul had to pass to Philippi from the province of Asia, where he may also have evangelized areas beyond Syria and Cilicia. Though the last point may be speculative, the rest of the evidence from Galatians and Philippians are details, sparse indeed, that tell about Paul's "preaching the faith" in the period prior to the "Council" and thus supply some correlation for the Lucan account of Mission I. In any case, Phil 4:15 does not mean that Macedonia was the first place that Paul had ever evangelized (*pace* M. J. Suggs, "Concerning the Date of Paul's Macedonian Ministry," *NovT* 4 [1960]: 60–68). Thus the Lucan account of Mission I in Acts is not in open conflict with the sparse details supplied by Paul himself about his activities in the period prior to the "Council."

(156) Related to the foregoing problem is that of the visits that Paul made to Jerusalem after his conversion. In the Lucan account these might number six: (a) 9:26, a visit after Paul has escaped from Damascus; (b) 11:30, the famine-relief visit; (c) 12:25, a service visit to Jerusalem, if *eis* is understood in a directional sense with the verb *hypestrepsan*, "they returned" (but see NOTE on this verse); (d) 15:4, a visit when Paul is sent by the Antiochene church for the "Council"; (e) 18:22, a visit to greet the church (of Jerusalem) at the end of Mission II; (f) 21:17, the visit to James and the presbyters of Jerusalem at the end of Mission III.

In the above list, visit (a) is to be equated with that mentioned by Paul in Gal 1:18 after his escape from Damascus (2 Cor 11:33), which took place three years after his experience on the road to Damascus. Visit (d) is to be equated with that mentioned by Paul in Gal 2:1, fourteen years after his experience on the road to Damascus. Visit (c) is not a visit *to* Jerusalem, but reports rather the return of Barnabas and Saul to Antioch after visit (b), after completing their service "in (*eis*) Jerusalem." The real problem is visit (b). The Pauline letters mention nothing of such an intermediate visit, i.e. between visits (a) and (d). One explanation of it is that Luke learned of a Pauline visit to Jerusalem in some source, which really referred to visit (d), but which he understood as related to famine relief sent from Antioch. In other words, so-called visits (b) and (c) may really be a doublet of visit (d). In Gal 2:10 Paul mentions that at the "Council" remembrance of the poor was recommended to him, which meant remembrance of the poor of Jerusalem, for which he tells us that he had collections taken up in the churches he founded. So Giet, Benoit, Pesch. Another explanation is drawn from the polemical character of Galatians, in which Paul was listing only those incidents in which he had relations with the church authorities of Jerusalem. So in Galatians he had no need or even opportunity to mention the famine-relief visit. So Polhill.

C. Extrabiblical Pegs for Pauline Chronology

(157) A.D. 14–37	Reign of the emperor Tiberius Julius Caesar Augustus, who had been born in 42 B.C. (see *Luke*, 455)
36	Pontius Pilate, prefect of Judea (A.D. 26–36), sent to Rome by Lucius Vitellius, legate of Syria (Josephus, *Ant.* 18.4.2 §89). Pilate arrived in Rome only after Tiberius died (16 March 37). See E. M. Smallwood, "The Date of the Dismissal of Pontius Pilate from Judaea," *JJS* 5 (1954): 12–21. Lynching of Stephen (Acts 7:58–60), and the call/conversion of Paul took place at this time (8:1, 3; 9:1–9)
41–54	Reign of the Roman emperor Tiberius Claudius Nero Germanicus, who had been born in 10 B.C.
44	Death of Herod Agrippa I, probably during the Vicennalia on 5 March (Josephus, *Ant.* 19.8.2 §§350–51; Acts 12:20–23)
46?	Famine in the time of the emperor Claudius (Acts 11:28), perhaps to be identified with that in Judea in the time of Tiberius Alexander, procurator (Josephus, *Ant.* 20.5.2 §101)
49	Edict of the emperor Claudius expelling Jews from Rome (Acts 18:2c; Suetonius, *Claudii Vita* 25: "He expelled from Rome Jews who were making constant disturbances at the instigation of *Chrestus*" [see COMMENT on 18:1–17]). It brought Aquila and Priscilla to Corinth, with whom Paul lodged
52–53	Proconsulate of L. Junius Gallio Annaeus in Achaia, before whose tribunal in Corinth Paul was haled (Acts 18:12). His proconsulate is mentioned in a Greek inscription from Delphi (discovered partly in 1905, partly in 1910) dated to the twelfth regnal year of Claudius (see COMMENT on 18:1–17)
52–60	M. Antonius Felix, appointed procurator of Judea by Claudius (Josephus, *J.W.* 2.12.8 §247; 2.13.2 §252; *Ant.* 20.7.1 §137)

54–68	Reign of emperor Nero Claudius Caesar, born 15 December A.D. 37.
60(?)–62	Porcius Festus succeeded M. Antonius Felix as procurator of Judea (Acts 25:9–12); precise dates cannot be established (Josephus, *Ant.* 20.8.9 §182–20.8.10 §188; 20.9.1 §§197, 200; *J.W.* 2.14.1 §271–72; see PW 22/1 [1953] 220–27)

D. Outline of Pauline Chronology

(158) This outline is intended to give a sketch of the relative chronology of Paul's life, making use of the extrabiblical pegs mentioned above and details that can be garnered from Paul's uncontested letters and the account of his career in Acts that agree with such details.

A.D. 1–10?	Born sometime in the first decade (Phlm 9), at Tarsus, Cilicia (Acts 22:3)
36	Paul persecuted "the church of God" (Gal 1:13) in Jerusalem (Acts 8:3); intended to do the same in Damascus, near which he was converted and called (Acts 9:3–19), after which he withdrew to Arabia (Gal 1:17b), then returned to Damascus (Gal 1:17c)
39	"After three years" (Gal 1:18), he escaped from Damascus (2 Cor 11:32–33; Acts 9:23–25); then he paid his first postconversion visit to Jerusalem for fifteen days (Gal 1:18); afterwards withdrew to regions of Syria and Cilicia (Gal 1:21) or to Tarsus (Acts 9:30)
43?	Vision of the Lord (2 Cor 12:2–4): 14 years before writing 2 Corinthians
44 or 45	Barnabas brought Paul from Tarsus to Antioch for a year's work there (Acts 11:25–26)
46–49	Mission I started from Antioch and ended there (Acts 13:4–14:28); Gal 1:21, 23; 2:2 probably refer to this missionary endeavor
49	Claudius expelled Jews from Rome (Acts 18:2c [see §157 above])
49	Paul visited Jerusalem once again during the 14 years from his conversion, to attend the "Council" (Gal 2:1–10; Acts 15:3–12)
49	Antioch incident: Paul rebuked Peter (Gal 2:11–14)

49–50	Jerusalem decree on dietary matters (Acts 15:22–29), about which Paul had to be told later by James (21:25)
50–52	Mission II started from Antioch and ended there (Acts 15:40–18:22)
51	Paul lodged in Corinth with Aquila and Priscilla (Acts 18:2)
51	1 Thessalonians written from Corinth (after Paul came there from Athens (1 Thess 3:1, 6)
52 (summer?)	Paul haled before proconsul Gallio (Acts 18:12)
52	Paul returned to Antioch (Acts 18:18–22), having greeted the church in Jerusalem before going down to Antioch
52 (winter)–54 (spring)	Paul based in Antioch (Acts 18:23a)
54–57	Mission III, during most of which Paul was based in Ephesus (Acts 18:23b–21:17)
54	Galatians written (Gal 1:6)
56	Letter to the Corinthians, now lost (see 1 Cor 5:9)
57 (before Pentecost)	1 Corinthians written (1 Cor 16:8)
57 (autumn)	Paul left Ephesus for Troas (Acts 20:1; 2 Cor 2:12); then went to Macedonia (2 Cor 2:13), where he wrote part of 2 Corinthians (Letter A)
57 (autumn)	Visited Illyricum (Rom 15:19), whence he probably wrote another part of 2 Corinthians (Letter B)
57–58	Paul spent "three months" (= winter) in Corinth (1 Cor 16:5–6; 2 Cor 1:16; Acts 20:2–3), whence he wrote to the Romans
58 (spring)	Left Greece, traveling overland through Macedonia and Philippi (Acts 20:3–6a)
58	After spending Passover in Philippi, Paul sailed for Troas; after seven days there he journeyed overland to Assos, whence he sailed for Caesarea Maritima (Acts 20:6b, 14; 21:1–8)
58	Paul arrived in Jerusalem before Pentecost (Acts 20:16; 21:17); paid a visit to James (21:18); faced uprising in Jerusalem against him (21:27–30); Paul arrested by the Roman commander (21:31–36); sent to the governor Felix in Caesarea Maritima (23:23–33)
58–60	Paul confined for two years in prison (Acts 24:27)
60?	Felix replaced by Festus as governor (Acts 25:1)
60	In Festus's court Paul appealed to Caesar (Acts 25:11–12)

60 (autumn)	Paul sent to Rome (Acts 26:32–27:1); voyage and shipwreck on island of Malta (27:2–28:10)
60–61	Paul spent three months (= winter) on Malta (Acts 28:11a); sailed from Malta to Puteoli (28:11b–13); traveled overland to Rome (28:14–16)
61–63	Paul under house arrest in Rome for two years (Acts 28:30)

(For further explanation of this chronology, see *PAHT*, 2–21 [§§P3–P54].)

E. The Threefold Lucan Account of Paul's Call

(159) Paul himself referred to the experience on the road to Damascus as a crucial turning point in his career. In Gal 1:16 he recorded, "God was pleased to reveal his Son to (*or* in) me so that I might preach him among the Gentiles." That sudden revelation came on the heels of what Paul spoke of as a faithful life, dedicated to the ideals of Judaism (Gal 1:14) and of a persecution of "the church of God" (Gal 1:13; cf. Phil 3:6; A. J. Hultgren, "Paul's Pre-Christian Persecutions of the Church: Their Purpose, Locale, and Nature," *JBL* 95 [1976]: 97–111). After that experience on the road to Damascus, Paul withdrew to "Arabia" and then returned to Damascus (Gal 1:17), from which he fled three years later. He supplies us, however, with none of the details of that experience on the road to Damascus. That experience proved to be an encounter with the risen Christ that Paul never forgot. When his apostolate was challenged, he expostulated, "Am I not an apostle? Have I not seen Jesus our Lord?" (1 Cor 9:1; cf. 15:8). As a result of the "revelation of Jesus Christ" (Gal 1:12), he became a "slave of Christ" (Gal 1:10), under a compulsion (*anankē*, 1 Cor 9:16) to preach the gospel of Christ; and for the sake of it he became "all things to all human beings" (1 Cor 9:22).

(160) Paul's conversion should not be regarded as something that developed from a human condition such as he described in Rom 7:7–8:2. That is not an autobiographical account of his experience, even though it has at times been so interpreted (see *Romans*, 463–64). Even as a Christian, Paul looked back on his Pharisaic past and boasted of his fidelity: "as for righteousness under the law, I was blameless" (Phil 3:6b). He was not crushed by the law, yet he did undergo a "reversal or transvaluation of values" (J. G. Gager), which led in time to a new understanding of himself as a Christian and as an apostle. That experience also led to a profound understanding of the Christ-event. See further, *PAHT*, §§PT 13–15.

(161) Details of that experience, however, are supplied by Luke in Acts. Indeed, it is given in threefold form: once as a narrative (9:1–19) and twice in speeches that Paul himself delivers, once before the mob in Jerusalem that

wanted to do away with him (22:1–21), and once before King Herod Agrippa II and Bernice (26:2–23). What is strange about the three forms is that they do not agree in minor details. One might have thought that Luke would be consistent, but that is not the case. Nevertheless, even apart from the minor differences, no modern attempt has succeeded in ascribing these accounts to different sources, as Haenchen (*Acts*, 325–27) has rightly shown.

(162) The Lucan threefold account serves to impress the reader of Acts with the importance of the call of Paul to be the apostle of the Gentiles. The Lucan message that comes across is that God has willed this mission to the Gentiles. What Luke inherited from the Christian tradition before him about the call of Paul is dramatized by him: the persecution of Christians as a continuation of the stoning of Stephen, the blinding of Paul, and his cure and baptism by Ananias all serve to depict how the Word of God spread to diaspora and Hellenistic Jewish communities, and eventually to Gentiles. Even though Luke cannot bring himself to depict Paul as one of the apostles, he endows him with the next best thing, a commission from the risen Christ himself to carry his name to the Gentile world.

(163) The basic story about Paul's experience on the road to Damascus is the same, save for the Greek wording, in the three accounts, but not the aftermath that deals with Ananias, who appears only in the first two accounts, and not in the third. In all three accounts, Paul is en route to Damascus and drawing close to it; a light shines about him from heaven; Paul hears a voice saying to him, "Saul, Saul, why are you persecuting me?" Paul answers, "Who are you, sir?" The answer comes, "I am Jesus, whom you are persecuting."

(164) The minor differences, however, are the following six: (a) The time of the day is not indicated in chap. 9, but it is about noon in 22:6 or about midday in 26:13. (b) At the shining of the heavenly light Paul falls to the ground in 9:4 and 22:7, but "all" fall in 26:14. (c) In 26:14 the question of the risen Christ, "Why are you persecuting me?" ends with the proverb about kicking against the goad, which is absent in chaps. 9 and 22. (d) In 26:14 that question is said to be posed "in Hebrew," a detail about the language in which the risen Christ speaks to Paul that is missing in chaps. 9 and 22. (e) In 22:8 Jesus' identification of himself includes "the Nazorean," which is not found in chaps. 9 and 26. (f) In 9:7 Paul's companions hear the voice but see no one, whereas in 22:9 they see the light, but hear nothing; and nothing about them is reported in chap. 26.

(165) In chap. 9 Luke has made use of an inherited tradition, a suspense-filled account of Paul's conversion, the main point of which is to present Paul as "a chosen instrument of mine to carry my name before Gentiles and kings, and the children of Israel" (9:15). His role in carrying the name to Gentiles will be recounted in the three missionary journeys to come (13:3–14:28; 15:36–18:22; 18:23–21:16); to kings in his appearance before King Herod Agrippa II and Bernice (25:26–26:27); and to the children of Israel in Rome (28:17–29), but also at times in the course of the missionary journeys. Luke introduces "the apostle of the Gentiles" just before he is going to present the first account of the conversion of Gentiles (Cornelius and his household in chap. 10); he is thus foreshadowing

the mission to the Gentiles. Indirectly, Luke also forestalls an objection: Why did not these new Christians content themselves with a mission to Jews? Luke's answer: God and the risen Christ have willed the evangelization of the Gentiles. Paul did not want to become a Christian or a missionary, but Christ has made him such. It was not a decision of a human being, but an act of God.

(166) In chap. 22 Paul's speech before the Jerusalem crowd purports to be a defense, but in reality it becomes expository and missionary in its own way. It is a rhetorical replay of the narrative of chap. 9. The speech presents Paul as a Jew, pious and devout in his background, a zealous persecutor of the church, but one now called through the agency of Ananias to be a witness of the risen Lord. Note especially Ananias's mandate in 22:14–16: Paul is now called to allegiance to the "Upright One" (the risen Christ) and summoned to testify to all human beings about what he has seen and heard. Added to this account is the vision in the Jerusalem Temple, which supplies the context of Paul's "call." From there he is to go afar, to the Gentiles. The risen Christ tells him to "depart" from this Jewish matrix and setting. Luke also weaves Paul's past into this form of the conversion story, because he is eager to show the continuity of Christianity with the Judaism that preceded it.

(167) In chap. 26 Paul's speech again purports to be a defense, when he tells of his experience to King Agrippa and Bernice. Paul's story, as known from chaps. 9 and 22, is now only alluded to in succinct fashion. The essentials are recounted, but Ananias disappears completely, and the mandate comes directly from the risen Christ (26:15–18). Paul refers to his past as a Pharisee, and the secondary motif in Luke-Acts begins to emerge: Christianity is a *religio licita* in the Roman empire, just as much as Judaism is, because it is the logical outgrowth of Pharisaic Judaism. There may be theological differences between Jews and Christians, but in this matter Roman competence has no say. In the form of the story in chap. 26 the blinding-healing sequence disappears, and there is no mention of Paul's baptism.

(168) The threefold repetition of the account in Acts is deliberate, for it comes at decisive moments in the story of testimony and the spread of the Word from Jerusalem. In chap. 9 the account is related to the spread of the Word to the Gentiles, sandwiched in between the story of the conversion of the Ethiopian eunuch (8:26–40) and that of the conversion of Cornelius (10:1–33). It thus precedes the mission to the Gentiles. In chap. 22 it will be related to the struggle of Christianity for liberty and independence from its Jewish matrix, and in chap. 26 it will be recounted when Rome's authority has been invoked to protect Christianity. Under such protection the testimony to the gospel and the spread of the Word will make their way "to the end of the earth" (1:8).

(169) Another way of characterizing the three accounts is to look at the way Luke has depicted Paul in each of them. Even though Luke is reluctant to give Paul the title "apostle" (used only in 14:4, 14), the way Paul is described in chap. 9 accords him certain features used of apostles. He may be "the chosen instrument," but he is indirectly compared with the others. Compare 9:15–17 with 1:9; 2:4, 40: Paul has seen the *Kyrios*, the risen Christ; he has been filled with the

Spirit; he has begun to proclaim Jesus. In effect, Luke is insinuating an equality of Paul with the apostles, even though he never puts it just that way. Paul has become a suffragan apostle. In chap. 22, Paul is the "witness" who sees, with various instances of *martys, martyrein* used of him (see vv 5, 12, 15, 18, 20 [compared to Stephen]), perceiving the "light" and the *doxa*, "glory" (vv 6, 9, 11), gazing on the "Upright One" (22:14). In chap. 26, the emphasis is rather on Paul as the prophet (vv. 16–18), with allusions to the inaugural vision of Ezekiel (2:1, 6) and Jeremiah (1:8); compare Isa 35:5; 42:7; 61:1. Moses and the prophets support his message about Christ (26:21); finally he asks whether Agrippa believes the prophets (16:27). Thus one detects the Lucan effort to present Paul as one who continues the work of Jesus, the Prophet (see *Luke*, 213–15). In the person of Paul he is at work, and so Paul becomes a worthy successor of the apostles, testifying to Christ and carrying his Word "to the end of the earth" (1:8). He bears it as the messenger of universal salvation.

F. PAUL'S ROMAN CITIZENSHIP

(170) Above I said that Paul's Roman citizenship is a detail that is almost universally admitted, even though nothing is said about it in Paul's letters. In the last decade or so, however, it has become a new issue of debate, because his Roman citizenship is known only from Acts. In an article published in 1987, W. Stegemann marshaled arguments against the status of Paul as a Roman citizen, maintaining that it was a Lucan literary creation, concocted to serve an apologetic purpose. He queries the entire Lucan story about Paul and his relation to Roman authority, insists that Paul's low social status (a craftsman) and Jewish background would have made it impossible for him to have such citizenship, and denies that Paul had it because he never mentions it in any of his letters. Stegemann's thesis, however, is overdrawn, and his radical skepticism is unwarranted. Noted experts in Roman history, such as Mommsen, Sherwin-Wright, and Hengel, have had no difficulty in admitting that Paul was a Roman citizen. The fact that Paul plied the trade of a tentmaker does not mean that he was of lower social standing, to say nothing of his boast of not depending on any of his communities for financial support (2 Cor 11:7–9) and his willingness to remember the poor (Gal 2:10). Paul would not have been the only Jew to have acquired Roman citizenship (see Josephus, *Ant.* 12.3.1 §§121–23; 14.10.13 §228; 14.10.18–19 §§237, 240). As for the failure of Paul's letters to mention his Roman citizenship, that may be sheer coincidence, since those letters are not autobiographical and in most instances were written to handle ad hoc problems, without any concern or opportunity to mention his Roman citizenship. He undoubtedly attached no importance to it (apart from occasions such as we learn about in Acts). To argue, then, as Stegemann does, is an instance of the worst kind of use of the argument from silence. Because Paul did not use his *tria nomina* (praenomen, nomen, and cognomen) in his letters means nothing, whereas the fact that he constantly called himself *Paulos*, and not *Saulos*, is sufficient indication of his Roman status. Finally, it is

significant that Lüdemann, an archskeptic when it comes to the historical value of Acts, has had to admit that Paul was indeed a Roman citizen; see *Early Christianity*, 240–41.

G. THE "PAULINISM" OF ACTS

(171) Apart from the way Paul's experience on the road to Damascus is depicted in Acts, there are other ways in which Luke has given a twist to the Pauline story. Even though the Lucan interpretation of Pauline teaching in Acts had been discussed in various ways earlier, in 1950 Philipp Vielhauer published an article, "Zum 'Paulinismus' der Apostelgeschichte" (in English, "On the 'Paulinism' of Acts"), which has become the modern formulation of the problem and the matter of much debate ever since. In it Vielhauer studied the way in which Luke presented "Paul's theology." Limiting himself to the Pauline speeches, he discussed four topics: natural theology, law, christology, and eschatology. These he compared with statements on the same topics in Paul's letters.

(172) (a) Under natural theology, Vielhauer compared Paul's speech on the Areopagus (Acts 17) mainly with Rom 1:18–32. The former used Stoic ideas about the true knowledge of God, emphasizing pagan ignorance of God, but also God's providence for and kinship with humanity, and his overlooking of such ignorance; the speech calls for an enlightened understanding of God and for repentance. The Lucan Paul thus espouses a Hellenistic natural theology. In Romans, however, Paul accuses pagans in that, though they had some knowledge of God (in a Stoic sense), they have failed to honor and thank him, and their consequent suppression of the truth has led to their ungodliness and wickedness. Consequently, pagans are inexcusable (1:20) and subject to God's wrath. Whereas Paul on the Areopagus stresses pagan ignorance that can lead to faith, Paul in Romans accuses pagans: their knowledge did not lead them to praise God and has led only to their degradation. Whereas for the Paul of Acts the natural knowledge of God needs only to be purified, corrected, and enlarged, for the Paul of Romans that defective knowledge reveals pagan responsibility for their consequent degradation. Paul in his letters never speaks of the kinship of God with humanity, for only "in Christ" is redeemed humanity united with God. Acts 17 does not mention "sin" or "grace," and the "word of the cross" has no place in it.

(173) (b) As for Paul and the law, Vielhauer maintains that Acts depicts Paul (i) preaching at first in synagogues and turning to Gentiles only on Jewish rejection; (ii) submitting to Jewish authorities; (iii) having Timothy circumcised (16:3); (iv) spreading the Jerusalem decree (16:4); (v) taking a vow (18:18); (vi) journeying to Jerusalem for Jewish feasts (18:21; 20:16) and bringing alms to the people of his race (24:17); (vii) participating in a purification ritual and paying the expenses of a Nazirite vow ceremony (21:18–28); (viii) stressing that he is a Pharisee and stands for the Jewish hope of resurrection (23:6; 26:5). Thus in Acts Paul is a missionary to Gentiles, but also a Jewish Christian, who accepts Jesus

as the Messiah, but who is also loyal to the law and stresses its validity for Jews. Contrast, however, Gal 2:9 ("we to the Gentiles, they to the circumcised"); 2 Cor 11:24 ("five times lashed by the Jews"); 1 Cor 9:21 ("to those outside the law I became as one outside it, but under the law of Christ"). Paul boasted of his freedom from the law, which might tolerate some Jewish observance, but he taught that the Mosaic law was not the way of salvation, that circumcision was not a condition for it, and that Jewish customs were of no relevance. Moses had introduced "the dispensation of death" (2 Cor 3:7). To submit to circumcision would be to admit that Christ has been of no avail (Gal 5:2–6). Acts, however, ascribes to Paul's opponents a motivation for their hostility that is everything but freedom from the law, and it depicts him preaching as if he never said anything about Judaism and its law. The statement about the circumcision of Timothy stands in direct contradiction of Paul's theology as expressed in Gal 5:2. Acts allows Paul to express himself negatively about the law only in 13:38–39, where Pauline justification is equated with forgiveness of sins (an idea that does not occur in uncontested Pauline letters), and this is tied to the messiahship of Jesus and his resurrection (bypassing his death). Luke never fully understood the central significance of Pauline justification, and though he may have understood the inadequacy of the law, he did not speak of its "end," as did Paul (Rom 10:4). There is no clear understanding of the Pauline antithesis of Christ and the law.

(174) (c) As for Paul's preaching in Acts, Vielhauer thinks that it concerns in general God's kingdom (19:8; 20:25; 28:23, 31) or Jesus (17:18; 19:13; 22:18; 25:19) or other vague topics. His christological statements are found in two speeches: to Jews at Pisidian Antioch (13:13–43) and to King Agrippa (26:22–23). In them Paul preaches that Jesus is the Messiah promised of old, the first to be raised from the dead, to bring light to his people and to Gentiles (26:22–23); the suffering and resurrection of Jesus fulfill all that was written about him in the OT, especially in Ps 16:10 (13:29). The Christian mission is related to his resurrection (13:32), for he is Savior and Son of God (cf. Ps 2:7). To such affirmations there are parallels, indeed, in Paul's letters, especially in Rom 1:3–4 and 1 Cor 15:3–4, but the upshot is that the christological formulations in Paul's speeches in Acts 13 and 26 are neither specifically Lucan nor specifically Pauline. Paul's speech in Acts 13 is akin to that of Peter in Acts 2, both having a kerygma in the form of a brief *vita Jesu*, a scripture proof, and a call for repentance. The christology ascribed to Paul in these speeches is in reality derived from that of the earliest congregations rather than from Paul. The christology is adoptionistic, not preexistence christology, and there is no theology of the cross or redemptive significance of the death of Jesus Christ (as in Rom 5:6–11; 2 Cor 5:14–21).

(175) (d) As for the eschatology of Paul, Vielhauer maintains that in Acts it disappears or leads only a modest existence on the periphery of the speeches. The return of Christ as judge is affirmed in 17:30–31 and becomes part of Lucan teaching on the last things. Eschatology has been removed from the center of Pauline faith, and in fact Lucan eschatology differs even from that of the earliest congregations. Contrast Gal 4:4; Rom 8:19–21; 1 Cor 7:29–31; 15:12–58, where

eschatology is a structural element of christology. Although Luke has some idea of the new aeon (Act 2:16–35), the important thing is that one must await the "restoration" (3:19–21). The Lucan "already" and "not yet" are understood quantitatively: the time between Pentecost and the parousia is the age of the Spirit and of progressive evangelization of the world. Luke's conception of history is that of a continuous salvific historical process. How uneschatologically Luke thinks is apparent from the fact of Acts itself; the earliest congregation, which expected the imminent end of the world, had no interest in leaving to posterity reports about its origin and development. Acts is not intended as kerygma or as "witness," but as a historically reliable account of the "witnesses of Jesus" and their "testimony to Jesus," which they set forth in the power of the Holy Spirit from Jerusalem to the end of the earth (1:8). This leads only to the early catholic church.

(176) Hence, according to Vielhauer, the author of Acts is in his christology pre-Pauline, in his natural theology, concept of the law, and eschatology, post-Pauline. He presents no specifically Pauline idea. His "Paulinism" consists in his zeal for the worldwide Gentile mission and in his veneration for the greatest missionary to the Gentiles.

This is, however, a clearly exaggerated view of the differences between the theology of Lucan Paul and that of the Paul of the uncontested letters, as many writers have since pointed out. Reaction to the Vielhauer view has come most strongly from Scandinavian and Dutch scholars. Lucan theology, even Luke's interpretation of Paul's teaching, may have to be regarded as a development beyond what is found in Paul's uncontested letters, but that does not mean that he has given us such a biased view of Paulinism, as Vielhauer implies.

(177) What Paul is made to utter in the Areopagus address may seem to be different from what Paul wrote in Rom 1:18–32, but that is not the only place in which Paul treats of pagans' knowledge of God. In 1 Cor 1:21 ("Since in God's wisdom the world did not know God through wisdom, it pleased God through the folly of what we preach to save those who come to believe"), one finds a differently nuanced statement that sounds more like the teaching of the Areopagus address. Moreover, in Romans 9–11 we see Paul coping with the rejection of the gospel by his former coreligionists in a way that is not unlike the narrative accounts that Luke presents of such rejection of Paul's preaching. Compare in particular Paul's use of Deut 29:4 (God giving a spirit of stupor and eyes that see not, ears that hear not) in Rom 11:7–8 with what the Lucan Paul preaches in Acts 28:26–28, quoting Isa 6:9–10. If Luke thinks so uneschatologically as Vielhauer contends, then how does one explain his depiction of "two men dressed in white robes" telling the Galileans that "this Jesus, who has been taken up from you into the heavens, will come in the same way you saw him go" (1:11)? Only Luke in the entire NT makes such an eschatological affirmation. As van Unnik once wrote apropos of the approach of Vielhauer and related interpretations of Luke-Acts, "The exegetical basis for many statements in the modern approach to Luke-Acts is often far from convincing" ("Luke-Acts, a Storm Center," 28).

BIBLIOGRAPHY

Barnikol, E., *Die drei Jerusalemreisen des Paulus* (Kiel: Mühlau, 1929).

Bondi, R. A., "Become Such as I Am: St. Paul in the Acts of the Apostles," *BTB* 17 (1997) 164–76.

Broughton, T.R.S., "Three Notes on Saint Paul's Journeys in Asia Minor," *Quantulacumque: Studies Presented to Kirsopp Lake* . . . (ed. R. P. Casey et al.; London: Christophers, 1937), 131–38.

Burchard, C., *Der dreizehnte Zeuge: Traditions- und kompositionsgeschichtliche Untersuchungen zu Lukas' Darstellung der Frühzeit des Paulus* (FRLANT 103; Göttingen: Vandenhoeck & Ruprecht, 1970).

———, "Paulus in der Apostelgeschichte," *TLZ* 100 (1975): 881–95.

Ch'en, Chia-shih, "The Role of Paul in the Acts of the Apostles," *Taiwan Journal of Theology* 1 (1979): 109–24.

Conzelmann, H., "Luke's Place in the Development of Early Christianity," *StLA*, 298–316.

Dibelius, M., "Paul in the Acts of the Apostles," *Studies*, 207–14.

Dobschütz, E. von, "Die Berichte über die Bekehrung des Paulus," *ZNW* 29 (1930): 144–47.

Dockx, S., "Luc a-t-il été le compagnon d'apostolat de Paul?" *NRT* 103 (1981): 385–400.

Dumais, M., "Les Actes des Apôtres: Bilan et orientations" (see p. 110), 317–22.

Dupont, J., "Notes sur les Actes des Apôtres," *RB* 62 (1955) 45–59; repr. *Études*, 163–71, 521–25.

———, "Pierre et Paul dans les Actes," *RB* 64 (1957) 35–47; repr. *Études*, 174–84.

Eltester, W., "Lukas und Paulus," *Eranion: Festschrift für Hildebrecht Hommel* (Tübingen: Niemeyer, 1961), 1–17.

Enslin, M. S., "Emphases and Silences," *HTR* 73 (1980): 219–25.

———, "'Luke' and Paul," *JAOS* 58 (1938): 81–91.

———, "Luke, the Literary Physician," *Studies in New Testament and Early Christian Literature: Essays in Honor of Allen P. Wikgren* (NovTSup 33; Leiden: Brill, 1972), 135–43.

Fitzmyer, J. A., *According to Paul: Studies in the Theology of the Apostle* (New York: Paulist, 1993), 36–46.

Foakes-Jackson, F. J., *The Life of St. Paul: The Man and the Apostle* (New York: Boni & Liveright, 1926; London: Jonathan Cape, 1927).

Franklin, E., *Luke: Interpreter of Paul, Critic of Matthew* (JSNTSup 92; Sheffield, UK: JSOT, 1994), 39–161.

Gasque, W. W., A *History of the Criticism*, 287–91.

Gnilka, J., *Paulus von Tarsus Apostel und Zeuge* (HTKNTSup 6; Freiburg im B.: Herder, 1996).

Goulder, M. D., "Did Luke Know Any of the Pauline Letters?" *PRS* 13 (1986): 97–112.

Ham, W., *Paul's First Missionary Journey* (Independence, MO: Herald Publ. House, 1989).

Harnack, A., *Date*, 30–89.

Hengel, M., *The Pre-Christian Paul* (London: SCM, 1991).

Hirsch, E., "Die drei Berichte der Apostelgeschichte über die Bekehrung des Paulus," *ZNW* 28 (1929): 305–12.

Howell, E., "St. Paul and the Greek World," *ExpTim* 71 (1959–60): 328–32; *GR* 11 (1964): 10–29.

Hurtado, L. W., "Convert, Apostate or Apostle to the Nations: The 'Conversion' of Paul in Recent Scholarship," *SR* 22 (1993): 273–84.

Jervell, J., "Paul in the Acts of the Apostles: Tradition, History, Theology," *Les Actes des Apôtres* (ed. J. Kremer), 297–306.

———, *The Unknown Paul: Essays on Luke-Acts and Early Christian History* (Minneapolis: Augsburg, 1984).

Knox, J., "Acts and the Pauline Letter Corpus," *StLA*, 279–87.

———, *Chapters in a Life of Paul* (Nashville: Abingdon, 1950).

Lentz, J. C., Jr., *Luke's Portrait of Paul* (SNTSMS 77; Cambridge: Cambridge University Press, 1993).

Löning, K., *Die Saulustradition in der Apostelgeschichte* (NTAbh 2/9; Münster in W.: Aschendorff, 1973).

Lohfink, G., *The Conversion of St. Paul: Narrative and History in Acts* (Herald Scriptural Library; Chicago: Franciscan Herald, 1976).

Lüdemann, G., *Early Christianity*, 106–20, 146–267.

Mattill, A. J., "The Value of Acts as a Source for the Study of Paul," *Perspectives on Luke-Acts* (ed. C. H. Talbert), 76–98.

Moessner, D. P., "Paul in Acts: Preacher of Eschatological Repentance to Israel," *NTS* 34 (1988): 96–104.

Morgado, J., "Paul in Jerusalem: A Comparison of His Visits in Acts and Galatians," *JETS* 37 (1994): 55–68.

Murphy-O'Connor, J., *Paul: A Critical Life* (Oxford: Clarendon, 1996).

———, *St. Paul's Corinth: Texts and Archaeology* (GNS 6; Wilmington, DE: Glazier, 1983).

Pervo, R. I., *Luke's Story of Paul* (Minneapolis: Fortress, 1990).

Radl, W., "Paulus traditus: Jesus und sein Missionar im lukanischen Doppelwerk," *EA* 50 (1974): 163–67.

Ramsay, W. M., *The Cities of St. Paul: Their Influence on His Life and Thought* (New York: Armstrong, 1908).

———, *St. Paul the Traveller and the Roman Citizen* (London: Hodder & Stoughton, 1896).

Rapske, B., *The Book of Acts and Paul in Roman Custody* (BAFCS 3, 1994).

———, "The Importance of Helpers to the Imprisoned Paul in the Book of Acts," *TynBull* 42 (1991): 3–30.

Rosenblatt, M.-E., *Paul the Accused: His Portrait in the Acts of the Apostles* (Zacchaeus Studies, NT series; Collegeville, MN: Liturgical, 1995).

Schenk, W., "Luke as Reader of Paul: Observations on His Reception," *Intertextuality in Biblical Writings: Essays in Honour of Bas van Iersel* (ed. S. Draisma; Kampen: Kok, 1989), 127–39.

Seidensticker, P., *Paulus, der verfolgte Apostel Jesu Christi* (SBS 8; Stuttgart: Katholisches Bibelwerk, 1965).

Slater, T. B., "The Presentation of Paul in Acts," *Bible Bhashyam* 19 (1993): 19–46.

Stolle, V., *Der Zeuge als Angeklagter: Untersuchungen zum Paulusbild des Lukas* (BWANT 102; Stuttgart: Kohlhammer, 1973).

Strecker, G. and T. Nolting, "Der vorchristliche Paulus: Überlegungen zum biographischen Kontext biblischer Überlieferung—zugleich eine Antwort an Martin Hengel," *Texts and Contexts: Biblical Texts in Their Textual and Situational Contexts: Essays in Honor of Lars Hartman* (ed. T. Fornberg and D. Hellholm; Oslo/Boston: Scandinavian University Press, 1995), 713–41.

Tajra, H. W., *The Trial of St. Paul.*

Thornton, C.-J., *Der Zeuge des Zeugen: Lukas als Historiker der Paulusreisen* (WUNT 56; Tübingen: Mohr [Siebeck], 1991).

The Chronology of Paul's Career

Dockx, S., "Chronologie de la vie de Saint Paul, depuis sa conversion jusqu'à son séjour à Rome," *NovT* 13 (1971): 261–304.

Duncan, G. S., "Chronological Table to Illustrate Paul's Ministry in Asia," *NTS* 5 (1958–59): 43–45.

———, "Paul's Ministry in Asia—The Last Phase: *autos epeschen chronon eis tēn Asian* (Acts xix. 22)," *NTS* 3 (1956–57): 211–18.

Hyldahl, N., *Die paulinische Chronologie* (Acta theologica danica 19; Leiden: Brill, 1986).

Jewett, R., *A Chronology of Paul's Life* (Philadelphia: Fortress, 1979).

Lüdemann, G., *Paul Apostle to the Gentiles: Studies in Chronology* (Philadelphia: Fortress, 1984).

Murphy-O'Connor, J., "Pauline Missions before the Jerusalem Conference," *RB* 89 (1982): 71–91.

Ogg, G., *The Chronology of the Life of Paul* (London: Epworth, 1968).

Slingerland, D., "Acts 18:1–17 and Lüdemann's Pauline Chronology," *JBL* 109 (1990): 686–90.

Suhl, A., *Paulus und seine Briefe: Ein Beitrag zur paulinischen Chronologie* (SNT 11; Gütersloh: Mohn, 1975), 299–345.

Paul's Visits to Jerusalem after His Conversion

Beare, F. W., "Note on Paul's First Two Visits to Jerusalem," *JBL* 63 (1944): 407–9.

Benoit, P., "La deuxième visite de saint Paul à Jérusalem," *Bib* 40 (1959): 778–92; repr. *Exégèse et théologie*, 3.285–99.

De Lacey, D. R., "Paul in Jerusalem," *NTS* 20 (1973–74): 82–86.

Funk, R. W., "The Enigma of the Famine Visit," *JBL* 75 (1956): 130–36.

Giet, S., "Nouvelles remarques sur les voyages de saint Paul à Jérusalem," *RevScRel* 31 (1957): 329–42.

———, "Le second voyage de saint Paul à Jérusalem, Actes xi, 27–30; xii, 24–25," *RevScRel* 25 (1951): 265–69.

Jeremias, J., "Sabbathjahr und neutestamentliche Chronologie," *ZNW* 27 (1928): 98–103.

Polhill, J. B., "Galatia Revisited, the Life-Setting of the Epistle," *RevExp* 69 (1972): 437–47.

Strecker, G., "Die sogenannte zweite Jerusalemreise des Paulus (Acts 11, 27–30)," *ZNW* 53 (1962): 67–77; repr. *Eschaton und Historie: Aufsätze* (Göttingen: Vandenhoeck & Ruprecht, 1979), 132–41.

Talbert, C. H., "Again: Paul's Visits to Jerusalem," *NovT* 9 (1967): 26–40.

Paul's Roman Citizenship

Hengel, M., *The Pre-Christian Paul,* 1–17.

Lüdemann, G., *Early Christianity,* 240–41.

Mommsen, T., "Die Rechtsverhältnisse des Apostels Paulus," *ZNW* 2 (1901): 81–96.

Sherwin-White, A. N., *Roman Society,* 144–93.

Stegemann, W., "War der Apostel Paulus ein römischer Bürger?" *ZNW* 78 (1987): 200–29.

Tajra, H. W., *The Trial of St. Paul,* 81–89, 197–201.

Wenger, L., "Bürgerrecht," *RAC* 2 (1954): 778–86.

The "Paulinism" of Acts

Bacon, B. W., *The Story of St. Paul: A Comparison of Acts and Epistles* (Boston/New York: Houghton, Mifflin and Co., 1904).

Barrett, C. K., "Acts and the Pauline Corpus," *ExpTim* 88 (1976–77): 2–5.

Bauernfeind, O., "Vom historischen zum lukanischen Paulus: Eine Auseinandersetzung mit Götz Harbsmeier," *EvT* 13 (1953): 347–53.

———, "Zur Frage nach der Entscheidung zwischen Paulus und Lukas," *ZST* 23 (1954): 59–88.

Borgen, P., "From Paul to Luke: Observations toward Clarification of the Theology of Luke-Acts," *CBQ* 31 (1969): 168–82.

Bornkamm, G., "The Missionary Stance of Paul in I Corinthians 9 and in Acts," *StLA,* 194–207.

Brawley, R. L., "Paul in Acts: Lucan Apology and Conciliation," *Luke-Acts: New Perspectives* (ed. C. H. Talbert), 129–47.

Bruce, F. F., "Is the Paul of Acts the Real Paul?" *BJRL* 58 (1975–76): 282–305.

Conzelmann, H., "Luke's Place in the Development of Early Christianity," *StLA,* 298–316.

Dahl, N. A., "Ordets Vekst: Skrevet til femtiårsjubileet i den eksegetiske forening, Clavis Veritas, 1940," *NorTT* 67 (1966): 32–46.

Haenchen, E., "The Book of Acts as Source Material for the History of Early Christianity," *StLA*, 258–87.

Harbsmeier, G., "Unsere Predigt im Spiegel der Apostelgeschichte," *EvT* 11 (1950–51): 352–68.

Jervell, J., "Zur Frage der Traditionsgrundlage der Apostelgeschichte," *ST* 16 (1962): 25–41.

Löning, K., "Paulinismus in der Apostelgeschichte," *Paulus in den neutestamentlichen Spätschriften: Zu Paulusrezeption im Neuen Testament* (QD 89; Freiburg im B.: Herder, 1981), 202–31.

Marshall, I. H., "Luke's View of Paul," *SwJT* 33 (1990): 41–51.

Müller, P. G., "Der 'Paulinismus' in der Apostelgeschichte: Ein forschungsgeschichtlicher Überblick," *Paulus in den neutestamentlichen Spätschriften* (see Löning above), 157–201.

Unnik, W. C. van, "Luke-Acts, a Storm Center in Contemporary Scholarship," *StLA*, 15–32, esp. 28–29.

Vielhauer, P., "Zum 'Paulinismus' der Apostelgeschichte," *EvT* 10 (1950–51): 1–15; "On the 'Paulinism' of Acts," *PSTJ* 17 (1963): 5–17; repr. *StLA*, 33–50.

Wenham, D., "The Paulinism of Acts Again: Two Historical Clues in 1 Thessalonians," *Themelios* 13 (1987–88): 53–55.

Wilckens, U., "Interpreting Luke-Acts in a Period of Existentialist Theology," *StLA*, 60–83.

———, "Lukas und Paulus unter dem Aspekt dialektisch-theologisch beeinflusster Exegese," *Rechtfertigung als Freiheit: Paulusstudien* (Neukirchen-Vluyn: Neukirchener-V., 1974), 171–202.

General Bibliography

◆

General Sources

◆

(178) Bibliography of Bibliographies

Hadidian, D. Y. (ed.), *A Periodical and Monographic Index to the Literature on the Gospels and Acts Based on the Files of the École Biblique in Jerusalem* (Pittsburgh: Pittsburgh Theological Seminary, 1971), 295–330.

Mattill, A. J., Jr. and M. B. Mattill, *A Classified Bibliography of Literature on the Acts of the Apostles* (NTTS 7; Leiden: Brill, 1966) [through 1961].

Metzger, B. M., *Index to Periodical Literature on the Apostle Paul* (NTTS 1; Leiden: Brill, 1960), 4–24.

Mills, W. E., *A Bibliography of the Periodical Literature on the Acts of the Apostles 1962–1984* (NovTSup 58; Leiden: Brill, 1986).

Stuehrenberg, P. F., "The Study of Acts before the Reformation: A Bibliographic Introduction," *NovT* 29 (1987): 100–36.

Wagner, G., *An Exegetical Bibliography of the New Testament: Luke and Acts* (Macon: Mercer University Press, 1985).

(179) Surveys

Allen, D. L., "Acts Studies in the 1990's: Unity and Diversity," *CrisTR* 5 (1990): 3–13.

Bovon, F., "Du côté de chez Luc," *RTP* 115 (1983): 175–89.

———, "Études lucaniennes: Rétrospective et prospective," *RTP* 125 (1993): 113–35.

———, *Luc le théologien: Vingt-cinq ans de recherches (1950–1975)* (Monde de la Bible; Neuchâtel/Paris: Delachaux et Niestlé, 1978), 89–117.

———, *Luke the Theologian: Thirty-three Years of Research (1950–1983)* (Allison Park, PA: Pickwick Publications, 1987), 82–108.

———, "Orientations actuelles des études lucaniennes," *RTP* 108 (1976): 161–90.

———, "Studies in Luke-Acts: Retrospect and Prospect," *HTR* 85 (1992): 175–96.

Bruce, F. F., "The Acts of the Apostles Today," *BJRL* 65 (1982–83): 36–56.

———, "The True Apostolic Succession: Recent Study of the Book of Acts," *Int* 13 (1959): 131–43.

Corsani, B., "Bulletin de Nouveau Testament: Etudes lucaniennes," *ETR* 64 (1989): 83–93.

Dumais, M., "Les Actes des Apôtres: Bilan et orientations," *"De bien des manières": Recherche biblique aux abords du XXIe siècle* (LD 163; ed. M. Gourgues et L. Laberge; Montreal: Fides; Paris: Cerf, 1995), 307–64.

Dupont, J., "Luc le théologien: Vingt-cinq ans de recherches (1950–1975): A propos d'un ouvrage de François Bovon," *RTL* 10 (1979): 218–25; repr. *Nouvelles études*, 13–23.

———, *Les problèmes du livre des Actes d'après les travaux récents* (ALBO 2/17; Louvain: Publications Universitaires de Louvain, 1950); repr. *Études*, 11–124.

Fuller, R. H., *The New Testament in Current Study* (New York: Scribner, 1962), 86–100 ("The Lucan Writings").

Gasque, W. W., "A Fruitful Field: Recent Study of the Acts of the Apostles," *Int* 42 (1988): 117–31.

———, *A History of the Criticism of the Acts of the Apostles* (BGBE 17; Tübingen: Mohr [Siebeck]; Grand Rapids, MI: Eerdmans, 1975); repr. as *History of the Interpretation of the Acts of the Apostles* (Peabody, MA: Henrickson, 1989).

Grässer, E., "Acta-Forschung seit 1960," *TRu* 41 (1976): 141–94, 259–90; 42 (1977): 1–68.

———, "Die Apostelgeschichte in der Forschung der Gegenwart," *TRu* 26 (1960): 93–167.

Guillet, J., "Bulletin d'exégèse lucanienne," *RSR* 69 (1981): 425–42.

Guthrie, D., "Recent Literature on the Acts of the Apostles," *Vox evangelica* 2 (1963): 33–49.

Jáuregui, J. A., "Historiografía y teología en Hechos: Estado de la investigación desde 1980," *EstBíb* 53 (1995): 97–123.

Kümmel, W. G., "Das Urchristentum," *TRu* 14 (1942): 81–95; 17 (1948–49) 3–50, 103–42; 18 (1950) 1–53; 22 (1954) 138–70, 191–211.

Plümacher, E., "Acta-Forschung 1974–1982," *TRu* 48 (1983): 1–56; 49 (1984) 105–69.

Powell, M. A., *What Are They Saying about Acts?* (New York: Paulist, 1991).

Schneider, G., "Literatur zum lukanischen Doppelwerk: Neuerscheinungen 1990/91," *TRev* 88 (1992): 1–18.

Unnik, W. C. van, "Luke-Acts: A Storm Center in Contemporary Scholarship," *StLA*, 15–32; repr. *Sparsa collecta*, 1.92–110.

Vouga, F., "Bulletin de Nouveau Testament," *ETR* 58 (1983): 537–49, esp. 544–49.

Windisch, H., "Urchristentum," *TRu* 5 (1933): 186–200, 239–58, 289–301, 319–34.

(180) COMMENTARIES

Bruce, F. F., "Commentaries on Acts," *Epworth Review* 8 (1981): 82–87.

———, "Commentaries on Acts," *BT* 40 (1989): 315–21.

Cowen, G., "Commenting on Commentaries on Acts," *CrisTReview* 5 (1990): 93–97.

Gasque, W. W., "Recent Commentaries on the Acts of the Apostles," *Themelios* 14 (1988–89): 21–23.

Ghidelli, C., "Tre recenti commenti in lingua tedesca agli Atti degli Apostoli," *ScCatt* 93 (1965): 371*–89*.

Neirynck, F., "Le Livre des Actes dans les récents commentaires," *ETL* 59 (1983): 338–49; 60 (1984) 109–17.

O'Neill, J. C., "Commentaries on the Acts of the Apostles," *Theology* 61 (1958): 140–43.

Ziesler, J. A., "Which Is the Best Commentary? V. The Acts of the Apostles," *ExpTim* 98 (1986–87): 73–77.

SOURCES PRESENTED BY PERIOD

◆

(181) I. PATRISTIC PERIOD

(Sections 181, 182, 183 list sources chronologically)

A. GREEK WRITERS

1. *General Items*

Cramer, J. A. (1793–1848), *Catena in Acta SS. Apostolorum e cod. nov. coll. descripsit et nunc primum edidit adiecta lectionis varietate e cod. coislin.* (Oxford: Typographeum Academicum, 1838).

———, *Catenae graecorum patrum in Novum Testamentum* (8 vols.; Oxford: Typographeum Academicum, 1840–44; repr. Hildesheim: Olms, 1967), 3.1–424.

2. *Specific Items*

Origen (184–ca. 253), "Homiliae in Acta Apostolorum," PG 14.829–32 (on Acts 1:16).

Athanasius of Alexandria, "Scholia in Actus," PG 26.1315–18.

Didymus of Alexandria, "Expositio in Actus Apostolorum," PG 39.1653–78.

John Chrysostom (344/54–407), "Homiliae in Actus," PG 51.65–112; "Commentarius in Acta Apostolorum," PG 60.13–384.

Euthalius of Alexandria (fourth century), "Elenchus capitum libri Actuum," PG 85.627–64; "Expositio capitum Actuum Apostolorum," PG 10.1549–58.

Theodore of Mopsuestia (350–428), "In Acta Apostolorum commentarii," PG 66.785–86.

Isidore of Pelusium (d. 435), "Epistularum libri V," PG 78.1671–74.

Cyril of Alexandria (d. 444), "Fragmenta in Acta Apostolorum," PG 74.757–74.

Theodotus of Ancyra (d. 446), "Fragmenta in Actus," PG 77.1431–32.

Hesychius of Jerusalem (d. ca. 450), "Fragmenta in Acta Apostolorum," PG 93.1387–90.

Ammonius of Alexandria (fifth century), "Commentaria in Vetus et Novum Testamentum," PG 85.1523–1608 (on Acts).

Ps.-Oecumenius (eighth century), *Hypomnēmata eis tēs Neas Diathēkēs pragmateias tasde: Commentaria in hosce Novi Testamenti tractatus: In Acta Apostolorum, in omnes Pauli epistolas, in epistolas catholicas omnes* (2 vols.; Paris: Sonn, 1631), 2.1–188; cf. PG 118.25–32, 43–308.

B. LATIN WRITERS

1. *Generic Items*

Stegmüller, F., *Repertorium biblicum medii aevi* (11 vols.; Madrid: Consejo Superior de Investigaciones Científicas, Instituto Francisco Suárez, 1950–80; vols. 8–11, with the assistance of N. Reinhardt; vols. 1–3, repr. 1981): *II–V: Commentaria.*

2. *Specific Items*

Eucharius of Lyons (d. 449), "Instructionum ad Salonium libri duo," CSEL 31.63–161.

Arator of Rome (500–50), "De Actibus Apostolorum," CSEL 72.9–149; PL 68.81–246. Cf. R. Hillier, *Arator on the Acts of the Apostles: A Baptismal Commentary* (Oxford Early Christian Studies; Oxford: Clarendon, 1993); R. J. Schrader, *On the Acts of the Apostles (De Actibus Apostolorum)* (Classics in Religious Studies 6; Atlanta: Scholars, 1987).

Cassiodorus, Senator (485–553), "Complexiones Actuum Apostolorum," PL 70.1381–1406.

Gregory I, Pope, "De expositione Veteris ac Novi Testamenti," PL 79.1085–96 (on Acts); "Expositio super Acta Apostolorum," PL 79.1269–92.

Isidore of Seville, "In libros Veteris ac Novi Testamenti prooemia," PL 83.155–80, esp. 178 (on Acts).

Bede the Venerable (673–735), *Expositio Actuum Apostolorum et retractatio* (MAA Publ. 35; ed. M.L.W. Laistner; Cambridge, MA: Medieval Academy of America, 1939; repr. New York: Kraus, 1970), 3–90. Cf. PL 92.937–1032. L. T. Martin (ed.), *Commentary on the Acts of the Apostles: Translated, with an Introduction and Notes* (Cistercian Studies 117; Kalamazoo: Cistercian Publications, 1989).

C. SYRIAC WRITERS

1. *Generic Items*

McCullough, J. C., "Early Syriac Commentaries on the New Testament," *Theological Review* (Beirut) 5 (1982): 14–33, 79–126.

2. *Specific Items*

Ephraem Syrus (306–373), *Commentary on the Acts of the Apostles* (ed. N. W. Akinian; Critical Editions of the Literature and Translations of the Ancient Armenians II/1; Venice: Mechitarist Brethren, 1921). Cf. F. C. Conybeare, "The Commentary of Ephrem on Acts," *Beginnings*, 3.373–453.

(182) II. Medieval Period

A. GREEK WRITERS

Theophylact of Ochrida (Bulgaria, 1050–1108), "Argumentum libri Actorum," PG 125.438–1132.

Theodore Prodromus (d. ca. 1166), "Epigrammata in Vetus et Novum Testamentum," PG 133.1101–1220, esp. 1209–20 (on Acts).

B. LATIN WRITERS

Ps.-Fulbert of Chartres (960–1028), "In illud Act. 12:1, Misit rex manus," PL 141.277–306.

Peter Damian (1007–1072), "Testimonia Actuum," PL 145.901–4.

Anselm of Laon (d. 1117), "Glossa ordinaria in Actus Apostolorum," PL 114.425–70. Cf. *Biblia latina una cum glossa ordinaria Walafridi Strabonis et interlineari Anselmi Laudunensis* (Strassburg: A. Rusch, 1479) 4.

Richard of St. Victor (?–1173), "De Actibus Apostolorum," PL 141.277–306.

Pierre de Poitiers (1130–1205), "Historia Actuum Apostolorum," PL 198.1645–1722.

Peter de Riga (1140–1209), *Aurora Petri Rigae biblia versificata* (2 vols.; ed. P. E. Beichner; Publications in Medieval Studies 19; Notre Dame: University of Notre Dame Press, 1965), 2.626–68.

Hugh of St. Cher (1200–1263), "Liber Actuum Apostolorum," *Opera omnia in universum Vetus et Novum Testamentum* (Venice: Pezzana, 1703), 7.278–309.

Robert de Sorbon (1201–1274), "Glossae divinorum librorum," *Commentarii totius S. Scripturae* (ed. G. S. Menochio; Paris: Robustel, 1719), 510–11.

Nicholas of Gorran (1232–ca. 1295), *In Acta Apostolorum et . . . epistulas & Apocalypsin commentarii* (Antwerp, 1620), 1–59.

Aureolus, Petrus (1280–1322), "Divisio libri Actuum Apostolorum," *Compendium sensus litteralis totius divinae Scripturae* (Strassburg: Schott, 1514; Quaracchi: Coll. S. Bonaventurae, 1896), 365–80.

Nicholas of Lyra (1270–1349), *Postilla super Actus Apostolorum* (Mantua: Paulus de Butzbach, 1480).

Denis the Carthusian (1402–1471), "Enarratio in Actus Apostolorum," *Dionysii Cartusiani opera omnia* (42 vols. in 44; Montreuil-sur-Mer: Cartusia S. M. de Pratis, 1896–1913), 14/1.81–220.

C. SYRIAC WRITERS

Theodore bar Konai (eighth century), "Liber scholiorum," CSCO 55, Scriptores Syri 19; CSCO 69, Scriptores Syri 26.

Isho'dad of Merv (ninth century), *The Commentaries of Isho'dad of Merv, Bishop of Ḥadatha (c. 850 A.D.) in Syriac and English: Vol. IV: Acts of the Apostles* (ed. M. D. Gibson; Horae Semiticae 10; Cambridge: Cambridge University Press, 1913) 1–35.

Dionysius bar Salibi (d. 1171), "In Acta Apostolorum," CSCO 53 and 60, Scriptores Syri 18 and 20.

Bar Hebraeus (Gregorios ibn al-'Ibri, 1226–1286), *In Actus Apostolorum et epistulas catholicas adnotationes syriacae* ... (ed. M. Klamroth; Göttingen: Dieterich, 1878), 1–23.

'Abdisho bar Berika (d. 1318), "Liber expositionis in textum Scripturae Veteris et Novi Testamenti," *Bibliotheca orientalis Clementino Vaticana* (Rome: Propaganda Fide, 1725), 3/1.325–61.

(183) III. Fifteenth- to Eighteenth-Century Writers

Tomaso de Vio Gaetani (Cajetan, 1469–1534), *Epistolae Pauli et aliorum apostolorum ad graecam veritatem castigatae ... Actus Apostolorum commentariis illustrati* (Paris: de Marnef & Cavellat, 1571), 459–513.

Erasmus, Desiderius (1469–1536), *Annotations on the New Testament: Acts, Romans, I and II Corinthians: Facsimile of the Final Latin Text with All Earlier Variants* (Leiden/New York: Brill, 1990).

———, *Paraphrasis ... in Acta Apostolorum* (Lyons: Seb. Gryphius, 1542).

Luther, Martin (1483–1546), *Luthers Episteln-Auslegung: Ein Commentar zur Apostelgeschichte* ... (Berlin: Verlag des Evangelischen Büchervereins, 1870).

Bugenhagen, J. (1485–1558), *Commentarius in Acta Apostolorum* (Wittenberg, 1524).

Calvin, Jean (1509–1564), *The Acts of the Apostles* (Calvin's Commentaries, ed. D. W. and T. F. Torrance; 2 vols.; Grand Rapids, MI: Eerdmans, 1965–66).

Bullinger, J. H., *In Acta Apostolorum ... commentariorum libri VI* (Zurich, 1540).

Hunnius, Aegidius (1550–1603), *Aegidii Hunnii, D., celeberrimi augustanae confessionis theologi, Thesaurus evangelicus, complectens commentarios in quatuor Evangelistas, et Actus Apostolorum* (ed. Jo. H. Feustking; Wittenberg: Meyer et Zimmermann, 1706).

Lapide, C. a (Cornelis Cornelissen van den Steen, 1567–1637), *In Actus Apostolorum* (Commentaria in Scripturam Sacram 17; ed. nova. A. Crampon; Paris: L. Vivès, 1877).

Grotius, H. (Huig de Groot, 1583–1645), *Annotationes in Novum Testamentum* (2 vols.; ed. nova C. E. de Windheim; Erlangen/Leipzig: Tetzchner, 1756–57), 2.1–178.

Bengel, J. A. (1687–1752), *Gnomon Novi Testamenti* (Tübingen: Fues, 1742; 4th ed. by J. Steudel; also London: David Nutt, 1855; 8th ed., 1915), 415–522. Cf. *Gnomon of the New Testament: Now First Translated into English* (tr. A. R. Fausset; 5 vols.; Edinburgh: Clark, 1858); *Gnomon of the New Testament: A*

New Translation (tr. C. T. Lewis and M. R. Vincent; 2 vols.; Philadelphia: Perkinpine and Higgins, 1862), 1.740–925; renamed and repr. *New Testament Word Studies* (Grand Rapids, MI: Kregel, 1971), 1.740–925.

Wettstein, J. J. (1693–1754), *Hē Kainē Diathēkē: Novum Testamentum graecum* . . . (2 vols.; Amsterdam: Dommer, 1751–52), 2.449–657.

Pyle, Thomas (1674–1756), *Paraphrase über die Apostelgeschichte und die apostolischen Briefe des Neuen Testaments* (ed. E. G. Kuster; Hamburg: C. E. Bohn, 1778).

Brugensis, F. L. (ed.), *Biblia Sacra vulgatae editionis . . . cum selectissimis litteralibus commentariis* . . . (28 vols.; Venice: M. Fentius, 1745–57), 25. 3–325.

Plevier, J., *De Handelingen der H. Apostelen beschreeven door Lukas, ontleedt, verklaardt* (Utrecht: Jac. Corn. ten Bosch, 1773).

Calmet, A., *Commentarius literalis in omnes libros Novi Testamenti* . . . (4 vols.; Würzburg: Rienner, 1787–88), 3.1–343.

IV. Nineteenth- and Twentieth-Century Writers

(Ordered alphabetically; the more important commentaries are marked*)

(184) A. COMMENTARIES

Abbott, L., *The Acts of the Apostles: With Notes, Comments* . . . (New York/Chicago: A. S. Barnes & Co., 1876).

Airhart, A. E., *Acts* (Beacon Bible Expositions 5; Kansas City, MO: Beacon Hill, 1977).

Alexander, J. A., *The Acts of the Apostles Explained* (2 vols.; London: Nisbet; New York: Scribner, 1857); repr. as *A Commentary on the Acts of the Apostles* (London: Banner of Truth Trust, 1963).

Alford, H., *The Greek Testament with a Critically Revised Text . . . and a Critical and Exegetical Commentary* . . . (4 vols.; Cambridge, UK: Deighton, Bell, 1849–61; repr. London: Longmans, Green, 1877, 1895, 1899), 2.1–31, 1–310; repr. as *The Greek Testament: An Exegetical and Critical Commentary* (Grand Rapids, MI: Guardian, 1976).

Amiot, F., *Gestes et textes des Apôtres: Actes—Epîtres—Apocalypse* (Paris: Arthème Fayard, 1950), 9–115.

Andel, J. van, *De Handelingen der Apostelen toegelicht* (n.p.: Traktaatgenootschap "Filippus", 1909).

Arrington, F. L., *The Acts of the Apostles: An Introduction and Commentary* (Peabody, MA: Hendrickson, 1988).

Ash, A. L. and R. Oster, *The Acts of the Apostles* (Living Word Commentary 6; 2 vols.; Austin: Sweet Publ. Co., 1979).

Baird, W., "The Acts of the Apostles," *The Interpreter's One-Volume Commentary on the Bible* (ed. C. M. Laymon; Nashville/New York: Abingdon, 1971) 729–67.

Baker, C. F., *Understanding the Book of Acts* (Grand Rapids, MI: Grace Bible College Publications, 1981).

Baker, S., *The Acts of the Apostles, Chapters 1–15: Notes* (Oxford: J. Thornton & Son, 1916).

Baljon, J.M.S., *Commentar op de Handelingen der Apostelen* (Utrecht: J. van Boekhoven, 1903).

Barclay, W., *The Acts of the Apostles* (rev. ed.; Philadelphia: Westminster, 1976).

Bard, B. T., *Apostelgeschichte: Auslegung* (Erzhausen: Leuchter, 1966).

Barde, E., *Commentaire sur les Actes des Apôtres* (Lausanne: Bridel, 1898).

Barker, C. J., *The Acts of the Apostles: A Study in Interpretation* (London: Epworth, 1969).

Barnard, W. J. and P. van't Riet, *Lukas de Jood, Een Joodse inleiding op het Evangelie van Lukas en de Handelingen der Apostelen* (Kampen: Kok, 1984).

Barnes, A., *Notes, Explanatory and Practical, on the Acts of the Apostles* (New York: Leavitt Lord & Co., 1834; 10th ed., London: Ward; New York: Harper & Bros., 1841; often repr.).

*Barrett, C. K., *A Critical and Exegetical Commentary on the Acts of the Apostles* (ICC; 2 vols.; Edinburgh: Clark, 1994, 199?).

Bartlet, J. V., *The Acts: Introduction . . . with Notes, Index and Map* (Century Bible; Edinburgh: Henry Frowde, 1900).

Bassi, D., *Gli Atti degli Apostoli* (Florence: Novissima Enciclopedia Monografica Illustrata, 1933).

*Bauernfeind, O., *Die Apostelgeschichte des Lukas* (THKNT 5; Leipzig: Deichert, 1939).

*———, *Kommentar und Studien zur Apostelgeschichte: Mit einer Einleitung von Martin Hengel* (WUNT 22; ed. V. Metelmann; Tübingen: Mohr [Siebeck], 1980).

Beelen, J. T., *Commentarius in Acta Apostolorum* . . . (2d ed.; Louvain: C.-J. Fonteyn, 1850–51, repr. 1870).

Belser, J. E., *Die Apostelgeschichte* (Kurzgefasster wissenschaftlicher Kommentar zu den Heiligen Schriften des Neuen Testaments 3/1; Vienna: Mayer, 1905; repr. in Biblische Zeitfragen 1/7; 3d ed.; Münster in W.: Aschendorff, 1910).

Beyer, H. W., *Die Apostelgeschichte übersetzt und erklärt* (NTD 5; Göttingen: Vandenhoeck & Ruprecht, 1933; 9th ed., 1959).

Bicknell, E. J., "The Acts of the Apostles," *A New Commentary on Holy Scripture, Including the Apocrypha* (3 parts; ed. C. Gore et al.; London: SPCK, 1928), 3.320–78.

Bisping, A., *Erklärung der Apostelgeschichte* (Exegetisches Handbuch zum Neuen Testament 4; Münster in W.: Aschendorff, 1866; 2d ed., 1871).

Blaiklock, E. M., *The Acts of the Apostles: An Historical Commentary* (TynNTC; London: Tyndale Press; Grand Rapids, MI: Eerdmans, 1959).

———, *Acts, the Birth of the Church: A Commentary* (Old Tappan, NJ: Revell, 1980).

Blass, F., *Acta Apostolorum, sive Lucae ad Theophilum liber alter: Editio philologica apparatu critico, commentario perpetuo, indice verborum illustrata* (Göttingen: Vandenhoeck & Ruprecht, 1895).

———, *Acta Apostolorum secundum formam quae videtur Romanam* (Leipzig: Teubner, 1896).

Blunt, A.W.F., *The Acts of the Apostles in the Revised Version with Introduction and Commentary* (Clarendon Bible; Oxford: Clarendon, 1923; repr. 1962).

Bock, D. L., *Acts* (BECNT; Grand Rapids, MI: Baker Book House, 1997).

*Boismard, M.-E. and A. Lamouille, *Les actes des deux Apôtres: I. Introduction—Textes; II. Le sens des récits; III. Analyses littéraires* (EBib ns 12–14; Paris: Gabalda, 1990).

Boles, H. L., A *Commentary on Acts of the Apostles* (Nashville: Gospel Advocate Co., 1941, repr. 1974).

Bonnet, L., *Actes des Apôtres* (Lausanne: Bridel, 1885).

Boor, W. de, *Die Apostelgeschichte* (Wuppertaler Studienbibel; Wuppertal: Brockhaus, 1965; 4th ed. 1977).

*Bossuyt, P. and J. Radermakers, *Témoins de la Parole de la Grâce: Lecture des Actes des Apôtres* (2 vols.; Brussels: Editions de l'Institut d'Études Théologiques, 1995).

Boudou, A., *Actes des Apôtres* (VS 7; 2d ed.; Paris: Beauchesne, 1933).

Browne, L. E., *The Acts of the Apostles: With Introduction and Notes* (Indian Church Commentaries; London: SPCK; Madras: Diocesan Press, 1925).

*Bruce, F. F., *The Acts of the Apostles: The Greek Text with Introduction and Commentary* (London: Tyndale, 1951; 3d ed., Leicester, UK: Apollos; Grand Rapids, MI: Eerdmans, 1990).

*———, *Commentary on the Book of the Acts: The English Text, with Introduction, Exposition, and Notes* (NICNT; London/Edinburgh: Marshall, Morgan & Scott; Grand Rapids, MI: Eerdmans, 1954; repr. 1988).

Burkitt, W., *Expository Notes with Practical Observations on the New Testament* . . . (2 vols.; Philadelphia: John Ball, 1849), 1. 565–725.

Burnside, W. F., *The Acts of the Apostles* (Cambridge: Cambridge University Press, 1916).

Callan, C. J., *The Acts of the Apostles: With a Practical Critical Commentary* . . . (New York: Wagner; London: B. Herder, 1919).

Camerlynck, A. and A. vander Heeren, *Commentarius in Actus Apostolorum* (Commentarii brugenses in S. Scripturam; 7th ed.; Bruges: Beyaert, 1923).

Carter, C. W. and R. Earle, *The Acts of the Apostles* (London: Oliphants, 1959; Grand Rapids, MI: Zondervan, 1973; repr. Salem, OH: Schmul, 1982).

Cecilia, Madame, *The Acts of the Apostles with Introduction and Annotations* (2 vols. in one; London: Burns, Oates and Washbourne, 1925).

Ceulemans, F. C., *Commentarius in Actus Apostolorum* (Mechlin: Dessain, 1903; 2d ed., 1924).

Charpentier, E., *Une lecture des Actes des Apôtres* (Cahiers Evangile 21; Paris: Cerf, 1977).

Cohausz, O., *Die Apostelgeschichte* (Die Heilige Schrift für das Leben erklärt 12; 2d ed.; Freiburg im B.: Herder, 1937).
*Conzelmann, H., *Acts of the Apostles: A Commentary on the Acts of the Apostles* (Hermeneia; Philadelphia: Fortress, 1987).
Cook, F. C. and W. Jacobson, "The Acts of the Apostles," *The Holy Bible according to the Authorized Version (A.D. 1611), with an Explanatory and Critical Commentary* . . . (12 vols.; ed. F. C. Cook; London: John Murray, 1872–1900); NT 2 (1899), 309–534; repr. in 10 vols. (without the Apocrypha; New York: Scribner, 1890), 8.309–534.
Corsani, B., *Atti degli Apostoli e Lettere* (Guida alla lettura della Biblia; Turin: Claudiana Editrice, 1978).
Cowles, H., *Acts of the Apostles: With Notes Critical, Explanatory, and Practical* . . . (New York: Appleton, 1881; repr. 1883).
Crelier, H. J., *Les Actes des Apôtres* (La Sainte Bible . . . avec commentaires 36; Paris: Lethielleux, 1883).
Criswell, W. A., *Acts, an Exposition* (3 vols.; Grand Rapids, MI: Zondervan, 1978–80; repr. in one vol., 1983).
Crowe, J., *The Acts* (NTM 8; Wilmington, DE: Glazier, 1979).
Delebecque, E., *Les Actes des Apôtres: Texte traduit et annoté* (Collection d'éptudes anciennes; Paris: Belles Lettres, 1982).
Dentler, E., *Die Apostelgeschichte übersetzt und erklärt* (Mergentheim: Ohlinger, 1912).
Denton, W., *A Commentary on the Acts of the Apostles* (2 vols.; London: G. Bell and Sons, 1874; 2d ed., 1888).
Dessain, C. S., "The Acts of the Apostles," *A Catholic Commentary on Holy Scripture* (ed. B. Orchard et al.; London: Nelson, 1953), 1018–44 (§814a–843i).
*DeWette, W.M.L., *Kurze Erklärung der Apostelgeschichte* (Kurzgefasstes exegetisches Handbuch zum Neuen Testament 1/4; Leipzig: Weidmann, 1838; 2d ed., 1841; 3d ed., 1848).
Dillon, R. J., "Acts of the Apostles," *NJBC*, 722–67 (art. 44).
Dillon, R. J. and J. A. Fitzmyer, "Acts of the Apostles," *JBC*, 2.165–214 (art. 45).
Diprose, R., *Il libro degli Atti: Introduzione e breve commento al libro degli Atti* (Rome: Istituto Biblico Evangelico, 1982).
Drioux, C. J., "Les Actes des Apôtres," *La Sainte Bible* . . . (8 vols.; Paris: Berche et Tralin, 1879), 7.362–484.
*Dunn, J.D.G., *The Acts of the Apostles* (Epworth Commentary; London: Epworth, 1996).
*Dupont, J., *Les Actes des Apôtres* (SBJ; Paris: Cerf, 1954; 3d ed., 1964).
Eaton, R., *The Acts of the Apostles* (2 vols.; London, 1938).
Eckermann, J.C.R., *Erklärung aller dunklen Stellen des Neuen Testaments* (3 vols.; Kiel, 1806–8).
Ellicott, C. J., *Ellicott's Bible Commentary in One Volume: A Verse-by-Verse Explanation* (ed. D. N. Bowdle; Grand Rapids, MI: Zondervan, 1971), 856–920.

Erdman, C. R., *The Acts: An Exposition* (Philadelphia: Westminster, 1919).
Ewald, H., *Die drei ersten Evangelien und die Apostelgeschichte* (2 vols.; Die Bücher des Neuen Bundes; 2d ed.; Göttingen: Dieterich, 1872).
Fabris, R., *Atti degli Apostoli* (Commenti biblici; Rome: Borla, 1977).
Farelly, M., *Les Actes des Apôtres* (Neuchâtel: Delachaux et Niestlé, 1958).
Faw, C. E., *Acts* (Believers Church Bible Commentary; Scottdale, PA: Herald, 1993).
Felten, J., *Die Apostelgeschichte übersetzt und erklärt* (Freiburg im B.: Herder, 1892).
Field, F., *Otium Norvicense, Pars Tertia: Notes on Select Passages of the Greek Testament Chiefly with Reference to Recent English Versions* (Oxford: Pickard Hall and Stacy, 1881); repr. as *Notes on the Translation of the New Testament* (2d ed., Cambridge: Cambridge University Press, 1899), 110–50; repr. Peabody, MA: Hendrickson, 1994.
Fillion, L.-C., "Les Actes des Apôtres," *La Sainte Bible (Texte latin et traduction française) commentée* . . . (8 vols.; Paris: Letouzey et Ané, 1904–12), 7.610–817.
Findlay, J. A., *The Acts of the Apostles: A Commentary* (London: SCM, 1934; 4th ed., 1952).
Flanagan, N. M., *The Acts of the Apostles* (NTRG 5; Collegeville, MN: Liturgical, 1960).
Fliedner, K. T., *Die Apostelgeschichte* (Stuttgarter Bibelhefte; Stuttgart: Quell-V., 1957).
*Foakes-Jackson, F. J., *The Acts of the Apostles* (Moffatt New Testament Commentary; London: Hodder and Stoughton; New York: R. R. Smith, 1931; repr. 1960).
*Foakes-Jackson, F. J., and K. Lake (eds.), *The Beginnings of Christianity: Part I, The Acts of the Apostles* (5 vols.; London: Macmillan, 1920–33; repr., Grand Rapids, MI: Baker, 1979).
Furneaux, W. M., *The Acts of the Apostles: A Commentary for English Readers* (Oxford: Clarendon, 1912).
Gatti, E., *Atti degli Apostoli: Il libro della missione* (Bologna: Editrice Missionaria Italiana, 1975; 2d ed., 1977).
Gerok, K., *Die Apostelgeschichte in Bibelstunden* (2 vols.; Stuttgart: S. G. Liesching, 1868; 3d ed., Gütersloh: Bertelsmann, 1896).
Ghidelli, C., *Atti degli Apostoli* (La Sacra Bibbia; Turin: Marietti, 1978).
Gilbert, G. H., *Acts, the Second Volume of Luke's Work on the Beginnings of Christianity, with Interpretative Comment* (New York: Macmillan, 1908).
Gloag, P. J., *A Critical and Exegetical Handbook of the Acts of the Apostles* (2 vols.; Edinburgh: Clark, 1870, 1877 [British transl. of H.A.W. Meyer]).
Goetz, B., *Die Apostelgeschichte* (Christus heute 17; Stuttgart: Kreuz, 1957).
Grant, F. C., "The Acts of the Apostles," *Nelson's Bible Commentary Based on the Revised Standard Version* (New York/Toronto/Edinburgh: Nelson, 1962), 6.414–518.

Grech, P., *Acts of the Apostles Explained: A Doctrinal Commentary* (Staten Island: Alba House, 1966).

Grosheide, F. W., *De Handelingen der Apostelen* (Kommentar op het Nieuwe Testament 5; 2 vols.; Amsterdam: Van Bottenburg, 1942, 1948).

———, *De Handelingen der Apostelen, opnieuw . . . vertaald* (Korte verklaring der Heilige Schrift; 2 vols.; Kampen: Kok, 1941, 1945; 3d ed., 1962, 1963).

Gutzke, M. G., *Plain Talk on Acts* (Grand Rapids, MI: Zondervan, 1966; repr. 1972).

Guy, H. A., *The Acts of the Apostles* (London: Macmillan; New York: St. Martin's Press, 1953; 2nd ed., 1975).

Hackett, H. B., *A Commentary on the Original Text of the Acts of the Apostles* (Boston: Jewett and Co., 1852; renamed and repr. Grand Rapids, MI: Kregel, 1992).

Hadorn, W., *Die Apostelgeschichte: Eine volkstümliche Erklärung* (Hamburg: Agentur des Rauhen Hauses, 1908).

*Haenchen, E. *The Acts of the Apostles: A Commentary* (Philadelphia: Westminster; Oxford: Blackwell, 1971).

Hamilton, R., *Acts* (Bryn Mawr Commentaries; Bryn Mawr: Thomas Library, Bryn Mawr College, 1986).

Hammond, H., *A Paraphrase and Annotations upon All the Books of the New Testament . . .* (4 vols.; Oxford: Oxford University, 1845), 1.465–602; 3.345–444.

Hanson, R.P.C., *The Acts in the Revised Standard Version: With Introduction and Commentary* (NClarB; Oxford: Clarendon, 1967).

Harrison, E. F., *Interpreting Acts: The Expanding Church* (Chicago: Moody, 1975; 2d ed., Grand Rapids, MI: Zondervan, Academie Books, 1986).

Harvey, A. E., *The New English Bible: Companion to the New Testament* (Oxford: Oxford University Press; Cambridge: Cambridge University Press, 1970) 399–500.

Heinrichs, I. H., *Novum Testamentum graece III/1–2: Acta Apostolorum* (2 vols.; Göttingen: Dieterich, 1809, 1812).

Hervey, A. C., *The Acts of the Apostles: Exposition and Homiletics* (2 vols.; London: Kegan Paul, Trench, 1884).

Hillard, A. E., *The Acts of the Apostles with Introduction, Notes, and Maps* (London: Rivington, 1905; 5th ed., 1918).

Hoennicke, G., *Die Apostelgeschichte* (Evangelisch-theologische Bibliothek; Leipzig: Quelle & Meyer, 1913).

Hoffmann, H., *Die Apostelgeschichte S. Lucä* (Neutestamentliche Bibelstunden; Leipzig: Deichert, 1903; 2d ed., 1907).

Holladay, C. R., "Acts," *Harper's Bible Commentary* (ed. J. L. Mays; San Francisco: Harper & Row, 1988) 1077–1118.

Holtzmann, H. J., *Die Apostelgeschichte* (Hand-Commentar zum Neuen Testament 1/2; 3d ed.; Tübingen/Leipzig: Mohr [Siebeck], 1899; 3d ed., 1901), 305–428.

Horton, S. M., *The Book of Acts* (Springfield, MO: Gospel Publ. House, 1981).

Howson, J. S. and H.D.M. Spence, *The Acts of the Apostles Explained* (International Revision Commentary on the New Testament 5; New York: Scribner, 1882).

Hückelheim, J. F., *Die Apostelgeschichte übersetzt und erklärt* (Paderborn: Schöningh, 1902).

Humphry, W. G., *A Commentary on the Book of the Acts of the Apostles* (London, 1847; 2d ed., 1854).

Jacobus, M. W., *Notes, Critical and Explanatory, on the Acts of the Apostles* (New York: R. Carter & Bros., 1859; repr. 1870)

*Jacquier, E., *Les Actes des Apôtres* (EBib; 2d ed.; Paris: Gabalda, 1926).

Jamieson, R., A. R. Fausset, and D. Brown, "The Acts of the Apostles," *Commentary Practical and Explanatory on the Whole Bible* (rev. ed.; Grand Rapids, MI: Zondervan, 1961; repr. 1968), 1080–1138.

*Johnson, L. T., *The Acts of the Apostles* (Sacra Pagina 5; Collegeville, MN: Liturgical, 1992).

Jonker, A.J.T., *De berichten van de Handelingen der Apostelen omtrent de gevangenschap van Paulus te Jerusalem, Cesarea en Rome, in hun historisch karakter beschouwd* (Utrecht: Kemink & Zoon, 1877).

Karris, R. J., *Invitation to Acts: A Commentary on the Acts of the Apostles with Complete Text from the Jerusalem Bible* (Image Books; Garden City, NY: Doubleday, 1978).

Kelly, W., *An Exposition of the Acts of the Apostles Newly Translated from an Amended Text* (2d ed.; London: F. E. Race, 1914; 3d ed.; London: C. A. Hammond; Denver: Wilson Foundation, 1952).

Kenrick, F. P., *The Acts of the Apostles, the Epistles of St. Paul, the Catholic Epistles, and the Apocalypse: Translated . . . with Notes, Critical and Explanatory* (New York: Dunigan, 1851) 21–161.

Kettenbach, G., *Das Logbuch des Lukas* (Frankfurt am M./New York: P. Lang, 1986).

Kilgallen, J. J., *A Brief Commentary on the Acts of the Apostles* (New York: Paulist, 1988).

Kistemaker, J. H., *Geschichte der Apostel* (Münster in W.: Theissing, 1821).

*Kistemaker, S. J., *Exposition of the Acts of the Apostles* (New Testament Commentary; Grand Rapids, MI: Baker, 1990).

Kliesch, K., *Apostelgeschichte* (Stuttgarter kleiner Kommentar, Neues Testament 5; Stuttgart: Katholisches Bibelwerk, 1986).

Knabenbauer, J., *Commentarius in Actus Apostolorum* (CSS 3/5; Paris: Lethielleux, 1899; repr. 1928).

Knapp, C., *The Acts of the Apostles, with Introduction, Maps and Explanatory Notes* (London: Thomas Murby & Co., 1914).

Knopf, R., *Die Apostelgeschichte* (Die Schriften des Neuen Testaments 3; Göttingen: Vandenhoeck & Ruprecht, 1906; 3d ed., 1917).

Knowling, R. J., *The Acts of the Apostles* (Expositor's Greek Testament; 5 vols.;

London: Hodder and Stoughton; New York: Dodd, Mead, 1900; 4th ed., 1912; repr. Grand Rapids, MI: Eerdmans, 1951), 2.3–554.

Krodel, G. A., *Acts* (Augsburg Commentary on the New Testament; Minneapolis: Augsburg, 1986).

———, *Acts* (Proclamation Commentaries; Philadelphia: Fortress, 1981).

Kühnöl (Kuinoel), C. T., *Commentarius in libros Novi Testamenti historicos: IV. Acta Apostolorum* (Leipzig: J. A. Barth, 1818; 2d ed., 1827).

Kürzinger, J., *The Acts of the Apostles* (NTSR 10–11; 2 vols.; London: Burns & Oates; New York: Herder and Herder, 1969, 1971).

———, *Die Apostelgeschichte* (Echterbibel NT 2; Würzburg: Echter-V., 1951; 3d ed., 1959).

Kurz, W. S., *The Acts of the Apostles* (Collegeville Bible Commentary 5; Collegeville, MN: Liturgical, 1983).

Ladd, G. E., "The Acts of the Apostles," *The Wycliffe Bible Commentary* (ed. C. F. Pfeiffer and E. F. Harrison; Chicago: Moody, 1962), 1123–78.

*Lake, K. and H. J. Cadbury, "Acts of the Apostles," *Beginnings*, 4 (1933).

Lampe, G.W.H., "Acts," *Peake's Commentary on the Bible* (ed. M. Black and H. H. Rowley; London: Nelson, 1962), 882–926 (§771a–803e).

Langenberg, H., *Apostelgeschichte: Das Werden der Gemeinde Gottes und das Werden des Apostels Paulus in gegenseitiger Bedeutung zu einander* (Wüstenrot, Kr. Heilbronn a. N.: "Wort und Geist," 1946).

LaSor, W. S., *Church Alive* (Layman's Bible Commentary; Glendale, CA: Regal Books, 1972).

Lattey, C., *The Acts of the Apostles* (London: Longmans, Green, 1933).

Leal, J., "Hechos de los Apóstoles," *La Sagrada Escritura* (BAC 211; Madrid: Editorial Católica, 1962), 2.1–170.

Lechler, G. V., *Der Apostel Geschichten* (Bielefeld/Leipzig: Velhagen und Kalsing, 1860; 3d ed., 1869).

Le Mouël, G., *Saint Luc médecin, collaborateur de saint Paul: l'Histoire des Apôtres: Texte, présentation et notes* (Paris: Editions Ouvrières, 1957).

Lenski, R.C.H., *The Interpretation of the Acts of the Apostles* (Columbus, OH: Lutheran Book Concern, 1934; repr. Columbus, OH: Wartburg, 1951; Minneapolis: Augsburg, 1962).

L'Eplattenier, C., *Les Actes des Apôtres* (Geneva: Labor et Fides, 1987).

Lightfoot, J., *Horae hebraicae et talmudicae: Hebrew and Talmudical Exercitations upon the Gospels, the Acts* . . . (4 vols.; new ed. R. Gandell; Oxford: Oxford University Press, 1859); renamed and repr., *A Commentary on the New Testament from the Talmud and Hebraica, Matthew—I Corinthians* (Grand Rapids, MI: Baker, 1979), 5–153.

Lindijer, C. H., *Handelingen van de Apostelen* (2 vols.; Nijkerk: Callenbach, 1975, 1979).

Lindsay, T. M., *The Acts of the Apostles, with Introduction, Notes, and Maps* (2 vols.; Edinburgh: Clark, 1884, 1885).

Livermore, A. A., *The Acts of the Apostles with a Commentary* (London: J. Chapman; Boston: J. Munroe and Co., 1841; repr. Boston: Lockwood, Brooks, 1881).

*Loisy, A., *Les Actes des Apôtres* (Paris: Nourry, 1920; repr. Paris: Rieder, 1925; Frankfurt am M.: Minerva, 1973).

*Longenecker, R. N., *The Acts of the Apostles* (Expositor's Bible Commentary 9; Grand Rapids, MI: Zondervan, 1981), 205–573.

Lüdemann, G., *Early Christianity according to the Traditions in Acts: A Commentary* (London: SCM; Minneapolis: Fortress, 1989).

Lüthi, W., *Die Apostelgeschichte ausgelegt für die Gemeinde* (Basel: Reinhardt, 1958).

Lumby, J. R., *The Acts of the Apostles with Maps, Notes and Introduction* (Cambridge Greek Testament for Schools and Colleges; Cambridge: Cambridge University Press, 1885; repr. 1937).

Lusseau, H. and M. Collomb, *Les Actes des Apôtres; Les grandes épîtres de Saint Paul* (Manuel d'études bibliques 5/1; Paris: Téqui, 1930), 1–241.

Macaulay, J. C., *Expository Commentary on Acts* (Chicago: Moody, 1978).

McBride, A., *The Gospel of the Holy Spirit: A Commentary on the Acts of the Apostles* (New York: Hawthorn Books, 1975).

MacEvilly, J., *An Exposition of the Acts of the Apostles, Consisting of an Analysis of Each Chapter and of a Commentary . . .* (New York: Benzinger, 1896; 3d ed., Dublin: M. H. Gill & Son, 1911).

Macgregor, G.H.C., "The Acts of the Apostles," *IB* 9 (1954): 1–352.

Maddox, R. L., *Acts* (Nashville: Broadman, 1979).

Maloney, L. M., *"All That God Had Done with Them": The Narration of the Works of God in the Early Christian Community as Described in the Acts of the Apostles* (American University Studies, Series 7: Theology and Religion; New York: Lang, 1991).

Manen, W. C. van, *De Handelingen der Apostelen* (Leiden: Brill, 1890).

*Marshall, I. H., *The Acts of the Apostles: An Introduction and Commentary* (TynNTC; Leicester: Inter-Varsity; Grand Rapids, MI: Eerdmans, 1980).

Martin, C. J., "The Acts of the Apostles," *Searching the Scriptures: Volume Two: Feminist Commentary* (New York: Crossroad, 1994), 763–99.

Martin, R. P., *Acts* (London: Scripture Union; Grand Rapids, MI: Eerdmans, 1968; repr. Philadelphia: Holman, 1978).

Martindale, C. C., *The Acts of the Apostles: With an Introduction and Commentary* (Stonyhurst Scripture Manuals; Westminster, MD: Newman, 1958).

Martini, C. M., *Atti degli apostoli* (2d ed.; Rome: Edizioni Paoline, 1972; 4th ed., 1977).

Menochio, J. E., *Totius Sanctae Scripturae commentarii ex optimis quibusque auctoribus collecti* (6 vols.; Lyons: Rusand, 1825), 5.514–624.

*Meyer, H.A.W., *Kritisch-exegetisches Handbuch über die Apostelgeschichte* (MeyerK 3; Göttingen: Vandenhoeck & Ruprecht, 1835; 4th ed., 1869).

———, *Critical and Exegetical Handbook to the Acts of the Apostles* (2 vols.; trans. from 4th Germ. ed.; Edinburgh: Clark, 1877; American ed. [ed. W. Ormiston], New York: Funk & Wagnalls, 1883; 2d ed., 1884).

Mezger, G., *Die Apostelgeschichte St. Lucä: Nebst kurzer Erklärung mit Berücksichtigung der Briefe der Apostel* (St. Louis, MO: Concordia Publ. House, 1913).

Michaelis, W., *Das Neue Testament verdeutscht und erläutert: II. Taten der Apostel, Briefe, Offenbarung* (Kröners Taschenausgabe 120–21; Leipzig: Kröner, 1934–35), 2.1–155.

Migne, J.-P., *Scripturae Sacrae cursus completus* . . . (28 vols.; Paris: Apud Editorem, 1839–41), 23.1125–1464.

Morgan, G. C., *The Acts of the Apostles* (New York: Revell, 1924; repr., London: Pickering & Inglis, 1946).

Munck, J., *The Acts of the Apostles* (AB 31; Garden City, NY: Doubleday, 1967).

*Mussner, F., *Apostelgeschichte* (Die neue Echter-Bibel, NT 5; Würzburg: Echter-V., 1984; 2d ed., 1988).

Neil, W., *Acts: Based on the Revised Standard Version* (NCB; London: Oliphants; Grand Rapids, MI: Eerdmans, 1973; repr. 1981).

Nösgen, C. F., *Commentar über die Apostelgeschichte des Lukas* (Leipzig: Dörffling und Franke, 1882).

Ogilvie, L. J., *Acts* (Communicator's Commentary 5; Waco, TX: Word Books, 1983).

Olshausen, H., *Biblischer Commentar über sämtliche Schriften des Neuen Testaments* . . . : *II/3. Die Apostelgeschichte* (7 vols. in 11; Königsberg: Unzer, 1830–62) 2 (1832); 4th ed. rev., A. Ebrard, 1853–62).

*Overbeck, F., *Kurze Erklärung der Apostelgeschichte* (Kurzgefasstes exegetisches Handbuch zum Neuen Testament 1/4; 4th ed.; Leipzig: Hirzel, 1870).

Packer, J. W., *Acts of the Apostles: Commentary* (CNEB; Cambridge: Cambridge University Press, 1966; rev. ed. 1973; repr. 1975).

Page, T. E., *The Acts of the Apostles, Being the Greek Text as Revised by Drs. Westcott and Hort, with Explanatory Notes* (London: Macmillan, 1886; new ed. with added introduction by A. S. Walpole, 1895).

Papa, B., *Atti degli Apostoli* (Collana Lettura pastorale della Bibbia; Bologna: EDB, 1981).

Pastor, F., *Hechos de los Apóstoles: Comentario* (El Mensaje del Nuevo Testamento 5; Estella [Navarra]: Verbo Divino; Salamanca: Sigueme; Madrid: Promoción Popular Cristiana, 1990).

Patrizi, F. X., *In Actus Apostolorum commentarium* (Rome: Civiltà Cattolica, 1867).

Pérez Gordo, A., *Hechos de los Apóstoles y cartas paulinas (I)* (Burgos: Ediciones Aldecoa [1989]), 11–102.

Perk, J., *Die Apostelgeschichte: Werden und Wachsen der jungen Kirche* (Stuttgart: Kepplerhaus, 1954).

*Pesch, R., *Die Apostelgeschichte* (EKKNT 5/1–2; Zurich/Einsiedeln/Cologne: Benziger; Neukirchen-Vluyn: Neukirchener-V., 1986).

Phillips, J., *Exploring Acts* (2 vols.; Chicago: Moody, 1986; repr. Neptune, NJ: Loizeaux Brothers, 1991).

Phillips, J. B., *The Young Church in Action: A Translation of the Acts of the Apostles* (London: G. Bles, 1955; New York: Macmillan, 1956).

Plumptre, E. H., *The Acts of the Apostles: With Commentary* (London/New York: Cassell and Co., 1877; new ed., by C. J. Ellicott, 1879).

*Polhill, J. B., *Acts* (New American Commentary 26; Nashville: Broadman, 1992).

Preuschen, E., *Die Apostelgeschichte erklärt* (HNT 4/1; Tübingen: Mohr [Siebeck], 1912).

Rackham, R. B., *The Acts of the Apostles: An Exposition* (Westminster Commentaries; London: Methuen, 1901; 14th ed., 1951; repr. Grand Rapids, MI: Baker, 1964).

Ramos, F. F., *Hechos de los Apóstoles* (Madrid: PPC. Edicabi, 1971).

Ravasi, G., *Gli Atti degli Apostoli all'origine del cristianesimo* (Bologna: EDB, 1988).

Reese, G. L., *New Testament History: A Critical and Exegetical Commentary on the Book of Acts* (Joplin, MO: College Press, 1976; repr. 1981).

Rendall, F., *The Acts of the Apostles in Greek and English, with Notes* (London: Macmillan, 1897).

Renié, J., *Les Actes des Apôtres traduits et commentés* (Sainte Bible de Pirot-Clamer 11/1; Paris: Letouzey et Ané, 1949; 2d ed., 1951).

Reuss, E., *Histoire apostolique: Actes des Apôtres* (Paris: Sandoz et Fischbacher, 1876).

Ricciotti, G., *The Acts of the Apostles: Text and Commentary* (Milwaukee: Bruce, 1958).

Rieu, C. H., *The Acts of the Apostles by Saint Luke Translated with an Introduction and Notes* (Penguin Books; Baltimore: Penguin, 1957).

Ripley, H. J., *The Acts of the Apostles: With Notes, Chiefly Explanatory . . .* (Boston: Gould, Kendall, and Lincoln, 1844; repr. 1854).

Rius-Camps, J., *El camino de Pablo a la misión de los paganos: Comentario lingüístico y exetico* [*sic*] *a Hch 13–28* (Madrid: Cristiandad, 1984).

*Roloff, J., *Die Apostelgeschichte übersetzt und erklärt* (NTD 5; 17th ed.; Göttingen: Vandenhoeck & Ruprecht, 1981).

Rose, V., *Les Actes des Apôtres: Traduction et commentaire* (Paris: Bloud & Cie., 1907).

Russ, H.-E., *Urkirche auf dem Weg in die Welt: Ein Kommentar zur Apostelgeschichte* (Würzburg: Arena-V., 1967).

Sadler, M. F., *The Acts of the Apostles, with Notes Critical and Practical* (New York: Pott, 1887; 3d ed. 1892).

Sargent, J. E., *Acts* (Nashville: Exodus Press, 1989).

*Schille, G., *Die Apostelgeschichte des Lukas* (THKNT 5; Berlin: Evangelische Verlagsanstalt, 1983; 3d ed., 1989).

Schiwy, G., *Weg ins Neue Testament: Kommentar und Material: II. Das Evangelium nach Johannes, Die Apostelgeschichte* (Würzburg: Echter-V., 1966) 155–314.

*Schlatter, A., *Die Apostelgeschichte: Ausgelegt für Bibelleser* (Erläuterungen zum Neuen Testament 4; Stuttgart: Calwer, 1913; 2d ed., 1948; reworked and repr. 1962).

Schmithals, W., *Die Apostelgeschichte des Lukas* (ZBKNT 3/2; Zurich: Theologischer-V., 1982).

*Schneider, G., *Die Apostelgeschichte* (HTKNT 5/1–2; Freiburg im B.: Herder, 1980, 1982).

Sitterly, C. F., *Jerusalem to Rome: The Acts of the Apostles, a New Translation and Commentary* . . . (New York/Cincinnati: Abingdon, 1915).

Smidt, U., *Die Apostelgeschichte übersetzt und ausgelegt* (Bibelhefte für die Gemeinde, NT Reihe 5; Hamburg, 1941; repr. Berlin: Evangelische Verlagsanstalt, 1951).

Smith, R. H., *Acts* (Concordia Commentary; Saint Louis, MO/London: Concordia Publ. House, 1970).

Smith, T. C., "Acts," *The Broadman Bible Commentary* (12 vols.; Nashville: Broadman, 1970), 10.1–152.

Södergren, C. J., *The Acts, with Commentaries* (Rock Island, IL: Augustana Book Concern, 1927).

Southward, W. T., *The Acts of the Apostles Edited with Critical, Grammatical and Explanatory Notes* . . . (7th ed.; Cambridge, UK: Hall & Son, 1890).

Stählin, G., *Die Apostelgeschichte überstezt und erklärt* (NTD 5; 11th ed.; Göttingen: Vandenhoeck & Ruprecht, 1966; 16th ed., 1980).

Steenkiste, J. A. van, *Actus Apostolorum breviter explicati* . . . (3d ed.; Bruges: Beyaert, 1875; 4th ed., 1882).

Steinmann, A., *Die Apostelgeschichte übersetzt und erklärt* (Die heilige Schrift des Neuen Testaments [= Bonner Bibel] 4; Berlin: Hermann Walther, 1913; 4th ed., Bonn: Hanstein, 1934).

Stern, W., *Erklärung der Apostelgeschichte* (Karlsruhe: C. T. Groos, 1872).

Stokes, G. T., *The Acts of the Apostles* (Expositor's Bible 34–35; 2 vols.; London: Hodder and Stoughton, 1891, 1892; 3d ed., 1897, 1899).

Stott, J.R.W., *The Spirit, the Church, and the World: The Message of Acts* (The Bible Speaks Today; Downers Grove, IL: InterVarsity, 1990).

Talbert, C. H., *Acts* (Atlanta: John Knox, 1984).

*Taylor, J., *Les Actes des deux Apôtres: Commentaire historique (Act 9, 1–18, 22)* (EBib ns 23; Paris: Gabalda, 1994).

Tourville, R. E., *The Acts of the Apostles: A Verse-by-Verse Commentary from the Classical Pentecostal Perspective* (New Wilmington, PA: House of Bon Giovanni, 1983).

Trenchard, E. H., "The Acts of the Apostles," *A New Testament Commentary* (ed. G.C.D. Howley; Grand Rapids, MI: Zondervan, 1969) 289–340.

———, *Los Hechos de los Apóstoles: Un comentario* (Madrid: Literatura Bíblica, 1977).

Turrado, L., "Hechos de los Apóstoles," *Biblia comentada: Texto de la Nácar-Colunga* (BAC; Madrid: Editorial Católica, 1965) 6.1–226.

Wade, J. W., *Acts: Unlocking the Scriptures for You* (Standard Bible Studies; Cincinnati: Standard Publ., 1987).

Walker, T., *Acts of the Apostles* (Indian Church Commentaries; London: SPCK, 1919; repr., Grand Rapids, MI: Kregel, 1984).

Wansbrough, H., "Acts of the Apostles," *A New Catholic Commentary on Holy Scripture* (ed. R. C. Fuller et al.; London: Nelson, 1969), 1075–1102.

*Weiser, A., *Die Apostelgeschichte* (Ökumenischer Taschenbuchkommentar zum Neuen Testament 5/1–2; Gütersloh: Mohn; Würzburg: Echter-V. 1981, 1985).

Weiss, B., *Die Apostelgeschichte, Katholischen Briefe, Apokalypse* . . . (Das Neue Testament 3; 2d ed.; Leipzig: Hinrichs, 1900).

———, *A Commentary on the New Testament* (4 vols.; New York/London: Funk & Wagnals, 1906) 2.416–637.

Wendt, H. H., *Die Apostelgeschichte* (MeyerK 3; Göttingen: Vandenhoeck & Ruprecht, 1880; 9th ed., 1913).

Whitham, A. R., *The Acts of the Apostles: The Text of the Revised Version with Introduction, Maps and Notes* (2 vols.; London: Rivingtons, 1920; 2d ed., 1962).

Whittaker, H., *Studies in the Acts of the Apostles* (Cannock, Staffordshire, UK: Biblia, 1985).

*Wikenhauser, A., *Die Apostelgeschichte übersetzt und erklärt* (RNT 5; Regensburg: Pustet, 1938; 4th ed., 1961).

Williams, C.S.C., *A Commentary on the Acts of the Apostles* (BNTC; London: Black, 1957; New York: Harper & Bros., 1958; 2d ed., 1969).

*Williams, D. J., *Acts* (Good News Commentaries; San Francisco: Harper & Row, 1985; repr. as part of New International Biblical Commentary; Peabody, MA: Hendrickson, 1990).

Williams, R. R., *The Acts of the Apostles* (Torch Bible Commentaries; London: SCM, 1953).

Williger, K., *Die Apostelgeschichte in Bibelstunden fur's Volk ausgelegt* (Halle a. S.: R. Muhlmann, 1847).

Willimon, W. H., *Acts* (Interpretation; Atlanta: John Knox, 1988; repr., Peabody, MA: Hendrickson, 1990).

Winn, A. C., *The Acts of the Apostles* (Richmond, VA: John Knox, 1960; repr. 1967).

Wise, I. M., *The Origin of Christianity, and a Commentary to the Acts of the Apostles* (Cincinnati: Bloch, 1868).

Witsch, A. W., *Die Apostelgeschichte: Vom historischen Christus über den eucharistischen Christus zum mystischen Christus* (Mainz: Grünewald, 1937).

Wittmann, G. M., *Erklärung der heiligen Evangelien, der Apostelgeschichte und einiger Briefe des heil. Paulus* (Regensburg: Manz, 1844).

Wordsworth, C., *The New Testament of Our Lord and Saviour Jesus Christ in the Original Greek with Notes: Part II. The Acts of the Apostles* (London: Rivingtons, 1857; 2d ed., 1877).

*Zahn, T., *Die Apostelgeschichte des Lucas* (2 vols.; KNT 5/1–2; Leipzig/Erlangen: Deichert, 1919–21; 4th ed., 1927).

———, *Die Urausgabe der Apostelgeschichte des Lucas* (FGNK 9; Leipzig: Deichert-Scholl, 1914; repr. 1916).

*Zmijewski, J., *Die Apostelgeschichte* (RNT; Regensburg: Pustet, 1994).

Zöckler, O., *Die Apostelgeschichte* (Kurzgefasster Kommentar zu den heiligen Schriften, Neues Testament II; Nördlingen, 1886; repr. Munich: Beck, 1894) 145–324.

Zwaan, J. de, *De Handelingen der Apostelen* (Het Nieuwe Testament, Tekst en Uitleg 2/5; Groningen: Wolters, 1920; 2d ed., 1931).

(185) B. MONOGRAPHS ON ACTS

Achtemeier, P. J., *The Quest for Unity in the New Testament Church: A Study in Paul and Acts* (Philadelphia: Fortress, 1987).

Amewowo, W. et al., *Les Actes des Apôtres et les jeunes églises: Actes du deuxième congrès des biblistes africains, Ibadan: 31 juillet–3 août 1984* (Kinshasa: Facultés Catholiques de Kinshasa, 1990).

Andrea, H., *Ursprung und erste Entwickelung der Kirche Christi: In Vorlesungen über die Apostelgeschichte des Lucas* (Frankfurt am. M.: Heyder & Zimmer, 1877).

Arnot, W., *Studies in Acts: The Church in the House* (Grand Rapids, MI: Kregel, 1978).

Aye, H., *Die Apostelgeschichte in religiösen Betrachtungen für das moderne Bedürfnis* (Gütersloh: Bertelsmann, 1908).

Barclay, W., *Turning to God: A Study of Conversion in the Book of Acts and Today* (London: Epworth, 1963).

Barnikol, E., *Personen-probleme der Apostelgeschichte, Johannes Markus, Silas und Titus: Untersuchungen zur Struktur der Apostelgeschichte und zur Verfasserschaft der Wir-Quelle* (Kiel: Muhlau, 1931).

Barsotti, D., *Meditazione sugli Atti degli Apostoli* (Brescia: Queriniana, 1977; 2d ed., 1979).

Bauer, B., *Die Apostelgeschichte: Eine Ausgleichung des Paulinismus und des Judenthums innerhalb der christlichen Kirche* (Berlin: Hempel, 1850).

Baumgarten, M., *The Acts of the Apostles, or the History of the Church in the Apostolic Age* (Clark's Foreign Theological Library ns. 2–4; Edinburgh: Clark, 1854).

———, *Die Apostelgeschichte oder der Entwickelungsgang der Kirche von Jerusalem bis Rom: Ein biblischhistorischer Versuch* (2 vols.; 2d ed.; Braunschweig: Schwetschke und Sohn, 1859).

Baur, A., *Apostelgeschichte und Apokalypse: Nach der Reich-Gottes-Bibel* (Donauwörth: Ludwig Auer, 1967).

Bieder, W., *Die Apostelgeschichte in der Historie: Ein Beitrag zur Auslegungsgeschichte des Missionsbuches der Kirche* (Theologische Studien 61; Zurich: EVZ-Verlag, 1960).

Blair, E. P., *The Acts and Apocalyptic Literature* (New York/Nashville: Abingdon-Cokesbury, 1946).

Boismard, M. E., *Literary Criticism of the Gospels and Acts: An Introduction* (Guilford, CT: Four Quarters Publ. Co., 1985).

Bornhäuser, K., *Studien zur Apostelgeschichte* (Gutersloh: Bertelsmann, 1934).

Bosworth, E. I., *New Studies in Acts* (New York/London: Association, 1913).

Bourguignon, J., *Ainsi nait l'Eglise: Actes des Apôtres hier et aujourd'hui* ("Chercheurs de Dieu"; Paris: Editions Ouvrières, 1977).

Brons, A., *Laienevangelium und erste Entwickelung des Christenthums: Nach der Apostelgeschichte mit Rücksicht auf die vorchristliche Zeit* (Emden und Aurich: Haynel, 1873).

Brown, St. C., *Evangelism in the Early Church: A Study in the Book of the Acts of the Apostles* (Grand Rapids, MI: Eerdmans, 1963).

Bruce, F. F., *Men and Movements in the Primitive Church: Studies in Early Non-Pauline Christianity* (Exeter: Paternoster, 1979) 97–101.

Cadbury, H. J., *The Book of Acts in History* (London: Black; New York: Harper & Bros., 1955).

Cannon, W. R., *The Book of Acts* (Nashville: Upper Room Books, 1989).

Cassidy, R. J., *Society and Politics in the Acts of the Apostles* (Maryknoll, NY: Orbis Books, 1987).

Cesari, A., *I fatti degli Apostoli: Ragionamenti* (2 vols in one; Verona: L'Erede Merlo 1821; repr. Florence: Angiolo Garinei, 1833).

Charlier, J.-P., *The Gospel of the Church's Infancy* (De Pere, WI: St. Norbert Abbey, 1969).

Chase, F. H., *The Credibility of the Book of the Acts of the Apostles: Being the Hulsean Lectures for 1900–1901* (London: Macmillan, 1902).

Clemen, C., *Die Apostelgeschichte im Lichte der neueren text-, quellen- und historisch-kritischen Forschungen* (Giessen: Töpelmann, 1905).

Cohausz, O., *Bilder aus der Urkirche: Eine gemeinverständliche Darbietung der Apostelgeschichte* (Betrachtungen über die Heilige Schrift 1; Leipzig: Vier Quellen V., [1921]).

Daniélou, J., *L'Eglise des Apôtres* (Paris: Editions du Seuil, 1970).

Dannenbaum, H., *Urchristliches Christentum: Gedanken die Einem beim Lesen der Apostelgeschichte kommen* (Gladbeck: Schriftenmissionsverlag, 1949).

Delarue, G., *Les Actes des Apôtres: Enfances de l'église . . .* (Sources de spiritualité 18; Paris/Colmar: Alsatia, 1968).

Delebecque, E., *Les deux Actes des Apôtres* (EBib ns 6; Paris: Gabalda, 1986).

Dibelius, M., *Aufsätze zur Apostelgeschichte* (FRLANT 60; 2d ed. H. Greeven; Göttingen: Vandenhoeck & Ruprecht, 1953); *Studies in the Acts of the Apostles* (London: SCM; New York: Scribner, 1956).

Dibelius, O., *Die werdende Kirche: Eine Einführung in die Apostelgeschichte* (5th ed.; Hamburg: Im Furche-V., 1951; 7th ed. 1967).

Dickson, K. A., *The Story of the Early Church as Found in the Acts of the Apostles* (London: Darton, Longman & Todd, 1976).

Dodd, C. H., *The Apostolic Preaching and Its Developments* (London: Hodder & Stoughton, 1936; 2d ed., 1944; New York: Harper, 1964).

Downing, F. G., *The Church and Jesus: A Study in History, Philosophy and Theology* (SBT 2/10; London: SCM; Naperville, IL: Allenson, 1968).

Drane, J. W., *Early Christians* (San Francisco: Harper & Row, 1982).

Dumais, M., *Communauté et mission: Une lecture des Actes des Apôtres pour aujourd'hui* (Relais — Etudes 10; Tournai/Paris: Desclée, 1992).

———, *Le langage de l'evangélisation: L'Annonce missionnaire en milieu juif (Actes 13,16–41)* (Tournai: Desclée; Montreal: Bellarmin, 1976).

Dumais, M. et al., *Cultural Change and Liberation in a Christian Perspective* (Rome: Gregorian University, 1987).

Dunn, J.D.G., *The Parting of the Ways between Christianity and Judaism and Their Significance for the Character of Christianity* (London: SCM; Philadelphia: Trinity Press International, 1991) 57–74.

Dupont, J., *Études sur les Actes des Apôtres* (LD 45; Paris: Cerf, 1967).

———, *Nouvelles études sur les Actes des Apôtres* (LD 118; Paris: Cerf, 1984).

———, *The Salvation of the Gentiles: Essays on the Acts of the Apostles* (New York: Paulist, 1979).

Easton, B. S., *Early Christianity: The Purpose of Acts and Other Papers* (London: SPCK, 1955).

Ehrhardt, A., *The Acts of the Apostles: Ten Lectures* (Manchester, UK: Manchester University, 1969).

Emmelius, J.-C., *Tendenzkritik und Formengeschichte: Der Beitrag Franz Overbecks zur Auslegung der Apostelgeschichte im 19. Jahrhundert* (FKDG 27; Göttingen: Vandenhoeck & Ruprecht, 1975).

Ferguson, E., *Acts of Apostles: The Message of the New Testament* (2 vols.; Abilene: Abilene Christian University Press, [1986]).

Filson, F. V., *Three Crucial Decades: Studies in the Book of Acts* (Richmond, VA: John Knox, 1963).

Fröhlich, R., *Das Zeugnis der Apostelgeschichte von Christus und das religiöse Denken in Indien* (Arbeiten zur Missionswissenschaft 2; Leipzig: Hinrichs, 1911).

Gewiess, J., *Die urapostolische Heilsverkündigung nach der Apostelgeschichte* (Breslauer Studien zur historischen Theologie 5; Breslau: Müller und Seiffert, 1939).

Gooding, D., *True to the Faith: A Fresh Approach to the Acts of the Apostles* (London: Hodder and Stoughton, 1990).

Goulder, M. D., *Type and History in Acts* (London: SPCK, 1964).

Gutbrod, K., *Die Apostelgeschichte: Einblick in ihre Anlage, Eigenart und Absicht* (Stuttgart: Calwer, 1968).

Hadorn, W., *Das Evangelium in der Apostelgeschichte* (Biblische Zeit- und Streitfragen 3/9; Berlin: Runge, 1907).

Harnack, A. von, *Beiträge zur Einleitung in das Neue Testament: III. Die Apostelgeschichte* (Leipzig: Hinrichs, 1908).

———, *The Expansion of Christianity in the First Three Centuries* (2 vols.; London: Williams & Norgate, 1904), 2.1–45.

———, *New Testament Studies, I: Luke the Physician; the Author of the Third Gospel and the Acts of the Apostles* (London: Williams & Norgate; New York: Putnam, 1911).

———, *New Testament Studies, III: The Acts of the Apostles* (London: Williams & Norgate; New York: Putnam, 1909).

———, *New Testament Studies, IV: The Date of Acts and the Synoptic Gospels* (London: Williams & Norgate; New York: Putnam, 1911).

Harrison, E. F., *The Apostolic Church* (Grand Rapids, MI: Eerdmans, 1985).

Hartshorn, C. B., *The Development of the Early Christian Church: A Study Based on the Acts of the Apostles and the Epistles* ([Independence, MO]: Reorganized Church of Jesus Christ of Latter Day Saints, 1967).

Hemer, C. J., *The Book of Acts in the Setting of Hellenistic History* (WUNT 49; ed. C. H. Gempf; Tübingen: Mohr [Siebeck], 1989; repr. Winona Lake, IN: Eisenbrauns, 1990).

Hengel, M., *Acts and the History of Earliest Christianity* (London: SCM, 1979; Philadelphia: Fortress, 1980).

———, *Between Jesus and Paul: Studies in the Earliest History of Christianity* (London: SCM; Philadelphia: Fortress, 1983).

Ironside, H. A., *Lectures on the Book of Acts* (Neptune, NJ: Loizeaux Brothers, 1943).

Jensen, I. L., *Acts: An Inductive Study: A Manual of Bible-Study-in-Depth* (Chicago: Moody, 1968).

Jervell, J., *The Theology of the Acts of the Apostles* (Cambridge: Cambridge University Press, 1996).

Johnson, L. T., *Decision Making in the Church: A Biblical Model* (Philadelphia: Fortress, 1983).

Jones, A.H.M., *Studies in Roman Government and Law* (Oxford: Blackwell, 1960; repr. New York: Barnes & Noble, 1968) 51–65.

Jovino, P., *La chiesa comunità di santi negli Atti degli Apostoli e nelle lettere di San Paolo* (Palermo: Edizioni 'O Theologos, 1975).

Keathley, N. H. (ed.), *With Steadfast Purpose: Essays on Acts in Honor of Henry Jackson Flanders, Jr.* (Waco, TX: Baylor University Press, 1990).

Keck, L. E., *Mandate to Witness: Studies in the Book of Acts* (Valley Forge: Judson, 1964).

Kent, H. A., Jr., *Jerusalem to Rome: Studies in the Book of Acts* (Grand Rapids, MI: Baker, [1972]).

Kinzie, F. E., *Salvation in the Book of Acts* (Hazelwood, MO: Word Aflame, 1988).

Klein, G., *Die zwölf Apostel: Ursprung und Gehalt einer Idee* (FRLANT 77; Göttingen: Vandenhoeck & Ruprecht, 1961).

Klostermann, A., *Probleme im Aposteltexte neu erörtert* (Gotha: Perthes, 1883).

Knox, W. L., *The Acts of the Apostles* (Cambridge: Cambridge University Press, 1948).

———, *St. Paul and the Church of Jerusalem* (Cambridge: Cambridge University Press, 1925).

———, *St. Paul and the Church of the Gentiles* (Cambridge: Cambridge University Press, 1939).

König, A., *Die Echtheit der Apostelgeschichte des heiligen Lucas: Ein Wort an deren Gegner* (Breslau: Aderholz, 1867).

Kremer, J. (ed.), *Les Actes des Apôtres: Traditions, rédaction, théologie* (BETL 48; Gembloux: Duculot; Louvain: Leuven University, 1979).

Krenkel, M., *Josephus und Lucas: Der schriftstellerische Einfluss der jüdischen Geschichtschreibers auf den christlichen nachgewiesen* (Leipzig: Haessel, 1894).

Kümmel, W. G., *Kirchenbegriff und Geschichtsbewusstsein in der Urgemeinde und bei Jesus* (2d ed.; Göttingen: Vandenhoeck & Ruprecht, 1968).

Lampe, G.W.H., *St Luke and the Church of Jerusalem* (London: Athlone, 1969).

Laurin, R. L., *Acts: Life in Action* (Grand Rapids, MI: Kregel, 1985).

Léon-Dufour, X., and C. Perrot, *L'Annonce de l'Evangile* (Paris: Desclée, 1976).

Lohfink, G., *Studien zum Neuen Testament* (SBA 5; Stuttgart: Katholisches Bibelwerk, 1989) 149–243.

Lohmeyer, E., *Gottesknecht und Davidsohn* (SBU 5; Copenhagen: Munksgaard, 1945; 2d ed., FRLANT 61; Göttingen: Vandenhoeck & Ruprecht, 1953).

McDonnell, J. J., *Acts to Gospels: A New Testament Path* (Lanham, MD: University Press of America, 1989).

Mackenzie, R., *The Word in Action: The Acts of the Apostles for Our Time* (Richmond, VA: John Knox, 1973).

Mann, C. S., *The Message Delivered* (New York: Morehouse-Barlow Co., 1973).

Mann, D., *Bis an die Enden der Erde: Eine Einführung in die Apostelgeschichte des Lukas* (Hermannsburg: Missionsbuchhandlung, 1978).

Marshall, I. H., *The Acts of the Apostles* (New Testament Guides; Sheffield, UK: JSOT, 1992).

Meeks, W. A., *The First Urban Christians: The Social World of the Apostle Paul* (New Haven/London: Yale University Press, 1983).

Menoud, P. -H., *La vie de l'église naissante* (Cahiers théologiques 31; Neuchâtel: Delachaux et Niestlé, 1952).

Meyer, E., *Ursprung und Anfänge des Christentums: III. Die Apostelgeschichte und die Anfänge des Christentums* (Stuttgard/Berlin: Cotta, 1921; repr. Darmstadt: Wissenschaftliche Buchgesellschaft, 1962).

Morton, A. Q., *A Critical Concordance to the Acts of the Apostles* (Wooster, OH: Biblical Research Associates, 1976).

Moule, C.F.D., *Christ's Messengers: Studies in the Acts of the Apostles* (2d ed.; London: National Board of the YMCA, 1957; New York: Association, 1963).

Moulton, W. F., *The Old World and the New Faith: Notes upon the Historical Narrative Contained in the Acts of the Apostles* (London: C. H. Kelly, [1896]).

Müller, P.-G., *Christos Archegos: Der religionsgeschichtliche und theologische Hintergrund einer neutestamentlichen Christusprädikation* (Europäische Hochschulschriften, 23/28; Bern/Frankfurt am M.: Lang, 1973).

Mulder, H., *Jakobus en de oudsten in de boeken van Lucas* (Exegetica ns 1; Amsterdam: T. Bolland, 1972).

Neander, A., *History of the Planting and Training of the Christian Church by the Apostles* (2 vols.; The Biblical Cabinet 35–36; Edinburgh: Clark, 1842).

Neil, W., *The Truth about the Early Church* (London: Hodder and Stoughton, 1970).

Nestle, E., *Philologica sacra: Bemerkungen über die Urgestalt der Evangelien und Apostelgeschichte* (Berlin: Reuther & Reichard, 1896).

Pache, R., *Notes sur les Actes des Apôtres* (4th ed.; Saint-Legier: Editions "Emmaus," 1979).

Papa, B., *La cristologia dei Sinottici e degli Atti degli Apostoli* ([n.p.]: EE, 1972).

Parker, E. M., *Introduction to the Acts of the Apostles and the Epistles of St. Paul* (London/New York: Longmans, Green and Co., 1927).

Parsons, M. C., and J. B. Tyson (eds.), *Cadbury, Knox, and Talbert: American Contributions to the Study of Acts* (SBLBSNA; Atlanta: Scholars, 1992).

Pervo, R. I., *Profit with Delight: The Literary Genre of the Acts of the Apostles* (Philadelphia: Fortress, 1987).

Pierson, P. E., *Themes from Acts* (Ventura, CA: Regal Books, 1982).

Plümacher, E., *Lukas als hellenistischer Schriftsteller: Studien zur Apostelgeschichte* (SUNT 9; Göttingen: Vandenhoeck & Ruprecht, 1972).

Ralph, M. N., *Discovering the First Century Church: The Acts of the Apostles, Letters of Paul, and the Book of Revelation* (Discovering the Living Word 2; New York/Mahwah, NJ: Paulist, 1991).

Ramsay, W. M., *Pictures of the Apostolic Church: Its Life and Teaching* (London: Hodder and Stoughton, 1910; repr., Grand Rapids, MI: Baker Book House, 1959).

Reicke, B., *Glaube und Leben der Urgemeinde: Bemerkungen zu Apg. 1–7* (ATANT 32; Zurich: Zwingli, 1957).

Reimer, I. R., *Women in the Acts of the Apostles: a Feminist Liberation Perspective* (Minneapolis: Fortress, 1995).

Resenhöfft, W., *Die Apostelgeschichte im Wortlaut ihrer beiden Urquellen: Rekonstruktion des Büchleins von der Geburt Johannes des Täufers Lk 1–2* (Europäische Hochschulschriften 23/39; Bern/Frankfurt am M.: Lang, 1974).

Rétif, A., *Foi au Christ et mission d'après les Actes des Apôtres* (Paris: Cerf, 1953).

Ricard, O., *Geistesfrühling in der ersten Gemeinde: Nach der Apostelgeschichte und den neutestamentlichen Briefen* (Basel: C. F. Spittlers Nachfolger, 1911).

Richards, L., *The Great Adventure: The First Days of the Church: Studies in Acts, James, Galatians, and Romans* (Leader's ed.; Elgin, IL: D. C. Cook Pub. Co., 1977).

Rusche, H., *Zeugnis für Jesus: Der Weg der Frohbotschaft nach der Apostelgeschichte* (Gedanken zur Schriftlesung 5; Stuttgart: KBW, 1964).

Saoût, Y., *Cette activité libératrice: Etudes des Actes des Apôtres: Les disciples de Jésus devant le pouvoir, l'avoir, le savoir* (Paris: Mame, 1984).

Schmidt, K., *Die Apostelgeschichte unter dem Hauptgesichtspunkte ihrer Glaubwürdigkeit* (Erlangen: Deichert, 1882).

Schmidt, P. W., *Die Apostelgeschichte bei DeWette-Overbeck und bei Adolf Harnack* (Basel: Helbing & Lichtenhahn, 1910).

Schmithals, W., *The Office of Apostle in the Early Church* (Nashville: Abingdon, 1969).

Schulz, M., *Der Arzt Lukas und die Apostelgeschichte* (Berlin: Evangelische Verlagsanstalt, 1959).

Segalla, G., *Carisma e istituzione a servizio della carità negli Atti degli Apostoli* (Padua: Euganea Editoriale, 1991).

Siegel, G., *Gespräche um die Bibel: Ausgewählte Stücke aus den Evangelien und der Apostelgeschichte* (Stuttgart: Calwer-V., 1951).

Sorof, M., *Die Entstehung der Apostelgeschichte: Eine kritische Studie* (Berlin: Nicolai, 1890).

Speer, R. E., *Studies in the Book of Acts* (New York: International Committee of YMCA, 1892).

Spitta, F., *Die Apostelgeschichte: Ihre Quellen und deren geschichtlicher Wert* (Halle a. S.: Waisenhaus, 1891).

Stagg, F., *The Book of Acts: The Early Struggle for an Unhindered Gospel* (Nashville: Broadman, 1955).

Stauderman, A., *Journey through Acts: Part I, The Awakening Apostles* (Lima, OH: C.S.S. Publ. Co., 1989).

Stegemann, W., *Zwischen Synagoge und Obrigkeit: Zur historischen Situation der lukanischen Christen* (FRLANT 152; Göttingen: Vandenhoeck & Ruprecht, 1991).

Stifler, J. M., *An Introduction to the Study of the Acts of the Apostles* (New York/Chicago: Revell, 1892).

Tajra, H. W., *The Trial of St. Paul: A Juridical Exegesis of the Second Half of the Acts of the Apostles* (WUNT 2/35; Tübingen: Mohr [Siebeck], 1989).

Torrey, C. C., *The Composition and the Date of Acts* (HTS 1; Cambridge: Harvard University Press, 1916).

Trocmé, E., *Le 'Livre des Actes' et l'histoire* (EHPR 45; Paris: Presses Universitaires de France, 1957).

Vaughan, C. J., *The Church of the First Days: Lectures on the Acts of the Apostles* (2d ed.; Cambridge, UK: Macmillan, 1865–66).

Venetz, H.-J., *So fing es mit der Kirche an: Ein Blick in das Neue Testament* (Zurich/Einsiedeln: Benziger, 1981).

Vosté, J.-M., *Theses in Actus Apostolorum* (Rome: Angelicum, 1931).

Weiss, J., *The History of Primitive Christianity* (New York: Wilson-Erickson, 1937); repr. as *Earliest Christianity: A History of the Period* A.D. *30–150* (2 vols. with new introduction by F. C. Grant; Gloucester, MA: Peter Smith, 1970).

Wellhausen, J., *Kritische Analyse der Apostelgeschichte* (AbhKGW, Philol.-histor. Kl. ns 15/2; Berlin: Weidmann, 1914; repr. 1989) 1–56.

Wendland, P., "Apostelgeschichten," *Die urchristlichen Literaturformen* (3d ed.; Tübingen: Mohr [Siebeck], 1912).

White, E. G., *The Acts of the Apostles in the Proclamation of the Gospel of Jesus Christ* (Mountain View, CA: Pacific Press, 1911).

Wiater, W., *Wege zur Apostelgeschichte: Ein Arbeitsbuch* (Topos Taschenbücher 31; Düsseldorf: Patmos, 1974).

Wildhaber, B., *Paganisme populaire et prédication apostolique: D'après l'exégèse de quelques séquences des Actes: Eléments pour une théologie lucanienne de la mission* (Le monde de la Bible; Geneva: Labor et Fides, 1987).

Winter, B. W. and A. D. Clarke (eds.), *The Book of Acts in Its Ancient Literary Setting* (BAFCS 1, 1993).

Witherington, B. (ed.), *History, Literature and Society in the Book of Acts* (Cambridge: Cambridge University Press, 1996).

Woiwode, L., *Acts* (San Francisco: HarperSanFrancisco, 1993).

Zeller, E., *The Contents and Origin of the Acts of the Apostles, Critically Investigated, to Which Is Prefixed F. Overbeck's Introduction to the Acts from DeWette's Handbook* (London/Edinburgh: Williams & Norgate, 1875–76).

Zettner, C., *Amt, Gemeinde und kirchliche Einheit in der Apostelgeschichte des Lukas* (Europäische Hochschulschriften 23/423; Frankfurt am M./New York: Lang, 1991).

Zimmer, F., *Galaterbrief und Apostelgeschichte: Eine exegetischer Beitrag zur Geschichte des Urchristentums* (Hildburghausen: F. W. Gadow, 1882).

(186) C. MONOGRAPHS ON TOPICS COMMON TO LUKE-ACTS

Asting, R., *Die Verkündigung des Wortes im Urchristentum: Dargestellt an den Begriffen "Wort Gottes," "Evangelium" und "Zeugnis"* (Stuttgart: Kohlhammer, 1939).

Bachmann, M., *Jerusalem und der Tempel: Die geographisch-theologischen Elemente in der lukanischen Sicht der jüdischen Kultzentrums* (BWANT 109; Stuttgart: Kohlhammer, 1980).

Barrett, C. K., *Luke the Historian in Recent Study* (London: Epworth, 1961; repr. Philadelphia: Fortress, 1970).

Bock, D. L., *Proclamation from Prophecy and Pattern: Lucan Old Testament Christology* (JSNTSup 12; Sheffield, UK: JSOT, 1987).

Bovon, F., *L'Oeuvre de Luc: Etudes d'exégèse et de théologie* (LD 130; Paris: Cerf, 1987).

Brawley, R. L., *Centering on God: Method and Message in Luke-Acts* (Literary Currents in Biblical Interpretation; Louisville: Westminster/John Knox, 1990).

Brown, S., *Apostasy and Perseverance in the Theology of Luke* (AnBib 36; Rome: Biblical Institute, 1969).

Cadbury, H. J., *The Making of Luke-Acts* (New York/London: Macmillan, 1927; 2d rev. ed., London: SPCK, 1958; repr. 1961).

———, *The Style and Literary Method of Luke* (HTS 6; Cambridge: Harvard University, 1920; repr. New York: Kraus Reprint Co., 1969).

Carroll, J. T., *Response to the End of History: Eschatology and Situation in Luke-Acts* (SBLDS 92; Atlanta: Scholars, 1988).

Casalegno, A., *Gesú [sic] e il tempio: Studio redazionale di Luca-Atti* (Brescia: Morcelliana, 1984).

Cassidy, R. J. and P. J. Scharper (eds.), *Political Issues in Luke-Acts* (Maryknoll, NY: Orbis, 1983).

Chance, J. B., *Jerusalem, the Temple, and the New Age in Luke-Acts* (Macon: Mercer University Press, 1988).

Darr, J. A., *On Character Building: The Reader and the Rhetoric of Characterization in Luke-Acts* (Louisville: Westminster/John Knox, 1992).

Degenhardt, H.-J., *Lukas, Evangelist der Armen: Besitz und Besitzverzicht in den lukanischen Schriften . . .* (Stuttgart: Katholisches Bibelwerk, 1965).

Delorme, J. and J. Duplacy (eds.), *La Parole de grâce: Etudes lucaniennes à la mémoire d'Augustin George* (= *RSR* 69/1; Paris: Recherches de science religieuse, 1981).

Dömer, M., *Das Heil Gottes: Studien zur Theologie des lukanischen Doppelwerkes* (BBB 51; Bonn: Hanstein, 1978).

Doeve, J. W., *Jewish Hermeneutics in the Synoptic Gospels and Acts* (Assen: Van Gorcum, 1954) 168–76.

Ernst, J., *Lukas: Ein theologisches Portrait* (Düsseldorf: Patmos, 1985).

Esler, P. F., *Community and Gospel in Luke-Acts: The Social and Political Motivations of Lucan Theology* (SNTSMS 57; Cambridge/New York: Cambridge University Press, 1987).

Fearghail, F. O., *The Introduction to Luke-Acts: A Study of the Role of Lk 1, 1–4,44 in the Composition of Luke's Two-Volume Work* (AnBib 126; Rome: Biblical Institute, 1991).

Fitzmyer, J. A., *Luke the Theologian: Aspects of His Teaching* (New York/Mahwah, NJ: Paulist, 1989).

Flender, H., *St. Luke: Theologian of Redemptive History* (London: SPCK; Philadelphia: Fortress, 1967).

Garrett, S. R., *The Demise of the Devil: Magic and the Demonic in Luke's Writings* (Minneapolis: Fortress, 1989).

George, A., *Études sur l'oeuvre de Luc* (Sources bibliques; Paris: Gabalda, 1978).

Gillman, J., *Possessions and the Life of Faith: A Reading of Luke-Acts* (Zacchaeus Studies: NT; Collegeville, MN: Liturgical, 1991).

Gowler, D. B., *Host, Guest, Enemy, and Friend: Portraits of the Pharisees in Luke and Acts* (Emory Studies in Early Christianity 2; New York/Bern: Lang, 1991).

Guillaume, J.-M., *Luc interprète des anciennes traditions sur la résurrection de Jésus* (EBib; Paris: Gabalda, 1979).

Hammer, P. L., *Interpreting Luke-Acts for the Local Church* (Lewiston/Queenston/Lampeter: Mellen Biblical Press, 1993).

Hastings, A., *Prophet and Witness in Jerusalem: A Study of the Teaching of Saint Luke* (London: Longmans, Green; Baltimore: Helicon, 1958).

Jervell, J., *Luke and the People of God: A New Look at Luke-Acts* (Minneapolis: Augsburg, 1972).

———, *The Unknown Paul: Essays on Luke-Acts and Early Christianity* (Minneapolis: Augsburg, 1984).

Johnson, L. T., *The Literary Function of Possessions in Luke-Acts* (SBLDS 39; Atlanta: Scholars, 1977).

———, *Luke-Acts: A Story of Prophet and People* (Chicago: Franciscan Herald, 1981).

———, *Sharing Possessions: Mandate and Symbol of Faith* (Overtures to Biblical Theology; Philadelphia: Fortress, 1981).

Juel, D., *Luke-Acts: The Promise of History* (Atlanta: John Knox, 1983; London: SCM, 1984).

Keck, L. E. and J. L. Martyn (eds.), *Studies in Luke-Acts: Essays Presented in Honor of Paul Schubert* (Nashville: Abingdon, 1966); repr. as *Studies in Luke-Acts* (Philadelphia: Fortress, 1980).

Kurz, W. S., *Reading Luke-Acts: Dynamics of Biblical Narrative* (Louisville: Westminster/John Knox, 1993).

Lampe, G.W.H., *St Luke and the Church of Jerusalem* (London: Athlone, 1969).

Luomanen, P., *Luke-Acts: Scandinavian Perspectives* (Publications of the Finnish Exegetical Society 54; Helsinki: Finnish Exegetical Society; Göttingen: Vandenhoeck & Ruprecht, 1991).

März, C.-P., *Das Wort Gottes bei Lukas: Die lukanische Worttheologie als Frage an die neuere Lukasforschung* (ErThS 11; Leipzig: St. Benno-V., 1974).

Marshall, I. H., *Luke: Historian and Theologian* (Contemporary Evangelical Perspective; Exeter, UK: Paternoster, 1970; Grand Rapids, MI: Eerdmans, 1971).

Minear, P. S., *To Heal and to Reveal: The Prophetic Vocation according to Luke* (New York: Seabury, 1976).

Monloubou, L., *La prière selon saint Luc: Recherche d'une structure* (LD 89; Paris: Cerf, 1976).

Muhlack, G., *Die Parallelen von Lukasevangelium und Apostelgeschichte* (Theologie und Wirklichkeit 8; Frankfurt am M./Bern: Lang, 1979).

Navone, J., *Themes of St Luke* (Rome: Gregorian University, [1970]).

Nellessen, E., *Zeugnis für Jesus und das Wort: Exegetische Untersuchungen zum lukanischen Zeugnisbegriff* (BBB 43; Cologne/Bonn: Hanstein, 1976).

Neyrey, J. H. (ed.), *The Social World of Luke-Acts: Models for Interpretation* (Peabody, MA: Hendrickson, 1991).

O'Toole, R. F., *The Unity of Luke's Theology: An Analysis of Luke-Acts* (GNS 9; Wilmington, DE: Glazier, 1984).

Pallis, A., *Notes on St Luke and the Acts* (London: Humphrey Milford, 1928).

Parsons, M. C. and R. I. Pervo, *Rethinking the Unity of Luke and Acts* (Minneapolis: Fortress, 1993).

Pilgrim, W. E., *Good News to the Poor: Wealth and Poverty in Luke-Acts* (Minneapolis: Augsburg, 1981).

Plymale, S. F., *The Prayer Texts of Luke-Acts* (New York: P. Lang, 1991).

Portefaix, L., *Sisters Rejoice: Paul's Letter to the Philippians and Luke-Acts as Seen by First-Century Philippian Women* (Coniectanea Biblica, NT series 20; Stockholm: Almqvist & Wiksell, 1988).

Radl, W., *Paulus und Jesus im lukanischen Doppelwerk: Untersuchungen zu Paral-*

lelmotiven im Lukasevangelium und in der Apostelgeschichte (Europäische Hochschulschriften 23/49; Bern/Franfurt am M.: Lang, 1975).

Richardson, N., *The Panorama of Luke: An Introduction to the Gospel of Luke and the Acts of the Apostles* (London: Epworth, 1982).

Schneider, G., *Lukas, Theologe der Heilsgeschichte: Aufsätze zum lukanischen Doppelwerk* (BBB 59; Konigsstein/Ts./Bonn: Hanstein, 1985).

Schweizer, E., *Luke: A Challenge to Present Theology* (Atlanta: John Knox, 1982).

Seccombe, D. P., *Possessions and the Poor in Luke-Acts* (SNTU B6; Linz: A. Fuchs, 1982).

Selwyn, E. C., *St Luke the Prophet* (London: Macmillan, 1901).

Sheeley, S. M., *Narrative Asides in Luke-Acts* (JSNTSup 72; Sheffield, UK: JSOT, 1992).

Siegel, G., *Gespräche um die Bibel: Ausgewählte Stücke aus den Evangelien und der Apostelgeschichte* (Stuttgart: Calwer, 1951).

Squires, J. T., *The Plan of God in Luke-Acts* (SNTSMS 76; Cambridge/New York: Cambridge University Press, 1993).

Stegemann, W., *Zwischen Synagoge und Obrigkeit: Zur historischen Situation der lukanischen Christen* (FRLANT 152; Göttingen: Vandenhoeck & Ruprecht, 1991).

Sterling, G. E., *Historiography and Self-Definition: Josephus, Luke-Acts, and Apologetic Historiography* (NovTSup 64; Leiden/New York: Brill, 1991).

Sweetland, D. M., *Our Journey with Jesus: Discipleship according to Luke-Acts* (GNS 30; Collegeville, MN: Liturgical, 1990).

Sylva, D. D. (ed.), *Reimaging the Death of the Lukan Jesus* (Monografien, Theologie 73; Frankfurt am Main: Hain, 1990).

Taeger, J.-W., *Der Mensch und sein Heil: Studien zum Bild des Menschen und zur Sicht der Bekehrung bei Lukas* (Gütersloh: Mohn, 1982).

Talbert, C. H., *Literary Patterns, Theological Themes and the Genre of Luke-Acts* (SBLMS 20; Missoula: Scholars, 1974).

——— (ed.), *Luke-Acts: New Perspectives from the Society of Biblical Literature Seminar* (New York: Crossroad, 1984).

———, *Luke and the Gnostics: An Examination of the Lucan Purpose* (Nashville: Abingdon, 1966).

——— (ed.), *Perspectives on Luke-Acts* (Special Studies Series 5; Danville VA: Association of Baptist Professors of Religion; Edinburgh: Clark, 1978; repr. Macon: Mercer University Press, n.d.).

Tannehill, R. C., *The Narrative Unity of Luke-Acts: A Literary Interpretation* (2 vols.; Philadelphia: Fortress, 1986, 1990).

Tiede, D. L., *Prophecy and History in Luke-Acts* (Philadelphia: Fortress, 1980).

Tyson, J. B., *The Death of Jesus in Luke-Acts* (Columbia: University of South Carolina, 1986).

———, *Images of Judaism in Luke-Acts* (Columbia: University of South Carolina, 1991).

——— (ed.), *Luke-Acts and the Jewish People: Eight Critical Perspectives* (Minneapolis: Augsburg, 1988).

Van Linden, P., *The Gospel of Luke & Acts* (Message of Biblical Spirituality 10; Wilmington, DE: Glazier, 1986).

Walaskay, P. W., *'And So We Came to Rome': The Political Perspective of St Luke* (SNTSMS 49; Cambridge: Cambridge University Press, 1983).

Wanke, J., *Beobachtungen zum Eucharistieverständnis des Lukas auf Grund der lukanischen Mahlberichte* (ErThS 8; Leipzig: St. Benno-V., 1973).

Wilson, S. G., *The Gentiles and the Gentile Mission in Luke-Acts* (SNTSMS 23; Cambridge: Cambridge University Press, 1973).

Zingg, P., *Das Wachsen der Kirche: Beiträge zur Frage der lukanischen Redaktion und Theologie* (OBO 3; Fribourg: Universitätsverlag; Göttingen: Vandenhoeck & Ruprecht, 1974).

(187) D. OTHER BOOKS FREQUENTLY CITED

Aland, K. and B., *The Text of the New Testament: An Introduction to the Critical Editions and to the Theory and Practice of Modern Textual Criticism* (Grand Rapids, MI: Eerdmans; Leiden: Brill, 1987).

Benoit, P., *Exégèse et théologie* (4 vols.; Paris: Cerf, 1961, 1961, 1968, 1982).

Braun, H., *Qumran und das Neue Testament* (2 vols.; Tübingen: Mohr [Siebeck], 1966) 1.139–68; 2.144–211.

Bultmann, R., *Exegetica: Aufsätze zur Erforschung des Neuen Testaments* (ed. E. Dinkler; Tübingen: Mohr [Siebeck] 1967).

Cerfaux, L., *Recueil Lucien Cerfaux* (3 vols.; BETL 6–7, 18; Gembloux: Duculot, 1954, 1954, 1962).

Conzelmann, H. and A. Lindemann, *Interpreting the New Testament: An Introduction to the Principles and Methods of N. T. Exegesis* (Peabody, MA: Henrickson, 1988), 229–44.

Finegan, J., *The Archeology of the New Testament: The Mediterranean World of the Early Christian Apostles* (Boulder, CO: Westview; London: Croom Helm, 1981).

———, *Handbook of Biblical Chronology* (Princeton: Princeton University Press, 1964).

———, *Light from the Ancient Past* (2d ed.; Princeton: Princeton University Press, 1959).

Gantois, R. (ed.), *A cause de l'Evangile: Etudes sur les Synoptiques et les Actes offertes au P. Jacques Dupont, O.S.B. à l'occasion de son 70e anniversaire* (LD 123; Paris: Publications de Saint-André/Cerf, 1985).

Haenchen, E., *Gott und Mensch: Gesammelte Aufsätze* (Tübingen: Mohr [Siebeck], 1965).

Jeremias, J., *Abba: Studien zur neutestamentlichen Theologie und Zeitgeschichte* (Göttingen: Vandenhoeck & Ruprecht, 1966).

Koester, H., *Introduction to the New Testament* (2 vols.; Philadelphia: Fortress; Berlin: de Gruyter, 1982).

Kümmel, W. G., *Introduction to the New Testament* (rev. ed.; Nashville: Abingdon, 1975).

Marxsen, W., *Introduction to the New Testament: An Approach to Its Problems* (Oxford: Blackwell, 1968).

Menoud, P. H., *Jesus Christ and the Faith: A Collection of Studies* (PTMS 18; Pittsburgh: Pickwick, 1978).

Millar, F., *The Roman Near East 32* BC–AD *337* (Cambridge: Harvard University Press, 1993).

Moule, C.F.D., *An Idiom Book of New Testament Greek* (Cambridge: Cambridge University Press, 1973).

Moulton, J. H., *A Grammar of New Testament Greek* (4 vols.; Edinburgh: Clark); vol. 1 (3d ed., 1949), vol. 2 (with W. F. Howard, 1929), vols. 3–4 (by N. Turner, 1963, 1976); repr. 1978–80.

Ramsay, W. M., *St. Paul the Traveller and the Roman Citizen* (11th ed.; London: Hodder and Stoughton, n.d.).

Schürer, E., *The History of the Jewish People in the Age of Jesus Christ (175* B.C.–A.D. *135)* (ed. G. Vermes et al.; 3 vols. in four; Edinburgh: Clark, 1973, 1979, 1986, 1987), 1.58–60, 357–98, 442–83.

Sherwin-White, A. N., *Roman Society and Roman Law in the New Testament* (The Sarum Lectures 1960–61; Oxford: Clarendon, 1963; repr. 1969).

Unnik, W. C. van, *Sparsa Collecta: The Collected Essays of W. C. van Unnik* (NovTSup 29–31; Leiden: Brill, 1973, 1980, 1983).

Translation, Commentary, and Notes

◆

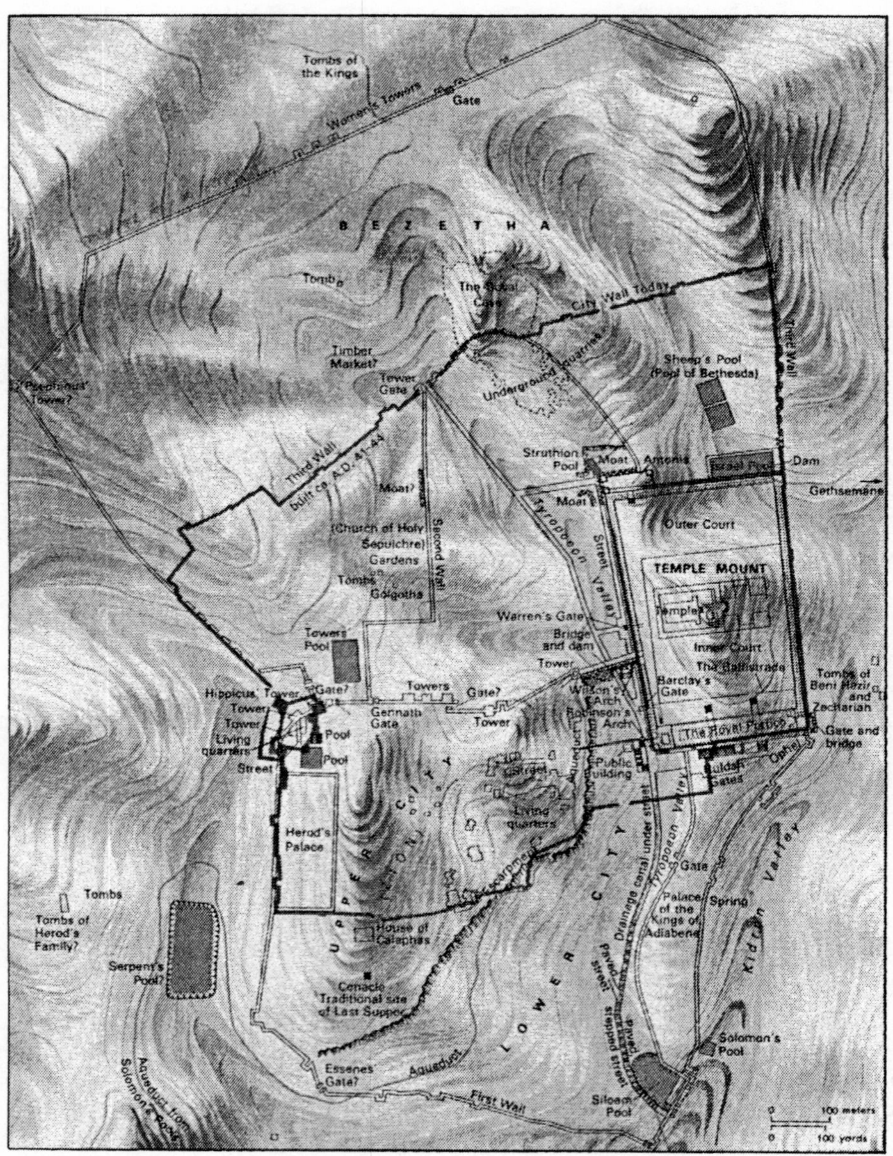

Map 3. Jerusalem

I. The Early Christian Community (1:1–26)

◆

A. Commission of Witnesses and Jesus' Farewell (1:1–14)

1. The Prologue (1:1–2)

1 [1]In my first account, Theophilus, I dealt with all that Jesus did and taught
from the beginning, [2]until the day that he was taken up, after he had instructed
through the Holy Spirit the apostles whom he had chosen.

WT: [2][some forms of WT omit "he was taken up, after"] . . . chosen, and he commanded (them) to preach the gospel.

✓ WT

COMMENT

Luke begins the Acts of the Apostles as he had begun the Third Gospel, with a literary prologue. Palmer ("The Literary Background"), Weiser (*Apg,* 46–47), and Barrett (*Acts,* 61) consider vv 1–14 to be Luke's literary introduction to Acts, and Johnson (*Acts,* 28) uses vv 1–11 as that. In a sense their reasoning may be better, because those verses (1–14 or 1–11) summarize details already presented in the Lucan Gospel and are all of clearly Lucan composition; however, the first two verses combine different literary forms and use some pre-Lucan tradition so that they have to be treated differently. They present the prologue, the risen Christ's farewell and commission, his ascension, and a description of the primitive community. So it is better to interpret them separately and consider the first two verses only as the prologue to Acts.

When did Luke compose this new prologue? That is a question not easy to answer. If, as seems likely, the Lucan account originally began at Luke 3:1–2 (*Luke,* 310–11, 1588) and was continued to the end of Acts and only subsequently divided into two volumes with the new prologue (Luke 1:1–4) and the addition of the infancy narrative (Luke 1:5–2:52), then the prologue to Acts may have been added at the same time. If there is any plausibility to this suggestion, one still has to cope with the problem of the double account of the ascension (Acts 1:2, 9). It might seem that Acts 1:3 followed directly on Luke 24:49. That would have made the division of the work fall at the end of Jesus' commission (24:44–49), roughly corresponding to Matt 28:16–20, and would have said nothing about the ascension; but then why would Luke have added 24:50–53 to the end of the Gospel, if he had already written Acts 1:9–11? It is perhaps more likely that Acts 1:3 originally followed on Luke 24:53 and that, as Benoit noted ("The Ascension," 242), Luke came upon the precise information about the interval between the resurrection and ascension only after he had finished the Gospel, and he intended Acts 1:9–11 to be a slight correction of what he had written earlier.

The prologue contains three elements: (1) the name of the person to whom the author dedicates his writing: Theophilus; (2) a brief description of the contents of the first volume, the Gospel, and its continuity with it; and (3) an allusion to the episodes that immediately follow.

This prologue, however, shares with the first volume the mode of literary presentation that Luke had used there in 1:1–4. It is neither as long as that of the Gospel nor as well constructed (as the periodic sentence composed for the first volume). The related prologues are similar to a convention found in Greek historical writers such as Herodotus, Thucydides, Josephus, and Polybius (*Historiae,* 2.1.1–2) and in such Hellenistic technical writers as Diodorus Siculus (*Bibliotheca Historica* 2.1), Dioscorides Pedanius (*De materia medica* 1.1), Hippocrates (*De prisca medicina* 1), and Aristeas (*Ep. ad Philocraten* 1). Josephus's apologetic work, Ag.*Ap.* 1.1 §§1–3; 2.1 §1, is particularly pertinent (see *Luke,* 288). Yet as Callan ("The Preface") has shown, Luke's double preface (prologue) resembles the prefaces of ancient histories more than those of biographies or other types of writing. Moreover, the first preface called attention to the assurance *(asphaleia)* that motivated the account that Luke was seeking to present. Whether Luke has achieved that assurance has to be judged by more than his protestation in such a prologue, which immediately raises the question of the degree of historical value to be accorded his account (see Introduction §§129–39).

In dedicating the second volume to the same person, Theophilus, to whom he had dedicated his "first account," Luke is clearly calling attention to the relation of the two parts of his literary work. In the prologue to Acts Luke continues to write as a third-generation Christian, who is composing his account in a period after the earthly ministry of Jesus and after his ascension. He again marks his distance from the "events," of which he had spoken in Luke 1:1. Now, however, he says nothing about his own involvement in any of the events to be narrated, which he seemed to imply in the prologue of his Gospel, when he spoke of "the events that have come to fulfillment among us" (1:1). There the "us" has to be distinguished from the "us" of v 2, but it has to include himself and other third-generation Christians, and especially what will be involved in the use of the first-person plural in the We-Sections of Acts (see Introduction, §§94–102).

Again, Luke makes his literary ambition serve a theological intention. The stated purpose expressed in Luke 1:1–4 has to be understood as governing the second volume as well as the first (*Luke*, 289–90). The differences between the two prologues, however, are not sufficient to reveal that the first prologue was not meant as the preface to the two-volume work, and the close literary association of Acts with the Third Gospel calls for such an interpretation of the first prologue. This has been denied at times (Conzelmann, *Theology*, 15 n. 1; Haenchen, *Acts*, 136 n. 3). See, however, E. E. Ellis, *The Gospel of Luke* (London: Nelson, 1966) 62; Marshall, "Acts and the 'Former Treatise,'" 172–74.

Luke writes the sequel to his first volume as a Hellenistic historian, but the mold in which he casts his narrative is still governed by what he intended when he projected his story of "the events that come to fulfillment among us" (Luke 1:1), i.e., with a theological program in mind. That is why "the Holy Spirit" is mentioned in the second prologue.

The new elements that appear in this second prologue are not only the mention of Jesus and the beginning of his deeds and words, but also his instruction of chosen apostles through the Holy Spirit. The first element sums up the Third Gospel, and the second calls attention to the role that the risen Christ will play through the Spirit in Acts. The Spirit of God will not only be responsible for the instruction of the apostles and other disciples, but will play a role in the developing narrative about the spread of the Word of God from Jerusalem to "the end of the earth" (1:8). There are only a few chapters in Acts in which the Spirit's influence is not evident in some way. It first appears in 1:2, and 56 times thereafter. Luke thus emphasizes the activity of the Spirit right from the very beginning of Acts as the driving force that launches the Period of the Church (see 9:31). It had been similarly depicted in the Period of Israel, and especially at the beginning of the Period of Jesus. The Spirit now becomes the dynamo of the narrative now about to unfold. Thus Acts presents the sequel to the Jesus-story of the Lucan Gospel and stresses the continuity between what was begun in the earthly ministry of Jesus and the Christian church, initiated by the risen Christ's instruction of the apostles through the Holy Spirit.

A minor textual problem is encountered here. Although the Codex Bezae basically agrees with the Alexandrian text-tradition, some witnesses of the WT read: ". . . until the day that he chose the apostles through the Holy Spirit and commanded (them) to preach the gospel." In this form there is no mention of the ascension. In Luke 24:51 the words *kai anephereto eis ton ouranon*, "and was carried up into heaven," are likewise omitted in MSS ℵ*, D, and the VL and Syriac Sinaitic versions (see *Luke*, 1590), i.e., in most of the WT. So Epp has raised the question that "if the 'Western' text *were* the original text of the gospels and Acts . . . could it then not be argued with considerable persuasion that the notion of the ascension of the risen Christ as a visible transfer from earth to heaven was only a secondary and later development in early Christian thought?" ("The Ascension," 144–45). That it may be a development in early Christian thought has to be admitted (see below), but this query gives too much play to the WT. After all, the same witnesses of the WT tradition, which omit the crucial words in v 2, record that a cloud took him up in v 9 and mention his going into the heavens. So the WT does not completely omit mention of the ascension in Acts. Zwiep ("The Text," 237), after examining the pros and cons in favor of the WT reading, concludes that one must prefer the Alexandrian text of vv 1–2 as original.

"Ascension" is a way we refer to what Luke means when he says, "he was taken up." It is his way of referring to what other (and earlier) NT writers have called Christ's "exaltation," a term that Luke will use in 2:33. The ascension functions in the Lucan account as the last appearance of the risen Christ from glory, as he takes visible leave of his assembled followers (see *Luke*, 1587–89). Luke has dramatized the exaltation as a visibly perceptible ascension of Christ into heaven. The ascension thus functions as the end of the Period of Jesus; once the risen Christ has taken his leave, the Period of the Church under Stress begins (see *Luke*, 181–87). No matter how the double reference to the same event, one at the end of the Gospel and the other at the beginning of Acts, is explained, it is clear that Luke makes of it an important caesura in his depiction of the phases of salvation history.

The editor, D. N. Freedman, has called my attention to a similar double reference to one event in 2 Chr 36:22–23 and Ezra 1:1–3, where the edict of Cyrus is mentioned twice, almost verbatim. If 1–2 Chronicles and Ezra-Nehemiah are the work of one author ("the Chronicler") and if that order of these books were original, the edict of Cyrus might also function as an important caesura between the story of the downfall of Israel in 1–2 Chronicles and that of its restoration in Ezra-Nehemiah. The comparison, however, may not walk on all fours, because this order of the four books differs from that in the *Kětûbîm* of the MT and also from the order in the LXX, where apocryphal *Esdras* A has been inserted before *Esdras B*, which is a version of canonical Ezra and Nehemiah.

The mention of Jesus' being "taken up" is an important christological affirmation, since it reflects the early Christian conviction that after his earthly ministry and death Jesus has become the risen Lord, who is in glory, in the presence of the Father, until he "comes again" (1:11). Even in this brief prologue Luke is emphasizing for the Christian reader of Acts how Jesus, who is now the risen and exalted Christ, has taken care through the Holy Spirit to train his apostles. The risen Christ does not leave his followers without assistance and instruction.

NOTES

1:1. *In my first account.* The *prōtos logos* refers to the Lucan Gospel. The same connotation of *logos,* "word," is found in Philo, who refers similarly to an earlier composition as *ho men proteros logos* in a dedicatory prologue (*Quod omnis probus liber sit* 1.1 §445). For *logos* = "book," see Plato, *Parmenides* 2.127D; Herodotus, *History* 5.36. The adj. *prōtos* is sometimes used in the sense of *proteros*, "former" (of two); see Acts 7:12; 12:10; Matt 21:28; John 1:15; Rev 20:5; 21:1; Diodorus Siculus, *Bibliotheca historica* 1.42.1. The use of *prōtos* does not imply that Luke was intending to write more than two volumes (BDF §62; ZBG §151). Nor was he referring to what some interpreters have called Proto-Luke, *pace* C.S.C. Williams ("The Date of Luke-Acts," *ExpTim* 64 [1952–53]: 283–84). Note the solitary *men*, the particle to which a *de* should correspond, but does not; it occurs also in Acts 3:13, 21; 27:21; 28:22 (BDF §447.3).

Theophilus. The same person to whom Luke dedicated his Gospel (see *Luke*, 299–300); though he is otherwise unknown, there is no reason to doubt his real existence. In the Gospel, he is hailed *kratiste Theophile*, "Your Excellency, Theophilus." The adj. *kratistos* was the Greek equivalent of Latin *egregius*, a title often used for the *ordo equester*, the "knights" of Roman society. It is used of the governor Felix in 23:26. It at least implies that Theophilus was socially respected and probably well off (L. Alexander [*The Preface*, 191–98] calls him the head of a house-church). He might have been Luke's *patronus*, one who would have financed the copying and publication of the Lucan work, even if dedication in ancient writings did not always imply that. Dedication to him hardly means that the work was intended solely for private reading. Theophilus may have been a catechumen or Christian neophyte and undoubtedly represents the kind of reader for whom Luke was writing.

I dealt with all that Jesus did and taught from the beginning. Lit., "concerning all that Jesus began to do and to teach." This statement describes the Lucan Gospel. "To do and to teach" is a description of Jesus' deeds of healing and words of instruction during his ministry, a summary of the impact that Jesus made, such as Luke has narrated in his Gospel (5:15; 6:18; 9:11; cf. 24:19). "Began" is a form of *archein*, the verb employed elsewhere (Luke 3:23; 23:5; Acts 1:22; 10:37) to refer to the inception of Jesus' ministry, i.e., from the baptism conferred by John, even though Luke's Gospel tells the story of Jesus' life from his conception. This verb is not pleonastic, so that it might be omitted in translation, as some commentators have done (Wendt, Boudou, Renié, Haenchen); it has rather to be given its normal force in Lucan writing, because it relates what becomes "the church" in Acts to what Jesus inaugurated in his public ministry. It is related to the noun *archē*, "beginning" (11:15), which describes the opening of the Period of the Church (cf. Luke 24:47). Note too its use in Acts 8:35; 11:4. See Feuillet, "Le 'commencement'"; E. Samain, "La notion de APXH."

2. *until the day that he was taken up.* The VL and Augustine omit "he was taken up," but the best Greek MSS read it; it is also the *lectio difficilior*. Its omission would eliminate mention of the ascension. Note the variants of the WT above; see J. M. Creed, "The Text and Interpretation of Acts i 1–2," *JTS* 35 (1934): 176–82; M. C. Parsons, "The Text of Acts 1:2 Reconsidered," *CBQ* 50 (1988): 58–71; *TCGNT*, 236–41.

Among NT writers Luke is the only one who demarcates the end of Jesus' ministry by the ascension, using the passive verb *anelēmphthē*, which echoes the passive *anephereto*, "was carried up" (Luke 24:51) and will be echoed in Acts 1:9,

11, 22; cf. 1 Tim 3:16; Mark 16:19. The same verb is used in 2 Kgs 2:11c (LXX) of Elijah's being taken up to heaven. Contrast John 20:17 (*oupō anabebēka,* "I have not yet ascended") and Eph 4:9 (*anebē,* "he went up").

Van Stempvoort ("'The Interpretation") tried to understand *anelēmphthē* as "to die, to be taken up in the sense of to pass away, removal out of this world," arguing that this is the normal sense of *analambanesthai* in Hellenistic Greek and is suggested by the noun *analēmpsis* (Luke 9:51). Dupont has shown that such an understanding is far from convincing and that the NT parallels to this verb reveal that it has to be understood in the traditional sense of ascension ("*Anelēmphthē* (Act. i.2)," *NTS* 8 [1961–62]: 154–57).

In this verse Luke does not indicate when that "day" was. In Luke 24:50–53 he depicted the taking up as an event on the evening of the day when the empty tomb was discovered. In vv 9–11 below Luke will depict the ascension itself as a visibly perceptible event occurring after an interval of "forty days." The ascension in these verses thus creates a notorious problem when it is related to Luke 24:50–53, raising the obvious question: When did the ascension really take place? Part of the answer to that question comes with a proper understanding of what the ascension really was (see COMMENT above).

after he had instructed through the Holy Spirit. Christ uses God's Spirit in the instruction of his apostles after his death and resurrection. Cf. Matt 28:19–20. Some commentators understand the phrase *dia pneumatos hagiou* to modify the rel. cl. that follows: "the apostles whom he had chosen through the Holy Spirit" (Dupont, *Actes,* 35; Weiser, *Apg,* 49). That, however, unduly forces the flow of the Greek text, and there is no mention of the Spirit in the choice of the apostles in Luke 6:12–13. Through this instruction the "apostles" become the official transmitters of the gospel that Jesus himself has preached. So Luke stresses the Spirit-guided apostolic character of the Christian gospel.

This is the first of 57 occurrences of "the Spirit" in Acts: 1:2, 5, 8, 16; 2:4, 17, 18, 33, 38; 4:8, 25, 31; 5:3, 9, 32; 6:5; 7:51, 55; 8:15, 17–19, 29, 39; 9:17, 31; 10:19, 38, 44, 45, 47; 11:12, 15, 16, 24, 28; 13:2, 4, 9, 52; 15:8, 28; 16:6, 7; 19:2, 6; 20:23, 28; 21:4, 11; 28:25. Luke does not tell us how the Spirit "instructed" the apostles, but that is something that we learn as we read between the lines of the developing story in Acts.

Luke takes over the portrayal of the Spirit from the OT: a way of expressing God's presence to human beings or to the world in the form of a breath or forceful wind active in creating (Ps 33:6), raising up leaders (Judg 6:34; 11:29), inspiring prophecy (Num 24:2; Ezek 2:2; Hos 9:7), judging (Isa 4:4), and renewing the face of the earth (Ps 104:30). See further *Luke,* 227–31.

the apostles whom he had chosen. This clause alludes to Luke 6:13, "he called his disciples and chose twelve of them whom he also named apostles," a reformulation of Mark 3:13–14. The last clause, "whom he also named apostles," is a peculiarly Lucan addition, which limits the "apostles" to the Twelve, and the Twelve to the apostles (see *Luke,* 614–16). This limitation will govern a number of details in the Lucan story as the sequel in Acts unfolds. Whereas "apostle" occurs only once in Mark, Matthew, and John, it is used often by Luke (six times in the Gospel and 28 times in Acts). As a title, it is scarcely to be traced back to Jesus himself, but represents rather an important title that developed in the early pre-Lucan and pre-Pauline church in Judea, where it was used of a group of Christian emissaries greater than the Twelve.

The title *apostolos* is derived from *apostellein*, "send," and in earlier Greek it denoted either someone or something sent: e.g., a naval expedition, an envoy (Herodotus, *History* 1.2), a bill of lading, a colonist (MM, 70); Josephus (*Ant.* 17.11.1 §300) uses it in an abstract sense for the "sending" of a delegation of Jews to Rome. It occurs only once in the LXX, translating the pass. ptc. *šālûaḥ*, "sent" (*RSV*: "charged"; *NAB*: "commissioned"), said of Abijah sent by God with a message for Jeroboam's wife. The religious connotation of the title in the NT may be analogous to and possibly influenced by the Palestinian Jewish institution of *šĕlûḥîm/šĕlîḥîn*, "emissaries," commissioned by the Sanhedrin or rabbis to act in their name to settle calendaric, fiscal, legal, or religious matters. *Apostolos* in the NT goes well beyond that Jewish institution and has even become a specific Christian word, transliterated in modern languages instead of being translated: *apostolus, apôtre, apóstol, Apostel, apostle.* See further *Luke*, 617–18. Cf. J. A. Kirk, "Apostleship since Rengstorf: Towards a Synthesis," *NTS* 21 (1974–75): 249–64; F. H. Agnew, "The Origin of the NT Apostle-Concept: A Review of Research," *JBL* 105 (1986): 75–96; G. Leonardi, "'I dodici' e 'gli apostoli' nei Vangeli sinottici e Atti — Problemi e prospettive," *StudPat* 42 (1995): 163–95.

After *anelēmphthē* (end of v 2), MS D and ancient Latin and Syriac versions add "and he commanded (them) to preach the gospel." This reading, possibly influenced by Luke 24:47, adds little to the comprehension of the verse and introduces a questionable further instance of *euangelion*, a term that Luke avoids in his Gospel and uses in Acts only at 15:7; 20:24 (see *Luke*, 172–74; cf. *TCGNT*, 236–41).

BIBLIOGRAPHY (1:1–2)

Alexander, L., *The Preface to Luke's Gospel: Literary Convention and Social Context in Luke 1.1–4 and Acts 1.1* (SNTSMS 78; Cambridge: Cambridge University Press, 1993).

Alfaric, P., "Les prologues de Luc," *RHR* 115 (1937): 37–52.

Brown, S., "The Role of the Prologues in Determining the Purpose of Luke-Acts," *Perspectives on Luke-Acts* (ed. C. H. Talbert), 99–111.

Callan, T., "The Preface of Luke-Acts and Historiography," *NTS* 31 (1985): 576–81.

Delebecque, E., "Les deux prologues des Actes des Apôtres," *RevThom* 80 (1980): 628–34.

Epp, E. J., "The Ascension in the Textual Tradition of Luke-Acts," *New Testament Textual Criticism: Its Significance for Exegesis: Essays in Honour of Bruce M. Metzger* (ed. E. J. Epp and G. D. Fee; Oxford: Clarendon, 1981), 131–45.

Feuillet, A., "Le 'commencement' de l'économie chrétienne d'après He ii.3–4; Mc i.1 et Ac i.1–2," *NTS* 24 (1977–78): 163–74.

Giesen, H., "Der heilige Geist als Ursprung und treibende Kraft des christlichen Lebens: Zu den Geistaussagen der Apostelgeschichte," *BK* 37 (1982): 126–32.

Goodspeed, E. J., "Some Greek Notes: I. Was Theophilus Luke's Publisher?" *JBL* 73 (1954): 84–92, esp. 84.

Higgins, A.J.B., "The Preface to Luke and the Kerygma in Acts," *Apostolic History and the Gospel: Biblical and Historical Essays Presented to F. F. Bruce* . . . (ed. W. W. Gasque and R. P. Martin: Grand Rapids, MI: Eerdmans, 1970), 78–91.

Marshall, I. H., "Acts and the 'Former Treatise,'" *The Book of Acts in Its Ancient Literary Setting* (BAFCS 1), 163–82.

Palmer, D. W., "The Literary Background of Acts 1.1–14," *NTS* 33 (1987): 427–38.

Parsons, M. C. and R. I. Pervo, *Rethinking the Unity of Luke and Acts* (Minneapolis: Fortress, 1993).

Rius-Camps, J., "Las variantes de la recensión occidental de los Hechos de los Apóstoles (Hch 1,1–3.4–14)," *FilNeot* 6 (1993) 59–68, 219–29.

Robbins, V. K., "Prefaces in Greco-Roman Biography and Luke-Acts," *SBLSP 1978* (Missoula: Scholars, 1978), 2.193–207.

Samain, E., "La notion de APXH dans l'oeuvre lucanienne," *L'Evangile de Luc: Problèmes littéraires et théologiques: Mémorial Lucien Cerfaux* (BETL 32; Gembloux: Duculot, 1973; repr. 1989), 299–328.

Stempvoort, P. A. van, "The Interpretation of the Ascension in Luke and Acts," *NTS* 5 (1958–59): 30–42.

Vögtle, A., "Was hatte Widmung des lukanischen Doppelwerks an Theophilus zu bedeuten?" *Tätigkeit im rechten Sinne: Festschrift für H. Rombach* (Freiburg im B.: Herder, 1969), 29–45; repr. *Das Evangelium und die Evangelien: Beiträge zur Evangelienforschung* (Düsseldorf: Patmos, 1971), 31–42.

Zwiep, A. W., "The Text of the Ascension Narratives (Luke 24.50–3; Acts 1.1–2,9–11)," *NTS* 42 (1996): 219–44.

2. SETTING: JESUS' FAREWELL AND COMMISSION (1:3–8)

[3]After he had suffered, he presented himself alive to them in many convincing ways, appearing to them throughout forty days and speaking about the kingdom
of God. [4]Once when he met with them, he bade them not to depart from Jerusalem, but to await the promise of my Father, about which you have already heard
from me. [5]For John baptized with water, but in a few days you will be baptized
with the Holy Spirit. [6]When they gathered together, they used to ask him, "Lord,
is this the time when you will restore the kingship to Israel?" [7]He said to them,
"It is not for you to know the times or seasons that the Father has determined by
his own authority. [8]You will receive power, when the Holy Spirit comes upon

you, and you will be witnesses to me in Jerusalem, [in] all Judea and Samaria, even to the end of the earth."

WT: [4]. . . heard from my mouth. [5]. . . a few days until Pentecost . . . Spirit, which you are going to receive. [7](Instead of "It is not for you to") No one can.

COMMENT

Luke begins his narrative proper with an account of appearances of the risen Christ to his followers and of the instructions that he imparted to them. Form-critically considered, the episode is a narrative into which a short speech of the risen Christ has been incorporated. The narrative is thus a combination of an epiphany and a commission scene (see Mullins, "New Testament Commission Forms"). The commission is partly given in indirect discourse and partly in the words of Christ. It is a free Lucan composition into which he has possibly incorporated elements of Palestinian tradition, but not a real source. One learns that the appearances took place during an interval of forty days. They and the instructions make up the risen Christ's farewell, of which the ascension in vv 9–11 will be the climax.

Christ's instructions are, in effect, his last will and testament to his chosen followers. They deal with four things: (1) the kingdom of God, a transitional topic introduced from the Gospel, which is not further developed; (2) the command that the apostles not depart from Jerusalem, a repetition of Luke 24:49b; (3) the explanation of "the promise" of the Father, mentioned in Luke 24:49a but not explained there; it is now interpreted as a coming baptism with the Holy Spirit; and (4) the commission of the apostles as his witnesses.

The first instruction about the kingdom reveals that the risen Christ still had to explain to his apostles implications of the topic that had been the major theme of his own preaching during his earthly ministry. It was the goal of his ministry: "I must proclaim the kingdom of God in other towns as well, for that is what I was sent for" (Luke 4:43). In the Gospel, Jesus was portrayed as one constrained to *proclaim* God's kingship over human beings, which summed up his whole role. Unlike the Matthean Jesus, whose kingdom preaching was preceded by that of John the Baptist (Matt 3:2; 4:17), the Lucan Jesus alone preached the kingdom. Nevertheless, even in Luke 4:43 no effort was made by the evangelist to explain what "the kingdom of God" meant. It is taken for granted that the reader will know what is meant; so too here in Acts. See B. Noack, *Das Gottesreich bei Lukas* (Uppsala: Almqvist, 1948).

The second instruction charges the apostles not to depart from Jerusalem. Jerusalem is thus emphasized, because in v 8 it will become the focal point: the city from which testimony must be carried by witnesses and from which the word that they will carry must go forth. Thus Luke links the beginning of Acts to the end of his Gospel. The risen Christ made it known that testimony to him must "begin from Jerusalem" (Luke 24:47), and the apostles were told "to remain here in the city until you are invested with power from on high" (24:49). Emphasis on Jerusalem becomes the way that Luke plays out his geographical perspective, which is part of his theological program (see *Luke*, 164–71).

The third instruction clarifies how the apostles are to be "invested with power" (Luke 24:49), when they will have received "the promise" of the Father, now explained as a baptism with the Holy Spirit. The baptism they are to receive will not be a water baptism such as John the Baptist administered, but the one that he also announced: "I am baptizing you with water, but someone more powerful than I is coming. . . . He will baptize you with a Holy Spirit and with fire" (Luke 3:16). The more powerful one is not just the earthly Jesus of Nazareth, but the risen Christ, who now makes known Spirit baptism. The Spirit will be the power given to disciples, the dynamic principle of their existence as Christians and of their role as witnesses in the new phase of salvation history. The Spirit thus becomes the dynamo of the Lucan story in Acts; the Spirit is behind all that the witnesses will do or proclaim.

The fourth instruction is the most important because it not only relates the Spirit to the power to be received, but also explains the commission that Christ gives to the apostles: they are to be witnesses of him as risen. Verse 8 is, in fact, the programmatic verse of Acts; it sets the scope of the spread of the Word of God, the goal that the commissioned apostles are to attain as they bring that Word from Jerusalem to "the end of the earth." It is important because it outlines the spread of the Word and gives a summary of the development of the narrative in Acts itself: testimony will be carried by these witnesses from Jerusalem to "all Judea and Samaria" and to "the end of the earth," from Jerusalem to Rome.

All these instructions are given by the risen Christ, "after he had suffered" (1:3). Thus Luke carefully reminds his readers about the passion and death of Jesus; he has not neglected the story of the cross. Though he makes no comment here about the significance of that suffering, Luke implicitly asserts in this way the identity of the crucified Jesus of Nazareth with the risen Christ, who now further instructs his followers.

Luke also insists that Jesus "presented himself alive to them in many convincing ways" (1:3). This is yet another way in which he emphasizes the reality of the experience of the apostles to whom the risen Christ has appeared. In Luke 24:38–43, the risen Christ challenged his disciples to look at his hands and feet and to touch him; as they watched, he ate a piece of fish (*Luke*, 1572–77). The risen Christ now appears from "glory," i.e., he is presenting himself alive from the glorious presence of the Father, whence he has already appeared to disciples on the road to Emmaus: "Was not the Messiah bound to suffer all this before entering into his glory?" (Luke 24:26). There Christ used the past tense *edei*, "was it not necessary," meaning that he had already made the transit to the glorious presence of his Father, even on the day of the discovery of the empty tomb. So when thereafter he "appeared," it means that he presented himself from "his glory," from the presence of his heavenly Father.

"Appearing to them throughout forty days" (1:3), i.e., to his "apostles" (1:2), or possibly "the Eleven and their companions" (Luke 24:33), among whom were at least Matthias and Joseph called Barsabbas (1:23). Cf. 13:31, "for many days thereafter."

The question that the apostles put to the risen Christ in this episode is likewise important: "Lord, is this the time when you will restore the kingship to Israel?" (1:6). Not only do the apostles address Christ as "Lord," by the title used repeatedly in the NT for the risen Christ, but they ask him about "the time" when the kingship will be restored to Israel. That "time" distinguishes the period just beginning in God's salvation history from what had preceded in the period of Jesus' earthly ministry. The apostles' question is formulated in terms of the restoration of self-rule to Israel, perhaps even of the theocratic kingship once enjoyed by Israel of old, and certainly of the elimination of the occupying power of the Romans. The question about "the time" makes it clear that Luke thinks of a period now beginning, the Period of the Church under Stress, as different from the Period of Jesus, the period of his earthly ministry. This is why the three-phase division of Lucan salvation history, advocated by Conzelmann, has to be maintained, even if it must be slightly modified (see *Luke*, 181–87). Although the risen Christ does not answer the apostles' query about "the time," their query reveals how the ascension of Christ acts as a caesura marking off another phase of salvation history that is now beginning. It marks the Period of the Church precisely as the time when all followers of Christ must bear witness to him.

The role that the apostles are to play, once they have been "invested with power from on high" (Luke 24:49), is again said to be testimony: "you will be witnesses to me" (1:8); recall Luke 24:48. They must carry the message about the risen Christ and his meaning for humanity to "the end of the earth." Their testimony must see to it that this new "Word of God" is proclaimed to all human beings, for Jesus' apostles are not only to follow him but are being sent to bear witness to him (see *Luke*, 241–43).

That testimony is to be borne, first of all, in "Jerusalem," then to "all Judea and Samaria," and eventually "to the end of the earth" (1:8). Thus Luke sums up the progress of his narrative in Acts. By stages he will record the spread of the Word of God in Jerusalem (2:1–8:1a), from Jerusalem to Judea, Samaria, and all Palestine (8:1b–11:18 [except for the account of Paul's conversion in chap. 9]), then to Cyprus and Syria (11:19–30), to the Roman provinces of Syria, Cilicia, Galatia, Asia (13:1–14:28; 15:40–16:8), to Macedonia and Achaia in Greece (16:9–19:22), and finally to Rome itself, the capital of the Roman empire and of the civilized world of Luke's day (27:1–28:31), "the end of the earth." The meaning of the last phrase is debated (see NOTE below), but it may explain why Acts ends where it does, with the house arrest of Paul in Rome and his testimony there. In any case, it reminds the reader of the Lucan geographical perspective in such testimony. In the next episode a temporal perspective will be added.

By the instructions that Christ here gives to his apostles and followers, he commissions them to bear witness to him unto the end of the earth. They are not to ask about "time" or persons, because their commission is to last through all times, until he "will come back in the same way you saw him go" (1:11). That means that Christian followers are always to proclaim the Word about him and bear witness to him until he comes.

NOTES

3. *After he had suffered.* Luke refers to the passion and death of Jesus of Nazareth; for use of *paschein* in this sense, see Luke 22:15; 24:26, 46; of Jesus as the Son of Man, Luke 9:22; 17:25; cf. Acts 3:18; 17:3. It is not a specifically Lucan word, occurring also in Heb 5:8; 13:12; 1 Pet 2:21. Luke, however, insists that the role of Jesus did not end with his ignominious death on the cross.

he presented himself alive to them in many convincing ways. Luke presupposes the description of the appearance of the risen Christ already given in Luke 24:36–43. He adds *en pollois tekmēriois,* "with many proofs," using the noun *tekmērion,* which Aristotle defined as *anankaion sēmeion,* "a compelling sign" (*Rhetoric* 1.2.16). Cf. Lysias, *Or.* 12.51: *amphotera tauta egō pollois tekmēriois parastēsō,* "both these points I shall present with many proofs."

appearing to them throughout forty days. Luke thus recounts multiple postcrucifixion epiphanies of the risen Christ, a detail inherited from the early tradition. This agrees with what Paul reports in 1 Cor 15:5–8, a passage generally regarded as a primitive pre-Pauline fragment of the early church's kerygma, which included the proclamation of such appearances, *pace* Walker ("Postcrucifixion Appearances"). Recall 2 Cor 12:1,7.

The verb *optanesthai,* "let oneself be seen," is attested in 1 Kgs 8:8 (LXX); Tob 12:19 (MSS A, B), and also in extrabiblical writings (see MM, 454; H. J. Cadbury, "Lexical Notes on Luke-Acts," *JBL* 44 [1925]: 214–27, esp. 218–19). For such appearances Luke otherwise uses the aor. pass. *ōphthē,* "was seen" (Luke 1:11; 9:31; 22:43; 24:34; Acts 7:2, 30; 9:17; 13:31; 26:16), often followed, as here, by the dat. of the person(s) to whom the appearance is accorded. The use of the passive of a verb "to see" with such a dative may be influenced by the contemporary Aramaic equivalent *'itḥăzî lî,* "was seen to me," i.e., appeared to me (1QapGen 21:8; 22:27). Cf. BDF §313.

About "forty days," Conzelmann says that we do not know where the number comes from (*Acts,* 5). Because in 13:31 Luke speaks of Christ's appearances "for many days," he introduces "forty days" as a round number for a vague interval, as in OT usage (1 Kgs 19:8; Exod 24:18; 34:28; cf. 2 Esdr 14:23) or in general Greek usage (Diodorus Siculus, *Bibilotheca historica* 17.111.6; Josephus, *Ant.* 18.8.3 §272). Other commentators seek to give the "forty days" a symbolic meaning, as in many instances in the OT. Cf. R. Poelman, *Times of Grace: The Sign of Forty in the Bible* (New York: Herder and Herder, 1964). In either case, "forty days" has to be related also to the coming "fifty days" of Pentecost (2:1); in the Lucan intention it helps to fill in events between Passover, when Jesus died, and the first major Jewish feast thereafter, the Feast of Weeks, when for the first time the reconstituted Twelve confront Jews gathered in Jerusalem with their testimony and proclamation about the risen Christ. See Fitzmyer, "The Ascension," 437–38.

For the use of *dia* + gen. to express time during which, see Luke 9:37; Gal 2:1 (often misconstrued as "after"); cf. BDF §223.1.

speaking about the kingdom of God. "Kingdom of God" was a constant theme in the Lucan Gospel (4:43; 6:20; 7:28; 8:1, 10; 9:2, 11, 27, 60, 62; 10:9, 11; 11:20; 13:18, 20, 28, 29; 14:15; 16:16; 17:20*bis*, 21; 18:16, 17, 24, 25, 29; 19:11; 21:31; 22:16, 18; 23:51; sometimes merely "the kingdom": 11:2; 12:31, 32; 22:29, 30; 23:42). It reappears occasionally in Acts (8:12; 14:22; 19:8; 20:25; 28:23, 31). As the prime kerygmatic theme of the Synoptic tradition, it occurs 55 times in Matthew and 14 times in Mark, whereas the Johannine Gospel uses it only five times. Surprisingly, the phrase is never explained.

Kingdom of God is a way of formulating what was meant in the OT when Yahweh was spoken of as king (1 Sam 12:12; Isa 6:5; 33:22; 43:15; Jer 8:19; Mic 2:13) or when kingship and regal authority were ascribed to God (Obad 21; Pss 103:19; 145:11–13). It expressed God's spiritual dominion over the minds and lives of his people and of human beings in general, and in time came to formulate also an eschatological hope when God's salvation of them would be fully realized. In the NT, it expresses the new way the kingship of God has entered into human experience through Jesus' ministry, passion, death, and resurrection (see *Luke*, 154–56). See M. Wolter, "'Reich Gottes' bei Lukas," *NTS* 41 (1995): 541–63.

Because the phrase occurs in 28:31, describing Paul's preaching in Rome, it may act as a literary *inclusio,* linking the end of the Lucan account in Acts with its beginning here.

4. *Once when he met with them.* Lit., "coming together with them," or possibly "eating (salt) with them." Luke uses *synalizomenos,* which, if understood as a pass. ptc. of *synālizein,* would mean "being assembled together with"; but, if understood as a mid. ptc. of *synălizein,* would mean "eating salt with" (related to *hals,* "salt"), supposedly referring to Luke 24:30–31, 42–43; cf. Acts 10:41. Some commentators, both ancient (Chrysostom, Ephraem) and modern (Barrett, Bossuyt and Radermakers, Goodspeed, Dupont, Johnson, Polhill, Weiser), have preferred the latter meaning. However, it ill suits the context; some (e.g., Schneider, *Apg.*, 1.196) have even queried whether that meaning is attested elsewhere. MS D strangely reads *synaliskomenos,* "being taken captive together"; and MSS 323, 614, 1241*, 1739 read *synaulizomenos,* which some interpreters regard as a mere alternate spelling of *synalizomenos,* whereas others understand it more literally as "spending the night together with." Farfetched is the explanation of C.F.D. Moule ("The Post-Resurrection Appearances in the Light of Festival Pilgrimages," *NTS* 4 [1957–58]: 58–61) that the ptc. refers to the festival lodging of the Galileans in Jerusalem. Equally farfetched is Torrey's explanation that the ptc. is a translation of Aramaic *mtmlḥ,* "eating salt in company with"; Wilcox (*Semitisms,* 106–9) shows that such a meaning of *mlḥ* is simply unattested. Cf. *TCGNT,* 241–42; H. J. Cadbury, "Lexical Notes on Luke-Acts: III. Luke's Interest in Lodging," *JBL* 45 (1926): 305–22, esp. 310–17.

he bade them not to depart from Jerusalem. This repeats the instruction given in Luke 24:49b: "you are to remain here in the city." As the Lucan Gospel began in Jerusalem (1:5), so does Acts; as the story of Jesus began there, so does the story of the spread of the Word of God, "beginning from Jerusalem" (Luke 24:47). For Luke, Jerusalem, the royal city of the Davidic dynasty and chief city of contemporary Judea, plays an important role in his geographical and theological perspective as the city where salvation for humanity was accomplished (see *Luke*, 164–71).

but to await the promise of my Father. The promise is explained in v 5 as the reception of the Holy Spirit. The risen Christ reiterates the source of this promised influence as his own heavenly Father. Cf. 2:33, 39.

about which you have already heard from me. The risen Christ is depicted in Luke 24:49 making this promise in the name of his Father, but there the promise is not explained. This remark thus creates another link between Acts and the end of the Lucan Gospel. The WT (MS D, Vg) changes the last phrase to "from my mouth," an unimportant modification, not necessarily an original Semitism.

5. *John baptized with water.* John's testimony, "I am baptizing you with water" (Luke 3:16b), was preparatory for the baptism by "someone more powerful" than he, who would baptize "with a Holy Spirit and with fire" (3:16c, e). The latter baptism is described in the rest of the verse. Cf. Acts 11:16. John's testimony is introduced by *hoti*, which may be recitative ("that") or less likely causative ("because, for"), as Barrett would have it (*Acts*, 73).

in a few days. Lit., "not after these many days," i.e., at the end of the interval mentioned in v 3. The same temporal phrase occurs in Luke 15:13. For parallels in extrabiblical Greek, see D. Mealand, "'After Not Many Days' in Acts 1.5 and Its Hellenistic Context," *JSNT* 42 (1991): 69–77. Cf. Acts 2:1, to which the WT (MS D*) refers with its addition, "until Pentecost."

you will be baptized with the Holy Spirit. The Greek verb *baptizein* can mean simply "wash, soak, dunk, plunge (into water)," but it developed a religious connotation among Greek-speaking Jews because of their ritual and purificatory washings, as 2 Kgs 5:14 (LXX), Sir 34:25 (LXX), and Mark 7:4 reveal. From this developed John's sense of "baptism," which even Josephus calls *baptisis* or *baptismos* (*Ant.* 18.5.2 §117), whence eventually the Christian use of the word developed. The prep. *en* is used here in an instrumental sense ("with," like Aramaic *bĕ-*) and stands in contrast to the simple dative (*hydati*) used in the first part of the verse about John's baptism (cf. BDF §195). This Spirit baptism also has an OT background: "I shall sprinkle clean water upon you . . . , and a new spirit I shall put within you" (Ezek 36:25–26). Cf. Isa 44:3. In the Lucan view, Christ, "exalted to God's right hand," will receive "from the Father the promised Holy Spirit" and will pour it forth (Acts 2:33). Such a baptism will thus be the Spirit principle by which Jesus' followers will live their new lives and bear witness to the risen Lord. The Spirit will be the dynamo that activates their testimony. The WT (D*) adds the unimportant modification "which you are going to receive."

6. *When they gathered together.* I.e., with the risen Christ, who has been appearing to them. Luke writes *hoi men oun synelthontes*, using *men oun* in a continuative sense, "then," as in 1:18; 2:41; 5:41; 8:4, 25; 9:31; 11:19; 12:5; 13:4;

14:3; 15:3, 30; 16:5; 17:12, 17, 30; 19:32, 39; 23:18, 22; 25:11; 26:4, 9; 28:5. It probably refers to the apostles of v 2.

they used to ask him, "Lord, is this the time when you will restore the kingship to Israel?" Lit., "when you are restoring," a futuristic present (BDF §323). Since Jesus did not wrest the governance of Judea from the Romans during his earthly ministry, it was a natural or logical question for his followers to put to him as the risen Lord. Cf. Luke 24:21, where a similar remark is made by Cleopas on the road to Emmaus. Kingship in Israel had been known in the remote past from the time of the monarchy before the Assyrian and Babylonian Captivities, in the more recent past in the Hasmonean priest-kings (before the Roman occupation of Judea under Pompey in 63 B.C.), and in the case of individuals like Herod the Great (37–4 B.C.) even in Roman times. The question formulates a hope for the restoration of an autonomous kingly rule for the Jews of Judea. Though the disciples who pose the question are Christians, they still speak as Judean Jews on behalf of "Israel." The ancient Jewish prayers, *Šĕmônēh 'Eśrēh* 14 and *Qaddîš* 2, called upon God for the restoration of the kingship to Israel and also of David's throne.

The conj. *ei,* "if," introduces a direct question, as in 7:1; it is a Septuagintism, not found in classical Greek (see Gen 17:7; Amos 3:3; cf. BDF §440.3; ZBG §401).

7. *He said to them.* Luke uses another Septuagintism, a verb of saying with *pros* + acc. instead of the dat. of indirect object; see *Luke,* 116. It occurs regularly hereafter (e.g., 2:29, 37; 4:8, 19, 23; 5:35; 7:3; 8:20, 26; 9:10, 15; 10:21; 11:14; 12:15; 15:36; 18:14; 21:37; 28:3). Cf. *IBNTG,* 52.

"It is not for you to know the times or seasons that the Father has determined by his own authority. The risen Christ refuses to answer the political question posed by his followers. His answer is not a rebuke or a reproach, but part of the instructions that he has to pass on to his followers. It is both negative (*ouch,* "not") and positive (*alla,* "but" [v 8]): only the heavenly Father knows the time when the definitive form of the kingdom will come. From what follows, it emerges that the kingdom awaits the testimony that must be borne about it to "the end of the earth." Cf. Mark 13:32; Matt 24:36; 1 Thess 5:2. Combined *chronoi* and *kairoi* is also found in 1 Thess 5:1; Dan 2:21; and in earlier Greek literature (Demosthenes, *Or.* 3.16; *Ep.* 2.3; Strato of Lampsacus, *Frg.* 10 [MM, 315, 694]). The WT changes the first clause to "No one can"; no NT MS contains that reading, but it is found in free patristic quotations belonging to that text-tradition (see *TCGNT,* 243–44).

8. *You will receive power, when the Holy Spirit comes upon you.* This is the "power *(dynamis)* from on high," of which Christ spoke in Luke 24:49. The witnesses to the risen Christ will not receive a kingship for Israel but rather the power of God's Spirit, the effect of the outpouring of which will enable those who receive it to give testimony and speak with boldness (Acts 4:29, 31). See 19:6 for its reception at baptism. Conzelmann (*Acts,* 7) strangely comments, "The Spirit is no longer the power of the endtime but its substitute." That is hardly the

way to put it, because for Luke it is precisely the Spirit that is "the power of the endtime"; the gift of the Spirit will inaugurate the endtime and enable its recipients to bear Christian testimony. Cf. Isa 32:15.

you will be witnesses to me. This statement sums up the main theme of Acts; the apostles are to give testimony to all peoples about what Jesus "did and taught" (1:1), in effect, about the Word of God that he preached: "In his name repentance for the forgiveness of sins shall be preached to all the nations—beginning from Jerusalem! You are witnesses of this!" (Luke 24:47–48). It must now spread abroad through such testimony borne by Jesus' followers, first of all by apostles, but then by others; they are all to become ministers of the Word, empowered by his Spirit. Testimony thus becomes a literary theme in Acts, reappearing in 1:22; 2:32; 3:15; 4:20, 33; 5:32; 8:25; 10:39, 41; 13:31; 18:5; 20:21, 24; 22:15, 18, 20; 23:11; 26:16; 28:23. See G. Schneider, "Die zwölf Apostel als 'Zeugen': Wesen, Ursprung und Funktion einer lukanischen Konzeption," in *LTH*, 61–85.

in Jerusalem, [*in*] *all Judea and Samaria, even to the end of the earth.*" Although the testimony must begin "from Jerusalem" and pass through "Judea and Samaria" (8:1), its goal is "the end of the earth."

Ioudaia, "Judea," means the southern part of Palestine as differentiated from Samaria, Galilee, Perea, and Idumea (so used in Luke 1:65; 2:4; and will be used in Acts 8:1; 9:31; 11:1, 29; 12:19; 21:10). It does not designate the wider territory occupied by the Jewish people and part of the Roman province of Syria, as in Luke 1:5 (see NOTE there); 3:1; 4:44; 6:17; 7:17; 23:5; Acts 2:9; 10:37; 15:1; 26:20; 28:21. See F. Millar, *Roman Near East,* 337–66.

Samareia, "Samaria," denotes the region south of Galilee, from the Plain of Esdraelon/Jezreel south to the northern border of Judea (see NOTE on Luke 17:11). Nothing should be made of the omission of "Galilee" here; Luke is simply using a stock phrase in mentioning the two (see 8:1).

The last phrase *heōs eschatēs tēs gēs* is noteworthy as sg., not pl. *eschata,* which is more usual in extrabiblical Greek (Herodotus, *History* 3.25; Aeschylus, *Prometheus Bound,* 665; Demosthenes, *Ep.* 4.7; Crates, *Ep.* 31; Apollonius Rhodius, *Argonautica* 2.418; Strabo, *Geography* 1.1.8; 1.2.31). The sg. often occurs in the LXX (Deut 28:49; Ps 135:7; Isa 8:9; 45:22; 48:20; 62:11; Jer 6:22; 10:13; 1 Macc 3:9). Luke may be deriving the phrase specifically from Isa 49:6, as Dupont has argued (*The Salvation,* 17–19 [where the pl. is wrongly used]); similarly Dillon (*From Eyewitnesses*); Ellis ("The End"). There God says of his servant: "I have made you a light of the Gentiles, that you may be a means of salvation to the end of the earth" (*'ad qĕṣēh hā'āreṣ;* LXX: *heōs eschatou tēs gēs*). This Isaian verse is quoted in 13:47 (cf. Luke 2:32). So Luke may be alluding to it here and casting the witnesses to the risen Christ in the role of servants of the Lord.

The allusion, however, is not certain, because the phrase *eschatos tēs gēs* not only occurs elsewhere in the LXX, but also in *Ps. Sol.* 8:15, where it is used to speak of God bringing the mighty Pompey from "the end of the earth," i.e., from Rome. As a result, some commentators (Baljon, *Handelingen,* 5; Loisy, *Actes,* 159; Foakes-Jackson, *Acts,* 4; Conzelmann, *Acts,* 7) maintain that Luke is alluding to Rome with this phrase. If so, this would explain why Acts ends where it does, with the story of Paul's testimony in the capital of the Roman empire. This seems to be the preferable interpretation.

Still other commentators take the phrase as referring to Spain (R. D. Aus, *NovT* 21 [1979]: 244–46; Ellis, "The End"), or even to Ethiopia, whence comes the eunuch of 8:27 (Cadbury, *The Book of Acts,* 15; Thornton, "To the End"), or simply to the furthest extent of the then-inhabited world (van Unnik, "Der Ausdruck," 401: "die ganze Welt"). D. R. Schwartz ("The End") argues rather that *gē* does not mean "earth," but only "land," i.e., Palestine; the phrase would refer only to the first stage of the development of the Lucan account, not to the whole book of Acts. That interpretation, however, limits the sweep of the expression unduly.

BIBLIOGRAPHY (1:3–8)

Applebaum, S., "Judaea as a Roman Province; the Countryside as a Political and Economic Factor," *ANRW* 25/II.8 (1977): 355–96.

Best, E., "Spirit-Baptism," *NovT* 4 (1960): 236–43.

Dillon, R. J., *From Eye-Witnesses to Ministers of the Word* (AnBib 82; Rome: Biblical Institute, 1978), 129–30, 208–9, 214–15.

Dupont, J., "*Anelēmphthē* (Actes 1,2)," *NTS* 8 (1961–62): 154–57; repr. *Études,* 477–80.

Ellis, E. E., "'The End of the Earth' (Acts 1:8)," *BBR* 1 (1991): 123–32; "'Das Ende der Erde' (Apg 1,8)," *Der Treue Gottes trauen: Beiträge zum Werk des Lukas: Für Gerhard Schneider* (ed. C. Bussmann and W. Radl; Freiburg im B.: Herder, 1991), 277–87.

Fitzmyer, J. A., "The Ascension of Christ and Pentecost," *TS* 45 (1984): 409–40.

Gaventa, B. R., "'You Will Be My Witnesses': Aspects of Mission in the Acts of the Apostles," *Missiology* 10 (1982): 413–25.

Grässer, E., "*Ta peri tēs basileias* (Apg 1,6; 19,8)," *A cause de l'évangile,* 709–25.

Günther, E., "Zeuge und Märtyrer," *ZNW* 47 (1956): 145–61.

Harrison, E. F., "The Ministry of Our Lord during the Forty Days," *BSac* 95 (1938): 45–55.

Keck, L. E., "Listening to and Listening for: From Text to Sermon (Acts 1:8)," *Int* 27 (1973): 184–202.

Menoud, P.-H., "'Pendant quarante jours' (Actes i 3)," *Neotestamentica et patristica: Eine Freundesgabe, Herrn Prof. Dr. Oscar Cullmann* . . . (NovTSup 6; Leiden: Brill, 1962), 148–56; tr. in *Jesus Christ and the Faith: A Collection of Studies* (PTMS 18; Pittsburgh: Pickwick, 1978), 167–79.

Mullins, T. Y., "New Testament Commission Forms, Especially in Luke-Acts," *JBL* 95 (1976): 603–14.

Ohm, T., "Die Unterweisung und Aussendung der Apostel nach Apg 1:3–8," *Zeitschrift für Missionswissenschaft und Religionswissenschaft* 37 (1953): 1–10.

Rétif, A., "Témoignage et prédication missionnaire dans les Actes des Apôtres," *NRT* 73 (1951): 152–65.

Schwartz, D. R., "The End of the *Gē* (Acts 1:8): Beginning or End of the Christian Vision?" *JBL* 105 (1986): 669–76.

Scott, J. M., "Luke's Geographical Horizon," *The Book of Acts in Its Graeco-Roman Setting* (BAFCS 2), 483–544.

Thornton, T.C.G., "To the End of the Earth: Acts 1:8," *ExpTim* 89 (1977–78): 374–75.

Unnik, W. C. van, "Der Ausdruck *heōs eschatou tēs gēs* (Apostelgeschichte 1:8) und sein alttestamentlicher Hintergrund," *Studia biblica et semitica Theodoro Christiano Vriezen . . . dedicata* (Wageningen: Veenman en Zonen, 1966), 335–49; repr. *Sparsa collecta,* 1.386–401.

Walker, W. O., Jr., "Postcrucifixion Appearances and Christian Origins," *JBL* 88 (1969): 157–65.

Wikenhauser, A., "Die Belehrung der Apostel durch den Auferstandenen nach Apg 1,3," *Vom Wort des Lebens: Festschrift für Max Meinertz . . .* (ed. N. Adler; NTAbh Ergbd. 1; Münster in W.: Aschendorff, 1951), 105–13.

3. Jesus' Ascension (1:9–11)

[9]When he had said this, as they were looking on, he was lifted up before their very eyes, and a cloud took him out of their sight. [10]While they were still staring at the heavens, as he was going, two men dressed in white robes suddenly stood beside them and said, [11]"Men of Galilee, why do you stand here looking at the heavens? This Jesus, who has been taken up from you into the heavens, will come back in the same way you saw him go into the heavens."

WT: [9] [omits "as they were looking on, he was lifted up"] a cloud took him up, and he was taken from them. [11] [omits "into the heavens"].

COMMENT

In this narrative Luke presents an account of the exaltation of the risen Christ: how he was carried up to the heavens and took final leave of his assembled followers. Whereas there is no description of the resurrection of Christ in any of the canonical Gospels, which otherwise recount the discovery of the empty tomb, Luke now describes Christ's ascension. In effect, he is doing for it what the apocryphal *Gospel of Peter* (§35–42) has done for the resurrection (see *Luke,* 1538). For the proper way to understand Christ's "ascension," see the COMMENT on 1:1–2 above.

This account is, in effect, a narrative, or better a description of the exaltation of Christ that uses apocalyptic stage props to present in visible form Christ's final departure from his assembled disciples. Luke stresses the visible perception of Christ's leave-taking. Five different verbs emphasize that: "as they were looking on," "out of their sight" (v 9); "staring" (v 10); "looking," and "saw" (v 11). Thus the apostles become eyewitnesses of Christ's exaltation. The apocalyptic stage props are the clouds, the passing up through the heavens, and the message of angelic interpreters. This last appearance of Christ from glory thus ends with his final leave-taking from his assembled followers in a visibly perceptible way.

The message of the angel interpreters stresses that these "men of Galilee" will see him thus no more until he returns at the parousia, when he will again come from "the heavens." It is important to relate to this angelic message that of the two disciples who had gone off to Emmaus. On their return to Jerusalem, they reported to the Eleven and their companions, explaining "what had happened on the road and how he [Christ] became known to them in the breaking of the bread" (Luke 24:35). The message of that episode instructs Christian readers that, once the risen Christ has taken his final visible leave of the community, they would know his presence among them henceforth "in the breaking of the bread." That is the Lucan way of referring to the Eucharist, and readers are being told that the risen Christ would hereafter be present among them, not in visible form, but in their eucharistic celebrations. Neither this angelic message nor the Emmaus scene makes any mention of Christ's presence to his followers in the outpouring of the Spirit, but that further aspect will eventually emerge in the message of Acts 2. The angelic message now assures Christ's followers that he will come again, but no indication is given when that will happen. Commentators have at times claimed that Luke has thereby played down the parousia. Conzelmann (*Theology*, 136) even maintains that Luke has substituted for the delayed parousia the gift of the outpoured Spirit in the history of the church. That is an exaggeration, because Luke is almost alone among NT writers to assert that the exalted Christ will "come in the same way you saw him go," i.e., with clouds and from the heavens. Compare Paul's affirmation in 1 Thess 4:16, equally accompanied by apocalyptic stage props. The message of the two men to the Galileans is intended to turn their attention to the future and to what will result from the exaltation of Christ and his outpouring of the Spirit.

The passage is again one of Lucan composition, in which he has possibly made use of Palestinian tradition about the exaltation of Christ from a probably oral but not written source.

"This Jesus," who has become the exalted Christ, is the one to whom the apostles, baptized with the Spirit, must now bear witness until he comes again. So the ascended Christ inaugurates the Period of the Church, when testimony must be borne to him during all its times of storm and stress, of peace and growth. The angel interpreters pass on this message not just to "apostles," but to "men of Galilee," to people from the area where the earthly Jesus worked and taught. That message is meant to be extended to all Christians.

NOTES

9. *When he had said this.* Thus, Luke closes off the instruction of the apostles by the risen Christ.

he was lifted up before their very eyes, and a cloud took him out of their sight.

MS D reads: "a cloud took him up, and he was taken from them." The pass. verb *epērthē* is to be understood as a theological passive (ZBG §236), i.e., by God. Borne up by God's cloud, Christ is seen no more and thus returns to glory at his Father's right hand (2:33). The cloud is used in the OT sense of an apocalyptic stage prop, an instrument of God's presence, power, or glory (cf. Exod 16:10; 19:9; 24:15–18; Ezek 10:3–4; Ps 18:11; Dan 7:13); also in the NT, Luke 9:34–35; 1 Thess 4:17; Rev 11:12. Josephus (*Ant.* 3.12.5 §290; 3.14.4 §310) explains the cloud hanging over the desert tabernacle as "God's presence" (*tēn epiphaneian tou theou*). See L. Sabourin, "The Biblical Cloud: Terminology and Traditions," *BTB* 4 (1974): 290–311.

10. *While they were still staring at the heavens, as he was going.* This detail explains why Christ was said to have been "lifted up." The exaltation of Christ was in reality his passage after death to "glory," to the glorious presence of his Father. That transit is expressed at times in terms of resurrection or of exaltation, which have different connotations. According to an ancient conception of the world, exaltation implies his being taken up or his passing through "the heavens" (in Greek, sg. *ouranos*) or through the concentric celestial spheres (Aristotle, *Metaphysica* 12.8 §1037a); recall Paul's rapture to the "third heaven" (2 Cor 11:2). A similar way of phrasing Christ's ascension is found in Eph 4:8–10. These are time-conditioned ways of speaking about the transit of Christ to the Father's presence, wherever that may be.

Luke uses for the first time in Acts his favorite verb *atenizein*, "stare, gaze intently at"; see 3:4, 12; 6:15; 7:55; 10:4; 11:6; 13:9; 14:9; 23:1; cf. Luke 4:20; 22:56. He thus stresses the apostles' staring that they might vouch for Christ's ascent.

two men dressed in white robes suddenly stood beside them and said. Cf. Luke 24:4, where one finds a similar description, "suddenly two men in gleaming robes happened to stand by them." Eventually, in the summary (Luke 24:23) the "two men" are identified as "angels." The "white robes" are meant to suggest their otherworldly nature. Thus the ascent of Christ is attended by heavenly figures, who act as apocalyptic *angeli interpretes.* Cf. Acts 10:30; 2 Macc 3:26.

11. "*Men of Galilee.* Lit., "Men, Galileans." See NOTE on 1:16 for *andres Galilaioi.* The apostles are designated by their geographical origin in a part of the district of Judea from which most of them came, but as the Lucan story develops "men of Galilee" may take on a wider extension (see vv 12–14). Cf. 13:31.

why do you stand here looking at the heavens? The final leave taking of the risen Christ is depicted. The angelic query implies that these Galileans have other things to do, but they are assured about Christ's return. Compare the corrective question addressed by "two men" to the women at Jesus' tomb (Luke 24:5). MSS P^{56}, $\aleph^{c}$, A, C, D, Ψ, and the *Koine*-text-tradition read *emblepontes*, whereas MSS P^{74}, ℵ*, B, E, 33, 81, 1739 have the simple verb *blepontes*, "looking." Luke's *tí hestēkate* [*em*]*blepontes* is perfectly good Greek, and *pace* Wilcox (*Semitisms*, 125), there is no reason to invoke a Semitism here.

This Jesus, who has been taken up from you into the heavens. The last phrase "into the heavens" is omitted by MSS D, 33^{c}, 242, 326, probably a scribal omission to avoid repetition of "the heavens." This appearance, in which Jesus is exalted to the heavens means that his earthly role has come to an end; from now he will be seen no more in visible form and will exert his influence on humanity from heavenly glory and through his Spirit.

will come in the same way you saw him go into the heavens." The corrective comment of the angelic interpreters informs the Galileans about Christ's parousiac return. Luke uses the simple verb *eleusetai,* "will come," in referring to that return with apocalyptic trappings, and his adv. *houtōs,* "so," describes the trappings: from the heavens, with clouds and attending angels, but it also means "so really and so certainly." If the time of the return is unknown, its certainty is not. Cf. Luke 21:27; 1 Thess 4:16, *katabēsetai ap' ouranou,* "will come down from heaven." Between Christ's exaltation and his parousia is the time for the testimony of his followers, the Period of the Church under Stress.

BIBLIOGRAPHY (1:9–11)

Benoit, P., "The Ascension," *Jesus and the Gospel 1* (New York: Herder and Herder, 1973), 209–53.

Davies, J. G., *He Ascended into Heaven* (London: Lutterworth, 1958).

Grässer, E., "Die Parusieerwartung in der Apostelgeschichte," *Les Actes des Apôtres* (ed. J. Kremer), 99–127.

Hahn, F., "Die Himmelfahrt Jesu': Ein Gespräch mit Gerhardt Lohfink," *Bib* 55 (1974): 418–26.

Larrañaga, V., *L'Ascension de Notre-Seigneur dans le Nouveau Testament* (Scripta Pontificii Instituti Biblici; Rome: Biblical Institute, 1938).

Lohfink, G., *Die Himmelfahrt Jesu: Untersuchungen zu den Himmelfahrts- und Erhöhungstexten bei Lukas* (SANT 26; Munich: Kösel, 1971).

Maile, J. P., "The Ascension in Luke-Acts," *TynBull* 37 (1986): 29–59.

Menoud, P.-H., "Remarques sur les textes de l'Ascension dans Luc-Actes," *Neutestamentliche Studien für Rudolf Bultmann* . . . (BZNW 21; ed. W. Eltester; Berlin: Töpelmann, 1954), 148–56; repr. *Jesus Christ and the Faith,* 107–20.

Metzger, B. M., "The Ascension of Jesus Christ," *Historical and Literary Studies Pagan, Jewish, and Christian* (NTTS 8; Leiden: Brill, 1968), 77–87.

———, "The Meaning of Christ's Ascension," *Search the Scriptures: New Testament Studies in Honor of Raymond T. Stamm* (Gettysburg Theological Studies 3; ed. J. M. Meyers et al.; Leiden: Brill, 1969), 118–28.

Parsons, M. C., *The Departure of Jesus in Luke-Acts: The Ascension Narratives in Context* (JSNTSup 21; Sheffield, UK: JSOT, 1987).

Ramsey, A. M., "What Was the Ascension?" *BullSNTS* 2 (1951–52): 43–50.

Schille, G., "Die Himmelfahrt," ZNW 57 (1966): 183–99.

Schnider, F., "Die Himmelfahrt Jesu — Ende oder Anfang? Zum Verständnis des lukanischen Doppelwerkes," *Kontinuität und Einheit: Für Franz Mussner* (ed. P.-G. Müller and W. Stenger; Freiburg im B.: Herder, 1981), 158–72.

Weiser, A., "Himmelfahrt Christi. I. Neues Testament," *TRE* 15 (1986): 330–34.

Wilder, A. N., "Variant Traditions of the Resurrection in Acts," *JBL* 62 (1943): 307–18.
See further *Luke*, 1591–92.

4. The Primitive Congregation in Jerusalem (1:12–14)

[12]Then they returned to Jerusalem from the hill called Olivet, which is near
Jerusalem, a sabbath day's journey away. [13]Entering the city, they went to the
upper room where they were staying, Peter, John and James, Andrew, Philip and Thomas, Bartholomew, Matthew and James son of Alphaeus, Simon the Zealot,
and Judas son of James. [14]They were all devoting themselves with one accord to
prayer, together with some women and Mary, the mother of Jesus, as well as his brothers.

WT: [14]Omits "with one accord."

COMMENT

Having described the final leave-taking of the risen Christ from his assembled followers, Luke informs us who constituted that primitive Christian community in Jerusalem. He recounts how Jesus' Galilean followers return from Mt. Olivet to the city and gather in the upper room: the Eleven, some women, Mary, the mother of Jesus, and his brothers. These Galilean men and women thus assembled make up the nucleus of the early Jerusalem community, the growth of which Luke will studiously depict.

This episode is one of the narratives of Acts, the purpose of which is to describe how the first Christian community gathered in the city where Jesus, regarded as the founder of the movement that gave rise to its gathering, had been put to death. The characteristics of their communal life were devotion to prayer and unanimity. The adv. *homothymadon*, "with one accord," appears for the first time, but it will recur regularly hereafter in the first half of Acts to mark the exemplary harmony of the first Christians resident in Jerusalem. Their constant communing with God is also stressed in v 14, the first of the minor summaries of Acts. The scene is intended also to set the stage for the reconstitution of the Twelve, because that number is now defective. The passage is another Lucan composition, in which Luke uses some Palestinian tradition, especially in recording the names of the Eleven.

Luke's picture of the early Jerusalem Christian community paints its communal prayer and harmony. The Eleven, Mary, Jesus' brothers, and the Galilean women gather together to manifest their dedication to the departed Lord, who has not abandoned them, but assured them of the coming Spirit and their testimonial role. Though they are bereft of the Jesus that they had known, they find union together and engage in communal prayer to their God.

NOTES

12. *Then they returned to Jerusalem.* So far in the Lucan narrative of Acts the only persons mentioned have been "apostles" (1:1), addressed as "Galileans" (1:11), so the "they" has to be understood at first as the apostles. As the narrative progresses, we learn that "they" includes others. Jerusalem is named as the scene of the following events that Luke is about to recount. What has preceded in his account is closely related to this city, as his next comment will reveal. Again, he is solicitous to emphasize the importance of this pivotal city in his overall story; recall his geographical perspective (*Luke*, 164–71).

from the hill called Olivet. Lit., "from the hill called 'the Olive Grove.'" Recall Luke 24:50, "Then Jesus led them out as far as Bethany," where the ascension took place at the end of the Lucan Gospel. Bethany was mentioned earlier in the account of Jesus' royal entry into the Jerusalem Temple (Luke 19:29), along with Bethphage, both of which, Luke notes, were on "the hill called the Mount of Olives" (lit., "the hill called 'the Olive Grove'"). Bethany was a small village situated about 2.7 km east of Jerusalem, on the eastern slope of the Mount (*Luke*, 1248). According to Josephus (*J. W.* 5.2.3 §70) the Mount "lies opposite the city to the east, being separated from it by a deep ravine called Kidron." The spot from which the Galileans return is said in Zech 14:4 to be the scene of the coming of Yahweh on the last day and the gathering of the nations, with whom he would do battle.

which is near Jerusalem, a sabbath day's journey away. The proximity of Mt. Olivet to Jerusalem is thus correctly marked by Luke. It would be within the space that an observant Jew would be allowed to walk on the sabbath, 2,000 cubits. The extent of a sabbath day's journey was regulated by Exod 16:29 ("let no one go out of his place on the seventh day") and Num 35:5 ("you shall measure, outside the city, for the east side two thousand cubits"). In time this was measured from the walls of Jerusalem; details of the later rabbinical understanding of this regulation are found in Str-B, 2.590–94. Luke is concerned to depict the apostles as Christians still observant of their Jewish obligations. Josephus tells us that the Mount was six *stadioi* from Jerusalem in *J. W.* 5.2.3 §70, but five *stadia* in *Ant.* 20.8.6 §169.

13. *Entering the city, they went to the upper room where they were staying.* In Luke 24:53 the followers of Jesus were said to return to the Temple, but here they go to the *hyperōon*, "upper room," which thus becomes the scene of their assembly and prayer and where the descent of the Spirit upon them will take place. Traditionally it has been identified with the place where Jesus took his Last Supper with the Twelve, the so-called Cenacle (called *anagaion* in Luke 22:12; Mark 14:15), with which later traditions have also associated the house of Mary, the mother of John Mark (Acts 12:12). See *HPG*, 326–34; *ELS* §§728–87.

Peter, John and James, Andrew, Philip and Thomas, Bartholomew, Matthew and

James son of Alphaeus, Simon the Zealot, and Judas son of James. The names of the Eleven are given in an order slightly different from that in Luke 6:14–16. As there and in Mark 3:16–19 and Matt 10:2–4, three groups of four names are preserved, despite the difference of order of names within each group (see parallels in *Luke,* 615) and the omission of Judas Iscariot. MS E reads: "Peter and Andrew and James and John." For the bearing of the order of the first three names on the authorship of Luke-Acts, see S. H. Price, "The Authorship of Luke-Acts," *ExpTim* 55 (1943–44): 194.

Peter. "Simon, whom he named Peter" is the first listed (Luke 6:14). Luke, however, never tells why Jesus called Simon "Peter" or relates that name to Aramaic *kēphā',* "rock." See Fitzmyer, "Aramaic Kepha' and Peter's Name in the New Testament," *Text and Interpretation: Studies in the New Testament Presented to Matthew Black* (ed. E. Best and R. M. Wilson; Cambridge: Cambridge University Press, 1979), 121–32. Peter is not only the first apostle named, but becomes in Acts the spokesman for the others. Even when he is paired with John, the latter is always the silent partner (1:15; 2:14, 38; 3:1, 3–4, 6, 11–12; 4:8, 13, 19; 5:3, 8–9, 15, 29; 8:14, 20). Peter is the sole actor in 9:32–43; 10:5–46; 11:2–13 and delivers an important address at the Jerusalem "Council" (15:7). After that he disappears from the Lucan story, which is thereafter devoted to Paul.

John and James. These are the Galilean fishermen, sons of Zebedee, companions of Peter; see NOTE on Luke 5:10. John will appear with Peter in 3:1–11; 4:13–19; 8:14; his brother will be put to death by Herod Agrippa I (12:2).

Andrew. He is identified in Luke 6:14 as "his (Peter's) brother."

Philip. Listed here as one of the Eleven, he is often called Philip the apostle. In later times he will be confused with "Philip the evangelist, one of the Seven" (Acts 21:8; cf. 6:5; 8:5–40), e.g., in Eusebius, *HE* 3.39.9.

Thomas. Cf. Luke 6:15. The Greek name *Thōmas* resembles Aramaic *Tĕ'ōma',* "the twin," and was often used as its equivalent; see John 11:16; 20:24, "who was called Didymus" (Greek for "twin"). Both *Thōmas* and *Didymos* were used as epithets; John 14:22 refers to a "Judas, not the Iscariot," who in the Curetonian Syriac version becomes "Judas Thomas," and in the apocryphal *Acta Thomae* appears as *Ioudas ho kai Thōmas,* "Judas, alias Thomas." In the Coptic *Gos. Thom.*, which is ascribed to him, he appears as "Didymus Judas Thomas" (see *ESBNT,* 365–68). Whether all these names refer to the same person is hard to decide.

Simon the Zealot. As in Luke 6:15, the epithet *zēlōtēs* is added; it serves to distinguish him from Simon Peter and to designate him as a Palestinian Jew zealously opposed to the Roman occupation of the country; it could, however, also mean that he was zealous in other ways. Shortly before the First Revolt against Rome (A.D. 66–70) a nationalist resistance movement emerged in Judea, called "the Zealots" (see Josephus, *J.W.* 2.22.1 §651; 4.3.9 §§160–61; 4.9.1 §490; 4.9.5–10 §514–58; 5.1.1–2 §3, 5, 7; 5.3.1 §§101–3; 5.6.1 §250; 5.9.2 §358; 5.13.1 §528; 6.1.8 §92; 6.2.6 §148; 7.8.1 §268). Despite contentions to the contrary, there is no real evidence that this movement antedates the year A.D. 66. So the epithet might mean that this one of the Twelve later became a member of "the

Zealots," when they eventually emerged. See K. Lake, "Simon Zelotes," *HTR* 10 (1917):57–63; M. Smith, "Zealots and Sicarii, Their Origins and Relation," *HTR* 64 (1971):1–19; cf. W. R. Farmer, *Maccabees, Zealots and Josephus* (New York: Columbia University Press, 1956); M. Hengel, *Die Zeloten* (AGSU 1; Leiden: Brill, 1961).

Judas, son of James. Lit., "Judas of James," which is usually understood as *huios Iakōbou*, but could be *adelphos Iakōbou*, "brother of James" (Jude 1); see BDF §162.4. He is often called Jude, to distinguish him from Judas Iscariot, but is otherwise unknown, as is his father James. He is not the same as "Thaddeus," whose name appears instead in Mark 3:18; Matt 10:3. In later Christian tradition the two names were often joined, "Jude Thaddeus," but that joining has no basis in the NT. The difference in names merely indicates that by the time the Gospels were composed, the names of the original Twelve were no longer accurately recalled. For further details on the Eleven, see *Luke*, 618–20.

14. *They were all devoting themselves with one accord to prayer.* The first minor summary in Acts begins the idyllic description of the early Christian community in Jerusalem. For Luke, prayer as a communing with God is a mark of Christian discipleship (see *Luke*, 244–47); cf. Acts 2:42, 46; 6:4 for Lucan stress on early Christian persistence. Persistent prayer is often the setting for major events in Lucan writings. Here the community's prayer of expectation (of the coming baptism with the Spirit) parallels that of Jesus before his baptism in Luke 3:21. The Lucan adv. used most frequently *homothymadon*, "unanimously, with one mind," describes the remarkable harmony and unanimity of early Christians. Apart from Rom 15:6, it is used by Luke only in Acts (1:14; 2:46; 4:24; 5:12; 7:57; 8:6; 12:20; 15:25); in 18:12; 19:29 it has another sense. MS C^3 and the *Koinē* text-tradition add *kai tē deēsei*, "and to supplication," a copyist's addition probably owing to Phil 4:6.

The Lucan clause *ēsan proskarterountes homothymadon proseuchē* (apart from the adv. *homothymadon*) is strikingly similar to a first-century A.D. Greek inscription from Kerch near the Black Sea, which tells of the emancipation of a slave on condition that *proskarterein tē proseuchē epitropeuousēs tēs synagōgēs tōn Ioudaiōn kai theon sebōn*, "he assiduously attend the prayer(s) of the synagogue of the Jews and Godfearers that protects (him)." See B. Lifshitz, "Notes d'épigraphie grecque," *RB* 76 (1969): 92–98, esp. 95–96; cf. T.C.G. Thornton, "Continuing."

together with some women. The "women" are presumably those "who had come up" with Jesus "from Galilee" and "stood at a distance" from his cross, "looking on" (Luke 23:49), who "noted the tomb and saw how his body had been placed," and prepared the spices and ointments for his burial (23:55–56); those too who had gone to the tomb after the Sabbath and discovered it empty (24:1–9; cf. 24:22–24). Some of them are named in Luke 8:2–3 as "Mary called Magdalene . . . , Joanna, the wife of Chuza, Herod's steward," and "Suzanna." The "women" might also include wives of the apostles (Luke 4:38; 1 Cor 9:5). MS D adds *kai teknois*, "and children."

Mary, the mother of Jesus. Mary is known from Luke 1:27–56; 2:1–52, esp.

2:34, where she is also referred to as "his mother." She is alluded to in Luke 8:19–21, where Jesus is portrayed substituting a spiritual family for his natural family. Now, however, Mary is depicted among the first community of believers. This represents a development beyond what was said of her in the beatitude pronounced over her by Elizabeth (Luke 1:45; see *Luke,* 358, 365, 723). In Mark 3:21 Jesus' mother is among those who are said to think that he was "beside himself" (omitted in Luke 8:19–21). Now, however, she is depicted by Luke among those who believe in him. Cf. A. George, *Études sur l'oeuvre de Luc* (Sources bibliques; Paris: Gabalda, 1978), 429–64, esp. 457–61. God's Spirit overshadowed her (Luke 1:35) that she might bring into this world him who would be Lord and Messiah (Luke 2:11; cf. Acts 2:36). Now she sits as a believer among those who are gathered together and will become the church of her son at its birth through the Spirit's outpouring.

as well as his brothers. Luke writes *kai tois adelphois autou,* and the meaning of *adelphos* is controverted. See Weiser, *Apg.,* 59–60 for the state of the question. Luke uses the same words that he used in the Gospel (8:19–20), where he took over a phrase from Mark 3:31, in which context *hoi adelphoi autou* at first sight suggests that blood brothers are meant.

In Mark 6:3 Jesus is said to be the *adelphos* of James, Joses, Judas, and Simon. The Marcan usage is complicated, because in 15:40, 47; 16:1 Mark mentions "Mary, the mother of James the Little and Joses" among the women standing at the cross. It is hardly likely that there Mark would have used such a circumlocution, if he meant thereby to indicate the presence of the mother of the person hanging on the cross. Because the "James" and "Joses" of Mark 15:40 are undoubtedly the same as those in 6:3, what relationship is being expressed by *adelphos* in those Marcan passages? That relationship is further complicated by what Paul says of James in Gal 1:19, "the brother of the Lord" (cf. 1 Cor 15:7), and of the Lord's brothers in 1 Cor 9:5. Significantly, Luke mentions no names of Jesus' *adelphoi* here, and later on he will speak of James (12:17; 15:13; 21:18) without any mention of kinship to Jesus. The meaning of *adelphos* is, then, not unambiguous in Luke 8:19–21; here in Acts it could simply mean "his relatives." Barrett (*Acts,* 90) concludes his discussion: "The present verse contributes nothing to the arguments for or against any of these theories, though it is fair to add that the most natural meaning of *adelphos* is blood-brother, that foster-brother is not impossible, and that cousin is very improbable. See J. B. Lightfoot, *Galatians* (Grand Rapids, MI: Zondervan, 1967), 252–91."

For evidence of *adelphos* expressing other relationships than "(blood) brother," e.g., "neighbor," "coreligionist," "relative," "kinsman," but not "cousin," see *Luke,* 723–24. See further J. Blinzler, *Die Brüder und Schwestern Jesu* (SBS 21; Stuttgart: Katholisches Bibelwerk, 1967); L. Oberlinner, *Historische Überlieferung und christologische Aussage: Zur Frage der "Brüder Jesu" in der Synopse* (FzB 19; Stuttgart: Katholisches Bibelwerk, 1975), 355; J. McHugh, *The Mother of Jesus in the New Testament* (London: Darton Longman & Todd, 1975), 200–54; J. P. Meier, *A Marginal Jew: Rethinking the Historical Jesus I* (ABRL; New York:

Doubleday, 1991) 316–32; P. Grelot, "Les noms de parenté dans le livre de *Tobie*," *RevQ* 17 (1996): 327–37.

In any case, the use of *adelphoi* in 1:14 has to be kept distinct from that in 1:15. See J. Beutler, "*Adelphos*," *EDNT* 1.28–30; H.-H. Schelkle, "Bruder," *RAC* 2.631–40; H. von Soden, "*Adelphos* . . . ," *TDNT* 1.144–46. On the added *syn* in MSS B, C^3, E, 33, 81, and 326, see *TCGNT*, 246–47.

BIBLIOGRAPHY (1:12–14)

Betori, G., *Perseguitati a causa del nome: Strutture dei raconti di persecuzione in Atti 1, 12–9, 4* (AnBib 97; Rome: Biblical Institute, 1981).
Lattey, C., "The Apostolic Groups," *JTS* 10 (1908–9): 107–15.
Mader, J., "Apostel und Herrenbrüder," *BZ* 6 (1908): 393–406.
Niccum, C., "A Note on Acts 1:14," *NovT* 36 (1994): 196–99.
Robinson, D. F., "A Note on the Twelve Apostles," *ATR* 26 (1944): 175–78.
Thiele, W., "Eine Bemerkung zu Act 1:14," *ZNW* 53 (1962): 110–11.
Thornton, T.C.G., "'Continuing Steadfast in Prayer' — New Light on a New Testament Phrase," *ExpTim* 83 (1971–72): 23–24.
Thurston, B., *Spiritual Life in the Early Church: The Witness of Acts and Ephesians* (Minneapolis: Fortress, 1993).
Trites, A. A., "The Prayer Motif in Luke-Acts," *Perspectives on Luke-Acts* (ed. C. H. Talbert), 168–86.
Weber, W., "Die neutestamentlichen Apostellisten," *ZWT* 54 (1912): 8–31.
See further *Luke*, 621.

B. Reconstitution of the Twelve (1:15–26)

15 During those days Peter stood up in the midst of the brothers (there must have
been about a hundred and twenty of them gathered together) and said, 16 "Brothers, that Scripture, which the Holy Spirit uttered long ago through David, had to
be fulfilled concerning Judas, who became the leader of those who arrested Jesus.
17 He had been numbered among us and was apportioned a share in this ministry
of ours. 18 But the wretch bought a plot of ground with ill-gotten money and fell
down on it head first so that his body burst open, and all his entrails spilled out.
19 This became known to all the inhabitants of Jerusalem, so that that plot came
to be called in their own language Akeldama, that is, Field of Blood. 20 For it
stands written in the book of Psalms,

Let his estate become desolate,
let there be no one to dwell on it.[a]

And,

Let another take his office.[b]

[21] So one of the men who have been part of our company all the while the Lord
Jesus moved in and out among us, [22] from the beginning when he was baptized
by John until the day when he was taken up from us, must become with us a
witness to his resurrection." [23] Then they nominated two, Joseph called Barsabbas, also known as Justus, and Matthias. [24] So they prayed, "Lord, you know the
hearts of all; make known to us which one of these two you choose [25] to take over
this apostolic ministry, which Judas deserted to go to his own place." [26] They cast
lots for them, and the lot fell on Matthias; and he was numbered with the
eleven apostles.

[a] Ps 69:26 [b] Ps 109:8

WT: [15] . . . in the midst of the disciples. [16] . . . that Scripture which said in advance through the Holy Spirit [with no mention of David]. [18] . . . his ill-gotten . . . and his [omits "all"]. [22] . . . become a witness [omits "with us"]. [23] . . . Joses [instead of Joseph]. [24] [omits "one"]. [26] [omits "for them"] . . . with the Twelve apostles.

COMMENT

The first episode that follows the Lucan idyllic description of the early Jerusalem Christian community recounts how Peter, its spokesman, marshalled it to reconstitute the Twelve. It is a narrative into which a speech of Peter has been inserted, which makes up the major part of the episode. Luke has composed this episode himself, making use of two Palestinian traditions about the death of Judas Iscariot and the choice of Matthias. Verses 15–17, 19a, 20–22, 24, 25a are of Lucan composition, vv 18, 19b, 23, 25b–26 are from pre-Lucan Palestinian tradition. Whereas most interpreters are willing to admit the use of an earlier tradition about Judas, some (Vielhauer, Klein) call that about Matthias in question. Fuller, however, has argued persuasively for the factual character of the tradition about Matthias ("The Choice"). With this I agree, even though I should hesitate to ascribe the two OT quotations to such a source.

Peter's speech is composite, beginning with a description of the situation and a scriptural justification for his proposal and ending with the criteria for membership in the Twelve and the proposal itself. In the midst of the speech two verses digress (vv 18–19) to tell of Judas's demise. That digression interrupts the flow of the speech itself and reveals the use of a different pre-Lucan tradition. The tradition about Judas originally had nothing to do with the choice of Matthias; it is Luke who has joined the two traditions. Whether Luke has inherited two or three traditions (Haenchen, *Acts*, 163) is debatable. The scriptural justification is not necessarily derived from tradition; it is rather a Lucan composition, since it does not agree with the OT passages that Matthew uses and depends on the LXX.

The tradition that tells of Judas's last days and death does not agree in detail with the account in Matt 27:3–10, which reads:

> [3]Then Judas who betrayed him, seeing that Jesus had been condemned, returned with deep regret the thirty pieces of silver to the chief priests and elders, [4]saying, "I have sinned in betraying innocent blood." They answered, "What is that to us? See to it yourself!" [5]Tossing the silver pieces into the Temple, he departed, went off, and hanged himself. [6]The chief priests took the silver pieces, but said, "It is not lawful to deposit them in the treasury, because it is the price of blood." [7]After a consultation, they bought with them a potter's field as a burial ground for foreigners. [8]For this reason that field has been called until today the Field of Blood. [9]Then was fulfilled what had been said by Jeremiah the prophet, "They took thirty pieces of silver, the value of a man with a price on his head, a price set by some Israelites; [10]they paid it out for a potter's field, as the Lord had ordered me."

Not only are different OT verses quoted, which is understandable in a different evangelist's account of the death and its meaning, but some details create a discrepancy. According to the Matthean story Judas "hanged himself," whereas in the Lucan story he "fell down on it [the plot of ground] head first so that his body burst open, and all his entrails spilled out." Moreover, in the Matthean form the priests bought the potter's field, whereas in the Lucan form, Judas "bought a plot of ground with ill-gotten money." Again, the Matthean Gospel introduces details about which Luke says nothing: the "potter's" field, thirty pieces of silver, and return of the money to those who paid it. In two respects the accounts agree: the field came to be known as Field of Blood, and both quote folkloric traditions (Matthew: "that field has been called until today the Field of Blood"; Acts: "that plot came to be called in their own language Akeldama, that is, Field of Blood"). Of the two NT accounts of Judas's death, Benoit thinks the Matthean is the less objectionable (*Exégèse,* 1.341).

The discrepancy, however, is compounded, because ecclesiastical tradition has preserved still another version of Judas's death. In book 4 of his *Logiōn kyriakōn exēgēseis,* Papias recounted Judas's death. This writing is not extant, but it was quoted by Apollinarius of Laodicea; unfortunately the quotation is preserved only in fragments and in different forms in the catena of Matthew 27 and in that of Acts 1 (J. A. Cramer, *Catenae graecorum patrum in Novum Testamentum* [8 vols.; Oxford: Oxford University Press, 1840–44; repr. Hildesheim: Olms, 1967], 1.231; 3.12–13). Basically, these forms recount how Judas, having become so swollen in flesh that he could not pass, when a wagon was coming by, was struck by the wagon, and all his inwards emptied out. See K. Lake, "The Death of Judas," where later forms of the tradition, mostly conflations of stories from Matthew, Luke, and Papias, are gathered.

All the different forms of the story of Judas's death are folkloric elaborations recounting his death in a stereotypical literary form, otherwise known as the horrible death of a notorious persecutor. It can be compared with the story of the death of Antiochus IV Epiphanes (2 Macc 9:7–12), Herod the Great (Josephus, *J.W.* 1.33.5–8 §§656–65; *Ant.* 17, 6, 5 §§168–69), and Herod Agrippa I (Acts 12:23). Luke thus passes on in the two verses, which interrupt the thrust of Peter's speech, a folkloric tradition about Judas. The association of his death with an area near Jerusalem and its Aramaic name are authentic reflections of such a tradition. To it Luke has joined the note of the fulfillment of OT prophecies and recast it all in his own vocabulary.

The way that Judas died is not important. More important for Luke is his having been chosen by Jesus as one of the Twelve and his dereliction of that post in becoming "the leader of those who arrested Jesus" (1:16). Luke is merely echoing the horror that early Christians sensed, whenever Judas was mentioned, a horror reflected in the various qualifying phrases added to his name, as one of the Twelve: "who became a traitor" (in the list of Luke 6:16); "Satan entered into Judas, who was called Iscariot and was numbered among the Twelve" (Luke 22:3); "one of the Twelve, the one named Judas" (Luke 22:47); "who betrayed him" (Mark 3:19; Matt 10:4; cf. Mark 14:10, 43; Matt 26:14, 25, 47; John 6:71; 12:4; 13:2; 18:2, 5). "He had been numbered among us and was apportioned a share in this ministry of ours" (Acts 1:17). That ministry Judas chose to desert.

As does Matthew in his story of Judas's death, so Luke relates Judas's dereliction to God's providence: what Judas has done was foreseen in Scripture of old. Luke associates Ps 69:26 and Ps 109:8 with Judas's defection. The implication is that God's providence will provide a replacement for him among the Twelve, and this is borne out in the selection of Matthias by lot. What is paramount is that Matthias is not democratically elected. He is rather chosen by lot, but not before the assembled community has prayed. After communing with God, they toss lots, and the implication is clear: God has selected Matthias as the replacement of Judas among the Twelve.

The account reveals the concern of the early community to fill up the gap left in the Twelve by Judas's death, but it remains a somewhat enigmatic account. On the one hand, it stresses the importance given by Luke to the Twelve at the beginning of Acts, undoubtedly because of the symbolic nature that he associated with that special group of disciples, whom according to his Gospel Jesus himself named "apostles" (6:13). At the Last Supper the Lucan Jesus tells "the apostles," who reclined at table with him (Luke 22:14), "I confer on you a kingship such as my Father has conferred on me, that you may eat and drink at my table in my kingdom and sit upon thrones as judges of the twelve tribes of Israel" (22:29–30). The imagery employed in the last clause probably reflects Ps 122:4–5, "Jerusalem . . . , to which the tribes go up, the tribes of the Lord, . . . There thrones for judgment were set, the thrones of David's house." In the Lucan context that allusion seats the apostles on kingly thrones, and "judging" has to be understood in the OT sense of "ruling" (1 Sam 8:20; Dan 9:12). Jesus' words promise that the apostles will thus become the leaders of reconstituted Israel, the people of God. The connection that Luke has seen between the Twelve and the twelve tribes of

Israel is noteworthy; this is the reason for the symbolic role of the Twelve. That connection, however, is not solely Lucan; indeed, it is probably pre-Lucan (see Matt 19:28), no matter what Luke makes of it both in his Gospel and in Acts. See further Horbury, "The Twelve."

On the other hand, once Matthias is chosen by lot to take his place with the Eleven and to stand with Peter on Pentecost (Acts 2:14), he disappears from the scene; nothing more is heard of him (except that he undoubtedly shared in the decision made in 6:2 and the imposition of hands in 6:6). Moreover, when James, son of Zebedee, is put to death by Herod Agrippa (12:1), no need is felt to replace him or to reconstitute the Twelve. At the time of the "Council," the Twelve are not mentioned, but are implied in the mention of the "apostles" (15:2, 4, 6, 22, 23); yet they too disappear from the story of Acts after 16:4. So the Twelve, which plays an important role at the beginning of the church's history, eventually disappears. In the developing tradition, bishops of the church are regarded as successors of the apostles (Council of Florence, *Decretum pro Armenis*; DH §1318; Council of Trent, *Doctrina de sacramento ordinis* 4; DH §1768; Vatican Council I, *Constitutio de Ecclesia* 3; DH §3061; Vatican Council II, *Lumen gentium* §24; DH §4148). Significantly, however, neither *apostolos* nor "the Twelve" ever became a title for a role, function, or office in the Christian church. Christians in general may be spoken of as "apostles," but that is a broader, extended use of the name.

Why, then, was a need felt at the beginning to reconstitute the Twelve, or why was Luke concerned to reconstitute the Twelve in the first important episode of Acts? The answer to that question comes not from this episode, but from its relation to what follows in chap. 2. The Twelve are reconstituted so that they can confront Israel assembled in Jerusalem on the first great feast day following Passover, the feast of Assembly or (in Greek) Pentecost. What Peter and the other eleven will proclaim at that important assembly is the first instance of testimony given by the apostles to the Twelve Tribes of God's people: despite the death of God's anointed one, God still addresses the message of salvation first to the children of Abraham, to the Twelve Tribes of Israel. To prepare the stage for that proclamation, "the Twelve" had to be reconstituted. Because Judas was no longer with them, the community seeks to replace him. Judas's defection is recounted in all four Gospels as well as here. Peter is portrayed seeing it as something foreseen in God's providence, indeed, as something foretold in the OT. This then is the justification for the proposal that Peter makes to the 120 early Christians.

The episode instructs Christian readers about two things: how followers of Christ can turn against their leader and in dependence on their own devices come to a sad end, but also how God can bring good out of such an incident in response to Christian prayer. The Lucan story recounts not only the end of him who betrayed his Lord, but supplies the reason why the name "Judas" has ever persisted in Christian parlance with opprobrium. To call someone "Judas" is the height of insult. The episode also shows how a human being, though chosen by the Lord for a dedicated ministry, can desert it "to go to his own place" (1:25).

NOTES

15. *During those days.* I.e., between the day of the Ascension and the Feast of the Assembly or Pentecost (2:1). Luke uses a favorite expression, often employed for joining episodes: Luke 1:39; 2:1; 4:2; 5:35; 6:12; 23:7; 24:18; Acts 1:15; 6:1; 7:41; 9:37; 11:27; cf. Acts 2:18 (from Joel); see *Luke*, 110.

Peter stood up in the midst of the brothers. Peter assumes the role of spokesman. This is a continuation of the esteem that he enjoyed in the Lucan Gospel (see *Luke*, 564). He is now seen carrying out the role of which Jesus spoke in Luke 22:32, strengthening his brothers.

Adelphoi is often the name for fellow Christians throughout Acts (1:16; 9:30; 10:23b; 11:1, 12, 29; 12:17; 14:2; 15:3, 22, 32, 33, 40; 17:6, 10, 14; 18:18, 27; 21:7, 17, 20; 28:14, 15; perhaps also in 15:7, 13, 23, where it may refer, however, solely to those assembled at the "Council"). In these instances it has nothing to do with blood relationship or kinship; it connotes rather the closeness experienced by those bonded together as followers of the risen Christ. In Acts 2:29; 3:17 Peter addresses Jews assembled in Jerusalem with the same title (also Stephen in 7:2, 26; Paul in Pisidian Antioch in 13:26, 38; in Jerusalem in 23:1, 5, 6; in Rome in 28:17), thus showing that early Jewish Christians took over such a designation from their former coreligionists, among whom it was also commonly used. Josephus describes Essenes enjoying a single patrimony "like brothers" (*J.W.* 2.8.3 §122). Hebrew *'aḥ*, "brother," is so used in 1QS 6:22; 1QSa 1:18; 2:13(?). Cf. Acts 7:23. The WT (MSS D, E, Ψ, and the *Koinē* text-tradition) reads "disciples"; MS P[74] has "apostles."

(there must have been about a hundred and twenty of them gathered together). Lit., "there was a crowd of persons in the same place, about one hundred and twenty." This statement is parenthetical and strange; Luke may be using it because it was part of the information he had received (Barrett, *Acts*, 95). The noun *onoma*, "name," is used in the sense of "person," as often in Greek writers (Phalaris, *Ep.* 128; Josephus, *Ant.* 14.2.1 §22) and papyrus texts (POxy 9.1188:8); cf. Rev 3:4; 11:13; MM, 451. The number mentioned is surprising, because to this point in Acts only the apostles, some women, Mary, and Jesus' brothers have been mentioned. Luke 24:33 had mentioned "the Eleven and their companions" (lit., the Eleven and those with them). So one learns about the early growth of the Jerusalem Christian community.

The phrase *epi to auto*, "together" or "in the same place," is problematic. In the LXX it often means "together" (Exod 26:9; Deut 12:15; 2 Sam 2:13; Ps 2:2; 4:9; Isa 66:17; Hos 2:2). It will occur further in 2:1, 44, 47; 4:26; see NOTES on 2:1, 47.

16. "*Brothers.* Luke writes *andres adelphoi*, "men, brothers." The combination of *andres* with another noun in apposition was a common mode of address in Greek oratory: *andres Athenaioi*, "Athenians" (Demosthenes, *Olynthiac* 1.1, 1.10; Lysias, *Or.* 6.8); *andres Israēlitai*, "Israelites" (Josephus, *Ant.* 3.8.1 §189).

See Acts 1:11; 2:14, 22, 29, 37; 3:12; 5:35; 7:2, 26; 13:16, 26; 15:7, 13; 17:22; 19:35; 21:28; 22:1; 23:1; 28:17. Cf. 4 Macc 8:19.

that Scripture, which the Holy Spirit uttered long ago through David. Lit., "through the mouth of David." Cf. Acts 4:25; 28:25. Or "uttered in advance," since Luke may be using *proeipen* in the sense of predicting. He cites the Holy Spirit as the one who inspired King David, the traditional author of the Psalter. Cf. 2:29–30 for a fuller expression. The statement echoes what Luke thinks about the OT in general: it was uttered by the Holy Spirit through its notable human writers. The WT omits mention of David.

Luke uses *hē graphē*, "the writing," in the sense of "Scripture" (as in Luke 4:21; Acts 8:32, 35). Cf. 4 Macc 18:14. More frequently he uses the pl. *hai graphai* (Luke 24:27, 32, 45; Acts 17:2, 11; 18:24, 28), as do Josephus (*Ag.Ap.* 2.4 §45) and Philo (*De fuga* 1 §4; *De specialibus legibus* 1.39 §214). Probably sg. *graphē* means merely "a passage of Scripture" (so Dupont, "La destinée," 41), which then refers to the two passages to be cited in v 20. It is, however, hardly likely that a covert reference is being made here to Ps 41:10 ("Even my friend, whom I trusted, who ate of my bread, has raised his heel against me"), as some have sought to understand it (e.g., Barrett, *Acts,* 96–97). Nor is it likely that the sg. refers only to one of the quotations of v 20. Rather, the sg. is used generically, and the two citations in v. 20 spell out the details.

had to be fulfilled concerning Judas. For similar notions about the fulfillment of Scripture in the Lucan writings, see Luke 4:21; 24:44; Acts 3:18. Such passages give in detail what Luke hinted at in his Gospel's prologue: "events that have come to fulfillment among us" (1:1). In what has happened to Judas, Scripture itself has seen fulfillment.

who became the leader of those who arrested Jesus. See Luke 22:3–4, 47, 54.

17. *He had been numbered among us.* I.e., as one of the Twelve, like Peter who speaks (cf. Luke 6:16). Because the Twelve had been chosen by Jesus, that group had significance for his followers. See C. Masson, "La reconstitution." Attempts to see this expression as dependent on a targumic version of Gen 44:18 (Wilcox, "Judas-Tradition") are misguided; there is no evidence that that targumic tradition existed in Luke's day. The expression is perfectly at home in the Greek language, as Philo shows in *De specialibus legibus* 23 §118; also 2 Chr 31:19.

was apportioned a share in this ministry of ours. In the Lucan Gospel Judas was one of those "sent out to proclaim the kingdom of God and to heal" (9:2), one of those on whom Jesus conferred "kingship such as my Father has conferred on me," and one appointed as a judge "of the twelve tribes of Israel" (22:29–30). He thus shared in the *klēros*, "lot, share," that the Twelve had received, which is now called *diakonia*, "ministry," and in v 25 will appear *diakonia kai apostolē*, "ministry and apostolate."

18. *But the wretch bought a plot of ground with ill-gotten money.* Lit., "with the reward of wrongdoing" or "with money paid for treachery." Thus Luke describes what in the Matthean story is called "thirty pieces of silver" (Matt 26:14–15; cf. 27:3–10), which Judas had received from the chief priests. In referring to Judas,

Peter uses the dem. pron. *houtos,* "that one," in a pejorative sense (B-A[6], 1208); cf. 6:13,14. What is here *chōrion,* "a plot of ground," is called *agron tou kerameōs,* "a potter's field," in Matt 27:7. The WT adds "his" to "ill-gotten money," probably alluding to the thirty silver pieces in the Matthean account. See J. M. Pfättisch, "Der Besitzer des Blutackers," BZ 7 (1909): 303–11.

fell down on it head first so that his body burst open, and all his entrails spilled out. Lit., "having become headlong (*or* prone), he (in the) middle burst apart, and . . ." The first clause is cryptic, because the adj. *mesos* modifies the subj. of the finite verb. Moreover, it may have been composed in dependence on Wis 4:19, which describes the demise of the wicked: they will become dishonored corpses, whom God will "hurl headlong" *(prēneis);* cf. 2 Sam 20:10 (LXX): *kai exechythē hē koilia autou* (said of Amasa's inwards). F. H. Ely ("On *prēnēs genomenos* in Acts i 18," *JTS* 13 [1911–12]: 278–85) tried unconvincingly to show that *prēnēs* was a medical term related to *pimprasthai,* "swell up." Torrey (*The Composition,* 24–25) tried to explain that *prēnēs genomenos* was the equivalent of Aramaic *nĕpal,* "fall," but that is hardly likely because it does not really correspond. On the variants of this part of the verse in the Latin versions, see *TCGNT,* 247–48.

Because Matt 27:5 says *apēnxato,* "he hanged himself," attempts have been made to harmonize the two descriptions of what Judas did to himself: that the rope broke or the branch of the tree on which he hanged himself cracked, and so he plunged headlong and burst in two. The texts, however, were not meant to be harmonized; they merely echo different legends about Judas's death.

The Papias story preserves another form of the legend: *prēstheis gar epi tosouton tēn sarka, hōste mē dynasthai dielthein, hamaxē rhadiōs dierchomenēs, hypo tēs hamaxēs ptaisthenta ta enkata ekkenōthēnai,* "he, having become so swollen in flesh that he could not pass when a wagon was easily coming by, was struck by the wagon, and all his inwards emptied out" (Catena *In Matt.* 27); or *prēstheis epi tosouton tēn sarka, hōste mēde hopothen hamaxa dierchetai rhadiōs ekeinon dynasthai dielthein,* "having become so swollen in his flesh that he was not easily able to pass where a wagon passes" (Catena *In Acta* 1).

19. *This became known to all the inhabitants of Jerusalem.* So Luke reveals the folkloric source of his information about Judas's death; cf. 4:16; 9:42; 19:17.

so that that plot came to be called in their own language. Peter is made to speak as if his native language were not Aramaic; the formula was undoubtedly inherited by Luke, who allows it to stand for the sake of his Greek readers.

Akeldama, that is, Field of Blood. This is "name etiology" (Conzelmann, *Acts,* 11), a story told to explain why a certain name exists in popular usage (cf. Num 21:3; Josh 5:9; Judg 2:5; 6:24; 15:19; 18:12). *Akeldamach* (MSS B, 1175) is the reading followed in critical editions of the Greek NT, but MSS P[74], א, A, and 81 have *Acheldamach,* an inconsequential variant of the foregoing. MS D has a strange variant, *Akeldaimach* (perhaps influenced by *haima,* Greek for "blood"). MSS C, Ψ, and *Koinē* text-tradition read *Akeldama,* which is closest to the Aramaic name, *ḥăqēl dĕmā',* "field of blood," given in the translation *chōrion haimatos;* cf. Matt 27:8, *agros haimatos.* The form of the name with the final *ch* is the *lectio difficilior* and similar to that found on the name *Seirach,* the LXX transcription of Hebrew *sîrāʾ* in the name Eleazar ben Sira, author of Ecclesiasticus, or on the name *Iōsēch* (= *Iōsē,* a short form of *Iōsēph*) in Luke 3:26. No one knows how the *ch* came to be added in either case. One strange explanation: Greek *chi* (χ) resembles the shape of Aramaic or Hebrew *aleph* (א), with which both Semitic names end. Another strange explanation has sought to interpret the name as *ḥăqēl dĕmāk,* "field of sleep," i.e., cemetery (see A. Klostermann, *Probleme im Aposteltexte,* 1–8). As Wilcox (*Semitisms,* 88) notes, evidence for a noun *dmk,* "sleep," has not been found, or for "cemetery" making use of it. Even worse are the interpretations of Derrett ("Akeldama") that the second part of the name is related to *dĕmê,* "blood" (= slaying, suicide) or *dāmê,* "compensation, retribution" (meanings unknown in Aramaic) and of the Ritmeyers that it is a "corruption of the Hebrew *aker dam,* which literally means Field of Blood" ("Akeldama"). It has nothing to do with a Hebrew expression.

Ecclesiastical tradition from the fourth century has located Akeldama to the south of Ge Hinnom, the Wadi er-Rababeh, running from west to east, south of Zion, before it joins the Kidron and Tyropoeon valleys. It was a potter's area; cf. Jer 19:2. See *ELS* §§871–85; *HPG,* 361–65; cf. L.-H. Vincent and F. M. Abel, *Jérusalem Nouvelle* (Paris: Gabalda, 1922), 4.864–66; P. Benoit, "La mort," 352–59. The traditional site is near the present-day Greek Orthodox monastery of St. Onuphrius, built in the nineteenth century at a burial site dating from the Herodian period (37 B.C.–A.D. 70), where many tombs of the wealthy have been found, among them the tomb of the high priest Annas.

20. *For it stands written in the book of Psalms.* Luke uses *gegraptai gar,* "for it has been written," a stereotyped formula for introducing OT quotations, also used in Luke 4:10; see NOTE on Luke 3:4; cf. *ESBNT,* 8–10. This is the Lucan double scriptural justification for Peter's proposal.

Let his estate become desolate, let there be no one to dwell on it. The first quotation of Scripture refers to the past; Judas's post has become desolate, with no one to hold it. The quotation comes from Ps 69:26 (LXX), which agrees with the MT: "Let their encampment become desolate; in their tents let there be no dweller." Luke changes "their" to "his" and "in their tents" to "on it," making it more applicable to Judas. The differences between the Lucan form of the verse and the LXX or MT cannot be ascribed to an inherited tradition, *pace* Haenchen (*Acts,* 161), Weiser (*Apg,* 65), et al.; it is simply a Lucan modification. The lengthy psalm of personal lament expresses a malediction (vv 22–28) over enemies who have opposed the psalmist. Peter in this speech thus quotes the psalm that early Christians often applied to Jesus' passion, using it as a biblical prediction of what has come to pass in Judas's defection and death: his post has become desolate and empty, with no one to occupy it.

Let another take his office. The second quotation of Scripture refers to the future. It comes verbatim from Ps 109:8 (LXX), which Luke modifies only by changing the optative mood to a 3d sg. imperative. The LXX translated Hebrew *pĕqûdātô,* "his overseeing office," with an apt equivalent *episkopēn,* which Luke understands of the task Judas deserted and which someone else must now assume. Psalm 109 is likewise a personal lament, a cry for deliverance from enemies. Peter applies it to Judas, the opponent of Jesus: Let another take over his overseeing office. The quotations from the two psalms thus provide the biblical basis for Peter's proposal to the early Christian community. Ps 109 is not otherwise quoted in the NT, even though it may be alluded to at times in the passion tradition (Matt 27:39; Mark 15:29); see Dupont, *Études*, 300.

21. *So one of the men who have been part of our company.* Peter's suggestion formulates two of the Lucan criteria for membership in the Twelve: one must be *anēr,* "a man," and *tōn synelthontōn hēmin,* "part of our company," lit., "of those who have come together with us." The next clause clarifies the latter criterion: he must be one who was an eyewitness of Jesus' ministry.

all the while the Lord Jesus moved in and out among us. Luke gives to Jesus the title normally reserved for the risen Christ, *ho Kyrios,* as often already in his Gospel (7:13, 19; 10:1, 29, 41; 11:39; 12:42a; 13:15; 17:5, 6; 18:6; 19:8a, 31, 34; 22:61bis; cf. *Luke,* 202–3). Here it is more justified, used by Peter with hindsight. See also 11:20; 16:31; 20:21, 24. Instead of "Jesus," MS D reads *Christos.*

22. *from the beginning when he was baptized by John.* Lit., "beginning from John's baptism," undoubtedly referring to Jesus, but it could mean simply from the time that John proclaimed baptism. If the former is meant, Luke would be calling attention again to the "beginning" of Jesus' Spirit-guided earthly career; see NOTE on 1:1 above. In his Gospel Luke never tells us that Jesus was baptized by John, as he may here; it is only implied in Luke 3:21 (see *Luke,* 479–86 for reasons why Luke so portrayed Jesus' baptism). Cf. 10:37.

until the day when he was taken up from us. I.e., until his ascension. See NOTES on 1:2, 9–11.

must become with us a witness to his resurrection." This clause formulates the third Lucan criterion for membership in the Twelve: one must be a "witness to his resurrection," i.e., a person to whom the risen Christ has appeared. This is the meaning of this criterion, which Luke formulates abstractly; he will use the same abstract phrase again in 4:33. It creates a problem of understanding in view of the fact that no NT writer has ever depicted or described Christ's resurrection; nor does any NT writer ever portray people witnessing that resurrection. The transit of Jesus to the glorious presence of his Father, which began with his death and burial, is often asserted in the NT, in a variety of formulations, but it is never depicted as something visibly perceptible. Cf. 2:32; 3:15; 5:32; 10:41; 13:31. The noun *martys,* "witness," marks a key role that the Twelve, and then later other disciples, are to play in Acts. The theme of their testimony is formulated here: the resurrection of Christ, "the one who was baptized, conducted the ministry described in the gospel, and subsequently was killed" (Barrett, *Acts,* 102).

23. *Then they nominated two, Joseph called Barsabbas, also known as Justus.* Lit., "they set up." MS E begins the verse with "then after this was said." MS D and Latin versions read the verb as sg. *estēsen,* "he (Peter) set up," thus enhancing the role of Peter. Christians propose, but God disposes. Through the lot they cast God chooses the one who will replace Judas, the betrayer.

Joseph is otherwise unknown, but Eusebius (*HE* 3.39.9) records a "wondrous tale" about him passed on to Papias by one of the daughters of Philip (the evangelist, whom Eusebius calls "the apostle"): He drank poison, but by the Lord's grace suffered no harm. Of the two other names by which Joseph was known, one is Semitic, the other Latin. *Ioustos* is Latin *Iustus,* a name often used by Gentiles and Jews in this period (Acts 18:7; Col 4:11). *Barsabbas* is the grecized form of Aramaic *bar Sabbā,* "son of Sabba" (the old man), a name now attested as *bršb'* in Mur 25 ar 1:4 (P. Benoit et al., *Les Grottes de Murabbaʿât* [DJD 2; Oxford: Clarendon, 1961], 135 [+ pl. XXXVIII]). *Pace* Polhill (*Acts,* 94), Johnson (*Acts,* 275), and Barrett (*Acts,* 102), the name cannot mean "son of the Sabbath" or "am Sabbat geboren" (Weiser, *Apg,* 71), Pesch (*Apg.,* 1.90), Roloff (*Apg.,* 34). Some MSS (D, 6), read *Barnaban,* "Barnabas," the second name of another Joseph (4:36), a copyist's harmonization that seeks to give this person a task later on in Acts.

Matthias. Otherwise unknown. His name is a shortened form of *Mattathias,* the grecized form of Hebrew *Mattityāh* (1 Chr 16:5) or *Mattityāhû* (1 Chr 15:18, 21), "gift of Yahweh." Though he was not chosen because his name means that, the name befits the nominee chosen by lot to replace Judas. Eusebius cites a tradition *(legetai)* that he was one of "the Seventy" called in Luke 10:1 (*HE* 1.12.3). After this episode we never hear of him again in Acts. Later an apocryphal Gospel was attributed to him, "Gospel according to Matthias," sometimes also called "The Traditions of Matthias," fragments of which are extant. See Eusebius, *HE* 3.25.6; Origen, *In Lucam hom.* 1.1 (GCS 49.5); cf. W. Schneemelcher, *New Testament Apocrypha* (2 vols.; Louisville: Westminster/John Knox, 1991), 1.382–85.

24. *So they prayed.* Luke describes the activity of the early community, carrying out what he already reported about their prayer in v 14. The implication is that they realize that the decision does not lie with them as to who will replace Judas, just as they had nothing to say about the selection of the original Twelve. They pray for God's choice in this matter.

"Lord, you know the hearts of all. God is addressed by the Christian community as *Kyrie,* a title used by Luke elsewhere for Yahweh of the OT (Luke 1:16, 32, 68; 4:8, 12; 10:27; 19:38; 20:37, 44; Acts 2:39; 3:22; 5:9). The title is thus understood by Conzelmann (*Acts,* 12), Pesch (*Apg.,* 90), Weiser (*Apg.,* 71); cf. 2 Macc 1:24; Wis 9:1.

God is also called *kardiognōstēs,* as again in 15:8. Although it is a title for God appearing only in Christian writings (*Herm. Man.* 4.3.4; Ps.-Clement, *Hom.* 10.13; *Acts of Paul and Thecla* 24), it expresses an OT teaching about God's omniscience or foreknowledge: one who knows, tests, or scrutinizes the human heart (Deut 8:2; 1 Sam 16:7; 1 Kgs 8:39; 1 Chr 28:9; Jer 11:20; 17:10; Ps 44:22). Clement of Alexandria (*Stromateis* 5.14.96.4) traced the idea to the Greek philosopher Thales. Barrett, following Bengel (*Acts,* 103), and Kistemaker (*Acts,* 67) think rather that Jesus is being so addressed.

make known to us which one of these two you choose. The WT omits the masc. pron. *hena,* "one."

25. *to take over this apostolic ministry.* Lit., "to take the place of this ministry

and apostolate." Luke uses hendiadys, *diakonia kai apostolē*. The place that Judas occupied was at once a ministry of service and apostleship. These joined notions express the function of the Twelve in the early community, a function that they will be depicted exercising as the Lucan account unfolds.

which Judas deserted to go to his own place." Luke uses *topos*, "place," in a different sense to express Judas's destiny; it thus makes a contrast between the place that God through Jesus chose for him and the place that he himself has chosen. It is a delicate way of referring to Judas's demise described in v 18. MSS P^{74}, A, B, C*, D, Ψ, and Vg read *topon*, "place," but א, C^3, E, and the *Koinē* text-tradition read *klēron*, "lot," a scribal change that depends on v 17.

26. *They cast lots for them.* Lit., "they gave lots to (*or* for) them," reading the dat. *autois* as in MSS א, A, B, C, D^1, 33, 81, etc.; but MSS D*, E, Ψ, etc., read rather the gen. *autōn*, "of them," an inconsequential variant. The dative is not, however, an indirect object, but a dative of advantage; the whole expression is probably a Hebraism (= *nātĕnû gôrālôt*, as in Lev 16:8). See G. Lohfink, "Der Losvorgang in Apg 1,26," *BZ* 19 (1975): 247–49.

Since practices of superstition and magic were forbidden to Israel (Deut 18:9–14), only the priestly Urim and Thummim could be used to ascertain an oracular decision (Exod 28:30; Lev 27:21; cf. 1 Sam 14:41). The word *klēros*, which has a broad basic meaning, "share, lot, portion," expresses a variety of nuances in the Greek OT. It can translate Hebrew *naḥălāh*, "inheritance, heritage, possession" (Num 16:14; 18:21; Isa 57:6) or Hebrew *gôrāl*, "lot" (Lev 16:8–10). It is being used here in the latter sense. Significantly, it is the means chosen by the early community to ascertain God's will in this matter, since not a democratic election but a divine choice is involved. Cf. Prov 16:33.

the lot fell on Matthias. Compare Jonah 1:7 (LXX), whence the terminology comes. See L. S. Thornton, "The Choice of Matthias," *JTS* 46 (1945): 51–59.

he was numbered with the eleven apostles. I.e., Matthias became one of the Twelve, and the group is duly reconstituted. The verb is *synkatapsēphizesthai*, "vote against (someone or something) along with." *Psēphos* denoted the "pebble" with which one cast one's vote (Plutarch, *Themistocles* 21). Here, however, the verb is used in a more generic sense; with the casting of lots, there was no voting for a person in the strict sense. The MS D and Eusebius read: "with the Twelve Apostles," which makes little sense. Matthias became the twelfth, not the thirteenth apostle.

BIBLIOGRAPHY (1:15–26)

Avni, G. and Z. Greenhut, "Akeldama: Resting Place of the Rich and Famous," *BARev* 20/6 (1994): 36–46.

Bauer, J. B. "*Kardiognōstēs*, ein unbeachteter Aspekt (Apg 1, 24; 15, 8)," *BZ* 32 (1988): 114–17.

Beardslee, W. A., "The Casting of Lots at Qumran and in the Book of Acts," *NovT* 4 (1960–61): 245–52.

Benoit, P., "La mort de Judas," *Synoptische Studien Alfred Wikenhauser . . . dargebracht* (Munich: Zink, 1954), 1–19; repr. *Exégèse et Théologie,* 1.340–59.

Derrett, J.D.M., "Akeldama (Acts 1:19)," *Bijdragen* 56 (1995): 122–32.

Dupont, J., "La destinée de Judas prophétisée par David (Actes 1, 16–20)," *CBQ* 23 (1961): 41–51.

———, "Le douzième apôtre (*Actes* 1, 15–26): À propos d'une explication récente," *BeO* 24 (1982): 193–98; repr. *The New Testament Age: Essays in Honor of Bo Reicke* (2 vols.; ed. W. C. Weinrich; Macon: Mercer University Press, 1984), 1.139–45; *Nouvelles études,* 186–92.

Enslin, M. S., "How the Story Grew: Judas in Fact and Fiction," *Festschrift to Honor F. Wilbur Gingrich* . . . (ed. E. H. Barth and R. E. Cocroft; Leiden: Brill, 1972), 123–41.

Flusser, D., "Qumran und die Zwölf," *Initiation* (NumenSup 12; ed. C. J. Bleeker; Leiden: Brill, 1965), 134–46.

Fuller, R. H., "The Choice of Matthias," *SE VI* (TU 112; Berlin: Akademie, 1973), 140–46.

Gaechter, P., "Die Wahl des Matthias (Apg. 1, 15–26)," *ZKT* 71 (1949): 318–46.

Haenchen, E., "Judentum und Christentum in der Apostelgeschichte," *ZNW* 54 (1963): 155–87, esp. 161–62.

Halas, R. B., *Judas Iscariot* (Washington, DC: Catholic University of America, 1946).

Hebert, A. G., *Apostle and Bishop: A Study of the Gospel, the Ministry and the Church-Community* (London: Faber and Faber, 1963).

Horbury, W., "The Twelve and the Phylarchs," *NTS* 32 (1986): 503–27.

Jansen, H. L., "Notes on the Ossuary Inscriptions of Talpioth," *SO* 28 (1950): 109–10.

Jaubert, A., "La symbolique des Douze," *Hommages à André Dupont-Sommer* (ed. A. Caquot and M. Philonenko; Paris: Adrien-Maisonneuve, 1971), 453–60.

Jáuregui, J. A., *Testimonio, apostolado-misión: Justificación teológico del concepto lucano apóstol-testigo de la resurrección: Análisis exegético de Act 1, 15–26* (Teología-Deusto 3; Bilbao: Universidad de Deusto, 1973).

Lake, K., "The Death of Judas," *Beginnings,* 5.22–30.

Lowther Clark, W. K., "The Election of St. Matthias," *Theology* 30 (1935): 230–32.

Lüthi, K., "Das Problem des Judas Iskarioth neu untersucht," *EvT* 16 (1956): 98–114.

Masson, C., "La reconstitution du collège des Douze: D'après Actes 1:15–26," *RTP* 3/5 (1955): 193–201.

Menoud, P.-H., "Les additions au groupe des douze apôtres, d'après le livre des Actes," *RHPR* 37 (1957): 71–80.

Moeser, A. G., "The Death of Judas," *TBT* 30 (1992): 145–51.

Mosbech, H., "Apostolos in the New Testament," *ST* 2 (1948–49): 166–200.

Nellessen, E., "Tradition und Schrift in der Perikope von der Erwählung des Matthias (Apg 1, 15–26)," *BZ* 19 (1975): 205–18.

Rengstorf, K. H., "The Election of Matthias: Acts 1.15ff.," *Current Issues in New Testament Interpretation: Essays in Honor of Otto A. Piper* (ed. W. Klassen and G. F. Snyder; New York: Harper, 1962), 178–92.

———, "Die Zuwahl des Matthias (Act 1,15 ff.)," *ST* 15 (1961): 35–67.

Renié, J., "L'Election de Matthias (Act. 1, 15–26): Authenticité du récit," *RB* 55 (1948): 43–53.

Ritmeyer, L. and K. Ritmeyer, "Akeldama: Potter's Field or High Priest's Tomb," *BARev* 20/6 (1994): 22–35, 76, 78.

Schwarz, G., *Jesus und Judas: Aramaistische Untersuchungen zur Jesus-Judas-Überlieferung der Evangelien und der Apostelgeschichte* (BWANT 123; Stuttgart: Kohlhammer, 1988).

Schweizer, E., "Zu Apg. 1, 16–22," *TZ* 14 (1958): 46.

Sickenberger, J., "Judas als Stifter des Blutackers; Apg 1,18 f.," *BZ* 18 (1928–29): 69–71.

Stauffer, E., "Jüdische Erbe im urchristlichen Kirchenrecht," *TLZ* 77 (1952): 201–6.

Weiser, A., "Die Nachwahl des Mattias (Apg 1, 15–26): Zur Rezeption und Deutung urchristlicher Geschichte durch Lukas," *Zur Geschichte des Urchristentums* (QD 87; ed. G. Dautzenberg et al.; Freiburg im B.: Herder, 1979), 97–110.

Wilcox, M., "The Judas-Tradition in Acts i.15–26," *NTS* 19 (1972–73): 438–52.

II. The Mission of Testimony in Jerusalem (2:1–8:4)

◆

A. Appeal to All Israel (2:1–3:26)

1. The Pentecost Event: Baptism in the Spirit (2:1–13)

2 1When the day of Pentecost came round, they all happened to be gathered
together in one place. 2Suddenly there was a noise from the heavens like a strong
wind sweeping along, and it filled the whole house where they were sitting.
3There appeared to them tongues like flames of fire that parted and rested on
each one of them. 4They were all filled with a Holy Spirit and began to speak in
other tongues, as the Spirit gave them to utter. 5Now there were sojourning in
Jerusalem devout men, Jews of every nation under the heavens. 6When that
sound was heard, they gathered in a large crowd and were confounded, because
each one heard them speaking in his own language. 7Bewildered, they asked in
amazement, "Are not all these who speak Galileans? 8How is it, then, that each
of us hears them speaking in the language in which we were brought up? 9We
are Parthians, Medes, and Elamites, inhabitants of Mesopotamia, Judea, and
Cappadocia, of Pontus and Asia, 10Phrygia and Pamphylia, of Egypt and the regions of Libya about Cyrene; even visitors from Rome 11(both Jews and proselytes), Cretans and Arabs, yet we hear them speaking in our own languages about
the mighty deeds of God." 12They were all bewildered and could make nothing
of it, saying to one another, "What does this mean?" 13But others scoffed and
said, "They have just had too much new wine."

WT: 1And it happened in those days that the day of Pentecost . . . ; 2[omits "and it . . . sitting"].
3There appeared to them something like fire that rested. . . . 4[first clause omitted]. They began to

speak in tongues, as . . . [5]In Jerusalem there were Jews, men of . . . [6]speaking in their languages. [7]. . . amazement, saying to one another. [8]. . . that we understand of them the language . . . [9][instead of Judea] Armenia. [11][omits "our own"]. [12]They were bewildered at what had happened, saying, "What . . . [13]"They are all heavy with new wine."

COMMENT

Having narrated the reconstitution of the Twelve as the first important event in the early Christian community, Luke now recounts the first instance of testimony given by the commissioned Twelve. They are depicted confronting Jews gathered in Jerusalem for the first great feast after the Passover, during which Jesus of Nazareth had been crucified. This important feast in the Jewish calendar, the Feast of Weeks, thus becomes for the followers of Jesus the first memorable public event in their history, and Luke is the only NT writer who tells us about it and its meaning.

It was memorable not only because it was the occasion when Jesus' disciples received "the promise of the Father" (Luke 24:49; Acts 1:4) and were baptized in the Spirit, but even more so because it was the first opportunity that the Twelve had to confront the twelve tribes of Israel in an official capacity and bear testimony to the risen Christ, having received the power from on high to do so. In fact, as far as the thrust of the story in Acts is concerned, this confrontation and testimony are far more important that the reception of Spirit baptism. That testimony, however, is begun and is carried out under the guidance of the Spirit; hence the two-pronged narrative that is recounted in this chapter (vv 1–13) is of supreme importance. Through the Spirit, which is the power received from on high, the apostles are emboldened to confront "the whole house of Israel." The gift of God's Spirit not only initiates their testimony but will guide the course of it to "the end of the earth." So Luke introduces the first great mission of the witnessing apostles on Pentecost.

Only Luke among NT writers, who was not himself present, makes much of this occasion. Paul was aware of the gift of the Spirit to Christians (Gal 3:2; Rom 8:4–11; cf. Eph 1:13), but he speaks of no significance of Pentecost. John speaks of the reception of the Spirit on the day of the discovery of the empty tomb (20:22), but knows nothing of a Pentecost. All of this raises the question, When did the apostles and other early Christians receive the gift of the Holy Spirit for the first time? The story of Pentecost may be Luke's historicization of aspects of Christ's resurrection/exaltation, as he did with the Ascension itself. See Fitzmyer, "The Ascension of Christ and Pentecost," *TS* 45 (1984): 409–40; cf. P-H. Menoud, "La Pentecôte lucanienne." Luke received from the tradition before him the date of Pentecost as the first time that the apostles confronted Jews assembled in Jerusalem with the Christian proclamation. He dramatized that tradition into the story of the outpouring of the Spirit on the apostles as the preliminary for Peter's proclamation in Jerusalem. Luke emphasizes the presence of the Spirit to the apostles through visible and audible signs, and especially through the speaking of Peter and his colleagues "in other tongues," who are understood by all the members of the diverse assembly of Jews in Jerusalem. This is "a special, 'founding' gift of the

Holy Spirit" (Barrett, *Acts*, 108). Thus is begun the church, which though at first is located only in Jerusalem, gradually becomes a universal society, hinted at in the gift of tongues enabling the apostles to speak to people of all nations.

"Pentecost" (*hē hēmera pentēkostē*, "the fiftieth day") was the name used by Greek-speaking Jews for the harvest feast called in Hebrew *ḥag šābūʿôt*, "Feast of Weeks" (Exod 23:16; 34:22; Deut 16:9–10, 16; 2 Chr 8:13). Originally it was a farmer's feast, "day of the first-fruits" (Num 28:26), of the wheat harvest (Exod 34:22), but it came eventually to be understood as the feast at the end of the harvest. According to Deut 16:9, one was to "count seven weeks from the time one first put the sickle to the standing grain." In time, this was understood as a counting "from the morrow after the sabbath *(mimmoḥŏrat haššabbāt)*, from the day that one brought the sheaf of wave-offering: seven full weeks shall they be, counting fifty days to the morrow of the seventh sabbath" (Lev 23:15–16). So 50 days after Passover, when *maṣṣôt*, "unleavened loaves," had been eaten, the Jews offered the wheat of leavened bread to the Lord. On it Jews celebrated the gifts of the grain harvest, thanking God for the blessings so received.

The date of the Feast of Weeks was not really fixed until the Priestly tradition joined the feasts of Passover and Unleavened Bread. Then debate among Palestinian Jews ensued. Sadducees started to count the 50 days from "the morrow after the Sabbath," understanding Sabbath generically as "feast day," and meaning Passover itself (14 Nisan, first month of the year). Reckoning from the day after Passover, they celebrated *Šābūʿôt* on 6 Siwan (third month). Pharisees counted from the Sabbath (understood strictly) after Passover, whenever that would come. Hence *Šābūʿôt* would vary, but would still be a feast in the third month. Essenes and others, who used the *Book of Jubilees* and a calendar in which the feasts fell every year on the same day of the week, held that the first sheaf was to be presented on the Sunday following the Passover octave (22 Nisan; cf. *Jub.* 15:1; 44:4–5). Reckoning from that date, they celebrated *Šābūʿôt* on 15 Siwan (middle of the third month). Debate about this reckoning among Jews persisted for centuries; echoes of it are found in the later rabbinic writings (see Str-B, 2. 598–600; cf. M. A. Sweeney, "Sefirah at Qumran: Aspects of the Counting Formulas for the First-Fruit Festivals in the Temple Scroll," *BASOR* 251 [1983]: 61–66).

Because Israel had arrived in its exodus wandering at Mt. Sinai in the third month after leaving Egypt (Exod 19:1), i.e., after Passover, this gave rise in time to the celebration of the giving of the Sinaitic covenant, the gift of the *Tôrāh*, even to a yearly renewal of it, in the third month. This celebration may be reflected in the assembly of Jews in Jerusalem in the fifteenth year of King Asa (2 Chr 15:10–12).

In recent decades, however, interpreters have tended to regard the association of that covenant renewal with the Feast of Weeks as a development within Judaism only in the Christian period (see Str-B, 2.601: it cannot be traced back *quellenmässig* before the second century of the Christian era). The *Book of Jubilees*, however, and certain Qumran texts reveal that in the pre-Christian period at least some Judean Jews were celebrating the Feast of Weeks in the middle of the third month precisely as the renewal of the Sinai covenant (*Jub.* 1:1; 6:17–19; 14:20; in 22:1–16 [even Abraham is depicted on the feast of firstfruits speaking of God "renewing his covenant" with Jacob]). The *Manual of Discipline* seems to record part of the ritual of that annual celebration (1QS 1:8–2:25), even though this passage makes no mention of the Feast of Weeks. It was a renewal of the covenant by which the community was regulated; that has often been understood as a renewal of the Sinaitic covenant of old, even if the community regarded itself as living out the "new covenant" (Jer 31:31; cf. CD 6:19; 8:21; 19:34; 20:12; 1QpHab 2:[3]). See J. T. Milik, *Ten Years of Discovery in the Wilderness of Judaea* (SBT 26; Naperville, IL: Allenson, 1959), 103, 116–18; G. Vermes, *The Dead Sea Scrolls: Qumran in Perspective* (Cleveland: Collins & World, 1978), 177–79; Kremer, *Pfingstbericht*, 232; *TDNT* 6.48–49.

When Josephus speaks of Pentecost, he says, *hē pentēkostē hēn Hebraioi asartha kalousi* (*Ant.* 3.10.6 §252), "the fiftieth (day), which Jews call Asartha." This can only be Aramaic *'ăṣartā'*, related to Hebrew *'ăṣeret*, "solemn assembly." The name reveals that by the first century A.D. Judean Jews were celebrating Pentecost as "the Feast of Assembly." Cf. *J.W.* 6.5.3 §299. Josephus, however, does not explain the reason why Jews would assemble on this day for this feast.

In the Lucan story of Pentecost there is no direct reference to the Sinaitic covenant, but indirect allusions reveal that Luke was aware of the association of Pentecost with the renewal of that covenant. First, Luke recounts the outpouring of the Spirit on an occasion when not only "Judeans" but "devout men, Jews of every nation under the heavens" (2:5; cf. Deut 2:25) had come to Jerusalem, for what Josephus called "the Assembly." He describes them as a *plēthos* that *synēlthen*, "a multitude that came together," undoubtedly meaning on their festive assembly. Second, when Peter "stood up with the Eleven" (2:14) and confronted the Jews, the "twelve apostles" confronted the "twelve tribes of Israel" (Luke 22:29; cf. Acts 2:36, "the whole house of Israel") and functioned as their judges, thus echoing what the Lucan Jesus predicted at the Last Supper. Here we see Lucan foreshadowing at work. Third, Dupont has worked out a list of verbal allusions in Acts 2 to Exodus 19–20, where the theophany at Sinai and the giving of the Torah are recounted, using the adv. *homou*, "together," or its variant *homothymadon* (2:1); cf. Exod 19:8, *pas ho laos homothymadon*, "all the people together"; the nouns *ēchos* and *phōnē* (2:2, 6) find their counterparts in Exod 19:16, *eginonto phōnai*, "there were sounds," and *phōnē tēs salpingos ēchei mega*, "a sound of the trumpet blasted loudly"; the source of the sound is *ek tou ouranou* (2:2); cf. Exod 20:22, *ek tou ouranou lalēka pros hymas*, "I have spoken to you from heaven." Yahweh's descent to Mt. Sinai in fire (Exod 19:18) gives the OT background to "the tongues of fire." Even if these allusions are not unambiguous, they at least associate the Lucan account of the giving of the Spirit to the Exodus account of the giving of the Torah on Sinai.

It has been customary to interpret the Pentecost of Acts 2 as related to the Jewish Feast of Weeks alone, but now we know that in the course of time other "pentecosts" came to be numbered by Judean Jews. Thus in the Temple Scroll from Cave 11 the Jews of Qumran celebrated three pentecostal feasts, and one of them may shed some light on the Lucan story of the first Christian Pentecost. The Temple Scroll texts read as follows:

> Feast of Weeks (New Grain), third month, fifteenth day (18:10–13): "You will count [for yourselves] seven Sabbaths complete from the day you bring the sheaf [of waving]; you will count until the morrow of the seventh Sabbath; you will count [fifty] days and you will bring a new meal-offering to Yahweh. . . ."
>
> Feast of New Wine, fifth month, third day (19:11–14): "You [will count] for yourselves from the day you bring the new meal-offering to Yahweh, [the] bread as the first fruit, seven weeks; seven Sabbaths complete [they will be un]til the morrow of the seventh Sabbath; you will count fifty days, and [will bring] new wine for a libation. . . ."
>
> Feast of New Oil, sixth month, twenty-second day (21:12–16): "You w[ill] count for y[ourselves] from this day seven weeks, seven times (seven), forty-nine days, seven Sabbaths complete they will be until the morrow of the seventh Sabbath; you will count fifty days, and you will offer new oil from the dwelling-places of [the] tribes of the Is[rael]ites, a half hin from each tribe, new oil crushed [ ] fresh oil upon the altar of holocaust as fresh-fruits before Yahweh."

In other words, 50 days from the morrow of the Sabbath of the Passover octave occurred the Pentecost of New Grain; 50 days from the morrow of the Pentecost of New Grain, the Pentecost of New Wine; and 50 days from the morrow of the Pentecost of New Wine, the Pentecost of New Oil (see Y. Yadin, *The Temple Scroll* 2 [Jerusalem: Israel Exploration Society, 1983], 78–96).

Given this evidence of three Pentecosts, one of which was of New Wine, one understands more clearly the mockery expressed in 2:13, "They have just had too much new wine" (cf. 2:15). It has always been a puzzle why "sweet new wine" would be mentioned in connection with the Feast of Weeks, because new grain and new wine were not harvested together. So the Temple Scroll shows how "new wine" could be associated with a Pentecost. Luke may have known of such multiple Pentecosts among contemporary Jews and alluded to the Pentecost of New Wine, when speaking more properly of the Pentecost of New Grain.

The Jewish feast of Pentecost, then, provides the occasion when the Twelve and other early Christians were endowed with the Spirit. This is their baptism. It is the moment when their apostolate becomes pneumatic or Spirit graced; from this point on all that the apostles do will be under the guidance of the Spirit. Important in the Lucan account are the symbols used for the Spirit: "a noise from the heavens like a strong wind sweeping along"; "tongues like flames of fire that parted and rested on each one of them." These symbols express the presence of the Spirit to the early Christians. The symbol plays on the meaning of Hebrew *ruaḥ*, which can mean "wind" or "spirit," and of Greek *pneuma*, "blowing, breath," which also means "wind" or "spirit." The symbols resemble the way Luke (and other evangelists) depicted the descent of the Spirit on Jesus at his baptism: "in bodily form like a dove" (Luke 3:22). They thus ascribe to God's Spirit an initiatory role, a function that launched not only the ministry of Jesus but that of testimony to be given about him by commissioned apostles. In this way Luke brings to the fore the work of the Spirit in the formation of the Christian church. "The Spirit's previous activity in Jesus is to be reproduced on a wider scale in the apostles and their converts until its operation reaches the heart of the Gentile world" (Lampe, "The Holy Spirit," 193).

Luke recounts in some detail the diaspora Jews who have come to Jerusalem for the feast of "the Assembly," and who are thus in the holy city for the Christian Pentecost, when the Spirit-guided apostles first confront Israel with their proclamation. Fifteen countries or peoples are mentioned in an order that seems to proceed from east to west, with Rome being mentioned last (and with "Cretans and Arabs" as an afterthought). No one knows for sure whence Luke might have derived this list of nations; many commentators think that the list in vv 9–10 has been derived from some source and modified by Luke, and with this I agree. The order of names is puzzling; perhaps some of them have been inserted by Luke himself. Judea seems out of place alongside Mesopotamia, and the last two, Cretans and Arabs, seem to have been added after the parenthetical remark, "both Jews and proselytes." If these are not counted, the list numbers twelve geographical regions, perhaps the number in the original list taken over from a source. However, would Rome have been part of that derived list?

The narrative with which Luke begins the story of apostolic testimony is also the first miracle story in Acts. It is not easy to say whether Luke intends it to be understood as an auditory miracle, because diaspora Jews are said to "hear" Galilean apostles speaking to them, "each one . . . in his own language," or as a speech miracle in that the apostles "began to speak in other tongues, as the Spirit gave them to utter." The phenomenon of speaking in tongues is also found in 10:46; 19:6, as well as elsewhere in the NT (1 Cor 12:10, 28, 30; 14:2, 4–6, 9), but only here does one find mention of "other tongues." This seems to refer to *xenologia*, "speaking in foreign tongues," as many patristic commentators understood it, and not *glōssolalia*, "ecstatic speech." See NOTE on 2:4. Luke seems to have modified the usual expression by adding "other" because of his concern for the universal scope of the salvation that the apostles were about to proclaim to Jews from all over.

In any case, Luke dramatically portrays the initial confrontation of Israel by the Spirit-guided Twelve with the heaven-sent miracle. They receive from the Father the promised Spirit, which enables them to inaugurate the mission of testimony, and they do this before "the whole house of Israel" on the first Jewish feast that followed Passover in Jerusalem. *Pace* S. M. Gilmour, there is no reason to identify this experience of the Spirit with the christophany to more than 500 people mentioned by Paul in 1 Cor 15:6, and Luke has thus not differentiated early Christian awareness of the risen Christ and the phenomenon of the Spirit. See C. F. Sleeper, "Pentecost."

This scene is basically a Lucan composition, in which Luke makes use of Palestinian tradition, possibly oral, about events that transpired in Jerusalem and mixes it with his own reflection. Verses 1–4 form a unit, a description of the reception of the Spirit, and vv 5–13 narrate the perception of it and the reaction of Jews to the event. Commentators debate whether Luke has joined independent traditions (see Schneider, *Apg,* 1. 243–47), but it is impossible to come to any certainty about that; vv 9–10 may come from a written source. What he has inherited, he has fashioned into his own account. Alone among NT writers, Luke has dramatized the reception of the Spirit as a perceptible event (contrast John 20:22).

Luke is not interested merely in recording historical details of the Pentecost assembly, but rather in stressing the theological significance of the historic occasion when the risen Christ bestowed on his followers the gift of the Holy Spirit. The Spirit thus becomes the source of the life and growth of the Christian church to be. The Pentecost miracle makes known the work of the Spirit: the gift of tongues enables the Twelve to proclaim the new Word of God to Israel, and eventually to all human beings.

It is important, however, to recall the christological aspect of Pentecost, because in effect the risen Christ is seen as the firstfruits of the ministry of Jesus; it is he who sends his apostles, now endowed with the Spirit, to reap the harvest, to gather in converts to the Christian proclamation. This passage in Acts is often called the Pentecostal descent of the Spirit on early Christians. Because of that outpouring of the Spirit, Pentecost has assumed a prominent role as a feast in the Christian calendar. It is often considered the birthday of the Christian church, even though another tradition has used that title for Good Friday. In any case, Pentecost has for centuries been celebrated as the feast of the gift of the Spirit to the church, precisely because of this Lucan account. Thus two feasts of the Jewish calendar have been adopted by Christians: Passover (called in English "Easter"; cf. 1 Cor 5:7–8) and Pentecost, the first Jewish feast to follow Passover. As Thomas Aquinas put it, "Other solemnities of the Old Law have been succeeded by solemnities of the new law, because benefits conferred on that people were a sign of those granted us by Christ. Thus the feast of Passover was succeeded by that of Christ's passion and resurrection. The feast of Pentecost, when the Old Law was given, has been succeeded by the Pentecost in which was given the law of the Spirit of life" (*Summa Theologiae* I–II, q. 103, a. 3 ad 4). Christians even in the twentieth century still live their lives in memory of that historic beginning.

NOTES

2:1. *When the day of Pentecost came round.* Lit., "in the coming of the fiftieth day to full number," i.e., the fiftieth day from the morrow of sabbath of Passover (Lev 23:15–16), Feast of New Grain. In Tob 2:1 it is "Pentecost, our feast, the festival of the seven weeks" (pap4QTob[a] ar 2:10: *ḥag šabûʿayyāʾ*, "Feast of Weeks"; cf. 2 Macc 12:32). It denotes the beginning of the term of fifty days, when the next Jewish feast after Passover was to be celebrated. Luke sees this day as important in salvation history, speaking of it as coming to full number, i.e., coming to fulfillment, just as he saw the beginning of the Travel Account in the story of Jesus' ministry (Luke 9:51). Luke uses the articular infin. with the prep.

en; see *Luke,* 110, 119–20; his phraseology is dependent on Jer 25:12; Gen 25:24; Lev 8:33 (LXX).

they all happened to be gathered together in one place. This may be the "upper room" (1:13), but in v 2 it is called *oikos,* "house." Zahn (*Apg.,* 77) maintained that this referred to the Temple, but Luke uses *to hieron* for that. A "house" that would hold 120 persons is seen to be a problem, but patristic and medieval interpreters understood the place to be the Cenacle, where Jesus ate the Last Supper with the apostles (*ELS* §§730–58; *HPG,* 330–34). Luke uses the phrase *epi to auto,* "together," which may say no more than the preceding adv. *homou,* but it can be used in the sense of "at the same place," which suits the context. It is found in other Greek writers (Josephus, *J.W.* 2.16.4 §346; Matt 22:34; 1 Cor 11:20; 14:23; see NOTE on 1:15). "All" presumably refers to the 120 (1:15), hence including those mentioned in 1:13–14 (so Chrysostom; Pesch, *Apg,* 102–3). On the text of MS D, see *TCGNT,* 250.

2. *Suddenly there was a noise from the heavens like a strong wind sweeping along.* Luke makes the reception of the Spirit perceptible, at first as something heard, then as something seen. The noun *ēchos,* "noise," may allude to the verb *ēchei* of Exod 19:16, part of the description of the theophany at Sinai. The "wind" symbolizes the Spirit's force now at work in the world.

it filled the whole house where they were sitting. The Spirit's presence was all-pervasive, filling the house. The wind symbolizing that presence gives unity to the group in it. See H. H. Muelenbelt, "*Holon ton oikon, NTStud* 1 (1918):168.

3. *There appeared to them tongues like flames of fire that parted and rested on each one of them.* Lit., "there were seen by them divided tongues as if of fire." For wind and fire of heavenly origin symbolizing the presence of God, see Ps 104:4; Exod 3:2; 14:20, 24; 1 Kgs 19:11–12. Cf. Iamblichus, *De mysteriis* 3.2. The symbolism is evident: "tongues" are the shape of the fire because the Spirit will enable the apostles to speak. Here the fire is clearly seen as a sign of the presence of the Spirit; it has nothing to do with the fire of judgment or of everlasting punishment often used for the "Holy Spirit and fire" of Luke 3:16; see Dunn, "Spirit-and-Fire Baptism." The tongues were distributed upon each of the disciples present and symbolize the diversified power of speech that comes upon them (C. H. Giblin). An interesting parallel is found in "three tongues of fire," mentioned in a poorly preserved Qumran liturgical text (1Q29 2:3; cf. 1:3). Cf. Philo, *De Decalogo* 11 §44.

The verb *ōphthēsan,* aor. pass. indic. of *horan,* "see," is often used (as in Luke 1:11; 24:34; Acts 7:2, 26, 30, 35; 9:17; 13:31; 16:9; 26:16) to denote various epiphanies or theophanies. It is a Septuagintism (Gen 12:7; 17:1; 18:1; Exod 3:2). Its Aramaic counterpart *('itḥāzî)* with an indir. obj. occurs in 1 QapGen 22:27 (rendering Gen 15:1); cf. 4QEn[a] 1 ii 2.

4. *They were all filled with a Holy Spirit.* Luke strangely uses no article with *pneumatos hagiou* (BDF §257.2). The first Christians are baptized (1:5) with a Spirit symbolized by the wind and the tongues of fire that rest on each one. Being "filled with" the Holy Spirit is a typically Lucan expression (Luke 1:15, 41, 67; Acts 4:8, 31; 9:17; 13:9), denoting the empowering gift of God's creative or pro-

phetic presence; it is an expression Luke derives from the LXX (Prov 14:4; Sir 48:12); see NOTE on 1:2; cf. *Luke*, 227–31. So empowered, the early Christians are suited for their ministry of testimony and emboldened to confront the Jews gathered in Jerusalem.

began to speak in other tongues. I.e., they started doing what they had not done before. The Lucan addition of "other" may be influenced by the LXX of Isa 28:11 *(dia glōssēs heteras)*; see Betz, "Zungenreden."

as the Spirit gave them to utter. So Luke presents the gift of the Spirit (now expressed with the anaphoric article, BDF §257.2). The verb *apophthengesthai* means to "speak out, declare boldly and loudly." It is the same Spirit that will fill Peter again to speak out boldly (2:14; 4:8), fill the disciples in prayer at the release of Peter and John (4:31), and fall upon the first Gentile converts (10:44–46).

"Speaking in tongues" is a gift of the Spirit in 1 Cor 12:10, 28, 30; 14:2, 4–6, 9. For many interpreters (e.g., Dupont, Giblin, Johnson, Martin) the gift meant here is *glōssolalia*, understood as "ecstatic utterance." For others, however, this is rather *xenologia*, "speaking in foreign tongues" (e.g., Davies; Gundry; Barrett, *Acts*, 109; Polhill, *Acts*, 99–100; Schneider, *Apg.*, 1.250; Weiser, *Apg.*, 85–86). In any case, only Luke makes it a miraculous gift to speak "in other tongues," i.e., other human tongues, not the "tongue of angels" (1 Cor 13:1). When the phenomenon is mentioned again in Acts 10:45–46; 19:6, the adj. *heterai* is not used. That may then be glossolalia, but it does not seem to be that here. In vv 6 and 11 there is mention of *dialektos* and *hai hemeterai glōssai*, which clearly point to different human languages, clarified further in the list of nations (2:9–11). Luke is not using different sources here; he rather modifies the tradition he inherits, transforming "tongues" into "other tongues," i.e., speaking in foreign languages, a miracle suited to the theological thrust of the episode, which is interested in the universality of salvation to which testimony is being made.

5. *Now there were sojourning in Jerusalem devout men, Jews of every nation under the heavens.* Luke now records the public reaction of people in Jerusalem to the phenomenon they have noticed. He calls them *andres eulabeis*, "men holding fast," i.e., observant of Jewish traditions. This is why they are present in Jerusalem for "the Assembly" (Josephus's *asartha* for the Feast of Weeks). To eliminate "Jews" from the verse, as Güting would have it ("Der geographische Horizont"), is to emasculate the Lucan story. The list in vv 9–11 mentions the nations not only as a sign of the eventual spread of apostolic testimony to such peoples, but also as a sign of the comprehensive testimony being borne to "all the house of Israel," now understood as "Jews of every nation." The testimony must be carried first of all to Israel; the Lucan story disregards any others in Jerusalem who might not be Jews. Note the characteristic Lucan hyperbole, "every nation"; see NOTE on 2:44. For parallels to "under the heavens," see Qoh 1:13; 3:1; Plato, *Timaeus* 23C; *Ep.* 7.326C.

6. *When that sound was heard.* I.e., the "noise" of v 2.

they gathered in a large crowd and were confounded. Their gathering was a form of "the Assembly," now suited to the Lucan purpose of apostolic confrontation and testimony. Their confusion is explained in the following clauses.

each one heard them speaking in his own language. This is the Pentecost miracle. As described, the miracle seems at first to have been auditory not vocal, in that the assembled Jews were each enabled to hear them speaking "in his own language," but v 4 has already described it as a vocal miracle, produced by the Spirit given to the Galileans. Whether auditory or vocal, the miracle conveys the idea that the gift of the Spirit transcends all bounds: the Christian message is to be borne to people of all languages and cultures.

7. *Bewildered, they asked in amazement, "Are not all these who speak Galileans?* This question is intended to advance the narrative; one should not ask how the crowd would have recognized them as Galileans. The remark made to Peter in Matt 26:73c should not be introduced here, because it is non-Lucan. For idle speculation about the apostles as Galileans, see Barrett, *Acts,* 120. In the Lucan story "Galileans" echoes "Men of Galilee" (1:11).

8. *How is it, then, that each of us hears them speaking in the language in which we were brought up?* Lit., "in which we were born."

9. *We are Parthians, Medes, and Elamites, inhabitants of Mesopotamia, Judea, and Cappadocia, of Pontus and Asia,* 10. *Phrygia and Pamphylia, of Egypt and the regions of Libya about Cyrene.* Luke uses such a list to show the wide areas from which diaspora Jews have come to Jerusalem for the feast and for the initial apostolic proclamation of the Christian gospel: from Asia, Asia Minor, and northeast Africa, but also (strangely) from Rome. Actually, the list mentions areas of a much earlier time than the first century A.D. Strikingly omitted are Achaia, Macedonia, Cilicia, Syria, Galatia, places about which there is mention elsewhere in Acts and the NT, especially as localities in the eastern Mediterranean where Jews lived. For other patristic readings instead of "Judea," see *TCGNT,* 254.

This catalogue of nations is scarcely a list composed at random by Luke (*pace* E. Güting, "Der geographische Horizont"), since it is difficult to show why he would list these names and not others, why in the order in which they occur, and why names of older localities. Rather the similarities it has with lists of nations found in Babylonian, Hellenistic, and other historians and writers such as Arrian (*Frg.* 1.5), Ps.-Callisthenes (2.4.9; 2.11.2), *Sibylline Oracles* (3.207–9), Philo (*In Flaccum* 7 §§45–46; *Legatio ad Gaium* 36 §§281–83), show that it is a list he has derived from some unknown source. Compare the list in Q. Curtius Rufus (*Historia Alexandri,* 6.3.3): "Cariam, Lydiam, Cappadociam, Phrygiam, Paphlagoniam, Pamphyliam, Pisidas, Ciliciam, Syriam, Phoenicen, Armeniam, Persidem, Medos, Parthienen habemus in potestate" (We have control over Caria, Lydia, Cappadocia, Phrygia, Paphlagonia, Pamphylia, the Pisidias, Cilicia, Syria, Phoenicia, Armenia, Persia, the Medes, and Parthiene).

Parthoi denotes people of Parthia, the region southeast of the Caspian Sea, which in NT times reached to the Euphrates River. The Parthians were the successors of ancient Persians and became adversaries of the Romans, on whose empire their land bordered to the east. Arsaces, king of the Parthians is mentioned in 1 Macc 15:22. Parthian rule ended in A.D. 227, when they were replaced by the Sassanids.

Mēdoi, "Medes," had been an ancient Indo-European people who inhabited the area southwest of the Caspian Sea and who warred against the Assyrians to the west of them in the seventh and sixth centuries B.C. Media had been a place to which Israelites had been deported by the Assyrians (2 Kgs 17:6; 18:11). In NT times the Medes were only a group of tribes who lived in Parthia. For Jews living in Media, see Tobit 3:7; Josephus, *Ant.* 11.5.2 §132.

Elamitai, "Elamites," were another ancient people who inhabited Elam (or Elymais), the district north of the Persian Gulf about the lower Tigris River and south of Media (see Isa 21:2 [LXX]; cf. Jer 25:25). The Elamites had been incorporated into the Parthian empire, but often asserted their autonomy.

Mesopotamia, "(the land) between the rivers," i.e., between the Tigris and the Euphrates; so the name was understood in Hellenistic times, but its boundaries varied, and it often extended beyond those rivers. It would have correspond roughly to the land of the ancient Assyrians and Babylonians, especially of the latter, to which Jews had been deported under Nebuchadnezzar in the sixth century (Josephus, *Ant.* 15.3.1 §39). The remains of a Jewish synagogue have been found at Dura Europos (see M. Rostovtzeff, *Dura Europos and Its Art* [Oxford: Clarendon, 1938], 100–130; J. Gutmann [ed.], *The Dura-Europos Synagogue: A Reevaluation (1932–1972)* [Religion and the Arts 1; Missoula: Society of Biblical Literature, 1973]).

Ioudaia designated the area (or possibly the province) in which Jerusalem itself was found. Though the name is found in all the Greek manuscripts, it appears to be an addition to the rest of the places from which diaspora Jews are supposed to have come. Its place in the list is striking, and since it is actually an adj., it should have an article when used as a substantive. It is odd that inhabitants of Judea should be astonished at hearing the apostles speaking in their own language. Not surprisingly, ancient writers have preserved a number of variants: *Armenia* (WT, Tertullian, Augustine); *Syria* (Jerome); *India* (Chrysostom). Modern conjectures have been proposed: Idumea, Ionia, Bithynia, Cilicia, Lydia, Adiabene. Eusebius, Harnack; and C.S.C. Williams considered it a scribal gloss. See *TCGNT*, 253–54.

Kappadokia, "Cappadocia," a territory in the eastern interior of Asia Minor, south of Pontus, and west of Armenia. It was devastated in the Mithridatic Wars but was restored by Pompey and eventually became a Roman province.

Pontos was originally the name of the Black Sea, but it came to designate the area bordering on that sea in the northeastern part of Asia Minor. The area was earlier an empire founded by Achaemenid Persians, reaching from the Black Sea to the Caucasus. After Pompey conquered it, part of it became the Roman province of Pontus. Many Greeks were known to have settled there, and with them Greek-speaking Jews (see Acts 18:2; Philo, *Legatio ad Gaium* 36 §281). Cf. 1 Pet 1:1.

Asia was the western Roman province in Asia Minor, which had been formed in 133 B.C., when the last king of Pergamum bequeathed his territory to the Romans. Alexander had conquered the area in 334 B.C., and after his death it came under Seleucid control until kings of Pergamum succeeded in wresting it from their domination. In time the province embraced areas of Mysia, Aeolis, Ionia,

Lydia, Phrygia, and Caria, i.e., the Anatolian peninsula from Propontis in the north to the Mediterranean in the south. From the time of Augustus it was a senatorial province, governed by proconsuls, who resided in Ephesus. See V. Chapot, *La province romaine proconsulaire d'Asie* (Paris: Bouillon, 1904); S. E. Johnson, "Early Christianity in Asia Minor," *JBL* 77 (1958): 1–17; P. Trebilco, "Asia," *The Book of Acts in Its Graeco-Roman Setting* (BAFCS 2), 291–362.

Phrygia was a large area in central Asia Minor; the borders of Phrygia varied from time to time. In 25 B.C. the eastern part of ancient Phrygia became part of the Roman province of Galatia, which also comprised the old "Galatian district" in northern Asia Minor. The western part of ancient Phrygia belonged to the Roman province of Asia. See H. Metzger, *St. Paul's Journeys in the Greek Orient* (SBA 4; London: SCM, 1955), 34–37.

Pamphylia was the coastal district in southern Asia Minor, to the east of Lycia and west of Cilicia, south of Pisidia. It was an independent province in the Roman empire from 25 B.C. until A.D. 43. Philo tells of the colonies of Jews sent from Judea to Pamphylia (*Legatio ad Gaium* 36 §281). See D. Magie, *Roman Rule in Asia Minor* (Princeton: Princeton University Press, 1950), 261–66.

Aigyptos, "Egypt," an ancient country in the African continent, home of the Pharaohs of old. From the time of the Ptolemies Egypt was the home of many Jews, especially in the eastern sector of Alexandria (Philo, *Legatio ad Gaium* 36 §281). It was the richest country in the Roman empire. See E. M. Smallwood, "The Jews in Egypt and Cyrenaica during the Ptolemaic and Roman Periods," in T. Ferguson (ed.), *Africa in Classical Antiquity: Nine Studies* (Ibadan: Ibadan University, 1969), 110–31.

"The regions of Libya about Cyrene" was a territory on the northern coast of Africa, the capital of which was Cyrene, which from 27 B.C. on formed with Crete the Roman province of Cyrenaica; it was an area where many Jews lived (see Josephus, *Ant.* 14.7.2 §§115–16).

Attempts have been made to see the influence of the zodiac or of astrology in this list of nations, especially the astrological speculations of Paulus of Alexandria's *Rudiments of Astrology* (see Cumont, "La plus ancienne géographie"; Weinstock, "Geographical Catologue"; Brinkman, "Literary Background") or the influence of the story of the Tower-of-Babel confusion of tongues (Gen 11:1–9; see Wikenhauser, *Apg.*, 38–41). None of these attempts, however, accounts for all the names in the Lucan list or the order of the names and the connectives (*kai* and *te kai*), which reveals undoubtedly that Luke has modified a different sort of list. See further Metzger, "Ancient Astrological Geography."

even visitors from Rome. This place is most likely another Lucan addition to the inherited list, since it is the name of a city, not a territory, and is not found in the eastern Mediterranean area, as are the other places. Whether an addition or not, it establishes a connection between Jerusalem and Rome and shows that Luke knew of Jews in Rome. Some of the visitors from Rome may have been among the Pentecost converts to Christianity and thus may have carried the Christian message to the capital of the empire, even before Rome itself was evangelized by an apostolic missionary and before Paul wrote his Epistle to the Romans (see Fitzmyer, *Romans*, 29).

11. *(both Jews and proselytes)*. This parenthetical remark modifies at least the foregoing phrase "visitors from Rome," but probably all the preceding places named too. Luke is concerned to include not only descendants of old Jewish families but even converts to Judaism.

The noun *prosēlytos*, "one who has come over," is used here in a technical sense, a "convert" to Judaism, one who has submitted to circumcision and been won over by Jewish missionary efforts among pagans. Cf. Matt 23:15; Acts 6:9; Philo, *De spec. leg.* 1.9 §51; 1.57 §308; *De somniis* 2.41 §273. In Acts 13:43 Luke links *prosēlytoi* with *sebomenoi*, a term that he otherwise uses independently (see NOTE there). In a less technical sense it occurs in the LXX as the translation of Hebrew *gēr*, "resident alien" (Exod 12:48; 22:21; Ezek 14:7). See H. Kuhli, *EDNT* 3.170–71; K. G. Kuhn, *TDNT* 6.727–44; K. G. Kuhn and H. Stegemann, "Proselyten," PWSup 9.1248–83; A. Paul, *DBSup* 8.1353–56; cf. P. Figueras, "Epigraphic Evidence for Proselytism in Ancient Judaism," *Immanuel* 24–25 (1990): 194–206; J. A. Loader, "An Explanation of the Term *prosēlutos*," *NovT* 15 (1973): 270–77; I. Levinskaya, *The Book of Acts in Its Diaspora Setting* (BAFCS 5), 19–49.

Cretans and Arabs. These added names give an expense not detected in the former names: from the west (inhabitants of the island of Crete) to the east (people from the Syrian Desert west of Mesopotamia and east of the Orontes and from the peninsula bounded by the Persian Gulf, Indian Ocean, and Red Sea).

yet we hear them speaking in our own languages. A repetition of v 8.

about the mighty deeds of God." Luke uses an OT expression (Deut 11:2; Ps 71:19; 105:1; Sir 36:7; 42:21) to characterize the message that Christian disciples announce: the salvific achievements of God. Cf. also 1QS 1:21; 1QM 10:8. Those who hear the Twelve, however, do not understand the precise content of what is being said and so characterize it in stereotypic OT language. The need for Peter's interpretive speech is here apparent.

12. *They were all bewildered and could make nothing of it, saying to one another, "What does this mean?"* Some ask the all-important question, to which Peter's speech will reply. The question sets the stage for Peter's testimony and proclamation of the gospel to these Jews gathered in Jerusalem. Note the Lucan hyperbole in "all," with which the *heteroi* of the next verse stands in conflict.

13. *others scoffed and said, "They have just had too much new wine."* Luke uses *gleukos*, "sweet new wine," sometimes called *moustos*, "must." *Gleukos* translates Hebrew *yayin*, "wine," in Job 32:19 (LXX), where Elihu claims a sort of prophetic inspiration (the divine Spirit making him speak, 33:4). When Josephus recounts the story of the chief butler's dream of Gen 40:9–10, he portrays the butler dreaming of having pressed grapes into the Pharaoh's cup to let *gleukos* run into it so that the Pharaoh may drink; but that detail corresponds to nothing in either the MT or the LXX of Genesis (*Ant.* 2.5.2 §64). Whatever the relation might be of *gleukos* to Hebrew *tîrôš*, "must, new wine" (see Fitzmyer, *TS* 45

[1984]: 436–37), the sense of the remark is clear: some of those listening simply write off the whole episode as a case of inebriated speakers. Such listeners stand in contrast to those who pose the real question in v 12. One should not ask how "new wine," still in the process of fermentation, could be obtained at Pentecost, which is just before, not after, the vintage (*Beginnings,* 4.20). Luke has undoubtedly mingled, perhaps unwittingly, allusion to the Jewish Pentecost of New Wine with that of New Grain (see COMMENT above). It makes little difference to him, since the only important thing is that 50 days have separated Christ's death and resurrection, about the time of Passover, from the Spirit-filled first proclamation of the Twelve to "the whole house of Israel," i.e., to Judeans and "Jews from every nation under the heavens."

BIBLIOGRAPHY (2:1–13)

Adler, N., *Das erste christliche Pfingstfest: Sinn und Bedeutung des Pfingstberichtes Apg 2, 1–13* (NTAbh 18/1; Münster in W.: Aschendorff, 1938).

Bavel, T. J. van, "La Pentecôte et le passage du Jésus terrestre au Christ de la prédication," *Expérience de l'Esprit: Mélanges E. Schillebeeckx* (Le Point théologique 18; ed. C. Kannengiesser; Paris: Beauchesne, 1976), 31–46.

Beare, F. W., "Speaking with Tongues: A Critical Survey of the New Testament Evidence," *JBL* 83 (1964): 229–46.

Betz, O., "Zungenreden und süsser Wein: Zur eschatologischen Exegese von Jesaja 28 in Qumran und im Neuen Testament," *Bibel und Qumran: Beiträge zur Erforschung der Beziehungen zwischen Bibel- und Qumran-wissenschaft: Hans Bardtke zum 22.9.1966* (ed. S. Wagner; Berlin: Evangelische Haupt-Bibelgesellschaft, 1968), 20–36.

Bleickert, G., "Ostern und Pfingsten: Lukanische und johanneische Schau," *WoAnt* 17 (1976): 33–37.

Brinkman, J. A., "The Literary Background of the 'Catalogue of the Nations' (Acts 2,9–11)," *CBQ* 25 (1963): 418–27.

Broer, I., "Der Geist und die Gemeinde: Zur Auslegung der lukanischen Pfingstgeschichte (Apg 2,1–13)," *BibLeb* 13 (1972): 261–83.

Causse, A., "Le pélerinage à Jérusalem et la première Pentecôte," *RHPR* 20 (1940): 120–41.

Cerfaux, L., "Le symbolisme attaché au miracle des langues," *ETL* 13 (1936) 256–59; repr. *Recueil Lucien Cerfaux,* 2.183–87.

Chevallier, M.-A., "'Pentecôtes' lucaniennes et 'Pentecôtes' johanniques," *RSR* 69 (1981): 301–13; repr. *La parole de grâce: Études lucaniennes à la mémoire d' Augustin George* (ed. J. Delorme et J. Duplacy; Paris: Recherches de Science Religieuse, 1981), 301–13.

Cumont, F., "La plus ancienne géographie astrologique," *Klio* 9 (1909): 263–73.

Dahl, N. A., "Nations in the New Testament," *New Testament Christianity for Africa and the World: Essays in Honour of Harry Sawyerr* (ed. M. E. Glasswell and E. W. Fasholé-Luke; London: SPCK, 1974), 54–68.

Davies, J. G., "Pentecost and Glossolalia," *JTS* 3 (1952): 228–31.
Dominy, B. B., "Spirit, Church, and Mission: Theological Implications of Pentecost," *SwJT* 35 (1993): 34–39.
Dunn, J.D.G., "Spirit-and-Fire Baptism," *NovT* 14 (1972): 81–92.
Dupont, J., "La nouvelle Pentecôte (Ac 2,1–11): Fête de la Pentecôte," *AsSeign* 30 (1970): 30–34; repr. *Nouvelles études,* 193–98.
———, "La première Pentecôte chrétienne (Actes 2,1–11)," *AsSeign* 51 (1963): 39–62; repr. *Études,* 481–502.
Etienne, A., "Étude du récit de l'événement de Pentecôte dans Actes 2," *FV* 80 (1981): 47–67.
Everts, J., "Tongues or Languages? Contextual Consistency in the Translation of Acts 2," *JPT* 4 (1994): 71–80.
Giblin, C. H., "Complementarity of Symbolic Event and Discourse in Acts 2, 1–40," *SE VI* (TU 112; Berlin: Akademie, 1973), 189–96.
Gilmour S. M., "Easter and Pentecost," *JBL* 81 (1962): 62–66
Grappe, C., "A la jonction entre Inter et Nouveau Testament: Le récit de la Pentecôte," *FV* 89 (1990): 19–27.
Güting, E., "Der geographische Horizont der sogenannten Völkerliste des Lukas (Acta 2,9–11)," *ZNW* 66 (1975): 149–69.
Gundry, R. H., "'Ecstatic Utterance' (N.E.B.)?" *JTS* 17 (1966): 299–307.
Haacker, K., "Das Pfingstwunder als exegetisches Problem," *Verborum Veritas: Festschrift für Gustav Stählin* . . . (ed. O. Böcher and K. Haacker; Wuppertal: Brockhaus, 1970), 125–31.
Harpur, T. W., "The Gift of Tongues and Interpretation," *CJT* 12 (1966): 164–71.
Harrisville, R. A., "Speaking in Tongues: A Lexicographical Study," *CBQ* 38 (1976): 35–48.
Horst, P. W. van der, "Hellenistic Parallels to the Acts of the Apostles (2.1–47)," *JSNT* 25 (1985): 49–60.
Jáuregui, J. A., "Pentecostés, fiesta de identidad cristiana," *EstEcl* 66 (1991): 369–96.
Johnson, S. L., Jr., "The Gift of Tongues and the Book of Acts," *BSac* 120 (1963): 309–11.
Kilpatrick, G. D., "A Jewish Background to Acts 2:9–11?" *JJS* 26 (1975): 48–49.
Kremer, J., "Biblische Grundlagen zur Feier der Fünfzig Tage," *Heiliger Dienst* 48 (1994): 3–15.
———, *Pfingstbericht und Pfingstgeschehen: Eine exegetische Untersuchung zu Apg 2, 1–13* (SBS 63–64; Stuttgart: Katholisches Bibelwerk, 1973).
Lake, K., "The Gift of the Spirit on the Day of Pentecost," *Beginnings,* 5.111–21.
Lampe, G.W.H., "The Holy Spirit in the Writings of St. Luke," *Studies in the Gospels: Essays in Memory of* R. H. *Lightfoot* (ed. D. E. Nineham; Oxford: Blackwell, 1957), 159–200.
Linton, O., "The List of Nations in Acts 2," *New Testament Christianity* (see above), 44–53.

Lohse, E., "Die Bedeutung des Pfingstberichtes im Rahmen des lukanischen Geschichtswerkes," *EvT* 13 (1953): 422–36.

Lyonnet, S., "De glossolalia Pentecostes eiusque significatione," *VD* 24 (1944): 65–75.

Marshall, I. H., "The Significance of Pentecost," *SJT* 30 (1977): 347–69.

Martin, I. J., "Glossolalia in the Apostolic Church," *JBL* 63 (1944): 123–30.

Menoud, P.-H., "La Pentecôte lucanienne et l'histoire," *RHPR* 42 (1962): 141–47.

Metzger, B. M., "Ancient Astrological Geography and Acts 2:9–11," *Apostolic History and the Gospel: Biblical and Historical Essays Presented to F. F. Bruce* . . . (ed. W. W. Gasque and R. P. Martin; Grand Rapids, MI: Eerdmans, 1970), 123–33; repr. *New Testament Studies: Philological, Versional, and Patristic* (NTTS 10; Leiden: Brill, 1980), 46–56.

Mínguez, D., *Pentecostés: Ensayo de semiótica narrativa en Hch* 2 (AnBib 75; Rome: Biblical Institute, 1976).

Neudecker, R., "'Das ganze Volk sah die Stimme . . .': Haggadische Auslegung und Pfingstbericht," *Bib* 78 (1997): 329–49.

Pfitzner, V. C., "'Pneumatic' Apostleship? Apostle and Spirit in the Acts of the Apostles," *Wort in der Zeit: Neutestamentliche Studien: Festgabe für Karl Heinrich Rengstorf* . . . (ed. W. Haubeck and M. Bachmann; Leiden: Brill, 1980), 210–35.

Potin, J., *La fête juive de la Pentecôte* (2 vols.; LD 65; Paris: Cerf, 1971).

Rétif, A., "Le mystère de la Pentecôte," *VSpir* 84 (1951): 451–65.

Ryrie, C. C., "The Significance of Pentecost," *BSac* 112 (1955): 330–39.

Sleeper, C. F., "Pentecost and Resurrection," *JBL* 84 (1965): 389–99.

Spicq, C., "Le Saint Esprit, vie et force de l'église primitive," *LumVie* 10 (1953): 9–28.

Stendahl, K., "Glossolalia and the Charismatic Movement," *God's Christ and His People: Studies in Honour of Nils Alstrup Dahl* (ed. J. Jervell and W. A. Meeks; Oslo: Universitetsforlaget, 1977), 122–31.

Stenger, W., "Beobachtungen zur sogenannten Völkerliste des Pfingstwunders (Apg 2,7–11)," *Kairos* 21 (1979): 206–14.

Thomas, J., "Formgesetze des Begriffs-Katalogs im N.T.," *TZ* 24 (1968): 15–28.

Unger, M. F., "The Significance of Pentecost," *BSac* 112 (1955): 1980.

Wedderburn, A.J.M., "Traditions and Redaction in Acts 2.1–13," *JSNT* 55 (1994): 27–54.

Weinstock, S., "The Geographical Catalogue in Acts II, 9–11," *JRS* 38 (1948): 43–46.

2. Peter's Discourse to Assembled Israel (2:14–36)

14 Peter stood up with the Eleven, raised his voice, and addressed them: "Fellow
Jews, and all who are sojourning here in Jerusalem! Let this be known to you
and listen, please, to what I have to say. 15 These people are not drunk, as you
suppose. After all, it is only nine o'clock in the morning! 16 No, it is rather what
was meant by Joel the prophet, when he said,

17 '*It shall happen* in the last days, God declares,
that I will pour out some of my Spirit upon all flesh;
your sons and daughters shall prophesy,
your young men shall see visions,
and your old men shall dream dreams.
18 *Yes, even upon my servants and my handmaids*
will I pour out some of my Spirit in those days, and they shall
speak like prophets.
19 *I will display wonders in the heavens* above
and signs *on the earth* below,
blood and fire and a cloud of smoke.
20 *The sun shall be turned to darkness, and the moon to blood,*
before that great and resplendent day of the Lord comes.
21 *Then everyone who calls upon the name of the Lord shall be saved.*'[c]

22 Fellow Israelites, listen to these words. Jesus the Nazorean was a man accredited to you by God with mighty deeds, wonders, and signs, which God wrought
through him in your midst, as you yourselves are well aware. 23 Though this man
was delivered up according to the set plan and foreknowledge of God, you used
lawless people to crucify and kill him. 24 But God raised him up, releasing him
from death's throes, since it was not possible for him to be held by it. 25 For David
says about him,

'*I have set the Lord ever before me,*
with him at my right hand I will not be perturbed;
26 *so my heart has been gladdened and my tongue has rejoiced,*
my flesh too shall live on in hope.
27 *For you will not abandon my soul to the nether world,*
nor will you allow your holy one to see decay.
28 *You have made known to me the paths of life;*
you will fill me with joy in your presence.'[d]

29 My brothers, one can speak frankly to you about the patriarch David: he died
and was buried, and his tomb is here in our midst to this very day. 30 But because
he was a prophet and knew that God *had sworn an oath* to him that he *would set*

one of his descendants upon his throne,[e] 31 he foresaw and spoke of the resurrection
of the Messiah, saying that he was *neither abandoned to the netherworld nor has*
his flesh seen decay.[f] 32 This Jesus God has raised up; of this we are all witnesses.
33 Exalted to God's right hand, he has received from the Father the promised Holy
Spirit and poured it forth. This is what you now [both] see and hear. 34 For it was
not David who went up into the heavens; yet it is he who says,

> *[The] Lord said to my Lord: 'Sit at my right hand*
> 35 *until I make your enemies a stool for your feet.'*[g]

36 Let all the house of Israel know for sure, then, that God has made him both
Lord and Messiah, this Jesus whom you crucified."

[c] Joel 3:1–5 [d] Ps 16:8–11 [e] Ps 132:11 [f] Ps 16:10 [g] Ps 110:1

WT: 14 Then Peter . . . with ten apostles. 17 I will pour out my Spirit . . . their sons . . . [omits "your" before "young men" and "old men"]. 18 my Spirit. 19 [omits "blood . . . smoke"]. 20 [omits "and splendid"]. 22 to my words . . . [omits "wonders"]. 24 from the nether world's throes . . . by them. 25 set my Lord. 30 would raise up the Messiah and set. 32 This Jesus, therefore, . . . [omits "all"]. 34 for it is he . . . Lord says to . . . 36 Let all Israel . . .

COMMENT

Peter acts as the spokesman for the Twelve and rises to the occasion to explain what has been seen and heard. Peter's speech is closely linked to the symbolic event that has preceded; it is, indeed, its complement, explaining the theological meaning of the event. He rejects the accusation of drunkenness and delivers for the first time the Christian proclamation to Jews assembled in Jerusalem. He explains the phenomenon that has drawn them together: the Spirit has not only come upon Christians, baptizing them with power from on high, but has enabled Jews gathered in Jerusalem for their Feast of Assembly to hear the new Christian proclamation. It is all the work of the Spirit and the fulfillment of ancient prophecy.

Peter thus delivers the first recorded sermon of the Christian church. It is the first of the missionary speeches in Acts, an address delivered to Jews, kerygmatic and christological in content. It is benevolent in its thrust, ending with an appeal for repentance and conversion. It proclaims the Christian message, encapsulated in v 36, and identifies Jesus as "Lord" and "Messiah." That important message is the climax of the speech, and the buildup to this affirmation calls upon the OT to explain the Spirit's work. Barrett (*Acts*, 131) thinks that "the speech shows no developed theology, especially when it is compared with the Pauline epistles." Why, however, should it be compared with Pauline theology? It is Lucan theology, put on the lips of Peter. Also why should Luke be faulted for failing to mention here or elsewhere in Acts that "Jesus Christ was the incarnation of the Son of God who shared equal divinity with his Father" (ibid., 132). That may be good Johannine theology, but it is not Lucan. Barrett, however, finally does recognize that "the speech . . . contains *Lucan* theology, the *Lucan* way of preaching the Gospel" (ibid. [Barrett's emphasis]).

Peter first invokes the prophet Joel (3:1–5) to explain the outpouring of the Spirit on this first Christian Pentecost. What Joel wrote about has now been fulfilled. The prophet's words, however, also provide Peter with numerous words and phrases with which he develops his sermon, as Evans has shown ("Prophetic Setting"). Moreover, in order to proclaim Christ's resurrection, Peter further invokes the words of Davidic psalms (16:8–11; 132:11), contrasting David, the king of Israel, whose tomb was nearby in Jerusalem itself, with the risen Christ. What David sang of has now come to pass in what God has brought about in the resurrection of Jesus. Peter calls further on Ps 110:1, a royal enthronement psalm, to explain Christ's present glorious status as *Kyrios* and *Christos:* God has exalted him and made him sit at his right hand.

The sermon is scarcely a verbatim report, since the composition of the speech is Lucan; Lucan style and formulation run throughout it. The extent to which it actually represents what Peter said will always remain problematic. Dodd regarded the speech as representative of "the *kerygma* of the Church of Jerusalem at an early period" (*Apostolic Preaching,* 21). Haenchen's skepticism about that view and his preference for Dibelius's judgment, that "Peter's speeches go back to Luke himself" (*Acts,* 185), do not resolve the problem, because the pattern in the early speeches of Peter and that of Paul in Acts 13 argues at least for something that Luke has inherited and has worked into the speeches that he has composed. They are not simply the way Luke would have preached or the way the church in his day would have proclaimed the kerygma. Nor are they simply Lucan theologoumena, *pace* Rese ("Die Aussagen"). Each speech has to be analyzed for traces of pre-Lucan material, as with Peter's speeches in general. This one in particular calls for the serious consideration that the early church preserved some recollection about how Peter proclaimed the Christian message on that first occasion, at least that he had appealed to Joel and the Davidic Psalter, called Jesus "Lord" and "Messiah," and summoned the Jews whom he addressed to repentance. The fact that Luke has composed the speech and made use of the LXX form of OT passages does not totally resolve the historicity problem; he seems to be dependent on some possibly Palestinian oral tradition. To resort to pre-Lucan material does not mean that Luke would have used an Aramaic source, as Torrey, Dodd, De Zwaan, and others have maintained. The alleged Aramaisms in it are highly dubious. The speech of Peter is dependent on the LXX and is otherwise composed in idiomatic, non-translation Greek.

The structure of the speech can be outlined as follows:

Introduction	2:14b–15
OT Quotation to Clarify the Situation	2:16–21
Kerygma	2:22–24, 32–33
OT Quotation to Relate Jesus to David	2:25–31, 34–35
Climactic Conclusion: Testimony	2:36
Hortatory Conclusion	2:38–39

Three important elements should be noted in the speech. The first is the explanation of the outpouring of the Spirit on the Christian community by the use of the words of Joel. Luke implies that a new age has dawned: this is now part of "the last days." Moreover, this outpouring of the spirit is what God meant of old when the prophet Joel was moved to speak about the Spirit: under that Spirit's guidance God's people will prophesy. This Spirit-guided prophetic utterance explains the phenomenon of speaking in tongues. This first element is set forth in the introduction of the speech (2:14b–15) and in the OT quotation from Joel (2:16–21).

In the OT Joel's words were uttered about Judah, the southern kingdom, after a cloud of locusts had consumed its produce. Although the locust plague was a heaven-sent condemnation of Judah's sins, what might be expected on the coming Day of Yahweh would make that plague picayune by comparison. So the prophet sought to warn Judah and call for its repentance, but he did so by promising God's blessings and deliverance (rain and abundant harvest) after the plague of locusts (Joel 2:18–27). "After that" there would be more: the outpouring of the Spirit "in those days," associated with the Day of Yahweh, which would come with cosmic cataclysms. Then men and women of all ages and classes would prophesy and call upon the name of Yahweh, warning the rest of Judah to seek salvation and deliverance from him who calls (3:1–5).

The second element is the kerygmatic proclamation of God's activity in raising Jesus from the dead and the application of David's words to Jesus. Thus the OT itself recorded elements of the divine plan of salvation according to which Jesus was to die, but that plan also foresaw what God would do in raising him from the dead: "God raised him up, releasing him from the throes of death." This was foreseen in what David sang about. Psalms 16 and 132 are quoted, and Peter stresses that David, king of Israel, could not have been speaking of himself, so they must refer to Jesus, who has not seen corruption. In so interpreting Psalm 16 especially, Peter supplies the basis for the historical origin of Christian faith (Boers, "Psalm 16").

The third element is the use of christological titles, *Kyrios* and *Christos*, for the risen Christ. They are found in the climactic v 36, which also points an accusing finger at the house of Israel: "God has made him both Lord and Messiah, this Jesus whom you crucified."

The major affirmation and the climax of the speech is found in vv 32–33 and 36: it portrays Peter testifying about the risen Christ to "the whole house of Israel," represented by the Jews assembled in Jerusalem from every nation, and calling Israel to repentance and conversion. Peter answers the question of v 12, "What does this mean?" and explains the Pentecost event that the assembled Jews have experienced by proclaiming that God through the risen Christ has poured out the Spirit on his people. Thus God's people will take a new shape under the guidance of the Spirit; Israel itself will be reconstituted.

Peter's testimony emphasizes for Christians of all ages what God has done in Christ and in the Spirit poured out on those who accept in faith such testimony. Scoffers may not agree with Christians, but God has sent Jesus the Nazorean and accredited him to people of all ages. His death on a cross in Jerusalem long ago has not been the end of him, for God "has raised him up, releasing him from death's throes" (1:24), and that aftermath has resulted in God making him "Lord and Messiah," a factor in the new mode of salvation with which people of all ages have to reckon.

NOTES

14. *Peter stood up with the Eleven, raised his voice, and addressed them.* MS D, Peshitta, and some MSS of VL read "with ten apostles." The difference would refer to Matthias being counted or not being counted. Haenchen (*Acts,* 178) strangely says that the phrase "with the Eleven" would "disregard the election of Matthias," but the opposite is precisely the case. MS D also adds *prōtos,* "first," thus enhancing Peter's prominence. The aor. pass. ptc. *statheis* is found again at 5:20; 11:13; 17:22; 25:18; 27:21, expressing the pose of one about to deliver a public speech or message in Hellenistic oratorical fashion. The expression *epēren tēn phōnēn,* "raised his voice," may be derived from the LXX (Judg 2:4; 9:7; 21:2; Ruth 1:9,14; 2 Sam 13:36), thus equaling Hebrew *nāśā' qôl,* but it is also known in both classical and Hellenistic Greek (Demosthenes, *Or.* 18.291; 19.336; Philostratus, *Vita Apollonii* 5.33); cf. Luke 11:27; Acts 14:11; 22:22.

"Fellow Jews, and all who are sojourning here in Jerusalem! Peter wants to include in his address not only Judeans in the proper sense, but all other Jews who have come from afar and are now staying for a time in the city for the Feast of Assembly *(asartha).* For *andres Ioudaioi,* "Fellow Jews," see NOTE on 1:16. Cf. Joel 1:2 (LXX).

Let this be known to you. The exact expression *gnōston estō* is found in the LXX (Dan 3:18; 1 Esdr 2:18; 6:8; 2 Esdr 4:12–13; 5:8) and has become a Lucan favorite (Acts 4:10; 13:38; 28:28); for similar uses of the verbal adj., see 1:19; 4:16; 9:42; 19:17; 28:22. Even though it corresponds to Aramaic *yĕdîă'* with the verb "to be," there is little reason to call it an Aramaism. Wilcox (*Semitisms,* 91) correctly recognizes it as "the normal stock-phrasing of letters and speeches." Ezek 36:32 (LXX) shows that it can render Hebrew *yiwwadēa' lākem,* "let it be known to you."

listen, please, to what I have to say. Lit., "give ear to my words," an expression occurring in the LXX of Job 32:11; Ps 5:2; cf. Joel 1:2. Peter calls for attention.

15. *These people are not drunk, as you suppose.* Peter begins by commenting on the mockery of some of his audience; he rejects a natural explanation of the experience of the Spirit. Cf. Joel 1:5 (LXX), which provides the background for the Joel passage to be quoted.

After all, it is only nine o'clock in the morning! Lit., "for it (is only) the third hour of the day." It is too early in the day for such carousing as the mockery supposes. Cicero (*Philippica* 2.41.104) decries as disgraceful such drinking: *ab hora tertia bibebatur, ludebatur, vomebatur,* "from the third hour one would drink, frolic, and vomit." The "day" was reckoned as lasting from dawn to dark (Pliny, *Naturalis Historia* 2.79.188) and divided into twelve hours (John 11:9).

See J. Finegan, *Handbook of Biblical Chronology* (Princeton: Princeton University Press, 1964), 8–12.

16. *No, it is rather what was meant by Joel the prophet, when he said.* Lit., "this is what was mentioned by the prophet Joel." This mode of introducing an OT quotation has its parallel in a Qumran text: *ky hw' 'šr 'mr,* "for that is what he said" (CD 10:16; 16:15; cf. 11QMelch 14); see Fitzmyer, *ESBNT,* 12. Peter quotes Joel not because of the mention of talking in tongues, as Haenchen (*Acts,* 178 n. 11) remarks, but because of the experience of the Spirit, even though such talk may be implied in the reference to prophecy. In the WT the name "Joel" is omitted.

Peter's introductory comment tells of the fulfillment of Joel's words. He does not cite Joel merely to illustrate his contention, because he sees what has just happened on this first Christian Pentecost to be the outpouring of the Spirit of which Joel spoke (even if it is not yet accompanied by all the cosmic events associated by the prophet with the Day of Yahweh). It is rather the "great and resplendent day of the Lord" for Peter in a sense that Joel never suspected. Peter sees it as the inauguration of the "last days"; for the time has come when the Christian message is about to move out from Jerusalem to "the end of the earth" (1:8).

17. *'It shall happen in the last days, God declares.* Luke changes the beginning of the Greek text of Joel from "after this" to "in the last days," a phrase also found in 2 Tim 3:1; Jas 5:3; and he adds, "God declares." Luke thus gives to the quotation a new eschatological orientation and ascribes the prophet's words to God himself. For Luke this is a new period in God's salvation history: the Period of the Church (*Luke,* 181–87, 227–31), under the guidance of the Spirit. It does not mean the "whole time since Jesus' ministry," *pace* Weiser (*Apg.,* 92), because Luke distinguishes the Period of the Church from the Period of Jesus (see *Luke,* 181–87).

Some MSS of the Alexandrian text-tradition (B, 076) and ancient versions read "after this," a scribal variant that harmonizes the Lucan text with the LXX. *Pace* Haenchen (*Acts,* 179), "after this" is not original, as Weiser (*Apg.,* 91) also rightly recognizes. Some Western MSS (D, E) read *Kyrios,* "the Lord," instead of "God."

I will pour out some of my Spirit upon all flesh. Lit., "I will pour out from my Spirit upon all flesh." The LXX, using the Greek prep. *apo,* reflects the partitive use of Hebrew *min* (hence "some of my Spirit"), which, however, is not found in the Hebrew text of Joel. "The fullness of the Spirit remains with God," but human beings only partake of it (Haenchen, *Acts,* 179).

The quotation of Joel 3:1–5a (in some English Bibles, 2:28–32) agrees for the most part with that found in the LXX. Luke transposes the sayings about young men and old men and adds a few words or phrases (see below). Apart from using *apo,* the LXX is an accurate rendering of the Hebrew original that sought to foretell the signs of the coming Day of the Lord, among which were to be the outpouring of the Spirit on all flesh, enabling people to prophesy, and also cosmic effects on the people of the land. In the original "all flesh" referred to all the people of Judah, but, as now used by Luke, its extension is greater: all human beings. On the different form of the quotation of Joel in MS D, see *TCGNT,* 255.

your sons and daughters shall prophesy. Joel's words speak of two sorts of phenomena attending the Day of the Lord, prophetic utterances and cosmic disturbances; both are invoked by Peter to explain what has occurred on the new Pentecost. The verb *prophēteusousin* in this Lucan context would be understood of the apostles' speaking in other tongues. This is the way Luke has identified their utterances as "prophetic," for they act as mouthpieces for God.

your young men shall see visions, and your old men shall dream dreams. Lit., "dream with dreams"; for the explanation of the dat. *enypniois,* see NOTE on 5:28. The Spirit will affect young and old alike, but in different ways.

18. *Yes, even upon my servants and my handmaids will I pour out some of my Spirit in those days.* A repetition of v 17b, but the Lucan addition of "my" changes the male and female "slaves" of the original into "servants" and "handmaids" of God. All human beings, male and female, young and old, free and slave, are to be affected by God's Spirit on the day of such a visitation. On "in those days," see NOTE on 1:15.

they shall speak like prophets. Lit., "they shall prophesy." These words are added by Luke to the quotation from Joel in order to emphasize prophetic utterance as a gift of the Spirit and its relation to speaking in other tongues. This is a special Lucan interest (Schneider, *Apg.,* 1.269). The words are omitted in MS D and the VL, perhaps by haplography or to make the quotation of Joel agree with the LXX; but see P. R. Rodgers, "Acts 2:18. *kai prophēteusousin,*" *JTS* 38 (1987): 95–97, who argues for the omitted words as more original.

19. *I will display wonders in the heavens above and signs on the earth below, blood and fire and a cloud of smoke.* Luke adds to the Greek text of Joel: "above," "signs," and "below." These additions do not change the sense of Joel's prophecy much, but they make clear how for Luke the cosmos itself warns of the coming Day of the Lord. In Joel this verse and the following were intended as an apocalyptic warning.

20. *The sun shall be turned to darkness, and the moon to blood, before that great and resplendent day of the Lord comes.* The "blood" refers to the red color that the moon will be seen to assume. Whereas the Hebrew spoke of *yôm Yhwh haggādôl wĕhannôrā',* "the great and awesome day of the Lord," the LXX rendered the last adj. as *epiphanē,* "resplendent," deriving the adj. not from *yārē',* "fear," but from *rā'āh,* "see, look at." Luke uses these words of Joel about cosmic disturbances to characterize the noise heard and the fire seen at the coming of the Spirit on the first Christian Pentecost. *Pace* Schneider (*Apg.,* 1.269), they are not to be understood as extraordinary natural features that will precede the end of time. They may have had that connotation in Joel, but Luke uses the description as a way of explaining what has accompanied the outpouring of the Spirit. *Kyrios* is used of Yahweh, as in the LXX.

21. *Then everyone who calls upon the name of the Lord shall be saved.'* Lit., "and it shall be that everyone . . ." In the context of Peter's speech, this concluding clause of Joel's prophetic utterance becomes climactic. Salvation is linked with invocation of the Lord. The words of Joel thus quoted prepare for the proclamation of the risen Christ as Lord and Messiah and also for the call to repentance

and baptism (Dillon, "Prophecy," 547). In the Hebrew text of Joel, "Lord" referred to Yahweh, but salvation as a consequence of the invocation of "the name of the Lord" appears again in Acts, with *Kyrios* as the risen Christ (4:10–12; 22:16). That too is the connotation of *Kyrios* here. *Pas hos*, "everyone who," is emphasized because Luke does not want to limit the quoted words only to the Jews assembled in Jerusalem: all human beings may call on the name of the Lord for salvation. This is his way of stressing an effect of the Christ-event in the first kerygmatic speech in Acts (see *Luke*, 222–23).

22. *Fellow Israelites, listen to these words.* For the mode of address, see NOTES on 1:16; 2:14. Peter directs his remarks to fellow Jews, using the honorific and sacred religious name "Israelites," and not merely "Jews" (as in 2:14; cf. 3:12; 5:35; 13:16; 21:28) or "Hebrews." "Israel" was the name bestowed by Yahweh on a patriarch of this people, Jacob (Gen 32:29). Cf. Rom 9:4 (*Romans*, 545). With these words Peter begins to announce the primitive kerygma, the proclamation about the risen Christ; it will be continued until v 24 and resumed in vv 32–33.

Jesus. Peter's proclamation centers on Jesus as an earthly being. He is not Jesus Christ or Jesus the Lord, but Jesus, the Nazorean, thus recalling to his listeners the Galilean origins of the one about whom he speaks.

the Nazorean. Whereas Jesus is called *Nazarēnos*, "Nazarene," in Luke 4:34; 24:19, the adj. *Nazōraios* occurs in Luke 18:37 and will appear again in Acts 3:6; 4:10; 6:14; 22:8; 26:9. In 24:5 it is employed to designate the Christian sect. This adj. is not, however, exclusively Lucan, being found also in Matt 2:23; 26:71; John 18:5,7; 19:19. Many commentators take the two forms as merely literary variants of the same name, "Nazarene," i.e., from Nazareth (H. Kuhli, *EDNT*, 2.454–56). Both forms have a typical ending for Greek proper adjs., *-aios* (as in *Pharisaios*, "Pharisee," *Saddoukaios*, "Sadducee," *Essaios*, "Essene" [Philo]); *-ēnos* (as in *Gerasēnos*, "Gerasene," *Essēnos*, "Essene" [Josephus]). *Nazōraios* does not simply = *Nazarēnos* (see *Luke*, 1215). At the moment, the best, but not certain, explanation is to regard *Nazōraios* as a gentilic adj. meaning "a person from Nazara/Nazareth," even if that does not explain the *ō*. See W. F. Albright, "The Names 'Nazareth' and 'Nazoraean,'" *JBL* 65 (1946): 397–401; H. H. Schaeder, *TDNT*, 4.874–79.

was a man. Peter calls Jesus *anēr*, "a man," like Latin *vir*, not *homo*, but adds an important qualification in the following phrase. As Barrett (*Acts*, 140) notes, this is the "starting point" of Lucan christology in Acts, for Luke has no idea of the preexistence or incarnation of Christ.

accredited to you by God. I.e., guaranteed by God and sent to you and all human beings. Luke uses the prep. *apo*, "from," instead of the more usual Greek prep. *hypo*, "by," to express agency with a passive verb. Though this use of *apo* is sometimes called a Semitism (reflecting *min* of agency in Aramaic and Hebrew), it is found occasionally in classical Greek, in the LXX (1 Macc 15:17; Sir 16:4) and in Philo (*Legum allegoriae* 3.19 §62). It occurs in Luke 1:26 (see NOTE there); 6:18b; 7:35; 8:43; 9:22; 17:25; Acts 4:36; 10:33; 15:4 and elsewhere in the NT (2 Cor 7:13; Jas 1:13; 5:4; Rev 12:6), where some MSS read *hypo* (cf. BAGD,

88; BDF §210.2). The Alexandrian text reads the ptc. *apodedeigmenon,* "displayed, attested, accredited," whereas MS D reads *dedokimasmenon,* "approved." Either ptc. reveals the heaven-blessed character of Jesus' ministry, which was used in later Adoptionist christology with dire consequences.

with mighty deeds, wonders, and signs, which God wrought through him in your midst. The divine accreditation is seen to come from Jesus' miracles, called *dynameis,* "powers, powerful deeds," the term regularly used for his miracles in the Gospels (Luke 10:13; 19:37; cf. *Luke,* 542–43, 581–82, 853); it will be used of Paul's miracles in Acts 19:11. To it Luke joins *terata kai sēmeia,* "portents and signs," a phrase occurring again in 2:43; 4:30; 5:12; 6:8; 7:36; 14:3; 15:12. This phrase is derived from the LXX, where it often describes God's mighty acts on behalf of Israel (e.g. Exod 7:3; Deut 4:34; 28:46; 29:2; 34:11; Ps 135:9; Isa 8:18). Cf. Josephus, *J.W.* 1.0.11 §28.

as you yourselves are well aware. By this Peter must mean that at least some of his listeners, those from Jerusalem, Judea, or Galilee, might have seen or at least heard of the miracles of Jesus.

23. *Though this man was delivered up according to the set plan and foreknowledge of God.* Peter relates Jesus' suffering and death to God's salvific plan. What happened to Jesus did not occur perchance; it was foreseen by God. Luke referred to God's *boulē,* "plan, design, will," in Luke 7:30 and will refer to it again in Acts 4:28; 13:36; 20:27 (*Luke,* 179). Now he spells out details of that plan. Luke is sometimes castigated for not having a "theology of the cross," but here he clearly refers to the death of Jesus and relates it to God's salvific plan. See further *Luke,* 219–21. The verbal adj. *ekdotos,* "given up," is employed in the sense of "handed over" (to death); cf. Ign. *Smyrn.* 4.2.

you used lawless people to crucify and kill him. Lit., "having fastened (him) to (the cross) through the hands of lawless ones, you did away with (him)." In Luke 23:33 the evangelist says only "they crucified Jesus there," without specifying the subject of the verb. In 23:26, however, one reads, "as they led Jesus away," the "they" can refer only to those who "asked for" the release of Barabbas and to whom Pilate handed Jesus over according to "their will" (23:25; see also 23:23–24). The Roman "soldiers" begin to appear in the Lucan passion narrative only at 23:36 so that they can hardly be the "they" of 23:33. Now Luke modifies his view, saying that Jesus was fastened to the cross by "lawless people," other than the "you" who "did away with (him)." This makes "lawless people" refer to the pagan Roman soldiers, whereas the "you" must mean the "fellow Israelites" addressed in 2:22. Perhaps Luke is using *anomoi,* "lawless, wicked, unjust," more etymologically as *a-nomoi,* "law-less," meaning pagan non-Jews, who live without the benefit of the Mosaic law. Barrett (*Acts,* 142) notes that "notwithstanding the crucifixion by Alexander Jannaeus . . . , crucifixion was not a Jewish punishment in the Roman period; yet with the main verb *aneilate* Luke fixes responsibility for the crucifixion of Jesus upon the Jews. Not however without qualification. The action took place *dia cheiros . . . anomōn.*" Josephus tells us that the Jewish leader Alexander Jannaeus crucified 800 Jews (*J.W.* 1.4.6 §97) at a time well before the Romans took control of Judea.

In this verse Luke refers to "the eternal paradox of the Cross; the Cross is at one and the same time the action of the purpose and the plan of God, and an unspeakably terrible crime at the hands of wicked men" (W. Barclay, "Great Themes," 245).

24. *God raised him up.* Lit., "whom God raised up (*anestēsen*)" from death. This statement becomes Peter's main affirmation in the speech so far; it is the essence of the primitive kerygma: the crucified Jesus of Nazareth has become the risen Lord, whom Peter and the Eleven now proclaim.

God's action stands in contrast to what was done to Jesus by wicked human beings. Luke ascribes the resurrection of Christ to the Father, as he will again in 2:32; 3:26; 13:33, 34; 17:31. In Luke 24:6, 34 the pass. of *egeirein,* "raise," is rather utilized; the act. of this verb with God as the subject recurs in 3:15; 4:10; 5:30; 10:40; 13:30, 37 (*Luke,* 195). The resurrection is thus depicted not as an achievement of Jesus, but the result of God's powerful action. Contrast Acts 10:41; 17:3. See G. Delling, "Die Jesusgeschichte."

releasing him from death's throes. Lit., "having loosed the pangs of death." Luke uses a phrase from 2 Sam 22:6 (LXX), *ōdines thanatou,* "pangs of death," which translates Hebrew *ḥeblê šĕ'ôl,* "the bonds of Sheol" (cf. Ps 18:5–6). Polycarp (*Phil.* 1.2) writes in a manner very similar to this verse: *hon ēgeiren ho theos, lysas tas ōdinas tou hadou,* "whom God raised up, having released the pangs of Hades." Did Polycarp know Acts? W. L. Knox (*Acts,* 1) thought so; Haenchen (*Acts,* 6) says no. See R. G. Bratcher, "'Having Loosed the Pangs of Death,'" *BT* 10 (1959): 18–20.

since it was not possible for him to be held by it. I.e., by death, or, with the WT, "by them," i.e., the throes. God released Jesus from death's hold because that was part of the divine "plan"; for this reason death could not hold him in its clutches.

25. *David says about him.* Peter now quotes the OT again as an indication of the divine plan. The psalm to be quoted is attributed in the OT Psalter to David *(miktām lĕDāwîd).*

'I have set the Lord ever before me, with him at my right hand I will not be perturbed. Luke's text quotes Ps 16:8–11 (LXX) exactly, which is for the most part an accurate rendering of the Hebrew original, but Greek *ep' elpidi,* "in hope," renders Hebrew *lābeṭaḥ,* "in security," and Greek *diaphthoran,* "corruption, decay," renders Hebrew *šaḥat,* "pit, grave." Most of the quotation has little pertinence to Peter's argument, but what appears in v 27 is crucial. Psalm 16 is a lament, actually a psalm of personal trust in God; it expresses the psalmist's faith in God's power to deliver from evil and personal troubles, as he calls upon God to recall his constant seeking of refuge in divine help and makes renewed recognition of that help. As Peter makes use of it in his speech, it is applied to the risen Christ's exaltation.

26. *so my heart has been gladdened and my tongue has rejoiced, my flesh too shall live on in hope.* What appears in the LXX as "my tongue" would be in the Hebrew "my liver," which modern translations often render as "my soul."

27. *For you will not abandon my soul to the netherworld, nor will you allow your holy one to see decay.* The important words are "the netherworld" *(hadēs),* "your

holy one" *(ton hosion sou)*, and "decay" *(diaphthora)*, which Peter applies from the Davidic psalm to the risen Christ, who is the preeminent "holy One," whose status is not in the netherworld, and who has not experienced decay.

28. *You have made known to me the paths of life; you will fill me with joy in your presence.'* Lit., "with your face," an exact rendering of Hebrew *'et pānêkā*. The "paths of life" would refer to the risen life that Christ now enjoys, and "your presence" to the association of Christ with the Father in glory. Cf. 3:15. See P. Ghiron-Bistagne, "L'Emploi du terme grec 'prosopon' dans l'*Ancien* et le *Nouveau Testament*," *Mélanges Edouard Delebecque* (Aix-en-Provence: Université de Provence, 1983), 155–74.

"Such a 'proof from Scripture' is strange to our way of thinking and does not satisfy us; but for the early church it was of fundamental importance that what had happened to Jesus had to be brought into harmony with the OT, because that was the Jews' book of belief" (Weiser, *Apg.*, 93).

29. *My brothers.* Peter addresses the Jews assembled as *adelphoi;* see NOTE on 1:15.

one can speak frankly to you about the patriarch David: he died and was buried, and his tomb is here in our midst to this very day. Having quoted the Davidic psalm, Peter begins to draw an argument from it: David not only died and was buried, as was true of Jesus too, but "his tomb" was not found empty. Peter appeals to the existence of David's tomb in their midst even as he speaks. He invokes implicitly the Davidic descent of Jesus as he addresses a Jewish audience, as will Paul in Pisidian Antioch (13:22–23). This was part of the early mode of preaching about Jesus the Christ.

According to 1 Kgs 2:10, the king "was buried in the city of David," usually identified with Zion, the southeastern hill of Jerusalem, south of the Temple area (2 Sam 5:7, 9; 6:10, 12, 16; 2 Kgs 9:28; 12:22; 1 Chr 11:5, 7). A later Christian tradition transferred the name Zion to the western hill of Jerusalem sometime in the fourth century, probably on the basis of Mic 3:12 ("Zion shall be plowed as a field, Jerusalem shall be reduced to ruins, and the mount of the Temple to a wooded hill"), when the fourth-century Bordeaux Pilgrim, the earliest known Christian pilgrim to the Holy Land from western Europe, understood it of the two hills of Jerusalem: since the mount of the Temple was the eastern, Zion had to be the western. Later, about the tenth century, possibly on the basis of Acts 2, David's tomb was located in the vicinity of where the Cenacle was thought to have been in western Jerusalem (*HPG*, 331–32, 334; *ELS* §§748, 756, 760, 768, 776.10, 777.5, 789.8, 790.2). Modern Jews also recognize this tradition (Z. Vilnay, *The Guide to Israel* [16th ed.; Jerusalem: Ahiever, 1973], 94–96).

Josephus too records that King David was buried "in Jerusalem" (*Ant.* 7.15.3 §392), but Bethlehem was also called "the city of David" (Luke 2:4, 11), because it was the city of his boyhood and youth. In addition, David is known in the OT as the son of "an Ephrathite of Bethlehem in Judah" (1 Sam 17:12) or of "Jesse the Bethlehemite" (1 Sam 17:58; cf. 20:6), whence grew up another tradition, traceable to Eusebius at least, that locates David's tomb in Bethlehem (*ELS*, §§91, 108.4, 110.4, 113.2, 129.2).

Peter cites Psalm 16 and interprets it in terms of Jesus, whom he will soon call "Lord" and "Messiah," thus giving a Christian messianic interpretation to the psalm. To explain why he can so interpret the psalm, Peter calls David "a prophet."

30. *because he was a prophet.* This description of David prepares for the implicit quotation that follows from another psalm and for the interpretation of Psalm 16: that is, why David knew of God's oath about one of his descendants (cf. 2 Sam 7:11b–14). David is never called a prophet in the OT, and there is little in the story of David that might serve as a springboard for such a title. The function of prophecy, however, is attributed to David in the Qumran text, "David's Compositions" (11QPs[a] 27:2–11), which tells of the 4,050 psalms and songs that he composed: *kwl 'lh dbr bnbw'h 'šr ntn lw mlpny h'lywn,* "all these he spoke through prophecy that was given to him before the Most High" (J. A. Sanders, *The Psalms Scroll of Qumran Cave 11 (11 QPs[a])* [DJD 4; Oxford: Clarendon, 1965], 48, 91–93). Josephus too speaks of David's prophetic role: ". . . the Deity abandoned Saul and passed to David, who, when the divine spirit had moved over to him, began to prophesy" (*Ant.* 6.8.2 §166). See Fitzmyer, "David, 'Being Therefore a Prophet . . .' (Acts 2:30)," *CBQ* 34 (1972): 332–39. This is but another example of the way that Luke interprets the OT, seeing even a psalm as a prediction of what will come to pass in the life and ministry of Jesus.

knew that God had sworn an oath to him that he would set one of his descendants upon his throne. Peter alludes to Ps 132:11, quoting implicitly a few words of it. It is a liturgical psalm, celebrating the dynasty of David, who is called in it God's "Anointed One." In the LXX, v 11 reads: *ōmosen Kyrios tō Dauid alētheian kai ou mē athetēsei autēn, Ek karpou tēs koilias sou thēsomai epi ton thronon sou,* "the Lord swore to David the truth, and he will not nullify it: (One) of your offspring I shall set upon your throne." This is almost an exact rendering of the Hebrew original. Thus, David, in his capacity as prophet, knew and sang in advance of the offspring who would sit upon his throne. Cf. 2 Sam 7:11b–14. Peter implies that, since David could not have been speaking of himself, he must have been speaking of a descendant of his.

31. *he foresaw and spoke of the resurrection of the Messiah.* Peter interprets David's words from Psalm 132, applying them specifically to Christ's "resurrection," as foreseen by David. This becomes clear when the following words from Ps 16:10 are joined to them. Peter's testimony thus identifies the crucified Jesus as the Christian Messiah. Though the christological title, *Christos,* was long in use by the time Luke wrote, Luke makes Peter use it of the crucified Jesus within 50 days of his death. See NOTE on 2:36 below.

he was neither abandoned to the netherworld nor has his flesh seen decay. This allusion to Ps 16:10 means that the dead Jesus, considered as the offspring of David, is not an inhabitant of *šĕ'ôl* or *hadēs;* he has not experienced death's "decay."

32. *This Jesus God has raised up.* I.e., from the dead. Again Peter uses *anestēsen* (see NOTE on 2:24) and proclaims Christ's risen status as a result of the Father's activity.

of this we are all witnesses. Peter does not mean that the Twelve actually witnessed the resurrection, but that they have become witnesses of the risen Christ, who has appeared to them (1:3). They have not only seen him "alive" (1:3), but have assumed the role of testifying to his risen status. They are thus carrying out the task that he assigned them: to bear witness to him "in Jerusalem" (1:8).

33. *Exalted to God's right hand.* Or "by God's right hand," if the dat. is to be taken in an instrumental sense, as Barrett (*Acts,* 149) prefers. In view of 5:31 the local sense of the dat. is preferable, as BDF §199, ZBG §57, Conzelmann (*Acts,* 21), and Schneider (*Apg.,* 1.275) have understood it. Peter asserts the risen Christ's privileged status: he sits in honor at God's right hand, whither he has been raised by God himself. Peter's statement does not mention "ascension," but preserves the more primitive way of expressing Jesus' transit to the Father's presence as "exaltation." Cf. 1 Tim 3:16g; Rom 1:4. See *Luke,* 194–96. Raised to the status of glory, he received from the Father the Spirit that he would pour out. The first words of this verse echo Ps 118:16 (LXX), *dexia Kyriou hypsōsen me,* "the right hand of the Lord has exalted me."

he has received from the Father the promised Holy Spirit and poured it forth. The "promise of the Holy Spirit" is known to the reader from 1:4–5. Peter's audience, however, would have had to understand the promise of the Spirit as something like that in Joel 3:1–2 (quoted earlier), or in Isa 32:15; 44:3; Ezek 11:19; 36:26–27; 37:14, the promise of new life through God's Spirit. Finally, Peter remarks that the Spirit has been poured out and that the effects of it have been manifested to his audience, the Jews assembled in Jerusalem.

The expression "has received from the Father" may seem strange, because the Holy Spirit came down on Jesus during his ministry according to the Lucan Gospel (3:21–22; 4:1, 4, 14, 18). Luke is concerned, however, to show the risen Christ subordinate to his heavenly Father. In vv 17–18 he has already depicted God saying that he would pour out his Spirit on human beings; in v 22 he has mentioned that God accredited Jesus through miracles and in vv 23, 32–33 that God raised him from the dead and exalted him. That Lucan way of expressing it, however, is a far cry from the later theological Subordinationism. See further Kilgallen ("A Rhetorical"), especially for the use of "Father" in this verse and also the possibility that it comes from a source that Luke may be using.

It is a matter of debate whether Luke alludes in this verse to Ps 68:19. Interpreters such as Barrett, Dupont, Kretschmar, Le Déaut, Lindars, Moule, Pesch, and Roloff think that this psalm, which influenced Eph 4:8, has also influenced Luke here. They are also influenced by the rabbinic tradition of later date, which saw an allusion in Ps 68:19 to Moses' ascent of Mt. Sinai to receive the law. As a parallel to Moses in that interpretation, Jesus would have ascended to receive the Spirit that he pours out. This suggestion, however, is eisegetical. When one compares the Greek of vv 33–34 with that of Ps 68:19 (LXX), the verbal echoes are minimal: *hypsōtheis* for *eis hypsos* of the psalm; *labōn para tou patros* for *elabes domata en anthrōpois;* in fact, they are so minimal as to be nonexistent. See Polhill, *Acts,* 115 n. 124.

This is what you now [both] see and hear. The audience in Jerusalem now sees the Galileans confronting them with a new message and hears it explained by Peter, the spokesman for the group.

34. *it was not David who went up into the heavens.* Peter reiterates his argument from v 29, using Psalm 110 instead in a negative sense. Nowhere in the OT does one read of an "assumption" of David, even though it tells of God's "taking" Enoch (Gen 5:24, i.e., his rapture), or of Elijah's going up to heaven in a whirlwind (2 Kgs 2:11).

yet it is he who says, [The] Lord said to my Lord: 'Sit at my right hand. Peter's argument uses and depends on the LXX form of Ps 110:1, which is quoted exactly. The Hebrew original reads rather *nĕ'ûm Yhwh la'dōnî, šēb lîmînî,* "Oracle of Yahweh to my Lord: Sit at my right hand." Psalm 110, ascribed to David, is a royal psalm commemorating the enthronement of a king of his dynasty, who is invited by Yahweh to ascend to the throne and assume a position of honor beside God. Peter argues: since David remains in his tomb, the words cannot refer to him. So David's words must refer to the exaltation and enthronement of the risen Christ, a descendant of David, thus exploiting a sense that goes beyond its OT meaning. This christological sense of Psalm 110 is found elsewhere in the NT, showing how the early church understood it particularly of the risen Christ. See M. Black, "Christological Use," 6–11.

35. *until I make your enemies a stool for your feet.'* In its OT context these words of the psalm would have expressed the victorious status acquired by the newly enthroned Davidic king. As applied to the risen Christ, they symbolize the victorious status of Christ that Peter will announce in the next verse.

36. *Let all the house of Israel know for sure, then, that God has made him both Lord and Messiah, this Jesus whom you crucified."* So Peter concludes his scriptural argument and proclaims its climax to the assembled Jews. As a result of God's raising/exalting him, the crucified Jesus has become a victor, both *Kyrios* and *Christos.* The risen Christ is now the "Lord," of whom David spoke in Ps 110:1 (LXX), and the "Messiah," which is mentioned in neither Psalm 16 nor Psalm 110, but implied in "one of your descendants" (Ps 132:11), the very psalm that speaks of the historical King David himself as God's "Anointed One" (132:10). In this way Peter affirms the victory of Christ over death and the installation of him in the glorious presence of the Father. This Peter proclaims to "all the house of Israel," the echo of an OT title; see Lev 10:6; Num 20:29; 1 Sam 7:2, 3; Jer 9:25; Ezek 37:11 (LXX). On *pas oikos Israēl,* "the whole house of Israel," see ZBG §190; *IBNTG,* 95.

The first of the two christological titles implies that Jesus in his risen status has been made the equal of Yahweh of the OT, for "Lord" was used by Palestinian Jews in the last pre-Christian centuries as a title for Yahweh: either *mārê'* or *māryā'* in Aramaic, or *'ādôn* in Hebrew, or *Kyrios* in Greek. All these forms are now attested in important contemporary extrabiblical texts (*Luke,* 200–204; *WA,* 115–42); so it is no longer right that "the un-modified expression 'the Lord' is unthinkable in Jewish usage" or that "'Lord' used of God is always given some modifier" (Bultmann, *TNT,* 1.51). Rather, Jewish Christians took over a title used of Yahweh by contemporary Jews of Judea and applied it to the risen Christ at an early date. Luke depicts Peter making use of that title in his first proclamatory testimony to Jews assembled in Jerusalem. See Fitzmyer, "*Kyrios*," *EDNT*, 2.328–31; *WA*, 115–42.

The second title means that God has made Jesus in his risen status the anointed agent (Hebrew *māšîăḥ* = Greek *christos*) to bring aid or deliverance to the people of Israel, who were looking forward to the coming of a Messiah—an expectation clearly attested in Qumran texts of the first centuries B.C. and A.D. (*Luke*, 197–200, 471–72). For the first Christians of Jerusalem this title was taken over from Jewish usage and applied to Jesus, who has thus become in a Christian sense "the Messiah." This too explains why a new stage in the realization or implementation of God's salvific plan has begun, with the coming of this "Messiah." It also shows why Luke has added to Joel's words "in the last days" (2:17). See D. L. Jones, "The Title *Christos* in Luke-Acts," *CBQ* 32 (1970): 69–76; C. C. Torrey, "*Christos*," *Quantulacumque: Studies Presented to Kirsopp Lake . . .* (ed. R. P. Casey et al.: London: Christophers, 1937), 317–24; F. Hahn, "*Christos*," *EDNT*, 3.478–86.

whom you crucified. The "you" refers above all to the Jews of Jerusalem who handed Jesus over to Pilate (see 2:23); it cannot refer to diaspora Jews visiting Jerusalem for the feast.

BIBLIOGRAPHY (2:14–36)

Argyle, A. W., "The Theory of an Aramaic Source in Acts 2,14–40," *JTS* 4 (1953): 213–14.

Barclay, W., "Great Themes of the New Testament: IV. Acts ii.14–40," *ExpTim* 70 (1958–59): 196–99, 243–46.

Best, E., "Spirit-Baptism," *NovT* 4 (1960): 236–43.

Black, M., "The Christological Use of the Old Testament in the New Testament," *NTS* 18 (1971–72): 1–14.

Boers, H. W., "Psalm 16 and the Historical Origin of the Christian Faith," *ZNW* 60 (1969): 105–10.

Buchanan, G. W., "Eschatology and the 'End of Days,'" *JNES* 20 (1961): 188–93.

Buis, P., "Le don de l'Esprit Saint et la prophétie de Joël," *AsSeign* 52 (1965): 16–28.

Constant, P., "Forme textuelle et justesse doctrinale de l'Ancien Testament dans le Nouveau: La citation du Psaume 16 dans le discours d'Actes 2," *Baptist Review of Theology* 2 (1992): 4–15.

Delling, G., "Die Jesusgeschichte in der Verkündigung nach Acta," *NTS* 19 (1972–73): 373–89.

Dillon, R. J., "The Prophecy of Christ and His Witnesses according to the Discourses of Acts," *NTS* 32 (1986): 544–56.

Dupont, J., "Ascension du Christ et don de l'Esprit d'après Actes 2:33," *Christ and Spirit in the New Testament: In Honour of Charles Francis Digby Moule* (ed. B. Lindars and S. S. Smalley; Cambridge: Cambridge University Press, 1973), 219–28; repr. *Nouvelles études,* 199–209.

———, "'Assis à la droite de Dieu': L'Interprétation du Ps 110,1 dans le Nouveau Testament," *Resurrexit: Actes du symposium international sur la résurrection de Jésus (Rome 1970)* (ed. E. Dhanis; Vatican City: Editrice Vaticana, 1974), 340–422; repr. *Nouvelles études,* 210–95.

———, "Les discours de Pierre dans les Actes et le chapitre xxiv de l'Evangile de Luc," *L'Evangile de Luc, The Gospel of Luke: Revised and Enlarged Edition* . . . (BETL 32; ed. F. Neirynck; Louvain: Leuven University/Peeters, 1989), 239–84, 328–30; repr. *Nouvelles études,* 58–111 (without added note).

———, "L'Interprétation des psaumes dans les Actes," *Études,* 283–308.

———, "Jésus, Messie et Seigneur dans la foi des premiers chrétiens," *VSpir* 83 (1950): 385–416; repr. *Études,* 367–90.

———, "L'Utilisation apologétique de l'AT dans les discours des Actes," *Études,* 245–82.

Ellis, E. E., "Midraschartige Züge in den Reden der Apostelgeschichte," *ZNW* 62 (1971): 94–104.

Evans, C. A., "The Prophetic Setting of the Pentecost Sermon," *ZNW* 74 (1983): 148–50.

Evans, C. F., "The Kerygma," *JTS* 7 (1956): 25–41.

Ghidelli, C., "Le citazioni dell'Antico Testamento nel cap. 2 degli Atti," *Il messianismo: Atti della xviii settimana biblica* (Brescia: Paideia, 1966), 285–305.

Gilmour, S. M., "Easter and Pentecost," *JBL* 81 (1962): 62–66.

Gourgues, M., "Lecture théologique du psaume cx et fête de la Pentecôte," *RB* 83 (1976): 5–24.

Hartman, L., "Baptism 'Into the Name of Jesus' and Early Christology," *ST* 28 (1974): 21–48.

Heather, B., "Early Christian Homiletics: 1. St. Peter's Discourse at Pentecost (Acts 2:14–36)," *ACR* 36 (1959): 149–54.

Hengel, M., "Psalm 110 und die Erhöhung des Auferstandenen zur Rechten Gottes," *Anfänge der Christologie: Festschrift für Ferdinand Hahn* . . . (ed. C. Breytenbach and H. Paulsen; Göttingen: Vandenhoeck & Ruprecht, 1991), 43–73.

Hull, J.H.E., *The Holy Spirit in the Acts of the Apostles* (London: Lutterworth; Cleveland: World Publishing Co., 1967).

Juel, D., "Social Dimensions of Exegesis: The Use of Psalm 16 in Acts 2," *CBQ* 43 (1981): 543–56.

Kaiser, W. C., Jr., "The Promise of God and the Outpouring of the Holy Spirit: Joel 2:28–32 and Acts 2:16–21," *The Living and Active Word of God: Essays in Honor of Samuel J. Schultz* (ed. M. Inch and R. Youngblood; Winona Lake, IN: Eisenbrauns, 1983), 109–22.

———, "The Promise to David in Psalm 16 and Its Application in Acts 2:25–33 and 13:32–37," *JETS* 23 (1980): 219–29.

Kerrigan, A., "The 'Sensus Plenus' of Joel, III, 1–5 in Act., II, 14–36," *Sacra Pagina* (2 vols.; Gembloux: Duculot, 1959), 2.295–313.
Kilgallen, J. J., "A Rhetorical and Source-traditions Study of Acts 2,33," *Bib* 77 (1996): 178–96.
———, "The Unity of Peter's Pentecost Speech," *TBT* 82 (1976): 650–56.
Kilpatrick, G. D., "Some Quotations in Acts," *Les Actes des Apôtres* (ed. J. Kremer), 81–97.
Kissane, E. J., "The Interpretation of Psalm 110," *ITQ* 21 (1954): 103–14.
Kretschmar, G., "Himmelfahrt und Pfingsten," *ZKG* 66 (1954–55): 209–53.
Lafferty, O. J., "Acts 2:14–36: A Study in Christology," *Dunwoodie Review* 6 (1966): 235–53.
Lake, K., "The Gift of the Spirit on the Day of Pentecost," *Beginnings*, 5.111–21.
Le Déaut, R., "Pentecôte et tradition juive," *Spiritus* 2 (1961): 127–44.
Lindars, B., *New Testament Apologetic: The Doctrinal Significance of the Old Testament Quotations* (London: SCM, 1961), 38–59.
Martini, C., "Riflessioni sulla cristologia degli Atti," *SacDoc* 16 (1971): 525–34.
Menoud, P.-H., "La Pentecôte lucanienne et l'histoire," *RHPR* 42 (1962): 141–47.
Mussner, F., "'In den letzten Tagen' (Apg 2,17a)," *BZ* 5 (1961): 263–65.
Noack, B., "The Day of Pentecost in Jubilees, Qumran and Acts," *ASTI* 1 (1962): 73–95.
O'Toole, R. F., "Acts 2:30 and the Davidic Covenant of Pentecost," *JBL* 102 (1983): 245–58.
Petzer, J. H., "Variation in Citations from the Old Testament in the Latin Version of Acts," *JNSL* 19 (1993): 143–57.
Refoulé, F., "Le discours de Pierre à l'assemblée de Jérusalem," *RB* 100 (1993): 239–51.
Rese, M., "Die Aussagen über Jesu Tod und Auferstehung in der Apostelgeschichte—Älteste Kerygma oder lukanische Theologoumena," *NTS* 30 (1984): 335–53.
Rodgers, P. R., "Acts 2:18. *kai prophēteusousin*," *JTS* 38 (1987): 95–97.
Rüger, H. P., "*Nazareth/Nazara Nazarēnos/Nazōraios*," *ZNW* 72 (1981): 257–63.
Sandt, H. van de, "The Fate of the Gentiles in Joel and Acts 2: An Intertextual Study," *ETL* 66 (1990): 56–77.
Schmitt, A., "Ps 16, 8–11 als Zeugnis der Auferstehung in der Apg," *BZ* 17 (1973): 229–48.
Sloan, R., "'Signs and Wonders': A Rhetorical Clue to the Pentecost Discourse," *EvQ* 63 (1991): 225–40.
Weiser, A., "Die Pfingstpredigt des Lukas," *BibLeb* 14 (1973): 1–12.
Zehnle, R. F., *Peter's Pentecost Discourse: Tradition and Lukan Reinterpretation in Peter's Speeches of Acts 2 and 3* (SBLMS 15; New York/Nashville: Abingdon, 1971).

3. Reaction to Peter's Discourse (2:37–41)

[37] Now when they heard this, they were cut to the quick and asked Peter and the
rest of the apostles, "What are we to do, Brothers?" [38] Peter [said] to them, "Reform your lives and be baptized, every one of you, in the name of Jesus the Messiah for the forgiveness of your sins, and you will receive the gift of the Holy
Spirit. [39] For to you and your children has the promise been made, yes, even to
all those still far off whom the Lord our God will call to himself." [40] With many
other explanations Peter bore witness and kept urging them, "Save yourselves
from this corrupt generation." [41] Those who accepted his message were baptized,
and some three thousand persons were added that day.

WT: [37] Then all those who had come together, [when they heard] . . . some of them asked Peter and
the apostles, "What then shall we do . . . show us." [38] . . . of the Lord Jesus. [41] accepted his message
gladly believed and were bap[tized. . . .

COMMENT

Peter's speech is interrupted by the reaction of those who listen to him. They have been affected by it and inquire what they might do. Peter's words in response constitute the continuation of his speech, its hortatory conclusion, in which he exhorts them to conversion. He calls for reform of their lives and invites them to baptism so that their sins might be forgiven and they too might receive the gift of the Spirit. In this way they might deliver themselves from "this corrupt generation." As in other missionary speeches in Acts, the call to conversion is its fitting conclusion.

Noteworthy in v 38 are the four elements of Peter's answer to the question posed by his listeners: They are to (1) reform their lives, (2) be baptized, (3) have their sins forgiven, and (4) receive the Holy Spirit. Peter's answer thus differs from the answer given by the Baptist in Luke 3:10, 12, 14, when he was asked what they were to do. Here one has a glimpse of Luke's understanding of Christian baptism. Two of the elements call for personal cooperation, and two reveal the effects of Christian conversion.

This episode is clearly of Lucan composition. If anything is traditional in it, it is only the inquisitive reaction of Peter's audience. The details are Lucan. It ends with a numerical summary.

So ends the initial testimony made by Peter to the assembled Jews of Jerusalem. To be noted is the way that Peter presents this reform and baptism to these Jews and their children: that they might thus share in the "promise" made by God to them and to all those still far off "whom the Lord our God will call to himself." In other words, Peter's testimony is directed not solely to the Jews assembled in Jerusalem and their offspring, but even to "those still far off." So

Luke foreshadows the carrying of Christian testimony to Gentiles, which will become the burden of his narrative in the later chapters of Acts.

The Petrine message continues to be addressed to "all those still far off," whom the Lord is calling to himself. To them "Jesus the Messiah" is still the anointed agent of God for the forgiveness of their sins. They too can still receive "the gift of the Holy Spirit" and join the long line of Christians who have heeded Peter's message across the centuries.

NOTES

37. *Now when they heard this.* Lit., "those listening," an aor. ptc. *akousantes,* which functions as the subject of the verb that follows. It refers to the Jews assembled in Jerusalem, who have gathered to listen to Peter.

they were cut to the quick. Lit., "they were cut to the heart." The expression is also found in Ps 109:16 (LXX).

asked Peter and the rest of the apostles. Lit., "said to Peter and the rest of the apostles." The WT omits the adj. *loipous,* "rest of."

"What are we to do, Brothers?" The Jews acknowledge Peter and the other apostles as *adelphoi* (see NOTE on 1:15). They ask about what is the proper reaction and response to the Christian proclamation. Their query echoes that of those who listened to the preaching of John (Luke 3:10, 12, 14); cf. Acts 4:16; 16:30.

38. *Peter [said] to them, "Reform your lives.* Peter challenges his listeners to a renewal of their conduct that would involve Christian engagement. He employs the verb *metanoein,* a favorite Lucan term (Luke 10:13; 11:32; 13:3, 5; 15:7, 10; 16:30; 17:3, 4; Acts 3:19; 8:22; 17:30; 26:20), with its corresponding noun *metanoia* (Luke 3:3, 8; 5:32; 15:7; 24:47; Acts 5:31; 11:18; 13:24; 19:4; 20:21; 26:20). Literally, it means "change of mind," and denoted in Greek philosophy the consciousness of one's own decline and consequent shame, which would make a person change one's life. This Greek notion entered into late OT writings and took on a religious sense of culpability toward someone, God or another human being; it came to mean a "reform of life," especially a change from sinful conduct (Wis 11:23; 12:19). Sometimes it is used along with "forgiveness of sins" (as here) or with *epistrephein, epistrophē,* "turning" (to God), the counterpart of reform (see 3:19; 9:35; 11:21; 14:15; 15:3, 19). The latter is the more Semitic way of phrasing conversion, often rendering *šûb,* "return" (to God); cf. Mal 2:6; Isa 6:9–10. See *Luke,* 459.

be baptized, every one of you. Peter counsels them to submit to the new washing by which they would become followers of Jesus Christ. Baptism is presented as the means of joining the Christian community, even though there is no mention in the NT of any of the apostles or the original 120 followers of Christ ever being baptized in this sense. Implied in the present context is the remission of sins by baptism and that one is enabled thereby to call upon the name of the Lord and so find salvation (2:21, quoting Joel 3:5). See NOTE on 1:5.

in the name of Jesus the Messiah. Or possibly, "in the name of Jesus Christ," if *Christos* is not being used in a titular sense. In the context of Peter's speech its original titular meaning is better retained, because so it would have been understood by Jews to whom he was preaching. By the time Luke writes, however, "Christ" has become Jesus' second name.

Commentators debate, however, about the sense of the phrase. Some believe that Luke knew of baptism being administered in the early church "in the name of Jesus Christ" (as in 8:16; 10:48; 19:5; 22:16) and not with the trinitarian formula derived from Matt 28:19. Others argue that the phrase is not so much a ritual formula but merely a Lucan way of describing baptism as a mode of ascription to Christ, to whom such persons are henceforth dedicated, whether the phrase "in(to) the name of Jesus" is an imitation of a banking or commercial expression or an imitation of Semitic *lšm* (1 Kgs 3:2; 1 Chr 6:10; Ezek 36:22). See L. Hartman, "La formule" (but beware of the late date of the rabbinic evidence adduced); *EDNT*, 2.519–22.

"The name of Jesus/Christ/the Lord" or "his name" or simply "the name" becomes a Lucan refrain in Acts (3:6, 16; 4:10, 17, 18, 30; 5:40; 8:12, 16; 9:14–16, 21, 27, 28; 10:48; 15:26; 16:18; 19:5, 13, 17; 21:13; 22:16; 26:9). Luke's use of it echoes the OT use of *šēm*, "name," which makes a person present to another: "For as is his name, so is he" (1 Sam 25:25). For Luke the "name of Jesus" connotes the real and effective representation of Jesus himself. One puts faith in it, is baptized into it; miracles are worked through it and salvation is found in it; disciples preach the name and suffer for it.

for the forgiveness of your sins. The verb *aphienai*, "pardon, forgive," is often used in the Synoptics with "sins," but *aphesis hamartiōn*, the abstract phrase (Luke 24:47; Acts 5:31; 10:43; 13:38; 26:18), is never used in the LXX and is found otherwise in the Synoptics only in Mark 1:4; Matt 26:28 and in Deutero-Pauline Col 1:14; Eph 1:7 (with "transgressions" instead of "sins"). It is a special Lucan formula expressing an effect of the Christ-event (*Luke*, 223–24). Here it is expressly related to baptism as its purpose, as it was related to the baptism of John (Luke 3:3; cf. 22:16). Pardon is thereby granted for the sinful transgressions of humanity. The image behind *aphesis* is commercial or financial, denoting the remission of a debt. Remission of the debt of sin is what has been achieved for human beings in God's sight by Jesus' death and resurrection. The prep. *eis* expresses purpose (*IBNTG*, 70).

you will receive the gift of the Holy Spirit. The Holy Spirit, the mark of the new phase of salvation history, will be shared by all those who reform their lives and are baptized. "Baptism in the name of Jesus Christ for the forgiveness of sins" has as its goal a share in the gift of this Spirit. *Tou hagiou pneumatos* is an epexegetic gen.: the Spirit is the gift (see ZBG §45).

39. *For to you and your children has the promise been made.* Peter refers to the "promise" mentioned in his speech (2:33), to be understood in terms of what has been promised in Joel, Isaiah, or Ezekiel mentioned in the NOTE on that verse, where God promised to give his people the Spirit in a new sense.

yes, even to all those still far off. The promised Spirit will not be limited to those present in Jerusalem. "Those still far off" could conceivably mean other Jews not present for the Assembly, but still in the diaspora; but from the thrust of the narrative in Acts it becomes clear that Luke is already hinting at the reconstitution of Israel as the people of God, which will incorporate the Gentiles. The phrase itself *tois eis makran* probably echoes Isa 57:19, "Peace, peace to those far off" (LXX: *eirēnēn ep' eirēnēn tois makran*).

whom the Lord our God will call to himself." This clause may echo the end of Joel 3:5 (not included in 2:17–21 above). Luke writes *hosous an proskalesētai Kyrios ho theos hymōn,* whereas Joel 3:5d (LXX) reads *hous Kyrios proskeklētai,* "whom the Lord has called to himself." The future divine call of Gentiles refers to reform of life, baptism, and the gift of the Spirit.

40. *With many other explanations Peter bore witness.* So Luke concludes his account of the first Christian Pentecost, with Peter fulfilling the role for which he has been commissioned, viz., bearing testimony about the risen Christ (cf. 8:25; 28:23). The verb *diemartyrato* might possibly mean rather, "he adjured (them)," or "he warned (them)," a meaning used in Luke 16:28; Acts 20:23. For parallels to Luke's summary statement, see Xenophon, *Hellenica* 2.4.42; Polybius, *Historiae* 21.14.4.

kept urging them, "Save yourselves from this corrupt generation." Peter exhorts his listeners to separate themselves from those who refuse to accept his message; these he characterizes with a phrase drawn from Deut 32:5 or Ps 78:8.

41. *Those who accepted his message were baptized, and some three thousand persons were added that day.* This is one of the numerical summaries with which Luke punctuates his narrative (see Introduction §93c). It marks the growth of the primitive Jerusalem community. Whereas they initially numbered 120 (1:15), now 3,000 have been added as a result of Peter's "word" (= preaching) and their subsequent baptism. In the Lucan story they are the first fruits of the new Pentecost. The verb "were added" is to be understood as a theological passive (ZBG §236), i.e., by God. For *psychai,* "souls," in the sense of "persons," see 7:14; 27:37; Exod 1:5 (LXX); cf. Euripides, *Andromache* 611; *Helena* 52.

BIBLIOGRAPHY (2:37–41)

Delling, G., *Die Zueignung des Heils in der Taufe: Eine Untersuchung zum neutestamentlichen "taufen auf den Namen"* (Berlin: Evangelische Verlagsanstalt, n.d.)

Glombitza, O., "Der Schluss der Petrusrede: Acts [2:]36–40," ZNW 52 (1961): 115–18.

Hartman, L., "La formule baptismale dans les Actes des Apôtres: Quelques observations relatives au style de Luc," *A cause de l'évangile,* 727–38.

———, "'Into the Name of Jesus': A Suggestion Concerning the Earliest Meaning of the Phrase," *NTS* 20 (1973–74): 432–40.

Heitmüller, W., *"Im Namen Jesu"* (FRLANT 1/2; Göttingen: Vandenhoeck & Ruprecht, 1903).

Tanton, L. T., "The Gospel and Water Baptism: A Study of Acts 2:38," *JGES* 3 (1990): 27–52.

4. First Major Summary: Unified Community Life (2:42–47)

[42]They continued to devote themselves to the teaching of the apostles, to a communal form of life, to the breaking of bread, and to the prayers. [43]Reverent awe characterized each of them; and many wonders and signs were wrought through the apostles. [44]All who believed lived together and held all things in common. [45]They would sell their property and belongings and divide them among all according to each one's need. [46]Each day with one accord they devoted themselves to meeting in the Temple, and, breaking bread in their homes, they kept taking their meals with glad and simple hearts, [47]praising God and winning the respect of all the people. Day by day the Lord added to the total those who were being saved.

WT: [42]to prayer. [43]. . . apostles in Jerusalem, and great awe came upon each one [omitted at the beginning of v 43].

COMMENT

After the numerical summary in v 41, Luke introduces his first major summary, vv 42–47a; it is followed by a minor summary in v 47b (see Introduction §93a, b). This statement is an idyllic description of the life of the primitive Christian community in Jerusalem, its spontaneity, harmony, and unity, its devotion to prayer and Temple worship. The picture it presents is a foil to the scandal and the squabble to be recounted in Acts 5 and 6.

The major summary is a Lucan composition. It is composite, as are the other two major summaries in 4:32–37; 5:12–16. In each case there is a coherent account, into which some detail, often derived from another major summary, has been inserted, so that they do not appear "to be logically constructed" (Conzelmann, *Acts*, xliii). In this case, the coherent account is found in vv 42, 46–47a; the insert, in vv 43–45. Verse 43 corresponds to 5:11–12a; vv 44–45 are a summary of 4:32, 34–35.

The composite nature of the major summaries has raised the question about the extent to which Luke may be dependent on pre-Lucan summaries; but there is no clear answer to such a question. Jeremias regarded vv 41–42 as the pre-Lucan original tradition to which vv 43–47 were later added, whereas Cerfaux considered vv 46–47a to be the original tradition, to which Luke added vv 41–45, 47b. Benoit thought that the early stratum of the summary recalled the prayer life and apostolic influence of the community (vv 41–42, 46–47), whereas vv 43–45 recount the thaumaturgic activity of the apostles and community of good, as in chaps. 4 or 5. Benoit's analysis sees a secondary hand at work in the three major summaries, which inserted in each case verses that were reminiscent of the other two. In contrast to such analyses is the position of Haenchen, who regards the major summaries as flowing "entirely from the pen of Luke" (*Acts*, 195); similarly Conzelmann (*Acts*, xliii).

Four things are noted as characteristic of Jerusalem Christians: their adherence to "the teaching of the apostles," "communal form of life," "the breaking of bread," and "prayers." The "teaching" of the apostles means more than the *kērygma*, "the proclamation" about the death, resurrection, and significance of Christ. What the apostles taught was the basis for what the church of Luke's own day was still teaching. *Koinōnia*, "communal form of life," is the first way that Luke names the Christian church in Acts; other designations will be used in addition to *ekklēsia*, the standard name for the Christian community. *Koinōnia* and the other designations undoubtedly preserve names employed by early Christians before they became fully aware of themselves as "church." "The breaking of bread," known from Luke 24:30, 35, is the abstract formulation that becomes the usual way Luke refers to the eucharistic celebration among early Christians. The "prayers" may echo the phrase *tē proseuchē* (1:14), but being plural, it may mean their continuing to share in Temple prayers (see 2:46). In either case, it depicts early Christians engaged in what Luke has considered an important element of discipleship: communing with God (*Luke*, 244–47).

For Jeremias the four elements "describe the sequence of an early Christian [worship] service" (*The Eucharistic Words of Jesus* [Philadelphia: Fortress, 1977], 118–21), but, as Schneider (*Apg.*, 1.285) notes, the "summary character" of these verses speaks against such a description.

In any case, the four elements underscore the common accord of Jerusalem Christians. In addition to these four things, Luke characterizes their life by *phobos*, "reverent awe," and the working of miracles. The insert of vv 43–45 introduces communal ownership of property, recounting how they "held all things in common." One gets the impression that such common pooling of property and possessions was obligatory; but later on this becomes less obvious, and in time the holding of all things in common completely disappears. It is not easy to determine how widespread this practice may have been, but it was at least noteworthy enough to bring Luke to mention it. It may merely be related to his desire to teach Christians how they should make use of wealth (*Luke*, 247–51).

Luke's idyllic description also notes the esteem that the Christians enjoyed among other inhabitants of Jerusalem. The passage ends with a minor summary (v 47b), which records that the Lord was constantly adding to their number each day.

Luke has included this description of early Christian life as an ideal that he would desire to be characteristic of all Christians. It may be an idyllic description, but it highlights the elements that should be part of genuine Christian life: harmony, reverent care for one another, formal and informal prayer in common, and celebration of the Lord's Supper.

NOTES

42. *They continued to devote themselves to the teaching of the apostles.* Luke employs *proskarterein,* "hold fast to," to stress the continuous and persistent tenacity of the disciples, who function almost like a self-enclosed group (see *EDNT,* 3.172). The *didachē,* "teaching," is to be distinguished from *kērygma,* the proclamation that the apostles made as they bore testimony to the risen Christ, and from *katēchēsis,* instruction given to catechumens. The teaching is the basis of Christian doctrine, built on the words and deeds of Jesus himself (1:1; see *Luke,* 826), on his instruction of the apostles (1:2) and those followers who would become his authenticated witnesses (10:41). This teaching, which appears again in 5:28; 13:12; 17:19, is the reason why Christian followers are called *mathētai,* "learners, disciples" (6:1; cf. 11:26). It is also the basis of the *asphaleia,* "assurance," about the teaching of the church in Luke's own day, which he himself stated as his purpose in the prologue (Luke 1:4). MS D adds "in Jerusalem."

to a communal form of life. Koinōnia, "communion (i.e., com-union), close association, partnership," was used in the contemporary Greek world to describe various close relationships among persons, as well as the mode of common life lived by followers of Pythagoras (Diodorus Siculus, *Bibliotheca historiae* 10.8.2), whence it came to denote specifically a "communal manner of life," as Luke uses it here.

The Essenes of Qumran, whom Josephus called "despisers of wealth" (*J.W.* 2.8.2 §122), characterized their mode of life as *yaḥad,* translated "community" and related to the root *'ḥd/yḥd,* "one" (1QS 1:1, 11–16; 5:1, 2, 16; 6:17, 21–25; 7:20; 1QSa 1:26, 27); see H. Braun, *Qumran und das Neue Testament,* 1.143–50. So the Christian *koinōnia* may be an imitation of such a model of communal life among pre-Christan Jews in Judea. The Essene *yaḥad,* however, was a form of community more structured than that of the early Christians as depicted in Acts. The Christian common ownership of property (2:44–45), which explains an aspect of this form of life, could also have been an imitation of such an Essene practice. The noun *koinōnia* occurs elsewhere in the NT with other meanings (Rom 15:26; 1 Cor 1:9; 10:16bis; 2 Cor 6:14; 8:4; 9:13; 13:13; Gal 2:9; Phil 1:5; 2:1; 3:10; Phlm 6; Heb 13:16; 1 John 1:3, 6, 7), none of which is related to its use here. It is never equated with *ekklēsia* or associated with it, and yet it designates the same group of people. Cf. S. Brown, "Koinonia as the Basis of New Testament Ecclesiology?" *One in Christ* 12 (1976) 157–67; J. Coppens, "La koinônia dans l'église primitive," *ETL* 46 (1970): 116–21; M. Manzanera, "Koinonia en Hch 2, 42: Notas sobre su interpretación y origen histórico-doctrinal," *EstEcl* 52 (1977): 307–29; A. C. Mitchell, "The Social Function of Friendship in Acts 2:44–47 and 4:32–37," *JBL* 111 (1992): 255–72.

to the breaking of bread. MSS ℵ[2], E, Ψ, 33, 1739, and the *Koinē* text-tradition insert *kai,* "and," before this phrase in order to separate it from the former word and distinguish it therefrom. This abstract formula occurred in Luke 24:35; its verbal form occurs in Acts 2:46; 20:7, 11; 27:35. It does not refer here only to the opening rite of a meal, as usually in Jewish meals, but to a whole meal.

Haenchen (*Acts*, 584) understands it not of the celebration of the Lord's Supper in 20:7, 11, but to ordinary (perhaps sumptuous) meals here and in 27:35; similarly Conzelmann, *Acts*, 23. Perhaps broken bread is not always said to have been distributed, but is that really necessary in each case? Moreover, in 2:46 common meals for nourishment seem to be explicitly mentioned in "taking their meals." Hence, even though *kyriakon deipnon*, "the Lord's Supper," *eucharistia*, "Eucharist," or *thysia* "sacrifice" is not found in Acts, *hē klasis tou artou* seems to be the formal reference to celebration of the Lord's Supper, as in 1 Cor 10:16: *ton arton hon klōmen*, "the bread that we break." By Luke's day (Stage III of the gospel tradition) it had become an abstract expression and perhaps has been read back by him into earlier stages of that tradition. This is the interpretation of many commentators: Johnson (*Acts*, 58), Polhill (*Acts*, 119), Roloff (*Apg.*, 67), Weiser (*Apg.*, 104). There is no reason to explain it as fellowship meals (of Essene or Pharisaic background), *agapē* meals, or even both ordinary meals and the Eucharist (so Pesch, *Apg.*, 130; Barrett, *Acts*, 165; Schneider, *Apg.*, 1.286). Cf. R. Orlett, "The Breaking of Bread in Acts," *TBT* 1 (1962): 108–13.

to the prayers. This may echo 1:14, or, because of the plural, it may refer to early Christians' participation in Temple prayers (3:1) or to their use of specific prayers (Barrett, *Acts*, 166). In any case, "prayers" seems to mean prayers offered by Christians in community, as in 1:24–25; 4:24–30; 12:12.

43. *Reverent awe characterized each of them*. Lit., "there was fear in every soul." Luke often uses *phobos*, "fear," but one wonders whether that is the precise connotation always meant. At times it suits his narrative, expressing reaction to divine or miraculous intervention (Luke 1:12, 65; 2:9; 8:37; 21:26; Acts 5:5, 11; 9:31[?]); at other times it seems rather to express "awe" (Luke 5:26; 7:16; Acts 19:17), and so it does here: "religious awe at the self-manifestation of the divine" (Haenchen, *Acts*, 192). Cf. Ps 105:38. The Greek wording of the verse is chiastic in its construction: a,b,c,c',b',a'.

many wonders and signs were wrought through the apostles. The text is variously transmitted: some MSS (33, 1409, 2344) add "in Jerusalem"; others (P^{74}, א) add a statement about awe after this clause, omitting it earlier in the verse: *phobos te ēn megas epi pantas*, "and great awe was on all (of them)." Luke again uses *terata kai sēmeia*, "wonders and signs," see NOTE on 2:22. What revealed the heavenly accreditation of Jesus is now used by Luke to confirm the heavenly approbation of the apostles' testimony. Cf. 3:1–11; 5:15–16; 9:32–35 for other instances of such "wonders and signs."

44. *All who believed lived together*. Lit., "all the believers were together (or in the same place)." Thus, Luke describes early Christian unity and harmony. Commentators debate about the extent to which the Lucan description of Christian common life has been influenced by Essene or Pythagorean customs or even by Greek ideas of friendship. *Hoi pisteuontes* (in MSS א, B, 36, 104: *hoi pisteusantes*), "the believers," is a Lucan way of saying "Christians"; see Fitzmyer, "The Designations of Christians in Acts and Their Significance," *Unité et diversité dans l'église* (ed. Biblical Commission; Vatican City: Editrice Vaticana, 1989), 223–36, esp. 225–26.

Lucan hyperbole twice makes use of *pas, hapas,* "all" (compare 1:14, 19; 2:5, 14, 43; 3:18, 24; 5:12; 8:1, 40; 9:32, 35, 40; 13:24, 44; 16:3, 15 [MS D]; 18:23; 19:10, 17 bis, 26; 21:18, 20, 21, 28; 25:24; 26:20; 28:2; contrast 10:12 [see NOTE there]). On *epi to auto,* "together," see NOTES on 1:15; 2:1.

held all things in common. The sense of this clause is not clear. It could mean that the early Christians pooled all that they owned, or it could mean that they remained owners of property, which they put to the common use of others. The first meaning would make them more like the Essenes, but the second may explain the subsequent stories in chaps. 4 and 5. See G. Theissen, "Urchristlicher Liebeskommunismus: Zum 'Sitz im Leben' des Topos *hapanta koina* in Apg 2,44 und 4,32," *Texts and Contexts: Biblical Texts in Their Textual and Situational Contexts: Essays in Honor of Lars Hartman* (ed. T. Fornberg and D. Hellholm; Oslo: Scandinavian University Press, 1995), 689–712.

45. *They would sell their property and belongings and divide them among all according to each one's need.* I.e., the proceeds of the sale just mentioned. The extent to which this custom was obligatory or voluntary is not clear. On the variants in vv 45–47 in MS D, see *TCGNT,* 263–64.

46. *Each day with one accord they devoted themselves to meeting in the Temple.* Lit., "daily persisting with one accord in the Temple." So Luke depicts another aspect of early Jewish Christian life together: frequenting the Temple together and sharing in its prayers, sacrifices, and services. Even though they had been baptized as followers of the risen Christ, they continued to be exemplary Jews, seeing no contradiction in this. See Schille, *Apg.,* 122; Barrett, "Attitudes," 364–65. This reflects Luke's concern to show the continuity of Christian life with that of Judaism. This they did *homothymadon,* "with one accord" (see NOTE on 1:14).

breaking bread in their homes. Lit., "breaking bread from home to home," they celebrated the Lord's Supper (see NOTE on 2:42). They had not yet developed what we call churches, separate buildings in which to celebrate the liturgy.

they kept taking their meals with glad and simple hearts. Their ordinary meals for sustenance were also taken together at times. Cf. 1 Cor 11:17–22, where Paul criticizes abuses of Corinthians in taking such common meals.

47. *praising God.* I.e., in prayer, which took the form of glorification and blessing.

winning the respect of all the people. Lit., "having favor with the whole people," as something experienced from them (so BAGD, 877, and many commentators; cf. Exod 11:3; 13:36; 33:12; 1 Esdr 6:5). A similar reaction of the people is recorded in 4:21; 5:13b. The respect they enjoyed stands in contrast to the reaction of religious authorities later in Acts. Luke's idyllic description again indulges in hyperbole, using *holos ho laos.*

Often *charin echein* with a following dative means "give thanks" (Luke 17:9; 1 Tim 1:12; 2 Tim 1:3; Josephus, *Ag.Ap.* 1.29 §270; *J.W.* 7.1.2 §9; *Ant.* 2.6.9 §162). This meaning, however, is not found with a prep. like *para* or *pros;* the latter with *charin echein* apparently occurs only here. For *charis pros* (alone, without *echein*), see Josephus, *Ant.* 6.5.5 §86 ("because of favor with others"); 14.8.5 §148. A similar use of *pros* is found in Rom 5:1; 1 Thess 1:8; 2 Cor 6:14; John 1:1. T. D.

Andersen ("The Meaning of *echontes charin pros* in Acts 2.47," *NTS* 34 [1988]: 604–10), however, understands the combination of words to mean "having good-will toward all the people." That would mean that "favor" was somehow bestowed by Christians on all Jerusalemites. Similarly F. P. Cheethan, "Acts ii.47: *echontes charin pros holon ton laon*," *ExpTim* 74 (1962–63): 214–15; G. G. Gamba, "Significato letterale e portate dottrinale dell'inciso participiale di Atti 2,47b: *echontes charin pros holon ton laon*," *Salmanticensis* 43 (1981): 45–70. This meaning is not impossible, but unlikely in the context.

Day by day the Lord added to the total those who were being saved. Lit., "added together," i.e., *epi to auto*, used now in a nonspatial sense (see NOTES on 1:15; 2:1). Torrey (*Composition and Date*, 10–14) claimed that it was a mistranslation of Aramaic *laḥdā'*, "exceedingly," and that the verse should be translated, "was greatly increased daily." This, however, is unlikely, as Cadbury (*AJT* 24 [1920]: 436–55, esp. 454 n.) and Burkitt (*JBL* 37 [1918]: 234) have noted.

Striking is the phrase *tous sōzomenous*, "those being saved," as a designation for new Christians. It echoes the last clause of Joel 3:5 cited in v 21 above; cf. Luke 13:23; 1 Cor 1:18. Cadbury ("Names for Christians and Christianity in Acts," *Beginnings*, 5.382–83) toyed with the idea of the ptc. as middle, "implying the initiative of believing," but the passive sense is preferred because of its LXX background and its use in the remnant passages of Isaiah (37:32; 45:20). Cf. Fitzmyer, "The Designations of Christians" (NOTE on v 44 above), 226. Given the Lucan emphasis on salvation as an effect of the Christ-event (*Luke*, 181–92, 222–23), the designation takes on added significance as a term for Christians as a group in Acts.

With this minor summary (2:47b) Luke concludes his narrative of the Pentecost event and its effect.

BIBLIOGRAPHY (2:42–47)

Barrett, C. K., "Attitudes to the Temple in the Acts of the Apostles," *Templum amicitiae: Essays on the Second Temple Presented to Ernst Bammel* (JSNTSup 48; ed. W. Horbury; Sheffield, UK: Academic, 1991), 345–67.

Benoit, P., "Remarques sur les 'sommaires' des Actes 2:42 à 5," *Aux sources de la tradition chrétienne: Mélanges M. Goguel* (Paris: Delachaux et Niestlé, 1950), 1–10; repr. *Exégèse et théologie*, 2. 181–92.

Bori, P. C., *Chiesa primitiva: L'immagine della comunità delle origini — Atti 2,42–47; 4,32–37 — nella storia della chiesa antica* (Testi e ricerche di scienze religiose 10; Brescia: Paideia, 1974).

Campbell, J. Y., "*Koinōnia* and Its Cognates in the New Testament," *JBL* 51 (1932): 352–80.

Capper, B., "The Palestinian Cultural Context of Earliest Christian Community of Goods," *The Book of Acts in Its Palestinian Setting* (BAFCS 4), 323–56.

Cerfaux, L., "La première communauté chrétienne à Jérusalem (*Act.* ii,41–v,42)," *ETL* 16 (1939): 5–31; repr. *Recueil Lucien Cerfaux*, 2.125–56.

Christiansen, E. J., "Taufe als Initiation in der Apostelgeschichte," *ST* 40 (1986): 55–79.

Daniélou, J., "La communauté de Qumrân et l'organisation de l'église ancienne," *RHPR* 35 (1955): 104–15.

Del Verme, M., "La comunione dei beni nella comunità primitiva de Gerusalemme," *RivB* 23 (1975): 353–82.

Delebecque, E., "Trois simples mots, chargés d'une lumière neuve (*Actes des Apôtres,* II,47b)," *RevThom* 80 (1980): 75–85.

Delling, G., "Die Heilsbedeutung der Taufe im Neuen Testament," *KD* 16 (1970): 259–81.

Dombrowski, B. W., "*Hyḥd* in 1QS and *to koinon:* An instance of Early Greek and Jewish Synthesis," *HTR* 59 (1966): 293–307.

Downey, J., "The Early Jewish Christians," *TBT* 91 (1977): 1295–1303.

Dupont, J., "L'Union entre les premiers chrétiens dans les Actes des Apôtres," *NRT* 91 (1969): 897–915; repr. *Nouvelles études,* 296–318.

———, "La communauté des biens aux premiers jours de l'église (Actes 2, 42.44–45; 4, 32.34–35)," *Études,* 503–19.

Elliott, J. H., "Temple versus Household in Luke-Acts: A Contrast in Social Institutions," *The Social World of Luke-Acts: Models for Interpretation* (ed. J. H. Neyrey; Peabody, MA: Hendrickson, 1991), 211–40.

Fitzmyer, J. A., "Jewish Christianity in Acts in the Light of the Qumran Scrolls," *StLA,* 233–57; repr. *ESBNT,* 271–303.

Grant, F. C., "Early Christian Baptism," *ATR* 27 (1945): 253–63.

Grelot, P., "Communion et prière dans le Nouveau Testament," *L'Année canonique* 25 (1981): 73–108.

Haufe, G., "Taufe und Heiliger Geist im Urchristentum," *TLZ* 101 (1976): 561–66.

Haulotte, E., "La vie en communion, phase ultime de la Pentecôte, Actes 2,42–47," *FV* 80/1 (1981): 69–75.

Herman, I. Z., "Un tentativo di analisi strutturale di *Atti* 2,41–4,35 secondo il metodo di A. J. Greimas," *Anton* 56 (1981): 467–74.

Kertelge, K., "'Kerygma und Koinonia: Zur theologischen Bestimmung der Kirche des Urchristentums," *Kontinuität und Einheit: Für Franz Mussner* (Freiburg im B.: Herder, 1981), 327–39.

Lake, K., "The Communism of Acts 2 and 4–6 and the Appointment of the Seven," *Beginnings,* 5.140–51.

Mealand, D. L., "Community of Goods at Qumran," *TZ* 31 (1975): 129–39.

———, "Community of Goods and Utopian Allusions in Acts ii–iv," *JTS* 28 (1977): 96–99.

Menoud, P.-H., "Les Actes des Apôtres et l'Eucharistie," *RHPR* 33 (1953): 21–36.

Meyer, B. F., "The Initial Self-Understanding of the Church," *CBQ* 27 (1965): 35–42, esp. 38.

Montagnini, F., "La comunità primitiva come luogo cultuale: Nota ad *At* 2,42–46," *RivB* 35 (1987): 477–84.

Murphy-O'Connor, J., "The Cenacle—Topographical Setting for Acts 2:44–45," *The Book of Acts in Its Palestinian Setting* (see above), 303–21.
Prieur, J.-M., "Actes 2,42 et le culte reformé," *FV* 94/2 (1995): 63–72.
Vööbus, A., "Kritische Beobachtungen über die lukanische Darstellung des Herrenmahls," *ZNW* 61 (1970): 102–10.
Zimmermann, H., "Die Sammelberichte der Apostelgeschichte," *BZ* 5 (1961): 71–82.

5. Peter's Miracle in the Temple (3:1–11)

3 [1]Once when Peter and John were going up to the Temple for the three
o'clock hour of prayer, [2]a man crippled from birth was being carried in. They
would put him each day at the gate of the Temple called Beautiful, to beg alms
from the people entering the Temple. [3]When he saw Peter and John about to go
into the Temple, he asked for alms. [4]Together with John, Peter looked intently
at him and said, "Look at us." [5]He gave them his attention, expecting to receive
something from them. [6]Then Peter said, "I have neither silver nor gold, but what
I have I give you: In the name of Jesus Christ the Nazorean [get up and] walk!"
[7]Taking him by the right hand, he drew him up. Immediately his feet and ankles
grew strong. [8]He jumped up, stood for a moment, and walked about. He went
into the Temple with them, walking about, jumping, and praising God. [9]When
all the people saw him walking about and praising God, [10]they recognized him
as "that beggar who used to sit at the Beautiful Gate of the Temple." They were
fully amazed and astonished at what had happened to him. [11]As he held fast to
Peter and John, all the people in excitement rushed over to them in the colonnade called Solomon's.

WT: [1]In those days Peter . . . Temple in the afternoon. [3]he, with his eyes staring (at them), saw Peter and John going . . . asked them for alms. [4]Peter gazed. [5]He expected. [6]said to him . . . [omits "Christ"]. [7]by his hand. Immediately he stood up and his feet . . . [8]walked about rejoicing and leaping . . . [10][omits "of the Temple"] . . . were all fully . . . at the cure that had . . . [11]As Peter and John were going out, he went out with them, holding on to them; but (the people) in excitement stood in Solomon's colonnade.

COMMENT

Luke continues his story about emerging Christianity with an example of how early Christians continued to frequent the Temple in Jerusalem; he tells how the apostles Peter and John went up there one day to join in the ninth hour of prayer. The narrative also recounts the first instance of a miracle performed by Peter, and it becomes the occasion of two further speeches of Peter (3:12–26 and 4:8–12), the first delivered on the heels of the miracle to people in Solomon's Portico within the Temple precincts. In effect, it begins Luke's story about the apostles coming into conflict with religious authorities in Jerusalem, a story that continues until the end of chap. 5.

Form-critically considered, this pericope is a narrative, including a miracle story, a healing worked by Peter, the spokesman, accompanied by a silent partner, John, son of Zebedee. The miracle is performed "in the name of Jesus Christ the Nazorean," continuing the important Lucan theme of healing wrought through the invocation of Jesus' name by one of those empowered by the pentecostal Spirit. It is thus the first explicit example of the "many wonders and signs wrought through the apostles" (2:43) and another example of the "signs" of Joel's words quoted in 2:19. Indirectly, it gives further proof of God's accreditation of Jesus himself (2:22), as the healing power of his name awakens faith in him.

The episode has the usual components of a miracle story known from the Synoptic tradition: (a) situation described (a beggar lame from birth, 3:2–3, 5); (b) word of command (3:4, 6); (c) restorative action (3:7a); (d) cure effected (3:7b–8); (e) reaction of the bystanders (3:10–11).

The account probably depends on a pre-Lucan story from Jerusalem that Luke has inherited, the miraculous cure of a lame man by Peter (alone). Though basically derived from a Palestinian source, one can detect in it certain Lucan features: Peter's silent companion, John (compare Luke 22:8; Acts 4:20; 8:14); "the three o'clock hour of prayer" (3:1); "look at us" (3:4); Peter's statement about silver and gold (3:6a); "immediately" (3:7).

In this episode Luke presents two main apostles, Peter and John, performing a cure in the name of the risen Christ. "The contrast between the silver and gold which Peter lacks and the gift in his power makes clear the surpassing value of what is peculiarly the Christians' possession: the healing power of the name of Jesus Christ" (Haenchen, *Acts*, 202). One must add also the role that faith plays in the episode, an aspect that the following speech of Peter rightly emphasizes (see 3:16).

This first miracle that Peter performs is followed by others: Ananias and Saphira (5:1–11); sick cured by Peter's shadow (5:14–16); Aeneas (9:32–34); Tabitha (9:36–41). There is, moreover, a certain parallelism with those to be performed by Paul: Elymas (13:8–11); cripple at Lystra (14:8–10); slave girl at Philippi (16:16–18); sick cured by Paul's handkerchiefs or aprons (19:11–12); Eutychus (20:7–12); father of Publius and other people on Malta (28:7–9). One notes the striking use of similar vocabulary in these parallel stories. Luke's literary hand is at work in the composition of these narratives; he presents the two major heroes of his account, Peter and Paul, as exemplary proclaimers of the power of the risen Christ among unfortunate human beings. See further J. Fenton, "The Order"; J. A. Hardon, "Miracle Narratives."

This miracle, however, stands out in Acts because of the two Petrine interpretations given to it in chaps. 3 and 4 and because of the symbolic aspect that it has in Acts as a whole. See further Hamm, "Acts 3, 1–10." Thus the miracle becomes a way in which the testimony of the apostles is further borne, the gospel is preached, and the Word of God is duly spread.

Peter cures the cripple "in the name of Jesus Christ." He is not concerned about the age or symptoms of the man, nor about his beggarly status. He sizes up the unfortunate condition of this human being and bestows on him what he can by invoking Jesus' name. Implicitly he elicits from the cripple faith in that name. Luke recounts this episode to elicit from the reader faith in the power of the risen Christ which can be invoked by calling on his name. Invocation of the name of Jesus should guide the concern of all Christians for unfortunate human beings (the sick, lame, paralyzed), for it is worth more than silver or gold.

NOTES

3:1. *Once when Peter and John were going up to the Temple.* Peter and John are portrayed as devout Jews going to the Temple for daily prayers (see 2:42). They appeared as a pair in Luke 22:8 and will so appear again in Acts 4:13, 19; 8:14. This clause introduces the occasion of the miracle to come. Luke uses the ordinary verb *anabainein,* "go up," for going to the Temple, because the Temple was situated on a height in Jerusalem (cf. Isa 37:1; 38:22 [LXX]; Luke 18:10; Josephus, *Ant.* 12.4.2 §164).

for the three o'clock hour of prayer. Lit., "for the ninth hour of prayer." This customary hour of afternoon prayer is explained in the OT as the "Tamid," the continual burnt offering (Exod 29:39; Num 28:3–4, 8; Ezek 46:13–15; Dan 9:21), when devout Jews would pause to pray or go to the Temple. Cf. Josephus, *Ant.* 3.10.1 §237; 14.4.3 §65. See NOTE on 2:15.

2. *a man crippled from birth was being carried in.* Lit., "crippled from his mother's womb," cf. 14:8. The cripple was clearly a hopeless case. This and the following verse describe the situation in which Peter's miracle will be performed. Luke uses *koilia* not in the sense of "belly," the organ of digestion, but of "womb," as in the LXX (Deut 28:4, 11; Job 1:21; 38:8; Isa 49:1; Jer 1:5; Ps 22:11), equalling Hebrew *beṭen.* One wonders why the cripple was being brought to the Temple only in the late afternoon; yet to ask that is to spoil the Lucan story. Obviously, the encounter of the apostles with the cripple is all important.

They would put him each day. "They" is generic or impersonal; the 3d pl. is used as a substitute for the passive (BDF §130.2). Cf. Acts 13:29, 42.

at the gate of the Temple called Beautiful. Hē thyra hōraia, "the Beautiful Gate," is not mentioned in Jewish descriptions of the Jerusalem Temple and its gates (Josephus, *J.W.* 5.5.2–5 §190–221; *Ant.* 15.11.5–7 §410–25; *m. Middoth* 1:1, 3–5). Where it was is a matter of debate. Three possibilities are usually mentioned: (1) the Shushan Gate (*m. Middoth* 1:3; *m. Kelim* 17:9), in the east wall of the Temple precincts, which gave access from the outside to the Court of the Gentiles and was located roughly where the modern Golden Gate is (*HPG,* 288); (2) the Nicanor Gate (*m. Middoth* 1:4; 2:3,6), also called the Corinthian or Bronze Gate (Josephus, *J.W.* 5.5.2–3 §201–4; 6.5.2 §293), which gave access on the east from the Court of the Gentiles to the Court of the Women; and (3) the "Nicanor" Gate (misnamed?) in rabbinic tradition (*b. Yoma* 38a), which gave access from the Court of the Women to the Court of Israel (the Men). See Str-B, 2.620–25; J. Jeremias, *TDNT,* 3.173; G. Dalman, *PJ* 5 (1909): 42; *EDNT* 3.508;

S. Corbett, "Some Observations on the Gateways to the Herodian Temple in Jerusalem," *PEQ* 84 (1952–53): 7–14 (+ pls.I–V); K. Lake, *Beginnings,* 5.479–86. The lack of an accurate description of the gate may be owing to Luke's defective knowledge of Judean geography, but the extra-Lucan tradition does not seem to be any better informed.

Ancient tradition identified the Beautiful Gate with the Shushan Gate (*ELS,* §660–69), which, as Barrett notes (*Acts,* 179–80), is more consistent with Luke's narrative; but today many commentators identify it with the Nicanor (Corinthian) Gate (so J. Murphy-O'Connor, *The Holy Land: An Archaeological Guide from Earliest Time to 1700* [Oxford: Oxford University Press, 1980], 65–66; J. A. Pattengale, "Beautiful Gate," *ABD,* 1.631–32; Polhill, *Acts,* 126–27). Schneider (*Apg.,* 1.300), however, following Stauffer and Jeremias, thinks it is the other "Nicanor" Gate, leading to the Court of the Men.

Perhaps the name of the gate is more important to the Lucan account than one normally realizes. It may be the "Beautiful" Gate because of what is going to happen to the cripple in the name of Jesus Christ. Luke depicts him carried into the Temple through the gate in order to stress the symbolic change that will come into his life.

to beg alms from the people entering the Temple. This was his sole source of livelihood. Luke uses the gen. of the articular infin. to express purpose (BDF §400.5).

3. *When he saw Peter and John about to go into the Temple, he asked for alms.* The beggar pursues his usual policy, recognizing nothing special in this pair of Temple visitors.

4. *Together with John, Peter looked intently at him and said, "Look at us."* The first prep. phrase is a Lucan addition, as is the formulation of Peter's remark, which calls for the attention of the beggar who is accustomed to being turned down or neglected. Luke hardly intends that Peter and John address the beggar in unison. Again, he uses *atenizein* of Peter's intent gaze; see NOTE on 1:10. Peter thus makes the meeting something personal for the beggar.

5. *He gave them his attention, expecting to receive something from them.* The ptc. *prosdokōn* explains why the beggar becomes attentive; he is in the long run not disappointed.

6. *Then Peter said, "I have neither silver nor gold, but what I have I give you: In the name of Jesus Christ the Nazorean [get up and] walk!"* Peter uses "Jesus Christ the Nazorean," employing *Christos* as Jesus' second name; on Nazorean, see NOTE on 2:22. He presents himself as one of the early Christians who are holding "all things in common" and so personally does not have "silver and gold." This phrase may have been inspired by the silver and gold used in constructing the gates of the Temple. Peter's first comment would have been disappointing to the beggar, but he continues by invoking "the name of Jesus" as the power for what he is about to say and do. The refrain of "the name" is thus again heard; see NOTE on 2:38. Barrett (*Acts,* 182) rightly rejects the idea that the name is used in Acts "as a magical formula," as some older commentators have suggested. See also Weiser, *Apg.,* 109. Peter cures the lame beggar in the name of him whom

he proclaims, "Jesus Christ, the Nazorean," and that cure is worth more than silver and gold. Indeed, the cure becomes a way of proclaiming the risen Christ. Some MSS read *egeire kai peripatei*, "get up and walk" (A, C, E, Ψ, 095, 33, 36, 81, etc., along with the *Koinē* text-tradition), but others (א, B, D) omit the first imperative.

7. *Taking him by the right hand, he drew him up. Immediately his feet and ankles grew strong.* Lit., "were strengthened," probably a theological passive (ZBG §236), meaning "by God." The right hand had been stretched out in expectation of the requested alms. The miracle takes place *parachrēma*, "immediately," an adverb that is characteristically Lucan (see Luke 1:64; 4:39; 8:44, 47, 55; Acts 5:10; 12:23; 13:11; 16:26, 33); elsewhere in the NT it appears only in Matt 2:19, 20.

8. *He jumped up, stood for a moment, and walked about. He went into the Temple with them, walking about, jumping, and praising* God. In a clumsy Greek sentence, Luke describes the complete cure of the beggar and his consequent reaction in almost the same way that Isaiah once proclaimed the restoration of Zion: "Then shall the lame one leap like a deer" (Isa 35:6). The allusion to Isaiah makes it clear that Luke sees this miracle as a fulfillment of the prophet's utterance, an event of salvation history. The lame man's praise of God is duly noted. So he passes from paralysis to joyful activity, from begging to praising God within the Temple.

9. *When all the people saw him walking about and praising* God. I.e., the inhabitants of Jerusalem, or at least all those gathered in the Temple for prayer; again Lucan hyperbole is at work (see NOTE on 2:44).

10. *they recognized him as "that beggar who used to sit at the Beautiful Gate of the Temple."* Luke records the reaction of Jerusalemites. The miracle has its effect not only on the beggar, but on inhabitants of the city who come to worship God in his Temple.

They were fully amazed and astonished at what had happened to him. Luke records the typical reaction to a miracle; cf. Luke 4:36; 5:9.

11. *As he held fast to Peter and John, all the people in excitement rushed over to them.* The beggar clutches Peter and John to show that it was through them that he is walking and jumping about. His action makes known the source of the miraculous cure that the people had not seen, and they react to its effect by rushing together. Their reaction becomes the occasion for Peter's speech.

In the colonnade called Solomon's. This portico is mentioned again in 5:12; it is also known from John 10:23 as a place where Jesus walked with his disciples. Its location is uncertain. *Stoa*, "colonnade," normally denoted a columned porch that provided shelter from sun and rain. It may have been on the inside of the eastern wall of the Herodian Temple in an area built on what was left of the Solomonic Temple (see Josephus, *J.W.* 5.5.1 §185; *Ant.* 20.9.7 §221; cf. *HPG*, 289). It seems to have been outside the Temple proper, perhaps in one of its forecourts.

The WT's variant reading—"As Peter and John were going out, he went out with them, holding on to them; but (the people) in excitement stood in Solomon's colonnade" — explains that Peter, John, and the cured beggar have left the Temple courts and are heading toward the colonnade of Solomon. See J. Duplacy, "À propose d'une variante 'occidentale' des *Actes des Apôtres* (iii 11)," *REAug* 2 (1956): 231–42; he thinks that the WT represents the original text of Luke; similarly K. Lake, *Beginnings*, 5.484. That view, however, does not solve the problem of the location of the colonnade. Cf. *TCGNT*, 267–69. Haenchen (*Acts*, 204) locates the colonnade on the "outer side of Nicanor's Gate"; similarly Weiser (*Apg.*, 115), outside the Beautiful Gate.

BIBLIOGRAPHY (3:1–11)

Cowton, C. J., "The Alms Trade: A Note on Identifying the Beautiful Gate of Acts 3.2," *NTS* 42 (1996): 475–76.

Crafer, T. W., *The Healing Miracles in the Book of Acts* (London: SPCK, 1925).

Fenton, J., "The Order of the Miracles Performed by Peter and Paul in Acts," *ExpTim* 77 (1965–66): 381–83.

Garner, G. G., "Jerusalem: Another Golden Gate!" *Buried History* 19 (1983): 28–32.

Hamm, D., "Acts 3,1–10: The Healing of the Temple Beggar as Lucan Theology," *Bib* 67 (1986): 305–19.

Hardon, J. A., "The Miracle Narratives in the Acts of the Apostles," *CBQ* 16 (1954): 303–18.

Holtzmann, O., "Tore und Terrassen des herodianischen Tempels," ZNW 9 (1908): 71–74.

———, "Die täglichen Gebetsstunden im Judentum und Urchristentum," ZNW 12 (1911): 90–107.

Horst, P. W. van der, "Hellenistic Parallels to Acts (Chapters 3 and 4)," *JSNT* 35 (1989): 37–46.

Lampe, G.W.H., "Miracles in the Acts of the Apostles," *Miracles: Cambridge Studies in Their Philosophy and History* (ed. C.F.D. Moule; London: Mowbray, 1965), 165–78.

Neirynck, F., "The Miracle Stories in the Acts of the Apostles: An Introduction," *Les Actes des Apôtres* (ed. J. Kremer), 169–213.

Sabugal, S., "La curación del 'cojo de nacimiento' por Pedro (Act 3,1–11): Análisis histórico-tradicional," *Revista agustiniana* 32 (1991): 595–613.

Stauffer, E., "Das Tor des Nikanor," ZNW 44 (1952–53): 44–66.

6. PETER'S TEMPLE DISCOURSE (3:12–26)

12 When Peter saw this, he turned to the people with these words: "Fellow Israelites, why are you amazed at this? Why do you stare at us, as if we had made this
man walk by some power or holiness of our own? 13 It is *the God of Abraham,* [*the
God*] *of Isaac, and* [*the God*] *of Jacob, the God of our ancestors,*[h] who has thus

honored his servant Jesus whom you handed over and disowned in Pilate's presence, when he had judged it right to release him. [14]You disowned the Holy and Upright One and begged that a murderer be released to you. [15]The author of life itself you put to death, but God raised him from the dead. Of this we are witnesses. [16]Indeed, because of faith in his name, that name has made this man strong whom you see and know well. The faith that comes through Jesus has given him the perfect health that is present before all of you. [17]Now I know, brothers, that you acted as you did out of ignorance, just as your leaders did too. [18]But God has thus brought to fulfillment what he announced long ago through all the prophets, that his Messiah would suffer. [19]So reform your lives and turn (to God) that your sins may be wiped out, [20]that times of recovery may be granted you by the Lord, and that he may send you the Messiah already appointed for you, Jesus, [21]whom heaven must retain until the time of universal restoration, about which God spoke through his holy prophets from of old. [22]For Moses said,

> 'A *prophet like me the Lord your God will raise up for you from among your kinsfolk; you must listen to him in everything that he may say*[i] to you. [23]*Everyone who does not listen to that prophet shall be ruthlessly cut off from the people.*'[j]

[24]All the prophets who have spoken, from Samuel on down, have also proclaimed these days. [25]You are the children of the prophets and of the covenant that God made with your ancestors, when he said to Abraham, *'Through your offspring shall all the families of the earth be blessed.'*[k] [26]For you, first of all, God raised up his servant and sent him, blessing you as each one of you turns from your evil ways."

[h]Exod 3:6, 15 [i]Deut 18:15–16 [j]Deut 18:19; Lev 23:29 [k]Gen 22:18; 26:4

WT: [12]Peter turned and said to them [omits "Why are you amazed at this"]. Why do you look at us as if by our own power we have done this? [13]whom you dishonored and disowned . . . who wished to release him. [14]You burdened . . . begged that a murderer might live and be released. [15]but he raised him. [16]. . . you know him that he (Jesus) has made (him strong). . . . [17]Now, brothers, we understand that you have done evil out of . . . [20]. . . by God . . . [omits "Jesus"]. [21]. . . about which he spoke . . . [omits "from of old"]. [22]said to the fathers, "A prophet God will raise up from . . ." [24][omits "also"]. [25]that he made with the ancestors . . . the tribes of the earth. . . . [26]he raised up . . . from their evil ways.

COMMENT

Peter's speech in the Temple precincts is occasioned by the cure of the lame beggar, the first of Peter's miracles recorded in Acts. It is linked to the foregoing story in Acts by the testimony that it again gives to the risen Christ (3:15; recall 1:8, 22); it interprets the miracle as a "sign" that accredits Jesus to the people of Jerusalem (3:13; recall 2:22); and it plays on the motif of "the name of Jesus" (3:16; recall 2:21, 27). Its purpose is to correct a misunderstanding on the part of bystanders, who are inclined to regard Peter and John as having cured the lame beggar with their own powers; but it has the consequence of involving Peter and

John with religious authorities, as the following speech of Peter in chap. 4 makes clear.

It is again a missionary speech, addressed to Jews, a kerygmatic sermon in which Peter repeats the basic Christian proclamation: God has glorified his servant Jesus by raising him from the dead, and in his name this beggar has been healed. In a special sense it is a christological speech, piling up a number of titles for the risen Christ but using "Messiah" in a different sense. It also makes its appeal for repentance.

Four parts can be discerned in the speech:

(1) 12b–13b	Explanation of the miracle as God's work
(2) 13c–19	Kerygmatic proclamation and admission of ignorance
(3) 20–21	Apocalyptic digression about Jesus the Messiah
(4) 22–26	Prophecy has been fulfilled.

Peter stresses that the miracle is God's work and that Jerusalem Jews are the first candidates for the reception of blessings promised to Abraham, which are now being channeled through Jesus the Messiah. These blessings constitute God's new mode of salvation, addressed to Jews first. Thus the fulfillment in Jesus of prophetic promises made of old is to be realized above all among his own people. Through them the promised blessings will be extended to all nations.

The kerygmatic elements in the speech can be seen in the following details: the age of fulfillment has dawned (3:18); the ministry and death of Jesus are recalled (3:13, 15), capped by his resurrection (3:15); he is God's appointed "Messiah" (3:20); a call is made for repentance (3:19, 25–26).

The speech, however, is unique in that it introduces the motif of Israel's ignorance (3:17), has an apocalyptic digression (3:20–21), uses once again the Lucan motif of the suffering Messiah (3:18), and utilizes several christological titles. These are seven: *pais*, "servant," *hagios*, "holy one," *dikaios*, "upright one," *archēgos tēs zōēs*, "author of life," *prophētēs*, "prophet," *Christos*, "Messiah" (suffering, and still to be sent), and *sperma Abraam*, "offspring of Abraham." Moreover, the speech provides the basis for the reaction of the Sanhedrin and other Jewish authorities in chap. 4.

For Dodd this Petrine speech preserves an example of the primitive Jerusalem kerygma (*Apostolic Preaching*, 21–24). A similar explanation was once given by Dibelius (*From Tradition to Gospel* [Scribner Library Books 124; New York: Scribner, n.d.), 16–18: "a primitive Christian message." Later, however, Dibelius regarded this type of Christian sermon as "customary in the author's day (about A.D. 90). This is how the gospel is preached and ought to be preached" (*Studies*, 165).

This sermon of Peter, however, is conflated. Some of the kerygmatic affirmations may well be pre-Lucan formulations, but they are joined with clearly Lucan affirmations. That "his Messiah would suffer" (3:18) is a Lucan insert into a statement about fulfillment, which refers to what has just been proclaimed in the preceding verses. Then on the heels of the following call for repentance comes an apocalyptic digression (3:20–21), which speaks of Jesus as the Messiah appointed and awaited (apparently at the parousia). J.A.T. Robinson has called this messianic formulation the "most primitive christology" in the NT, an embryonic christology not fully compatible with what one finds in 2:36. This too may be the reason why such early christological titles as "servant" and "prophet" emerge here. Along with the primitive messianic formulation, Luke would have also inherited such titles from the early tradition. Jesus is described as "prophet," the fulfillment of God's promise to raise up a prophet like Moses (Deut 18:15–18). Although that prophet has come and was put to death, God raised him up and will send him as the Messiah. Thus he is the Messiah designate, the Christ-elect. That "his Messiah would suffer" (3:18) seems to upset the rest of Peter's affirmations. That is because of the Lucan insert into an otherwise pre-Lucan formulation. As Robinson admits, we seem to have here remnants of an older christological formulation that did not win out over the more standard christology, according to which the Messiah had already come. Likewise of Lucan formulation is the attribution of Jesus' death to ignorance (3:17).

"The times of recovery" (3:20) and "the time of universal restoration" (3:21) must also be inherited from pre-Lucan tradition. Those peculiar expressions fit little into Lucan eschatology, and it is difficult to understand their real function in the appeal for conversion that Peter's speech makes at this point. Whether they have anything to do with an Elijah tradition, as Bauernfeind (*Apg.*, 66–69) and others would have it, is doubtful. Even though the verb *apokatastēsai* is found in a passage about Elijah (Mal 3:23) and may seem to be related to Luke's *apokatastasis*, its object is quite different. Malachi speaks of Elijah turning the hearts of fathers to their children, whereas Luke thinks in terms of a "renewal of all things." To bring an allusion to Elijah into this speech of Peter is eisegetical. Apart from such items, the speech as a whole is of Lucan composition.

What is strikingly absent in this speech of Peter is any reference to the Spirit, the driving force of the apostolic community and its mission of testimony. The speech, however, is important for Lucan eschatology, for, together with what is said in 1:11, it shows that Luke has not wholly dismissed the idea of a parousia (see *Luke*, 231–35). Likewise, it reiterates the fulfillment of prophecy (3:18–26), a favorite Lucan theme.

The speech makes much of conversion and faith in human life. Peter in effect challenges Jerusalem Jews to call upon "the name of Jesus Christ," i.e., to put their faith in this person whom God had sent into their midst for their benefit. It seeks to teach all Christians about their dependence on God and his Messiah, and their need of a strong faith in him.

Peter rejects the idea that he and John have cured this cripple by their own power and affirms that God's influence has once again been invoked by calling on the name of Jesus to alleviate the affliction of an unfortunate human being. The ancestral God of Israel is thus accessible to those who invoke this name. Peter insists on the necessity of faith, both faith in God and faith in the agent of salvation that he has sent. Peter acknowledges this agent, hailing him with seven titles or epithets. "Faith in his name" has made this lame man walk and has restored him to "perfect health." One can react with ignorance, as did the religious leaders of Jerusalem, who disowned this agent and handed him over to Pilate, but such ignorance stands in contrast to the faith that is called for. God, whose power has made this lame man walk, is the one who promised to send a prophet like Moses and a Messiah; what he promised has come to pass in Jesus, about whom all the prophets have spoken. So all children of Abraham must now reckon with this servant of God, Jesus of Nazareth, and believe in the power of his name.

NOTES

12. *When Peter saw this, he turned to the people with these words.* Lit., "Seeing this, Peter replied to the people." At the sight of Jerusalemites in the Temple rushing over to them in Solomon's colonnade, Peter is moved to address them. The verb *apokrinesthai,* "answer," is used absolutely to introduce direct discourse, in the sense of "speaking up" (in reaction to something, in this case the gathering of the crowd); cf. Luke 13:14; Acts 5:8; 10:46.

"*Fellow Israelites.* See NOTE on 2:22.

why are you amazed at this? Why do you stare at us, as if we had made this man walk by some power or holiness of our own? Peter begins by referring to the preternatural event that has just occurred, as he did in his speech on Pentecost (2:16–21), seeking again to correct a misunderstanding. He and John are not *theioi andres,* "divine men." His answer to the amazed reaction of the people stresses that the cure of the lame beggar was not the result of some naturally possessed power or even the piety of the apostles; God has wrought this through them.

13. *It is the God of Abraham, [the God] of Isaac, and [the God] of Jacob, the God of our ancestors.* Peter uses a traditional formula for speaking of God's power and authority, making it clear that no new god or mysterious power has intervened. He alludes to Exod 3:6, 15, where the LXX follows the MT. In other words, none other than the God of Israel, known from the Hebrew Scriptures, has intervened on behalf of Jesus. It is the God whom his Jewish listeners have always worshiped. Through the invocation of Jesus' name, their God has acted on behalf of the lame beggar. With this OT allusion Luke stresses the continuity between historic Israel and the new Christian movement.

Some MSS (B, E, Ψ, 0236) omit *ho theos* twice, whereas many (P[74], ℵ, A, C, D, 36, 104, 1175) read it in all three instances; hence the brackets.

who has thus honored his servant Jesus. Lit., "who has glorified." Although Haenchen (*Acts,* 205) thinks that "the glorification which Luke has in mind is not that of the resurrection but that of the miracle performed in Jesus' name," that is far from certain, as Weiser (*Apg.,* 116) rightly notes. *Doxazein* is not used elsewhere in Lucan writing to express a reaction to a miracle. Moreover, since this verb is used with *pais,* "servant," in Isa 52:13 (*ho pais mou . . . hypsōthēsetai kai doxasthēsetai sphodra,* "my servant . . . shall be exalted and glorified exceedingly"), there seems to be an allusion to the Servant Song. In this Lucan context *edoxasen* would mean, then, that God has bestowed on Jesus the status of "glory," a share in his own presence, as in Rom 8:30; cf. Luke 24:26; 1 Tim 3:16; John 7:39; 12:16. That is the status of the risen Christ. Luke uses as a christological title, *pais*, derived either from the Greek translation of *'ebed* in the Servant Songs (Isa 42:1; 49:6; 50:10; 52:13) or less likely from that used of great agents of God in the OT (Abraham, Gen 18:17 [LXX]; Moses, Josh 1:7, 13; 11:12; David, Isa 37:35). Apart from this verse and v 15, no connection is otherwise made between this title and resurrection.

See O. Cullmann, "Jésus serviteur de Dieu," *Dieu vivant* 16 (1950): 17–34; A. von Harnack, "Die Bezeichnung Jesu als 'Knecht Gottes' und ihre Geschichte in der alten Kirche," *SPAW* phil.-hist. Kl. 28 (1926): 212–38; J.-E. Ménard, "*Pais Theou* as Messianic Title in the Book of Acts," *CBQ* 19 (1957): 83–92; "Un titre messianique propre au livre des Actes: Le *pais theou*," *SMR* 1 (1958): 213–24; "Le titre *pais theou* dans les Actes des Apôtres," *Sacra Pagina* (BETL 12–13; ed. J. Coppens et al.; Gembloux: Duculot, 1959), 2.314–21; D. L. Jones, "The Title 'Servant' in Luke-Acts," *Luke-Acts: New Perspectives* (ed. C. H. Talbert), 148–65. Barrett (*Acts*, 190) rightly recognizes that "servant" is not to be identified with "Messiah"; they are distinct titles in the OT.

whom you handed over and disowned in Pilate's presence. Peter thus points an accusing finger at the people he addresses: you handed over Jesus to Pilate. By "you" he must mean those Jews of Jerusalem who were involved in Jesus' arrest, thereby heaping responsibility for Jesus' death on such Jerusalemite Jews. Compare 4:27.

Luke employs the verb *paradidonai*, "hand over," which is said of Pilate in Luke 23:25, as he delivers Jesus to them. It is often used of Judas's betrayal (Luke 22:4, 6, 21, 22, 48; 1 Cor 11:23), and from such usage it developed its traditional meaning for the arrest or betrayal of Jesus. "In Pilate's presence" refers to the trial of Jesus (Luke 23:1–5, 13–16, 18–25).

Pontius Pilate was the sixth "prefect of Judea" (Luke 3:1), having been appointed by Sejanus, Tiberius's anti-Jewish adviser. He governed Judea from A.D. 26–36 and so was the Roman official in the country at the time of Jesus' crucifixion. See J.-P. Lémonon, *Pilate et le gouvernement de la Judée: Textes et monuments* (EBib; Paris: Gabalda, 1981), 189.

Luke records in his Gospel that "the whole assembly of them ['the elders of the people, the chief priests, and the Scribes,' 22:66] arose and led Jesus to Pilate" (23:1). Even though in the Lucan Gospel Pilate declared Jesus to be innocent, he finally "handed Jesus over to their will" (Luke 23:25). In this way, he became involved in Jesus' death and so is mentioned here.

when he had judged it right to release him. In the Lucan passion narrative Pilate is depicted three times over declaring Jesus innocent or trying to release him (23:4, 14–15, 22). Luke seeks to disengage Roman authorities from responsibility for Jesus' death.

14. *You disowned the Holy and Upright One.* Peter repeats his accusation of v 13, now using the verb *arneisthai*, "deny, disown," which appears in the passion narratives of the Gospels only concerning Peter's denials. The implication of Pe-

ter's accusation is that Jerusalem Jews rejected Jesus and refused to recognize him as "the Holy and Upright One." These titles are derived from OT usage. *Hagios*, "holy," is employed of Aaron (Ps 106:16) and Elisha (2 Kgs 4:9); *dikaios*, "upright, righteous," of Noah (Gen 6:9; Sir 44:17). The combination designates Jesus as a dedicated and righteous agent sent to God's people and stands in contrast to the title *phoneus*, "murderer," in the next clause. In Mark 6:20 the double titles were used of John the Baptist.

begged that a murderer be released to you. Peter alludes to the demand made by the chief priests, leaders, and people (Luke 23:13) that Pilate release Barabbas (Luke 23:18–19), who "had been imprisoned for murder." The contrast between the "murderer" favored by their request and "the Holy and Upright One" disowned by them is noteworthy. It brings out the enormity of the crime involved.

15. *The author of life itself you put to death.* Peter repeats his accusation in its most extreme form, *apekteinate*, "you killed." Another christological title heightens the contrast.

Archēgos tēs zōēs is not easy to translate. Basically, *archēgos* means "pathfinder, pioneer" and was used of patrons, founders, and eponymous heroes. Here it must mean something like "originator, author." The title will appear again at 5:31; cf. Heb 2:10; 12:2. In 26:23 Luke will identify Christ as "the first to rise from the dead," and that notion explains the title used here. See G. Johnston, "Christ as Archegos," *NTS* 27 (1980–81): 381–85, who would translate it "Prince of life." Cf. T. Ballarini, "ARCHEGOS (*Atti* 3:15, 5:31; *Ebr.* 2:10, 12:2) Autore o condottiero?" *SacDoc* 16 (1971): 535–51; I. de la Potterie, "Gesù il capo che conduce alla vita (At 3,15)," *PSV* 5 (1982): 107–26.

"Life" is another Lucan way of expressing an effect of the Christ-event (see *Luke*, 225–26). The contrast between "life" and "death" is again not to be missed.

God raised him from the dead. This is Peter's kerygmatic testimony, derived from an earlier tradition, which ascribes to God the resurrection of Christ. See NOTE on 2:24. By raising Jesus from the dead, God has "glorified" him (2:13). In 5:31 Luke will say that God "has exalted (him) to his right hand as leader and savior." That is but another way of formulating what is asserted here.

Of this we are witnesses. Peter again proclaims his role as an apostle commissioned and sent to bear witness to the risen Christ; see 1:8, 22; 2:32; cf. Luke 24:48.

16. *because of faith in his name, that name has made this man strong whom you see and know well.* This sentence is not well written, and the WT has tried to improve it: "because of faith in his name, you know him (the beggar), that he (Jesus) has made (him strong)." Luke associates "faith" with his motif of "the name of Jesus" (see NOTE on 2:38). It is not clear whose faith is involved. One might think that it is the beggar's faith, but that is not expressed, save indirectly in his subsequent praise of God (3:8–9). So it might refer to the faith of Peter and John who, believing in the power of Jesus' name, were able to cure the lame beggar. In any case, *pistis* expresses an effective allegiance to the risen Christ, and through it the miracle has taken place.

According to Torrey (*Composition and Date*, 14–16), "that name has made this man strong" would be a mistranslation of *tqp šmh* (understood as *taqqēp šĕmēh*); it should read *taqqîp śāmēh*, "he (God) made him strong." This is hardly the right solution for a cumbersome passage; and there is no likelihood that Luke used an Aramaic source.

The faith that comes through Jesus has given him the perfect health that is present before all of you. Lit., "the faith that is through him (*or:* through it, viz., the name) has given him the perfect health." It is not easy to interpret *hē pistis hē di' autou. Pistis* followed by the prep. *dia* (+ gen.) is found again in 20:21 (MS D). Possibly it means "faith which is caused by him (Christ)" (Moule, *IBNTG,* 58).

17. *Now I know, brothers.* Again, *adelphoi* is used in the sense of fellow Jews; see NOTE on 1:15. Peter employs it to introduce the conclusion that he draws from the foregoing.

that you acted as you did out of ignorance, just as your leaders did too. In ignorance, the Jerusalemites failed to understand who Jesus really was. Cf. 1 Cor 2:8: "they would not have crucified the Lord of glory." This is an interesting Lucan comment, because the evangelist often distinguishes the people from their leaders (Luke 22:2, 52–53, 66; 23:27 [distinguished from "they"], 48), but now Peter includes ordinary people of Jerusalem in his accusation. See C. Escudero Freire, "'Kata agnoian' (Hch 3,17): ¿Disculpa o acusación?" *Communio* 9 (1976): 221–31.

Jesus's death, explained in Acts as a misunderstanding on the part of Jews, leads to a peculiarly Lucan idea of the soteriological value of that death. Luke never speaks of Jesus' death as expiation, atonement, reconciliation, and only once as justification. This motif of the ignorance of the Jews, excusing them from guilt in the death of Jesus, appears in three speeches: 3:17; 13:27; 17:30. See Epp and Barrett on Codex Bezae in this matter.

18. *God has thus brought to fulfillment what he announced long ago through all the prophets.* Lit., "through the mouth of all the prophets," using a Septuagintal phrase *dia stomatos* (1 Kgs 17:1; Deut 8:3). Peter comments on what he has just said, explaining how in God's plan (2:23) Jesus was "put to death" and how "God raised him from the dead" (3:15). God has not only reversed the unintentional sin and evil of putting Jesus to death by raising him from the dead, but he has actually used such ignorance and folly to bring about his own purpose. It is another example of Luke's global christological understanding of the OT (see Luke 24:25, 44), even though a pre-Lucan idea may be echoed here. To it Luke adds the following clause, again a Lucan hyperbole in "all" the prophets (see NOTE on 2:44); cf. Luke 1:76; Acts 3:21.

that his Messiah would suffer. I.e., that Jesus precisely as Messiah would undergo death, as *paschein* is understood in Luke 22:15; Acts 1:3; 17:3; 1 Pet 3:17–18, 21, 23. Luke implies that the OT spoke of a "suffering Messiah." Such a notion, however, is not found in the Hebrew Scriptures; in fact, in the NT the idea is found exclusively in Lucan writings: Luke 24:26, 46; Acts 17:3; 26:23 (*Luke,* 197–200, 1565–66). Luke adds this clause to the inherited material with which he is composing Peter's speech in order to sum up what God has fulfilled. He adds it in order to relate the suffering and death of Jesus to the new mode of salvation which comes to humanity through them. These things have happened to Jesus not arbitrarily or without relation to the divine plan of salvation.

19. *So reform your lives and turn (to God) that your sins may be wiped out.* Luke joins *metanoēsate,* "reform," and *epistrepsate,* "turn," with the wiping away of sins. See NOTE on 2:38. Together the two imperatives express the call to conversion, a turning to God who offers the possibility of a change of heart. Thus Peter calls for recognition of the need of reform on the part of the Jerusalem Jews who listen to him.

20. *that times of recovery may be granted you by the Lord.* Lit., "that times of refreshment may come from the face of the Lord." Peter admits that God in mercy will pardon such Jews for what his Messiah has suffered, and especially that God will grant them a respite, i.e., times when they will be able to repent and convert before the end. *Kyrios* is used of Yahweh, the God of the OT, as in 2:39; Luke 1:16, 32, 68; 4:12; 10:27; 20:37.

The noun *anapsyxis,* "breathing space, relaxation, recovery," is related to the verb *anapsychein,* "cool by blowing" (Homer, *Odyssey* 4.569; Herodotus, *History* 7.59.3). It is used in Exod 8:11 (LXX) of the "breathing space" granted after the plague of the frogs, in consequence of which Pharaoh again hardened his heart. Here the breathing space is accorded for Israel's repentance and salvation. Repentance will be a preparation for the definitive stage of salvation (see v 21), but Luke says nothing about such repentance hastening that stage. He insists only that God in his mercy provides for suitable reactions of repentance. See G. Ferraro, "*Kairoi anapsyxeōs:* Annotazioni su Atti 3,20," *RivB* 23 (1975): 67–78; E. Schweizer, *TDNT,* 9.664–65.

that he may send you the Messiah already appointed for you, Jesus. Peter speaks not only of Jesus as "the Messiah," but as one still to come, apparently alluding to his parousia (not mentioned, but cf. 1:11). Peter is aware of the conviction of many Jews of the last pre-Christian century that a Messiah was expected (*Luke,* 197–200, 471–72). Now he says that Jesus has been appointed in advance *(procheirismenon),* destined as a Messiah still to come. This is a new Christian interpretation of existing Jewish messianic expectations, according to which the Messiah already exalted is destined to come at the parousia in his glorious advent. This has been planned or appointed of old by God for "you," i.e., for Jews of Jerusalem.

21. *whom heaven must retain.* Heaven must keep him because that is where Christ now is: with the Father in glory (1:9–11; 2:32–33; 3:13, 15).

until the time of universal restoration. Lit., "until the times of the restoration of all (things)," i.e., to their former state. *Chronoi apokatastaseōs pantōn* must be another way of saying *kairoi anapsyxeōs* (3:20); they are related and mutually explain each other. *Kairoi* would indicate the beginning of the period, and *chronoi* the duration of it. It is hardly likely that *pantōn* is to be taken as masc., "restoration of all men," for that makes little sense in the context, and it is hardly likely that *apokatastasis* is to be understood as "conversion," referring to that of human beings or Satan. Josephus (*Ant.* 11.3.8 §63) used *apokatastasis* of the "restoration" or "return to a former status" of the Jews under Cyrus after the Babylonian

Captivity. Here it might refer to the restoration of "the kingship to Israel" (1:6, where the verb *apokathistanein* occurs); but more probably it refers generically to an awaited universal cosmic restoration, often mentioned vaguely in Jewish prophetic and apocalyptic writings, e.g., as a new creation of heaven and earth (Mal 3:24; Isa 62:1–5; 65:17; 66:22; *1 Enoch* 45:4–5; 96:3; *2 Esdr* 7:75, 91–95; *Assumptio Moisis* 10.10). In this Lucan context it would be associated with the coming of the Messiah and would seem to connote a messianic restoral of everything to pristine integrity and harmony. Cf. J. Kremer, *EDNT*, 1.95.

On this text Origen built his theory of *Apokatastasis*, the doctrine about the restoration of all creation to its original, purely spiritual state before the end of the world (*De principiis* 1.6.1–4; 2.3.1–5; 3.5–6; GCS 27.78–85, 113–20, 271–91; *Contra Celsum* 8.72; GCS 3.288–90). He was followed by Gregory of Nyssa (*Or. catechetica* 26; GCS 45.68–69), Scotus Erigena, Bengel, Schleiermacher et al.; but that doctrine goes far beyond what Peter means here. Cf. J. Quasten, *Patrology* (3 vols.; Westminster, MD: Newman; Utrecht: Spectrum, 1950, 1953, 1960), 2.87–91; 3.289–91; A. Oepke, *TDNT* 1.392–93; P.-G. Müller, *EDNT*, 1.130.

about which God spoke through his holy prophets from of old. Lit., "through the mouth of . . ." See NOTE on 3:18. The antecedent of relative pron. *hōn* can only be *pantōn*, "all (things)." Peter seeks to root the destination of a Messiah still to come in the OT itself, as he quotes Moses in the Pentateuch.

22. *For Moses said, 'A prophet like me the Lord your God will raise up for you from among your kinsfolk; you must listen to him in everything that he may say to you.* 23. *Everyone who does not listen to that prophet shall be ruthlessly cut off from the people.'* Lit., ". . . it will be that every soul that does not listen will be cut off. . . ." As an example of what God has said of old, Peter quotes a saying of Moses, who is thus classed with the prophets, as David was said to prophesy in 2:30. Peter thus identifies Jesus, not as a Messiah but as a "prophet," indeed as the prophet like Moses promised of old. He has come to preach to Israel with all the authority that Moses enjoyed of old. On the relation of an expected prophet to Messiah(s), see the Essene teaching in 1QS 9:11.

What is quoted is a form of Deut 18:15–16a, 19, in which some words are inverted and to which words from Lev 23:29 are joined. The LXX of Deut 18:15–16a reads thus: "A prophet like me from among your brothers the Lord your God will raise up; you must listen to him in everything that you asked of the Lord your God in Horeb on the day of the assembly." That is a fairly accurate translation of the MT, the only difference in the Hebrew being "from your midst, from among your brothers." The LXX of Deut 18:19 reads: "As for the one who does not listen to all that the prophet will say in my name, I will require (it) of him" (i.e., I will take vengeance on him). This Greek version agrees with Deut 18:19 as preserved in 4QTestim 7, which includes *hnby*, "the prophet" (J. M. Allegro, *Qumrân Cave 4: I (4Q158-4Q186)* [DJD 5; Oxford: Clarendon, 1968], 58). The MT omits this word. Cf. J. de Waard, "The Quotation from Deuteronomy in Acts 3,22.23 and the Palestinian Text: Additional Arguments," *Bib* 52 (1971): 537–40.

The LXX of Lev 23:29 reads: "Every soul that does not mortify itself on that day shall be ruthlessly cut off from its (fem.) people," an exact translation of the MT, which prescribes the fast of *Yôm hakkippûrîm*. From this prescription Peter draws a few words for his ominous conclusion about people refusing to listen to the prophet like Moses whom God has raised up. Moses is thus portrayed as the one who has announced the coming of Jesus the prophet; his words are cited as a warning against those who refuse to listen to this new heaven-sent prophet.

The Samaritan tradition derived from God's promise to Moses about a "prophet like me" (Deut 18:15) its teaching about the awaited *tā'ēb*, or *tāhēb*, "Returning One." In that tradition the expected figure is more or less the equivalent of an awaited Messiah in the Jewish tradition.

As Haenchen (*Acts*, 209) notes, a difficulty may be sensed in this verse from the OT passage quoted, which in reality refers not to the parousiac coming of Jesus as Messiah, but to his first coming as a prophet like Moses. But v 22 is not to be understood as picking up on the immediately preceding v 21, but rather on v 19, as Schneider (*Apg.*, 1.327) rightly notes.

24. *All the prophets who have spoken, from Samuel on down, have also proclaimed these days.* Lit., "from Samuel and those in order (after him)." The phrase *apo Samuēl kai tōn kathexēs* is strange; it means "Samuel and (his) successors." The adv. *kathexēs*. "in order," was used in Luke 1:3 and will appear again in Acts 11:4; 18:23. This strained expression makes Peter say that all the prophets of Israel have uttered a message about this new age, which is just beginning. Samuel is singled out because in a sense he was the first of the prophets in the OT. As a result of his call by God, "all Israel, from Dan to Beer-sheba, came to know that Samuel was a prophet accredited to the Lord" (1 Sam 3:20). Cf. 2 Chr 35:18; Sir 46:13–20; *1 Esdras* 1:20. See further R. Press, "Der Prophet Samuel," ZAW 56 (1938): 177–225. The OT, however, records little of Samuel's sayings, and nothing that could be understood eschatologically as referring to this new age. As for other prophets after him, they uttered at times vague eschatological sayings that could in some sense be taken as referring to "these days"; but that is the most one can say. This is another instance of Luke's global interpretation of the OT, whereby he implies that some reference to Christ is to be found in every OT prophet. Cf. Luke 24:25. Again note the Lucan hyperbole in "all the prophets"; see NOTE on 2:44.

25. *You are the children of the prophets.* Lit., "the sons of the prophets." In the OT, the prophetic guild was often called *bĕnê hannĕbî'îm* (1 Kgs 20:35; 2 Kgs 2:3, 5, 7, 15), but the phrase is not being used here in that sense. Peter means rather that his audience, as part of the people to whom God sent his prophets of old, is indebted and tributary to the prophetic heritage. Therefore, they above all have an obligation to heed what the prophets have said, for they are descendants of those who were mouthpieces of God himself; but they are more, because they are also "children" of the covenant that God made with Abraham.

of the covenant that God made with your ancestors. Similarly, Peter wants his audience to realize their relationship to the covenant that God established of old with their *pateres*, "ancestors." Hence they, as children of the covenant, are obligated to that pact of old. Luke uses an expression, "sons of the covenant," found in Ezek 30:5 (LXX: *tōn huiōn tēs diathēkēs mou*), which differs from the MT in wording and in sense. The Essenes of Qumran were also called *bĕnê bĕrîtô*, "sons of his [God's] covenant" (1QM 17:8); *bĕnê bĕrîtĕkāh*, "sons of your covenant" (4Q501 1 i 2; 4Q503 7–9 iv 3). Cf. CD 12:11 (*bbryt ʾbrhm*, "in the covenant of Abraham"); *Ps. Sol.* 17:15.

when he said to Abraham, 'Through your offspring shall all the families of the earth be blessed.' Peter regards Abraham as the primary example of the "ancestors" he has just mentioned. The pact that God made with Abraham became the way of life (dedication to the God of the covenant) for all his descendants, and the blessings that came to the patriarch were to continue for his offspring for centuries. Moreover, through Abraham's offspring blessings were to come upon all the families of the earth. This quotation in Peter's speech foreshadows the spread of the Christian message to non-Jewish families as well. First, however, that message has to be addressed to the Jewish people of Jerusalem. The promise made to Abraham was important for Luke; see Luke 1:55, 73; Acts 7:5–6.

Peter understands *sperma Abraam*, "offspring of Abraham," in a twofold way: not just generically of all the Jewish people, but more specifically as a reference to an individual descendant of Abraham, the risen Christ, from whom all these blessings are to come to Jewish families as well as to those of all the earth. The note of universalism is struck by this quotation.

Peter quotes a form of the LXX of Gen 22:18 or 26:4c. It reads in both cases: *eneulogēthēsontai en tō spermati sou panta ta ethnē tēs gēs*, "there will be blessed through your seed all the nations of the earth," which is a tolerable translation of the MT. The Greek version of Genesis that Luke was using may have substituted *patriai*, "families," for *ethnē*, "nations," but, more likely, Luke himself has substituted it for the latter term, which he normally uses for "Gentiles." Peter means that those blessings promised to Abraham will come through the one who is now recognized as God's "servant" (3:26) and "offspring of Abraham" (3:25). Paul similarly understands the collective *sperma* of the individual, Christ Jesus (Gal 3:16). Cf. Gen 12:3; 18:18.

26. *For you, first of all, God raised up his servant and sent him.* Peter thus insists that it was, above all, to the Jewish people whom he is addressing that God, despite their "ignorance," sent Jesus of Nazareth and his message. Peter is made to enunciate a principle that Luke will continue to advocate in Acts: that the word of God has to be preached first of all to Jews. See also Rom 1:16; 2:9–10.

The ptc. *anastēsas*, "having raised (him) up," is ambiguous. Because it is followed by *apesteilen*, "he sent," it could mean no more than that he brought Jesus onto the stage of Judean and Jerusalemite history, but in view of the way Luke has used *anistanai* to mean "raise up" from the dead (see NOTE on 2:24), he probably means it so here too, especially since he has employed *pais*, "servant," in connection with the resurrection of Christ (3:13, 15). In either case, God has "raised up" Jesus of Nazareth, constituting him in a special way as his "servant," and sent him to preach to Jews of Judea. Thus Peter sees that God has conferred a special "blessing" on his own people. See R. F. O'Toole, "Some Observations on *anistēmi*, 'I Raise,' in Acts 3:22–26," *ScEsp* 31 (1978): 84–92.

blessing you as each one of you turns from your evil ways." The blessing that was to come to and through Abraham's offspring is still offered by God to the Jewish people "first of all," because they are still "Abraham's offspring," and then through them to all others. Peter presumes that they are individuals willing to turn from the evil that has marked their past. To such a conversion he now summons them; they must put their faith in Jesus Christ, the object of apostolic proclamation.

BIBLIOGRAPHY (3:12–26)

Barbi, A., *Il Cristo celeste presente nella chiesa: Tradizione e redazione in Atti 3, 19–21* (AnBib 64; Rome: Biblical Institute, 1979).

Barrett, C. K., "Faith and Eschatology in Acts 3," *Glaube und Eschatologie: Festschrift für Werner Georg Kümmel* . . . (ed. E. Grässer und O. Merk; Tübingen: Mohr [Siebeck], 1985), 1–17.

———, "Is There a Theological Tendency in Codex Bezae?" *Text and Interpretation: Studies in the New Testament Presented to Matthew Black* (ed. E. Best and R. M. Wilson; Cambridge: Cambridge University Press, 1979), 15–27.

Bauernfeind, O., "Tradition und Komposition in dem Apokatastasisspruch, Apg. 3,20f.," *Abraham unser Vater: Festchrift für Otto Michel* (ed. O. Betz et al.; Leiden: Brill, 1963), 13–23.

Beel, A., "Sermo s. Petri ad populum post sanationem claudi nati (Act. Apost. iii, 12–26)," *CollBrug* 31 (1931): 390–94.

Berger, K., "Zum traditionsgeschichtlichen Hintergrund christologischer Hoheitstitel," *NTS* 17 (1970–71): 391–425.

Carrón Pérez, J., *El Mesías escondido y su manifestación (Tradición literaria y trasfondo judío de Hch 3,19–26* (Madrid: Editorial Ciudad Nueva, 1991).

———, *Jesús, el Mesías manifestado: Tradición literaria y trasfondo judío de Hch 3,19–26* (Studia semitica Novi Testamenti 2; Madrid: Editorial Ciudad Nueva — Fundación San Justino, 1993).

Comiskey, J. P., "'All the Families of the Earth Will Be Blessed,'" *TBT* 83 (1976): 753–62.

Dahl, N. A. "The Story of Abraham in Luke-Acts," *StLA*, 139–58; repr. *Jesus in the Memory of the Early Church* (Minneapolis: Augsburg, 1976), 66–86.

Davies, P. E., "Jesus and the Role of the Prophet," *JBL* 64 (1945): 241–54.

Dixon, L. E., "*Apokatastasis* and the Kingdom of Christ: Will There Be Any Finally *Outside*," *EvJ* 10 (1992): 65–80.

Doeve, J. W., "Apokatastasis in Act. 3:21, een voorbereiding?" *Vox theologica* 18 (1947–48): 165–69.

Dupont, J., "Repentir et conversion d'après les Actes des Apôtres," *ScEccl* 12 (1960): 137–73; repr. *Études*, 421–57.

———, "La conversion dans les Actes des Apôtres," *LumVie* 47 (1960): 47–70; repr. *Études*, 459–80.

Epp, E. J., "The 'Ignorance Motif' in Acts and Anti-Judaic Tendencies in Codex Bezae," *HTR* 55 (1962): 51–62.

Hahn, F., "Das Problem alter christologischer Überlieferungen in der Apostelgeschichte unter besonderer Berücksichtigung von Act 3,19–21," *Les Actes des Apôtres* (ed. J. Kremer), 129–54.

Heimerdinger, J., "Unintentional Sins in Peter's Speech: Acts 3:12–26," *RCT* 20 (1995): 269–76.

Hengel, M., "Christologie und neutestamentliche Chronologie: Zu einer Aporie in der Geschichte des Urchristentums," *Neues Testament und Geschichte: Oscar Cullmann zum 70. Geburtstag* (ed. H. Baltensweiler und B. Reicke; Zurich: Theologischer-V.; Tübingen: Mohr [Siebeck], 1972), 43–67.

Jonge, M. de, "*Apokatastasis pantōn* in Handelingen 3:21," *Vox theologica* 18 (1947–48): 68–71.

Juel, D., "Hearing Peter's Speech in Acts: Meaning and Truth in Interpretation," *WordW* 12 (1992): 43–50.

Kilpatrick, G. D., "Three Problems of New Testament Text," *NovT* 21 (1979): 289–92.

Lohfink, G., "Christologie und Geschichtsbild in Apg 3, 19–21," *BZ* 13 (1969): 223–41.

Lowther Clarke, W. K., "'A Prophet Like unto Me,'" *New Testament Problems: Essays — Reviews — Interpretations* (London: SPCK; New York: Macmillan, 1929), 39–47.

MacRae, G. W., "'Whom Heaven Must Receive until the Time': Reflections on the Christology of Acts," *Int* 27 (1973): 151–65; repr. *Studies in New Testament and Gnosticism* (GNS 26; ed. D. J. Harrington and S. B. Marrow; Wilmington, DE: Glazier, 1987), 47–64.

Martini, C. M., "L'Esclusione dalla comunità del popolo di Dio e il nuovo Israele secondo Atti 3,23," *Bib* 50 (1969): 1–14; *Communio* 12 (1972): 63–82.

Moessner, D. P., "'The Christ Must Suffer': New Light on the Jesus-Peter, Stephen, Paul Parallels in Luke-Acts," *NovT* 28 (1986): 220–56.

Moule, C.F.D., "The Christology of Acts," *StLA*, 159–85.

Mudge, L. S., "The Servant Lord and His Servant People," *SJT* 12 (1959): 113–28.

Müller, G., *Apokatastasis Pantōn: A Bibliography* (Basel: Basler Missionsbuchhandlung, 1969).

Mussner, F., "Die Idee der Apokatastasis in der Apostelgeschichte," *Lux tua veritas: Festschrift für Hubert Junker . . .* (ed. H. Gross and F. Mussner; Trier: Paulinus, 1961) 293–306; repr. in *Praesentia salutis: Gesammelte Studien . . .* (Düsseldorf: Patmos, 1967), 223–34.

Parker, J., *The Concept of* apokatastasis *in Acts: A Study in Primitive Christian Theology* (Austin: Schola, 1978).

Rasco, E., "La gloire de la résurrection et ses fruits, Acts 2,14.22–28; 3,13–15.17–19; 5,27b–32.40b–41," *AsSeign* 24 (1969): 6–14.

Rius-Camps, J., "Cuatro paradigmas del Pentateuco refundidos en los Hechos de los Apóstoles," *EstBíb* 53 (1995): 25–54.

Robinson, J.A.T., "The Most Primitive Christology of All?" *JTS* 7 (1956): 177–89;

repr. *Twelve New Testament Studies* (SBT 34; London: SCM, 1962), 140, 148–53.

Schlosser, J., "Moïse, serviteur du kérygma apostolique d'après Ac 3,22–26," *RevScRel* 61 (1987): 17–31.

Schmitt, J., "L'Eglise de Jérusalem ou la 'restoration' d'Israël d'après les cinq premiers chapitres des Actes," *RevScRel* 27 (1953): 207–18.

Scobie, C.H.H., "The Use of Source Material in the Speeches of Acts III and VII," *NTS* 25 (1978–79): 399–421.

Teeple, H. M., *The Mosaic Eschatological Prophet* (SBLMS 10; Philadelphia: Society of Biblical Literature, 1957).

Ternant, P., "Repentez-vous et convertissez-vous (Ac 3,19)," *AsSeign* 21 (1963): 50–79.

B. Life and Trials of the Primitive Jerusalem Community (4:1–8:4)

1. Peter and John before the Sanhedrin (4:1–22)

4 1 While they were still addressing the people, the priests, the captain of the
Temple guard, and the Sadducees confronted them, 2 annoyed that Peter and
John were teaching the people and proclaiming in Jesus the resurrection of the
dead. 3 They arrested them and put them in jail for the night, for it was already
evening. 4 But many of those who had heard the word came to believe, and [the]
number of men grew to [about] five thousand. 5 The next day their leaders, elders,
and scribes happened to assemble in Jerusalem, 6 with Annas, the high priest,
and Caiaphas, John, and Alexander, and all who were of high-priestly class.
7 They brought Peter and John in before them and questioned them: "By what
authority or what name have such as you done this?" 8 Then Peter, filled with the
Holy Spirit, said to them, "Leaders of the people and elders, 9 if we must answer
today for a good deed done to a cripple (and explain) how he has been restored
to health, 10 then let it be known to all of you and to all the people of Israel that
it was in the name of Jesus Christ the Nazorean, whom you crucified and whom
God raised from the dead. In virtue of that name this man stands before you
perfectly well. 11 This Jesus is *the stone rejected by* you *builders, which has become
the cornerstone.*[1] 12 There is salvation in no one else, for there is no other name in
the whole world given to human beings through which we are to be saved."
13 Seeing the bold self-assurance of Peter and John and realizing that they were

uneducated, ordinary men, they were amazed; they recognized that they had
been with Jesus. [14]When they looked at the man who had been cured standing
there with them, they had nothing to say in reply. [15]So they ordered them out of
the Sanhedrin and held a consulation among themselves: [16]"What are we going
to do with these people? For it is known to all who live in Jerusalem that a remarkable sign has been done through them; we cannot deny it. [17]But that it may not
spread further among the people, we must warn them never to speak again about
that name to anyone." [18]They called them back in and ordered them not to speak
or teach in the name of Jesus under any circumstances. [19]But Peter and John
said to them in reply, "Judge for yourselves whether it is right in God's sight for
us to obey you rather than God. [20]We cannot help but speak of what we have
seen and heard." [21]So when they had threatened them further, they dismissed
them, finding no way to punish them, because of the people, who were all honoring God for what had happened. [22]For it was for a man more than forty years
old that this sign of healing had been performed.

[l]Ps 118:22

WT: [1]addressing these words to the people . . . the priests and the Sadducees. [3]They apprehended them and delivered (them) to the jail [omits "for the night"]. [4][omits "the word"]. [5][omits "their" . . . "happened to" . . . "in Jerusalem"]. [6]Caiaphas, Jonathas [*sic*], and. [7]have they acted [omits "this"]. [8]elders of Israel. [9]Look, we are being examined by you about a good deed. [10][omits "to all of you and" . . . "Christ"] . . . before you today perfectly well, and in no other. [12]There is no other name . . . one is to be saved. [13]As all (of them) listened to the bold . . . convinced that they . . . ; some of them recognized that they used to gather with Jesus. [14]the sick man . . . [omits "standing there with them"] . . . nothing to do. [15]Then they conferred among themselves and ordered Peter and John to be led out . . . and they inquired among themselves. [16]"What shall we do . . . men? It is known . . . them; it is more than evident, and we . . . [17]But that these things may . . . , we shall warn them . . . [18]Because all found themselves in agreement with this opinion, they ordered them . . . [19][omits "to them"]; whether this seems right to you for . . . [22]the sign of healing.

COMMENT

Luke's story now moves to another episode as he recounts how Peter and John are haled before Jerusalem religious authorities because they have been explaining to the people how the lame beggar had been cured in the Temple area. The pretext for their arrest is the annoyance of the authorities at the teaching of the people by Peter and John and their maintaining that in Jesus' case there has been an instance of "resurrection of the dead" (4:2). The apostles are arrested and put in jail for the night.

When the authorities realize how the number of Christians has increased to "five thousand" men (*andres,* 4:4), a formal meeting of the high priest and Sanhedrin is called. Peter and John, brought before them, are queried by what authority or in whose name they have done what they did. Again, Peter makes his official and apostolic testimony: "in the name of Jesus Christ the Nazorean, whom you crucified and whom God raised from the dead; in virtue of that name this man stands before you perfectly well" (4:10). The boldness of Peter in bearing witness even to them, the highest religious authorities in Jerusalem, astounds them. After a consultation the authorities decide to forbid the apostles ever "to speak or teach in the name of Jesus" again (4:18). Peter boldly retorts: "Judge for yourselves whether it is right in God's sight for us to obey you rather than God. We cannot help but speak of what we have seen and heard" (4:19–20). With further threats, Peter and John are dismissed.

Form-critically assessed, the episode is basically a narrative, in which a conversation between Peter and the religious authorities is inserted, but Peter's answer to the query of the authorities becomes a short speech (4:8b–12, 19–20). As such it is a Lucan composition, an apologetic oration, in which Peter defends the miracle and again proclaims the Christian message, this time to Jewish authorities. Thus, it is partly defensive and partly a missionary and kerygmatic discourse. Related to the miracle in 3:1–11, it echoes the sentiments of the speech in 3:12b–26 and also the kerygma of 2:32, 36. A new element, however, is introduced: the OT idea of the stone rejected that becomes the cornerstone. In effect, Peter's speech becomes yet another missionary speech in the story of Acts.

The cure of the lame beggar, who stands with Peter and John before the authorities, is used as the occasion to proclaim the kerygma, which reasserts the death and resurrection of Jesus, repeating what Peter had said in 2:32, 36 (without the christological titles). Jesus is now implicitly proclaimed as Savior: "There is salvation in no one else, for there is no other name in the whole world given to human beings through which we are to be saved" (4:12). The Lucan emphasis on salvation as an effect of the Christ-event reemerges (*Luke*, 222–23). Now salvation is directly linked to the refrain of "the name of Jesus" (see NOTE on 2:38). It is all related indirectly to God's will and salvific plan; this is why Peter quotes Ps 118:22. What has happened to Jesus of Nazareth at the hands of such authorities is nothing more than a fulfillment of the "rejected stone" of that psalm. God has symbolically made it into a "cornerstone," a stone of supreme importance in the structure of the new mode of salvation for humanity. For the importance of this speech of Peter in Luke's kerygma, see *Luke*, 11–14, 145–62.

The episode is basically derived from a Palestinian source, into which Luke has introduced a speech and some of his favorite terms, especially in 4:8b–12, 19–20. To the pre-Lucan tradition belong the fact of the appearance of Peter and John before the Sanhedrin, the makeup of the Sanhedrin, and the names of the members. The clearly Lucan modifications begin with his literary suture and continue with the interruption of the speech (after it has already been terminated), and the number of new believers (5,000).

The episode is important in that it gives a dramatic presentation of apostolic courage or boldness. The term *parrhēsia* has already appeared in 2:29, where it is used with little significance; but now it becomes a mark of Peter's character, his bold self-assurance, and a characteristic of Christian testimony. Like *homothymadon* (see NOTE on 1:14), this term, along with the related verb *parrhēsiazesthai*, is a Lucan favorite for describing the boldness and self-assurance of early Christian disciples and their united activity.

What is noteworthy in the episode is the lack of reference to the resurrection of Jesus apart from the brief kerygmatic statement in v 10. Nothing more is really made of it, even though Peter and John are arrested for having been "teaching the people and proclaiming in Jesus the resurrection of the dead." The apostles are not charged explicitly with having preached about resurrection; instead, all is made to turn on "the name" of Jesus and its implied power in the cure of the cripple.

There is a certain parallelism that Luke used in this episode with the passion narrative of his Gospel. In both instances the religious authorities gather to adjudicate in the morning (Luke 22:66; Acts 4:6); Peter plays a special role (Luke 22:56; Acts 4:13); there is lack of evidence of guilt (Luke 23:4, 14–15, 22; Acts 4:21) and a similar reaction of the people (Luke 19:47; Acts 4:21).

The Lucan teaching on Christ as Savior is presented in this episode, when Peter boldly declares, "There is salvation in no one else, for there is no other name in the whole world given to human beings through which we are to be saved" (4:12). From Peter's statement, one realizes how incorrect is the assertion of Bultmann that Luke has "surrendered the original kerygmatic sense of the Jesus-tradition" (*TNT*, 2.117). Luke has not deformed the Christian kerygma, but has rather proclaimed Jesus as the sole agent of eschatological salvation for all humanity. Peter's declaration is kerygmatic indeed and no less a challenge to those who listen to it. Peter accosts his immediate audience, but also all those who seek salvation, both in a physical sense (a healing, a cure) and a spiritual sense (eschatological deliverance). Only through Christ can human beings find peace with God.

NOTES

4:1. *While they were still addressing the people.* The interrupted speech is now ascribed to both Peter and John, even though Peter alone has spoken. The "people" are those mentioned in 3:11, who had rushed to the colonnade of Solomon, within the Temple precincts. In the Lucan story the *laos* is the foil to the religious authorities who oppose the apostles.

the priests, the captain of the Temple guard, and the Sadducees confronted them. Three groups represent the religious authorities of the Jerusalem Temple; they are classed together here as opponents of the apostles. *Hiereis* is the reading in the important MSS ℵ, A, D, E, Ψ, 0165, 1739, etc.; but MSS B and C have *archiereis*, "chief priests," the term often used with the next phrase (Luke 22:4, 52; Acts 5:24), which is for that reason usually regarded as a harmonizing reading. *Ho stratēgos tou hierou* was the "(military) officer of the Temple," mentioned in Luke 22:52; Acts 5:24, 26, i.e., probably the head of the Temple police, made up of Levites serving in the Temple. The "captain" would have been second in importance, after the high priest. In the rabbinic tradition he was called *sĕgan hakkôhănîm*, "prefect of the priests."

The name *Saddoukaioi*, "Sadducees," is related to the Hebrew proper noun *Ṣādôq*, "Zadok," which appears in LXX with a double delta: *Saddouk* (2 Sam 8:17; Ezek 40:46; 43:19). In Josephus one finds *Saddōk* or *Saddouk* (depending on the MS, see *Ant.* 18.1.1 §4). Descendants of Zadok *(bĕnê Ṣādôq)* were granted the privilege of officiating as priests in the Temple after the return from the Babylonian Captivity. These "Zadokites" traced their lineage to Zadok, the Aaronid priest under Solomon, who replaced Abiathar (1 Kgs 2:26–27, 35), and even further back to Zadok, elder son of Aaron (1 Chr 5:30–35 [6:4–10E]; cf. Sir 51:12 [Hebrew]). As a group within Judaism distinct from the Pharisees and the Essenes, the "Sadducees" emerged in the Maccabean period (see Josephus, *J.W.* 2.8.2 §119; 2.8.14 §§164–65; *Ant.* 13.5.9 §173; 18.1.4 §§16–17). These were priestly and lay aristocrats, considerably Hellenized. Luke depicts them among the authorities in Jerusalem, but of them Josephus writes, "The Sadducees have the confidence of the well-to-do but no following among the people" (*Ant.* 13.10.6 §298); "this teaching [of the Sadducees] has reached but few of the people, yet they are men of highest esteem" (*Ant.* 18.1.4 §17). In Luke's view the Sadducees are the archenemies of Christianity. They appear only once in the Lucan Gospel (20:27–33), but they will appear again in Acts 5:17; 23:6–8. In the Gospel Luke describes them as "those denying there is a resurrection"; cf. Acts 23:8. They held for a strict interpretation of the *written* Torah and would have nothing to do with the oral law *(tôrāh še-bĕ-ʿal peh)* and the *hălākāh* of the Pharisees, "regulations handed down by former generations" (*Ant.* 13.10.6 §297). Since there is no mention of the resurrection in the Torah, they found no need to believe in it. Josephus records that the Sadducees maintain that "souls perish with their bodies" (*Ant.* 18.1.4 §16; *J.W.* 2.8.14 §165) and so disagreed with the Pharisees in this regard. See *HJPAJC*, 2.404–14; J. Le Moyne, *Les Sadducéens* (EBib; Paris: Gabalda, 1972), 123–35. Sadducees also rejected "fate" (i.e., predestination) and maintained the freedom of the will and individual responsibility for conduct (*J.W.* 2.8.14 §§164–65; *Ant.* 13.5.9 §173). Cf. Fitzmyer, "The Qumran Community: Essene or Sadducean?" *HeyJ* 36 (1995): 467–76.

2. *annoyed that Peter and John were teaching the people and proclaiming in Jesus the resurrection of the dead.* Two reasons are stated for the annoyance of the authorities and their confrontation of Peter and John: they, "as uneducated, ordinary men" (4:13), have been teaching the people; and they have been claiming that there was "resurrection from the dead" in the case of Jesus of Nazareth. The latter reason would have been particularly annoying to the Sadducees. The phrase *en tō Iēsou*, "in Jesus," is difficult. Barrett (*Acts*, 220) takes it as instrumental: "by means of (the story of) Jesus." Cf. BDF §219; *IBNTG*, 77.

3. *They arrested them and put them in jail for the night, for it was already evening.* Lit., "they laid hands on them and put them in custody for the morrow." Cf. 5:18. The postponement of the hearing of the apostles enables people to learn more about the episode and Peter's speech and to react to it.

4. *many of those who had heard the word came to believe, and* [*the*] *number of men grew to* [*about*] *five thousand. Ho logos* is used in the pregnant sense of "the Christian message," which Peter has been preaching, as it will appear elsewhere (6:4; 8:4). The absolute usage is a Lucan favorite in the story of the spread of the Word. This verse also contains one of the numerical summaries, with which Luke has punctuated his narrative (see Introduction §93c). Luke passes over the mention of women in this summary. As in 2:41, Peter is made to address thousands once again. The question of how his voice would have been heard by so

many on these occasions is taken up by B. C. Crisler, "The Acoustics and Crowd Capacity of Natural Theaters in Palestine," BA 39 (1976): 128–41.

5. *The next day their leaders, elders, and scribes happened to assemble in Jerusalem.* The three groups mentioned are those that make up the Jerusalem Sanhedrin *(synedrion)*, which numbered seventy-one. In the Lucan Gospel "the chief priests, the scribes, and the elders" (9:22; 20:1) are so mentioned, in a phrase derived from Mark 8:31; they were the components of the Sanhedrin of 4:15 (see NOTE there). Those called *archontes* are clarified by the names given in v 6 and by the phrase, "all who were of high-priestly class." Thus a formal session of the Jerusalem Sanhedrin was called; it was the highest group of religious authorities in Jerusalem, made up of *kôhănîm gĕdōlîm* or *archiereis*, "(chief) priests," *zĕqēnîm* or *presbyteroi*, "elders," and *sôpĕrîm* or *grammateis*, "scribes." The last named were called "teachers of the law" (Luke 5:17), lawyers *(nomikoi)* of the Pharisaic party (Luke 7:30; see *Luke*, 583). They will reappear in 6:12; 19:35; 23:9. Luke again uses *egeneto de* with an infin.; see *Luke*, 118.

6. *with Annas, the high priest.* Annas, or Ananus (Hebrew *Ḥānān*), son of Seth, was appointed high priest by the Roman governor, P. Sulpicius Quirinius, in A.D. 6 and held this position until he was deposed by Valerius Gratus in A.D. 15. He was succeeded by Ishmael, son of Phiabi (A.D. 15), Eleazar, his own son (16–17), Simon, son of Camith (17–18), and eventually by his son-in-law, Joseph, called Caiaphas (Josephus, *Ant.* 18.2.2. §§33–34; 20.9.1 §198). Here Luke shows that he knows correctly about Annas's prestige in giving him the title "high priest" (as does John 18:13a, 19), at a time when he would scarcely have been high priest any longer. It seems to have been a custom to refer in this way to an ex-high priest. The gospel tradition gives us the impression that Annas was a powerful figure, and this is the reason why he above all would have been called to such a session of the Sanhedrin. See P. Gaechter, "The Hatred of the House of Annas," *TS* 8 (1947): 3–34; cf. A. Wikenhauser, *Geschichtswert*, 303–4.

Caiaphas. Joseph, surnamed Caiaphas, was appointed high priest by Valerius Gratus in A.D. 18 and continued as such until he was deposed by Vitellius in 36. The Fourth Gospel refers to him twice as "the high priest that year" (John 11:49; 18:13b), i.e., in the year of Jesus' death. Here Luke correctly names him along with others of the "high-priestly family." The mention of him gives a *terminus ante quem* for the appearance of the apostles before him. It must have been before A.D. 36.

The burial cave of the Caiaphas family and inscribed ossuaries, one of which bears the name *Yhwsp br qyp'*, "Joseph, son of Caiaphas," were recently found in Jerusalem; see Z. Greenhut, "Burial Cave of the Caiaphas Family," *BARev* 18/5 (1992): 28–36, 76; R. Reich, "Caiaphas Name Inscribed on Bone Boxes," ibid., 38–44, 76; "Ossuary Inscriptions from the Caiaphas Tomb," *JerusPersp* 4/4–5 (1991): 13–22.

John, and Alexander, and all who were of high-priestly class. Instead of *Iōannēs*, which is read in MSS P^{74}, ℵ, A, B, 0165, MS D and the VL, read *Iōnathas*, "Jonathan," who may be the same as *Iōnathēs*, mentioned by Josephus (*Ant.*

18.4.3 §95) as the son of Ananas, the high priest; he succeeded Caiaphas as high priest (A.D. 36–37). Alexander is otherwise unknown. The *genos archieratikon* was made up of the chief priests in Jerusalem, those from whom the high priest was normally chosen. See E. M. Smallwood, "High Priests"; E. Schürer, "Die *archiereis* im Neuen Testamente," *TSK* 45 (1872): 593–657; D. Barag and D. Flusser, "The Ossuary," esp. 42–43.

7. *They brought Peter and John in before them and questioned them: "By what authority or what name have such as you done this?"* Lit., "stationing them in (their) midst, they questioned, 'In what power or in what name . . .'" The pron. "you" is put emphatically at the end of the question. The topic of resurrection disappears, and the apostles are questioned only about the miraculous cure of the lame beggar.

8. *Peter, filled with the Holy Spirit, said to them.* Luke introduces the Spirit in its role of inspiring prophetic utterance at a crucial moment; see NOTE on 2:4. Cf. Luke 12:11–12; 21:14–15, which explain the activity of the Spirit given on such an occasion. Again, Peter acts as the spokesman.

"Leaders of the people and elders. Peter addresses the Sanhedrin with respect. *Archontes* picks up the term used in v 5. Some MSS (D, E, Ψ, 33, 36) read "elders of Israel," an unimportant addition.

9. *if we must answer today for a good deed done to a cripple (and explain) how he has been restored to health.* Lit., "done to a sick person, in what he has been saved (from disease)." Peter uses the verb *sōzein,* which can mean "save" in either a physical sense (as here) or a spiritual sense, which may also be connoted, because of what he adds. Peter's answer concentrates on the cure of the cripple; he does not try to defend himself against the charge of "proclaiming in Jesus the resurrection of the dead" (4:2). See B. H. Throckmorton, "*Sōzein.*"

10. *then let it be known to all of you and to all the people of Israel.* Peter directs his explanation not only to the religious authorities of Jerusalem but to all Israel; thus he continues his apostolic testimony in Jerusalem (see 1:8) but broadens it into a missionary speech directed to all Israel as well. For the introductory formula, see NOTE on 2:14; cf. 13:38; 28:28.

it was in the name of Jesus Christ the Nazorean. In thus answering the question put to him, Peter implies that the name of Jesus is the source of the "power" about which they have been asked. The refrain of the "name of Jesus" appears again, as Peter answers the query; see NOTE on 2:38. Peter employs *Christos* as Jesus' second name (see NOTE on 2:36); on Nazorean, see NOTE on 2:22.

whom you crucified and whom God raised from the dead. In this double rel. cl., Peter repeats the essence of the primitive kerygma (crucifixion, death, and resurrection); see NOTE on 2:24; cf. 2:36. Note the contrast between "you" and "God," between guilty human conduct and corrective divine activity. This contrast will be repeated in a different form in v 11 ("Jesus" and "you"). Peter relates the healthy condition of the lame beggar to the status of him whom God has raised from the dead. See L. Schenke, "Die Kontrastformel," 11.

In virtue of that name this man stands before you perfectly well. The WT (MS E and the VL) adds: "stands before you today perfectly well, and in no other (name)," the last phrase being borrowed from v 12. Note the different referents of the pron. *houtos*, "this," in this and the following verse: here the man just cured, and in v 11, "Jesus" (supplied in the translation), who is mentioned earlier in this verse. Cf. ZBG §214.

11. *This Jesus is the stone rejected by you builders, which has become the cornerstone.* As part of his kerygmatic proclamation, Peter introduces an allusion to the OT to reveal the divine plan according to which all that has happened really belongs. He alludes to Ps 118:22 (LXX): *lithon, hon apedokimasan hoi oikodomountes, houtos egenēthē eis kephalēn gōnias*, "the stone that the builders rejected has become the head of the corner," an accurate translation of the Hebrew, but it is cited here with some modification. Instead of the active verb *apedokimasan*, Luke uses the pass. ptc. *exouthenētheis;* he also introduces *hyph' hymōn*, "by you," and changes *houtos egenēthē* to *ho genomenos.* Whether Luke is quoting from memory or using a different Greek version of the Psalter is hard to say.

Peter alludes to the last of the Hallel psalms in the Psalter, originally a thanksgiving hymn addressed to God for deliverance in battle. His modified use of it disregards its original meaning and applies its words to Jesus, thus introducing the motif of divine reversal. Peter implies that in God's view Scripture has already told of the rejection of Jesus by his contemporaries. The stone that did not measure up to the expected estimate of builders has become the most important stone in the edifice. It is accorded the place of honor by the function that it now plays in the whole structure.

"Cornerstone" is not to be understood in the modern sense (the stone of a principal part of the building, usually laid at its inauguration, with a date on it and often some inscription). It expresses rather the function of a main, often oversized, stone used at an important spot in the joining of two walls of a building, to bear their weight and stress. It would function somewhat like a "keystone" or "capstone" in an arch, but is used in a more primitive mode of construction as a sort of copingstone.

In death Jesus was "rejected" by leaders of Jerusalem, but by his resurrection he has become the key figure in God's new building, reconstituted Israel. In the structure of God's salvific plan Jesus has become its "cornerstone," its main element, as Peter's following remark makes clear. Luke quoted this verse of Psalm 118 similarly in the Gospel (20:17); it had already become part of the pre-Lucan kerygma (being used also in Mark 12:10; 1 Pet 2:4–7). See M. Lattke, *EDNT*, 2.284–86.

12. *There is salvation in no one else.* For the first time Luke introduces *sōtēria*, "salvation," the most important term among his various ways of expressing effects of the Christ-event (*Luke*, 222–23). By it he means deliverance of human beings from evil, whether physical, political, cataclysmic, moral, or eschatological, and the restoration of them to a state of wholeness. The term will appear again in 7:25; 13:26, 47; 16:17; 27:43 (cf. Luke 1:69, 71, 77; 19:9); in 28:28 he uses the alternate form, *to sōtērion tou theou*, as in Luke 2:30; 3:6. Other NT writers make use of it as well (Paul, John, Hebrews), but only Luke emphasizes the exclusive

nature of this new mode of divine salvation. What Peter announces here, Paul will also proclaim to the Gentiles, as Luke's story develops.

there is no other name in the whole world given to human beings through which we are to be saved." Lit., "there is no other name under heaven given among humans by which we must be saved." MS D and Latin versions omit the prep. *en* so that it would mean, "given to humans." Barrett (*Acts,* 232) understands "given" as "provided, as a means of salvation." It means "given by God," a theological passive (ZBG §236). This part of the verse simply reiterates what has just been said, now relating salvation to the motif of "the name of Jesus" and insisting on the universality of salvation available in Christ for all human beings who turn to him. This note of universality grows gradually throughout Acts, as one learns of the rejection of the Christian message and its extension to others than the Jewish people. Indeed, the motif of reconstituted Israel, by which Gentiles become part of Israel, is the precise way that God's salvation is further extended. Luke depicts Peter proclaiming the exclusive role of Jesus Christ in that divine plan for human salvation. He does not envisage the modern problem of salvation for human beings who have never heard of Christ or who are devotees of other religions, like Hinduism, Buddhism. Cf. M. Dumais, "Le salut universel par le Christ selon les Actes des Apôtres," *SNTU* 18 (1993): 113–31.

Whether Luke is here playing on the meaning of the name of Jesus as related to "salvation" is hard to say. Those who accept the popular etymology of "Jesus" used in Matt 1:21 would see this implied, but Luke never gives that meaning to the name. See *Luke,* 347, for the etymology of "Jesus."

13. *Seeing the bold self-assurance of Peter and John.* Luke describes the reaction of the Jerusalem leaders to what Peter has said. The stance of the apostles has been one of *parrhēsia,* "frankness, outspokenness, courage," by which he means Spirit-inspired eloquence. The term had been used in 2:29, but now it recurs in a special way and, along with its related verb, will characterize Christian boldness (4:13, 29, 31; 9:27, 28; 13:46; 14:3; 18:20, 26; 19:8; 26:26). In classical Greek literature *parrhēsia* was the noted characteristic of free citizens in Attic democracy (Demosthenes, *Or.* 9.111.3–4; Euripides, *Hippolytus* 422; *Ion* 672; Aristophanes, *Thesmophoriazusae* 541). See M. Radin, "Freedom of Speech in Ancient Athens," *AJP* 4 (1927): 215–20. In time it came to denote a moral concept that was important in Cynic philosophy, related to *eleutheria,* "freedom," and connoting the mark of a person morally free and able to resist public attention or opposition. See H. Schlier, *TDNT,* 5.87–75; H.-C. Hahn, *NIDNTT,* 2.734–37. In using the idea for Peter and John, Luke is adopting Greek thought forms to make comprehensible the apostles' defiance of the Jerusalem authorities. The comparison of Peter with Socrates has often been made (see M. Adinolfi, "Il Socrate").

realizing that they were uneducated, ordinary men, they were amazed. The assurance and eloquence of the apostles do not seem to accord with their background and surprise the Sanhedrin. Peter and John are depicted as *agrammatoi,* "unlettered, unable to write," and *idiōtai,* "amateurs, nonspecialists." Josephus uses the latter term to describe those unskilled in speaking (*Ant.* 2.12.2 §271), as does Paul (2 Cor 11:6). This condition explains the authorities' amazement. The reader has already been told the source of the assurance and eloquence in v 8.

they recognized that they had been with Jesus. I.e., were companions of his earthly ministry. In this way Luke expresses the special relation of Peter and John to the Jesus that they are now proclaiming. How the Sanhedrin would have recognized this association is not explained.

14. *When they looked at the man who had been cured standing there with them, they had nothing to say in reply.* Peter's words have had some effect on the members of the Sanhedrin, but it is the cured cripple standing before them who is the living proof of what Peter has said, a proof that the Sanhedrin cannot ignore.

15. *So they ordered them out of the Sanhedrin and held a consulation among themselves.* The Sanhedrin adjourns so that it can consider privately what it must do. Luke identifies the assembled authorities as *synedrion,* "the Sanhedrin." This Greek word means "conference, session, meeting" (lit., "group of those sitting together"); it was transcribed into Hebrew as *sanhedrîn* and became the official designation of the Jerusalem religious council (*m. Sanhedrin* 1:6; see *Luke,* 1466), a body of 71 (70 members plus their president). As a technical name, it occurs only once in Luke (22:66 [*Luke,* 1466]); but it will appear again in Acts 5:21, 27, 34, 41; 6:12, 15; 22:30; 23:1, 6, 15, 20, 28; 24:20. For a full description of its legal prerogatives, see H. W. Tajra, *The Trial of St. Paul,* 98–103. See NOTE on 4:5; cf. F. E. Meyer, "Einige Bemerkungen."

16. "*What are we going to do with these people?* I.e., at least Peter and John; but the question may refer to the rest of the early Christians in Jerusalem, since Luke uses simply the generic *tois anthrōpois,* "human beings." He records the Sanhedrin's consultation as though he had been present at it.

it is known to all who live in Jerusalem that a remarkable sign has been done through them. Or "that a notable sign has been performed through them is manifest to all the inhabitants of Jerusalem" *(RSV).* Luke's sentence is not pellucid, but the general sense is clear. Even the Sanhedrin cannot deny the obvious: the cure of the lame beggar has become a matter of public knowledge in Jerusalem. The miraculous cure is called a "sign," which echoes 2:22, 43.

we cannot deny it. Even the Sanhedrin has to admit that a miracle has been wrought. In effect, this reveals the Sanhedrin's hardness of heart.

17. *But that it may not spread further among the people, we must warn them never to speak again about that name to anyone.*" It is not clear what is meant by "it," the subject of the verb. Possibly the "sign," but more probably "it" refers to the knowledge of the miracle or the influence that the apostles have been having on the people of Jerusalem as a result of the sign. The authorities are depicted as reluctant to mention Jesus and simply refer to him as "that name," thus ironically using the Lucan motif of the name. The name is thus proscribed; it is not to be mentioned to any human being hereafter.

18. *They called them back in and ordered them not to speak or teach in the name of Jesus under any circumstances.* Peter and John are forbidden to "proclaim" (*phthengesthai,* "utter loudly") or to teach anyone, using "the name of Jesus." Cf.

Acts 5:28. Luke uses the adv. *katholou,* attested in classical Greek in the sense of "wholly, entirely," but it is preceded here by the neut. of the definite article (used as an adverbial acc.); cf. BDF §160.

19. *Peter and John said to them in reply.* Luke uses for the first time the stereotyped formula of response, *apokrithentes eipon,* inherited from the LXX; see *Luke,* 114. He again makes it seem as though both of the apostles speak in unison.

"Judge for yourselves whether it is right in God's sight for us to obey you rather than God. Lit., "to listen to you." The impv. *krinate,* "judge," is put emphatically at the end of the sentence; my translation has transposed it to the front. Peter's reply stakes out the bounds of the issue at hand: God or human beings! Whom does one obey? Again the contrast is noteworthy. It makes clear that obedience to one's conscience is supreme. Peter and John do not fail to recognize the authority of the religious leaders, but they will not surrender their consciences to such authorities. The same argument will reappear in 5:29. Peter's answer resembles that of the seven brothers and their mother in 2 Macc 7:2; cf. Josephus, *Ant.* 17.6.3 §§158–59. Compare too the answer of Socrates in Plato, *Apology* 29D: "Athenians, I respect and love you, but I shall obey God rather than you." A similar condition had been proposed to Socrates that he pursue his inquiry and speculation no more in any way (29C). See M. Adinolfi, "Il Socrate."

20. *We cannot help but speak of what we have seen and heard."* Peter refers to the visions of the risen Christ that he and other apostles have been accorded (1:3) and to the commission orally given them by Christ (Luke 24:47–48a; Acts 1:8). They have been eyewitnesses and earwitnesses, and they refuse to be silenced. So with due respect they boldly defy the authorities.

21. *when they had threatened them further, they dismissed them.* I.e., from the Sanhedrin. Freedom under threats is their lot. The Sanhedrin is reluctant to consider who speaks for God.

finding no way to punish them, because of the people, who were all honoring God for what had happened. So Luke records once again the reaction of the ordinary people in Jerusalem to the apostles and the other Christian disciples. It is a reaction with which the Sanhedrin has to reckon.

22. *For it was for a man more than forty years old that this sign of healing had been performed.* The forty years are significant when one recalls that he was lame from birth (3:2), but Luke scarcely means to suggest that people would not have been thus honoring God if the man were only twenty.

BIBLIOGRAPHY (4:1–22)

Adinolfi, M., "'Obbedire a Dio piuttosto che agli uomini': La comunità cristiana e il sinedrio in Atti 4,1–31; 5,17–42," *RivB* 27 (1979): 69–93.

———, "Il Socrate dell'Apologia platonica e il Pietro di Atti 4–5 di fronte alla libertà religiosa," *Anton* 65 (1990): 422–41.

Ambroggi, P. de, "S. Petri loquentis *parrēsia,*" *VD* 9 (1929): 269–76.

Bammel, E., "Jewish Activity against Christians in Palestine according to Acts," *The Book of Acts in Its Palestinian Setting* (BAFCS 4), 357–64.
Barag, D. and D. Flusser, "The Ossuary of Yehoḥanah Granddaughter of the High Priest Theophilus," *IEJ* 36 (1986): 39–44.
Cullmann, O., "Tutti quelli che invocano il nome del Signor Gesù Cristo," *Protestantesimo* 16 (1961): 65–80.
Gowen, H. H., "The Name," *ATR* 12 (1929–30): 275–85.
Manson, T. W., "Sadducee and Pharisee—the Origin and Significance of the Names," *BJRL* 22 (1938): 144–59.
Mason, S., "Chief Priests, Sadducees, Pharisees and Sanhedrin in Acts," *The Book of Acts in Its Palestinian Setting* (see above), 115–77.
Meyer, F. E., "Einige Bemerkungen zur Bedeutung des Terminus 'Synhedrion' in den Schriften des Neuen Testaments," *NTS* 14 (1967–68): 545–51.
Schenke, L., "Die Kontrastformel Apg 4,10b," *BZ* 26 (1982): 1–20.
Smallwood, E. M., "High Priests and Politics in Roman Palestine," *JTS* 13 (1962): 14–34.
Throckmorton, B. H., "*Sōzein, sōtēria* in Luke-Acts," *SE VI* (TU 112; Berlin: Akademie, 1973), 515–26.
Villiers, P.G.R. de, "The Medium Is the Message: Luke and the Language of the New Testament against a Graeco-Roman Background," *Neotestamentica* 24 (1990): 247–56.

2. The Prayer of Jerusalem Christians (4:23–31)

[23] After their release, Peter and John went back to their friends and reported to
them all that the chief priests and elders had told them. [24] On hearing it, they
raised their voices with one accord in prayer to God: "Sovereign Lord, *who have
made the heaven and earth, the sea and all that is in them,*[m] [25] it is you who spoke
by the Holy Spirit through our ancestor David, your servant:

Why have nations raged
and peoples plotted folly?
[26] *Kings of the earth have drawn up in hostile array,*
and rulers have gathered together
against the Lord and against his Anointed.[n]

[27] For truly in this very city there have indeed gathered together against your holy
servant Jesus, whom you have anointed, Herod and Pontius Pilate, together with
Gentiles and peoples of Israel, [28] to do the very things that your designing hand
planned long ago. [29] But now, O Lord, look at their threats and grant your servants
the courage to preach your word with all boldness, [30] as you stretch forth [your]
hand to cure, and as signs and wonders are performed in the name of your holy
servant Jesus." [31] As they prayed, the place trembled in which they were gathered

together; all were filled with the Holy Spirit and they continued to speak about the word of God with boldness.

[m]Ps 146:6 [n]Ps 2:1–2

WT: [24][omits "on hearing it"] they, knowing the working of God, raised . . . [omits "with one accord"] . . . "Sovereign Lord God. [27][omits "For," "Jesus," "Pontius," and "Gentiles"] . . . people of Israel. [29][omits "all"]. [30]hand that cures, signs, and wonders be performed . . . [31]together; they were filled with the Spirit . . . boldness to everyone who was willing to believe.

COMMENT

This passage serves as a climax of the narrative that began at 3:1 and conveys Luke's real intention: Peter and John have not been acting on their own, but rather as God's agents on behalf of the rest of Jerusalem Christians. They are said now to return to "their friends," with whom they pray, and only afterwards is the narrative resumed.

The early Christian community's reaction to the release of Peter and John from arrest by the Sanhedrin is one of prayer. The episode with the recorded prayer gives yet another instance of Luke's emphasis on that element in Christian life (*Luke*, 244–47). Just as Luke had depicted Jesus often at prayer, so now he depicts early Christian disciples of Jesus (recall 1:14; 2:42). In this case, it is an example of Christians praying in common, publicly acknowledging with one accord their thanksgiving for the deliverance of Peter and John, but also turning to God in an hour of need and persecution. In their prayer they recognize that what has happened to the two apostles is a fulfillment of what was already recorded in Ps 2:1–2. Their prayer is not only one (implicitly) of thanksgiving, but mainly of praise, because they acknowledge God's sovereignty, wisdom, and counsel, and also of petition, as they invoke God's support for their coming need to proclaim the Christian message with boldness and courage. They do not pray to be spared persecution but beg rather for the grace of *parrhēsia*, "courageous speech," and ask for a confirmation of their message through "signs and wonders." In their prayer they recall the actions of Herod and Pontius Pilate against Jesus, God's anointed servant, the conspiring of Gentiles and peoples of Israel in his death. All that has happened is recognized as having been done in accord with God's salvific plan. The miracles that Jesus performed were also an implementation of that plan and are acknowledged as such. Now these Christians seek God's further support for the proclamation of their message about this anointed servant of God. Thus, with God's help they will be able to circumvent the attempt of Jerusalem authorities to thwart their preaching.

The prayer of these Christian disciples resembles that of Hezekiah recorded in Isa 37:16–20 and 2 Kgs 19:15–19, which may have served as Luke's model, but the conclusion is Lucan, making it suit the present situation. "With the Isaiah prayer as model Luke has cunningly recast in prayer-form an early Christian exegesis of Psalm 2" (Haenchen, *Acts*, 228). Also interesting is the parallel to this prayer in Josephus, *Ant.* 4.3.2 §§40–50, which records an earthquake as a result of Moses' prayer. Some of the same elements are used in the two prayers.

The result of the prayer of these early Christians is yet another manifestation of God's Spirit. Their prayer is heard and is efficacious. The place where they were gathered for common prayer shakes, and they are all filled with God's Spirit once again, in virtue of which they are emboldened anew for the proclamation of God's Word. The Spirit is thus depicted once more as the prophetic presence of God, strengthening the disciples to go forth and proclaim the Word. No speaking in tongues is associated with this prayer or reception of the Spirit. The prayer is intellectually formulated, based on Scripture and addressed to God; the implication of the account is that the Spirit has likewise enabled these disciples so to pray.

This episode is one of Lucan composition, which may incorporate a few details inherited from a Palestinian tradition, such as the fact of the prayer and intervention of the Spirit and the mention of Herod and Pilate.

This Lucan episode reveals how prayer marks the early Jerusalem community. It lives not only in the vicinity of where its Lord has been crucified, but also near the Temple of Israel. It is constantly in communion with God, who is now addressed in prayer as Sovereign Lord and Creator, the one who controls all human life and destiny. God who has acted on behalf of his Son Jesus and vindicated him by raising him from the dead is now being invoked to reassure and vindicate the preaching of those who proclaim his Son. God is being asked to embolden those who proclaim him. They do not selfishly ask for benefits for themselves, but for the grace to carry out what God has called them to accomplish in frankness and unity.

NOTES

23. *After their release, Peter and John went back to their friends.* Lit., "having been released, they went to their own." No indication is given about where this might be. Luke describes them as gathered in one place. It is hardly likely that the whole Christian community in Jerusalem, now numbering more than 8,000, would be meant.

reported to them all that the chief priests and elders had told them. See NOTES on 4:1, 5. Their report would have concentrated on the prohibition imposed by the Sanhedrin "not to speak or teach in the name of Jesus under any circumstances" (4:18) and its threats.

24. *On hearing it, they raised their voices with one accord in prayer to God.* "They" would refer to *hoi idioi*, "their own" (4:23), i.e., their friends who, having heard the report, pray together with Peter and John. Again Luke significantly stresses the unity of the Jerusalem congregation, using "with one accord"; see NOTE on 1:14.

"*Sovereign Lord.* The prayer of these early Christians is addressed to God as *despotēs*, "lord, master," the word from which we get English "despot," a connotation that the Greek word does not usually have. God is so addressed, precisely as Creator. *Despotēs* occurs as an address for God in Luke 2:29, but elsewhere in the NT it is rare (Jude 4; Rev 6:10; 2 Pet 2:1[?]). It may be derived from Greek literature, where it is often used of gods (Euripides, *Hippolytus* 88; Xenophon, *Anabasis* 3.2.13), but it is also found in the LXX (Job 5:8; Wis 6:7; 8:3; Sir 36:1). In the writings of Philo (*Quis rerum divinarum heres* 6 §§22–23) and of Josephus it is often used, sometimes even where the MT has *Yhwh* (*J.W.* 7.8.6 §323; *Ant.* 8.4.1 §107; 18.1.6 §23). Cf. *1 Clem.* 59.4; 61.1–2.

In many important MSS (P[74], ℵ, A, B, 2495) and some ancient versions (VL, Vg, Coptic) *despota* is followed by the pron. *sy*, "you" (2d sg.). In my translation I have incorporated it into the beginning of v 25. Some MSS read rather *sy ei ho theos*, "You are God" (D, E, Ψ, 36, 307, 593, 608); a few have *Kyrie ho theos*, "Lord, God," a harmonization derived from the LXX of Ps 146:6 or Exod 20:11, the source of the next clause.

who have made the heaven and earth, the sea and all that is in them. This OT allusion manifests the sovereignity of the Lord God as creator. God is regarded as the one who guides human life and its destiny. See Ps 146:6; Exod 20:11; Neh 9:6; cf. Acts 14:15. Early Christians so pray to God, aware of their own creaturely dependence. Cf. Josephus, *Ant.* 4.3.2 §40 for a parallel in Moses' prayer.

25. *it is you who spoke by the Holy Spirit through our ancestor David, your servant.* Lit., "who spoke through the mouth of David, your servant, our ancestor, by the Holy Spirit" (or something similar; see below on the garbled transmission of this verse). In this case the psalm to be quoted does not bear an ascription to David in the MT; yet like the rest of the Psalter, it has been traditionally attributed to David, whose words are now ascribed to God, speaking through the Spirit. Implied is that what David has said, God has said. Cf. 2 Tim 3:16. David is called *patēr hēmōn*, "our father," i.e., forefather (cf. Luke 1:32) and *pais sou*, "your [God's] servant" (cf. Luke 1:69; Acts 9:2a [MS D]). The latter title is derived from the LXX of Ps 18:1; Isa 37:35.

The text of this introductory clause in the Alexandrian text is garbled: "one of the most impossible clauses in the entire Book of Acts" (Dibelius). In MSS P[74], ℵ, A, B, E, Ψ, 33, 36, etc., it reads: *ho tou patros hēmōn dia pneumatos hagiou stomatos Dauid paidos sou eipōn.* It begins with the def. art. *ho,* which governs the ptc. *eipōn,* "speaking," at the end of the clause; but that art. is immediately followed by the phrase *tou patros hēmōn,* "of our ancestor," a genitive phrase, which modifies *stomatos Dauid paidos sou,* "the mouth of David, your servant." Moreover, there is only one prep. *dia* that governs both *pneumatos hagiou,* "Holy Spirit" and the immediately following *stomatos . . . sou,* making it say, "through (the) Holy Spirit of the mouth of David, our ancestor"! Codex D and some ancient versions try to ameliorate the situation, reading: *hos dia pneumatos hagiou dia tou stomatos lalēsas Dauid paidos sou,* "who through the Holy Spirit has spoken through the mouth of David, your servant," which is a bit of an improvement, but still places the ptc. *lalēsas* in a peculiar position. A few MSS of lesser importance (181, 614, and the Byzantine tradition) read: *ho dia stomatos Dauid paidos sou eipōn,* "who spoke through the mouth of David, your servant," eliminating all reference to the Spirit. See Dibelius, *Studies*, 90; he would expunge both "Holy Spirit" and "of our ancestor." Torrey claimed that Luke, in writing *ho tou patros hēmōn*, has mistranslated Aramaic *hî' dî 'abûnā' lěpûm* . . . , "this is that which our father, thy servant David, said by . . . the command . . ." (*Composition and Date*, 16–18). That solves nothing.

Why have nations raged and peoples plotted folly? 26. *Kings of the earth have drawn up in hostile array, and rulers have gathered together against the Lord and against his Anointed.* Ps 2:1–2 (LXX) is quoted verbatim; it is also an exact translation of the MT. Psalm 2 is a royal psalm, composed for the enthronement of some (unknown) historical king of the Davidic dynasty, whose subject peoples are plotting against their new ruler. Their action is understood as a conspiracy against God and the king, who is called God's "Anointed." Because v 2 uses *měšîḥô*, "his Anointed," it is easily applied in this early Christian interpretation of the psalm to Jesus, already hailed as *Christos* in 2:36. This is a Christian understanding of the psalm. Despite its use of *měšîḥô*, there is little evidence that it was ever understood as a messianic psalm (in the strict sense: of an expected, coming Messiah) in pre-Christian Judaism, unless one is prepared to admit that *Ps. Sol.* 17:21–33; 18:5–9 is already a reflection of Psalm 2—a dubious contention at best. In the following verse, "kings," "rulers," "nations," and "peoples" are interpreted as those who had a share in Jesus' death.

27. *For truly in this very city.* In Jerusalem (see 4:5), where Jesus of Nazareth was crucified (Luke 23:7, 28, 33). Luke uses *ep' alētheias*, "in truth, truly," as a mode of asseveration; see also 10:34; Luke 4:25; 20:21; 22:59 (*Luke*, 537).

there have indeed gathered together against your holy servant Jesus. The early Christians realize that Jesus' death was the result of a conspiracy of different elements, a disciple (Judas), Jews (Jerusalem leaders), and pagans (Romans). Again Luke uses of Jesus *hagios*, "holy" (see NOTE on 3:14) and *pais*, "servant" (see NOTE on 3:13). Compare 2 Chr 32:16.

whom you have anointed. One looks in vain in the Lucan Gospel for any indication of the anointing of Jesus by God, apart from Luke 4:18, where the quotation of Isa 61:1 uses it and would imply such an anointing; but in Acts 10:38 Luke interprets the baptism of Jesus by John the Baptist as an anointing: "how God anointed Jesus of Nazareth with a Holy Spirit and with power."

Herod. Herod Antipas represents "the kings of the earth" mentioned in the psalm. He was the younger son of Malthace and Herod the Great, who received part of his father's realm at his death and ruled over Galilee and Perea from 4 B.C. until A.D. 39. In Luke 3:1 he is called "tetrarch of Galilee." See NOTES on Luke 2:2; 3:1. He is mentioned now because of his involvement in Jesus' trial before Pilate in the Lucan passion narrative (Luke 23:6–12, 15). The Herodian family was considered by Josephus to be "half-Jewish" (*Ant.* 14.15.2 §403), and this Jewish connection is probably part of the reason why Herod Antipas is mentioned along with the Roman Pilate. See J. Jervell, "Herodes Antipas og hans plass i evangelieoverleveringen," *NorTT* 61 (1960): 28–40.

Pontius Pilate. Pilate represents the "rulers" mentioned in the psalm. See NOTE on 3:13. He figures in the passion narratives as involved in Jesus' death, but as one who tried to release Jesus (Luke 23:4, 14–15, 22). Here, however, Pilate is more involved as responsible for the death of Jesus.

together with Gentiles and peoples of Israel. "Gentiles" may refer to the Roman soldiers involved in the crucifixion of Jesus (see NOTE on Luke 23:36), or more broadly the Roman occupiers of Judea at the time. *Laoi Israēl* lacks the def. art. in the Alexandrian text, and it may be Luke's way of being vague about the number of Jews involved; possibly it refers to the tribes of Israel (so Haenchen, *Acts,* 227); cf. Johnson, *Acts,* 85. The WT emends the plural to a singular: either "people" (MSS E, 326) or "the people" (MS Ψ). That would implicate more than just a few Jews. See G. D. Kilpatrick, "*Laoi* at Luke ii. 31 and Acts iv.25, 27," *JTS* 16 (1965): 127. In any case, Luke uses for the first time *ethnē* in the sense of "Gentiles," a meaning that will take on significance as his story progresses; see 10:45; 11:1, 18.

28. *to do the very things that your designing hand planned long ago.* Lit., "to do what your hand and [your] plan determined beforehand would happen." Peter ascribes to God's "hand" what has been determined, using an OT phrase (see Exod 13:3, 14, 16; Ps 55:21) to denote God's sovereign control. What the just-named adversaries of Jesus have accomplished is something that was foreseen in God's providence; indeed, it has fitted into the implementation of the divine salvific plan. The prayer repeats what Peter has said in his Pentecostal speech (2:23).

This is the first reference in Acts to the divine "plan" or God's providence, a notion that Luke shares with other Hellenistic historiographers such as Diodorus Siculus, Dionysius of Halicarnassus, and Josephus. It will continue elsewhere in Acts. See J. T. Squires, *The Plan of God.*

29. *now, O Lord, look at their threats.* The phrase *kai ta nyn* introduces the supplication in the prayer; compare 2 Kgs 19:19. The Christians call upon God to take notice of the threats that the Sanhedrin has leveled against Peter and John, and through them against all the rest of their number. They beseech God to be concerned about the "threats" leveled against them. MS D strangely introduces the adj. *hagias,* "holy ones" (fem. pl.) for *apeilas,* "threats."

grant your servants the courage to preach your word with all boldness. Lit., "grant to your servants to speak." This is the main request in the petition made by the Christians: that they may have *parrhēsia* (see NOTE on 4:13) in their preaching and proclamation. On "your word," see NOTE on 4:31.

30. *as you stretch forth* [*your*] *hand to cure, and as signs and wonders are performed.* They also ask that further healings and other signs and wonders may accompany and give credit to their preaching of the Word. See NOTE on 2:22. Cf. Acts 5:12 for the confirmation so given.

in the name of your holy servant Jesus." The role that the name of Jesus plays here is particularly important because the Sanhedrin has forbidden Peter and John "to speak or teach in the name of Jesus under any circumstances" (4:17). Moreover, the prayer ends significantly with that name. Thus, Luke introduces once more the refrain of "the name of Jesus"; see NOTE on 2:38. Jesus is again called *hagios pais sou;* see NOTES on 3:13, 14.

31. *As they prayed, the place trembled in which they were gathered together.* Now heaven's response to their prayer is given by a different symbol of the presence of the Spirit, the trembling or rattling of the place where they are gathered, a sign of the power that will accompany their preaching of the Word. Exod 19:18b speaks of Mt. Sinai quaking greatly at the descent of Yahweh; similarly Isa 6:4. Cf. Josephus, *Ant.* 7.4.1 §§76–77, who knows of the divine presence in terms of a shaking of a grove.

all were filled with the Holy Spirit. The Spirit is given again as the inspirer of prophetic preaching; see NOTE on 2:4. What was promised at Pentecost is now being accorded.

they continued to speak about the word of God with boldness. The Spirit thus spurs on their public testimony, endowing them with the requisite *parrhēsia*. The Christian message is designated *ho logos tou theou*, "the Word of God," as it will be again in 6:2, 7; 8:14; 11:1; 12:24; 13:5, 7, 44, 46, 48; 16:32; 17:13; 18:11. This is a development beyond what it meant in the Lucan Gospel, where it denoted Jesus' own preaching (Luke 5:1; 8:11, 21; 11:28). Now it includes the "word" carried abroad about Jesus Christ and his significance for humanity. The phrase is derived from the OT (LXX of Jer 1:2; 9:19), where *logos Kyriou*, "the word of the Lord," is far more frequent. This too is used by Luke; see 8:25; 12:24 (in some MSS); 13:44; 15:35; 16:32 (in some MSS); 19:10, 20. See C.-P. März, *Das Wort Gottes bei Lukas: Die lukanische Worttheologie als Frage an die neuere Lukasforschung* (ErThS 11; Leipzig: St. Benno, 1974), 24–27.

BIBLIOGRAPHY (4:23–31)

Conn, H. M., "Luke's Theology of Prayer," *ChrT* 17 (1972): 290–92.

Dibelius, M., "'Herodes und Pilatus,'" ZNW 16 (1915): 113–26.

Doohan, H. and L., *Prayer in the New Testament* (Collegeville, MN: Liturgical, 1992).

Downing, F. G., "Common Ground with Paganism in Luke and in Josephus," *NTS* 28 (1982): 546–59.

Dupont, J., "Notes sur les Actes des Apôtres," *RB* 62 (1955): 45–59, esp. 45–47; repr., *Études*, 521–22.

Hamman, A., "La nouvelle Pentecôte (Actes 4,24–30)," *BVC* 14 (1956): 82–90.

Laplace, J., *Prayer according to the Scriptures* (San Francisco: Ignatius, 1991).

LeRoux, L. V., "Style and the Text of Acts 4:25(a)," *Neotestamentica* 25 (1991): 29–32.

O'Brien, P. T., "Prayer in Luke-Actds," *TynBull* 24 (1973): 111–27.

Rimaud, D., "La première prière liturgique dans le livre des Actes, 4:23–31 (Ps. 2 et 145)," *La Maison Dieu* 51 (1957): 99–115.

Squires, J. T., *The Plan of God in Luke-Acts* (SNTSMS 76; Cambridge: Cambridge University Press, 1993).

Thurston, B., *Spiritual Life in the Early Church: The Witness of Acts and Ephesians* (Minneapolis: Fortress, 1993), 55–65.

Trites, A. A., "The Prayer Motif in Luke-Acts," *Perspectives on Luke-Acts* (ed. C. H. Talbert), 168–86.

Wahlde, U. C. von, "Acts 4,24–31: The Prayer of the Apostles in Response to the Persecution of Peter and John—and Its Consequences," *Bib* 77 (1996): 237–44.

———, "The Theological Assessment of the First Christian Persecution: The Apostles' Prayer and Its Consequences in Acts 4,24–31," *Bib* 76 (1995): 523–31.

Webber, R. C., "'Why Were the Heathen So Arrogant?' The Socio-Rhetorical Strategy of Acts 3–4," *BTB* 22 (1992): 19–25.

3. SECOND MAJOR SUMMARY: A SHARING COMMUNITY (4:32–35)

32 The community of believers was of one heart and mind; none of them ever
claimed any possession as his own, but they held all things in common. 33 With
great forcefulness the apostles continued to bear witness to the resurrection of
the Lord Jesus, and much favor was accorded them all. 34 There was never a
needy person among them, for those who owned property or houses would sell
them, bring the proceeds of what was sold, 35 and lay them at the feet of the
apostles; and it was distributed to each according to one's need.

WT: 32 mind, and there was no difference among them. 33 [omits "all"]. 34 [omits "for," "property or," and "of what was sold"].

COMMENT

Luke introduces his second major summary, which presents the early Christian community mainly in terms of its common ownership of material goods. See COMMENT on 2:42–47. The summary is again composite or conflated. Its main theme stresses common ownership (4:32, 34–35), but the insert (4:33) expresses their testimony to the risen Christ. From this summary may have been drawn the insert that was made in the first major summary (2:43–45). Reference to common meals is completely absent in the present summary.

The summary is a Lucan composition. Jeremias claimed that vv 32, 34–35 represent the original stratum of this summary, and that v 33, which echoes 5:42 and 2:47b, is the secondary insert. For Cerfaux, v 33 belonged originally to the third major summary and has been moved here. Benoit too regarded v 33 as the insert of a later editorial hand. Zimmermann considers vv 32b, 34–35 to be the older account, into which Luke inserted vv 32ac and 33. Haenchen, who will have none of such analysis, regards it all as Lucan composition. For him vv 34–35 are a generalization made by Luke on the information that he has about

Barnabas and Ananias. As Weiser (*Apg.*, 135) notes, it is really impossible in this instance to distinguish Lucan and pre-Lucan material. According to Conzelmann (*Acts*, 36), the summary describes the inner life and the outer situation of the early Jerusalem Christians, and v 33 is extraneous to that.

What is not wholly clear is the extent to which common ownership was obligatory or voluntary. Even within this passage there is a difference between what is asserted in v 32 about holding all things in common, and the selling of property in v 34, which seems to imply that some members still hold some private property that they can sell.

The insert in v 33 continues the testimony to the risen Christ and also records the favor that the early Christians enjoyed with the rest of the populace of Jerusalem.

NOTES

32. *The community of believers was of one heart and mind.* Lit., "the heart and soul of the multitude of believers was one," the numerical adj. being placed at the end of the sentence for emphasis. This generic statement idyllically describes the unity and harmony of the Jerusalem Christians. See 1 Chr 12:39 *(psychē mia)*. Even though the following clauses give an instance of this unity in terms of common ownership, the initial statement should probably not be so restricted. The *plēthos* will be mentioned again in 6:2, "the community (lit., multitude) of disciples," and 6:5; 15:12. It is here made up of *hoi pisteusantes,* those who have come to faith (see NOTE on 2:44). The term *plēthos* may be a reflection of various Hebrew terms used to describe the assembly of the Essene community, such as *rab, rôb,* and *rabbîm* (1QS 5:2, 9, 22; 6:1, 7–9, 11–19, 21, 25). See Fitzmyer, "Jewish Christianity," *StLA*, 246. Note the addition in the WT.

none of them ever claimed any possession as his own, but they held all things in common. This description repeats that of 2:44b, merely rephrasing it differently. Nothing is said about how long common ownership of property was so practiced, or even how widespread it was among Christians. Compare the Greek saying, "Among friends everything is common" (Aristotle, *Nicomachean Ethics* 9:8 §1168B). Luke may well be idealizing the situation. Cf. Deut 15:4. MS D adds at the end of the verse: *kai ouk ēn diakrisis en autois oudemia,* "and there was no difference among them."

33. *With great forcefulness the apostles continued to bear witness to the resurrection of the Lord Jesus.* Whereas Luke usually characterizes the testimony of the apostles as courageous or bold, he speaks here of the "force" *(dynamis)* with which they bore witness. Again, he expresses abstractly the testimony borne to "the resurrection" of the Lord, which no one really witnessed (see NOTE on 1:22). He means that the apostles bear witness to the risen Christ who has appeared to them alive (1:3).

much favor was accorded them all. See 2:47b, which is here rephrased. This is a more likely interpretation than that of Barrett (*Acts*, 254), who toys with the idea that *charis* might refer to God's "active favour" or "divine aid bestowed in unusual measure." Similarly Haenchen (*Acts,* 231 n.4); Schneider (*Apg.,* 1.356), referring to Luke 2:40. Weiser (*Apg.,* 137) understands *charis* in a threefold way: the favor of the people, God's grace, and the effect of the Holy Spirit.

34. *There was never a needy person among them.* Luke's phraseology borrows words from Deut 15:4, 11 (LXX), which imply that the ideal stated there was actually governing the life of Jewish Christians in Jerusalem.

for those who owned property or houses would sell them, bring the proceeds of what was sold, 35. *and lay them at the feet of the apostles.* This was a sign of their divesting themselves of material goods and of the sacrifice that early Christians made for one another in the *koinōnia;* it was also a sign of their unanimity and their oneness of mind with the rest of their Christian *adelphoi.* As the story progresses, it is implied that they gave up 100 percent of the proceeds; that seems to be meant here and seems to be the implication in the following stories of two examples of those who did sell property. Nevertheless, this notice does not mean that all gave up their property or that it was a universal practice. The notice stands in a certain tension with what Luke said in v 32 about their holding "*all things* in common." Even Haenchen (*Acts,* 237) admits that the laying of the proceeds at the apostles' feet was derived by Luke from "the tradition." The money was brought to the apostles, who continued to act as administrators of the dole. Cf. 1QS 6:19–20: *'el yad hamměbaqqēr,* "to the hand of the overseer" (a parallel idea, if not exact in wording).

it was distributed to each according to one's need. The proceeds so contributed became the source of the dole to all in the community according to their need. This implies that the need was not equal among all; but the inequality is not explained. On the use of the particle *an* with the impf. *eichen,* see ZBG §358 (a substitute for the classical optative to express generality).

BIBLIOGRAPHY (4:32–35)

Combet-Galland, A. & C., "Actes 4,32–5,11," *ETR* 52 (1977): 548–53.

Dupont, J., "L'Union entre les premiers chrétiens dans les Actes des Apôtres," *NRT* 91 (1969): 897–915; repr. *Novelles études,* 296–318.

Gerhardsson, B., "Einige Bemerkungen zu Apg 4,32," *ST* 24 (1970): 142–49; repr. *The Shema in the New Testament* (Lund: Nova Press, 1996), 239–46.

Grelot, P., "La pauvreté dans l'Ecriture Sainte," *Christus Cahiers Spirituels* 8 (1961), 306–30.

Hauck, F., *Die Stellung des Urchristentums zu Arbeit und Geld* (BFCT 2/3; Gütersloh: Bertelsmann, 1921).

Kato, T., "Le caractère lucanien de l'image de la communauté primitive de Jérusalem en Act 4,32–35," *AJBI* 20 (1994): 79–95.

Noorda, S. J., "Scene and Summary: A Proposal for Reading Acts 4,32–5,16," *Les Actes des Apôtres* (ed. J. Kremer), 475–83.

Sudbrack, J., "Die Schar der Gläubigen war ein Herz und eine Seele (Apg 4,32)," *GuL* 38 (1965): 161–68.

Verheijen, L., *Saint Augustine's Monasticism in the Light of Acts 4,32–35* (Villanova, PA: Villanova University Press, 1979).
See further bibliography on 2:42–47 (esp. Benoit and Zimmermann).

4. Individual Examples of Christian Conduct (4:36–5:11)

[36]Thus there was Joseph, surnamed by the apostles Barnabas (which is interpreted "Son of Consolation"), a Levite, a Cypriot by birth, [37]who owned a farm
that he sold and brought the money and put it at the feet of the apostles. 5 [1]But
there was also a certain Ananias, who with his wife Sapphira sold a piece of property. [2]With the knowledge of his wife, he put aside for himself some of the proceeds; he brought only a part of them and laid them at the feet of the apostles.
[3]But Peter said, "Ananias, why have you let Satan so fill your heart that you would
lie to the Holy Spirit and put aside for yourself some of the proceeds of that field?
[4]Was it not yours so long as it remained unsold? Even when you had sold it, was
it not still at your disposal? What gave you the idea of such a thing? You have
lied not to human beings, but to God." [5]When Ananias heard these words, he
dropped dead. Great fear came upon all those who heard about it. [6]Some of the
young men came forward, wrapped him up, and carried him out for burial.
[7]About three hours later Ananias's wife came in, unaware of what had happened.
[8]Peter addressed her, "Tell me, did you sell that piece of property for such and
such an amount?" She answered, "Yes, for that amount." [9]Then Peter said to her,
"What made you agree to put the Lord's Spirit to the test? Listen, the footsteps
of those who have buried your husband are at the door, and they will carry you
out too." [10]She collapsed at once at his feet and died. The young men who had
just returned, finding her dead, carried her out too and buried her next to her
husband. [11]And great fear came upon the whole church and on all those who
heard about these things.

WT: [36][omits "a Levite"]. [5:3]Peter said to Ananias, "Why . . . [4]idea to do evil. [8][omits "Tell me" and "Yes"]. [10][omits "at once"].

COMMENT

Luke's story now descends to particulars after the generic idyllic description drawn in the second major summary (4:32–35). Two specific examples are given of the conduct of some early Christians. They tell of the actions of two of the well-to-do in the community that now numbers more than 8,000 (1:15; 2:41; 4:4); the names of Barnabas, Ananias, and Sapphira were remembered specifically. The first example is edifying, but the second is not; in fact, it sounds the knell of deceit and dispute that begin to ring through the community, as its human side comes to the fore.

My relating the story about Joseph Barnabas to that of Ananias and Sapphira disregards the conventional chapter division, usually attributed to Stephen Langton, the archbishop of Canterbury (d. A.D. 1228). His division separates unduly the examples that Luke has introduced at this point in the narrative. One is clearly the foil of the other; so they should be treated together.

The first example is that of Barnabas, as he will be called consistently later on in Acts. He is recalled as one of the first Christians, who was not one of the Twelve but a good example of a Christian who sacrifices property for the benefit of the *koinōnia,* all the community. What is told of him is a only a brief introduction; it foreshadows the more important role that he will play in the story of Paul. Luke strangely says that his name means "son of consolation," by which he may mean to hold up Barnabas as a source of comfort to the Christian community in Jerusalem. So consoled, it can weather storms such as that of the following incident.

The second example is that of Ananias and Sapphira, a wealthy husband and wife who practice deceit. Their names are undoubtedly recalled from earlier days and come from a "pre-Lucan tradition" (Haenchen, *Acts,* 237). They apparently seek to have the good reputation of being among those Christians who own property and sell it in order to "bring the proceeds of what was sold and lay them at the feet of the apostles" (4:34–35). They seek the glory of that reputation, however, without being willing to make the sacrifice that it entails, and with an ulterior motive of having some of the proceeds for themselves. Though they provide some money for the needs of the poor in the community, they in effect lie to it, given the existing convention. Peter, however, sees through their action and denounces Ananias for what he has done: "You have lied not to human beings, but to God" (5:4). At that Ananias drops dead. The same thing happens to his wife Sapphira, who unwittingly arrives on the scene some time after her husband has been buried, is questioned by Peter, and likewise dies. The Lucan lesson drawn from this incident: "Great fear came upon the whole church and on all those who heard about these things" (5:11; cf. 5:5). Such salutary fear recognizes how divine retribution swiftly sets in to reckon with deception. This fear stands in contrast to the consolation that Barnabas brought.

Form-critically considered, the episode is a double narrative, and the second part of it is a sort of miracle story, recounting a punitive miracle, or what has been called a rule miracle of punishment (G. Theissen). Such a description of the second part of the episode seems unsatisfactory, because this account does not have the usual elements of a miracle story known from the Synoptic tradition. Nevertheless, there is hardly any other way of categorizing the narrative, because Peter is depicted saying to Sapphira, "they will carry you out too," at which she collapses and dies (5:9–10). The instant death of the two of them occurs at the words of Peter; so it is a sort of miracle, even though Peter's words are not like the direct curative command in Synoptic miracle stories.

Interpreters usually distinguish vv 1–6 (story about Ananias) from vv 7–11 (story about Sapphira), in effect a diptych-like composition. Even if one regards the episode as a miracle story, it should be noted that the Lucan emphasis is not on the deaths of Ananias and Sapphira, but rather on how God works through the apostles, and especially through Peter in this case, within the new community to handle a scandalous activity.

Many commentators recognize that there is undoubtedly some traditional Palestinian story that Luke has inherited and wants to pass on about early Christians. The extent, however, to which he has embellished the deception of Ananias and Sapphira is not clear, despite all attempts to sort out what may be Lucan additions. Conzelmann (*Acts*, 37) believes that Luke received the story "already in written form, as is evident from his insertions" (i.e., Lucan reflections). Such a reflection would be found in v 4. Weiser (*Apg.*, 143) goes so far as to reconstruct the pre-Lucan story: vv 1, 2b, 8, 3a, 4a, 5a, 6, 5b, an account restricted to Ananias alone, which would run thus:

> There was also a certain Ananias, who with his wife Sapphira sold a piece of property. He brought only part of the proceeds and laid them at the feet of the apostles. Peter addressed him, "Tell me, did you sell that piece of property for such and such an amount?" He answered, "Yes, for that amount." But Peter said, "Ananias, why have you let Satan so fill your heart that you would lie? Was not the property yours so long as it remained unsold? Even when you had sold it, was it not still at your disposal?" When Ananias heard these words, he dropped dead. Some of the young men came forward, wrapped him up, and carried him out for burial. Great fear came upon all those who heard about it.

The rest would be a Lucan reworking that makes Sapphira as guilty as her husband. This interesting analysis, however, is far from certain. The one element that argues for an independent inherited tradition that Luke has used is v 4, which stands in tension with what Luke himself has recorded in 4:32, 34–35.

In itself, it is a good tale, dramatically composed by Luke, and serves a hortatory purpose. It is, however, the main incident in Acts that raises questions about the historical value of the Lucan narrative as a whole. Certain details in the story are strange: how does one square vv 7–10 (about Sapphira) with vv 2–6 (about Ananias)? Did Peter and those with him just sit there for "three hours" waiting for Sapphira to come? Would not someone have told her that her husband had died and been carried out for burial? The harshness of Peter's words stands in contrast to the way he is portrayed in chaps. 2–4. Why does Peter not give the two a chance to repent, as Jesus recommended in Luke 17:3–4, or to do something in reparation? Were not Ananias and Sapphira merely moral weaklings, not transgressors worthy of death and eternal damnation? What sort of church does Luke envisage here, the purity of which has to be preserved by the removal of sinners by death? Lastly, how does one relate 5:4 to 4:32, 34–35?

For these and other reasons the account has been regarded as legendary. O. Pfleiderer (*Primitive Christianity* [2 vols.; New York: Putnam, 1906, 1909], 2.210) says: it "proves itself by its physical and moral impossibility to be a legend." Similarly Dibelius (*Studies*, 15–16). Conzelmann (*Acts*, 37) says, "No historical kernel can be extracted." Haenchen (*Acts*, 241) expresses himself ambiguously. Others think that it was a cautionary paradigm recounted to neophytes to show how God watches over the purity of his community and regards sin as an affront to it (Schmitt, "Contribution," 103).

Other aspects of the story, however, have to be considered. Modern interpretation of the episode has been divided into six different modes: (1) an etiological reading, based on 1 Thess 4:13–17: divine judgment against Ananias and Sapphira explains the death of Christians before the parousia (Menoud, Boismard and Lamouille); (2) a Qumran reading, comparing the punishment of Ananias and Sapphira with that of the candidate for membership in the Essene community who deceives it in concealing property (Schmitt, Trocmé, Capper); (3) a typological interpretation, drawing its inspiration from a comparison of this episode with that of Achan in Joshua 7 (Prete and others); (4) an institutional reading, which interprets the episode as an excommunication from the institutional church, as in 1 Cor 5:13 or Matt 18:15–17 (Perrot, Schille); (5) a history-of-salvation reading, understanding the episode as an obstacle to the progress of the Spirit's guidance of the Christian testimony announced in 1:8 (P. B. Brown); (6) an "original sin" reading, which sees the episode as an example of sin at the beginning of the Christian community's existence (Marguerat).

(1) The so-called etiological reading seeks to explain the episode in terms of the question that Paul sought to answer in 1 Thess 4:13–17: why have Christians perished before the parousia, when it was thought that death had already been conquered. Ananias and Sapphira were the first Christians to die (before the parousia!), and people wanted to know why they so died. The answer: they sinned in lying to the Spirit. In other words, death was not the punishment for sin, but the sin has been proposed as the explanation for their death (Menoud, "La Mort").

(2) The Qumran reading: The story of Ananias and Sapphira has been compared with the regulations about personal property in the Essene community of Qumran. The Manual of Discipline, the community's rule book, states the following about a candidate who has gone through the two years of probation: "They shall enroll him among his brethren in the order of his rank for the Law, for justice, for the pure meal, and for the merging of his property. . . . If there be found among them anyone who lies about property and (does this) knowingly, he shall be excluded from the pure meal of the Many for a year and shall be fined a quarter of his food" (1QS 6:22–25; cf. CD 14:20–21 [punishment for six days]). At Qumran the handing over of property was obligatory in a highly structured communal mode of life; deception about property on the part of a candidate was punishable, but the punishment for such an infraction was not death, as in Acts (Schmitt, "Contribution," 104; Trocmé, *Le 'Livre'*, 198–99).

Haenchen (*Acts*, 241) stresses the difference in the two communities: not only is the punishment different, but "it is quite wrong to say that Peter acts like a Mebaqqer of Qumran: the Overseer did not execute judgments of God. . . ." Cf. CD 13:9: "He [the Overseer of the Camp] shall show mercy to them as a father *does to his children*." Moreover, there is no indication in Acts that Ananias and Sapphira had "fraudulently" taken a "vow" of dispossession in some "inner circle" of Christians, which might resemble the Essene obligation, *pace* Johnson, "The Dead Sea Manual," 131–32.

(3) The typological interpretation is based on instances in the OT that resemble this episode. The punitive miracle has a background in the story of Achan in Josh 7:1, 24–25. At the time when the Hebrews were entering the Promised Land and had taken Jericho, Achan sequestered for himself some spoils of the conquered city (a mantle from Shinar, 200 silver shekels, and a bar of gold), which should have remained among the Jericho goods that were to be consecrated to Yahweh (by *ḥērem*, "ban" [or removal from ordinary use]). All Israel stoned him to death for it, because violation of the oath taken at the destruction of Jericho resulted in Israel losing the battle for the town of Ai (Josh 7:5). Yahweh had demanded the consignment of the Jericho property, and so Joshua put all the people under oath (Josh 6:26). Achan's deed violated that oath; in effect, he stole from Yahweh. Similarly, Ananias and Sapphira misappropriate material goods and are subsequently punished; but there is no miracle in the case of Achan (Prete, "Anania e Saffira").

Other OT instances of punitive deaths have been invoked. Two of Aaron's sons, Nadab and Abihu, sought to make an unauthorized incense offering to the Lord, defying the desert community's regulations, and "fire came forth from the presence of the Lord and devoured them" (Lev 10:2). Similarly, the sick Abijah, son of King Jeroboam, died at the word of Ahijah the prophet, whom the wife of Jeroboam had sought to deceive. The prophet thus brought down evil on the royal house and the death of its male members, because of the king's wickedness and idolatry (1 Kgs 14:1–18).

Such OT incidents provide a certain typology: if that could happen at the beginning of Israel's possession of the Promised Land, so something similar could come to pass at the beginning of the Christian community's existence. The trouble with such interpretations is that, save for the verb *nosphizein*, "misappropriate" (Josh 7:1 and Acts 5:2, 3), there is little relation between the two accounts. Who is seeing the connection between them, Luke or the modern commentator?

(4) The institutional reading seeks to interpret the episode as an excommunication similar to the case of incest that Paul handled in 1 Cor 5:13 (Perrot, "Ananie et Saphire").

(5) The salvation-history reading of the episode interprets it as an obstacle to the Spirit-guided spread of the Word of God as forecast in Acts 1:8 (P. B. Brown, *The Meaning*).

(6) The so-called original-sin reading of the episode relates it to accounts of other OT instances of sin at the "beginnings": Adam and Eve in Eden (Genesis 3); the sons of God and the daughters of men, as humanity began to spread (Gen 6:1–4); the golden calf at Sinai (Exodus 32); David's treatment of Uriah shortly after his anointing as king (2 Samuel 11). Now a husband and wife again sin at an early stage of the Christian church and disrupt the idyllic story of the church's beginnings. Satan is said to be at work once again.

Some commentators have even compared the episode with that of the punitive death of a Libyan servant recounted by the second-century A.D. satirist, Lucian of Samosata (*Philopseudes* 19–20). In this case, however, there is so little similarity that it is simply farfetched. Likewise the supposed parallels from the Greco-Roman world cited by Weiser, *Apg.*, 141–42; they shed little light on the meaning of this passage.

Say what one will about such precedents in the OT, in contemporary Judaism, or the Greco-Roman world, the story of Ananias and Sapphira reveals how evil and deception finally manifest themselves among God's new people and disrupt the idyllic existence that Luke has so far depicted. Whether one can determine anything about the historicity of the incident, whether it be folkloric or legendary, it effectively teaches the lesson that Luke wants to achieve by incorporating it into his account of the early days of the Christian community: The "fear" that Luke says came upon the whole church as a result (5:11) of the deception has to be understood as salutary fear, derived from the realization of what sin can do to *koinōnia*, especially the sin of individuals involving material possessions or money. In effect, it is but another episode in the Lucan writings that teaches a lesson about how Christian disciples should use such possessions (*Luke*, 247–51). Luke dramatizes the incident by showing how Satan, and not the Holy Spirit, has dominated two early Christians and the whole episode. The play on opposites in the episode is noteworthy: life/death, Spirit/satan, truth/falsehood, need/freedom, divine/antidivine, harmony/fear. Barrett (*Acts*, 264) rightly ends his comment: "Luke used the tradition for edification . . . [but] he may not have perceived all the implications of his account."

"One must not pass the story off, however, as a unique phenomenon of the primitive church or an adjunct to Luke's ideal portrait of the church. If the incident makes us uncomfortable, it should. For one, it deals with money. Luke, who . . . probably had known personally the pitfalls of wealth, of all the Gospel writers gave the strongest treatment of money's dangers" (Polhill, *Acts*, 162).

NOTES

36. *Thus there was Joseph.* The name *Yôsēp*, "Joseph" (Gen 30:24), is not only a contraction of *Yĕhôsēp* ("May [God] add" [Ps 81:6]), but also a form shortened (by the dropping of the theophoric element) from a name like *Yôsipyāh*, "Josiphiah" (Ezra 8:10). It means, "May Yahweh add" (another child to the one just born). Many MSS (Ψ, 22, and the *Koinē* text-tradition) read *Iōsēs*, "Joses," a different Greek shortening of the same name (BDF §53.2).

surnamed by the apostles. Apostles had given Joseph a *supernomen* according to a custom in contemporary Greco-Roman society. See Cerfaux "Le 'supernomen.'" Luke again uses the prep. *apo* instead of *hypo* to express agency (see NOTE on 2:22), but MSS D, 33, 323, 2495 read *hypo*.

Barnabas (which is interpreted "Son of Consolation"). Luke's comment about the meaning of the *supernomen* "Barnabas" is problematic. "Son of Consolation" may have been a contemporary folk etymology of the name, but neither in Greek nor in Aramaic or Hebrew does the second part *nabas* suggest anything like "consolation."

Greek *Barnabas* seems to be a combination of Aramaic *bar*, "son of," and a patronymic. Of what patronymic? A Babylonian god *nb'*, "Nabu," is known from an eight-century B.C. Aramaic inscription (Sefire I A 8). This name appears in the Hebrew OT as *Něbô* (Isa 46:1), so that a personal name could have developed from it (cf. Jer 39:3; also J. K. Stark, *Personal Names in Palmyrene Inscriptions* [Oxford: Clarendon, 1971], 12, 79). This explanation of the name has been preferred by Cadbury, who attributes it also to Deissmann, Dalman, Gray; it is widely used today. The Greek ending *-as*, however, is still problematic, and one could question whether such a name, involving a pagan god, would be borne by a Jewish Levite. *Pace* Bossuyt and Radermakers (*Témoins*, 196), Barrett (*Acts*, 259), and Weiser (*Apg.*, 138), it does not reflect *bar něbû'āh*, "son of prophecy." That combination would never have produced *Barnabas*, and it is unrelated to Luke's folk etymology; nor would it reflect *bar něwāḥā'*, "son of soothing" (ascribed to A. Klostermann, *Probleme*, 8–11), which fails to explain the second *b* of Barnabas. Or *bar nuḥā'*, "son of rest" (Zahn, *Apg.*, 187–88). Or *bar nḥm'* (G. Dalman, *GJPA*, 178 n. 2), which retroverts Luke's folk-etymology into Aramaic but has no relation to Greek *Barnabas*. Or *bar nbayya* (Brock), an impossible late Syriac form. The Peshitta NT translates the name as *běrā' děbuyyā'ā'*, "son of consolation," using the root *by'*, which does not explain the initial *n*. The Syriac translator was as puzzled by it as all others.

See S. Brock, "*Barnabas: huios paraklēseōs*," *JTS* 25 (1974): 93–98; C. H. van Rhijn, "Barnabas d.i. *huios paraklēseōs* 'zoon der vertroosting' (Hand. 4:36)," *Theologische Studiën* 17 (1899): 81–82; J.-D. Burger, "L'Enigme de Barnabas," *Museum Helveticum* 3 (1946): 180–93, esp. 191–92; H. P. Rüger, "Barnabas," *TRE* 3 (1978): 604.

A few MSS of Acts (181, etc.) read rather *Barsabbas*, the second name of another Joseph (1:23), a copyist's error or harmonization.

a Levite, a Cypriot by birth. Or "by descent." I.e., a diaspora Jew who was either born on Cyprus or came from a Cypriot Jewish family belonging to the tribe of Levi. The Levites were entrusted with lowlier services in the Jerusalem Temple, but not all Levites performed such Temple functions. The fact that he is related to Cyprus may indicate that. The phrase *tō genei* can mean "native of," as in 18:2; Josephus, *Ant.* 20.7.2 §142, or "by descent," as in 4:6; Josephus, *Ant.* 15.3.1 §40. Before he became a Christian, however, he must have been resident in Jerusalem. Later on in Acts Barnabas brings consolation to the converted Saul, by introducing him to the apostles (9:27). Still later he seeks out Saul for ministry in Antioch (11:25–26), after which Saul becomes his collaborator. The two are commissioned for Saul's first missionary journey (13:1–4) and are later sent by the Antiochene church to the Jerusalem "Council" (15:2). Eventually they part, disagreeing about John Mark as a companion on further missionary journeys (15:36–40; cf. Gal 2:13). Barnabas thus becomes the first-named non-apostle in this period of salvation history, probably a Hellenist, who lives an exemplary life. On Levites, see J. Jeremias, *Jerusalem in the Time of Jesus* (Philadelphia: Fortress, 1969), 207–13.

Kypros, "Cyprus," is a Mediterranean island about 80 km south of Cilicia and

96 km west of northern Syria. Originally inhabited by Phoenicians, it came under Assyrian control in the eighth century B.C., under Persian domination in 525, and under Greek authority toward the end of the fifth century. It was annexed by the Romans in 58 B.C. It is a place that will be evangelized by Barnabas and Saul in Acts 13. Josephus tells of the flourishing Jewish community there (*Ant.* 13.10.4 §§285–88).

37. *who owned a farm that he sold.* According to Num 18:20; Deut 10:9, Levites could not own land in Israel. This may be the reason why the WT has omitted "Levite" in the description of him. The farm that he sold may have been in Cyprus, not in Israel; but see Jer 1:1; 32:7–9.

brought the money and put it at the feet of the apostles. He conformed to the convention that existed among the Jerusalem Christians, which Luke has described in vv 34–35a. He made the sacrifice to help the *koinōnia.* See further R.O.P. Taylor, "What Was Barnabas?" *CQR* 136 (1943): 59–79.

5:1. *There was also a certain Ananias, who with his wife Sapphira sold a piece of property.* Lit., "a possession," which in v 3 becomes *chōrion,* "piece of land, field." The couple is otherwise unknown, but they are used by Luke as the foil to Barnabas; they are not good examples of Christians who were "of one heart and mind" (4:32). Some commentators (Capper, Schmitt, Trocmé) have claimed that Ananias and Sapphira belonged to an inner group of Christians for whom communal ownership of goods was obligatory; but there is nothing in the Lucan story to suggest this. *Pace* Derrett, nothing in the story shows that it had anything to do with Sapphira's *ketubbāh,* "marriage contract"; to read the story that way is eisegetical.

Ananias is the grecized form of either *'Ananyāh* (Neh 3:23), meaning "Yahweh has shown himself(?)," or *Ḥănanyāh* (1 Chr 25:4), meaning "Yahweh has shown favor" (in the birth of the child so named). His wife's name is the Greek transcription of *Šappîrāh,* "Beautiful One," a substantivized Aramaic fem. adjective. Her name is not found in the OT, but the Aramaic adj. is used in Dan 4:9, 18, and the name is attested on first-century Jerusalem ossuaries (*MPAT* §§73, 117, 147; cf. J. Naveh, *Atiqot* [English Series] 14 [1980]: 55–59).

2. *With the knowledge of his wife, he put aside for himself some of the proceeds.* This is meant to implicate Sapphira in the deception of Ananias. Luke uses *nosphizein,* "misappropriate, put aside for oneself, purloin" the same verb that occurs in the Achan story in Josh 7:1 (LXX). Cf. Titus 2:10. The verb is often employed in extrabiblical Greek texts for sequestering part of a large sum belonging to a community (Lake and Cadbury, *Beginnings,* 4.50). Because this has been done with Sapphira's knowledge, there has to be a second part of the story (vv 7–9).

he brought only a part of them and laid them at the feet of the apostles. Ananias carries out publicly the act of sacrifice that other early Christians have made; but he does so only in part, not in whole, as the others have done.

3. *Peter said, "Ananias, why have you let Satan so fill your heart.* Lit., "why has Satan filled your heart?" Peter acts as the spokesman of the community, and the reader has as yet no suspicion about how Peter will react in this situation. *Pace*

Conzelmann (*Acts*, 38), Peter is not cast as a *theios anēr*, "a divine man," even though he does read Ananias's heart. Instead of the verb *eplērōsen*, MS א* and a few others read *epērōsen*, "blinded" (your heart); this is probably a mere scribal omission of *l*. P^{74} has *epeirasen*, "tempted," like the Vg *temptavit*.

"Satan" is to be understood as the personification of evil seduction, as elsewhere in Lucan writings (Luke 10:18; 11:18; 13:16; 22:3, 31; Acts 26:18); see *Luke*, 514. Just as Satan played an important role at the beginning of the Period of Jesus (Luke 4:1–13), so he plays a parallel role now at the beginning of the Period of the Church under Stress. Whereas the disciples, after their prayer, were all "filled" with the Holy Spirit (4:30), Ananias is rather "filled" with Satan; he has become Satan's plaything.

that you would lie to the Holy Spirit and put aside for yourself some of the proceeds of that field? Peter dramatizes the action of Ananias and his wife. Their knowing deception was a lie to the *koinōnia* and, even more, a lie to the Holy Spirit, i.e., to God, present to the community through the Spirit. Ananias may have thought that he was dealing only with human beings. If, as some commentators think, a vow was involved in the transaction, this might explain the "lie" about which Peter speaks. Nothing, however, in the Lucan story suggests that a vow was involved, and what Peter says in the next verse undermines that explanation. *Pace* Polhill (*Acts*, 157), mention of the Spirit is hardly "inspired" by the Spirit's role in the story of Gehazi and Naaman in 2 Kgs 5:26.

4. *Was it not yours so long as it remained unsold? Even when you had sold it, was it not still at your disposal?* Peter emphasizes the right of ownership that Ananias and his wife had of the property and still had over the proceeds of the sale, even after they had sold it. This suggests that the surrender of property or money was voluntary in the early community, unlike that of Qumran, despite what Luke affirms in 4:32b. The spontaneous decision to give it up to the community was that of Ananias and Sapphira, but their "lie" consists in the retention of part of the proceeds, when it was customary to give up all of the proceeds and they are believed to be conforming to such a custom. Their retention of part of the proceeds was thus hypocritical make-believe.

What gave you the idea of such a thing? Lit., "For what (reason was it) that you put this deed in your heart?" Peter now ascribes the deception, not to Satan, but to Ananias himself. The expression, "put (something) in one's heart" in the sense of considering or resolving, is used in 1 Sam 21:12; 29:10; Hag 2:19; Mal 2:2; Jer 12:11; Dan 1:8. Cf. Luke 1:66; 21:14.

You have lied not to human beings, but to God." This is the problem in Ananias's action. Peter's accusation merely repeats v 3c in another form. The apostles, before whose feet part of the proceeds would have been laid, are the "human beings," and Peter reacts accordingly. His query will be reformulated in v 9a, when in the second part of the episode he questions Sapphira.

5. *When Ananias heard these words, he dropped dead.* Lit., "falling down, he expired." The pres. ptc. *akouōn* expresses simultaneous action with the words of the apostle. Peter's words do not directly condemn Ananias to death, but they imply something similar, because Ananias's punitive death follows upon them,

as a result of God's judgment. It is God who strikes down the guilty. This is a sort of "shock therapy" for the community; see vv 5b, 11. Cf. Jerome, *Ep.* 130.14.5; CSEL 56.194, who maintained that Peter merely announced with prophetic spirit God's judgment so that "the punishment of two persons might be a lesson to many."

Great fear came upon all those who heard about it. Luke uses *phobos,* "fear," no longer in the sense of reverent awe, but of the salutary fear that the death of Ananias is meant to inculcate. See NOTE on 2:43; compare 19:17.

6. *Some of the young men came forward, wrapped him up, and carried him out for burial.* Ananias is wrapped in a shroud and taken out for interment. The burial is carried out even before Sapphira is informed of his death; thus, the dramatic action of the episode achieves its effect. The young men are called *neōteroi,* whereas in v 10 they are *neaniskoi,* "youths." There is no relation between them and candidates for membership in the Essene community, *pace* Schmitt ("Contribution," 104: "novices").

7. *About three hours later Ananias's wife came in, unaware of what had happened.* These details add dramatic effect to the narrative that Luke is telling. No reason is given why Sapphira comes on the scene three hours later or why those present are still assembled. Luke begins this part of the episode with *egeneto de* + *kai* + a finite verb, as in Luke 5:1; see *Luke,* 119. Haenchen's analysis of this grammatical construction (*Acts,* 238) is wrong; *diastēma* is not a nominative absolute, but an adverbial accusative, "at an interval of three hours."

8. *Peter addressed her.* Luke uses *apekrithē* in an absolute sense; see NOTE on 3:12. Peter seeks to lay bare Sapphira's involvement in the deception of her husband.

"Tell me, did you sell that piece of property for such and such an amount?" Lit., "whether for so much you sold the property." One wonders why a specific amount is not mentioned by Peter, but that is only a part of the story-telling technique. Peter seeks to get the woman to reflect on what she and her husband have done.

She answered, "Yes, for that amount." Lit., "for so much."

9. *Then Peter said to her, "What made you agree to put the Lord's Spirit to the test?* Lit., "what (was it) that it was agreed upon by you (pl.) together to test. . . ." Peter queries about the motivation that made Sapphira comply with the deception of Ananias. His words imply that she could have disagreed and dissuaded her husband from such a course of action. The deception was not merely a "lie" to God or the Holy Spirit (5:3, 4), but a putting of God's Spirit to the test. The "testing" of God has an OT background in Exod 17:2; Num 20:13, 24 (Israel's rebellious tempting of God in the desert); Ps 106:32. Luke uses the same verb (*peirazein*) as is used of Israel in Deut 33:8 (LXX). *Kyrios* refers to Yahweh, whose Spirit has been put to the test. See NOTE on 1:24; cf. Luke 4:18; Acts 8:39.

Listen, the footsteps of those who have buried your husband are at the door, and they will carry you out too." Peter refers to the return of the "young men" of 5:6. His words to Sapphira, introduced by *idou,* "behold," imply a punitive death.

They are not, however, like the curative command of the Synoptic miracles; the immediate execution is divine. Haenchen (*Acts,* 239) clearly exaggerates: "Peter *kills* her by announcing her husband's demise and her own imminent death" (his italics); similarly C. H. Rieu (*Acts,* 124). For the OT figurative use of *podes,* "feet," see Isa 59:7; 52:7.

10. *She collapsed at once at his feet and died.* Sapphira shares the same fate as her husband Ananias; compare v 5. Sapphira does not die of "shame," as Reicke (*Glaube,* 89) would have it. That sort of psychological explanation seeks to rid the story of the punitive miracle. Sapphira collapses at the feet of an apostle, where the full sum of the money should have been deposited.

The young men who had just returned, finding her dead, carried her out too and buried her next to her husband. Sapphira shared her husband's deception in life, and now she shares burial with him in death.

11. *great fear came upon the whole church and on all those who heard about these things.* Luke repeats the reaction recorded in v 5b, now extending it beyond the immediate community.

For the first time in Acts one meets *ekklēsia,* "church," as the designation of the Christian community in Jerusalem; Luke is using the standard term current in his day, as he reflects on this incident and records with hindsight the community's reaction to it. *Ekklēsia* now begins to appear regularly in Acts, especially after 8:1b. See 8:3; 9:31; 11:22, 26; 12:1, 5; 13:1; 14:23, 27; 15:3, 4, 22, 41; 16:5; 18:22; 19:32, 39, 40; 20:17, 28. It is not found in the Lucan Gospel. Three things are significant in the Lucan use of *ekklēsia:* (1) The emergence of the term in a context that mentions Saul (Paul), whose use of it in his writings did much to popularize it. (2) It is not necessarily the oldest or most primitive title for the community (see NOTES on 2:42; 9:2), despite what one might be tempted to conclude from Matt 16:18; 18:17, the only two places where the word is found in the gospel tradition. (3) The frequency with which it designates a local or particular Christian community; in time, even in narratives of Acts, it begins to assume the connotation of the universal church transcending local boundaries.

A different sense of *ekklēsia* is found in 7:38, "congregation assembly," reflecting its OT usage. In the LXX it designates the Hebrews wandering in the desert (e.g. Deut 4:10; 9:10; 18:16; 31:30), or the assembly of returned exiles (Ezra 10:8), or the cultic assembly of Israel (2 Chr 6:3). There it often translates Hebrew *qāhāl,* which is found occasionally also in Qumran writings for the Essene community (e.g., 1QM 4:10 [*qĕhal 'ēl*]; 1QSa 1:25; 2:4; CD 7:17; 11:22; 12:6). This usage shows its aptness for describing a group of persons holding the same religious convictions. For older discussions of the term, see L. Rost, *Die Vorstufen von Kirche und Synagoge im Alten Testament: Ein wortgeschichtliche Untersuchung* (BWANT 76; Stuttgart: Kohlhammer, 1938; repr. Darmstadt: Wissenschaftliche Buchgesellschaft, 1967); J. L. Murphy, "'Ekklesia' and the Septuagint," AER 139 (1958): 381–90; K. L. Schmidt, "Die Kirche des Urchristentums: Eine lexikographische und biblisch-theologische Studie," *Festgabe für Adolf Deissmann . . .* (Tübingen: Mohr [Siebeck], 1927): 258–319.

BIBLIOGRAPHY (4:36–5:11)

Boismard, M.-E. and A. Lamouille, *Les Actes des deux Apôtres,* 2.165.

Brown, P. B., *The Meaning and Function of Acts 5:1–11 in the Purpose of Luke-Acts* (Boston: Boston University Press, 1969).

Cadbury, H. J., "Four Features of Lucan Style," *StLA,* 87–102.

———, "Some Semitic Personal Names in Luke-Acts," *Amicitiae Corolla: A Volume of Essays Presented to James Rendel Harris* . . . (ed. H. G. Wood; London: University of London Press, 1933) 45–56.

Capper, B. J., "The Interpretation of Acts 5.4," *JSNT* 19 (1983): 117–31.

Cerfaux, L., "St. Barnabé, apôtre des gentiles," *CollDiocTor* 23 (1927–28): 209–17.

———, "Le 'supernomen' dans le livre des Actes," *ETL* 15 (1938): 74–80.

D'Alès, A., "Actes, V, 3," *RSR* 24 (1934): 199–200.

Derrett, J. D. M., "Ananias, Sapphira, and the Right of Property," *DownRev* 89 (1971): 225–32.

Hannam, W. L., "Ananias and Sapphira," *London Quarterly and Holborn Review* 169 (January 1944): 19–24.

Johnson, S. E., "The Dead Sea Manual of Discipline and the Jerusalem Church of Acts," *The Scrolls and the New Testament* (ed. K. Stendahl; rev. J. H. Charlesworth; New York: Crossroad, 1991), 129–42, 273–75.

Marguerat, D., "Ananias et Saphira (Actes 5,1–11): Le viol du sacré," *LumVie* 42/5 (1993): 51–63.

———, "La mort d'Ananias et Saphira (Ac 5.1–11) dans la stratégie narrative de Luc," *NTS* 39 (1993): 209–26.

———, "Terreur dans l'église: Le drame d'Ananias et Saphira (Actes 5,1–11), *FV* 91 (1992): 77–88.

Menoud, P.-H., "La mort d'Ananias et de Saphira (Actes 5. 1–11)," *Aux sources de la tradition chrétienne: Mélanges offerts à M. Maurice Goguel* . . . (Bibliothèque théologique; ed. O. Cullmann and P.-H. Menoud; Neuchâtel/Paris: Delachaux et Niestlé, 1950), 146–54.

O'Toole, R. F., "'You Did Not Lie to Us (Human Beings) but to God' (Acts 5,4c)," *Bib* 76 (1995): 182–209.

Perrot, C., "Ananie et Saphire: Le jugement ecclésial et la justice divine," *L'Année canonique* 25 (1981): 109–24, esp. 119–20.

Prete, B., "Anania e Saffira (*At* 5,1–11): Componenti letterarie e dottrinali," *RivB* 36 (1988): 463–86.

Reicke, B., *Glaube und Leben der Urgemeinde: Bemerkungen zu Apg. 1–7* (ATANT 32; Zurich: Zwingli-V., 1957).

Reimer, I. R., *Women in the Acts of the Apostles,* 1–29.

Scheidweiler, F., "Zu Acta 5,4," *ZNW* 49 (1958): 136–37.

Schmitt, J., "Contribution à l'étude de la discipline pénitentielle dans l'église primitive à la lumière des textes de Qumran," *Les manuscrits de la Mer Morte:* Colloque de Strasbourg *25–27 mai 1955* (Paris: Presses Universitaires de France, 1957), 93–109 (cf. *RevScRel* 30 [1956]: 273–80).

Trocmé, E., *Le 'Livre des Actes' et l'histoire*, 197–99.
Weiser, A., "Das Gottesurteil über Hananias und Saphira: Apg 5,1–11," *TGl* 69 (1979): 148–58.

5. Third Major Summary: A Caring Community (5:12–16)

12 Many signs and wonders were wrought among the people at the hands of the
apostles. All of them used to meet with one accord in Solomon's Colonnade.
13 No one else dared to join them, yet the people held them in high esteem.
14 More than ever, believers in the Lord were added to them, great numbers of
men and women. 15 As a result, they would even carry the sick out into the streets
and lay them on cots and mats so that, when Peter would pass by, his shadow
might fall at least on one or another of them. 16 Then too a great number of
people from towns around Jerusalem would gather, bringing the sick and those
troubled by unclean spirits, who were all cured.

WT: 12 [omits "Many" and "All"]. 13 [omits "else"]. 15 [adds at the end of the verse:] and they were cured of every disease with which each of them was afflicted. 16 [omits "too"] . . . and all of them were healed.

COMMENT

On the heels of the story about Ananias and Sapphira Luke introduces his third major summary, yet another description of the Christian community in Jerusalem. It is again a Lucan composition, an idyllic, generalizing description resembling the two earlier summaries (2:42–47; 4:32–35) and revealing that the prayer of the community, that God might stretch forth his hand to cure and perform signs and wonders (4:30), has been heard. This summary is likewise conflated, consisting of a unit that tells of the coming together of Christians and people in meetings (vv 12b–14, 16a), into which notices about wonder working have been inserted (vv 12a, 15, 16b). These notices repeat in different wording the one already found in 2:43. The esteem for the apostles and other Christians among people, who apparently have not yet been convinced by the Christian message, continues to grow.

Jeremias regarded the original tradition to be found in vv 11–14, to which vv 15–16, influenced by 8:6–8 and 19:11–12, were added later. Benoit identified the original stratum as vv 12a, 15–16, to which a later hand has added vv 12b–14 to the cohesive summary. Zimmermann took vv 12a, 15 to be the original tradition, into which the other elements have been secondarily introduced. Again, Haenchen regards the whole summary as a Lucan composition, a generalization of the effects of the Petrine miracle.

In the summary, the miracles of the apostles again come to the fore; it is not just Peter but other apostles as well who perform them. For the first time one finds in this summary a mention of the reaction of people to the Christian message outside of Jerusalem, as it tells how great numbers of people brought the sick "from towns around Jerusalem" to Peter (5:16). Also new is the mention of the sick in great numbers; they stand in contrast to the individual man lame from birth cured in chap. 3.

The Lucan summary makes much of the miraculous cures wrought by Peter and other apostles among the people of Jerusalem and surrounding towns. The people who bring their sick to the Christians have obviously put their trust in them. Many must have been moved by faith in the Word that the apostles have been preaching. These people were moved too by what they saw in the Christians who gathered "with one accord in Solomon's Colonnade" (5:12). The faith and the good example of the apostles and other Christians have moved people to esteem them highly and put trust in them. Such traits manifest the Christians as a caring community.

NOTES

12. *Many signs and wonders were wrought among the people at the hands of the apostles.* See Note on 2:22; cf. 2:43, where a similar report is made about apostolic wonder working.

All of them used to meet with one accord in Solomon's Colonnade. Lit., "and they were all with one accord in . . ." See Notes on 1:14; 3:11. The "all" refers to the apostles, who have been working miracles among the people, from whom they seem to be distinguished in v 13. The Lucan hyperbole again comes to the fore; see Note on 2:44.

13. *No one else dared to join them.* Lit., "of the rest no one dared to join them," i.e., the apostles. It is not clear, however, to whom the term *hoi loipoi,* "the rest," refers. Since *ho laos,* "the people," occurs in the next clause, "the rest" seems to be different from "the people." Perhaps it refers to members of the three classes mentioned in 4:5, the leaders, elders, and scribes. Conzelmann (*Acts,* 39) sees an "apparent contradiction" between vv 13 and 14 and attributes it to the clumsiness of the narrator. But Weiser (*Apg.,* 150) may be right in suggesting that a spatial distance from the Christians in Solomon's Colonnade is meant. Those who held them in esteem were nevertheless reluctant to associate closely with them. Pesch (*Apg.,* 206) sees "the rest" as Christians who were not apostles, as does Johnson (*Acts,* 95), but Haenchen and Conzelmann take the term to refer to non-Christians. Schneider (*Apg.,* 381) considers "the rest" to be the same as "the people," which may the option to be preferred.

yet the people held them in high esteem. Lit., "the people made much of them," viz., the apostles. "The people" must refer to inhabitants of Jerusalem who have not yet become Christians. This remark echoes what was said in 2:47 and 4:33.

14. *More than ever, believers in the Lord were added to them, great numbers of men and women.* Lit., "believers in the Lord were added to a greater degree, multitudes of men and women." Or possibly, "more than ever believers were

added to the Lord" *(RSV)*. Here *Kyrios* refers to the risen Christ (see NOTE on 2:36). The great number of such believers (Christians) remains unspecified. The verb "were added" is undoubtedly to be understood as a theological passive, pointing to God's activity in adding believers to the Jerusalem community (ZBG §236). It too would be responsible for the miraculous cures of the apostles.

15. *As a result, they would even carry the sick out into the streets and lay them on cots and mats.* This verse, though introduced by the consecutive conj. *hōste*, does not logically follow from what precedes in vv 12–14. In this summary Luke is simply piling up varying motifs (see Haenchen, *Acts*, 243–45), which idyllically describe the increase in numbers of Christians and the effect that they are having on the populace of Jerusalem. The noun *klinarion*, "cot," occurs only here in the NT; it is the diminutive of *klinē*, "bed," used in Luke 5:18; 8:16; 17:34. *Krabattos*, "mattress, pallet," occurs only here and in 9:33 in the Lucan writings. Both are mentioned to connote the portable character of the bedding on which the sick lay.

so that, when Peter would pass by, his shadow might fall at least on one or another of them. This is a new mode of miracle working, not found in the Gospels, healing by an efficacious shadow. The shadow is understood as something more than merely the spot where the sunlight cannot fall. Because it reflects the shape of the person, it is regarded in some primitive thinking as something powerful, a vital part of a person. See van der Horst, "Peter's Shadow."

A cure by Peter's shadow is strange, but it is something similar to what Luke recounts about handkerchiefs or aprons in Paul's cures (19:12). Luke has no qualms about apostolic power, especially in a context of faith (v 14). To read this detail about the effectiveness of Peter's shadow as an instance in which Luke reveals his leaning toward "early catholicism" *(Frühkatholizismus)* borders on the absurd, *pace* W. Bieder; see the remarks of B. Reicke, *Int* 13 (1959): 168–69. Luke is not recounting such miracles *ad maiorem apostolorum gloriam*. "In the shadow the *dynamis* [power] of a person can be effective, when God stands behind it; in that way wondrous things can happen" (Schneider, *Apg*., 1.382).

The last clause is introduced by the conj. *hina*, which expresses purpose, stating the reason why people brought out the sick. It ends the sentence introduced by the consecutive conj. *hōste* at the head of the verse. The whole verse reveals the conviction that the people of Jerusalem had concerning the apostles and their power and shows why they were held in great esteem.

The WT adds the effect of this Petrine miracle: "and they were cured of every disease with which each of them was afflicted." MSS of this text-tradition, however, differ slightly in the wording of the addition: MS D has, *apēllassonto gar apo pasēs astheneias hōs eichen hekastos autōn*, whereas MS E reads, *kai rhysthōsin apo pasēs astheneias hēs eichon*.

16. *Then too a great number of people from towns around Jerusalem would gather.* Lit., "the multitude from the towns in the vicinity would also gather (at) Jerusalem." The Alexandrian text-tradition uses *Hierousalem* as an adv., "at Jerusalem," whereas MSS D, E, Ψ, 36, 181, etc., read *eis H.*, which precedes the ptc. *pherontes* so that it means, "would also gather, bringing to Jerusalem the sick . . ."

bringing the sick and those troubled by unclean spirits, who were all cured. I.e., both bodily and mentally ill people were healed. "Troubled by unclean spirits" is a phrase also used in Luke 6:18. Luke uses a Palestinian Jewish expression, "unclean spirit," which has its Aramaic counterpart in 1 QapGen 20:16–17 (see NOTE on Luke 4:33). The ancients used such terms to explain serious psychic disturbances, whose causes they were unable to diagnose. Cf. Acts 19:12. What is described in this verse leads to the reaction of the religious authorities, which begins in 5:17. Note the Lucan hyperbole in "all"; see NOTE on 2:44.

BIBLIOGRAPHY (5:12–16)

Bieder, W., "Der Petrusschatten, Apg. 5,15," *TZ* 16 (1960): 407–9.

Horst, P. W. van der, "Peter's Shadow: The Religio-Historical Background of Acts v.15," *NTS* 23 (1976–77): 204–12.

Schwartz, D. A., "Non-Joining Sympathizers (Acts 5,13–14)," *Bib* 64 (1983): 550–55.

6. FURTHER PERSECUTION OF THE APOSTLES (5:17–42)

17 Then the high priest reacted, he and his colleagues, the party of the Sadducees;
they were filled with jealousy 18 and arrested the apostles and put them in the
public jail. 19 But during the night the angel of the Lord opened the gates of the
prison, led them out, and said, 20 "Go, take your place in the Temple, and tell
the people all about this Life." 21 Hearing this, they entered the Temple about
dawn and continued their teaching. When the high priest and his colleagues
arrived, they convened the Sanhedrin, the full senate of the Israelites, and sent
to the prison to have the apostles brought in. 22 When the officers arrived, they
did not find them in the prison; they returned and reported, 23 "We found the
prison securely locked, with sentries posted at the gates, but when we opened
them, we found no one inside." 24 Now when the captain of the Temple guard
and the chief priests heard this report, they could make nothing of it, or what it
might become. 25 Then someone arrived and reported, "Look, the men whom
you put in prison are standing in the Temple, even teaching the people."
26 Whereupon the captain went off with his officers and brought them in, but
without using force, for they feared the people, that they might be stoned.
27 When they had brought them in and made them stand before the Sanhedrin,
the high priest interrogated them, saying, 28 "We ordered you, [did we not], not
to teach in that name? Yet you have filled Jerusalem with your teaching, and you
seek to bring that man's blood upon us." 29 But Peter and the apostles said in reply,
"One must obey God rather than human beings! 30 The God of our ancestors has
raised up Jesus, whom you had killed by hanging him on a tree. 31 It is he whom
God has exalted to his right hand as leader and savior, [to] grant Israel repentance
and forgiveness of sins. 32 We are witnesses of these things, and so is the Holy

Spirit that God has given to those who obey him." 33 When they heard this, they were infuriated and wanted to do away with them. 34 But a certain Pharisee, Gamaliel by name, a teacher of the law esteemed by all the people, stood up in the Sanhedrin and ordered these men out of court for a short time. 35 He said to them, "Fellow Israelites, be careful about what you are going to do to these men. 36 Not long ago there appeared Theudas, trying to pass himself off as somebody important, and about four hundred men joined him. But he was killed, and all those who were duped by him were disbanded, and they came to nothing. 37 After him, at the time of the census, there appeared Judas the Galilean, and he drew away some of the people to follow him. But he too perished, and all those who were duped by him were dispersed. 38 So in the present case I say to you, keep your distance from these men and let them be. For if this scheme or this undertaking is of human design, it will destroy itself. 39 But if it is of God, you will not be able to destroy them; you may even find yourselves fighting against God." They were won over by him. 40 After calling in the apostles and having them flogged, they ordered them not to speak again in the name of Jesus and let them go. 41 These then left the presence of the Sanhedrin full of joy that they had been judged worthy of ill-treatment for the sake of that name. 42 Day after day, both in the Temple and in house after house, they never stopped teaching and preaching Jesus as the Messiah.

WT: 17 Annas, the high priest. 18 [adds at the end of the verse] and each one went to his own quarters. 19 [omits "led them out"]. 21 [instead of "hearing this"] going out . . . When the high priest and his colleagues awoke at dawn, they . . . 22 arrived, having opened the prison, they . . . [omits "in the prison"]. 23 posted before the gates . . . [omits "inside"]. 25 someone reported. 26 force, fearing they might be stoned by the people. 27 [omits "and made them stand"] brought them before the Sanhedrin, the captain began to say. 29 in reply to them . . . [adds at the end of the verse] They said, "God." Then Peter said to them. 31 exalted to his glory . . . sins through him. 32 of all these things, and so is the Spirit that he has given . . . 34 But someone from the Sanhedrin stood up, a Pharisee, Gamaliel . . . [omits "all"] . . . ordered the apostles [omits "for a short time"]. 35 said to the whole Sanhedrin. 36 a certain Theudas . . . as somebody great, and four hundred men followed him. But he was destroyed, and through him they came to nothing. 37 Then there appeared, at the time . . . a large number of people . . . and as many as were duped . . . 38 in the present case, brothers, . . . let them be; do not defile your hands. For if this power is of human device, its force will destroy itself. 39 destroy them, neither you nor kings nor tyrants. So keep away from these men, lest you find yourselves . . . 40 flogged, they dismissed them, ordering them . . . 41 These then, having been dismissed, went from the presence . . . 42 Jesus as the Lord.

COMMENT

After the foregoing summary, Luke resumes the narrative proper with an account of further persecution of the apostles by religious authorities in Jerusalem. The account begins almost in medias res, as Luke opens it with a reference to the high priest's reaction. The high priest is hardly reacting to the summary just given, but rather to the effect that the apostles were having among the people through their teaching and healing recounted in the last verse of the summary. Into the narrative Luke inserts once again a short speech of Peter (5:29–32). It is supposed to be the reply that Peter and the apostles make to the charge of the high priest, but in effect it is another Petrine speech, resembling that in 4:8–12. In reaction to Peter's words, the Pharisee Gamaliel rises in the Sanhedrin, puts the apostles outside, and counsels his colleagues to be prudent. He cites other examples of individuals who tried to dupe the people in the past, all of which came to nothing. He introduces a consideration not heard before: "If this scheme or this undertaking is of human design, it will destroy itself. But if it is of God, you will not be able to destroy them; you may even find yourselves fighting against God" (5:39). The Sanhedrin is persuaded by his words, and, having flogged the apostles, they order them once more "not to speak again in the name of Jesus" (5:40). Luke's conclusion is typical: the apostles rejoice in such persecution.

The structure of the episode can be seen in this way:

Verses 17–18	Narrative Introduction
19–21a	Miracle: The Angelic Deliverance of the Apostles
21b–26	Setting for Judicial Transaction
27–40	The Judicial Transaction
28	High-Priestly Charge
29–32	Reply: Peter's Speech
33–34	Reaction of the Sanhedrin
35–39ab	Advice: Gamaliel's Speech
39c–40	Reaction of the Sanhedrin
41–42	Reaction of the Apostles

The question that this episode raises is whether it is merely a doublet of that recounted in 4:1–22. Commentators such as Harnack, Bauernfeind, and Reicke have considered it such: Luke would have made two episodes out of what he found in independent sources, which actually were accounts of the one appearance of Peter and John before the Sanhedrin. Not all interpreters, however, agree with such an analysis. Jeremias, for instance, insists on the difference of the accounts and on the progress that chap. 5 makes over chap. 4. As would have been required in criminal trials, a warning had to be given before punishment was meted out. In 4:17 the warning is given, and in 5:40 the apostles are flogged and warned yet again ("Untersuchungen," 205–21).

Jeremias's analysis has problems, some of which are mentioned by Conzelmann (*Acts*, 41), but Jeremias has stressed at least a difference in the two accounts with which one has to reckon. Moreover, this episode incorporates another kind of miracle story; it is not like those of the gospel tradition, but it is an angelic deliverance of the apostles. Nothing like that, however, was recounted in chap. 4. The episode further introduces Gamaliel and the advice that he gives to the Sanhedrin, a significant difference from chap. 4. No matter what one might decide about the use of sources in chaps. 4 and 5, the two episodes should be reckoned for what they are: independent accounts of confrontations of the apostles with religious authorities in Jerusalem, undoubtedly derived by Luke from Palestinian sources. To the latter, one should undoubtedly ascribe in this episode at least the imprisonment of the apostles, their appearance before the Sanhedrin, and Gamaliel's intervention. Peter's speech and Gamaliel's advice may well be largely Lucan compositions.

The miracle, the angelic deliverance of the apostles from prison, manifests once again heavenly protection for God's emissaries, but it plays no part in the rest of the account, being almost passed over. The two most important elements in the episode are the speech of Peter (vv 29–32) and that of Gamaliel (vv 35–39). One is the foil to the other. Peter's speech is again apologetic and kerygmatic; it defends the apostles' stand and their activity and proclaims anew the Christian message: "you had killed (Jesus) by hanging him on a tree," but God "has raised him up," and we are witnesses to him (5:30, 32). It scarcely advances the Lucan story. The only new elements that this Petrine speech introduces are the allusion to Deut 21:22–23 and the description of Jesus' crucifixion as a hanging on a tree.

In the speech of Gamaliel, which is one of judicial advice and counsel, one hears a Pharisee counseling prudence. After the speech of the risen Christ (1:4–5, 7–8), it is the first speech in Acts by a non-Christian. It is a minatory speech: Gamaliel warns the Sanhedrin and thereby implicitly defends the apostles. Three parts of it can be distinguished: (1) a prudent warning (5:35b); (2) historical examples of other leaders who gathered followers (5:36–37); (3) a conclusion (5:38–39). There is no allusion to anything in the OT; historical examples replace that in this speech. Luke thus depicts a prominent Jewish authority showing tolerance of Christianity: what Gamaliel proposes is the apologetic concern of Luke himself. Gamaliel is not a Jewish religious authority who accepts the Christian message, but one who can find in his way of thinking a way to cope with it. Coming from such a respected Pharisee, the advice contributes to the Lucan picture of Christianity as the logical outgrowth of Pharisaic Judaism. The relevance of his counsel has to be seen, then, in the course of the larger development of this theme in the narrative of Acts. What is implied here will only come to full understanding toward the end of Acts. Luke thus makes Gamaliel utter a supreme irony. As the leading Pharisee of the day, he counsels the Jerusalem religious leaders to tolerate a movement that Luke sees as the logical continuation of Pharisaism itself.

The speech of Gamaliel contains a notorious problem, which calls in question Luke's knowledge of Palestinian history. He makes Gamaliel at this early stage of church history, speak of Theudas, who only appeared almost a decade later, in the time of the procurator C. Cuspius Fadus (A.D. 44–46). Moreover, Luke thinks that Theudas's uprising was followed by that of Judas the Galilean "at the time of the census" (5:37). The problem was well stated by Dibelius:

> Here, two revolutionary movements are mentioned, the risings of Theudas and of Judas of Galilee. Their example is intended to show that in some circumstances, when the leader is dead, the adherents cease to be dangerous. Gamaliel cannot have spoken in this way for, at the time of this speech, Theudas had not yet appeared on the scene. Besides, the historical sequence is reversed here; it was not Theudas who appeared first, and then *(meta touton)*

> Judas, but first Judas 'at the time of the census' and then Theudas under the procurator Cuspius Fadus, who assumed office in A.D. 44. (*Studies*, 186)

It is to be noted that Josephus speaks similarly of the incident of Theudas (*Ant.* 20.5.1 §§97–98) and *then*, when speaking about the procurator Alexander's crucifixion of James and Simon (*Ant.* 20.5.2 §102), introduces a flashback about the revolt under Judas the Galilean, who was their father. In other words, Josephus too has the order Theudas, Judas; but he does not insert the phrase "after him," as does Luke, and knows their correct dates. One has to admit with Dibelius that "Luke has obviously recorded these incidents as freely as he composed the whole speech" (ibid., 187). Gamaliel's speech suits the setting given to it in Acts and for that reason has a bit of verisimilitude, in the manner of Thucydidean speeches.

Many attempts have been made to explain this confusion. Some have maintained that there was another rebel named Theudas in the last days of Herod the Great (37–4 B.C.); but no real evidence supports such a claim. There is little likelihood that Luke was dependent on Josephus and his way of referring to the two incidents, so that one cannot so explain the confusion. The understanding of Swain ("Gamaliel's Speech") is even less convincing: that Gamaliel's speech was misplaced by Luke; that it should have been used in chap. 12 after Peter was once again imprisoned. Whatever one says about Gamaliel's speech, one has to live with it in its present form, despite the confusion it causes. We have no real answer as to why Luke so composed it, but as Hemer (*Book of Acts*, 163) has put it, "one such slip on his [Luke's] part would not entitle us to argue for his general unreliability. The fact that Luke's background information can so often be corroborated may suggest that it is wiser to leave this particular matter open rather than to condemn Luke of a blunder."

NOTES

17. *Then the high priest reacted.* Lit., "the high priest standing up," an abrupt beginning for this episode. *Anastas de* is the reading in MSS P^{45}, P^{74}, ℵ, A, B, D, 0189, and 33, but some Western MSS read *Annas de,* thus introducing the name of Annas, called the "high priest" in 4:6. MS E and some VL texts read rather, *kai tauta blepōn anastas,* "Seeing these things, the high priest stood up."

he and his colleagues, the party of the Sadducees. See NOTE on 4:1. The Sadducees are called *hairesis,* "party, school, sect," the very word that Josephus uses to describe the different kinds of Jews of his day (*Ant.* 13.5.9 §171; 20.9.1 §199; *Life* 2 §§10, 12; 38 §191; *J.W.* 2.8.2 §118). Luke will use it again, both of Jewish parties (15:5; 26:5) and of "Nazoreans" (= Christians, 24:5, 14; 28:22).

they were filled with jealousy 18. *and arrested the apostles and put them in the public jail.* Jealousy is aroused by the success of these unlettered and ordinary men among the Jerusalem people. The authorities treat the apostles again as they did in 4:3. At the end Luke adds *dēmosia,* "public," which may modify *tērēsei,* "public jail, prison" but may be used as an adv., "publicly (put them in jail)"; compare 16:37; 18:28; 20:20.

19. *during the night the angel of the Lord opened the gates of the prison, led them out.* *Angelos Kyriou* is the Greek translation of a standard Hebrew expression *mal'ak Yhwh,* used in older OT books as a theophanic element to express the presence of God to his people or to bring them messages (Gen 16:7–11; 21:17; 22:10–18; 31:11–13; Exod 3:2–6; Judg 2:1–5). Used in Luke 1:11 (see NOTE there); 2:9; 12:8–9; 15:10, it appears again in Acts 8:26; 10:3; 12:7, 23. For other instances of angelic deliverance from prison, see 12:6–11; 16:25–26. Conzelmann (*Acts,* 41) maintains that the miraculous opening of the gates is "artificial" but fails to explain what is meant by that.

20. *"Go, take your place in the Temple, and tell the people all about this Life."* Lit., "speak all the words of this life." The angel's instruction to the liberated apostles is an encouragement to proclaim the message about an effect of the Christ-event, "this Life." Recall 3:15, where Christ is called "the author of life." In 13:26 it will be phrased as "this salvation." See *Luke,* 225–26.

21. *Hearing this, they entered the Temple about dawn and continued their teaching.* Obedient to the angel's instruction, the apostles return to the Temple area at early morning and begin once again to evangelize the people there. So they continue their apostolic testimony. The prep. *hypo* is used in a temporal sense, as in classical Greek, with *ton orthron,* "the dawn" (BDF §232.1).

When the high priest and his colleagues arrived, they convened the Sanhedrin, the full senate of the Israelites. Lit., "the high priest arriving and those with him." The Sanhedrin (see NOTE on 4:15) is now possibly identified as *gerousia,* "body of elders." Because Luke adds *kai pasan tēn gerousian tōn huiōn Israēl,* "and all the body of elders of the sons of Israel," some commentators think that this may be a group different from the Sanhedrin (Schneider, *Apg.,* 1.390), but *kai* seems to be used as an adv. "even"; it is merely another way of designating the Sanhedrin (*EDNT,* 1.245; Polhill, *Acts,* 167; ZBG §455ζ). See Exod 3:16; 12:21 for the origin of the explanatory phrase; cf. Ezra 5:9; 6:7; 1 Macc 12:6, 35; 14:20; 2 Macc 1:10; and Josephus, *Ant.* 13.5.8 §166 for the use of *gerousia.*

sent to the prison to have the apostles brought in. Whereas the prison was called *tērēsis dēmosia,* "public custody" (5:18), and *phylakē,* "guard-house" (5:19), it is now called *desmōtērion,* "place of binding." Cf. 12:19. The apostles are sent for so that the interrogation might begin. The pass. infin. *achthēnai,* "to be brought in," is used with a verb of commanding (BDF §392.4).

22. *When the officers arrived, they did not find them in the prison; they returned and reported,* 23. *"We found the prison securely locked."* Lit., "closed with all security." The officers rush back with the surprising news. Luke writes *en pasē asphaleia,* using hyperbolically a Greek expression that has found its Aramaic counterpart in a letter of Bar Cochba, *b'splyh* (*IEJ* 11 [1961]:41–42).

with sentries posted at the gates, but when we opened them, we found no one inside." The officers know nothing of the angelic deliverance of the apostles.

24. *Now when the captain of the Temple guard and the chief priests heard this report.* See NOTES on 4:1, 6.

they could make nothing of it, or what it might become. The perplexity of the authorities is thus recorded. Cf. 10:17.

25. *Then someone arrived and reported, "Look, the men whom you put in prison are standing in the Temple, even teaching the people."* Lit., "behold, the men are in the Temple, standing and teaching. . . ." So it is reported to the authorities that the apostles had not run off but were within the Temple precincts, where they were dutifully carrying out the angel's instruction.

26. *Whereupon the captain went off with his officers and brought them in, but without using force.* One cannot miss the irony of the situation.

for they feared the people, that they might be stoned. So reads the clumsy Alexandrian text-tradition. Codex Bezae clarifies the statement, reading the ptc. *phoboumenoi,* "fearing (lest they might be stoned)."

27. *When they had brought them in and made them stand before the Sanhedrin, the high priest interrogated them.* Finally the action that the religious leaders planned is achieved: the apostles stand trial before the Sanhedrin a second time.

28. *"We ordered you, [did we not], not to teach in that name?* Lit., "Did we not order you with an order," i.e., did we not strictly order you? Thus, the high priest refers to the threats recorded in 4:18, 21. The name of Jesus is studiously avoided by him. The dat. *parangeliā* functions as an intensifier of the verb. It is the way the LXX often translates the Hebrew intensifying infin. absol., with a Greek abstract noun that modifies a verb of the same root (BDF §198.6). Cf. the same usage in 2:17, 30; 16:28; 23:14; Luke 22:15.

Yet you have filled Jerusalem with your teaching. Lucan hyperbole serves to underline the success of apostolic preaching. Not only the news about the miraculous cure, but even the teaching of the apostles, has spread thoroughly abroad in the city.

you seek to bring that man's blood upon us." The high priest does not interrogate Peter or ask how the apostles escaped from prison; rather he seeks to set in sharp relief their disobedience of the commands given them. Again the high priest avoids mention of Jesus' name. This is the apostles' main accusation against the Jewish authorities (see 2:36c; 3:14–15; esp. 4:10). The high priest insinuates that the apostles "seek divine retribution for the killing of Jesus" (Haenchen, *Acts,* 251), with which he obviously does not agree. For "blood" as a metaphor for the taking of life, see 2 Sam 1:16; Ezek 33:4 (LXX). Cf. Lev 20:9; Josh 2:19; Matt 27:25.

29. *Peter and the apostles said in reply.* This and the next three verses constitute Peter's answer to the charge of the high priest; in effect, in this speech he again bears testimony. Recall Jesus' words in Luke 21:13. Persecution provides the occasion for bearing witness.

"One must obey God rather than human beings! So Peter repeats substantially what he said in 4:19. He does not deny that he and John have disregarded the commands given them, but he seeks rather to put them in their proper perspective: they come only from human beings! Recall the answer of Socrates quoted in NOTE on 4:19.

30. *The God of our ancestors has raised up Jesus, whom you had killed.* In mentioning "the God of our ancestors," Peter reformulates the way he described God in 3:13. Again the verb *egeirein* is used to express God's bringing about Jesus'

resurrection (see NOTE on 2:24). Peter once again points his accusatory finger at the religious authorities in Jerusalem for the death of Jesus, as he did in 2:36c; 3:14–15; 4:10.

by hanging him on a tree. This new element in Peter's accusation will reappear in 10:39. *Kremasantes epi xylou,* "hanging (him) on a tree," is an allusion to Deut 21:22–23, which stipulated that the body of a criminal executed in a capital case and hanged on a tree (LXX: *kremasēte auton epi xylou*) should not remain there over night. It was so hanged as a deterrent to crime, but it was to be buried the same day, because such a person, "accursed by God," would defile the land. In the last pre-Christian centuries "hanging on a tree" became a way of referring to execution by crucifixion in Judea.

Deuteronomy 21:22–23 is used in the Qumran Cave 4 pesher (commentary) on Nahum, as it comments on Nah 2:12–13: "The interpretation of it concerns the Lion of Wrath, [who has found a crime punishable by] death in the Seekers-after-Smooth-Things (= Pharisees), whom he hangs as live men [on a tree, as was done] in Israel from of old, for of one hanged alive on the tree (Scripture) re[ads] . . . " (4QpNah 3–4 i 6–8). "The Lion of Wrath" is an allusion to the bellicose Sadducee high priest, Alexander Janneus (103–76 B.C.). He punished the Jews who had opposed him and had invited the Seleucid ruler, Demetrius III Eucerus (who is mentioned earlier in the pesher), to come and take Jerusalem. Josephus tells how, after the unsuccessful Demetrius withdrew, Alexander Janneus "ordered about 800 Jews to be crucified, and slaughtered their children and wives in the sight of the still living wretches" (*Ant.* 13.14.2 §§379–80; cf. *J.W.* 1.4.5–6 §§93–98).

Moreover, the Qumran Temple Scroll speaks of two crimes in Israel punishable by such death: treason (passing on information to an enemy or betraying one's people) and evasion of due process of law (in a case of capital punishment). In the former case it says, "you shall hang him on the tree and he shall die" (11QTemple 64:7–8). In the same passage Deut 21:22–23 is quoted, making clear that hanging on the tree was understood as an application of what was said there (in lines 10–12). In both Qumran texts, then, hanging on the tree is a phrase derived from Deuteronomy. The first text, 4QpNah, when understood in light of what Josephus tells us about the incident, shows that "hanging on the tree" was already understood in pre-Christian Palestine as crucifixion, a mode of execution used among Jews even prior to the coming of the Romans (63 B.C.). See further Fitzmyer, "Crucifixion in Ancient Palestine, Qumran Literature, and the New Testament," *TAG,* 125–48.

Contrast Haenchen (*Acts,* 251), who recognizes the allusion to Deut 21:22–23 LXX, but wrongly adds, "which the Christians have applied to the crucifixion of Jesus." See Wilcox, M., "'Upon the Tree'—Deut 21:22–23 in the New Testament," *JBL* 96 (1977): 85–99; T.C.G. Thornton, "Trees, Gibbets, and Crosses," *JTS* 23 (1972): 130–31.

Thus, Peter echoes this idea in speaking of the death of the crucified Jesus as a "hanging on a tree"; Paul refers to the same OT passage in Gal 3:13.

31. *It is he whom God has exalted to his right hand as leader and savior.* Peter's

kerygma proclaims the exaltation of Jesus (recall 2:33) and uses two titles of the risen Christ, *archēgos* (see NOTE on 3:15) and *sōtēr*, "savior." The latter, already used in Luke 2:11, appears now for the first time in Acts; see 13:23. The title has been used of Yahweh in Luke 1:47, as often in the OT, translating Hebrew *môšîăʿ* (1 Sam 10:19; Isa 45:15, 21). It denotes one who delivers from evil, physical, psychic, national, cataclysmic, or moral (see further *Luke*, 204–5). Here it would connote the last-named nuance: a deliverer from moral evil (sin), as the next clause makes clear. In this way Peter casts the exalted Christ in a salvific role: God has made him a helper and a savior of human beings. *Pace* Roloff (*Apg.*, 104), the nuance of this role is not Hellenistic, because the idea of "salvation" has an OT background as well as a Greek one.

[*to*] *grant Israel repentance and forgiveness of sins.* I.e., to give Israel the opportunity to repent. Peter expresses the purpose of God's exaltation of Jesus and the functions that the risen Christ plays in God's salvific plan. Cf. 17:30. For *metanoia* and *aphesis hamartiōn*, see NOTE on 2:38.

32. *We are witnesses of these things.* Peter reaffirms his role of witness and that of the other apostles; see 2:32; 3:15. He thus acknowledges the commission that was given them by the risen Christ (Luke 24:48; Acts 1:8).

so is the Holy Spirit that God has given to those who obey him." Just how the Holy Spirit bears witness is explained in the rel. cl.: God has bestowed his Spirit on those who are willing to accept his message, and so the Spirit testifies through those who welcome the Christian message. Not only was the Spirit given to early Christians on their first Pentecost, but it also filled Peter as he was about to testify before the Sanhedrin (4:8). In 2:38 it is described as a "gift" to those who reform and are baptized.

33. *When they heard this, they were infuriated and wanted to do away with them.* Lit., "they were sawn through," a similar but fuller expression occurs in the reaction to Stephen's speech in 7:54. The reaction of the Sanhedrin has grown. At first it was warning and threats (4:17, 21); now it is a desire or a scheme to put the apostles to death. Some MSS (A, B, E, Ψ, 36, and 614) read *eboulonto*, "they wanted," but others (א, D, 181, 307, 453, etc.) read *ebouleuonto*, "they were deciding, plotting"; still others (1175, 1409) have the aor. of the same verb, *ebouleusanto*, "they plotted."

34. *a certain Pharisee.* Luke seeks to differentiate Gamaliel from the chief priests and Sadducees already mentioned among the religious leaders of Jerusalem. The Pharisees were another of the three "philosophies" among the Jews of Judea when Josephus wrote (*Ant.* 18.1.2 §11), which he sometimes called *haireseis*, "sects" (see NOTE on 5:17). The Pharisees were nonpriestly interpreters of the Torah in postexilic Judea; they first emerged as an organized group in the Maccabean period, perhaps shortly before the time of John Hyrcanus (*Ant.* 13.5.9 §171). They were staunch defenders of observance of the Mosaic law, ancestral customs, and the resurrection of the dead (Acts 23:8; cf. Josephus, *J.W.* 2.8.14 §§162–63; *Ag.Ap.* 2.30 §218; *Ant.* 18.1.3 §14). They also maintained that all was governed by fate (i.e., predestination), even while affirming human re-

sponsibility for conduct. They enjoyed great influence among the ordinary people. The name *Pharisaios* is a grecized form of Aramaic *Pĕrîšāyê*, "separated ones," probably used of them by others who differed with them in interpretation. See *Luke*, 580–81. For a different explanation of the name, see J. M. Baumgarten, "The Name of the Pharisees," *JBL* 102 (1983): 411–28.

Gamaliel by name. This is Rabban Gamaliel, the Elder, who will appear again in 22:3 as the Jewish teacher at whose feet Paul sat to learn Torah. He was the grandson of Hillel and was the grandfather of R. Gamaliel II, and was probably the father of Jesus the high priest (A.D. 63–65 [Josephus, *Ant.* 20.9.4 §213: *Iēsous ho tou Gamaliēlou*]). Gamaliel's floruit was roughly A.D. 25–50 (Str-B, 2.636–39), during which time he presided over the *bêt dîn*, "house of judgment," a Pharisaic tribunal. He is depicted here interceding on behalf of Peter and John some time prior to A.D. 44 (death of Herod Agrippa I, Acts 12:20–23). *Gamaliēl* is the Greek form of Hebrew *Gamlî'ēl*, "God is my reward," a name found in the OT (Num 1:10; 2:20). See G. C. Glanville, "Gamaliel," *ExpTim* 30 (1918–19): 39–40. Cf. Phil 3:5e.

a teacher of the law esteemed by all the people. Gamaliel was an exemplary Jewish teacher and man of authority. His title, *rabbān*, "our Master," was given to him, the first of many great Jewish teachers. The later rabbinic tradition also records his fame: "When Rabban Gamaliel the Elder died, the glory of the law ceased, and purity and abstinence died" (*m. Sotah* 9:15).

stood up in the Sanhedrin and ordered these men out of court for a short time. Lit., "gave order to put these men outside for a short time." Such an order reveals the authority that Gamaliel had in the Sanhedrin.

35. *He said to them.* I.e., to the members of the Sanhedrin. The WT reads rather "to the leaders and those of the Sanhedrin."

"Fellow Israelites. See NOTE on 2:22.

be careful about what you are going to do to these men. Lit., "look to yourselves about . . ." So Gamaliel formulates generically his caution and proceeds to cite historic incidents to support it. Conzelmann (*Acts*, 42) mentions parallels of citing historical examples as arguments in speeches: Jer 26:17–23; Josephus, *J.W.* 5.9.4 §§376–98; Sallust, *Catilina* 51.5–6.

36. *Not long ago there appeared Theudas.* Gamaliel appeals to contemporary popular uprisings to explain by way of comparison what Peter and John are doing (see R. A. Horsley, "Popular Prophetic Movements"). Theudas is also mentioned by Josephus (*Ant.* 20.5.1 §§97–98):

> An impostor named Theudas persuaded a considerable crowd of people to take along their belongings and follow him to the Jordan River, for he said that he was a prophet and that, having parted the river-waters with a command, he would provide them easy passage. With such talk, he duped many. Fadus [C. Cuspius Fadus, the procurator of Judea, A.D. 44–46], however, did not let them profit from their folly; he sent against them a squadron of cavalry, which fell on them unexpectedly, killed many of them, and took many captive.

Theudas himself they captured alive, cut off his head, and brought it to Jerusalem.

trying to pass himself off as somebody important. I.e., as a prophet who would split the waters of the Jordan. MS D reads *megan,* "somebody great."

about four hundred men joined him. The number is not found in Josephus's account. This aspect of the Theudas incident is important for the point that Gamaliel wants to make: Theudas gathered a following, just as Peter, John, and the apostles have.

he was killed, and all those who were duped by him were disbanded, and they came to nothing. Thus far Luke's account substantially agrees with that of Josephus, even though Luke does not mention that many of Theudas's followers were also killed. The mention of Theudas is, however, problematic because he only appeared sometime after Gamaliel could have made this plea.

37. *After him.* I.e., after Theudas's unsuccessful attempt to stir up trouble in the time of Cuspius Fadus (A.D. 44–46).

at the time of the census, there appeared Judas the Galilean. This incident is also mentioned by Josephus, who, having finished his account about the procuratorship of Fadus, tells of his successor, Tiberius Julius Alexander (A.D. 46–48). Alexander ordered the crucifixion of James and Simon, the sons of "Judas the Galilean" (using the same phrase that Luke does). Josephus identifies the latter thus: "While Quirinius was taking the census of Judea, he [Judas the Galilean] drew the people into revolt against the Romans" (*Ant.* 20.5.2 §102). This agrees with the date that Luke assigns to Judas, "at the time of the census." Josephus also speaks of Judas in the time of the prefect Coponius: "a Galilean named Judas incited a revolt of his countrymen, upbraiding them for paying tribute to the Romans . . ." (*J.W.* 2.8.1 §118). These Josephus passages refer to the same incident, but Coponius was prefect of Judea (A.D. 6–9), while P. Sulpicius Quirinius was governor of the province of Syria (A.D. 6–7?), of which Judea was a district. Hence the first-mentioned notice in Josephus's *Antiquities* contains a flashback to an earlier period. This creates a problem in the interpretation of this verse of Acts, only because Luke writes *meta touton,* "after him," i.e., after Theudas. That would mean that Luke understood the revolt inspired by Judas as happening after the incident of Theudas. See the COMMENT above.

he drew away some of the people to follow him. This detail is important to Gamaliel's argument: Judas too had a group of followers.

But he too perished, and all those who were duped by him were dispersed. Luke uses the same verb *(apestēsen)* that Josephus uses in §102 *(apostēsantos),* but it is undoubtedly sheer coincidence. As does Josephus, Luke mentions Judas after Theudas; but since Luke speaks of Judas as "having perished" *(apōleto),* he is not dependent on the same source as Josephus, who says rather that Judas's sons were put to death.

38. *So in the present case I say to you, keep your distance from these men and let them be.* This is the burden of Gamaliel's counsel. Through Gamaliel, Luke makes it clear that Jesus is not to be likened to Judas the Galilean or Theudas

despite historical outward appearances, especially that all three had followers and were somehow looking for eschatological deliverance. See J. A. Trumbower, "Historical Jesus."

For if this scheme or this undertaking is of human design, it will destroy itself. As did the incidents of Theudas and Judas just cited, even though in those cases authorities moved in, i.e., political authorities, the Roman prefects Fadus and Coponius. Luke uses a future more vivid condition (*ean* + subjunctive, with future indicative in the apodosis); cf. ZBG §307.

39. *But if it is of God, you will not be able to destroy them; you may even find yourselves fighting against God."* Lit., "lest you even find yourselves to be God-fighters." Gamaliel's advice is like that of the pentateuchal counsel about how one is to distinguish a God-sent prophet from one who is not: "The prophet who presumes to speak a word in my name, which I have not ordered him to speak, or who speaks in the name of other gods, that prophet shall die. If you say in your heart, 'How shall we know the word that the Lord has not spoken?'—When a prophet speaks in the name of the Lord, if the word does not come to pass or come true, that is a word that the Lord has not spoken. That prophet has uttered it presumptuously; you need not be afraid of him" (Deut 18:20–22). In contrast to v 38, Luke uses here a simple condition (*ei* + indicative, with future indicative in the apodosis); cf. ZBG §307. The last adj. *theomachoi*, "God-fighting," is known in classical Greek literature (Euripides, *Bacchae* 45). Cf. 2 Macc 7:19. See A. Vögeli, "Lukas und Euripides," *TZ* 9 (1953): 415–38, esp. 429–36.

"Them" is the reading in MSS P^{74}, ℵ, A, B, C^2, Ψ, 36, but some MSS (C*, 1409, 1739) read *auto*, "it," a correction that makes better sense, which is for that reason suspect. After this word the WT has different additions; see above.

They were won over by him. Lit., "they were persuaded by him." This strange note about the rest of the Sanhedrin being persuaded by Gamaliel nevertheless has to cope with its decision to flog the apostles. In any case, it shows how God's judgment has prevailed, not the Sanhedrin's. It does not make of Gamaliel a Christian disciple; he is still a Jewish authority figure, but one who rightly assesses the situation and prudently distances himself from others who have authority over "these men" (5:34, 35, 38). Gamaliel does not defend them outright, but he shrewdly sizes up their situation.

40. *After calling in the apostles and having them flogged.* The persecution of the apostles by the Jerusalem authorities has thus moved from threats to physical mistreatment. Flogging is mentioned as a punishment in Deut 22:18 for a man who has defamed a woman as not a virgin. In Deut 25:3, flogging is limited to 40 stripes. Consequently, in the later rabbinic tradition "forty stripes" were prescribed for various offenses (*m. Kilaim* 8:3; *m. Makkoth* 1:1), and "forty stripes save one" is already known in the first century (see 2 Cor 11:24; Josephus, *Ant.* 4.8.21 §238).

they ordered them not to speak again in the name of Jesus and let them go. The Sanhedrin repeats its prohibition of apostolic preaching and testimony; recall 4:18, 21; 5:28. Again the refrain "in the name of Jesus" is used; see NOTE on 2:38.

41. *These then left the presence of the Sanhedrin full of joy that they had been*

judged worthy of ill-treatment for the sake of that name. The joyful reaction of the apostles to this persecution by Jerusalem authorities is a typically Lucan note; they rejoice that they have been deemed worthy of such treatment for the name of Christ.

42. *Day after day, both in the Temple and in house after house.* Lit., "every day in the Temple and by house," i.e., in different houses. Luke uses the prep. *kata* in a distributive sense (BDF §224.3).

they never stopped teaching and preaching Jesus as the Messiah. So the apostolic testimony is continued both by the teaching of the apostles and by their proclamation. On Messiah, see NOTE on 2:36. For the first time Luke uses the verb *euangelizesthai*, "preach," and its object is significantly "Jesus." It will appear again with an object (of what is preached) in 8:4, 35; 10:36; 11:20; 13:32; 15:35; 17:18; with an object (of those evangelized) in 8:25, 40; 14:15, 21; 16:10; absolutely (with no object) in 14:7; and with the prep. *peri* in 8:12. On the relation of this verb to the Lucan use and nonuse of *euangelion*, "gospel," see *Luke*, 173–74.

BIBLIOGRAPHY (5:17–42)

Baumbach, G., "Zeloten und Sikarier," *TLZ* 90 (1965): 727–40.

Black, M., "Judas of Galilee and Josephus's 'Fourth Philosophy,'" *Josephus — Studien: Untersuchungen zu Josephus, dem antiken Judentum und dem Neuen Testament: Otto Michel zum 70. Geburtstag gewidmet* (ed. O. Betz et al.; Göttingen: Vandenhoeck & Ruprecht, 1974), 45–54.

Böhlig, H., "Der Rat des Gamaliel in Apg. 5,38–39," *TSK* 86 (1913): 112–20.

Burhop, W. C., "Was Gamaliel's Counsel to the Sanhedrin Based on Sound Reasoning?" *CTM* 10 (1939): 676–83.

Campeau, L., "Theudas le faux prophète et Judas le Galiléen," *ScEccl* 5 (1953): 235–45.

Dehandschutter, B., "La persécution des chrétiens dans les Actes des Apôtres," *Les Actes des Apôtres* (ed. J. Kremer), 541–46.

Horsley, R. A., "Popular Prophetic Movements at the Time of Jesus: Their Principal Features and Social Origins," *JSNT* 26 (1986): 3–27.

Iglesias, E., "El libro de los Hechos: Las primeras persecuciones," *Christus: Revista Mensual* 5 (1938): 555–63.

Jeremias, J., "Untersuchungen zum Quellenproblem der Apostelgeschichte," *ZNW* 36 (1937): 205–21; repr. *Abba*, 238–55.

Kingsbury, J. D., "The Pharisees in Luke-Acts," *The Four Gospels 1992: Festschrift Frans Neirynck* (3 vols.; BETL 100; ed. F. van Segbroeck et al.; Louvain: Leuven University/Peeters, 1992), 2.1497–1512.

Lohfink, G., "'Wir sind Zeugen dieser Ereignisse' (Apg 5,32): Die Einheit der neutestamentlichen Botschaft von Erhöhung und Himmelfahrt Jesu," *BK* 20 (1965): 49–52.

Sanders, J. T., "The Pharisees in Luke-Acts," *The Living Text: Essays in Honor of*

Ernest W. Saunders (ed. D. E. Groh and R. Jewett; Lanham, MD: University Press of America, 1985), 141–88.

Schwartz, G. D., "The Pharisees and the Church," *TBT* 31 (1993): 301–4.

Spencer, K. J., Jr., "Judas of Galilee and His Clan," *JQR* 36 (1945–46): 281–86.

Swain, J. W., "Gamaliel's Speech and Caligula's Statue," *HTR* 37 (1944): 341–49.

Trumbower, J. A., "The Historical Jesus and the Speech of Gamaliel (Acts 5.35–39)," *NTS* 39 (1993): 500–17.

7. Community Restructured: Commission of the Seven (6:1–7)

6 [1]In those days, as the disciples continued to grow more numerous, there was
a complaint of the Hellenists against the Hebrews that their widows were being
neglected in the daily distribution of food. [2]So the Twelve summoned the community of the disciples and explained, "It is not right for us to neglect the word
of God to wait on tables. [3]So look about among you, brothers, for seven men of
good reputation, filled with the Spirit and with wisdom, whom we may appoint
to this task, [4]whereas we shall continue to devote ourselves to prayer and the
ministry of the word." [5]The proposal proved acceptable to the whole community,
and they selected Stephen, a man full of faith and the Holy Spirit, Philip, Prochorus, Nicanor, Timon, Parmenas, and Nicolaus, a proselyte of Antioch.
[6]These men they presented to the apostles, who prayed and laid their hands on
them. [7]The word of God continued to spread, and the number of disciples in
Jerusalem greatly increased; a large number of the priests became obedient to
the faith.

WT: [1]as the number of the disciples continued to increase . . . [omits "of the Hellenists against the Hebrews"] . . . the widows of the Hellenists were . . . food by the ministers of the Hebrews. [2]summoned all the community. [3]What is it, then, brothers? Look about . . . Spirit of the Lord [omits "and with wisdom"]. [5]This proposal. [7]word of the Lord . . . [omits "in Jerusalem"].

COMMENT

The Lucan narrative has passed from an account of difficulties that early Christians experienced from external forces to difficulties within their community. The story of the persecution of Christians by religious authorities has been left for the moment in order to recount some of the internal strife. Luke has told of scandalous conduct in the community in the story of Ananias and Sapphira and now begins to reveal other internal problems. Whereas he has depicted Jerusalem Christians as believers one in "heart and mind" (4:32), this episode gives a different picture of the reality of Christian life, for the idyllic peace and harmony described in the three major summaries have been disturbed. There have been persecution from religious authorities, deception in the ranks of the community, and now internal division on a different scale. As the apostles have coped with the earlier problems, so they do now in another way.

In 4:35b Luke recounted how proceeds of the sale of property laid at the feet of the apostles were "distributed to each according to one's need." Apparently, that distribution was not always made as it should have been, for "there was a complaint of the Hellenists against the Hebrews that their widows were being neglected in the daily distribution of food" (6:1).

To handle this problem, the Twelve do not hesitate to restructure the early community, proposing to set up seven persons who would "wait on tables" and handle the dole. This is done so that the more important tasks, "prayer and the ministry of the word," may continue without distraction for those of the Twelve. The proposal made by the Twelve finds approval in the community as a whole, and seven are appointed. They are commissioned for their task by the apostles, who pray and impose hands on them. Unity and peace have to be preserved, but not by having the Twelve spend time on such trivia; the Twelve are depicted manifesting a proper sense of priority. So is solved a conflict within the Jerusalem "church," as it was called in 5:11.

The episode ends with another minor summary (6:7). That verse tells of the spread of the Word of God throughout Israel, and, even though the religious authorities have reacted against the Christian movement, "the number of disciples in Jerusalem greatly increased" and "a large number of the priests became obedient to the faith."

The noun *diakonia* is used for "the ministry" of the word (6:4), the ministry of the Twelve (1:17, 25), and now it is employed for that of the Seven (6:1–2). They are appointed to "wait on" or "serve" tables, and the verb is *diakonein* (6:2). The dole that they are to administer is *hē diakonia hē kathēmerinē,* "the daily service" (6:1). Because of the occurrence of this term in various ways here, the Seven have often been regarded as the first "deacons" of the church, even though the name *diakonoi,* which otherwise appears for special functionaries in the NT (Phil 1:1; Rom 16:1; 1 Tim 3:8, 12; 4:6), is not employed for them here. "The Seven," substantivized in 21:8, is developed as a name from the number in v 3; it stands in contrast to "the Twelve."

Form-critically assessed, the episode is another narrative in Acts, a straightforward account with only minor problems of interpretation. This account of the first rift in the Jewish Christian community in Jerusalem foreshadows the rift to come between Christians and the rest of the Jerusalem populace with its authorities.

As Conzelmann recognizes (*Acts,* 44), Luke undoubtedly inherited a written form of this account, but the details behind it are only vaguely perceived. The role assigned to the Seven does not fit well with subsequent episodes in Acts. In a minor way this episode serves as an introduction to the execution of Stephen, one of the Seven and the first martyr; it enables the reader to see how Stephen came to occupy a prominent place in the Jerusalem community and thus prepares for the Stephen story.

Commentators have sometimes suggested that the appointment of the Seven was a means to care for the needs of proselytes, whereas the Twelve would care for those of Jews. Still others wonder about the Hellenists as those involved in a coming schism (Haenchen, *Acts*, 264–65). All that is sheer speculation. Since there is no more mention of common ownership of property, now that the major summaries have come to an end, that may signal the demise of such an institution on a wide scale, and the institution of the Seven may reflect a later remedial development in the community (see Lake, *Beginnings*, 5.140–51). In time, when the Twelve disappear, that title, along with "apostles," is no longer continued. What eventually developed in the Christian church from the Seven is a new class of ministers, commissioned by the Twelve with prayer and the laying on of hands, and subordinate to them, the "deacons," as known from Ignatius of Antioch (*Eph.* 2.1; *Magn.* 2; 6.1; 13.1; *Did.* 15.1) and the diaconate (Irenaeus, *Adversus haereses* 1.26.3; 3.12.10; 4.15.1; SC 264.348; 211.224; 100/2.550). Eventually it became part of the Sacrament of Orders. For details and problems in the development, see Bihel, "De septem diaconis"; Gaechter, "Die Sieben"; Domagalski, "Waren?"

Luke seems to be making use of a new source of information; the subject matter is new, and the name *mathētai* for Christians has not been used before. Part of the source material is the list of seven names associated with an account of the charitable work the Seven did. From that source would have come also the selection of the Seven by the community and their commission by the apostles. Because of the sort of information that now appears it is thought that Luke is dependent on an Antiochene source.

As Jesus chose the Twelve (Luke 6:13), so the community and the Twelve now choose the Seven. As the risen Christ commissioned the Twelve (Acts 1:8) to be witnesses to him, so the Twelve commission the Seven to wait on tables.

Chapters 6 and 7 are important in the Lucan story, because they introduce Stephen and his speech just before the story begins about the second hero in Acts, Saul of Tarsus. Stephen's speech and his subsequent martyrdom thus provide the setting for the story of Saul and his mission to the Gentiles. Though Stephen suffers eventually the same fate as did Jesus, he never intended to alienate Israel; nor did Saul. See G. N. Stanton, "Stephen."

An earlier episode (5:12–16) described the Jerusalem Christians as a caring community, and now this one shows how they care for their widows. Widows were often in particular need and vulnerable to abuse and neglect, because they had lost their main source of companionship and support, their husbands, in a society that was male dominated (cf. Luke 7:12). The lot of the widow, often reduced to poverty by the death of her husband, was a topic to which the law and the prophets often spoke (Deut 14:29; 24:17; 26:12; Isa 1:23; 10:2; Jer 7:6; 22:3; Mal 3:5). The Lucan story now reveals how Christians of Jerusalem develop their own dole to aid such women, but his account is really the springboard for the restructuring of the early community. It manifests too a concern for the proper service of the Word of God. Nothing is to distract the Twelve from that service.

NOTES

6:1. *In those days.* This Lucan formulation (Luke 1:39; 6:12; Acts 1:15; 11:27) links what the author is about to narrate concerning the early Christian church in Jerusalem with what has preceded. The same phrase appears in 1:15 (see NOTE there), at the beginning of the Matthias episode, which enjoys a certain parallelism with this episode, in which the Twelve are again active.

as the disciples continued to grow more numerous. As the number of Christians grow, so do the problems. Cf. 5:42. The verb *plēthynein,* "grow numerous," is Lucan (see 9:31; 12:24), as is the use of the gen. absolute.

For the first time Luke utilizes *mathētēs,* "disciple"; it will appear in the same sense in 6:2, 7; 9:1, 10, 19, 26bis, 38; 11:26, 29; 13:52; 14:20, 22, 28; 15:10; 16:1; 18:23, 27; 19:1, 9, 30; 20:1, 30; 21:4, 16bis; fem. *mathētria* appears in 9:36. It was often employed in the Lucan Gospel (e.g., 5:38; 6:1). In a religious sense the term is, practically speaking, a Christian word.

The Hebrew counterpart *talmîd* is almost absent from the OT, occurring only in 1 Chr 25:8 and denoting pupils in the Temple choir. *Limmûd,* often mistranslated "disciple" (Isa 8:16; 50:4; 54:13; cf. Jer 13:23), never has *mathētēs* as its LXX counterpart. This word occurs in the LXX of Jer 13:21; 20:11; 46:9, but always with variant readings, so that it is difficult to discern how it came to be used. *Talmîd* is likewise absent from QL. "Disciple" is, however, found abundantly in the Gospels, used of the "followers" of Jesus the "teacher." Otherwise it is conspicuously absent from the rest of the NT. Its emergence in the Gospels may be explained by the growing Hellenistic influence on that tradition. By contrast, one often reads in the OT of "followers": sons of the prophets (1 Kgs 20:35; 2 Kgs 2:3, 5, 7, 15; 5:22; 6:1; 9:1); Elisha, who "followed after" Elijah (1 Kgs 19:20); Baruch and Jeremiah; but Elisha and Baruch are never called "disciples." In the Greek world, "disciples" of eminent teachers appear from the fifth century B.C. on: of the Sophists, Pythagoras, the Stoics, and Epicurus. Socrates would not allow his companions to be called *mathētai,* and in this he was followed by Plato and Aristotle; but many others encouraged the idea, and among them the idea of *mimēsis,* "imitation," emerged. The abundant use of *akolouthein,* "follow," in the Gospels suggests that this was the primitive term, adopted from OT usage, to designate the relation of companions of Jesus to him. The gradual adoption of Greek *mathētēs* reveals the reinterpretation of that relationship as "discipleship," as the Gospels were being composed in the Greco-Roman world. See Fitzmyer, "The Designations of Christians in Acts and Their Significance," *Unité et diversité dans l'église* (ed. Biblical Commission; Vatican City: Libreria Editrice Vaticana, 1989), 223–36, esp. 227–29; L. O. Richards, "The Disappearing Disciple: Why Is the Use of 'Disciple' Limited to the Gospels and Acts?" *EvJ* 10 (1992):3–11. Thus, it is hardly likely that *mathētai* was "a Palestinian self-designation which Luke found in a source," *pace* Conzelmann (*Acts,* 44).

there was a complaint of the Hellenists against the Hebrews. Lit., "there developed a murmuring." The *gongysmos,* "complaint," echoes that of the Hebrews in the desert (Num 11:1); cf. Luke 5:30; John 6:41, 43, 61; 7:12, 32. For the first time we learn in Acts about a difference among Jewish Christians in Jerusalem, some called "Hellenists," others "Hebrews." *Hellēnistai* is used of Jews in 9:29.

Hebraioi, which occurs in the LXX of the Pentateuch a few times for "Hebrews" (Gen 40:15; 43:32; Exod 1:15), becomes more frequent in the deuterocanonical and apocryphal books (Jdt 10:12; 14:18; 2 Macc 7:31; 11:13; 4 Macc 4:11; 8:2; 9:18; 17:9). The OT usage, however, does not explain its occurrence here, as a designation of one of two groups of Jewish Christians in Jerusalem. Neither name, however, can be traced to a solely Christian usage, as 9:29 reveals.

Hellēnistai, which is not found in the LXX, Philo, or Josephus, is a proper noun developed from the verb *hellēnizein*, the meaning of which is controverted. Cadbury maintained that *hellēnizein* meant "live like a Greek," and not "speak like a Greek." Consequently, for him *Hellēnistai* denoted Gentile members of the Jerusalem Christian church (*Beginnings*, 5.59–74).

It does mean, however, "speak Greek," as in Plato, *Meno* 82b; *Charmides* 159a; Aeschines, *Or.* 3.172. Chrysostom understood *Hellēnistai* to mean "those speaking Greek" (*In Acta hom.* 21.1; PG 60.164). Following him, many modern commentators (e.g., Hengel, "Die Ursprünge," 26; Haenchen, *Acts*, 260; Pesch, "'Hellenisten'") understand "Hellenists" merely as "Greek-speaking Jews," whereas the "Hebrews" are "Aramaic-speaking Jews." The matter is not so simple, because this distinction does not explain the Pauline use of *Hebraios*. Paul, a diaspora Jew, never calls himself *Hellēnistēs*, but rather *Hebraios* (Phil 3:5; 2 Cor 11:22). Moreover, we have not yet learned in Acts that there were Gentile Christians in Jerusalem.

So the best solution is that suggested by C.F.D. Moule ("Once More, Who Were the Hellenists?" *ExpTim* 70 [1958–59]: 100–2): *Hellēnistai* in Acts denotes Jews (and Jewish Christians) "who spoke *only* Greek" and *Hebraioi* "Jews who, while able to speak Greek, knew a Semitic language *also*," i.e., Hebrew or Aramaic. Cf. Conzelmann, *Acts*, 45. "Hellenists" would refer, then, to Jerusalem Jews who pray and read their Scriptures in Greek, whereas "Hebrews" means Jews, who can speak Greek, but who pray and read in Aramaic or Hebrew. It would be an exaggeration to call the Hellenists "a sect" within Judaism, as did M. Simon (cf. Delorme, "Note"); they are not a formal group like Pharisees, Sadducees, or Essenes. Hellenists and Hebrews in the Jerusalem church would rather have been Jewish Christians, converts from any of these backgrounds who thus distinguished themselves linguistically. Cf. Philo, *De confusione linguarum* 26 §129. In other words, the distinction is not ethnic, but linguistic. As Johnson notes (*Acts*, 105), "The suggestion that Luke meant by *hellēnistēs* 'Greek Gentiles' in the present passage has little to recommend it." Schneider (*Apg.*, 1.423) understands "Hellenists" to refer to "Greek-speaking Jews from the diaspora," but the last phrase is nowhere intimated in the text, *pace* N. Walter ("Apostelgeschichte 6.1"). Ossuaries found in Jerusalem, the largest number of which bear Greek inscriptions, reveal that Greek was used by many Jews in Jerusalem in the first centuries B.C. and A.D.

Cullmann, who favored Cadbury's definition, called the Hellenists "a bridge between the Essenes and the early Christians," because they "belonged to the original Palestinian church from the beginning"; hence they were not from the diaspora and "must have played a far greater role in the beginnings of Christianity than is immediately apparent from Acts." In other words, early Christian Hellenists were "in some way *in contact with the kind of Judaism we find in the Qumran texts*" ("The Significance" [his italics]). Similarly P. Géoltrain ("Esséniens et Hellénistes"): "The Hellenists of Acts are to be located in the same line as the Essene movement." Such a relation of the Hellenists of Jerusalem with Qumran Essenes, however, grows ever more tenuous as one learns more about the Qumran community. How such strict Palestinian Jews would ever have been thought to "live like Greeks" is hardly intelligible. See further Haenchen, *Acts*, 260 n. 3. Even less likely is the view that "Hellenists" were Jewish proselytes converted to Christianity (E. C. Blackman; G. Rinaldi). That would make the identification of Nicolaus in v 7 superfluous.

their widows were being neglected in the daily distribution of food. Lit., "in the daily service." The distribution, which was mentioned in 4:35b, apparently was not always carried out with equity. Hence the complaint of the Hellenist Christians against the Hebrew Christians. This complaint may record only a surface tension between the two groups in Jerusalem, who differed in other ways too, but further differences would be a matter of speculation, since Luke says nothing about them. Much of the wording of this verse is non-Lucan, which suggests that he has derived it from a source.

Jeremias (*Jerusalem in the Time of Jesus* [Philadelphia: Fortress, 1969], 129–34) claimed that there was an organized system of public assistance or relief for the Jewish poor in pre-Christian Jerusalem, but his interpretation of the later Mishnaic evidence may not be applicable to this period and has been contested by Seccombe ("Was There"; cf. Strobel, "Armenpflege"; Schneider, *Apg.*, 1.424). The evidence does not permit such an anachronistic interpretation.

2. *the Twelve summoned the community of the disciples and explained.* Lit., "the Twelve, having summoned the multitude of the disciples, said." The Twelve are presented as having authority to summon the community, to counsel action, and to determine criteria for those to be selected. Since the selection of Matthias, the Twelve have not been mentioned; this is the last time that they will appear in Acts under this name, even though they will still be mentioned as "the apostles" (6:6; 8:1, 14, 18; 9:27; 11:1; 14:4, 14; 15:2, 4, 6, 22, 23; 16:4). After 16:4 "apostles" too disappears from the story. See *Luke*, 617–18. The Twelve summon the *plēthos*, "multitude, community" (see NOTE on 4:32), a designation of the Christians as a religious group.

"It is not right for us to neglect the word of God to wait on tables. Lit., "it is not desirable . . . to minister to (*or:* serve) tables." *Trapeza*, "table," is that from which a meal is taken (Homer, *Odyssey* 17.333; Herodotus, *History* 1.162; 5.20), which is undoubtedly what is meant here. It can also mean that on which money changers piled their coins (Plato, *Apology* 17c; Mark 11:15), and even in a financial

sense, "bank" (Luke 19:23). Thus, it might possibly mean "to administer the (financial) tables" in the distribution of the dole. Haenchen rightly rejects this interpretation (*Acts*, 215). In any case, the Twelve do not think that they should be distracted from the ministry of preaching and testimony by such a problem. The Christian message is again designated the Word of God; see NOTE on 4:31.

3. *look about among you, brothers, for seven men of good reputation, filled with the Spirit and with wisdom, whom we may appoint to this task.* The community is to select the candidates, but the commission of them rests with the apostles. Cf. Exod 18:21; Num 27:18–19 (LXX). The criteria for the choice of the Seven are different from those for the reconstitution of the Twelve in 1:21–22 (see NOTES there). The Seven must be men of whom one speaks well *(martyroumenoi)*, filled with spirit (*or:* the Spirit [see 6:5b]) and with wisdom so that they can carry out the task with discernment and respect. Why seven are chosen is anyone's guess; it is not necessarily an imitation of a Jewish institution, for none of the evidence for it brought forward by Str-B (2.641) comes from pre-Christian Judaism. When Josephus interprets Deut 16:18 (*Ant.* 4.8.14 §214) about the administration of justice in each city, he introduces "seven men"; this is a parallel to the Lucan statement, but hardly has any bearing on this issue. Seven, being a prime number and an odd number (important if decisions had to be made by a vote), is often used for crucial matters in the OT and developed into a customary number in Jewish society (Josh 6:4; Jer 52:25; Esth 1:14; cf. Josephus, *J.W.* 2.20.5 §571), which is now imitated. Cf. S.J.K. Pearce, "Flavius Josephus as Interpreter of Biblical Law: The Council of Seven and the Levitical Servants in *Jewish Antiquities* 4.214," *HeyJ* 36 (1995): 477–92.

4. *we shall continue to devote ourselves to prayer and the ministry of the word."* "Prayer" undoubtedly means the common celebration of the Christian liturgy (recall 1:14; 2:42), or possibly participation in Jewish cultic prayers (see 3:1). To speak of Christian prayer as a "meritorious act of piety," as does Haenchen (*Acts*, 263), is to introduce a consideration far from Luke's mind. *Diakonia tou logou* means the proclamation of the Christian message, the testimony for which the apostles have been commissioned (Luke 24:47–48; Acts 1:8). In the Lucan story it is the Word of God that, in the last days, proceeds from Jerusalem (see B. Gerhardsson, *Memory*, 243). Perhaps Luke subordinates the "menial" forms of *diakonia*, such as feeding widows, to the more "spiritual" pursuits of teaching, preaching, and prayer, as F. S. Spencer ("Neglected Widows") would have it, but the episode seems rather to provide simultaneously for both, and in due proportion. The promotion of the ministry of teaching and preaching is not a Lucan "proclivity"; nor is to be done "at the expense of the service of food at table." To read the episode that way is to turn the Lucan story on its head.

5. *The proposal proved acceptable to the whole community.* Lit., "the word was pleasing before all the multitude" (of disciples [6:2]), i.e., the proposal formulated in vv 3–4. Luke uses an expression *ēresen enōpion*, "was pleasing before," found in 2 Sam 3:36; Jer 18:4 (LXX).

they selected Stephen, a man full of faith and the Holy Spirit. Stephanos means "crown, wreath," often connoting the garland of laurel or the crown of victory in games and athletic contests; it was also a personal name commonly used in the Greco-Roman world (POxy 3.517:14; Josephus, *J.W.* 2.12.2 §228: of a slave of Caesar). We are not told how the selection of the Seven was made, but it was not by a casting of lots, as it had been for Matthias (1:26).

Stephen's name heads the list undoubtedly because of the role he will play in the next chapter and a half in Acts; he is an important figure in Luke's story, even though he is not one of the Twelve, an apostle, or a presbyter. He was probably a converted Hellenist, originally a Jewish settler in Jerusalem coming from somewhere in the diaspora, "an almost solitary figure among the leaders of the first Christian generation" (Simon, *St Stephen*, 98). He will be the first to bear witness to the risen Christ by giving up his life. *Pace* Spiro ("Stephen's Samaritan Background"), he is hardly a Samaritan, for there is nothing in the Lucan account to suggest this, as Scharlemann has correctly noted (*Stephen*, 19–22).

Accordingly, Stephen is characterized as a man "full of faith" in the risen Christ, i.e., a robust Christian; and "full of the Holy Spirit," i.e., endowed with Spirit-given force and eloquence (as the story will eventually reveal; cf. 7:55). In v 8 he will be further described as "full of grace and power," and in v 10, as a speaker with "wisdom and spirit." Haenchen (*Acts*, 263–64) is inclined to understand "faith" as that of 1 Cor 13:2, faith that moves mountains, because of the mention of Stephen's miracles in v 8, but such a sense is far from obvious; the more obvious meaning is that of essential Christian belief and commitment.

Philip. Philip "the evangelist, one of the Seven," as he is called in 21:8, where he is the father of "four unmarried daughters," who were able to prophesy. He figures prominently in chap. 8 (vv 5–40). Eusebius (*HE* 2.1.10) speaks of him as one "ordained to the diaconate" *(cheiristheis eis tēn diakonian)*, but later seems to consider him one of the "apostles" (*HE* 3.31.5–6). See F. S. Spencer, *The Portrait of Philip in Acts: A Study of Roles and Relations* (JSNTSup 67; Sheffield, UK: Academic, 1992). *Philippos*, "fond of horses," was a commonly used Greek name, borne by the Macedonian father of Alexander the Great; cf. Luke 3:1 (see NOTE there).

Prochorus, Nicanor, Timon, Parmenas, and Nicolaus, a proselyte of Antioch. These five are otherwise unknown. Since the time of Irenaeus (*Adversus haereses* 1.26.3; SC 264.348), Nicolaus has been identified with the Nicolaitans of Rev 2:6, 15, a case of *ignotum per ignotius*, "the unknown (explained) by what is more unknown." All seven bear good Greek names, but it is hard to say whether they were from among the Hellenists or the Hebrews, because many Jews of that period bore Greek names, as would have been true also of Jewish Christians. Most of them were probably Hellenists and probably originally diaspora Jews. Nicolaus, "a proselyte of Antioch," was probably born in Antioch on the Orontes, but is now resident in Jerusalem. On "proselyte," see NOTE on 2:11. Because of the last identification, Haenchen (*Acts*, 264) insists that all seven were Jewish Christians; so far we have not heard in Acts of Gentile Christians in Jerusalem; the first mention of them comes in Acts 10.

6. *These men they presented to the apostles.* I.e., to the Twelve, who made the proposal in vv 3–4. MS D reads the pass., "these were presented."

who prayed and laid their hands on them. The commissioning of the Seven as a group to handle the dole is made by the Twelve with prayer and the laying on of hands. Prayer or communing with God preceded the choosing of Matthias (1:24–25); it now becomes part of the commissioning of these men. "Laying on of hands" is known in the OT, where it usually expresses a solidarity between persons, a self-identification of one with the other in some blessing, spiritual gift, or office or rank. Thus Moses is told by God to commission Joshua, son of Nun, as his successor (Num 27:18–23); the Levites are so commissioned in Num 8:10. In the NT the laying on of hands has diverse significance (see W. Radl, "*Cheir,*" *EDNT,* 3.462–63). In Acts 19:6 it accompanies baptism and is a means whereby the Spirit is given. Denoting installation in a role or office, as here, it also occurs in 13:3; 1 Tim 4:14; 5:22; 2 Tim 1:6. Those so installed are considered the recipients of divine assistance for their work, what later theologians called *gratia gratis data,* "a grace freely given," the grace to carry out an ecclesial function. See further J. Behm, *Die Handauflegung im Urchristentum in religionsgeschichtlichem Zusammenhang untersucht* (Naumburg: Pätz, 1911); J. Coppens, *L'Imposition des mains et les rites connexes dans le Nouveau Testament et dans l'église ancienne: Etude de théologie positive* (Dissertationes Universitatis Lovaniensis 2/15; Wettern: de Meester et Fils; Paris: Gabalda, 1925); "L'Imposition des mains dans les Actes des Apôtres," *Les Actes des Apôtres* (ed. J. Kremer), 405–38; E. Ferguson, "Laying on of Hands: Its Significance in Ordination," *JTS* 26 (1975): 1–12; E. Lohse, *Die Ordination im Spätjudentum und im Neuen Testament* (Berlin: Evangelische Verlagsanstalt, 1951), 74–79.

7. *The word of God continued to spread.* This minor summary may be a description of the continued activity of preaching the Word by the apostles, or it may denote the effect of that preaching, as the following clause suggests. The Christian church continues to develop and grow. Cf. 12:24.

the number of disciples in Jerusalem greatly increased. The original number was 120 (1:15b), to which about 3,000 converts were added on Pentecost (2:41), and later on "[about] five thousand men" (4:4). Now the increase of Jerusalem Jewish Christians, whether Hebrews or Hellenists, is left indefinite.

a large number of the priests became obedient to the faith. I.e., members of Jewish priestly families, some of whom may have been serving in the Temple. Because the original nucleus of the Qumran Essenes were members of priestly families, it is sometimes thought that this notice would refer to Essene priests. That is not impossible, but Luke's words cannot be restricted to them, since he seems to be speaking of Jerusalem priests. Qumran Essenes were critical of the "last priests of Jerusalem, who amass money and wealth by plundering the people" (1QpHab 9:4); so it is not easy to see how only Essenes would have been such priests. Josephus tells us of Essenes resident in Jerusalem (*Ant.* 13.11.2 §311), and some of their priestly members might have been among those who "became obedient to the faith." "The faith" is employed in the content sense of that which Christians believed *(fides quae creditur)*; as such it = the Christian religion. Cf. 13:8; Gal 1:23; Rom 12:6; Eph 4:5; 1 Tim 1:19; 2:7; 3:9; 4:1, 6; 6:21; Titus 1:1.

BIBLIOGRAPHY (6:1–7)

Barnikol, E., "Die ersten Diakonen, die Zwölf nach Apg. 1.25," *TJb* (1941): 88–89.

Bihel, S., "De septem diaconis (Act. 6,1–7)," *Anton* 3 (1928): 129–50.

Black, M., "Qumran and the 'Hebraists' of Acts," *The Scrolls and Christian Origins* (New York: Scribner, 1961), 75–81.

Blackman, E. C., "The Hellenists of Acts vi.1," *ExpTim* 48 (1936–37): 524–25.

Bowman Thurston, B., *The Widows: A Women's Ministry in the Early Church* (London: SCM, 1983).

Cerfaux, L., "La composition de la première partie du livre des Actes," *ETL* 13 (1936): 667–91, esp. 681–83; repr. *Recueil Lucien Cerfaux*, 2.63–91, esp. 79–81.

Cullmann, O., "Secte de Qumran, Hellénistes des Actes et quatrième évangile," *Les manuscrits de la Mer Morte: Colloque de Strasbourg* (Paris: Presses Universitaires de France, 1957), 61–74.

———, "The Significance of the Qumran Texts for Research into the Beginnings of Christianity," *JBL* 74 (1955): 213–26; repr. *The Scrolls and the New Testament* (ed. K. Stendahl; New York: Harper & Bros., 1957; repr. New York: Crossroad, 1992), 18–32, 251–52.

———, "Von Jesus zum Stephanuskreis und zum Johannesevangelium," *Jesus und Paulus: Festschrift für Werner Georg Kümmel* . . . (ed. E. E. Ellis and E. Grässer; Göttingen: Vandenhoeck & Ruprecht, 1975), 44–56.

Delebecque, E., "Etienne, le premier diacre, et le texte dit occidental des Actes (Actes 6,6 et 10–11)," *Mélanges offerts en hommage au Révérend Père Etienne Gareau* (Ottawa: Université d'Ottawa, 1982), 187–90.

Delorme, J., "Note sur les Hellénistes des Actes des Apôtres," *L'Ami du clergé* 71 (1961): 445–47.

Domagalski, B., "Waren die 'Sieben' (Apg 6,1–7) Diakone?" *BZ* 26 (1982): 21–33.

Dupont, J., "Les ministères de l'église naissante d'après les Actes des Apôtres," *Nouvelles études*, 133–85, esp. 151–57.

Ferguson, E., "The Hellenists in the Book of Acts," *ResQ* 12 (1969): 159–80.

Foerster, W., "Stephanus und die Urgemeinde," *Dienst unter dem Wort: Eine Festgabe für Professor D. Dr. Helmuth Schreiner* (ed. K. Janssen; Gütersloh: Bertelsmann, 1953), 9–30.

Fox, K. A., "The Nicolaitans, Nicolaus and the Early Church," *SR* 23 (1994): 485–96.

Gaechter, P., "Die Sieben (Apg 6,1–6)," *ZKT* 74 (1952): 129–66.

Gager, J. G., "Jews. Gentiles, and Synagogues in the Book of Acts," *Christians*

among Jews and Gentiles: Essays in Honor of Krister Stendahl . . . (ed. G.W.E. Nickelsburg and G. W. MacRae; Philadelphia: Fortress, 1986), 91–99.
Géoltrain, P., "Esséniens et Hellénistes," *TZ* 15 (1959): 241–54.
George, A., "Les ministères," *Études sur l'oeuvre de Luc*, 369–94, esp. 375–76.
Gerhardsson, B., *Memory and Manuscript* (ASNU 22; Uppsala: Almqvist & Wiksells, 1961).
Giles, K., "Is Luke an Exponent of 'Early Protestantism'? Church Order in the Lukan Writings (Part 1)," *EvQ* 54 (1982): 193–205; (Part 2), ibid. 55 (1983): 3–20.
Glombitza, O., "Zur Charakterisierung des Stephanus in Act 6 und 7," *ZNW* 53 (1962): 238–44.
Grundmann, W., "Das Problem des hellenistischen Christentums innerhalb der Jerusalemer Urgemeinde," *ZNW* 38 (1939): 45–73.
Hahn, F., "Zum Problem der antiochenischen Quelle in der Apostelgeschichte," *Rudolf Bultmanns Werk und Wirkung* (ed. B. Jaspert; Darmstadt: Wissenschaftliche Buchgesellschaft, 1984), 316–31.
Hengel, M., "Between Jesus and Paul: The 'Hellenists', the 'Seven' and Stephen," *Between Jesus and Paul: Studies in the Earliest History of Christianity* (London: SCM; Philadelphia: Fortress, 1983), 1–29.
———, "Die Ursprünge der christlichen Mission," *NTS* 18 (1971–72): 15–38.
Hill, C. C., *Hellenists and Hebrews: Reappraising Division within the Earliest Church* (Minneapolis: Fortress, 1992).
Keck, L. E., "The Poor among the Saints in the New Testament," *ZNW* 56 (1965): 100–29.
———, "The Poor among the Saints in Jewish Christianity and Qumran," *ZNW* 57 (1966): 54–78.
Kodell, J., "'The Word of God Grew': The Ecclesial Tendency of *Logos* in Acts 6:7; 12:24; 19:20," *Bib* 55 (1974): 505–19.
Larsson, E., "Die Hellenisten und die Urgemeinde," *NTS* 33 (1987): 205–25.
Lienhard, J. T., "Acts 6:1–6: A Redactional View," *CBQ* 37 (1975): 228–36.
Pathrapankal, J., "The Hellenists and Their Missionary Dynamism in the Early Church and Its Message for Our Times," *Bible Bhashyam* 8 (1982): 216–26.
Pesch, R. et al., "'Hellenisten' und 'Hebräer': Zu Apg 9,29 and 6,1," *BZ* 23 (1979): 87–92.
Richard, E., *Acts 6:1–8:4: The Author's Method of Composition* (SBLDS 41; Missoula: Scholars, 1978).
Rinaldi, G., "Stefano," *BeO* 6 (1964): 153–62.
Scharlemann, M. H., *Stephen: A Singular Saint* (AnBib 34; Rome: Biblical Institute, 1968).
Scroggs, R., "The Earliest Hellenistic Christianity," *Religions in Antiquity: Essays in Memory of Erwin Ramsdell Goodenough* (SHR 14; ed. J. Neusner; Leiden: Brill, 1968), 176–206.
Seccombe, D., "Was There Organized Charity in Jerusalem before the Christians?" *JTS* 29 (1978): 140–43.

Simon, M., *St Stephen and the Hellenists in the Primitive Church* (London/New York: Longmans, Green and Co., 1958).
Spencer, F. S., "Neglected Widows in Acts 6:1–7," *CBQ* 56 (1994): 715–33.
Spiro, A., "Stephen's Samaritan Background," Appendix V in J. Munck, *Acts*, 285–300.
Stanton, G. N., "Stephen in Lucan Perspective," *Studia Biblica III: Papers on Paul and Other New Testament Authors: Sixth International Congress on Biblical Studies Oxford 3–7 April 1978* (JSNTSup 3; ed. E. A. Livingstone; Sheffield, UK: JSOT, 1980), 345–60.
Strobel, A., "Armenpfleger 'um des Friedens willen' (Zum Verständnis von Act 6,1–6)," *ZNW* 63 (1972): 271–76.
Trudinger, P., "Stephen and the Life of the Primitive Church," *BTB* 14 (1984): 18–22.
Tyson, J. B., "Acts 6:1–7 and Dietary Regulations in Early Christianity," *PRS* 10 (1982): 145–61.
Walter, N., "Apostelgeschichte 6. 1 und die Anfänge der Urgemeinde in Jerusalem," *NTS* 29 (1983): 370–93.
Zimmermann, H., "Die Wahl der Sieben (Apg 6, 1–6): Ihre Bedeutung für die Wahrung der Einheit in der Kirche," *Die Kirche und ihre Ämter und Stände: Festgabe . . . Joseph Kardinal Frings . . .* (Cologne: Bachem, 1960), 364–78.

8. Testimony of Stephen (6:8–7:1)

8 Now Stephen, full of grace and power, was performing great wonders and signs
among the people. 9 Some members of the Synagogue of Freedmen, as it was
called, of Cyrenians and Alexandrians, and of people from Cilicia and Asia, came
forward to debate with Stephen, 10 but they were no match for the wisdom and
spirit with which he spoke. 11 So they put up some men to claim, "We have heard
him uttering blasphemous words against Moses and against God." 12 They stirred
up the people, the elders, and the scribes, confronted him, seized him, and led
him off to the Sanhedrin. 13 They also brought in false witnesses who maintained,
"This man never stops saying things against [this] sacred place and the law. 14 We
have heard him claim that this Jesus the Nazorean will destroy this place and
change the customs that Moses handed down to us." 15 All those who sat in the
Sanhedrin kept staring at him, and they saw that his face was like that of an angel.
7 1 Then the high priest asked, "Is this so?"

WT: 8 [omits "great"]. 9 other Cyrenians, and people from Alexandria, Cilicia. . . . 10 who were . . . wisdom that was in him and the spirit . . . [adds at end] so that they were refuted by him with all boldness. 13 witnesses against him. 15 [omits "who sat"] . . . [adds at end] an angel of God who stood in their midst. 7:1 the high priest said to Stephen.

COMMENT

The preceding episode told of the election of the Seven and of their commission by the apostles to wait on tables. What is strange about what ensues is that two of the Seven, Stephen and Philip, will never be depicted waiting on tables, but rather engaging in the ministry of the apostles themselves, in "the ministry of the word" (6:4). In this episode Stephen's ministry is narrated in summary fashion, in an incident of debate with diaspora Jews sojourning or resident in Jerusalem. Though they prove to be no match for his eloquence and argumentation, they eventually bring about his summons before the same religious authorities that had arrested Peter and John and forbidden them to preach or teach in the name of Jesus.

The charges brought against Stephen are three: (1) he has uttered blasphemies against Moses and God; (2) he has spoken against this "sacred place" (the Temple) and the law; and (3) he has maintained that Jesus the Nazorean will destroy "this place" and change Mosaic customs. The charges are supported by witnesses whom Luke labels from the start as "false." Again, however, heaven comes to the defense of the Christian minister: members of the Sanhedrin look at him and think that they are gazing at an angel. The story of Stephen forms a climax to the persecution of Jerusalem Christians: the first episode ended in a warning to the apostles (4:17, 21), the second in a flogging of them (5:40), and the third will end in Stephen's death (7:60).

So far it has been the apostles who have been preaching and have been persecuted by Sadducees and the Sanhedrin, but now Luke introduces another early Christian tradition about Stephen, who appears alone, speaks his piece, and is put to death as the result of action against him coming from diaspora Jews. Into the latter account the Sanhedrin has been also introduced, perhaps by Luke himself, who is concerned to continue the theme of persecution from such a source (recall 4:17, 21; 5:33, 40).

Luke has again freely composed this passage, but undoubtedly is using source material, which explains the multiple charges and the interweaving of verses that seem to be doublets. For a long time commentators have sorted out two sets of verses: (a) 6:9–11 and 7:54–58a, which are supposed to be a pre-Lucan account of the lynching of Stephen; (b) 6:12–14 and 7:58b–60, which are supposed to be a pre-Lucan account of an official trial and its outcome (see Foakes Jackson and Lake, *Beginnings*, 2.148–49; Barrett, *Acts*, 380). Verse 8 is clearly Lucan, as would be v 1a. As in all source analysis of Acts, however, the opinions of commentators go in many diverse directions. Conzelmann (*Acts*, 48) says that "it is not possible . . . to distinguish two sources" in 6:8–15; but then later (*Acts*, 61) he says, "literary seams in the account (between 6:11 and 12; the unevenness of 7:54–8:4) indicate that Luke is using a source document." What Luke uses is an Antiochene tradition about Stephen.

Form-critically, this episode is another narrative in Acts, which sets the stage for the coming speech of Stephen, one of the most important in the book. This episode, however, is directly continued in 7:54–8:3; into such a narrative complex Luke has inserted Stephen's speech. The story of Stephen seems to begin with a judicial proceeding, but it ends with the lynching of Stephen (7:54–8:3). The *martyria*, "testimony," of Stephen, which begins in this episode, ends eventually with his martyrdom. Stephen's speech will enable Luke to formulate clearly the position of Christianity vis-à-vis Judaism before the Jerusalem religious authorities.

Moreover, this account depicts the penultimate crisis that the Word of God encounters in Jerusalem, for on the heels of it will come the ultimate crisis, a general persecution of Christians in the city, and Jerusalem Christians will find it necessary to disperse.

Stephen, now singled out by Luke, is depicted as an early Christian commissioned by the community to serve tables, but gifted by heaven with "grace and power," which enable him to engage in an effective ministry with diaspora Jews resident in Jerusalem. He is thus a remarkable example of what solid Christian faith can become. Though he annoys diaspora Jews, who maintain that he has been uttering blasphemous things against Moses and God and criticizing Temple worship, he is not cowed by such opposition. He displays his faith, his wisdom, and a good Christian spirit in the face of it all.

NOTES

8. *Stephen, full of grace and power, was performing great wonders and signs among the people.* The signs of heaven's support for the apostles, for which the community prayed (4:30), now continue to be bestowed on one of the Seven, Stephen, described as endowed with God's favor and power. Luke at first depicts Stephen's public ministry as one of performing miracles, but he tells of no specific miracles. That does not mean that he did not know of them, *pace* Conzelmann *Acts*, 47, for this verse affirms just the opposite. MSS P^{8}, P^{45}, P^{74}, ℵ, A, B, D, 0175, and 33 read "full of grace," whereas the *Koinē* text-tradition reads "full of faith"; MS E has "full of grace and faith"; and MS Ψ has "full of faith (and) grace of the Spirit." "The people" refers to the populace of Jerusalem, not just to Christians. On Stephen, see NOTE on 6:5; on "signs and wonders," see NOTE on 2:22.

9. *Some members of the Synagogue of Freedmen, as it was called.* Luke uses *Libertinoi*, a Greek transliteration of Latin *Libertini*, to designate a group of Jews originally from Italy who had settled in Jerusalem and had their own synagogue. The name *Libertini* is known from Pompeii in Italy (see G. B. de Rossi, *Bolletino di archeologia cristiana* [1864], 70, 92–93). The name is a substantivized adj. developed from *libertus*, "freedman," the designation of an emancipated slave, or a descendant of such. Philo (*Legatio ad Gaium* 23 §155) tells of Jews who lived across the Tiber in Rome, "most of whom were emancipated Roman citizens," originally captives brought to Italy. Tacitus (*Annales* 2.85) tells of 4,000 *libertini* who became infected with the "superstition" (of Judaism). Such synagogue members must have been among the Jerusalem Hellenists.

The meaning of *synagōgē* is problematic: "congregation" or "place of congregating, synagogue" (in the modern sense)? Either meaning would be suitable, since in this instance nothing is decisive one way or the other. It may denote an assembly of Jews for the reading and interpretation of Scripture, for prayer, and other instruction or social activity—or the place where they assembled for such purposes. *Pace* Kee, there is enough evidence, literary and archaeological, for the latter meaning, even in Judea itself, as Oster has shown.

See E. L. Sukenik, *Ancient Synagogues in Palestine and Greece* (Schweich Lectures 1930; London: Humphrey Milford, 1934), 69–78; S. Stowers, "The Synagogue in the Theology of Acts," *ResQ* 17 (1974): 129–43; B.W.W. Dombrowski, "Synagōgē in Acts 6:9," *Intertestamental Essays in Honour of Jósef Tadeusz Milik* (Qumranica mogilanensia 6; ed. Z. J. Kapera; Cracow: Enigma, 1992), 53–65; N. Fernández Marcos, "Sinagoga e iglesia primitiva: Arquitectura e institución," *Sefarad* 53 (1993): 41–58; L. L. Grabbe, "Synagogues in Pre-70 Palestine: A Re-assessment," *JTS* 39 (1988): 401–10; R. Hachlili, "The Origin of the Synagogue: A Re-assessment," *JSJ* 28 (1997): 34–47; F. Hüttenmeister and G. Reeg, *Die antiken Synagogen in Israel* (BTAVO B12; 2 vols.; Wiesbaden: Reichert, 1977), 192–95; F. G. Hüttenmeister, "'Synagoge' und 'Proseuche' bei Josephus und in anderen antiken Quellen," *Begegnungen zwischen Christentum und Judentum in Antike und Mittelalter: Festschrift für Heinz Schreckenberg* (Schriften des Institutum Judaicum Delitzschianum 1; ed. D.-A. Koch und H. Lichtenberger; Göttingen: Vandenhoeck & Ruprecht, 1993), 163–81; H. C. Kee, "The Transformation of the Synagogue after 70 C.E.: Its Import for Early Christianity," *NTS* 36 (1990): 1–24; "Early Christianity in the Galilee: Reassessing the Evidence from the Gospels," *The Galilee in Late Antiquity* (ed. L. I. Levine; New York: Jewish Theological Seminary of America, 1992), 3–22; L. I. Levine, "The Nature and Origin of the Palestinian Synagogue Reconsidered," *JBL* 115 (1996): 425–48; R. E. Oster, Jr., "Supposed Anachronism in Luke-Acts' Use of *synagōgē*: A Rejoinder to H. C. Kee," *NTS* 39 (1993): 178–208; H. C. Kee, "The Changing Meaning of Synagogue: A Response to Richard Oster," *NTS* 40 (1994): 281–83; D. Urman and P.V.M. Flesher (eds.), *Ancient Synagogues: Historical Analysis and Archaeological Discovery*, Vol. 1 (SPB 47/1; Leiden: Brill, 1995); R. Riesner, "Synagogues in Jerusalem," *The Book of Acts in Its Palestinian Setting* (BAFCS 4), 179–211.

In 1913–14 excavations on the hill of Ophel uncovered a synagogue inscription, which tells of the building of a synagogue by Theodotos, (son) of Vettenos, "for the reading of the law and for the teaching of the commandments," along with a hostel for those coming from abroad (see *CIJ* 2.332–35 §1404; C. K. Barrett, *NTB*, §53). Whether this inscription refers actually to the Synagogue of Freedmen of Acts is debated: L.-H. Vincent (*RB* 30 [1921]: 247–77) thought it was the same, but H. Lietzmann (*ZNW* 20 [1921]: 171–73) and A. Deissmann denied it. Sukenik (*Ancient Synagogues*, 70) and Hemer (*Book of Acts*, 176) consider it a possible, but not certain, identification. The date of the inscription, moreover, is not agreed on. See H. C. Kee, "Defining the First-Century CE Synagogue: Problems and Progress," *NTS* 41 (1995): 481–500.

Cyrenians and Alexandrians. Such diaspora Jews came from Cyrene in northern Africa, the district of Cyrenaica, which with the island of Crete formed a senatorial province in the Roman Empire ruled by a proconsul. In Acts 2:10 Libya is mentioned as near Cyrene, i.e., Libya Cyrenaica. Actually Cyrene was the capital of Libya. The burial place of a Jewish family from Cyrene was discovered in Jerusalem (N. Avigad, "A Depository of Inscribed Ossuaries in the Kidron Valley," *IEJ* 12 [1962]: 1–12). Diaspora Jews also came from Alexandria, where they created many problems for their Egyptian neighbors and Roman authorities (see Philo, *Legatio ad Gaium*). In Jerusalem, they would probably all have been members of the same Synagogue of Freedmen, but some commentators understand *synagōgē* before each of the names so that there might be mention of three or even five synagogues. I prefer to take the names as designating different diaspora Jews who were members of the one "Synagogue of Freedmen," understanding *kai* in the first instance as adverbial.

of people from Cilicia and Asia. From two areas of Asia Minor. *Asia* was the most westerly Roman province in this region, bordering on the Aegean Sea; it was a senatorial province governed by a proconsul resident in Ephesus. *Kilikia*, "Cilicia," mentioned again in 15:23, 41; 21:39; 22:3; 23:34; 27:5, was an area on the southern coast of Asia Minor, mainly to the southeast and around the Gulf of Alexandretta and the town of Tarsus. This district had been a Roman province in 102 B.C., when the Romans sought to control the pirates who were based there. Toward the end of the first century B.C. its area was divided between the provinces of Syria and Galatia. In A.D. 72 the province of Cilicia was reconstituted by Vespasian (including Pedias and Tracheia). So it is not clear in what sense Luke may be using the name, as that of a province or a district. Diaspora Jews had lived in both these areas for a long time.

came forward to debate with Stephen. Lit., "rose up, debating with Stephen." The initiative for the debate comes from such synagogue members, not from Stephen. Compare Saul's activity in 9:29. Stephen may have visited the synagogue and presumably would have insisted on the messiahship and lordship of Christ (recall Peter's words in 2:36), which the Jews of the synagogue would have considered an abomination. He may also have argued with them about the Scriptures as relating to Jesus.

10. *they were no match for the wisdom and spirit with which he spoke.* Lit., "they were unable to withstand . . ." Or "the wisdom and the Spirit, with which . . . ," i.e., the wisdom with which the Spirit endowed him. Cf. Luke 21:15, the promise made there is now fulfilled. MS D ends the verse so: *tō pneumati hagiō hō elalei dia to elenchesthai autous hyp' autou meta pasēs parrhēsia. mē dynamenoi oun antophthalmein tē alētheia*, "the Holy Spirit with which he spoke with all boldness so that they were refuted by him. Being unable to face the truth, they . . ."

11. *they put up some men to claim, "We have heard him uttering blasphemous words against Moses and against God."* The accusation comes from synagogue members who have suborned such agents to utter them. This is the first charge made against Stephen. "Blasphemy" (proper) against "the name of the Lord" was punishable by death (stoning) according to Lev 24:11–16; it meant blaspheming God or cursing his name. Later rabbinic tradition specified, "'The blasphemer' [of Lev 24:11–16] is not guilty unless he pronounces the Name itself," i.e., the

tetragrammaton (*m. Sanh.* 7:5). That "blasphemous words" against God mentioned here are meant in that strict sense is far from certain; the accusation of the Jews seems to have a different connotation. Blasphemy against Moses might have been a violation of Exod 22:27b, "You shall not curse a ruler of your people" (*nāśî' bĕʿammĕkā*), but what its specific form may have been is not clear.

12. *They stirred up the people, the elders, and the scribes, confronted him, seized him, and led him off to the Sanhedrin.* The people (*ho laos*) are involved for the first time along with the religious leaders. On Sanhedrin, see NOTE on 4:15. Haenchen (*Acts*, 271) wrongly ascribes the arrest of Stephen to "the people" alone, whereas Luke states that both the synagogue members and leaders (elders and Scribes) were involved in bringing Stephen before the Sanhedrin. The implication is that Stephen is to be tried officially by Jerusalem authorities; the "people" may or may not be involved in the outcome of the trial, Stephen's execution (see NOTE on 7:57).

13. *They also brought in false witnesses who maintained, "This man never stops saying things against [this] sacred place and the law.* Luke makes sure that the reader understands the falsity of the second charge by putting it on the lips of "false witnesses." The adj. *pseudeis* is added for the sake of the reader; they would not have been known as "false" by the religious authorities at that time. Cf. Mark 14:57; Prov 24:28; Pss 27:12; 35:11. "Bearing false witness" was proscribed by the Decalogue (Exod 20:16; cf. Deut 19:16–18). Luke again uses the dem. *houtos* in a pejorative sense, "this one," as again in v 14 below; see NOTE on 1:18. As the story develops, the reader realizes that "[this] place" is the Jerusalem Temple, which becomes even more evident in Stephen's speech, in which he does speak against it. The phrase occurs again in 21:28 with the same meaning; cf. Jer 7:14; 2 Macc 5:17–20. It is never explained in what way Stephen has been speaking against the Torah. As the story of Stephen goes on, one realizes how Luke has made it parallel at times to the accusations leveled against Jesus in the Gospel and other details in the Lucan passion narrative. Cf. Acts 7:53, and compare the generic accusation in Josephus, *Ant.* 20.9.1 §200 (*hōs paranomēsantōn*). MSS E, Ψ, and the *Koinē* text-tradition add *blasphēma* to *rhēmata*, "blasphemous things."

The use of "place" as a reference to the Temple or to God himself may imitate the Jewish practice of referring to them as *ham-māqôm*, "the place," e.g., a surrogate for God's name (see Esth 4:14).

14. *We have heard him claim that this Jesus the Nazorean will destroy this place and change the customs that Moses handed down to us."* The third charge against Stephen finally introduces Jesus, who in the gospel tradition was charged with saying that he would destroy the Temple (Mark 14:57–58; Matt 26:60–61; omitted in Luke). The phrase *ta ethē*, "the customs," inherited from Moses, might again refer to "the law" (v 13), but more probably refers to what the Pharisaic-rabbinic tradition identified as the oral law (*tôrāh še-bĕ-ʿal peh*). Josephus speaks of it as *ta patria nomima*, "the ancestral regulations" (*Life* 38 §191) or *ta patria ethē* (*J.W.* 7.10.2 §424), which grew up around the *nomos*, "law," and which assumed in Pharisaic life the force of law. It is what the Mishnah eventually called *Pirqê 'ābôt*, "Sayings [lit., Chapters] of the Fathers" (*m. Aboth* 1:1). Cf. Plato's

remark: *ethos esti nomos agraphos,* "custom is unwritten law" (*Leges* 7.793a). Jesus is depicted in Mark 7:1–13 as criticizing such customs as not coming from Moses. On "Nazorean," see NOTE on 2:22.

15. *All those who sat in the Sanhedrin kept staring at him, and they saw that his face was like that of an angel.* The implication is that Stephen's face is illumined by God's glory; see 7:55. MS D and some MSS of the VL add at the end: "standing in their midst." The sequel to this remark is 7:55–56. Again the Lucan verb *atenizein,* "stare," is used; see NOTE on 1:10.

7:1. *the high priest asked, "Is this so?"* The high priest in effect asks Stephen whether the charges made against him are true or not. His query gives Stephen the opportunity to address the Sanhedrin. He never answers the question directly, but turns the attention of the assembled members to other considerations. MS D and the VL read: *eipen . . . tō Stephanō,* "said to Stephen."

BIBLIOGRAPHY (6:8–7:1)

Amos, C., "Renewal in the Likeness of Christ: Stephen the Servant Martyr," *IBS* 16 (1994): 31–37.

Arai, S., "Zum 'Tempelwort' Jesu in Apostelgeschichte 6.14," *NTS* 34 (1988): 397–410.

Bihler, J., "Der Stephanusbericht (Apg 6,8–15 und 7,54–8,2)," *BZ* 3 (1959): 252–70.

———, *Die Stephanusgeschichte im Zusammenhang der Apostelgeschichte* (MTS 1/30; Munich: Hueber, 1963).

Boismard, M.-E., "Le martyre d'Etienne: Actes 6,8–8,2," *RSR* 69 (1981): 181–94.

Brodie, T. L., "The Accusing and Stoning of Naboth (1 Kgs 21:8–13) as One Component of the Stephen Text (Acts 6:9–14; 7:58a)," *CBQ* 45 (1983): 417–32.

Daube, D., "Neglected Nuances of Exposition in Luke-Acts," *ANRW* II/25.3 (1985): 2329–56.

Gutmann, J., *Ancient Synagogues: The State of Research* (Chico, CA: Scholars, 1981).

Hanson, R.P.C., "Studies in Texts (Acts 6.13–14)," *Theology* 50 (1947): 142–45.[ch]

Harris, J. R., "A New Witness for a Famous Western Reading," *ExpTim* 39 (1927–28): 380–81.

Légasse, S., *Stephanos: Histoire et discours d'Etienne dans les Actes des Apôtres* (LD 147; Paris: Cerf, 1992).

Levine, L. I., "The Nature and Origin of the Palestinian Synagogue Reconsidered," *JBL* 115 (1996): 425–48.

———, *The Synagogue in Late Antiquity* (Philadelphia: American Schools of Oriental Research, 1987).

Neudorfer, H.-W., *Der Stephanuskreis in der Forschungsgeschichte seit F. C. Baur* (Giessen: Brunnen, 1983).

Schneider, G., "Stephanus, die Hellenisten und Samaria," *Les Actes des Apôtres* (ed. J. Kremer), 215–40; repr. *LTH*, 227–52.
See also the bibliography on 6:1–7.

9. Stephen's Discourse (7:2–53)

2 Stephen replied, "Brothers and fathers, listen to me. The God of glory appeared
to our father Abraham when he was still in Mesopotamia and before he settled
in Haran. 3 *He said to him, 'Leave your country and your relatives and go to the*
land that I shall show you.'[o] 4 So he left the land of the Chaldeans and settled in
Haran. After his father died, (God) made him move from there to this land where
you now dwell. 5 But he did not give him any of it as his inheritance, not even a
foot of ground, yet (God) promised *to give it to him and his descendants after him*
as a possession,[p] to him who was childless! 6 These were the words God used: '*His*
descendants will be aliens in a foreign land, where they will be enslaved and op-
pressed for four hundred years. 7 *But I will pass judgment on that nation to which*
they will be enslaved,[q] God said, *and after that they shall leave it and shall worship*
me in this place.'[r] 8 Then (God) gave him the covenant of circumcision. So it was
that he became the father of Isaac, whom he circumcised on the eighth day, as
Isaac became the father of Jacob, and Jacob the father of the twelve patriarchs.
9 Out of jealousy, the patriarchs sold Joseph into (slavery in) Egypt. Yet God was
with him 10 and rescued him from all his hardships. He granted him favor and
wisdom in the presence of Pharaoh, the king of Egypt, who made him governor
over Egypt and [over] all his palace. 11 But when famine and great hardship came
upon all Egypt and Canaan, our ancestors could find no sustenance. 12 Hearing
that there was grain in Egypt, Jacob sent our ancestors there for the first time.
13 The second time, Joseph made himself known to his brothers, and Joseph's
family became known to the Pharaoh. 14 Then Joseph sent and summoned his
father Jacob and the whole clan, seventy-five persons in all. 15 Jacob went down
to Egypt and died there, as our ancestors did too. 16 But they were brought back
to Shechem and laid in the tomb, which Abraham had bought for a sum of
money from the sons of Hamor in Shechem. 17 When the time drew near for the
fulfillment of the promise that God had made to Abraham, our people in Egypt
spread and grew more numerous, 18 until *a different king came to power [in*
Egypt], who knew nothing of Joseph.[s] 19 This one dealt treacherously with our
people and forced [our] ancestors to expose their infants so that they might not
survive. 20 In this crisis Moses was born, a child handsome in God's sight. For the
first three months he was nursed in his father's house, 21 but when he was exposed,
Pharaoh's daughter adopted him and reared him as her own son. 22 Moses was
educated [in] all the wisdom of the Egyptians and became mighty in words and
deeds. 23 When he was forty years old, the thought came to him to visit his fellow
Israelites. 24 Seeing one of them being mistreated, he went to his aid and avenged
the oppressed man by striking down the Egyptian. 25 He assumed that [his] kins-

folk would understand that God was offering them deliverance through him, but
they did not understand. 26 The next day he appeared to some of them who were
fighting and tried to reconcile them peacefully, saying, 'Men, you are brothers!
Why do you do wrong to one another?' 27 But the man who was wronging his
neighbor thrust Moses aside with the jibe, '*Who has appointed you ruler and
judge over us?* 28 *You do not plan to kill me as you killed the Egyptian yesterday,
do you?*'[t] 29 At that remark Moses fled and settled as an alien in the land of Midian,
where he became the father of two sons. 30 When forty years had passed, *an angel appeared to him in the flame of a burning bush in the desert near Mount* Sinai.[u] 31 When Moses saw it, he was amazed at the sight; as he drew near to look
better (at it), the voice of the Lord was heard. 32 '*I am the God of your ancestors,
the God of Abraham, Isaac, and Jacob.*'[v] Moses trembled and dared to look no
more. 33 *But the Lord said to him, 'Remove the sandals from your feet, for the place
where you are standing is holy ground.*[w] 34 *I have seen indeed the ill-treatment of
my people in Egypt and I have heard their cry, and I have come down to rescue
them.*[x] *Now come, I shall send you to Egypt.*'[y] 35 That Moses, whom they had disowned with the words, '*Who has appointed you ruler and judge?*',[z] God then sent
as [both] ruler and deliverer through the angel that appeared to him in the bush.
36 That one led them forth, performing wonders and signs in the land of Egypt,
at the Red Sea, and for forty years in the desert. 37 That is the Moses who said to
the Israelites, '*A prophet like me God will raise up for you from among your kinsfolk.*'[a] 38 That is the one who was in the congregation in the desert, was with our
ancestors, and with the angel who spoke to him on Mount Sinai, and who received living oracles to give to us. 39 Our ancestors were unwilling to obey him,
thrust him aside, and hankered in their hearts after Egypt. 40 They said to Aaron,
'*Make us gods that will go before us. As for that fellow Moses, who brought us out
of the land of Egypt, we do not know what has happened to him.*'[b] 41 So they made
a calf in those days, offered sacrifice to that idol, and celebrated over a product
of their own hands. 42 But God turned and handed them over to the worship of
the hosts of heaven, as it stands written in the book of the prophets,

'Did you bring me sacrifices and offerings
for forty years in the desert, O house of Israel?
43 *No, you took along the tent of Moloch*
and the star of [*your*] *god Rephan,*
images that you made to worship.
So I shall exile you beyond Babylon.'[c]

44 In the desert our ancestors had the tent of testimony, just as the One who had
spoken to Moses had ordered him to make it, after the model that he had seen.
45 Our ancestors who inherited it brought it in with Joshua, when they took the
land from the nations that God had driven out before our ancestors. (So it was)
until the time of David, 46 who found favor with God and begged that he might
provide a habitation for the house of Jacob. 47 But it was Solomon who built the

house for it. [48]Yet the Most High dwells not in buildings made by human hands, as the prophet says,

> [49]*'The heavens are my throne,*
> *the earth is my footstool.*
> *What kind of a house will you build for me? asks the Lord.*
> *Or what is to be my resting-place?*
> [50]*Did not my hand make all these things?'*[d]

[51]You stiff-necked people, uncircumcised in hearts and ears, you are always resisting the Holy Spirit; as your ancestors did, so do you. [52]Which of the prophets did your ancestors not persecute? Why, they even put to death those who foretold the coming of the Upright One, of whom you have now become the betrayers and murderers — [53]you who received the law as transmitted by angels, but have not observed it."

[o]Gen 12:1 [p]Gen 17:8; 48:4 [q]Gen 15:13–14 [r]Exod 3:12 [s]Exod 1:8
[t]Exod 2:14 [u]Exod 3:2 [v]Exod 3:6 [w]Exod 3:5 [x]Exod 3:7–8
[y]Exod 3:10 [z]Exod 2:14 [a]Deut 18:15 [b]Exod 32:1, 23 [c]Amos 5:25–27
[d]Isa 66:1–2

WT: [2][omits "when . . . Haran"]. [4][omits "So he . . . died"; and "now"]; [adds at the end] and (y)our ancestors before us are dwelling. [5][omits "to him who was childless"]. [6][instead of "God used"] he spoke to him. [10][omits "Pharaoh"]. [11]all the land of Egypt. [14][omits "Jacob"]. [16]but he was brought back . . . Hamor of Shechem. [17]he had announced to Abraham. [18]a king who did not remember Joseph. [19]so that the males might not. [21]exposed in the river. [24]one of his people being. [25]that he was. [26]he saw some of them doing violence to each other. [29]With that remark he made him flee, and he settled. [30]When after that forty years had passed for him . . . [omits "near Mount Sinai"]. [34][omits "come"]. [35]sent even as deliverer. [41]sacrifices. [42]turned them and. [44]that he saw. [49][omits "asks the Lord"] . . . Or what kind of a place is. [51]in heart and ears . . . [omits "Holy"] Spirit, as your ancestors did. [52][omits "now"].

COMMENT

Luke now portrays Stephen, arraigned before the Sanhedrin in Jerusalem, having his say, as he delivers one of the most important speeches in Acts. The speech hardly answers the high priest's question, "Is this so?" but it does purport to answer the charges brought by the "false witnesses," suborned by diaspora Jews resident in Jerusalem against this Christian already described as one of the "seven men of good reputation, filled with the Spirit and with wisdom" (6:3). At least it so begins, but further analysis shows that its purpose is to accomplish something else.

Stephen has been charged with three things: (1) "uttering blasphemous words against Moses and against God" (6:11); (2) "saying things against [this] sacred place and the law" (6:13); and (3) claiming that "Jesus the Nazorean will destroy this place and change the customs that Moses handed down to us" (6:14). These are new charges, which have not been leveled against the Twelve or other Christians up to this point in the Lucan story.

This speech, delivered by a minor character in Acts, by a Hellenist, one of those appointed to "serve tables," is not kerygmatic or missionary, even though addressed to Jews. It purports rather to be a defense speech, even if it does not really answer all the charges. Though it touches on the Temple, i.e., "this sacred place," it never answers the charges of Stephen's blasphemy against God and Moses or his attacks on the law, except indirectly in its appeal to Moses as God's agent. As Dibelius noted, it is hardly the type of speech that someone about to be martyred would utter in defense, for it turns out to be anything but a defense. It is rather (a) historical or typological, as it presents a thumbnail sketch of Israel's history, in deuteronomic style, depicting the reaction of Israel of old to God's actions on its behalf, and it thus achieves a polemic and apologetic purpose; (b) didactic, as it interprets the Scriptures for Jewish religious authorities who listen to it; and (c) accusatory, as it indicts those listening and condemns those who are trying Stephen with "resisting the Holy Spirit" and with being as intolerant of prophets sent to them as were their ancestors of old. More than halfway through, it becomes an open attack on their Temple-centered cult (and implicitly on the law, vv 38, 44).

Written like a *cento* of OT passages, the speech recounts Israel's history in the stories of Abraham, Joseph, Moses, and of the Chosen People's defection. In effect, it imitates summaries of such history found in Joshua 24; Ezek 20:5–44; Neh 9:7–27; and Psalms 78 and 105. They are meditative reflections on the history of salvation for various literary purposes. In this speech the résumé is used for instruction and warning, but the recital is fitted out with polemical and accusatory inserts. It can also be compared with the first part of the Essene Damascus Document (CD 2:14–6:1), in which a recital of Israel's history is similarly used, but in an attempt to convert Judean Jews to the tenets of the Essene community.

The speech seeks to make the point that God has been constantly at work in the history of his people and has constantly brought good out of evil. The pattern of this divine action has been seen in the choice of individual agents whom the people have rejected but who have eventually been vindicated (Barrett, *Acts*, 337). Israel's reaction to God's chosen leaders and to the divine promises of the past has foretold the people's corporate rejection of what God wants of them now: The disobedience and defection of Israel of old are continued in its opposition to Jesus of Nazareth and to those who now preach in his name. Stephen, who is eventually martyred, is the one who becomes, by his speech and his martyr's death, the faithful devotee of the God of their ancestors. What he stands for is only the outgrowth of all that God has achieved in the past through Abraham, Joseph, and Moses. Or as Stephen puts it: "as your ancestors did, so do you. . . . they even put to death those who foretold the coming of the Upright One, of whom you have now become the betrayers and murderers."

M. Simon has maintained that Stephen's speech has been wholly inherited by Luke from some source, whereas many other commentators insist rather that it comes wholly from Luke's pen (so Bihler). It is, however, likely that Luke has passed on to us an inherited form of Stephen's speech, into which he has introduced modifications (e.g., *topō* instead of *orei* [from LXX of Exod 3:12] in 7:7, and others. In its present form it is certainly a Lucan composition, but it builds on inherited tradition, possibly Antiochene. Moreover, the speech itself has been secondarily inserted into the account about Stephen and his martyrdom, for it breaks the connection of 7:1 and 7:54. Haenchen (*Acts*, 289) argues that Lucan polemical additions are found in vv 35, 37, 39–43, and 48–53; to these Conzelmann has added parts of vv 25, 27 (*Acts*, 57). These verses read so, but how can one be sure that the polemical inserts stem solely from Luke's pen? Once again, the problem of the source material in Acts emerges. Roloff (*Apg.*, 117) rightly maintains that the speech differs too much from Luke's own ideas about the Temple so that it cannot all stem from him; but Roloff is not right in ascribing all the negative Temple criticism to Jesus. Torrey sought to ascribe "every part of the first half" of Acts to an Aramaic source (*Composition and Date*, 6), but his views are based on incorrect, late Aramaic evidence and are highly questionable. See H.F.D. Sparks, "The Semitisms of Acts," *JTS* 1 (1950): 16–28; M. Wilcox, *Semitisms*, 158–64.

The structure of the speech can be outlined thus:

2a Introduction (appeal for a hearing)
2b–8a *Part I*: Story of Abraham (God's promise to an obedient Abraham, to whom he gave "this place/land" and a "covenant of circumcision")
8b Transition (from Abraham to the patriarchs)
9–16 *Part II*: Story of Joseph (jealous patriarchs sold Joseph; but God was with him and he became the one who rescued the patriarchs from affliction)
17–19 Transition (stories of Abraham and Joseph are linked; the "promise" draws near—deliverance from Egypt)
20–38 *Part III*: Story of Moses (handsome before God and educated in all Egyptian wisdom, Moses became the one through whom God brought "deliverance"; yet he was rejected by Israelites as their ruler and judge. Called again by God in a holy place, Moses became the agent of deliverance [v 34]. "This Moses" Israel thrust aside and returned in their hearts to Egypt; but he promised them a prophet like himself)
39–40 Transition (rejection of Moses led to idolatry)
41–43 *Part IV*: Israel's First Falling Away (its desert idolatry: hosts of heaven worshiped)
44–50 *Part V*: Israel's Second Falling Away (substitution of a man-made Temple for the desert Tabernacle)
51–53 Conclusion: Stephen's Indictment (Israel's guilt continues: As your ancestors did, so do you! You have betrayed and murdered the Upright One)

In part I, the story of Abraham (vv 2b–8a), the speech opens with a typical Greek rhetorical device and quickly assumes the character of a *cento,* as many OT phrases are built into its allusions. The "God of glory" (7:2) becomes the chief actor in the account of divine ways with Abraham. Luke depicts God calling Abraham from "Mesopotamia" to leave his land in order to worship "in this place" (7:7). So Abraham becomes a wanderer, and the reader learns that the worship of God is not tied to any individual place. The wandering Abraham thus becomes important for diaspora Jews, who have come to worship in "this place" (a phrase that assumes another connotation as the speech progresses). Then God's "promise" comes to Abraham, the wanderer, not yet settled in Canaan (cf. Gen 11:32; 15:7). Abraham has neither land nor offspring of his own when the promise comes to him, but it comes to realization in the birth of Isaac, through whom Abraham becomes the father of the "patriarchs" and of many "descendants."

After the transitional verse (8b), the speech continues in part II with the story of Joseph (vv 9–16). Joseph, sold into slavery in Egypt by his brothers, settles in a land belonging to others, the sign of the great diaspora. Indirectly, Stephen begins his accusation against those listening to him with Joseph, who is the type of Jesus, the rejected one. Rejected by his own, "the patriarchs" who sold him into slavery, Joseph is protected by God, who shows him favor and brings it about that Jacob, Israel's eponymous ancestor, though he died in a foreign land, is buried in "this place," viz., in Israel. God's deliverance is thus contrasted with human mistreatment: the "hardships" that Joseph suffered at the hands of the patriarchs stand in contrast to his God-given "favor and wisdom" before Pharaoh. Thus God achieved a saving work in spite of human fumbling and opposition to his agents.

The drawing near of the "time of the promise" (7:17) links the stories of Abraham and Joseph; it shows the similarity of the way God dealt with Abraham and with Joseph. It also introduces the story of Moses in part III (vv 20–38), which becomes the main and central part of the speech. Moses and the rejection of him by Israel are likewise typological of Jesus, the "prophet like me." At first, Stephen's recital stresses that the agent of salvation and deliverance of Yahweh's people was born and raised outside of "this place." Moses lived to the age of 120 (Deut 34:7), and his life is here divided into three periods of forty years (vv 23, 30, 36). In the second period the forty-year-old Moses appears as an agent of deliverance for his people, as he first comes to the aid of an oppressed individual Israelite, "by striking down the Egyptian" (7:24). This leads to his rejection by his own people: "Who has appointed you ruler and judge over us?" (7:27). In the third period God appears to Moses, the deliverer, in the burning bush at Sinai and gives him the law, the "living oracles" (7:38); but "our ancestors were unwilling to obey him" and "thrust him aside." In the transition (vv 39–40) this Moses says to the Israelites, "A prophet like me God will raise up for you from among your kinsfolk" (7:39), as yet unexplained. The rejection of Moses, the God-sent deliverer of Israel, however, leads to Aaron-led idolatry (Exod 32:23).

In part IV (vv 41–43) Israel's falling away is at first recounted in its worship of idols of its own making (the golden calf) and the hosts of heaven; thus did it rebel against God's Spirit in the course of its desert wanderings. From its historic beginnings as God's Chosen People in Egypt and its desert wanderings, "the house of Israel" constantly has gone astray, and as a result it suffered exile in Babylon.

In part V (vv 44–50) Israel's falling away is further recounted in its substitution of a temple of its own making for the tabernacle made after the divine pattern and given to it by God through Moses in the desert. "Yet the Most High dwells not in buildings made by human hands" (7:48). This misguided act has made Yahweh like a heathen idol. So Stephen criticizes the Jerusalem Temple.

Finally, in part VI (vv 51–53) Stephen concludes his speech by indicting contemporary leaders of Israel. He bursts into an invective that is indirectly related to the central argument of his defense, but after rehearsing Israel's past stubbornness and its reluctance to fulfill its true calling, he accuses these leaders of resisting the Holy Spirit. "As your ancestors did, so do you" (7:51). That is why they have not recognized "the coming of the Upright One," Jesus of Nazareth. The notion that the contemporary Judeans have consummated the rebellion of previous generations in Israel thus becomes a point of controversy between Christians and Jews, and it will continue long beyond Luke's day. Yet Stephen's accusation is hardly different from the accusations uttered by the Essenes of Qumran against the rest of the people in Judea (see CD 8:9).

Stephen's speech, then, reviews the history of Israel, extols the patriarchs, Abraham and Joseph, and enhances the role of Moses (and indirectly the law that he passed on), but it reserves its criticism for the Temple and its cult. Such criticism has often been regarded as "a 'Hellenist' sermon" (see Barrett, *Acts,* 338). But the "Hellenists" among Jerusalem Jews would presumably have been as much centered on the Temple as the "Hebrews." Even the criticism of the Temple by the Essenes of Qumran was centered on the mode of cult carried out by the "last priests of Jerusalem" (1QpHab 9:4–11), which they considered tainted and in need of restoration to ritual purity; it was not per se anti-Temple or anti-cult. See H. Braun, *Qumran,* 1.159, who is rightly reluctant to ascribe any affinity of Stephen's speech to Qumran ideas. Stephen's criticism of the Temple and its cult stems from a different attitude. Opposition to Stephen has come from Jews of the diaspora sojourning or resident in Jerusalem. Those who have brought Stephen before the Sanhedrin have come to worship "in this place," but he counters their opposition to him by attacking that for which they stand most. His attitude might be seen as akin to that of the Therapeutae in Egypt, about whom Philo reports: "In each house there is a sacred room, which is called a sanctuary [*semneion*] or closet [*monastērion*], in which they gather alone and are initiated into the mysteries of consecrated life [*ta tou semnou biou mystēria*]" (*De vita contemplativa* 3 §25). As Stephen sees it, diaspora Jews should be more critical of the Jerusalem Temple made by human hands.

No matter how one judges the historicity of the speech of Stephen, in its present Lucan form it records an invaluable first-century testimony about the way some Christians had begun to consider the relation of the Christian church to contemporary Judaism. Even though it is put on the lips of Stephen, it reveals how some Jewish Christians were trying to interpret the Christ-event in light of their traditional biblical religion and esteem for the law of Moses.

The story of Stephen and especially this speech represent the beginning of Luke's account of the break of Christianity from its Jewish matrix. Even though the mission to the Gentiles does not begin before Peter's activity in Acts 10, Stephen, an originally Jewish settler in Jerusalem coming from the diaspora and a converted Hellenist, is now in controversy with diaspora Jews who have haled him before the Jerusalem Sanhedrin. The controversy arose from those who have come from outside the Palestinian Jewish matrix of Christianity. Stephen's stinging indictment of his Jewish adversaries initiates the break of Christianity from that matrix. Though it begins as an apologia, a defense against the charges made against him, it leads to a judgment against his Jewish opponents. The ending of Stephen's speech in 7:51–53 contrasts with that of Peter in 2:32–36, where the tone is quite different. The history of Israel described in parts I to V of Stephen's speech only prepares for the concluding indictment: the misunderstanding of Israel of old, its disobedience, its rejection of God-sent leaders, its failure to listen to God's promises have all prepared it for the present rejection of God's Upright One and the message about him.

Some have tried to see Samaritan traits in the speech, especially in its opposition to the Jerusalem Temple, but most of them are not convincing (see M. H. Scharlemann, *Stephen*, 20, 45–51). As Bruce has noted, it cannot be convincingly said that

> Stephen's speech expresses a Samaritan as against a Jewish attitude. So far as the temple was concerned, the issue between Samaritans and Jews was whether Gerizim or Zion was the place where God was to be worshiped. But Stephen's argument would exclude the Samaritan viewpoint as emphatically as the Jewish. ("Stephen's Apologia," 40)

The attitude toward the Temple that Stephen represents in this speech is not entirely that of Luke himself, because he has already depicted the apostles worshiping in the Temple along with Jerusalem Jews. This is the best reason for saying that at least some details of Stephen's speech have been inherited by Luke from a preexisting source.

Stephen's speech is a good example of his "wisdom and spirit" (6:10). He aligns himself with "father Abraham" (7:2), Joseph the guardian of Israel, and Moses, its liberator. In recounting the historic reaction of the Chosen People called by God, he recounts their proclivity to idolatry in worshiping the golden calf and in building a man-made Temple. He thus extols the privilege of historic Israel, which enjoyed the favors shown by God to this people in the call of Abraham, the guidance of Joseph, and the sending of Moses. Following such leaders, Stephen insists that God has now sent another Upright One to call people through such an agent to a renewed allegiance to himself. If Israel does not respond as it should, it will become as stiff-necked as its ancestors, a fate that can be met by all who react against God's chosen messengers.

NOTES

2. "*Brothers and fathers, listen to me.* Stephen calls for attention, employing the usual rhetorical address formula (see NOTE on 1:16); in this case *adelphoi* refers to "fellow Jews" (see NOTE on 1:15) and implies that both Stephen and the Sanhedrin are children of the patriarch he is about to mention. The addition of *pateres* to the formula is a mark of respect for the members of the Sanhedrin (which Paul will also use in 22:1). Stephen thereby tries to render his hearers benevolent.

The God of glory. Stephen borrows a title from Ps 29:3, which echoes the resplendent theophanies of Israel's desert wanderings (Exod 16:10; 24:16–17). He thus alludes to the God of Israel, the God whom his listeners acknowledge and worship.

appeared to our father Abraham. Lit., "was seen by" (see NOTE on 2:3). Abraham has already been mentioned in 3:13, 25. He is now invoked by a loyal Jew (Stephen) as "our father" and as an example of how God dealt with the forebears of Israel (cf. Luke 1:73). Stephen begins his recital of its history by appealing to the "patriarch" par excellence. See Gen 12:1, 7 for God's appearance to Abraham; cf. 1QapGen 22:27 for an Aramaic account of the vision. In bearing witness to Jesus sent by God to his people, Stephen wants to relate this latest emissary of heaven to the primary call given to "Father Abraham."

Abraham, whose name was at first Abram, the son of Terah, was born in Ur, an ancient town in southern Mesopotamia (Gen 11:26–27).

when he was still in Mesopotamia and before he settled in Haran. On Mesopotamia, see NOTE on 2:9. Haran was in northwest Mesopotamia, in Amorite country, to the east of Canaan; it was an important trade center, the crossroads of caravan routes (from Egypt to Persia and from Babylonia to Asia Minor).

According to Gen 11:28–31, after Terah's son Haran died in Ur, Terah took Abram and other members of his family and departed from there, "to go into the land of Canaan; but when they came to Haran, they settled there." Terah eventually died there at the age of 205 (Gen 11:32). Then the Lord addressed Abram (Gen 12:1) and called him to leave Haran, i.e., his "land, kindred, and father's house" (see Gen 12:5; 24:10; 29:4).

Stephen speaks of God's call of Abraham according to a form of the Abraham story current in contemporary Judaism, which depended more on Gen 15:7, "I am Yahweh who brought you forth from Ur of the Chaldeans" (cf. Neh 9:7). So Philo too understood Abraham's call (*De Abrahamo* 14 §62; but cf. *De migratione Abrahami* 32 §177); also Josephus, *Ant.* 1.7.1 §154: "being seventy-five years old, he left Chaldea, when God ordered him to move to Canaan." See Str-B, 2.666–67; W. Mundle, "Die Stephanusrede." Luke's preoccupation with Mesopotamia comes from this later understanding of the Abraham story. *Pace* Haenchen (*Acts*, 278), Abraham's departure from Mesopotamia is not "wrongly" related by Luke. He is simply following a different interpretation of the Abraham story. In any case, the Lucan emphasis falls on God's initiative in calling Abraham to leave his country.

3. *'Leave your country and your relatives and go to the land that I shall show you.'* Lit., "go out from your land and from your kin, and come to the land . . ." Stephen quotes part of Gen 12:1 in a form close to the LXX, which employs the adv. *deuro*, "hither," as an impv. "come!" Though the LXX paraphrases, it catches the sense of the original Hebrew. Luke also omits the LXX phrase, "and from your father's house," because Abraham departs from Haran in the form of the story that he uses. *Pace* Wilcox (*Semitisms*, 26–27), this omission and the use of *deuro* do not form a "point of contact between a Targumic tradition and a text in Acts." The similarity with the late Targum Pseudo-Jonathan, which Wilcox nowhere dates, is at best coincidental.

The impv. *exelthe* expresses God's call of Abraham, to which the patriarch responded in obedience. His response made of him a wanderer in the Genesis story, without an inheritance of his own, going first to Shechem in Canaan, and then through the length of that land even as far as Egypt, whence he would be summoned back to the promised land. Abraham, not knowing what he would encounter, obediently set out as God had asked of him.

4. *he left the land of the Chaldeans and settled in Haran.* I.e., Abraham went forth from the land (Ur), which would be called many centuries after him "the land of the Chaldeans." Abraham left Ur with his father Terah (Gen 11:31). Centuries later southern Babylonia, in which Ur had been situated, came to be ruled by the last dynasty of Babylonian kings (Nabopolassar, Nebuchadrezzar II, Evil-Merodach, Nergal-sharezer, and Nabonidus, 626–539 B.C.), who were called Chaldeans. Assyrian royal inscriptions from the ninth century on, however, refer to that southern land as *Kaldu* and to its inhabitants as *Kaldai*, dwellers in the land between the Tigris and Euphrates just north of the Persian Gulf. Some exilic or postexilic scribe undoubtedly added the Hebrew name *Kaśdîm* to the end of Gen 11:28 to explain for his contemporaries where the city of *'Ûr* was located (see Neh 9:7); from v 28 it spread to Gen 11:31; 15:7. The LXX does not mention Ur in any of these places, using rather *chōra (tōn) Chaldaiōn*, "land of the Chaldeans." Luke writes *ek gēs Chaldaiōn*, a literary variant of the same. See Jer 24:5 (LXX: *gē Chaldaiōn*).

After his father died. According to Gen 11:26, Terah was seventy years old when Abraham was born, and he died in Haran at the age of 205 (Gen 11:32). Gen 12:4, however, says that Abraham "was seventy-five years old when he left Haran." That would mean that Terah was at that time 145 years old, when Abraham departed (as the Samaritan Pentateuch has it, 11:32). Luke, however, is apparently following a contemporary Jewish understanding of the Abraham story. Philo also says that Abraham moved from Haran "after his father had died there" (*De migratione Abrahami* 32 §177). That form of the tradition did not want to admit that Abraham had abandoned his elderly father; see Str-B, 2.667. Though there might be some agreement here with the Samaritan tradition, what lies behind it is the harmonizing tendency of the Palestinian recension of the Pentateuch found in the Samaritan text (Bruce, "Stephen's Apologia," 41).

(God) made him move from there to this land where you now dwell. Lit., "into which you are dwelling." The same prep. *eis* is used twice; in the second instance

one would expect rather *en* (see NOTE on 2:5). Stephen makes a summary statement, mentioning only the starting point and the end of Abraham's wanderings, Haran and Canaan, but he stresses God's influence in Abraham's movements and in the choice of the final place where he and his descendants would reside. MSS D and E add: *kai hoi pateres hymōn* [or *hēmōn*] *hoi pro hēmōn,* "and (y)our ancestors before us."

5. *he did not give him any of it as his inheritance, not even a foot of ground.* Because "the Canaanites were in the land" (Gen 12:6), when Abraham first passed through Canaan, none of it became his. Stephen's phraseology echoes that of Deut 2:5, which actually has nothing to do with Abraham.

(God) promised to give it to him and his descendants after him as a possession. Stephen alludes to Gen 17:8, which in the LXX reads, "I will give to you and to your descendants (lit., your seed) after you the land where you are sojourning, all the land of Canaan, as an everlasting possession," an exact translation of the MT. Most of the promise is also found in Gen 48:4; cf. Gen 12:7; 13:15; 15:18–20; 24:7. This is the first mention in Acts of the famous "promise" made by God to Abraham and his posterity, the people of Israel; it will assume even greater importance later (see 7:17; 13:32; 26:6). It is introduced now in view of the following phrase at the end of the verse. Recall Luke 1:55.

to him who was childless! Lit., "there being to him no child." Though Abraham was married, when God first called him, Sarah his wife was barren (Gen 11:29–30). Stephen adds this detail to the allusion just made to Gen 17:8, because it is important in view of the promise. Luke uses the negative *ou* with a ptc., instead of the more correct *mē*, as in Luke 6:42; Acts 19:11; 26:22; 28:2, 17; see BDF §430.2. The clause is actually a gen. absol., with concessive force and with a reference to a preceding word (BDF §423.5).

6. *These were the words God used.* Lit., "so God spoke."

'His descendants will be aliens in a foreign land, where they will be enslaved and oppressed for four hundred years. 7. *But I will pass judgment on that nation to which they will be enslaved.* Lit., "where they will enslave and oppress them. . . ." Stephen alludes to Gen 15:13–14, which in the LXX reads, "Know for sure that your descendants will be sojourning in a land not their own, and they [the rulers] will enslave them and oppress them and humiliate them for four hundred years, but I will pass judgment on that nation to which they will be in servitude." Save for the addition of "and humiliate them," the LXX agrees with the MT; the Lucan form is closer to the MT. Possibly Exod 2:22 has also influenced the wording of Acts.

The MT of Exod 12:40–41 speaks of Israel's stay "in Egypt" as 430 years, a tradition that Paul echoes in Gal 3:17, whereas the LXX of Exod 12:40 gives those years for its stay "in the land of Egypt and in the land of Canaan." For the later rabbinic version of the tradition, see Str-B, 2.668–71. Stephen refers to the time of the Hebrews' bondage in Egypt in order to show that God brought the promise made to Abraham to realization precisely through a crisis that his people faced. Divine judgment on Egypt brought about Israel's exodus from its land of bondage.

after that they shall leave it and shall worship me in this place.' Stephen loosely paraphrases the LXX of Exod 3:12, which reads, "As you lead my people out of Egypt, and you (pl.) will worship God on this mountain." He also changes *en tō orei toutō*, "on this mountain" (Horeb), to *en tō topō toutō*, "in this place." The meaning of the last phrase is debated. Now at its first occurrence it must be understood as "Canaan" (so too Schille, *Apg.*, 181). Eventually it will come to mean Jerusalem, in the context of Stephen's coming argument about the Temple. Schneider (*Apg.*, 1.455 n. 72) and Barrett (*Acts*, 345), however, think that it already refers to Jerusalem, and Weiser (*Apg.*, 184) to the Temple; but that introduces a specification not yet known in Stephen's speech, despite 6:13–14. The change from *orei* to *topō* does not necessarily show that the passage was composed in Jerusalem (*pace* Holtz, *Untersuchungen*, 98), but only reveals Lucan composition, as Conzelmann rightly notes (*Acts*, 52). Stephen's exposé began with the wanderings of Abraham through Canaan and Egypt and has shifted to the sojourning of Israel, his descendants, in Egypt, after which they came to enter Canaan, the promised land, where they were to worship God.

8. *Then (God) gave him the covenant of circumcision.* Stephen alludes to Gen 17:2, 10–14. Circumcision, the ritualistic removal of the male foreskin, was to be "the sign of the covenant" (Gen 17:11; cf. *Jub.* 15:28) between Abraham and God, in effect, the visible sign of the ongoing pact between Israel and God. That is why it is called here "the covenant of circumcision." This is cited as another example of the obedience of the patriarch of Israel, who circumcised himself, Ishmael, and all the men of his household (Gen 17:22–27; 21:4). Circumcision came to be understood in Judaism as the mark of salvation. See further *Romans*, 320–21.

So it was that he became the father of Isaac, whom he circumcised on the eighth day. This part of the verse marks a transition to the story of the patriarchs after Abraham. The force of the adv. *houtōs*, "so," is elliptical. It does not mean that through circumcision Abraham begat Isaac, but rather that Abraham, in his circumcised state, became the father of Isaac, through whom the Chosen People would be descended (Gen 21:2–4). Circumcision on the eighth day is prescribed in Gen 17:12; it became part of Mosaic legislation in Lev 12:3. Though Stephen's speech will become quite critical of the Jerusalem Temple, it implicitly at least admits the validity of the law and its prescription of circumcision.

as Isaac became the father of Jacob. Though Jacob was the younger of the twins born to Isaac and Rebekah, only Jacob received his father's blessing, not Esau (Gen 27:27–37); and so Jacob became the one through whom Abraham's line and the promise made to Abraham would continue (cf. Rom 9:10–13).

Jacob the father of the twelve patriarchs. See Gen 29:31–30:24 for the birth of eleven of the sons of Jacob (Reuben, Simeon, Levi, Judah, Dan, Naphtali, Gad, Asher, Issachar, Zebulun, Joseph) and Gen 35:16–18 for the twelfth (Benjamin).

9. *Out of jealousy, the patriarchs sold Joseph into (slavery in) Egypt.* See Gen 37:11, 26–28, 36; 45:4; Philo, *De Iosepho* 4 §15; 40 §238. The selling of Joseph and the carrying of him to Egypt introduce the settlement of descendants of Abraham in a land belonging to others; it is the sign of the diaspora. The "patriarchs"

who were to be the bearers of the promise to the coming generations of Hebrews are the ones who introduce crisis into its continuation. The enslaving of Joseph connotes the rejection of him by his own kin, by "patriarchs" of Israel itself. Joseph thus becomes the type of Jesus, the rejected one, in Stephen's argument. See G. D. Kilpatrick, "The Land of Egypt in the New Testament," *JTS* 17 (1966): 70.

Yet God was with him and rescued him from all his hardships. See Gen 39:2: "Yahweh was with Joseph, and he became successful; he was in the house of his master, the Egyptian." Cf. Gen 39:21; 50:20. Joseph is the innocent one who suffers, but who is eventually victorious, because God is with him and brings good out of evil. So Stephen stresses God's providential guidance of Joseph in spite of the evil action of the other sons of Jacob. Cf. Ps 105:16–22.

10. *He granted him favor and wisdom in the presence of Pharaoh, the king of Egypt, who made him governor over Egypt and [over] all his palace.* See Gen 39:4–6, 21; 41:37–45. Joseph suffered in slavery and imprisonment in Egypt for thirteen years (Gen 37:2; 41:46), before his interpretation of the Pharaoh's dream about the coming famine brought him deliverance and a place of honor in Pharaoh's land and palace. God's activity on his behalf brought him the favor and esteem that he eventually won with the Egyptian ruler. So he became a regent in the land of his bondage. Cf. Ps 105:21–22, the wording of which may be considered closer to what Luke writes. *Pace* Wilcox (*Semitisms*, 28), the Lucan text may be related to "the textual tradition" preserved in the late targum Pseudo-Jonathan of Gen 41:41, 43b, but that tradition may rather be affected by the Lucan reading.

11. *when famine and great hardship came upon all Egypt and Canaan, our ancestors could find no sustenance.* See Gen 41:53–54, 57: "there was famine in all lands . . . the famine was severe over all the earth." Cf. Gen 42:5.

12. *Hearing that there was grain in Egypt.* See Gen 42:1–2; cf. 1QapGen 19:10. For the prep. *eis*, see NOTE on 2:5; some MSS (D, Ψ, and the *Koinē* text-tradition) read more correctly *en Aigyptō*.

Jacob sent our ancestors there for the first time. Jacob sent at first only ten of his sons, keeping the youngest, Benjamin, with him, "fearing that harm might come to him" (Gen 42:3–5). On the arrival of the ten sons in Egypt, Joseph recognized them, without revealing himself to them, and demanded that one of them (Simeon) remain in Egyptian prison, while the rest would return to Canaan with food and come back again, bringing their youngest brother (Benjamin) along with them (Gen 42:7–20). Luke passes over other details (Gen 42:21–38).

13. *The second time, Joseph made himself known to his brothers.* See Gen 43:13–15; 45:1–3. On their second descent to Egypt, Joseph revealed himself to his brothers and told them that what they had done to him was providential: "God sent me before you to preserve for you a remnant on the earth" (Gen 45:7). MSS P^{74}, ℵ, A, B, C, Ψ, and the *Koinē* text-tradition read *anegnōristhē*, "he was made known again," which uses the same verb as Gen 45:1 (LXX). Other MSS (A, B, Vg) read the simple verb *egnōristhē*, "he was made known." In both cases, the pass. voice has to be understood in a middle sense.

Joseph's family became known to the Pharaoh. See Gen 45:16.

14. *Then Joseph sent and summoned his father Jacob and the whole clan.* See Gen 45:9–13, 23–28; 46:1–7: "Jacob and all his offspring with him."

seventy-five persons in all. Lit., "amounting to seventy-five souls." The prep. *en* is used in a peculiar sense (see BDF §198.1), perhaps derived from Deut 10:22 (LXX). See Gen 46:26 ("sixty-six persons"), to which one must add Jacob, Joseph, and Joseph's two sons (46:20), or "seventy persons" (Gen 46:27; cf. Exod 1:5; Deut 10:22). Cf. *Jub.* 44:33. The LXX of the first two of these passages reads "seventy-five" (= 66 + 9 sons of Joseph), as do 4QGen-Exod[a] 17–18:2; 4QExod[b] 1:5 (DJD 12.18, 84; cf. *ESBNT*, 87–88 n. 75). Luke follows the LXX tradition, but not all 75 would have come to Egypt on this visit. See Philo, *De migratione Abrahami* 36 §§199–201 for an allegorical explanation of the difference in the traditions of Exodus and Deuteronomy.

15. *Jacob went down to Egypt and died there.* This is the third visit of Jacob's family to Egypt. See Gen 46:5–6, 28–29; 47:28; 49:33. Luke makes Stephen abridge the story of Jacob's descent to Egypt.

as our ancestors did too. I.e., the rest of the family of Jacob.

16. *they were brought back to Shechem and laid in the tomb.* Lit., "memorial," a word commonly used in the contemporary Greek-speaking world for a "grave, tomb." It was a place where the dead were remembered. Jacob, Israel's eponymous ancestor, though he died in a foreign land, was thus buried in his own land, Israel.

which Abraham had bought for a sum of money from the sons of Hamor in Shechem. Stephen's speech confuses the land of Jacob's burial with the land bought by Jacob from the sons of Hamor at Shechem (Gen 33:19). Jacob was buried in the field of Machpelah at Mamre near Hebron (Gen 50:13; cf. 49:30–31), in ground bought by Abraham from Ephron the Hittite (Gen 23:16–20), where Abraham, Sarah, Isaac, Rebekah, Leah were also buried (cf. Josephus, *J.W.* 4.9.7 §532). According to Josephus (*Ant.* 2.8.2 §199), Joseph's brothers were also buried in Hebron; so too *Jub.* 46:9; *T. Reuben* 7:2. In the land bought by Jacob at Shechem, however, Joseph was buried (Josh 24:32; cf. Exod 13:19).

17. *When the time drew near for the fulfillment of the promise that God had made to Abraham.* Lit., "as the time of the promise drew near." I.e., the promise to Abraham's descendants about inheriting the land of Canaan, mentioned in vv 5–7 (Gen 17:8; 48:4; cf. Gen 12:7; 13:15; 15:18–20; 24:7). In this context, the "promise" forms a transition between the Joseph story in Stephen's speech and the Moses story, between the way God dealt with Joseph and with Moses. As Joseph was an instrument in God's providential care of his people, so Moses will be too. The verse begins with a conjunction *kathōs* used in an unusual temporal sense, "when," a meaning that occurs rarely elsewhere (2 Macc 1:31; Neh 5:6; *Ep. Aristeas* 310).

our people in Egypt spread and grew more numerous. See Exod 1:7: "the Israelites were fruitful and increased; they multiplied and grew very strong so that the land was filled with them." *Ho laos* refers to the people who were descended from Jacob and his family.

18. *until a different king came to power* [*in Egypt*], *who knew nothing of Joseph.* Luke begins with *achri hou,* which is elliptical for *achri tou chronou hō,* "until the time in which" (BDF §216.3). Stephen alludes to Exod 1:8 ("there arose a new king over Egypt, who did not know Joseph"), the LXX of which agrees with the MT. It may refer to Seti I (1308–1290), of the nineteenth Egyptian dynasty, who moved the royal throne from Thebes in Upper Egypt to the Nile Delta region in the hope of recapturing control over western Asia and there began a vast building program; or it may refer to Ramesses II (1290–1224), under whom the building continued. The WT (MSS D, E; VL and Chrysostom) read *emnēs-thē,* "(Joseph) was (not) remembered."

19. *This one dealt treacherously with our people.* Lit., "taking advantage of our race by trickery." Stephen alludes to Exod 1:10–14, using the ptc. of the same verb *katasophizesthai* (Exod 1:10). The new Pharaoh imposed forced labor on the Israelites to build the store-cities, Pithom and Raamses, in the delta.

forced [*our*] *ancestors to expose their infants so that they might not survive.* The LXX of Exod 1:22 records Pharaoh's command to all his people: "Every male born to the Hebrews you shall throw into the Nile, but you shall let every female live." The MT, however, lacks "to the Hebrews." Cf. LXX Num 20:15. For *ka-koun,* "force," followed by the articular infin. *(tou poiein),* see LXX 1 Kgs 17:20; cf. DBF §400.8.

20. *In this crisis Moses was born, a child handsome in God's sight.* Moses, born in a foreign land, was favored by God and would become his agent to deliver the Hebrews from the land of their oppression. He would bring God's promise to various stages of its realization. Moses too would be rejected eventually and would thus become another type of Jesus, the rejected one. See Exod 2:1–10 for the account of his birth, his concealment in the bulrushes of the Nile, and the discovery of him by the Pharaoh's daughter.

In 2:2 (LXX) Moses is called *asteion,* "beautifully formed," which adj. Luke takes over and to which he adds *tō theō,* a phrase not easy to translate, perhaps as an ethical dative, "(handsome) unto God." The addition in any case emphasizes the divine providence for the child. His exceptional beauty was a sign of his voca-tion (cf. Heb 11:23). Cf. Philo, *De vita Mosis* 1.3 §9; 1.5 §18, who uses the same adj.; Josephus, *Ant.* 2.9.5 §224.

His name in Hebrew is *Mōšeh.* As given to the child by Pharaoh's daughter, it undoubtedly stands for a shortened form of Egyptian names like Ah-mose ("Ah is born"), Har-mose ("Horus is born"), Thut-mose ("Thut is born"). Exod 2:10de, however, records a Hebrew folk etymology, even ascribing it to the Pharaoh's daughter: "Because I drew him *(mĕšîtihû)* from the water." The author of Exodus saw divine providence at work in that the very daughter of the Pharaoh, who had ordered the death of male Hebrew infants, became the instrument of the salva-tion of Moses, drawing him from the waters of the Nile and naming him. His name was written in Greek as *Mōysēs* or *Mōsēs,* whence comes the English spell-ing. See Josephus, *Ant.* 2.9.6 §228, where the name is explained as derived from Egyptian *mōy,* "water," and *esēs,* "those saved," another folk etymology. Similarly Philo, *De vita Mosis* 1.4 §17.

the first three months he was nursed in his father's house. See Exod 2:2c–4. Moses' father is not named in Exodus 2, but only described as "a man from the house of Levi." In Exod 6:20 his name is recorded, Amram, married to Jochebed. Through the intervention of Miriam, Moses' older sister, Moses was nursed by his own mother (Exod 2:4, 7–8; 15:20). "Three months" denotes the length of time it was possible to hide the newborn child.

21. *when he was exposed, Pharaoh's daughter adopted him and reared him as her own son.* Lit., "and reared him for herself as/for a son." The prep. *eis* expresses a predicate accusative, imitating the Greek of Exod 2:10 (LXX). See Exod 2:5–10c for the full story of the finding of the hidden child and his adoption. Josephus (*Ant.* 2.9.5–7 §§224–37) gives the name of the daughter as Thermuthis (cf. *Jub.* 47:5) and greatly embellishes the story of her finding the infant and saving him from Pharaoh's counselors, who wanted to kill him. So God brings it about that a daughter of the Pharaoh saves and protects the Hebrew whom God has chosen to liberate his people.

22. *Moses was educated [in] all the wisdom of the Egyptians.* Stephen stresses the foreign birth and upbringing of Moses. Such was the character of the one who would lead God's people to "this place." Cf. Philo, *De vita Mosis* 1.5 §§20–24; 2.1 §1; Josephus, *Ant.* 2.9.7 §236.

became mighty in words and deeds. So Stephen describes Moses, employing the phrase used of Jesus by the disciples on the way to Emmaus (Luke 24:19; cf. Acts 2:22). Compare Exod 4:10, Moses' own description of himself as lacking in eloquence, "slow of speech and tongue." Cf. Sir 45:3 ("by his words he causes signs to cease"); Philo, *De vita Mosis* 1.14 §80; Josephus, *Ant.* 2.12.2 §271. None of the ancient traditions about Moses testifies to his eloquence, save this part of Stephen's speech.

23. *When he was forty years old, the thought came to him to visit his fellow Israelites.* Lit., "when the time of forty years was fulfilled for him, it mounted in his heart to visit his brothers, the sons of Israel," i.e., in their forced labor under Egyptian taskmasters. Despite his Egyptian upbringing, Moses never forgot his background and his own people. The "forty years" are not mentioned in the OT; this place in the NT is probably the earliest extant dating of Moses' age when he left Egypt; see Str-B, 2.679–80 for the later rabbinic debate about his age when this happened; also *Sifre* §357. The expression *anebē epi tēn kardian,* "it mounted in his heart," is derived (*pace* Wilcox, *Semitisms,* 63) from the LXX of 2 Kgs 12:5 (MS A.); Isa 65:16; Jer 3:16; 51:21 (= MT 44:21), where it is sometimes a translation of Hebrew *'lh 'l lb.*

24. *Seeing one of them being mistreated, he went to his aid and avenged the oppressed man by striking down the Egyptian.* See Exod 2:11b–12. The OT story records that Moses looked about and saw no one before he struck the Egyptian. Stephen's speech assumes that the reader is familiar with the Moses story and does not explain "the Egyptian." Cf. Philo, *De vita Mosis* 1.8 §§43–44.

25. *He assumed that [his] kinsfolk would understand that God was offering them deliverance through him, but they did not understand.* This is Stephen's interpre-

tive embellishment of the Exodus story in order to build on it later (in vv 33–38): deliverance through Moses and lack of understanding.

26. *The next day he appeared to some of them who were fighting.* Exod 2:13 (LXX) specifies "them" as *dyo andras Hebraious diaplēktizomenous,* "two Hebrew men fighting," i.e., two of Moses' own people were caught by him mistreating each other.

tried to reconcile them peacefully, saying, 'Men, you are brothers! Why do you do wrong to one another?' Again Stephen embellishes the story, for in Exod 2:13c Moses simply asks, "Why do you strike your fellow?" Stephen wants to present Moses as a peacemaker among his own people.

27. *the man who was wronging his neighbor thrust Moses aside with the jibe, 'Who has appointed you ruler and judge over us? 28. You do not plan to kill me as you killed the Egyptian yesterday, do you?'* Stephen's words adapt some of the initial phraseology of Exod 2:14, but quote the jibe exactly as it is in the LXX; it agrees with the MT. So Moses is "thrust aside" and rejected by some of his own people; cf. vv 35, 39.

29. *At that remark Moses fled.* So Stephen curtails the story in Exod 2:14d–15. It records rather that Moses feared, thinking that the deed was surely known and learning that Pharaoh had heard about it and was seeking to kill him, and so he fled. Stephen understands Moses' flight as occasioned merely by the remark of his fellow Hebrew, not directly by Pharaoh, as in Exod 2:15.

settled as an alien in the land of Midian, where he became the father of two sons. Again Stephen curtails the Exodus story; see 2:15b for Moses' flight to Midian, where he marries Zipporah, a daughter of the priest of Midian, who bore him two sons, Gershom and Eliezer (Exod 2:21–22; 18:3–4). Little is known about Midian (Hebrew *Midyān*); even its location is contested. See H.S.J. Philby, *The Land of Midian* (London: E. Benn, 1957). The Midianites seem to have been a tribal group related to the early Hebrews (see Gen 25:2–4).

30. *When forty years had passed.* Lit., "forty years being fulfilled." This is a Lucan embellishment, not found in the Exodus account. See COMMENT.

an angel appeared to him in the flame of a burning bush in the desert near Mount Sinai. Stephen's words are a loose paraphrase of Exod 3:2 (LXX). At the end of 3:1 the LXX names the place as "the mountain of Horeb," following the MT. Then the LXX of v 2 reads: "The angel of the Lord appeared to him in a flame of fire from the bush, and he saw that the bush was not burned by the fire," which is a slight curtailment of the MT. Stephen's words locate the incident "in the desert" and "near Mount Sinai" and speak of "an angel" instead of "the angel of the Lord." Some MSS (D, H, P, S, 614) and some ancient harmonizing versions add *Kyriou,* "of the Lord." See P. Katz, "*En pyri phlogos,*" ZNW 46 (1955): 133–38.

31. *When Moses saw it, he was amazed at the sight.* See Exod 3:3: "I shall turn aside to look at this great sight; why is it that the bush is not burned?" Or possibly (with D. N. Freedman), "that the bush is indeed burning?"

as he drew near to look better (at it), the voice of the Lord was heard. Lit., "there occurred the voice of the Lord." Again *Kyrios* is used for Yahweh; see NOTE on 2:36. Exod 3:4 is loosely paraphrased.

32. *'I am the God of your ancestors, the God of Abraham, Isaac, and Jacob.'* Exod 3:6ab (LXX) is quoted, with pl. *paterōn*, "fathers," instead of the sg.; with "God of" mentioned only once, whereas it occurs three times in the LXX of Exod 3:6 and 3:15. See NOTE on 3:13.

Moses trembled and dared to look no more. Exod 3:6c (LXX) reads, "Moses turned his face away, for he was afraid to gaze before God."

33. *the Lord said to him.* This introductory clause is derived from Exod 3:7, but the following words come from 3:5, followed by parts of 3:7–8, 10.

'Remove the sandals from your feet, for the place where you are standing is holy ground. See Exod 3:5bc, quoted almost exactly as in the LXX. The removal of the sandals is a form of recognition of "holy ground." Neither Temple nor sacrifice was required for the theophanies of Abraham, and so neither of them is required now for the theophany to Moses. "The place" where it occurs is holy because God manifests himself there. Moses does not build there a shrine or a temple, and this has a bearing on Stephen's argument to come. See L. Dürr, "Zur religionsgeschichtlichen Begründung der Vorschrift des Schuhausziehens an heiliger Stätte," *OLZ* 41 (1938): 410–12.

34. *I have seen indeed the ill-treatment of my people in Egypt and I have heard their cry.* God's words in Exod 3:7b are quoted exactly as in the LXX; the last clause is the same in sense, but not in wording. The LXX has *kai tēs kraugēs autōn akēkoa,* a literary variant with the same meaning.

I have come down to rescue them. See the divine oracle in Exod 3:8a (LXX), quoted exactly.

I shall send you to Egypt.' Exod 3:10 (LXX) reads: "I shall send you to the Pharaoh, king of Egypt."

35. *That Moses, whom they had disowned with the words, 'Who has appointed you ruler and judge?'* Stephen begins to draw his conclusion from the foregoing Moses story, and his change of rhetorical phraseology, especially "that Moses," calls attention to the shift in his argument. He alludes to the words quoted in v 27 above (Exod 2:14, omitting *eph' hēmōn*). The rejected Moses is now to become God's chosen agent. Stephen, who respects Moses, thus answers indirectly the charge about his "blasphemous words against Moses" (6:11). The phrase "that Moses" will be echoed again in vv 36, 37, 38.

God then sent as [both] ruler and deliverer. Three important ideas appear here: God's sending, Moses as ruler, and Moses as deliverer. The verb "sent" echoes that quoted from Exod 3:10 in v 34c above. The title "ruler" *(archōn)* is derived from the jibe in v 27. The new title is *lytrōtēs*, "deliverer, redeemer," i.e., one who will ransom or buy back God's people from bondage. Two titles were denied Moses by a fellow Hebrew, but God has bestowed two others on him. Thus he has become God's commissioned agent, one with authority over God's people and one who will deliver them.

through the angel that appeared to him in the bush. A reference to v 30, where

Exod 3:2 is loosely paraphrased. Though God is behind all this, his commissioning of Moses comes through the mediation of an angel.

36. *That one led them forth, performing wonders and signs in the land of Egypt.* The exodus of the Hebrews from the land of bondage and servitude was guided by Moses, who brought the Pharaoh to allow them to depart. Moses as the thaumaturge or wonder-worker becomes the type of Jesus. The "wonders and signs in the land of Egypt" allude to God's words to Moses in Exod 7:3, where he tells of the hardening of Pharaoh's heart and the ten plagues that are to follow in Exod 7:8–11:10. Cf. Ps 105:27; Josephus, *Ant.* 2.12.4 §276; *Assumption of Moses* 3.11. Recall the use of "wonders and signs" in the description of Jesus in Peter's Pentecostal speech (2:22).

at the Red Sea. See Exod 14:21–31, for the routing of the Egyptians at the Sea as Moses stretched his hand over it. The "Sea" is not named in these verses of Exodus; but shortly before, Exod 13:18 mentions *yam sûp*, "Sea of Reeds" (also found in Exod 15:4). In later Jewish tradition it became known as the "Red Sea," as Exod 13:18 (LXX) understands it, *hē erythra thalassa.* Luke follows this tradition, which is also found in Wis 10:18; 1 Macc 4:9; Heb 11:29; Philo, *De vita Mosis* 1.29 §165; 2.1 §1; *1 Clem.* 51.5.

"Red Sea," however, was the ancient name for the Persian Gulf, as is evident from 1QapGen 21:17–18, where *yammā' śimmōqā'*, "Red Sea" (the Persian Gulf and the Indian Ocean), is distinguished from *liššān yam sûp*, "the tongue of the Reed Sea" (the tongue-shaped Gulf of Suez emerging from the body of water usually called today the Red Sea). Josephus (*Ant.* 1.1.3 §39) knows that the Tigris and Euphrates Rivers empty into the Red Sea. See M. Copisarow, "The Ancient Egyptian, Greek and Hebrew Concept of the Red Sea," *VT* 12 (1962): 1–13; N. H. Snaith, "*Yam Sôp:* The Sea of Reeds," *VT* 15 (1965): 395–98; Fitzmyer, *The Genesis Apocryphon of Qumran Cave 1: A Commentary* (BibOr 18A; Rome: Biblical Institute, 1971), 68, 153–54; cf. B. F. Batto, "The Reed Sea: *Requiescat in Pace,*" *JBL* 102 (1983): 27–35; "Red Sea or Reed Sea," *BARev* 10/4 (1984): 57–63; J. R. Huddlestun, "Red Sea," *ABD* 5.633–42.

for forty years in the desert. The phrase is derived from Num 14:33, which tells in God's words how the children of Israel were to suffer because of their murmuring. A similar threefold description of the things that Moses did "in Egypt," "at the Red Sea," and "throughout the desert" is found in Philo, *De vita Mosis* 2.1 §1; *T. Moses* 3:11.

37. *That is the Moses who said to the Israelites, 'A prophet like me God will raise up for you from among your kinsfolk.'* Lit., "to the sons of Israel." Stephen moves on to another episode in the Moses story, as he quotes Deut 18:15 (LXX) with a slight transposition of phrases. Compare the wording used in Acts 3:22 and see NOTE there. Here we have only "God" as the subject, instead of "the Lord, your God," but the scribes of some MSS (C, E, H, P) harmonized the text, adding *kyrios* before *ho theos* and either *hēmōn* or *hymōn* after that. In using this promise made by Moses to the Israelites, Stephen is preparing for his identification of Jesus as that "prophet like me." Moses, the "prophet" (= mouthpiece of God), is

thus the type of Jesus. That Stephen's words carry a Samaritan nuance or are related to the Samaritan Taheb (see NOTE on 3:22) is far from certain; see Simon, *St Stephen*, 61–62; Weiser, *Apg.*, 186.

38. *That is the one who was in the congregation in the desert, was with our ancestors, and with the angel who spoke to him on Mount Sinai, and who received living oracles to give to us.* Stephen now recalls four characteristics of Moses: (1) he was the leader of the *ekklēsia*, "congregation," in the desert; (2) he was with our "fathers" of old; (3) he was with the angel who spoke at Sinai; and (4) he was the one who received God's oracles to pass them on to Israel. The last characteristic stresses the mediatory role of Moses as the redeemer of Israel, who thus becomes the type of Christ, and his story becomes the pattern for the Christian story of redemption. Stephen speaks of the law given to Moses on Mt. Sinai as "living oracles" (cf. Rom 3:2), which Moses was "to give to us." In "us" Stephen includes himself and thus indirectly answers the charge about speaking against the law. In 7:53 he will speak of that law as promulgated by "angels," referring to this statement, which implicitly says that the "angel who spoke to him on Mount Sinai" also gave him the "living oracles" for Israel. Compare Philo, *De vita Mosis* 2.1 §3: "By the providence of God he became king, lawgiver, high priest, and prophet; and in each role he achieved the first rank." The "living oracles" were the God-given directives of the law, and by observing them Israel would find life; cf. Lev 18:5; Deut 32:46–47.

The order of Greek text of v 38 is disturbed. The phrase *kai tōn paterōn hēmōn*, "and our fathers," is also the object of the prep. *meta*, "with," which stands before *tou angelou*, but it is out of place and immediately precedes the sg. rel. pron. *hos*. The phrases have to be transposed in translation.

39. *Our ancestors were unwilling to obey him, thrust him aside, and hankered in their hearts after Egypt.* Lit., "whom our ancestors did not want to obey." Cf. Acts 7:27. So ends Stephen's use of the Moses story. This verse is transitional to his recital of the defection of Israel. See Exod 16:3; Num 14:2–3, for the hankering of the Israelites after "the fleshpots of Egypt" against their precarious freedom in the desert. Stephen's words understand the "hankering" of their ancestors on a broader scale: the Egypt that had become home to them, despite their servitude; cf. Ezek 20:8.

40. *They said to Aaron, 'Make us gods that will go before us. As for that fellow Moses, who brought us out of the land of Egypt, we do not know what has happened to him.'* Stephen's words quote the LXX of Exod 32:1 or 32:23 with insignificant variations; they reflect the substance of the MT. The Israelites did not know what had happened to Moses, who had gone up the mountain to consult Yahweh, the real God of Israel, the God of their ancestors (Exod 24:15–18). So they thrust Moses aside and turned to Aaron, from whom they begged gods made by human hands, who would lead them.

41. *So they made a calf in those days, offered sacrifice to that idol, and celebrated over a product of their own hands.* Lit., "over works of their hands." See Exod 32:4–6. Their celebration consisted of eating, drinking, and playing before the calf. This was their desert idolatry, an act of rebellion against the God of their

ancestors. Stephen cites this incident to stress that from its origins this people of God has been rebellious and prone to turn to idols of its own making. Cf. Ps 115:4; Wis 13:10. He tones down Aaron's involvement and accuses "them." See A. Pelletier, "Une création de l'apologétique chrétienne: *moschopoiein*," *RSR* 54 (1966): 411–16. On "in those days," see NOTE on 1:15.

42. *God turned.* This clause is ambiguous: The verb could be taken intransitively and mean that God himself "turned" from Israel, i.e., would have nothing more to do with it. Or it could be taken transitively and mean that God "turned" Israel to the cult of heavenly hosts, expressing in different words only what will be stated in the next clause.

handed them over to the worship of the hosts of heaven. In Stephen's view, Israel not only worshiped the golden calf but also "the hosts of heaven," a phrase derived from 1 Kgs 22:19; Jer 7:18; 19:13; Neh 9:6 (LXX), which denotes stars and other heavenly bodies, and sometimes spirits or angels thought to govern their movements. As did Paul in Rom 1:24, 26, 28, Stephen is depicted indulging in protological thinking, as he speaks of God "handing over" the people of Israel to idolatry (see *Romans*, 108, 272). Cf. Wis 11:16: "that they might learn that one is punished by the very things by which one sins." Also Deut 4:16; Hos 13:2–4.

as it stands written. Luke uses the introductory formula *kathōs gegraptai*, "as it has been written," as in Luke 2:23 (see NOTE there); it occurs again in Acts 15:15. The formula is derived from Dan 9:13 (Theodotion), a translation of Hebrew *ka'ăšer kātûb*, or from 2 Kgs 14:6 (LXX), a translation of Hebrew *kakkātûb*), where it is also used of Scripture. The former of these Hebrew formulas introducing OT quotations is found in QL (e.g., 1QS 5:17; 8:14; CD 7:19; 4QFlor 1–2 i 12; 4QpIsa[c] 4–7 ii 18; 4QCatena[a] 10–11:1; 4Q178 3:2; see Fitzmyer, *ESBNT*, 3–58, esp. 8–9). Contrast B. M. Metzger, "The Formulas Introducing Quotations of Scripture in the NT and the Mishnah," *JBL* 70 (1951): 297–307; repr. *Historical and Literary Studies: Pagan, Jewish, and Christian* (NTTS 8; Leiden: Brill, 1968), 52–63.

in the book of the prophets. I.e., in the *dōdekaprophēton*, "the (book of the) Twelve Prophets." The twelve minor prophets were usually thought of as one book in antiquity. See Josephus, *Ag.Ap.* 1.8 §40 (one of "thirteen" post-Mosaic prophetic writings); Epiphanius, *De mensuris* 4.

'Did you bring me sacrifices and offerings for forty years in the desert, O house of Israel? 43. *No, you took along the tent of Moloch and the star of* [*your*] *god Rephan, images that you made to worship. So I shall exile you beyond Babylon.'* Stephen quotes Amos 5:25–27 (LXX), transposing a phrase in the first verse, substituting *proskynein autois*, "to worship them," for *heautois*, "for yourselves," and changing "Damascus" to "Babylon." The prophet's words had reproached the house of Israel for its idolatry and had threatened banishment and exile as a consequence. Amos recalled that Israel's relation to God during its desert experience was direct and did not have to depend on sacrificial offerings. Stephen repeats such prophetic words as he builds up his invective against the Jerusalem Temple and attributes apostasy to Israel even during that desert experience. Because of the preference for idols of their own making, God's judgment of them took the

form of abandonment to even greater idolatry. Israel was carted off to "Babylon" in Stephen's estimation, a reference to the Babylonian Captivity, because of Israel's idolatry.

Rhaiphan is found in MSS P[74], ℵ[2], A, C, E, Ψ, 33, and 453; but a variety of other spellings occur: *Rhompha* in MS B; *Rhomphan* in ℵ*; *Rhemphan* in D, 323, 945, and 1739; *Rhepha* in 81, 104. At the end, instead of *epekeina Damaskou* (LXX of Amos 5:27), MS D reads *epi ta merē Babylōnos,* "to the regions of Babylon," which harmonizes the Lucan text with the LXX.

In the Hebrew original of Amos 5:26 Israel was accused of taking along *sikkût malkĕkem,* "Sakkuth, your king," the name of an Assyrian god. The consonants *skt,* however, could also be understood as the cst. sg. of *sukkāh,* "booth, tent," i.e., "the tent of your king." So the LXX understood the word; but the consonants *mlk* were then taken as *Mōlek,* "Molech," the name of the god to whom people of Judah offered infants in sacrifice (Jer 32:35; 2 Kgs 23:10). In the LXX the phrase became "the tent of *Moloch.*" Thus for Stephen the prophet's words still accuse the house of Israel of idolatry.

Similarly, in the Hebrew of Amos 5:26 Israel was accused of taking along *kiyyûn kôkab 'ĕlōhêkem,* "Kaiwan, your star-god," another Assyrian god (= Saturn). That was translated in the LXX as *ton astron tou theou hymōn Rhaiphan,* "the star of your god," which Luke uses too. This is cited by Stephen as another example of Israel's idolatry. Where this divine name comes from is uncertain. See R. Borger, "Amos 5,26, Apostelgeschichte 7,43 und Šurpu II, 180," *ZAW* 100 (1988): 70–81. Whether the two names, Hebrew *sikkût* and *kiyyûn* in Amos and *Sakkud* and *Kaywan* in Akkadian, refer to the same star-god, Saturn, is debatable.

These words of Amos are also quoted in the Damascus Document in QL (CD 7:14–15) and given an interpretation that suits that Jewish community, being there joined to Amos 9:11. It has little bearing on this passage in Acts, except in that it interprets the consonants *skt* as a sg., *swkt hmlk,* "the tent of the king," which supports the sg. understanding of the LXX.

See W. L. Knox, *Some Hellenistic Elements in Primitive Christianity* (Schweich Lectures 1942; London: Humphrey Milford, 1944), 14–15; S. A. Meier, "Sakkuth and Kaiwan," *ABD,* 5.904.

44. *In the desert our ancestors had the tent of testimony. Hē skēnē tou martyriou* is the name for the desert tabernacle derived from the LXX (Exod 27:21; 28:43; 33:7; Num 1:50; 12:4; Deut 31:14), rendering Hebrew *'ōhel mô'ēd,* "tent of meeting." It was a portable sanctuary, the sign of God's "testimony": that God was present to Israel and in its midst (Exod 25:8). Its main furnishing was the "ark of the covenant," i.e., the "testimony that I shall give you" (Exod 25:21); "there I will meet with you" (25:22). This verse is joined to the preceding by the catchword bond of "tent," but the logic of the two verses is difficult to follow, as Conzelmann (*Acts,* 55) has recognized.

just as the One who had spoken to Moses had ordered him to make it, after the model that he had seen. Stephen refers to God's instructions to Moses about the building of the desert tabernacle in Exod 25:9, 40. He understands that tabernacle as God given, and not the product of human craftsmanship, because it was constructed according to the heavenly pattern. Contrast the explanation given by Philo: how Moses made the "handmade" *(cheiropoiēton)* tabernacle out of the four elements (earth, water, air, fire), as befitted one dedicated to the Father and Ruler of All (*De vita Mosis* 2.18 §88). This sign to Israel of God's presence sufficed until the time of David.

45. *Our ancestors who inherited it brought it in with Joshua.* See Josh 3:11–4:18 for the story of the bringing of the ark across the Jordan into Canaan. This movable tabernacle, which housed the ark, preceded the house of Israel wherever it went (Deut 31:8–9), until it came to rest at Shiloh (Josh 18:1).

Joshua's name may be significant here, because its Hebrew form in Josh 1:1 is *Yĕhôšūăʿ* ("Yahweh, help!" the cry of a woman in birth pangs). Later on, the name was contracted to *Yēšûăʿ*, which becomes in the LXX *Iēsous*, "Jesus," to whom Stephen will refer as the "Upright One" in v 52. See *Luke*, 347.

when they took the land from the nations that God had driven out before our ancestors. Joshua counseled the people of Israel: "By this you shall know that the living God is in your midst: He shall dispossess the Canaanite, the Hittite, the Hivite, the Perizite, the Girgashite, the Amorite, and the Jebusite before you" (Josh 3:10). These are the names of the pre-Israelite inhabitants of Canaan. During all the conquest God was present to his Chosen People in the movable tabernacle.

(So it was) until the time of David. I.e., Israel was content that God was present to it in the portable tabernacle, which was not tied to one place. David brought the ark of the covenant to Jerusalem and placed it in a tent that he had pitched for it (2 Sam 6:1–17).

46. *who found favor with God.* See 1 Sam 16:13; 18:12, 14: "the Lord was with him." Cf. 2 Sam 5:10; 7:1; 15:25.

begged that he might provide a habitation for the house of Jacob. MSS P^{74}, א*, B, D, and 2344 read *oikō*, whereas others (א^{2}, A, C, E, Ψ, 33, 36, 81, 1739) read *theō*, "for the God" (of Jacob; see LXX of Ps 132:5). The latter reading makes better sense, but is for that reason suspect. It is also possible that homoeoteleuton has influenced copyists; the original may have been "for the God of the house of Jacob."

See 2 Sam 7:1–16, where David raises the question with Nathan, the prophet, about building a house for God. In that passage there is a play on the word "house." At first it means "palace" (vv 1–2), then "temple" (house of God, vv 5–7, 13), then "household, dynasty" (vv 11, 16). Cf. 1 Chr 17:1–14. David's desire was not found acceptable (1 Kgs 8:17–19; 2 Chr 6:7–8).

47. *it was Solomon who built the house for it.* Or "for him," depending on the reading of v 46. See 1 Kgs 5:5; 6:1–2, 14, 37–38; 8:20; 2 Chr 2:1; 3:1; 5:1; 6:10. So in Stephen's view Israel substituted a human construction for the divinely inspired desert tabernacle, and this will now become the focus of his further remarks and conclusion. His argument: You had a tent of testimony, which signified God's presence among you for generations; it was made by Moses according

to the divine pattern given to him. Then your kings replaced it with a Temple made by human craft. You preferred a structure made by human hands to what God had given you.

48. *Yet the Most High dwells not in buildings made by human hands, as the prophet says.* Lit., "dwells not in handcrafted (things)." Even Solomon in his dedicatory prayer acknowledged this (1 Kgs 8:27; cf. Josephus, *Ant.* 8.4.2 §107). Stephen, however, draws his own conclusion from the preceding exposé: Israel's decision was a misguided act in that it made Yahweh like a heathen idol. This is Stephen's main polemic contention, which he bolsters up with a prophetic statement. The same argument will reappear in Paul's speech at the Areopagus (17:24).

(Theos) hypsistos or *ho hypsistos*, "the Most High," as a divine name is found in many Greek writings. It is used of Zeus in the Greco-Roman world (Pindar, *Nemean Odes* 1.90; 11.2; Aeschylus, *Eumenides* 28); also in inscriptions, esp. from Cyprus (PGM 4.1068; 5.46) and Cyrene, where it was employed even as a designation for Egyptian Isis. In the LXX (e.g., Gen 14:18, 19, 22; Ps 46:4) it is applied to Yahweh, translating *'ēl 'elyôn*, "God, Exalted One." Philo (*In Flaccum* 7 §46; *Legatio ad Gaium* 36 §278) and Josephus (*Ant.* 16.6.2 §163) also use it of Yahweh. *Hypsistos* is found for God in Mark 5:7 and Heb 7:1, but otherwise in the NT only in Lucan writings (Luke 1:32, 35, 76; 6:35; 8:28; Acts 16:17); see NOTE on Luke 1:32. Cf. C. Roberts, T. C. Skeat, and A. D. Nock, "The Guild of Zeus Hypsistos," *HTR* 29 (1936): 39–88.

49. *'The heavens are my throne, the earth is my footstool. What kind of a house will you build for me? asks the Lord. Or what is to be my resting-place?* 50. *Did not my hand make all these things?'* Stephen quotes the LXX of Isa 66:1–2, transposing the introductory *legei Kyrios* to the end of the first question, changing *poios topos*, "what kind of a place," to *tís topos*, "what is the place," and making a question out of the last clause. He cites Isaiah's words, which sought to make Israel aware that a human construction of stone and wood, no matter how beautiful, could not really contain God; it could not even compare with the things that he has created. Yet Solomon himself, in the course of the dedication of the Temple that he had built, reflected on it and similarly expressed the ideas of Trito-Isaiah (see 1 Kgs 8:27; 2 Chr 6:18). The prophet wanted Israel to learn that a "humble and contrite spirit, one that trembles at the divine word" was far more acceptable to God than the one who would slaughter an ox (Isa 66:2–3). Stephen now comes to an answer of the charge brought against him in 6:13–14. See T.C.G. Thornton, "Stephen's Use of Isaiah lxvi.1," *JTS* 25 (1974): 432–34. For a development of Stephen's argument against the Temple, see *Ep. Barn.* 16:1–2.

51. *You stiff-necked people.* After the recital of Israel's stubborn resistance to Yahweh in various stages of its history, Stephen turns to address the Jewish leaders of the Sanhedrin. The religious authorities who challenge him are no better than the stiff-necked Israelites who demanded of Aaron the golden calf for their idolatry. He borrows an OT adj. *sklērotrachēloi*, found in Exod 33:3, 5; Deut 9:6, 13 (LXX); its Hebrew counterpart is also in Exod 32:9. Cf. Neh 9:29–30.

uncircumcised in hearts and ears. Another description is drawn from Lev 26:41, where it depicts Israel's unresponsive reaction to the Holiness Code (Lev 17–26; cf. Deut 10:16). The uncircumcised heart or ear is also a favorite topic of the prophet Jeremiah (4:4; 6:10; 9:26); see Ezek 44:7, 9. In QL, see 1QpHab 11:13; 1QS 5:5.

you are always resisting the Holy Spirit. In his indictment of the contemporary religious leaders in Jerusalem, Stephen echoes the ideas of Trito-Isaiah, who composed a psalm of intercession with a historical prologue reflecting on the deliverance of Israel from Egyptian bondage and God's blessings on it: "they rebelled and provoked his Holy Spirit to wrath" (Isa 63:10).

as your ancestors did, so do you. So Stephen concludes his argument, uttered with wisdom and the Spirit (6:10). Cf. Neh 9:34–36.

52. *Which of the prophets did your ancestors not persecute?* The murder of the prophets was a Jewish motif, even though most OT books do not speak of it. It began to surface in 1 Kgs 18:4, 13; 19:10, 14 (Elijah's complaint to God) and is continued in Jer 2:30; 26:20–24 (Uriah of Kirjath-jearim, who prophesied against Jerusalem and Judah); 2 Chr 24:20–21 (Zechariah, son of Jehoiada); the apocryphal *Martyrdom of Isaiah* (*OTP*, 2.143–76). Cf. Neh 9:26; 2 Chr 36:16; Luke 13:34; Matt 23:31; 1 Thess 2:15; Heb 11:32, 36–37; Str-B, 1.943. Stories about martyrs who were considered prophets continued in the rabbinic tradition. See B. H. Amaru, "The Killing of the Prophets: Unraveling a Midrash," *HUCA* 54 (1983): 153–80; H.-J. Schoeps, *Die jüdischen Prophetenmorde* (SBU 2; Uppsala: Wretman, 1943; repr. *Aus frühchristlicher Zeit: Religionsgeschichtliche Untersuchungen* (Tübingen: Mohr [Siebeck], 1950), 126–43.

Why, they even put to death those who foretold the coming of the Upright One. Stephen charges that the religious authorities of Jerusalem are like their forebears, those who put to death the prophets, even those who predicted the coming of Jesus, again called "the Upright One" (see NOTE on 3:14). Thus Stephen is made to echo a Lucan global interpretation of the OT (Luke 24:25–27: "all that the prophets have said"). In other words, their ancestors murdered not only prophets who exposed their stubborn reaction to God's message, but also those who foretold the coming of Jesus. Cf. 1 Thess 2:15. See G. D. Kilpatrick, "Acts vii.52 *Eleusis*," *JTS* 46 (1945): 136–45, who regards *eleusis* as a "messianic term." The Christian "Upright One" may be the Messiah, but the terms and connotations of the two are different.

of whom you have now become the betrayers and murderers. This is the climax of Stephen's charge: the authorities who listen to his words are the *prodotai kai phoneis*, "betrayers and murderers," of the heaven-sent Upright One. Stephen's words echo those of Peter in 3:14c: "his servant Jesus whom you handed over and disowned in Pilate's presence."

53. *you who received the law as transmitted by angels.* Stephen adds this clause to compound the guilt of such religious authorities, who, he knows, would boast of their fidelity to the Mosaic law. He also echoes a contemporary Jewish belief that the law was given to Moses by angels, not by Yahweh himself; see the LXX of Deut 33:2; *Jub.* 1:27–29; Josephus, *Ant.* 15.5.3 §136. Cf. Acts 7:38; Gal 3:19; Heb 2:2. For the use of this idea in the later rabbinic tradition, see Str-B, 3.554–

56. The phrase *eis diatagas angelōn* is strange and difficult to translate, probably "by directions of angels" (BAGD, 189), i.e., by God's directing of angels to transmit it. The prep. *eis* is understood as = *en,* used in an instrumental sense (ZBG §101; BDF §206.1).

have not observed it." Stephen's indictment ends, with a note familiar to Paul (Rom 2:13, 23, 25). What Stephen means is that they have not really understood what this law was teaching—another covert reference to the Lucan global understanding of the OT. Luke uses *phylassein* in the sense of obediently keeping the law, as in Luke 11:28; 18:21; Acts 16:4; 21:24.

BIBLIOGRAPHY (7:2–53)

Aarde, A. G. van, "The Most High God Does Live in Houses, but not 'Houses Built by Men . . .': The Relativity of the Metaphor 'Temple' in Luke-Acts," *Neotestamentica* 25 (1991): 51–64.

Arndt, W., "Some Difficulties in the Speech of Stephen, Acts 7," *TM* 4 (1924): 33–37.

Bacon, B. W., "Stephen's Speech: Its Argument and Doctrinal Relationship," *Biblical and Semitic Studies* (Yale Bicentennial Publications; New York: Scribner, 1901), 213–76.

Barnard, L. W., "Saint Stephen and Early Alexandrian Christianity," *NTS* 7 (1960–61): 31–45.

Barrett, C. K., "Old Testament History according to Stephen and Paul," *Studien zum Text und zur Ethik des Neuen Testaments: Festschrift . . . Heinrich Greeven* (BZAW 47; ed. W. Schrage; Berlin/New York: de Gruyter, 1986), 57–69.

Bruce, F. F., "Stephen's Apologia," *Scripture: Meaning and Method: Essays Presented to Anthony Tyrrell Hanson* (Hull: Hull University Press, 1987), 37–50.

Carrez, M., "Présence et fonctionnement de l'Ancien Testament dans l'annonce de l'évangile," *RSR* 63 (1975): 325–42.

Charlier, C., "Le manifeste d'Etienne (Actes 7)," *BVC* 3 (1953): 83–93.

Coggins, R. J., "The Samaritans and Acts," *NTS* 28 (1982): 423–34.

Colmenero Atienza, J., "Hechos 7,17–43 y las corrientes cristológicas dentro de la primitiva comunidad cristiana," *EstBíb* 33 (1974): 31–62.

Cullmann, O., "L'Opposition contre le Temple de Jérusalem, motif commun de la théologie johannique et du monde ambiant," *NTS* 5 (1958–59): 157–73.

Dahl, N. A., "The Story of Abraham in Luke-Acts," *StLA*, 139–58.

Daniélou, J., "L'Etoile de Jacob et la mission chrétienne à Damas," *VC* 11 (1957): 121–38.

Davies, W. D., "A Note on Josephus, Antiquities 15:136," *HTR* 47 (1954): 135–40.

Donaldson, T. L., "Moses Typology and the Sectarian Nature of Early Christian Anti-Judaism: A Study in Acts 7," *JSNT* 12 (1981): 27–52.

Downing, F. G., "Ethical Pagan Theism and the Speeches in Acts," *NTS* 27 (1980–81): 544–63.
Dupont, J., "La structure oratoire du discours d'Etienne (Actes 7)," *Bib* 66 (1985): 153–67.
Elliott, J. H., "Response to van Aarde's Article . . . ," *Neotestamentica* 25 (1991): 171–73.
Esler, P. F., "Response to van Aarde's Article . . . ," *Neotestamentica* 25 (1991): 173–74.
Foakes Jackson, F. J., "Stephen's Speech in Acts," *JBL* 49 (1930): 283–86.
Fridrichsen, A., "Zur Stephanusrede," *Le Monde Oriental* 25 (1931): 44–52.
Hannay, T., "The Temple," *SJT* 3 (1950): 278–87.
Kilgallen, J. J., "The Function of Stephen's Speech (Acts 7,2–53)," *Bib* 70 (1989): 173–93.
———, *The Stephen Speech: A Literary and Redactional Study of Acts 7,2–53* (AnBib 67; Rome: Biblical Institute, 1976).
Klijn, A.F.J., "Stephen's Speech—Acts vii.2–53," *NTS* 4 (1957–58): 25–31.
Koivisto, R. A., "Stephen's Speech: A Theology of Errors?" *GTJ* 8 (1987): 101–14.
Larsson, E., "Temple-Criticism and the Jewish Heritage: Some Reflections on Acts 6–7," *NTS* 39 (1993): 379–95.
Le Déaut, R., "*Actes* 7,48 et *Matthieu* 17,4 (par.) à la lumière du targum palestinien," *RSR* 52 (1964): 85–90.
Lorenzi, L. de, "Gesù *lytrotes:* Atti 7:35," *RevBib* 7 (1959): 294–321; 8 (1960): 10–41.
Mare, W. H., "Acts 7: Jewish or Samaritan in Character?," *WTJ* 34 (1971): 1–21.
Mundle, W., "Die Stephanusrede Apg. 7: Eine Märtyrerapologie," *ZNW* 20 (1921): 133–47.
Mussner, F., "Wohnung Gottes und Menschensohn nach der Stephanusperikope (Apg 6,8–8,2)," *Jesus und der Menschensohn: Für Anton Vögtle* (ed. R. Pesch et al.; Freiburg im B.: Herder, 1975), 283–99.
Nestle, E., "Sirs, Ye Are Brethren," *ExpTim* 23 (1911–12): 528.
Paulo, P.-A., *Le problème ecclésial des Actes à la lumière de deux prophéties d'Amos* (Recherches ns 3; Montreal: Editions Bellarmin, 1985).
Pincherle, A., "Stefano e il tempio 'manufatto,'" *RicRel* 2 (1926): 326–36.
Pummer, R., "The Samaritan Pentateuch and the New Testament," *NTS* 22 (1975–76): 441–43.
Ravanelli, V., "La testimonianza di Stefano su Gesù Cristo," *SBFLA* 24 (1974): 121–41.
Reinmuth, E., "Beobachtungen zur Rezeption der Genesis bei Pseudo-Philo (LAB 1–8) und Lukas (Apg. 7.2–17)," *NTS* 43 (1997): 552–69.
Richard, E., "Acts 7: An Investigation of the Samaritan Evidence," *CBQ* 39 (1977): 190–208.
———, "The Creative Use of Amos by the Author of Acts," *NovT* 24 (1982): 37–53.
———, "The Polemical Character of the Joseph Episode in Acts 7," *JBL* 98 (1979): 255–67.

Ropes, J. H., "Bemerkungen zu der Rede des Stephanus und der Vision des Petrus," *TSK* 102 (1930): 307–15.

Sandt, H. van de, "Why Is Amos 5,25–27 Quoted in Acts 7,42f.?" *ZNW* 82 (1991): 67–87.

Scharlemann, M. H., "Acts 7:2–53: Stephen's Speech: A Lucan Creation?" *CJ* 4 (1978): 52–57.

Scobie, C.H.H., "The Origins and Development of Samaritan Christianity," *NTS* 19 (1972–73): 390–414.

———, "The Use of Source Material in the Speeches of Acts III and VII," *NTS* 25 (1978–79): 399–421.

Scott, J. J., Jr., "Stephen's Speech: A Possible Model for Luke's Historical Method?" *JETS* 17 (1974): 91–97.

Simon, M., "Retour du Christ et reconstruction du Temple dans la pensée chrétienne primitive," *Aux sources de la tradition chrétienne: Mélanges offerts à M. Maurice Goguel* (Bibliothèque théologique; Neuchâtel/Paris: Delachaux et Niestlé, 1950), 247–57.

———, "La prophétie de Nathan et le temple (Remarques sur II Sam. 7)," *RHPR* 32 (1952): 41–58.

———, "Saint Stephen and the Jerusalem Temple," *JEH* 2 (1951–52): 127–42.

Soffriti, O., "Stefano, testimone del Signore," *RivB* 10 (1962): 182–88.

Sweet, J.P.M., "A House Not Made with Hands," *Templum Amicitiae: Essays on the Second Temple Presented to Ernst Bammel* (JSNTSup 48; ed. W. Horbury; Sheffield, UK: Academic Press, 1991), 368–90.

Sylva, D. D., "The Meaning and Function of Acts 7:46–50," *JBL* 106 (1987): 261–75.

Synge, F. C., "Studies in Texts: Acts 7:46," *Theology* 55 (1952): 25–26.

Thornton, T.C.G., "Stephen's Use of Isaiah lxvi.1," *JTS* 25 (1974): 432–34.

Trudinger, P., "Stephen and the Life of the Primitive Church," *BTB* 14 (1984): 18–22.

Unité de Recherche Associée, "Sur le discours d'Etienne en Actes 7," *A cause de l'évangile*, 739–55.

Via, J., "An Interpretation of Acts 7,35–37 from the Perspective of Major Themes in Luke-Acts," *PRS* 6 (1979): 190–207.

Weinert, F. D., "Luke, Stephen and the Temple in Luke-Acts," *BTB* 17 (1987): 88–90.

Wiens, A., "Luke on Pluralism: Flex with History," *Direction* 23 (1994): 44–53.

Wolfe, R. F., "Rhetorical Elements in the Speeches of Acts 7 and 17," *JOTT* 6 (1993): 274–83.

Young, F. M., "Temple Cult and Law in Early Christianity: A Study in the Relationship between Jews and Christians in the Early Centuries," *NTS* 19 (1972–73): 325–38.

See further bibliography on 6:8–15.

10. Reaction to Stephen's Testimony; His Martyrdom (7:54–8:1a)

54 As they listened to this, they were infuriated and were grinding their teeth at
him. 55 But Stephen, filled with the Holy Spirit, stared at the heavens and saw the
glory of God and Jesus standing at God's right hand. 56 He exclaimed, "I see the
heavens open and the Son of Man standing at God's right hand." 57 But they
shouted aloud, covered their ears, and together they rushed at him; 58 they
dragged him out of the city and began to throw stones. Witnesses piled their
cloaks at the feet of a young man named Saul. 59 They kept stoning Stephen, as
he called out and prayed, "Lord Jesus, receive my spirit." 60 Falling to his knees,
he shouted aloud, "Lord, do not hold this sin against them." Having said this, he
passed away. 8 1a And Saul was there, giving approval to his execution.

WT: 55 But he, being in the Holy Spirit . . . [omits "standing" and "God's"]. 57 When the people heard this, they shouted . . . and they all rushed at him. 58 began to stone him. [omits "their"] . . . man, whose name was called Saul.

COMMENT

Luke now resumes the Stephen story, which has been interrupted by the speech just recorded. The narrative, which this episode represents from a form-critical standpoint, picks up from 7:1 and records the reaction of the diaspora Jews and the Jerusalem authorities who have listened to Stephen's speech. Luke now adds a further remark about a vision that Stephen has been accorded of the Son of Man in glory, "standing at God's right hand." As Haenchen puts it, "If Jesus stands on the right hand of God, this must show that the Christians are right in the sight of God and that the High Council is virtually God's enemy. And so the opposition breaks loose" (*Acts*, 295). All those listening are infuriated even more; they pounce upon Stephen, drag him out of the city, and stone him to death. Thus an official, possibly legal proceeding in Jewish law, becomes a lynching process. As Stephen dies, he begs God to forgive those who execute him. Those who watch the proceeding pile their cloaks at the feet of a young man, Saul, who is mentioned here for the first time and is said to approve of Stephen's execution.

Stephen's vision and what happens are not to be separated radically from the speech, for the vision gives the real interpretation to those listening about why the Most High does not dwell in temples made by human hands: the transcendent God dwells in heaven. That interpretation excites those listening even more, especially when Stephen adds that "the Son of Man stands at God's right hand."

The episode tells of the martyrdom of Stephen, the first Christian to die for Christ and his message to humanity. Thus Stephen the "witness" has become Stephen the "martyr." That is the implication of this episode, in which the two senses of *martys* are exploited. In his speech (7:2–53), Stephen has given his testimony, just as Peter and the Eleven did on Pentecost as they confronted Jews assembled in Jerusalem (2:14), and as did Peter and John before the religious authorities in the same city (3:12; 4:8; 5:29). Now a Christian disciple, not one of the Twelve, adds his testimony to the risen Christ, recalling Christ's commission of the apostles (Luke 24:47–48). The pl. "you" used there (24:48) was addressed also to others, actually to "the Eleven and their companions" (24:33); Stephen is seen as one of "those with them." The episode is concerned not only with the suffering of Stephen, but also with the spread of the Word of God and the rift between the Christian community and Judaism that soon develops.

The death that Stephen suffers, stoning, was the penalty for blasphemy in the OT (Lev 24:11–16, 23) and is probably to be related to the first of the three charges leveled against him (6:11). Luke has recorded a historical incident from an inherited pre-Lucan Christian tradition, probably an Antiochene source, but he has dramatized it in his own manner.

Lucan literary endeavor is seen in the parallel of Stephen's death to that of Jesus in the Lucan Gospel: As Jesus "uttered a loud cry" (Luke 23:46), so Stephen "shouted aloud" (Acts 7:60). The vision that Stephen is accorded of "the Son of Man" standing "at the right hand of God" (Acts 7:56) echoes the words of Jesus on trial before the Sanhedrin (Luke 22:69). The vision introduces Stephen's prayer, "Lord, do not hold this sin against them," reminding the reader of the Lucan Jesus' prayer, preserved unfortunately only in some MSS, "Father, forgive them; they do not realize what they are doing" (see *Luke*, 1503–4). After that Stephen "passed away" (Acts 7:60) just as Jesus "breathed his last" (Luke 23:46). This is another instance of the parallelism with which Luke has fitted out his entire story; it is part of his imitative historiography, the way he has chosen to present his historical narrative.

At the end of the episode the name of Saul is introduced (7:58; 8:1). At the first mention, the name appears to be adventitious, added at the end of the sentence that records that "witnesses piled their cloaks at the feet of a young man." Whether the name was originally part of the inherited pre-Lucan source may be doubted, but it has become Luke's way of relating Saul to the martyrdom of Stephen, to which Paul's speech in 22:20 will again allude. Saul's approval of the execution of Stephen is duly noted in 8:1a, undoubtedly a Lucan notice. On the question of pre-Lucan sources in this episode, see COMMENT on 6:8–7:1.

The historical problem that this episode causes is twofold. First, by what sort of death did Stephen die: by legal execution following an official trial or by a lynching? In the discussion of the sources possibly underlying 6:8–15 and 7:54–8:1a, the separating out of doublet verses gives rise to this sort of question. It is compounded by the fact that the Sanhedrin is mentioned in 6:12, which suggests an official trial, but that comes right after the mention of opposition to Stephen from diaspora Jews in 6:9–11. Moreover, in 26:10 Paul himself admits that when Christians were sentenced to death, he cast his vote against them. This seems to suggest that Luke presumed that an official trial against Stephen was held. Second, the first question gives rise to another: How could a lynch mob succeed in Jerusalem during Roman occupation? Or how could there have been an official trial ending with capital punishment under Roman authorities? In the discussion of this second question one always finds mention of John 18:31: "It is not lawful for us to put anyone to death." That introduces a question about the legal competence of the Sanhedrin in capital cases, a question too intricate to be discussed here (see R. E. Brown, *The Gospel according to John* [AB 29, 29A; Garden City, NY: Doubleday, 1966, 1970], 849–50; *The Death of the Messiah: From Gethsemane to the Grave* [2 vols.; New York: Doubleday, 1994], 363–72). What Luke says in this episode about it contributes nothing as an answer to that question.

The Lucan account of the Stephen story (6:8–15 and 7:54–8:1a), as it now stands, seems more like a mob reaction or lynching than an official trial, despite the mention of the Sanhedrin. How could anything like that have happened? It might have taken place in the interregnum after Pilate, prefect of Judea for ten years (A.D. 26–36), had been ordered by Vitellius, the Roman governor of Syria, to return to Rome to give the emperor Tiberius an account of his governance, because of accusations made against him by Samaritans (Josephus, *Ant.* 18.4.2 §89). Pilate arrived in Rome only after Tiberius had died (6 March A.D. 37), and no one knows when he may have left Judea. It could have been before the winter of A.D. 36–37, which accords with the probable date of the conversion of Saul (see COMMENT on 9:19b–25). This explanation, using the interregnum after Pilate's departure and before the arrival of the acting prefect, Marcellus, as the occasion of the lynching of Stephen, is not without its problems (see Barrett, *Acts,* 382). They are minor, however, and hardly of the sort that seriously undermines this explanation. In any case, the execution of Stephen is plausibly understood as "lynch-justice" (Haenchen, *Acts,* 296), *pace* S. Dockx ("Date de la mort d'Etienne le Protomartyr," *Bib* 55 [1974]: 65–73).

Luke does not describe the stoning with details concerning the mode of such execution set forth in the Mishnah (*Sanhedrin* 6:3–4); that, however, does not mean that he "had no idea how judicial stonings were carried out" (Haenchen, *Acts,* 296). Haenchen naively predicates Mishnaic judicial prescriptions of pre-70 Judea without a word to justify such gratuitous extrapolation.

Stephen, the first Christian martyr, suffered death for the testimony that he had borne to Jerusalemites about the Upright One (7:52), who has now appeared to him "standing at God's right hand" (7:55). Testimony borne to the risen Christ can encourage his followers to give up their lives for that cause. Stephen leads the way not only in professing his faith in Christ even unto death, but also in begging God's mercy for his persecutors. He has criticized Jerusalem Jews of being obdurate and resisting the Holy Spirit, but in death he bears further witness to the power of Christ and his Spirit in a dedication that is a fitting end to his Christian life. He likewise calls down God's mercy on those who stone him.

NOTES

54. *As they listened to this, they were infuriated.* Lit., "they were sawn through to their hearts." Luke graphically describes the initial inward reaction of the Sanhedrin and others to Stephen's speech, repeating that of 5:33. Their fury centers not only on his indictment, but also on the arguments used that build up to it.

were grinding their teeth at him. This description of their further rage is drawn from the LXX (Job 16:9; Pss 35:16; 37:12; 112:10; Lam 2:16). Gnashing of teeth as an emotional reaction is also found extrabiblically in *Sib. Or.* 2.203, 305; 8.105.

55. *Stephen, filled with the Holy Spirit.* Cf. 6:3, 5, 10. Stephen is again accorded the assistance of the Spirit, as was Peter in 4:8 (see NOTE there). The gift of the Spirit enables Stephen to perceive God's glory and to face his coming death. The Spirit is with Stephen, not against him. The real "place" of God's dwelling, heaven itself, is thus on Stephen's side.

stared at the heavens and saw the glory of God and Jesus standing at God's right hand. So Luke describes Stephen's vision: as he stands in the presence of the Sanhedrin and gazes upward, Stephen sees "God's glory." The anarthrous phrase *doxa theou* reveals its Semitic background (Ezek 9:3; 10:19), expressive of the resplendent aspect of Yahweh's majestic presence. It more frequently appears in the LXX as *doxa Kyriou* (Exod 40:34–35; Lev 9:23; 1 Kgs 8:11; 2 Chr 5:14); cf. Isa 58:8; Bar 4:37; 5:7; Luke 2:9; *TDNT*, 2.232–49. On *atenizein*, "stare," see NOTE on 1:10.

Stephen beholds the risen Christ standing in a position of honor, "at God's right hand," expressed by another OT phrase (Ps 110:1, quoted in Acts 2:34; cf. Exod 14:22, 29; 2 Sam 24:5; 2 Chr 18:18; Luke 20:42). *Ek dexiōn*, "from the right" (pl. *merōn*, 'sides'), is an idiom found in Greek literature (e.g., Xenophon, *Cyropaedia* 8.5.15; Hero, *Automatapoetica* 6.24). Conzelmann (*Acts*, 59) compares the visions of martyrs in *Ascension of Isaiah* 5:7; *Martyrium Carpi* 39, 42.

56. *He exclaimed, "I see the heavens open and the Son of Man standing at God's right hand."* The terminology in this verse is heavily Lucan: *theōrein*, "see" (used by Luke 21 times); *dianoigein*, "open" (used eight times, almost exclusively Lucan in the NT); and perhaps even the pl. *ouranoi*, "heavens" (as in 2:34). The vision that Stephen sees is described in terms reminiscent of Luke 22:69, where the words of Jesus on trial echo Dan 7:13 ("son of man") and Ps 110:1 ("Sit at my right hand").

Now the risen Christ, as the Son of Man, "stands," instead of being seated (as elsewhere in the NT: Mark 14:62; Matt 26:64; Luke 22:69), which may suggest his readiness to receive or welcome Stephen (*Beginnings*, 4.84; Polhill, *Acts*, 208; Wikenhauser, *Apg.*, 92) or to come to Stephen's aid as an advocate (H. P. Owen, "Stephen's Vision in Acts vii. 55–6," *NTS* 1 [1954–55]: 224–26), or possibly his role as a witness to the martyrdom of Stephen (O. Cullmann, *The Christology of the New Testament* [Philadelphia: Westminster, 1963], 157–58), or even more significantly as one who rises in judgment against Stephen's own people, as Isa 3:13 may suggest (Conzelmann, *Acts*, 60; Pesch, *Die Vision*, 38, 53; Weiser, *Apg.*,

194). Whatever the meaning of the Son of Man's "standing" might be, Stephen is accorded a vision of the risen Christ, who has been exalted to a position of honor next to God (2:33), and the vision confirms the accusations Stephen has expressed in his speech. *Pace* S. Légasse ("Encore *hestōta* en Actes 7,55–56," *FilNeoT* 3 [1990]: 63–66), the ptc. *hestōta* does not simply mean "to be" ("se tenir, se trouver"), for that would completely weaken Stephen's affirmation. On the opening of the heavens, see Luke 3:21; Acts 10:11; cf. Matt 3:16; John 1:51; Rev 19:11.

The title, *ho huios tou anthrōpou*, "Son of Man," for the risen Christ is taken over from the Gospels, where it appears as a title for Jesus during his earthly ministry. Anyone familiar with the gospel tradition would recognize Stephen's use of the title as a reference to Christ. In most of the Gospel instances the title appears on Jesus' lips; here Luke puts it on Stephen's lips, thus extending the use to another speaker. *Pace* Conzelmann (*Acts*, 59), Polhill (*Acts*, 207), Weiser (*Apg.*, 193), and others, this is not the only place in the NT where "Son of Man" occurs on the lips of someone other than Jesus; see Luke 5:24 and parallels (*Luke*, 579, 584–85), where the evangelists themselves use it of him. Perhaps because of the problem that Conzelmann sees involved here, the scribes of some MSS (P^{74}, 614) and an ancient Coptic version read *tou theou*, "of God." See G. D. Kilpatrick, "Acts vii.56: Son of Man?" *TZ* 21 (1965): 209. For a discussion of the Aramaic background of the title and its use elsewhere in biblical and extra-biblical texts, see *Luke*, 208–11; Fitzmyer, "The New Testament Title."

57. *they shouted aloud, covered their ears, and together they rushed at him.* Thus, the authorities and his other opponents manifest their blind rage at and furious reaction to Stephen's words. Cf. LXX Job 16:10, "they have massed together against me." They rush at Stephen because they think he is lying and, in effect, blaspheming. Once again Luke utilizes the adv. *homothymadon* to express the concerted move of listeners against Stephen; see NOTE on 1:14.

58. *they dragged him out of the city and began to throw stones.* Execution was not to be carried out within the holy city itself (a development beyond the prescription in Lev 24:11–13; Num 15:35; cf. *m. Sanhedrin* 6:1). The "dragging" outside the city is part of the reason why Stephen's death is regarded as an unauthorized action, a lynching. Luke records no formal verdict against Stephen. Moreover, the indefinite "they" is to be noted; it cannot be limited to members of the Sanhedrin.

Stoning as a mode of punishment was set down in the OT for such offenses as the worship of alien gods (Deut 17:2–7), sacrifice of children to Molech (Lev 20:2–5), prophesying in the name of an alien god (Deut 13:2–6), divination (Lev 20:27), blasphemy (Lev 24:14–16), violation of the Sabbath (Num 15:32–36), adultery (Deut 22:22–23), filial insubordination (Deut 21:18–21), and violation of the ban on spoil dedicated by *ḥērem* (Josh 7:25). For later mishnaic regulations governing the procedure, see *m. Sanhedrin* 6:1–7:10, especially 6:4, which mentions stoning by witnesses. Stoning, however, was also the fate of prophets (2 Chr 24:21). See R. Hirzel, *Die Strafe der Steinigung* (Darmstadt: Wissenschaftliche Buchgesellschaft, 1967); W. Michaelis, *TDNT* 4.267–68.

Witnesses piled their cloaks at the feet of a young man. Lit., "put off their cloaks near the feet of . . ." See Acts 22:20, where Paul refers to this detail. The "witnesses" were those who heard Stephen's words of testimony and were now executing him. According to Deut 17:7, "witnesses" were to be the first to execute a culprit. The piling of cloaks at the feet of someone seems to have been a symbolic act, whose meaning escapes us today. Recall the symbolic act of depositing proceeds "at the feet of the apostles" (4:35, 37; 5:2). *Neanias,* "young man, youth," could designate anyone from 24 to 40 years of age (see Diogenes Laertius 8.10; Philo, *De Cherubim* 32 §114).

named Saul. This is the first mention of Luke's hero of the second half of Acts, the beginning of his story about Saul/Paul of Tarsus. He is called *Saulos,* a grecized form of the name that also appears as *Saoul* (9:4, 17; 22:7, 13; 26:14). Both are attempts to write Hebrew *Šā'ûl,* "(the child) asked for" (from God), the name of King Saul (13:21). See NOTE on 13:9. In Phlm 9, Paul calls himself *presbytēs,* "an old man," which would have meant anyone from 50 years up (see Dio Chrysostom 57[74].10). That may suggest that Paul was born sometime in the first decade A.D. If the stoning of Stephen took place in the year A.D. 36 (see COMMENT), Saul would well have been *neanias.*

Witnesses probably piled their cloaks at the feet of Saul, because he was known to them personally and probably attended the synagogue of the Freedmen (6:9), and because he was a Roman citizen. Compare Paul's own references to his activity as a persecutor in Gal 1:13, 23; 1 Cor 15:9; Phil 3:6; he himself never utters a word about Stephen or his death. Cf. Acts 22:20.

59. *They kept stoning Stephen, as he called out and prayed, "Lord Jesus, receive my spirit."* This may be a doublet recording of the execution already mentioned in v 58. As the dying Jesus confided his spirit to his Father (Luke 23:46), so Stephen confides his to *Kyrie, Iēsou,* thus firmly expressing his faith in Christ. As he dies, he utters a traditional evening prayer, based on Ps 31:6 (see Str-B, 2.269) and acknowledges his own destiny to be with the risen Lord (recall Luke 23:43; 1 Thess 4:17b; Phil 1:23b).

60. *Falling to his knees, he shouted aloud.* Lit., "having placed the knees, he shouted with a great voice." Stephen has been standing, but now kneels in prayer for his enemies before he dies. The phrase *tithenai ta gonata* is sometimes thought to be a Latinism (= *genua ponere* [Ovid, *Fasti* 2.438]); it occurred in Luke 22:41 and will appear again in Acts 9:40; 20:36; 21:5.

"Lord, do not hold this sin against them." Lit., "do not set this sin on them." Stephen magnanimously prays that those who are stoning him may not incur the guilt of his murder. He thus expresses his concern for those who are stoning him. Cf. Luke 23:34 in some MSS.

Having said this, he passed away. Lit., "he fell asleep," the aor. pass. indic. is used in an intrans. sense. For *koimasthai* in the sense of the "sleep of death," see 13:36; 1 Cor 7:39; 11:30; 15:6, 51; 2 Pet 3:4; Matt 27:52. It was also so used in the LXX (Gen 47:30; Deut 31:16; Isa 14:8) and in extrabiblical Greek (Homer, *Iliad* 11.241; Sophocles, *Electra* 509).

8:1a. *Saul was there, giving approval to his execution.* Saul is involved by association in the death of Stephen, the first Christian martyr.

BIBLIOGRAPHY (7:54–8:1a)

Barrett, C. K., "Stephen and the Son of Man," *Apophoreta: Festschrift für Ernst Haenchen* . . . (BZNW 30; ed. W. Eltester and F. H. Kettler; Berlin: Töpelmann, 1964), 32–38.

Bornhäuser, K., "Zur Erzählung von der Steinigung des Stephans: Apostelgesch. 7:54–8:3," *Beth-El* 22 (1930): 313–21.

Brodie, T. L., "The Accusing and Stoning of Naboth (1 Kgs 21:8–13) as One Component of the Stephen Text (Acts 6:9–14; 7:58a)," *CBQ* 45 (1983): 417–32.

Caragounis, C. C., *The Son of Man: Vision and Interpretation* (WUNT 38; Tübingen: Mohr [Siebeck], 1986), 25, 142–43, 164, 191.

Doble, P., "The Son of Man Saying in Stephen's Witnessing: Acts 6.8–8.2," *NTS* 31 (1985): 68–84.

Fitzmyer, J. A., "The New Testament Title 'Son of Man' Philologically Considered," *WA*, 143–60.

Langevin, P.-E., "Etienne, témoin du Seigneur Jésus: Ac 7,55–60," *AsSeign* 29 (1973): 19–24.

Légasse, S., "Paul's Pre-Christian Career according to Acts," *The Book of Acts in Its Palestinian Setting* (BAFCS 4), 365–90.

Lentzen-Deis, F., "Das Motiv der 'Himmelsöffnung' in verschiedenen Gattungen der Umweltliteratur des Neuen Testaments," *Bib* 50 (1969): 301–27.

Michel, O., "Zur Lehre vom Todesschlaf," *ZNW* 35 (1936): 285–90.

Moule, C.F.D., "Sanctuary and Sacrifice in the Church of the New Testament," *JTS* 1 (1950): 29–41.

Pesch, R., "Der Christ als Nachahmer Christi: Der Tod des Stephanus (Apg 7) im Vergleich mit dem Tode Christi," *BK* 24 (1969): 10–11.

———, "Die Vision des Stephanus Apg 7,55f. im Rahmen der Apostelgeschichte," *BibLeb* 6 (1965): 92–107, 170–83.

———, *Die Vision des Stephanus: Apg 7,55–56 im Rahmen der Apostelgeschichte* (SBS 12; Stuttgart: Katholisches Bibelwerk, 1966).

Robinson, B. W., "Influences Leading toward the Conversion of Paul: A Study in Social Environment," *Festgabe für Adolf Deissmann* . . . (Tübingen: Mohr [Siebeck], 1927), 108–15.

Sabbe, M., "The Son of Man Saying in Acts 7,56," *Les Actes des Apôtres* (ed. J. Kremer), 241–79.

Selwyn, E. G., "St. Stephen's Place in Christian Origins," *Theology* 5 (1922): 306–16.

See also bibliography on 6:8–7:1 and 7:2–53.

11. Further Persecution in Jerusalem (8:1b–4)

8 [1b]On that day a great persecution broke out against the church in Jerusalem,
and all except the apostles were scattered throughout the countryside of Judea
and Samaria. [2]Devout men buried Stephen and mourned him greatly. [3]But Saul
continued to ravage the church, entering house after house and dragging out
both men and women, whom he handed over for imprisonment. [4]Now those
who had been scattered went about preaching the word.

WT: [1b]a great distress . . . apostles, who remained in Jerusalem, . . . throughout the villages. . . . [3]the churches . . . [omits "dragging out"] handing over both men and women . . . [4]scattered, going about through towns and villages, preached . . .

COMMENT

As a result of the accusatory speech of Stephen and as a follow-up to his death by stoning outside the city, the opposition to the Christian movement by inhabitants of Jerusalem takes on a new form, that of public persecution of the followers of Jesus. Luke describes it as "a great persecution of the church in Jerusalem." Actually, it is a continuation of what began with the opposition of Jerusalem religious authorities to the apostles Peter and John in chap. 4. The effect is to make most of the Jerusalem Christians, especially the Hellenists, flee the city. Strangely, however, the apostles themselves, who were those first opposed, choose to stay behind. In any case, this is the beginning of the rift that will grow between early Christians and their Jewish contemporaries.

After Stephen is buried and mourned, the leader of the persecution of Christians becomes none other than Saul, who witnessed and consented to the stoning death of Stephen. His action is described as "ravaging the church" in dragging men and women from their homes and imprisoning them. Thus, Luke records Saul's persecution of the Christian church in the Jerusalem area.

Nevertheless, all is not dark and gloomy. The Christians made to flee from Jerusalem by such persecution now become witnesses to the risen Christ, carrying the message about him abroad to other parts of Judea, and even to Samaria. The testimony of the persecuted spreads the Word. In this episode Luke undoubtedly used information derived from his Antiochene source.

NOTES

1b. *On that day a great persecution broke out against the church in Jerusalem.* Lit., "there came to be a great persecution." Luke writes *diōgmos*, "pursuit," a term used in the NT only of religious persecution; cf. 2 Macc 12:23; possibly Lam 3:19. In the context of persecution, *ekklēsia* appears as the name for the Christian community in Jerusalem; see NOTE on 5:11. Eusebius recounts this persecution (*HE* 2.1.8–9) in dependence on Luke.

all except the apostles were scattered throughout the countryside of Judea and Samaria. Jerusalem Christians flee from the form of persecution that will be described in v 3. They spread abroad not only to neighboring Judea, in which the city of Jerusalem was located, but also to the land of the Samaritans to the north, and eventually to Phoenicia, Cyprus, and Antioch (11:19). One can only wonder why "the apostles" did not flee. Luke records a historical recollection, and it gives his story the picture of unflinching apostolic reaction to persecution, a characteristic that he gladly records: it is the way Christians should react to persecution. It also establishes a linkage between Jerusalem Christianity and other evangelized areas, for Jerusalem will remain the mother church. On "Judea" and "Samaria," see NOTE on 1:8. Lucan hyperbolic use of *pas* reappears; see NOTE on 2:44.

2. *Devout men buried Stephen and mourned him greatly.* Who they were is not said. They could conceivably be Jewish inhabitants of Jerusalem, whose opposition to Christians was not intense (so Schneider, *Apg.*, 1.479); but they more likely were sympathetic Christians who buried and mourned Stephen before their flight. Later Jewish tradition permitted burial only in a common grave and no public lamentation for someone executed by stoning, "for mourning has place in the heart alone" (*m. Sanhedrin* 6:6).

3. *Saul continued to ravage the church, entering house after house and dragging out both men and women, whom he handed over for imprisonment.* Saul, who witnessed and consented to the death of Stephen, becomes the archpersecutor of the Jerusalem church. Haenchen (*Acts*, 294) finds Luke's picture of Saul "breathtaking, to say the least," because in 7:58 he was "a youth," but now he is "the archpersecutor" who invades Christian homes but does "not arrest the apostles."

Paul's own statements support this detail of the Lucan story: "I persecuted the church of God violently" (Gal 1:13), "as to zeal, a persecutor of the church" (Phil 3:6). The details, however, are Lucan. Under what pretext Saul could cart Christians off to prison is not said. "Imprisonment" for Christians is not new to the Lucan story, for the apostles Peter and John have already been so treated (4:3; 5:18). Nothing is said about Saul's activity against the apostles still in Jerusalem, either because he did not come across them or could not find them. Luke mentions Saul's persecution of Christians in Jerusalem as a background for the continuation of it to be recounted in 9:1, but more importantly for what he says in the verse following this.

4. *those who had been scattered went about preaching the word.* The persecution of Christians, an evil in itself, is now seen to have a good effect, enabling Christians to carry their testimony to a wider area. This notice is linked to 11:19, where scattered Christians arrive in Antioch. The verse is undoubtedly a Lucan juncture in the story. *Ho logos* again appears as the succinct way of describing the Christian "message"; see NOTES on 2:41; 4:4. It is the obj. of *euangelizesthai*, "preach"; see NOTE on 5:42.

BIBLIOGRAPHY (8:1b–4)

Cullmann, O., "Samaria and the Origins of the Christian Mission," in *The Early Church* (London: SCM; Philadelphia: Westminster, 1956), 183–92.

Dana, H. E., "Where Did Paul Persecute the Church?" *ATR* 20 (1938): 16–26.

Dehandschutter, B., "La persécution des chrétiens dans les Actes des Apôtres," *Les Actes des Apôtres* (ed. J. Kremer), 541–46.

Haudebert, P., "La Samarie en *Luc-Actes*: Lc 9,51–56—Ac 8,4–8," *Impacts* (Anger) 1 (1994): 25–34.

Thomas, W.H.G., "New Testament Evangelism," *The Biblical Review* 1 (1916): 592–603.

III. The Mission of Testimony in Judea and Samaria (8:5–40)

◆

1. Philip in Samaria Encounters Simon (8:5–25)

5 Philip went down to [the] town of Samaria and preached about the Messiah to
the people. 6 With one accord, crowds paid attention to what was said by Philip,
as they listened and saw the signs that he performed. 7 Unclean spirits that
possessed many people came out, shrieking loudly; many others, paralyzed or
crippled, were cured. 8 So there was much joy in that town. 9 Now a man named
Simon had been practicing magic in the town and fascinated the people of Samaria, 10 pretending to be someone great. All of them, from the least to the greatest,
paid attention to him, saying, "This man is the 'Power of God' that is called
great." 11 They paid attention to him because he had fascinated them with his
magic for quite some time. 12 But when they began to believe Philip who
preached about the kingdom of God and the name of Jesus Christ, they were
baptized, men and women alike. 13 Simon too came to believe, was baptized,
and became a devoted follower of Philip. When he saw signs and great wonders
occurring, he too was fascinated. 14 When the apostles in Jerusalem heard that
Samaria had accepted the word of God, they sent Peter and John to the people
there. 15 These went down and prayed for them that they might receive the Holy
Spirit. 16 For it had not yet come upon any of them; they had only been baptized
in the name of the Lord Jesus. 17 Then Peter and John laid their hands on them,
and they received the Holy Spirit. 18 Seeing that the Spirit was conferred through
the laying on of the apostles' hands, Simon offered them money, 19 saying, "Give
me that power too, so that anyone on whom I lay my hands will receive the Holy
Spirit." 20 But Peter said to him, "May your money perish with you! You think
that you can buy God's gift with money. 21 You can have no part or share in this
matter, for your heart is not right with God. 22 Repent of that wickedness of yours,
and beg the Lord that you may possibly be pardoned for thinking as you have.
23 For you are, I see, filled with bitterness and caught in the shackles of iniquity."
24 Simon said in reply, "Pray to the Lord for me, that nothing you have said may
happen to me." 25 So when they had borne witness and proclaimed the word of

the Lord, they gradually made their way back to Jerusalem, preaching in many of the villages of Samaria.

WT: [5] [omits "to the people"]. [6] [adds at the beginning:] when they heard. [7] From many of them unclean spirits came out. [10] [omits "all of them" and "called"]. [11] [omits "with his magic"]. [13] [omits "was baptized, and"]. [16] [omits "Lord"]. [19] urging and saying . . . on whom I too lay. [21] [omits "for"]. [22] [omits "beg the Lord"]. [24] "I urge you, pray to God . . . [adds at end of verse:] and he did not stop shedding many tears." [25] [omits "and proclaimed"].

COMMENT

Luke begins his account of the spread of the Word of God outside of Jerusalem with the activity of Philip the evangelist. Once again the Lucan geographical perspective comes into play as the Word is spread under stress of persecution. This is a new phase in the Period of the Church under Stress. The persecution was launched at first against the apostles by Jerusalem leaders (4:1, 5–6; 5:17), then by diaspora Jews against Stephen (6:12; 7:58), and now by Saul against all Christians (8:1, 3). That stress gives rise to missionary endeavor (8:5–8), the testimony that Philip bears about the Messiah in Samaria.

Thus another of the Seven, appointed "to wait on tables" (6:2, 6), turns out to be a preacher, the evangelist of Samaria, in a way that resembles Stephen and his testimony in Jerusalem. The episode shows, then, how others than the Twelve become involved in bearing testimony to Christ. Not only does Philip successfully evangelize Samaria, but he also works wonders of the sort already ascribed to apostles (2:43; 4:30; 5:12). He preaches to Samaritans, to people who were not Jews in the strict sense but remotely related to Judaism.

At first, the main interest in this episode is Philip's encounter with Simon who is skilled in magic (8:9–13). He is often called Simon Magus, a title that Luke does not use of him. That became his sobriquet in patristic explanations of this episode. He has fascinated the people of Samaria for some time before Philip arrives on the scene; but when he sees what Philip is accomplishing through "the name of Jesus Christ," he too submits to baptism, becomes a Christian, and follows Philip.

The testimony of Philip in Samaria becomes the occasion for sending two apostles, Peter and John, to the people there. When they arrive, they pray for the Samaritans "that they might receive the Holy Spirit" (8:15). This detail in the passage seems strange: How could they have been baptized, even "in the name of the Lord Jesus," and not have received the Spirit? The episode is not meant to convey that Philip was actually baptizing with a formula that used only "in the name of the Lord Jesus" and not the customary trinitarian formula (derived in liturgical usage from Matt 28:19). Baptism "in the name of the Lord Jesus" means only Christian baptism (not some other ritual washing, Jewish or Baptist). Rather, the episode brings out the Lucan teaching that the gift of the Spirit comes only through the apostles (or, in time, through those sent forth by them; cf. 10:44–48; 18:25–27; 19:2–6; 20:29–30). This is an important Lucan teaching in this episode concerning the role of the Spirit-guided institutional church of Acts. Such a spiritual gift is mediated by the apostles. It also tells of the incorporation of splinter groups into the mainstream church; Samaritans who are baptized become fully Christian by such an apostolic relationship. As Barrett has put it,

> From the beginning it [the Christian community] enjoys the gift of the Spirit, and as new converts are added they are not only incorporated into the institution by institutional means but receive the Holy Spirit just as the apostles did at the beginning, and with the same manifest results . . . ; the church is a Spirit-filled community, and possesses the power, which no wealth or other resource can acquire, of passing on the Spirit to others. ("Light," 295)

This aspect of the narrative is further enhanced by Peter's reaction to Simon's offer to buy the power to confer the Spirit from the apostles. Simon probably made his offer because in the Greek world of the time pagans could buy a role as priests in various religions; it was often sold to the highest bidder (see Derrett, "Simon Magus"). This spiritual gift, however, cannot be bought with silver or gold (recall 3:6). It is not for sale, and so Peter reacts to the offer of Simon: "May your money perish with you! You think that you can buy God's gift with money" (8:20). From this encounter Simon learns his lesson, and the episode ends with his repentance and the mention of the continued evangelization of Samaria.

The picture that Luke paints of Simon is a salutary one for all Christians, showing that salvation is not dependent solely on faith and baptism, but on one's conduct too, and even more on one's desires. These can lead to "perdition." In the postconversion activity of Simon, Philip plays no role; only Peter is involved.

Form-critically, the passage is another of the narratives in Acts, an account with an important message about the role of the Spirit in Christian life. The information that Luke uses in this episode has undoubtedly come to him from a prior tradition, most likely of Palestinian origin. It teaches, by its contrast with the magic arts of Simon, that the gift of the Spirit and what can be accomplished by the Spirit's power have nothing to do with magic. The Spirit as the manifestation of God's presence to his people transforms them into the reconstituted people of God; it revitalizes Israel of old, associating with it people with a new God-given vitality.

The episode about Philip's evangelization of Samaria recounts his success and cures there but more importantly relates how the converted and baptized Samaritans receive the Spirit through the prayer of the apostles Peter and John. In the Lucan story the Spirit is conferred through the activity of the Twelve or their emissaries. In the bestowal of the Spirit Peter and John play an important role. In the second part of the episode the encounter of Peter with Simon brings out another important aspect of the Spirit's activity in Christian life: no outsider can acquire the power to bestow the Spirit, which has no part with magic or money. That is why Simon is rebuffed. The Spirit is not for sale and is not available at the beck and call of a magician. It is indeed the dynamo of Christian life, but is bestowed only by apostolic invocation.

NOTES

5. *Philip went down to [the] town of Samaria.* This is not the Philip mentioned in 1:13, one of the Twelve, nor the one mentioned in John 12 (*pace* Haenchen, *Acts,* 301, following Wellhausen). It is Philip, the evangelist, one of the Seven (see NOTE on 6:5). Though he travels north, Philip goes "down" from the high city of Jerusalem (over 800 m. above sea level). Cf. Luke 10:30–31; Acts 11:27; 12:19; 15:30; 24:1, 22; 25:1, 7; 1 Macc 16:14.

His destination may be "a town of Samaria," because, though the art. *tēn* is read in MSS P[74], ℵ, A, B, 181, 1175, 2344, many others omit it (C, D, E, Ψ, 33, 36, 81, 1739). From 8:14 it might seem that the first meaning, "the town of Samaria," is to be preferred; but perhaps for that very reason the reading with the article is suspect. "Samaria" was the name of both a town and a region (on the latter, see NOTE on 1:8). Originally it was the name of a city (Hebrew *Šōmĕrôn;* Aramaic *Šomrayin*); from there the name spread to a district in Israel. The city was rebuilt under Herod the Great in the Roman period and renamed *Sebastē,* the "august" (city), after Caesar Augustus. See A. Parrot, *Samaria* (New York: Philosophical Library, 1958); J. A. Montgomery, *The Samaritans: The Earliest Jewish Sect: Their History, Theology and Literature* (Philadelphia: Winston, 1907; repr. New York: Ktav, 1968); R. Pummer, *The Samaritans* (Iconography of Religions 23/5; Leiden: Brill, 1987).

preached about the Messiah to the people. Lit., "and proclaimed the Messiah to them," or possibly "preached Christ to them." Cf. 9:20, 22. Philip carries Christian testimony about the risen Christ to people of Samaria, i.e., to Samaritans (see 8:25). Among the Synoptic evangelists, only Luke depicts Jesus dealing with Samaritans (Luke 9:52; 10:30–37; 17:11–19; cf. Acts 9:31; 15:3); in this he manifests a certain affinity to the Johannine Gospel (John 4:4–42), which traces the evangelization of the Samaritans to Jesus himself. In part, this stems from Luke's concern to show the universality of salvation now available through Jesus Christ (see *Luke,* 189; and NOTE on Luke 9:51).

How the Samaritans would have understood the risen Christ being preached to them is problematic, because Samaritans did not share a messianic expectation with the Jews. That difference stemmed from the Samaritan use of the Pentateuch only as their Scriptures (and rejection of the Prophets and the Writings). The coming of a "Messiah" is not found in the Pentateuch. The Samaritans believed rather in the coming of a "prophet like Moses" (see NOTE on 3:22), who in their extrabiblical literature was eventually called "Taheb" (= Aramaic *Tāʾēb,* "Returning One"). Luke makes no mention of this difference of belief; see John 4:25, for a similar glossing over of the difference. See M. S. Enslin, "Luke and the Samaritans," *HTR* 36 (1943): 278–97.

6. *With one accord, crowds paid attention to what was said by Philip.* Luke depicts the success of Philip's preaching. Eusebius (*HE* 2.1.10) attributes Philip's success to the grace of God working in him. Again Luke uses the adv. *homothymadon;* see NOTE on 1:14.

as they listened and saw the signs that he performed. Again Luke portrays miracles as *sēmeia*, "signs"; see NOTE on 2:22. As with the preaching of the apostles, whose evangelization was accompanied by miracles (4:30; 5:12), so now that of Philip is similarly attended.

7. *Unclean spirits that possessed many people came out, shrieking loudly.* Lit., "many of those having unclean spirits, shouting in a great voice, came out." This is a Lucan way of speaking about mental illnesses. Since he, like most of his contemporaries, could not diagnose afflictions properly, he attributes them to demon possession, and the cures are exorcisms. See NOTE on Luke 4:33. Haenchen (*Acts*, 302) maintains that "the identification of the sick with their devils is in conflict with the distinction between them (the sick man has the unclean spirit)." That, however, is a modern way of thinking about the situation, not an ancient way, which could well describe it as Luke does. The WT sought to tidy up Luke's Greek: MSS Ψ, 33, 614, 945, 1739, and the *Koinē* text-tradition read *apo pollōn echontōn*, "from many having (them) unclean spirits came out."

many others, paralyzed or crippled, were cured. Philip's miracles were not only exorcisms, but also cures of physical ailments. This verse and the following are, in effect, like a minor summary.

8. *there was much joy in that town.* The joy resulted not only from the miracles but also from Philip's proclamation of Jesus as the Messiah.

9. *a man named Simon had been practicing magic in the town.* Nothing more is said about this Simon in the NT beyond what is recorded in this episode. He is usually presumed to be a Samaritan, since he is depicted as active in this town, but whether he espoused Samaritan tenets is unknown. Because he is said to be *mageuōn*, "a practicer of magic" (cf. v 11), he acquires in later church tradition the name "Simon Magus" (Eusebius, *HE* 2.1.10).

Magos will be used in 13:6, 8 of "a Jew whose name was Bar-Jesus, who posed as a prophet," and is later called "Elymas the magician (for that is what his name means)." *Magos* is related to Persian *magha*, "power," and the name denoted originally a member of a tribe of priests among the Medes, who carried out a daily worship of fire. The borrowed name came to denote in Greek in the Hellenistic period not only the Persian "fire priest," but also "teacher," "magician," and even "quack." In Acts the name means "magician," and *mageia* would denote the magician's arts. None of these meanings, however, suits the occurrence of the word *magoi* in Matt 2:1, where "wise men" is normally used instead. Cf. R. P. Casey, "Simon Magus," *Beginnings*, 5.151–63; A. D. Nock, "Paul and the Magus," ibid., 164–88; G. Delling, *TDNT*, 4.356–59.

Because of what is said about Simon in v 10, he has often been called "Simon Magus" and the first Gnostic, indeed a representative of "pre-Christian gnosis" (Haenchen, "Gab es," 298), an identification that Luke himself does not make. In the later tradition he also becomes the first heretic, founder of the sect of Simonians. Justin Martyr, himself originally a Samaritan and born in Flavia Neapolis (= ancient Shechem, modern Nablus), records that Simon came from a Samaritan town, Gitta, and otherwise embellishes the Lucan text; but not even he calls Simon a Gnostic (*Apology* 1.26.1–6; 1.56.2; *Dialogue with Trypho* 120.6). Cf. Irenaeus, *Adversus haereses* 1.23.1–2; 1.16; 1.20; Eusebius, *HE*

2.13.1–8; Tertullian, *De anima* 34; *Adversus omnes haereses* 1; Clement of Alexandria, *Stromata* 2.52.2; Epiphanius, *Panarion* 21.1–4. To all of this K. Beyschlag (*Simon Magus*, 7–98) rightly reacts, maintaining that there was no such early Gnosticism and that Simon was not a Gnostic. Similarly R. Bergmeier ("Quellen vorchristlicher Gnosis?" *Tradition und Glaube . . . Festgabe für Karl Georg Kuhn* . . . [ed. G. Jeremias et al.; Göttingen: Vandenhoeck & Ruprecht, 1972], 202–8). Gnosticism reared its head in the middle of the second century, and though there might be protognostic elements in the NT, none of them is clearly evident in this episode or in Lucan writings. Some commentators have tried to use this episode as evidence that this Simon is not the same as the one mentioned by Justin Martyr and other patristic writers (R. M. Grant, *Gnosticism & Early Christianity* [New York: Harper & Row, 1966], 75). That view, however, is highly unlikely. Justin certainly dates Simon to the reign of Claudius.

Going beyond such ancient embellishments of the account, Conzelmann adds (*Acts*, 63) that Simon "appears as a *theios anēr*, 'divine man,' with miraculous powers and teachings about redemption." All that is being read into the Lucan text, which identifies Simon only as a magician.

fascinated the people of Samaria. I.e., he had attracted many followers by his magic arts before Philip's arrival. He is introduced into the Lucan story to offset any identification of the effect of the Spirit with magic practices.

10. *pretending to be someone great.* Lit., "saying that he was someone great." This is explained by what is said later in the verse.

All of them, from the least to the greatest, paid attention to him. This notice merely expands on the fascination mentioned at the end of v 9.

"This man is the 'Power of God' that is called great." The ptc. *kaloumenē* is read by MSS P[74], ℵ, A, B, C, D, E, 33, and 1739, but omitted by MSS Ψ, 36, 307, and 453. The omission of it strengthens the identification of Simon, because the adj. *megalē* is fem., referring to *dynamis*, "power." The implication is that Simon was not just called that but was such, or at least was giving himself off as such: "I am the Great Power of God." The title "Power of God" is not explained by Luke. It may be like the title used of a pagan god: *heis theos en ouranois, Mēn ouranios, megalē dynamis tou athanatou theou*, "one god in heaven, the heavenly Mēn, the great power of the immortal god" (said of the Anatolian moon god Men, in the Inscription of Saïttaï in Lydia; cf. *PGM* 4.1275–77; see *DKP*, 3.1194). One of the Hebrew words for "God" in the OT is *'ēl*, which as a common noun means "powerful, mighty one" (Ezek 31:11; 32:21). Perhaps Simon's title is playing on that idea.

"The 'Power of God' that is called great" may be found in later gnostic texts, but there is no guarantee that gnosticism was already evident in the time of Luke, *pace* G. Lüdemann ("Acts of the Apostles"). His main argument, built on a questionable interpretation of *epinoia tēs kardias*, "intention of the heart," is basically untenable, as the parallels that he himself cites show. As Torrey noted, Gnosticism "is quite outside the atmosphere of the Book of Acts" (*Composition and Date*, 18). Torrey, however, claimed that the expression is another mistranslation from Aramaic, because *houtos* is masc. and *dynamis* is fem., whereas Aramaic *dēn Ḥaylā'* would be perfectly natural in Aramaic, where the noun is masc. (ibid., 19–20). That is too facile a solution for the problematic Greek text.

11. *They paid attention to him because he had fascinated them with his magic for quite some time.* Lit., "with magic arts." So Luke explains the Samaritan following Simon had; it stems from fascination, not belief.

12. *when they began to believe Philip who preached about the kingdom of God and the name of Jesus Christ, they were baptized, men and women alike.* Philip not only bears witness to the risen Christ, but also preaches about "the kingdom of God." What the risen Christ spent time teaching his apostles, when he appeared to them (1:3), now becomes part of the Christian message borne abroad by Jesus' disciples. For the Lucan refrain, "the name of Jesus Christ," see NOTE on 2:38. The reaction of the people of this Samaritan town is to accept the testimony of Philip in faith and receive baptism, as did the Jews assembled in Jerusalem on the first Christian Pentecost (see NOTES on 1:5; 2:38). See E. A. Russell, "They Believed Philip Preaching (Acts 8, 12)," *IBS* 1 (1979): 169–76; J.D.G. Dunn, "They Believed Philip Preaching: A Reply," *IBS* 1 (1979): 177–83.

13. *Simon too came to believe, was baptized, and became a devoted follower of Philip.* Thus Simon becomes a Christian through faith and baptism. Luke apparently knows nothing more about him as a Christian. Later tradition understood Simon as having feigned "faith in Christ even to the point of baptism" (Eusebius, *HE* 2.1.11; cf. Irenaeus, *Adversus haereses* 1.23.1). This, however, is not the Lucan picture, as Barrett (*Acts*, 409), Pesch (*Apg.*, 275), and Schneider (*Apg.*, 1.491) recognize.

When he saw signs and great wonders occurring, he too was fascinated. Philip's miracles are expressed in the usual Lucan way; see NOTE on 2:22. The fascination of Samaritans with Simon gives way to the fascination of Simon himself with Philip's deeds. This note about Simon's "fascination" is an added Lucan afterthought that explains Simon's belief and baptism. After this we hear no more of Philip's involvement with Simon; the story shifts to the apostles, Peter and John.

14. *When the apostles in Jerusalem heard that Samaria had accepted the word of God.* Recall 8:1c, which explains why "the apostles" are still in Jerusalem. "Acceptance of the Word" would mean that those Samaritans have become Christians (see 11:1; 17:11; Luke 8:13; cf. 1 Thess 1:6; 2:13; Jas 1:21), and so Jerusalem Christians learn about the spread of the Word to Samaria. On "the Word of God," see NOTE on 4:31.

they sent Peter and John to the people there. Peter and John are sent by "the apostles," i.e., the Twelve; they are thus the emissaries of the apostles. The verb *apostellein* is used, implying an official mission, as Jesus "sent" the Twelve and other disciples out on missions (Luke 9:2; 10:1). As earlier (Acts 3:1–11; 4:13, 19), John is Peter's silent partner.

15. *These went down.* See NOTE on 8:5.

prayed for them that they might receive the Holy Spirit. The Spirit is given through the prayer of Peter and John, emissaries of "the apostles." The presence of God imparted through the Spirit (see NOTE on 1:2) to these new Christians is not accompanied by any external manifestation, as it was on Pentecost (2:4) and later (4:31).

16. *it had not yet come upon any of them; they had only been baptized in the name of the Lord Jesus.* For Bultmann (*TNT*, 1.139) this meant that the Samaritans had received "no proper baptism." Is that the right understanding of this enigmatic statement? It certainly does not mean that they have received a baptism like that of John (19:3), and it should not be understood in terms of a ritual formula used by Philip in baptizing these new Christians. There is no evidence that Christian baptism was ever performed with a formula different from the traditional one. See N. Adler, *Taufe*, 58–59. For the refrain, "the name of the Lord Jesus," see NOTE on 2:38.

17. *Peter and John laid their hands on them.* Prayer and the imposition of hands denoted the commissioning of the Seven in 6:6; now the same double action, mentioned in vv 15 and 17, conveys the gift of the Spirit, enabling the baptized to become full Christians. From this notice will develop in time the laying on of hands at the time of Christian baptism. Cf. Acts 19:6; Tertullian, *De baptismo* 8.1–2; CCLat 1.283. It was apparently so understood in the community of which Luke was a part. Still later it will be separated from baptism and continue as the rite of Confirmation.

they received the Holy Spirit. So God's presence is thus manifested to these converted Samaritans, as it was to the Jewish converts of Jerusalem (2:38, 41). No mention is made of a perceptible sign of that presence through the Spirit.

18. *Seeing that the Spirit was conferred through the laying on of the apostles' hands, Simon offered them money.* Many MSS (P^{45}, P^{74}, A, C, D, E, Ψ, etc.) read "the Holy Spirit," a reading undoubtedly influenced by v 19.

19. *"Give me that power too, so that anyone on whom I lay my hands will receive the Holy Spirit."* Simon does not offer to buy the Spirit, but rather the "power" to confer it by the laying on of hands. His offer to buy a spiritual power with money gave rise to the term "simony" as the name for the acquisition of spiritual power, ecclesiastical benefices, or preferment by such means.

20. *Peter said to him, "May your money perish with you!* Lit., "your money be with you to perdition," or colloquially, "To hell with your money!" (J. B. Philipps). For the Greek expression *einai eis apōleian*, see Dan 2:5c; 3:29 (Theodotion). Again Luke uses a verb of saying with the prep. *pros* and the acc.; see *Luke*, 116.

You think that you can buy God's gift with money. 21. *You can have no part or share in this matter, for your heart is not right with God.* Peter rejects Simon's offer and sets the matter straight. Even though Simon has put his faith in Christ and been baptized as a Christian, he could still find himself disoriented from God. With spiritual insight, Peter warns about requisite Christian conduct. A Christian who is not on guard about his or her actions or designs may still end in "perdition" *(apōleia)*, the opposite of salvation. Baptized Christians must still have their "hearts right with God," because "wickedness can stifle even the

Spirit" (Conzelmann, *Acts*, 66). Cf. Ps 78:37. The phrase "no part or share" is an echo of Deut 12:12; 14:27. Haenchen (*Acts*, 305) thinks that Peter's words ("no share *en tō logō toutō*") is "a form of excommunication," understanding *logos* to be "Christianity." That, however, is far from certain, because *logos*, like Hebrew *dābār*, can mean generically "matter, subject, thing" as well as "word" (Acts 15:6; Mark 8:32; 9:10; cf. BAGD, 477).

22. *Repent of that wickedness of yours, and beg the Lord that you may possibly be pardoned for thinking as you have.* Lit., "that the intent of your heart may be pardoned/canceled." Peter calls for repentance, a change of heart (see NOTE on 2:38). He realizes that Christian baptism has not wholly removed from Simon a tendency to wickedness; that has manifested itself in Simon's intent to acquire with crass materialism something wholly spiritual.

23. *you are, I see, filled with bitterness and caught in the shackles of iniquity."* Cf. Deut 29:17; Isa 58:6 (LXX), from which the Lucan phraseology comes. Thus Peter sums up Simon's spiritual state: bitterness at the success of Philip's preaching and the ability of the apostles to confer the Spirit. It is a bitterness that stems from his bondage to iniquity *(adikia)*.

24. *Simon said in reply, "Pray to the Lord for me, that nothing you have said may happen to me."* Simon repents, taking Peter at his word. He begs, moreover, for Peter's prayers on his behalf. Contrary to the later tradition about the apostasy of Simon, Luke's story of him ends on a favorable note.

25. *when they had borne witness and proclaimed the word of the Lord.* The episode ends with another summary-like statement. It records once again the testimony to the risen Christ given by the apostles Peter and John and their proclamation of the Word (see NOTE on 4:31).

they gradually made their way back to Jerusalem, preaching in many of the villages of Samaria. Lit., "villages of the Samaritans." Although some commentators limit this notice to the apostles, Peter and John (Pesch, *Apg.*, 278; Schneider, *Apg.*, 1.495), it seems to refer also to Philip (Barrett, Acts, 418; Polhill, Acts, 221), who apparently accompanies the apostles to Jerusalem, for in the next episode he will set out again from Jerusalem, but in a different direction.

BIBLIOGRAPHY (8:5–25)

Adler, N., *Taufe und Handauflegung: Eine exegetisch-theologische Untersuchung von Apg 8, 14–17* (NTAbh 19/3; Münster in W.: Aschendorff, 1951).

Barrett, C. K., "Light on the Holy Spirit from Simon Magus (Acts 8,4–25)," *Les Actes des Apôtres* (ed. J. Kremer), 281–95.

Bergmeier, R., "Die Gestalt des Simon Magus in Act 8 und in der simonianischen Gnosis—Aporien einer Gesamtdeutung," *ZNW* 77 (1986): 267–75.

Beyschlag, K., *Simon Magus und die christliche Gnosis* (WUNT 16; Tübingen: Mohr [Siebeck], 1974).

Casalegno, A., "Evangelizaçâo e práticas mágicas nos Atos dos Apóstolos," *PerspTeol* 24 (1992): 13–28.

Cerfaux, L., "La gnose simonienne: Nos sources principales," *RSR* 15 (1925):

489–511; 16 (1926): 5–20, 265–85, 481–503; repr. in *Recueil Lucien Cerfaux*, 1.191–258.
———, "Simon le magicien à Samarie," *RSR* 27 (1937): 615–17; repr. in *Recueil Lucien Cerfaux*, 1.259–62.
Derrett, J.D.M., "Simon Magus (Act 8,9–24)," *ZNW* 73 (1982): 52–68.
Drane, J. W., "Simon the Samaritan and the Lucan Concept of Salvation History," *EvQ* 47 (1975): 131–37.
Frickel, J., *Die Apophasis Megale in Hippolyts Refutatio VI,9–18: Eine Paraphrase zur Apophasis Simons* (OrChrAnal 182; Rome: Oriental Institute, 1968).
Gourgues, M., "Esprit des commencements et esprit des prolongements dans les *Actes:* Note sur le 'Pentecôte des Samaritans' (*Act.*, viii, 5–25)," *RB* 93 (1986): 376–85.
Grundmann, W., "Die Apostel zwischen Jerusalem und Antiochia," *ZNW* 39 (1940): 110–37.
Haenchen, E., "Gab es eine vorchristliche Gnosis?" *ZTK* 49 (1952): 316–49; repr. *Gott und Mensch*, 265–98.
Haar, S., "Lens or Mirror: The Image of Simon and Magic in Early Christian Literature," *LTJ* 27 (1993): 113–21.
Koch, D. A., "Geistbesitz, Geistverleihung und Wundermacht: Erwägungen zur Tradition und zur lukanischen Redaktion in Act 8,5–25," *ZNW* 77 (1986): 64–82.
Lüdemann, G., "The Acts of the Apostles and the Beginnings of Simonian Gnosis," *NTS* 33 (1987): 420–26.
———, *Untersuchungen zur simonianischen Gnosis* (GTA 1; Göttingen: Vandenhoeck & Ruprecht, 1975).
Meeks, W. A., "Simon Magus in Recent Research," *RelSR* 3 (1977): 137–42.
Ory, G., *La "conversion" de Simon le magicien* (Cahiers du Cercle Ernest Renan 3/9; Paris: Cercle Ernest-Renan, 1956).
Pummer, R., "New Evidence for Samaritan Christianity?" *CBQ* 41 (1979): 98–117.
Rudolph, K., "Simon — Magus oder Gnosticus? Zur Stand der Debatte," *TRu* 42 (1977): 279–359.
Unnik, W. C. van, "Die Apostelgeschichte und die Häresien," *ZNW* 58 (1967): 240–46.
Waitz, H., "Simon Magus in der altchristlichen Literatur," *ZNW* 5 (1904): 121–43.
———, "Die Quelle der Philippusgeschichten in der Apostelgeschichte 8,5–40," *ZNW* 7 (1906): 340–55.
Wilkens, W., "Wassertaufe und Geistempfang bei Lukas," *TZ* 23 (1967): 26–47.
Wilson, R. M., "Gnostic Origins Again," *VC* 11 (1957): 93–110.
———, "Simon and Gnostic Origins," *Les Actes des Apôtres* (ed. J. Kremer), 485–91.

2. PHILIP AND THE ETHIOPIAN EUNUCH ON THE GAZA ROAD (8:26–40)

[26]Now the angel of the Lord said to Philip, "Get up and head south on the road
that goes down from Jerusalem to Gaza, the desert route." [27]So he got up and set
out. Now there was an Ethiopian eunuch, a court official in charge of all the
treasury of Candace (that is, the Queen) of the Ethiopians. He had come to
Jerusalem to worship, [28]and was returning home. Seated in his carriage, he was
reading the prophet Isaiah. [29]The Spirit said to Philip, "Run and catch up with
that carriage." [30]Philip ran up and heard the man reading Isaiah the prophet. He
said to him, "Do you really understand what you are reading?" [31]He replied,
"How should I be able, unless someone guides me?" So he invited Philip to get
in and sit with him. [32]Now this was the passage of Scripture that he was reading:

He was led like a sheep to the slaughter,
and as a lamb before its shearer is silent,
so he opened not his mouth.
[33]*In [his] humiliation justice was denied him.*
Who will ever speak of his posterity?
For his life is taken away from this earth.[e]

[34]Then the eunuch said to Philip, "Please, sir, about whom does the prophet say
this? About himself or about someone else?" [35]Then Philip spoke up, and beginning with that very passage of Scripture, he preached about Jesus to him. [36]As
they moved along the road, they came to some water, and the eunuch asked,
"Look, there is some water. What prevents me from being baptized?" [37] [38]He
ordered the carriage to stop, and both of them, Philip and the eunuch, went
down into the water, and he baptized him. [39]When they came up out of the
water, the Spirit of the Lord snatched Philip away, and the eunuch saw him no
more, but continued on his way quite happy. [40]Philip, however, found himself at
Azotus and went about preaching in all the towns until he reached Caesarea.

[e]Isa 53:7–8

WT: [27][omits "a court official"]. [28][omits "his"]. [29][omits "that"]. [30]Philip came up. [31]How can I. [34][omits "to Philip"] . . . about another? [35][omits "and" and "to him"]. [36][omits "Look, there is some water."] What is preventing me. [37][whole verse is added] "He (Philip) said to him, 'If you believe with all your heart, it is possible.' He said in reply, 'I believe that Jesus Christ is the Son of God.' " [38][omits "Philip and the eunuch"] . . . and Philip baptized him. [39]the Holy Spirit fell upon the eunuch, but the angel of the Lord snatched. [40]himself to be present in Azotus, and returning from there, he preached throughout the towns until.

COMMENT

The preceding episode told of the Hellenist Philip's evangelization of Samaria to the north of Jerusalem; now Philip is told to turn his attention to the south, to the road that goes from Jerusalem to Gaza. The episode creates something of a problem because Philip is now depicted evangelizing an important individual, a eunuch of the Ethiopian royal court. How is one to understand this individual? Is he a Gentile? Or a diaspora Jew? Eusebius regarded the eunuch from Ethiopia as "the first of the Gentiles" to be converted to Christianity (*HE* 2.1.13). Similarly Conzelmann (*Acts,* 67), Schneider (*Apg.,* 1.498), Tannehill (*Narrative Unity,* 2.110), Barrett (*Acts,* 425–26), Polhill (*Acts,* 222). This, however, would be to assign a major development in the Lucan story to a minor character (Philip) in Acts. It creates a problem with what Peter says in 15:7. So far in the development of the story line in Acts, however, we have read of the testimony to the risen Christ borne to Palestinian Jews, diaspora Jews, and Samaritans, to all of whom the Word of God has been preached in Jerusalem, Judea, and Samaria. Now we learn about the testimony to an Ethiopian, and soon to Cornelius and other Gentiles. The spread of the Word to the Gentiles, however, begins only in chap. 10 with Peter's evangelization of them and in the conversion of Cornelius, after the call of Saul, "a chosen instrument of mine to carry my name before Gentiles," has been narrated. So in the Lucan story line the Ethiopian eunuch is to be understood as a Jew, or possibly a Jewish proselyte, who comes from a distant land, despite the difficulty that this understanding may create. There is no room for the ambiguous position that Haenchen (*Acts,* 314) assumes; most of the arguments he proposes are in favor of the eunuch as a Jew or a proselyte. See further Pesch, *Apg.,* 288.

A difficulty arises because Deut 23:2 seems to exclude a eunuch from entering "the assembly of the Lord"; cf. Lev 21:17–21. However, Trito-Isaiah later developed a different view, which may explain how Luke understands this eunuch from a far-off country as a diaspora Jew: "Let not the eunuch say, 'Look, I am a dry tree.' For thus says the Lord: 'For eunuchs, who observe my sabbaths, choose what is pleasing to me, and hold fast to my covenant, I will put in my house and within my walls a monument and a name'" (Isa 56:3–4). This seems to be the way Luke has understood this prominent Ethiopian, for he depicts him making a pilgrimage from distant Ethiopia to Jerusalem "to worship" and reading Isaiah, presumably in Hebrew or Greek, but not in Ethiopic, because Philip recognizes the passage.

At any rate, Philip instructs the eunuch in the meaning of the Servant Song of Isaiah 53, interpreting it for him christologically. The eunuch accepts the instruction and asks to be baptized; Philip makes a Christian of him. After that, the Spirit removes the evangelist from the scene.

Form-critically judged, this episode is another of the narratives in Acts. Haenchen (*Acts,* 314) rightly recognizes that it is not a miracle story. Luke probably makes use here of information that he derived from some Palestinian source.

Some interpreters see in this episode a parallel to the story of Jesus on the road with the two disciples going to Emmaus. If convincing, it would show how Luke has made his story of the early Christian community follow his story of Jesus. A parallel has already been noted in the story of the death of Stephen, and this may be yet another in the Lucan composition, if the comparison is valid. See further Dupont, "Le repas"; D'Sa, "The Emmaus Narrative"; Grassi, "Emmaus Revisited."

A major problem that the episode creates is the historicity of Philip's movements. Beginning mainly with Harnack, a "psychological" interpretation of this episode has often been proposed: Philip moves about "in a state of ecstasy and hardly knows how he goes from place to place" (Lake, *Beginnings*, 4.99). Whatever the explanation, the Lucan emphasis in this episode falls on how the Word of God has spread even to an influential individual of different background, from a far-off country, who has come to Jerusalem on pilgrimage. This too at the testimony of Philip the evangelist.

After this episode we hear no more of the Ethiopian eunuch. Presumably he continues on his journey, returns home, and spreads the good news there about Jesus the Christ, but the beginnings of Christianity in Nubia and Ethiopia cannot be traced back earlier than the fourth century A.D.

The episode of Philip's converting the Ethiopian eunuch presents the risen Christ above all as the new Servant of the Lord who tolerated what was done to him as a silent sheep before its shearers. It emphasizes the Lucan understanding of the suffering and death of Jesus as a humiliation silently accepted: his life was taken away and justice was denied him. This christological understanding of the Isaian Servant is important for Lucan theology, for it teaches Christians how they must learn to interpret the Hebrew Scriptures and learn from others, even as the eunuch sought understanding from Philip.

NOTES

26. *the angel of the Lord said to Philip.* Luke introduces the heavenly messenger to bring word to Philip, presumably at Jerusalem. With most commentators I take this "Philip" to be the same as the Hellenist evangelist of the preceding episode. There is nothing in the Lucan text to make one think that it is rather the "Apostle Philip" of 1:13, as Pesch (*Apg.*, 288, 290) would have it. On "angel of the Lord," see NOTE on 5:19. The angel is introduced to make clear that this mission of Philip is God-inspired. Again a verb of saying is followed by the prep. *pros* with the acc.; see *Luke*, 116.

Get up and head south on the road that goes down from Jerusalem to Gaza. Philip is instructed to head toward Gaza, which was one of the five old cities of the Philistines, in southwest Palestine. At the time that Luke writes, it was on a caravan route leading to Egypt, which someone traveling from Jerusalem to Ethiopia would naturally take. For *mesēmbria,* "midday, noon," as meaning the "south," see Dan 8:4, 9 (LXX).

the desert route. I.e., by way of Bet-Govrin (Betogabris of Ptolemy's *Geography*). This addition creates a problem, because the route from Jerusalem to Gaza would not be through a desert. Some ancient writers, however, did call Gaza itself *erēmos.* See W. J. Pythian-Adams, "The Problem of 'Deserted' Gaza," *PEFQS* (1923): 30–36. It may be another instance of Luke's defective knowledge of Palestinian geography.

27. *he got up and set out.* In obedience to the heavenly command, Philip immediately undertakes the journey. Luke describes Philip's obedience in OT phraseology, repeating the same verbs; cf. Gen 43:13–15 (LXX).

there was an Ethiopian eunuch. Lit., "and behold, an Ethiopian man, a eunuch." Physically castrated men often served in the ancient Near East as keepers of a royal harem (Esth 2:14) and often became highly placed officials or "chamberlains" in a royal court (Herodotus, *History* 8.105; Plutarch, *Demetrius* 25.5; Philostratus, *Life of Apollonius* 1.33–36). Greek *eunouchos* (in the LXX) and Hebrew *sārîs* did not always connote a castrated man (Gen 39:1; 40:2; 1 Sam 8:15); sometimes it meant merely "chamberlain," even if he were still capable of begetting children (*TDNT* 2.766). So it is not really possible to say in which sense the term is used here.

Ethiopia was an ancient name used for countries in Africa, south of Egypt and the modern Sudan, for example, Nubia, Abyssinia, and other regions, since *Aithiops* meant "people with a burnt face." In the MT, Ethiopia is called *Kûš* (Gen 2:13; 10:6; 1 Chr 1:8; Isa 11:11; Ezek 38:5), and in the LXX either *Aithiopia* or *Chous* (with much confusion). It is not surprising that an Ethiopian would be a Jew or a proselyte, because Ethiopic is a Semitic language related to Hebrew and Aramaic.

a court official in charge of all the treasury of Candace (that is, the Queen) of the Ethiopians. Luke describes the eunuch as *dynastēs,* "a powerful man," a term often employed of rulers, chamberlains, or court officials. In LXX Jer 41:19 (= MT 34:19) it translates Hebrew *sārîs,* "eunuch." The noun *Kandakē* is not the queen's name, but the transcription of a Nubian word for "queen," *Kntky;* hence Luke juxtaposes it with the Greek word for queen, *basilissa.* Reference is being made to a queen in Meroe (Nubia), who has no connection with Sheba, "the queen of the South" (Matt 12:42; Luke 11:31), despite later legends that so conflate them. See E. Ullendorff, "Candace (Acts viii.27) and the Queen of Sheba," *NTS* 2 (1955–56): 53–56. Cf. Pliny, *Naturalis Historia* 6.35.186; Strabo, *Geography* 17.1.54; G. Roeder, "Die Geschichte Nubiens und des Sudans," *Klio* 12 (1912): 51–82, esp. 72–73; S. Lösch, "Der Kämmerer der Königin Kandake (Apg. 8, 27)," *TQ* 111 (1930): 477–519; B. G. Trigger, "La Candace, personnage mystérieux," *Archéologie* 77 (1974): 10–17.

He had come to Jerusalem to worship. This implies that he was a Jew or at least a proselyte coming from the diaspora. Luke uses the fut. ptc. *proskynēsōn* with a verb of motion as a substitute for a final clause, as in classical Greek; it is rare in NT Greek, almost exclusively Lucan; see 22:5; 24:11, 17 (BDF §351.1).

28. *was returning home. Seated in his carriage, he was reading the prophet Isaiah.* I.e., presumably in Hebrew, or less likely in Greek. At least the story demands something like that so that Philip may recognize what he has been read-

ing (v 30), because, if the eunuch were reading it in Ethiopic, Philip would scarcely have recognized the passage. Luke describes the Ethiopian riding in a *harma*, which often means "war chariot," a meaning that is unlikely here; rather it is a "traveling carriage," as in Gen 41:43; 46:29.

29. *The Spirit said to Philip, "Run and catch up with that carriage."* Although the command at first came to Philip from "the angel of the Lord" (8:26), now "the Spirit" takes over; or else it means that "the angel of the Lord" has spoken for "the Spirit."

30. *Philip ran up and heard the man reading Isaiah the prophet.* Philip heeds the Spirit's directive and comes upon the eunuch reading the prophet Isaiah. The Book of Isaiah was always a well-read book of the OT among Jews, as the number of copies of it found in Qumran caves reveals. The eunuch was reading to himself aloud, as was the custom in antiquity. See G. L. Hendrickson, "Ancient Reading," *CJ* 25 (1929): 182–96; J. Balogh, "Voces paginarum: Beiträge zur Geschichte des lauten Lesens und Schreibens," *Philologus* 82 (1926–27): 84–109, 202–40.

He said to him, "Do you really understand what you are reading?" Philip's query is a leading question.

31. *He replied, "How should I be able, unless someone guides me?"* Luke frames the eunuch's answer with a potential optative with *an* (see BDF §385), but the WT changes it to the pres. indic., "How can I?" The eunuch's answer to Philip poses the classic problem about the interpretation of Scripture. One needs guidance to understand it. That gives Philip the opportunity to bring out the christological meaning of the words of the prophet. Recall Luke 24:25–27, 44–49 for the Lucan global interpretation of the OT in terms of Christ.

So he invited Philip to get in and sit with him. 32. *Now this was the passage of Scripture that he was reading.* Lit., "the pericope of Scripture that he was reading was this." On *hē graphē* for "Scripture," see NOTE on 1:16.

He was led like a sheep to the slaughter, and as a lamb before its shearer is silent, so he opened not his mouth. 33. *In [his] humiliation justice was denied him. Who will ever speak of his posterity? For his life is taken away from this earth.* The words of Isa 53:7–8 (LXX) are quoted exactly, with the addition only of *autou* (at the beginning of v 33) in some MSS (C, E, Ψ, 33, the Koine text-tradition; omitted by MSS P[74], ℵ, A, B, 1739) and with the suppression of the last clause of v 8. The LXX is not an accurate rendering of the MT, which in v 8 differs considerably. In the LXX form, the words of the prophet describe the silent suffering of the Servant of the Lord; he is compared to a mute animal about to be shorn or slaughtered; for he was unjustly condemned and executed, and no one would ever hear of his posterity. Luke understands these words of Isaiah to refer to the crucifixion and death of Jesus. *Pace* Conzelmann (*Acts*, 69), he scarcely understood "the 'taking away of justice' as referring to the resurrection"; similarly Haenchen (*Acts*, 312. See NOTE on 8:35. Cf. P. B. Decock, "The Understanding of Isaiah 53:7–8 in Acts 8:32, 33," *Neotestamentica* 14 (1981): 111–33; E. Fascher, *Jesaja 53 in christlicher und jüdischer Sicht* (AVTRW 4; Berlin: Evangelische Verlagsanstalt,

1958), 8–13. What is noteworthy is that Luke does not quote the verse about the vicarious suffering of the Servant, which would have been so important for the interpretation that Philip would give to the eunuch.

34. *Then the eunuch said to Philip, "Please, sir, about whom does the prophet say this? About himself or about someone else?"* The eunuch poses the question that has been asked ever since Isaiah penned those words. The eunuch's question can be illustrated from 1QpHab 2:1–15, where the words of the prophet Habakkuk are interpreted in terms of individuals.

Jeremias (*TDNT,* 5.684–89) has shown that three different interpretations were used in Palestinian Judaism in the first millennium A.D.: (a) the collective interpretation, in which *pais theou* was understood of Israel as a whole; (b) an individual interpretation, in which it was understood (esp. in Isa 49:5 and 50:10) to refer the prophet himself; and (c) an individual interpretation, in which it came to be applied to *Elias redivivus* (Sir 48:10) or to the Messiah (esp. Isa 52:13 and 53:11, phrases of which are used in *1 Enoch* 37–71 and in the late Targum of Isaiah); so too in the (Christian) Peshitta. Today many interpreters understand the Isaian Servant Songs to refer to Israel or Israel and its leaders. See C. R. North, *The Suffering Servant in Deutero-Isaiah* (London: G. Cumberlege, 1948); J. Lindblom, *The Servant Songs in Deutero-Isaiah* (Lund: Gleerup, 1951); C. Westermann, *Isaiah 40–66* (OTL; Philadelphia: Westminster, 1969), 253–69.

35. *Philip spoke up, and beginning with that very passage of Scripture, he preached about Jesus to him.* Lit., "Philip, opening his mouth and beginning . . ." For the same expression, see 10:34; 18:14. The Christian Philip applies the words of the Servant Song to Jesus. In effect, he identifies Jesus as the Servant of the Lord. Parts of the Lucan passion narrative bear out Philip's christological interpretation: "In [his] humiliation justice was denied him," see Luke 23:2–4, 14–15, 22, 41 and esp. 23:23c–24; "His life is taken away from this earth," see Luke 23:33, 44–46. In this sense Luke composes this part of Acts. Cf. 5:42.

The christological interpretation of the Servant Song is ancient among Christians (see Rom 10:16; John 12:38; 1 Pet 2:21–15), even if one cannot show that it derives from Jesus himself (see M. D. Hooker, *Jesus and the Servant,* 149). It is hardly to be described as originating with Luke.

36. *As they moved along the road, they came to some water, and the eunuch asked, "Look, there is some water. What prevents me from being baptized?"* Philip must have included in his instruction of the eunuch the ideas of faith in Jesus Christ and baptism. In any case, the eunuch understands Philip's message and asks to become a Christian. Haenchen (*Acts,* 312) comments: "The attempts to identify the *hydōr* with a particular water-course are as touching as they are in vain."

[37.] This verse is not found in MSS P[45], P[74], ℵ, A, B, C, P, Ψ, 049, 33, 81, 614, or in ancient versions (Vg, Syriac, Coptic). In the WT (MS E, 36, 307, 453, 610, 1739 [with minor variants]) and in many patristic quotations it runs thus: "He (Philip) said to him, 'If you believe with all your heart, it is possible.' He said in reply, 'I believe that Jesus Christ is the Son of God.'" Metzger (*TCGNT,* 315–16) notes that *ton Iēsoun Christon* is not a Lucan expression and believes that the verse is a formula from early baptismal ceremonies that was written as a gloss on the margin of some copies of Acts, which eventually was copied into the text itself. The eunuch's confession, however, is attested from the end of the second century; see Irenaeus, *Adversus haereses* 3.12.8. So it is an ancient reading.

38. *He ordered the carriage to stop, and both of them, Philip and the eunuch, went down into the water, and he baptized him.* Thus the Ethiopian eunuch became a Christian. Luke provides no details about the baptism.

39. *When they came up out of the water, the Spirit of the Lord snatched Philip away.* Compare vv 26, 29: "The angel of the Lord" became "the Spirit," and now it becomes "the Spirit of the Lord," who is directing Philip. This lack of consistency is removed in the WT: "the Holy Spirit fell upon the eunuch, but the angel of the Lord snatched Philip away." This reading, in MSS A, 36, 94, 103, 307, 322, 323, 385, 467, and 1739, would mean that the baptized eunuch also receives the gift of the Spirit, whereas "the angel of the Lord" removes Philip from the scene. This introduces a strange note into the ending of the story of the eunuch's conversion, but it serves the Lucan motif of the Spirit-directed spread of the Word of God, which Philip has been preaching. Cf. 2 Kgs 2:16; Ezek 11:24 for OT precedents of the snatching.

the eunuch saw him no more, but continued on his way quite happy. Lit., "rejoicing." So Luke introduces once again "joy" at Christian conversion. Recall 5:41.

40. *Philip, however, found himself at Azotus.* As in Isa 20:1 (LXX), *Azōtos* stands for Ashdod, one of the five ancient towns of the Philistines, 15 km north of Ashkelon and about 4 km inland from the Mediterranean Sea, almost due west of Jerusalem. Through it passed the *Via Maris,* "Sea Road." It was about halfway between Gaza and Joppa. Cf. 1 Macc 4:15; 10:70–84; Josephus, *Ant.* 13.4.4 §92.

went about preaching in all the towns until he reached Caesarea. I.e., Caesarea Maritima, a seaport on the coast of Palestine, to the northwest of Jerusalem, about 50 km north of Tel Aviv, where Philip has his home (according to the We-Passage of 21:8). Again Luke indulges in hyperbole, "all the towns"; see NOTE on 2:44.

Kaisareia was apparently first settled in the fourth century B.C. and was often called Strato's Tower (after Strato, King of Sidon, whose settlement seems to have been about 300 m. to the north). It was completely rebuilt as a port city by Herod the Great in the manner of a Roman provincial capital about 10 B.C., with an aqueduct and amphitheater, which made of it a very important city in the Judea of that time (see Josephus, *Ant.* 15.9.6 §§331–41). In A.D. 6 it became the seat of the Roman prefect, and its population was chiefly "Greek"; two Roman legions were quartered there (Josephus, *J.W.* 3.9.1 §§409–12), one being the *cohors Italica* (see 10:1). Pontius Pilate, prefect of Judea, constructed a building there in honor of the emperor Tiberius, called *Tiberieum.* A fragment of an inscription on that building, mentioning the prefect Pilate, has recently been discovered. The city and its port have been under recent excavation. See R. L. Hohlfelder, "Caesarea," *ABD,* 1.798–803; A. Frova et al., *Scavi di Caesarea Maritima* (Rome: "L'Erma" di Bretchneider, 1966); R. J. Bull, "Caesarea Maritima: The Search for Herod's City," *BARev* 8/3 (1982): 24–40; K. G. Holum et al., *King Herod's*

Dream: Caesarea on the Sea (New York: Norton, 1988), 108, 111, 156–58; A. Raban and K. G. Holum, *Caesarea Maritima: A Retrospective after Two Millennia* (DMOA 21; Leiden: Brill, 1996); L. I. Levine, *Caesarea under Roman Rule* (SJLA 7; Leiden: Brill, 1975); L. Haefeli, *Cäsarea am Meer: Topographie und Geschichte der Stadt nach Josephus und Apostelgeschichte* (NTAbh 10/5; Münster in W.: Aschendorff, 1923).

BIBLIOGRAPHY (8:26–40)

Bishop, E.F.F., "Which Philip?" *ATR* 28 (1946): 154–59.

Brodie, T. L., "Towards Unraveling the Rhetorical Imitation of Sources in Acts: 2 Kgs 5 as One Component of Acts 8,9–40," *Bib* 67 (1986): 41–67.

Bruce, F. F., "Philip and the Ethiopian," *JSS* 34 (1989): 377–86.

Campenhausen, H. von, "Taufen auf den Namen Jesu?" *VC* 25 (1971): 1–16.

Charbel, A., "La fontana di Filippo di Ain el-Haniyah (Act 8,26–40)," *Terra Santa* 53 (1978): 150–54.

Corbin, M., "Connais-tu ce que tu lis? Une lecture d'Actes 8, v. 26 à 40," *Christus* 93 (1977): 73–85.

Das, A. A., "Acts 8: Water, Baptism, and the Spirit," *ConcJ* 19 (1993): 108–34.

Dinkler, E., "Philippus und der *anēr aithiops* (Apg 8,26–40)," *Jesus und Paulus: Festschrift für Werner Georg Kümmel* . . . (ed. E. E. Ellis and E. Grässer; Göttingen: Vandenhoeck & Ruprecht, 1975), 85–95.

D'Sa, T., "The Emmaus Narrative, A Missionary Journey from a Missionary Pastor's Point of View," *Vidyajyoti* 57 (1993): 147–56.

Dupont, J., "Le repas d'Emmaüs," *LumVie* 31 (1957): 77–92.

Gage, W. A. and J. R. Beck, "The Gospel, Zion's Barren Woman and the Ethiopian Eunuch," *Crux* 30 (1994): 35–43.

Gibbs, J. M., "Luke 24:13–33 and Acts 8:26–39: The Emmaus Incident and the Eunuch's Baptism as Parallel Stories," *Bangalore Theological Forum* 7 (1975): 17–30.

Grassi, J. A., "Emmaus Revisited (Luke 24,13–35 and Acts 8,26–40)," *CBQ* 26 (1964): 463–67.

Hooker, M. D., *Jesus and the Servant: The Influence of the Servant Concept of Deutero-Isaiah in the New Testament* (London: SPCK, 1959), 113–14, 147–54.

Lindijer, C. H., "Two Creative Encounters in the Work of Luke: Luke xxiv, 13–35 and Acts viii, 26–40," *Miscellanea Neotestamentica* (NovTSup 48; ed. T. Baarda; Leiden: Brill, 1976), 77–85.

Meester, P. de, "'Philippe et l'eunuque éthiopien' ou 'le baptême d'un pèlerin de Nubie'?" *NRT* 103 (1981): 360–74.

Mínguez, D., "Hechos 8,25–40: Análisis estructural del relato," *Bib* 57 (1976): 168–91.

O'Toole, R. F., "Philip and the Ethiopian Eunuch (Acts viii, 25–40)," *JSNT* 17 (1983): 25–34.

Rapuano, Y., "Did Philip Baptize the Eunuch at Ein Yael?" *BARev* 16/6 (1990): 44–49.

Rosica, T. M., "Encounters with Christ: Word & Sacrament," *Church* 10 (1994): 9–13.

———, "The Road to Emmaus and the Road to Gaza: Luke 24:13–35 and Acts 8:26–40," *Worship* 68 (1994): 117–31.

———, "Two Journeys of Faith," *TBT* 31 (1993): 177–80.

Sauter, G., "Die Kunst des Bibellesens," *EvT* 52 (1992): 347–59.

Smith, A., "'Do You Understand What You Are Reading?' A Literary Critical Reading of the Ethiopian (Kushite) Episode (Acts 8:26–40)," *JITC* 22 (1994): 48–70.

Stroumsa, G. G., "Le couple de l'ange et de l'esprit: Traditions juives et chrétiennes," *RB* 88 (1981): 42–61.

Trummer, P., "'Verstehst du auch, was du liest?' (Apg 8,30)," *Kairos* 22 (1980): 103–13.

Unnik, W. C. van, "Der Befehl an Philippus," *ZNW* 47 (1956): 181–91; repr. *Sparsa collecta*, 1.328–39.

Wolff, H. W., *Jesaja 53 im Urchristentum* (3rd ed.; Berlin: Evangelische Verlagsanstalt, 1952).

Young, E. J., "Of Whom Speaketh the Prophet This?" *WTJ* 11 (1949): 133–55.

IV. The Word Is Carried Further: Testimony Even to Gentiles (9:1–14:28)

◆

A. The Persecutor Becomes a Christian Witness (9:1–31)

1. The Call of Saul (9:1–19a)

9 1 Now Saul, still breathing murderous threats against the Lord's disciples,
went to the high priest 2 and asked him for letters to the synagogues in Damascus,
that, if he should find any men or women belonging to the Way, he might bring
them back to Jerusalem as prisoners. 3 As he traveled along, he happened to draw
near to Damascus, and a light from the heavens suddenly flashed about him.
4 He fell to the ground and heard a voice saying to him, "Saul, Saul, why are you
persecuting me?" 5 He asked, "Who are you, sir?" The reply was, "I am Jesus,
whom you are persecuting. 6 Get up and go into the city, and you will be told
what you must do." 7 The men traveling with him stood there speechless; they
heard the voice but saw no one. 8 Saul got up from the ground, and though he
opened his eyes, he could see nothing. Leading him by the hand, they brought
him into Damascus. 9 For three days he could not see, and he neither ate nor
drank. 10 There was a certain disciple in Damascus, Ananias by name, and the
Lord said to him in a vision, "Ananias." "Yes, Lord," he answered. 11 The Lord
continued, "Go at once to the street called Straight and look for a man of Tarsus
named Saul in the house of Judas. He is there praying, 12 and [in a vision] he has

seen a man named Ananias entering and laying [his] hands on him that he might
recover his sight." [13]But Ananias protested, "Lord, I have heard from many
people about this man and how much harm he has done to your dedicated
people in Jerusalem. [14]He is here now with authority from the chief priests to
arrest all those who call upon your name." [15]But the Lord said to him, "Go! This
man is a chosen instrument of mine to carry my name before Gentiles and kings,
and the children of Israel. [16]I myself shall show him how much he will have to
endure for the sake of my name." [17]So Ananias went and entered the house. He
laid his hands on him, saying, "Saul, my brother, the Lord Jesus, who appeared
to you on the road as you were coming here, has sent me that you might recover
your sight and be filled with the Holy Spirit." [18]Immediately, something like
scales fell from his eyes, and he recovered his sight. He got up and was baptized;
[19]when he had taken some food, he regained his strength.

WT: [2]to this Way. [3][omits "as he traveled along"]. [4]to the ground with great confusion and heard. [5]He said in reply, "Who are you, Sir?" And the Lord said to him. [adds at the end:] "It is useless for you to kick against the goad." He was trembling and becoming afraid because of what had happened to him, he said, "Sir, what do you want me to do?" The Lord said to him. [6]city, there it will be shown to you what . . . [7]saw no one speaking. [8]He said to them, "Pick me up from the ground." When they had picked him up, he saw nothing, though his eyes were open. [9]And so he remained for three days, [12][whole verse is omitted]. [13][omits "from many people"]. [14]And look, he is here now. [17]So Ananias got up and went to the house. . . . He laid his hand on him.

COMMENT

Here begins another great section of Acts, which describes the spread of the Word from Jerusalem, the geographic center of sacred history, to the third stage of missionary endeavor indicated in Jesus' command to the apostles to carry the testimony to the end of the earth (see 1:8 and its NOTE). Two important features are to be noted: the influential activity of Peter, the leader of the Twelve, and the breakaway of Christianity from its Jewish matrix. The story of Saul's call, with which this section begins, is an important factor in the spread of the Word to Gentiles, for he is being called to bring his testimony to these people.

Luke has foreshadowed the spread of the Word of God to others than Jews in Judea in the activity of the evangelist Philip in Samaria and on the road to Gaza. Now he continues his narrative of the spread of the Word by recounting how Saul the persecutor becomes a witness to Jesus Christ. Luke has already depicted Saul persecuting Christians in Jerusalem. The sequel to that persecution is the way Saul plans to carry this distress even to Christians in Damascus. For the first time we learn of Christians outside of the immediate vicinity of Jerusalem, Judea, or Samaria.

This is an important incident in the Lucan story, because it narrates how Saul, who will become the hero of the second half of Acts, is transformed by the risen Christ himself. Before testimony is carried by Christians to Gentiles, Luke must incorporate this hero into the Christian community. This is the story of the call of Saul. It is not an account of his psychological "conversion," as it is often characterized, but the story of how divine grace transforms even the life of a persecutor.

Modern interpreters of Paul's letters and of Acts often raise the question whether Paul's experience on the road to Damascus should be labeled a "conversion" or a "call." Stendahl has rightly seen that it was a misreading of Paul's letters to understand it as something like the experience of Augustine or Luther or as an example of the "introspective conscience," since Paul himself speaks of his Jewish past with a robust conscience in Phil 3:4–6; Gal 1:13–14 ("The Apostle Paul"). If one uses "conversion" of the account in Acts, it should not bear all the nuances of a psychological experience in the Augustinian sense, even if Luke has depicted Saul's call as an experience that has changed or transformed him from a persecutor to a witness of the risen Christ. That is all that should be meant by his "conversion." It is not the story of the conversion of a great sinner, but rather of how heaven can upset the persecution of God's people.

The incident is important to Luke, because he is not content to narrate it only once (here in 9:1–19a), but will present two further accounts in the form of speeches (22:1–16; 26:9–18). Thus, three times over in Acts one reads the story of Saul's conversion. They represent a single tradition, derived ultimately from Saul himself. Luke's vocabulary and style in all three forms are quite similar, despite his tendency to vary phrases and details.

The triple account of Saul's call is Luke's way of telling the story. For Paul's own description of the experience, see Gal 1:11–16; 1 Cor 9:1c; 15:8–10; Phil 3:6–8. There Paul himself tells how God revealed his Son to him that he might preach him to the Gentiles and how he received the "gospel" that he has been preaching; nothing is said about the gospel in the Lucan account. Rather, Saul is directed to the church, which becomes the way he learns about the Jesus-story.

The first Lucan account of Saul's call, form-critically considered, is a narrative that tells how the experience took place. It might also be called a commissioning narrative, since the stress falls not so much on what took place as on the election of Saul by the Lord Jesus as an instrument of evangelization. Hedrick would have us believe that this episode is "a traditional miracle story . . . adapted as a commissioning narrative" ("Paul's Conversion/Call," 432), but that is hardly the way to describe it. The episode does not have the traits of a miracle story, even if it resembles the form of the OT prophetic call.

The narrative undoubtedly has been derived by Luke from his Pauline source. It tells about Saul journeying to Damascus, empowered with authority from the high priest in Jerusalem to synagogues in Damascus, his encounter with the risen Christ a short distance from that city, his subsequent temporary blindness, his being cared for by a Christian disciple in Damascus itself, and about his eventual baptism, recovery of sight, and reception of the Spirit.

The episode recounts a revelatory Christophany, a "manifestation of God's Son" to Saul, which impresses him with the need of faith in Christ as the way to salvation for all human beings. It relates how the power of the risen Christ transforms even the archpersecutor of his church into its most ardent defender and prominent witness. In the course of the episode the risen Christ instructs Ananias: Saul is to become "a chosen instrument of mine to carry my name before Gentiles and kings, and the children of Israel" (9:15). He is thus the vessel of election, chosen by Christ himself, to bear witness on his behalf. He it is who will carry that testimony "to the end of the earth" (1:8). This is the only episode in the NT that tells of a postpentecostal appearance of the risen Christ to anyone. In 1 Cor 15:8, Paul himself speaks of this appearance of Christ and relates it to prepentecostal appearances accorded to others. It thus forms part of Paul's insistence on his right to be called an "apostle" (see 1 Cor 9:1–2).

See Haenchen (*Acts*, 325–27) for earlier attempts of Spitta, Wendt, Hirsch, Drews, and von Dobschütz to analyze the three accounts on a source basis. None of them has really succeeded. What we have in chap. 9 is Luke's dramatization (not a legendary account, *pace* Hirsch) of what he has learned (from his Pauline source) about Saul's experience on the road to Damascus: how God provided that Saul would go to Damascus in his persecutory role, be encountered by the risen Christ, cured by Ananias, and become the "chosen instrument"; how the archpersecutor is commissioned to carry the "name" of Jesus to Jews, kings, and Gentiles. Cf. 1 Tim 1:12–14, for a still later description of the conversion-call.

Ananias is the means whereby the Lucan Saul is incorporated into the existing Christian church. In Galatians Paul makes no mention of Ananias, for he is there stressing that his vocation is directly from God and not from human beings; that too is the reason why he insists on his right to be called an "apostle." That stress resembles the way Saul's vocation is presented in chap. 26. Yet Luke has dramatized the very call made by Jesus himself. It is "the Lord" who has spoken to Saul (9:27). Even though Ananias is a mediator for the healing, baptism, and reception of Saul into the church, the risen Christ has called him, a detail that does agree with Gal 1:12, 16, although there Paul ascribes the call to God the Father. Moreover, it is the risen Christ who commissions Ananias so to act. Earlier commentators who were eager to exaggerate the difference between the Lucan story of Saul's conversion and Saul's own account have often overlooked or deliberately played down these details.

The Lucan account of Saul's call has often been compared with the call of prophets in the OT (e.g., 1 Kgs 22:19b–22; Isa 6:1–10; Jer 1:4–10), but it is important too to note a difference. In the OT the call stories are recounted as a commission for a special mission, but not as a call to change one's way of life, which is the burden of the call of Saul: he is to become the risen Christ's chosen instrument for the evangelization of Gentiles, indeed, but he is also called to recognize that the crucified King of the Jews has become God's Messiah now in glory. He is called to become a witness to that Christ, to change from his role as persecutor. Saul is thus called to surrender his previous understanding of himself and to submit to God's will manifested in the cross of Christ Jesus. As a Jew, Saul may well have looked forward to the coming of a Messiah, but he has been called to recognize Jesus as that Messiah, now raised to glory as the risen Christ. In that sense his "call" involves indeed a "conversion." See O. H. Steck, "Formgeschichtliche Bemerkungen."

The significance of this episode in Acts about Saul's call has been well caught by A.D. Nock:

> This community [of Jerusalem Christians] was joined by Paul, who had earlier attached himself to the Christian movement under circumstances which gave him a new attitude. The Twelve in Jerusalem, and no doubt most of their early adherents, had found in the Gospel of Jesus and the Gospel which took shape around Jesus the integration and completion of the religious traditions in which they had always lived. For them he came to fulfil, and not to destroy. Paul, on the other hand, had regarded them and theirs as apostates and had thrown himself heart and soul into the struggle to suppress them. For him to become a Christian meant in the first instance a complete change of face. It is the first conversion to Christianity of which we have knowledge. He brought to it not merely a fresh enthusiasm but also an imperious inner need to discover an interpretation and reconciliation of the old and the new in his religious life. (*Conversion: The Old and the New in Religion from Alexander the Great to Augustine of Hippo* [Oxford: Clarendon, 1933], 190–91)

Noteworthy in this account of Saul's call is the omission by Luke of any mention of his journey to "Arabia" (Gal 1:17b) and subsequent return to Damascus (1:17c).

The call of Saul to be "a chosen instrument" of the risen Christ to carry his name before Gentiles, kings, and the children of Israel remains one of the great wonders of divine grace in the history not only of Christianity but of the world. The archpersecutor of Christians was transformed by the call of Christ into the "apostle of the Gentiles" (Rom 11:13). The Lucan story of that call and transformation proclaims the power of the risen Christ in the life of a human being. "Man proposes, but God disposes!" so runs the proverb.

NOTES

9:1. *Now Saul, still breathing murderous threats against the Lord's disciples.* Lit., "still breathing threat and murder against . . ." Luke's formulation may depend on the Greek of Ps 18:16. His hendiadys continues the description of Saul, the persecutor of those who have followed the Lord, which was begun in 8:3; cf. 26:10. The description implies that Saul has indeed been persecuting Christians in Jerusalem and its environs, despite what some interpreters have said (J. Knox, *Chapters*, 35–36). This and the following verse provide the geographical and chronological setting for the experience that Saul is about to have. On "disciples," see NOTE on 6:1; on *Kyrios* as a title for the risen Christ, see NOTE on 2:36. Cf. P. W. van der Horst, "Drohung und Mord schnaubend (Acta ix 1)," *NovT* 12 (1970): 257–69.

went to the high priest. The high priest is unnamed. He may have been Caiaphas, the high priest from A.D. 18–36, or Jonathan, son of Ananus, who was the high priest for a short time during A.D. 36–37 (Josephus, *Ant.* 18.4.3 §95). Much depends on how the chronology of the life of Paul is reconstructed (Introduction §157). The driving force of the persecution is not the high priest, but Saul. Cf. NOTE on 4:6.

2. *asked him for letters to the synagogues in Damascus.* The letters would have been documents authorizing the work that Saul was to carry out in Damascus, where diaspora Jews had settled. Acts 26:11 implies that Paul succeeded in getting the letters of authorization. The letter in 1 Macc 15:16–21 shows that Roman authorities had granted the Jewish high priest, as leader of the Sanhedrin, power to pursue fugitives with letters of extradition. It is not certain, however, to what extent that would be applicable to Jews in the diaspora, and much less to those who might have become Christians. Josephus (*J.W.* 1.24.2 §474) seems to suggest that only King Herod had enjoyed such a privilege of extradition. Luke's story presumes that Christians are already among the diaspora Jews of Damascus. In any case, his comment indicates that leaders of synagogues in the diaspora were thought to have authority even over Christian Jews, who perhaps still frequented those synagogues.

Damaskos was an important city in Syria, situated in the plain east of the Anti-Lebanon range, at the foot of Mt. Hermon on the western edge of the Syrian Desert, at the crossroads of important caravan routes. It was an old city, already mentioned in the story of Abraham (Gen 14:15; 15:2) and later controlled by Egyptians under Thutmoses III. After Alexander the Great, it was dominated by the Ptolemies and later by the Seleucids, but when Antiochus XII Dionysus was defeated by the Nabatean King Aretas III (85–60 B.C.), Damascus came under Nabatean control (Josephus, *Ant.* 13.15.1–2 §§387–92; *J.W.* 1.4.7–8 §§99–103). It eventually became part of the Roman Empire in 64 B.C., after the defeat of the Damascenes by Metellus, and was one of the cities of the Decapolis (Pliny, *Naturalis historia* 5.16.74). On the death of the emperor Tiberius (16 March 37), it came again under the control of the Nabateans. About the time of Saul's conversion it was governed by the Nabatean ethnarch of King Aretas IV Philopatris (8 B.C.–A.D. 40, mentioned in 2 Cor 11:32). Josephus (*J.W.* 2.20.2 §561; 7.8.7 §368) reports that the number of Jews resident there was considerable; thus Saul was undoubtedly on his way to their synagogues. To get to Damascus, Saul would have had to travel from Jerusalem along the Great North Road. See E.F.F. Bishop, "The Great North Road," *TToday* 4 (1947–48): 383–99. Cf. J. Finegan, *Archeology of the New Testament*, 55–63; W. T. Pitard, *Ancient Damascus* (Winona Lake, IN: Eisenbrauns, 1987); F. Millar, *Roman Near East*, 310–19.

In Gal 1:17 Paul himself implied that his call occurred in the vicinity of Damascus, the city to which he returns after his journey to "Arabia."

if he should find any men or women belonging to the Way. For the first time, *hē hodos* appears as a designation for the Christian church and its teaching; it will reappear in 19:9, 23; 22:4; 24:14, 22. An exclusively Lucan name, it designates those whom Paul is persecuting (here and 22:4) and is even put on Paul's lips (22:14). It is known in Ephesus (19:9, 23), and knowledge of it is ascribed to the procurator Felix (24:22). Haenchen (*Acts*, 320) says: "We do not know for certain—despite Repo's fine study—the origin of the absolute use of *hodos* for

Christianity." He relates the term to "the Way of the Lord" (18:25) and to "the Way of God" (18:26), which fill out its meaning. The former of these references echoes the phrase of Isa 40:3, used in the preaching of John the Baptist, "make ready the way of the Lord" (Luke 3:4), but neither of them nor the OT background of the phrase explains its absolute usage. Haenchen rightly recognized that the references to rabbinic literature in Str-B, 2.690 are irrelevant. Yet, even before Repo's study, the agnosticism of Haenchen was excessive. Acts 24:14 implies that "the Way" was a term that the Christian community was using of itself in contrast to the name *hairesis*, "sect," undoubtedly applied by outsiders who associated Christianity with other movements in Judaism (see NOTE on 24:14).

The absolute term "(the) Way" (*derek* or *hadderek*) occurs in QL as a designation of the mode of Jewish life lived by Essenes, which involved a strict observance of the Mosaic law as understood in that community: *bwḥry drk*, "those who have chosen the Way" (1QS 9:17–18); *'lh tkwny hdrk lmśkyl*, "these are the regulations of the Way for the Master" (1QS 9:21); *hm sry drk*, "these are they who turn away from the Way" (CD 1:13; cf. CD 2:6; 1QS 10:21). See further 1QS 4:22; 8:10, 18, 21; 9:5, 9; 11:11; 1QM 14:7; 1QH 1:36; 1QSa 1:28. "The way of the Lord" (Isa 40:3) is interpreted as *mdrš htwrh*, "the study of the law" (1QS 8:12–15). This plausibly explains the source of the absolute usage in Acts. Both the Essene community and the Christian community could have independently derived this designation from Isa 40:3, but more likely Luke has preserved a genuine recollection of an early historical name for Christianity, borrowed from earlier Essene usage. See Fitzmyer, "Jewish Christianity," 240–42; "The Designations," 229–30; E. Repo, *Der "Weg" als Selbstbezeichnung des Urchristentums* (Annales Academiae Scientiarum Fennicae B132/2; Helsinki: Suomalainen Tiedeakatemia, 1964); S. V. McCasland, "'The Way,'" *JBL* 77 (1958): 222–30; J. Pathrapankal, "Christianity as a 'Way' according to the Acts of the Apostles," *Les Actes des Apôtres* (ed. J. Kremer), 533–39; G. Wingren, "'Weg,' 'Wanderung,' und verwandte Begriffe," *ST* 3 (1949–51): 111–23.

he might bring them back to Jerusalem as prisoners. Lit., "bring them back bound to Jerusalem." As in 8:3, no reason is given for Paul's carting Christian Jews off to prison. Presumably he considered such Christians as heretics or apostates from orthodox Judaism. Saul is opposing Christianity not because it is a rival of Judaism, but because it is a heterodox movement within Judaism.

3. *As he traveled along, he happened to draw near to Damascus.* So Luke begins the account of the great experience in Saul's life that will turn him from the persecutor of the church to its main witness and missionary. For Paul's own brief description of the Christophany, see Gal 1:15–16. Luke uses the articular infin. with *en* (see NOTE on 2:1) and the *egeneto* construction with the infin. *engizein*, "draw near" (see *Luke*, 118–19). The place near Damascus may be identified with Kaukab; see O. F. Meinardus, "The Site of the Apostle Paul's Conversion at Kaukab," *BA* 44 (1981): 57–59. Even though "Damascus" may have a symbolic meaning in QL, there is no guarantee that it is a code name for Qumran or that it can mean Qumran as the place of Saul's call in the Lucan story, *pace* S. Sabu-

gal ("La conversión de S. Pablo en Damasco: ¿Ciudad de Siria o región de Qumrân?" *Aug* 15 [1975]: 213–24).

a light from the heavens suddenly flashed about him. Compare Luke's description in 22:6, 9; 26:13; cf. 4 Macc 4:10. Saul undoubtedly perceived this light; but the more important aspect of his experience on the road to Damascus is described in the next verse. Cf. Ezek 1:28.

4. *He fell to the ground and heard a voice saying to him.* Cf. 22:7; 26:14. In all three descriptions of what happened to Saul on the road to Damascus the emphasis is on its auditory aspect. This will, however, be interpreted in time as a vision of the Lord; see 9:27 and NOTE there. Cf. Ezek 1:28; 3:23–24; 43:3; Dan 8:15, for the reaction of OT prophets to a theophany. Cf. Josephus, *Ant.* 10.11.7 §269.

"Saul, Saul, why are you persecuting me?" The risen Christ addresses the archpersecutor as *Saoul* (see NOTE on 7:58); only he and Ananias use this Greek form of the name (see 9:17; 22:7, 13; 26:14). For the doubling of the name in an address, compare Exod 3:4; 1 Sam 3:4, 10; Luke 8:24; 10:41; 22:31. Note the equivalence of "me" and "the Way" mentioned in v 2 as the object of Saul's persecution. For OT antecedents of this epiphanic dialogue, see Gen 31:11–13; 46:2–3; Exod 3:4–10; *Jub.* 44:5. Cf. G. Lohfink, "Eine alttestamentliche Darstellungsform."

5. *He asked, "Who are you, sir?"* Saul uses *Kyrie*, as in 22:8 and 26:15, but at this stage of his career, it could not yet have had for him the connotation of "Lord," with which he would so often later use it. So Weiser, *Apg.*, 224; Roloff, *Apg.*, 149. *Pace* Johnson (*Acts*, 163), it should not "be taken at full value."

The reply was, "I am Jesus, whom you are persecuting. So the risen Christ identifies himself with his disciples, in effect with his church (cf. 22:8; 26:15; 1 Cor 15:8–9; Gal 1:12, 16). To persecute Christians is to persecute him who founded the movement. Cf. Luke 10:16. The way of thinking here is akin to that of Matt 25:35–40, 42–45.

One should not read into this Lucan verse the Pauline notion of the church as the body of Christ, as did Augustine (*Ennarrationes in Psalmos* 30.2.3; CCLat 38.192). That Pauline designation of the Christian community has no place in Lucan theology. Moreover, it is highly unlikely that Paul came to such a characterization of the Christian church immediately as a result of this experience on the road to Damascus. It was rather the result of his missionary endeavors, since it only gradually appears in his letters, being absent in the earliest of them.

The Sixto-Clementine Vg adds *durum est tibi contra stimulum calcitrare. Et tremens ac stupens dixit: Domine, quid me vis facere?* ("It is difficult for you to kick against the goad. Trembling and shocked, he said, 'What do you want me to do, sir?'"). This is clearly a modified borrowing from 26:14, but it is used by Hilary, Ambrose, and Augustine in their interpretation of the text. See J. Doignon, "Le dialogue de Jésus et de Paul *Actes* 9,4–6: Sa 'pointe' dans l'exégèse latine la plus ancienne (Hilaire, Ambroise, Augustin)," *RSPT* 64 (1980): 477–89. The addition, however, is not found in modern critical editions of the Vg. Cf. K. Lowther Clarke, "Acts 9.5," *Theology* 6 (1923): 100–1.

6. *Get up and go into the city, and you will be told what you must do."* The risen Christ uses the mediation of a faithful Jewish Christian in dealing with Saul, as in 22:10; but this mediation disappears in chap. 26. Compare Ezek 2:1.

7. *The men traveling with him stood there speechless; they heard the voice but saw no one.* Lit., "hearing the voice, but seeing no one." Contrast 22:9 ("Those who were with me saw the light but did not hear the voice speaking to me") and 26:14 ("We all fell to the ground, and I heard a voice saying to me"). Here the verb *akouein* occurs with the gen. *tēs phōnēs,* and since it is not specified whose voice is meant, debate surrounds the phrase. John Chrysostom interpreted it: "For there were two voices, Paul's and the Lord's; there [i.e., in 9:7] it is the voice of Paul, and here [22:9] that of the Lord, and he adds, 'They did not hear the voice speaking to me'" (*Hom. 47 in Act.* 2; PG 60.328). That *tēs phōnēs* refers to Paul's voice, however, cannot be right; it has to refer to the "voice" speaking to Saul in v 4. Luke, like many other Greek authors, used *akouein* with gen. and acc. "without a differentiation in meaning" (H. R. Moehring, "The Verb *akouein* in Acts ix 7 and xxii 9," *NovT* 3 [1959]: 80–99, esp. 81). But J. H. Moulton insisted on the distinction: the acc. of the thing heard and the gen. of the person heard from (*Grammar of New Testament Greek,* 1.66). Moulton, consequently, would translate *tēn de phōnēn ouk ēkousan* (22:9), "they did not understand the voice" (see BAGD, 32). This distinction may be valid for Greek in general (*TDNT,* 1.216), but it "does not accord with Lukan usage" (Bruce, *Acts,* 236). See 10:46; 11:7; 14:9; 15:12; 22:7. Similarly R. G. Bratcher, "*akouō* in Acts ix.7 and xxii.9," *ExpTim* 71 (1959–60): 243–45. Cf. G. Steuernagel, "*Akouontes men tēs phōnēs*" (Apg 9.7): Ein Genetiv in der Apostelgeschichte," *NTS* 35 (1989): 619–24 for a less likely explanation.

8. *Saul got up from the ground, and though he opened his eyes, he could see nothing. Leading him by the hand, they brought him into Damascus.* Paul arrives blind at the city of his destination. Conzelmann (*Acts,* 72) rightly notes that the blinding is not a punishment, but an indication of the helplessness of the one who was formerly a powerful opponent. Cf. 22:11.

9. *For three days he could not see, and he neither ate nor drank.* Thus Luke describes Saul's plight: blindness and fasting. The blindness comes from God, but God will heal it in time. It indicates the psychological effect that Saul's call has had on him; it may also be understood as that whereby he repents and prepares for what faces him in the future. Though physically blind, Saul's eyes are being opened spiritually. For fasting as a preparation for baptism, see *Did.* 7.4. See W. Ameling, "*Phagōmen kai piōmen:* Griechische Parallelen zu zwei Stellen aus dem Neuen Testament," *ZPE* 60 (1985): 35–43.

10. *There was a certain disciple in Damascus, Ananias by name.* He is an otherwise unknown Jewish Christian (see 22:12), who bears the same name as the notorious Ananias of 5:1 (see NOTE there); he is called *mathētēs,* "disciple" (see NOTE on 6:1). How he, a Christian, would already have come to Damascus is not explained; he would actually have been among those whom Saul intended to cart off to prison in Jerusalem. The Lord uses an opponent of Saul as an instrument in the latter's conversion.

the Lord said to him in a vision, "Ananias." "Yes, Lord," he answered. From vv 15 and 17 it will become clear that *Kyrios* is used of the risen Christ, not of Yahweh of the OT. See NOTE on 2:36. Note the parallel of vv 10–11 with Gen 22:1–2. As in vv 4–6 above, Luke has imitated OT style in his composition, but he has also made use of the literary device of double visions in thus depicting both Saul and Ananias accorded a vision of the risen Christ. For extrabiblical parallels of accounts of double visions in Greek and Latin writings, see A. Wikenhauser, "Doppelträume," *Bib* 29 (1948): 100–11.

11. *The Lord continued, "Go at once to the street called Straight and look for a man of Tarsus named Saul in the house of Judas.* There is still an east-west street so called (Derb el-Mustaqim) in the eastern part of the Old City of Damascus; see *Moyen-Orient: Liban, Syrie, Jordanie, Irak, Iran* (Guides Bleus; ed. F. Ambrière; Paris: Hachette, 1956), 204. For the first time we learn that Saul is a diaspora Jew, *Tarseus*, "a man of Tarsus." See further 11:25; 21:39; 22:3. Judas is otherwise unknown, but may have been a Jewish Christian resident in Damascus.

Tarsos was an ancient town in the Plain of Cilicia, just north of the Bay of Alexandretta, near the crossroad of important trade roads, one coming from the Euphrates to the west and the other from Antioch to the north. According to Greek legends it was founded by Perseus or Heracles; but it seems to have been a Phoenician foundation. Some, like C. B. Welles, have identified it with Tarshish of Gen 10:4. It is first attested as *Tarzi* in the ninth-century Black Obelisk of Shalmaneser III (line 138; see D. D. Luckenbill, *Ancient Records of Assyria and Babylonia* [2 vols.; Chicago: University of Chicago Press, 1926–27; repr. New York: Greenwood, 1968], 1.207). In the fourth century Xenophon called it *polis megalē kai eudaimōn*, "a great and prosperous city" (*Anabasis* 1.2.23), and its Greek coins of the fifth–fourth centuries attest to its hellenization. It was more heavily hellenized by the Seleucid ruler, Antiochus IV Epiphanes (175–164 B.C.), who also established a colony of Jews there (ca. 171 B.C.) to foster its commerce and industry (2 Macc 4:30–31), although this further hellenization has sometimes been queried. In 64 B.C. Pompey made Cilicia a Roman province, and Tarsus became the seat of the Roman governor. From the time of Mark Antony it was accorded the status of *municipium*, "free city," and *civitas libera et immunis*, "a city free and exempt [from taxation]" (see Appian, *Bellum Civile* 5.7). In effect, this amounted to Roman citizenship for many of its people (see Dio Chrysostom, *Discourses* 34.23). This status was later confirmed by Augustus. Then it became densely populated and more wealthy. It was in Saul's day a renowned cultural and intellectual center (see Strabo, *Geography* 14.5.9–15). The most famous philosopher of Tarsus was the Stoic Athenodorus, teacher of Caesar Augustus. In 21:39 Paul will claim that he is "a citizen of no mean city in Cilicia."

See W. M. Ramsay, "The Tarsian Citizenship of St. Paul," *ExpTim* 16 (1904–5): 18–21; A. N. Sherwin-White, *Roman Society*, 144–93; H. Böhlig, *Die Geisteskultur von Tarsos im augusteischen Zeitalter mit Berücksichtigung der paulinischen Schriften* (FRLANT 19; Göttingen: Vandenhoeck & Ruprecht, 1913); C. B. Welles, "Hellenistic Tarsus," *MUSJ* 38 (1962): 41–75; A.H.M. Jones, *The Cities of the Eastern Roman Provinces* (Oxford: Clarendon, 1937), 192–209;

D. Magie, *Roman Rule in Asia Minor to the End of the Third Century after Christ* (2 vols.; Princeton: Princeton University Press, 1950; repr. New York: Arno, 1975), 2.1146–48; J. Finegan, *Archaeology of the New Testament*, 51–55; J. Tischler, "Der Ortsname *Tarsos* und Verwandtes," *ZVS* 100 (1987): 339–50; W. Ruge, "Tarsos," *PW* 2/4.A.ii (1932): 2413–39.

He is there praying, 12. *and [in a vision] he has seen a man named Ananias entering and laying [his] hands on him that he might recover his sight."* Saul, who has been confronted by the risen Christ, is depicted as not only fasting, but also communing with God in prayer. He practises ordinary Jewish acts of piety as he awaits further guidance. To him heaven has made known that Ananias is coming to help him.

13. *Ananias protested, "Lord, I have heard from many people about this man and how much harm he has done to your dedicated people in Jerusalem.* Lit., "to your saints in Jerusalem." How Ananias has learned about Saul and his persecution in Jerusalem is not explained. *Hagioi*, the substantivized adj. "saints," is often used as a designation for the early Christians of Jerusalem or Judea; see 9:32, 41; 1 Cor 16:1; 2 Cor 8:4; Rom 15:25, 26, 31. In time it was extended to others; see Phil 1:1; 1 Cor 1:2; 6:1; 2 Cor 1:1; Rom 1:7; 8:27; 12:13; Eph 1:1.

14. *He is here now with authority from the chief priests to arrest all those who call upon your name."* We are not told how Ananias knows that Saul has come with authority from the "chief priests," now used in the pl., whereas in 9:1 *archiereus* was used in the singular. Again, the refrain of the "name" is played upon in this and two following verses; see NOTE on 2:38. Cf. 1 Cor 1:2.

15. *the Lord said to him, "Go!* The risen Christ commissions Ananias, who is thus involved intimately in the call of Saul, as he is in 22:21; but the role of Ananias will disappear in the account of Saul's conversion in chap. 26.

This man is a chosen instrument of mine. Lit., "this one is for me a vessel of election." This explains why Saul has been accorded a unique postpentecostal appearance of the risen Christ, whereas all the other appearances preceded the "ascension" of Christ. Christ's words resume those of Ananias: the persecutor of those who call upon "the name" is to become the instrument for spreading that "name." Saul will have to suffer for that name. The instrumental sense of *skeuos*, "object, vessel," comes to the fore in that Christ has chosen Saul to be the means of missionary endeavor that will spread his name especially among the Gentiles. Polybius also uses *skeuos* of human beings as "instruments" referring to others (*Frg.* 13.5.7; 15.25.1). Cf. Ps.-Clem., *Recognitions* 3.49.5 *(vas electionis factus est maligno)*; Rom 9:22–23.

to carry my name before Gentiles and kings, and the children of Israel. Luke formulates the call of Saul, who will become a "Christian," bearing the name of Christ, and will proclaim that name. Compare 22:15; 26:17–18 and the call of the prophet in Isa 6:9; Jer 1:9–10 (LXX); Ezek 2:3–4. Christ makes sure that Saul will be depicted not only as "an apostle of the Gentiles," as Paul calls himself (Rom 11:13), but also as one who will evangelize "kings" and "the children of Israel" as well. In this way Luke will portray Saul later in Acts: he will preach to Jews in synagogues of Cyprus, Antioch in Pisidia, and Iconium (13:5, 15–41; 14:1), and to King

Agrippa (25:23–26:29), as well as to Gentiles (14:8–20; 15:3). See G. Lohfink, "'Meinen Namen zu tragen . . .' (Apg 9,15)," *BZ* 10 (1966): 108–15, who argues rightly for this interpretation instead of that given by many commentators: "bear my name to Gentiles and kings, and the children of Israel." Although the latter translation is grammatically possible (understanding *enōpion* as an answer to "whither?" rather than "where?"), the rest of the Lucan story in Acts almost demands the first translation given above. So the Vg understands it, as did Luther ("vur den Heiden, und vur den Königen, und vur den Kindern von Israel").

16. *I myself shall show him how much he will have to endure for the sake of my name."* The risen Christ makes known that Saul will have to suffer as his witness and in giving testimony about him. Christ stresses the fellowship of suffering that there must be between him and his followers. Saul who has made others suffer for "the name" must now learn to suffer for it too. See L. Legrand, "How Much He Must Suffer for My Name," *ClerM* 31 (1967): 109–11.

17. *Ananias went and entered the house. He laid his hands on him.* Ananias goes in obedience to the Lord's command and lays his hands on Saul. The imposition of hands takes on a curative aspect; see NOTE on 6:6. As a gesture of healing, it is unknown in the OT or in rabbinical literature but has turned up in 1QapGen 20:28–29, where Abram prays, lays his hands on the head of Pharaoh, and exorcises the evil spirit afflicting him and his household for having carried off Sarai, Abram's wife. See *Luke*, 553.

"Saul, my brother, the Lord Jesus, who appeared to you on the road as you were coming here. The sense of *adelphe* is debatable; it is probably used by one Jew addressing another, as in 2:29, 37; 7:2, 26 (see NOTE on 1:15). Since Ananias, however, is depicted as a Christian, he may be using it proleptically of Saul, about to become one. The risen Lord is clearly identified as "Jesus." Luke does not tell us how Ananias came to know about the appearance of Jesus to Saul a few days before, but the reader of Acts understands that Ananias has learned this from the risen Christ himself.

has sent me that you might recover your sight and be filled with the Holy Spirit." So Saul receives through the mediation of Ananias the gift of the Spirit as well as the cure of his blindness by the imposition of hands. Cf. 8:17.

18. *Immediately, something like scales fell from his eyes, and he recovered his sight.* "Something like scales (or films)" is a primitive way of describing the cause of blindness; cf. Tob 2:10; 11:13. Pliny the Elder speaks similarly of *squama* in the eyes (*Naturalis historia* 29.8.21).

He got up and was baptized; 19. *when he had taken some food, he regained his strength.* Saul was baptized by Ananias and thus became a Christian. Though Paul never mentions his baptism explicitly in any of his letters, he may refer to it implicitly in 1 Cor 12:13 *(ebaptisthēmen);* Rom 6:3. Certainly the lack of a mention of the Spirit being received by him says nothing against the baptism by Ananias. Ananias has thus been the means whereby Saul is legitimized as a Christian and becomes a witness to Christ in the Lucan story. With it Saul ends the fast mentioned in v 9. Cf. R. H. Fuller, "Was Paul Baptized?" *Les Actes des Apôtres* (ed. J. Kremer), 505–8; E. Fascher, "Zur Taufe des Paulus," *TLZ* 80 (1955): 643–48.

Ananias's role in the call of Saul is repeated (with some modification) in 22:12–16, but it is completely absent in the speech of chap. 26. There the commission is given to Saul at the time of Jesus' appearance to him, and there is no mention of his blindness. He goes immediately to Damascus and starts to preach. This accords with Galatians, where there is no mention of Ananias either. There, in fact, Paul insists on his call without the mediation of any human being.

BIBLIOGRAPHY (9:1–19a)

Baracaldo, R., "La Cristofanía de Damasco (Actos de los Apóstoles 9,1–29; 22,3–21; 26,9–20)," *Virtud y Letras* 13 (1954): 3–11.

Bruston, E., "Saul de Tarse: Influence de l'Ancien Testament sur sa conversion et sa vocation," *ETR* 12 (1937): 282–301.

Burchard, C., "Paulus in der Apostelgeschichte," *TLZ* 100 (1975): 881–95.

Denny, R. E., *Wind in the Rigging: A Study of Acts 9–12 and Its Meaning for Today* (Kansas City, MO: Beacon Hill, 1985).

Dietzfelbinger, C., *Die Berufung des Paulus als Ursprung seiner Theologie* (WMANT 58; Neukirchen-Vluyn: Neukirchener-V., 1985), 12–14, 75–82.

Dobschütz, E. von, "Die Berichte über die Bekehrung des Paulus," *ZNW* 29 (1930): 144–47.

Dunn, J. D. G., "'A Light to the Gentiles': The Significance of the Damascus Road Christophany for Paul," *The Glory of Christ in the New Testament: Studies in Christology in Memory of George Bradford Caird* (Oxford: Clarendon, 1987), 251–66.

Dupont, J., "The Conversion of Paul and Its Influence on His Understanding of Salvation by Faith," *Apostolic History and the Gospel: Biblical and Historical Essays Presented to F. F. Bruce . . .* (ed. W. W. Gasque and R. P. Martin; Grand Rapids, MI: Eerdmans; Exeter, UK: Paternoster, 1970), 176–94.

Fletcher, R. J., *A Study of the Conversion of St. Paul* (London: Bell & Sons, 1910).

Gager, J. G., "Some Notes on Paul's Conversion," *NTS* 27 (1980–81): 697–704.

Gill, D., "The Structure of Acts 9," *Bib* 55 (1974): 546–48.

Girlanda, A., "De conversione Pauli in Actibus Apostolorum tripliciter narrata," *VD* 39 (1961): 66–81, 129–40, 173–84.

Guignebert, C., "La conversion de saint Paul," *Revue historique* 175 (1935): 465–81.

Hamm, D., "Paul's Blindness and Its Healing: Clues to Symbolic Intent (Acts 9; 22 and 26)," *Bib* 71 (1990): 63–72.

Hedrick, C. W., "Paul's Conversion/Call: A Comparative Analysis of the Three Reports in Acts," *JBL* 100 (1981): 415–32.

Hirsch, E., "Die drei Berichte der Apostelgeschichte über die Bekehrung des Paulus," *ZNW* 28 (1929): 305–12.

Holtz, T., "Zum Selbstverständnis des Apostels Paulus," *TLZ* 91 (1966): 321–30.

Hultgren, A. J., "Paul's Pre-Christian Persecutions of the Church: Their Purpose, Locale, and Nature," *JBL* 95 (1976): 97–111.

Inglis, G. J., "The Problem of St. Paul's Conversion," *ExpTim* 40 (1928–29): 227–31.

———, "St. Paul's Conversion in His Epistles," *Theology* 34 (1937): 214–28.

Jervell, J., "Paul in the Acts of the Apostles: Tradition, History, Theology," *Les Actes des Apôtres* (ed. J. Kremer), 297–306.

Kelly, J., "The Conversion of St. Paul," *Emmanuel* 88 (1982): 563–65, 576.

Kietzig, O., *Die Bekehrung des Paulus religionsgeschichtlich und religionspsychologisch untersucht* (UNT 22; Leipzig: Hinrichs, 1932).

Klein, G., *Die zwölf Apostel: Ursprung und Gehalt einer Idee* (FRLANT 77; Göttingen: Vandenhoeck & Ruprecht, 1961), 120–27, 144–59.

Lake, K., "The Conversion of Paul and the Events Immediately Following It," *Beginnings*, 5.188–95.

Leenhardt, F. J., "Abraham et la conversion de Saul de Tarse, suivi d'une note sur 'Abraham dans Jean viii,'" *RHPR* 53 (1973): 331–51.

Lilly, J. L., "The Conversion of Saint Paul: The Validity of His Testimony to the Resurrection of Jesus Christ," *CBQ* 6 (1944): 180–204.

Linton, O., "The Third Aspect: A Neglected Point of View: A Study in Gal. i–ii and Acts ix and xv," *ST* 3 (1949–50): 79–95.

Lohfink, G., "Eine alttestamentliche Darstellungsform für Gotteserscheinungen in den Damaskusberichten (Apg 9; 22; 26)," *BZ* 9 (1965): 246–57.

———, *The Conversion of St. Paul: Narrative and History in Acts* (Herald Scriptural Library; Chicago: Franciscan Herald, 1976).

———, "Meinen Namen zu tragen . . . (Apg 9,15)," *BZ* 10 (1966): 108–15.

Loisy, A., "La conversion de Paul et la naissance du christianisme," *Les mystères païens et le mystère chrétien* (Paris: Nourry, 1930), 293–332.

Lundgren, S., "Ananias and the Calling of Paul in Acts," *ST* 25 (1971): 117–22.

Lyonnet, S., "'La Voie' dans les Actes des Apôtres," *La parole de grâce: Etudes lucaniennes à la mémoire d'Augustin George* (= *RSR* 69/1–2; Paris: Recherches de science religieuse, 1981), 149–64.

Michel, O., "Das Licht des Messias," *Donum gentilicium: New Testament Studies in Honour of David Daube* (ed. E. Bammel et al.; Oxford: Clarendon, 1978), 40–50.

Munck, J., "La vocation de l'Apôtre Paul," *ST* 1 (1947): 131–45.

———, "Paul, the Apostles, and the Twelve," *ST* 3 (1949–50): 96–110.

Oliver, A. B., "Did Paul's Companions Hear the Voice?" *RevExp* 37 (1940): 63–66.

Pesch, W., "Die Bekehrung des Apostels Paulus nach dem Zeugnis seiner Briefe," *BK* 16 (1961): 36–38.

Prentice, W., "St. Paul's Journey to Damascus," *ZNW* 46 (1955): 250–55.

Prokulski, W., "The Conversion of St. Paul," *CBQ* 19 (1957): 453–73.

Rist, M., "Visionary Phenomena and Primitive Christian Baptism," *JR* 17 (1937): 273–79.

Rongy, H., "Une divergence dans les récits de la conversion de S. Paul," *Revue ecclésiastique de Liège* 17 (1925): 150–54.

Sabugal, S., *Análisis exegético sobre la conversión de san Pablo: El problema teológico e histórico* (Barcelona: Editorial Herder, 1976).
Schilling, F. A., "Why Did Paul Go to Damascus?" *ATR* 16 (1934): 199–205.
Smend, F., "Untersuchungen zu den Acta-Darstellungen von der Bekehrung des Paulus," *Angelos* 1 (1925): 34–45.
Squillaci, D., "La conversione di San Paolo (Att. 9,1–19)," *PC* 40 (1961): 233–39.
Stanley, D. M., "Paul's Conversion in Acts: Why the Three Accounts?" *CBQ* 15 (1953): 315–38; repr. *The Apostolic Church in the New Testament* (Westminster, MD: Newman, 1965), 285–311, 441–47.
Steck, O. H., "Formgeschichtliche Bemerkungen zur Darstellung des Damaskusgeschehens in der Apostelgeschichte," *ZNW* 67 (1976): 20–28.
Stendahl, K., "The Apostle Paul and the Introspective Conscience of the West," *HTR* 56 (1963): 199–215.
Unnik, W. C. van, "Tarsus or Jerusalem: The City of Paul's Youth," *Sparsa collecta,* 259–320; "Once again: Tarsus or Jerusalem," ibid., 321–27.
Vosté, J.-M., "S. Pauli conversio," *Angelicum* 8 (1931): 469–514.
Wetter, G. P., "Die Damaskusvision und das paulinische Evangelium," *Festgabe für Adolf Jülicher* . . . (Tübingen: Mohr [Siebeck], 1927), 80–92.
Wikenhauser, A., "Die Wirkung der Christophanie vor Damaskus auf Paulus und seine Begleiter nach den Berichten der Apostelgeschichte," *Bib* 33 (1952): 313–23.
Wilckens, U., "Die Bekehrung des Paulus als religionsgeschlichtliches Problem," *ZTK* 56 (1959): 273–93.
Windisch, H., "Die Christusepiphanie vor Damaskus (Act 9, 22 und 26) und ihre religionsgeschichtliche Parallelen," *ZNW* 31 (1932): 1–23.
Witherup, R. D., "Functional Redundancy in the Acts of the Apostles: A Case Study," *JSNT* 48 (1992): 67–86.
Wood, H. G., "The Conversion of St Paul: Its Nature, Antecedents and Consequences," *NTS* 1 (1954–55): 276–82.

2. SAUL'S PREACHING AND PROBLEMS IN DAMASCUS (9:19b–25)

[19] Saul stayed some days with the disciples in Damascus [20] and at once began to
preach about Jesus in the synagogues, that he was the Son of God. [21] All who
heard him were bewildered and kept saying, "Is not this the one who caused such
havoc in Jerusalem among those who invoke this name? Did he not come here
purposely to bring such people back as prisoners to the chief priests?" [22] Yet Saul
grew steadily more powerful and kept confounding [the] Jews who dwelled in
Damascus with proofs that Jesus was the Messiah. [23] After considerable time had
passed, the Jews began to conspire to kill Saul, [24] but their plot became known to
him. Day and night they were keeping close watch even at the city gates in order

to kill him. [25]But some of his disciples took him one night and let him down through an opening in the wall, lowering him in a hamper.

WT: [19]many days . . . in the city of Damascus. [20][omits "at once"] and entering into the synagogues of the Jews he preached with all boldness . . . [22]powerful in word . . . [25][omits "through an opening in the wall"].

COMMENT

Luke continues his story about the converted Saul, recounting how he stays for some time in Damascus and begins to preach that Jesus was the Son of God or the Messiah to the bewilderment of many. Luke says nothing about Paul's journey to Arabia or his return from there to Damascus (see Gal 1:17). Nor does he indicate that the "considerable time" (9:23) was actually "three years" (Gal 1:18). As Saul's influence in Damascus grows, Jews there seek to do away with him and keep watch to capture him, but Christian disciples enable him to escape from them and from Damascus itself. Nothing is said about Saul trying to preach to Gentiles, despite the character of his call (9:15). The reason is that Luke has not yet told about the inauguration of the Gentile mission; that comes with the mission of Peter in chap. 10.

The Lucan story about Saul's escape from Damascus is confirmed by what Paul himself has narrated in 2 Cor 11:32–33: "In Damascus the ethnarch of Aretas the King kept guarding the city of the Damascenes to capture me; but I was lowered in a basket through a window in the city wall, and I escaped his hands." That occurred at the end of Paul's sojourn of three years in Damascus after his conversion (Gal 1:17c–18). Damascus was apparently under Roman rule until the death of Tiberius (16 March 37; cf. Josephus, *Ant.* 18.5.3 §124). Then the Nabatean ruler, King Aretas IV Philopatris, who ruled from 8 B.C. to A.D. 39/40, seems to have been given control over Damascus by the emperor Gaius Caligula (*PW* 2/1 [1895]: 674). At least Damascus had an *ethnarchēs*, "sheikh of an ethnic group," appointed by Aretas to control the caravan routes leading to that city, since a colony of Nabatean merchants was resident there, whether or not he was actually the governor of the city. Some scholars, however, think it unlikely that Aretas would have been in control of Damascus at this time (so M. Harding, "On the Historicity"). Even if it is not certain, it is more likely than not that the ethnarch had some control, as Bruce, Hemer, Hengel, Marshall, and Wainwright have argued. This problem of chronology affects the Pauline story more than the Lucan. See E. Schürer, *HJPAJC*, 1.574–86, esp. 581–83; J. Starcky, "Pétra et la Nabatène," *DBSup*, 7.886–1017, esp. 913–16.

If Saul fled from Damascus sometime in A.D. 39, before Aretas died, that would mean that his experience on the road to Damascus would have taken place some time in A.D. 36, possibly during the interregnum after the departure of Pilate (see COMMENT on 7:54–8:1; Introduction §§156–57).

The difference between the Lucan and the Pauline accounts is that Luke ascribes the reason for the escape and flight of Saul from Damascus to Jews there who were seeking to kill him, whereas Paul himself ascribes it to the ethnarch of Aretas who wanted to capture him. Luke says nothing, and apparently knew nothing, about the involvement of the ethnarch of Aretas in Saul's flight from Damascus; nor does Paul ever tell us why the ethnarch would have been on the lookout for him. Since we do not know what Paul did in "Arabia" or how long he stayed there (Gal 1:17b), it is sheer speculation on Haenchen's part (*Acts,* 331) to say that Paul had become suspect to Aretas through what he had done in Arabia. Would the ethnarch in Damascus have known of what Paul did in "Arabia"? Even though they differ, the two reasons given by Luke and Paul are not incompatible, because Saul's Jewish opponents might have convinced the ethnarch to side with them. Pesch thinks that the Jews of Damascus denounced Saul before the ethnarch (*Apg.,* 315); yet even though that is nowhere so explained by either Luke or Paul, "different opponents may make common cause" (Hemer, *Book of Acts,* 182). This difference, moreover, is scarcely sufficient to undermine the historicity of the Lucan account of Saul's flight from Damascus and of his subsequent coming to Jerusalem, or to justify the redactional speculations and psychologizing of Haenchen (*Acts,* 333–36). In fact, it is one of the rare items in Acts and in the Pauline corpus that supplies something of an absolute chronological peg for the reconstruction of Paul's life and career. Presumably the Lucan and Pauline accounts describe the same situation from different perspectives. As Barrett remarks (*Acts,* 466), "It is surely correct to identify the two occasions; it is too much to suppose that Paul twice left Damascus in a basket."

To argue thus, however, does not mean that Luke would have derived his information from 2 Cor 11:32–33, *pace* Masson ("À propos"). There is no substantial evidence that Luke had ever read any of Paul's letters. Rather, the information that Luke has about Saul and his ministry has come to him from other sources, esp. his Pauline source.

Luke depicts the Christian Saul preaching in Damascus that Jesus was "the Son of God" and "the Messiah." Thus Saul the persecutor has become another Christian witness proclaiming the new Word of God. The latter title, "Messiah," has already been met in 2:31, 36 (see NOTE on 2:36), but the former occurs now for the first time (cf. NOTE on 8:37, a verse read by the WT, but omitted by the Alexandrian text). It will be reflected in the quotation of Ps 2:7 in Acts 13:33. What Peter proclaimed on Pentecost in Jerusalem, Saul is now depicted proclaiming in Damascus.

This Lucan passage, then, reveals how Saul's influence is exerted on others and is confirmed by the way he is portrayed in his own letters.

This episode portrays Saul preaching the risen Christ as both "Messiah" and "Son of God." Such christological titles are found in Paul's own letters: Rom 9:5; 1:3–4; 2 Cor 1:19. These are expressions of his own faith in Jesus Christ and what God has wrought in and through Christ. In effect, Luke depicts Saul proclaiming the basic Christian message, the gospel about the Son of God (Rom 1:1–3) and what that Messiah and Son of God means for humanity.

NOTES

19. *Saul stayed some days with the disciples in Damascus.* Lit., "and he was with the disciples in Damascus some days," whereas P[45] reads *hēmeras hikanas,* "many days," undoubtedly an attempt to harmonize this verse with v 23. According to Gal 1:17c–18, Saul would not have left Damascus for Jerusalem before three years were up. Luke says nothing about Saul's going off to "Arabia," of which Paul himself speaks in Gal 1:17b. "Arabia" is usually interpreted as the area of Nabatea in Transjordan, to the east and south of Damascus and stretching westward to the south of Judea toward the Suez. No one knows what the Apostle would have done in Arabia or how long he stayed there; so Luke's passing over it is scarcely significant. See G. W. Bowersock, "A Report on Arabia Provincia," *JRS* 61 (1971): 219–42; *Roman Arabia* (Cambridge: Harvard University Press, 1983). On "disciples" as Christians, see NOTE on 6:1.

20. *at once began to preach about Jesus in the synagogues.* The object of Saul's preaching is identified as "Jesus," the way the risen Christ identified himself to Saul on the road to Damascus (9:5). Saul begins his preaching by proclaiming Jesus to Jews of Damascus and thus begins to carry out his role as the "chosen instrument" to carry Jesus' name to "the children of Israel" (9:15).

that he was the Son of God. The title *ho huios tou theou* now appears for the first time in Acts; but cf. the WT of 8:37. It first appeared in the Lucan Gospel in the message of Gabriel to Mary in Luke 1:35, and several times thereafter (see *Luke,* 205–8 for its background and OT use). It was almost certainly an early kerygmatic title, since it is reflected in pre-Pauline fragments of the kerygma in 1 Thess 1:10; Rom 1:3–4. See M. Hengel, *The Son of God* (Philadelphia: Fortress, 1976). It is implied in Paul's speech in 13:33, where Ps 2:7 is cited.

The title expressed a unique relationship of Jesus to Yahweh, the God of the OT (recall Luke 10:22), even though one has to recognize that, as used in Acts, it does not yet carry the connotation of physical or metaphysical sonship that it will have in the later Nicene and Constantinopolitan creeds. Luke, however, does not mean that Jesus was recognized as God's son merely in the adoptive sense in which a king on David's throne would be called his son (2 Sam 7:14; 1 Chr 17:13); the use of the title at the time of Jesus' conception (Luke 1:35) connotes much more. *Pace* Haenchen (*Acts,* 331), the title is not "synonymous with the Messianic epithet of verse 22." Both in OT origin and in Palestinian usage and connotation the two titles were different. For their proper understanding in the NT, they should be kept distinct and not equated or conflated. See further Fitzmyer, "The Palestinian Background."

21. *All who heard him were bewildered and kept saying, "Is not this the one who caused such havoc in Jerusalem among those who invoke this name?* Cf. 9:13–14. As Ananias was bewildered about Saul, so now Jews of Damascus who hear him preaching Jesus as the Son of God share the same reaction. Luke alludes to what he reported about Saul's persecution of Jerusalem Christians in 8:3. Again the refrain of the "name" reappears; see NOTE on 2:38. The havoc would have been wrought through Saul's attempt to imprison Christians who were invoking that

"name" (see 8:3). Simply because Luke uses the verb *porthein*, "ravage," is no proof that he had read Gal 1:13, 23, where it is similarly used by Paul. See P.-H. Menoud, "Le sens du verbe *porthein*: Gal 1,13.23; Act 9,21," *Apophoreta: Festschrift für Ernst Haenchen* . . . (BZNW 30; ed. W. Eltester and F. H. Kettler; Berlin: Töpelmann, 1964), 178–86.

Did he not come here purposely to bring such people back as prisoners to the chief priests?" See 9:1,14.

22. *Saul grew steadily more powerful.* MSS C and E add *(en) tō logō*, "in word," i.e., his rhetorical ability grew steadily. Luke implies that this growth in influence and power is the reason why the opposition rises against Saul.

kept confounding [*the*] *Jews who dwelled in Damascus.* Josephus tells that the number of Jews resident in Damascus was considerable (*J.W.* 2.20.2 §561; 7.8.7 §368).

with proofs that Jesus was the Messiah. Lit., "demonstrating that he was the Messiah." Luke employs the ptc. *symbibazōn*, "bringing together," i.e., marshaling arguments (from the Hebrew Scriptures) to establish his contention. On "Messiah," see NOTE on 2:36. Cf. Acts 17:3; 18:5.

23. *After considerable time had passed.* Lit., "when many days were filled," i.e., had elapsed. Compare the similar modes of expressing the passage of time in 7:23, 30; 24:27.

Jews began to conspire to kill Saul. Lit., "plotted together to do away with him." Cf. 23:12. Thus begins the suffering of which the risen Christ spoke in his words to Ananias that Saul would have to endure (9:16).

24. *their plot became known to him.* How we are not told.

Day and night they were keeping close watch even at the city gates in order to kill him. Compare 2 Cor 11:32, and Josephus, *Life* 11 §53 for an extrabiblical parallel to guarding exits of a town.

25. *some of his disciples took him one night and let him down through an opening in the wall, lowering him in a hamper.* 2 Cor 11:33 mentions that Saul was let down "through a window," and the object used to lower him is called *sarganē*, "(woven) basket," instead of the Lucan *spyris*, "hamper." Compare Josh 2:15 (LXX), where similar language is used of the Hebrew spies lowered down the wall of Jericho from Rahab's house. One can only ask who "his disciples" might have been. Conzelmann (*Acts*, 74) wonders whether the gen. *autou* might be a mistake for the acc. *auton*, which is the reading of MSS E, Ψ of the WT. Similarly, Haenchen (*Acts*, 332) calls *autou* an early corruption.

BIBLIOGRAPHY (9:19b–25)

Barnikol, E., "War Damaskus um 38 n. Chr. arabisch? 2. Kor. 11:32–33 und Gal. 1:17," *TJb* 1 (1933): 93–95.

Dupont, J., "Les trois premiers voyages de Saint Paul à Jérusalem," *Études*, 167–71.

Fitzmyer, J. A., "The Palestinian Background of 'Son of God' as a Title for Jesus,"

Texts and Contexts: Biblical Texts in Their Textual and Situational Contexts: Essays in Honor of Lars Hartman (ed. T. Fornberg and D. Hellholm; Oslo/Boston: Scandinavian University Press, 1995), 567–77.

Harding, M., "On the Historicity of Acts: Comparing 9.23–5 with 2 Corinthians 11.32–3," *NTS* 39 (1993): 518–38.

Kremer, J., "'Dieser ist der Sohn Gottes' (Apg 9,20): Bibeltheologische Erwägungen zur Bedeutung von 'Sohn Gottes' im lukanischen Doppelwerk," *Der Treue Gottes trauen: Beiträge zum Werk des Lukas: Für Gerhard Schneider* (ed. C. Bussmann and W. Radl; Freiburg im B.: Herder, 1991), 137–58.

Masson, C., "À propos de Act. 9.19b–25: Note sur l'utilisation de Gal. et de 2 Cor. par l'auteur des Actes," *TZ* 18 (1962): 161–66.

Steinmann, A., *Arethas IV, König der Nabatäer* (Freiburg im B.: Herder, 1909).

Taylor, J., "The Ethnarch of King Aretas at Damascus: A Note on 2 Cor 11,32–33," *RB* 99 (1992): 719–28.

Wainwright, A. W., "The Historical Value of Acts 9:19b–30," *SE VI* (TU 112; Berlin: Akademie, 1973), 589–94.

Zahn, T., "Zur Lebensgeschichte des Apostels Paulus," *NKZ* 15 (1904): 23–41, esp. 34–41.

3. Saul's First Visit to Jerusalem (9:26–31)

26 When Saul arrived in Jerusalem, he tried to associate with the disciples, but
they were all afraid of him, not believing that he was a disciple. 27 Finally Barnabas took charge of him, brought him to the apostles, and explained to them how
on the way he had seen the Lord, how the Lord had spoken to him, and how in
Damascus he had been preaching fearlessly in the name of Jesus. 28 Saul stayed
on with them, freely moving about in and out of Jerusalem, preaching fearlessly
in the name of the Lord. 29 He also used to speak and debate with the Hellenists,
but they kept trying to kill him. 30 When the brothers learned of this, they took
him down to Caesarea and sent him off to Tarsus. 31 Meanwhile, the church was
at peace throughout all Judea, Galilee, and Samaria. It was gradually being built
up and advanced in the fear of the Lord. With the encouragement of the Holy
Spirit, it grew in numbers.

WT: [27] took him by the hand, brought. [28] in the name of Jesus. [31] the churches [with pl. verbs throughout the verse].

COMMENT

Luke continues the story of Saul, telling of his arrival back in Jerusalem and his attempt to associate with Christians there, who recognize him only as the archpersecutor. Barnabas intervenes and explains Saul's new Christian status. In that context Saul resumes his preaching and debates with Jewish Hellenists, who become his fierce opponents. When it is learned that they are trying to kill him, some Christians accompany Saul to Caesarea Maritima, where he takes off for Tarsus, his hometown. The episode ends with another minor summary, which records the peace that the Christian community now enjoys throughout Judea, Galilee, and Samaria.

There is a certain similarity in the description of the events in Jerusalem to those in Damascus: Ananias's hesitation to believe (9:13–14) is paralleled by that of the Jerusalem disciples (9:26); the Lord's reassurance (9:15–16) and Barnabas's reassurance (9:27); Saul's association with disciples in Damascus (9:19b) and his association with disciples in Jerusalem (9:28a); Saul's immediate preaching in the Damascene synagogues (9:20–22) and his speaking out boldly in Jerusalem (9:28b–29a); the plot against Paul in Damascus (9:23–24) and that of Hellenists in Jerusalem (9:29b); the escape of Paul in both places (9:25, 30). See D. Gill, "The Structure of Acts 9," *Bib* 55 (1974): 546–48.

Luke reports the first visit of Saul to Jerusalem after his flight from Damascus (9:26–29; cf. 22:17; 26:20). It is the first of five, or possibly six, postconversion visits to Jerusalem that will be enumerated (the counting depends on a problematic variant reading). Whether they are all individually historical is problematic. It may be that Luke, dependent on different sources, has historicized and individualized some of the visits, when he should rather have realized that he had inherited more than one record of the same visit (see Introduction §156).

The information about this first visit of Saul to Jerusalem after his call is derived from Luke's Pauline source, to which he has added a minor summary in v 31.

In any case, this first postconversion visit of Saul to Jerusalem in Acts is to be taken as that reported in Gal 1:18: "Then after three years I went up to Jerusalem to consult Cephas, and I stayed with him for fifteen days." That means "three years" after his experience on the road to Damascus.

Conzelmann (*Acts,* 75), in comparing this episode with Gal 1:17–24, claims that the historical Paul in Galatians maintains his own independence, whereas the Lucan Paul is linked to and legitimized by Jerusalem. That is reading far too much into the Lucan story, which says nothing of a legitimatization of Saul. Nor is it evident why Conzelmann is reluctant to assimilate this Lucan episode with Gal 1:18–19.

The example of Barnabas is noteworthy. As his name is explained in 4:36, "Son of Consolation," he now brings that consolation to the Christians of Jerusalem in acting as the bridge whereby Saul is brought into their midst and reconciled with them. Barnabas reaches out to the converted Saul and welcomes him as a fellow Christian. He explains to the others what God's grace has produced in the life of an individual who is open to it. Consolation and encouragement come from the Holy Spirit, who makes Barnabas the mediator of it. Under such guidance of the Spirit the Christians of Jerusalem advance in "the fear of the Lord" and grow in numbers.

NOTES

26. *When Saul arrived in Jerusalem, he tried to associate with the disciples.* This would have been sometime in A.D. 39. What Luke describes is Saul's first attempt to associate with other Jerusalem Christians, who are again called *mathētai*; see NOTE on 6:1. This implies that disciples are once again in Jerusalem, where the persecution of Christians has abated.

they were all afraid of him, not believing that he was a disciple. The ordinary Christians of Jerusalem still recognize him as the archpersecutor and cannot believe that he has become one of them.

27. *Finally Barnabas took charge of him.* Lit., "taking hold of (him), Barnabas brought." Barnabas acts as a chaperone for the newly arrived Saul. The verb *epilambanesthai* usually governs the gen., and the masc. pron. *auton* is actually the obj. of the main verb *ēgagen*, "he led him." On Barnabas, see NOTE on 4:36.

brought him to the apostles. There were "apostles" in Jerusalem (see 8:1), but who is meant beyond Peter is not clear. According to Gal 1:19 Saul saw "no other of the apostles," save Cephas, but did consult "James, the brother of the Lord," who was not one of the Twelve. Luke would not have considered James one of that group, eleven of whom he named in 1:13. In Gal 2:9 Paul does mention "James, Cephas, and John," but that was on a later visit to Jerusalem. Yet even there it is not clear that the James so mentioned was any other than the one named in Gal 1:19. In any case, the three are designated "pillars," not "apostles," the term used here.

explained to them how on the way he had seen the Lord. I.e., how he was accorded an appearance of the risen Christ on the road to Damascus. The logic of the sentence would suggest that Barnabas is the subject of the verb *diēgēsato*, "explained," and so I have taken it above, along with Barrett (*Acts*, 469), Dupont (*Actes*, 94), Roloff (*Apg.*, 156), Schneider (*Apg.*, 2.33 [but cf. 38]), and Weiser (*Apg.*, 234); but some commentators maintain that there is a change of subject and that Saul is really the subject (so Pesch, *Apg.*, 313; Wikenhauser, *Apg.*, 91). In other words, when Barnabas brought Saul to the apostles, Saul explained. That would answer the question about how Barnabas would have known about Saul's experience on the road to Damascus; he would have learned about it from Saul along with the apostles. Luke now interprets Saul's auditory experience described in v 4 as a vision. Recall 1 Cor 9:1, where Paul himself says, "Have I not seen (*heōraka*) our Lord?" Cf. 1 Cor 15:8, but contrast Gal 1:15–16: "God was pleased . . . to reveal his Son to me." Whether that revelation was visual or auditory is not said there.

how the Lord had spoken to him. See 9:4b–6.

how in Damascus he had been preaching fearlessly in the name of Jesus. See 9:20, 22. Again the refrain of "the name of Jesus"; see NOTE on 2:38. The verb *eparrhēsiasato*, "spoke fearlessly," is related to the Lucan favorite noun *parrhēsia*; see NOTES on 2:29; 4:13. Cf. 9:28; 18:26; 19:8; 26:26. Paul himself uses the noun in 2 Cor 3:12; 7:4; Phil 1:20; Phlm 8.

28. *Saul stayed on with them, freely moving about in and out of Jerusalem, preaching fearlessly in the name of the Lord.* Thus Lucan summarily describes the effect of Barnabas's intervention and the resultant intimate dealings Saul had with apostles and other disciples. He was thus accepted by Jerusalem Christians and continued his own fearless independent proclamation and testimony among Jerusalemites. Nevertheless, Paul in Gal 1:22 insists that he was "still not known by sight to the churches of Christ in Judea." This may be read as a Lucan contradiction of what Paul has stated; but perhaps one has to distinguish Saul's activity in Jerusalem, described here, from what became known about him in "the churches in Judea." Haenchen (*Acts*, 332 n. 5) rightly notes that Luke makes no mention of Saul's activity outside of Jerusalem. If one takes the time of "fifteen days" (Gal 1:18) into consideration, then Paul's statement in Gal 1:22 becomes intelligible.

29. *He also used to speak and debate with the Hellenists.* I.e., with Greek-speaking Jews, perhaps even from the diaspora. In 6:1 *Hellēnistai* was used of Greek-speaking Jewish Christians. The latter are certainly not meant here, because of the following clause. Yet these "Hellenists" react against Saul, as diaspora Jews had reacted against Stephen (8:10–13). *Pace* Lake and Cadbury (*Beginnings*, 4.106), "Hellenists" here cannot mean "heathen." That makes little sense in this context.

they kept trying to kill him. Saul meets with the same reaction to his preaching Christ to Jews in Jerusalem as he did to those in Damascus; recall 9:23. This reaction to Saul is repeated in 22:18.

30. *When the brothers learned of this.* Again Jewish Christians in Jerusalem are referred to as *adelphoi;* see NOTE on 1:15. They are Saul's fellow Christians.

they took him down to Caesarea. I.e., overland to Caesarea Maritima, on the seacoast, to the northwest of Jerusalem (see NOTE on 8:40). Christians of Jerusalem thus get Saul off the scene, because he was stirring up trouble among Jews there, with whom they had come to some amicable understanding.

sent him off to Tarsus. Presumably by ship, although he could have made the journey overland northward through Syria to Cilicia, which may be what Gal 1:21 suggests, "into the regions of Syria and Cilicia." That, however, is not likely, because it would mean that Saul had to traverse all the rest of Palestine alone. See E.M.B. Green, "Syria and Cilicia—A Note," *ExpTim* 71 (1959–60): 52–53. Thus Saul is sent back as a Christian by fellow Christians to his hometown. On Tarsus, see NOTE on 9:11. In his hometown Saul carries out a missionary role for a good period of time; see Gal 1:23, which speaks of his "preaching the faith" in the region of Cilicia.

31. *the church was at peace throughout all Judea, Galilee, and Samaria.* MSS E, 614, 1409, 2344, and the *Koinē* text-tradition read rather the pl. *ekklēsiai*, "churches," with the following verbs and ptcs. in the plural. This difference raises the question whether the sg. *ekklēsia* in the Alexandrian text is to be understood in the sense of the universal church. Because Luke elsewhere uses *ekklēsia* of local churches (8:11; 11:22; 13:1), the pl. in some MSS may be suspect, and the sg. is the *lectio difficilior.* Actually one could still understand it of the local church represented in these different regions. See NOTE on 5:11; cf. K. N. Giles,

"Luke's Use of the Term '*ekklēsia*' with Special Reference to Acts 20.28 and 9.31," *NTS* 31 (1985): 135–42.

Luke introduces another of his minor summaries (see Introduction §92b). It stresses the peace and growth of the church and emphasizes the role of the Spirit in that growth. "Peace" is one of the effects of the Christ-event as seen by Luke (*Luke,* 224–25). What is noteworthy is the "peace" that the Christians of Judea and elsewhere enjoy in contrast to the reaction of Jerusalem Jews to Saul.

On "Judea" and "Samaria," see NOTES on 1:8; 8:5. Galilee is now mentioned for the first time in Acts; it will appear again in 10:37; 13:31. It has been mentioned several times in the Lucan Gospel (1:26; 2:4, 39; 3:1; 4:14, 31, 44; 5:17; 8:26; 23:5, 49, 55). The Greek name *Galilaia* is found in the LXX as the translation of Hebrew *Gālîl* (Josh 20:7; 21:32; 1 Kgs 9:11; 1 Chr 6:76) or *Gālîlāh* (2 Kgs 15:29), meaning "circle, circuit, district." In the postexilic period it was the name for the northern part of Palestine, surrounded by the Jordan River, the plain of Jezreel/Esdraelon, Mt. Carmel, Ptolemais, Tyre, and Syria. Pliny (*Naturalis historia* 5.15.70) speaks of Galilee as "part of Judea adjoining Syria." Does the invective against Galilean towns (Luke 10:12–15) and the symbolic obstacle to Jesus' preaching in Nazareth (Luke 4:16–30) really make one conclude that there were no groups of Christians in Galilee "in apostolic times," as Haenchen (*Acts,* 333 n. 2) maintains?

It was gradually being built up and advanced in the fear of the Lord. Thus was the Christian movement being consolidated as "church." A new element is introduced into the description of the Christian church: the OT idea of "the fear of the Lord" (Prov 1:7, 29; 2:5; 9:10; 19:23; Ps 19:9; Sir 9:16; 25:6), the beginning of knowledge. Luke introduces that idea to enhance the wisdom that characterized early Palestinian Christians.

With the encouragement of the Holy Spirit, it grew in numbers. The growth of the church is thus ascribed to the *paraklēsis,* "encouragement, exhortation, consolation" of the Spirit. See NOTE on 1:2.

BIBLIOGRAPHY (9:26–31)

Barnikol, E., "Kam Paulus vor Pfingsten zu Petrus? Die Entstehung der Hellenisten-Gemeinde in Jerusalem nach 40 n. Chr. um 42 n. Chr. und ihre Zerstreuung nach dem Martyrium des Stephanus vor 45 n. Chr.," *TJb* 24 (1956): 16–20.

Beare, F. W., "Note on Paul's First Two Visits to Jerusalem," *JBL* 63 (1944): 407–9.

———, "The Sequence of Events in Acts 9–15 and the Career of Peter," *JBL* 62 (1943): 295–306.

Cambier, J., "Le voyage de S. Paul à Jérusalem en Act. ix. 26ss. et le schéma missionnaire théologique de S. Luc," *NTS* 8 (1961–62): 249–57.

De Lacey, D. R., "Paul in Jerusalem," *NTS* 20 (1973–74): 82–86.

Dockx, S., "Chronologie de la vie de Saint Paul, depuis sa conversion jusqu'à son séjour à Rome," *NovT* 13 (1971): 261–304.

Giet, S., "Les trois premiers voyages de Saint Paul à Jérusalem," *RSR* 41 (1953): 321–47.

———, "Novelles remarques sur les voyages de Saint Paul à Jérusalem," *RevScRel* 31 (1957): 329–42.

———, "Un procédé littéraire d'exposition: l'anticipation chronologique," *Mémorial Gustave Bardy* (= *REAug* 2 [1956]): 243–49.

Greydanus, S., *Is Hand. 9 (met 22 en 26) en 15 in tegenspraak met Galaten 1 en 2? Eene verglijkende, exegetische studie* (Kampen: Kok, 1935).

Langevin, P.-E., "Les débuts d'un apôtre: Ac 9,26–31," *AsSeign* 26 (1973): 32–38.

Liechtenhan, R., "Die beiden ersten Besuche des Paulus in Jerusalem," *Harnack-Ehrung: Beiträge zur Kirchengeschichte, ihrem Lehrer Adolf von Harnack . . .* (Leipzig: Hinrichs, 1921), 51–67.

Lowther Clarke, W. K., "St. Paul's Conversion and the Beginnings of Gentile Christianity," *New Testament Problems: Essays — Reviews — Interpretations* (London: SPCK; New York: Macmillan, 1929), 132–35.

Parker, P., "Once More, Acts and Galatians," *JBL* 86 (1967): 175–82.

Pesch, R., "'Hellenisten' und 'Hebräer': Zu Apg 9,29 und 6,1," *BZ* 23 (1979): 87–92.

Reiser, M., "Hat Paulus Heiden bekehrt?" *BZ* 39 (1995): 76–91.

Robinson, D. F., "A Note on Acts 11:27–30," *JBL* 63 (1944): 169–72.

B. Peter Initiates the Mission to Gentiles (9:32–11:18)

1. Peter's Miracles in Lydda and Joppa (9:32–43)

[32]Once Peter happened to be traveling about the country and came to God's
dedicated people living in Lydda. [33]There he found a man named Aeneas, bedridden for eight years because he was paralyzed. [34]Peter said to him, "Jesus Christ
heals you, Aeneas! Get up and make your bed." He got up at once. [35]All the
inhabitants of Lydda and Sharon who saw him were converted to the Lord.
[36]Now in Joppa there was a disciple named Tabitha (which translated means
Dorcas). She lived a life full of good deeds and almsgiving. [37]Just about that time
she happened to become sick and died; after washing her, they laid [her] out in
an upstairs room. [38]Since Lydda was near Joppa, the disciples, who had heard
that Peter was there, sent two men to him with the request, "Please come over to
us without delay." [39]Peter got up and went with them. On his arrival, they took
him upstairs to the room, where all the widows came up to him in tears and

showed him the tunics and robes that Dorcas had made, while she was still with them. [40]Peter made them all go out of the room; then he knelt down and prayed. Turning to her body, he said, "Tabitha, get up!" She opened her eyes, looked at Peter, and sat up. [41]He gave her his hand and helped her to her feet. Then he called in God's dedicated people and the widows and presented her to them alive. [42]It became known all over Joppa, and many people began to believe in the Lord. [43]Then Peter stayed on in Joppa for many days with Simon, a tanner.

WT: [34][omits "to him" and "Aeneas"]. [38][omits "two men"]. [39]that Dorcas had made for them. [41][omits "God's dedicated people and"]. [42]This became known. [43][omits "in Joppa"].

COMMENT

Luke's story about the conversion of Saul has come to an end, and he has laid the groundwork for the Pauline missions in the second half of Acts. Now Luke prepares to introduce the story of the spread of the Word of God to Gentiles. In order to do that, since it is important for him that Peter, the spokesman and leader of the apostles, be the one to inaugurate that mission, Luke begins by telling about Peter's journeys outside of Jerusalem. Two episodes in which Peter evangelizes and performs miracles become the connecting link between the story about Saul, the "chosen instrument" for the Gentile mission, and the actual start of that mission, which Peter inaugurates.

Luke first recounts how Peter came to Lydda and worked a miracle there, curing a man paralyzed and bedridden for eight years. This results in many conversions to Christianity in Lydda and the neighboring plain of Sharon. Then Peter goes on to Joppa and there performs another miracle, raising a woman who has just died; many people in that town too become believers.

Form-critically considered, the episode is again a narrative, in fact, a double miracle story, which contains the usual elements of Synoptic miracle stories. Its main purpose is to present Peter curing a paralyzed man in the name of "Jesus Christ" and later praying that a dead woman may be revived. It thus reveals Peter's apostolic power at work among Jews and Jewish Christians of Judea to the northwest of Jerusalem. Luke may well have joined here two inherited reports that circulated originally independently, but it is not impossible that they were already joined in the Palestinian source that he is now using.

Luke's account of Peter's tour of ministry in Lydda and Joppa is intended as a buildup to his coming missionary activity in the conversion of Cornelius and his household. The miracles of healing and resuscitation that he performs in these towns of Judea are means whereby he stirs up faith in Christ. "Jesus Christ heals you, Aeneas!" (9:34). That makes it clear that Jesus, not Peter himself, is the origin of the miraculous power expended on Aeneas. It is the power of God's Son that heals and vivifies, for he has already been proclaimed as "the author of life" (3:15). As Jesus himself once said, "*Talitha koum,* little girl, get up" (Mark 5:41), so now Peter says, "Tabitha, get up!" (9:40). In virtue of Jesus' power, Peter heals and resuscitates.

NOTES

32. *Peter happened to be traveling about the country and came to God's dedicated people living in Lydda.* Peter, the spokesman (see NOTE on 1:14), undertakes either a missionary journey or an inspection tour on his own. Luke describes his activity as *dierchomenon dia pantōn*, "going through all (places)." *Pace* Torrey, the prep. phrase *dia pantōn* is not a mistranslation of Aramaic *bĕkōllāʾ*, "(through) the whole (region)." That Aramaic phrase would make no sense here. There is another instance of Lucan hyperbole (see NOTE on 2:44). On "saints," see NOTE on 9:13.

Lydda was an old town, called in the OT *Lōd* (Ezra 2:33; 1 Chr 8:12), to the northwest of Jerusalem on the crossroads leading from Jerusalem to Joppa (about seventeen km southeast of it) and from Egypt to Babylon. Later on, probably in the third century, Lydda became known as Diospolis ("City of Zeus") and became a heavily Christian town.

By using *hagioi*, "saints," or "dedicated people," already used in 9:13 and to be used again in 9:41, Luke suggests that Christians are already living in Lydda, even though one has learned nothing about missionary activity in that area, unless one is to presume that Philip the evangelist has been active there. In 8:40 he is said to have evangelized all the towns from Azotus to Caesarea Maritima. *Hagioi*, however, might denote religious Jews, as in LXX Dan 7:18, 21; Isa 4:3; but there is no reason to see this term as a specific reference to Essenes, *pace* H. Kosmala (*Hebräer—Essener—Christen* [SPB 1; Leiden: Brill, 1959], 35). Barrett (*Acts*, 480) observes that a Christian writer, who on occasion uses this term of Christians, would hardly use it of others, unless this were already part of the source used by Luke.

33. *There he found a man named Aeneas, bedridden for eight years because he was paralyzed.* Lit., "lying for eight years on a mat." Aeneas is otherwise unknown. Though a Judean Jew, he bears a Greek name known from Homer (*Iliad* 13.541) on. *Pace* Barrett (*Acts*, 480) and Weiser (*Apg.*, 242), he was not already a Christian; Luke's failure to remark on his becoming one does not support that. The implication of the episode is that he did become one.

34. *Peter said to him, "Jesus Christ heals you, Aeneas!* Peter attributes his healing power to Jesus Christ, the one about whom he preaches. So he makes known the curative effect of the preached Word. See Cadbury, "A Possible Perfect in Acts 9:34," *JTS* 49 (1948): 57–58.

Get up and make your bed." Lit., "stand up and spread out (your mat) for yourself." This is to put some responsible activity on the healed person, to make clear the effectiveness of the miracle.

He got up at once. The cure is efficacious. Luke adds the typical conclusion to a miracle story in the next verse: the reaction of the people.

35. *All the inhabitants of Lydda and Sharon who saw him were converted to the Lord.* Lit., "all . . . turned to the Lord," again an instance of Lucan hyperbole; see NOTE on 2:44. Luke uses *Kyrios* as a title for the risen Christ; see NOTE on 2:36. The believers were not only fellow inhabitants of Lydda, but also dwellers

in Sharon, the plain that stretches along the coast of Palestine northwest of Lydda from Joppa to Caesarea Maritima.

36. *Now in Joppa.* Joppa (= modern Jaffa) was an ancient Philistine city on the coast of Palestine, in the Plain of Sharon; it served as a seaport for travel on the Mediterranean Sea and was about 50 km south of Caesarea.

a disciple named Tabitha (which translated means Dorcas). Luke uses the fem. noun *mathētria,* designating her as a Christian woman (see NOTE on 6:1). Her Aramaic name is *Ṭabyĕtā'* or *Ṭĕbîtā',* "gazelle" (fem.), which is in Greek *Dorkas.* It is related to the fem. Hebrew name *Ṣibyāh,* "Zibiah" (2 Chr 24:1), which means "gazelle."

She lived a life full of good deeds and almsgiving. Lit., "she was full of good deeds and alms which she made," i.e., she was concerned about the poor and gave to the needy.

37. *Just about that time she happened to become sick and died.* Luke uses *egeneto de* with an infin. (see *Luke,* 118). The time indication is expressed by *en de tais hēmerais ekeinais;* see NOTE on 1:15.

after washing her, they laid [her] out in an upstairs room. I.e., fellow citizens of Joppa performed the customary ritual and prepared her for burial. From v 39 one concludes that "they" refers to widows, but the indef. 3d pl. may be no more than a substitute for the passive: she was laid out.

38. *Since Lydda was near Joppa.* I.e., about sixteen km away.

the disciples, who had heard that Peter was there, sent two men to him with the request, "Please come over to us without delay." Lit., "sent two men to him, urging, 'Do not delay in coming to us.' " The request comes from other Christians, again called "disciples" (see NOTE on 6:1).

39. *Peter got up and went with them. On his arrival, they took him upstairs to the room.* See v 37b.

where all the widows came up to him in tears and showed him the tunics and robes that Dorcas had made, while she was still with them. The middle ptc. *epideiknymenai* indicates that the widows were "showing themselves" in the robes that they were actually wearing, which Dorcas had made for them (ZBG §234; BDF §316.1).

40. *Peter made them all go out of the room.* Lit., "expelling them all (masc.)," which would imply that more than widows were there. Cf. 2 Kgs 4:33.

he knelt down and prayed. Turning to her body, he said, "Tabitha, get up!" Luke insists that Peter revives the woman through prayer, and not some other power. Cf. the similar words of Jesus in Mark 5:41, *talitha koum,* "maiden, arise!" which Luke renders as *hē pais, egeire,* "Get up, child!" (8:54). Peter kneels (*theis ta gonata,* "having placed (his) knees (on the floor)" and prays. See NOTE on 7:60.

She opened her eyes, looked at Peter, and sat up. Peter's prayer is efficacious, and Tabitha is revived. Cf. 2 Kgs 4:35.

41. *He gave her his hand and helped her to her feet.* Lit., "caused her to stand up." Luke uses *anistanai,* a verb often employed to denote resuscitation of the dead or resurrection; 2:24, 32; 3:26; 13:33, 34; cf. Lucian, *Alexander* 24.

Then he called in God's dedicated people and the widows and presented her to them alive. From this it becomes clear why Luke uses the masc. pron. in v 40, because there are *hagioi,* "saints" (masc.), along with the widows; see NOTE on 9:13.

42. *It became known all over Joppa, and many people began to believe in the Lord.* The miracle has had its desired effect; many come to believe in the Lord, the risen Christ. This miracle has the same effect as the first one that Peter performed (9:35).

43. *Peter stayed on in Joppa for many days with Simon, a tanner.* Lit., "he happened to remain many days in Joppa with a certain Simon, a tanner," who will reappear in 10:6, 32. Peter is depicted lodging with a man whose trade was often scorned by ancient Pharisees because of the odors associated with it. See the reactions of later rabbis to such a trade in Str-B, 2.695. See J. McConnachie, "Simon a Tanner *(Byrseus)* (Acts ix.43; x.6, 32)," *ExpTim* 36 (1924–25): 90. *Egeneto de* with the infin. is used; see *Luke,* 118.

BIBLIOGRAPHY (9:32–43)

Beare, F. W., "The Sequence of Events in Acts 9–15 and the Career of Peter," *JBL* 62 (1943): 295–306.

Crum, W. E., "Schila and Tabitha," *ZNW* 12 (1911): 352.

Fenton, J., "The Order of the Miracles Performed by Peter and Paul in Acts," *ExpTim* 72 (1965–66): 381–83.

Harvey, P. B., "The Death of Mythology: The Case of Joppa," *JECS* 2 (1994): 1–14.

Kreyenbühl, J., "Ursprung und Stammbaum eines biblischen Wunders," *ZNW* 10 (1909): 265–76.

Nestle, Eb., "Schila et Tabitha," *ZNW* 11 (1910): 240.

Schwartz, J., "Ben Stada and Peter in Lydda," *JSJ* 21 (1990): 1–18.

Smit Sibinga, J., "Acts 9,37 and Other Cases of ellipsis objecti," *Text and Testimony: Essays on New Testament and Apocryphal Literature in Honour of A.F.J. Klijn* (Kampen: Kok, 1988), 242–46.

Tannehill, R. C., "'Cornelius' and 'Tabitha' Encounter Luke's Jesus," *Int* 48 (1994): 347–56.

2. CONVERSION OF CORNELIUS AND HIS HOUSEHOLD IN CAESAREA (10:1–11:18)

a) CORNELIUS'S VISION (10:1–8)

10 [1]There was in Caesarea a man named Cornelius, a centurion of the Cohort
called Italica, [2]a devout and God-fearing man, along with his whole household.

He used to give many alms to the (Jewish) people and pray to God constantly.
[3]One afternoon about three o'clock he saw clearly in a vision an angel of God
come to him and say, "Cornelius." [4]He stared at him and said in fear, "What is
it, sir?" The angel said to him, "Your prayers and your alms have mounted before
God as a memorial offering. [5]Now send some men to Joppa and summon a certain Simon, who is called Peter. [6]He is staying with another Simon, a tanner,
whose house is by the sea." [7]When the angel who spoke to him had left, he called
two servants and a devout soldier from his staff, [8]recounted everything to them,
and sent them to Joppa.

WT: [3][omits "of God"]. [4][omits "at him"]. Who are you, sir? [5][omits "some men"]. [6]He has been lodging with a certain Simon. [8]recounted to them the vision, and.

COMMENT

Luke begins the story of the actual spread of the Word to Gentiles, as he recounts how Peter is summoned by God to Cornelius, a Roman centurion in Caesarea Maritima, who is converted along with his household. Thus under heaven's direction Peter, the spokesman of the Twelve, officially inaugurates the mission to the Gentiles.

The episode that involves Cornelius is lengthy, and there is no unanimity among commentators as to how one should divide it. It may be helpful to discuss it in five subsections: (a) 10:1–8, Cornelius's Vision; (b) 10:9–16, Peter's Vision; (c) 10:17–23a, Welcome for Messengers from Cornelius; (d) 10:23b–48, Peter's Testimony in Cornelius's House; (f) 11:1–18, Peter's Self-Defense at Jerusalem. This outline of the episode brings out not only the way the episode develops, but even its aftermath as Luke recounts how news of what Peter has done reaches Jerusalem and how he is queried about his activity in Caesarea. For a different outline, see H. de Lubac, "De vocatione"; F. Bovon, *De Vocatione Gentium*.

This story is a crucial development in the Lucan story of the spread of the Word of God. It reflects the Lucan view of history and his idea of the church, but Conzelmann's view that it "does not fit the facts" (*Acts*, 80) is extreme; his analysis of possible sources is no basis for such a conclusion.

This account raises the question of the legitimacy of the mission to Gentiles who are not made to observe the Mosaic law. It is thus an important episode that prepares for the decision of the "Council" in chap. 15. Up to this episode Peter's speeches, though christological and kerygmatic, have been benevolent. Stephen's speech broke with that tradition in Acts, and with its indictment it sounded the knell of the split of Christianity from its Jewish matrix. This episode further develops the story of that split, but in a more irenic way. At the end of Peter's speech the Spirit is given to Gentiles, and one realizes that it is the equivalent of Pentecost for them.

The Cornelius episode is not just another conversion story, like that of the Ethiopian eunuch (8:26–40), for Cornelius and his household symbolize Gentiles, to whom testimony about the Christ-event now spreads, not just under the aegis of the leader of the Twelve, but at the direction of heaven itself. The story of Cornelius's conversion and that of Peter's justification of his missionary activity both stress the heavenly direction now being given to this spread. The explicit formulation of the policy that guides it does not come until the "Council," when Peter will insist that "some time ago God chose me from your number to be the one from whose lips the Gentiles would hear the word of the gospel and come to believe in it" (15:7). Instead of such an explicit formulation, Luke now presents it dramatically; hence the double vision of Cornelius and Peter. The vision accorded Peter is not meant for his glorification, but rather to make clear that it is God's will that Gentiles become part of God's people without the obligation of obeying prescriptions of the Mosaic law. The repetition of the vision is emphatic in serving this purpose: the vision accorded to Cornelius is recounted in 10:3–8 and that to Peter in 10:9–16 (with a summary of it in 11:7–9).

Form-critically considered, the episode is a narrative, but into it Luke has inserted an important speech in which Peter bears testimony once again (10:23b–48) and adds an explanatory speech in Jerusalem (11:5–16). This story about Cornelius's conversion has been inherited by Luke from a prior tradition, as Dibelius (*Studies*, 109–22) showed long ago. It is undoubtedly derived from a Palestinian source. There is probably a Lucan insertion in vv 27–29, because v 30 seems to flow naturally from v 26. Peter's companions (v 23b) are probably also a Lucan addition.

The episode begins in the first subsection (10:1–8) with the story of a vision accorded to Cornelius, a Roman centurion stationed in Caesarea Maritima, who is instructed to send for Simon Peter from Joppa, where he has last been seen. This first subsection is merely introductory, setting the stage for Peter's complementary vision.

The episode shows how a person sympathetic to Judaism and praying to the God of Israel has already manifested a basic faith. Cornelius's faith, prayers, and alms are all acceptable in God's sight; indeed, they are a sign of his openness to divine grace, which is now about to reveal to him that his salvation comes through Jesus Christ. Nothing in the episode shows that Cornelius has merited such salvation because of his prayers and almsgiving. Nevertheless, they manifest his basic attitude and have become in God's sight a memorial of him.

NOTES

10:1. *There was in Caesarea.* Caesarea Maritima was the town where the Roman prefect, and later the procurator, normally resided; see NOTE on 8:40. So it is not surprising that Luke chooses this important town as the site of the inauguration of the mission to the Gentiles. It becomes for him a station midway between Jerusalem and Antioch in Syria (Conzelmann, *Acts*, 81).

a man named Cornelius. The first Gentile to whom the Word is carried bears a Latin name, *Cornelius*, the name of a famous Roman clan. The name became common after P. Cornelius Sulla freed many slaves; many of them so emancipated took the name Cornelius in gratitude or by custom. The historian Livy knows of another military tribune called A. Cornelius Cossus (*Ab Urbe Condita* 4.19.1). The use of the *nomen* alone "reflects an older Roman practice which persisted into the Julio-Claudian period" (Hemer, *Book of Acts*, 177; cf. Sherwin-White, *Roman Society*, 160–61).

a centurion of the Cohort called Italica. As a centurion, Cornelius would have been a Roman citizen. In Roman military service a *centurio*, a noncommissioned officer, commanded a *centuria* or *curia*, a division of a hundred soldiers. There were 59 centurions in a legion, which in the Augustan period normally numbered 6,000 men, the first centurion being in command of 200. Whereas Mark uses the Greek transliteration of the Latin name, *kentyriōn* (15:39, 44, 45) and Matthew has the Attic Greek equivalent, *hekatonarchos* (8:5, 8), Luke uses the Hellenistic Greek form, *hekatonarchēs* (Luke 7:2, 6; Acts 10:22); there are often variants of these forms in different NT MSS. In addition to his military command, Cornelius probably served in some administrative capacity that brought him into contact with Jews who also lived there. See F. G. Untergassmair, "*Hekatonarchēs*," *EDNT*, 1.405.

The Greek term *speira*, which occurs again in 21:31; 27:1, normally translates the Latin *cohors* (Polybius, *History* 11.23.1) but can also render *manipulus* (Polybius, *History* 6.24.5), another subdivision of the legion. The cohort was usually one-tenth of a legion and comprised 600 soldiers. This would mean that Cornelius belonged to the "Cohort called Italica" but was not in charge of all of it. Roman historians are not all in agreement about the total number of a Roman legion in the Augustan period. Cf. T.R.S. Broughton, "The Roman Army," *Beginnings*, 5.427–45; H.M.D. Parker and G. R. Watson, "Legion," *OCD*, 591; A. R. Neumann, "Legio," *DKP*, 3.538–46.

Speira hē kaloumenē Italikē was undoubtedly the *Cohors II miliaria Italica civium romanorum voluntariorum*, a contingent of auxiliary archers known to have served in the Roman province of Syria from various Latin inscriptions (*CIL* 6.3528; 11.6117; *ILS* 3.2:9168). It served in Syria from 69 B.C. on into the second century A.D. It is a matter of debate whether such Roman troops would have been stationed in Caesarea during the reign of Herod Agrippa I (A.D. 41–44; see Josephus, *Ant.* 19.8.2 §343); cf. Haenchen, *Acts*, 346 n. 2; T.R.S. Broughton, *Beginnings*, 5.437, 440. Bruce (*Acts*, 215) dates this episode "before 41," which would agree with my chronology (Introduction §157).

2. *a devout and God-fearing man, along with his whole household.* Cornelius is said to be *eusebēs*, "devout, godly, pious," an adj. often used in the Greek world for someone who revered the gods. He is also said to be *phoboumenos ton theon*, "fearing God," a quasi-technical phrase that occurs again in 10:22, 35; 13:16, 26 and undoubtedly reflects the Septuagintal expression, *hoi phoboumenoi ton Kyrion* (Pss 115:11 [LXX 113:19]; 118:4; 135:20), which was used of Jews. It is often taken as the equivalent of the more Hellenistic *sebomenos ton theon*, "worshiping God," "God worshiper" (13:50; 16:14; 17:4, 17; 18:7; cf. 18:13; 19:27). As quasi-technical phrases, both seem to have been employed to denote "Godfearers," non-Jews sympathetic to Judaism, those who did not submit to circumcision or observe the Torah in its entirety, but who did agree with the ethical monothe-

ism of the Jews and attended their synagogue services. Josephus uses the second term in the same sense (*Ant.* 14.7.2 §110). In Greek inscriptions such persons are often referred to as *theosebeis,* a term that can refer to both Jews and non-Jewish sympathizers. This seems clear even if one cannot establish that such individuals were viewed as a distinct class. Even though some scholars (e.g., A. T. Kraabel) have queried whether there were such people among ancient non-Jews, recent evidence has piled up to show that there were indeed people like the Cornelius whom Luke depicts here. In the later rabbinic tradition they are called *yir'ê šāmayim,* "Heaven Fearers" (see *TDNT,* 6.741).

Cf. K. Lake, "Proselytes and God-Fearers," *Beginnings,* 5.74–96; L. H. Feldman, "Jewish 'Sympathizers' in Classical Literature and Inscriptions," *TPAPA* 81 (1950): 200–8; R. Marcus, "The Sebomenoi in Josephus," *Jewish Social Studies* 14 (1952): 247–50; K. Romaniuk, "Die 'Gottesfürchtigen' im Neuen Testament: Beitrag zur neutestamentlichen Theologie der Gottesfrucht [*sic*]," *Aegyptus* 44 (1964): 66–91; B. Lifshitz, "Du nouveau sur les 'sympathisants,'" *JSJ* 1 (1970): 77–84; F. Siegert, "Gottesfürchtige und Sympathisanten," *JSJ* 4 (1973): 109–64; M. J. Mellink, "Archaeology in Asia Minor," *AJA* 81 (1977): 289–321, esp. 306; M. Wilcox, "The God-Fearers in Acts—A Reconsideration," *JSNT* 13 (1981): 102–22; A. T. Kraabel, "The Disappearance of the 'God-Fearers,'" *Numen* 28 (1981): 113–26; T. M. Finn, "The God-fearers Reconsidered," *CBQ* 47 (1985): 75–84; R. S. MacLennon and A. T. Kraabel, "The God-Fearers—A Literary and Theological Invention," *BARev* 12/5 (1986): 46–53, 64; R. F. Tannenbaum, "Jews and God-Fearers in the Holy City of Aphrodite," *BARev* 12/5 (1986): 54–57; L. H. Feldman, "The Omnipresence of the God-Fearers," *BARev* 12/5 (1986): 58–63; J. Reynolds and R. Tannenbaum, *Jews and God-fearers at Aphrodisias: Greek Inscriptions with Commentary* (Proceedings of the Cambridge Philological Society Sup. 12; Cambridge: Cambridge Philological Society, 1987); J. A. Overman, "The God-fearers: Some Neglected Features," *JSNT* 32 (1988): 17–26; L. H. Feldman, "Proselytes and 'Sympathizers' in the Light of the New Inscriptions from Aphrodisias," *REJ* 148 (1989): 265–305; A. Levinskaya, "The Inscription from Aphrodisias and the Problem of God-fearers," *TynBull* 41 (1990): 312–18; *The Book of Acts in Its Diaspora Setting* (BAFCS 5), 51–126; P. Figueras, "Epigraphic Evidence for Proselytism in Ancient Judaism," *Immanuel* 24–25 (1990): 194–206; P. W. van der Horst, "A New Altar of a Godfearer?" *JJS* 43 (1992): 32–37; J. Murphy-O'Connor, "Lots of God-Fearers? *Theosebeis* in the Aphrodisias Inscription," *RB* 99 (1992): 418–24; *NDIEC,* 3.54, 125.

He used to give many alms to the (Jewish) people and pray to God constantly. These two activities are singled out to show not only Cornelius's attachment to Judaism, but also his active involvement in its piety; see Tob 12:8–9. Prayer and almsgiving are also recommended to Christians in *Did.* 15:4. For *ho laos* as a term designating the Jewish people or Israel, see *SIG* §1247; cf. G. Kittel, *TLZ* 69 (1944): 13.

3. *One afternoon about three o'clock.* Lit., "as it were, about the ninth hour of the day." Cf. 3:1, for this Jewish hour of prayer, and see NOTE on 2:15. See

H. Cadbury, "Some Lukan Expressions of Time (Lexical Notes on Luke-Acts VII)," *JBL* 82 (1963): 272–78.

he saw clearly in a vision an angel of God come to him and say, "Cornelius." Cf. 9:10, 12. The heavenly messenger addresses the centurion by name. The origin of the instruction that will be given Cornelius is thus made clear; a messenger from God brings it. Compare 10:30, where the "angel" is said to be "a man (*anēr*) robed in dazzling clothes."

4. *He stared at him and said in fear, "What is it, sir?"* Cornelius does not understand who is appearing to him and, as did Saul (9:5), addresses the angel respectfully as *kyrie*, "sir."

The angel said to him, "Your prayers and your alms have mounted before God as a memorial offering. Cornelius's prayers and generosity are interpreted by the heavenly visitor in terms that recall the "memorial portions" of OT sacrifices (see Lev 2:2, 9, 16; 5:12; 6:15). This is a common understanding of the value of prayer and almsgiving in Judaism; see Tob 12:12, 15; Sir 35:6; 38:11; 45:16. The prayers and alms memorialize the devout Jew in God's presence. Cf. Acts 10:31. See W. C. van Unnik, "The Background and Significance of Acts x 4 and 35," *Sparsa Collecta*, 1.213–58.

5. *Now send some men to Joppa.* See NOTE on 9:36.

summon a certain Simon, who is called Peter. I.e., someone whom Cornelius does not know personally. This double appellation will appear again in 10:18, 32; 11:13. Luke 6:14 explains that Jesus named Simon "Peter." Though "Simon Peter" occurred earlier in Luke 5:8, *Petros* is the only name used after 6:14 in the Gospel and in Acts up to this point. The Greek name *Simōn* = Hebrew *Šimĕʿôn* (see *Luke*, 426).

6. *He is staying with another Simon, a tanner, whose house is by the sea."* See 9:43. This is an added detail, explaining Joppa as a town on the coast of the Mediterranean Sea.

7. *When the angel who spoke to him had left, he called two servants and a devout soldier from his staff.* Lit., "two house slaves and a devout soldier from those who were faithfully attached to him," i.e., one of his underlings in the *centuria*, whom he had learned he could trust. Like Cornelius (10:2), this soldier too is *eusebēs*.

8. *recounted everything to them, and sent them to Joppa.* I.e., told them all that he had been told by the angel. Though they are sent directly by Cornelius, he acts under heaven's guidance.

BIBLIOGRAPHY (10:1–11:18)

Barthes, R., "L'Analyse structurale du récit: À propos d'Actes x–xi," *RSR* 58 (1970): 17–37.

Bovon, F., *De Vocatione Gentium: Histoire de l'interprétation d'Act. 10,1–11,18 dans les six premiers siècles* (BGBE 8; Tübingen: Mohr [Siebeck], 1967).

———, "Tradition et rédaction en Actes 10,1–11,18," *TZ* 26 (1970): 22–45.

Catrice, P., "Réflexions missionnaires sur la vision de Saint Pierre à Joppé: Du judéo-christianisme à l'église de tous les peuples," *BVC* 79 (1968): 20–39.

Courtès, J., "Actes 10,1–11,18 comme système de représentations mythiques," *Exégèse et herméneutique* (Paris: Editions du Seuil, 1971), 205–11.

Dibelius, M., "The Conversion of Cornelius," *Studies*, 109–22.

Dietrich, W., *Das Petrusbild der lukanischen Schriften* (BWANT 94; Stuttgart: Kohlhammer, 1972), 268–95.

Haacker, K., "Dibelius und Cornelius: Ein Beispiel formgeschichtlicher Überlieferungskritik," *BZ* 24 (1980): 234–51.

Haulotte, E., "Fondation d'une communauté de type universel: Actes 10,1–11,18," *RSR* 58 (1970): 63–100.

Löning, K., "Die Korneliustradition," *BZ* 18 (1974): 1–19.

Lubac, H. de, "De vocatione gentium," *RTP* 19 (1969): 331–32.

Lukasz, C., *Evangelizzazione e conflitto: Indagine sulla coerenza letteraria e tematica della pericope di Cornelio (Atti 10,1–11,18)* (European University Studies 23/484; Frankfurt/New York: P. Lang, 1993).

Marin, L., "Essai d'analyse structurale d'Actes 10,1–11,18," *RSR* 58 (1970): 39–61.

Müller, P.-G., "Die 'Bekehrung' des Petrus: Zur Interpretation von Apg 10,1–11," *Herder Korrespondenz* 28 (1974): 372–75.

Pesch, R., "Das Jerusalemer Abkommen und die Lösung des antiochenischen Konflikts: Ein Versuch über Gal 2, Apg 10,1–11,18, Apg 11,27–30; 12,25 und Apg 15,1–41," *Kontinuität und Einheit: Für Franz Mussner* (ed. P.-G. Müller and W. Stenger; Freiburg: Herder, 1981), 105–22.

Schoonheim, P. L., "De centurio Cornelius," *NedTT* 18 (1963–64): 453–75.

Scott, J. J., "The Cornelius Incident in the Light of Its Jewish Setting," *JETS* 34 (1991): 475–84.

Templeton, E., "Reflecting on Acts: Acts 10: 'God Shows No Partiality,'" *One in Christ* 28 (1992): 97–105.

Witherup, R. D., "Cornelius Over and Over and Over Again: 'Functional Redundancy' in the Acts of the Apostles," *JSNT* 49 (1993): 45–66.

BIBLIOGRAPHY (10:1–8)

Jervell, J., "Das gespaltene Israel und die Heidenvölker: Zur Motivierung der Heidenmission in der Apostelgeschichte," *ST* 19 (1965): 68–96.

Kurz, W. S., "Effects of Variant Narrators in Acts 10–11," *NTS* 43 (1997): 570–86.

Lieu, J. M., "The Race of the God-fearers," *JTS* 46 (1995): 483–501.

Lönnqvist, K.K.A., "New Vistas on the Countermarked Coins of the Roman Prefects of Judaea," *INJ* 12 (1992–93): 56–70 (+ pls. 14–15).

Wall, R. W., "Peter 'Son' of Jonah: The Conversion of Cornelius in the Context of Canon," *JSNT* 29 (1987): 79–90.

b) Peter's Vision (10:9–16)

[9]The next day, while they were traveling along and drawing near to the town,
Peter went up to the roof terrace about noon to pray. [10]He happened to get hungry and wanted something to eat. While they were preparing some food, he fell
into a trance. [11]He saw the heavens open and an object resembling a big sheet
come down, being lowered to the ground by its four corners. [12]On it were all the
four-legged creatures and reptiles of the earth, and birds of the sky. [13]A voice said
to him, "Peter, get up! Slaughter these things and eat!" [14]But Peter said, "Not on
your life, sir, for I have never eaten anything common or unclean." [15]The voice
said to him again, a second time, "What God has made clean, you are not to call
common." [16]Three times this happened, and the object was suddenly snatched
up to the heavens.

WT: [9]to the upper room. [11]an object tied by its four corners being lowered to the ground. [12][omits "of the earth"]. [13][omits "Peter"]. [14][omits "not on your life"]. [16][omits "suddenly"].

COMMENT

The Lucan story of the inauguration of the mission to the Gentiles continues with the complementary vision of Peter, the second subsection of the Cornelius episode. Not only has Cornelius been accorded a vision, but Simon Peter, who is to be sent to him, is likewise instructed by heaven about this mission. Luke thus makes use of the literary device of the double vision or double dream, attested elsewhere in Greek literature (see A. Wikenhauser, "Doppelträume").

In this vision the instruction comes to Peter in symbolic form. On the surface, he is instructed by heaven about food: none of it is common or unclean. Its further meaning, which will dawn upon Peter in due time, is heaven's instruction about human beings: none of them is beyond the pale of salvation by Christ. So Peter must associate with all human beings.

Again we are dealing with a narrative, which recounts a vision that Peter has and which conveys an interpretive saying from heaven. In fact, it resembles a pronouncement story of the Synoptic Gospel tradition (see *Luke*, 436). It may be that the story that Luke has inherited from his Palestinian source originally had no symbolic meaning; it may have been an instruction about food (so Conzelmann, *Acts*, 80). Luke would then have used it to give it a symbolic nuance, but it is not easy to think that that is even probable. There is, indeed, a certain redundancy in the story, in which slight differences are introduced; but they all have their own significance. In these instances it is not easy to sort out Lucan modifications from inherited information.

Though this vision is about clean and unclean food, God uses it to prepare Peter for bearing testimony to Gentiles. Cornelius and his pagan household are understood as representatives of such Gentiles. Their acceptance into the Christian church will not be formally recognized until the "Council" in chap. 15, but in order that Peter, who has been the chief spokesman of Jerusalem Christians, may bring authoritative word about this matter to that "Council," he must now inaugurate such a ministry among Gentiles. To guide Peter himself rightly, God's Spirit first uses the symbolism of clean and unclean food to teach Peter a proper understanding of Gentiles in the divine plan of salvation. As no food that God has provided for his created people can be called unclean, so no human beings can be considered unclean, i.e., unworthy of a share in that plan.

NOTES

9. *The next day, while they were traveling along and drawing near to the town.* I.e., the three men mentioned in 10:8 are drawing near to Joppa, where Peter is lodging. They were not dispatched by Cornelius until late afternoon; so it is "the next day" as they approach Joppa.

Peter went up to the roof terrace about noon to pray. Lit., "about the sixth hour," perhaps the time for the midday meal, as in Greece and Rome. It was not an ordinary time for Jewish prayer. See NOTE on 2:15. The roof terrace would provide sufficient isolation for communing with God privately. Compare Jer 19:13; 32:29; Zeph 1:5.

10. *He happened to get hungry and wanted something to eat.* The vision about to be accorded Peter is related to his physical condition, but that condition undoubtedly symbolizes his spiritual status. Luke uses *prospeinos*, "hungry," an adj. that was previously considered a *hapax legomenon* in Greek literature. It is now attested in a sixth-century A.D. medical writer, Aëtius of Amida (Armenia), but it still does not prove that Luke was a physician; cf. F. W. Dillistone, "*Prospeinos* (Acts 10.10)," *ExpTim* 46 (1934–35): 380.

While they were preparing some food, he fell into a trance. Lit., "there came upon him an ecstasy." See Acts 22:17; cf. Gen 2:21; 15:12, where the LXX uses *ekstasis* to translate Hebrew *tardēmāh*, "deep sleep," that came upon Adam and Abraham.

11. *He saw the heavens open.* See 7:56 and Luke 3:21. Peter is accorded a *horama*, "vision" (10:17), by heaven.

an object resembling a big sheet come down, being lowered to the ground by its four corners. Lit., "a vessel" *(skeuos)*, now used in a concrete sense, whereas it was used of Saul in a symbolic sense in 9:15.

12. *On it were all the four-legged creatures and reptiles of the earth, and birds of the sky.* I.e., representatives of the entire animal world, according to the usual classes mentioned in the OT (Gen 1:24; 6:20; Lev 11:46–47). They have been given according to Gen 1:30 to human beings as food. Note the absence of fish, undoubtedly a coincidental omission. The emphasis falls on the adj. "all," which in this case is more than the usual Lucan hyperbole (see NOTE on 2:44). Compare 11:6.

13. *A voice said to him.* I.e., an instruction comes from the same realm from which the sheetlike object descends, from heaven.

"Peter, get up! Slaughter these things and eat!" Heaven instructs the hungry Peter to make a meal of the animals that he sees in the vision, without regard for their cleanness or uncleanness. Though the verb *thyein* often has a cultic or sacrificial connotation, it lacks that here, *pace* Sint ("Schlachten und opfern") and Barrett (*Acts,* 507).

14. *Peter said, "Not on your life, Sir, for I have never eaten anything common or unclean."* Lit., "common and unclean." Compare 11:8. In Lev 11:1–47; Deut 14:3–20 one finds lists of the animals that a Jew was not supposed to eat, and the distinction between ritually "clean" and "unclean" foods. In the LXX of 11:47; Deut 14:10 the forbidden or defiling foods are called *akatharta,* "unclean," but in the Greek-speaking world they came to be called "common," i.e., profane, or permissible to all, the food that ordinary non-Jews would eat. Hence the double descriptive adjs. used. Cf. Ezek 4:13–14, for a protestation similar to Peter's. Cf. F. Hauck, *"Koinos," TDNT,* 3.790–91.

15. *The voice said to him again, a second time, "What God has made clean, you are not to call common."* The main point of the vision is thus stated. The implication is not that God has brought about a purification of food through this vision, but that all food given to human beings comes from a clean source and so has always been clean (cf. 1 Tim 4:4). So Peter is not to categorize it as common, profane, or "unclean." Recall Mark 7:19 for the evangelist's comment on a declaration of Jesus about food being clean.

16. *Three times this happened, and the object was suddenly snatched up to the heavens.* So divine guidance overcomes human resistance. The repetition is meant to emphasize the importance of the instruction given to Peter. In time he will realize the implications of the vision.

BIBLIOGRAPHY (10:9–16)

Döller, J., *Die Reinheits- und Speisegesetze des Alten Testaments in religionsgeschichtlicher Beleuchtung* (ATAbh 7/2–3; Münster in W.: Aschendorff, 1917).

Gispen, W. H., "The Distinction between Clean and Unclean," *OTS* 5 (1948): 190–96.

House, C., "Defilement by Association: Some Insights from the Usage of *koinós/koinóō* in Acts 10 and 11," *AUSS* 21 (1983): 143–53.

Kornfeld, W., "Reine und unreine Tiere im Alten Testament," *Kairos* 7 (1965): 134–47.

Paschen, W., *Rein und Unrein: Untersuchung zur biblischen Wortgeschichte* (SANT 24; Munich: Kösel, 1970).

Sint, J. "Schlachten und opfern: Zu Apg 10,13; 11,7," *ZKT* 78 (1956): 194–205.

Wikenhauser, A., "Doppelträume," *Bib* 29 (1948): 100–111.

c) WELCOME FOR MESSENGERS FROM CORNELIUS (10:17–23a)

[17]While Peter was trying to make something out of the vision he had seen, the men sent by Cornelius suddenly arrived at the gate, inquiring after the house of Simon. [18]They called out, asking whether Simon, called Peter, was staying there. [19]As Peter was still pondering over the vision, the Spirit said [to him], "Look, three men are here, looking for you. [20]Get up, go downstairs, and go along with them without hesitation, because I have sent them." [21]Peter went down and said to the men, "I am the one you are looking for. What is the reason for your coming?" [22]They answered, "The centurion Cornelius, an upright and God-fearing man, well spoken of among all the Jewish people, was instructed by a holy angel to summon you to his house and to listen to what you have to say." [23a]So he invited them in and treated them as guests.

WT: [17][omits "inquiring after the house of Simon"]. [18][omits "they called out" and "called Peter"]. [19]was still perplexed by the vision . . . [omits "three"]. [20][omits "go downstairs"]. [21][adds as first question]: What do you want? [22]They said to him. [23]Then Peter brought them in and.

COMMENT

Luke continues in this third subsection of the Cornelius episode (10:17–23a) with a narrative that joins the two visions of Cornelius and Peter just recounted. The men sent by Cornelius arrive in Joppa, seek out the house of Simon the tanner, and meet Simon Peter. The important element in this section is the Spirit's instruction to Peter that he is to go along with the men who have come to bring him to the Gentile Cornelius in Caesarea. Thus heaven's guidance moves the story a step further. The account is otherwise without complications, being derived from the same Palestinian source. Peter is not only ready to accompany them, but even invites these Gentiles into his lodging to be his guests.

NOTES

17. *While Peter was trying to make something out of the vision he had seen.* Lit., "While Peter was puzzling within himself as to what the vision that he had seen might be." Because it had to do with eating animals of various kinds, its implication was not fully clear to him. This verse is a transitional Lucan seam, joining the two visions. It explains the vision to Christian readers: the abolition of Jewish dietary regulations for those of Gentile background, but also the abolition of the deeper distinction between Jews and non-Jews.

the men sent by Cornelius suddenly arrived at the gate, inquiring after the house of Simon. I.e., the house of Simon, the tanner; see 9:43; 10:6.

18. *They called out, asking whether Simon, called Peter, was staying there.* On Simon, called Peter, see NOTE on 10:5.

19. *As Peter was still pondering over the vision, the Spirit said [to him], "Look, three men are here, looking for you.* The pondering Peter is confronted with a direct command of the Spirit. The vision that he has seen may not have been clear to him, but the Spirit's directive is. MS B reads rather *dyo*, "two" (men), and the WT omits the number (MSS D, Ψ, and the *Koinē* text-tradition). Apparently, in such a counting the devout soldier of 10:9 is not included.

20. *Get up, go downstairs, and go along with them without hesitation.* Lit., "debating (about it) in no way." Peter is thus informed by God's Spirit that there is no room for dispute in this matter.

because I have sent them." I.e., the men who have come seeking him have been dispatched by God's Spirit. Peter is to go along with them, even though he, a Jew, may not yet realize the implications of his accompanying these men to a Gentile's house.

21. *Peter went down and said to the men, "I am the one you are looking for. What is the reason for your coming?"* 22. *They answered, "The centurion Cornelius, an upright and God-fearing man, well spoken of among all the Jewish people.* Lit., "all the Jewish nation," an official term (used in 1 Macc 10:25; 11:30, 33; Josephus, *Ant.* 12.3.3 §135; 14.10.22 §248). In v 2 Cornelius was called *eusebēs kai phoboumenos ton theon*, but now he is said to be *dikaios kai phoboumenos ton theon*; see NOTES on 10:1–2. *Dikaios*, "upright," means that he was living as a Jew would, carrying out the precepts of the Mosaic law (see 10:35).

was instructed by a holy angel to summon you to his house and to listen to what you have to say." So Peter learns about Cornelius's vision and instruction by a heaven-sent messenger. The important thing in this statement is the invitation coming to Peter to come to the "house" of the Gentile Cornelius. This would be a source of defilement in Jewish thinking, as the later rabbinic tradition makes clear: "The dwelling-places of Gentiles are unclean" (*m. Oholot* 18:7). Cf. Luke 7:6; Str-B 4.353–414. The problem, however, is solved because the men also tell Peter that the angel has instructed Cornelius "to listen to what" Peter has to say. This accords with the instruction that Peter himself has received from the Spirit.

23a. *So he invited them in and treated them as guests.* Peter responds with magnanimity, but also with boldness, in treating these Gentiles as guests in a Jewish house, where he himself is a guest. His invitation becomes the first effect of the vision; he has no hesitation in dining with such guests.

d) PETER'S TESTIMONY IN CORNELIUS'S HOUSE (10:23b–48)

[23b]The next day he got up and went off with them, and some of the brothers from Joppa accompanied him. [24]The following day he arrived in Caesarea, where Cornelius was waiting for them; he had even called in his relatives and close friends. [25]As Peter was about to enter, Cornelius went to meet him, fell at his feet, and

paid him homage. [26]But Peter pulled him up and said, "Get up! After all, I too
am only a human being." [27]Peter went in, talking with him the while, and found
many people gathered there. [28]He said to them, "You are aware that it is unlawful
for a Jew to associate with or visit a Gentile, but God has shown me that no one
should call a human being common or unclean. [29]So in response to your summons, I have come without any objection. May I ask, then, why you summoned
me?" [30]Cornelius replied, "Four days ago, at this very hour, three o'clock in the
afternoon, I was praying at home, when a man robed in dazzling clothes suddenly stood before me. [31]He said, 'Cornelius, your prayer has been heard, and
your alms have been remembered before God. [32]Send someone to Joppa and
invite here Simon who is called Peter. He is staying at the house of Simon, a
tanner, by the sea.' [33]So I sent for you immediately, and you have been kind
enough to come. Now, then, we are all here in the presence of God to listen to
all the instructions that the Lord has given you." [34]Then Peter spoke up, "Now I
realize how true it is that God shows no partiality. [35]Rather, in every nation whoever reverences him and acts uprightly is acceptable to him. [36]You know the
word [that] he sent to the children of Israel, as he proclaimed peace through
Jesus Christ, who is Lord of all; [37]you know what has happened throughout Judea, starting from Galilee after the baptism that John preached— [38]how God
anointed Jesus of Nazareth with a Holy Spirit and with power; how he went about
doing good and healing all who were in the power of the devil, because God was
with him. [39]We are witnesses of all that he did in the country of the Jews and [in]
Jerusalem. They put him to death, hanging him on a tree. [40]This man God raised
up [on] the third day and made manifest, [41]not to all the people, but to us, witnesses chosen by God beforehand, who ate and drank with him after he rose
from the dead. [42]He ordered us to preach to the people and to bear witness that
he is the one appointed by God to be judge of the living and the dead. [43]To
him all the prophets bear witness, that everyone who believes in him receives
forgiveness of sins through his name." [44]While Peter was still saying these things,
the Holy Spirit came down upon all who were listening to the word, [45]and the
circumcised believers, who had come along with Peter, were bewildered because
the gift of the Holy Spirit had been poured out on Gentiles too. [46]For they heard
them speaking in tongues and extolling God. Then Peter spoke up, [47]"Can anyone withhold from these people, who have received the Holy Spirit just as we
have, the water with which they are to be baptized?" [48]He ordered them to be
baptized in the name of Jesus Christ. Then they invited him to stay for some
days.

WT: [24]they arrived . . . [adds at end:] he was waiting for (them). [25]As Peter was drawing close to
Caesarea, one of the slaves reported that he was at hand, and Cornelius sprang up quickly and went
to meet . . . [26]Peter said to him, "What are you doing? I am a human being like you." [27]When Peter
went in, he found many people. [28][omits "God"]. [30]Four days ago now, I was fasting and praying.
[32][adds at end:] He will come here and speak to you. [33]. . . immediately, urging you to come to us,
and . . . to come in haste. Now then we are all here in your presence, eager to listen to you about all
the instructions given by God to you. [35]reverences God. [38]healing those who. [39]his witnesses, of

what he did . . . Jerusalem. The Jews rejected him and put him to death . . . [40]after the third day. [41][omits "by God"] . . . who ate, drank, and gathered together with him for forty days after. [42]He commanded us . . . [omits "by God"]. [45]who were with Peter [omits "Holy"]. [47][omits "Holy"]. [48][omits "Christ"]. Then they urged him to remain. . . .

COMMENT

Of the various subsections of this Cornelius episode, this fourth one is the most important, because although it continues the narrative, which had been begun in v 1, it introduces the discourse of Peter in vv 34–43. It depicts Peter, having been asked to come to Cornelius's house in Caesarea Maritima, complying with that request and arriving on the scene, to be greeted by Cornelius and those whom he had invited to be present in honor of his guest.

The discourse (10:34–43) is another missionary speech, which repeats a bit of the kerygma. It has, then, affinity with the missionary speeches already addressed by Peter to Jews. Now, however, it is addressed to a Palestinian Gentile, a Jewish sympathizer and Godfearer, and those whom he has invited to be present. They are presumably of like mind with Cornelius, Gentiles on good terms with Jews, perhaps Godfearers too. In effect, however, even though it is the last great missionary speech that Peter delivers in Acts, it is the beginning of apostolic testimony being borne to Gentiles without insistence on the obligation to obey the Mosaic law. In Peter's activity in Caesarea the mission to the Gentiles is thus formally inaugurated. For the Lucan story it is important that Peter, the spokesman of the early Christian community, be seen in this role.

In its kerygmatic section the speech presents the fullest formulation of the early proclamation about Jesus in Acts. It is the primary one to which Dodd appealed for what he regarded as the apostolic preaching that developed into the Synoptic Gospels (*Apostolic Preaching,* 27). The speech, however, includes another important element of apostolic testimony, viz., an explanation of God's impartiality: the Word sent to Israel is now preached to others. Dibelius maintained that the speech had nothing really to do with the topic of the episode as such and followed the pattern of other speeches of Peter in Acts and of Paul in Pisidian Antioch: "By developing the same scheme several times Luke wants to show what Christian preaching is and ought to be. It is a literary-theological, not a historical task, which he wants to fulfill here" (*Studies,* 111). Wilckens, too, believes that the speech is a wholly Lucan composition (ZNW 49 [1958]: 223–37; *Missionsreden,* 46–50).

This Petrine speech may be another Lucan composition, like other speeches in Acts, but it bears clearer marks of source material than others. The suture is most evident in v 37, where *rhēma,* "word, thing, matter," stands in apposition to *ton logon,* "the word," which in the Greek text stands at the head of v 36. One would have expected that the same word would be used; the different word is probably the mark of source material. The syntax of the parenthetical remark, "who is Lord of all," is also difficult, so that one has to reckon with Palestinian source material not perfectly integrated. If this part of the speech were merely a résumé of the Lucan Gospel and nothing more, one would have to explain why Luke has written such miserable Greek at this point (vv 36–38). The syntax of these verses, coupled with allusions to Isa 52:7 and 61:1, points much more to an echo of primitive kerygmatic preaching, undoubtedly derived from Palestinian tradition, than to a wholly Lucan composition. For a further treatment of this matter, see Weiser, *Apg.*, 253–62, where the discussion is carried to an extreme with little certain outcome.

The structure of the speech can best be seen thus:

1. 10:34–36, Introduction: The impartial God has sent Jesus as Lord of all.
2. 10:37–41, Kerygma: What Jesus has done for humanity.
3. 10:42–43, Conclusion: We are his witnesses and announce forgiveness of sins in his name

The last missionary speech of Peter in Acts is the classic proclamation of the gospel to Gentile sympathizers. Though Peter will speak again in 15:7–11, on a topic that is related to the subject at issue here, the extent of that speech cannot compare with the missionary discourse put on his lips by Luke in this section.

After the speech, the narrative is resumed, and Peter's listeners are baptized and receive the Spirit. In effect, it recounts a "Pentecost of the Gentiles."

"God shows no partiality" (10:34), so Peter proclaims. God calls both Jews and non-Jews to salvation through Jesus Christ, respecting all human beings, from any nation, who reverence the Deity and seek to conduct themselves with uprightness and righteousness. All can thus find acceptance in the sight of God, who has sent the word of salvation to all through Jesus Christ, who was put to death on the cross but raised now to his Father's glorious status. In God's design Jesus has been sent to bring forgiveness of sins to all who are willing to accept him and put faith in "his name" (10:43). Cornelius and his household become people who welcome this message; they are baptized and receive the Spirit, sharing in the Pentecost accorded to the Jews in Jerusalem at the outset.

NOTES

23b. *The next day he got up and went off with them.* Peter goes off from Joppa with the three men sent by Cornelius; see 10:7. His destination is Caesarea Maritima.

some of the brothers from Joppa accompanied him. "Brothers" is again used of Christians (see NOTE on 1:15); they are Jewish Christians who will reappear in 10:45; in 11:12 we shall learn that they are six in number.

24. *The following day he arrived in Caesarea, where Cornelius was waiting for them.* Caesarea was 50 km north of Joppa; see NOTE on 9:35.

he had even called in his relatives and close friends. I.e., mainly other Gentiles, although some Jews may have been among those invited, since Cornelius was on good terms with Jewish people there (10:2, 22). At the end of this section the assembled group is characterized as "Gentiles" (10:45).

25. *As Peter was about to enter.* The syntax of this introductory clause is clumsy.

It is an *egeneto de* construction but introduced by the conj. *hōs* and followed by the gen. of an articular infin., *tou eiselthein ton Petron,* which Moule (*IBNTG,* 129) understands as the subject of *egeneto,* "when Peter's entry took place." This is a highly strange construction. See the rewriting of the verse in the WT above.

Cornelius went to meet him, fell at his feet, and paid him homage. Cornelius meets Peter at the door of his house and prostrates himself in honor of his guest. Luke uses of Cornelius's action the verb *proskynein,* which can mean "adore, worship." That nuance is behind Peter's reaction expressed in the next verse. Cornelius's reception of Peter in this manner shows his esteem for the heavenly authority attached to Peter's visit and mission.

26. *Peter pulled him up and said, "Get up! After all, I too am only a human being."* Peter rejects the implication of the homage, which should be reserved for God, as Jesus once said (Luke 4:8), quoting Deut 6:13. Cf. Rev 19:10.

27. *Peter went in, talking with him the while, and found many people gathered there.* I.e., the relatives and friends mentioned in v 24. Peter's entrance into the house of a Gentile is the second effect of the vision that Luke carefully notes.

28. *He said to them.* Peter's conversation with Cornelius changes to a remark addressed to the assembled people.

"You are aware that it is unlawful for a Jew to associate with or visit a Gentile. Peter still thinks like a Jew, as he addresses the assembled Gentiles, who are presumed to know enough about Judaism to sense that something unusual is happening. See the NOTE on 10:22. As expressed here, visiting the house of a Gentile is not only a source of ritual uncleanness, but *athemiton,* "unlawful," a word used in 2 Macc 6:5; 7:1; 10:34; 3 Macc 5:20. The adj., derived from alpha privative and *themis,* "right," is a Greek notion, not a Semitic expression. Luke makes Peter state that it was unlawful for a Jew, not only to visit the house of a Gentile, but even to come into close contact with one. He uses *kollan,* a verb that means "cling to, join oneself to" (BAGD, 441).

God has shown me that no one should call a human being common or unclean. Peter has by now understood the import of the vision of the animals accorded him in vv 11–16. Not only does food not defile, but contact with a non-Jew does not either. The abolition of dietary regulations has a further consequence; it explains why Peter has been instructed by the Spirit to accompany Cornelius's messengers, whom he himself has hosted, and to come to Cornelius's house. The sequels in 11:9 and 15:9 confirm this conclusion.

29. *So in response to your summons, I have come without any objection.* Lit., "without contradicting." Peter is thus depicted as obedient to God's Spirit (10:20); cf. 11:12.

May I ask, then, why you summoned me?" Recall 10:21. Peter repeats his request.

30. *Cornelius replied, "Four days ago, at this very hour, three o'clock in the afternoon.* The indication of time is not easily translated; it says literally, "from the fourth day until this hour I was performing the ninth[-hour] prayer." It seems to result from a combination of different time references in an attempt to say, "Three days ago," "at this very hour," "I was praying at the ninth hour." As did

many ancients, Cornelius counts both ends of the time span so that he says "from (the) fourth day." See Moule, *IBNTG,* 34.

I was praying at home, when a man robed in dazzling clothes suddenly stood before me. Lit., "in my house." Compare 10:3–6, where the one who appears to Cornelius is called "an angel of God."

31. *'Cornelius, your prayer has been heard.* We are not told for what Cornelius had been praying; this repeats 10:4 (see NOTE there). Compare Luke 1:13, where the same formula is used by Gabriel speaking to Zechariah.

your alms have been remembered before God. Instead of saying that God has remembered Cornelius's alms, the recollection is phrased impersonally out of respect for God.

32. *Send someone to Joppa and invite here Simon who is called Peter. He is staying at the house of Simon, a tanner, by the sea.'* See 10:5–6.

33. *So I sent for you immediately.* MS D and a Syriac version add "urging you to come to us."

you have been kind enough to come. Lit., "and you have done well, making yourself present." Luke uses the aor. ptc. of *paraginesthai.*

Now, then, we are all here in the presence of God. Cornelius emphasizes the gathering in his house as coming together in the sight of God in order to listen to Peter. MS D and Latin and Syriac versions read rather "in your presence," which Dupont (*Actes,* 103) prefers. The same text witnesses also add "wishing to hear from you."

to listen to all the instructions that the Lord has given you." Lit., "to all the instructions given to you by the Lord," or, as MSS P^{45}, P^{74}, $\aleph^{2}$, A, C, D read *apo,* "from the Lord." *Kyrios* may refer to the risen Christ, but on the lips of Cornelius who has not yet heard the Christian proclamation, it is probably better understood as referring to Yahweh; see NOTES on 2:20, 36.

34. *Then Peter spoke up.* Lit., "opening (his) mouth, Peter said." The same introductory expression was used of Philip in 8:35; it will occur again in 18:14. It solemnly introduces an important pronouncement. Compare Job 3:1. Verses 34–35 serve as the introduction to Peter's discourse and relate the speech to the situation in which he finds himself.

"Now I realize how true it is that God shows no partiality. Lit., "I understand in truth that God is no respecter of persons." Peter characterizes God negatively as not being *prosōpolēmptēs.* Recall Rom 2:10–11, where the abstract noun *prosōpolēmpsia,* "partiality," is used. Both words are found only in Christian writings, being fashioned on the LXX phrase *prosōpon lambanein,* which translates the Hebrew *pānîm nāśā',* "lift up, raise the face (of someone)." Cf. Lev 19:15. *lō' tiśśā' pěnê dāl,* "you shall not lift up the face of (the) poor," i.e., you shall not show partiality to the poor; you shall not recompense unfairly because of selfish motives. Cf. Deut 10:17, which denies that God respects persons or accepts bribes; 2 Chr 19:7; Sir 35:12–13; *Ps. Sol.* 2:18. It denotes the gracious act of someone who lifts up a person's face by showing him favor. According to ancient Near Eastern customs the greeting to a superior would include the bowing of the head, if not full prostration; and lifting up the face would mean full acceptance

of such obeisance. As used by Peter, it means that God does not favor only Jews, but also respects Gentiles who call upon him. In this regard both Luke and Paul basically agree about God's impartiality toward Jews and law-free Gentiles and the justified evangelization of the Gentiles, *pace* Haenchen (*Acts,* 112) and S. G. Wilson (*The Gentiles,* 251). See further J. M. Bassler, "Luke and Paul on Impartiality," *Bib* 66 (1985): 546–52. For "in truth," see NOTE on 4:27.

35. *Rather, in every nation whoever reverences him and acts uprightly.* Lit., "practises righteousness." Emphasis falls on the phrase "in every nation," and Peter means that this could be done even if one were not a Jew. Recall Rom 3:29: "Is God the God of Jews only? Is he not also the God of Gentiles?" Cf. M. Dumais, "Le salut universel par le Christ selon les Actes des Apôtres," *SNTU* 18 (1993): 113–31.

is acceptable to him. The terminology is cultic, as in Lev 1:3 (*dekton enantion Kyriou,* "acceptable before the Lord"); cf. Lev 19:5; Isa 56:7 (said even of Gentile offerings).

36. *You know the word* [*that*] *he sent to the children of Israel.* The syntax of vv 36–37 is difficult and variously explained. The phrase *ton logon,* "the word, message," is put for emphasis at the very head of the sentence and is assimilated to the acc. case of the following rel. pron. (BDF §295). Moreover, it stands in apposition to the preceding clause (10:34b–35), which is the obj. of the verb *katalambanomai,* "I realize." God sent the message about the new mode of salvation first of all to the "children of Israel," to the Jews, to his chosen people of old. This is again a Lucan theme: the Word preached first to Israel. The next clause will tell how God sent that word. The syntax is a bit garbled, because the ptc. *euangelizomenos,* which is masc. nominative, seems to agree with God, the subject of "sent." Cf. Ps 107:20. See F. Neirynck, "Acts 10,36a *ton logon hon,*" *ETL* 60 (1984): 118–23; G. Rinaldi, "*Lógos* in *Atti* 10,36," *BeO* 12 (1970): 223–25. My translation has introduced the verb *oidate* (from v 37) in front of *ton logon* because of the implied apposition.

as he proclaimed peace through Jesus Christ. God's message was one of "peace," and thus Luke plays on an effect of the Christ-event (see *Luke,* 224–25). "Peace" expresses not just the absence of war (in a social or military sense), but *šālôm,* the state of bounty or well-being that comes from God and includes concord, harmony, order, security, and prosperity. For its OT background, see Isa 48:18; 54:10; Ezek 34:25–29; Pss 29:11; 85:8–10. That state of bounty comes through Jesus Christ: the basic apostolic proclamation. This clause alludes to Isa 52:7, which describes the function of the herald of the good news that was to be made known to Jerusalem (cf. Nah 1:15).

who is Lord of all. Lit., "that one is Lord of all." In a parenthetical statement Peter applies to Jesus this ancient title. It may have been used in Palestinian Judaism. The phrase *'dwn hkwl,* "Lord of all," is found in 11QPs[a] 28:7, but its syntax is disputed; cf. 1QapGen 20:13. It seems to occur in Josephus, *Ant.* 20.4.2 §90 as *tōn pantōn . . . kyrios.* It was also used in the Greek world. Plutarch uses it of the Egyptian god Osiris: (*hōs ho pantōn kyrios eis phōs proeisin,* "when the Lord of all came forth to the light (of day)," i.e., was born (*De Iside* 12 [355E]). It is also found in Epictetus (*Discourses* 4.1.12), used of Caesar. It seems to have been originally an Egyptian title, used of the sun god.

The problem is whether one should take *pantōn* as a gen. of neuter *panta* ("all things," i.e., all the world) or as gen. of masc. *pantes* ("all people"). In this Lucan context, Schneider (*Apg.*, 2. 75), Dupont ("'Le Seigneur de tous' [Ac 10:36; Rm 10:12]: Arrière-fond scripturaire d'une formule christologique," *Tradition and Interpretation in the New Testament: Essays in Honor of E. Earle Ellis* . . . [ed. G. Hawthorne et al.; Grand Rapids, MI: Eerdmans; Tübingen: Mohr (Siebeck), 1987], 229–36), Barrett (*Acts*, 522), and Polhill (*Acts*, 261) prefer the latter.

The syntax is further complicated by the pron. *houtos*, "he, that one," which one would expect to refer to *ton logon*, "the word" (10:36), but that is nigh impossible. So its antecedent has to be "Jesus Christ."

37. *you know.* The words *hymeis oidate* are to be understood as addressed to the Christian reader of Acts, not to Cornelius; they are clearly Lucan in their formulation (Dibelius, *Studies*, 111). Compare 10:1–6, which implies that Cornelius, as a Godfearer, might be expected to have known something about the OT. That he should know the essence of the Christian message now being made known is another matter, yet Haenchen (*Acts*, 352) claims that "it is presupposed that even every 'Godfearing' person in Palestine knows of the events involving Jesus." With that Weiser agrees (*Apg.*, 268).

what has happened throughout Judea. Lit., "the word/thing that has occurred throughout all Judea." *Rhēma*, "word, saying," reflects the meaning of the Septuagintal translation of Hebrew *dābār* and is used to explain *ton logon* at the head of v 36. It refers globally to the ministry, death, burial, and resurrection of Jesus. See C. Burchard, "A Note on *rhēma* in JosAs 17:1 f.; Luke 2:15, 17; Acts 10:37," *NovT* 27 (1985): 281–95. *Rhēma*, in apposition to *ton logon* at the beginning of v 36, is a sign of a source that Luke is using.

"Throughout Judea" denotes a district of the Roman province of Syria, to which it belonged and which was usually so designated (see Luke 23:5). As used here, "Judea" includes "Galilee," as the next clause shows. See *Luke*, 322.

Verses 37–39 give a résumé of the kerygma, a recital of Jesus' ministry that is very close to the thrust of the Lucan Gospel itself. See Dodd, "The Framework of the Gospel Narrative," *New Testament Studies* (Manchester: University of Manchester Press, 1953), 1–11, esp. 9; D. E. Nineham, "The Order of Events in St. Mark's Gospel—an Examination of Dr. Dodd's Hypothesis," *Studies in the Gospels: Essays in Memory of R. H. Lightfoot* (Oxford: Blackwell, 1957), 223–39; J. Dupont, "Les discours missionnaires des Actes des Apôtres d'après un ouvrage récent," *RB* 69 (1962): 37–60, esp. 43–44; repr. *Études*, 133–55, esp. 139–40.

starting from Galilee after the baptism that John preached. Jesus' public ministry started in Galilee on the heels of the preaching of John the Baptist; see Luke 3:23, following upon 3:1–18; cf. Luke 4:14 and Mark 1:1–15. Possibly the nom. ptc. *arxamenos*, "starting," represents a frozen, pre-Lucan formula, which originally applied to Jesus, but in this context it can refer only to "the Word," i.e., early Christian preaching; it also bears a Lucan nuance (see NOTE on 1:1).

38. *how God anointed Jesus of Nazareth with a Holy Spirit and with power.*

Barrett (*Acts*, 524): this "presumably means that God made him *christos*." Although the gospel tradition never speaks of the baptism of Jesus by John as an "anointing," Luke so interprets it here. In his Gospel, Luke depicted Jesus' ministry influenced by the Spirit (see 3:22 [descent of the Spirit on him at his baptism]; 4:1 [led by the Spirit in the desert]; 4:14 [armed with the Spirit, he withdraws to Galilee]; see *Luke*, 227–31). Now he implies that Jesus' "power" stemmed from the Spirit with which he had been anointed; in Luke 5:17 it is "power of the Lord," i.e., Yahweh. See J. Berchmans, "Anointed with Holy Spirit and Power," *Jeevadhara* 8 (1978): 201–17; G. D. Kilpatrick, "The Spirit, God, and Jesus in Acts," *JTS* 15 (1964): 63.

how he went about doing good and healing all who were in the power of the devil. So Peter sums up Jesus' healing and exorcising activity. See Luke 4:31–41 for instances of Jesus' curative activity. Elsewhere, Luke never describes any of those exorcised as being under the influence of "the devil," as he does here. *Ho diabolos* occurs in Luke 4:2, 3, 6, 13 (temptations of Jesus); 8:12 (parable of the sowed seed). Recall, however, how "Satan" has entered into Judas (Luke 22:3), wants to sift the apostles like wheat (Luke 22:31), and has filled Ananias's heart (Acts 5:3); and even how Paul has been called to rescue people from Satan's dominion (26:18). Demon sickness is otherwise ascribed to evil spirits (*Luke*, 514, 544–45, 810).

because God was with him. The source of the power that Jesus exercised during his ministry came from God; see Luke 5:17c.

39. *We are witnesses of all that he did in the country of the Jews and* [*in*] *Jerusalem.* Peter uses a generic first plural, referring to himself and other apostles, who were commissioned by the risen Christ as his "witnesses" (Luke 24:48; Acts 1:8, 22; 2:32; 3:15; 5:32; 10:41; 13:31; 22:15; 26:16). The testimony bears, first of all, on Jesus' earthly ministry (recall 1:21), and then it becomes testimony about Jesus' death and resurrection. "The country of the Jews" would mean Galilee and Judea in Luke's geographical perspective (see *Luke*, 166): from Galilee to Jerusalem. Jesus' ministry "in Jerusalem" is recounted at greater length in Luke (19:28–21:38) than in either the Marcan or Matthean Gospel.

They put him to death, hanging him on a tree. Peter reiterates what he said earlier in 2:36; 3:15; 4:10; 5:30. There his accusation was couched in the second plural, as he addressed Jews of Jerusalem. Now "they" can only refer to the "Jews" of v 39a. On "hanging on a tree" as a way of saying "crucifixion," see NOTE on 5:30.

40. *This man God raised up* [*on*] *the third day.* Peter dates the resurrection of Christ on the "third day" after his death. Actually no one knows when the "resurrection" occurred. The tomb in which Jesus was buried was discovered on the "third day" after his death, when one counts both ends (day of death, sabbath, day after the sabbath). From that mode of counting grew up a way of speaking: When he was raised from the dead to the Father's glorious presence, he was "raised on the third day." In the Lucan Gospel, however, the crucified Jesus tells the penitent thief, "Today you shall be with me in Paradise" (23:43), and "today" must refer to the day of Jesus' death. See further Fitzmyer, "'Today You Shall Be

with Me in Paradise' (Luke 23:43)," *LTAHT*, 203–33. Cf. Matt 27:52–53; Eusebius, *HE* 5.23.1–2 (on Quartodeciman practice). The date of the "raising" is not important; the fact that the Father raised him is! See S. V. McCasland, "The Scripture Basis of 'On the Third Day,'" *JBL* 48 (1929): 124–37.

made manifest. As Peter phrases it, it sounds as though the Father has caused the risen Christ to appear and be seen by his apostles, but in Acts 1:3 "he presented himself alive to them in many convincing ways, appearing to them throughout forty days."

41. *not to all the people, but to us, witnesses chosen by God beforehand.* This might seem to limit appearances of the risen Christ to the apostles, but recall Luke 24:33, "the Eleven and their companions," to whom the two disciples return from Emmaus. That is the group to whom the risen Christ appears that same evening (24:36) and the group from whom he takes his final leave (25:50–53). That group must be considered the "witnesses chosen by God beforehand." The commission to be "witnesses" is addressed to them (24:48; cf. Acts 1:8, 22). Now we learn that the commissioning of them as witnesses was part of the Father's salvific plan, conceived "beforehand." Luke is careful to state that the witnesses were not indiscriminate (1:8; Luke 24:48). The risen Christ did not appear "to all the people."

who ate and drank with him after he rose from the dead. This may refer to Luke 24:41–43, or perhaps to Acts 1:4, depending on how the verb there is translated (see NOTE on 1:4). See *Luke*, 1574–75.

42. *He ordered us to preach to the people and to bear witness.* Verses 42–43 are the conclusion of Peter's speech. See Luke 24:47–48, where the command of the risen Christ is recorded. Barrett, however, prefers to think that God is the subject of the verb *parēngeilen* (*Acts*, 527). "To the people" means first of all the people of Israel; in this incident we see the extension of the meaning of "people." The commission of the risen Christ thus sets up a distinction between those sent to preach and testify and those to whom they are sent. Compare 13:31.

that he is the one appointed by God to be judge of the living and the dead. Jesus was sent not only to preach and minister to humanity during his earthly life, but also to sit in judgment over all of them. See 17:31, where this motif is repeated in a different form in a speech delivered to pagans. This role of judge will be exercised by the risen Christ, precisely as *Kyrios*. Cf. Rom 14:9; 2 Tim 4:1; 1 Pet 4:5; *2 Clem.* 1:1.

43. *To him all the prophets bear witness.* No prophetic passages are cited in a speech addressed to Gentiles. Again, we would love to know to which OT prophets Peter refers, in making such a statement (cf. 3:18). It is another instance of the Lucan global way of interpreting the OT; see Luke 24:25–27, 44; Acts 8:35.

that everyone who believes in him receives forgiveness of sins through his name." A Lucan effect of the Christ-event, *aphesis hamartiōn*, "forgiveness of sins," is accorded to the one who puts faith in Christ and "his name." Again the refrain of "the name" appears; see NOTE on 2:38 for both notions. Cf. *Luke*, 223–24 (on forgiveness of sins), 235–37 (on faith).

44. *While Peter was still saying these things, the Holy Spirit came down upon all who were listening to the word.* Lit., "fell upon all." Cf. 11:15, where Peter reports the same. The gift of the Spirit is accorded to the Gentiles who were listening to Peter's message and welcoming it. They immediately become part of those "who believe in him" (v 43).

45. *the circumcised believers, who had come along with Peter.* Lit., "the faithful from the circumcision," a way of speaking about Jews or Jewish Christians; see 11:2; cf. Rom 4:12; Gal 2:12; Col 4:11; Titus 1:10. In 10:23b Peter's companions were "some of the brothers from Joppa." Now we learn they were Jewish Christians.

were bewildered because the gift of the Holy Spirit had been poured out on Gentiles too. The bewilderment stems from the fact that up to this time in Acts only Jewish converts have received it. The reception of it by Gentiles shows that the preaching of the Word among Gentiles has the same effect as it had among Jews earlier (cf. 2:38; 8:20).

46. *they heard them speaking in tongues.* Although this is a sign of the reception of the Spirit, the people do not speak "in other tongues," as in 2:4 (see NOTE there); cf. 2:11; 19:6.

extolling God. Praise of God is the purpose for which they are endowed with the Spirit and glossolalia (compare 2:11). Recall what Paul had to say about "speaking in tongues" in 1 Cor 14:2, 4, and especially his ironic statement in 14:18–19, that he so spoke more than others for all the good his preaching sometime did!

Then Peter spoke up. Luke uses *apokrinesthai* to introduce direct discourse; see NOTE on 3:12.

47. *"Can anyone withhold from these people, who have received the Holy Spirit just as we have, the water with which they are to be baptized?"* See 8:36 for a similar expression in a baptismal context. The Spirit was received as a result of their faith (implicitly expressed in their acceptance of Peter's message). Now baptism is to be joined to their faith and the Spirit received. One should not ask how they might have received the Spirit without having been baptized; that would be to miss the point of the Lucan story. Gentiles are baptized, because that is part of the process by which one becomes a Christian. Luke is interested in the complex of faith, baptism, and reception of the Spirit; see *Luke,* 235–37, 239–41.

48. *He ordered them to be baptized in the name of Jesus Christ.* See NOTE on 2:38. Peter ordered them to be received as Christians, followers of Christ. Again the refrain of "the name" appears.

Then they invited him to stay for some days. Presumably Peter did so. This Lucan notice stresses again the effect of the vision on Jewish Christian Peter, who prolongs his stay with Gentile converts.

BIBLIOGRAPHY (10:23b–48)

Corell, J., "Actos 10,36," *Estudios Franciscanos* 76 (1975): 101–13.

Dumais, M., "Le salut en dehors de la foi en Jésus-Christ?: Observations sur trois passages des Actes des Apôtres," *Eglise et théologie* 28 (1997): 161–90.

Dupont, J., "Dieu l'a oint d'Esprit Saint (Ac 10,34–38)," *AsSeign* 2/12 (1969): 40–47; repr. *Nouvelles études*, 319–28.

———, "Les discours de Pierre dans les Actes et le chapitre xxiv de l'évangile de Luc," *L'Evangile de Luc: Problèmes littéraires et théologiques: Mémorial Lucien Cerfaux* (BETL 32; ed. F. Neirynck; Gembloux: Duculot, 1973), 329–74; repr., *Nouvelles études*, 58–111.

———, "La conversion de Corneille," *Études*, 75–81.

———, "Ressuscité 'le troisième jour' (1 Co 15,4; Ac 10, 40)," *Études*, 321–36.

———, "Saint Pierre et le centurion de Césarée," *Études*, 409–12.

Ellis, E. E., "'Those of the Circumcision' and the Early Christian Mission," *SE IV* (TU 102; Berlin: Akademie, 1968), 390–99.

Esler, P. F., "Glossolalia and the Admission of Gentiles into the Early Christian Community," *BTB* 22 (1992): 136–42.

Fenasse, J.-M., "Pierre et Corneille, le centurion," *BTS* 41 (1961): 4–5.

Kraabel, A. T., "Greeks, Jews, and Lutherans in the Middle Half of Acts," *Christians among Jews and Gentiles: Essays in Honor of Krister Stendahl* (ed. G.W.E. Nickelsburg and G. W. MacRae; Philadelphia: Fortress, 1986): 147–57.

MacKenzie, R. S., "The Western Text of Acts: Some Lucanisms in Selected Sermons," *JBL* 104 (1985): 637–50, esp. 638–41.

Mussner, F., "'Das Wesen des Christentums ist *synesthiein*': Ein authentischer Kommentar," *Mysterium der Gnade: Festschrift für Johann Auer* (ed. H. Rossmann and J. Ratzinger; Regensburg: Pustet, 1975), 92–102.

Neirynck, F., "Le livre des Actes: 6. Ac 10,36–43 et l'Evangile," *ETL* 60 (1984): 109–17.

Perrot, C., "Un fragment christo-palestinien découvert à Khirbet Mird (Actes des Apôtres, x, 28–29; 32–41)," *RB* 70 (1963): 506–55.

Riesenfeld, H., "The Text of Acts x.36," *Text and Interpretation: Studies in the New Testament Presented to Matthew Black* (ed. E. Best and R. M. Wilson; Cambridge: Cambridge University Press, 1979), 191–94.

Schlier, H., "Die Entscheidung für die Heidenmission in der Urchristenheit," *Die Zeit der Kirche: Exegetische Aufsätze und Vorträge* (5th ed.; Freiburg im B.: Herder, 1972), 90–107.

Schneider, G., "Die Petrusrede vor Kornelius: Das Verhältnis von Tradition und Komposition in Apg 10,34–43," *LTH*, 253–79.

Schürmann, H., "Es tut not, der Worte des Herrn zu gedenken," *Katechetische Blätter* 79 (1954): 254–61.

Segal, A. F., "The Costs of Proselytism and Conversion," *SBL Seminar Papers 1988* (Atlanta: Scholars, 1988), 336–69.

Squillaci, D., "La conversione del centurione Cornelio (Atti cap. 10)," *PC* 39 (1960): 1265–69.

Villiers, P. de, "'God Raised Him on the Third Day and Made Him Manifest . . . and He Commanded Us to Preach to the People . . .' (Acts 10:34–40)," *JTSA* 70 (1990): 55–63.

Völkel, M., "Der Anfang Jesu in Galiläa: Bemerkungen zum Gebrauch und zur Funktion Galiläas in den lukanischen Schriften," *ZNW* 64 (1973): 222–32.

Weiser, A., "Tradition und lukanische Komposition in Apg 10,36–43," *A cause de l'évangile*, 757–67.

Wilckens, U., "Kerygma und Evangelium bei Lukas (Beobachtungen zu Acta 10,34–43)," *ZNW* 49 (1958): 223–37.

e) PETER'S SELF-DEFENSE AT JERUSALEM (11:1–18)

11 [1]Now the apostles and brothers who were in Judea heard that Gentiles too
had welcomed the word of God. [2]So when Peter came up to Jerusalem, circumcised believers confronted him, [3]saying, "You entered the house of uncircumcised men and ate with them." [4]Peter explained it to them step by step from the
beginning. [5]"I was at prayer in the town of Joppa, when in a trance I had a vision.
I saw an object resembling a big sheet come down, being lowered from the heavens by its four corners, and it moved up to me. [6]As I stared at it, I could see and
make out four-legged creatures of the earth, wild beasts and reptiles, and birds of
the sky. [7]I also heard a voice say to me, 'Get up, Peter! Slaughter and eat.' [8]But I
said, 'Not on your life, sir, for nothing common or unclean has ever entered my
mouth!' [9]A second time the voice from the heavens spoke out, 'What God has
made clean, you are not to call common.' [10]Three times this happened, and
everything was drawn up again to the heavens. [11]Just then three men arrived at
the house where we were, sent to me from Caesarea. [12]The Spirit told me to go
with them without hesitation. These six brothers also accompanied me, and we
entered that man's house. [13]He informed us how he had seen [the] angel standing in his house and saying, 'Send someone to Joppa and summon Simon, who
is called Peter. [14]He will tell you things by which you and all your household will
be saved.' [15]As I began to address them, the Holy Spirit came down upon them,
just as it did on us at the beginning. [16]Then I remembered the word of the Lord,
how he said, 'John baptized with water, but you will be baptized with a Holy
Spirit.' [17]So if God gave them the same gift he gave us when we came to believe
in the Lord Jesus Christ, who was I to be able to stop God?" [18]When they heard
this, they stopped objecting; instead they began to honor God, saying, "So God
has granted life-giving repentance even to Gentiles."

WT: [1]It was heard among the apostles . . . and they praised God. [2]Therefore after some time Peter wanted to proceed to Jerusalem; he addressed the brothers, and having strengthened them, he left; making many a discourse throughout the area, he taught them. [3]saying, "Why did you enter . . . and eat with them?" [4][omits "step by step"]. [5][omits "at prayer," "in a trance," "an object resembling," and "come down"]. [6][omits "and make out" and "of the earth"]. [9]A voice from the heavens said to me. [10][omits "everything" and "again"]. [11]Look, three men . . . where I was. [12][omits "without hesitation"]. [13]an angel . . . saying to him. [15][omits "Holy"]. [17]He gave . . . [omits "Christ" and adds at end:] from giving them the Holy Spirit?

COMMENT

Luke now recounts the aftermath of what Peter has done in Caesarea. The inauguration of the mission to the Gentiles eventually becomes known in Judea, and when Peter returns to Jerusalem, he is confronted by Jewish Christians taken aback by his activity, especially by his consorting with non-Jews. In reply to their reaction at what he has done, Peter defends himself and gives a brief résumé of the events recounted in chap. 10. This enables Luke to retell the story of Peter's inauguration of the mission to the Gentiles, because it was an event of such importance for his whole story. Peter sums it up: "The Spirit told me to go with them without hesitation" (11:12); "if God gave them the same gift he gave us when we came to believe in the Lord Jesus Christ, who was I to be able to stop God?" (11:17). The mission to the Gentiles is thus God inspired. Peter's explanation satisfies all who have inquired. Luke ends the episode by recording in Peter's words, "God has granted life-giving repentance even to Gentiles." Thus the mission to Gentiles is officially inaugurated and defended by no less a person than Peter.

The episode begins as a narrative, but most of it is a recapitulatory speech (11:5–17). It is a defense speech, in which Peter explains God's initiative. At first portrayed as baptizing a Gentile, he explains how that is God's will: "What God has made clean, you are not to call common" (11:9, echoing 10:15, 28). Peter's explanation enables the Jerusalem Christians to accept the mission to Gentiles. All of Peter's activity and explanation prepares for the story to be told in chap. 15. As elsewhere, Peter's speech is a Lucan composition, merely recapitulating chap. 10.

"God gave the same gift to Gentiles as he gave us when we came to believe in the Lord Jesus Christ" (11:17), i.e., the gift of the Spirit. This Spirit is the dynamo of Christian life, inspiring faith in all and undoing age-old patterns of obsolete and obstinate conduct, even bringing about repentance. No one should try to thwart the work of God's Spirit, for one cannot stop God who can bring even cooperation out of human opposition. So Peter has learned from this encounter with the Roman Cornelius, and so have Jerusalem Christians learned from Peter.

NOTES

11:1. *the apostles and brothers who were in Judea.* Christians other than the twelve apostles have come back to live in Jerusalem after the persecution (8:1). On "apostles" and "brothers," see NOTES on 1:12 and 15. Here "Judea" is used in the narrow sense of the country about Jerusalem (see NOTE on 1:8).

heard that Gentiles too had welcomed the word of God. The welcoming of the

Word by Gentiles is now explicitly recorded for the first time; the inauguration of a mission to them is thus officially announced. It will have repercussions in the "Council" in chap. 15. Recall 8:14. On "Gentiles," see NOTE on 4:27; on "the word of God," see NOTE on 4:31.

2. *So when Peter came up to Jerusalem.* In returning to Jerusalem, Peter had to mount up to the high city; see NOTE on 8:5.

circumcised believers confronted him. Lit., "those of the circumcision," see NOTE on 10:45. Jewish Christian inhabitants of Jerusalem are meant.

3. *"You entered the house of uncircumcised men.* Lit., "men having a foreskin," a phrase used in Gen 34:14 (LXX) to denote uncircumcised non-Jews.

and ate with them." The Jewish Christians are scandalized at what they have heard about Peter, who is one of their own. Their objection says nothing about Peter's having baptized Gentiles and concentrates on his consorting with them. See NOTE on 10:22; cf. Gal 2:12; Luke 15:2.

4. *Peter explained it to them step by step from the beginning.* Lit., "beginning, Peter set it forth for them in order," i.e., giving a résumé of his experience in Joppa and Caesarea.

5. *"I was at prayer in the town of Joppa, when in a trance I had a vision.* Recall 10:9–16, and see NOTES there.

I saw an object resembling a big sheet come down, being lowered from the heavens by its four corners, and it moved up to me. 6. As I stared at it, I could see and make out four-legged creatures of the earth, wild beasts and reptiles, and birds of the sky. 7. I also heard a voice say to me, 'Get up, Peter! Slaughter and eat.' Thus, Peter recounts the basic part of his vision, 10:11–13.

8. *I said, 'Not on your life, sir, for nothing common or unclean has ever entered my mouth!' 9. A second time the voice from the heavens spoke out, 'What God has made clean, you are not to call common.' 10. Three times this happened, and everything was drawn up again to the heavens. 11. Just then three men arrived at the house where we were, sent to me from Caesarea.* A summary of 10:17–18.

12. *The Spirit told me to go with them without hesitation.* Recall 10:19–20. The Spirit's message was, "I have sent them." Peter says nothing about his inviting the Gentile emissaries in and his treating them as guests where he was lodging in Joppa.

These six brothers also accompanied me. This is a new detail, that the "brothers" from Joppa are six (see 10:23c), who have been with Peter and were witnesses of what took place. For *adelphoi* = Christians, see NOTE on 1:15.

we entered that man's house. Peter does not apologize to his fellow Jewish Christians about his entry into the house of a Gentile.

13. *He informed us how he had seen [the] angel standing in his house and saying, 'Send someone to Joppa and summon Simon, who is called Peter. 14. He will tell you things by which you and all your household will be saved.'* Peter summarizes the heavenly message given to Cornelius and his household. He introduces the mention of "salvation," because the issue of debate is not merely one of fellowship with Gentiles. It concerns the very purpose of the ministry of Jesus and

the testimony of his disciples. As an effect of the Christ-event, salvation is an important issue for Luke (see *Luke*, 222–23).

15. *As I began to address them, the Holy Spirit came down upon them, just as it did on us at the beginning.* If Peter's words were to be pressed, he would be exaggerating, because the descent of the Spirit on Cornelius and his household followed Peter's speech (10:44). The descent of the Spirit is thus depicted by Luke in order to emphasize that the Spirit has indeed been accorded Cornelius and his gathered friends. Dibelius understood the opening words of this verse *en de tō arxasthai me lalein* to mean that the Spirit came down "just as he had begun to speak," and so "there would be no place for Peter's speech" (*Studies*, 110). That is stretching a point too far, because *archesthai* is sometimes used in Greek, classical, Hellenistic, and Lucan (Luke 7:24; 20:9), in a pleonastic sense, meaning "to proceed to do something"; so here (see BDF §392.2; Moulton, *Grammar*, 2.455; J. J. Kilgallen, "Did Peter"). Luke is concerned with stressing God's initiative in this affair, and so he speaks of the effect before narrating its occasion.

16. *I remembered the word of the Lord, how he said, 'John baptized with water, but you will be baptized with a Holy Spirit.'* Peter recalls the substance of what Luke has recorded in 1:5 and ends his explanation with a quotation of Jesus himself (Luke 3:16). Thus, he interprets the descent of the Spirit on Cornelius and his guests; they have been "baptized" with the Spirit, just as Jerusalem Jews were on the first Christian Pentecost.

17. *if God gave them the same gift he gave us.* Recall 10:47 and 2:1–4.

when we came to believe in the Lord Jesus Christ. Peter speaks in the name of all Jewish Christians, not just of his own personal coming to faith. The ptc. *pisteusasin*, "coming to faith," actually has to be understood as modifying both *autois*, "them," and *hēmin*, "us" (translated as nom. above). Conzelmann (*Acts*, 86) rightly argues against the interpretation of Schweizer (*TDNT*, 6.413), who tried to sever the connection between baptism and the gift of the Spirit. Cf. Schneider, *Apg.*, 2.83.

who was I to be able to stop God?" I.e., how could I think that *I* could oppose God? For Peter, the Spirit's descent upon Cornelius and his household is an act of God, which no human being, especially one who has been accorded the same gracious gift, can think of thwarting.

18. *When they heard this, they stopped objecting.* Lit., "they grew silent," as in 21:14; Luke 14:4. Words coming from the leader of Jewish Christians of Jerusalem are enough to put an end to all further criticism, especially since Peter has shown how the authority of God has been involved.

instead they began to honor God. The reaction of the Jewish Christians of Jerusalem is one of praise, glorifying God for such an inauguration of the mission to the Gentiles.

"God has granted life-giving repentance even to Gentiles." Lit., "repentance unto life." Recall 5:31, where repentance was granted to Israel. Now it is said to lead to "life," one of the effects of the Christ-event (*Luke*, 225–26). Luke again makes use of the crucial term *metanoia*, "repentance"; see NOTE on 2:38.

BIBLIOGRAPHY (11:1–18)

Beel, A., "Sermo s. Petri ad fratres post conversionem Cornelii (Act. Ap. xi, 4–18)," *CollBrug* 32 (1932): 3–10.

Boismard, M.-E., "The Text of Acts: A Problem of Literary Criticism?" *New Testament Textual Criticism: Its Significance for Exegesis: Essays in Honour of Bruce M. Metzger* (ed. E. J. Epp and G. D. Fee; Oxford: Clarendon, 1981), 147–57.

Delebecque, E., "La montée de Pierre de Césarée à Jérusalem selon le *Codex Bezae* au chapitre 11 des *Actes des Apôtres*," *ETL* 58 (1982): 106–10.

Dupont, J., "L'Apôtre comme intermédiaire du salut dans les Actes des Apôtres," *RTP* 112 (1980): 342–58; repr. *Nouvelles études*, 112–32.

Haacker, K., "Dibelius und Cornelius: Ein Beispiel formgeschichtlicher Überlieferungskritik," *BZ* 24 (1980): 234–51, esp. 240.

Kilgallen, J. J., "Did Peter Actually Fail to Get a Word In? (Acts 11,15)," *Bib* 71 (1990): 405–10.

C. Spread of the Word to Gentiles Elsewhere (11:19–12:25)

1. Greeks in Antioch Evangelized by Barnabas (11:19–26)

[19] Now those who had been scattered by the hardship that arose because of Stephen traveled as far as Phoenicia, Cyprus, and Antioch, addressing the word to none but Jews alone. [20] Among them, however, were some Cypriots and Cyrenians who came to Antioch and began to address the Greeks as well, preaching to them about the Lord Jesus. [21] The hand of the Lord was with them, and a great number believed and turned to the Lord. [22] News about this came to the ears of the church in Jerusalem, and they sent Barnabas [to go] to Antioch. [23] When, on his arrival, he saw the grace of God, he rejoiced and encouraged all of them to remain steadfast in their dedication to the Lord. [24] He was a good man, full of the Holy Spirit and of faith, and a large number of people was added to the Lord. [25] Then Barnabas went off to Tarsus to look for Saul. [26] When he found him, he brought him back to Antioch, and for a whole year they met with the church and instructed a large number of people. It was in Antioch that the disciples were first called Christians.

WT: [19] [omits "the word" and "alone"]. [20] [omits "some"]. [25] Then Barnabas, hearing that Saul was in Tarsus, went (there) to look for him. [26] When he met him, he urged him to come to Antioch. When they got there, and . . . people. Then for the first time, in Antioch, the disciples were called Christians.

COMMENT

The third subsection of this part of Acts now begins; Luke continues his account of the spread of the Word of God from its starting point in Jerusalem to other areas. Now that the mission to the Gentiles has been officially inaugurated by Peter, Luke begins with a generic statement about the aftermath of the persecution that has followed on the death of Stephen. One of the good things that has resulted from such trouble is the spread of testimony about the risen Christ to the important town of Antioch in Syria, to Phoenicia, and even as far as the island of Cyprus. For the first time the Word is carried by disciples beyond the bounds of Palestine itself. This is the activity of Hellenists, Greek-speaking Jewish Christians, who bring the kerygma to important non-Jewish areas, or areas of the Jewish diaspora. When news of the success of these disciples, even among Greeks or Gentiles, is brought back to Jerusalem, the church decides to send Barnabas, a prominent disciple, who is not himself a member of the Twelve, to strengthen and confirm those working in Antioch. When Barnabas arrives and has worked for some time there, he realizes the need of a coworker and goes off to get Saul. The episode ends with the notice that there in Antioch the disciples are called "Christians" for the first time, i.e., recognized as followers of "the Christ," of Jesus of Nazareth, whom they have acknowledged as "the Messiah." There where Greek was widely spoken, a Greco-Latin name was given them, and that has been used of such followers ever since.

The episode is a narrative, when it is considered form-critically. Probably derived from Luke's Antiochene source, it gives a summary description of the spread of the Word beyond Palestine. It is more than a mere summary, because it reintroduces Saul to active collaboration in ministry, after his withdrawal to his hometown (9:20). From this point on he will play an active role in the Lucan story.

Up to this point in Acts followers of Christ have been called believers, disciples, brothers, and saints. They are members of the *koinōnia*, followers of "the Way." None of these titles has really suggested any difference from Jews. Now that the Word has spread beyond Judea (in the broad sense) we are not surprised to learn that a distinctive name for them comes into play: followers of Jesus Christ are called "Christians." The Lucan refrain of "the name" thus comes to the fore in a new way. Such followers now bear the name: they are Christ-ians. Apart from this passage and 26:28, where Herod Agrippa II uses it ironically, it occurs in the NT only in 1 Pet 4:16: "If (one suffers) as a Christian, let him not be ashamed, but under that name let him glorify God." This is the heritage associated with the name "Christian," even if we cannot tell whether early followers of Christ so designated themselves that way in Antioch, or whether opponents of their allegiance and heritage so labeled them in a form of mockery.

NOTES

19. *those who had been scattered by the hardship that arose because of Stephen.* Recall the notice about the persecution in 8:1, 4, which told of the scattering of Christians of Jerusalem to "the countryside of Judea and Samaria." Now we learn that some Hellenists have carried the Word even farther. Luke calls the persecution *thlipsis,* "hardship," the word used of the Hebrews in Egypt in 7:10, 11.

traveled as far as Phoenicia, Cyprus, and Antioch. I.e., to the relatively nearby diaspora, where Jews are living.

Phoinikē was the name of the Mediterranean seacoast area of the Roman province of Syria, in which Tyre and Sidon were the two most important towns, but where Ptolemais, Acco, Sarepta, Berytus, Tripolis, and Arvad were also located. It was cut off from the Syrian inland by the Taurus mountain range. The name *Phoinikē* is related to the adj. *phoinos,* "red-purple," the color of the famous dye of Tyre, which was called in Akkadian *kinaḫḫu* and is related to the Hebrew name *Kĕnaʿan,* "Canaan," which *Phoinikē* translates in Exod 16:35 (LXX). See NOTE on 21:3. Cf. F. Millar, *Roman Near East,* 264–95, esp. 285–95.

Kypros, "Cyprus," was the large island to the south of Asia Minor, about 100 km west of northern Syria. It became a senatorial province of the Roman empire in 22 B.C., the place from which Barnabas originally came (4:36 [see NOTE there]). There was a large colony of Jews on Cyprus (see 13:5; Philo, *Legatio ad Gaium* 36 §282; Josephus, *Ant.* 13.10.4 §284–87). Cf. A. Nobbs, "Cyprus," *The Book of Acts in Its Graeco-Roman Setting* (BAFCS 2), 279–89.

Antiocheia, "Antioch," was the name given to many towns over which Seleucid kings ruled after the death of Alexander the Great. The one meant here was the capital of the Seleucid empire, "Antioch on the Orontes (River)," or "Antioch near Daphne," i.e., near the spring of Daphne, a sanctuary of the god Apollo. It had been founded about 300 B.C. by Seleucus I Nicator (312 to 281 B.C.), about 32 km inland from its port, Seleucia (13:4). Situated about 480 km north of Jerusalem, it was the third most important town in the Roman Empire at that time (after Rome and Alexandria) and was the seat of the Roman *legatus,* "legate" or governor of the province of Syria. Josephus called it "the metropolis of Syria" (*J.W.* 3.2.4 §29), a phrase that also appears on its municipal coins. Tacitus called it *Syriae . . . caput,* perhaps "the capital of Syria" (historians debate the sense of *caput*). In any case, it became the site of famous philosophical, rhetorical, and medical schools, the home of a renowned library, and was noted for its architectural monuments, theaters, gymnasia, and baths. Many Jews lived there (Josephus, *J.W.* 7.3.3 §§43–44; *Ant.* 12.3.1 §§119–20). Citizens of Antioch were known for their scurrilous wit and invention of nicknames. See Finegan, *Archeology of the New Testament,* 63–78; K. Bauer, *Antiochia in der ältesten Kirchengeschichte* (Tübingen: Mohr [Siebeck], 1919); B. M. Metzger, "Antioch-on-the-Orontes," *BA* 11 (1948): 69–88; R. E. Brown and J. P. Meier, *Antioch and Rome: New Testament Cradles of Catholic Christianity* (New York/Ramsey, NJ: Paulist, 1983), 11–86; G. Downey, A *History of Antioch in Syria from Seleucus to the*

Arab Conquest (Princeton: Princeton University Press, 1961), 163–207, 272–92; *Ancient Antioch* (Princeton: Princeton University Press, 1963), 120–42; I. Levinskaya, "Antioch," *The Book of Acts in Its Diaspora Setting* (BAFCS 5), 127–35; A. Dauer, *Paulus und die christliche Gemeinde im syrischen Antiochia: Kritische Bestandsaufnahme der modernen Forschung mit einigen weiterführenden Überlegungen* (BBB 106; Weinheim: Beltz Athenäum, 1996).

addressing the word to none but Jews alone. Probably because they were "Hellenists," Greek-speaking Jewish Christians from Jerusalem (6:1), who were not accustomed to dealing with others than Jews (recall Peter's remark in 10:28). This preaching to Jews in Phoenicia is the origin of the Christian community there to which reference will be made in 15:3. The Lucan motif in Acts, to depict the Word being preached first to the Jews and only subsequently to Gentiles, appears here.

20. *Among them, however, were some Cypriots and Cyrenians.* I.e., among the Christian Hellenists from Jerusalem were some who originally came from the island of Cyprus and from Cyrene in northern Africa (see NOTE on 2:10). Because they were originally Jews from the diaspora, they would have been more accustomed to speak to and deal with Gentiles.

who came to Antioch and began to address the Greeks as well. The Greek text of Acts is problematic. MSS P[74], ℵ[2], A, D*, and 1518 read *Hellēnas,* "Greeks," but MSS B, D[2], E, Ψ, 33, 81, 614, 1739, and the *Koinē* text-tradition read *Hellēnistas,* "Hellenists," and MS ℵ* strangely has *euangelistas,* "evangelists." I follow the first reading; in doing so, I depart from the reading in N-A[27] and GNT[4], which prefer the second, probably as *lectio difficilior.* In this situation the reading "Hellenists" makes little sense. See P. Parker, "Three Variant Readings in Luke-Acts," *JBL* 83 (1964): 165–70, esp. 167–68, who argues (unconvincingly) for "Hellenists," understood as "Greek-speaking Jews only," to whom "the mission of Acts 11" is directed. But is it? How could *Hellēnistas* stand in contrast to *Ioudaiois* of v 19? Similarly D. R. Fotheringham, "Acts xi.20," *ExpTim* 45 (1933–34): 430. Cf. *TCGNT,* 340–42.

preaching to them about the Lord Jesus. See 8:35, where the same expression is employed of Philip. Hellenists of Jerusalem thus bring the Christian kerygma to Gentiles of Antioch. What Peter has begun in chap. 10 is now furthered.

21. *The hand of the Lord was with them.* It is not easy to say to whom *Kyrios* refers in this case, since it was used of Jesus at the end of v 20, but the expression, actually an OT anthropomorphism (1 Chr 28:19; 4:10; Isa 66:2), is used in Luke 1:66 to describe Yahweh's protection of young John the Baptist. It could, then, be merely a way of expressing divine assistance.

a great number believed and turned to the Lord. Luke joins faith to a turning to the Lord; see NOTES on 2:38; 3:19. Again *Kyrios* is ambiguous, because of the Gentiles being converted. Weiser (*Apg.,* 277) understands it of Christ.

22. *News about this came to the ears of the church in Jerusalem.* Luke uses *ho logos,* "the word," in the generic sense of "news." Just as Philip's evangelization of Samaria became known to the apostles in Jerusalem (8:14), so now the evange-

lization of Cypriots and Cyrenians in Antioch. In this case, however, it becomes known to the "church," and "apostles" are not singled out.

they sent Barnabas [*to go*] *to Antioch.* MSS D, E, Ψ, 33, and the *Koinē* text-tradition read the infin. *dielthein,* "go," but MSS P[74], ℵ, A, B, 81, and 1739 omit it. Its omission may be owing to homoeoteleuton, since both *Barnaban* and *dielthein* end in *n.* In this case, the reading in N-A[27] and GNT[4] seems to agree more with the WT than the Alexandrian. Now Barnabas, not an apostle, is despatched to the newly evangelized Antioch, and the important Lucan detail is that he is "sent" by the "church" in Jerusalem. In other words, he bears a commission of the mother church.

23. *When, on his arrival, he saw the grace of God.* I.e., the effects of God's grace in the lives and conduct of recent converts, both Jewish and Greek.

he rejoiced and encouraged all of them to remain steadfast in their dedication to the Lord. Barnabas seeks to strengthen the newborn faith of Antiochene converts.

24. *He was a good man, full of the holy Spirit and of faith.* Recall the description of Stephen in 6:5, 8; 7:55. Such qualities of Barnabas help to account for the success of his evangelization.

a large number of people was added to the Lord. Compare 2:47. *Kyrios* means Christ. This is a Lucan summary statement about the growth of the Christian church. So Conzelmann (*Acts,* 88), Pesch (*Apg.,* 350), Johnson (*Acts,* 202), Roloff (*Apg.,* 176); but Schneider (*Apg.,* 2.91) understands it to refer to God, with a dat. of agency, "by the Lord." Similarly Weiser, *Apg.,* 278.

25. *Then Barnabas went off to Tarsus to look for Saul.* Barnabas, who "brought Saul to the apostles" (9:27), was probably among the "brothers" who took Saul and sent him to Tarsus (9:30). That at least would be the implication of the Lucan story. Though sent by the church in Jerusalem, Barnabas now acts on his own. See further C. Burchard, "Fussnoten zum neutestamentlichen Griechisch II," ZNW 69 (1978): 143–57, esp. 153–55.

26. *When he found him, he brought him back to Antioch.* Barnabas thus associates Saul with his own ministry in this important city. It foreshadows the work that the two will do together.

for a whole year they met with the church. Lit., "it happened that they were both brought together for a whole year in the church and . . ." Luke uses *egeneto de* with an infin. (see *Luke,* 118), actually with three infinitives. It is a clumsy way of expressing the collaboration of Barnabas and Saul. This must have been about A.D. 44 (see Introduction §158).

instructed a large number of people. Lit., "a goodly crowd."

It was in Antioch that the disciples were first called Christians. In 12:1 Luke will speak of Jesus's followers as *hoi apo tēs ekklēsias,* "some (members) of the church"; but now he reveals where the name *Christianoi* was actually coined, where the followers of Christ were first clearly recognized as distinct from Jews. Christians had now become so numerous that they had to be distinguished from the Jewish population, and so the name emerged. *Christos* was recognized no longer as a title, but as a name for Jesus, after whom his followers are now named.

This clause is another acc. with the aor. act. infin. *chrēmatisai* dependent on *egeneto de* at the beginning of the verse. Codex D, however, makes a full clause out of it: *kai tote prōton echrēmatisan en Antiocheia hoi mathētai Christianoi,* "and then for the first time in Antioch the disciples were called Christians."

The name is a grecized form of Latin *Christianus,* which raises a question about its origin and who might have used it first. It is like other grecized Latin names: *Hērōdianoi* (Mark 3:6; 12:13), *Kaisarianoi, Asianoi, Nerōnianoi.* MSS א*, 28, and 81 spell the name *Chrēstianous,* but its best attested spelling is with an *iota,* relating it clearly to *Christianus.*

The name is also found in Josephus, *Ant.* 18.3.3 §64; Pliny the Younger, *Ep.* 10.96–97; Tacitus, *Annales* 15.44: *quos per flagitia invisos vulgus Christianos appellabat,* "those people, loathed for (their) vices, whom the rabble used to call Christians"; and *auctor huius nominis Christus,* "the originator of this name (was) Christ"; Lucian, *Alexander* 25 and 38. See E. Gibson, *The "Christians for Christians" Inscriptions of Phrygia* (HTS 32; Missoula: Scholars, 1978), 16–17.

The translation of the infin. *chrēmatisai* is problematic. It may mean: "in Antioch disciples first were called Christians." See Rom 7:3 for a similar passive sense of the verb; cf. Philo, *Quod Deus immutabilis sit* 25 §121; Josephus, *Ant.* 8.6.2 §157. Cadbury ("Names," 385 n. 4) maintained that the "intransitive active in the sense 'be named' is abundantly illustrated by the papyri," referring to F. Preisigke, *Wörterbuch der griechischen Papyrusurkunden* . . . (ed. E. Kiessling; 3 vols.; Berlin: Privately published, 1925–31), 2.753–54. That would mean that others gave the disciples this name, either Jews who did not accept the Christ, or Gentiles who perhaps wanted to heap scorn on the disciples, or perhaps even Roman authorities who wanted to distinguish them from Jews (Peterson, "Christianus"; Taylor). See Conzelmann, *Acts,* 88–89.

Bickerman contested the pass. meaning of the act. infin., maintaining rather that it has a middle meaning, "to style oneself"; hence it would mean "in Antioch disciples first came to call themselves Christians," i.e., agents or representatives of the Messiah ("The Name," 123). Similarly Spicq (*Vie chrétienne,* 13 n. 1; "Ce qui signifie," 68); Moreau ("Le nom"); P. Zingg, *Das Wachsen der Kirche* (Göttingen: Vandenhoeck & Ruprecht, 1974), 221. Karpp, however, has rejected Bickerman's arguments ("Christennamen," 1132), as have Shepherd ("The Occasion," 709) and Mattingly ("The Origin," 28 n. 3). Cf. B. Reicke, "*Chrēma, chrēmatizō, chrēmatismos,*" *TDNT,* 9.480–82.

BIBLIOGRAPHY (11:19–26)

Bickerman, E. J., "The Name of Christians," *HTR* 42 (1949): 109–24.

Cadbury, H. J., "Names for Christians and Christianity in Acts," *Beginnings,* 5.375–92, esp. 383–86.

Cecchelli, C., "Il nome e la 'setta' dei Cristiani," *Rivista di archeologia cristiana* 31 (1955): 55–73.

Delebecque, E., "Saul et Luc avant le premier voyage missionnaire: Comparaison des deux versions des *Actes* 11,26–28," *RSPT* 66 (1982): 551–59.

Fitzmyer, J. A., "The Designations of Christians in Acts and Their Significance," *Unité et diversité dans l'église* (ed. Pontifical Biblical Commission; Vatican City: Libreria Editrice Vaticana, 1989), 223–36.

Gercke, A., "Der Christenname ein Scheltname," *Festschrift zur Jahrhundertfeier der Universität Breslau* . . . (ed. Schlesischer Philologenverein; Breslau: Trewendt & Granier, 1911), 360–73.

Grundmann, W., "Die Apostel zwischen Jerusalem und Antiochia," ZNW 39 (1940): 110–37.

Horsley, G.H.R., "Name Change as an Indication of Religious Conversion in Antiquity," *Numen* 34 (1987): 1–17.

Judge, E. A., "Judaism and the Rise of Christianity: A Roman Perspective," *TynBull* 45 (1994): 355–68.

Karpp, H., "Christennamen," *RAC*, 2.1114–38.

Kraeling, C. H., "The Jewish Community at Antioch," *JBL* 51 (1932): 130–60.

Kretzmann, P. E., "The Earliest Christian Congregations at Rome and Antioch," *TM* 6 (1926): 129–36.

Labriolle, P. de, "Christianus," *Bulletin du Cange: Archivum latinitatis medii aevi* 5 (1929–30): 69–88.

Lifshitz, B., "L'Origine du nom des Chrétiens," *VC* 16 (1962): 65–70.

Mattingly, H. B., "The Origin of the Name *Christiani*," *JTS* 9 (1958): 26–37.

Michaelis, W., "Judaistische Heidenchristen," ZNW 30 (1931): 83–89.

Moreau, J., "Le nom des chrétiens," *La nouvelle Clio* 1–2 (1949–50): 190–92.

Murillo, L., "El ministerio de san Pablo en Antioquía," *EstEcl* 1 (1922): 273–96.

Pasinya, M., "Antioche, berceau de l'église des Gentils, Act 11,19–26," *RAT* 1 (1977): 31–66.

Peterson, E., "Christianus," *Miscellanea Giovanni Mercati* (6 vols.; ed. A. M. Albareda; Vatican City: Bibliotheca Apostolica Vaticana, 1946), 1.355–72; repr. *Frühkirche, Judentum und Gnosis: Studien und Untersuchungen* (Freiburg im B.: Herder, 1959), 64–87.

Robert, L., *Hellenica: Recueil d'épigraphie, de numismatique et d'antiquités grecques, Volume I* (Limoges: Bontemps, 1940), 72; *Hellenica, Volume II* (Paris: Maisonneuve, 1946), 148; *Hellenica, Volume XI-XIII* (1960), 454.

Shepherd, M. H., "The Occasion of the Initial Break between Judaism and Christianity," *Harry Austryn Wolfson Jubilee Volume* . . . (3 vols.; Jerusalem: American Academy for Jewish Research, 1965), 2.703–17.

Spicq, C., "Ce que signifie le titre de chrétien," *ST* 15 (1961): 68–78.

———, *Vie chrétienne et pérégrination selon le Nouveau Testament* (LD 71; Paris: Cerf, 1972), 13–57.

Taylor, J., "Why Were the Disciples First Called 'Christians' at Antioch? (Acts 11,26)," *RB* 101 (1994): 75–94.

2. Prophet Agabus and the Collection for Jerusalem (11:27–30)

[27] In those days some prophets came down from Jerusalem to Antioch, [28] and one of them named Agabus got up and through the Spirit predicted that there was going to be a severe famine all over the world. In fact, it happened under Claudius. [29] So the disciples, each according to one's ability, determined to send something for the support of the brothers living in Judea. [30] This they did, sending it to the presbyters in the care of Barnabas and Saul.

WT: [28] [adds at beginning:] and there was much rejoicing. When we gathered together, one . . . [omits "through the Spirit"]. [30] They did (so), sending.

COMMENT

Luke's narrative continues with an episode about the Christians of Antioch. When prophets from Jerusalem arrive, one of them, Agabus, predicts the coming of a severe famine, which moves the disciples in Antioch to gather support for their colleagues in Judea. Luke thus emphasizes the close connection and solidarity of the young Antiochene church with the mother church of Jerusalem. The latter has sent Barnabas to this new church (11:22), and now it seeks to acknowledge its solidarity with Jerusalem. What Antiochene Christians have put aside is entrusted to Barnabas and Saul to take to Jerusalem as famine relief.

According to the Lucan story, this would be Saul's second visit to Jerusalem since his conversion (recall 9:26). Some commentators would identify this visit of Saul and Barnabas with that mentioned by Paul in Gal 2:1–10 (so Bruce, *Acts* [NICNT], 244; Marshall, *Acts*, 205; D. R. De Lacey, *NTS* 20 [1973–74]: 82–86), but that identification is far from certain, since Gal 2:1 is undoubtedly the same as the visit for the "Council" in Acts 15:4. The issue is far more complicated; see Introduction §156 and COMMENTS on 15:1–2, 3–12.

In this narrative Luke continues to make use of his Antiochene source in vv 27–29. Verse 30 is most likely a Lucan summary. Strecker ("Die sogenannte zweite Jerusalemreise") regarded this episode as coming wholly from Luke's pen.

In the face of the famine that is coming upon vast regions, Antiochene Christians do not hesitate to send aid to their colleagues in Jerusalem via their esteemed leaders and teachers, Barnabas and Saul. The latter is thus returning to the city from which he has had to take flight, not from the Christians there but from Hellenist Jews who have opposed his teaching (9:29–30). He and Barnabas are to carry the famine relief to "presbyters" in Jerusalem, who are probably different from the Seven who have been commissioned to handle the dole (6:3–6).

NOTES

27. *In those days.* See NOTE on 1:15. Reference is made to the year of collaboration of Barnabas and Saul in Antioch (11:26).

some prophets came down from Jerusalem to Antioch. For the descent from Jerusalem, see NOTE on 8:5. This is the first mention of Christian "prophets"; see further 13:1; 15:32; 21:10. Mention is made of them elsewhere in the NT: 1 Cor 12:28–29; 14:29, 32, 37; Eph 2:20; 3:5; 4:11. In the OT a prophet was the mouthpiece of God, uttering oracles on behalf of God (see Exod 4:14–16). Luke, however, often thinks of an OT prophet as a predictor of the future; indeed, he sometimes makes use of OT passages in a predictive way, which per se have no reference to the future. From this stems in part the Lucan idea of promise and fulfillment. It is not easy, however, to determine precisely what function "prophets" played in the early Christian community; they may have been more like inspired or gifted preachers. For Paul, a prophet could read the secrets of the heart of another person (1 Cor 14:24–25). In this case, the prophets may have been itinerants passing through Antioch to a mission elsewhere. See *Did.* 11:7–12.

28. *one of them named Agabus got up.* He is apparently the same as the one mentioned in the We-Passage of 21:10. The meaning of his name is unknown. A woman from Palmyra in Syria bore the name *ʿgbʾ* (RES 2.1086), which may mean something like "Love, lover." Haenchen (*Acts,* 374), following H. H. Wendt, thinks that the name is related to Hebrew *Hāgāb,* "locust," which is unlikely. See H. Patsch, "Die Prophetie des Agabus," *TZ* 28 (1972): 228–32.

At the beginning of this verse the WT adds "and there was much rejoicing. When we gathered together, one of them spoke, predicting. . . ." That reading in MS D is a unique instance of a We-Section in an account in which Saul does not yet appear. Bultmann once defended it as original, but it is hardly so, even though it is not easy to explain how it would have got secondarily into this context, even in MS D.

through the Spirit predicted that there was going to be a severe famine all over the world. Lit., "throughout all the inhabited (earth)" *(oikoumenē),* on which see *Luke,* 400; cf. O. Michel, *TDNT,* 5.157. The term occurs elsewhere in Luke 2:1; 4:5; 21:26; Acts 17:6, 31; 19:27; 24:5. Torrey (*Composition and Date,* 21) maintains that *oikoumenē* is a Lucan mistranslation of Aramaic *ʾarʿāʾ,* "the land," meaning Judea. If so, then it might more easily refer to the famine noted in Josephus (see below). But the matter is not so simple, because a "worldwide famine" seems to be a literary hyperbole used in speaking of a severe famine and shortage of food. An inscription from Asia Minor (*CIG* 3973:5–6) also speaks of "a famine in the land, flesh-eating, terrible, and bearing inescapable death, [that] gripped the whole world" *(kosmon epesche[th]e panta).* See B. W. Winter, "Acts and Food Shortages," *The Book of Acts in Its Graeco-Roman Setting* (BAFCS 2), 59–78, esp. 65–67.

In fact, it happened under Claudius. This is Luke's parenthetic statement, not really part of his narrative account. It is meant to show the fulfillment of Agabus's prophecy.

Klaudios was the Roman emperor Tiberius Claudius Nero Germanicus, who was born in 10 B.C. and reigned A.D. 41–54. He was acclaimed *imperator* in A.D. 41 by accident, after the emperor Gaius Caligula had been murdered. Claudius was discovered by a Roman soldier in the palace hiding behind a curtain for fear of being murdered too. Dragged to the Praetorian camp, he was hailed *imperator* by the Praetorian Guard in Rome, while the Roman Senate was debating about the restoration of the Republic. He ignored the senate, sided with the military, and was acclaimed *imperator* twenty-seven times by the end of his principate (A.D. 54). He was eventually "consecrated" emperor (i.e., deified), the first since Augustus. Hence Seneca's ironic *Apocolocyntosis*, the "Pumpkinification" of Claudius, which spoofed his *apotheōsis*. He will appear again in 18:2.

See Suetonius, *Claudii Vita;* cf. E. M. Smallwood, *Documents Illustrating the Principates of Gaius, Claudius and Nero* (Cambridge: Cambridge University Press, 1967), 2–4; A. Momigliano, *Claudius: The Emperor and His Achievement* (Oxford: Clarendon, 1934; rev. ed., New York: Barnes & Noble, 1961); V. M. Scramuzza, *The Emperor Claudius* (Cambridge: Harvard University Press, 1940).

Famines seem to have occurred in various places during Claudius's reign (Suetonius, *Claudii Vita* 18.2; Tacitus, *Annales* 12.43; Dio Cassius, *History* 40.11), but there seems to be no record of what has often been called "a worldwide famine." A particularly severe famine occurred in Judea in the time of the procurator Tiberius Alexander (A.D. 46–48), recorded by Josephus (*Ant.* 20.2.5 §51; 20.5.2 §101), when Queen Helen of Adiabene had grain brought from Egypt and dried figs from Cyprus to help the poor there (possibly A.D. 47–48). The dating of it is problematic in that Josephus also speaks of a famine in Judea "shortly before the war, when Claudius was ruling the Romans and Ishmael was the high priest" (*Ant.* 3.15.3 §320). Ishmael ben Phiabi was high priest about A.D. 59–61, when Nero was emperor, which could be understood as "shortly before the war" (i.e., of A.D. 66–70); but no high priest bore that name in the time of Claudius, who died in A.D. 54. So the famine to which Luke alludes may be simply unknown, or unattested elsewhere, but K. S. Gapp thinks that there is evidence of a severe famine in Egypt ca. 45–46, more or less about the time of that mentioned by Josephus. This might support Luke's contention, at least in a general way, because Egypt was the source of grain for many lands in the eastern Mediterranean area ("The Universal Famine under Claudius," *HTR* 28 [1935]: 258–65). See also J. Dupont, "Notes sur les Actes des Apôtres," *RB* 62 (1955): 45–59, esp. 52–55 ("La famine sous Claude [*Actes*, xi, 28]"); repr. *Études*, 163–71; K. S. Lake, "The Famine in the Time of Claudius," *Beginnings*, 5.452–55.

29. *the disciples, each according to one's ability, determined to send something for the support of the brothers living in Judea.* Agabus's words stirred them to immediate activity, and they gathered what they could for the Christians of Judea.

30. *This they did, sending it to the presbyters in the care of Barnabas and Saul.* Lit., "through the hand of Barnabas and Saul." *Presbyteroi* occurs in 4:5, 8, 23;

6:12; 23:14; 24:1; 25:15 as "elders," authority figures in the Jewish community. Now we meet it for the first time as a designation for officials of Christian communities in Judea, "presbyters." In this sense, it further appears in 14:23; 15:2, 4, 6, 22, 23; 16:4; 20:17; 21:18, in some of these instances along with "apostles," not mentioned here. The latter are not to be understood here as among the "presbyters" of Jerusalem. Luke gives no indication of how these officials originated in the Christian community or how they might be related to either the apostles or the Seven of 6:3. This designation may well have been borrowed from Judaism, for the OT speaks of "elders" (Josh 20:4; Ruth 4:2; Isa 24:23). In extrabiblical texts they are known to have been in the Jerusalem Jewish community (*SEG* 8.170:9). There were "elders" also in the Hellenistic world, and the Greek use of that term may also have influenced Christians in their adoption of the title for authority figures in their communities. Barnabas and Saul are chosen by "disciples" in Antioch to bring the relief to Judean Christians, and presumably they traveled to Jerusalem to turn it over to the "presbyters" there.

BIBLIOGRAPHY (11:27–30)

Beare, F. W., "Note on Paul's First Two Visits to Jerusalem," *JBL* 63 (1944): 407–9.

Benoit, P., "La deuxième visite de Saint Paul à Jérusalem," *Bib* 40 (1959): 778–92; repr. *Exégèse et théologie*, 3.285–99.

Funk, R. W., "The Enigma of the Famine Visit," *JBL* 75 (1956): 130–36.

Giet, S., "Nouvelles remarques sur les voyages de saint Paul à Jérusalem," *RevScRel* 31 (1957): 329–42.

———, "Le second voyage de saint Paul à Jérusalem, Actes xi, 27–30; xii, 24–25," *RevScRel* 25 (1951): 265–69.

Hoerber, R. G., "Galatians 2:1–10 and the Acts of the Apostles," *CTM* 31 (1960): 482–91.

Holtzmann, O., "Die Jerusalemreisen des Paulus und die Kollekte," ZNW 6 (1905): 102–4.

Jeremias, J., "Sabbathjahr und neutestamentliche Chronologie," ZNW 27 (1928): 98–103.

Keck, L. E., "The Poor among the Saints in the New Testament," ZNW 56 (1965): 100–29.

Robinson, D. F., "A Note on Acts 11:27–30," *JBL* 63 (1944): 169–72.

———, "A Reply," *JBL* 63 (1944): 411–12.

Strecker, G., "Die sogenannte zweite Jerusalemreise des Paulus (Act 11, 27–30)," ZNW 53 (1962): 67–77; repr. *Eschaton und Historie: Aufsätze* (Göttingen: Vandenhoeck & Ruprecht, 1979), 132–41.

Strobel, A., "Lukas der Antiochener," ZNW 49 (1958): 131–34.

Talbert, C. H., "Again: Paul's Visits to Jerusalem," *NovT* 9 (1967): 26–40.

Tornos, A. M., "*Kat' ekeinon de ton kairon* en Act 12,1 y simultaneidad de Act 12 con Act 11,27–30," *EstEcl* 33 (1959): 411–28.

3. HEROD'S PERSECUTION OF JAMES AND PETER; HEROD'S DEATH (12:1–23)

12 1 About the same time King Herod arrested some members of the church in
order to mistreat them. 2 He had James, the brother of John, put to the sword,
3 and when he saw that that pleased the Jews, he proceeded to arrest Peter too.
That was during [the] Feast of Unleavened Bread. 4 He had him seized and put
in prison with four squads of four soldiers to guard him. Herod intended to bring
him before the people after Passover. 5 So Peter was kept in prison, while the
church prayed fervently to God on his behalf. 6 During the very night before
Herod was going to bring him forth, Peter was sleeping between two soldiers,
secured by double chains. Outside the door sentries were also guarding the
prison. 7 Suddenly the angel of the Lord stood by him, and the cell glowed with
light. He tapped Peter on the side and woke him up, saying, "Hurry, get up!" and
the chains dropped from his wrists. 8 Then the angel said to him, "Fasten your
belt and put on your sandals." This he did, and he said to him again, "Put on
your cloak and follow me." 9 He went out following the angel, not realizing what
was really happening with the angel's help; he thought he was seeing a vision.
10 Having passed the first sentinel and then the second, they came to the iron gate
leading to the city, which opened for them of itself. They went out and moved
along a narrow alley, and suddenly the angel left him. 11 Peter then came to himself and said, "Now I know for sure that [the] Lord has sent his angel and rescued
me from Herod's clutches and from all that the Jewish people had been expecting." 12 When he realized this, he went to the house of Mary, the mother of
John, who is called Mark, where many people were gathered in prayer. 13 When
he knocked at the door of the gateway, a maid named Rhoda came to answer it.
14 She recognized Peter's voice and was so overjoyed that she did not stop to open
the gate but ran back and reported that Peter was standing at the gate. 15 They
said to her, "You're crazy!" But she insisted that it was so, and they kept saying,
"It must be his angel." 16 Yet Peter continued to knock. When they finally opened
the gate and saw him, they were bewildered. 17 He motioned to them to be quiet
and explained [to them] how the Lord had brought him out of prison. Then he
said, "Report this to James and the brothers." Then he departed and went off to
another place. 18 When it was day, no little confusion ensued among the soldiers
over what had become of Peter. 19 Herod, after instituting a search for him and
not finding him, had the sentries tried and ordered their execution. Then he
went down from Judea to Caesarea and spent some time there. 20 Now Herod was
infuriated with the people of Tyre and Sidon, but they came to him in a body,
having won over Blastus, the royal chamberlain, and sued for peace, because
their country was usually supplied with food from the king's territory. 21 On an
appointed day, when Herod arrayed in his royal robes took his seat on the rostrum
and publicly addressed them, 22 the assembled crowd shouted back, "This is the

voice of a god, not of a human being!" [23]At once the angel of the Lord struck him down, because he did not ascribe the honor to God. Eaten with worms, he breathed his last.

WT: [1][omits "King" and adds after "church":] in Judea. [3]that his attack on the believers pleased. [6]Outside the door there were also soldiers. [7]Suddenly an angel stood by him . . . and a light shone. He nudged Peter. [9]He took hold of him and went before him, leading him out, and he did not realize . . . [omits "with the angel's help"]. [10][omits "leading to the city"] . . . They went out and went down the seven steps, and immediately the angel left him. [11][omits "Peter" and "people"]. [12][omits "when he realized this"]. [13][omits "at the door of the gateway" and "to answer it"]. [14][omits "Peter's" and "the gate"]. [16][omits "Peter"]. [17]and entered and explained . . . [omits "the Lord"]. [19][omits "and ordered their execution" and "spent some time there"]. [20]came to the king in a body from both towns . . . from his territory. [22]when he was reconciled to them, the assembled crowd. [23]an angel struck him . . . Having descended from the rostrum, he was eaten.

COMMENT

Luke's story of the Church under Stress now continues in a different vein, as he shows that persecution came not only from religious authorities in Jerusalem or archpersecutors like Saul, but even from the ruling political authority, King Herod. The episode is actually double. The first tells about the persecution of James and Peter, and the second about the fate of King Herod. In the first, the king arrests and mistreats members of the church and even has James put to the sword. When he sees that that has pleased the Jewish element of his people, he moves against Peter, the spokesman of the new group. He imprisons him, intending to bring him before the people in due time. Peter, however, is freed miraculously from prison, visits Christians in the house of the mother of John Mark, and eventually leaves Jerusalem for an unspecified place. In the second part, King Herod goes down to Caesarea and, after being reconciled with the townspeople of Tyre and Sidon, is struck with a deadly disease and dies, ostensibly as a punishment for his opposition to God's new people.

The episode is basically a narrative, and part of the first section is another miracle story, which recounts the angelic deliverance of Peter from prison. The episode is, as Marshall has noted (*Acts,* 206), "at first sight . . . unnecessary to the developing theme of the expansion of the church; had it been omitted, we should not have noticed the loss." It may have been merely part of the tradition about Peter that Luke inherited from his Palestinian source; it may be intended to tell how Peter, having to leave Jerusalem, turns over direction of the church there to James, the "brother of the Lord" (Gal 1:19). The episode recounts the persecution of two of the Twelve: of James, son of Zebedee and brother of the apostle John (3:1–11; 4:13–19; 8:14), and of Peter. Whereas James is put to death, Peter is delivered by heavenly assistance from Herod's clutches. This is important for Luke's story because Peter must be saved for his role in chap. 15 at the "Council." The episode also explains the transition from Peter's importance in the Jerusalem community to that of James, who eventually takes over from him as the chief authority in that community.

Where Luke got these stories is hard to say, apart from a generic derivation from a Palestinian source. Certainly, it is an exaggeration to say with Ramsay that "Luke had listened to" Rhoda, the slave girl mentioned in the episode (*Bearing*, 212).

What is remarkable is that no effort is made by the early church to reconstitute the Twelve on the death of the apostle James, as was done after the death of Judas Iscariot. The role of the Twelve has come to an end in Acts, but the "apostles" (who in the Lucan understanding are the same as the Twelve [see Luke 6:13]) will continue to be influential until 16:4. After that they too will disappear; nor is there in the history of the church any continuation of the titles "apostle" or "the Twelve." Bishops are said to be the successors of the apostles, but they do not bear either of those early titles. Luke's failure to recount a reconstitution of the Twelve at this point merely reflects the historical disappearance of that group.

One should note the parallelism between vv 20–23 in this passage and Ezek 28:17–20. In Ezekiel the nations oppose Israel, especially Tyre, and in the NT it is the Herods who oppose Christianity, the climax of which comes in the murder of James by Herod Agrippa I, who had relations with Tyre and Sidon. See further M. R. Strom, "An Old Testament Background."

The actions of Herod Agrippa stand in contrast to the prayer of the early Christian community on Peter's behalf. In answer to that prayer, God sends his angel to deliver Peter from Herod's clutches and to make known to the king the evil in his mistreatment of the apostles. When in his frustration over Peter's escape, Herod leaves Jerusalem and returns to his palace in Caesarea, he goes to his own fate. Basking in his royal glory and being hailed by adulant admirers, he is struck down and suffers the horrible death of the classic persecutor. So heaven protects its own, especially in response to the fervent prayer of the church on Peter's behalf (12:5). For Luke the episode is important, not only because it reveals the power of Christian faith and prayer, but also the fidelity of God who stands by his chosen agents.

NOTES

12:1. *About the same time.* Lit., "at that critical moment," i.e., about the time of the famine in Judea (11:28).

King Herod. This is Herod Agrippa I, the son of Aristobulus IV and Bernice I, the brother of Herodias (see Mark 6:15–28), and grandson of Herod the Great and Mariamne I. He was born in 10 B.C. and reigned from A.D. 37 until his death in 44. He was a friend of the emperor Gaius Caligula, who assigned him in 37 to rule over the territory of Philip the tetrarch in northern Transjordan and accorded him the title *rex*, "King." When Herod Antipas was exiled in A.D. 39, his territory (Galilee and Perea) was added to the domain of Herod Agrippa I. In 41 his territory was expanded to include all of Judea. As a descendant of Herod the Great, he was Idumean-Jewish, but sided with the Pharisees. See Josephus, *Ant.* 19.6.1–4 §§292–316 for an account of his reign.

arrested some members of the church in order to mistreat them. Lit., "laid hands upon some from the church." We are not told why Herod takes such action against Christians in Judea. As described by Luke, Herod's actions are marked by caprice. They serve as a foil to the miraculous deliverance of the early community, especially of another of the Twelve, viz., Peter in the rest of this episode.

2. *He had James, the brother of John, put to the sword.* This is James, son of Zebedee, one of the Twelve (see NOTE on 1:13). He is often called James the Great to distinguish him from James the Less (Mark 15:40) and from James, son of Alphaeus (Acts 1:13). He is not to be confused with "James, the brother of the Lord" (Gal 1:19). The killing of James is recounted merely as the buildup to the angelic release of Peter. No reason is given for the killing of James.

3. *when he saw that that pleased the Jews, he proceeded to arrest Peter too.* MS D reads *hē epicheirēsis autou epi tous pistous,* "his attack on the believers (pleased the Jews)." Christians are called *hoi pistoi,* as in 10:45. More common is the participial designation *hoi pisteuontes,* "those believing" (2:44; 4:32; 10:43; 11:21; 18:27; 19:18).

That was during [*the*] *Feast of Unleavened Bread.* Lit., "they were the days of Unleavened Bread." In Luke 22:1 the evangelist speaks of "the Feast of Unleavened Bread, called the Passover." Actually they were two feasts. Passover was celebrated on the 14 Nisan (the first month of the Babylonian/Jewish calendar), when the Passover lamb was sacrificed and eaten. In the late hours of 13 Nisan everything leavened had to be removed from the house before the slaying of the lamb (Deut 16:4). Unleavened bread continued to be eaten for seven days after Passover (Exod 12:17–20; 23:15; 34:18); this seven-day period was actually "the Feast of Unleavened Bread." In time, however, "Passover" became the name for all eight days (Deut 16:1–4; Ezek 45:21–25; Josephus, *Ant.* 6.9.3 §423; 20.5.3 §106). The two feasts are mentioned together in 2 Chr 35:17. Although Josephus still distinguished the two feasts (*Ant.* 3.10.5 §249), he sometimes referred to the whole period as the Feast of Unleavened Bread (*J.W.* 2.14.3 §280; *Ant.* 17.9.3 §213), as does Luke in the Gospel (22:1, 7) and here (in vv 3–4). Cf. Acts 20:6.

4. *He had him seized and put in prison with four squads of four soldiers to guard him.* Recall 4:3, where Peter was imprisoned with John by Jerusalem religious authorities. On the four squads, see Philo, *In Flaccum* 13 §111; also Vegetius, *De re militari* 3.8.

Herod intended to bring him before the people after Passover. See NOTE on v 3. What Herod intended by bringing Peter before "the people" is not explained. Probably a public trial of some sort is meant, at which crowds might be present, as was the case with Jesus (Luke 23:1–5). This action stands in contrast to his summary execution of James by "the sword" in v 2.

5. *Peter was kept in prison, while the church prayed fervently to God on his behalf.* Luke is concerned to record the proper reaction of the Christian church in Jerusalem to Peter's imprisonment: they fervently beseech God for intervention on Peter's behalf. Such petitionary prayer suits a common Lucan theme (see *Luke,* 244–47).

6. *During the very night before Herod was going to bring him forth, Peter was sleeping between two soldiers, secured by double chains. Outside the door sentries were also guarding the prison.* Compare 5:23. Seneca (*Ep.* 5.7) also knows of this mode of chaining a prisoner to soldiers; cf. Josephus, *Ant.* 18.6.7 §196.

7. *Suddenly the angel of the Lord stood by him.* See NOTE on 5:19. MS D supplies the name, "by Peter." In v 17 Peter ascribes his deliverance to "the Lord," not to an angel.

the cell glowed with light. Recall Luke 2:9.

He tapped Peter on the side and woke him up, saying, "Hurry, get up!" and the chains dropped from his wrists. Thus, the angel miraculously delivers Peter. For the dropping of the chains, compare Euripides, *Bacchae* 447–48; for the rousing of Peter, compare Homer, *Iliad* 24.88. Cf. P. Hofrichter, "Parallelen."

8. *Then the angel said to him, "Fasten your belt and put on your sandals." This he did, and he said to him again, "Put on your cloak and follow me."* 9. *He went out following the angel, not realizing what was really happening with the angel's help; he thought he was seeing a vision.* I.e., in a dream of the night. So runs Luke's dramatic presentation of the angelic deliverance of Peter from prison.

10. *Having passed the first sentinel and then the second, they came to the iron gate leading to the city, which opened for them of itself.* Compare Ovid, *Metamorphoses* 3.699–700: "of their own accord the doors opened wide."

They went out and moved along a narrow alley, and suddenly the angel left him. Compare 5:19. MS D reads at the beginning of the verse *katebēsan tous z' bathmous,* "they went down the seven steps."

11. *Peter then came to himself and said.* Lit., "becoming to himself," a way of saying, "coming to his senses," an expression found in Sophocles, *Philoctetes* 950; Xenophon, *Anabasis* 1.5.17; Polybius, *History* 1.49.8.

"Now I know for sure that [the] Lord has sent his angel and rescued me from Herod's clutches. For the phraseology, see Dan 3:95; 6:23 (Theodotion); LXX of Exod 18:4. Peter realizes that heaven has delivered him. As earlier, it shows how the divine salvific plan is working itself out, in this case on behalf of the leader of Jerusalem Christians.

from all that the Jewish people had been expecting." Lit., "and from all the expectation of the people of the Jews." Luke does not even hint at what that expectation might be. See v 4 above.

12. *When he realized this, he went to the house of Mary, the mother of John, who is called Mark.* Nothing more is known of Mary. Her son, John Mark, will reappear in 12:25; 13:5, 13; 15:37, 39. He is usually identified with Mark mentioned in Phlm 24; Col 4:10 (the cousin of Barnabas); 2 Tim 4:11; 1 Pet 5:13, and in the ecclesiastical tradition with Mark the evangelist (*SQE,* 531–48). See S. J. Case, "John Mark," *ExpTim* 26 (1914–15): 372–76; B. T. Holmes, "Luke's Description of John Mark," *JBL* 54 (1935): 63–72. See *HPG,* 327–30, for the traditional location of this house.

where many people were gathered in prayer. Compare 1:14. The implication is that these people are Christians, again depicted at prayer, probably on Peter's behalf (v 5), according to the common Lucan motif.

13. *When he knocked at the door of the gateway, a maid named Rhoda came to answer it.* The *pylōn*, "gateway," separated the street from the inner courtyard.

14. *She recognized Peter's voice.* I.e., without even having seen him.

and was so overjoyed that she did not stop to open the gate but ran back and reported that Peter was standing at the gate. This narrative detail heightens the effect of the miraculous deliverance of Peter.

15. *They said to her, "You're crazy!" But she insisted that it was so, and they kept saying, "It must be his angel."* Many of those present are incredulous and react by invoking a spirit to explain what Rhoda has heard. By "his angel" is meant Peter's guardian angel. The expression preserves the ancient popular belief in guardian angels, considered as the double of the person guarded (cf. Ps 91:11; Matt 18:10; Heb 1:14; *EDNT*, 1.14; Str-B, 2.707–8). Compare *Herm. Vis.* 5.7. See J. H. Moulton, "'It Is His Angel,'" *JTS* 3 (1901–2): 514–27.

16. *Yet Peter continued to knock. When they finally opened the gate and saw him, they were bewildered.* They did not understand how he might have been released from prison.

17. *He motioned to them to be quiet and explained* [*to them*] *how the Lord had brought him out of prison.* Cf. 13:16; 19:33; 21:40. In v 7 it was "the angel of the Lord."

Then he said, "Report this to James and the brothers." So Peter acknowledges the leadership of James, who will function as the head of the church in Jerusalem. He is James, "the brother of the Lord" (Gal 1:19; cf. Gal 2:9,12). He was not one of the Twelve but will reappear in 15:13; 21:18. Josephus knows of him as "James, the brother of Jesus, who was called the Christ" (*Ant.* 20.9.1 §200). He is never given the title *episkopos* in the NT, but Eusebius will later regard him as the first bishop of Jerusalem (*HE* 2.23.1): ". . . to whom the throne of the bishopric in Jerusalem had been allotted by the apostles." James acquired such a status in the Jerusalem church because of his kinship to Jesus. See G. Kittel, "Die Stellung des Jakobus zum Judentum und Heidenchristentum," *ZNW* 30 (1931): 145–57; W. K. Prentice, "James the Brother of the Lord," *Studies in Roman Economic and Social History in Honor of Allan Chester Johnson* (Princeton: Princeton University Press, 1951), 144–51; E. Joyce, "James, the Just," *TBT* 1 (1963): 256–64; R. Bauckham, "James and the Jerusalem Church," *The Book of Acts in Its Palestinian Setting* (BAFCS 4), 415–80.

Again Luke refers to other Christians as "brothers"; see NOTE on 1:15. From this it is clear that not all the Christians in Jerusalem were present.

he departed and went off to another place. I.e., he left Jerusalem for security, perhaps to a hiding place in some other city of the Roman Empire. What is meant by "another place" has been the subject of much speculation. It is thought to be a Lucan way of saying that Peter made his way to Rome, which he does not want to mention, because it will be the hero of the second part of Acts who will bring testimony to Rome. It has often been so interpreted (e.g. Eusebius, *HE* 2.14.5). There is no guarantee that that traditional interpretation is correct. Actually Peter seems to have become a traveling apostle (see 1 Cor 9:5; Gal 2:11) who reappears in Jerusalem in chap. 15 for the "Council." Where he has been in the interval is anybody's guess. For Foakes-Jackson, Peter would have gone to Mesopotamia (*Peter,* 117), for Osborne, to the eastern diaspora centered in Edessa ("Where").

See A. Fantoli and M. Ambrosi, "Una ipotesi circa il primo viaggio di s. Pietro a Roma," *ANL cl. di sc. mor., stor. e filol., Rendiconti* 8/22 (1967): 3–15; C. P. Thiede, "Babylon, der andere Ort: Anmerkungen zu 1 Petr 5,13 und Apg 12,17," *Bib* 67 (1986): 532–38; C. F. Nesbitt, "What *Did* Become of Peter?" *JBR* 27 (1959): 10–16; D. F. Robinson, "Where and When Did Peter Die?" *JBL* 64 (1945): 255–67; W. M. Smaltz, "Did Peter Die in Jerusalem?" *JBL* 71 (1952): 211–16; R. E. Osborne, "Where Did Peter Go?" *CJT* 14 (1968): 274–77; J. Wenham, "Did Peter Go to Rome in A.D. 42?" *TynBull* 23 (1972): 94–102; F. J. Foakes-Jackson, *Peter: Prince of Apostles: A Study in the History and Tradition of Christianity* (New York: Doran, 1927).

18. *When it was day, no little confusion ensued among the soldiers over what had become of Peter.* Compare 5:21–24.

19. *Herod, after instituting a search for him and not finding him, had the sentries tried and ordered their execution.* Lit., "ordered them to be led off." Cf. Luke 23:26, which uses the same verb *apagein,* "lead off, away," i.e., to execution. MS D reads *apoktanthēnai,* "to be put to death." The implication is that the soldiers set to guard the prison have proved to be irresponsible.

he went down from Judea to Caesarea and spent some time there. I.e., he went down from the high city of Jerusalem in Judea; see NOTE on 8:5. Herod goes to the town where Herod the Great had built a sumptuous palace. Josephus (*Ant.* 19.8.2 §343) also tells of Herod Agrippa coming to Caesarea, where he conducted spectacles and games in honor of the Roman emperor. Luke's transitional statement thus supplies a chronological peg for his story about the death of James.

20. *Herod was infuriated with the people of Tyre and Sidon.* Lit., "he was furiously angry with the Tyrians and Sidonians." These were inhabitants of the two most important towns in Phoenicia (see NOTES on 11:19; 21:3). This relationship of Herod and the Phoenicians is nowhere else reported. Perhaps Herod Agrippa was waging some sort of economic war against Phoenicia, and Phoenicians had come to Blastus begging his intervention on their behalf, as they confronted the king.

they came to him in a body, having won over Blastus, the royal chamberlain, and sued for peace. Nothing more is known of this official at the court of Herod Agrippa.

because their country was usually supplied with food from the king's territory. For other ancient trade between Judah and Tyre and Sidon, see 1 Kgs 5:11, 23; Ezek 27:17.

21. *On an appointed day, when Herod arrayed in his royal robes took his seat on the rostrum and publicly addressed them.* Herod Agrippa was attending a spectacle (the *Vicennalia*) in honor of Caesar. Josephus (*Ant.* 19.8.2 §344) tells how on the second day of the spectacle Herod, clad in a garment wondrously woven

of silver, entered the theatre at dawn, and his garment was so radiant in the early sunlight that it instilled fear and awe in all who gazed at him.

22. *the assembled crowd shouted back.* MS D adds: *katallagentos de autou tois Tyriois,* "when he was reconciled to the Tyrians." The shout was a form of royal acclamation. Compare Dio Cassius, *History* 62.5.

"This is the voice of a god, not of a human being!" Josephus (*Ant.* 19.8.2 §345) records: "Immediately the flatterers raised their voices from different directions . . . addressing him as a god, 'May you be well-disposed toward us,' adding, 'if we have up to now feared you as a human being, we acknowledge henceforth that you are more than mortal in your being.'" Cf. Ezek 28:2 (LXX). See M. R. Strom, "An Old Testament Background to Acts 12.20–23," *NTS* 32 (1986): 289–92.

23. *At once the angel of the Lord struck him down, because he did not ascribe the honor to God.* The "angel of the Lord" who delivered Peter from Herod Agrippa's prison now strikes the king in retaliation for what he had done and because he failed to reckon with God. In the Lucan context this would include his persecution of the early church. Josephus's version runs thus: "The king did not reprove them; nor did he reject their flattery as impious. A little later he looked up and saw an owl perched on a rope above his head; immediately he recognized it as a messenger of woe, just as it had once been a harbinger of weal. He then suffered a heart attack and was caught by a pain in his stomach that was intense in its onset, and he sensed it all over" (*Ant.* 19.8.2 §346). Eventually, after five days of intense suffering Herod Agrippa died in his seventh regnal year (A.D. 44), three years after the accession of Claudius (*Ant.* 19.8.2 §343; cf. *J.W.* 2.11.6 §219).

Eaten with worms, he breathed his last. So Luke describes the demise of Herod Agrippa I, using a genre well known in Greek literature. Compare 2 Macc 9:5–28 (death of Antiochus IV Epiphanes); Josephus, *Ant.* 17.6.5 §§168–79 (death of Herod the Great); Herodotus, *History* 4.205 (death of Pheretime); Pausanias, *Descriptio Graeciae* 9.7.2 (death of Cassander). The gruesome details are supposed to enhance the account of the death deserved by those who despise God (or the gods).

BIBLIOGRAPHY (12:1–23)

Black, C. C., "The Presentation of John Mark in the Acts of the Apostles," *PRS* 20 (1993): 235–54.

Blinzler, J., "Rechtsgeschichtliches zur Hinrichtung des Zebedäiden Jakobus (Apg xii, 2)," *NovT* 5 (1962): 191–206.

Böhlig, A., "Zum Martyrium des Jakobus," *NovT* 5 (1962): 207–13.

Cullmann, O., "Courants multiples dans la communauté primitive: A propos du martyre de Jacques fils de Zébédée," *RSR* 60 (1972): 55–68.

Dupont, J., "Pierre délivré de prison (Ac 12,1–11)," *AsSeign* 1/84 (1967): 14–26; repr. *Nouvelles études,* 329–42.

———, "La mission de Paul 'à Jérusalem' (Actes xii 25)," *NovT* 1 (1956): 275–303; repr. *Études*, 217–41.

Eulenstein, R., "Die wundersame Befreiung des Petrus aus Todesgefahr, Acta 12,1–23," *WD* 12 (1973): 43–69.

Garrett, S. R., "Exodus from Bondage: Luke 9:31 and Acts 12:1–24," *CBQ* 52 (1990): 656–80.

Hengel, M., "Jakobus der Herrenbruder—der erste 'Papst'?," *Glaube und Eschatologie: Festschrift für Werner Georg Kümmel* . . . (ed. E. Grässer and O. Merk; Tübingen: Mohr [Siebeck], 1985), 71–104.

Hofrichter, P., "Parallelen zum 24. Gesang der Ilias in den Engelerscheinungen des lukanischen Doppelwerkes," *PzB* 2 (1993): 60–76.

Holmes, B. T., "Luke's Description of John Mark," *JBL* 54 (1935): 63–72.

Lake, K., "The Death of Herod Agrippa I," *Beginnings*, 5.446–52.

Maciel del Río, C., "Pedro dormía en medio de dos soldados (Análisis narrativo estilístico de Act 12,1–23)," *EfMex* 13 (1995): 27–46.

Priero, G., "Circa la morte d'Erode Agrippa I," *PC* 18 (1939): 70–72, 256–60.

Radl, W., "Befreiung aus dem Gefängnis: Die Darstellung eines biblischen Grundthemas in Apg 12," *BZ* 27 (1983): 81–96.

Ramsay, W. M., *The Bearing of Recent Discoveries on the Trustworthiness of the New Testament* (London: Hodder and Stoughton, 1915), 209–21.

Rius-Camps, J., "Qüestions sobre la doble obra lucana: II. Qui és Joan, l'anomenat 'Marc'?" *RCT* 5 (1980): 297–329.

Strobel, A., "Passa-Symbolik und Passa-Wunder in Act. xii.3ff.," *NTS* 4 (1957–58): 210–15.

Veldhuizen, A. van, *Markus: De Neef van Barnabas* (Kampen: Kok, 1933).

Wall, R. W., "Successors to 'the Twelve' according to Acts 12:1–17," *CBQ* 53 (1991): 628–43.

Zuckschwerdt, E., "Das Naziräat des Herrenbruders Jakobus nach Hegesipp (Euseb. h. e. ii 23, 5–6)," *ZNW* 68 (1977): 276–87.

4. Summary and Lucan Suture (12:24–25)

[24] But the word of God continued to spread and increase. [25] Barnabas and Saul returned, when their ministry to Jerusalem was complete, bringing with them John, who was called Mark.

WT: [25] [omits "to Jerusalem"].

COMMENT

Luke now adds a minor summary to his account (Introduction §92b), one that tells about the increase or growth of the Word of God. To it he adds a verse that is unrelated to the summary. That corresponds to 11:30 and tells of the aftermath of the visit of Barnabas and Saul to Jerusalem with the collection that had been taken up by Christians of Antioch. It is another problematic verse that may refer to Saul's visits to Jerusalem after his conversion (see Introduction §156). In this case it is even more of a problem, because of the textual variants involved.

Bultmann (*Exegetica* [Tübingen: Mohr (Siebeck), 1967], 421–22) assigned v 25 to the Antiochene source. Whatever the source of the information, it is a Lucan suture about the so-called Famine Visit and is related to 11:30.

NOTES

24. *the word of God continued to spread and increase.* See 6:7 and 19:20, where a similar statement is made. Cf. Luke 8:4–15. Thus, Luke stresses the dynamism of the Word, the apostolic testimony about Jesus, which like a seed "grows." MS B reads rather *Kyriou*, "(the word of) the Lord," but MSS P^{74}, ℵ, A, D, E, Ψ, 33, 1739, and the *Koinē* text-tradition read *Theou*, "God."

25. *Barnabas and Saul returned.* Their return was from Jerusalem to Antioch, whence they started out in 11:30. MS 614 and a few other minor MSS read *hos epeklēthē Paulos*, "who was surnamed Paul," a reading influenced by 13:9.

when their ministry to Jerusalem was complete. After the verb *hypestrepsan*, "returned," the Alexandrian Greek text of Acts (MSS ℵ, B, H, L, P) and the *Koinē* text-tradition have *eis Ierousalēm*, which has been understood at times as the destination of the movements of Barnabas and Saul, "returned to Jerusalem." That creates a problem, because 11:30 implies that Barnabas and Saul have gone to Jerusalem, so that they could not now be returning "*to* Jerusalem." Consequently, copyists of various MSS (P^{74}, A, 33, 945, 1739) changed the prep. to *ex*, "from," and those of other MSS (D, E, Ψ, 36, 323, 453, 614) changed it to *apo*, "from." Both of these would make good sense ("returned from Jerusalem"), but they are for that reason suspect. Some MSS (E, 104, 323, 945, 1175, 1739), in addition to the change to "from," also add "to Antioch": "returned from Jerusalem to Antioch." Commentators such as Bruce (*Acts*, 257), Conzelmann (*Acts*, 97), Polhill (*Acts*, 285–86), Roloff (*Apg.*, 191) prefer to read *ex*.

The better solution, however, is to take the prep. phrase *eis Ierousalēm* not with the verb *hypestrepsan*, but with the following ptc. *plērōsantes* and to understand *eis* as the equivalent of *en* (often so used in Lucan Greek [Luke 4:23; 14:8, 10; Acts 2:5; 8:40]): "having completed their ministry in Jerusalem." See Dupont, "La mission de Paul 'à Jérusalem' (Actes xii, 25)," *NovT* 1 (1956): 275–303; repr. *Études*, 217–41; cf. P. Benoit, "La deuxième visite," 786; repr. 293; P. Parker, "Three Variant Readings in Luke-Acts," *JBL* 83 (1964): 165–70, esp. 168–70. Such a solution eliminates the interpretation of the aor. ptc. *plerōsantes* as "futuristic" or expressing purpose, as Howard and Robertson would have it. For a history of the various proposals of readings and interpretations, see B. M. Metzger, *TCGNT*, 350–52.

bringing with them John, who was called Mark. See NOTE on 12:12. Jerusalem was the site of his home. Mark is brought along to Antioch so that he can accompany Barnabas and Saul at the outset of Mission I.

BIBLIOGRAPHY (12:24–25)

Beare, F. W., "Note on Paul's First Two Visits to Jerusalem," *JBL* 63 (1944): 407–9.

Black, M., "Notes on the Longer and the Shorter Text of Acts," *On Language, Culture, and Religion: In Honor of Eugene A. Nida* (ed. M. Black and W. A. Smalley; The Hague/Paris: Mouton, 1974), 119–31, esp. 123–24.

Chambers, C. D., "On a Use of the Aorist Participle in Some Hellenistic Writers (Acts 12.25; 25.13)," *JTS* 24 (1922–23): 183–87.

Dockx, S., "Chronologie de la vie de Saint Paul, depuis sa conversion jusqu'à son séjour à Rome," *NovT* 13 (1971): 261–304.

Howard, W. F., "On the Futuristic Use of the Aorist Participle in Hellenistic," *JTS* 24 (1922–23): 403–6.

Kodell, J., "'The Word of God Grew': The Ecclesial Tendency of *Logos* in Acts 1,7 [read 6,7]; 12,24; 19,20," *Bib* 55 (1974): 505–19.

Nairne, A., "Two Questions of Text and Translation," *JTS* 11 (1909–10): 560–62.

Robertson, A. T., "The Aorist Participle for Purpose in the *Koinē*," *JTS* 25 (1923–24): 286–89.

Simcox, G. A., "A Point in Pauline Chronology," *JTS* 2 (1900–1901): 586–90.

D. Paul's First Missionary Journey to Gentiles in Asia Minor (13:1–14:28)

1. Mission of Barnabas and Saul (13:1–3)

13 [1]In the church at Antioch there were prophets and teachers: Barnabas, Simeon called Niger, Lucius of Cyrene, Manaen, who had been raised with Herod
the tetrarch, and Saul. [2]Once while they were holding the Lord's service and
fasting, the Holy Spirit spoke to them, "Set apart for me Barnabas and Saul, for
the work to which I have called them." [3]Then, having completed their fasting
and prayer, they laid hands upon them and sent them off.

WT: [1]among whom (were) Barnabas . . . , and Paul. [2][omits "and fasting" and "holy"] Paul.

COMMENT

Luke begins the story of the first missionary journey of Saul, who becomes the hero of the second part of Acts. With Saul's mission the testimony that was to be carried to "the end of the earth" (1:8) now moves into a new stage. The Lucan geographical perspective is no longer limited to Palestine or Judea, even though Jerusalem remains the mother church and will at times reappear as such. Saul's activity is to carry the Word of God to Gentiles. Luke's story first focuses on the problematic Mission I (13:4–14:28) of Saul with Barnabas prior to the "Council," which is to take place in Jerusalem (A.D. 49); see Introduction §155.

The first episode is preparatory, as Luke describes how Barnabas and Saul are set apart for this missionary work by the church in Antioch at the explicit behest of the Spirit. The mission takes place roughly from A.D. 46 to 49. Neither Barnabas nor Saul makes a decision to undertake this mission on his own. They are the chosen instruments of the Spirit, which continues to be the dynamo inaugurating the further spread of the Word of God. Emphasis is thus put on the role of the Spirit, which is behind the *mission* of Barnabas and Saul: they are "sent forth by the Holy Spirit" (13:4). Now we see how the call of Saul by the risen Christ (9:15) is being worked out in the concrete. The Lucan preparatory setting is one of prayer, fasting, worship, and laying on of hands.

This is the first of three blocks of episodes that form accounts of Saul's missionary journeys. The first one sets the pattern for all three. It is important to realize, however, that neither the apostle nor Luke has so numbered them. The numbering stems from modern commentators on Acts, who divide up the episodes into three blocks. Mission I runs from Acts 13:4–14:28.

The route that Barnabas and Saul will take leads first to Seleucia, the port of Antioch, then to Salamis on the eastern coast of Cyprus, to Paphos on its western coast, then to Perga in Pamphylia (in southern central Asia Minor), to Antioch in Pisidia, Iconium, Lystra, Derbe; then to Lystra, Iconium, Antioch, Perga, Attalia, and back to Antioch in Syria. The places through which Paul passes on Mission I raise a question about the lack of anything to correspond to them in Paul's letters. This raises in turn the question of the historicity of Mission I. More than the other two, Mission I is the one that some commentators claim to be a Lucan construct, with no basis in the ministry of the historical Paul. That mode of interpreting Mission I, however, is far from certain. There are good reasons to think that Luke merely spells out in detail a missionary journey, to which Paul himself makes only brief reference in Gal 1:21–23 and Phil 4:15. See Introduction §155 for a discussion of the problems involved.

This missionary journey is important for Luke as a preparation for what will be recounted in Acts 15, the "Council" in Jerusalem. The first journey begins and ends in Antioch, which functions in the Lucan story as the matrix of the Christian Gentile mission.

So far in the Lucan story Barnabas has been mentioned ahead of Saul; he was the one sent from the Jerusalem church to Antioch and later sought out Saul to help him in his evangelical work. Soon the order of names will change, and priority will be given to Saul in his relation to the communities to be founded.

The question of sources used by Luke in this account of Mission I is a matter of debate. Bultmann assigned vv 3–4, 13–14, 43–44, 48–49, and 52(?) to the Itinerary source. I prefer to assign vv 1–3 in this episode to the Pauline source.

The inauguration of Saul's missionary work is Spirit guided. Saul's preaching activity has been mentioned in 9:20–22, 29; 11:26, but now the story of his extensive missionary work is about to begin formally. Luke describes how the Spirit is behind that work, as Antiochene Christians are instructed in a liturgical setting to single out and ordain Barnabas and Saul for such a mission: for the work of proclamation, healing, and founding ecclesial communities in different towns. Thus the Spirit is the dynamo at the beginning of Pauline Mission I.

NOTES

13:1. *In the church at Antioch there were prophets and teachers.* MSS E, Ψ, and the *Koinē* text-tradition add *tines,* "some." About "prophets," who came from Jerusalem, we have already heard in 11:27 (see NOTE there). Now we learn also about *didaskaloi,* "teachers," in the church of Antioch, possibly another group entrusted with passing on "the teaching of the apostles" (2:42). Holtzmann and Harnack once tried to distinguish the first three of those named as prophets and the last two as teachers, and Dockx believed they were all teachers, but few other commentators have followed them. The five to be named undoubtedly constitute leaders in the Antiochene church. Such leaders as "teachers" and "prophets" are mentioned in 1 Cor 12:28–29 and Eph 4:11, along with other functionaries. Whereas the church leaders at Antioch are prophets and teachers, no mention is made of apostles or elders, as in the church at Jerusalem. Perhaps one could say with Filson that a "teacher" is in a biblical sense one called by God to aid others to understand the meaning of life in a God-centered world and guide them in finding and fulfilling the divine will.

Barnabas. Already known from 4:36; 9:27; 11:22, 30; 12:25 (see NOTES there). The list begins with a strange *ho te* before the name of Barnabas, for which MS D and the Vg read rather *en hois,* "among whom (were)." See Benoit, *Bib* 40 (1959): 782 n. 3.

Simeon called Niger. I.e., the Black One, a simple Greek transcription of Latin *niger.* The name *Symeōn* is a grecized form of Hebrew *Šimĕʿôn,* a name commonly used among Jews of first-century Palestine. The Hebrew name was an abridged form of *Šĕmaʿʾēl,* "God has heard," or of *Šĕmaʿyāh,* "Yahweh has heard," shortened to *Šimĕʿôn,* for which the more common Greek equivalent was *Simōn,* "Simon." See NOTE on 15:14.

Lucius of Cyrene. He is otherwise unknown, and hardly the same as the *Loukios* of Rom 16:21, or Luke himself *(Loukas),* with whom he has been identified at times, ever since Origen (e.g., R. C. Ford). The evangelist may use the def. art. incorrectly here before the proper adj.; see BDF §268.1. On Cyrene, see NOTE on 2:10.

Manaen, who had been raised with Herod the tetrarch. Lit., "one brought up with," or "friend from youth" of Herod. This is Herod Antipas, son of Herod the Great and Malthace, the tetrarch of Galilee during the ministry of Jesus (see Luke 3:1, 19; 8:3; 9:7, 9; 13:31; 23:7–15), and not to be confused with Herod the king or Herod Agrippa I (12:1). Herod Antipas was an adult when he became tetrarch in 4 B.C.; he reigned for 42 years until his banishment in A.D. 39. Though Manaen was such a confidant of young Herod Antipas, he is now a Christian and one of the prophets or teachers of Antioch. *Manaēn* is a Greek form of Hebrew *Menaḥēm*, "Menahem" (2 Kgs 15:14 [LXX]), meaning "Comforter."

Saul. See NOTE on 7:58. Because Barnabas and Saul are both mentioned, this is not sufficient reason to think that their presence now in Antioch is the same as the occasion of which Paul speaks in Gal 2:11, *pace* Hemer (*Book of Acts*, 183). That occasion is quite different, for there is no indication here that Cephas was on hand.

2. *Once while they were holding the Lord's service and fasting.* Lit., "while they were rendering service to the Lord and were fasting." Again, *Kyrios* is used in the sense of the God of Israel, not the risen Christ. The ptc. *leitourgountōn* is a form of the verb *leitourgein*, which in the Greek world denoted "rendering public service" or "rendering service to the people" *(tō laō)*. It came to be used, especially in Christian writings, in a religious sense to denote "liturgical service." See N. Lewis, "*Leitourgia* and Related Terms," *GRBS* 3 (1960): 175–84; E. Peterson, "La *leitourgia* des prophètes et des didascales à Antioche," *RSR* 36 (1949): 577–79; A. Romeo, "Il termine *leitourgia* nella grecità biblica," *Miscellanea liturgica in honorem L. Cuniberti Mohlberg* (Bibliotheca "Ephemerides Liturgicae" 23; 2 vols.; Rome: Edizioni Liturgiche, 1949), 467–519. That this service included prayer is clear from v 3. Cf. 10:30.

The Holy Spirit spoke to them, "Set apart for me Barnabas and Saul, for the work to which I have called them." Thus, the Spirit-guided missionary journey of Barnabas and Saul is inaugurated; compare 20:28 and 1 Tim 4:14. The risen Christ has called Saul, and the Jerusalem church has sent Barnabas to Antioch. Now the Spirit takes over and inaugurates the joint missionary work of the two, and especially of Saul, who becomes "the apostle to the Gentiles" (Rom 11:13). "The work" is a reference to the mission of Saul proposed in 9:15.

3. *having completed their fasting and prayer, they laid hands upon them and sent them off.* The laying on of hands is duly accompanied by prayer and fasting as a ritual means of invoking God's blessing on the commission about to be given to Saul and Barnabas; see NOTE on 6:6. The attempt to describe the laying on of hands solely as a blessing and not an ordination (Conzelmann, *Acts*, 99; Schneider, *Apg.*, 2.115); Weiser, *Apg.*, 307–8) is meaningless. It is not a question of a transfer of power, but of a Spirit-guided commission. The Antiochene community acts in the name of the Spirit and designates two individuals for a specific task in the Christian church, to whom the grace of the Spirit is accorded. The notion of "office" is not so developed in Lucan writings as it becomes in the Pastoral Epistles, but one should not deprive the action of its proper meaning. See S. Dockx, "L'Ordination de Barnabé et de Saul d'après *Actes* 13,1–3," NRT 98 (1976): 238–50.

BIBLIOGRAPHY (13:1–3)

Bertalot, R., "Il digiuno nella chiesa primitiva," *Protestantesimo* 11 (1956): 107–10.

Best, E., "Acts xiii.1–3," *JTS* 11 (1960): 344–48.
Bishop, E.F.F., "Simon and Lucius: Where Did They Come from? A Plea for Cyprus," *ExpTim* 51 (1939–40): 148–53.
Cadbury, H. J., "Lucius of Cyrene," *Beginnings*, 5.489–95.
Fain, J., "Church-Mission Relationships: What We Can Learn from Acts 13:1–4," *Stulos Theological Journal* 2 (1994): 19–39.
Filson, F. V., "The Christian Teacher in the First Century," *JBL* 60 (1941): 317–28.
Ford, R. C., "St. Luke and Lucius of Cyrene," *ExpTim* 32 (1920–21): 219–20.
Greeven, H., "Propheten, Lehrer, Vorsteher bei Paulus: Zur Frage der 'Ämter' im Urchristentum," *ZNW* 44 (1952–53): 1–43.
Klauck, H. J., "With Paul in Paphos and Lystra: Magic and Paganism in the Acts of the Apostles," *Neotestamentica* 28 (1994): 93–108.
Kunst, P. G., "Bidden en vasten," *Arcana revelata: Een bundel Nieuw-Testamentische studiën aangeboden aan Prof. Dr. F. W. Grosheide* . . . (ed. N. J. Hommes et al.; Kampen: Kok, 1951), 53–58.
Lempriere, P. C., "Studies in Texts: Acts xiii.1–3," *Theology* 14 (1927): 94–96.
Miesner, D. R., "The Missionary Journeys Narrative: Patterns and Implications," *Perspectives on Luke-Acts* (ed. C. H. Talbert), 199–214.
Mullins, T. Y., "New Testament Commission Forms, Especially in Luke-Acts," *JBL* 95 (1976): 603–14.
Murphy-O'Connor, J., "Pauline Missions before the Jerusalem Conference," *RB* 89 (1982): 71–91.
Peterson, E., "Zu Apostelgeschichte 13:1f.," *Nuntius sodalicii neotestamentici upsaliensis* 2 (1949): 9–10.
Rius-Camps, J., "La misión hacia el paganismo avalada por el Señor Jesús y el Espíritu Santo (Hch 13–15)," *EstBíb* 52 (1994): 341–60.
Schille, G., *Anfänge der Kirche: Erwägungen zur apostolischen Frühgeschichte* (BEvT 43; Munich: Kaiser, 1966), 53–64.
Schürmann, H., ". . . und Lehrer": Die geistliche Eigenart des Lehrdienstes und sein Verhältnis zu anderen geistlichen Diensten im neutestamentlichen Zeitalter," *Dienst der Vermittlung: Festschrift zum 25jährigen Bestehen des philosophisch-theologischen Studiums im Priesterseminar Erfurt* (ErThS 37; ed. W. Ernst et al.; Leipzig: St. Benno-V., 1977), 107–47.
Sevenster, G., "De wijding van Paulus en Barnabas," *Studia Paulina in honorem Johannis de Zwaan septuagenarii* (ed. J. N. Sevenster and W. C. van Unnik; Haarlem: Erven F. Bohn, 1953), 188–201.

2. EVANGELIZATION OF CYPRUS (13:4–12)

[4]Sent forth thus by the Holy Spirit, these two went down to Seleucia and set sail
from there for Cyprus. [5]On their arrival in Salamis, they proclaimed the word of

God in the synagogues of the Jews. They also had John along as an assistant. [6]When they had traveled through the whole island, even as far as Paphos, they met a certain magician, a Jew whose name was Bar-Jesus, who posed as a prophet. [7]He was in the service of the proconsul Sergius Paulus, a man of intelligence, who had summoned Barnabas and Saul and was anxious to hear the word of God. [8]But Elymas the magician (for that is what his name means) opposed them, seeking to turn the proconsul away from the faith. [9]However, Saul, also known as Paul, filled with the Holy Spirit, stared at him and said, [10]"You shyster and thoroughgoing fraud, son of the devil, and enemy of all that is right, will you never stop making crooked the straight ways of [the] Lord? [11]Look, even now the Lord's hand is upon you! You will be blind, unable to see even the sunlight for a time!" At once a dark mist fell upon him, and he went groping about for someone to lead him by the hand. [12]When the proconsul saw what had happened, he became a believer, astonished at the teaching of the Lord.

WT: [4]by the dedicated people of God. [5][omits "of God" and adds at end:] to them. [6]traveled about through . . . a Jew called by the name Bar-Jesus [omits "who posed as a prophet"]. [8]Etoimas the magician . . . [adds at the end:] since he was gladly listening to them. [12]he was amazed and became a believer.

COMMENT

The initial episode of the first missionary journey that Saul undertakes with Barnabas recounts the evangelization of the island of Cyprus. From there, after they have gone through the island, they will pass on to Asia Minor proper. Accompanied by John Mark, the two missionaries visit first Cypriot synagogues and announce the Christian message to Jews; but their evangelization is not limited to them. The missionaries encounter two prominent men of Cyprus, Bar-Jesus or Elymas, a Cypriot magician, and the Roman proconsul, Sergius Paulus, in whose service Bar-Jesus is active. The latter tries to hinder the proconsul from being captivated by the words of Saul, who eventually subdues the magician, causing him to become blind. The punitive miracle has the effect of converting the proconsul.

Form-critically considered, the episode is again a narrative, and part of it is a miracle story, recounting another punitive miracle, as in chap. 5. The information that Luke uses in this episode comes to him from the Pauline source.

In this episode Luke mentions Saul's double name: "Saul, also known as Paul" (13:9). Commentators, following Jerome, have tried at times to suggest that Saul adopted this name from the proconsul, Sergius Paulus, the first Gentile whom the apostle brings to the Christian faith. That, however, is fanciful. It is sheer coincidence that Saul happens to bear the same Roman name as the proconsul. "Paul" is the only name that the apostle ever uses in his letters, and if it were not for the Lucan usage in Acts up to this point, we would never have known that Paul was also called Saul. From this point on in the Lucan story only "Paul" will be used, save in the episodes in which Luke recounts the apostle's experience on the road to Damascus, when the risen Christ addresses him as *Saoul* (22:7; 26:14), as he did in 9:4, or when Ananias so speaks (9:17; 22:13).

The change of name is hardly intended to be "the water-shed in the Book of *Acts* and the turning point in the ministry of St Paul," as Synge ("Studies") would have it: "Up to this point . . . you have been reading about Saul the Jew. . . . From this point onwards you are to read of Paul, who turned his face to the Gentiles." That is to make far too much out of this minor detail.

In any case, the episode describes the first part of Saul's missionary endeavors in Cyprus, where he and Barnabas have some success. As they begin this Spirit-guided mission, they preach the Word of God to Jews and Gentiles in Salamis, Paphos, and throughout the island of Cyprus. They convert even the proconsul, Sergius Paulus, despite the machinations of a Jew who posed as a prophet, Bar-Jesus or Elymas. The spread of the Word of God is not hampered by tricks of a magician; rather Saul, now called Paul, performs a punitive miracle and blinds the magician. This he does as one "filled with the holy Spirit" (13:9) so that we realize once again the power of the Spirit in fostering the spread of the Word of God. In other words, though sent off formally by the Antiochene church on this mission, Barnabas and Saul are not left to themselves. The Spirit continues to guide their work and them.

NOTES

4. *Sent forth thus by the Holy Spirit.* The Spirit is again mentioned as the one who has commissioned the missionary journey of Barnabas and Saul. Recall 13:2.

these two went down to Seleucia. Several ancient towns were called *Seleukeia;* the one meant here was a port on the Mediterranean seacoast of Syria, at the mouth of the Orontes River, about 20 km west of Antioch, and north of Mt. Casius. It was founded ca. 300 B.C. by Seleucus I Nicator and served as the port of Antioch on the Orontes, the capital of the province. It was the natural crossing point to the island of Cyprus. See Strabo, *Geography* 7.5.8; Polybius, *History* 5.58.4.

set sail from there for Cyprus. Cyprus was the island in the Mediterranean, slightly southwest of Seleucia in Syria. See NOTE on 11:19.

5. *On their arrival in Salamis.* Salamis was an important port town on the east coast of Cyprus. Under the Ptolemies it was the seat of the governor of Cyprus, but that changed to Paphos under the Romans.

they proclaimed the word of God in the synagogues of the Jews. MS D reads "the word of the Lord." The proclamation of it is consonant with the Lucan narrative motif of depicting the Christian missionaries evangelizing diaspora Jews first (W. Schrage, *TDNT,* 7.835). Recall Paul's activity in the the synagogue of Damascus (9:20); it will be repeated in Pisidian Antioch (13:14), Iconium (14:1), Philippi (16:13 [see NOTE]), Thessalonica (17:1–2), Beroea (17:10), Athens (17:17), Corinth (18:4–6), Ephesus (18:19; 19:8). As Barnabas and Saul bear witness to such Jews, the Word of God spreads to Cyprus, and the Lucan geographical perspective is again noted. Philo (*Legatio ad Gaium* 36 §282) knew of colonies of Jews who dwelt on the island of Cyprus; similarly Josephus, *Ant.* 13.10.4 §284. On synagogue, see NOTE on 6:9.

They also had John along as an assistant. This is John Mark, last mentioned in 12:25. See NOTE on 12:12. John Mark is called *hypēretēs,* "assistant." This common Greek term is often said to have meant originally an "under-rower" on an ancient ship, but that is far from clear. It seems to have denoted a "member of an organized team of oarsmen" (L.J.D. Richardson) and was extended to the sense of a general "helper" or "servant." It was often used to designate a "public servant" who dealt with legal or civil documents (B. T. Holmes). Among Greek-speaking Jews it came to mean the *ḥazzān,* a "synagogue attendant," who was active at the time of lectionary reading. See Luke 4:20. In Christian usage it further acquired another specific meaning in the phrase *hypēretēs tou logou,* "minister of the word" (Luke 1:2). That may be the nuance intended here. Cf. Ignatius, *Trall.* 2; *Pol.* 6, describing the function of deacons. See L.J.D. Richardson, "*Hypēretēs,*" *ClassQ* 37 (1943): 55–61; A. Feuillet, "'Témoins oculaires et serviteurs de la parole' (Lc i 2[b])," *NovT* 15 (1973): 241–59; R.O.P. Taylor, "The Ministry of Mark," *ExpTim* 54 (1942–43): 136–38.

6. *When they had traveled through the whole island, even as far as Paphos.* Paphos was about 175 km from Salamis. It was actually the name of two port towns on the southwest coast of Cyprus: Old Paphos had a famous sanctuary of Aphrodite. Fifteen km away, New Paphos, which also bore the name Augusta, became the seat of the Roman governor, a proconsul, at the time of Augustus. See E. Meyer, "Paphos," *DKP* 4.484–87.

they met a certain magician, a Jew whose name was Bar-Jesus, who posed as a prophet. Lit., "a Jewish false prophet." The description of Bar-Jesus borders on the fantastic: a Jew, who was a magician, a "false prophet," and in the service of the Roman proconsul. Why he was called a "false prophet" is not explained. Luke calls him *magos,* which is probably to be understood as "magician," and not a member of the ancient order of *magoi* (see Matt 2:1 and NOTE on 8:9). He bears a good Jewish name, Bar-Jesus, "son of Jesus/Joshua," but in the Syriac Pešitta this becomes *Baršuma',* "son of the Name" (probably meaning Yahweh) and used in an effort to avoid saying he was "son of Jesus."

7. *He was in the service of the proconsul Sergius Paulus, a man of intelligence.* Lit., "who was with the proconsul." Only Luke among NT writers uses the Greek proper title *anthypatos* for the Latin *proconsul,* who was the governor of a senatorial province (see also 13:8, 12; 18:12; 19:38). This historically correct title is given to Sergius Paulus and also Gallio (18:12), both of whom were proconsuls of the second grade, ex-praetors *(praetorii),* who had not yet risen to the consular rank. See *IGRR* 3.933, 947.

Sergius Paulus (or Sergius Paullus) was the proconsul of Cyprus A.D. 46–48. He may be known from a fragmentary dedicatory Greek inscription from Kithraia in northern Cyprus (*IGRR* 3.935 = *SEG* 20.302), presently housed in the Metropolitan Museum of New York, which on line 10 may preserve part of his name: *Koïntou Serg*[*iou* . . .], after mentioning Claudius Casesar Augustus in the preceding line. Unfortunately the restoration is not certain, and the restored name is contested. This possible mention of Sergius Paulus would accord well with the date given above for Paul's Mission I as A.D. 46–49, prior to the "Council" in Jerusalem (A.D. 49). Two other Greek inscriptions have been associated with this proconsul, but neither of them is certainly connected with him. They are an inscription from Soloi in northern Cyprus (*IGRR* 3.930) and a Tiber inscription from Rome (*CIL* 6.31545; *ILS* 2.5926). The latter was set up in the time of Claudius and may refer to an earlier stage in the career of Sergius Paulus before he became proconsul, but he is called in it L. Sergius Paullus. Sergius was the *nomen gentilicium* and Paulus the *cognomen* of this Roman governor. See Lake, "The Proconsulship of Sergius Paulus," *Beginnings,* 5.455–59; Hemer, *Book of Acts,* 109 and n. 17; A. Nobbs, "Cyprus," *The Book of Acts in Its Graeco-Roman Setting* (BAFCS 2), 279–89, esp. 282–87.

who had summoned Barnabas and Saul and was anxious to hear the word of God. The proconsul shows interest in what the missionaries have to say and takes the initiative of inviting them.

8. *Elymas the magician.* MS D reads the name as *Etoimas.*

(for that is what his name means). This is a Lucan explanation of the Greek name *Elymas*, but that that name means *magos*, "magician," is far from clear. No one knows what it means. Ancient versions have simply transliterated the name: thus, Vg *Elimas;* Pešitta *'Ellumas;* Bohairic *Elumas.* Some modern commentators (e.g., J. Lightfoot) have invoked Arabic *'alîm*, "wise man, magician," but that too is problematic, because its relationship is still unexplained. L. Yaure ("Elymas—Nehelamite—Pethor," *JBL* 79 [1960]: 297–314) interprets it as a form of Aramaic *ḥālômā'*, "dreamer," which is no better, *pace* Schneider, *Apg.*, 2.122, because *ḥālôm* is the Hebrew word for "dream," not Aramaic.

opposed them, seeking to turn the proconsul away from the faith. I.e., from Christianity. Luke uses *pistis* in the content sense of what Christians believe, what later theologians have called *fides quae* (see NOTE on 6:7).

9. *Saul, also known as Paul.* According to Conzelmann (*Acts,* 100), Luke uses the opportunity provided by Paul's first convert (Sergius *Paulus*) to introduce Paul into the mission under his own name (similarly Ramsay, *Paul the Traveller,* 81–88). The connection is purely literary, not historical. In fact, it is a sheer literary coincidence and mentioned even before the conversion of the proconsul.

The apostle undoubtedly bore two names, one Greco-Roman, *Paulos* (= Roman name *Paul*[*l*]*us*), the other a grecized Semitic name, *Saulos* (= Hebrew *Šā'ûl,* "[the child] asked for"). *Saulos* was Paul's *supernomen*, and *Paulos* was undoubtedly his Roman *cognomen* (G. A. Harrer). It is the one thing in Paul's letters that supports the Lucan identification of him as a Roman citizen, *pace* Lake and Cadbury, *Beginnings,* 4.145. Augustine (*De Spiritu et littera* 7.12) thought that Paul took that name out of modesty because Latin *paulus* means "little" (*ut se ostenderet parvum tamquam minimum apostolorum,* "that he might present himself as little, as the least of the apostles"). It is not a question of a change of name, either at his conversion (as many have often maintained), or at the time of his commission or ordination (as John Chrysostom thought [*Hom.* 28.13; PG 60.209]), or at the conversion of Sergius Paulus (as Jerome thought [*De viris illustribus* 5; TU 14/1.9]). It is not impossible, however, that Luke, being aware of the connotation of Greek adj. *saulos,* "loose, wanton," a term describing the gait of courtesans and effeminate males, decided to avoid the Semitic name that he had been using and preferred the Greco-Roman name in the rest of the story of Paul's evangelization (cf. Anacreon, 168; Scholiast on Aristophanes, *Vespae,* 1169). That, however, does not explain why the double name appears first here.

filled with the Holy Spirit. As were the apostles on Pentecost (2:4), or Peter before the Sanhedrin (4:8).

stared at him and said. Luke's favorite verb *atenizein* recurs; see NOTE on 1:10.

10. *"You shyster and thoroughgoing fraud.* Lit., "O one full of deceit and all villainy." Paul's words are not kind. Whereas he is said to be filled with the Spirit, he recognizes that Bar-Jesus is filled with deception and hostility. See A. Wikenhauser, "Zum Wörterbuch des Neuen Testaments," *BZ* 8 (1910): 271–73. Cf. Sir 1:30 ("full of deceit").

son of the devil. Cf. 1 John 3:10. Paul ascribes the influence on Bar-Jesus to the devil. See NOTE on 10:38.

enemy of all that is right. Lit., "enemy of all righteousness."

will you never stop making crooked the straight ways of [the] Lord? Paul sees the machinations of Bar-Jesus as perverting the divine guidance of human beings, especially the conversion of the proconsul, but in a wider sense even the Christian mission. His accusation makes use of biblical phrases; see Prov 10:9; Hos 14:10. It is not easy to say who is meant by *Kyrios*: God or the risen Christ; probably the former, as in v 11.

11. *Look, even now the Lord's hand is upon you!* Paul indulges in biblical anthropomorphism, which is intended to assert God's power in coping with this opposition. See NOTE on 11:21. God will punish such hostility.

You will be blind, unable to see even the sunlight for a time!" The second clause expresses the extent of Bar-Jesus's blindness. The important qualification is *achri kairou,* "for a time" (cf. Luke 4:13). Paul curses Bar-Jesus and, in effect, calls upon the Lord to cause the blindness. The punitive miracle wrought by Paul is reminiscent of the parallel miracle of Peter in the episode of Ananias and Sapphira (5:1–11).

At once a dark mist fell upon him, and he went groping about for someone to lead him by the hand. The curse that Paul has laid on the magician is instantaneous in its effect. One should recall Paul's own blindness in 9:8. That too was heaven sent, but for a different reason. Cf. 22:11.

12. *When the proconsul saw what had happened, he became a believer.* Sergius Paulus becomes the first convert that Paul is recorded making on Mission I. Lake and Cadbury question whether Sergius Paulus was actually converted, because

"there is no mention of his baptism" (*Beginnings,* 4.147). That is merely idle speculation and contradicts what is said in this verse. To say that it expresses "courtesy" and not "conversion" is awry.

astonished at the teaching of the Lord. This may mean that the proconsul was amazed at the teaching about the Lord implied in the words of Paul; that would make *tou Kyriou* an objective genitive. If it is rather to be taken as a subjective gen., then it would mean that the proconsul was captivated by what the Lord was teaching him through Paul by this incident. In any case, Luke insists that the reason for the conversion of Sergius Paulus is not the blinding of the magician Bar-Jesus but the "teaching of the Lord" being given by Paul and Barnabas, which caused him no little astonishment.

BIBLIOGRAPHY (13:4–12)

Blevins, J. L., "Acts 13–19: The Tale of Three Cities," *RevExp* 87 (1990): 439–50.

Burkitt, F. C., "The Interpretation of *Bar-Jesus,*" *JTS* 4 (1902–3): 127–29.

Elderen, B. van, "Some Archaeological Observations on Paul's First Missionary Journey," *Apostolic History and the Gospel: Biblical and Historical Essays Presented to F. F. Bruce* . . . (ed. W. W. Gasque and R. P. Martin; Grand Rapids, MI: Eerdmans, 1970), 151–61.

Foster, J., "Was Sergius Paulus Converted? Acts xiii.12," *ExpTim* 60 (1948–49): 354–55.

Grimme, H., "Elym, der Astrolog," *OLZ* 12 (1909): 207–11.

Halfmann, H., *Die Senatoren aus dem östlichen Teil des Imperium Romanum bis zum Ende des 2. Jahrhunderts n. Chr.* (Hypomnemata 58; Göttingen: Vandenhoeck & Ruprecht, 1979), 101–6, 163.

Harrer, G. A., "Saul Who Is Also Called Paul," *HTR* 33 (1940): 19–33.

Harris, J. R., "A Curious Bezan Reading Vindicated," *Expos* 6/5 (1902): 189–95.

Hemer, C. J., "The Name of Paul," *TynBull* 36 (1985): 179–83.

Holmes, B. T., "Luke's Description of John Mark," *JBL* 54 (1935): 63–72.

Howell, E. B., "St. Paul and the Greek World," *GR* 11 (1964): 7–29.

Klauck, H. J., "With Paul in Paphos and Lystra: Magic and Paganism in the Acts of the Apostles," *Neotestamentica* 28 (1994): 93–108.

Leary, T. J., "Paul's Improper Name," *NTS* 38 (1992): 467–69.

Molthagen, J., "Die ersten Konflikte der Christen in der griechisch-römischen Welt," *Historia* 40 (1991): 42–76.

Nock, A. D., "Paul and the Magus," *Beginnings,* 5.164–88.

Rius-Camps, J., *El camino de Pablo a la misión de los paganos: Comentario lingüístico y exetico a Hch 13–28* (Lectura del Nuevo Testamento, Estudios críticos y exegéticos 2; Madrid: Cristiandad, 1984; Córdoba: Ediciones Almendro, 1989), 42–65.

———, "La misión hacia el paganismo avalada por el Señor Jesús y el Espíritu Santo (Hch 13–15)," *EstBíb* 52 (1994): 341–60.

Robinson, B. P., "Paul and Barnabas in Cyprus," *Scripture Bulletin* 26 (1996): 69–72.

Saffrey, H. D., "Sergius Paullus (Quintus)," *DBSup* 12 (fasc. 68, 1993): 693–99.

Synge, F. C., "Studies in Texts: Acts 13.9: Saul, Who Is Also Paul," *Theology* 63 (1960): 199–200.

Unnik, W. C. van, "Die Apostelgeschichte und die Häresien," ZNW 58 (1967): 240–46; repr. *Sparsa Collecta*, 1.402–9.

3. Evangelization of Pisidian Antioch; Paul's Discourse (13:13–52)

13 From Paphos Paul and his companions put out to sea and came to Perga in
Pamphylia, but John left them and returned to Jerusalem. 14 They continued their
journey from Perga and came to Pisidian Antioch. On the sabbath they entered
the synagogue and sat down. 15 After the reading of the law and the prophets, the
synagogue leaders sent word to them, "Brothers, if you have a word of exhortation
to address to the people, please speak up." 16 So Paul got up and with a gesture
began to speak.

"Fellow Israelites and you who are Godfearers, listen to me! 17 The God of this
people of Israel once chose our ancestors and made the people great during its
sojourn in the land of Egypt. With uplifted arm he led them forth from it. 18 For
some forty years he put up with them in the desert. 19 Then he overthrew seven
nations in the land of Canaan and gave them that land as a heritage 20 for about
four hundred and fifty years. Later on he set up judges to rule until Samuel [the]
prophet. 21 Then, when they asked for a king, God gave them Saul, son of Kish,
a man of the tribe of Benjamin, for forty years. 22 Then God removed him and
raised up David as their king, about whom he testified, '*I have found David*[f] son
of Jesse *a man after my own heart*;[g] he will do all that I desire.' 23 From this man's
descendants God has brought forth for Israel a Savior, Jesus, according to his
promise. 24 John heralded his coming, preaching a baptism of repentance to all
the people of Israel. 25 As John was finishing his course, he used to say, 'What do
you suppose me to be? That I am not! No, someone is coming after me, the
sandal of whose feet I am not worthy to unfasten.'

26 "Brothers, children of the family of Abraham, and you who are Godfearers,
to us the message of this salvation has been sent. 27 Those who live in Jerusalem
and their leaders failed to recognize Jesus, and, in condemning him, they have
fulfilled the oracles of the prophets that are read sabbath after sabbath. 28 Though
they found no charge against him worthy of death, they demanded of Pilate that
he be put to death. 29 When they thus brought about all that was written about
him, they took him down from the tree and laid him in a tomb. 30 But God raised
him from the dead, 31 and for many days thereafter he appeared to those who had

come up with him from Galilee to Jerusalem. They are [now] his witnesses before the people. 32 We too are proclaiming to you that the promise made to our
ancestors has been realized: 33 God has fulfilled this promise for us, [their] children, by raising up Jesus, even as it stands written in the second psalm,

You are my son,
this day I have begotten you.[h]

34 As proof that he raised him from the dead, who is never again to return to
decay, he thus declared, 'I will give *you the covenant benefits assured to David.*'[i]
35 That is why he also says in another place, '*You will not allow your holy one to
see decay.*'[j] 36 For David indeed, after he had served God's purpose in his own
generation, fell asleep and was buried with his ancestors, and did see decay. 37 But
the one whom God raised up has not seen decay.

38 So let it be known to you, Brothers, that through him forgiveness of sin is
being proclaimed to you, 39 [and] through him everyone who believes is justified
from everything from which you could not be justified by the law of Moses. 40 Beware, then, lest what was said in the prophets becomes true of you:

41 '*Look, you scoffers,*
be amazed, and then disappear!
For I am doing a deed in your days,
a deed *which you will not believe, even if someone tells you about it.*'[k]

42 As they were leaving, the people begged them to speak further on this topic
again on the following sabbath. 43 After the meeting of the synagogue had finally
broken up, many Jews and devout converts to Judaism followed Paul and Barnabas, who continued to speak to them and urge them to hold fast to the grace of
God. 44 The next sabbath almost the whole town gathered to hear the word of the
Lord. 45 When the Jews saw the crowds, they became very jealous and with violent
abuse countered what was said by Paul. 46 Both Paul and Barnabas, however,
spoke out fearlessly, "To you, first of all, the word of God had to be proclaimed.
Since you reject it and thus judge yourselves unworthy of eternal life, we now
turn to the Gentiles. 47 For so the Lord has instructed us,

'*I have made you a light of the Gentiles,*
that you may be a means of salvation to the end of the earth.'"[l]

48 The Gentiles who heard this were delighted and were continually honoring
the word of the Lord. All who were destined for eternal life became believers.
49 The word of the Lord continued to be carried through that whole area. 50 The
Jews, however, stirred up well-to-do women worshipers and the leading men of
the town and started a persecution against Paul and Barnabas, whom they expelled from their district. 51 So they shook its dust from their feet in protest against
them and went on to Iconium. 52 The disciples were filled with joy and the
Holy Spirit.

[f]Ps 89:21 [g]1 Sam 13:14 [h]Ps 2:7 [i]Isa 55:3
[j]Ps 16:10 [k]Hab 1:5 [l]Isa 49:6

WT: [14]Antioch of Pisidia . . . [omits "and sat down"]. [15]if there is in you any wisdom, address (it) to the people. [16]gesture to be silent began to speak. [17]chose our ancestors throughout the people and made (them) great. [omits "this" and "the land of"]. [18]For forty years he cared for them. [19][omits "seven"] he parceled out the land of foreigners by lot. [20][omits "about" and "later on"]. [21]he gave them Saul. [22][omits "all"]. [23][omits "for Israel" and "Jesus"]. [24][omits "all" and "of Israel"]. [25]Whom do you suppose. [26]this message of salvation. [27]and its leaders, failing to understand the writings of the prophets that are read sabbath after sabbath, fulfilled (them) [omits "in condemning him"]. [28]Though . . . deaths, they judged him and handed him over to Pilate to have him put to death. [29]After he was crucified, they asked Pilate to take him down from the tree; having obtained him, they laid him in a tomb. [30][omits "from the dead,"]. [31]This one appeared . . . for many days thereafter. [32]made to the ancestors. [33]by raising up the Lord, Jesus Christ. For thus it stands written in the first psalm [or in some MSS: "in the psalms"; after the quotation there is added: "Ask of me, and I will make nations your heritage, and the ends of the earth your possession"]. [34]When he raised him. [35]He otherwise says. [36][omits "For" and "fell asleep and"]. [37]But the one whom he raised. [41][adds after the quotation:] And he became silent. [43]and Barnabas, asking to be baptized; and they continued . . . [adds at the end:] The message happened to go through the whole city. [44]. . . to listen to Paul who made many an address about the Lord. [45]and with violent abuse and contradiction countered. [46][omits "first of all"]. But since you judged yourselves unworthy (of it), we now turn. [47]*Look, I have made you a light for the Gentiles.* [48]were continually praising God. [49][omits "of the Lord"]. [50]started distress for Paul. [51]and came to Iconium.

COMMENT

Having finished the evangelization of the island of Cyprus, Barnabas and Paul pass on to the mainland of Asia Minor. They travel from Paphos to Perga in Pamphylia and gradually make their way to Pisidian Antioch, where they enter the synagogue of the Jews. The first major address of Paul in Acts is now recorded, being delivered in the synagogue of Pisidian Antioch (13:16b–41).

The episode, form-critically considered, is basically a narrative, into which Luke has incorporated a Pauline speech. He is again using information from his Pauline source, and even some of that tradition is incorporated in the speech itself, which is mainly a Lucan composition.

In some respects Paul's address is reminiscent of Peter's speech in Jerusalem on the first Christian Pentecost (2:14–36) and of that of Stephen (7:1–53), but it has its own distinctive elements. It is another missionary, kerygmatic sermon addressed this time to diaspora Jews and Gentile sympathizers. The structure of the speech is indicated by the threefold use of *andres Israēlitai* or *andres adelphoi*, the form of address used in vv 16, 26, 38; hence the three parts: (1) 16b–25; (2) 26–37; (3) 38–41. The structure is so understood by Schneider, *Apg.*, 2.130; deSilva, "Paul's Sermon," 34–35; Pesch, *Apg.*, 2.30–31; Polhill, *Acts*, 300; Roloff, *Apg.*, 202–3. For a four-part division (16b–25, 26–31, 32–37, 38–41), see Weiser, *Apg.*, 322–23. As Barrett (*Acts*, 623) notes, it makes little difference if the second part is divided in two or not.

The first part of the discourse (13:16b–25) is a recital of salvation history. It differs from the recital in Stephen's speech (7:2–47) in being positive in its exposé, and not negative as a buildup for an indictment. It makes no mention of the patriarchs and Moses, and Paul emphasizes God's guidance, which leads from the election of Israel to Jesus, "the continuity between Israel and the church" (Conzelmann, *Acts,* 103). God has provided for Israel even before he raised up "judges" (charismatic leaders) and "kings" for it. Such divine providence was exercised on behalf of Israel of old.

The second part (13:26–37) is a proclamation made to contemporary Israel: To us, "children of the family of Abraham" (v 26), the message of this salvation has been sent, "God raised him [Jesus] from the dead" (v 30). The kerygma itself is found in vv 26–31, and an argument from Scripture supports it in vv 32–37. The Lucan themes of Jewish ignorance and Christian testimony appear again (in vv 27, 30–31).

The third part (13:38–41) is the concluding exhortation: Through Christ come forgiveness of sins and justification, a message not to be spurned. This is the climax of Paul's address to the people in the synagogue. It is the only time in Acts, when Paul's teaching about justification by faith is mentioned, the topic that is prominent in his letters to the Galatians and Romans. One should note how Luke has recast the Pauline teaching in vv 38–39. The prime effect of the Christ-event in Pauline theology, justification by faith, is adjusted as an explanation of forgiveness of sins. The latter is a prominent Lucan way of expressing an effect of the Christ-event, which, however, is absent in Paul's uncontested letters. It is found in the Deutero-Pauline Col 1:14 and Eph 1:7. Such a treatment of this Pauline topic introduces part of the problem of the Paulinism of Acts; see Introduction §§171–77. The entire episode thus presents Pauline testimony in a certain parallelism with that of Peter, both in the speech and in the miracles.

In this important "word of exhortation," which the Lucan Paul addresses to Jews in Pisidian Antioch, we see how he interprets the OT and uses the written Word of God to his rhetorical purpose. He recalls how the God of Israel once dealt with their ancestors, leading the Hebrews of old out of Egypt and into the land of Canaan, giving them prophets and kings, even establishing the Davidic dynasty. This God still addresses contemporary Israel, speaking to it now about the Savior that he had promised to raise up from David's line. This he has now done in Jesus whom he has sent. Jerusalemites and their leaders failed to recognize him and delivered him to Pilate to have him put to death. God has raised Jesus from the dead and has fulfilled his promise in him, of whom God in the psalter says, "You are my son; this day I have begotten you." This is the one in whom we are all to find salvation, justification, and forgiveness of sins. So the Lucan Paul has proclaimed the word of the cross.

NOTES

13. *From Paphos.* See NOTE on 13:6.

Paul and his companions. Lit., "those around Paul," which might seem to say that Paul himself was not with them; but from what follows it is clear that that is merely a Lucan literary way of stating that Paul was not traveling alone.

put out to sea. Lit., "having been carried up (onto the high sea) they came."

Luke uses the technical nautical term *anagein*, "put (a ship) to sea," as also in 16:11; 18:21; 20:3, 13; 21:1, 2; 27:2, 4, 12, 21; 28:10, 11.

came to Perga in Pamphylia. This would have been done in two stages, because the ship would have brought them first to Attalia (14:25), the logical destination of a ship sailing from Paphos on Cyprus. *Pergē* was a river port near the central southern coast of Asia Minor, about 13 km north of Attalia, within the district of Pamphylia (see NOTE on 2:10). Whether the same ship could have navigated the sea and the river is problematic. In any case, their immediate destination is Perga.

John left them and returned to Jerusalem. John Mark has been part of the Lucan story since 12:12, 25. He probably returns to the house of his mother, Mary, in Jerusalem (12:12; see NOTE there). Weiser (*Apg.*, 330) ascribes John's desertion to the dangerous journey that had to be taken from Perga to Pisidian Antioch, 160 km away. The desertion of John Mark will cause a problem when Paul is about to begin Mission II (15:37, 39).

14. *They continued their journey from Perga and came to Pisidian Antioch.* MSS P^{45}, P^{74}, ℵ, A, B, C, 453, and 1175 read *Antiocheian tēn Pisidian*, using the otherwise unattested proper adj. *Pisidios*, but the WT (MSS D, E, Ψ, 33, 1739) and the *Koinē* text-tradition read *Antiocheian tēs Pisidias*, "Antioch of Pisidia." This Antioch was called more properly *Antiocheia hē pros Pisidian*, "Antioch facing Pisidia," and was actually in the district of Phrygia (see Strabo, *Geography* 12.6.4; 12.8.14; *OGIS* §536) of the Roman province of Asia. Because it lay close to the border of Pisidia, it was called "Pisidian" to distinguish it from Phrygian Antioch on the Meander River. It was wrongly assigned to Pisidia by Pliny (*Naturalis Historia* 5.24.94), and the text of Acts may reflect the same confusion. This Pisidian Antioch lay in a mountainous area west of the Taurus Mountains, which became part of the Roman Empire in 25 B.C. and in time a Roman colony (*Pisidarum Colonia Caesarea Antiochia*). See B. Levick, *Roman Colonies in Southern Asia Minor* (Oxford: Clarendon, 1967), 12–41. In traveling from Perga to Antioch, Paul and Barnabas would have traveled along an old paved highway, the *Via Sebaste*, which led through Colonia Comama to Colonia Antiochia. See D. H. French, *Roman Roads and Milestones of Asia Minor* (2 fascicles; Oxford: BAR, 1981, 1988), 2.183.

On the sabbath they entered the synagogue and sat down. Lit., "on the day of the sabbath." This manifests again Luke's concern to depict Barnabas and Paul evangelizing the Jews first, a concern that will dominate this episode and Paul's speech at the end (see NOTE on 13:5). Compare the exclusively Lucan account of Jesus' arrival in the synagogue of Nazareth (Luke 4:16–30). On "synagogue," see NOTE on 6:9.

15. *After the reading of the law and the prophets.* This is a description of the basic part of the synagogue service, which normally consisted of the recitation of the *Šĕma'*, the *Tĕphillah* (or *Šĕmôneh 'Eśreh*, "Eighteen Blessings") with a priestly blessing, then the reading of the *Tôrāh* (Law of Moses) and a *Haphtārāh* (a reading from the Prophets), after which a sermon was preached; see Str-B, 4/1.153–88.

the synagogue leaders sent word to them. The *archisynagōgoi* are leaders responsible for the organization of the synagogue service; they normally designate someone to lead the congregation in prayer. They invite Paul or Barnabas to address the congregation instead of having the usual sermon. Their title will reappear at 18:8, 17.

"Brothers, if you have a word of exhortation to address to the people, please speak up." Luke uses *logos paraklēseōs*, "a word of exhortation," the expression used at the end of Hebrews (13:22), which characterizes its hortatory message. Pillai (*Early Missionary Preaching*, 55) interprets the phrase as a technical term for a unit of tradition made up of a liturgical credo that recounts God's saving acts, a unit that would have been passed on from rabbi to disciple. It would then refer to vv 17–22. Pillai does not offer any evidence, however, for such a restricted meaning of the phrase, and the use of it in Heb 13:22 seems to tell against such an interpretation. From the way it is used here, it would have to refer to Paul's sermon as a whole, as Kilgallen more correctly remarks ("Acts 13,38–39," 482). Note the explanatory phrase *logos sōtērias* in v 26.

16. *Paul got up and with a gesture began to speak.* The gesture was a sign given for silence and attention; see the WT reading and 12:17; 19:33; 21:40. There follows the missionary and kerygmatic speech of Paul to the Jews of Pisidian Antioch, in which he seeks to exhort and encourage them, telling about the fulfillment of the divine promise made of old.

"Fellow Israelites and you who are Godfearers, listen to me! Paul realizes that his audience is mixed: there are Jews like himself present, but also those who were Gentile sympathizers *(hoi phoboumenoi ton theon)*, such as Cornelius (see NOTE on 10:2). To all of them he calls for a hearing. Compare the form of address in vv 26 and 38.

17. *The God of this people of Israel.* The WT smooths out the Greek of this clause by omitting the dem. adj. "this," perhaps by homoeoteleuton *(laou toutou)*. For "God of Israel," see Josh 7:19–20; 8:30; 1 Sam 1:17.

once chose our ancestors. Paul begins his recital of salvation history with a recollection of God's mighty acts in the election of Israel (Exod 6:6–7; Deut 4:37; 10:15; Jer 31:33). Because of that election Israel became the Chosen People.

made the people great during its sojourn in the land of Egypt. Lit., "exalted the people." Paul passes over the bondage in which the Hebrews in Egypt had to live and work; he regards it all as a way in which God made this people great.

With uplifted arm he led them forth from it. I.e., from Egypt at the time of the Exodus. This clause alludes to Exod 6:1. Cf. Exod 6:6, 8; 12:51; Deut 4:34; 5:15; 9:26 for further OT background.

18. *For some forty years he put up with them in the desert.* Lit., "for about a forty-year period." The MSS ℵ, B, C^2, D, 36, 81, 307, 453, and 1739 read the verb *etropophorēsen*, "he put up with (their moods)," but other MSS (P^{74}, A, C*, E, Ψ, 33, 181) read *etrophophorēsen*, "he cared for them," i.e., bore them in his arms, a reading borrowed from Deut 1:31 (LXX). That, however, may be a copyist's harmonization of the text of Acts with Deuteronomy. Each one makes good sense in the context of Paul's speech. The latter may be an allusion to Exod 16:35. See Num 14:33–34, for the mention of forty years. R. P. Gordon ("Tar-

gumic Parallels to Acts xiii 18 and Didache xiv 3," *NovT* 16 [1974]: 285–89) calls attention to parallels in Tg. Onqelos of Deut 2:7 and 32:10 and in Tg. Jonathan of Hos 13:5, but those Aramaic translations date from a later period and only questionably represent a "community of tradition" that already existed prior to Luke.

19. *Then he overthrew seven nations in the land of Canaan.* Lit., "and having overthrown." See Deut 7:1, where the following seven are named: Hittites, Girgashites, Amorites, Canaanites, Perizzites, Hivites, and Jebusites, "seven nations greater and mightier than yourselves." Some MSS (B, 6, 81) omit the first *kai.*

gave them that land as a heritage. It means that the land of Canaan became the inheritance of the Hebrews. Cf. Josh 14:1–2. This is the meaning of this part of the verse, whether one reads *tēn gēn autōn,* as in MSS P[74], ℵ, B, Ψ, 33, 81, 181, and 1175, or *autois tēn gēn autōn,* as in MSS A, C, D[2], E, and 1739 (see *TCGNT,* 358).

20. *for about four hundred and fifty years.* The position and pertinence of this phrase are problematic. Though read as the first part of the printed text of v 20 (NA[27], GNT), it is sometimes made the end of v 19 *(RSV),* to which it really belongs. When so used (as in MSS P[74], ℵ, A, B, C, 33, 36, and 81), it is understood to refer to 400 years in Egypt (Gen 15:13 [cf. Acts 7:6]), 40 in the desert (Num 14:33–34), and 10 in the conquest of Canaan (Joshua 14) before the rule of the judges. This reading is preferred by Bruce (*Acts,* 272), Weiser (*Apg.,* 319), Johnson (*Acts,* 231), Polhill (*Acts,* 300), Schneider (*Apg.,* 2.132), Barrett (*Acts,* 633).

The phrase, however, is often put in v 20 and after *meta tauta* (in MSS D[2], E, P, Ψ, 945, and 1739); then it would refer to 450 years of the rule of the judges. This more or less agrees with the reckoning in Josephus, *Ant.* 8.3.1 §61. This reading is preferred by Conzelmann (*Acts,* 104).

1 Kgs 6:1 mentions 480 years as having elapsed since the exodus until Solomon's beginning to build the Temple, and the LXX there reads 440 years. See *TCGNT,* 358–59; E. H. Merrill, "Paul's Use of 'About 450 Years' in Acts 13:20," *BSac* 138 (1981): 246–57.

Later on he set up judges to rule until Samuel [*the*] *prophet.* See Judg 2:16. Those who are called *kritai,* "judges," were actually military leaders who because of their successes were entrusted with governance; they became, in effect, charismatic leaders of God's Chosen People. Samuel was eventually born to Elkanah and his wife Hannah, who had been barren (1 Sam 1:20), and in time "all Israel, from Dan to Beer-sheba, learned that Samuel had been established as a prophet to Yahweh" (1 Sam 3:20). Thus God provided judges and a prophet for the guidance of the people.

21. *when they asked for a king.* See 1 Sam 8:5–10. At first the prophet Samuel would have nothing to do with the request of the elders of Israel for a king to rule over them; but eventually at the word of Yahweh, he yielded to their request (1 Sam 8:22).

God gave them Saul, son of Kish, a man of the tribe of Benjamin, for forty years. Saul was chosen by lot to be the first anointed king in Israel (1 Sam 9:1–2 gives his family and tribe; cf. 1 Sam 10:1, 20–21, 24; 11:15; 13:1). Information about Saul in 1 Samuel is problematic; see P. K. McCarter, Jr., *I Samuel* (AB 8; Garden City: Doubleday, 1980), 222–23. Josephus notes that Saul reigned for 18 years during the time of Samuel and 22 years thereafter (*Ant.* 6.14.9 §378; but cf. *Ant.* 10.8.4 §143, where Saul's reign is 20 years). In any case, God manifested his providence over Israel, even when it demanded a king to rule over it. This Saul is the apostle's namesake; his tribe is the same as that mentioned in Phil 3:5: "of the tribe of Benjamin, a Hebrew born of Hebrews." On the "undesigned coincidence" between Acts and a genuine letter of Paul, see Hemer, *Book of Acts*, 183.

22. *Then God removed him.* See 1 Sam 13:13–14, where Samuel informs Saul that he had acted foolishly and disobeyed God and that his kingship would not continue forever. Also 1 Sam 15:11–35; 16:1, which ends with the note that God regretted having made Saul king over Israel.

raised up David as their king. David was the youngest son of Jesse, the Bethlehemite (1 Sam 16:11); God chose him and bade Samuel to anoint him as king over Israel (1 Sam 16:12–13).

about whom he testified, 'I have found David, son of Jesse, a man after my own heart.' This part of the verse is conflated from Ps 89:20 (LXX: *heuron Dauid*) and 1 Sam 13:14 (LXX: *kata tēn kardian autou*). God thus bore witness to the people of Israel about the character of the king who would rule over them.

he will do all that I desire. Lit., "all my desires." The clause is an echo of Isa 44:28 (LXX), where the words are applied to the Persian king, Cyrus, called "my shepherd" and the Lord's "anointed one" (45:1), the only figure in the Book of Isaiah to whom the Hebrew title *māšîaḥ* is accorded. The clause explains, however, why David, a shepherd and one also called *māšîaḥ* (2 Sam 19:22), is said to be a man after God's heart. Wilcox (*Semitisms*, 21–26) claims that "a Targumic tradition" found in Tg. Jonathan (1 Sam 13:14) is involved in this clause. That is hardly likely because the noun *(r'wtyh)* is singular; see E. Richard, *CBQ* 42 (1980): 331–32.

23. *From this man's descendants God has brought forth for Israel a Savior, Jesus.* David is thus regarded as the type of Jesus, who was born of this king's descendants. For Jesus' Davidic descent elsewhere in the NT, see Rom 1:3; 2 Tim 2:8; Matt 1:1; Luke 3:23, 31; Mark 12:35. See E. Vallauri, "La filiazione davidica di Gesù negli Atti degli Apostoli," *Laurentianum* 19 (1978): 38–88. The title *sōtēr*, "Savior," is added by Luke to the OT promises, because that is a distinctive Lucan title for Jesus or the risen Christ (see *Luke*, 204–5). The title designates Jesus as the deliverer of Israel from evils that beset it. MSS P^{74}, H, L, and a number of minuscules read simply *sōtērian*, "has brought forth for Israel salvation." This is generally recognized to be a confusion of two abbreviated words CPA IN (= *sōtēra Iēsoun*), read as if they were one word, CPIAN (= CΩTHPIAN). See *TCGNT*, 359.

according to his promise. The OT background for this promise is found in 2 Sam 7:12, 16, the oracle of Nathan, which mentions the offspring that God would raise up to succeed David and thus "establish the throne of his kingdom forever" (cf. 2 Sam 22:51). In time this promise was reformulated in terms of a *future* "David" (Jer 30:9; Hos 3:5; Ezek 37:24–25) and even of a *coming* "Messiah" (Dan 9:25; *Ps. Sol.* 17:21–34). Now Paul proclaims to Jews of Pisidian Antioch that implementation of the divine promise in Jesus, who has been born of Davidic lineage and has come as Savior of Israel and of all humanity; but he has been "raised" in a different sense.

24. *John heralded his coming.* Lit., "With John proclaiming beforehand, before the face of his entering/coming." This is actually a gen. absol., dependent on v 23. Although John the Baptist is never mentioned in any letter of the Pauline corpus, Luke depicts Paul preaching about him. This advance heralding agrees with the historical role of John and with the way it is described in the Lucan Gospel. There the infancy narrative presents in parallel form the coming of both John and Jesus (Luke 1–2), and the story of the public ministry of Jesus begins with a prior description of the preaching and ministry of John (Luke 3:1–22). As in the Gospel, so too here: Luke presents John as the precursor of Jesus (recall Luke 16:16; Acts 1:5, 22; 10:37; 11:16; cf. 18:25; 19:3–4). For further details about the understanding of John's role in salvation history, see *Luke,* 181–86. The phrase *pro prosōpou,* "before the face," is strange before *tou eisodou,* "the entering," but it may be dependent on the LXX of Mal 3:1, a text often associated with the coming of John in the gospel tradition (see NOTES on Luke 1:17 and 7:27).

preaching a baptism of repentance. See Luke 3:3, where the same phrase *baptisma metanoias* was first used of the ritual washing that John proclaimed to fellow Jews, a washing that connoted a "change of mind" and a reform of one's life (see NOTES on Luke 3:3 and Acts 5:31). John's baptism was known also to Josephus (*Ant.* 18.5.2 §§116–17): John, "called the Baptist," exhorted Jews to live upright lives and "join in baptism." So John prepared the way for Jesus's ministry.

to all the people of Israel. I.e., to all Jews who would listen to his message in contemporary Judea. Again, Lucan hyperbole is at work; see NOTE on 2:44.

25. *As John was finishing his course.* One should note in these verses how Luke plays on the geographical perspective of his two-volume story (see *Luke,* 164–71, esp. 169). In v 24 he mentioned Jesus's coming, *eisodos* (= *eis* + *hodos*), "coming in, entrance," before which John was already preaching his baptism. Now he speaks of John's *dromos,* "running, course," an apt way of describing his precursor ministry: he ran on ahead of Jesus to herald his entrance on the scene. This suits the way Luke speaks of Jesus' ministry as *hodos,* "a way" (Luke 3:4; 7:27; 9:57; 18:35), to which the description of Christianity as "the Way" also corresponds (see NOTE on 9:2).

he used to say, 'What do you suppose me to be? That I am not! Or "What you suppose me to be that I am not!" The Alexandrian text, represented by MSS P^{74}, ℵ, A, B, E, 33, 81, and 1175, read *tí eme hyponoeite einai,* whereas the WT, in MSS P^{45}, C, D, Ψ, 36, 181, and 1739, read *tína me,* "Whom do you suppose me to be?" The latter makes better sense, but it is for that reason suspect, seeming to be a copyist's correction. There is no recollection of such a saying of John in the Lucan Gospel; but recall the Baptist's saying in John 1:20; 3:28, as he rejects the title *Christos*. Compare Luke 3:15.

No, someone is coming after me. See Luke 3:16c, where Luke has taken over from Mark 1:7 only the verb *erchetai*, "is coming," without the *opisō mou*, "behind me." Now, however, Luke has a corresponding prep. phrase *met' eme*. See NOTE on Luke 3:16.

the sandal of whose feet I am not worthy to unfasten.' This echoes the Baptist's statement in Luke 3:16d, but its wording is not exact. Here Luke writes, *hou ouk eimi axios to hypodēma tōn podōn lysai*; in the Gospel he wrote, *hou ouk eimi hikanos lysai ton himanta tōn hypodēmatōn autou*, "I am not fit to unfasten even the strap of his sandals," a statement derived from Mark 1:7. Compare John 1:27 (especially in P^{66} and P^{75}). So Paul preaches about John's recognition of his precursor status in reference to Jesus as the One-Who-Is-to-Come. John's preaching is thus a christological proclamation in itself, announced in advance of Jesus' "coming." On whether John thus belongs to the Period of Israel, as Conzelmann once proposed (followed by Schneider, *Apg.*, 2.134), or is a transitional figure ending that period and inaugurating the Period of Jesus in salvation history, see *Luke*, 181–87.

26. *Brothers, children of the family of Abraham, and you who are Godfearers.* Lit., "and those among you who fear God." With the direct address in this verse the second part of Paul's speech begins. Compare the form of address in v 16b above; Paul now calls them all "brothers," not only his fellow Jews (see NOTE on 1:15), but Gentile sympathizers as well (see NOTE on "fearing God," 10:2). The new element is "children of the family of Abraham," a way of acknowledging Israel's descent from Father Abraham (see 7:2 and compare Luke 3:8).

to us the message of this salvation has been sent. I.e., by God (theological passive; cf. 10:36; ZBG §236). In v 23 Paul proclaimed Jesus as the savior; now he speaks of the message (lit., "the word") of salvation that Jesus himself has brought and the message about it that is now announced by his disciples.

This message is sometimes thought to be an allusion to Ps 107:20, "He sent forth his word and healed them." It is at least a Lucan literary variant for other expressions that he has already used in 5:20; 6:2, 7 and will use in 16:32; 19:10, all descriptions of the Christian gospel and the benefits that it brings. The pron. *hēmin*, "to us," is put in emphatic position at the head of the clause. The first pl. is read in MSS P^{74}, ℵ, A, B, D, Ψ, 33, 81, and 614, whereas MSS P^{45}, C, E, 36, 181, 1175, and 1739 read the second pl., *hymin*, "to you." The variant is the result of itacism in the pronunciation of the vowels, both being pronounced *hîmin*.

27. *Those who live in Jerusalem and their leaders failed to recognize Jesus.* Luke introduces again the ignorance motif, as he writes *agnoēsantes*, "failing to know, acknowledge," applying it to Jerusalem Jews (see NOTE on 3:17). Compare the similar notice in Jesus's words used in John 16:3. By "their leaders" is meant the chief priests, elders, and scribes (4:5, 8, 23).

in condemning him, they have fulfilled the oracles of the prophets that are read sabbath after sabbath. The Greek text of vv 27–29 is not uniformly transmitted in the MSS. The simplest form of v 27 is that given here, as in MSS P^{45}, P^{74}, ℵ, A, B, C, D^2 (*agnoountes*), Ψ, 33, 36, 81, 1818, and 1739, but some other MSS read "in condemning him, they have not understood the writings of the prophets that are read sabbath after sabbath" (D*, Vetus Itala). See *TCGNT*, 360–61. Cf. Acts 3:15, 18.

Luke ascribes to inhabitants of Jerusalem and their (or in WT: its) leaders the condemnation of Jesus to death. Practically all the MSS read a form of the verb *krinein*, "judge," which, *pace* Schneider (*Apg.*, 2.135), has to be understood as *katakrinein*, "judge adversely, condemn," as in Luke 19:22; 20:47 (see NOTES there); Acts 23:3; 24:6 v.l. (BAGD, 451).

The unwitting fulfillment of prophetic oracles is again an instance of Luke's global interpretation of the OT; he fails to indicate which prophets or what oracles. See NOTES on Luke 24:27, 44. In the sabbath synagogue service, passages of OT prophets were read; see NOTE on 13:15.

28. *Though they found no charge against him worthy of death.* "They" must be understood of the inhabitants of Jerusalem and their leaders mentioned in v 27. Paul's statement implies that their condemnation of Jesus was unfounded. See Luke 23:4, 14–15, 22, where a triple declaration of Jesus' innocence is uttered by Pilate. Cf. John 18:38; 19:4, 6.

they demanded of Pilate that he be put to death. See Luke 23:21, 23, where "they" refers to "the chief priests, leaders, and people" of 23:13; cf. 23:18 (see *Luke*, 1488–89); cf. John 19:6, 7, 15. On Pilate, see NOTE on 3:13. Thus Pilate as well as Jerusalem inhabitants and their leaders are implicated in the death of Jesus.

29. *When they thus brought about all that was written about him.* I.e., in the oracles of the prophets (see v 27 and the NOTE there). Luke uses *telein* in the sense of "carrying out, fulfilling" (BAGD, 811).

they took him down from the tree. "They" in this case must be indefinite or generic (= French *on* or German *man*), as a substitute for the passive, "he was taken down" (BDF §130.2; ZBG §1). In the gospel tradition the people, to whom the crucifixion of Jesus is ascribed (Luke 23:25–26; John 19:16–17), are not the same as those who take him down from the cross, Joseph of Arimathea (Luke 23:50–52; John 19:38). On "tree" as a way of expressing the cross of crucifixion, see NOTE on 5:30. Cf. 10:39.

laid him in a tomb. Not only the death of Jesus, but the burial of his body is duly recorded; see Luke 23:53; John 19:41–42.

30. *God raised him from the dead.* The contrast is evident between what human beings have done to Jesus and what God has done. The resurrection of Christ is part of the implementation of the divine plan of salvation. Luke stresses that salvation, which is available to Israel and all human beings, comes precisely through the resurrection of Jesus. The verb *egeirein*, "raise," appears here explicitly with *ek nekrōn*, "from the dead," as in 3:15; 4:10. Again, the efficiency of that resurrection is ascribed to God; see also 2:24, 32; 3:15; 4:10; 5:30; 10:40; 13:37; 17:31. Cf. 1 Thess 1:10; Gal 1:1; 1 Cor 6:14; 15:4, 12, 13, 15, 17, 20; 2 Cor 4:14; Rom 4:24–25; 6:4, 9; 7:4; 8:11, 34; 10:9; Col 2:12; Eph 1:20.

31. *for many days thereafter.* In 1:3 "forty days" are mentioned, a round number, not used here.

he appeared to those who had come up with him from Galilee to Jerusalem. Recall 1:3 for the multiple appearances of the risen Christ to his disciples. There Luke records that he showed himself alive to them after his crucifixion. "From Galilee to Jerusalem" sums up the movement of Jesus in the Lucan Gospel from the area of Palestine where his ministry began (Galilee) to the city of destiny (Jerusalem); see *Luke,* 165–66. Cf. Luke 8:1–3; 9:51–53.

They are [*now*] *his witnesses before the people.* Luke recalls the role of disciples who have been called to testify to Jesus's risen status. See Luke 24:48; Acts 1:8; 2:32; 3:15; 5:32; 10:39, 41. The "people" are not only the inhabitants of Jerusalem (13:27), but also those of Judea, Samaria, and areas of the eastern Mediterranean to which the Word has already spread.

32. *We too are proclaiming to you.* I.e., Paul and Barnabas are announcing to you, Jews of the diaspora, who are also "children of the family of Abraham" (13:26), and to sympaihetic Godfearers.

that the promise made to our ancestors has been realized. I.e., the "promise" made to David and mentioned in v 23: a Davidic descendant would be raised up and become a Savior for Israel. Paul proclaims that that promise has now been implemented.

33. *God has fulfilled this promise for us,* [*their*] *children, by raising up Jesus.* The promise was not made to Jesus, but to the people of Israel, among whom Paul numbers himself. By *anastēsas,* "raising up," Luke may be echoing *anastēsō* of 2 Sam 7:12b, but he means something different, since he applies it to the resurrection of Christ. The Jews of Pisidian Antioch are also among "the children" born of those "ancestors." MSS C^3, E, 33, 36, 81, 181, 614, and 1739 read *autōn hēmin,* "for us, their (children)," but MSS P^{74}, ℵ, A, B, C*, and D read simply *hēmōn,* "for our (children)," a most improbable reading; see *TCGNT,* 362. Instead of "Jesus," the WT reads "the Lord, Jesus Christ" (MS D and Ambrose).

even as it stands written in the second psalm. MSS P^{74}, ℵ, A, B, C, Ψ, 33, 36, 81, 181, and 1739 read the text thus, but MS D has "in the first psalm" (*tō prōtō psalmō*), and P^{45} has simply "in the psalms" (*tois psalmois*). It is not known when the numbering of the psalms was introduced. Some MSS of Tertullian's *Adversus Marcionem* 4.22.8 also read *primo psalmo,* but the critical editions of Tertullian's text (CCLat 1.602; CSEL 47.494) have *secundo psalmo;* see also Origen, *Comm. in Psalmos* 2.1; PG 12.1100. In the later rabbinic tradition Psalms 1 and 2 were at times treated as one (see Str-B, 2.725; cf. G. D. Kilpatrick, "Acts xiii.33 and Tertullian, *Adv. Marc.* IV. xxii. 8," *JTS* 11 [1960]: 53).

You are my son, this day I have begotten you. This is an exact quotation of Ps 2:7 (LXX), which is also used in Heb 1:5; 5:5. Psalm 2 is a royal psalm, originally composed for the installation of a king on the Davidic throne. In v 2 of the psalm, "his anointed" refers to an unnamed historical king, and it did not yet have a messianic connotation in the strict sense, i.e., referring to an expected or awaited anointed figure. As the words are now applied to the risen Christ, they take on in this context a Christian messianic connotation. Through the resurrection of Jesus (see v 34), God is said to have begotten Jesus, just as it was said of old that God had begotten the historical unnamed king of the Davidic dynasty at his enthronement. Cf. 2 Sam 7:14.

The sonship expressed in the psalm takes on Christian connotations by its application here and its use in the Epistle to the Hebrews. Such NT uses of Psalm 2 lead eventually to the Nicene Creed's confession about the Son as One in being with the Father, a mode of expression not yet current in NT times.

34. *As proof that he raised him from the dead, who is never again to return to decay.* The words of Psalm 2 are clearly interpreted in terms of the resurrection of Christ. Recall Peter's similar affirmation in 2:31. The "decay" is that of death.

he thus declared. I.e., God is understood to have offered proof in what he affirmed through the prophet Isaiah about to be quoted.

'I will give you the covenant benefits assured to David.' This declaration is part of a quotation of Isa 55:3 (LXX), which reads, *kai diathēsomai hymin diathēkēn aiōnion, ta hosia Dauid ta pista,* "I shall bequeath to you (pl.) an everlasting covenant, the assured holy things of David." The Greek form of the LXX is a fairly accurate translation of the Hebrew MT and of 1QIsa[a] 45:22–23. Only the last five Greek words are used by Luke, who introduces "the covenant benefits assured to David" with his own verb. Those "benefits" refer to covenant blessings promised to David. As used by Paul in this speech, they are concretized now in the risen Christ. It is but another way of saying that the promise made to David has been fulfilled in the resurrection of Christ. Thus Luke brings out God's intention with respect to Gentiles: the covenant benefits assured to David will be rejected by his people and will be offered to Gentiles. Haenchen (*Acts,* 412) thinks that the two quotations (Ps 2:7 and Isa 55:3) were already paired in the pre-Lucan tradition because the abridged form of the latter would otherwise be scarcely intelligible. For him the Isaiah text implies that "I will give you Christians the scion of David together with the immortal life of the Resurrection."

35. *That is why he also says in another place.* I.e., God says in a different psalm.

'You will not allow your holy one to see decay.' Paul cites verbatim Ps 16:10 (LXX), which is an accurate translation of the MT, save for the last word. In Hebrew it is *šaḥat,* "pit," often used as a euphemism for *šĕʾôl,* "Sheol, realm of the dead." The Greek *diaphthora,* "decay," gets across more or less the same idea as "pit," but it is more suited to Paul's argument as he refers to Christ's resurrection. The implication is that Jesus's body did not decay in the tomb. Peter used the same argument in his speech to Jews of Jerusalem on the first Christian Pentecost (2:27b).

36. *David indeed, after he had served God's purpose in his own generation.* The two datives, *idiā geneā,* "in his own generation," and *tē tou theou boulē,* "God's purpose," flank the ptc. *hypēretēsas,* "having served," so that they can be taken in different senses, either as translated above, or "having served God's purpose, he fell asleep in his own generation."

fell asleep and was buried with his ancestors. Lit., "fell asleep and was added to his fathers," which uses a well-known OT expression (see Judg 2:10; 2 Kgs 22:20;

1 Macc 2:69). 1 Kgs 2:10 reports: "David fell asleep with his ancestors and was buried in the city of David."

did see decay. Cf. Ps 16:10 for the expression. Paul does not use Peter's argument, referring to the presence of David's tomb in Jerusalem even in his day (2:29), because Paul is not preaching in Jerusalem. Both of them, however, appeal to the decay of the remains of the dead David in contrast to those of the dead Jesus.

37. *the one whom God raised up has not seen decay.* I.e., Jesus has become the risen Christ. Cf. 2:31.

38. *So let it be known to you, Brothers.* With this address the third part of Paul's speech begins. Paul again addresses his synagogue audience as "brothers" (see NOTES on 13:16, 26). In this instance, the form of address is peculiar, because in v 16 he employed "Fellow Israelites and Godfearers." Thus "brothers" seems to have a comprehensive meaning that includes the Gentile sympathizers. In these verses, in which he will speak about justification, he may be directing his comments more specifically to the Jews in the synagogue audience. The climax of the speech in this third part draws an important conclusion from the recital just presented, as it proclaims effects of the Christ-event and utters a warning: such effects are not to be spurned.

through him forgiveness of sin is being proclaimed to you. The Lucan Paul announces to the synagogue audience of Antioch the first effect of the Christ-event: Jesus has accomplished for humanity *aphesis hamartiōn*, "forgiveness of sins." He has brought about the pardon of human sin (see NOTE on 2:38). This proclamation is the answer that Paul gives to the request for a "word of exhortation" (13:15). He duly makes it known that such forgiveness comes "through him," the risen Christ, or through his name (10:43).

39. [*and*] *through him everyone who believes is justified.* Or "is acquitted." The second effect of the Christ-event is justification. The Jews who listen to him can come to a status of uprightness and rectitude in God's sight by faith. The image behind "justification" is drawn from a judicial setting, in which sinful human beings find themselves standing before the tribunal of the divine Judge. Paul thus proclaims here what he advocated in Gal 2:16 and Rom 3:28: "We maintain that a human being is justified by faith apart from deeds prescribed by the law." Luke has not seen fit to include the final phrase of the Pauline declaration, because he is not recording the Pauline battle over *erga nomou*, "deeds of the law," vs. *pistis*, "faith." Luke, however, only secondarily introduces justification, making it almost a form of "forgiveness of sins." Justification never acquires in Lucan teaching the prominence that it has in Pauline theology. Herein is part of the problem of the "Paulinism" of Acts; see Introduction §§171–77.

from everything from which you could not be justified by the law of Moses. This is Luke's way of expressing the contrast of faith and deeds. He makes Paul declare the inadequacy of the pursuit of uprightness or righteousness in God's sight by performing deeds prescribed by the Mosaic Law.

It is sometimes said that Luke is here introducing a nuance, as he makes Paul declare that the Mosaic law would justify people from some things but not from all and that, where the law falls short, faith in Jesus takes over. That, however, is hardly the view of justification that one finds in the Pauline letters themselves, and it may be a misreading of Luke to insist on that nuance, as some interpreters have done. Haenchen (*Acts*, 412 n.4) notes: "Anyone who . . . makes the author here develop a doctrine that an incomplete justification through the law is completed by a justification through faith imputes to him a venture into problems which were foreign to him." See W. H. Bates, "A Note."

40. *Beware, then, lest what was said in the prophets becomes true of you.* To the proclamation just made about what can be appropriated through faith in Christ, Paul adds a warning drawn from the prophetic writings of the OT. He warns against spurning the Christian message as he calls upon one of the prophets of Israel of old.

41. *Look, you scoffers, be amazed, and then disappear! For I am doing a deed in your days, a deed which you will not believe, even if someone tells you about it."* Paul cites Hab 1:5 (LXX), curtailing it slightly and repeating the word, "a deed." The LXX runs thus: "Look, you scoffers, gaze well and be amazed at wondrous things, and then disappear! For I am doing a deed in your days, which you will not believe even if someone tells you." The Hebrew MT is different: "Look among the nations and see; be amazed and astounded! For I am doing a deed in your days that you would not believe, if it were told." The MT reads *baggôyim*, "among the nations," instead of the LXX's *hoi kataphronētai*, "scoffers." A Qumran Hebrew text of Habakkuk reads instead of *baggôyim*, "among the nations," the word *habbôgĕdîm*, "scoffers" (1QpHab 2:1–2), the very term that the LXX and Luke presuppose. The words of the prophet Habakkuk were directed in the MT form against the Neo-Babylonians or Chaldeans (= "the nations"), a tyrannical nation that sought to dominate ancient Judah, probably sometime between 608 and 598 B.C. Paul now cites the LXX form of the words of Habakkuk as a warning to the Jews of Pisidian Antioch. They must not scoff at God's message to which they are now listening. In effect, it is Luke's way of stressing how God's intentions concerning the Gentiles will indeed be played out.

The crucial word, however, in the climactic ending of this sermon is *ergon*, "deed," which Luke inserts a second time into the OT quotation. It has been interpreted of the "resurrection" of Christ (Pillai, *Apostolic Interpretation*, 72–73), or of what God "has done in Christ" (Barrett, *Acts*, 652). It should more likely be understood of the goal and purpose of Paul's speech, the "work" that God is now performing, viz., the missionary proclamation of the Christ-event to Jews and Gentiles (cf. 13:2). In effect, Paul is saying to the synagogue audience that they should not spurn the "word of salvation" now being addressed to them, but should respond to it with faith in Christ.

So ends the major speech of Paul in the synagogue of Pisidian Antioch.

42. *As they were leaving.* I.e., as Paul and Barnabas were leaving the synagogue. Some MSS (the *Koinē* text-tradition) add *ek tēs synagōgēs Ioudaiōn*, "(going out) of the synagogue of the Jews." This verse begins the sequel to Paul's speech (13:42–48), which records the conversion of many Jews and proselytes.

the people begged them to speak further on this topic again on the following sabbath. Lit., "they (indefinite) kept urging that these things be addressed to them (again) on the sabbath in between," a cumbersome sentence. Luke uses *eis to metaxy sabbaton* to say "on the next sabbath" (BAGD, 513). This is the immediate reaction to Paul's speech.

43. *After the meeting of the synagogue had finally broken up, many Jews and devout converts to Judaism followed Paul and Barnabas.* A further reaction is found in those who have been attracted by Paul's speech and are said to be *polloi tōn Ioudaiōn kai sebomenōn prosēlytōn,* "many of the Jews and devoted proselytes." At the end, MS 614 adds "asking to be baptized." The ptc. *sebomenos,* "worshiping," is often used as a substantive to denote pagans who sympathized with the Jewish religion (see NOTE on 10:2); Luke uses it in 13:50; 16:14; 17:4, 17; 18:7; 19:27 in that sense. Here the ptc. modifies "proselytes," a different group (on proselytes, see NOTE on 2:11).

who continued to speak to them. I.e., Paul and Barnabas continued to converse with Antiochenes about the topic of Paul's speech.

urge them to hold fast to the grace of God. This Lucan comment finally introduces a main element of Pauline teaching, the role of divine grace in the process of conversion and justification. Paul urges them to cooperate duly with such divine guidance and assistance.

MS D and some other MSS add "The message happened to go through the whole city" at the end of this verse. It provides a detail that explains the following verse.

44. *The next sabbath almost the whole town gathered to hear the word of the Lord.* Lit., "on the coming sabbath almost all the town." Again Lucan hyperbole comes to the fore; see NOTE on 2:44. One wonders how the "whole town" could have fitted into the synagogue. Luke is not worried about such details. MSS P^{74}, ℵ, A, B^2, 33, 36, 81, 181, and 1739 read *ton logon tou Kyriou,* but MSS B*, C, E, Ψ, and 614 have *ton logon tou theou,* "the word of God." At the end of the verse MS D adds: ". . . to listen to Paul who made many an address about the Lord."

45. *When the Jews saw the crowds, they became very jealous and with violent abuse countered what was said by Paul.* A similar reaction will be found in 14:2.

46. *Both Paul and Barnabas, however, spoke out fearlessly.* Luke again introduces the theme of bold and frank proclamation; see NOTE on *parrhēsia* in 4:13. Paul and Barnabas are not deterred by the denial and abuse.

"To you, first of all, the word of God had to be proclaimed. The Lucan principle of proclaiming the Word first to Jews emerges once more; see NOTES on 3:26 and 13:5. The necessity comes from God's providence for his Chosen People, to which Paul alluded at the beginning of his discourse.

Since you reject it. I.e., the Word of God. *Auton* is masc. and refers to *ton logon tou theou,* "God's word."

and thus judge yourselves unworthy of eternal life. Lucan irony comes forth. "Eternal life" is closely linked to acceptance of "the word of God" in faith. Paul is made to mince no words in speaking to his Jewish opponents in Pisidian Antioch. The phrase *zōē aiōnios* occurs only here and in v 48 in Acts; cf. Luke 10:25; 18:18, 30. It is a phrase inherited from Palestinian Judaism, either as *ḥayyê ʿôlām* (Dan 12:2; Sir 37:26; 4Q181 1:4, 6); or as *ḥayyê neṣaḥ* (1QS 4:7; CD 3:20; 4Q511 2 i 4; 6Q18 2:2), to describe life in the blessed period of final consummation. The phrase would be equivalent to "salvation."

we now turn to the Gentiles. This might sound like a new principle that Paul is adopting, which might govern his dealings with people in the future, leaving Jews to their own fate and confining his attention to Gentiles. However, he will continue to try to address himself first to fellow Jews (see 18:4–6, 19; 19:8). If they continue to reject his message, then he will turn to Gentiles. In effect, this verse may seem like a turning point in Acts, but the reader already knows from the episode about the call of Paul (9:15) that his evangelization of Gentiles is not solely motivated by the rejection of his message by fellow Jews.

47. *so the Lord has instructed us.* Paul recalls the instruction rooted in the call of the risen Christ on the road to Damascus: he was to become "a chosen instrument of mine to carry my name before Gentiles and kings, and the children of Israel" (9:15). Although he was told that he should preach to "the children of Israel," he realizes that his main role was to preach to Gentiles, and now he bases that instruction on a prophetic word of Scripture.

"I have made you a light of the Gentiles, that you may be a means of salvation to the end of the earth.'" At first sight, it seems that Paul explains his turning to Gentiles by citing Isa 49:6d (LXX), i.e., that he is a light for the Gentiles because of the Christ whom he preaches. The full text of Isaiah reads: *idou tetheika se eis diathēkēn genous, eis phōs ethnōn tou einai se eis sōtērian heōs eschatou tēs gēs*, "Look, I have set you as a covenant for a race, a light for Gentiles, that you may be a means of salvation to the end of the earth." Luke omits "as a covenant for a race" and so eliminates all reference to the Jewish people. Moreover, the quotation in Acts corresponds better, but not exactly, to phrases in the MT. The quotation comes from the second Servant Song in the Book of Isaiah, and Paul seems to be applying the Servant's words to himself (and Barnabas). The trouble is that the Isaiah passage speaks of someone in the 2d sg., but it is being applied to Paul and Barnabas, who speak as "we" or "us" (v 47a). So the quoted part of the Servant Song may in reality refer to Christ, who through Barnabas and Paul is making known to the Jews of Pisidian Antioch this "light of the Gentiles" and "means of salvation to the end of the earth," i.e., a light that will shine on Gentiles and bring salvation everywhere. Cf. 28:16. The last phrase of the quotation echoes Acts 1:8. Luke is stressing once again God's intention in regard to Gentiles. Isaiah's words reveal that that intention is being realized in a way different from what one might have expected from the words of Habakkuk quoted in v 41.

48. *Gentiles who heard this were delighted and were continually honoring the word of the Lord.* Cf. 11:18. So God's intention is realized and his plan of salvation is seen to be implemented in the case, not of Jews in Antioch, but of some Gentiles. Their existence is characterized by joy and praise of God.

All who were destined for eternal life became believers. Lit., "and as many as were destined . . ." Eternal life (see NOTE on 13:46) becomes the destiny of those who put faith in the risen Christ, who has been sent by the Father for the salvation of human beings.

49. *The word of the Lord continued to be carried through that whole area.* This minor summary statement records the radiating spread of the Word. The "area" would be the southern central part of Asia Minor.

50. *The Jews, however, stirred up well-to-do women worshipers and the leading men of the town and started a persecution against Paul and Barnabas.* In contrast to the spread of the Word there emerges trouble. What was done to Peter and John earlier now becomes the fate of Paul and Barnabas. Persecution begins. On *sebomenas,* see NOTES on 10:2; 13:43.

whom they expelled from their district. The persecution takes the form of banishment of the two missionaries. Cf. 16:37.

51. *So they shook its dust from their feet in protest against them.* Cf. Luke 9:5; 10:11. They sought to get rid of anything of that district that might still cling to them, by an act symbolizing the severance of all association with it. Jews returning to Palestine from pagan territory were expected to do the same (see Str-B, 1.571; cf. H. J. Cadbury, "Dust and Garments," *Beginnings,* 5.269–77. Compare 18:6.

went on to Iconium. The town of *Ikonion* was in Phrygia according to Xenophon (*Anabasis* 1.2.19), but according to Pliny the Elder (*Naturalis Historia* 5.25.95) it was *urbs celeberrima,* "most famous city," of Lycaonia. Strabo (*Geography* 12.6.1) too says that it was a prosperous town in Lycaonia. See W. M. Ramsay, *Cities,* 317–84. Cf. 2 Tim 3:11 for a further reference to these sufferings in Antioch, Iconium, and Lystra.

52. *The disciples were filled with joy and the Holy Spirit.* Presumably Paul and Barnabas are meant by the "disciples," even though the term could mean other Christians as well in that region. Their reaction to persecution is reminiscent of that of Stephen (7:55).

BIBLIOGRAPHY (13:13–52)

Bates, W. H., "A Note on Acts, 13:39," *SE VI* (TU 112; Berlin: Akademie, 1973), 8–10.

Bérard, J., "Recherches sur les itinéraires de Saint Paul en Asie Mineure," *RArch* 6/5 (1935): 57–90.

Billerbeck, P., "Ein Synagogengottesdienst in Jesu Tagen," *ZNW* 55 (1964): 143–61.

Broughton, T.R.S., "Three Notes on Saint Paul's Journeys in Asia Minor," *Quantulacumque: Studies Presented to Kirsopp Lake . . .* (London: Christophers, 1937), 131–38.

Bruce, F. F., "Justification by Faith in the Non-Pauline Writings of the New Testament," *EvQ* 24 (1952): 66–77.

———, "Paul's Use of the Old Testament in Acts," *Tradition and Interpretation in the New Testament: Essays in Honor of E. Earle Ellis . . .* (Tübingen: Mohr [Siebeck]; Grand Rapids, MI: Eerdmans, 1987), 71–79, esp. 71–73.

Buss, M. F.-J., *Die Missionspredigt des Apostels Paulus im pisidischen Antiochien: Analyse von Apg 13,16–41 im Hinblick auf die literarische und thematische Einheit der Paulusrede* (Stuttgart: Katholisches Bibelwerk, 1980).

Delling, G., "Israels Geschichte und Jesusgeschehen nach Acta," *Neues Testament und Geschichte: Historisches Geschehen und Deutung im Neuen Testament: Oscar Cullmann zum 70. Geburtstag* (ed. H. Baltensweiler and B. Reicke; Zurich: Theologischer V.; Tübingen: Mohr [Siebeck], 1972), 187–97.

Downing, F. G., "Ethical Pagan Theism and the Speeches in Acts," *NTS* 27 (1980–81): 544–63.

Dumais, M., *Le langage de l'évangélisation: L'Annonce missionnaire en milieu juif (Actes 13,16–41)* (Recherches 16; Tournai/Paris: Desclée; Montreal: Bellarmin, 1976).

Dupont, J., "'Filius meus es tu': L'Interprétation de Ps. II, 7 dans le Nouveau Testament," *RSR* 35 (1948): 522–43; repr. *Etudes*, 294–97.

———, "Je t'ai établi lumière des nations Ac 13,14.43–52," *AsSeign* 2/25 (1969): 19–24; repr. *Nouvelles études*, 343–49.

———, "*Ta hosia Dauid ta pista* (Ac xiii 34 = Is lv 3)," *RB* 68 (1961): 91–114; repr. *Etudes*, 337–59.

———, *The Salvation of the Gentiles: Essays on the Acts of the Apostles* (New York: Paulist, 1979), 11–33.

———, "L'Interprétation des psaumes dans les Actes des Apôtres," *Le Psautier: Ses origines. Ses problèmes littéraires. Son influence* (Orientalia et biblica lovaniensia 4; Louvain: Publications universitaires, 1962), 357–88; repr. *Etudes*, 283–307.

Ellingworth, P., "Acts 13.38—A Query," *BT* 45 (1994): 242–43.

Ellul, D., "Antioche de Pisidie: Une prédication . . . trois credos? (Actes 13,13–43)," *FilNeot* 5 (1992): 3–14.

French, D., "Acts and the Roman Roads of Asia Minor," *The Book of Acts in Its Graeco-Roman Setting* (BAFCS 2), 49–58.

Ghidelli, C., "Un saggio di lettura dell'AT nel libro degli Atti (Atti 13,33–35)," *Parole di Vita* 9 (1964): 83–91.

Glombitza, O., "Akta xiii.15–41: Analyse einer lukanischen Predigt vor Juden: Ein Beitrag zum Problem der Reden in Akta," *NTS* 5 (1958–59): 306–17.

Goldsmith, D., "Acts 13:33–37: A *Pesher* on II Samuel 7," *JBL* 87 (1968): 321–24.

Green, H. B., "Matthew, Clement and Luke: Their Sequence and Relationship," *JTS* 40 (1989): 1–25, esp. 18–21.

Grelot, P., "Note sur Actes, xiii,47," *RB* 88 (1981): 368–72.

Grobel, K., "'He That Cometh after Me,'" *JBL* 60 (1941): 397–401.

Harnack, A., *Date*, 68.

Hartman, L., "Davids son: Apropå Acta 13,16–41," *SEA* 28–29 (1963–64): 117–34.

Kaiser, W. C., Jr., "The Promise to David in Psalm 16 and Its Application in Acts 2:25–33 and 13:32–37," *JETS* 23 (1980): 219–29.

———, "The Unfailing Kindnesses Promised to David: Isaiah 55.3," *JSOT* 45 (1989): 91–98.
Kilgallen, J. J., "Acts 13,38–39: Culmination of Paul's Speech in Pisidia," *Bib* 69 (1988): 480–506.
Klein, G., "Der Synkretismus als theologisches Problem in der ältesten christlichen Apologetik," *ZTK* 64 (1967): 40–82.
Lövestam, E., *Son and Saviour: A Study of Acts 13,32–37: With an Appendix, 'Son of God' in the Synoptic Gospels* (ConNT 18; Lund: Gleerup, 1961).
Mackenzie, R. S., "The Western Text of Acts: Some Lucanisms in Selected Sermons," *JBL* 104 (1985): 637–50, esp. 641–46.
Macleod, J., "The Sure Mercies of David," *EvQ* 14 (1942): 128–38.
Menoud, P.-H., "Justification by Faith According to the Book of Acts," *Jesus Christ and the Faith: A Collection of Studies* (PTMS 18; Pittsburgh: Pickwick, 1978), 202–27.
Michaels, J. R., "Paul and John the Baptist: An Odd Couple?" *TynBull* 42 (1991): 245–60.
O'Toole, R. F., "Christ's Resurrection in Acts 13,13–52," *Bib* 60 (1979): 361–72.
Pillai, C.A.J., *Apostolic Interpretation of History: A Commentary on Acts 13:16–41* (Hicksville, NY: Exposition, 1980).
———, *Early Missionary Preaching: A Study of Luke's Report in Acts 13* (Hicksville, NY: Exposition, 1979).
Ramsay, W. M., *The Cities of St. Paul* (London: Hodder and Stoughton; New York: Armstrong, 1908).
Sandt, H. van de, "The Quotations in Acts 13,32–52 as a Reflection of Luke's LXX Interpretation," *Bib* 75 (1994): 26–58.
Schmitt, J., "Kerygma pascal et lecture scripturaire dans l'instruction d'Antioche (Act. 13,23–37)," *Les Actes des Apôtres* (ed. J. Kremer), 155–67.
Schweizer, E., "The Concept of the Davidic 'Son of God' in Acts and Its Old Testament Background," *StLA*, 186–93.
Silva, D. A. de, "Paul's Sermon in Antioch of Pisidia," *BSac* 151 (1994): 32–49.
Turner, M.M.B., "The Sabbath, Sunday and the Law in Luke/Acts," *From Sabbath to Lord's Day* (ed. D. A. Carson; Grand Rapids, MI: Zondervan, 1982), 99–157.
Wilckens, U., *Die Missionsreden der Apostelgeschichte* (WMANT 5; Neukirchen-Vluyn: Neukirchener-V., 1961), 50–55, 70–71.
Williamson, H.G.M., "'The Sure Mercies of David': Subjective or Objective Genitive?" *JSS* 23 (1978): 31–49.

4. Evangelization of Iconium (14:1–7)

14 [1]In Iconium Paul and Barnabas happened to enter together into the synagogue of the Jews; they spoke in such wise that a good number of Jews and Greeks became believers. [2]But Jews who remained unbelieving stirred up the Gentiles

and poisoned their minds against the brothers. [3]So they stayed there for a considerable time, speaking out fearlessly about the Lord, who confirmed the word about his grace, by causing signs and wonders to be performed by them. [4]Most of the townspeople were divided: some siding with the Jews, others with the apostles. [5]But when an attempt was made by Gentiles and Jews, together with their leaders, to mistreat and even stone them, [6]Paul and Barnabas became aware of it and fled to the Lycaonian towns of Lystra and Derbe and the surrounding countryside. [7]There they continued to preach.

WT: [1][omits "In Iconium"]. Jews and Greeks were surprised and became believers. [2]The leaders of the synagogue of the Jews and (other) leaders stirred up a persecution of them against the upright and poisoned . . . [4]others associating with the apostles because of the word of God. [5]Again the Jews with some Gentiles stirred up a persecution a second time; having stoned them, they drove them out of the town. [6]They fled and came to Lycaonia, to a certain town called Lystra. [7]They continued to preach, and all the populace was aroused by their teaching. Paul and Barnabas continued to spend time in Lystra.

COMMENT

At the end of the last episode Paul and Barnabas had moved on from Pisidian Antioch, where a persecution had arisen against them, and they came to the town of Iconium (13:51). Now they undertake the evangelization of this town, making converts of a good number of Jews and also of Greeks. The effect of this evangelization is the same as that in Pisidian Antioch, for Jews who do not accept their message stir up antagonism against Paul and Barnabas and bring it about that the townspeople are divided. Some of them support the apostles, and others the Jews. The opposition grows more violent, when an attempt is made even to stone them, and so the two of them pass on to other towns in the Lycaonian region.

From a form-critical point of view, the episode is another narrative with little complication in its account. The source behind this chapter is, however, problematic. Dibelius ascribed it to what he called the Itinerary source, whereas Barrett (*Acts*, 672) and Weiser (*Apg.*, 348) speak of it as coming from an Antiochene source. I consider it to be an episode that Luke has derived from his Pauline source, but it has undergone some Lucan redaction, traces of which are seen in the special Lucan phrases (on which see Lüdemann, *Early Christianity*, 156–64). In particular, the chapter stands out because of the way Luke presents the work of Paul and Barnabas in spite of the opposition to it from Jews of Iconium. Luke makes it clear that the transition of Paul's missionary activity from the synagogue to Gentiles is divinely inspired.

The real problem in the paragraph is the position of v 3. To many commentators it seems out of place. Ramsay simply eliminated it, whereas Moffatt placed it before v 2; for others vv 3–5 are only an enlarged account of vv 1–2, perhaps derived from a different source. Codex Bezae also sought to resolve some of the problem (see WT above). Michael ("The Original Position") may be right in saying that v 3 originally stood in the middle of 13:48. In any case, one has to interpret it where it is in the Alexandrian text today.

One other item calls for special comment: Paul and Barnabas are called "apostles" in vv 4 and 14. Apart from these occurrences Luke never accords Paul the title *apostolos*. Even though Paul will become the hero of the second part of Acts and is already playing an important role in preaching to Gentiles on Mission I, Luke seems to have been reluctant to use that title for him. We know from Paul's letters how he had to insist on his apostolic role and the right to be called *apostolos* (Gal 1:1–17; 1 Cor 9:1–2). Apart from that struggle, a reason for Luke's reluctance to use the title for him is the way he has equated the Twelve with the apostles and the apostles with the Twelve and the way he has portrayed Jesus in Luke 6:13, he "called his disciples and chose twelve of them whom he also named apostles." Only Luke among the evangelists ascribes that name for the Twelve to Jesus himself. Elsewhere in the NT one reads about others who may well have had that title in the early church: "Andronicus and Junia . . . who are outstanding among the apostles" (Rom 16:7 [see *Romans*, 737–39 for the problems of interpreting this verse]); and about unnamed "apostles" (2 Cor 8:23). In Acts itself Matthias has been added to the Eleven in the place of Judas Iscariot (1:26), so that he too would have been called an apostle. Strangely enough, however, in Acts 14 Luke uses the pl. *apostoloi* of Barnabas and Paul. This designation probably comes from the source he is using, in which the two were so named, and he has not bothered to make the source conform to his otherwise usual practice. So Roloff, *Apg.*, 211; Weiser, *Apg.*, 348–49. If this explanation is not considered valid, and Barrett (*Acts*, 671) considers that it is not, then it is difficult to explain why Luke would refer to Paul as an "apostle" only in this chapter. Becker thinks that Luke uses the title in these two instances only in the sense of "a church missionary" and that it does not have the same sense as that implied in 1:21–22 (*Paul*, 59, 79). That, however, is a dubious distinction. In 1:21–22 Luke has listed his criteria for membership in the Twelve, and otherwise he never regards either Paul or Barnabas as part of that group. There were, in fact, in the early church other persons beyond the Twelve who bore the title *apostolos*.

The episode describes the experience of Paul and Barnabas in Iconium as they dutifully proclaim the Word of God and fearlessly announce the message of salvation. It is a mixed experience, at once one of acceptance and of rejection. Paul and Barnabas are thus good examples of the Church under Stress, as they boldly preach about the Lord who confirms their message with his grace and various signs and wonders. Their flight to other towns in the Lycaonian area is the result of their prudent reaction to their rejection and to the persecution and opposition being stirred up against them. That flight enables them to continue the preaching of the gospel elsewhere.

NOTES

14:1. *In Iconium Paul and Barnabas happened to enter together into the synagogue of the Jews.* Even though Paul has enunciated in 13:46 his principle of turning "to the Gentiles," he continues to try to preach to Jews as well. In fact, Paul and Barnabas go to the Jewish synagogue in Iconium as their first-mentioned visit. Recall the formulation of 9:15, where the risen Christ speaks of Paul as "a chosen instrument . . . to carry my name before Gentiles and kings, *and the children of Israel.*" Even though Paul in his letters speaks of God revealing his Son to him on the road to Damascus "that I might preach him among the Gentiles" (Gal 1:16) and calls himself "an apostle of the Gentiles" (Rom 11:13), he nevertheless thought that he was obligated to all human beings: "To Jews I became as a Jew, in order to win over Jews; to those under the law I became as one under the law—though not being myself under the law—that I might win those under the law" (1 Cor 9:20). This then explains why Luke depicts him entering "the synagogue of the Jews." Instead of "together," used above as the translation of *kata to auto,* one could also translate it "in the same way," i.e., as Barnabas and Paul had done in Antioch; so now they do in Iconium. See E. Nestle, "Acts 14:1," *ExpTim* 24 (1912–13): 187–88. On "synagogue," see NOTE on 6:9. Luke again uses *egeneto de* with an infin. (see *Luke,* 118).

they spoke in such wise that a good number of Jews and Greeks became believers. Success among the Jews of Iconium attends their evangelization at first, but it also includes Greeks. Where the latter are found we are not told. MS D adds "to them" to the verb.

2. *Jews who remained unbelieving stirred up the Gentiles and poisoned their minds against the brothers.* Christians are again called *adelphoi*; see NOTE on 1:15. Paul and Barnabas are persecuted by Iconium Jews who refuse to accept the Christian message and proceed to stir up even Greeks against not only the two of them, but also against other Christians as well.

3. *they stayed there for a considerable time.* In this case Paul and Barnabas do not take flight, but face the opposition on the spot. The conj. *men oun,* omitted in my translation, could be rendered, "Nay rather," because it expresses the contrast between flight and facing the opposition. See D. S. Sharp, "The Meaning of *men oun* in Acts 14:3," *ExpTim* 44 (1932–33): 528.

speaking out fearlessly about the Lord. The motif of frank and fearless testimony reappears; see NOTE on 4:13. *Kyrios* is used of the risen Christ; see NOTES on 1:21; 2:21.

who confirmed the word about his grace. Or "who bore witness to the word of his grace." The message that Paul and Barnabas preach is characterized as *logos tēs charitos,* "a word of grace," i.e., a message of how God's favor manifests itself in Christ and in the preaching about him toward those who are open to it.

by causing signs and wonders to be performed by them. The same expression, "signs and wonders," occurs in 2:22 as the way God authenticated the ministry of Jesus himself (see NOTE there). Now divine intervention attends the preaching about him by Paul and Barnabas. It is a sign of God's support for their missionary endeavors.

4. *Most of the townspeople were divided: some siding with the Jews, others with the apostles.* On the use of *apostoloi,* see the COMMENT above.

5. *when an attempt was made by Gentiles and Jews, together with their leaders,*

to mistreat and even stone them. This reveals the extent to which the opposition to Paul and Barnabas has grown in Iconium.

6. *Paul and Barnabas became aware of it and fled to the Lycaonian towns of Lystra and Derbe and the surrounding countryside.* Luke's text implies that Iconium was not in Lycaonia, but that merely reflects the changing boundaries of Phrygia and Lycaonia in the first century, for which there is little historical control at present. *Lystra* was a Roman colony situated about 40 km south-southwest of Iconium in Lycaonia, which was a district in Asia Minor bounded by Cappadocia, Galatia, Phrygia, Pisidia, and Cilicia. *Derbē* was another town in Lycaonia, situated some 96 km southeast of Lystra, at modern Kerti Hüyük. Cf. M. Ballance, "The Site of Derbe; a New Inscription," *Anatolian Studies* 7 (1957): 147–51. It is said by Strabo (*Geography* 12.6.3 p. 569) to be in the province of Galatia, and he was followed by Ramsay, but that location is now questionable. See G. Ogg, "Derbe," *NTS* 9 (1962–63): 367–70. Cf. W. Ruge, "Lykaonia," PW 13/2. 2253–65.

7. *There they continued to preach.* Luke uses the verb *euangelizesthai* absolutely (without an object); see NOTE on 5:42.

BIBLIOGRAPHY (14:1–7)

Becker, J., *Paul: Apostle to the Gentiles* (Louisville: Westminster/John Knox, 1993), 59, 79.

Beutler, J., "Die paulinische Heidenmission am Vorabend des Apostelkonzils: Zur Redaktionsgeschichte von Apg 14,1–20," *TP* 43 (1968): 360–83.

Bludau, A., "Paulus in Lystra: Ac 14,7–21," *Der Katholik* 87 (1907): 91–113, 161–83.

Dupont, J., "L'Apôtre comme intermédiaire du salut dans les Actes des Apôtres," *RTP* 30 (1980): 342–58; repr. *Nouvelles études*, 112–32.

Elderen, B. van, "Some Archaeological Observations on Paul's First Missionary Journey," *Apostolic History and the Gospel: Biblical and Historical Essays Presented to F. F. Bruce* . . . (ed. W. W. Gasque and R. P. Martin; Grand Rapids, MI: Eerdmans, 1970), 151–61, esp. 156–60.

Michael, J. H., "The Original Position of Acts xiv.3," *ExpTim* 40 (1928–29): 514–16.

Roberts, J. E., "Acts 14:3," *ExpTim* 22 (1910–11): 329–31.

Verheul, A., "Kent sint Paulus buiten 'de Twaalf' nog andere apostelen," *StudCath* 22 (1947): 65–75.

5. EVANGELIZATION OF LYSTRA AND DERBE (14:8–20)

[8]In Lystra there sat a cripple, lame from birth, who had never walked. [9]He listened to Paul as he was talking. When Paul looked intently at him and saw that he had the faith to be saved, [10]he said to him in a loud voice, "Stand up!" The

man jumped up and started to walk around. [11]When the crowds saw what Paul had done, they cried out in Lycaonian, "Gods have come down to us in human form." [12]They called Barnabas Zeus, and Paul Hermes because he was the chief speaker. [13]The priest of the temple of Zeus, which stood just outside the town, brought oxen and garlands to the gates and, accompanied by the crowds, intended to offer sacrifice. [14]When the apostles Barnabas and Paul heard of this, they tore their garments and rushed out into the crowd, shouting, [15]"Friends, why do you do this? We are human beings like you, trying to preach to you to turn from such folly to the living God, who made the heavens, the earth, the sea, and all that is in them. [16]In bygone generations he allowed all nations to go their own way; [17]yet, in bestowing his benefits, he did not leave himself without a trace, for he has sent you rains from the heavens and seasons of fruitfulness; he has filled you with food and your hearts with gladness." [18]Even with such words they hardly kept the crowds from sacrificing to them. [19]Then some Jews from Antioch and Iconium came there and won over the crowds. They stoned Paul and dragged him out of the town, leaving him there for dead. [20]But his disciples formed a circle about him, and soon he got up and went back into the town. The next day he left with Barnabas for Derbe.

WT: [8][omits "In Lystra"]. There was a man sitting there, with crippled feet, who had never walked since birth. [9]He listened to Paul talking, being struck with awe. [11]When the crowd saw. [13]The priests of the temple of Zeus. [14][omits "the apostles"] . . . into the crowd, saying. [15]Friends, what are you doing? . . . trying to preach God to you that you may turn to him who made . . . [16]allowed every nation of humans to go its own way. [18]they scarcely persuaded the crowds not to sacrifice to them, but to make their way, each one to his own home. [19][adds at the beginning:] While they were spending time (there) and were teaching, (some) Jews came from Antioch and Iconium. Though they debated with them fearlessly, they persuaded the crowds to dissociate themselves from them, maintaining that they were saying nothing true, but were lying about everything. [20]and in the evening they led him into the town of Lystra.

COMMENT

Having left Iconium and fled to Lystra, Paul and Barnabas continue their evangelization. Their ministry includes a miracle wrought for a man crippled from birth. The reaction to the cure among the people is to regard Paul and Barnabas as "gods." That is rejected, and their reaction becomes the occasion for Paul's first speech to pagans. It is a short address (vv 15–17), in which Paul introduces no christological kerygma, but seeks to inculcate belief in the living and true God.

After the summary-like description of vv 1–7, Luke now comes to individual details. The episode is basically a narrative, including a miracle story of healing, which becomes the occasion for a speech, a Lucan composition. One notes the parallelism of miracles performed on behalf of a cripple by Peter (chap. 3) and Paul (chap. 14). The speech itself is a protest, theological (and not christological) in its thrust, addressed to Gentiles outside of Palestine. It makes a proclamation: turn to the living God who has not left himself without a trace. Paul does not blame the pagans here, as he does in Rom 1:20. The Lucan message is that witnesses to the Christian Gospel fear no comparison with the *theioi andres* of paganism; they turn all attention to the living God. In this regard, the speech resembles what Paul himself wrote in 1 Thess 1:9b–10.

The miraculous cure of the cripple of Lystra incites the pagan populace there to regard Paul and Barnabas as gods. To prevent the people and their priest from sacrificing to them, Paul utters a short discourse in which he tries to turn the people to acknowledge "the living God." Instead of beginning with the patriarchs of Israel, as Paul had done in his address to the Jews of Pisidian Antioch (13:17), he now begins with creation in this address to pagans. He teaches them that the living God is the creator and provider of all that is good for human life. This God sends them rain, seasons of fruitfulness, food, and all that gladdens the heart. This message that Paul preaches to such pagan people is basic, and Paul does not hesitate to affirm such fundamental truths. The good that Paul might have been achieving with such people is interrupted by "some Jews from Antioch and Iconium" who arrive on the scene and begin turning the people against Paul and Barnabas; that opposition ends in the stoning of Paul, who manages to survive it. So ends the good that Paul was able to do in Lystra, and so continues the story of Jewish opposition to him. In spite of it, he marches on to preach the good news elsewhere, for it is not yet time for him to leave this world.

NOTES

8. *In Lystra there sat a cripple, lame from birth, who had never walked.* Lit., "Incapacitated in (his) feet, a cripple from his mother's womb, who had never walked, was sitting (there)." The word order in the Greek text is strange: the phrase "in Lystra" occurs between "incapacitated" and "in (his) feet." For this reason, the WT alters the order, but its meaning is not really changed. A threefold description is given of the man's condition.

9. *He listened to Paul as he was talking.* He attends to the testimony being borne to the risen Christ. MS D adds "being in fear."

When Paul looked intently at him and saw that he had the faith to be saved. Paul is the one who gazes intently, whereas in 3:5 the cripple is the one who stares. Again Luke links "faith" to the cure, as in 3:16; 4:9–12.

10. *he said to him in a loud voice, "Stand up!"* Lit., "stand up straight on your feet." Paul performs the miracle with a word of command, and his cure reminds the reader of that of Peter in 3:6, another cure by word of mouth.

The man jumped up and started to walk around. I.e., showing that he was indeed cured. Cf. 3:8.

11. *When the crowd saw what Paul had done, they cried out in Lycaonian.* The adv. *Lykaonisti* must refer to a dialect, spoken in that remote and less developed district of Anatolia, possibly a developed form of Luwian, related to ancient Hittite. Cf. G. Neumann, "Das Weiterleben hethitischen und luwischen Sprachguts in hellenistischer Zeit," *Proceedings of the Eighth International Congress of Lin-*

guists (Oslo: Oslo University Press, 1958), 609–10. All surviving inscriptions from the area are in either Greek or Latin.

Gods have come down to us in human form. A Greek myth, known in Phrygia in Asia Minor, tells of Zeus (Jupiter) and Hermes (Mercury) visiting the elderly Philemon and his wife Baucis "in the likeness of human beings" and rewarding them for their hospitality by telling them to climb a mountain in view of a coming flood that destroys other inhospitable people (see Ovid, *Metamorphoses* 8.617–725; cf. J. Fontenrose, *Philemon, Lot, and Lycaon* [University of California Publications in Classical Philology 13/4; Berkeley: University of California Press, 1945], 93–119). Such a myth, perhaps not in its precise Ovidian form, may well explain the reaction of the Lystrans to Paul and Barnabas and their comparing them to the same two Greek gods. Cf. 28:6, where Paul is thought to be divine by the Maltese.

12. *They called Barnabas Zeus.* Zeus was the chief deity of the ancient Greek pantheon, the ruler of the heavens (corresponding to Latin Jupiter). Though Lystra was a Roman colony, the gods are given Greek names, Zeus and Hermes; and though the deities were so worshiped with classical Greek names in Lystra, they were probably older local gods linked to better known Greek gods. The hellenization of native gods as Zeus and Hermes is known also from inscriptions from Lystra. See D.W.J. Gill and B. W. Winter, "Acts and Roman Religion," *The Book of Acts in Its Graeco-Roman Setting* (BAFCS 2), 79–102.

and Paul Hermes because he was the chief speaker. Hermes was the messenger of the gods in the Greek pantheon (corresponding to Latin Mercury). In other words, the people of Lystra accord Paul and Barnabas the customary welcome of their culture, receiving them almost as deified ambassadors; see Plato, *Leges* 941A. Cf. W. M. Calder, "Zeus and Hermes." In Greek mythology, however, Hermes was not considered to be a healing god, and so, if the Lycaonians attempt to deify Paul, it must have been for the reason stated in this verse. Compare Iamblichus, *De Mysteriis* 1.1: *theos ho tōn logōn hēgemōn,* "the god (who is) the leader in speaking" or "of words."

13. *The priest of the temple of Zeus, which stood just outside the town.* Luke has curtailed his expression, writing *ho te hiereus tou Dios tou ontos pro tēs poleōs,* "the priest of Zeus who is before the town," where "Zeus before the town" is undoubtedly a short way of speaking of a temple of Zeus outside the town limits. This mode of expression is found elsewhere. MS D reads "the priests," which is said to be historically more accurate, because the Anatolian god grecized as Zeus was served by a collegium of priests. See W. M. Calder, "The 'Priest.'"

brought oxen and garlands to the gates and, accompanied by crowds, intended to offer sacrifice. I.e., to Barnabas and Paul, as v 18 makes clear, since the Lycaonians regard them as gods in human form. "The gates" might refer to those of the town, or possibly to a precinct surrounding the temple of Zeus.

14. *When the apostles Barnabas and Paul heard of this.* Luke again refers to the two of them as "apostles"; see COMMENT above. Cf. W. M. Green, "Apostles—Acts," *ResQ* 4 (1960): 245–47.

they tore their garments and rushed out into the crowd, shouting. For the ancient practice of tearing of garments as a sign of horror, see LXX of Gen 37:29; Esth 4:1; Jdt 14:16, 19.

15. *Friends.* Lit., "men" *(andres)*, compare 7:26; 19:25; 25:24; 27:10, 25.

"why do you do this? We are human beings like you. So they try to dissuade the people from sacrificing to them as if they were gods.

trying to preach to you to turn from such folly to the living God. This is usually regarded as another Pauline speech, even though it is only three verses long. It is neither kerygmatic nor christological, as were the missionary speeches addressed to Jews, but rather *theo*logical, as the apostles preach about "the living God." This sample address made to pagans foreshadows the speech that Paul will deliver on the Areopagus in Athens (17:22–31). Yet in it Paul does not argue as Greek philosophers might have about the existence of God, who is rather described in OT terms as "living" (2 Kgs 19:4, 16; Isa 37:4, 17; Hos 2:1 [LXX]; Dan 6:21 [Theodotion]). The implication is that other gods are not.

who made the heavens, the earth, the sea, and all that is in them. This description of God the creator may be drawn from Exod 20:11. It is an allusion by which Paul validates his mission to the Gentiles. Compare Ps 146:6 (LXX), which is echoed in 4Q521 2 ii 2, where the final phrase is also preserved.

16. *In bygone generations he allowed all nations to go their own way.* So Paul expresses bygone divine tolerance of pagan worship; he insinuates that God will suffer it no longer. Cf. Acts 17:30; 1 Cor 1:20–21.

17. *yet, in bestowing his benefits, he did not leave himself without a trace.* Lit., "and yet he did not leave himself untestified (*or* witness-less) in doing good," a litotes. Luke depicts Paul using some of the same arguments that Paul employs in Rom 1:19–21. God has made himself manifest in the good things that he has made in creation or given to humanity. In such natural blessings God has left traces of his deity.

he has sent you rains from the heavens and seasons of fruitfulness; he has filled you with food and your hearts with gladness." Lit., "filling your hearts with food and gladness," which is somewhat problematic, if one tries to understand how hearts can be filled with food. Luke's expression is elliptical. Compare Acts 23:6. The terminology echoes that of Ps 147:8; Jer 5:24. Such gifts from heaven should make humans aware of the source of them, or at least should make them inquire into whence such blessings of nature come. The noun *euphrosynē*, "gladness," may have the nuance of joy in sharing the bountiful table of God, who provides the rain, fruit, and food.

18. *Even with such words they hardly kept the crowds from sacrificing to them.* Inveterate habits of people resist change and especially advice, even when it is enlightening.

19. *Then some Jews from Antioch and Iconium came there and won over the crowds.* Lit., "persuading the crowds." Recall 14:2; perhaps the same people are meant.

They stoned Paul and dragged him out of the town, leaving him there for dead. Lit., "stoning Paul, they were dragging him out of the town, thinking him to have died." In the Greek text the subject is clearly *Ioudaioi*, who have come the considerable distance from Antioch and Iconium. Now they succeed, whereas in Iconium they only tried to stone the two missionaries. See 2 Cor 11:25, for Paul's own recollection of having been stoned. Cf. 2 Tim 3:11.

20. *his disciples formed a circle about him, and soon he got up and went back into the town.* "His disciples" probably refers to the Lystrans who have become convinced of the message that he and Barnabas have been preaching in their town.

The next day he left with Barnabas for Derbe. The implication is that Paul did not suffer badly. On Derbe, see NOTE on 14:6.

BIBLIOGRAPHY (14:8–20)

Breytenbach, C., "Zeus und der lebendige Gott: Anmerkungen zu Apostelgeschichte 14.11–17," *NTS* 39 (1993): 396–413.

Calder, W. M., "Acts 14[12]," *ExpTim* 37 (1925–26): 528.

———, "The 'Priest' of Zeus at Lystra," *Expos* 7/10 (1910): 148–55.

———, "Zeus and Hermes at Lystra," *Expos* 7/10 (1910): 1–6.

Delebecque, E., "L'Eglise d'Antioche et le sanctuaire de Zeus à Lystres en l'année 45," *REG* 95 (1982): 74–84.

Downing, F. G., "Common Ground with Paganism in Luke and in Josephus," *NTS* 28 (1982): 546–59.

Eitrem, S., "De Paulo et Barnaba deorum numero habitis (Act. xiv, 12)," *ConNT* 3 (1938): 9–12.

Festugière, A. J., "Notules d'exégèse: *Euphrosynē, mystērion, kyrios*," *RSPT* 23 (1934): 359–62.

Gärtner, B., "Paulus und Barnabas in Lystra: Zu Apg. 14,8–15," SEA 27 (1962): 83–88.

Imschoot, P. van, "S. Paul à Lystre (Act. 14,8–20)," *CollGand* 16 (1929): 155–61.

Kearsley, R. A., "Acts 14.13: The Temple Just outside the City," *NDIEC* 6 (1992): 209–10.

Lackmann, M., *Vom Geheimnis der Schöpfung: Die Geschichte der Exegese von Römer 1,18–23, 2,14–16 und Acta 14,15–17, 17,22–29 vom 2. Jahrhundert bis zum Begin der Orthodoxie* (Stuttgart: Evangelisches Verlagswerk, 1952).

Lagercrantz, O., "Act 14,17," ZNW 31 (1932): 86–87.

Lerle, E., "Die Predigt in Lystra (Acts xiv.15–18)," *NTS* 7 (1960–61): 46–55.

Martin, L. H., "Gods or Ambassadors of God? Barnabas and Paul in Lystra," *NTS* 41 (1995): 152–56.

Quirmbach, J., *Die Lehre des hl. Paulus von der natürlichen Gotteserkenntnis und der natürlichen Sittengesetz: Eine biblisch-dogmatische Studie* (Strassburger theologische Studien 7/4; Freiburg im B.: Herder, 1906).

Schierling, S. P. and M. J. Schierling, "The Influence of the Ancient Romances on Acts of the Apostles," *ClassBull* 54 (1978): 81–88.

Schwank, B., "Wenn Steine zu reden beginnen: Archäologie zum Verständnis des Neuen Testaments," *BK* 50 (1995): 40–47.

Slater, T. B., "The Possible Influence of LXX Exodus 20:11 on Acts 14:15," *AUSS* 30 (1992): 151–52.
Traill, D. S., "St Paul's Estimate of Paganism," *CJRT* 7 (1930): 130–38, 239–49.
Trémel, B., "Voie du salut et religion populaire: Paul et Luc face au risque de paganisation," *LumV* 30 (1981): 87–108.
Williams, A. M., "St. Paul's Speech at Lystra," *ExpTim* 31 (1919–20): 189.

6. Paul's Return to Antioch in Syria (14:21–28)

[21] Having evangelized that town and made many disciples, they retraced their
steps to Lystra, Iconium, and Antioch. [22] They strengthened the spirits of the disciples, encouraging them to remain steadfast in the faith, because "we must undergo many hardships to enter the kingdom of God." [23] In each church they installed presbyters and with prayer and fasting commended them to the Lord,
in whom they had put their faith. [24] They traveled through Pisidia and came to
Pamphylia; [25] after preaching the word in Perga, they came down to Attalia.
[26] From there they sailed back to Antioch, where they had first been commended
to the grace of God for the task that they had now completed. [27] On their arrival,
they called together the church and related all that God had accomplished with
them, and how he had opened the door of faith to the Gentiles. [28] They then
spent no little time there with the disciples.

WT: [21] having evangelized those in the town. [22] because "one must . . ." [25] [adds at end:] and preached to them.

COMMENT

Luke brings to an end the account of Paul's Mission I, as he tells how Paul retraces his steps with Barnabas through the towns of Lystra, Iconium, and Pisidian Antioch. As they pass through these towns, they encourage and strengthen the new Christians there, urging them to be steadfast in the faith and to endure the hardships that may come to them because of it. Then they return to Perga in Pamphylia and eventually to the port of Attalia, whence they take a ship to return to Antioch on the Orontes, where they are received by the church that listens to the story of all that God has accomplished through them on this first missionary journey.

The episode is again a narrative, with little complication in its details. Details of it come to Luke from his Pauline source.

NOTES

21. *Having evangelized that town and made many disciples.* So Luke records the success of the evangelization of Derbe in Lycaonia; see NOTE on 14:6.

they retraced their steps to Lystra, Iconium, and Antioch. See NOTES on 13:14, 51; 14:6.

22. *They strengthened the spirits of the disciples.* Lit., "the souls of the disciples," i.e., of the Christians whom they have converted on their earlier visit. For similar reports of encouragement, see 15:32, 41; 18:23. Paul is thus depicted playing the role that Peter was to play for his fellow Christians according to Jesus' prayer in Luke 22:32.

encouraging them to remain steadfast in the faith. The noun *pistis* is probably to be understood in the sense of the practice of Christian belief, not in its content sense. Recall similar encouragement in 11:23; 13:43.

because "we must undergo many hardships to enter the kingdom of God." Lit., "through many hardships we must enter the kingdom of God." The conj. *hoti* may be causal (as translated here); but it may also simply introduce direct discourse. On kingdom, see NOTES on 1:3; 19:8. "Entering" the kingdom is to be understood as another way of saying salvation. The expression has its roots in Jesus' teaching (Luke 18:25; John 3:5; Mark 9:47; 10:23–25).

23. *In each church they installed presbyters.* Lit., "appointing for them presbyters church by church." On the Christian sense of *presbyteroi,* see NOTE on 11:30. The verb *cheirotonein* actually means to "choose or vote for someone (something) by raising the hand," but it came to mean generically "choose, appoint," as here. Compare Philo, *De praemiis* 9 §54; *De Josepho* 41 §248; Josephus, *Ant.* 6.13.9 §312. *Ekklēsia* is used of different individual churches; see NOTE on 5:11.

This notice creates something of a problem, because in neither the uncontested letters of Paul nor the Deutero-Paulines does the apostle ever speak of *presbyteroi* in the churches to which he writes, nor does he install such persons. In 1 Thess 5:12 Paul writes about "those who are over you" *(proistamenoi)*; in Phil 1:1 about "overseers and deacons" *(episkopois kai diakonois)*; and in Rom 16:1 about Phoebe the *diakonos,* but never about *presbyteroi.* These are mentioned, indeed, in the Pastoral Letters (Titus 1:5; 1 Tim 5:17, 19) and undoubtedly were a fixture in local churches by the time Luke writes. So the notice may simply be a Lucan anachronism as he ascribes to Paul and Barnabas such care for the structure of these newly founded communities.

with prayer and fasting commended them to the Lord, in whom they had put their faith. Paul and Barnabas intercede with the risen Christ for the protection of the churches so constituted. The Lucan refrain of prayer appears again; see 13:3 and NOTE there.

24. *They traveled through Pisidia and came to Pamphylia.* See NOTE on 13:13. Undoubtedly they stopped at Pisidian Antioch en route, as v 23 implies.

25. *after preaching the word in Perga, they came down to Attalia.* Some MSS (א, A, C, Ψ, 81, 181, 614, etc.) read "the word of the Lord." The town of *Attaleia* was not mentioned before. It would have been the seaport on the southern coast of Asia Minor, to which Paul and Barnabas first came (13:13) in order to get to Perga and to which they now come to get a ship that would sail along the coast

toward Syria. The port was named after Attalos II Philadelphus of Pergamum (ca. 150 B.C.).

26. *From there they sailed back to Antioch.* I.e., to Antioch on the Orontes in Syria. Actually they would have sailed to Seleucia, whence they originally embarked for Cyprus (13:4), to go overland to Antioch.

where they had first been commended to the grace of God for the task that they had now completed. Recall 13:2–3, the inauguration of Mission I under the guidance of Holy Spirit, which is now called God's grace. Such ambivalent expressions led in time to the later theological distinction of God's uncreated grace (the Spirit) and created grace (communicated to humans).

27. *On their arrival, they called together the church.* The word *ekklēsia* is used again in the sense of the individual church in Syrian Antioch.

related all that God had accomplished with them. Cf. 15:4. This seems to have been a custom in the early church, when missionaries returned to their home bases.

how he had opened the door of faith to the Gentiles. I.e., how God had made it possible for Gentiles to enter the kingdom. Cf. 11:28; 13:47–48. "Faith" is probably meant in the sense of the exercise of Christian belief and conduct. The "door of faith" is that whereby one "enters the kingdom" (14:22). This opening of the door to the Gentiles creates the problem that must be discussed at the coming "Council."

28. *They then spent no little time there with the disciples.* I.e., with the Christians of Syrian Antioch. See NOTE on 6:1.

BIBLIOGRAPHY (14:21–28)

Cadbury, H. J., "Lexical Notes on Luke-Acts, IV," *JBL* 48 (1929): 412–25.

Cheung, A.T.M., "A Narrative Analysis of Acts 14:27–15:35: Literary Shaping in Luke's Account of the Jerusalem Council," *WTJ* 55 (1993): 137–54.

Detwiler, D. F., "Paul's Approach to the Great Commission in Acts 14:21–23," *BSac* 152 (1995): 33–41.

Dupont, J., "Les ministères de l'église naissante d'après les Actes des Apôtres," *Sacramentum 1* (Studia anselmiana 61; Rome: Editrice Anselmiana, 1973), 94–148; repr. *Nouvelles études*, 133–85.

———, "La première organisation des églises (Ac 14,21–27): Cinquième dimanche de Pâques," *AsSeign* 2/26 (1973): 60–66; repr. *Nouvelles études*, 350–57.

Gebhardt, H., "Die an die Heiden gerichtete Missionspredigt der Apostel . . . ," ZNW 6 (1995): 235–49.

Matute, A., "La puerta de la fe (Act 14,21–28)," *Helmantica* 21 (1970): 421–39.

Nellessen, E., "Die Einsetzung von Presbytern durch Barnabas und Paulus (Apg 14,23)," *Begegnung mit dem Wort: Festschrift für Heinz Zimmermann* (BBB 53; ed. J. Zmijewski and E. Nellessen; Bonn: Hanstein, 1980), 175–93.

———, "Die Presbyter der Gemeinden in Lykaonien und Pisidien (Apg 14,23)," *Les Actes des Apôtres* (ed. J. Kremer), 493–98.

Pohlenz, M., "Paulus und die Stoa," ZNW 42 (1949): 69–104, esp. 82–98.
Ross, J. M., "The Appointment of Presbyters in Acts 14.23," *ExpTim* 63 (1950–51): 288.
Vögtle, A., "Exegetische Reflexionen zur Apostolizität des Amtes und zur Amtssukzession," *Die Kirche des Anfangs: Festschrift für Heinz Schürmann . . .* (ed. R. Schnackenburg et al.; Leipzig: St. Benno, 1977), 529–82.
Whitley, W. T., "Luke of Antioch in Pisidia," *ExpTim* 21 (1909–10): 164–66.

V. The Jerusalem Decision about Gentile Christians (15:1–35)

◆

1. Prehistory (15:1–2)

15 [1] Some people came down from Judea and were teaching the brothers, "Unless you have been circumcised according to Mosaic practice, you cannot be saved." [2] Because this created dissension and no small controversy between them and Paul and Barnabas, it was decided that Paul, Barnabas, and some others of their number should go up to Jerusalem to see the apostles and the presbyters about this controversial matter.

WT: [1] circumcised and conduct yourselves according to Mosaic practice. [2] Barnabas—for Paul kept insisting and maintaining that they should so remain as they had come to believe—those who had come from Jerusalem commanded them, Paul and Barnabas, and some others to go up to Jerusalem to the apostles and presbyters in order that a decision might be made for them about this controversial matter.

COMMENT

The peace that reigned in the church of Antioch is eventually disturbed, this time by Christians of Jewish background who come from Judea to Antioch and insist on the circumcision of Gentile Christians and on their having to observe the Mosaic law. In fact, they insist on these matters as necessary for salvation. Some Christians of Antioch are consequently reluctant to yield to the view of Paul and Barnabas that Gentile Christians have no need to submit to circumcision or observe the Mosaic law.

The issue that the incident in the Antiochene church raises sparks what is for Luke a very important development in his story of the early church. It falls designedly in the center of Acts. In my translation, chaps. 1–14 have 12,385 words; chaps. 15–28, 12,502 words. So what is now recounted is the turning point of Luke's story, when the apostolic and presbyteral college of Jerusalem officially recognizes the evangelization of Gentiles, which has been initiated by Peter and carried out on a wide scale by Barnabas and Paul. It leads to the definitive break of the Christian church from its Jewish matrix. It is also the last act that Luke records about Peter and the apostles. During the persecution mentioned in 8:1, only the apostles were said to have remained in Jerusalem; the flight of the rest led to the preaching of the Word to Jews and others in the diaspora. In the Lucan story the Antiochene church seeks doctrinal guidance from the mother church of Jerusalem. The controversial issue is to be laid before the apostles and the presbyters of Jerusalem, and the testimony borne to Gentiles is officially accepted and approved.

Up to this point in Acts Jerusalem has been a focal point, as the mother church and the doctrinal center. To it appeal is again made. The mother church will continue to be predominantly Jewish Christian and will exert its influence under the guidance of James. Paul, in particular, becomes hereafter in the Lucan story the hero of the second part of Acts. He will bear testimony "to the end of the earth" (1:8), even though he was not actually the only one to carry it there historically. Paul's influence will be exerted mostly in the diaspora and in areas where Gentiles are dominant. Even Paul's Mission I, already described in 13:1–14:28, was in reality preparatory for Acts 15, bringing to a head the problem that has to be the subject matter of a Jerusalem decision. Luke has been at pains to depict the influence of the mother church on areas in Palestine and Syria that have been evangelized by its emissaries, by Peter and John (8:14) and by Barnabas (9:27; 11:22). Once the Jerusalem decision is made, the last mention of the Jerusalem apostles will be found in 16:4. After that they disappear from the Lucan story in Acts, but the Word continues to be carried freely and maturely to "the end of the earth."

The controversy that Luke now introduces into his account was a historic incident in the early church. It is also recorded by Paul himself in Gal 2:1–10. His account of it runs as follows:

> [1]Then once again within fourteen years I went up to Jerusalem with Barnabas, taking along Titus too. [2]I went up because of a revelation; and I laid before them the gospel that I preach to the Gentiles—privately before those of repute—lest perchance I was running or had been running in vain. [3]But even Titus who was with me, Greek though he was, was not compelled to be circumcised. [4]Then because of some false brothers, who had slipped in to spy on the freedom that we have in Christ Jesus in order that they might enslave us—[5]to them we did not yield in submission even for a moment, in order that the truth of the gospel might continue to remain with you. [6]From those who were reputed to be something (what they were makes no difference to me; God shows no partiality)—those, indeed, who were of repute added nothing to me. [7]On the contrary, when they saw that I had been entrusted with the gospel for the uncircumcised, as Peter had been for the circumcised [8](for he who worked in Peter for the apostolate of the circumcised worked in me for that of the Gentiles), [9]and when they recognized the grace that had been granted to me, James, Cephas, and John, reputed to be pillars, gave me and Barnabas the right hand of fellowship, so that we might go to the Gentiles and they to the circumcised. [10]They would only have us remember the poor, a thing that I was glad to do.

This double attestation, in Acts and in Galatians 2, reveals that we are dealing with a historic debate in the early church, as, among others, H. Schlier has well shown (*Der Brief an die Galater* [MeyerK 7; 13th ed.; Göttingen: Vandenhoeck & Ruprecht, 1965], 11–17).

There are, however, differences of detail in the two accounts. First, Paul says that he went up to Jerusalem on this occasion (14 years after his conversion) "because of a revelation" (Gal 2:2), whereas Luke attributes the reason for this Jerusalem visit to a decision of the Antiochene church to consult "the apostles and presbyters" in Jerusalem about the controversial matter that has arisen between Barnabas and Paul and those Jewish Christians who have come to Antioch from Judea. Second, on reading the Pauline account, one gets the impression that the controversy first arose in Jerusalem itself, whereas the Lucan story locates the beginning of the controversy in Antioch. Third, in the Lucan account those who oppose Paul and Barnabas in Antioch are said to be merely "some people who came down from Judea" (15:1); they might have been related to those who are later called "some from the party of the Pharisees, who had become believers" (15:5), i.e., Jerusalem Christian converts of Pharisaic background. When Paul speaks of them, however, he calls them simply "some false brothers, who had slipped in to spy out the freedom that we have in Christ Jesus" (Gal 2:4). Fourth, no mention is made in Acts either of Titus accompanying Paul to Jerusalem or of John in Jerusalem (see Gal 2:3, 9). None of these differences, however, is significant enough to undermine the substantial agreement of the two reports, Lucan and Pauline. The differences come from reports (sources) that Luke has inherited and hence reflect slightly different versions of the story. See Weiser, *Apg.*, 368–76; Pesch, *Apg.*, 2.71–74.

Some interpreters of Acts, however, think that chap. 15 does not treat of the same matter as Galatians 2. For instance, D. R. De Lacey ("Paul in Jerusalem") claims that Acts 9:26–30 corresponds to Gal 2:1–10. Or V. Weber, following an earlier view of Ramsay, maintains the equation of Galatians 2 with the visit of Paul to Jerusalem mentioned in 11:30 and 12:25. See Introduction §156. Cf. R. H. Stein, "The Relationship of Gal 2:1–10 and Acts 15:1–35: Two Neglected Arguments," *JETS* 17 (1974): 239–42.

The question of the source(s) used in Acts 15 has been a matter of no little debate. Commentators such as Dibelius (*Studies,* 93–101) and Haenchen ("Quellenanalyse," 160; *Acts,* 440–72) interpret chap. 15 without any recourse to sources; they regard the whole chapter as a Lucan composition. Ever since the analysis of Harnack, many commentators have ascribed the account in chap. 15 in some way to the Antiochene source that Luke has been using. This seems to be the best solution, but one has to modify it a bit.

The solution adopted here is that vv 1–2 are a Lucan suture, joining the material found in vv 3–33, which comes from Antiochene sources that Luke has come upon, with the Pauline source that he had been using in 13:1–14:28, the description of Paul's Mission I. The last material that Luke used from an Antiochene source was that of 11:19–29, to which the Antiochene material in chap. 15 was originally the sequel (see Benoit, *Bib* 40 [1959]: 778–92). See further the COMMENTS on 15:13–21 and 22–33.

NOTES

15:1. *Some people came down from Judea.* The vagueness of *tines*, "some people," reveals the suturelike character of this introduction. MSS Ψ and 614 add "of those who had come to believe from the party of the Pharisees," a variant that has been added by copyists from 15:5. According to Haenchen (*Acts*, 442–43), Luke has written "Judea," because he wants to avoid the impression that the *tines* are "a Jerusalem delegation." If Haenchen means by that the Jerusalem church would have sent such a delegation, one might agree, but that may be making too much depend on what is no more than a stylistic variant. Certainly the collection sent to "the brothers living in Judea" (11:29) would not be an attempt to avoid saying "in Jerusalem." In any case, "some people" are not to be taken as the same as "some people from James" (Gal 2:12), which refers rather to an incident that happens after the "Council." See Conzelmann, *Acts*, 115; Pesch, *Apg.*, 2.75.

were teaching the brothers. I.e., the Gentile Christians in Syrian Antioch. Those who have come from Judea seem to be Jewish Christians, perhaps like those described in 15:5, of Pharisaic background.

"Unless you have been circumcised according to Mosaic practice, you cannot be saved." Two related issues are singled out for mention: the necessity of circumcision (see Lev 12:3) and the need to observe the Mosaic law. The WT, esp. MS D, clarifies the issues, reading "and conduct yourselves according to the practice of Moses." The practice and obligation of circumcision are related in Jewish tradition not to Moses but to Abraham (Gen 17:9–14). In other words, according to the people from Judea, Gentile Christians had to become like Jewish Christians. On circumcision, see NOTE on 7:8. "Salvation" has to be understood in its eschatological sense, as in 2:21, 40; 4:12; 11:4; 14:9; see *Luke*, 222–23.

2. *Because this created dissension and no small controversy between them and Paul and Barnabas.* Paul and Barnabas take issue with the people from Judea. The order of the names, "Paul and Barnabas," reveals the Lucan composition of this verse, as in 13:43, 46, 50; 15:22; contrast 14:14; 15:12, 25.

it was decided that Paul, Barnabas, and some others of their number should go up to Jerusalem to see the apostles and the presbyters about this controversial matter. The officials of the Jerusalem church are thus specified; they are distinguished from "the church" (15:4, 22). According to Gal 2:9 Peter and John would have been the "apostles" among these officials; James too is mentioned, but he was not an apostle. MS D and some other witnesses of the WT read rather: "for Paul kept insisting and maintaining that they should so remain as they had come to believe—those who had come from Jerusalem commanded them, Paul and Barnabas, and some others to go up to Jerusalem to the apostles and presbyters in order that a decision might be made for them about this controversial matter."

In the Lucan account this controversy provides the reason why Paul and Barnabas go up to Jerusalem, but according to Gal 2:2 Paul went up to Jerusalem "because of a revelation," which is not further explained there.

BIBLIOGRAPHY (15:1–2)

Bammel, E., "Der Text von Apostelgeschichte 15," *Les Actes des Apôtres* (ed. J. Kremer), 439–46.

Benoit, P., "La deuxième visite de saint Paul à Jérusalem," *Bib* 40 (1959): 778–92; repr. *Exégèse et théologie,* 3.285–99.

Burgos Núñez, M. de, "Asamblea de Jerusalén (Hch xv) y Gal 2,1–14 en la obra *Les Actes de Deux Apôtres* de M.-E. Boismard y A. Lamouille," *Communio* 23 (1990): 405–28.

De Lacey, D. R., "Paul in Jerusalem," *NTS* 20 (1973–74): 82–86.

Féret, H.-M., *Pierre et Paul à Antioche et à Jérusalem: Le "conflit" des deux Apôtres* (Paris: Cerf, 1955).

Gaechter, P., "Geschichtliches zum Apostelkonzil," *ZKT* 85 (1963): 339–54.

Haenchen, E., "Quellenanalyse und Kompositionsanalyse in Act 15," *Judentum, Urchristentum, Kirche: Festschrift für Joachim Jeremias* (BZNW 26; ed. W. Eltester; Berlin: Töpelmann, 1960), 153–64.

Parker, P., "Once More, Acts and Galatians," *JBL* 86 (1967): 175–82.

Ravarotto, E., "De hierosolymitano concilio (Act. cap. 15)," *Anton* 37 (1962): 185–218.

Strecker, G., "Die sogenannte zweite Jerusalemreise des Paulus (Act 11,27–30)," *ZNW* 53 (1962): 67–77.

Talbert, C. H., "Again: Paul's Visits to Jerusalem," *NovT* 9 (1967): 26–40.

Weber, V., "Die Frage der Identität von Gal 2,1–10 und Apg 15," *BZ* 10 (1912): 155–67.

———, *Galater 2 und Apostelgeschichte 15 in neuer Beleuchtung* (Würzburg: Becker, 1923).

2. CONVOCATION AND PETER'S APPEAL TO PRECEDENT (15:3–12)

[3]Those sent off by the church traveled through Phoenicia and Samaria, telling everyone about the conversion of the Gentiles, and they caused great joy among all the brothers. [4]On their arrival in Jerusalem, they were welcomed by that church, and by the apostles and presbyters, to whom they related all that God had accomplished with them. [5]Some from the party of the Pharisees, however, who had become believers, stood up and demanded, "One must circumcise them and order them to observe the law of Moses." [6]So the apostles and presbyters gathered together to look into this matter. [7]After much controversy, Peter took the floor and said to them, "Brothers, you know that some time ago God

chose me from your number to be the one from whose lips the Gentiles would
hear the word of the gospel and come to believe in it. 8 God who reads the heart
has given testimony, granting to them the Holy Spirit, just as to us. 9 He has made
no distinction between us and them, but has purified their hearts too by faith.
10 Why then should you now put God to the test, by imposing on the shoulders
of these disciples a yoke that neither we nor our ancestors have been able to bear?
11 Rather, through the grace of the Lord Jesus we believe that we are saved, just
as they do." 12 At that the whole assembly grew silent. Then they listened to Barnabas and Paul recounting how many signs and wonders God had performed
among the Gentiles through them.

WT: 3 [omits "great"]. 4 they were heartily welcomed. 5 Those who had ordered them to go up to the
presbyters stood up, saying, "One must . . ." 6 gathered together with the assembly . . . this controversial matter. 7 As they were even more perplexed, Peter under the guidance of the Spirit took the floor
. . . [omits "from your number"]. 10 And now why do you try to impose a yoke which not even our
ancestors were able to bear? 11 [omits "the Lord"]. 12 [adds at the beginning of the verse:] Since the
presbyters agreed with what had been said by Peter, the whole assembly . . . [omits "God"].

COMMENT

This episode, which now narrates the initial reaction of the Jerusalem community to the coming of Paul and Barnabas to the mother church, recounts another postconversion visit of Paul to Jerusalem. It would have been in year A.D. 49, the fourteenth year after his experience on the road to Damascus.

On their arrival in Jerusalem, Paul, Barnabas, and the others are greeted by the church, the apostles, and the presbyters. The controversy is continued with demands made by Jerusalem Jewish Christians of Pharisaic background that Gentile Christians be circumcised and made to observe the Mosaic law. The apostles and presbyters of the mother church decide to convene over the matter, because it is an issue of importance, as is apparent also in Paul's record of it (Gal 2:4–6).

This meeting has often been referred to as the Apostolic Council. That is really a misnomer, because the meeting as described is not a solemn assembly of authorities from all over the church. Moreover, it is never counted as one of the councils in the history of Christianity. Yet when one reflects on the issue that is discussed and its doctrinal significance for the future of the church, one can see why it might be regarded as a sort of "Council." (So I retain the name and put it in quotation marks.) It is, in effect, the episode in the early church that eventually leads to the convening of official councils of later date.

The episode begins as a narrative, but incorporates a decisive speech of Peter in vv 7–11. His speech is neither missionary nor kerygmatic, but rather a judicial or constitutive discourse, addressed to Christians, which enables the assembly to come to a doctrinal decision. Peter's words appeal, in effect, to his experience in the Cornelius episode, but they are really devoted to a larger issue. In Acts 10 the mission to the Gentiles was justified by the miracles confirming it (10:44–46) and the principle that what matters is that human beings reverence God and do what is right in his sight. Now a further justification is added: the purification of Gentiles (15:9) and the role of divine grace (15:11).

Peter's words still the debate; the silent acquiescence of the assembly conveys their decision. It is later confirmed by the address of James, even if he adds qualifications.

This raises the question about the unity of the Lucan account in Acts 15. Above in the COMMENT on vv 1–2, it was noted that Luke most likely was using Antiochene sources in vv 3–33. It is now necessary to make a further distinction, because in vv 3–12 we have in effect the counterpart of what Paul himself refers to in Galatians 2. In both of these accounts, Lucan (Acts 15:3–12) and Pauline (Gal 2:4–6), the issue is the requirement of circumcision for Gentile converts and their observance of the Mosaic law. The negative decision about this requirement recorded in both accounts reveals that the Jerusalem "Council" was devoted to these questions alone. Information about this "Council" decision has come to Luke from an Antiochene source.

To this decision Luke has joined another story that deals with a decision that James and others have made in Jerusalem about dietary and other matters. That story too has come to him from an Antiochene source; information that is concerned with this further question will be discussed in vv 13–33. Even though Luke is elsewhere dependent on a Palestinian source for his account of Jerusalem events in Acts, it seems unlikely that the information combined in this chapter stems from such a source. That is the reason for assigning the basic account in both vv 3–12 and vv 13–33 to Antiochene sources. Moreover, this would also be the reason why Luke has combined them and presented them as Jerusalem decisions made on one occasion. The decisions, however, seem rather to have been originally made on different occasions, whereas Luke now recounts them together in chap. 15. He has undoubtedly modified the first story drawn from the Antiochene source with references to Peter's experience in chap. 10, especially in the speech of Peter, which is basically of Lucan composition.

The significance of this episode is that the "Council" decides that to be a Christian one does not have to be circumcised or have to obey all the prescriptions of the Mosaic law. This decision comes about through the intervention of Peter, who up to this point in Acts has been the spokesman for the Jerusalem Christian church. He contributes to the debate on the matter as a result of his own experience in the conversion of Cornelius and his household. There it was sufficient that they be baptized in order to receive the Spirit; they did not have to be circumcised or assume the obligation to observe all the Mosaic law. In effect, Peter was confirming the practice of Paul, who had been founding Gentile Christian churches and not demanding of his converts that they be circumcised or assume that obligation. So Peter's word intervenes and silences the objections of converted Pharisees who were seeking to impose such burdens on Gentile converts. In effect, Peter was simply carrying out the commission imposed on the Eleven by the risen Christ to preach in his name repentance for the forgiveness of sins "to all the nations" (Luke 24:47), which said nothing about the necessity of circumcision or obligation of observing all the Mosaic law. Such customary observances may continue among Jewish Christians, but they have often been a yoke that even the ancestors of Jewish Christians were unable to bear. The significance of Peter's voice at the Jerusalem "Council" is lost on no Christians today.

NOTES

3. *Those sent off by the church traveled through Phoenicia and Samaria.* This verse could well have been the natural sequel to 11:29. "The church" that sends them off is that of Antioch in Syria. Only two of the areas through which the emissaries would have traveled overland are mentioned; Galilee is not. They pass through the Christian community already started in Phoenicia (11:19; see NOTE there). On Samaria, see NOTES on 1:8 and 8:5.

telling everyone about the conversion of the Gentiles. Recall 14:27.

they caused great joy among all the brothers. Luke describes idyllically the rejoicing of Christians over the news of Gentile conversions. On *adelphoi* = Christians, see NOTE on 1:15.

4. *On their arrival in Jerusalem, they were welcomed by that church, and by the apostles and presbyters.* In the church of Jerusalem the officials are "apostles" and "presbyters," in contradistinction to the "prophets" and "teachers" of the church in Antioch. See NOTES on 1:2; 11:30; 13:1. The *Didascalia Apostolorum* (ed. R. H. Connolly, 206) paraphrases this verse so: "When they were come to Jerusalem, they related to us the controversy which they had in the church of Antioch." For the dubious relevance of this paraphrase, see the comments of J. Taylor, "Ancient Texts."

to whom they related all that God had accomplished with them. They repeat what they had recounted to the Christians in Phoenicia and Samaria (v 3) about Gentile conversions. These reports will be repeated in the apostolic and presbyteral assembly to be convoked; see v 12. Compare 14:27.

5. *Some from the party of the Pharisees, however, who had become believers, stood up and demanded.* Lit., "some who had come to believe (perf. ptc.) from the sect *(hairesis)* of the Pharisees," i.e., Jewish Christians of Pharisaic background; see NOTES on 5:17, 34. These may be related to "some people" (15:1) and may even be the "false brothers" of whom Paul speaks in Gal 2:4. It is not said that these Jewish Christians "stood up" in the "Council" (*pan to plēthos*, v 12); the occasion of their demand is rather the welcoming reception of the visitors from Antioch. Their demand follows on the report mentioned at the end of v 4. Conzelmann (*Acts*, 116) maintains that there is only one "plenary assembly," to which both vv 4–5 and vv 6–12 refer; similarly Weiser, *Apg.*, 380, but that is far from certain, as Schneider (*Apg.*, 2.179) recognizes. Cf. Pesch, *Apg.*, 2.76.

"One must circumcise them and order them to observe the law of Moses." Former Pharisees insist that such Gentile Christians have to become, in effect, Jewish proselytes (see NOTE on 2:11). The reason for their insistence has been set forth in 15:1: circumcision and observance of the Mosaic law are conditions necessary

for salvation. Their demands are based on the way they interpret God's words to Abraham in Gen 17:10–14 (cf. Josh 5:2–9) and to Moses in Deut 5:28–33.

6. *the apostles and presbyters gathered together to look into this matter.* The demand of such converted Pharisees of the Jerusalem church gives rise to the decision of the apostles and presbyters to convoke a meeting (*pan to plēthos,* v 12) about the matter. This decision by officials in the Jerusalem church reminds the reader of the similar decision made because of the dispute between the Hellenists and Hebrews in 6:1–2. There the Twelve summoned "the community of the disciples" to a decision; here "the apostles and presbyters" gather to make a decision. The former of this twosome include the unnamed members of the Twelve still in Jerusalem; now they are called simply "apostles," because their number is no longer complete after the death of James (12:2) or possibly after the departure of others from Jerusalem. The latter are the "presbyters," about whom we learned first in 11:30. In both instances, the important element is the decision made by the officials of the Jerusalem church. In Gal 2:2, 6, 9 Paul refers to them as those who "were of repute," "pillars" of the church, and numbers among them "James, Cephas, and John." What is noteworthy is the inactivity of Paul and Barnabas in the account of the decision making. Even though in Galatians 2 Paul maintained that he resisted the "false brothers," he implied that the "pillars" of the Jerusalem church came to a decision with which he agreed; and they added nothing to him. See J. L. North, "Is *idein peri* (Acts 15.6 cf. 18.15) a Latinism?" *NTS* 29 (1983): 264–66.

7. *After much controversy.* Lit., "there being much debate," i.e., about the contention raised by Christian Pharisees (v 5). The controversy conveys the conciliar nature of the gathering.

Peter took the floor and said to them. Peter addresses his words to the assembly in view of the experience that he has had in the conversion of Cornelius (10:1–11:18). In the Lucan story Peter has been seen so far as an important spokesman in the Jerusalem church. His voice is not necessarily meant now to carry weight because of who he is, but rather because he is the only one of the apostolic and presbyteral college who has had experience in dealing with Gentiles. To this he now appeals. The issue to which he addresses himself has actually been settled in 11:18, but it does not yet have the approval of the apostles and presbyters in Jerusalem, which is now the point of the Lucan story. MSS D*, 257, and 614 read "Peter arose in the Spirit and said," a form of the text that enhances Peter's role even more. The references to the Cornelius episode would be Lucan modifications of what he may have learned from the Antiochene source about Peter's speech.

Peter's speech has two parts: (1) 15:7–9, Report of what has happened; (2) 15:10–11, Appropriate conclusions.

"*Brothers.* I.e., fellow Christians. For Peter's mode of address, see NOTES on 1:11, 15.

you know that some time ago God chose me from your number. Lit., "from bygone days." Peter alludes to his experience with Cornelius as heaven-directed, singling him out to be the instrument of the coming of the first Gentile in the

Lucan story to Christian faith (10:1–11:18). The time reference makes the story of Cornelius a "'classic' prototype," as did *en archē*, "at the beginning," in 11:15 (Conzelmann, *Acts*, 116). The somewhat strange construction *eklegesthai en*, "to choose among," is a Septuagintism (1 Sam 16:10; 1 Kgs 8:16, 44; 11:32; 2 Chr 6:5, 34).

to be the one from whose lips the Gentiles would hear the word of the gospel. Lit., "from my mouth." This the first time in his two-volume work that Luke uses *euangelion*, "gospel"; it will appear only once again, on the lips of Paul in 20:24. The phrase "the word of the gospel" occurs only here in the NT. For some reason that escapes us, Luke generally seems to have avoided *euangelion*, which otherwise so aptly sums up the Christian message about Jesus Christ, especially as announced to Gentiles; see *Luke*, 172–74. Schneider's explanation (*Apg.*, 2.179 n. 46) runs: "Gospel is for Luke the proclamation of the apostles among the heathen."

and come to believe in it. The reaction expected of human beings to the "gospel" is faith, which Luke expresses by the purpose infin. *pisteusai* (BDF §390).

8. *God who reads the heart.* So Luke makes Peter describe the all-knowing God. This characteristic of God is the basis of the testimony that is given (see NOTE on 1:24). Cf. Luke 16:15.

has given testimony. The all-knowing God has seen to it that testimony be borne even to Gentiles, beyond that which was carried to Jews in Judea. Thus, heaven has directed the spread of testimony to the gospel.

granting to them the Holy Spirit, just as to us. Peter refers to the aftermath of his speech to Cornelius and his household in 10:44–47; cf. 11:15–17; recall 2:4. The fact that the Spirit descended on Gentiles is interpreted by Peter as a form of heavenly testimony to Christians of Jewish background about the acceptability of the Gentiles' share in the divine plan of salvation. God makes no distinction between Jews and Gentiles.

9. *He has made no distinction between us and them, but has purified their hearts too by faith.* I.e., God has granted the Gentiles the grace to come to belief in Jesus Christ and his salvific message, just as he had earlier granted such grace to Jews. This coming to faith is now regarded as a purification of human hearts. Peter is saying in other words what he has already said in 10:34: "God shows no partiality." He is again offering an interpretation of the vision shown to him in 10:9–16.

10. *Why then should you now put God to the test.* I.e., to see whether God really makes no distinction between Jew and Gentile or whether God will make manifest his salvific intention to save Gentiles as well as Jews. Peter draws a conclusion from what he has said by using the OT idea of putting God to the test (see Exod 15:22–27; 17:2, 7; Num 14:22; Isa 7:12; Ps 77:18, 41, 56; Wis 1:2). To "put God to the test" would mean to approach God in a spirit of unbelief and mistrust; those who would so test him show that they cannot trust a deity who would free Gentiles from such Jewish obligations. God's gracious treatment of Gentile Christians stands in contrast to the imposition of circumcision and observance of the Mosaic law. To impose that now would be to put God to the test.

by imposing on the shoulders of these disciples a yoke. I.e., by making Gentile converts to Christianity take up the "yoke" of the law. The "yoke," as a symbol of the religious obligation of the Jews, denoted the linking together of Yahweh and Israel in the covenant of Sinai (Exod 19:5; 34:10); it was not thought of as an unbearable yoke, but as a privilege of Israel and a symbol of its election. The image is drawn from the harnessing of animals together for common labor, but it connotes an instrument that enables obedience. The later rabbinic tradition often spoke of *'ôl tôrāh*, "the yoke of the Torah" (*m. Aboth* 3:5; see Str-B, 1.608–10), but that Jewish tradition did not regard it as an unbearable burden. See Josephus, *Ag.Ap.* 2.37 §§271–80. Peter accords Gentile converts the title *mathētai*, "disciples"; see NOTE on 6:1.

that neither we nor our ancestors have been able to bear? Peter as a Jewish Christian recognizes the impossibility of human beings ever being able to carry out *(bastazein)* all the demands of the Mosaic law. Cf. 13:38–39; Rom 2:25–27. Paul too referred to the obligation of observing the Mosaic law as a yoke, but as "a yoke of slavery" (Gal 5:1; cf. 3:19). His view of the law says far more than Peter does here. Haenchen comments (*Acts*, 446): "Here . . . we have the law seen through Hellenistic Gentile Christian eyes, as a mass of commandments and prohibitions which no man can fulfill. Luke here is obviously speaking for himself and transmitting the view of his age and milieu," quoted approvingly by Schneider (*Apg.*, 2.181). See J. Nolland, "A Fresh Look at Acts 15.10," *NTS* 27 (1980–81): 105–15.

11. *Rather, through the grace of the Lord Jesus we believe that we are saved.* Luke uses the timeless aor. infin. *sōthēnai*, to express "salvation" in the eschatological sense. The Lucan Peter thus sums up the essence of the Christian gospel: salvation comes to human beings by the grace that God has accorded them to believe in what Jesus Christ has accomplished for humanity by his life, death, and resurrection. He voices a form of what Paul proclaimed in 13:38–39 and what Deutero-Pauline Eph 2:5–8 teaches, but without any mention of the famous Pauline distinction of "faith" and "deeds." The all-important factor in the salvation of humanity is "the grace of the Lord Jesus," given for saving faith, and not the yoke of the law. The present Lucan formula, *dia tēs charitos tou Kyriou Iēsou*, is never found of salvation or justification in Paul's letters, even though it occurs in other contexts (blessing, calling). See S. A. Panimolle, "La *charis* negli Atti e nel quarto vangelo," *RivB* 25 (1977): 143–58, esp. 143–51.

just as they do." In saying "we," Peter refers to the conviction of Jewish Christians about the role of God's grace in salvation and then applies it to converts of Gentile background. Cf. Gal 2:16.

12. *At that the whole assembly grew silent.* I.e., the controversy or debate mentioned in v 7 comes to an end with Peter's words, which in effect counsel against the imposition of circumcision and the obligation to observe the Mosaic law on Gentile converts. The apostles and elders accept the view of Peter in this matter (see the WT above). "Silence gives consent" (Goldsmith, *Goodnatured Man*), or, as the Latin proverb has it, "Qui tacet consentire videtur." See too Roloff, *Apg.*, 231; Pesch, *Apg.*, 2.78; Johnson, *Acts*, 263; but also Weiser, *Apg.*, 381.

Then they listened to Barnabas and Paul recounting how many signs and wonders God had performed among the Gentiles through them. The assembly now turns its attention to another topic, the report of all the good that God has wrought through Barnabas and Paul among the Gentiles (recall v 4). It is a fitting conclusion to the effect of Peter's speech upon the assembly, for their report confirms what Peter has been saying. Luke describes the work of Barnabas and Paul as accompanied by "signs and wonders" (see NOTE on 2:22). The mighty deeds that God has worked among Gentiles manifests divine approval not only of the evangelization of them but also of what Peter has said. Note the order of names, Barnabas and Paul, a sign of Luke's Antiochene source, as in 14:14; 15:25, whereas Luke himself writes Paul and Barnabas (15:2, 35).

BIBLIOGRAPHY (15:3–12)

Beel, A., "Concio s. Petri in concilio hierosolymitano (Act. Ap., xv, 7–11)," *Coll-Brug* 32 (1932): 30–34.

Borse, U., "Kompositionsgeschichtliche Beobachtungen zum Apostelkonzil," *Begegnung mit dem Wort: Festschrift für Heinrich Zimmermann* (BBB 53; ed. J. Zmijewski and E. Nellessen; Bonn: Hanstein, 1980), 195–212.

Cerfaux, L., "Le chapitre xve du livre des Actes à la lumière de la littérature ancienne," *Studi e Testi* 121 (1946): 107–26; repr. *Recueil Lucien Cerfaux*, 2.105–24.

Crehan, J. H., "Peter according to the D-Text of Acts," *TS* 18 (1957): 596–603.

———, "Peter at the Council of Jerusalem," *Scripture* 6 (1953–54): 175–80.

Dibelius, M., "Das Apostelkonzil," *TLZ* 72 (1947): 193–98; *Studies*, 93–101.

Dockx, S., "Chronologie de la vie de Saint Paul, depuis sa conversion jusqu'à son séjour à Rome," *NovT* 13 (1971): 261–304.

Dupont, J., "Pierre et Paul à Antioche et à Jérusalem," *RSR* 45 (1957): 42–60; repr. *Etudes*, 185–215.

Fahy, T., "The Council of Jerusalem," *ITQ* 30 (1963): 232–61.

Goguel, M., "Le récit des Actes 15, l'histoire de Corneille et l'incident d'Antioche," *RHPR* 3 (1923): 138–44.

Hirsch, E., "Petrus und Paulus," *ZNW* 29 (1930): 63–76.

Jefford, C. N., "Tradition and Witness in Antioch: Acts 15 and Didache 6," *PRS* 19 (1992): 409–19.

Kalu, O., "Luke and the Gentile Mission: A Study on Acts 15," *AJBS* 1 (1986): 59–65.

Katzenmayer, B., "Das sogenannte Apostelkonzil von Jerusalem," *IKZ* 31 (1941): 149–57.

Klein, G., "Galater 2,6–9 und die Geschichte der Jerusalemer Urgemeinde," *ZTK* 57 (1960): 275–95.

Lake, K., "The Apostolic Council of Jerusalem," *Beginnings*, 5.195–212.

———, "The Council of Jerusalem Described in Acts xv," *Jewish Studies in Memory of Israel Abrahams* . . . (ed. G. A. Kohut; New York: Jewish Institute of Religion, 1927), 244–65.

Léturmy, M., *Le concile de Jérusalem: Chronique* (Paris: Gallimard, 1969).

Linton, O., "The Third Aspect: A Neglected Point of View: A Study in Gal. i–ii and Acts ix and xv," *ST* 3 (1949): 79–95.

Martin, R. P., *New Testament Foundations II* (Exeter, UK: Paternoster, 1978), 109–17.

Menoud, P.-H., "Justification by Faith according to the Book of Acts," *Jesus Christ and the Faith: A Collection of Studies* (Pittsburgh: Pickwick, 1978), 202–27.

Miguens, M., "Pietro nel conciglio apostólico," *RevBíb* 10 (1962): 240–51.

Mussner, F., *Petrus und Paulus: Pole der Einheit* (QD 76; Freiburg im B.: Herder, 1976), 36–39.

Nolland, J., "Acts 15: Discerning the Will of God in Changing Circumstances," *Crux* 27 (1991): 30–34.

Panimolle, S. A., *Il discorso di Pietro all'assemblea apostolica: Il concilio di Gerusalemme (Atti 15,1–35)* (Bologna: Dehoniane, 1976).

Reicke, B., "Der geschichtliche Hintergrund des Apostelkonzils und der Antiochia-Episode, Gal. 2,1–14," *Studia paulina in honorem Johannis de Zwaan septuagenarii* (ed. J. N. Sevenster and W. C. van Unnik; Haarlem: Bohn, 1953), 172–87.

Sanders, J. N., "Peter and Paul in the Acts," *NTS* 2 (1955–56): 133–43.

Sandt, H. van de, "An Explanation of Acts 15.6–21 in the Light of Deuteronomy 4.29–35 (LXX)," *JSNT* 46 (1992): 73–97.

Schmidt, A., "Das historische Datum des Apostelkonzils," *ZNW* 81 (1990): 122–31.

Šagi, J., *Textus decreti concilii hierosolymitani lucano opere et antiquioris ecclesiae disciplina illustratus* (Temi e testi 25; Rome: Edizioni di storia e letteratura, 1977).

Sieben, H.-J., "Zur Entwicklung der Konzilsidee: Zehnter Teil: Die Konzilsidee des Lukas," *TP* 50 (1975): 481–503.

Squillaci, D., "Il primo concilio e San Paolo (Atti 15:1–34)," *PC* 40 (1961): 829–34.

Suhl, A., "Der Beginn der selbständigen Mission des Paulus: Ein Beitrag zur Geschichte des Urchristentums," *NTS* 38 (1992): 430–47.

———, "Ein Konfliktlösungsmodell der Urkirche und seine Geschichte," *BK* 45 (1990): 80–86.

Taylor, J., "Ancient Texts and Modern Critics: Acts 15,1–34," *RB* 99 (1992): 373–78.

Zuntz, G., "An Analysis of the Report about the 'Apostolic Council,'" *Opuscula selecta: Classica, Hellenistica, Christiana* (Manchester, UK: Manchester University; Totowa, NJ: Rowman & Littlefield, 1972), 216–51.

3. James's Confirmation and Proposals (15:13–21)

13 After they stopped talking, James spoke up, "Brothers, listen to me. 14 Simeon
has recounted how God first concerned himself with acquiring from among the
Gentiles a people to bear his name. 15 With this the words of the prophets agree,
as it stands written:

16 *I will return hereafter*
and rebuild the fallen hut of David;
from its ruins will I rebuild it
and set it up again,
17 *that the rest of humanity may seek out the Lord*
even all the nations among whom my name is invoked.
Thus says the Lord who does these things[m] —
18 that have been known from of old.

19 So my judgment is that we ought to stop causing trouble for Gentiles who are
turning to God. 20 We should merely write, telling them to abstain from food
contaminated by idols, from illicit marital unions, from meat of strangled animals, and from eating blood. 21 For in every town, for generations now, Moses has
had preachers, and he has been read aloud in the synagogues every sabbath."

[m] Amos 9:11–12

WT: 13 James stood up and said. 15 Thus the words of the prophets. 16 I shall turn hereafter. 17 seek God. 18 from of old to the Lord his work is known. 20 [omits "from meat of strangled animals"]. 21 [omits "in every town"].

COMMENT

The Lucan story of the assembly at the "Council" in Jerusalem continues with the intervention of James. As the Lucan text stands today, James's speech has to be understood as a further development at the "Council" itself. James's voice is that of an independent judge in the matter; he joins Peter as one of "two witnesses" who testify about what must be adopted by the assembly of the apostles and presbyters and what they must decide. Moreover, James bolsters up the position advocated by Peter by citing Scripture itself; he thus provides the biblical background for that decision. Some commentators think that James is actually disagreeing with Peter; but that is a forced way of reading the text. James is depicted basically agreeing with Peter, but winning his own way about some restrictions for Gentile Christians who live in close proximity to Jewish Christians.

The proposals that James makes about the avoidance of certain foods and illicit marital unions (and the letter that is formulated about these matters in vv 22–29) have often been called the "apostolic decree." In the Lucan context in which they both now appear that title is acceptable, but one should use it with care, for there is a sense in which it is not "apostolic." This part of chap. 15 introduces the classic problems with which every interpreter of the chapter has had to cope. What Luke has written in vv 13–21, James's speech, undoubtedly depends in part on an Antiochene source, perhaps the same source that he has used in vv 3–12, but more likely on another Antiochene source of information, from which vv 22–33 also come (see the COMMENT on these verses below).

Even if the question of sources for this chapter in Acts is not certain—they are debated—the reader should at least keep this question in mind, because of the obvious nature of chap. 15. Its conflated character is widely admitted, even if agreement in analysis is not found. In this chapter one has to distinguish the historical background of what is recounted from the Lucan literary presentation of it and what seems to have been the Lucan telescoping of materials, and to reckon also with the relation of what is recounted here not only to other things yet to come in Acts, but also to Galatians 2.

As Luke presents the event, the "Council" dealt with two issues: (1) circumcision of Gentiles and their obligation to observe the Mosaic law; and (2) dietary and other restrictions for Gentile Christians living among Jewish Christians. He has done this to stress the inevitable break with Judaism that ensued (probably in his lifetime), with and without certain conditions being laid on Gentile converts by the apostolic and presbyteral college of Jerusalem. Luke has just depicted Peter as the one whose voice has prevailed in the debate about circumcision and the Mosaic law; in effect, this is what Peter has learned from his experience at the conversion of Cornelius. Now Luke presents James, another influential figure in the Jerusalem church, who basically supports Peter, but who qualifies the assembly's decision in some details, about dietary problems and illicit marital unions. The Lucan Paul's contribution to the "Council" is at most implied and indirect. He is depicted as simply acquiescing to a decision, after having played an important preliminary part leading up to the Jerusalem meeting.

Luke has, however, most likely telescoped two incidents that were historically distinct in topic and in time. This emerges from the following considerations: First, from the composite nature of the chapter, which is seen in the suture function of vv 1–2 (the joining of material from two different sources, Pauline and Antiochene) and in v 34, which is absent in the best Greek MSS but added in the WT and Latin versions in an effort to explain where Silas was at the beginning of Mission II. When v 34 is omitted, as it is in the Alexandrian text, the location of Silas is problematic: When does he join Paul on Mission II?

Second, who is Simeon *(Symeōn)* in 15:14? He is often simply identified with Simon Peter, who has just spoken in vv 7–11. That is probably the way Luke intends the reader to understand it in the context of the "Council." Elsewhere in Acts, however, Peter is called either *Simōn Petros* (10:5, 18, 32) or *Petros* (15:7), and never *Symeōn*. Moreover, in the whole NT this name is given to Peter only in 2 Pet 1:1, and even there the transmission of the text is not uniform; the oldest text of that letter (P^{72}) reads *Simōn*. Moreover, John Chrysostom, a witness to the traditions of the Antiochene church, did not identify *Symeōn* of 15:14 with Simon Peter but knew that some people thought that he was the old man of Luke 2:25 (*In Acta Apostolorum hom.* 33.1; PG 60.239; see E. R. Smothers, "Chrysostom and Symeon (Acts xv, 14)," *HTR* 46 [1953]: 203–15). Because of this situation, some scholars have suggested that Luke has taken the *Symeōn* of the Antiochene source he is using to be Simon Peter here, whereas the source in reality spoke of *Symeōn ho kaloumenos Niger*, "Simeon called Niger" (13:1). He would have been one of the emissaries sent by the Antiochene church to consult James and the Jerusalem church about dietary problems, as a result of the fracas that arose in Antioch after the incident between Paul and Peter described in Gal 2:11–14. See S. Giet, "L'Assemblée apostolique." This is for me a highly plausible explanation.

Third, the lack of harmony between Peter's speech in 15:7–11, which deals with circumcision and the Mosaic law, and the purported summary of it made by James (15:14–21), in which the topic is rather disciplinary problems.

Such reasons, therefore, suggest that chap. 15 is a conflation of reports about two separate incidents when the Antiochene church consulted officials of the Jerusalem church about certain problems: (1) a report about the Jerusalem "Council," when apostles and presbyters handled the question of circumcision and the obligation of Gentile Christians to observe the Mosaic law (the issue reported by Paul in Gal 2:1–10); and (2) a report about the Jerusalem "Decree," in which James and the presbyters settled a different problem, giving instructions in a letter about diet and marital unions for the local churches of Antioch, Syria, and Cilicia. These instructions are not mentioned and are apparently unknown to Paul in Galatians 2. Indeed, how could that Antioch incident have occurred, if the issue of dietary matters had been settled at the "Council"? Moreover, even in Acts Paul is informed about these instructions, apparently for the first time, by James in 21:25, on his return to Jerusalem after Mission III. See further the next COMMENT. Undoubtedly Luke has joined these two reports and made them part of his story about the "Council" because he inherited them both from Antiochene sources.

In vv 13–21 the important element is James's speech, which is, again, neither missionary nor kerygmatic, but clarificatory and constitutive, offering an interpretation of an OT passage. Amos 9:11 is quoted to show how the prophet's words are actually fulfilled in Jesus and his relation to the nations. James's speech can be divided into two parts: (1) vv 13b–18: a doctrinal section, in which James formulates the principle about the call of Gentiles based on Amos; (2) vv 19–21: a juridical section, in which he proposes a solution to practical problems, justifying it by an appeal to Mosaic law.

This part of chap. 15 shows us another important figure in the Jerusalem church who is concerned for the church at large. There are, indeed, many Gentile Christians in the church, but there are also Jewish Christians; and the church has to accommodate both sorts of Christians. James is the broadminded leader who, while basically agreeing with Peter about no circumcision and no obligation to observe the Mosaic law for Gentile Christians, seeks to preserve the unity and peace of the church. The first Christians were Jewish, and their background, culture, and sentiments have to be respected. This is the reason why he proposes the dietary and marital regulations for Gentile Christians who live among such Jewish Christians. Luke presents James as a church official who seeks a reasonable compromise in the interest of the church at large.

NOTES

13. *After they stopped talking.* I.e., Barnabas and Paul, who were last mentioned in v 12 reporting on their heaven-blessed mission to Gentiles. The clause is another Lucan suture, which joins the two reports, apparently derived from different Antiochene sources.

James spoke up. This "James" has been mentioned in 12:17, the Jerusalem leader who was not one of the Twelve, but to whom Peter's release from prison was to be reported (see NOTE there). His intervention now reveals the important role that he begins to play in the Jerusalem church. Paul in Gal 1:19; 2:9, 12 also recognizes his importance in the Jerusalem church as "the brother of the Lord."

"Brothers, listen to me. James's mode of address is the same as that of Peter in 1:16 (see NOTE there).

14. *Simeon.* As "Simeon" stands in the present Lucan account, it is an apt way for an Aramaic-speaking Jewish Christian like James to refer to Peter. The name *Symeōn* is a grecized form of Hebrew *Šimĕʿôn,* a name commonly used among Jews, for which the Greek equivalent was *Simōn. Pace* Conzelmann (*Acts,* 117), there is nothing Aramaic about it, even if it is "archaic." See Fitzmyer, *ESBNT,* 105–12. Whether it referred to Peter in the Antiochene source that Luke is using is another question; see COMMENT above.

has recounted how God first concerned himself with acquiring from among the Gentiles a people to bear his name. I.e., Gentiles, who have accepted the Christian message in faith, are now said to become "a people of God." James's words allude to the OT, which recounted how Yahweh had acquired a people of old; see Deut 14:2 (LXX): "the Lord your God has chosen you to be a people set apart from all the nations" *(laon periousion apo pantōn tōn ethnōn);* 7:6; 26:18–19; Exod 19:5; 23:22. Luke omits the adj. *periousion,* "chosen, special," found in all the LXX passages, where it specifies *laos* as Israel; he also inverts the order of words, writing *ex ethnōn laon.* This transposition stresses the new way in which God has acquired a people, as Gentiles are now destined "to bear his name." For the background of the latter phrase, see Jer 13:11 (LXX): *tou genesthai moi eis laon onomaston,* "to be for me a people of name," i.e., of my name (cf. Zech 2:11 [LXX 2:15]). From such an OT text was developed the idea of Israel as *ʿam ʾēl,* "the people of God" (1QM 1:5; 3:13), a title that is now extended even to Gentiles. For Luke it has become a way of singling out who belongs to God. In targums of the 3d–4th centuries A.D. one also finds the very phrase that Luke uses: *wʾprś ytkwn lšmy lʿm qdyš,* "I shall set you apart as a holy people for my name" (Palestinian Tg. Exod 6:7 [ed. P. Kahle, frg. D]). See Dupont, "*Laos*"; Dahl, "'A People.'"

15. *With this the words of the prophets agree.* This is the important affirmation in James's speech: OT prophets have foreseen this event of God acquiring a people from among Gentiles. The term "the prophets" may seem to be plural because both Amos and Isaiah are to be quoted, but it is more likely a formulaic plural, which introduces only one prophetic saying (the main quotation from Amos), as the plural does in 7:42; 13:40.

as it stands written. See NOTE on 7:42.

16. *I will return hereafter and rebuild the fallen hut of David; from its ruins will I rebuild it and set it up again,* 17. *that the rest of humanity may seek out the Lord, even all the nations among whom my name is invoked. Thus says the Lord who does these things —* 18. *that have been known from of old.* Save for what appears in v 18, which is a Lucan addition drawn from Isa 45:21, the prophetic utterance is derived from a Greek form of Amos 9:11–12. The Jewish Christian head of the Jerusalem church might have been expected to quote Amos according to the Hebrew original, but what is put on James's lips depends on a wording of Amos that does not agree with either the Hebrew or the LXX. At its beginning, the Greek text is also influenced by the *meta tauta,* "hereafter," possibly of Jer 12:15 (LXX).

In the Hebrew original, Amos 9:11–12 reads: "'On that day I shall raise up the hut of David that is fallen, and I shall repair its breaches; I shall raise up its ruins and rebuild it as in days of old, that they may possess the remnant of Edom and all the nations that are called by my name' — oracle of Yahweh, who does this." Amos was referring to the restoration of the Davidic dynasty. The fallen "hut of David" would have meant the dynasty that came to an end, when Jehoiachin and Zedekiah, the last kings of Judah, were carted off to Babylonian Captivity (2 Kgs 24:15–25:7; cf. Jer 36:30). Yahweh promises the prophet that the Davidic line will be restored, and God's people will inherit what is left of Edom and other nations that will come to be called God's people.

In the LXX these verses of Amos read: "'On that day I shall raise up the tent of David that is fallen and rebuild the ruins of it, and the parts thereof that have been broken down I shall set up, and I shall rebuild it as (in) the days of old, that the rest of humanity may seek (it), even all the nations, upon whom my name has been invoked' — says the Lord, who does all these things." Hebrew *šĕ'ērît 'ĕdôm,* "the remnant of Edom," has become in Greek *hoi kataloipoi tōn anthrōpōn,* "the rest of human beings." The Hebrew name *'ĕdôm,* with the triconsonantal root *'dm,* looks like *'dm* = *'ādām,* "man," and so has been rendered in Greek by the pl. of *anthrōpos,* "humanity."

The text of Amos, as used by James, curtails that of the LXX and does not agree with the sense of the original Hebrew; but it suits James's purpose, because he wants to show that words of an OT prophet have already provided for Gentiles becoming part of a reconstituted "people of God," for an incorporation of them into Israel. So Lohfink, *Sammlung,* 59; Roloff (*Apg.,* 232), Weiser (*Apg.,* 382). Haenchen (*Acts,* 448), however, thinks that Luke interprets the restoration of the fallen hut of David as "adumbrating the story of Jesus, culminating in the

Resurrection, in which the promise made to David has been fulfilled: the Jesus event that will cause the Gentiles to seek the Lord." Similarly Schneider (*Apg.*, 2.183). Either interpretation is possible, but the former is more likely.

that have been known from of old. These words, perhaps derived from the LXX Isa 45:21 (not a verbatim quotation), are added to the quotation from Amos to support Peter's use of "some time ago" (15:7). Thus the whole speech of James is related to the Lucan view of God's salvation history.

The same passage of Amos 9:11 is used in CD 7:16 and again in 4QFlor 1–2 i 12–13, but in different senses. In the latter instance it stresses the restoration of the Davidic dynasty by the one "who will arise to save Israel," by which is meant "the scion of David" *(ṣemaḥ Dāwîd)*, mentioned in the preceding context (derived from Jer 23:5). In CD 7:16 "the books of the Law" are identified with "the hut," as a way of affirming a renewed promulgation of the Mosaic law. Here, however, James uses the words of Amos in a sense quite different from either way in which it was interpreted in the Essene community of Qumran.

19. *So my judgment is that we ought to stop causing trouble for Gentiles who are turning to God.* Lit., "therefore I judge that we should not trouble." The verb *krinein* is used not in the sense of a formal judicial decision, as Lake and Cadbury (*Beginnings*, 4.177), Johnson (*Acts*, 264,266) have understood it, but of James's opinion, as he concludes from the Scripture just quoted. Compare the less formal use of *krinein* in 13:46; 16:15; 21:25; 25:25; 26:8, as Schneider (*Apg.*, 2.183) and Weiser (*Apg.*, 383) have taken it. James's conclusion thus supports Peter's position, even though he adds a stipulation that is not contradictory of that fundamental position.

20. *We should merely write, telling them to abstain from food contaminated by idols, from illicit marital unions, from meat of strangled animals, and from eating blood.* The mention and order of these elements follow the reading of MSS P[74], ℵ, A, B, C, D, E, Ψ, 33, 36, and 81; some MSS (945, 1739, 1891) have *porneia* after the last two. MSS P[74], A, C, E, Ψ, 33, 1739, and the *Koinē* text-tradition add the prep. *apo*, "from," which does not change the meaning of the compound verb, "abstain from." MS P[45] omits *kai tēs porneias*, so that there are only three elements. MS D and some MSS of the VL omit *kai tou pniktou*, but (along with other MSS [323, 945, 1739, 1891, and Irenaeus]) add a form of the Golden Rule: "and whatever they do not wish to be done to them, they should not do to others." The form with the four elements (without the Golden Rule) is most likely original, as Conzelmann (*Acts*, 118) rightly notes. The form in the WT is merely another of its usual vagaries, *pace* T. Boman ("Das textkritische Problem"). Since the elements are connected by *kais*, the omitted words may be owing to haplography, as a copyist's eye jumped from one *kai* to another.

These are the four regulations that James would impose on Gentile Christians who live among Jewish Christians, considering them like the "aliens" of old in Israel. James thus appeals for a sympathetic understanding of Jewish Christian sensitivities. As Conzelmann recognizes (*Acts*, 118), James's intention is not "to retain the Law as valid, not even symbolically or 'in principle.'" Rather, it enables

Jewish Christians to have contact with Gentile Christians. James's regulations seek only a *modus vivendi* of Gentile among Jewish Christians and imply no salvific purpose in them.

The four things that James would impose are derived from part of the Holiness Code in Lev 17–18, which proscribed certain things not only for "anyone of the house of Israel," but also for "the aliens that sojourn among them" (*ûmin haggēr ʾăšer yāgûr bĕtôkām*, Lev 17:8). Laws that apply to both Israel and the *gēr* are also known from Exod 12:48–49; Lev 24:16, 22; Num 9:14; 15:14–16, 26, 29–30, as are those that mention the sojourner specifically in Exod 20:10; Lev 16:29; Num 19:10; 35:15; Deut 5:14; 16:11, 14; 26:11; Josh 20:19; but the four things named are found mainly in Lev 17–18. See T. Callan, "Background."

Pace H.-J. Schoeps (*Theologie*, 259–60), the four are not derived from the so-called Noachic regulations, which numbered seven: prohibition of idolatry, blasphemy, bloodshed, sexual immorality, theft, eating from a living animal, and need to establish a legal system. Those regulations were a rabbinic development, probably unknown in the first century, from the pact made with Noah in Gen 9:8–18. They laid down far more comprehensive details than the four things mentioned here. See Str-B, 3.37–38; G. Strecker, "Noachische Gebote," *RGG* 45.1500–1501; S. S. Schwarzschild and S. Berman, "Noachide Laws," *EJ* 12.1189–91.

The four things are (1) *ta alisgēmata tōn eidōlōn*, "the polluted things of idols," i.e., food ritually unclean, contaminated by having been offered to idols in pagan sacrifice (see Lev 17:7–9; cf. Lev 20:2–3; Ezek 14:7–8). They are called *eidōlothyta*, "things sacrificed to idols" in 15:29; 1 Cor 8:1–13; 10:19–30. (2) *hē porneia*, "fornication" (see below). (3) *to pnikton*, "what has been strangled," i.e., meat from animals improperly or not ritually butchered, without having the blood properly drained from them (Lev 17:15; cf. 7:24; Exod 22:31). (4) *to haima*, "blood," i.e., eating of food made from the blood of animals (Lev 17:10–11; cf. Lev 3:17; 7:26–27). Cf. Josephus, *Ant.* 3.11.1 §260; Philo, *De specialibus legibus* 4.23 §§122–23.

The element that upsets the unity of the four as dietary tabus is *hē porneia.* Etymologically, it means "fornication, prostitution," but because it was often used in a wider sense of other forms of sexual aberration, it is often translated simply as "unchastity" (*RSV*). In the LXX it regularly renders Hebrew *zĕnût, taznût*, or *zĕnûnîm*, different abstract nouns, derived from the Hebrew root *zny*, "fornicate." Sometimes in the OT *zĕnût* takes on the symbolic meaning of "idolatry" (Num 14:33; Hos 6:10; Jer 3:2), a nuance scarcely intended here. In Lev 18:6–18 (LXX) of the Holiness Code, where *porneia* does not occur, various forms of marriage within close degrees of kinship are proscribed. In time, Jewish teachers and rabbis came to describe such illicit marital unions as *zĕnût.* This specific meaning of *zĕnût* is found in QL, showing that such a meaning was current among Jews of pre-Christian Palestine. In CD 4:12b–5:14a three nets of Belial are described in which Israel has been ensnared: *hahôn*, "wealth" (not further explained), *ṭammēʾ hammiqdāš*, "defilement of the sanctuary" (i.e., by failure to avoid intercourse with a woman considered unclean in Lev 15:19), and *hazzĕnût.* When *zĕnût* is explained, two forms of it are mentioned: "taking two wives in their lifetime" (4:20–21 [polygamy and divorce, a contravention of Gen 1:27; 7:9; Deut 17:17]); and "taking (as wives), each one (of them), the daughter of his brother, and the daughter of his sister" (5:7–8 [marriage within close degrees of kinship, a contravention of Lev 18:13]). The Damascus Document thus provides the missing link for this specific understanding of Hebrew *zĕnût.* This seems, then, to be the meaning along with the other three things proscribed in Lev 17–18. Hence it is to be taken as the meaning of *porneia* in Acts 15:20. (The LXX of Jer 3:2, 9 shows that *zĕnût* could be translated into Greek as *porneia.*) See further Fitzmyer, "The Matthean Divorce Texts"; Weiser, *Apg.*, 383.

However, as do some others, B. W. Bacon ("The Apostolic Decree against *porneia,*" *Expos* 8/7 [1914]: 40–61) understood *porneia* to mean "adultery," as in *Ps.-Clementine, Homilies* 3.68. That, however, seems impossible, because there was an explicit word for "adultery," *moicheia,* and because it makes no sense to proscribe that for Gentile Christians alone. H. H. Johnson ("The Acts, xv.29," *CR* 33 [1919]: 100–101) would emend the text to read *porkeia,* "food made of pork." Though that would nicely make all four things dietary, it is more ingenious than correct. Sometimes *haima* has been understood as "shedding blood," especially in the WT form of the verse; but that changes the legal proscriptions into moral stipulations, as does the thrust of this verse in the WT. For that reason it is suspect and scarcely original.

21. *in every town, for generations now, Moses has had preachers, and he has been read aloud in the synagogues every sabbath."* After the quotation of one of the prophets, James might have drawn a conclusion from the words. Instead, he appeals to "Moses," meaning thereby the law of Moses or the Pentateuch, which has both been read every sabbath in synagogues all over and explained in expository preaching. The implication is that even Gentile Christians, who have read the Jewish Scriptures or have heard them explained, would know about regulations of the Holiness Code in the Pentateuch of "Moses," to which allusion is made as a confirmation of the Jerusalem decree just cited in the speech. James implies that Gentile Christians would know of the four things that he is proscribing for them in order to avoid friction with Jewish Christians. He probably also implies that "Moses" is the basis for not imposing any more burdens on such Gentiles and that "Moses" will suffer no loss if they do not impose his law on Gentiles. An even better explanation is that James refuses to impose Mosaic law on Gentile converts to Christianity, because he knows from experience that only a few would agree to believe in the living God under such conditions. The Mosaic law is thus an obstacle to the worship of God by Gentile Christians, and a Jewish Christian attempt to impose it on other Christians will not succeed. In effect, James is telling the converted Pharisees that they are wrong in principle. See D. R. Schwartz, "The Futility."

Philo similarly noted that "in every city" thousands of schools stand open every seventh day, where students sit learning about the piety, holiness, and virtue that Moses taught (*De specialibus legibus* 2.15 §§61–64).

BIBLIOGRAPHY (15:13–21)

Aldrich, W. M., "The Interpretation of Acts 15:13–18," *BSac* 111 (1954): 317–23.

Baltensweiler, H., *Die Ehe im Neuen Testament: Exegetische Untersuchungen über Ehe, Ehelosigkeit und Ehescheidung* (Zurich: Zwingli, 1967), 87–103.

Barrett, C. K., "Things Sacrificed to Idols," *NTS* 11 (1964–65): 138–53.

Bartsch, H.-W., "Traditionsgeschichtliches zur 'goldenen Regel' und zum Aposteldekret," *ZNW* 75 (1984): 128–32.

Bockmuehl, M., "The Noachide Commandments and New Testament Ethics: With Special Reference to Acts 15 and Pauline Halakhah," *RB* 102 (1995): 72–101.

Boman, T., "Das textkritische Problem des sognannten Aposteldekrets," *NovT* 7 (1964–65): 26–36.

Braun, M. A., "James' Use of Amos at the Jerusalem Council: Steps toward a Possible Solution of the Textual and Theological Problems," *JETS* 20 (1977): 113–21.

Brun, L., "Apostelkoncil und Aposteldekret," *Paulus und die Urgemeinde* (ed. L. Brun and A. Fridrichsen; Giessen: Töpelmann, 1921), 1–52.

Callan, T., "The Background of the Apostolic Decree (Acts 15:20, 29; 21:25)," *CBQ* 55 (1993): 284–97.

Catchpole, D. R., "Paul, James and the Apostolic Decree," *NTS* 23 (1976–77): 428–44.

Dahl, N. A., "'A People for His Name' (Acts xv.4)," *NTS* 4 (1957–58): 319–27.

Dupont, J., "*Laos ex ethnōn* (Act. xv.14)," *NTS* 3 (1956–57): 47–50; rep. *Etudes*, 361–65.

———, "Un peuple d'entre les nations (Actes 15.14)," *NTS* 31 (1985): 321–35.

Ferrarese, G., *Il concilio di Gerusalemme in Ireneo di Lione: Ricerche sulla storia dell'esegesi di Atti 15,1–29 (e Galati 2,1–10) nel II secolo* (Testi e ricerche di scienze religiose 17; Brescia: Paideia, 1979).

Fitzmyer, J. A., "The Matthean Divorce Texts and Some New Palestinian Evidence," *TS* 37 (1976): 197–226; repr. *TAG*, 79–111.

Gavin, F., "A Further Note on *Porneia*," *Theology* 16 (1928): 102–5.

Geyser, A. S., "Paul, the Apostolic Decree and the Liberals in Corinth," *Studia paulina in honorem Johannis de Zwaan septuagenarii* (ed. J. N. Sevenster and W. C. van Unnik; Haarlem: Bohn, 1953), 124–38.

Giet, S., "L'Assemblée apostolique et le décret de Jérusalem: Qui était Siméon?" *RSR* 39 (1951): 203–20.

———, "Les trois premiers voyages de Saint Paul à Jérusalem," *RSR* 41 (1953): 321–47.

———, "Nouvelles remarques sur les voyages de Saint Paul à Jérusalem," *RevScRel* 31 (1957): 329–42.

Harnack, A., *New Testament Studies, III: Acts*, 248–63.

Hayward, C. E., "A Study in Acts 15:16–18," *EvQ* 8 (1936): 162–66.

Jervell, J., "Das Aposteldekret in der lukanischen Theologie," *Texts and Contexts: Biblical Texts in Their Textual and Situational Contexts: Essays in Honor of*

Lars Hartman (ed. T. Fornberg and D. Hellholm; Oslo/Stockholm/Boston: Scandinavian University Press, 1995), 227–43.

Kaiser, W. C., Jr., "The Davidic Promise and the Inclusion of the Gentiles (Amos 9:9–15 and Acts 15:13–18): A Test Passage for Theological Systems," *JETS* 20 (1977): 97–111.

Klijn, A. F. J., "The Pseudo-Clementines and the Apostolic Decree," *NovT* 10 (1968): 305–12.

Klinghardt, M., *Gesetz und Volk Gottes: Das lukanische Verständnis des Gesetzes nach Herkunft, Funktion und seinem Ort in der Geschichte des Urchristentums* (WUNT 2/32; Tübingen: Mohr [Siebeck] 1988), 181–89.

Kümmel, W. G., "Die älteste Form des Aposteldekrets," *Heilsgeschehen und Geschichte: Gesammelte Aufsätze 1933–1964* (MarTSt 3; Marburg: Elwert, 1965), 278–88.

Lohfink, G., *Die Sammlung Israels: Eine Untersuchung zur lukanischen Ekklesiologie* (SANT 39; Munich: Kösel, 1975).

Manns, F., "Remarques sur Actes 15,20–29," *Anton* 53 (1978): 443–51.

Mauro, P., "Building Again the Tabernacle of David," *EvQ* 9 (1937): 398–413.

Nägele, S., *Laubhütte Davids und Wolkensohn: Eine auslegungsgeschichtliche Studie zum Amos 9,11 in der jüdischen und christlichen Exegese* (AGJU 24; Leiden: Brill, 1995).

Perrot, C., "Les décisions de l'assemblée de Jérusalem," *RSR* 69 (1981): 195–208.

Philonenko, M., "Le décret apostolique et les interdits alimentaires du Coran," *RHPR* 47 (1967): 165–72.

Richard, E., "The Creative Use of Amos by the Author of Acts," *NovT* 24 (1982): 37–53.

Richards, H. J., "Christ on Divorce," *Scripture* 11 (1959): 22–32.

Sanday, W., "The Apostolic Decree (Acts XV.20–29)," *Theologische Studien Theodor Zahn . . . dargebracht* (Leipzig: Deichert, 1908), 317–38.

———, "The Text of the Apostolic Decree," *Expos* 8/6 (1913): 289–305.

Schoeps, H.-J., *Theologie und Geschichte des Judenchristentums* (Tübingen: Mohr [Siebeck], 1949), 188–96.

Schwartz, D. R., "The Futility of Preaching Moses (Acts 15,21)," *Bib* 67 (1986): 276–81.

Simon, M., "The Apostolic Decree and Its Setting in the Ancient Church," *BJRL* 52 (1969–70): 437–60.

———, "De l'observance rituelle à l'ascèse: Recherches sur le décret apostolique," *RHR* 193 (1978): 27–104.

Turner, C. H., "Jewish Christianity: The Apostolic Decree of Acts xv and the Apostolic Church Orders-I," *Theology* 20 (1930): 4–14.

Waitz, H., "Das Problem des sog. Aposteldekrets und die damit zusammenhängenden literarischen und geschichtlichen Probleme des apostolischen Zeitalters," *ZKG* 55 (1936): 227–63.

Wedderburn, A.J.M., "The 'Apostolic Decree': Tradition and Redaction," *NovT* 35 (1993): 362–89.

Wilson, S. G., *Luke and the Law*, 73–102.
Winter, P., "Miszellen zur Apostelgeschichte," *EvT* 17 (1957): 398–406.
See further bibliography on 15:22–29.

4. The Jerusalem Letter to Local Gentile Churches (15:22–29)

22 Then it was resolved by the apostles and presbyters, in agreement with the
whole church, to choose representatives from their number and send them to
Antioch along with Paul and Barnabas: Judas, called Barsabbas, and Silas, leading men among the brothers. 23 They were to deliver this letter: "The apostles
and presbyters, your brothers, to the brothers of Gentile origin in Antioch, Syria,
and Cilicia: Greetings! 24 Since we have heard that some of our number, who
[went out] without any instruction from us, have upset you with their talk and
disturbed your peace of mind, 25 it has been resolved by us with one accord to
choose representatives and send them to you along with our friends Barnabas
and Paul, 26 who have dedicated their lives to the name of our Lord Jesus Christ.
27 We send you, therefore, Judas and Silas, who will also convey this message by
word of mouth: 28 'It is the decision of the Holy Spirit, and ours too, not to lay on
you any burden beyond what is strictly necessary: 29 to abstain from meat sacrificed to idols, from blood, from meats of strangled animals, and from illicit marital unions.' You will do well to avoid these things. Farewell."

WT: 22 [omits "from their number"] . . . Paul and Barabbas. 23 writing a letter through their hand (that) contained this . . . [omits "of Gentile origin"]. 24 [omits "who went out . . . from us"]. 26 of the Lord Jesus in every trial. 27 [omits "this message"]. 29 [omits "from meats of strangled animals" and adds:] and whatever you do not wish to be done to you, do not do to others. Being moved by the Holy Spirit, you will do well.

COMMENT

As the Lucan form of this chapter now stands, the apostolic and presbyteral assembly in Jerusalem has acquiesced to the proposal of Peter and likewise to that of James. The practical regulations that James considers advisable for Gentile Christians living among Jewish Christians are formulated in a letter that the Jerusalem church sends to the local churches of Antioch, Syria, and Cilicia. In it the four things that have been mentioned in James's speech are now incorporated. Noteworthy in the text is the guidance of the Spirit that is mentioned. The assembly admits that this letter comes as a result of its deliberation, but it also insists that it is "the decision of the Holy Spirit" (15:28).

Just when this Jerusalem decree would actually have been drawn up and sent to the local churches of Antioch, Syria, and Cilicia is a matter of debate. Historically, it must have been a short time after the "Council" itself. The letter might have been sent ca. A.D. 49–50. The Antioch Incident that is mentioned in Gal 2:11–14 is undoubtedly part of this background of the Jerusalem decree. In any case, that incident cannot be taken as part of the reason that the "Council" was called. In Galatians 2 the incident takes place after Paul's visit to Jerusalem (2:1–10).

Pace Weiser (*Apg.*, 385), the text of the letter that Luke incorporates here (vv 23b–29) was undoubtedly the main thing that he acquired from his Antiochene source along with a recollection of James's intervention. On it he built the formulation of much of the preceding episode that tells of James's intervention and the substance of his speech. The following comparison will make clear the parallel between the letter (v 25) and the Lucan introduction to it (v 22):

Letter (v 25)	*Lucan Introduction (v 22)*
It has been resolved by us	Then it was resolved by the apostles and presbyters,
with one accord	in agreement with the whole church
to choose representatives and send them to you	to choose representatives from their number and send them to Antioch
along with our friends Barnabas and Paul	along with Paul and Barnabas

Luke has composed an introduction to the letter itself, which goes beyond the few words here compared, but the letter has been the guide for his composition. In the parallel just cited, the meaning of the prep. *syn*, "(along) with," is problematic, especially as Luke has used it in v 22. This preposition sometimes develops the nuance merely of "and," as it does at the beginning of v 22; see also 14:5; 16:32; 21:18; Luke 20:1. It is used now in v 25, and one sees how a misunderstanding could arise. According to v 25, the letter and representatives are being sent "to you [Christians of Antioch, Syria, and Cilicia] along with our friends Barnabas and Paul," i.e., to you and to Barnabas and Paul. That would mean that Barnabas and Paul were thought to be still in Antioch and were intended as corecipients of the letter about dietary matters.

Luke, finding the letter in his Antiochene source, read the prep. *syn* to mean that the church in Jerusalem was sending representatives to Antioch, Judas and Silas, "along with Paul and Barnabas," i.e., was sending Judas, Silas, Paul, and Barnabas. Note too the order of the names: Luke, in composing his introduction to the letter, puts his hero Paul before Barnabas, whereas his source has the order "Barnabas and Paul." Compare A.J.M. Wedderburn, "The 'Apostolic Decree.'" This mode of reading the letter from the Antiochene source and the Lucan introduction to it gives rise to the further problem about where Silas joins Paul for Mission II, and why some MSS include v 34 that offers an explanation.

The letter offers a solution to the problem in the Antiochene church that rose out of the incident of Paul's public rebuke of Peter there (Gal 2:11–14). In other words, after the departure of Peter and Paul from Antioch subsequent to that rebuke, a problem developed about Gentile Christians living and eating with Jewish Christians. So the church in Antioch eventually sent emissaries (among them Simeon Niger, 13:1) to Jerusalem and sought advice about it from James and the church there. The Jerusalem church responded in the letter sent. Luke, however, because he found the letter in an Antiochene source, as he had also learned about the Jerusalem "Council," joined the two accounts and presented the two (originally independent) Jerusalem decisions as events of the "Council."

In any case, we see that the Jerusalem church tries to settle the problem of dietary and marital disputes among Gentile and Jewish Christians in the daughter churches by invoking regulations from the OT Code of Holiness (Lev 17–18) and passing them on to Christians of Antioch, Syria, and Cilicia in the form of a letter. This is the so-called Jerusalem Decree. It is a decision that did not stem historically from the "apostles and elders" at the Jerusalem "Council," but rather from the church of Jerusalem under the guidance of James. Luke, however, has joined the two decisions, the apostolic and presbyteral negative decision of the "Council" about circumcision and obligation to obey the Mosaic law and the positive decision of the Jerusalem mother church about dietary matters and illicit marital unions. He has joined them in order to explain how the Christian church eventually achieves its own independent status and mode of living as it emancipates itself from its Jewish matrix.

One also notes the Lucan emphasis on the Spirit-guided institutional church in Jerusalem guiding like a mother its daughter churches, especially those where Gentile and Jewish Christians have come to live together otherwise in peace and harmony. The same four elements that appeared in v 20 reappear in the letter in v 29, which is actually the source from which Luke would have learned about them.

Patristic writers also record the Jerusalem decree in various forms: Justin, *Dialogue with Trypho* 34.8; Minucius Felix 30.6; Tertullian, *Apologeticum* 9.13; Eusebius, *HE* 5.1.26. See G. Resch, *Das Aposteldecret nach seiner ausserkanonischen Textgestalt* (TU 28/3; Leipzig: Hinrichs, 1905); K. Six, *Das Aposteldekret (Act 15,28.29): Seine Entstehung und Geltung in den ersten vier Jahrhunderten* (Veröffentlichungen des biblisch-patristischen Seminars zu Innsbruck 5; Innsbruck: Rauch, 1912).

The letter sent by the Jerusalem church to the local churches of Antioch, Syria, and Cilicia counsels Gentile Christians there to respect the background of those Jewish Christians among whom they may live and thus preserve the unity of the church. The Gentile Christians are not to think that their observance of such regulations will guarantee their salvation, for God grants salvation only on the merits of Jesus Christ's death and resurrection. That is why the letter ends, "You will do well to avoid these things" (15:29b). It thus inculcates a crucial distinction, one that Christians of all ages have to recall: there are demands of Christian life that are essential, and others that, while nonessential, may preserve harmony and peace.

NOTES

22. *it was resolved by the apostles and presbyters.* See NOTE on 15:2.

in agreement with the whole church. The sense of this phrase could be debated. It may mean no more than "the whole church" of Jerusalem, i.e., the church that greeted Paul and Barnabas along with the apostles and presbyters on their arrival (15:4), but that seems to conflict with v 6, which says that "the apostles and presbyters gathered together to look into this matter," where there is no involvement of "the whole church." Luke may, however, be implying more: an involvement of "church" that transcends particular locales.

to choose representatives from their number and send them to Antioch along with Paul and Barnabas. See the COMMENT for the ambiguity of the prep. *syn.* Although the letter is destined for more areas than Antioch, Luke in his introduction to it, singles out only Antioch as its destination. This is probably because the emissaries sent to consult Jerusalem authorities have come from Antioch (14:26–28; 15:1–2) and the letter is first of all to be carried there.

Judas, called Barsabbas. He is otherwise unknown. On his second name, see NOTE on 1:23. MS D reads *Barabbas!*

Silas. This future companion of Paul on Mission II appears now for the first time in the Lucan story. See further 15:27, 32, 34, 40; 16:19, 25, 29; 17:4, 10, 14, 15; 18:5, after which he disappears. *Silas* is a grecized form of the Aramaic name *Šĕʾîlāʾ*, known from Palmyrene inscriptions; it is the counterpart of Hebrew *Šāʾûl* (see NOTE on 7:58). He undoubtedly is the same as *Silouanos,* "Silvanus" (derived from the Latin name of a Roman forest god), whom Paul mentions (1 Thess 1:1; 2 Cor 1:19). Cf. 2 Thess 1:1; 1 Pet 5:12. "Silvanus" may be his *supernomen;* "Silas" occurs only in Acts.

leading men among the brothers. Thus they are described here, but in v 32 they are identified as "prophets" in the Christian church.

23. *They were to deliver this letter.* Lit., "writing (a letter) through their hand," i.e., the hand of Judas and Silas. The nom. ptc. *grapsantes* dangles; it agrees with the logical subject of v 22. MS D and some ancient versions read rather "(writing) a letter through their hand (that) contained this," but MS 614 has "(writing) and sending a letter through their hand (that) contained this." The epistolary form that is used in the following text is characteristic of ancient Greek letters, especially in its opening greeting and concluding farewell; see *NJBC,* 768–71 (art. 45).

"The apostles and presbyters, your brothers, to the brothers of Gentile origin in Antioch, Syria, and Cilicia: Greetings! The letter of James and his colleagues is destined for three local Christian churches (joined under one article to stress its limited destination, ZBG §184); it does not have the scope or bearing of the apostolic and presbyteral decision set forth in Peter's speech (15:7–11). *Antiocheia* (see NOTE on 11:19) was the capital of Syria, a Roman province, whereas Cilicia was the name of a district in Syria at this time, or better Syria-Cilicia was still the double province, which was only split when Vespasian reestablished the

province of Cilicia in A.D. 72. On Cilicia, see NOTE on 6:9; on brothers, see NOTE on 1:15.

Syria is mentioned for the first time; it will appear again in 15:41; 18:18; 20:3; 21:3. It denotes that part of western Asia that is bounded on the north by the Taurus mountains, on the south by Judea, on the west by the Mediterranean, and on the east by lands of the Euphrates. It became a Roman province in 64 B.C., the seat of its governor was Antioch on the Orontes. See R. Tracey, "Syria," *The Book of Acts in Its Graeco-Roman Setting* (BAFCS 2), 223–78. Cf. Gal 1:21; Xenophon, *Anabasis* 1.4.4; Ignatius, *Phld.* 11:1, where Syria and Cilicia are mentioned together.

Luke uses the common opening formula of a Greek letter: X to Y, *chairein.* The last word is the infin. of the verb meaning "be glad, rejoice," the stereotyped abbreviation of a longer salutation, which in letters came to mean simply "Greetings!" (see *NJBC*, 769, art. 25:6). It occurs again in 23:26. See E. R. Goodspeed, "The Origin of Acts," *JBL* 39 (1920): 83–101, esp. 87.

24. *Since we have heard that some of our number.* In the Lucan account, as it now stands, this would refer to "some people" of 15:1. Historically, however, it might more likely refer to "some people from James" (Gal 2:12), i.e., people who sided with James in Jerusalem, but who may not have been authorized to act as they did. Conzelmann (*Acts*, 120) notes that vv 24–26 contain the only periodic sentence in Luke-Acts outside of the prologue to the Gospel (Luke 1:1–4). This may be a sign of its derivation from an Antiochene source.

who [went out] without any instruction from us, have upset you with their talk and disturbed your peace of mind. The troublemakers went on their own to Antioch. The aftermath of Paul's rebuke of Peter at Antioch (Gal 2:11–14) would have provided the opportunity for such trouble.

25. *it has been resolved by us with one accord.* Lit., "it has seemed good to us being of one accord." "Us" would refer to James and his colleagues. Again Luke uses his favorite adv. *homothymadon*; see NOTE on 1:14.

to choose representatives and send them to you along with our friends Barnabas and Paul. In the source that Luke has been using this prep. phrase, "along with our beloved Barnabas and Paul," was meant to be understood as "and to Barnabas and Paul." In other words, Barnabas and Paul were thought of as being in Antioch, and hence the corecipients of this letter. The Lucan introduction in v 22, however, understood it to mean that the representatives are accompanying Barnabas and Paul. The translation of this clause is dependent on the reading of the ptc. *eklexamenois* in MSS P[45], A, B, L, Ψ, 33, 81, 614, 945, and 1739, but other MSS (א, C, D, E, H, P, 36, 323) read the acc. ptc. *eklexamenous*, "having chosen," which would correctly function as the subject of the infin. *pempsai*, "to send," but it strangely follows on a dat. *hēmin*, "to us" (cf. BDF §410).

26. *who have dedicated their lives to the name of our Lord Jesus Christ.* This eulogy in the letter from Jerusalem implicitly sounds a paean for Luke's hero, Paul. Cf. Rom 16:4. Once again the Lucan refrain of "the name" appears; see NOTE on 2:38.

27. *We send you, therefore, Judas and Silas.* See NOTE on 15:22.

who will also convey this message by word of mouth. According to Conzelmann (*Acts,* 120), this would better suit a "fictitious letter" than a real one, but that is clearly an exaggeration.

28. *'It is the decision of the Holy Spirit, and ours too.* The Spirit-guided church of Jerusalem passes on its instructive decision to its daughter churches. Compare the parallel formulation of a decree of Caesar Augustus quoted in Josephus, *Ant.* 16.6.2 §163: "it has been decided by me [Caesar Augustus] and my council under oath."

not to lay on you any burden. In the present Lucan context, that would refer to the decision of the apostolic and presbyteral assembly, viz., about no circumcision and no need to observe the Mosaic law. In the Antiochene source document it would have been a general demurrer introducing the exceptions that follow.

beyond what is strictly necessary. I.e., for Gentile Christians living among Jewish Christians. The necessary matters are those drawn from the Holiness Code of Leviticus.

29. *to abstain from meat sacrificed to idols, from blood, from meats of strangled animals, and from illicit marital unions.'* See NOTE on 15:20. MSS P^{74}, $\aleph^2$, A^c, E, Ψ, 33, and 1739 read the sg. *tou pniktou,* as in v 20; but MSS $\aleph^*$, A^*, B, C, 81, 614, and 1175 read the pl. *tōn pniktōn,* "strangled things." MS D omits all mention of this item, but adds a form of the Golden Rule, as in v 20, couched in the 2d plural. The order of the four elements follows the order of their proscription in Lev 17–18; contrast v 20. Note too that the first element is *eidōlolytha,* whereas in v 20 it was called *alisgēmata.*

You will do well to avoid these things. Lit., "you will do well, keeping yourselves free of these things." MS D adds, "being moved by the Holy Spirit."

Farewell." Lit., "be well" (*errōsthe*), the conventional closing greeting in a Hellenistic letter. Compare 2 Macc 11:21, 33; 3 Macc 7:9; Josephus, *Life* 44 §227.

BIBLIOGRAPHY (15:22–29)

Campbell, J. Y., "The Apostolic Decree in Acts 15:29," *CJRT* 3 (1926): 315–22.

Coppieters, H., "Le décret des Apôtres (Act. xv, 28–29)," *RB* ns 4 (1907): 34–58, 218–39.

Hunkin, J. W., "The Prohibitions of the Council at Jerusalem (Acts xv 28, 29)," *JTS* 27 (1925–26): 272–83.

Jones, M., "The Apostolic Decrees in Acts xv: A Compromise or a Triumph?" *Expos* 8/5 (1913): 242–55.

Kaye, B. N., "Acts' Portrait of Silas," *NovT* 21 (1979): 13–26.

Kümmel, W. G., "Die älteste Form des Aposteldekrets," *Spiritus et veritas* (Fest. K. Kundsiņš; Eutin: Ozolins, 1953), 83–98; repr. *Heilsgeschehen und Geschichte: Gesammelte Aufsätze 1933–64* (MarTS 3; Marburg: Elwert, 1965), 278–88.

Lake, K., "The Judaistic Controversy, and the Apostolic Council," *CQR* 71 (1910–11): 345–70.
Lietzmann, H., "Der Sinn des Aposteldekretes und seine Textwandlung," *Amicitiae corolla: A Volume of Essays Presented to James Rendel Harris* . . . (ed. H. G. Wood; London: University of London Press, 1933), 203–11; repr. *Kleine Schriften II* (TU 68; ed. K. Aland; Berlin: Akademie-V., 1958), 292–98.
Ploiij, D., "The Apostolic Decree and Its Problems," *Expos* 8/25 (1923): 21–40, 81–100, 223–38.
Porter, J. R., "The 'Apostolic Decree' and Paul's Second Visit to Jerusalem," *JTS* 47 (1946): 169–74.
Suggit, J. N., "'The Holy Spirit and We Resolved . . .' (Acts 15:28)," *JTSA* 79 (1992): 38–48.
Witherington, B., "Not So Idle Thoughts about *eidololuthon*," *TynBull* 44 (1993): 237–54.
See further bibliography on 15:13–21.

5. Aftermath of the Jerusalem Decision and Letter (15:30–35)

30 The representatives were sent off and traveled down to Antioch, where they
called a meeting of the community to deliver the letter. 31 When it was read, there
was great delight at the encouragement it gave. 32 Judas and Silas, who themselves
were prophets, encouraged the brothers and strengthened them with many a discourse. 33 After passing some time there, they were sent off again with a blessing
of peace from the brothers to those who had sent them.[34] 35 But Paul and Barnabas spent their time in Antioch teaching and proclaiming the word of the Lord,
along with many others.

WT: 30 were sent off in a few days. 31 Judas and Silas read (the letter) and encouraged. . . , being themselves prophets. 33 After passing some time there (sg.), [after which v 34 follows immediately:] Judas returned to Jerusalem (but see NOTE).

COMMENT

Luke concludes his account of the important Jerusalem decisions and letter by describing the reception of the representatives of the Jerusalem church in Antioch, where the problems originally began. Judas and Silas bring the message and encourage the Christians there. The prosaic ending of this dramatic chapter records the delight and the encouragement that the message from Jerusalem brings to the Christians in Antioch. In some form vv 30–33 undoubtedly came to Luke from his Antiochene source, but one notes Lucan composition in the idyllic account of the reception of the letter received in Antioch. Verse 34 is missing in the Alexandrian text-tradition (see NOTE below), and v 35 may be a Lucan suture.

The episode describes the continuation of the church in the aftermath of the "Council" and the Jerusalem decree. The decisions made in Jerusalem launch the Christian church on its way after establishing its independence from its Jewish matrix. Those decisions are welcomed by the Christians of Antioch, and the prophets Judas and Silas encourage them in many ways. The story of Paul's missionary activities that now begins again spreads the Christian church among still other Gentiles so that it can become the world entity that is known in history.

NOTES

30. *The representatives were sent off and traveled down to Antioch.* MS D adds "in a few days." See NOTE on 8:5.

where they called a meeting of the community to deliver the letter. Lit., "gathering together the assembly/multitude (*plēthos* of Christians)."

31. *When it was read, there was great delight at the encouragement it gave.* Lit., "reading (it), they rejoiced at the encouragement." Again one meets Luke's idyllic description of the Christian community, this time in Antioch.

32. *Judas and Silas, who themselves were prophets.* See NOTES on 15:27 and 13:1. Even though they come from Jerusalem, they are called "prophets" and thus put on a par with officials in the Antiochene church.

encouraged the brothers and strengthened them with many a discourse. I.e., they exercised their prophetic role among the Antiochene Christians. Cf. 14:22; 1 Cor 14:3.

33. *After passing some time there, they were sent off again with a blessing of peace.* Lit., "with peace," a phrase probably derived from Gen 26:29 (LXX).

from the brothers to those who had sent them. Judas and Silas thus leave the Christians of Antioch and return to Jerusalem. Verse 40 will report that Paul chose Silas as a companion for his coming missionary journey as he departs from Antioch. That notice, however, creates a difficulty about where Silas joins Paul on Mission II. Hence the addition of v 34 in various forms of the WT (MSS C, D, the Vg, etc.): "But Silas decided to stay there, and only Judas left for Jerusalem." MSS P^{74}, ℵ, A, B, E, Ψ, and the *Koinē* text-tradition omit v 34, and that omission is one of the important signs of the conflation of chap. 15. See K. and B. Aland, *The Text of the New Testament,* 299; *TCGNT,* 388.

35. *Paul and Barnabas spent their time in Antioch teaching and proclaiming the word of the Lord, along with many others.* This is a Lucan transitional verse that tells of the further aftermath of the Jerusalem decisions in the Antiochene church. In effect, it is a sort of summary, similar to 5:42. The two missionaries of Mission I continue to evangelize Gentile inhabitants of the capital of the province of Syria. Who the "many other" teachers are we never learn, unless we are to understand those of 13:1. On "the word of the Lord," see NOTE on 4:31.

BIBLIOGRAPHY (15:30–35)

Delebecque, E., "Silas, Paul et Barnabé à Antioche selon le texte 'occidental' d'Actes, 15,34 et 38," *RHPR* 64 (1984): 47–52.

Meinertz, M., "Apg 15,34 und die Möglichkeit des antiochenischen Streitfalles (Gal 2,11ff) nach den Apostelkonzil," *BZ* 5 (1907): 392–402.

VI. Paul's Universal Mission and Testimony (15:36–22:21)

◆

A. Paul's Further Missionary Journeys (15:36–20:38)

1. Paul and Barnabas Differ and Separate (15:36–40)

[36] Some time later, Paul said to Barnabas, "Let us go back and see how the brothers are getting on in each of the towns where we proclaimed the word of the
Lord." [37] Barnabas wanted to take John, who was called Mark, along with them,
[38] but Paul kept insisting that, since he had deserted them at Pamphylia and had
refused to go along with them, he was not fit to be taken along for this task. [39] So
sharp a disagreement about it ensued that they decided to separate from each
other. Barnabas took Mark and sailed for Cyprus, [40] but Paul chose Silas and set
out on his journey, commended by the brothers to the grace of the Lord.

WT: [36] what the brothers are doing . . . [omits "of the Lord"; adds at end:] The decision was pleasing to Barnabas too. [38] but Paul was unwilling, saying that . . . with them for the task for which they had been sent, he should not be with them (now). [39] Then Barnabas took Mark along. [40] the grace of God.

COMMENT

The sixth major division of Acts begins here. Luke's account of a critical episode in the history of the early church has come to an end, and he begins the second half of his story: the testimony that Paul bears to the Gentiles of the eastern Mediterranean world and the beginning of his mission beyond Asia, even to what we call Europe today. Luke concentrates on further missionary journeys of the apostle to the Gentiles, now that such missionary endeavors have received the official blessing of the mother church of Jerusalem.

Before he starts his account, however, Luke explains how the two missionaries of Mission I come to part ways. As they are about to begin Mission II, Barnabas and Paul think it wise to revisit the churches established on Mission I in order to strengthen the Christians there. Barnabas wants to take his cousin John Mark along, but Paul, annoyed that he had deserted them just as the evangelization of Asia Minor was to begin (13:13), disagrees and is reluctant to take Mark with him. So Paul and Barnabas separate. Barnabas takes Mark and sails for Cyprus, whereas Paul finds a new companion for Mission II, Silas who has just been mentioned (15:22, 27).

The episode is again a narrative, which ends with the actual beginning of Pauline Mission II under the blessing of the church in Antioch and the grace of the Lord God. Mission II (15:40–18:22) begins in Antioch and will end there. It covers the period of A.D. 50–52.

What Luke recounts now (15:36–17:21) comes to him from the Pauline source, excerpts from which will become frequent. The verb *dietribon*, "spent their time" (15:35), resumes that of 14:28, the last place that the Pauline source has appeared (Benoit, *Bib* 40 [1959]: 786; *Exégèse et théologie*, 3.293). There is, however, some Lucan composition, especially in transitions.

This episode, which inaugurates Pauline Mission II, reveals that, even though the decisions made at Jerusalem contributed to the harmony and peace of the church, dissension may still be part of Christian life. That life has its ups and downs, and this episode gives an instance of that. Now the difference of opinion that develops has nothing to do with doctrine, but with personalities. The story of the collaboration of Paul and Barnabas up to this point in Acts has been exemplary, but now a conflict arises between them. Part of it may be owing to the fact that John Mark, whom Barnabas was defending, was a cousin *(anepsios)* of Barnabas, as we know from Col 4:10, but Luke is silent about that relationship. He rather ascribes the conflict to Paul's angry reluctance to take John Mark along on further missionary work because he had deserted them in the middle of Mission I. The episode reveals that even a great missionary, such as Paul was, can still allow a human side of himself to show. His anger over the earlier conduct of John Mark dissolves the collaborative work of Barnabas and himself. Yet it has a good side to it, because Barnabas and Mark go off to evangelize further the island of Cyprus (about which we learn nothing more), whereas Paul gets a new collaborator, Silas, with whom he sets out on Mission II.

NOTES

36. *Some time later.* Lit., "after some days," i.e., an indefinite period after the "Council" and its aftermath. Paul and Barnabas are still in Antioch.

Paul said to Barnabas, "Let us go back and see how the brothers are getting on in each of the towns where we proclaimed the word of the Lord." The towns evangelized in Mission I were Salamis and Paphos in Cyprus, Pisidian Antioch, Iconium, Lystra, Derbe, and Perga im Pamphylia (13:5–6, 14, 51; 14:1, 8, 20, 25). As the story develops, Paul does not include the two Cypriot towns in Mission II, because Barnabas and Mark have set out for Cyprus.

37. *Barnabas wanted to take John, who was called Mark, along with them.* See NOTE on 12:12 and recall 13:13. According to Col 4:10 Mark was the cousin of Barnabas, and this relationship was undoubtedly involved in Barnabas's desire. The last we heard was that Mark was in Jerusalem; since Paul and Barnabas are now in Antioch, we never hear how Mark came from Jerusalem to join Barnabas. Phlm 24 indicates that there must have been a later reconciliation between Paul and Mark, *pace* Haenchen (*Acts,* 474), who questions the identity of the Mark of Acts and the Mark of Phlm 24 and Col 4:10.

38. *Paul kept insisting that, since he had deserted them at Pamphylia and had refused to go along with them.* Whereas the Alexandrian text reads *ēxiou,* "he (Paul) was considering it fitting," MS D reads rather *ouk ebouleto legōn,* "he (Paul) did not want to, saying (that)." MS D also adds (at the end) *eis ho epemphthēsan,* "for (that for) which they had been sent." On Pamphylia, see 13:13 and NOTE there.

he was not fit to be taken along for this task. Lit., "that (they) should not take him along." MS D reads "that he should not be with them." Unfortunately, Luke does not tell us what the nature of the disagreement between Mark and Paul really was; it may be that Mark basically differed with Paul over the judaizing problem, whether Gentiles should be made to observe the Mosaic law.

So sharp a disagreement about it ensued that they decided to separate from each other. Conzelmann (*Acts,* 115, 123) thinks that this verse echoes the conflict in Gal 2:12. That, however, is hardly correct, because the conflict in Gal 2:12 is mainly between Paul and Peter, who misled Barnabas. What happened in Antioch is never related in Galatians 2 to a split between Paul and Barnabas.

Barnabas took Mark and sailed for Cyprus. That means that they would have sailed from Seleucia, the port of Antioch, which was roughly 20 km west on the shore of the Mediterranean (see NOTE on 13:4). On Cyprus, see NOTE on 11:19.

40. *Paul chose Silas and set out on his journey.* See NOTES on 15:22 and 33. Thus begins Pauline Mission II.

commended by the brothers to the grace of the Lord. Luke makes sure that readers understand that Mission II and its further evangelization of Gentiles are also blessed by the Lord at the prayer of the Antiochene community; recall 13:1–3. MSS P^{45}, C, E, Ψ, 1739 and the *Koinē* text-tradition read rather "of God." On brothers, see NOTE on 1:15.

BIBLIOGRAPHY (15:36–40)

Bailey, J. W., "Paul's Second Missionary Journey," *BW* 33 (1909): 414–23.

Bruzzone, G. B., *Il dissenso tra Paolo e Barnaba in Atti 15,39* (Collectio Ianuensis 1; Genoa: Centro Studi Francescani per la Liguria, 1973).

Dupont, J., "La question du plan des Actes des Apôtres à la lumière d'un texte de Lucien de Samosate," *NovT* 21 (1979): 220–31; repr. *Nouvelles études,* 24–36.

Holmberg, B., *Paul and Power: The Structure of Authority in the Primitive Church as Reflected in the Pauline Epistles* (Lund: Gleerup, 1978), 18–32.

Schepens, G., "Lucas, hellenisme en christendom: Beschouwingen over 'De Handelingen der Apostelen,'" *Collationes* 31 (1984): 31–55.

2. Paul's Second Missionary Journey (15:41–18:22)

a) In Derbe and Lystra: Timothy as Companion (15:41–16:5)

41 Paul traveled through Syria and Cilicia, bringing strength to the churches.
16 1 He [also] arrived at Derbe and at Lystra, where there was a disciple named
Timothy, the son of a believing Jewish woman and a Greek father. 2 The brothers
in Lystra and Iconium spoke highly of him, 3 and Paul wanted him to come along
with him on the journey. So he took him and had him circumcised because of
the Jews of those regions, for they all knew that his father was a Greek. 4 As they
made their way from town to town, they passed on to the people for observance
the decisions made by the apostles and presbyters in Jerusalem. 5 The churches
grew stronger in faith, and day by day they increased in numbers.

WT: 41 They traveled . . . [adds at end:] (and) passing on the instructions of the presbyters. 16 1 Passing
through all the nations, they arrived at Derbe and Lystra . . . a believing Jewish widow. 3 knew his
father, that he was a Greek. 4 they preached and passed on to the people with all boldness the Lord
Jesus Christ, at the same time passing on as well the instructions of the apostles and presbyters in
Jerusalem. 5 [omits "in faith"].

COMMENT

The story of Pauline Mission II starts now. It is the beginning in Acts of the account of a major missionary endeavor of Paul. Having passed overland with Silas through Syria and Cilicia, he comes again to Derbe and Lystra. In the latter place he finds still another collaborator, Timothy, whom he has circumcised because he was born of a convert Jewish mother. With his two companions Paul continues his evangelization of the area in the southern part of the province of Galatia, passing on to the churches already founded there the decisions made at Jerusalem. These are the "decisions" made by "the apostles and presbyters in Jerusalem" concerning no circumcision and no obligation to observe the Mosaic law for Gentile Christians. They do not include the regulations made by James and the Jerusalem church, about which Paul will have to be told by James for the first time in 21:25. This Mission II will eventually lead Paul to what we call Europe, and his main base of evangelization will be Corinth. The episodes to be recounted will describe dramatically the further spread of the Word to Europe.

Again, the first episode is a narrative, which recounts the missionary activity of Paul and his companions throughout southern Asia Minor. Their activity is one of evangelization, bolstering up the faith of those already converted, and teaching them about the decisions of the Jerusalem "Council." The Lucan narrative is again idyllic, emphasizing the growth of churches evangelized. Recall the "grace" with which Paul begins this Mission II (15:40), to which the growth and increase are ultimately due. In v 4 we read for the last time of "the apostles," who disappear thereafter from the Lucan story. Jerusalem presbyters will be mentioned again in 21:18 (at the end of Mission III).

The episode ends with v 5, another of the minor summaries in Acts. For the rest of the episode Luke is making use of information from his Pauline source.

For the first time in Acts we read about Timothy as one of Paul's coworkers; he is otherwise well known from various letters of Paul. Timothy was well spoken of in Lystra and Iconium and so Paul was anxious to have him as a collaborator. "Because of the Jews of those regions" Paul has Timothy circumcised, which is surprising, especially in light of what has been decided at the "Council" in chap. 15. This move on Paul's part may be explained by what he himself says in 1 Cor 9:20 that "to Jews I became as a Jew in order to win Jews over." In any case, Luke thus paints a picture of Paul that upsets some of our ideas about him, and perhaps that is the real message of this episode in Acts. For as Luke notes at the end of it in his summary, "The churches grew stronger in faith" (16:5) as a result of the work of Paul and his collaborators.

NOTES

41. *Paul traveled through Syria and Cilicia.* I.e., he retraced his steps through territory already evangelized in Mission I, through areas mentioned together in 15:23.

bringing strength to the churches. I.e., as Paul is reported having done in Lystra, Iconium, and Pisidian Antioch (14:22; see NOTE there).

16:1. *He [also] arrived at Derbe and at Lystra.* See NOTE on 14:6. Coming from the Cilician Gates, he would arrive first at Derbe and then at Lystra; so Luke's order is correct.

where there was a disciple named Timothy. We learn for the first time about this Lycaonian Christian *mathētēs* (see NOTE on 6:1), whom Paul meets here in Lystra and who becomes his noted friend and collaborator.

Timotheos is a good Greek name, found in the writings of Aristophanes and Xenophon, and often interpreted as meaning "one who honors God." He will appear again in 17:14–15; 18:5; 19:22; 20:4 and is mentioned as an important collaborator of Paul in his letters: 1 Thess 1:1; Phil 1:1; 2 Cor 1:1; Phlm 1 (in these four as the coauthor); cf. 1 Thess 3:2, 6; Phil 2:19; 1 Cor 4:17 ("my beloved and faithful child in the Lord"); 16:10; 2 Cor 1:19; Rom 16:21. Also in the Deutero-Paulines: Col 1:1; 2 Thess 1:1; and in the Pastoral Letters: 1 Tim 1:2, 18; 6:20; 2 Tim 1:2, 5 (where Timothy's mother Eunice and grandmother Lois are mentioned). Cf. Heb 13:23. See P. Trummer, *EDNT*, 3.359–60.

the son of a believing Jewish woman and a Greek father. According to the Lucan context, his birth to a Jewish mother married to a pagan husband may be the reason why he has not been circumcised. She was probably converted, because she is called *pistē*, "believing," along with her son. Timothy would then be a *Jewish* Christian, and this would provide the background for Paul's decision to have him circumcised. Children born to such a mixed marriage, which was not recognized as normal in Jewish practice, would have been considered Jewish, according to a later Mishnaic tradition (*m. Kidd.* 3:12: "the offspring is of her own standing"; cf. Str-B, 2.741). Conzelmann (*Acts*, 125) so understands Timothy's status; similarly Bruce (*Acts*, 322), Pesch (*Apg.*, 2.96–97), Polhill (*Acts*, 343).

However, Cohen ("Was Timothy") argues that the "vast majority of ancient and medieval exegetes did not think" that Timothy was Jewish. "There is no evidence that Paul or the Jews of Asia Minor thought so. Ambrosiaster and his medieval followers did think so, but in all likelihood this interpretation is wrong because there is no evidence that any Jew in premishnaic times thought that the child of an intermarriage followed the status of the mother" (268). From the mixed NT data (see 2 Tim 1:5) arose the debate in patristic times about Timothy's background. See also C. Bryan, "A Further Look."

2. *The brothers in Lystra and Iconium spoke highly of him.* Lycaonian Christians, undoubtedly converts made by Paul on Mission I, have recommended Timothy to Paul. The towns of Lystra and Iconium were relatively close so that Christians of both towns could easily have known Timothy. See NOTES on 13:51; 14:6.

3. *Paul wanted him to come along with him on the journey.* I.e., as a collaborator on Mission II.

he took him and had him circumcised Lit., "taking him, he circumcised him." The import of the last phrase in this part of the verse escapes us, unless one admits with Conzelmann (*Acts*, 125) that the circumcision of Timothy was necessary for the story of Paul's missionary endeavors that often begin with a visit to Jewish synagogues.

This Lucan statement, however, creates one of the biggest problems about the Paulinism of Acts, as Vielhauer and others have noted (see Introduction §173). It stands in contrast to what Paul himself says about circumcision in 1 Cor 7:18–19 and about Titus in Gal 2:3 as it is usually understood: that Titus was not circumcised. Cf. Gal 5:3, 6.

There are some who read Gal 2:3 differently, "Titus, . . . though he was a Greek, was not compelled to be circumcised," putting emphasis on the main verb, "was not compelled," and implying thereby either that Titus voluntarily agreed to be circumcised or that Paul had consented to the circumcision of Titus. That, however, sounds like an attempt to harmonize Paul and Acts. Not even 1 Cor 9:20, where Paul himself admits, "to Jews I became as a Jew in order to win Jews over," necessarily argues for such an interpretation.

Haenchen (*Acts*, 482) thinks that Luke simply took the story over "from tradition," "an unreliable tradition," based on a rumor reflected in Gal 5:11, where Paul reveals that he is still accused of preaching circumcision. The Lucan account has been called "a confused and perhaps erroneous memory" of the episode alluded to in Gal 2:3–5 (Lake and Cadbury, *Beginnings*, 4.184), whose position is supported by Walker, "Timothy-Titus Problem." See Harnack, *Date*, 42–44.

Some commentators query the historicity of the circumcision of Timothy: Roloff (*Apg.*, 240) and Weiser (*Apg.*, 402). Its historicity is accepted by Wikenhauser and Marshall (*Acts*, 260). Schneider (*Apg.*, 2.200–1) understands it as an exceptional measure that Paul took; this may be the best answer to the problem.

because of the Jews of those regions. This is the main reason that Luke gives, the advantage that Paul would gain in having a circumcised Jewish Christian collaborator when he would be dealing with Jews of the area. Paul is obviously not contravening the decision of the "Council" (15:10–12).

they all knew that his father was a Greek. "Greek" would mean that his father was a heathen, not a Jew. As a Greek, his father may have opposed the circumcision of Timothy; by this time he may have died. MSS P^{45}, D, E, and the *Koinē* text-tradition read rather "they all knew his father, that he was a Greek," a variant that does not substantially change Luke's meaning. Again, Lucan hyperbole is employed; see NOTE on 2:44.

4. *As they made their way from town to town, they passed on to the people for observance the decisions made by the apostles and presbyters in Jerusalem.* The *dogmata* are the "decisions" made by the apostolic and presbyteral college, which acquiesced to the advice of Peter in 15:7–11, that circumcision and observance of the Mosaic law were not to be required of Gentile converts to Christianity. These decisions are now passed on as "apostolic" teaching.

5. *The churches grew stronger in faith, and day by day they increased in numbers.* This is another of the minor summaries with which Luke has punctuated his account. It stresses the steadfastness and growth of local churches. Cf. 14:22.

BIBLIOGRAPHY (15:41–16:5)

Belkin, S., "The Problem of Paul's Background," *JBL* 54 (1935): 41–60, esp. 43–47.

Bryan, C., "A Further Look at Acts 16:1–3," *JBL* 107 (1988): 292–94.

Cohen, S.J.D., "Was Timothy Jewish (Acts 16:1–3)? Patristic Exegesis, Rabbinic Law, and Matrilineal Descent," *JBL* 105 (1986): 251–68.

Delebecque, E., "De Lystres à Philippi (Ac 16) avec le codex Bezae," *Bib* 63 (1982): 395–405.

Linton, O., "The Third Aspect: A Neglected Point of View: A Study in Gal. i–ii and Acts ix and xv," *ST* 3 (1949): 79–95.

Rius-Camps, J., "Jesús y el Espíritu Santo conducen la misión hacia Europa (Hch 16, 1–18,22)," *Est-Bíb* 52 (1994): 517–34.

Tissot, Y., "Les prescriptions des presbytres (Actes, xv, 41, D)," *RB* 77 (1970): 321–46.

Walker, W. O., "The Timothy-Titus Problem Reconsidered," *ExpTim* 92 (1980–81): 231–35.

White, N.J.D., "Note on Acts xvi.1–8," *Hermathena* 12 (1903): 128–35.

b) Paul Crosses Asia Minor (16:6–10)

6 They passed through Phrygia and Galatian territory, having been prevented by
the Holy Spirit from going to preach the word in Asia. 7 When they came to
Mysia, they tried to go on into Bithynia, but again Jesus' Spirit would not allow
them. 8 So they traversed Mysia and came down to Troas. 9 There Paul had a
vision one night: a man of Macedonia stood beckoning him and saying, "Come
over to Macedonia and help us!" 10 When he had seen this vision, we immediately made efforts to get over to Macedonia, concluding that God had summoned
us to preach to them.

WT: 6 [omits "holy"] . . . to preach the word to anyone in Asia. 7 When they were at Mysia, they wanted to go. 8 they passed through Mysia and arrived at Troas. 9 [omits "one night"] . . . stood before him . . . [omits "him"]. 10 So when he woke up, he recounted his vision to us and we realized that he had summoned us to preach to the people in Macedonia.

COMMENT

Luke continues the story of the first part of Paul's Mission II. After leaving the area of Iconium, Derbe, and Lystra, towns in southern Galatia, Paul makes his way with Silas and Timothy northward through Phrygia and Galatian territory and comes to Mysia. Having tried to go still further north into Bithynia and been prevented by the Spirit, the three of them turn westward, cross through Mysia, and come to Troas in northwest Asia Minor. In Troas Paul dreams that a Macedonian has been summoning him to cross over to Macedonia and preach the gospel there.

The episode is again a narrative, but Luke's information about this part of Mission II is not very satisfying; he writes as one with little firsthand acquaintance of the area. His real interest is expressed in v 9, where the evangelization of what we call Europe is itself proposed as the Spirit-guided goal of Paul's missionary journey. This evangelization is under divine guidance; it is the work of God, not of human beings. Note the crescendo in vv 6–10: "Holy Spirit," "Jesus' Spirit," and lastly "God" (apropos of the vision that Paul has).

In this episode Luke has been dependent on his Pauline source, but suddenly in v 10 he injects himself into the story of Acts. For the first time the Alexandrian text of Acts records a verse from the We-Sections (see Introduction §§94–102), as the narrative account changes from the third person to the first plural. It will be continued in the next episode as well. Some commentators regard the We-Sections as part of the Itinerary source. In a generic sense that may be right, but I prefer to keep the We-Sections separate from other so-called sources.

This episode stresses the Spirit-guided ministry of Paul, as he is prevented from swerving either to the right or the left and eventually arrives at the important seaport town of Troas. There Paul learns in a dream that he is to carry his testimony to Greece, a very important part of the Mediterranean world of his day: "Come over to Macedonia and help us!" (16:9). In response to that invitation Paul begins the evangelization of Europe. This call of Paul is like that of OT calls: Isaiah in Isa 6:8; Jeremiah in Jer 1:5–10. Paul responds to heaven's call and so understands why the Spirit was preventing him from going to Asia and Bithynia. The Lucan Paul thus gives the readers of Acts a view of how the Christian disciple must patiently await heaven's instructions.

NOTES

6. *They passed through Phrygia and Galatian territory.* Phrygia was in central Asia Minor; see NOTE on 2:10. *Galatikē chōra,* "Galatian district/region," is undoubtedly the name, not for the Roman province of Galatia, but for the ancient district of Galatia in northern Asia Minor. The preceding episode (15:41–16:5) has depicted Paul and his companions in Iconium, Derbe, and Lystra, which were towns in southern Galatia; now they are said to pass from them through Phrygia and Galatian territory, which must mean the area often called North Galatia, the main towns of which were Ancyra, Pessinus, and Tavium.

Some commentators understand *Phrygian* as an adj. and translate "through Phrygian and Galatian territory." Then the meaning would not be radically different. The word order in 18:23, where the names recur, seems to argue for *Phrygian* being a noun. See *JBC,* 2.236–37 (art. 49 §4). Cf. G. W. Hansen, "Galatia," *The Book of Acts in Its Graeco-Roman Setting* (BAFCS 2), 377–95.

having been prevented by the Holy Spirit from going to preach the word in Asia. Paul and his companions may have wanted to go directly to the province of Asia, i.e., to Ephesus, the seat of the Roman governor, via the Roman post road. Although Paul's missions were inaugurated by the Spirit (13:2, 4, 9; 19:2, 6), we are not told how the Spirit now prevents Paul's immediate move from South Galatia to the west. In any case, he now heads north, and in time we learn the reason for the prevention. See ZBG §265; cf. *IBNTG,* 100. MS D adds *mēdeni* and *tou theou,* "(from preaching) the word of God to anyone (in Asia)." On Asia, see NOTE on 2:10.

7. *When they came to Mysia.* This was an area in northwest Asia Minor, part of the province of Asia (Strabo, *Geography* 12.564–65, 571).

they tried to go on into Bithynia. Since 64 B.C. the area of Bithynia formed along with Pontus a senatorial Roman province in northwestern Asia Minor. Cf. 1 Pet 1:1. It was actually to the east of Mysia, and perhaps for that reason the direction of Paul's mission is changed by the Spirit. The Spirit prevents them from swerving either to the right (Bithynia) or to the left (Asia).

again Jesus' Spirit would not allow them. The direction of Paul's missionary journey continues to be guided by the Spirit. This is the only time in the Lucan writings that the Spirit is described as that of Jesus; it stands in parallelism with the "Holy Spirit" (v 6). Cf. Rom 8:9; Gal 4:6; Phil 1:19; 1 Pet 1:11.

8. *they traversed Mysia and came down to Troas. Trōas* was in a mountainous

area of northwestern Asia Minor, dominated by the Ida massif and surrounded on three sides by the Aegean Sea, not far from the site of ancient Troy. It was an important port because of a great artificial harbor constructed there. At first the town was called *Antigoneia*, founded in 310 B.C. by Antigonus I (382–301), one of the successors of Alexander the Great. After Antigonus's death in 301, it was renamed *Alexandreia* in honor of Alexander, and in order to distinguish it from other Alexandrias, it became known as "Alexandria Troas." In time it was made a Roman colony by Augustus (*Colonia Augusta Troadensium* or *Colonia Augusta Troas*). It served as a port of embarkation for those sailing to Greece. See 20:5–6; 2 Cor 2:12–13; 2 Tim 4:13. Paul's route through Asia Minor to Troas is not too clear in this account, when one tries to follow it according to known ancient Roman roads that crisscrossed the land, but Luke does speak correctly of Troas and its place in the Roman system of roads, communication, and embarkation. See W. P. Bowers, "Paul's Route"; C. J. Hemer, "Alexandria Troas," *TynBull* 26 (1975): 79–112; J. M. Cook, *The Troad: An Archaeological and Topographical Study* (Oxford: Clarendon, 1973), 198–204; P. Trebilco, "Asia," *The Book of Acts in Its Graeco-Roman Setting* (BAFCS 2), 291–362, esp. 357–59.

9. *There Paul had a vision one night.* I.e., a dream, which the context implies was Spirit instilled; it has symbolic meaning: Paul is being summoned to a still larger area of missionary endeavor.

a man of Macedonia stood beckoning him and saying. Paul recognizes the figure as Macedonian from what he says.

Come over to Macedonia and help us! Further Spirit-guided direction is given to Paul's missionary endeavor, this time in the form of a dream.

Makedonia was the region in mountainous, northern Greece, bordering on Illyria and the Nestos River. It had been founded as a political area in the seventh century B.C. by kings residing in Edessa and Pella. Under Philip II (359–336 B.C.) it became the leading power in Greece. In 293 B.C. the Antigonids gained control, and their last king, Perseus, was defeated in 168 B.C. by the Romans. Then Macedonia was divided into four regions. In 148 B.C. it became a Roman province and from A.D. 15–44 was governed by an imperial legate resident in Moesia; later it became a senatorial province. Roman colonies were established in Dyrrhachium, Pella, and Philippi.

See P. E. Davies, "The Macedonian Scene of Paul's Journeys," *BA* 26 (1963): 91–106; P. Lemerle, *Philippes et la Macédoine orientale à l'époque chrétienne et byzantine* (Bibliothèque des écoles françaises d'Athènes et de Rome 158; 2 vols.; Paris: de Boccard, 1945); C. Edson, *Macedonia* (Harvard Studies in Classical Philology 51; Cambridge: Harvard University Press, 1940), 125–36; B. Barr-Sharrar and E. N. Borza, *Macedonia and Greece in Late Classical and Early Hellenistic Times* (Studies in the History of Art 10; Washington, DC: National Gallery of Art, 1982); D.W.J. Gill, "Macedonia," *The Book of Acts in Its Graeco-Roman Setting* (BAFCS 2), 397–417; I. Levinskaya, "Macedonia and Achaia," *The Book of Acts in Its Diaspora Setting* (BAFCS 5), 153–66.

10. *When he had seen this vision.* MS D begins this verse thus: "So when he

woke up, he recounted his vision to us and we realized that he [the Macedonian or possibly God] had summoned us to preach to the people in Macedonia." This WT addition introduces the "we" in the rest of the verse.

we immediately made efforts to get over to Macedonia. The first We-Section (16:10–17) in the Alexandrian text of Acts now begins. It reads like an eyewitness account and has often been regarded as an indication that the author has joined Paul and his other companions for part of Mission II. The inclusion of Luke in the first person plural is contested, however, as Haenchen (*Acts,* 430) notes, and other explanations are given for the shift to the first person plural (see Introduction §§94–102). That Luke includes himself still remains the best explanation (Dupont, *Sources,* 75–165). Luke would have accompanied Paul as far as Philippi, where the We-Section resumes, when Paul later finds him on his return journey to Jerusalem at the end of Mission III (see NOTE on 20:5).

concluding that God had summoned us to preach to them. Paul and his companions finally understand the directions supplied by the Spirit in vv 6–7. God's summons was leading them to the evangelization of Europe. Paul's evangelization of Asia is temporarily suspended in the interest of the evangelization of another field.

BIBLIOGRAPHY (16:6–10)

Bowers, W. P., "Paul's Route through Mysia: A Note on Acts xvi.8," *JTS* 30 (1979): 507–11.

Broughton, T.R.S., "Three Notes on Saint Paul's Journeys in Asia Minor," *Quantulacumque: Studies Presented to Kirsopp Lake* . . . (ed. R. P. Casey et al.; London: Christophers, 1937), 131–38, esp. 133–34.

Glombitza, O., "Der Schritt nach Europa: Erwägungen zu Act 16,9–15," ZNW 53 (1962): 77–82.

Greene, A., Jr., "The North-South Galatia Theory Controversy," *BSac* 92 (1935): 478–85.

Hemer, C. J., "The Adjective 'Phrygia,'" *JTS* 27 (1976): 122–26.

Lake, K., "Paul's Route in Asia Minor," *Beginnings,* 5.224–40.

McDonald, W. A., "Archaeology and St. Paul's Journeys in Greek Lands," *BA* 3 (1940): 18–24.

Penna, R., "Lo 'Spirito di Gesù' in *Atti* 16,7: Analisi letteraria e teologica," *RivB* 20 (1972): 241–61.

Rius-Camps, J., "L'Aparició/desaparició del 'nosaltres' en el llibre dels Fets: Un simple procediment teològicoliterari?" *RCT* 6 (1981): 33–75.

Schwank, B., "'Setz über nach Mazedonien und hilf uns!' Reisenotizen zu Apg 16,9–17,15," *EA* 39 (1963): 399–416.

Steinmann, A., "Nordgalatien," *BZ* 8 (1910): 274–77.

Wikenhauser, A., "Religionsgeschichtliche Parallelen zu Apg 16, 9," *BZ* 23 (1935–36): 180–86.

———, "Die Traumgesichte des Neuen Testaments in religionsgeschichtlicher Sicht," *Pisciculi: Studien zur Religion und Kultur des Altertums: Franz Joseph*

Dölger . . . dargeboten (ed. T. Klauser and A. Rücker; Antike und Christentum Ergänzungsband 1; Münster in W.: Aschendorff, 1939), 320–33.

c) EVANGELIZATION OF PHILIPPI (16:11–40)

11 So we put out to sea from Troas and set a course straight for Samothrace and
the next day for Neapolis; 12 from there we traveled on to Philippi, which is a
leading city of the district of Macedonia and a Roman colony. We spent several
days in that city. 13 On the sabbath we went outside the city gate along the bank
of the river, where we thought a place of prayer would be. As we sat there, we
engaged in conversation with women who had also gathered there. 14 One
woman, who was listening, was named Lydia, a dealer in purple cloth from the
town of Thyatira, who already worshiped God. The Lord opened her heart to
follow what Paul was saying. 15 When she and her household were baptized, she
extended us an invitation, "If you have judged me to be one who believes in the
Lord, come and stay at my house." And she prevailed upon us. 16 Once as we
were on our way out to the place of prayer, a slave girl with a spirit of clairvoyance
happened to meet us; her fortune-telling used to bring in considerable profits for
her masters. 17 She began to follow Paul and the rest of us, shouting, "These men
are slaves of the Most High God; they are proclaiming to you a way of salvation."
18 This she did for several days, until Paul became annoyed, turned around, and
said to the spirit within her, "In the name of Jesus Christ I order you to come out
of her!" It left her then and there. 19 When the girl's masters saw that their hope
of making money was gone, they seized Paul and Silas and dragged them to the
main square before the authorities. 20 They turned them over to the magistrates
with the complaint, "These men are disturbing the peace of our city; they are
Jews 21 and are advocating practices unlawful for us Romans to adopt or observe."
22 The crowd joined in the attack against them, and the magistrates had them
stripped of their clothes and ordered them to be flogged. 23 After they had lashed
them many times, they threw them into prison and ordered the warden to guard
them securely. 24 He took this order to heart and locked them up in the inmost
cell, even securing their feet to a stake. 25 About midnight, while Paul and Silas
were praying and singing hymns to God, and their fellow prisoners were listening, 26 such a severe earthquake occurred that the prison was shaken to its
foundations. All the doors suddenly flew open, and the chains of all were loosened. 27 When the warden woke up and saw the prison gates standing open, he
drew [his] sword to kill himself in the belief that the prisoners had escaped. 28 But
Paul shouted out, "Don't do yourself any harm! We are all still here." 29 The warden asked for a light, rushed in, and fell trembling at the feet of Paul and Silas.
30 When he had led them out, he said, "Sirs, what must I do to be saved?" 31 Their
answer was, "Believe in the Lord Jesus, and you will be saved, you and your
household." 32 So they explained to him and all the members of his house the
word of the Lord. 33 At that very hour of the night he took them and bathed their

wounds. Thereupon he and his whole household were baptized. [34]He brought them up into his house, spread a table before them, and with his whole household rejoiced at having found faith in God. [35]When it was day, the magistrates dispatched officers with orders, "Release those men!" [36][This] information the warden conveyed to Paul, "The magistrates have sent orders that you are to be released. Now then get out and go in peace." [37]Paul, however, said to the officers, "They flogged us in public without even a trial, though we are Roman citizens, threw us into prison, and now they want to get rid of us quietly. No, indeed! Let them come here in person and lead us out." [38]The officers reported these words to the magistrates, who were alarmed when they heard that they were Roman citizens. [39]So they came, tried to placate them, and led them out with the request that they leave the city. [40]Once outside the prison, they made their way to Lydia's house, where they saw and encouraged the brothers, and then departed.

WT: [11]The following day we put out to sea. [12]a city of the first district of Macedonia. [13]where a place of prayer was thought to be. [14]who listened. [15]and all her household . . . to be a believer, come. [16]happened to come upon us . . . for the masters. [17]they are preaching to you. [18]It left her immediately. [19]that they had been deprived of the moneymaking they had through her. . . . [omits "before the authorities"]. [20][omits "adopt or"]. [22]A great crowd joined in . . . shouting against them. Then the magistrates. [23]that they be securely guarded. [25]About the middle of the night. [26]were loosed. [27][omits "prison"]. [29]When the warden heard that, he searched for a light. [30]He led them out, and having secured the rest, he said to them. [32][omits "of the Lord"]. [33][omits "thereupon"]. [34]in the Lord. [35]When it was day, the magistrates gathered together in the main square and, remembering with fear the earthquake that had occurred, dispatched . . . those men, whom you put in custody yesterday. [36]The warden went in and conveyed this information to Paul . . . Now then go. [37]without cause. [38]these words which had been spoken . . . When they heard that they were Roman citizens, they were alarmed. [39]So they arrived at the prison with many friends and urged them to leave: "We did not understand your situation, that you were upright men." Leading them out, they urged them, "Leave the city, lest those who have cried out against you gang together again." [40]where they saw the brothers and explained what the Lord had done for them. Having encouraged them, they departed.

COMMENT

Luke now recounts the story of Paul's first visit to Philippi, where he establishes a Christian community, to which he eventually sent his Letter to the Philippians. From that letter we know that this community was one of which Paul thought highly. Little in that letter, however, corresponds to the account that we now read in Acts, save perhaps Phil 1:5.

In this episode, Paul, having sailed from Troas, reaches Neapolis, the port serving inland Philippi. Again he seeks out fellow Jews in an effort to evangelize them first. At a place of prayer he meets Lydia, a dealer in purple goods from Thyatira, who is converted to Christianity. An encounter with a slave girl leads to the flogging and eventual imprisonment of Paul and his companions by the city authorities, from which they are miraculously delivered by an earthquake. The authorities, frightened by the earthquake, send word to the warden to release them, but Paul protests on the basis of his Roman citizenship. If they have jailed him, a Roman, they must come in person and release him. Paul is thus released and, having visited the Christians in Lydia's house, departs from Philippi.

The Lucan story succeeds once again in depicting the Spirit-guided missionary efforts of Paul and his companions in an important Roman town in the eastern Mediterranean area. It is the first place evangelized by Paul in Europe. The exorcism of the possessed slave girl is used by Luke to depict the triumph of Christianity over pagan Greco-Roman practices. A pagan religious practice is made to acknowledge that salvation comes from the Most High God of Christianity. Again the refrain of "the name of Jesus" is introduced, as Paul frees the girl of the python spirit (16:18). This exorcism results again in persecution, as Paul and his companions are flogged and imprisoned. Under such stress the Word continues to spread.

Thus, Luke begins his account of the evangelization of major urban areas in Greece; all of them will be important cities in the contemporary Roman empire. The first is actually a colony where many Roman soldiers lived along with others. This is part of Luke's account of how Christianity became in the Roman world *religio licita*.

The episode is basically a narrative, and part of it is a double miracle story, recounting how Paul exorcises the slave girl and how an earthquake brings about his release from prison. It starts with the continuation of the We-Section, which began in v 10b and ends in v 17. After that Luke makes use again of information from his Pauline source. One has to distinguish in this episode five different accounts: (1) In vv 11–15 there is the continuation of the travel narrative, which includes the meeting of Paul and his companions with Lydia, whose hospitality they accept. (2) In vv 16–18 there is the first miracle story, the exorcism of the slave girl. (3) In vv 19–24 there is the account of the aftermath of the exorcism, the troubles that befall Paul and his companions. (4) In vv 25–34 there is the second miracle story, in which Paul is rescued from imprisonment by a heaven-sent earthquake, an account that differs strikingly from the preceding and following sections. (5) In vv 35–40 there is the account of the reaction of the Philippian authorities to the earthquake and of the justification that Paul and his companions seek from the authorities.

NOTES

11. *So we put out to sea from Troas and set a course straight for Samothrace.* Luke again uses the technical nautical term *anagein*; see NOTE on 13:13. *Samothrakē* is an island in the northeastern part of the Aegean Sea, dominated by a mountain over 1,500 m high that served as a mariner's landmark. Under Roman administration a city on the island with the same name was considered *civitas libera*, "a free city." It was also the cultic seat of the non-Hellenic twin fertility gods, Cabiri, with a famous temple dedicated in their honor. See K. Lehmann, *Samothrace* (2 vols. in 3; New York: Bollingen Foundation, 1958, 1960, 1960).

the next day for Neapolis. Neapolis or *Nea polis*, read as two words in the best

MSS, means "New City." It was the port serving Philippi in Macedonia, called today Kavalla. Cf. Strabo, *Geography* 7, frg. 36; Pliny, *Naturalis historia* 4.11.42. During the battle of Philippi (42 B.C.) it served as the naval base for Brutus and Cassius (Appian, *Bellum Civile* 4.13 §106).

12. *from there we traveled on to Philippi, which is a leading city of the district of Macedonia.* Here I read *hētis estin prōtē tēs meridos tēs Makedonias polis* with MSS P^{74}, ℵ, A, C, Ψ, 33, 36, 81, 323, 945, 1175, and 1891, which has been called "the oldest form of text in the extant Greek witnesses" (*TCGNT*, 393). NA^{27} and GNT^{4}, however, think that a dittography of *-tē tēs* is involved: *hētis estin prōtē[s] meridos tēs Makedonias polis,* "a city of the first district of Macedonia." This conjecture is based on the reading *prōtē tēs meridos* of MSS B, 614, 1241, 1505, 1739, and the *Koinē* text-tradition. Part of the problem is that Thessalonica was the capital of Macedonia, whereas the chief city of the district of Macedonia, in which Philippi was located, was Amphipolis. Another part of the problem is the nuance to be understood for the adj. *prōtē,* "first," because it can denote not only order, but also rank or dignity (LSJ, 1535). See also *TCGNT,* 395; BA^{6}, 1023. Some commentators have tried to say that it means the "first" city to which Paul came in the district of Macedonia. That would not be accurate, because he came first to Neapolis, and it otherwise strains the Greek syntax.

The Roman province of Macedonia was divided into four districts *(merides),* and *Philippoi* was a city in eastern Macedonia, situated east of Mt. Pangaeus on the Via Egnatia, which led from Byzantium to Dyrrhachium on the Adriatic. Founded on the site of an older Thracian town of *Krēnides* ("Springs") by Philip of Macedonia in 356 B.C., it was a gold-mining center in the area. In 167 B.C., after Aemilius Paulus defeated the Macedonians, Philippi came under Roman control and was heavily populated by Romans (Appian, *Bellum Civile* 4.13–17 §§105–31; Dio Cassius, *Roman History* 47.42–49). In 42 B.C. it was the scene of a double battle, in which Mark Antony defeated Brutus and Cassius. In addition to Romans, many Macedonian Greeks and a contingent of diaspora Jews dwelled there. See W. Elliger, *Paulus in Griechenland: Philippi, Thessaloniki, Athen, Korinth* (SBS 92–93; Stuttgart: Katholisches Bibelwerk, 1978), 23–77; P. Pilhofer, *Philippi: 1. Die erste christliche Gemeinde Europas* (WUNT 87; Tübingen: Mohr [Siebeck], 1995); P. Lemerle, *Philippes et la Macédoine orientale* (see above); P. Collart, *Philippes, ville de Macédoine* (Paris: de Boccard, 1937); J. Schmidt, "Philippoi," PW 19/2 (1938): 2206–44.

a Roman colony. This Lucan description of Philippi is historically correct. *Kolōnia* is a grecized Latin word, *colonia.* M. Antony founded a colony in Philippi for Roman veterans of the battles of 42 B.C. After the battle of Actium (31 B.C.), Octavian settled still more veterans there, as well as the partisans of M. Antony evicted from Italy. He named it *Colonia Iulia Augusta Philippensis,* granting it *libertas* (self-government), *ius italicum* (same right as citizens of an Italian city), and *immunitas* (exemption from taxation).

We spent several days in that city. The amount of time is only vaguely stated.

13. *On the sabbath we went outside the city gate along the bank of the river.*

Many commentators identify the river as the Gangites, which is 2.4 km from Philippi. A. J. Festugière (*RB* 54 [1947]: 133) queried that identification, because that distance would have been too far for a sabbath-day journey (see Acts 1:12; *m. Erubin* 4:3: 2,000 cubits or 880 m.). So he proposed to identify the "river" as the closer creek, Crenides.

where we thought a place of prayer would be. So read MSS A[c], C, Ψ, 33, and 81; but MSS P[74], E, 1739, and the *Koinē* text-tradition read rather *enomizeto proseuchē,* "a place of prayer was thought to be." *Proseuchē,* "prayer," is sometimes used as a technical term for a place where Jews gathered to pray (cf. 3 Macc 7:20, *topon proseuchēs*). It sometimes denoted a synagogue building (Philo, *In Flaccum* 6 §41); but this is scarcely meant in a town where so few Jews were living. Cf. Dan 8:2; 10:4; Ezek 1:1. See S. M. Zarb, "De Iudaeorum *proseuchē* in Act. xvi, 13, 16," *Ang* 5 (1928): 91–108; M. Hengel, "Proseuche und Synagoge: Jüdische Gemeinde, Gotteshaus und Gottesdienst in der Diaspora und in Palästina," *Tradition und Glaube: Das frühe Christentum in seiner Umwelt: Festgabe für Karl Georg Kuhn . . .* (ed. G. Jeremias et al.; Göttingen: Vandenhoeck & Ruprecht, 1971), 157–84; D. Noy "Jewish Place"; I. Levinskaya, "The Meaning of *proseuchē,*" *The Book of Acts in Its Diaspora Setting* (BAFCS 5), 207–25. The implication is that Paul and his companions sought out first the Jewish community at Philippi; this is the reason for their going to a place of prayer on a sabbath.

As we sat there, we engaged in conversation with women who had also gathered there. Some of them at least would have been Jewish women, or at least sympathizers with Judaism.

14. *One woman, who was listening, was named Lydia.* As a woman's name, Lydia is found in Latin literature (Horace, *Odes* 1.8.1; 1.13.1; 1.25.8). Her name corresponds to the land from which she came, for Thyatira was in a district called Lydia in Asia Minor.

a dealer in purple cloth from the town of Thyatira. She sold wool or cloth that had been dyed purple. The noun *porphyra,* "purple," denoted actually the shellfish *(Murex trunculus),* from which one form of the ancient precious purple dye was obtained. The mollusks were harvested from the Mediterranean, and Tyre in Phoenicia was a very important place for the production of purple goods; its twice-dyed *(dibaphos)* Tyrian purple was an ancient luxury (see Josephus, *J.W.* 6.8.3 §390). Purple cloth, however, was also produced in other Greek cities in Asia Minor, among which was Thyatira, the Lydian town on the Lycus River, situated on the road from Pergamum to Sardis and called today Akhisar. It was originally settled by Macedonian Greeks in pre-Hellenistic time (Strabo, *Geography* 13.4.4), but became a military colony under Seleucus I Nicator in 281 B.C.; it was noted for its production of purple goods (*CIG* §§3496–98). In 129 B.C. it came under Roman control. Thyatira is mentioned in Rev 1:11; 2:18, 24. See W. H. Buckler, "Monuments de Thyatira," *Revue de philologie* 37 (1913): 289–331; E. Ziebarth, "Zur Epigraphik von Thyateira," *RhMP* 51 (1896): 632–36; D. Magie, *Roman Rule in Asia Minor to the End of the Third Century after Christ* (2 vols.; Princeton: Princeton University Press, 1950), 123–24, 977–78.

Possibly Lydia's purple was not that derived from the Tyrian *murex,* but rather from *rubia,* the madder plant, from which came so-called Turkey red, an ancient dye used especially in the Thyatira area. Cf. *NDIEC,* 3.53–55.

who already worshiped God. Lit., "being a worshiper of God." See NOTE on 13:43. She was a Jewish sympathizer, which accounts for her being at the place of prayer on a sabbath.

The Lord opened her heart to follow what Paul was saying. Lit., "to attend to the things being said by Paul." So Lydia put faith in the Christian gospel preached by Paul. The opening of the heart is known from 2 Macc 1:4.

15. *When she and her household were baptized.* Whether the baptism took place then and there (by the river), we are not told; Luke is interested only in recording Lydia's becoming a Christian, along with her household. Cf. 16:33. MS D introduces the adj. *pas,* "all," which would be another instance of Lucan hyperbole; see NOTE on 2:44. On baptism, see NOTES on 1:5; 2:38.

she extended us an invitation, "If you have judged me to be one who believes in the Lord, come and stay at my house." And she prevailed upon us. Paul and his companions sojourn in the house of Lydia; thus Jewish Christians accept the hospitality of a Gentile Christian host. Luke depicts Paul doing what Peter has done (Acts 10).

16. *Once as we were on our way out to the place of prayer, a slave girl with a spirit of clairvoyance happened to meet us.* Lit., "a little girl having a python spirit" or "a python as spirit" (*pneuma pythōna*). So read MSS P^{74}, ℵ, A, B, C*, D*, 81, and 326; but MSS P^{45}, C^{3}, D^{1}, E, Ψ, 33, 1739, and the *Koinē* text-tradition have rather *pneuma pythōnos,* "the spirit of a python." In Greek mythology, *Pythōn* was the serpent or dragon that guarded the Delphic oracle at the base of Mt. Parnassus; it was slain by Apollo. Later on, its name came to denote a "spirit of divination," or "soothsaying," and even of "ventriloquism." See Strabo, *Geography* 9.3.12; Plutarch, *De defectu oraculorum* 8 (= *Moralia* 414E); cf. A. J. Festugière, *RB* 54 (1947): 133. *Paidiskē,* fem. diminutive of *pais,* "child," was often used to denote a slave in a Greek household.

her fortune-telling used to bring in considerable profits for her masters. Lit., "she, (in) soothsaying, was providing much profit for her masters." The verb *manteuesthai* means to act as a *mantis,* "soothsayer, diviner." Presumably her ability attracted gullible people who paid for her services.

17. *She began to follow Paul and the rest of us, shouting, "These men are slaves of the Most High God.* What the phrase "the Most High God" would have meant on the lips of a pagan slave girl is hard to say: probably Zeus, the highest god of the Greek pantheon (Pindar, *Nemean Odes* 1.60; 11.2). For Luke it would have meant Yahweh, as in Stephen's speech (see NOTE on 7:48). With "us," the We-Section ends; another will begin at 20:5.

they are proclaiming to you a way of salvation." So the slave girl divines the import of the Christian message, using the distinctively Lucan *hodos sōtērias,* "way of salvation" (see *Luke,* 169). She thus announces a prominent motif of Lucan redemptive history. Cf. 4:12.

18. *This she did for several days, until Paul became annoyed, turned around,*

and said to the spirit within her. To ask how Paul would have discerned that a spirit was at work in her is to miss the point of the story. He rebukes the spirit and so exorcises the girl; that is the Lucan intention.

"In the name of Jesus Christ I order you to come out of her!" The name is clearly a sign of the power that Paul commands. Once again the refrain of "the name" appears; see NOTE on 2:38.

It left her then and there. Lit., "that very hour." See *Luke*, 117; cf. J. Jeremias, "*En ekeinē tē hōra, (en) autē tē hōra,*" ZNW 42 (1949): 214–17. The exorcism is successful.

19. *When the girl's masters saw that their hope of making money was gone.* Luke stresses the monetary advantages the girl's masters had in her; their greed incites their revenge. MS D reads, "that they had been deprived of the money-making they had through her."

they seized Paul and Silas and dragged them to the main square before the authorities. In a Greek city the *agora*, "market place, main square," was usually the center of public life (see 17:17), where the *archontes*, "rulers, authorities," in charge of law and order would be found. So Luke resumes his story of persecution, the characteristic of the Period of the Church under Stress (see *Luke*, 181–87).

20. *They turned them over to the magistrates with the complaint.* Lit., "leading them to the chief magistrates, they said." *Stratēgoi* usually means "military leaders," but now "chief magistrates," used of the official *duoviri* of Philippi, as they are named on inscriptions (*PWSup* 6.1071–1158). Cf. Josephus, *Ant.* 14.10.22 §247; 20.6.2 §131. They were responsible for maintaining peace and adjudicating legal and political cases, because they held magisterial *coercitio*, the power to inflict punishment, but they could not execute or flog a Roman citizen. See F. Haverfield, "On the *stratēgoi* of Philippi," *JTS* 1 (1899–1900): 434–35; W. M. Ramsay, "The Philippians and Their Magistrates," *JTS* 1 (1899–1900): 114–16.

"These men are disturbing the peace of our city; they are Jews. Lit., "these men, being Jews, are throwing our city into confusion." The reason for the confusion is stated in the following clause. Luke describes such Philippians stirring up opposition against Paul on the pretext that he is a Jew, hence exploiting the Roman suspicion of Jews in general. The Roman historian Tacitus once wrote of Jews, *adversus omnis alios hostile odium*, "of all others (they have) a hostile hatred" (*Histories* 5.5); cf. Juvenal, *Satires* 14.96–106.

21. *advocating practices unlawful for us Romans to adopt or observe."* Paul is charged with preaching a non-Roman cult, a mode of worship and practices that Romans do not welcome. A Roman could not adopt Judaism without liability according to Roman penal code; Cicero, *De legibus* 2.8.19: "No one shall have gods for himself, either new or foreign gods, unless they are officially recognized" (*nisi publice adscitos*, i.e., acknowledged by the state); cf. Dio Cassius, *Roman History* 67.14.2; 57.18.5. Paul and Silas, however, have not been proselytizing for Judaism, but the magistrates in Philippi at that time would scarcely have known the difference between Judaism and Christianity. Luke so formulates the charge

that Paul and Silas can easily repudiate it. The charge, however, raises a question about the legitimacy of Christianity then in the Roman empire: Was it *religio licita,* a licit religion?

22. *The crowd joined in the attack against them.* MS D reads, "A great crowd joined in the attack, shouting against them."

the magistrates had them stripped of their clothes and ordered them to be flogged. The magistrates are said to act on the basis of such accusations, that Paul and his companions are a threat to civil order, and without really looking into the matter, proceed against them. Though none of the charges are valid, the owners of the slave girl and the crowd win their way. See 1 Thess 2:2; Phil 1:30; 2 Cor 11:25 for Paul's own testimony about mistreatment at Philippi and about flogging. The magistrates were attended by *rhabdouchoi* (16:35), "rod-bearers," i.e., *lictores,* "lictors," who would have stripped Paul and were preparing to administer the flogging.

23. *After they had lashed them many times, they threw them into prison and ordered the warden to guard them securely.* MS D reads, "that they be securely guarded." Cf. 1 Thess 2:2.

24. *He took this order to heart and locked them up in the inmost cell, even securing their feet to a stake.* The details are stressed in order to heighten the climax of their deliverance.

25. *About midnight.* MS D* reads, "About the middle of the night." The tone in this section (vv 25–34) changes from the preceding straightforward account to these verses that resound with folkloric elements. It is an idyllic description of the deliverance of Paul and his companions.

while Paul and Silas were praying and singing hymns to God, and their fellow prisoners were listening. Luke introduces the motif of prayer as the background for the deliverance of Paul and Silas. For an extrabiblical parallel, see Epictetus 2.6.26–27; cf. J. Moffatt, "Exegetica: Acts 16:25," *Expos* 8/7 (1914): 89–96, esp. 93–94.

26. *such a severe earthquake occurred that the prison was shaken to its foundations. All the doors suddenly flew open, and the chains of all were loosened.* The earthquake is the means whereby heaven miraculously liberates its servants. As Peter was delivered from prison (12:6–11), so now Paul. As Peter confronted Samaritan magic (8:9–24), so Paul confronts Greco-Roman divination. "Even today, earth tremors are not rare at Philippi; but it is evident that the author does not intend to speak of a natural phenomenon. It is a question of the manifestation of God's presence and of testimony that he is making for his servants" (Dupont, *Actes,* 148).

27. *When the warden woke up and saw the prison gates standing open, he drew [his] sword to kill himself in the belief that the prisoners had escaped.* The warden so acts because he realizes that he would be judged as irresponsible and incompetent by higher Roman authorities.

28. *Paul shouted out, "Don't do yourself any harm! We are all still here."* Paul reassures the warden and brings it about that he does not kill himself; so the prisoner Paul delivers his jailer from self-inflicted death.

29. *The warden asked for a light, rushed in, and fell trembling at the feet of Paul and Silas.* Luke dramatically depicts the reaction of the Roman warden.

30. *When he had led them out, he said, "Sirs, what must I do to be saved?"* The Roman warden's question echoes that of Jerusalem Jews on the first Christian Pentecost (2:37). It is the classic question of everyone on the threshold of faith; it is the beginning of a response to the gospel. What a Roman would have meant by such a question about being "saved" is hard to say; but in the Lucan story he is made to query an effect of the Christ-event.

31. *Their answer was, "Believe in the Lord Jesus, and you will be saved, you and your household."* The answer given by Paul is likewise classic; it briefly formulates the "way of salvation" (16:17; cf. 2:21; 11:14) and calls for faith in "the Lord Jesus," a succinct reformulation of the basic Christian proclamation. Compare Mark 16:16; Matt 9:22; John 4:53; Rom 10:9–13. It probably reflects the way early Christians proclaimed the Word of God: the message that God was sending to all humanity. MSS C, D, E, Ψ, 1739, and the *Koinē* text-tradition add "Christ" to "the Lord Jesus."

32. *they explained to him and all the members of his house the word of the Lord.* I.e., they developed further the implications of their brief answer (v 31). MSS ℵ* and B read "the word of God." See NOTE on 4:31.

33. *At that very hour of the night he took them and bathed their wounds.* Not only does the warden become a Christian along with his household, but he seeks to give aid to the prisoners who have been flogged.

Thereupon he and his whole household were baptized. Again baptism follows immediately on the implied profession of faith; compare 16:15.

34. *He brought them up into his house, spread a table before them, and with his whole household rejoiced at having found faith in God.* A festive meal is shared in celebration of their baptism and faith. In v 31 it was faith in "the Lord Jesus."

35. *When it was day, the magistrates dispatched officers with orders, "Release those men!"* Verses 35–40 supply the sequel to vv 15–24, without any reference to the miraculous deliverance of Paul and Silas. The "officers" are called *rhabdouchoi*; see NOTE on 16:22. MS D reads, "When it was day, the magistrates gathered together in the main square and, recalling with fear the earthquake that had occurred, dispatched . . . those men, whom you put in custody yesterday." The WT supplies the reason for the magistrates' decision.

36. *[This] information the warden conveyed to Paul, "The magistrates have sent orders that you are to be released. Now then get out and go in peace."* The magistrates officially seek to get rid of a bothersome case.

37. *Paul, however, said to the officers, "They flogged us in public without even a trial, though we are Roman citizens.* Paul may refer to this incident in 2 Cor 11:25, where he speaks of having been beaten with rods three times. He thus defends himself, not by declaring his innocence in the matter of which he was accused (recall vv 20–21), but by appealing to his right as *civis romanus.* Cf. 22:25. The *Lex Porcia de provocatione* forbade under severe penalty the flogging of a Roman citizen (Livy, *Historia* 10.9.4; Cicero, *Pro Rabirio* 4.12–13; Appian, *Bellum Civile* 2.26 §98; *OCD*, 604). Paul compounds the matter by adding that

the flogging was done without a proper public trial or examination; they were *akatakritoi*, "uncondemned." MS D calls them *anaitious*, "guiltless." That Silas was also a Roman citizen is stated nowhere else. Paul includes him in saying, "They flogged us," and that is hardly meant to be an editorial we. So one must assume that Silas was also a Roman citizen.

From elsewhere in Acts (22:28b) we know that Paul was born a Roman citizen, but he never speaks of this status in any of his letters. His name *Paulos*, however, is undoubtedly a sign of that Roman identity. See A. N. Sherwin-White, *The Roman Citizenship* (Oxford: Clarendon, 1939), 266.

threw us into prison. Recall 5:18.

now they want to get rid of us quietly. No, indeed! Let them come here in person and lead us out." Paul thus puts the magistrates on the defensive.

38. *The officers reported these words to the magistrates, who were alarmed when they heard that they were Roman citizens.* Their alarm stems from the possible consequences of their hasty and inconsiderate treatment of Roman citizens, a violation of the Roman law mentioned in NOTE on v 37.

39. *they came, tried to placate them, and led them out with the request that they leave the city.* The action of the Philippian authorities implies that they have been wrong and that what Paul and his companions have done is not something against Roman custom and law. The issue may be gray, and their treatment of Paul, the Roman citizen, may possibly have evil consequences for them. So they want him off the scene.

40. *Once outside the prison, they made their way to Lydia's house.* Recall 16:15.

where they saw and encouraged the brothers, and then departed. So ends the story of Paul's activity in Philippi, where he has made some converts; see NOTE on 1:15 for "brothers" = Christians.

BIBLIOGRAPHY (16:11–40)

Arndt, W. F., "A Note Concerning the Text and the Meaning of Acts 16:12," *CTM* 16 (1945): 697–98.

Barnikol, E., "Paulus im Kerker zu Philippi," *TJb* (1956): 21–29.

Bormann, L., *Philippi, Stadt und Christengemeinde zur Zeit des Paulus* (NovTSup 78; Leiden: Brill, 1995).

Cannon, H. J., *Liebe Brüder, was soll ich thun, dass ich selig werde? (Apostelgeschichte 16,30): Eine kurze Erklärung der für jeden Menschen zur Seligkeit notwendigen Grundsätze des Evangeliums Jesu Christi* (Hamburg: Stern, 1900).

Cherry, R. S., "Acts xvi.14f.," *ExpTim* 75 (1963–64): 114.

Gillman, J., "Hospitality in Acts 16," *LS* 17 (1992): 181–96.

Kelso, J. L., "Paul's Roman Citizenship as Reflected in His Missionary Experiences and His Letters," *BSac* 79 (1922): 173–83.

Lowther Clarke, W. K., "St Luke and the Pseudepigrapha: Two Parallels," *JTS* 15 (1914): 597–99.

Martin, F., "Le géolier et la marchande de pourpre: Actes des Apôtres 16,6–40 (première partie)," *Sémiotique et Bible* 59 (1990): 9–29.

Noy, D., "A Jewish Place of Prayer in Roman Egypt," *JTS* 43 (1992): 118–22.

Redalié, Y., "Conversion ou libération? Notes sur les Actes 16,11–40," *BCPE* 26 (1974): 7–17.

Rees, W., "St Paul's First Visit to Philippi (Acts of the Apostles xvi.11–40)," *Scripture* 7 (1955): 99–105.

Rius-Camps, J., "Pablo y el grupo 'nosotros' en Filipos: Dos proyectos de evangelización en conflicto (Hch 16, 11–40)," *Laurentianum* 36 (1995): 35–59.

Schille, G., *Anfänge der Kirche: Erwägungen zur apostolischen Frühgeschichte* (BEvT 43; Munich: Kaiser, 1966), 43–53.

Schwartz, D. R., "The Accusation and the Accusers at Philippi (Acts 16,20–21)," *Bib* 65 (1984): 357–63.

Sherwin-White, A. N., "The Early Persecutions and Roman Law Again," *JTS* 3 (1952): 199–213.

Sihler, E. G., "St. Paul and the Lex Julia de vi," *Theological Quarterly* 18 (1914): 23–31.

Torrance, T., "St. Paul at Philippi: Three Startling Conversions," *EvQ* 13 (1941): 62–64.

Trémel, B., "Voie du salut et religion populaire: Paul et Luc face au risque de paganisation," *LumVie* 30/153–54 (1981): 87–108.

Unnik, W. C. van, "Die Anklage gegen die Apostel in Philippi (Apostelgeschichte 16,20g)," *Mullus: Festschrift Theodor Klauser* (JAC Ergänzungsband 1; Münster in W.: Aschendorff, 1964), 366–73; repr. *Sparsa Collecta*, 1.374–85.

Veillé, M., "Actes 16/16–24," *ETR* 54 (1979): 271–78.

Vos, C. S. de, "The Significance of the Change from *oikos* to *oikia* in Luke's Account of the Philippian Gaoler (Acts 16.30–4)," *NTS* 41 (1995): 292–96.

d) Paul in Thessalonica and Beroea (17:1–15)

17 1 They took the road through Amphipolis and Apollonia and came to Thessalonica, where there was a synagogue of the Jews. 2 Following his usual custom,
Paul went to their services, and for three sabbaths conducted discussions with
them about the Scriptures, 3 explaining and demonstrating that the Messiah had
to suffer and rise from the dead: "This Jesus, whom I am proclaiming to you, is
the Messiah!" 4 Some of the Jews were convinced and threw in their lot with Paul
and Silas, as did a great number of Greeks who were worshipers, and not a few
prominent women. 5 But Jews who resented this engaged some worthless loafers
in the public square to form a mob and start a riot in the city. They marched on
the house of Jason, demanding that Paul and Silas be brought out before the
popular assembly. 6 When they did not find them there, they dragged Jason himself and some of the brothers before the city magistrates, shouting, "These men

have been causing trouble all over the world; and now they have come here,
[7]and Jason has taken them in. They all act in defiance of Caesar's decrees and
claim instead that there is another king, a certain Jesus." [8]So they threw into
confusion the populace and even the city magistrates, who, on hearing this,
[9]would only release Jason and the others after they had posted bond. [10]The brothers immediately sent Paul and Silas off to Beroea during the night. On their arrival they went to the Jewish synagogue. [11]These Jews were better disposed than
those in Thessalonica and welcomed the word with great enthusiasm, reading
the Scriptures each day and checking to see whether it was all so. [12]Many of
them came, then, to believe, as did many of the influential Greek women, and
not a few men. [13]But when Jews from Thessalonica learned that God's word had
been proclaimed by Paul in Beroea too, they came there to stir up trouble and
to throw the populace into confusion. [14]So the brothers immediately sent Paul on
his way to the seacoast, but Silas and Timothy stayed behind. [15]Paul's attendants
escorted him as far as Athens and then left, with instructions for Silas and Timothy that they were to join him as soon as possible.

WT: [1]and descended to Apollonia, and from there to Thessalonica. [3][omits "from the dead" and "the Messiah"]: "This is Jesus, whom I am proclaiming to you." [4]were convinced by the teaching, and many of the devout threw. [5]But Jews who did not believe gathered together some . . . square and started a riot in the city. [6]shouting and saying. [7]in defiance of Caesar and claim Jesus is a king. [8]So by saying this, they have thrown . . . magistrates. [9]The city magistrates would only release. [10][omits "immediately" and "during the night"] . . . and they arrived at the Jewish synagogue. [11]it was all as Paul was reporting. [12]Some of them came, then, to believe, but some did not believe. Many of the Greeks, even influential ones, both men and women, became believers. [13]that the word had been proclaimed in Beroea too . . . and did stop throwing the populace into confusion. [14]to go to the seacoast. [15]Paul passed by Thessaly, for he was prevented from proclaiming the word to people there, and his attendants escorted . . . without delay.

COMMENT

Luke continues his account of Pauline Mission II. Having evangelized Philippi in Macedonia and leaving Luke behind there, Paul and his companions, Silas and Timothy, make their way to the western part of the province. They travel along the famous ancient road, the Via Egnatia. Passing through Amphipolis, the most important town in the first district of Macedonia, and then through Apollonia, Paul comes to the capital of the province, Thessalonica, the next object of his evangelization. This he begins, according to his custom, by preaching first in the synagogue of the Jews in Thessalonica. There for three sabbaths he proclaims Jesus as the Messiah. Some Jews and many Greeks are won over by his testimony, but other Jews are annoyed at him and stir up a riot against him and his collaborators. The adversaries accuse Paul and his companions of three things: (1) "causing trouble all over the world"; (2) "acting in defiance of Caesar's decrees"; and (3) "claiming that there is another king," to whom one should show loyalty. Though the account of these charges is somewhat garbled, it conveys their seriousness. As a result, Paul and Silas flee to Beroea, another town in Macedonia, where they are accorded a better reception.

The mention of "three sabbaths" does not necessarily mean that Paul's sojourn in Thessalonica would have totaled a mere three weeks or a month. Conzelmann (*Acts*, 135) finds it to be a description of "the brevity of Paul's stay," and that it "does not fit well with 1 Thessalonians and Phil 4:9 [read 4:16]," which suggest rather that Paul would have spent a considerable amount of time there. But that is not the only way to read Luke's report.

The episode is another narrative, and Luke is making use of information from his Pauline source. It can be divided into three sections: (1) vv 1–4, the arrival of Paul in Thessalonica and evangelization in its synagogue; (2) vv 5–9, the reaction of Thessalonian Jews to his preaching; and (3) vv 10–15, Paul's flight from Thessalonica and evangelization of Beroea before going on to southern Greece.

This episode recounts Paul's arrival in the important Macedonian town of Thessalonica, where he evangelizes both Jews and Greeks before he has to flee from there because of opposition to him. In the course of his evangelization Paul proclaims that Jesus, the Messiah, had to suffer and rise from the dead. He thus implicitly invokes the divine plan of salvation that has been working itself out in the earthly ministry of Jesus, his death, and resurrection. All of this the Lucan Paul preaches on the basis of his understanding of "the Scriptures." Those in Thessalonica who oppose him accuse him of acting in defiance of Caesar's decrees, maintaining that he is preaching allegiance to "another king, a certain Jesus" (17:7). This opposition, which stems from "Jews who resented" Paul's successful preaching, eventually makes him flee. What he thus suffers is the fulfillment of what the risen Christ predicted in 9:16: "I myself shall show him how much he will have to endure for the sake of my name." Suffering attends success.

NOTES

17:1. *They took the road through Amphipolis and Apollonia.* So Luke recounts the departure of Paul and his companions from Philippi, where they arrived in 16:11–12. *Amphipolis,* originally called *Ennea Hodoi* (Nine Ways), was colonized by Athenians and founded in 436 B.C. It became the capital of the first (southern) district of Macedonia, being situated about 50.5 km west of Philippi, and an important commercial center. It was encircled by the Strymon River and built on both sides of it; hence its name (Thucydides, *Histories* 4.102.3). The Via Egnatia, running from Neapolis to Dyrrhachium on the Adriatic, passed through Amphipolis, and along this road Paul and his companions would have traveled.

Apollōnia (modern Pollina) was another town in Macedonia, on the Via Egnatia about 40 km to the southwest of Amphipolis.

came to Thessalonica. I.e., modern Saloniki. The city of *Thessalonikē,* founded by Cassander, one of the generals under Alexander the Great, in 315 B.C. and named after Alexander's half-sister, was the capital of the second district of Macedonia. In 167 B.C. it became the seat of the Roman governor. Situated on the Thermaic Gulf and on the Via Egnatia, it was almost 50 km due west of Apollonia (see Polybius, *History* 23.11.2; Strabo, *Geography* 7.frg. 24). It is mentioned in Phil 4:16; 2 Tim 4:10. Cf. W. Elliger, *Paulus in Griechenland: Philippi, Thessa-*

loniki, Athen, Korinth (SBS 89–93; Stuttgart: Katholisches Bibelwerk, 1978), 78–116; J. Finegan, *The Archeology of the New Testament*, 106–16.

where there was a synagogue of the Jews. See NOTE on 6:9. Luke uses the rel. adv. *hopou* (not the simple *hou*), which implies that Paul did not stop at Amphipolis or Apollonia, because he knew there was no synagogue there (ZBG §217).

2. *Following his usual custom, Paul went to their services.* Lit., "according to what was customary for Paul, he went in to be with them." Recall 13:5, 14; 14:1; 16:13; 17:10, 17; 18:4, 19; 19:8; 28:17, 23. For Paul's own report about his activity in Thessalonica, see 1 Thess 1:5–2:16.

for three sabbaths conducted discussions with them about the Scriptures. Lit., "he discussed with them from the writings." See NOTE on *graphē,* meaning "Scripture" in 1:16. Unfortunately Luke does not tell us what passages of the Hebrew Scriptures Paul would have been using; what follows in v 3 explains the gist of his arguments. It is another instance of Luke's global christological interpretation of the OT in terms of Jesus as the Messiah (see *Luke*, 200, 1558).

3. *explaining and demonstrating that the Messiah had to suffer and rise from the dead.* Lit., "opening (its meaning) and setting (it) before (them) that . . ." On the suffering Messiah, see NOTE on 3:18; on the necessity of the Messiah suffering, see 2:23, "according to the set plan and foreknowledge of God." To the idea of a suffering Messiah, Luke now adds that of a "rising" Messiah, a notion that is equally foreign to the Hebrew Scriptures; neither of these notions is found in QL. Conzelmann (*Theology*, 153 n. 3) speaks of the phrase as a formula and a usage "that is already stereotyped": "it is from Scripture that the correct idea of the Messiah as a suffering Messiah is derived. The fulfillment is then confirmed in the historical Jesus." Unfortunately, Conzelmann never tells us how this formula is derived from Scripture or from what part of the OT it comes. If it is, indeed, "stereotyped," it is only so in Lucan theology. Compare the futile attempt of R. A. Rosenberg to derive the notion from Dan 9:26; Zech 12:10–11; 2 Chr 35:25, applying ideas from these disparate verses to the Suffering Servant of Isaiah 52–53 and Zech 3:8; Jer 23:5 ("The Slain Messiah in the Old Testament," ZAW 99 [1987]: 259–61). In the OT, however, the Isaian Suffering Servant is never called a Messiah; that title is found in the Book of Isaiah only for the pagan King Cyrus (Isa 45:1), who is not said to "suffer" or "rise from the dead." Compare, however, Tg. Jonathan of Isa 52:13: *ʿabdî mĕšîḥāʾ*, "my Servant, the Messiah" (an Aramaic translation not earlier than A.D. 300).

Note the important phrase "from the dead," which the WT omits; it leaves no doubt about the sense of the infin. *anastēnai*, "rise."

"This Jesus, whom I am proclaiming to you, is the Messiah!" Lit., "this is the Messiah, Jesus, whom . . ." Compare 18:28. Paul proclaims to Jews of Thessalonica that their expected Anointed One has arrived on the scene. He is Jesus, who has suffered and is now the risen Christ. On the meaning of Messiah, see *Luke*, 197–200. The predicate is expressed with the article, *ho Christos* (ZBG §172).

4. *Some of the Jews were convinced and threw in their lot with Paul and Silas.* Lit., "some of them." The indefinite *tines* is clarified by the following clause that

tells about Greek worshipers; so the *tines* must refer to a few Jews. MS B omits "and Silas."

as did a great number of Greeks who were worshipers. The *plēthos poly* used of Greeks stands in contrast to the *tines* of Thessalonian Jews. The Greeks were *sebomenoi,* Gentiles who were sympathetic to Judaism; see NOTE on 13:43. However, some MSS (P^{74}, A, D, 33) read "a great number of *sebomenoi kai* Greeks." This would mean not only Greek sympathizers, but also pagan Greeks who were not *sebomenoi.* In this case three groups of men would be meant, not counting the women.

not a few prominent women. Lit., "not a few of the first women." Luke uses again the adj. *prōtos* in the sense of rank or dignity; see NOTE on 16:12. Paul's own first letter to the Thessalonians gives the impression that more Gentiles than Jews were among his converts. Both Haenchen (*Acts,* 507) and Conzelmann (*Acts,* 135) find it strange that such prominent women would not have been able to avert the persecutions of Christians; but to query that is to miss the thrust of the Lucan account. Luke recounts the favorable reaction to Paul's evangelization as a preparation for what is next narrated.

5. *Jews who resented this engaged some worthless loafers in the public square to form a mob and start a riot in the city.* Lit., "Jews, being jealous and taking along some worthless market people and forming a mob, set the city in riot." MS D reads, "Jews, who did not believe, gathered together some . . ." Luke now describes the conduct of Thessalonian Jews, their reaction, motivation, and helpers. The opposition to Paul and Silas comes from their fellow coreligionists, who get support from Gentiles. Luke uses *hoi Ioudaioi* in a pejorative sense, as in 12:3; 13:45; 14:2; 17:13. Compare 1 Thess 2:14–15. A similar instigation to rioting in an agora is recounted by Plutarch, *Aemilius Paulus* 38.3.

They marched on the house of Jason. He is otherwise unknown, but probably is to be understood as a diaspora Jew of Thessalonica, who furnished Paul and his companions with hospitality. He is hardly the same as Jason of Rom 16:21.

demanding that Paul and Silas be brought out before the popular assembly. I.e., before the *dēmos,* which in many Greek towns was the gathering of citizens for the transaction of public business. From this word comes the first part of the English word "democracy."

6. *When they did not find them there, they dragged Jason himself and some of the brothers before the city magistrates, shouting.* I.e., did not find Paul and Silas in Jason's house, in which there were other Christians, among whom may have been Aristarchus and Secundus (20:4; 27:2). The non-Roman civic magistrates are called *politarchai,* five (or later, six) of whom formed an administrative council in Thessalonica and other Macedonian cities. Such magistrates are not known from Greek literature, but do appear in a number of Macedonian inscriptions. See E. D. Burton, "The Politarchs," *AJT* 2 (1898): 598–632; F. Gschnitzer, "Politarches," *PWSup* 13 (1973): 483–99; G.H.R. Horsley, "The Politarchs," *The Book of Acts in Its Graeco-Roman Setting* (BAFCS 2), 419–31; cf. *CIG* 2.1967; *BCH* 18 (1894): 420; 21 (1897): 161–63. On *adelphos* as "Christian," see NOTE on 1:15.

"These men have been causing trouble all over the world. Lit., "these (are) the inhabited (world) upsetters." This is the first charge that is made against Paul and his companions. Luke again uses *oikoumenē*, "inhabited (world, earth)"; see NOTE on 11:28. Cf. 16:20; 24:5. Similar accusations against Jews upsetting the *oikoumenē* are found in Pap. London 1912:96–100; *Acts of Isidore* (Pap. Berolinensis) 8877:22–24. Earlier the emperor Claudius had issued a decree about Jews in Alexandria, which ended with the order that both parties [Alexandrian Greeks and Jews] were to take "the greatest precaution that no disturbance arise after the posting of the decree" (Josephus, *Ant.* 19.5.3 §285). Claudius was generally concerned about such disturbances in his realm.

now they have come here, 7. *and Jason has taken them in.* Lit., "has entertained (them) as guests." This is incidental to the charge that they make in the following statement.

They all act in defiance of Caesar's decrees. See NOTE on 16:21; cf. 25:8. This is the second charge against Paul and his companions, but unfortunately it is not specific. It could be a repetition of the first in different terminology, because Claudius had included in some of his decrees warnings about disturbances of world order, but it may have a broader connotation. Espousal of Christianity may be seen as a contravention of Caesar's *dogmata*, "decrees," but how? That may be expressed in the next clause.

Kaisar is the Greek form of Latin *Caesar*, which was originally the cognomen of Gaius Julius Caesar. When Julius Caesar died, his will revealed that C. Octavius had been adopted by him and designated as his successor; thereupon he was recognized by the Roman Senate as Gaius Julius Caesar Octavianus. So the name Caesar passed to the first *princeps*. In 27 B.C. the Senate bestowed on Octavian the title *Augustus* (in Greek *Sebastos*), and he became known as Caesar Augustus. Successors of Caesar Augustus in the principate often bore these names: e.g., Tiberius Julius Caesar Augustus, Gaius Julius Caesar Germanicus (nicknamed Caligula). From this developed the custom of referring to the head of the Roman empire as "Caesar." The "Caesar" who was reigning at this time would have been Claudius (A.D. 41–54; see NOTE on 11:28).

claim instead that there is another king, a certain Jesus." This is the third charge: instead of loyalty to Caesar in Rome, Paul and his companions are charged with advocating loyalty to some other *basileus*, "king." The name *Iēsous* stands in emphatic position at the end (compare 2:36; 3:20; 4:27; 13:23; 18:5, 28). Because Paul has proclaimed Jesus as "the Messiah" (17:3), his opponents deduce that Jesus must be regarded as *basileus*, knowing how ill the title "king" would sit with Romans. The implication is sedition and high treason. For indications in Lucan writings that Jesus was a kingly figure, see Luke 1:32–33; 19:38; 23:2, 38. *Pace* Johnson (*Acts*, 307), *basileus* should not be translated "emperor," since that term as a title did not then exist in Roman history.

Compare the so-called Oath of Gangra from 3 B.C., in which the one who swears promises to support "Caesar Augustus, his children and descendants throughout my life in word, deed, and thought . . . that whenever I see or hear of anything being said, planned, or done against them I will report it . . ."

(V. Ehrenberg and A.H.M. Jones, *Documents Illustrating the Reigns of Augustus & Tiberius* [Oxford: Clarendon, 1949], §315:9–21; cf. §311:II). See "Rex," OCD, 918–19; cf. E. A. Judge, "Decrees of Caesar."

8. *they threw into confusion the populace and even the city magistrates.* Luke expresses the success of the Jews who oppose Paul and his preaching.

who, on hearing this. I.e., when the *politarchai* hear the confusing reports, they are not clear what is at stake, but react by taking some official measures at least against Jason.

9. *would only release Jason and the others after they had posted bond.* Lit., "having taken security from Jason and the others." The phrase *labontes to hikanon* is a Latinism, equaling *satis accipere,* "receive bail, bond, security." Implied is that Jason and the others would be legally responsible for Paul and Silas, lest they might flee from due process. This mistreatment is mentioned by Paul himself in 1 Thess 2:14, comparing it to the persecution of Christians of the churches in Judea. He speaks of it there as a hindrance provided by Satan (2:18).

10. *The brothers immediately sent Paul and Silas off to Beroea during the night.* Thessalonian Christians realize the danger of the situation and quickly see to it that Paul, Silas, and Timothy are escorted out of town and taken to Beroea. *Beroia,* modern Verria, was an ancient city in Macedonia on the Astraeus River at the foot of Mt. Bermius, about 80 km southwest of Thessalonica, on the road leading to central and southern Greece. It was the seat of the Macedonian *koinon* (commonalty) and the center of the imperial cult in the province, but it was outside the authority of the Thessalonian politarchs. It came under Roman control in 168 B.C. In the time of Nero, Beroea was given the title *mētropolis,* which implied no little importance.

On their arrival they went to the Jewish synagogue. As in 17:2.

11. *These Jews were better disposed than those in Thessalonica.* The Greek comparative adj. *eugenesteroi,* "more well born," really denotes nobility of origin, but as it is used in this context, it ascribes to Beroean Jews a more noble attitude.

welcomed the word with great enthusiasm. I.e., they accepted the Christian proclamation about Jesus the Christ; see NOTE on 8:14. This is the first of three reactions of Beroean Jews to Paul's preaching; the second follows in the next clause, and the third in the next verse.

reading the Scriptures each day and checking to see whether it was all so. See NOTE on 1:16. Luke uses the rare "oblique optative" as the mood in the subordinate clause (*ei echoi tauta houtōs,* "whether these things might be so"). See ZBG §346. MS 614 adds, "as Paul was reporting."

12. *Many of them came, then, to believe, as did many of the influential Greek women, and not a few men.* The *polloi,* "many," said of Beroean Jews, stands in contrast to the *tines,* "some," of Thessalonica (17:4). So Luke records the success of Pauline missionary endeavors in Beroea, among Jews and Gentile women and men. MS D reads, "Some of them . . . , but some did not believe," which is a more negative report about the Jews. At the end MS D* adds, "Many of the Greeks, even influential ones, both men and women, became believers."

13. *when Jews from Thessalonica learned that God's word had been proclaimed*

by Paul in Beroea too, they came there to stir up trouble and to throw the populace into confusion. They try to cause the same trouble that they have already stirred up against Paul in Thessalonica.

14. *the brothers immediately sent Paul on his way.* See NOTE on 1:15.

to the seacoast. The Greek text is not clear; if one reads *heōs epi tēn thalassan* with the best MSS (P^{74}, A, B, E, 33, 81, 323, 945, 1175, and 1739), it could mean that Paul sails from some point in northern Greece to Athens. If, however, *hōs* is read instead of *heōs*, as in MSS Ψ, H, and L, it would mean, "as it were, toward the sea," expressing a subterfurge to mislead Paul's adversaries, because he is escorted overland to Athens. The confused state of the text continues in v 15.

Silas and Timothy stayed behind. We learn at length that Timothy has been accompanying Paul and Silas. In 1 Thess 3:1–2, however, Paul indicates that Timothy has escorted him to Athens and then has been sent back by Paul to Thessalonica, which he eventually leaves again in order to be with Paul in Corinth (compare Acts 18:5). Luke's information is either abridged or inaccurate.

15. *Paul's attendants escorted him as far as Athens.* MS D adds, "Paul passed by Thessaly, for he was prevented from proclaiming the word to people there, and his attendants escorted . . . without delay." So Paul passes from the Roman province of Macedonia to that of Achaia.

then left, with instructions. MS D adds, "from Paul."

for Silas and Timothy that they were to join him as soon as possible. MS D reads at the end, "without delay."

BIBLIOGRAPHY (17:1–15)

Barclay, J.M.G., "Conflict in Thessalonica," *CBQ* 55 (1993): 512–30.

Delebecque, E., "Paul à Thessalonique et à Bérée selon le texte occidental des Actes (xvii, 4–15)," *RevThom* 82 (1982): 605–15.

Judge, E. A., "The Decrees of Caesar at Thessalonica," *RTR* 30 (1971): 1–7.

Kemmler, D. W., *Faith and Human Reason: A Study of Paul's Method of Preaching as Illustrated by 1–2 Thessalonians and Acts 17,2–4* (NovTSup 40; Leiden: Brill, 1975), 11–143.

Kremer, J., "Einführung in die Problematik heutiger Acta-Forschung anhand von Apg 17,10–13 *anakrinontes tas graphas*," *Les Actes des Apôtres* (ed. J. Kremer), 11–20.

Meers, A., "Who Went Where and How? A Consideration of Acts 17.14," *BT* 44 (1993): 201–6.

Nigdelis, P. M., "Synagoge(n) und Gemeinde der Juden in Thessaloniki: Fragen aufgrund einer neuen jüdischen Grabinschrift der Kaiserzeit," *ZPE* 102 (1994): 297–306.

e) PAUL EVANGELIZES ATHENS; AT THE AREOPAGUS (17:16–34)

16 While Paul was waiting for them in Athens, he became quite annoyed at the
sight of idols everywhere in the city. 17 In the synagogue, he used to hold discussions with the Jews and their Gentile worshipers; and every day in the public
square, with ordinary passersby. Some of the Epicurean and Stoic philosophers
would confer with him; 18 and some of them would ask, "What would this chatterer be trying to say to us?" Others commented, "He seems to be lobbying for
foreign deities," because he was preaching about "Jesus" and the "Resurrection."
19 So they took him and led him to the Areopagus with the request, "May we
know what this new teaching is that is being proposed by you? 20 You are bringing
up subjects unfamiliar to our ears, and so we want to know what this is all about."
21 Now all Athenians, as well as the aliens residing with them, used to spend their
time in nothing else but telling about or listening to something new. 22 Then Paul
rose in the meeting of the Areopagus and said: "People of Athens, I see that you
are in every respect religiously exact." 23 For as I walked about and looked carefully at your objects of worship, I even came upon an altar inscribed, 'To a God

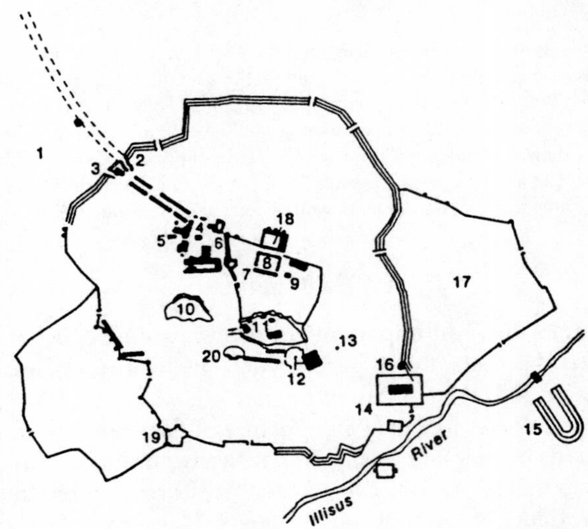

1. Outer Ceramicus; *2.* Dipylon Gate; *3.* Sacred Gate; *4.* Agora; *5.* Hephaesteum; *6.* Stoa of Attalus; *7.* Gate of Athena Archegetis; *8.* Roman Agora; *9.* Horologion; *10.* Areopagus; *11.* Acropolis; *12.* Theater of Dionysus; *13.* Monument of Lysicrates; *14.* Temple of Olympian Zeus; *15.* Stadium; *16.* Arch of Hadrian; *17.* New Athens; *18.* Library of Hadrian; *19.* Monument of Philopappus; *20.* Theater of Herodes Atticus.

Map 4. Athens

Unknown.' Now what you thus worship unknowingly I would proclaim to you.
[24]The God who made the world and all that is in it, this Lord of the heavens and
the earth, does not live in temples made by human hands. [25]Nor is it because he
lacks something that he is served by human hands. It is rather he who gives everyone life and breath and everything else. [26]From one stock he made the whole
human race dwell on the face of the whole earth. He it is who has fixed the dates
of their epochs and the boundaries of their habitation, [27]so that people might
seek for God, perhaps even grope for him, and eventually find him, even though
he is not really far from any one of us. [28]For in him we live and move and have
our being. As some of your own poets have put it: 'For we too are his offspring.'
[29]If we are really God's offspring, we ought not to think that divinity is something
like a statue of gold, of silver, or of stone, a work of human art and conception.
[30]God may well have overlooked bygone periods of human ignorance, but now
he orders all people everywhere to repent, [31]because he has set a day on which
he is going to judge the world with justice through the man whom he has appointed and whom he has endorsed before all, by raising him from the dead."
[32]When they heard about resurrection of the dead, some of them sneered, but
others said, "We'll listen to you about this topic some other time." [33]So Paul withdrew from their meeting. [34]A few of them, however, did join him and become
believers; among these were Dionysius, a member of the Areopagus, a woman
named Damaris, and some others.

WT: [16]While he was waiting. [17]In the synagogue of the Jews . . . [omits "and their Gentile worshipers"]. [18][omits "because . . . "Resurrection"]. [19][adds at the beginning:] After some days . . . Areopagus, inquiring, "May we know what this is that you are saying?" [21]Now Athenians and those residing
with them. [23]was wandering about and examining your objects of worship. [26]From one blood.
[27]might seek for the deity . . . even grope and find (it). [28]have our being every day. [30]have passed over
. . . he commands. [31]set a day to judge. [32][omits "some other time"]. [34][omits "and became believers"] . . . a certain Dionysius . . . , a prominent woman . . . , and many others.

COMMENT

Luke now recounts the most important episode in Pauline Mission II, the evangelization of what had been the most renowned city in ancient Greece. In Paul's day Athens was no longer the glory of the ancient world, as it had been in the fifth and fourth centuries B.C. The architecture of fifth-century Athens, its temples and deities, its theater and poetry, its politicians, historians, and orators had all contributed to that glory. In the fourth century its renown continued because of its prosperity, trade, industry, its philosophers (Plato, Aristotle), and its philosophical schools (Stoic, Epicurean). Toward the end of that century, Macedonia began to dominate Greece with the rise of the dynasty of Philip, and then with the exploits of Alexander the Great. After 228 B.C. Athens became a free-city state, which lived on its past glory. In 88 Athens sided with Mithridates VI against Rome, but it was reduced by Sulla to Roman occupation and control in 87–86. The people of Athens pleaded with him to respect its past glory, but Sulla retorted that he had come to punish rebels, not to learn ancient history. In time, Corinth, or rather Neocorinth, came to outshine Athens and had become politically more important in the eastern Mediterranean world. The Roman poet Horace speaks of "vacuas Athenas" (*Epist.* 2.2.81), empty Athens.

Luke, however, still regards Athens as the historical, cultural, and philosophical center of the ancient world. It is thus for him the ideal setting for a sermon that his hero preaches to educated Gentiles of the Greco-Roman world. He depicts Paul evangelizing Athens and delivering in it a major speech, as he waits for his companions, Silas and Timothy, to join him for the further evangelization of Greece (see 16:14–15). Christianity is depicted in this episode in direct confrontation with pagan idolatry, Greek philosophy, and Athenian intellectual curiosity, and there is no opposition to Paul from Jews or their sympathizers.

The episode begins and ends as a narrative (vv 16–22a and 32–34), but it incorporates a major Pauline discourse (in vv 22b–31). The speech itself is well integrated into the narrative; it is not intrusive, but constitutes an essential element of the narrative, even though it is an insertion into the Pauline source that Luke is otherwise using at this point in 17:1–22a and 17:32–34.

The introductory narrative (vv 16–22a) is important and sets the tone for this unique speech of Paul in Acts. His observation of the many objects of Athenian worship and his discovery of a monument erected "To a God Unknown" (17:23) provide him with the spring-board for teaching the Athenians about "the God who made the world and all that is in it, this Lord of the heavens and the earth" (17:24). He emphasizes divine forbearance of human failure to acknowledge God's existence. Luke's account of Paul's activity in Athens thus typifies the encounter of the preaching of the gospel with the culture of a pagan city, i.e., Christianity's contact with paganism. The Lucan Paul is made to announce the Christian gospel by connecting it with the religiosity and curiosity of Greek Athens.

One should note the impression made on the Athenians by the Lucan Paul: he is a "chatterer" or "babbler" and a preacher of "foreign deities," specifically of "Jesus" and his consort "Anastasis." Paul has little success with the learned audience of the Areopagus in Athens, which dismisses his words about "resurrection" with the promise, "We'll listen to you about this topic some other time." Contrast this Lucan description and speech with Paul's own impressions of the pagan world recorded in 1 Cor 1:18–25.

Luke makes of Paul's discourse (17:22b–31) one of the highlights of Acts and of the apostle's missionary activity. It is the second most important Pauline speech in Acts. It is once again a Lucan composition, another example of an inserted speech, a missionary speech, addressed not to Jews, but to pagan Athenians and alien Greek-speaking sojourners. It is a more developed presentation of the missionary propaganda used in 14:15–17. As there, its message is mainly theological, not christological, but there is an indirect reference to Christ at the end in v 31. There is, moreover, none of the usual kerygmatic elements found in other missionary speeches of Peter or Paul. It mirrors rather the reaction of a Jewish Christian missionary confronted with Greco-Roman culture, Greek intellectual curiosity, and pagan piety. It reflects a mild line of Hellenistic Jewish missionary propaganda, viz., God's forbearance of paganism, but it is christianized at the end of it.

After Paul's introductory words in vv 22–23, three parts of the speech and a conclusion can be discerned: (1) 17:24–25, Relation of the unknown God to the world, as creator and preserver; (2) 17:26–27, Proximity of this God, who has made human beings; (3) 17:28–29, Kinship of this God to humanity; and (4) 17:30–31, Conclusion alluding to God's judgment through the risen Jesus. In thus analyzing the speech, I follow Dibelius (*Studies,* 27) and Marshall (*Acts,* 282); for a bipartite division of the body of the speech, see Conzelmann (*Acts,* 141) or Dupont.

Commentators have debated about the source material used in the writing of the speech. There is no explicit quotation of the OT in this speech; instead a Greek poet, Aratus, is quoted. For Dibelius, it is a Hellenistic speech about the true knowledge of God to be derived from the world, which is really a foreign body in the NT and comparatively independent of the thrust of Acts itself: "the theology of the Areopagus speech is absolutely foreign to Paul's own theology, . . . it is, in fact, foreign to the entire New Testament" (*Studies,* 71). Norden went so far as to regard it as composed by a foreign hand and inserted into Acts. The great classicist Wilamowitz maintained that the religious sentiment of the speech was not that of Paul of Tarsus, who never adopted any of the elements of Greek education. This sort of analysis of the speech has often been repeated; for the speech does sound different from the Pauline teaching about human beings estranged from God by sin (Romans 1–3), yet reconciled to God "in Christ," justified and saved by divine grace, which is announced in the gospel about his Son that the apostle otherwise preaches.

Nevertheless, there are in it some echoes of Pauline teaching, even if allusions to phrases found in the LXX (especially Isa 45:18–25) make the source analysis of the speech complicated. Some expressions do resemble Hellenistic philosophical teaching (see the NOTES that follow), but other elements in the speech echo not only Jewish belief, but OT phraseology. In effect, Luke makes Paul sound like a Jewish preacher addressing a pagan audience about the true God (save for the indirect reference to Christ at the end). Even the idea of "resurrection" would be a more Jewish way of speaking about the afterlife, whereas "immortality" would be the more Greek way of phrasing it, but that does not appear in the speech. True, the "word of the cross" (1 Cor 1:18) does not occur in the speech, but that is because the speech is more *praeparatio* than *evangelium.* If Paul himself could write to the Thessalonians, "You turned to God from idols, to serve a living and true God" (1 Thess 1:9), he could well have preached as Luke depicts him here in Acts. So the real Paul might well have tried to meet pagans halfway.

One should also note the Lucan buildup in Acts for this speech. Its remote context can be seen in the promise in 2:39 ("to you and your children has the promise been made, yes, even to *all those still far off* whom the Lord our God will call to himself"); the promise in 3:25 ("through your offspring shall all the families of the earth be blessed"); in what Stephen asserts in 7:48 ("the Most

High dwells not in buildings made by human hands"); in what Peter affirms in 10:34 ("God shows no partiality"). Its more proximate context is found in Paul's speech to pagans in 14:15–17; in Peter's words in 15:7 ("God chose me from your number to be the one from whose lips the Gentiles would hear the word of the gospel and come to believe in it"); in James's agreement in 15:14 ("how God first concerned himself with acquiring from among the Gentiles a people to bear his name"). The climax of all this is seen in the quotation of a Greek poet (17:28) instead of a quotation from Scripture. The Jewish elements in the speech have been well worked out by Gärtner in *The Areopagus Speech.* One has to reckon with the mixed character of the speech.

In this episode we see Paul preaching to pagan Greeks in their renowned city of Athens. He begins with their own respect for an "unknown God" and builds on it, to bring them to a proper understanding of the living God, who is the creator of the world, is close to human beings, and even related to them. This God, he maintains, will judge human beings. Into such a challenge that Paul presents to these Greek intellectuals, he finally introduces a reference to the risen Christ, through whom God will carry out this judgment. Thus, in an indirect way, Paul preaches his gospel even in Athens, his message "about 'Jesus' and the 'Resurrection'" (17:18). In this Paul is true to his apostolic commission. He has little success in Athens, because his address is interrupted when he mentions divine judgment of the world "through the man whom he [God] has appointed and whom he has endorsed before all, by raising him from the dead" (17:31). This lack of success is again part of what Paul has to suffer on behalf of Jesus' name.

NOTES

16. *While Paul was waiting for them.* I.e., for Silas and Timothy (see 17:14–15). This transitional verse introduces the setting for the Pauline address to come and its topic of Athenian idols and shrines.

in Athens. Paul himself tells us of his being in Athens (1 Thess 3:1), thus corroborating this detail in Luke's account of this mission. He let no opportunity of evangelization pass him by, as he awaited his companions.

Athēnai, the city of the patron goddess Athena, was the capital of ancient Attica, situated in the Roman province of Achaia. Its acropolis was first fortified in the thirteenth century B.C. A Doric temple had been constructed on it ca. 525, and a newer marble temple was begun in 480 B.C. on the southern end of the acropolis. Most of these buildings were destroyed by the Persians along with many votive statues in 480–479. In the 450s a colossal statue of Athena Promachos (the work of Phidias) was erected in token of the defeat of the Persians. Under Pericles the acropolis was further beautified with the Parthenon and the Propylaeum. The environs of the acropolis and the Athenian agora were all enhanced. In the first century B.C., Cicero still sang its praises (*Pro Flacco* 26.62), as the place in which humanity, learning, religion, produce, rights, and laws had their origin. It was the site of a famous ancient university: *doctae Athenae,* "learned Athens" (Ovid, *Ep.* 2.38).

See Pausanias, *Description of Greece* 1.2.1–1.17.6; I. T. Hill, *The Ancient City of Athens: Its Topography and Monuments* (Cambridge: Harvard University Press, 1953); W. B. Dinsmoor, *The Architecture of Ancient Greece* (rev. W. J. Anderson and R. P. Spiers; New York: Biblo and Tannen, 1973), 265–336; W. S. Ferguson, *Hellenistic Athens: An Historical Essay* (London: Macmillan, 1911), 415–59; J. Day, *An Economic History of Athens under Roman Domination* (New York: Columbia University Press, 1942); P. Graindor, *Athènes sous Auguste* (Cairo: Imprimerie Misr, 1927); *Athènes de Tibère à Trajan* (Cairo: Imprimerie Misr, 1931); W. Elliger, *Paulus in Griechenland,* 117–99.

he became quite annoyed at the sight of idols everywhere in the city. Lit., "his spirit within him was provoked to anger, as he saw the city full of idols." Luke describes Paul reacting as a Jewish Christian repulsed by such idolatry. His annoyance stems from his Jewish monotheistic background and his conviction that what pagans "sacrifice they offer to demons and not to God" (1 Cor 10:20). The adj. *kateidōlos,* "idol-rife," i.e., with idols well distributed throughout it. Ancient Latin and Greek authors recount the same impression of Athens; see Livy, *Hist.* 45.27.11 ("Athenas . . . habentis . . . simulacra deorum hominumque, omni genere et materiae et artium insignia"); Pausanias, *Description of Greece* 1.17.1–2 (altars to *Eleos,* "Mercy," *Aidos,* "Shame," *Phēmē,* "Reputation," *Hormē,* "Effort," *Hermai,* "Hermae," etc.); Strabo, *Geography* 9.1.16. See O. T. Broneer, "Athens, City of Idol Worship," *BA* 21 (1958): 2–28.

17. *In the synagogue, he used to hold discussions with the Jews and their Gentile worshipers.* Lit., "with the Jews and the worshipers." Recall 17:2 and NOTES there. On *sebomenoi,* see NOTES on 10:2 and 13:43. This probably describes Paul's activity on sabbaths. No opposition is recorded coming from Athenian Jews or Jewish sympathizers.

every day in the public square, with ordinary passersby. These people Paul encountered during the week in the Athenian agora, which lay to the north of the acropolis. See *The Athenian Agora: A Guide to the Excavations* (Athens: American School of Classical Studies at Athens, 1954).

Some of the Epicurean and Stoic philosophers would confer with him. Only two of the famous philosophical schools of Athens are mentioned. The first are members of the philosophical school traced to Epicurus (341–270). He had opened a school at Mitylene in 311 and another at Lampsacus. When he came to Athens in 306, he bought a house with a garden, which became the site of his teaching. His followers lived a materialist, spartan, and austere type of life on the Epicurean property, secluding themselves from city affairs. They were often criticized because of their aloofness and even accused of hedonism and profligacy. They maintained that philosophical discussion was the way to a happy life, that humans were mortal, that the cosmos was the result of chance, and that there was no such thing as a provident god; some of them regarded pleasure as the criterion of a good life. See Diogenes Laertius, *Epicurus* 10.1–21; E. Zeller, *The Stoics, Epicureans and Sceptics* (rev. ed.; New York: Russell & Russell, 1962),

404–513; A. A. Long, *Hellenistic Philosophy: Stoics, Epicureans, Sceptics* (2d ed.; Berkeley: University of California Press, 1986), 107–209; J. Brunschwig, *Etudes sur les philosophes hellénistiques: Epicurisme, stoïcisme, scepticisme* (Paris: Presses Universitaires de France, 1995), 15–112.

The Stoics were members of the philosophical school, founded ca. 320 by Zeno (340–265) of Citium (Cyprus). It was named after the *Stoa Poikilē*, a public colonnade in Athens, in which Zeno used to teach. In Paul's day such philosophers would have been members of the Late Stoa (e.g., L. Annaeus Seneca, C. Musonius Rufus, and Epictetus). For the Stoics virtue was based on knowledge, and the aim of the philosopher was to live in harmony with nature *(kata physin)*. The formative and guiding principle of nature was *ho logos*, "reason," often deified or manifested as *heimarmenē*, "fate." Their ethical teaching emphasized self-sufficiency *(autarkeia)* and obedience to the dictates of reason and duty. See Diogenes Laertius, *Zeno* 7.1–160; E. Zeller, *The Stoics* (above), 36–403; A. A. Long, *Hellenistic Philosophy*, 14–74; J. Brunschwig, *Etudes*, 113–268.

18. *some of them would ask, "What would this chatterer be trying to say to us?"* The derogatory Athenian slang term for Paul was *spermologos*, "seed picker," i.e., one who picks up bits of news as a bird pecks at seeds. See M. A. Robinson, "Spermologos: Did Paul Preach from Jesus' Parables?" *Bib* 56 (1975): 231–40.

Others commented, "He seems to be lobbying for foreign deities." The comment of such Athenians foreshadows the discourse that Paul is soon to deliver. Their comment echoes one of the charges brought against Socrates (Plato, *Apology* 11 §24B: he believes not in the gods the city believes in, but in other strange deities [*hetera daimonia kaina*]); Xenophon, *Memorabilia* 1.1.1). Josephus (*Ag.Ap.* 2.37 §§266–67) knows of Athenian regulations against teaching or propagating "foreign gods" *(xenous theous)*: "This was prohibited by law among them, and the penalty decreed for those who introduced a foreign god was death."

because he was preaching about "Jesus" and the "Resurrection." It is not easy to determine the nuance that Luke associates with these words. An obvious sense is the one that any Christian reader of Acts would understand (about the resurrection of Christ), but that would scarcely have been the meaning a pagan Athenian would have comprehended. Perhaps such a person would have understood the fem. Greek noun *anastasis* as the name of a consort for the foreign deity, Jesus, "Jesus and Anastasis." So John Chrysostom understood it (*Hom. in Acta* 38.1; PG 60.267), and many after him.

19. *they took him and led him to the Areopagus. Areios pagos* once denoted the hill to the west-northwest of the acropolis in Athens, the "hill of Ares" (Greek god of war) or "Mar's Hill." It was an open-air space, where speakers often held forth. From it came the name for the ancient supreme judicial council of the city, which originally met on the hill, but which in Paul's day held its sessions in the *Stoa Basileios*, "Royal Colonnade," or at the Stoa of Zeus Eleutherios (see H. J. Cadbury, *The Book of Acts in History*, 52, 57). It is impossible to say in which sense Luke would be using the prep. *epi* with the name. If it means "on," that Paul was led to the hill, as Dibelius thought, it would be the ideal place for his speech. A bronze plaque on the hill today presents the ancient Greek text of

Paul's speech, which still preserves a popular understanding of the phrase. It could, however, mean that Paul was led "to" the council of the Areopagus, which is the more likely meaning. Then, however, the motive of that action is less clear, unless we are to understand the council as the supervisor and judge of public instruction. Paul would then be asked to explain his novel ideas before it. The latter meaning of Areopagus seems to be called for by v 22. For the role of the Areopagite Council in Greek history, see Haenchen, *Acts*, 519 n. 1. Cf. B. Keil, *Beiträge zur Geschichte des Areopags* (Leipzig: Teubner, 1920); H. M. Martin, Jr., "Areopagus," *ABD*, 1.370–72.

with the request, "May we know what this new teaching is that is being proposed by you? It is "new" in the sense of "strange" to Athenian ears. Compare Euripides, *Bacchae* 650: "For you are bringing in sayings ever new," i.e., strange *(logous . . . kainous).*

20. *You are bringing up subjects unfamiliar to our ears, and so we want to know what this is all about."* The interest of the Athenians is polite, but it is not without serious concern; so they are depicted as skeptical.

21. *Now all Athenians, as well as the aliens residing with them, used to spend their time in nothing else but telling about or listening to something new.* This is Luke's parenthetical remark, which helps to explain the foregoing request. Compare the query of Demosthenes in the fourth century, "Or do you want . . . to run around and ask one another, 'Is anything new being said?' Could there be anything newer . . .?" (*Or.* 4.10 §43). Also Thucydides, *Histories* 3.38.4–7. Luke uses *akouein ti kainoteron*, which is not easily translated because *kainoteron* is the comparative degree of the adj., used either as a positive (as translated above), or possibly as a superlative, "the latest news" (ZBG §150).

22. *Then Paul rose in the meeting of the Areopagus and said.* Lit., "Paul, standing up in the midst of the Areopagus." The phrase *en mesō tou A.*, "in the midst of the A.," creates the problem of the meaning of the name Areopagus. See NOTE on v 19. Conzelmann (*Acts*, 140) all too quickly says that it means "'in the middle,' that is, of the place."

"People of Athens. On *andres Athēnaioi*, see NOTE on 1:11.

I see that you are in every respect religiously exact. Lit., "rather demon fearing," in which the Greek *daimōn* is not to be immediately understood of "evil spirits"; rather *daimōn* in the Greek world would have been understood as "deity, divinity." So *deisidaimonia* would basically mean "reverence for deities," whence it developed a generic sense of "religious devotion" (cf. 25:19); but it also carried at times the idea of "superstition." See H. A. Moellering, "Deisidaimonia: A Footnote to Acts 17:22," *CTM* 34 (1963): 455–71. Luke uses the comparative *deisidaimonesterous*, which should be taken as a superlative, "very religious" (ZBG §148).

At the outset of his address, Paul seeks to win over his audience with *captatio benevolentiae*, "a currying of favor," but for the Christian reader his words bear an unmistakable irony. In the fifth century Sophocles had described Athens as *theosebestatas*, "most god-revering" (*Oedipus Colonus* 260); compare Josephus,

Ag.Ap. 2.11 §130, who knew of the reputation of Athenians as *tous eusebestatous tōn Hellēnōn*, "the most devout of the Greeks."

23. *For as I walked about and looked carefully at your objects of worship.* The *sebasmata* would have included statues, shrines, sanctuaries, and temples set up in honor of gods of the Greek pantheon. The same Greek word has a pejorative connotation in Wis 14:20; 15:17, expressing the criticism of such objects by the Jewish author.

I even came upon an altar inscribed, 'To a God Unknown.' No altar at Athens has yet been discovered with precisely this inscription, *Agnōstō Theō*. Ancient Greek authors, however, tell of Athenian *bōmoi theōn onomazomenōn agnōstōn*, "altars of gods called unknown" (Pausanias, *Descr. Graec.* 1.1.4; cf. 5.14.8; Philostratus, *Vita Apollonii* 6.3.5 [*agnōstōn daimonōm bōmoi*]; Diogenes Laertius, *Vitae* 1.110). Some commentators think that by such words ancient writers would have meant altars erected without a dedication to some named god. In any case, Luke may have been aware of such literary references and have recast the phrase in the singular to make it the starting point of Paul's address. Thus Paul would be beginning his address to Athenians with a reference to popular Greek piety. Such altars were apparently set up under the direction of Epimenides of Crete (see Diogenes Laertius, *Epimenides* 1.10.110 [*Athēnaiōn bōmoi anōnymoi*, "altars of Athenians with no name on them"]). Jerome may well have caught the implication, when he wrote: "The altar's inscription was not, as Paul stated, 'To the unknown god,' but 'To the gods of Asia, Europe, and Africa, unknown and foreign gods'" (*Comm. in Titum* 1.12; PL 26.607).

See P. W. van der Horst, "The Unknown God (Acts 17:23)," *Knowledge of God in the Graeco-Roman World* (EPRO 112; ed. R. van den Broek et al.; Leiden: Brill, 1988), 19–42; K. Lake, "The Unknown God," *Beginnings*, 5.240–46; E. des Places, "'Au Dieu inconnu' (Act 17,23)," *Bib* 40 (1959): 793–99; A. Wikenhauser, "'Ignoto Deo,'" *Oberrheinisches Pastoralblatt* 14 (1912): 193–200; T. Birt, "*Agnōstoi theoi* und die Areopagrede des Apostels Paulus," *RhMP* 69 (1914): 342–92; J. P. Dunn, "The Unknown God," *BW* 42 (1913): 351–61; T. Plüss, "*Agnōstō theō*," *Wochenschrift für klassische Philologie* 30 (1913): 553–58; P. Corssen, "Der Altar des unbekannten Gottes," ZNW 14 (1913): 309–23; L. Legrand, "The Unknown God of Athens: Acts 17 and the Religion of the Gentiles," *IJT* 30 (1981): 158–67; H. Külling, "Zur Bedeutung des Agnostos Theos: Eine Exegese zu Apostelgeschichte 17,22.23," TZ 36 (1980): 65–83.

Now what you thus worship unknowingly I would proclaim to you. Paul engages in a proclamation, not a reasoned philosophical argument; yet it differs from the kerygma proclaimed to Israel. As a Jewish Christian, he realizes that pagan Greeks do not worship the "true" God of Jews and Christians, but he tries to show that the God whom he proclaims is in reality no stranger to the Athenians, if they would only rightly reflect. His starting point is Athenian religious piety, and he tries to raise them from such personal experience to a sound theology. Their piety, in his view, does not go far enough.

24. *The God who made the world and all that is in it.* In part I of his address

(vv 24–25), Paul makes known to the Athenians the God who created the universe. This God is the maker and preserver of the *kosmos*, "the universe, (ordered) world." The terminology that Paul employs is common to both Greek philosophical speculation and the OT. For the latter, see the LXX of Gen 1:1; 14:19, 22; Exod 20:11; Ps 146:6; Isa 42:5; Wis 9:9; 11:17; 2 Macc 7:23, 28 (and NOTE on 14:15). For the former, see the teaching of Pythagoras, who in the sixth century first designated the "ordered world" as *kosmos* (Plutarch, *De placitis philosophorum* 2.1); for the Maker and Father of the Universe, see Plato, *Timaeus* 28C, 76C; and "God" as its maker, see Epictetus, *Arrian's Discourses* 4.7.6. Paul will not allow, however, Greek philosophical distinctions about a demiurge or a master workman; he insists that "God" is the supreme being. Recall the way Philo reformulated OT teaching about the creator God in Greek philosophical terminology in *De opificio mundi* 2 §§7–12; *De specialibus legibus* 1.16 §81.

this Lord of the heavens and the earth. This title is found in Tob 7:17 (MSS A, B); 1QapGen 22:16, 21, an interpretative Aramaic paraphrase of Gen 14:19. Cf. Matt 11:25; Luke 10:21. The implication is that the maker of the universe is its *kyrios*, "lord," and that characteristic evokes how he should be acknowledged and worshiped.

does not live in temples made by human hands. Recall Stephen's strictures on the Jerusalem Temple (7:48). What Paul now proclaims echoes OT teaching (cf. 1 Kgs 8:27; Isa 57:15), and he does it in the presence of famous Greek temples that surround him in Athens itself. He is also only repeating what the Stoic philosopher Zeno had taught: "It is Zeno's teaching that one should not build temples of the gods" (Plutarch, *Moralia* 1034B). This is echoed in a fragment of Euripides (968): "What house fashioned by builders can contain the divine form within enclosing walls?" Cf. Lactantius, *Divinae Institutiones* 6.25.

25. *Nor is it because God lacks something that he is served by human hands.* The God of whom Paul speaks is not just the creator of all but lacks nothing that human beings can supply. Paul echoes a motif common to the OT (Ps 50:9–12; Amos 5:12–23; 2 Macc 14:35) and to Greek philosophy (Aristobulus, frg. 4; cf. Eusebius, *Praeparatio evangelica* 13.12.3); Euripides, *Hercules Furens* 1345–46: "For God, if indeed God he be, is in need of nothing." See the similar ideas attributed to the Stoic philosopher Zeno in Clement of Alexandria, *Stromateis* 5.76.1.

It is rather he who gives everyone life and breath and everything else. See Gen 2:7; Isa 42:5; 2 Macc 7:23. Though God needs nothing and takes nothing from human beings, he is the one who sustains all life, human, animal, and plant. God is the creator of the human race; human beings are not autochthonous, and Athenians are not sprung from Attic soil.

Even though Luke makes Paul trace all the ordered universe back to God as its maker, creator, and preserver, there is no mention of how this has been done. The Lucan teaching is not espousing creationism and says nothing about the geological age of earth; what is being taught is compatible with a sane view of scientific development and evolution.

26. *From one stock he made the whole human race dwell on the face of the whole*

earth. Or, "he made every race of mankind to dwell." Lit., "from one," the pron. *henos* (neuter? masculine?) is used absolutely, without a noun, which it might modify as an adjective. This is the reading of MSS P[74], ℵ, B, and the Alexandrian tradition. Two basic translations have been proposed: (1) "From one he made every nation of mankind dwell on the face of the earth." In this understanding the verb *epoiēsen,* "made," is modal, governing the infin. "to dwell." This would mean, "from one nation," or "from one stock," every other one is derived. To support this understanding, MSS D, E, P, and the *Koinē* text-tradition insert after *henos* (neut.): *haimatos,* which would mean, "from one blood"; and MS Ψ reads rather *stomatos,* "from one mouth." (2) "From one he made the whole human race, to dwell on the face of the earth." In this case, *epoiēsen* is absolute ("made" = "created"), and the infin. *katoikein* is epexegetical or final, explaining why God created humanity. It is also parallel to the purpose infin. *zētein,* "seek," in v 27. In this case, *ex henos* (masc.) could mean "from one man" (e.g., "from Adam"). Despite the cumbersome syntax, the latter interpretation is often preferred, because of its allusion to Gen 1:27–28: so Johnson (*Acts,* 315), Kistemaker (*Acts,* 634), Marshall (*Acts,* 287), Pesch (*Apg.,* 2. 137), Polhill (*Acts,* 374), Roloff (*Apg.,* 261), Schneider (*Apg.,* 2.240), Weiser (*Apg.,* 471). It is also in accord with Greek philosophical thinking about the one and the many, even though the Greeks did not have the idea of a First Man from whom all humanity was descended (see A. D. Nock, *Essays,* 831).

In either case, in part II of his address, Paul stresses the unity of all humanity and its nearness to this creator God. He does this, by insisting that God has put all human beings on this earth and is thus countering the idea that the universe came into being by chance, emphasizing rather the divine design and intention that lie behind all human existence.

He it is who has fixed the dates of their epochs and the boundaries of their habitation. I.e., the regular periods in the history of nations and their set geographical boundaries. So God is close to human beings. The historic limitations set upon humanity, the times and places where they dwell, are all the object of divine determination. See Genesis 10; Deut 32:8; Ps 74:12–14; Job 38:8–11; IQM 10:12–15. The words have, however, been understood more in the sense of a philosophy of nature: "He ordered the seasons and the boundaries of their habitations," i.e., the habitable zones (Dibelius, *Studies,* 38, 53). In any case, divine determination seeks to guide human beings: so they are to seek out the God who is near to them. This distinction, between a historical and a philosophical interpretation, is idle; see Conzelmann, *Acts,* 143–44. Cf. R. Lapointe, "Que sont les *kairoi* d'*Act* 17,26? Etude sémantique et stylistique," *EgT* 3 (1972): 323–38.

27. *so that people might seek for God, perhaps even grope for him, and eventually find him.* Luke makes Paul formulate the purpose of human existence or the destiny of humanity. This seeking and groping may connote a philosophical quest, as in Seneca, *Ep.* 95.47; Cicero, *De natura deorum* 2.153; or it may involve something less intellectual, a more emotional endeavor. Cf. Deut 4:28–29; and esp. 32:8; Amos 5:6; Isa 55:6; Philo, *De specialibus legibus* 1.7 §36 ("Nothing is better

than to seek the true God, even if the discovery of him eludes human capability, since even the endeavor to wish to learn produces unspeakable joys and pleasures"). MS D reads *zētein to theion,* "seek for the divinity," using the word that appears toward the end of v 29. What Paul is speaking about here is not just the quest of God with the eyes of faith, but the instinctive searching of the human mind and heart for God in the traces that God has left in the creation and disposition of humanity in this world and on this earth. It is a form of natural theology.

even though he is not really far from any one of us. This sums up Paul's argument in part II of his address: the proximity of God. Cf. Ps 145:18: God "is near to all who call upon him." Also Jer 23:23. Compare Seneca, *Ep.* 41.1: "God is near you, with you, within you"; Dio Chrysostom, *Or.* 12.27–28; 30.26; Philo, *Legum allegoria* 2.2 §4; Josephus, *Ant.* 8.4.2 §108.

28. *For in him we live and move and have our being.* So Luke makes Paul sum up human existence: in God is rooted all human existence, all human movement, and all human life. "We live" refers to physical life; "have our being," to spiritual-intellectual life; and "move," to a transfer of both to a cosmic level (so H. Hommel, "Platonisches"). In any case, this is not a pantheistic formula, *pace* Conzelmann (*Acts,* 144) and Weiser (*Apg.,* 474), or one that expresses the immanence of human beings in God; it merely formulates the dependence of all human life on God and its proximity to him. Luke makes use of a tricolon, which has been shown to be an old and frequent pattern in the Greek language, with nothing particularly philosophical about it, even though the tricolon was also used in Greek philosophical writing (Plato, *Soph.* 248E–249A; Aristotle, *De anima* 414a 12–13). This Lucan tricolon is an echo of neither Platonic nor Stoic philosophy, despite the attempt of Norden to argue for the latter (*Agnostos Theos,* 22) and Haenchen's contention (*Acts,* 524 n. 3: "a received Stoic formulation"). For farfetched and alleged Greek parallels, see Conzelmann, *Acts,* 144. If Luke had any model for the tricolon he uses, it has not survived. See R. Renehan, "*Acts,* 17.28," *GRBS* 20 (1979): 347–53. *Pace* P. Colaclides, it is not even "in part" a parallel to Euripides, *Bacchae,* 506.

That the tricolon is modeled on words of the sixth-century Epimenides of Knossos in Crete is highly unlikely, *pace* K. Lake, "'Your Own Poets,'" *Beginnings,* 5.246–51; P. Courcelle, "Un vers d'Epiménide dans le 'discours sur l'Aréopage,'" *REG* 76 (1963): 404–13; J. R. Harris, "St. Paul and Epimenides," *Expos* 8/4 (1912): 348–53; Bruce, *Acts,* 359.

As some of your own poets have put it. This is the normal Greek way of introducing a single quotation from a specific writer. In this case, it introduces the quotation from Aratus found in the next clause. The fact that the pl. *tines* is used does not mean that more than one poet or writer is being cited, *pace* Lake and Cadbury, *Beginnings,* 4.218; Bruce, *Acts,* 359.

For similar introductory formulas, see Lycurgus, *In Leocratem* c. 92, 132; Aristotle, *Politica* 7.14.11 §1335b 32–34; *Magna moralia* 2.15.1 §1212b 27–29; Philo, *De specialibus legibus* 1.8 §48; 1.13 §74; cf. R. Renehan, "Classical Greek Quotations in the New Testament," *The Heritage of the Early Church: Essays in Honor of . . . Georges Vasilievich Florovsky* (OrChrAn 195; Rome: Oriental Institute, 1973), 17–46, esp. 40–42; also Dibelius, *Studies*, 50–51 n. 76; M. Pohlenz, "Paulus," 101–4.

'For we too are his offspring.' These words are quoted from the third-century astronomical poem of the Stoic, Aratus, who was born in Soli (in Cilicia) ca. 315 B.C.: *tou gar kai genos eimen*, "of him we too are offspring" (*Phaenomena* 5). Luke may have changed the Ionic *eimen* to Attic *esmen*, but he more likely found it so in a source, because the Attic form was current. It appears also in frg. 4 of the second-century B.C. Jewish apologist, Aristobulus, quoted in Eusebius, *Praeparatio evangelica* 13.12.6 (GCS 8/2.194). In quoting this verse, the Lucan Paul makes a new point in part III of his address: God is not only near to human beings, but they are related to him as kin. Paul understands the Stoic idea in a biblical sense; cf. Psalm 139; Luke 3:38 (Adam as God's son).

See D. A. Frøvig, "Das Aratoszitat der Areopagrede des Paulus," *SO* 15–16 (1936): 44–56; M. Zerwick, "Sicut et quidam vestrorum poetarum dixerunt: 'Ipsius enim et genus sumus' (Act 17,28)," *VD* 20 (1940): 307–21; M. J. Edwards, "Quoting Aratus: Acts 17,28," ZNW 83 (1992): 266–69.

This quotation from Aratus is often said to resemble a line from Cleanthes' *Hymn to Zeus* 4: *ek sou gar genos esmen*, "from you we are offspring," but for all its similarity it is not what Luke quotes. It addresses Zeus and does not speak of him. To introduce it is a distraction in the interpretation of Acts; the words quoted come from Aratus and from no one else, even though one can point to similar statements in other Greek writers. The quotation from Aratus may be part of the information that Luke has inherited from his Pauline source about this discourse in Athens.

29. *If we are really God's offspring.* Thus, Paul begins his conclusion from the Aratus quotation.

we ought not to think that divinity is something like a statue of gold, of silver, or of stone, a work of human art and conception. Cf. Acts 19:26, where the same idea reappears. The Lucan Paul is giving voice to stock Jewish arguments against idolatry and polytheism; see Deut 4:28; Isa 40:18–20; 44:9–10; 46:5–6; Ps 115:4; Wis 13:10. Instead of "God," Luke uses neuter substantivized *to theion*, "the deity, divinity," a term commonly used in classical and Hellenistic Greek writings (Herodotus, *History* 3.108; Thucydides, *Histories* 5.70; Xenophon, *Cyropaedia* 4.2.15; Josephus, *Ant.* 1.11.1 §194; 2.12.4 §275). It is not found in the LXX, where *theios* occurs only as an adjective.

30. *God may well have overlooked bygone periods of human ignorance.* Cf. 3:17; 13:27. Paul concludes his address at the Areopagus, stressing divine forbearance of past human failure to recognize God. The failure is regarded as culpable (recall Rom 1:20; 3:23), but God has mercifully overlooked that culpable failure; for, Paul says again, God "in bygone generations allowed all nations to go their own way" (14:16). Recall too Rom 3:25; 11:32; and esp. 1 Cor 1:19–22, where one sees that what the Lucan Paul here preaches is not so very different from what Paul himself on occasion maintained, *pace* Dibelius (*Studies*, 55–56).

now he orders all people everywhere to repent. Paul preaches eschatological repentance to the philosophers of Athens. Such Athenians are to recognize their idolatry and turn from it. Paul's recommendation to them is that of a change of mind and a break with the past. On "repentance," see NOTE on 2:38. *Pace* Vielhauer ("Paulinism," 36), the repentance called for does not "consist entirely in the self-consciousness of one's natural kinship to God," since there is no reason to limit it to such a notion, given the way the term is understood elsewhere in Lucan writings (see *Luke*, 237–39).

31. *because he has set a day on which he is going to judge the world with justice.* This statement echoes Peter's speech at the conversion of Cornelius, which ended with a similar allusion to God's coming judgment of human activity (cf. Pss 9:9; 96:13; 98:9). That judgment will be concerned with all who populate the *oikoumenē*, "the inhabited (world, earth)" (see NOTE on 11:28). We are not told when that "day" will be, just as it is generally kept hidden in Jewish and Christian apocalyptic writings (see Mark 13:32), but it is the basis of Paul's call for eschatological repentance.

through the man whom he has appointed and whom he has endorsed before all. Lit., "furnishing proof to all (of his fitness for the task) by. . . ." Recall 2:22–24; cf. Rom 14:9; 2 Tim 4:1. MS D adds "Jesus" to "the man" *(andri)*. Paul is thus made to assert the mediation of Christ in the divine judgment of all human activity and conduct. He views world history only from one perspective, viz., from that of the risen Christ.

by raising him from the dead." The resurrection is the way that God has endorsed the role of Christ in human history. The efficiency of Jesus' resurrection is again attributed to God, now to God the Judge, for the risen Christ is seen as sharing in divine judicial activity. See NOTE on 2:24. In 1 Thess 1:10 Paul counseled the Thessalonians, ". . . to await his Son from heaven, whom he raised from the dead, Jesus who delivers us from the wrath to come." Cf. Acts 10:40–42; Heb 6:1–2.

32. *When they heard about resurrection of the dead, some of them sneered.* Although "resurrection of the dead" would have been at home in Judaism at least since the second century B.C. (Dan 12:2), it would not have been a tenet of Greek philosophy. This is why some pagan Athenians sneer. Half a millennium earlier the tragedian Aeschylus had put on the lips of Apollo the statement, "When the dust has soaked up the blood of a man, once he has died, there is no resurrection" (*outis est' anastasis, Eumenides* 647–48).

others said, "We'll listen to you about this topic some other time." I.e., Your new idea is fascinating, but we shall have to hear you on this topic on some other occasion. Commentators debate whether this should be understood as a polite but firm rejection of Paul's message (Haenchen, *Acts*, 526; Roloff, *Apg.*, 256; Schneider, *Apg.*, 2.244) or whether it should be an expression of genuine interest (Barrett, "Paul's Speech," 71; Johnson, *Acts*, 317; Marshall, *Acts*, 291; Polhill, *Acts*, 378). In favor of the latter understanding is the contrast expressed by *hoi men, . . . hoi de.*

33. *Paul withdrew from their meeting.* Lit., "so Paul withdrew from their midst." See NOTES on 17:19, 22.

34. *A few of them, however, did join him and become believers; among these were*

Dionysius, a member of the Areopagus. This is neither the St. Denys of Paris nor the fifth-sixth century Syrian writer, Pseudo-Dionysius. Eusebius (*HE* 3.4.10) identifies this Dionysius as the first "shepherd of the diocese of the Corinthians."

a woman named Damaris. Otherwise unknown. MS D adds a description of her, *euschēmōn*, "respectable"; MS E adds *timia*, "honorable." See a farfetched explanation of her name by J. G. Griffiths, "Was Damaris an Egyptian? (Acts 17,34)," *BZ* 8 (1964): 293–95.

and some others. Lit., "and others with them."

BIBLIOGRAPHY (17:16–34)

Adams, J. M., "Paul at Athens, Acts 17:15–33," *RevExp* 32 (1935): 50–56.

Auffret, P., "Essai sur la structure littéraire du discours d'Athènes (Ac xvii 23–31)," *NovT* 20 (1978): 185–202.

Baldwin, C. S., *God Unknown: A Study of the Address of St. Paul at Athens* (London: Mowbray; Milwaukee: Morehouse, 1920).

Barrett, C. K., "Paul's Speech on the Areopagus," *New Testament Christianity for Africa and the World: Essays in Honour of Harry Sawyerr* (ed. M. E. Glasswell and E. W. Fasholé-Luke; London: SPCK, 1974), 69–77.

Bieder, W., "Zum Problem Religion—christlicher Glaube," *TZ* 15 (1959): 431–45.

Bossuyt, P., and J. Radermakers, "Rencontre de l'incroyant et inculturation: Paul à Athènes (Ac 17,16–34)," *NRT* 117 (1995): 19–43.

Bruce, F. F., "Paul and the Athenians," *ExpTim* 88 (1976–77): 8–12.

———, "Paul's Use of the Old Testament in Acts," *Tradition and Interpretation in the New Testament: Essays in Honor of E. Earle Ellis* . . . (ed. G. F. Hawthorne and O. Betz; Grand Rapids, MI: Eerdmans; Tübingen: Mohr [Siebeck], 1987), 71–79, esp. 73–76.

Bruston, C., "Le poète Epiménide et l'apôtre Paul," *Revue de théologie et des questions religieuses* 21 (1912): 533–35.

Bultmann, R., "Anknüpfung und Widerspruch," *TZ* 2 (1946): 401–18.

———, "Prédication: Actes 17/22–32," *ETR* 59 (1984): 453–62.

Calloud, J., "Paul devant l'Aréopage d'Athènes: Actes 17,16–34," *RSR* 69 (1981): 209–48.

Charles, J. D., "Engaging the (Neo-)Pagan Mind: Paul's Encounter with Athenian Culture as a Model for Cultural Apologetics (ACTS 17:16–34)," *TrinJ* 16 (1995): 47–62.

Colaclides, P., "Acts 17,28A and Bacchae 506," *VC* 27 (1973): 161–64.

Conzelmann, H., "The Address of Paul on the Areopagus," *StLA*, 217–30.

Curtius, E., "St. Paul in Athens," *Expos* 7/4 (1907): 436–55.

Delage, M., "Résonances grecques dans le discours de saint Paul à Athènes," *Bulletin de l'Association Guillaume Budé* 4/3 (1956): 46–69.

Delebecque, E., "Les deux versions du discours de saint Paul à l'Aréopage (*Actes des Apôtres*, 17,22–31)," *EtClass* 52 (1984): 233–50.

Dibelius, M., "Paul in Athens," *Studies*, 78–83.

———, "Paul on the Areopagus," *Studies*, 26–77.

Dubarle, A.-M., "Le discours à l'Aréopage (*Actes* 17,22–31) et son arrière-plan biblique," *RSPT* 57 (1973): 576–610.

Dupont, J., "Le discours à l'Aréopage (Ac 17,22–31): Lieu de rencontre entre christianisme et hellénisme," *Bib* 60 (1979): 530–46; repr. *Nouvelles études*, 380–423.

———, "La rencontre entre christianisme et hellénisme dans le discours à l'Aréopage (Actes 17,22–31)," *Fede e cultura alla luce della Bibbia* (ed. Biblical Commission; Turin: Elle di Ci, 1981), 261–86; repr. *Nouvelles études*, 380–423.

———, "Le salut des Gentiles et la signification théologique du livre des Actes," *NTS* 6 (1959–60): 132–55, esp. 152–53 n. 4; repr. *Etudes*, 393–419, esp. 416 n. 79

Elliger, W., "Die Rede des Apostels Paulus auf dem Areopag (Apg 17,16–34)," *Altsprachliche Unterricht* 25 (1982): 63–79.

Eltester, W., "Gott und die Natur in der Areopagrede," *Neutestamentliche Studien für Rudolf Bultmann . . .* (BZNW 21; Berlin: Töpelmann, 1954), 202–27.

———, "Schöpfungsoffenbarung und natürliche Theologie im frühen Christentum," *NTS* 3 (1956–57): 93–114.

Enslin, M. S., "Once Again, Luke and Paul," *ZNW* 61 (1970): 253–71, esp. 258.

Fascher, E., "Gott und die Götter: Zur Frage von Religionsgeschichte und Offenbarung," *TLZ* 81 (1956): 279–308.

Fudge, E., "Paul's Apostolic Self-Consciousness at Athens," *JETS* 14 (1971): 193–98.

Fürbringer, L., "Paulus in Athen (Act. 17,16–34)," *CTM* 1 (1930): 735–42, 804–10, 881–87.

Gärtner, B., *The Areopagus Speech and Natural Revelation* (ASNU 21; Uppsala: Almqvist & Wiksell; Lund: Gleerup, 1955).

Gangel, K. O., "Paul's Areopagus Speech," *BSac* 127 (1970): 308–12.

Garland, R., *Introducing New Gods: The Politics of Athenian Religion* (London: Duckworth; Ithaca: Cornell University Press, 1992).

Gatti, V., *Il discorso di Paolo ad Atene: Studio su Act. 17,22–31* (Brescia: Paideia, 1982).

Gaugusch, L., "Die Areopagrede des Apostels Paulus (Apg. 17,16–34)," *TPQ* 72 (1919): 553–61.

Grant, F. C., "St. Paul and Stoicism," *BW* 45 (1915): 268–81.

Given, M. D., "Not Either/Or but Both/And in Paul's Areopagus Speech," *BI* 3 (1995): 356–72.

Halstead, S., "Paul in the Agora," *Quantulacumque: Studies Presented to Kirsopp Lake . . .* (ed. R. P. Casey et al.; London: Christophers, 1937), 139–43.

Hamm, D., "The Rich Fool and the Speech on Mars Hill: From the Comic to the Cosmic in Luke's Creator-Centered Theology," *An Ecology of the Spirit: Religious Reflection and Environmental Consciousness* (ed. M. Barnes; Annual Publication of the College Theology Society 36; Lanham, MD: University Press of America, 1990), 85–95.

Harnack, A., *Ist die Rede des Paulus in Athen ein ursprünglicher Bestandteil der Apostelgeschichte?* (TU 39/1; Leipzig: Hinrichs, 1913), 1–46.

Hemer, C. J., "Paul at Athens: A Topographical Note," *NTS* 20 (1973–74): 341–50.

Hommel, H., "Neue Forschungen zur Areopagrede Acta 17," *ZNW* 46 (1955): 145–78.

———, "Platonisches bei Lukas: Zu Act 17,28a (Leben—Bewegung—Sein)," *ZNW* 48 (1957): 193–200.

Horn, R. C., "Classical Quotations and Allusions of St. Paul," *LCQ* 11 (1938): 281–88.

Horst, P. W. van der, "The Altar of the 'Unknown God' in Athens (Acts 17:23) and the Cult of 'Unknown Gods' in the Hellenistic and Roman Period," *ANRW* II/18.2 (1989): 1426–56.

Jagu, A., "Saint Paul et le stoïcisme," *RevScRel* 32 (1958): 225–50.

Kinsey, R. S., "Was Paul Thinking of a Statue? (Acts 17)," *Studies Presented to David Moore Robinson* (2 vols.; ed. G. E. Mylonas; St. Louis: Washington University Press, 1951, 1953), 2.1247–48.

Kisil, P., "Die Areopagrede des heiligen Paulus—Eine apologetische Rede," *TPQ* 77 (1924): 674–86.

Kragerud, A., "Itinerariet i. Apostlenes gjerninger," *NorTT* 56 (1955): 255.

Külling, H., *Geoffenbartes Geheimnis: Eine Auslegung von Apostelgeschichte 17,16–34* (ATANT 79; Zurich: Theologischer-V., 1993).

Lattey, C., "Paul at Athens," *ClR* 33 (1950): 392–98.

Lebram, J.-C., "Der Aufbau der Areopagrede," *ZNW* 55 (1964): 221–43.

Leonard, W., "St. Paul at Athens," *ACR* 12 (1935): 364–71.

Lindemann, A., "Die Christuspredigt des Paulus in Athen (Act 17,16–33)," *Texts and Contexts: Biblical Texts in Their Textual and Situational Contexts: Essays in Honor of Lars Hartman* (ed. T. Fornberg and D. Hellholm; Oslo/Stockholm: Scandinavian University Press, 1995), 245–55.

Luque, S., "San Pablo en Atenas frente al paganismo," *CB* 10 (1953): 148–51, 180–86.

McKay, K. L., "Foreign Gods Identified in Acts 17:18?" *TynBull* 45 (1994): 411–12.

Marth, A., "Die Zitate des hl. Paulus aus der Profanliteratur," *ZKT* 37 (1913): 889–95.

Menoud, P.-H., " 'Jésus et Anastasie': Actes xvii, 18," *RTP* 32 (1944): 141–45.

Morrice, W. G., "Where Did Paul Speak in Athens—On Mars' Hill or before the Court of the Areopagus? (Acts 17^{19})," *ExpTim* 83 (1971–72): 377–78.

Mussner, F., "Anknüpfung und Kerygma in der Areopagrede (Apg 17,22b–31)," *TTZ* 67 (1958): 344–54; repr. *Praesentia salutis: Gesammelte Studien zu Fragen und Themen des Neuen Testaments* (Düsseldorf: Patmos, 1967), 235–43.

———, "Einige Parallelen aus den Qumrântexten zur Areopagrede (Apg 17,22–31)," *BZ* 1 (1957): 125–30.

Nauck, W., "Die Tradition und Komposition der Areopagrede: Eine motivgeschichtliche Untersuchung," *ZTK* 53 (1956): 11–52.

Nock, A. D., Review of M. Dibelius, *Aufsätze zur Apostelgeschichte*, *Gnomon* 25 (1953): 497–506; repr. *Essays on Religion and the Ancient World* (2 vols.; ed. Z. Stewart; Cambridge: Harvard University Press, 1972), 821–32.

Norden, E., *Agnostos Theos: Untersuchungen zur Formengeschichte religiöser Rede* (Leipzig/Berlin: Teubner, 1913; 2d ed. 1923; 4th ed.: Darmstadt: Wissenschaftliche Buchgesellschaft, 1956).

O'Toole, R. F., "Paul at Athens and Luke's Notion of Worship," *RB* 89 (1982): 185–97.

Owen, H. P., "The Scope of Natural Revelation in Romans i and Acts xvii," *NTS* 5 (1958–59): 133–43.

Parente, P., "St. Paul's Address before the Areopagus," *CBQ* 11 (1949): 144–50.

Places, E. des, "Actes 17,25," *Bib* 46 (1965): 219–22.

———, "Actes 17,27," *Bib* 48 (1967): 1–6.

———, "Actes 17,30–31," *Bib* 52 (1971): 526–34.

———, " 'Ipsius enim et genus sumus' (Act 17,28)," *Bib* 43 (1962): 388–95.

———, " 'Quasi superstitiosiores' (A 17,22)," *Studiorum Paulinorum Congressus Internationalis Catholicus* (AnBib 17–18; Rome: Biblical Institute, 1963), 2.183–91.

———, *La religion grecque: Dieux, cultes, rites et sentiment religieux dans la Grèce antique* (Paris: Picard, 1969), 327–61.

———, " 'Des temples faits de main d'homme' (Actes des Apôtres, 17,24)," *Bib* 42 (1961): 217–23.

Pohlenz, M., "Paulus und die Stoa," *ZNW* 42 (1949): 69–104, esp. 82–98, 101–4.

Prior, K.F.W., *The Gospel in a Pagan Society: The Relevance for Today of Paul's Ministry in Athens* (London: Hodder and Stoughton, 1975).

Reicke, B., "Natürliche Theologie nach Paulus," *SEA* 22–23 (1957–58): 154–67.

Reitzenstein, R., "Die Areopagrede des Paulus," *Neue Jahrbücher für das klassische Altertum* 31 (1913): 393–422.

Rüther, J., "Stoisches zur Areopagrede des Paulus," *TGl* 3 (1911): 228–30.

Sabugal, S., "El kerygma de Pablo en el Areópago ateniense (Act 17,22–31): Análisis histórico-tradicional." *Revista agustiniana* 31 (1990): 505–34.

Sandnes, K. O., "Paul and Socrates: The Aim of Paul's Areopagus Speech," *JSNT* 50 (1993): 13–26.

Schmid, W., "Die Rede des Apostels Paulus vor den Philosophen und Areopagiten in Athen," *Philologus* 95 (1942–43): 79–120.

Schneider, G., "Anknüpfung, Kontinuität und Widerspruch in der Areopagrede Apg 17,22–31," *Kontinuität und Einheit: Für Franz Mussner* (ed. P.-G. Müller and W. Stenger; Freiburg im B.: Herder, 1981), 173–78; repr. *LTH*, 297–302.

———, "Urchristliche Gottesverkündigung in hellenistischer Umwelt," *BZ* 13 (1969): 59–75; repr. *LTH*, 280–96.

Schrenk, G., "Urchristliche Missionspredigt im 1. Jahrhundert," *Auf dem Grunde der Apostel und Propheten: Festgabe für Landesbischof D. Theophil Wurm* . . . (ed. M. Loeser; Stuttgart: Quell, 1948), 51–66; repr. *Studien zu Paulus* (ATANT 26; Zurich: Zwingli, 1954), 131–48.

Schubert, P., "The Place of the Areopagus Speech in the Composition of Acts,"

Transitions in Biblical Scholarship (Essays in Divinity 6; ed. J. C. Rylaarsdam; Chicago: University of Chicago Press, 1968), 235–61.

Sciberras, P., "The Figure of Paul in the Acts of the Apostles: The Areopagos Speech," *Melita theologica* 43 (1992): 1–15.

Shields, B. E., "The Areopagus Sermon and Romans 1:10ff: A Study in Creation Theology," *ResQ* 20 (1977): 23–40.

Stonehouse, N. B., *The Areopagus Address* (London: Tyndale, 1049); repr. *Paul before the Areopagus and Other New Testament Studies* (London: Tyndale; Grand Rapids, MI: Eerdmans, 1957), 1–40.

Thyen, H., *Der Stil der jüdisch-hellenistischen Homilie* (FRLANT 65; Göttingen: Vandenhoeck & Ruprecht, 1955).

Wilkinson, T. L., "Acts 17: The Gospel Related to Paganism: Contemporary Relevance," *Vox reformata* 35 (1980): 1–14.

Winter, B. W., "On Introducing Gods to Athens: An Alternative Reading of Acts 17:18–20," *TynBull* 47 (1996): 71–90.

Wolfe, R. F., "Rhetorical Elements in the Speeches of Acts 7 and 17," *JOTT* 6 (1993): 274–83.

Wycherley, R. E., "St. Paul at Athens," *JTS* 19 (1968): 619–21.

Zuntz, G., "Zum Hymnus des Kleanthes," *RhMP* 94 (1951): 337–41.

Zwaan, J. de, "Semitica semitice (Act. 17,16–34)," *NThSt* 19 (1936): 73–80.

Zweck, D., "The *Exordium* of the Areopagus Speech, Acts 17.22,23," *NTS* 35 (1989): 94–103.

f) PAUL EVANGELIZES CORINTH; HALED BEFORE GALLIO (18:1–17)

18 [1]After that Paul left Athens and went to Corinth. [2]There he found a Jew
named Aquila, a native of Pontus who had recently arrived from Italy, and his
wife Priscilla; for Claudius had ordered all Jews to leave Rome. Paul went to
them, [3]and since he was trained in the same trade as they, made his lodging with
them and worked together, for they were tent makers by trade. [4]Every sabbath
Paul would lead discussions in the synagogue and tried to convince both Jews
and Greeks. [5]When Silas and Timothy came down from Macedonia, Paul continued to occupy himself with preaching the word, bearing witness to Jews that
Jesus was the Messiah. [6]When they would oppose him and insult him, he would
shake his cloak at them in protest and say, "Your blood be on your own heads! I
am not to blame; from now on I shall go to the Gentiles." [7]So Paul withdrew
from there and went to the house of a certain man named Titius Justus, who
worshiped God and lived next door to the synagogue. [8]Crispus, the leader of the
synagogue, put his faith in the Lord, together with all his household, and many
were the Corinthians who also listened (to Paul), came to believe, and were baptized. [9]One night the Lord said to Paul in a vision, "Do not be afraid! Speak out

and do not become silent, [10]because I am with you. No one will attack you or
harm you, for there are many of my people in this city." [11]So Paul settled there
for a year and six months, teaching the word of God among them.

[12]While Gallio was proconsul of Achaia, the Jews rose up in a body against
Paul and brought him to court, [13]charging, "This fellow is influencing people to
worship God in ways that are against the law." [14]As Paul was about to speak up,
Gallio said to the Jews, "If it were a crime or some serious evil trick, I would
tolerate the complaint of you Jews, [15]but since this is a dispute about words and
titles and your own law, you must see to it yourselves. I refuse to judge such
matters." [16]So he dismissed the case from court. [17]Then they all pounced on
Sosthenes, the leader of the synagogue, and beat him in full view of the court.
But none of this was of concern to Gallio.

WT: [1]Having left Athens, he went. [2][omits "named"] . . . with Priscilla, his wife; he greeted them, who had just departed from Rome . . . and they had just settled in Achaia. [omits "Paul went to them"]. [3]Paul was known to Aquila, since he was . . . and of the same tribe [omits "for they were tent makers by trade"]. [4]Having entered the synagogue, Paul would lead . . . He introduced the name of the Lord Jesus and tried to convince not only Jews, but also Greeks. [5]Then there arrived from Macedonia Silas and Timothy, and Paul continued . . . that the Lord Jesus was the Messiah. [6]But with much discussion and interpretation of the Scriptures, some Jews opposed (him) and insulted (him). Then shaking his cloak, Paul would say to them . . . , "Now I am going to the Gentiles." [7]So Paul withdrew from Aquila and went off to the house of Justus, who. [8]A certain leader of the synagogue, named Crispus . . . and a great number of Corinthians listened to the word of the Lord and were

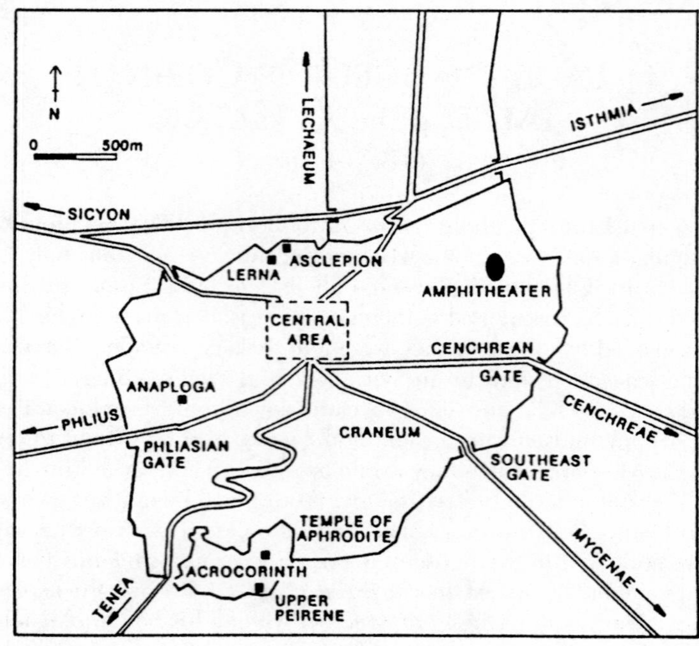

Map 5. Corinth

baptized, believing in God through the name of Jesus Christ. [9][omits "One night"]. [11]teaching them the word of God. [12][omits "in a body"; adds:] having spoken against Paul among themselves, they laid hands on him and brought him to the proconsul. [13]shouting and charging. [omits "this fellow"]. [15]I do not want to be a judge of such matters. [17]Then the Greeks pounced . . . Gallio pretended not to notice (it).

COMMENT

Luke continues with the rest of his account of Mission II, telling how Paul goes on from Athens to Corinth, where he finds Aquila and Priscilla, Jewish Christians who had to leave Italy when the emperor Claudius expelled Jews from Rome (A.D. 49). Paul resides at first with them, because they are workers in the same trade. He frequents the Jewish synagogue and preaches as well to Corinthian Gentiles. Soon he is joined by Silas and Timothy who have come from Thessalonica. Opposition to his preaching arises among Corinthian Jews, which makes Paul decide again to turn to Gentiles. He changes his residence to dwell with Titius Justus, who lives next door to a synagogue. When Paul is assured of heaven's assistance in a dream, he stays on in Corinth for a year and a half. At the end of that time, he is haled by Corinthian Jews before Lucius Junius Gallio, proconsul of the province of Achaia, and charged by them with preaching a form of worship prohibited by law. Gallio, however, sees through the charge and refuses to hear the case against Paul. In reaction, Paul's opponents pounce on Sosthenes, a synagogue leader.

The scene is important for Luke's story of Mission II, because it records Paul's departure from Athens in his disappointment at the reaction of Athenians to his preaching. It also tells of his founding of the church in Neocorinth, capital of the Roman province of Achaia. Moreover, it recounts a Roman reaction to nascent Christianity: the proconsul treats it as if it were but a form of Judaism, which has already been accorded tolerance in the Roman empire.

When Paul comes to Corinth (probably in A.D. 51), he resides with Aquila and Priscilla. They become his fellow workers (18:26) and are mentioned by Paul himself in 1 Cor 16:19; Rom 16:3 (cf. 2 Tim 4:19).

They had to leave Rome because of an edict of the emperor Claudius (A.D. 41–54), about which one learns in Suetonius, *Claudii vita* 25: "Iudaeos impulsore Chresto assidue tumultuantis Roma expulit" (He expelled Jews from Rome, who were constantly making disturbances at the instigation of Chrestus). Greek *Chrēstos* means "good, worthwhile" and was often used as a name for a slave. It would have been pronounced *Christos* in Suetonius's day (by itacism). As a result, the reason given by Suetonius's *impulsore Chresto* probably refers to a controversy that arose in Rome between Jews and Jewish Christians over "the Christ," i.e., whether Jesus of Nazareth was indeed the "messiah" or not. Not understanding the Greek name *Christos*, "anointed (one)," equivalent of Hebrew *māšîaḥ*, "messiah," Suetonius seems to have confused it with the more commonly used name, *Chrēstos*, which he writes in Latin as "Chrestus." So his report is interpreted by many modern Roman historians (A. Momigliano, *Claudius: The Emperor and His Achievement* [New York: Barnes & Noble, 1961], 31–34;

V. M. Scramuzza, *The Emperor Claudius* [Cambridge: Harvard University Press, 1940], 151; A. Piganiol, *Histoire de Rome* [Clio; Paris: Presses Universitaires de France, 1949], 258).

A fifth-century Christian writer, P. Orosius (*Historia adversus paganos* 7.6.15–16; CSEL 5.451), quoted Suetonius's text and dated the expulsion of the Jews to Claudius's ninth regnal year. That would have been 25 January 49 to 24 January 50. Orosius said that Josephus recorded the same expulsion, but the Jewish historian had written not a word about it. For this reason Orosius's testimony, even about the date, is queried by some modern scholars. No one knows where Orosius got the information about the ninth year, but it remains not unlikely, and a number of interpreters rightly accept it (E. M. Smallwood, *The Jews under Roman Rule* [SJLA 20; Leiden: Brill, 1976], 211–16; R. Jewett, *A Chronology of Paul's Life* [Philadelphia: Fortress, 1979; E. Schürer, *HJPAJC*, 3.77–78; S. Benko, "The Edict," 417; G. Howard, "The Beginnings of Christianity in Rome: A Note on Suetonius, Life of Claudius xxv. 4," *ResQ* 24 [1981]: 175–77).

Some scholars, however, have sought to interpret Suetonius's testimony as referring to a decision made by Claudius in his first regnal year (A.D. 41), which is reported by Dio Cassius (*Roman History* 60.6.6). According to this writer, the emperor, noting the growing number of Jews in Rome, "did not drive them out," but ordered them "not to hold meetings." In other words, both Suetonius and Dio Cassius are said by these scholars to be referring to the same Claudian decision, and the expulsion of Jews because of Chrestus would have occurred eight years earlier. See G. Lüdemann, *Paul, Apostle to the Gentiles: Studies in Chronology* (Philadelphia: Fortress, 1984), 165–71; J. Murphy-O'Connor, *St. Paul's Corinth*, 130–40; R. Penna, "Les Juifs à Rome au temps de l'apôtre Paul," *NTS* 28 (1982): 321–47, esp. 331. Lüdemann (*Early Christianity*, 11) even says that "most scholars all over the world are agreed" about this date (A.D. 41). That is exaggerated nonsense.

Such an interpretation is unconvincing, because Dio Cassius says explicitly that Claudius did *not* expel Jews at that time (*Roman History* 60.6.6). Claudius may have expelled *some* Jews later on (A.D. 49–50), as Suetonius actually affirms, without indicating the date. Dio Cassius's history for the year 49 exists only in a Byzantine epitome, and the lack of reference to such an expulsion in that year may be owing to the summary nature of the epitome. Moreover, Dio Cassius makes no mention of *Chrestos*, which is a major obstacle to the identification of the two events. See further Hemer, *Book of Acts*, 168; H. W. Tajra, *The Trial of St. Paul*, 53; Hengel, *Acts*, 108.

One must, however, prescind from the Lucan hyperbole, "all the Jews" (18:2) and ask how recently Aquila and Priscilla would have come from "Italy" (or specifically from "Rome"), despite the WT of 18:2. If the edict were issued by Claudius in his ninth regnal year, their arrival in Corinth would have taken place some time after A.D. 49, whereas Paul would have arrived somewhat later (see Introduction §158).

In v 12 Luke recounts another important episode in the life of Paul: the haling of Paul before the proconsul Gallio. This episode in Acts is accorded historical credence by almost all interpreters of Acts today. A dissenting voice was once raised against its historicity by J. Juster (*Les Juifs,* 2. 154 n. 4), but he has had little or no following. Strangely enough, the appearance before Gallio is never mentioned by Paul himself in any of his letters, but this Lucan detail has become the most important item in the study of Pauline chronology and missionary activity. In fact, it supplies a rare peg on which to hang their absolute chronology.

Lucius Junius Gallio is mentioned as a friend of the emperor Claudius and as the proconsul of Achaia in a Greek inscription that records the text of a letter sent by Claudius to the people of Delphi about a depopulation problem. Since the text is dated in the customary Roman fashion, one can determine from it the time when Gallio was proconsul in Achaia. The inscription had been set up in a temple of Apollo in Delphi, where it was discovered by E. Bourguet in fragmentary form in 1905 and 1910. The nine fragments, however, were not fully published until 1970: A. Plassart, "Lettre de l'empereur Claude au gouverneur d'Achaie (en 52)," *Les inscriptions du temple,* 26–33 §286. See also his article, "L'Inscription de Delphes"; cf. J. H. Oliver, "The Epistle of Claudius."

The main part of the inscription runs as follows:

1 *Tiber[ios Klaudios Kais]ar S[ebast]os G[ermanikos, dēmarchikēs exou]*
2 *sias [to IB, autokratōr t]o KZ, p[atēr p]atri[dos . . . chairein].*
3 *Pal[ai men t]ēi p[olei tē] tōn Delph[ōn ēn o]u mo[non eunous all' epimelēs ty]*
4 *chēs aei d' etērē[sa t]ēn thrēskei[an t]ou Apo[llōnos tou Pythiou. epei de]*
5 *nyn legetai kai [pol]eitōn erē[mo]s einai, hō[s moi arti apēngeile L. Iou]*
6 *nios Galliōn ph[ilos] mou ka[i anthy]patos, [boulomenos tous Delphous]*
7 *eti hexein ton pr[oteron kosmon entel]ē e[tellomai hymein kai ex al]*
8 *lōn poleōn kal[ein eu gegonotas eis Delphous hōs neous katoikous kai]*
9 *autois epitre[pein ekgonois te ta] pres[beia panta echein ta tōn Del]*
10 *phōn hōs pole[itais ep' isē kai homoia. e]i men gar ti[nes . . . hōs polei]*
11 *tai metōkis[anto eis toutous tou]s topous, kr[. . .]*

[1]Tiber[ius Claudius Caes]ar A[ugust]us G[ermanicus, invested with tribunician po]wer [2][for the 12th time, acclaimed imperator for t]he 26th time, F[ather of the Fa]ther[land . . . sends greetings to . . .]. [3]For a l[ong time I have been not onl]y [well disposed toward t]he ci[ty] of Delph[i, but also solicitous for its [4]pros]perity, and I have always sup[ported th]e cul[t of Pythian] Apol[lo. But] [5]now [since] it is said to be desti[tu]te of [citi]zens, as [L. Jun][6]ius Gallio, my fri[end] an[d procon]sul, [recently reported to me, and being desirous that Delphi] [7]should continue to retain [inta]ct its for[mer rank, I] ord[er you (pl.) to in]vite [well-born people also from [8]ot]her cities [to Delphi as new inhabitants and to] [9]all[ow] them [and their children to have all the] privi[leges of Del]phi

[10]as being citi[zens on equal and like (basis)]. For i[f] so[me . . .] [11]were to trans[fer as citi]zens [to those regions . . .*

From the text of the letter one sees that Gallio was proconsul of Achaia during the twelfth regnal year of Claudius (A.D. 41–54) and after the twenty-sixth acclamation of him as *imperator.* The emperor was invested with *potestas tribunicia* each year, and that investment marked his regnal years. The emperor's name and the twelfth year of this tribunician power have in large part been reconstructed in this inscription, but the reconstruction is certain, being based on other known inscriptions of Claudius (see M. P. Charlesworth, *Documents Illustrating the Reigns of Claudius & Nero* [Cambridge: Cambridge University Press, 1951], 11–14). His twelfth regnal year began on 25 January A.D. 52. Acclamation as imperator was sporadic, because it depended on military victories in which the emperor was engaged or at least indirectly involved. To date an event by such acclamations, one has to learn when a given acclamation occurred. From other inscriptions it is known that the twenty-second to the twenty-fifth acclamations took place in Claudius's eleventh regnal year (25 January 51 to 24 January 52) and that the twenty-seventh acclamation occurred in his twelfth regnal year before 1 August 52. Theoretically, then, the twenty-sixth acclamation could have occurred during the winter of 51 or in the spring or early summer of 52. The matter is settled by a Greek inscription often neglected in the discussion of Pauline chronology and the Delphi inscription: an inscription of Kys in Caria (published 1887). It combines the twenty-sixth acclamation with the twelfth regnal year: *dēmarchikēs exousias to dōdekaton, hypaton to penpton, autokratora to eikoston kai hekton,* "(invested with) tribunician power for the twelfth time, consul for the fifth, imperator for the twenty-sixth time" (see G. Cousin and G. Deschamps, "Emplacement et ruines," esp. 306–8; cf. *CIL* 6.1256; 8.14727; Frontinus, *De Aquis* 1.13; A. Brassac, "Une inscription"). So the combination of the twenty-sixth acclamation of Claudius as imperator and his twelfth regnal year points to a time between 25 January 52 and 1 August 52. Claudius would have written the letter, in which he mentions Gallio, to the people of Delphi in this period.

Since Achaia was a senatorial province of praetorian rank, it was governed by a proconsul (Greek *anthypatos,* Acts 18:12; 13:7; Josephus, *Ant.* 14.10.21 §244). Such a provincial governor normally ruled for a year and was expected to assume his task by 1 June (Dio Cassius, *Roman History* 57.14.5) and to leave for the province by 1 April or mid-April at the latest (ibid., 60.11.6; 60.17.3). Claudius's letter mentions that Gallio had reported to him about conditions in Delphi on his arrival. This would mean that Gallio was already in Achaia by late spring or early summer of A.D. 52 and had written to Claudius about the situation that he found there. See B. Reicke, *EDNT,* 1.234.

The problem has always been to determine whether Gallio's proconsular year

* (The remainder of the fragmentary inscription is inconsequential. My reading of the text and translation of it follow that of Oliver. Square brackets enclose reconstructed parts of the text, most of which are restored with certainty.)

stretched from a time in 51–52 or 52–53. A. Deissmann (*Paul,* 272), Finegan (*Handbook,* 317–18), and Hemer (*Book of Acts,* 119, 214, 244–76) espouse the former view and have influenced many others.

However, Seneca, Gallio's younger brother, writes that Gallio developed a fever in Achaia and "took ship immediately," insisting that the disease was not of the body, but of the place (*Ep.* 104.2). Thus it seems that Gallio cut short his proconsular stay in Achaia and hurried home. Thus, having arrived in Achaia in the spring of 52 and reported on conditions there to Claudius, he spent the summer in Achaia, but departed from the province not later than the end of October 52, before *mare clausum* (the closed sea), when ship travel on the Mediterranean became impossible because of winter storms (see Acts 27:9). Hence it follows that Paul would have been haled before Gallio either in the late spring, summer, or even early fall of A.D. 52.

Not all interpreters reckon the year of Gallio's proconsulship correctly, often neglecting the Carian inscription, and so they use A.D. 51–52 instead of A.D. 52–53. The suggestion of Lüdemann (*Paul,* 163–64) that Claudius's letter was actually sent to Gallio's successor and that Gallio's term should be reckoned as falling "in the years 51/52 C.E." is farfetched and based on sheer speculation.

In this episode Luke has also incorporated a speech of Gallio to the Jews of Corinth. It is another speech of a non-Christian in Acts. As for its type, it is a judicial explanation, which passes on legal counsel. The Roman proconsul of Achaia refuses to get involved in matters pertaining to Jewish religion, regarding the dispute between Jews and Christians as a matter of hairsplitting that does not concern Roman law or governance. The details of this episode have come to Luke from his Pauline source, but the speech of Gallio is largely of Lucan composition.

Sometime during this sojourn in Corinth Paul would have written 1 Thessalonians, after he has come from Athens (ca. A.D. 51); see 1 Thess 3:1,6.

This episode tells us more about Paul's collaborators in Corinth: about Aquila and Priscilla and about Silas and Timothy. Together they support his efforts to preach to Corinthian Jews that Jesus of Nazareth is the Messiah. When the Jews refuse to accept his message, he turns to "the Gentiles" in the city. Paul is not allowed to become discouraged, for the Lord appears to him and assures him that he is not to be deterred by such opposition: "I am with you" and "there are many of my people in this city" (18:10). Thus the Christian missionary is encouraged in his work. A concrete instance of the Lord's assistance is seen in the way the Roman proconsul Gallio dismisses the case against Paul, when his opponents claim that he has been influencing people to worship God in ways that are against the law (18:13). Gallio's reaction to these opponents becomes, in effect, a manifestation of the help that is accorded Paul in his missionary work.

NOTES

18:1. *After that Paul left Athens and went to Corinth. Korinthos* was a city in Greece on the isthmus of Corinth, which funneled traffic from northern Greece to the southern Peloponnesus. It lay roughly 60 km from Athens and was situated between two ports, Cenchreae, seven km to the southeast on the Saronic Gulf, serving trade with Asia (see Rom 16:1), and Lechaion, three km to the north on the Gulf of Corinth, serving trade with Italy. Its strategic position made it *bimaris Corinthus*, "Corinth on two seas," an important ancient city in the eastern Mediterranean area.

Old Corinth lay to the north of a lofty citadel, called Acrocorinth, which was inhabited as early as Mycenean, pre-Homeric times. Corinth came under the control of the Dorians as they invaded from the north about 1000 B.C. At the time of Temenus's conquest, it became part of his territory, Argos. A Dorian oligarchy (Bacchiadae) ruled there for a considerable time from the eight century on, when Corinth became a famous shipbuilding city and manufacturer of pottery. About 657 B.C. a tyrant, Cypselus, came to power, and during his rule Corinth reached its greatest fame and prosperity. The tyranny was eventually replaced by a constitutional government, headed by eight executive magistrates and an eighty-member council. In the sixth century, Corinth often acted as a mediator between the rising Athens to the north and Sparta to the south. Athenian interference at Megara and in the Gulf of Corinth led to battles between Athens and Corinth in 459 B.C. and to the outbreak of the Peloponnesian Wars in 431, in which Corinth suffered greatly. After the fall of Athens in 404, Corinth joined with Athens, Argos, and Boeotia against the tyranny of Sparta. During the Corinthian War (395–386) a democratic form of government was developed, only to be replaced by an oligarchy. In the Hellenistic period Corinth became a center of industry, commerce, and commercialized pleasure and vice, and eventually rose to prominence as the chief city of the Aegean Confederacy. As such it suffered heavily, when the Romans moved against that confederacy. Old Corinth was sacked and destroyed by the Romans in 146 under L. Mummius, who shipped all its treasures to Italy. After that it lay fallow for over a century.

Corinth was refounded by the Romans as a colony (*Colonia Laus Iulia Corinthiensis*) in 44 B.C. (often called Neocorinth in popular parlance) and became the capital of the senatorial province of Achaia and seat of the proconsul in 27 B.C. (see Pausanias, *Descriptio Graeciae* 2.1–5). This would have been the Corinth that Paul visited, where he founded its Christian community. At that time it was in the course of reconstruction. Still preserved today is the road from the port, Lechaion, into the Corinthian agora in the center of the city, about which important civic and religious buildings (basilicas, temples, and stoas) had been erected.

See J. Murphy-O'Connor, *St. Paul's Corinth: Texts and Archaeology* (GNS 6; Wilmington, DE: Glazier, 1983); "Corinth," *ABD*, 1.1134–39; W. Elliger, *Paulus in Griechenland*, 200–51; O. Broneer, "Corinth: Center of St. Paul's Missionary Work in Greece," *BA* 14 (1951): 78–96; *Ancient Corinth: A Guide to the Excavations* (6th ed.; Athens: American School of Classical Studies at Athens, 1954); E. Will, *Korinthiaka: Recherches sur l'histoire et la civilisation de Corinthe des origines* (Paris: de Boccard, 1955); J. T. Dean, *Saint Paul and Corinth* (London: Lutterworth, 1947).

2. *There he found a Jew named Aquila, a native of Pontus.* The name *Akylas* is a grecized form of the Latin cognomen *Aquila* (meaning "eagle"); cf. Cicero, *Philippic Orations* 11.6.14. This name is borne by a Jewish tradesman, who becomes a collaborator of Paul. He will appear again in vv 18, 22 (MS 614), 26; Rom 16:3–5a; 1 Cor 16:19; cf. 2 Tim 4:19. He is described as a *Pontikos tō genei*, "a man of Pontus by race/nation," i.e., originally a diaspora Jew from Pontus on the Black Sea (see NOTE on 2:9). Cf. R. Schumacher, "Aquila und Priscilla," *TGl* 12 (1920): 86–99; F. X. Pölzl, *Die Mitarbeiter des Weltapostels Paulus* (Regensburg: Manz, 1911), 371–81; J. Murphy-O'Connor, "Prisca and Aquila," *BRev* 8/6 (1992): 40–51, 62.

who had recently arrived from Italy. Though the land of *Italia* denoted originally only a southwestern part of the peninsula, with the colonization of the Greeks it came to be the name for the whole peninsula. On *Italia*, see B. Andreae, "Italien," *Lexikon der alten Welt* (ed. C. Andresen et al.; Zurich/Stuttgart: Artemis, 1965), 1418–22.

his wife Priscilla. The name *Priskilla* (also vv 18, 26) is the diminutive of *Priska*, the form that Paul always writes (1 Cor 16:19; Rom 16:3; cf. 2 Tim 4:19). *Priska* is a grecized form of a fem. Latin adj. *prisca*, meaning "primitive, ancient." Aquila and Priscilla are people well known to Corinthian Christians, as is evident from Paul's greetings (1 Cor 16:19).

Claudius had ordered all Jews to leave Rome. I.e., Jews and Jewish Christians; see the COMMENT above and NOTE on Claudius in 11:28.

This is the first mention in Acts of *Rōmē* (= Latin *Roma*). It is the goal of Paul's testimony, where the story of Acts will end in chap. 28. Originally it was a shepherd's village, founded as an offshoot of Alba Longa, but in time its villagers surpassed the neighboring tribes because of its geographical position in central Italy, not far from the sea, and in command of a ford of the Tiber River. Legend has it that it was founded by descendants of Aeneas, Romulus and Remus (about 753 B.C.). By the sixth century shepherd villages had coalesced to form one town, which was at first ruled by kings. It became a republic in 510 and was governed by two magistrates called consuls, elected each year. By 275 Rome had gained control of the Italian peninsula and then waged war on Carthage, gradually acquiring provinces (Sicily in 241, Sardinia in 238, Spain in 206). Then it began to spread its control over the eastern Mediterranean world; in 146 Corinth was conquered. Class struggle and slave wars marred its subsequent history. Eventually Rome became a dictatorship set up by Marius (107–100), which lasted until Sulla marched against Rome at the head of Roman legions (88–79). In time Rome was governed by a triumvirate (Pompey, Crassus, and Julius Caesar), which broke up when Caesar was assassinated in 44 and C. Octavius (later called Gaius Julius Caesar Octavianus) and Mark Antony vied for power. The latter was defeated at Actium in 31, and Octavian became the sole master of the Roman world in 27 B.C., when the Roman Senate conferred on him the title *Augustus* (Greek *Sebastos*, "Venerable"). He then ruled as *princeps*. When Paul finally makes his way to Rome, Nero is the reigning Caesar.

See M. Cary, *A History of Rome down to the Reign of Constantine* (2d ed.;

London: Macmillan, 1960); T. Frank, *A History of Rome* (New York: Holt, 1923); T. Mommsen, *The History of Rome* (5 vols.; New York: Scribner's Sons, 1908); R. Syme, *The Roman Revolution* (Oxford: Clarendon, 1939); R. E. Brown and J. P. Meier, *Antioch and Rome: New Testament Cradles of Catholic Christianity* (New York: Paulist, 1983), 89–104; G. Edmundson, *The Church in Rome in the First Century* (Bampton Lectures; London: Longmans, Green, 1913); E. G. Hinson, *The Evangelization of the Roman Empire: Identity and Adaptability* (Macon: Mercer University Press, 1981); I. Levinskaya, "Rome," *The Book of Acts in Its Diaspora Setting* (BAFCS 5), 167–93.

Paul went to them. I.e., went to lodge with them.

3. *since he was trained in the same trade as they, made his lodging with them and worked together, for they were tent makers by trade.* The meaning of *skēnopoios* is debated. Literally, it seems to mean "tent maker," its traditional meaning, a weaver of tent fabric. Sometimes it is said to mean *skyotomos*, "leather worker"; so patristic interpreters, who considered tents to be made of leather. In Roman times, however, many were made of *cilicium*, "(goat's) haircloth," of Cilician provenience. Hence the debate about Paul's handicraft. See Acts 20:34; 1 Cor 4:12; 1 Thess 2:9, which suggest that Paul's work was technical and carried out in a metropolitan area. It shows that, though Paul came from a socially privileged class in ancient society, he did not hesitate to turn to a menial trade for his own sustenance.

See R. F. Hock, "Paul's Tentmaking and the Problem of His Social Class," *JBL* 97 (1978): 555–64; *The Social Context of Paul's Ministry: Tentmaking and Apostleship* (Philadelphia: Fortress, 1980); H. Szesnat, "What Did the *skēnopoios* Paul Produce?" *Neotestamentica* 27 (1993): 391–402; R. Silva, "'Eran, pues, de oficio, fabricantes de tiendas *[skēnopoioi]*' (Act. 18,3)," *EstBíb* 24 (1965): 123–34; P. Kost, "Der heilige Paulus als Handarbeiter," *TPQ* 77 (1924): 271–78, 432–38.

4. *Every sabbath Paul would lead discussions in the synagogue.* See NOTES on 6:9; 17:2. A marble stone found on the Lechaion road leading into the Corinthian agora bears a fragmentary inscription: *[Syn]agōgē Hebr[aiōn]*, "Synagogue of the Hebrews" (*CIJ* §718). It is probably the remains of a lintel once set over the entrance of a building. The style of its lettering is said to be later than Paul's time. It may have marked a building subsequently erected in the vicinity of the one in which Paul preached on this visit to Corinth. See B. Powell, "Greek Inscriptions from Corinth," *AJA* 7 (1903): 26–71, esp. 60–61; G. A. Deissmann, *LAE*, 14; J. Finegan, *Archeology of the New Testament*, 151–52.

tried to convince both Jews and Greeks. I.e., Jews in their synagogues and Greeks in their agora or other gathering places, unless one is to understand "Greeks" as Jewish sympathizers (see NOTE on 13:43).

5. *When Silas and Timothy came down from Macedonia.* Recall 17:14–16; see NOTES there. Cf. 2 Cor 1:19, which similarly refers to the association of Silas and Timothy with Paul in preaching to the Corinthians.

Paul continued to occupy himself with preaching the word. I.e., he continues to do in Corinth what he has already been doing, giving testimony to Jesus the Christ. See NOTE on 4:31.

bearing witness to Jews that Jesus was the Messiah. This explains the message of his synagogue discussions (v 4). His message would have been differently formulated in his attempt to convert pagan Greeks in the Corinthian agora. On Messiah, see NOTE on 2:36.

6. *When they would oppose him and insult him, he would shake his cloak at them in protest.* MS D begins v 6 thus: "But with much discussion and interpretation of the Scriptures, some Jews opposed (him)." P^{74} omits "and insult him." The verb *blasphēmein* means "speak ill of, calumniate," which would amount to a personal insult. Shaking one's cloak at opponents was considered a gesture protesting innocence and disavowing any agreement with them (cf. Neh 5:13). Compare Paul's action in Pisidian Antioch, 13:51.

"Your blood be on your own heads! Paul's words about blood and responsibility echo those of various OT passages: Josh 2:19; Judg 9:24; 2 Sam 1:16; 1 Kgs 2:32; Ezek 33:4. In echoing them, Paul divests himself of any responsibility for the refusal of fellow Jews to accept the testimony about Jesus the Messiah. Cf. Matt 27:25; Acts 5:28.

I am not to blame; from now on I shall go to the Gentiles." Lit., "(Being) clean, from now on I shall go to the Gentiles," i.e., in turning to Gentiles, Paul is not guilty of neglect of duty. Paul repeats what he has said to Jews in Pisidian Antioch (13:46c–d); compare 20:26. So Luke makes Paul formulate what he himself once wrote about being "the apostle of the Gentiles" (Rom 11:13). This is a further determination to carry out the role he was destined to play according to the call of the risen Christ (Acts 9:15).

7. *Paul withdrew from there.* To what the adv. *ekeithen,* "from there," refers is not clear. It could mean "from the synagogue of the Jews," to another teaching locale, but the rest of the verse implies that Paul moves to another residence in Corinth. If this is the correct understanding of the rest of the verse, one wonders why he moves from the house of Aquila and Priscilla and prefers the house of a Jewish sympathizer to that of Jewish Christians. Perhaps it was to give him better entrée among indigenous Corinthian Gentiles.

went to the house of a certain man named Titius Justus, who worshiped God. Titius Justus is otherwise unknown. He is described as *sebomenos ton theon,* which meant that he was sympathetic to Judaism; see NOTE on 13:43. E. J. Goodspeed ("Gaius Titius Justus," *JBL* 69 [1950]: 382–83) argued that Titius Justus was the same as Paul's host Gaius in Rom 16:23. Possibly, but that may be sheer speculation. MSS א, E, 36, 453, and 945 read rather *Titou,* "of Titus."

lived next door to the synagogue. Paul thus remains in the proximity of Corinthian Jews and their synagogue. See NOTE on 6:9.

8. *Crispus, the leader of the synagogue, put his faith in the Lord.* This is possibly the same *Krispos* who is mentioned in 1 Cor 1:14. By believing, Crispus joins many others said to have put their faith in the Lord (recall 5:14; 16:34). On *archisynagōgos,* see NOTE on 13:15.

together with all his household. Cf. 11:14; 16:15, 31–32 for the association in faith (and baptism) of a household with the head of it.

many were the Corinthians who also listened (to Paul), came to believe, and were baptized. I.e., Corinthian Gentiles. Cf. 1 Cor 1:14–16, where Crispus and Gaius are mentioned, and in an afterthought "the household of Stephanas," as baptized by Paul. On baptism, see NOTE on 2:38. So Luke ascribes some success to Paul's evangelization in Corinth.

9. *One night the Lord said to Paul in a vision, "Do not be afraid! Speak out and do not become silent,* 10. *because I am with you.* Thus, the risen Christ encourages his chosen instrument for the evangelization of Gentiles in the important city of Corinth. "Being with" echoes an OT phrase that describes Yahweh assisting or doing battle on behalf of his people (Gen 21:22; 26:3; 31:3, 5; Exod 3:12; Josh 1:5). Cf. Josh 1:9; Isa 41:10; Jer 1:8; Matt 28:20.

No one will attack you or harm you, for there are many of my people in this city." Cf. Jer 1:19. "Many of my people" probably refers to the Gentile Christians to be. On their behalf Paul prolongs his sojourn in Corinth, as the following verse makes clear.

11. *Paul settled there for a year and six months.* As will become evident from vv 12–17, this would mean roughly from the beginning of A.D. 51 to mid-52. MS D reads "settled in Corinth."

teaching the word of God among them. I.e., not only did Paul function as a missionary but also as an inner-church teacher passing on the heaven-sent message about Jesus the Messiah and Savior of humanity. See NOTE on 4:31.

12. *While Gallio was proconsul of Achaia.* I.e., from the late spring to the late autumn of A.D. 52. The name of the proconsul was actually Lucius Annaeus Novatus. He was the son of M. Annaeus Seneca, a Roman *eques* and *rhetor,* and the older brother of the philosopher Seneca, who was the tutor of emperor Nero. Lucius Junius Gallio was the name that Seneca's older brother assumed, when he was adopted by a wealthy senator friend and introduced into political life. Pliny the Elder tells about his consulship (*Naturalis Historia* 31.62), and Dio Cassius (*Roman History* 61.20.1) about his connections with the imperial court of Rome. His brother Seneca dedicated some of his writings to him, and after his brother came into political disfavor in the unsuccessful Pisonian Conspiracy, he too was compelled to commit suicide. On his relation to the emperor Claudius and a Delphi inscription that mentions him in Achaia, see the COMMENT above. Gallio is correctly called *anthypatos,* the Greek equivalent of Latin *proconsul;* see NOTE on 13:7.

Achaia was the most important part of Greece in Paul's day. Situated north of the Peloponnesus, it was the center of political life especially from 280 to 146 B.C. In the latter year it became part of the Roman province of Greece created after the conquest of the Aegean Confederacy and the fall of Corinth to L. Mummius (see Pausanias, *Descriptio Graeciae* 7.16.7–10). Augustus made it an independent senatorial province in 27 B.C., with Neocorinth as the governor's seat. The province included Attica, Boeotia, Thessaly, and the Peloponnesus; perhaps also Epirus. From A.D. 15 to 44 it was administered along with Macedonia as one imperial province. Later it became an independent province again, and Nero accorded it freedom in A.D. 67, which status it retained until A.D. 73 under emperor Vespasian. This is the province that Paul mentions in 1 Thess 1:7, 8; 1 Cor 16:15; 2 Cor 1:1; 9:2; 11:10; Rom 15:26. See B. Reicke, *EDNT*, 1.185–86.

the Jews rose up in a body against Paul and brought him to court. Lit., "to the step, platform *(bēma)*," i.e., the tribunal from which a magistrate addresses an assembly. The *bēma* was located in the center of the Corinthian agora and was flanked by rows of shops. Adornment of the *bēma* or Latin *rostra* (pl.), overlooking the forum, is still in evidence today. See Broneer, *BA* 14 (1951): 91–92. Again Luke uses the adv. *homothymadon* (see NOTE in 1:14); here it does not express the harmony and unanimity of Christians, but a concerted uprising of Jews in Corinth against Paul.

These Jews were at least residents in Corinth, but not certainly Corinthian citizens; if they were indeed citizens, they might have had a better basis to be heard by Gallio. The privileges accorded Jews in the Roman empire by Julius Caesar are listed by Josephus, *Ant.* 14.10.2–8 §§190–216; many of them were continued after the death of Caesar (cf. *Ant.* 19.5.2–3 §§278–91). Some of them applied to Jews resident outside of Judea; thus, for example, Claudius's edict cited by Josephus, *Ant.* 19.5.3 §290: "Therefore it is right that Jews throughout the whole world that is under our domination should observe their ancestral customs without hindrance. I hereby order them too to avail themselves reasonably of this benefaction and not set at nought beliefs about gods held by other peoples, but to keep their own laws." In general, such Roman decisions reckoned with the legitimacy of the Jewish religion, the authority of its high priests, freedom from taxation, and protection from interference by Hellenistic authorities in religious and social customs; but they gave no guarantee that Roman authority would adjudicate intramural disputes.

See H. R. Moehring, "The *Acta pro Judaeis* in the *Antiquities* of Flavius Josephus," *Christianity, Judaism, and Other Greco-Roman Cults I–IV: Studies for Morton Smith at Sixty* (ed. J. Neusner; Leiden: Brill, 1975), 3.124–58; M. Pucci ben Zeev, "Did the Jews Enjoy a Privileged Position in the Roman World?" *REJ* 154 (1995): 23–42; T. Rajak, "Jewish Rights in the Greek Cities under Roman Rule: A New Approach," *Approaches to Ancient Judaism V* (Brown Judaic Studies 32; ed. W. S. Green; Atlanta: Scholars, 1985), 19–35; T. Rajak, "Was There a Roman Charter for the Jews?" *JRS* 74 (1984): 107–23.

13. *charging, "This fellow is influencing people to worship God in ways that are against the law."* The charge echoes that brought against Stephen (6:13), but on a different topic and in a different setting; cf. 21:28; 25:8. Paul is charged with violation of Roman law, because he is said to be influencing, not only Jews, but *tous anthrōpous*, "people," i.e., even Greeks or Romans in this *colonia civium romanorum*, "colony of Roman citizens." Recall 16:20–21; cf. 17:7. In other words, these Jews in Corinth were hoping to obtain the aid of the Roman proconsul against a fellow Jew who was interfering with their customary beliefs and status. Judaism was *religio licita* in the eyes of Roman authorities, and for fear that that status might be jeopardized, the Jews in Corinth wanted Gallio to determine that what Paul stood for was something new and had nothing to do with orthodox

or official Judaism. If the charge mentioned here is indeed historical, it is not clear what Roman law would have been involved.

14. *As Paul was about to speak up.* Lit., "was about to open his mouth," in his defense or *apologia.*

Gallio said to the Jews, "If it were a crime or some serious evil trick. Luke phrases Gallio's comment as a contrary-to-fact condition. Gallio is thus depicted as failing to see the charges brought against Paul as a violation of Roman law and considers it an intramural dispute among Jews of differing views. In effect, as a Roman authority, he fails to see a distinction between Judaism and Christianity. Gallio's reaction is the first official recognition in Acts by a Roman governor that Christianity is not a crime (*adikēma,* "wrongful deed, injurious act") or some serious evil trick (*rhadiourgēma,* "wicked act easily done").

I would tolerate the complaint of you Jews. Lit., "I would put up with your complaint, O Jews." The verb *anechesthai* is used in the technical, legal sense of having to accept a complaint for further consideration (*TDNT,* 1.359 n. 2).

15. *since this is a dispute about words and titles and your own law, you must see to it yourselves.* The "words" may refer to the charge about *sebesthai ton theon,* "to worship God." The "titles" may refer to the use of "Messiah/Christ" for Jesus. "Your own law" is a striking admission for a Roman proconsul; it reflects the edict of Claudius cited above in the NOTE on v 12. Gallio is, in effect, admitting that he sees no distinction between Jews who live according to a certain law, which the Christian reader of Acts would recognize as the Mosaic law, and Christians. It reflects a period prior to the Neronian persecution of Christians in A.D. 64. Provincial governors were apparently sensitive to attempts of minority groups to have Roman authorities decide disputes for them. Cf. 23:29; 25:18–19.

I refuse to judge such matters." Lit., "I do not wish to be a judge of these matters." This has been recognized as the precise reply of a Roman magistrate who refuses judgment (*arbitrium iudicantis*) in a legal case, which is *cognitio extra ordinem* (see Sherwin-White, *Roman Society,* 102). Mosaic legislation was a religious law not recognized as such by Greeks or Romans; so the proconsul, being a civil political authority, refuses to adjudicate the matter. Because no specific wrong that violates Roman law is cited, Gallio refuses to take cognizance of the charge that is made.

16. *he dismissed the case from court.* Lit., "he expelled them from the tribunal" (*bēma*), i.e., the bar before which the Jews of Corinth have appeared to plead their case against Paul. He probably gave orders that the lictors remove them.

17. *they all pounced on Sosthenes, the leader of the synagogue.* According to the Alexandrian text, the *pantes,* "all," would refer to the Jews of v 14; MSS 36 and 453 add *hoi Ioudaioi,* "all the Jews," but the WT (MSS D, E, Ψ, 33, 1739) and the *Koinē* text-tradition add *hoi Hellēnes,* "all the Greeks," which is indeed strange and may have evoked Gallio's intervention. *Sōsthenēs* may be the same as the one named in 1 Cor 1:1; if so, he was subsequently converted to Christianity. Luke gives no explanation of why Sosthenes is so treated; if Paul had been the victim, it would be an intelligible reaction to Gallio's dismissal of the case. Sosthenes may have been the leader of the Jewish delegation that has failed

to get its way with Gallio, and the failure is why the Jews have pounced on him.

beat him in full view of the court. But none of this was of concern to Gallio. I.e., the proconsul ignores the actions of the Jews seeking to wreak revenge on a prominent Corinthian, because he regards it as an inner-Jewish strife.

BIBLIOGRAPHY (18:1–17)

Benko, S., "The Edict of Claudius of A.D. 49 and the Instigator Chrestus," *TZ* 25 (1969): 406–18.

Braun, F., "Paulus als Seelsorger zu Korinth," *KZ* 33 (1909): 99–114, 203–21.

Buzy, D., "Un cas de syllepse historique (*Act.* xviii, 5)," *RB* 45 (1936): 66–71.

Dockx, S., "Silas a-t-il été le compagnon de voyage de Paul d'Antioche à Corinthe?" *NRT* 104 (1982): 749–53.

Goguel, M., "La vision de Paul à Corinthe et sa comparution devant Gallion: Une conjecture sur la place originale d'*Actes* 18,9–11," *RHPR* 12 (1932): 321–33.

Gutbrod, W., "Zur Predigt des Paulus in Korinth: Nach Apostelgeschichte 18," *EvT* 3 (1936): 379–84.

Hoerber, R. O., "The Decree of Claudius in Acts 18:2," *CTM* 31 (1960): 690–94.

———, "Evangelism in Acts," *ConcJ* 7 (1981): 89–90.

Juster, J., *Les Juifs dans l'empire romain* (2 vols.; Paris: Geuthner, 1914; repr. New York: B. Franklin, 1965).

Lüdemann, G., "Das Judenedikt des Claudius (Apg 18,2)," *Der Treue Gottes trauen: Beiträge zum Werk des Lukas: Für Gerhard Schneider* (ed. C. Bussmann and W. Radl; Freiburg im B.: Herder, 1991), 289–98.

McDonald, W. A., "Archaeology and St. Paul's Journeys in Greek Lands: Part III—Corinth," *BA* 5 (1942): 36–48.

Pherigo, L. P., "Paul and the Corinthian Church," *JBL* 68 (1949): 341–50.

Pujol, A., "'Egressus ab Athenis venit Corinthum' (Act. 18.1)," *VD* 12 (1932): 273–80, 305–8.

Schmidt, P., "Der Aufruhr in Korinth," *Wahrheitszeuge* 5 (1929): 1–5.

Scramuzza, V. M., *The Emperor Claudius* (HHS 44; Cambridge: Harvard University Press, 1940).

Slingerland, D., "Acts 18:1–17 and Luedemann's Pauline Chronology," *JBL* 109 (1990): 686–90.

———, "Suetonius *Claudius* 25.4, Acts 18, and Paulus Orosius' *Historiarum adversum paganos libri VII:* Dating the Claudian Expulsion(s) of Roman Jews," *JQR* 83 (1992–93): 127–44.

———, "Suetonius *Claudius* 25.4 and the Account in Cassius Dio," *JQR* 79 (1988–89): 305–22.

White, N. J. D., "The Visits of St. Paul to Corinth," *Hermathena* 12 (1903): 79–89.

Winter, B. W., "The Achaean Federal Imperial Cult II: The Corinthian Church," *TynBull* 46 (1995): 169–78.

Works on the Delphi Inscription

Bourguet, E., *De rebus delphicis imperatoriae aetatis capita duo* (Montpellier: C. Coulet et Fils, 1905).

Brassac, A., "Une inscription de Delphes et la chronologie de saint Paul," *RB* 10 (1913): 36–53, 207–17.

Cantarelli, L., "Gallione proconsule di Acaia e S. Paolo," *ANL, Rendiconti* (Classe di scienze morali, storiche e filologiche 5/32; Rome: Accademia Nazionale dei Lincei, 1923), 157–75.

Cousin G. and G. Deschamps, "Emplacement et ruines de la ville de KYC en Carie," *BCH* 11 (1887): 305–11, esp. 306–8.

Deissmann, A., *Paul: A Study in Social and Religious History* (2d ed.; New York: Doran, 1926), 272.

Fitzmyer, J. A., *According to Paul,* 43–46.

Groag, E., *Die römischen Reichsbeamten von Achaia bis auf Diokletian* (Akademie der Wissenschaften in Wien, Schriften der Balkankommission, Antiquarische Abteilung 9; Vienna/Leipzig: Hölder-Pichle-Tempsky, 1939; repr. Nendeln, Liechtenstein: Kraus, 1976), col. 3 §123.

Haacker, K., "Die Gallio-Episode und die paulinische Chronologie," *BZ* 16 (1972): 252–55.

Hennequin, L. "Delphes (Inscription de)," *DBSup,* 2.355–73 (with older bibliography).

Lake, K., "The Proconsulship of Gallio," *Beginnings,* 5.460–64.

Larfeld, W., "Die delphische Gallioinschrift und die paulinische Chronologie," *NKZ* 34 (1923): 644.

Murphy-O'Connor, J., "Paul and Gallio," *JBL* 112 (1993): 315–17.

———, *St. Paul's Corinth: Texts and Archaeology* (GNS 6; Wilmington, DE: Glazier, 1983), 141–52, 173–76.

Oliver, J. H., "The Epistle of Claudius Which Mentions the Proconsul Junius Gallio," *Hesperia* 40 (1970): 239–40.

Plassart, A. "L'Inscription de Delphes mentionnant le proconsul Gallion (Act 18,12–17)," *REG* 80 (1967): 372–78.

———, *Les inscriptions du temple du iv siècle* (Ecole Française d'Athènes, Fouilles de Delphes III/4; Paris: Boccard, 1970): 26–32 (§286).

Rees, W., "Gallio the Proconsul of Achaia (Acts 18:12–17)," *Scripture* 4 (1949–51): 11–20.

Schlatter, T., "Gallio und Paulus in Korinth," *NKZ* 36 (1925): 500–513.

Schwank, B., "Der sogenannte Brief an Gallio und die Datierung des 1 Thess," *BZ* 15 (1971): 265–66.

Slingerland, D., "Acts 18:1–18, the Gallio Inscription, and Absolute Pauline Chronology," *JBL* 110 (1991): 439–49.

Wohlenberg, G., "Eine Klaudiusinschrift von Delphi in ihrer Bedeutung für die paulinische Chronologie," *NKZ* 23 (1912): 380–96.

g) Paul Returns to Antioch (18:18–22)

18 Paul stayed on in Corinth for a considerable time; eventually he took leave of
the brothers and sailed for Syria in the company of Priscilla and Aquila. At
Cenchreae he had his hair cut off because he had made a vow. 19 They landed at
Ephesus, where he left Priscilla and Aquila; he himself entered the synagogue
and held discussions with the Jews. 20 Although they asked him to stay longer, he
declined. 21 As he said goodbye, he promised, "God willing, I shall come back to
you again." Then he set sail from Ephesus. 22 On landing at Caesarea, he went
up and paid his respects to the church; then he went down to Antioch.

WT: 18 He made a vow at Cenchreae and had his hair cut off. 19 at Ephesus the following sabbath,
and Paul entered the synagogue [omits "he left them there"]. 21 He bade them goodbye, saying, "It is
quite necessary that I spend the coming feast in Jerusalem; God willing . . ." Then he left Aquila in
Ephesus; but he himself set sail. 22 He came to Caesarea and went up.

COMMENT

With this episode Luke concludes the story of Paul's second missionary journey, which began at 15:40, probably in the year A.D. 50. Luke now tells how Paul remains for a time in Corinth, but then leaves via its port of Cenchreae, being accompanied by Aquila and Priscilla, whom he later leaves at Ephesus (18:19), as he continues his way to Caesarea Maritima. From there he goes up to Jerusalem to pay his respects to the church of that city (18:22b) and then makes his way north to Syrian Antioch (18:22c), which will be his base (18:23a) from the winter of A.D. 52 until the spring of A.D. 54, when he will decide to set out on Mission III.

We are dealing in this episode with a simple narrative, which is based on Luke's Pauline source. The controversial detail in this episode is the mention of Paul having his hair cut in fulfillment of a vow that he had made. It is one of the details that create the special Lucan portrait of Paul and affects the "Paulinism" of Acts (see Introduction §173). That detail may well come from Luke's compositional pen.

Once again we see in this episode Paul carefully planning his missionary endeavor. He not only continues his work among the Corinthians after having been haled into court, but seeks to bring this phase of his activity to an end, as he leaves Corinth to return to Antioch in Syria. He makes a vow in Corinth, and though we are not told what relevance that has to his missionary work, he fulfills part of the obligation entailed by it by having his hair cut off in Cenchreae (18:18). He is dutiful in his obligation to God in that, having made the vow, he carries through with it. His journey back to Antioch includes also a visit to the church in Jerusalem, a visit that suits his character as a Jewish Christian.

NOTES

18. *Paul stayed on in Corinth for a considerable time.* Just how long that would have been is not stated, and there is no way of determining it.

eventually he took leave of the brothers and sailed for Syria in the company of Priscilla and Aquila. Corinthian Christians are again called *adelphoi* (see NOTE on 1:15). The destination of Paul's return journey is Antioch in Syria, whence he started off on Mission II with Silas (15:40). We are not told whether Silas and Timothy accompany Paul on this return, but Aquila and Priscilla, with whom he has lodged and worked in Corinth (18:2–3), do so. On Syria, see NOTE on 15:23. Here it must mean the Roman province of Syria, which would include Jerusalem (see v 22) as well as Antioch, which more properly lay in the area of ancient Syria.

At Cenchreae he had his hair cut off because he had made a vow. Lit., "having shorn his head in Cenchreae, for he had a vow." *Kenchreiai* was the port on the eastern side of the isthmus of Corinth; see NOTE on 18:1; also *Romans,* 730–31. Luke does not further explain the *euchē*, "vow," but it is usually understood to be the Nazirite vow that Jews sometimes made. *Nāzîr* means "someone vowed," i.e., consecrated to God by a vow. Originally, it denoted a person dedicated to the service of Yahweh for a certain period of time (Num 6:2; Judg 13:5–7). The details required of the person so vowing are set forth in Num 6:2–21, one of which was the shaving of the head (Num 6:9, 18; cf. Acts 21:24; Philo, *De Ebrietate* 1.2; Str-B, 2.80–89). The cutting of the hair prior to a voyage is, however, strange. Perhaps all that one is to gather from this notice is that the Lucan Paul somehow carries out requirements of a Jewish vow; he is again a model Jew in his conduct. See Weiser, *Apg.*, 498.

19. *They landed at Ephesus, where he left Priscilla and Aquila.* They will still be located at Ephesus when the next chronological reference is made to them. Cf. 1 Cor 16:19; Rom 16:3.

Ephesos was the seat of the governor of the Roman province of Asia; see NOTES on 2:9; 6:9. In Paul's day it was an Aegean seaport near the mouth of the Cayster River. The river was then navigable up to the city, which lay about 5 km to the east, but which during the course of the centuries since then has silted up, so that it no longer seems to be a seaport town. It was a place where Jews had been granted Ephesian citizenship (Josephus, *Ant.* 12.3.2 §§125–26). For many Greek inscriptions from Ephesus at this period, see I. Levinskaya, "Asia Minor," *The Book of Acts in Its Diaspora Setting* (BAFCS 5), 137–52, esp. 143–48. Because Ephesus was the chief market for Asia Minor, it was a city of enormous wealth. It is now mentioned for the first time in Acts and will appear again in 18:21, 24,27; 19:1, 17, 26; 20:16, 17. It becomes the center of Paul's evangelizing activity on Mission III.

See R. Tonneau, "Ephèse au temps de Saint Paul," *RB* 38 (1929): 5–34; F. V. Filson, "Ephesus and the New Testament," *BA* 8 (1945): 73–80; J. Keil, *Ephesos: Ein Führer durch die Ruinenstätte und ihre Geschichte* (Vienna: A. Hölder, 1957); F. Miltner, *Ephesos, Stadt der Artemis und des Johannes* (Österreichisches archäologisches Institut; Vienna: Deuticke, 1964); E. Lessing and W. Oberleitner, *Ephesos: Weltstadt der Antike* (Vienna: Ueberreuter, 1978); J. T. Wood, *Discoveries at Ephesus: Including the Site and Remains of the Temple of Diana* (Hildesheim/New York: Olms, 1975); H. Koester (ed.), *Ephesos Metropolis of Asia: An Interdisciplinary Approach to Its Archaeology, Religion, and Culture* (HTS 41; Valley Forge: Trinity Press International, 1995), 1–25, 119–40; R. Oster, "Ephesus as a Religious Center under the Principate: I. Paganism before Constantine," ANRW II/18.3 (1990): 1661–728, esp. 1699–726; W. Thiessen, *Christen in Ephesus: Die historische und theologische Situation in vorpaulinischer und paulinischer Zeit und zur Zeit der Apostelgeschichte und der Pastoralbriefe* (Texte und Arbeiten zum neutestamentlichen Zeitalter 12; Tübingen/Basel: Francke, 1995).

he himself entered the synagogue and held discussions with the Jews. Again Luke makes Paul pursue a consistent policy of evangelizing the Jewish people of the town first. Recall 17:2–3 (see NOTE there) and what Paul said in v 6 above.

20. *Although they asked him to stay longer, he declined.* MSS D, E, and the *Koinē* text-tradition add to the subordinate clause *par' autois*, "among them."

21. *As he said goodbye, he promised.* The WT begins, "He bade them goodbye, saying, 'It is quite necessary that I spend the coming feast in Jerusalem.'" So read MSS D, Ψ, and the *Koinē* text-tradition, but the sentence is omitted in MSS P^{74}, ℵ, A, B, E, 33, 36, 945, 1739, and 1891. J. M. Ross ("The Extra Words in Acts 18:21," *NovT* 34 [1992]: 247–49) argues that the longer form is the more original, but most modern critical-text editors do not agree.

"God willing, I shall come back to you again." Lucan foreshadowing is at work; Paul fulfills the promise in 19:1. Phrases like *tou theou thelontos*, "Deo volente," were often used in antiquity (in the NT: 1 Cor 4:19; 16:7; Heb 6:3; Jas 4:15; extrabiblically: Josephus, *Ant.* 2.15.5 §333; 2.16.5 §347; 7.14.9 §373; Plato, *Alcibiades* 1.31 §135D).

he set sail from Ephesus. Luke again uses the technical nautical term *anagein*; see NOTE on 13:13.

22. *On landing at Caesarea.* I.e., Caesarea Maritima; see NOTE on 8:40.

he went up and paid his respects to the church. I.e., went up to the church of Jerusalem. Although Jerusalem is not mentioned, it is implied in the ptc. *anabas*, "having gone up." See NOTE on 8:5; 11:2. This is another visit of Paul to Jerusalem after his conversion; see Introduction §156. The added clause in the WT of v 21 makes Paul go to Jerusalem to celebrate a feast there.

he went down to Antioch. I.e., to Antioch on the Orontes in Syria, whence he started out on Mission II; see 15:40.

BIBLIOGRAPHY (18:18–22)

Barnikol, E., "Apostelgeschichte 18:18," *TJb* 1 (1933): 96.
Gray, G. B., "The Nazirite," *JTS* 1 (1899–1900): 201–11.
Jastrow, M., "The 'Nazir' Legislation," *JBL* 33 (1914): 266–85.

3. Paul's Third Missionary Journey (18:23–20:38)

a) Apollos in Ephesus and Achaia (18:23–28)

23 After spending some time there, he set out again and traveled systematically
through the Galatian territory and Phrygia, strengthening all the disciples.
24 Meanwhile there landed at Ephesus a Jew named Apollos, a native of Alexandria, an eloquent speaker, learned in the Scriptures. 25 He had been instructed in
the Way of the Lord and, being ardent in spirit, he spoke and taught accurately
enough about Jesus, even though he knew only the baptism of John. 26 He too
began to speak out boldly in the synagogue there, but when Priscilla and Aquila
heard him, they took him home and explained to him the Way [of God] more
accurately. 27 Because he wanted to go on to Achaia, the brothers encouraged
him by writing to the disciples there to welcome him. On his arrival, he contributed much to those who through grace had become believers, 28 for he vigorously
refuted the Jews in public, demonstrating from the Scriptures that Jesus was the
Messiah.

WT: 23 [omits "all"]. 24 Apollonius, an Alexandrian. 25 who had been instructed in his homeland in
the word of the Lord. 26 but when Aquila heard him, he took him home and explained to him the
Way more accurately. 27 Now there were some Corinthians sojourning at Ephesus who listened to
him, and they urged him to go with them to their homeland. Since he agreed, the Ephesians wrote
to the disciples in Corinth that they might welcome the man. He traveled to Achaia and contributed
much to the churches. 28 debating and demonstrating.

COMMENT

Luke now begins the story of the journeys of Pauline Mission III (18:23–20:38), during the years A.D. 54–58. We are not told who, if anyone, accompanies Paul on this mission; the Lucan account speaks only of Paul in the third singular. Having first offered support and encouragement to the Christian disciples in Galatian territory and Phrygia, Paul makes his way to Ephesus, which becomes his base during Mission III. Early during this time in Ephesus Paul writes his letter to the Galatians (A.D. 54), a letter to the Corinthians that is now lost (see 1 Cor 5:9), and toward the end of his stay 1 Corinthians (A.D. 56 or early 57, before Pentecost [see 1 Cor 16:8]), and possibly also the letter(s) to the Philippians (A.D. 56 or 57).

Before Paul gets to Ephesus, however, a noteworthy convert to Christianity arrives there, a Jewish orator named Apollos, a man skilled in the interpretation of Scripture. Although he was accurate in his teaching about Jesus, he "knew only the baptism of John" (18:25). Thus, Priscilla and Aquila see to his further instruction in the Way of God. Because he desires to go on to Achaia, Christians of Ephesus write a letter of recommendation for him to Christians of Achaia. When he arrives there, Apollos strengthens the Corinthian Christians and argues with Jews, seeking to show that Jesus of Nazareth was indeed the Messiah.

This episode is another Lucan narrative, derived from the Pauline source, in which attention is concentrated on Apollos (called "Apollonius" in the WT). He is the same as the Apollos known from 1 Cor 1:12; 3:4–6, 22; 4:6; 16:12. There Paul regards him as a brother and a coworker, but says little more about him. This Lucan episode introduces him and explains his background. Luke does not tell us how this Alexandrian Jew has come to a form of Christian faith, but he describes the anomaly of a learned orator who speaks accurately about Jesus yet has never heard of Christian baptism: "he knew only the baptism of John" (18:25). An analogous situation will be encountered in the next episode. In both instances Luke is concerned to incorporate such "Johannine Christians" into the mainstream Christian fold. In this case, it is accomplished by Paul's collaborators, Priscilla and Aquila (in the WT by Aquila alone). When Christians of Ephesus realize the contribution that Apollos can make to the spread of the Christian message, they gladly send him on with a letter of recommendation to Achaia. So the deficiency of the "Johannine Christian" is remedied by instruction and teaching, whereas in chap. 19 it will be remedied by baptism.

Anomalies in the episode give rise to questions about the historicity of Luke's account. In 1 Cor 16:12, Paul intimates that he and Apollos worked together in Ephesus, but in the Lucan story they never meet in Ephesus. 1 Cor 3:4–9 also suggests that Apollos arrived in Corinth after Paul and then came to Ephesus, where he is when 1 Corinthians is being written; but Luke's account brings Apollos to Ephesus first and then to Achaia. How could Apollos, who knows about Jesus, have known only "the baptism of John" some twenty years after the beginning of the Christian movement? Such anomalies raise questions about both the historicity and the accuracy of the source material of the Lucan account of this incident. If the episode is indeed essentially historical, its information must come from Luke's Pauline source.

Paul is not the only one to preach Jesus of Nazareth as the Messiah in Corinth. From his own first letter to the Corinthians we learn about another famous preacher there, Apollos, about whom Luke also tells us in this brief episode. Coming from a town noted for its rhetorical studies and practice, Alexandria in Egypt, Apollos is thus "an eloquent speaker." But he is also one "learned in the Scriptures" (18:34). We are surprised at his knowing "only the baptism of John," but that deficiency is remedied by the work of Aquila and Priscilla so that he continues on to Corinth, where he "demonstrates from the Scriptures that Jesus was the Messiah" (18:28). The Lucan story recounts how God provides eloquent witnesses to bring the testimony about his Son to renowned centers in the contemporary Greek world.

NOTES

23. *After spending some time there.* I.e., in Antioch on the Orontes in Syria (see 18:22), whither Paul had gone at the end of Mission II.

he set out again. I.e., on Mission III, the story of which will run until 20:38.

traveled systematically through the Galatian territory and Phrygia. I.e., through southern and northern Galatia, already evangelized on Mission II (see 16:6 and NOTE). Cf. Gal 4:13, which implies a second visit of Paul to Galatia.

strengthening all the disciples. Recall the similar support given to Christians of Asia Minor mentioned in 14:22. Again Lucan hyperbole appears in "all" (see NOTE on 2:44).

24. *Meanwhile there landed at Ephesus a Jew named Apollos. Apollōs* is a shortened form of the name *Apollōnios,* which is used in MS D. MSS ℵ*, 36, 307, 431, 453, 610, and 1175 name him rather *Apellēs,* which G. D. Kilpatrick maintains might well be "original" in Acts ("Apollos—Apelles," *JBL* 89 [1970]: 77). He was a diaspora Jew, who bore the name of the Greek god Apollo, but had already become a follower of Jesus. See H. Offermann, "Apollos, Apelles, Apollonios," *LCR* 39 (1919): 145–50.

a native of Alexandria. Lit., "an Alexandrian by birth," a phrase also met in 4:36; 18:2. *Alexandreia* was a prominent city on the Mediterranean Sea at the western edge of the Nile delta, founded by Alexander the Great after his conquest of Egypt. Under his successors, the Ptolemies, it became the capital of Egypt, when the seat of government was transferred from Memphis. It grew rapidly and became a center of learning, commerce, and industry. Opposite it was the island of Pharos, which was linked to Alexandria by a causeway 1.25 km long; it provided the city with a double harbor. In the city were famous buildings: to the east, the Ptolemaic palace, a theater, the Caesareum, and the renowned library and museum; to the west, a temple of Serapis. Under Roman occupation it was the seat of the governor of the province of Egypt. In the first century A.D. it was, along with Rome, Syrian Antioch, and Corinth, one of the four most important cities in the Mediterranean world.

an eloquent speaker. Or "a cultured man." The meaning of the adj. *logios* is debated, either "eloquent" (as understood in ancient versions [e.g., Vg, *vir eloquens*]) or "learned, cultured." See BAGD, 476.

learned in the Scriptures. Lit., "being powerful/capable in the writings," i.e., well-versed in OT writings. On *graphē,* "Scripture," see NOTE on 1:16.

25. *He had been instructed in the Way of the Lord.* MS D reads, "who had been instructed in his homeland in the word of the Lord." "The Way of the Lord" reflects an OT phrase (Isa 40:3; Jer 5:4) but is meant as a designation for Christianity, as the rest of the verse makes clear. "The word of the Lord" in the WT is simply a harmonization of the verse with 8:25; 12:24; 13:44, 48 (in some MSS). From the phrase, "the way of the Lord," was developed the absolute designation for Christianity, "the Way" (see NOTE on 9:2).

being ardent in spirit. I.e., burning with zeal. The sense of the phrase is debated. "Fervent in spirit," i.e., of fiery temperament, is the meaning preferred by

Loisy, Zahn, Bruce, and Marshall. "Boiling with the Spirit," i.e., with God's Spirit, is preferred by Dibelius, Käsemann, Polhill, and Weiser. Cf. Rom 12:11, where the phrase is used in Christian exhortation. In either case, it is hard to say whether this description is meant of Apollos as a Jew or a Christian, probably the latter.

he spoke and taught accurately enough about Jesus. Lit., "the (things) concerning Jesus." This must mean that Apollos had been rightly informed about the words and deeds of the earthly Jesus, but how he would have come to know about him is not mentioned.

even though he knew only the baptism of John. The "baptism of John" is known from 1:22; 10:37 and will be met again in 19:3. In these instances it refers to the ritual washing administered by John the Baptist (Luke 3:3: "a baptism of repentance for the forgiveness of sins"). It was undoubtedly carried abroad by disciples of John (Mark 2:18; 6:29; Luke 11:1). This would make of Apollos a "Johannine" Christian at most, to use Conzelmann's term, or an adept of "an immature form of Christianity" (Käsemann, "Disciples of John"). Indeed, Käsemann insists that the last two descriptions are Luke's additions to the account he inherited, by which he meant to demote Apollos beneath Paul. Nothing is said about Apollos being baptized again, in contrast to the "disciples" in Acts 19.

26. *He too began to speak out boldly in the synagogue there.* I.e., in Ephesus. As a Jew, Apollos goes on the sabbath to the gathering of his own people, but even there he speaks out about Jesus. On synagogue, see NOTE on 6:9; also NOTES on 4:13; 9:27.

when Priscilla and Aquila heard him. See 18:2–3, 19. These coworkers of Paul are presumed to be in the synagogue too and so undertake the fuller instruction of this eloquent preacher. Through their instruction Apollos becomes a mature Christian.

they took him home and explained to him the Way [of God] more accurately. "The way of God" is a literary variant of "the way of the Lord" (v 25), which some MSS (323, 945, 1739, 1891) read even here. It is used as a way of describing Christianity. The more accurate explanation of the Way would have included its relation to baptism in the Spirit (Christian baptism) and the role it was playing in the implementation of the divine plan of salvation. Cf. CD 20:18.

27. *Because he wanted to go on to Achaia.* See NOTE on 18:12. MSS P^{38} and D begin the verse thus: "Now there were some Corinthians sojourning at Ephesus who listened to him, and they urged him to go with them to their homeland. Since he agreed with them, the Ephesians wrote to disciples in Corinth that they might welcome the man. He traveled to Achaia and contributed much to the churches." See 1 Cor 1:12; 3:4–6, 22; 4:6, where Apollos's activity in Corinth is alluded to; in 1 Cor 16:12, Paul says that he has been urging Apollos to return to Corinth.

the brothers encouraged him by writing to the disciples there to welcome him. For an example of a letter of recommendation in the NT, see Rom 16:1–23; cf. 2 Cor 3:1–3. "Brothers" suggests that there were already Christians in Ephesus prior to Paul's arrival. That they are the same as the "disciples" to be mentioned in 19:1 is likely, but not certain. In any case, Christians of Ephesus communicate with Christians of Corinth on Apollos's behalf. See NOTES on 1:15; 6:1.

On his arrival, he contributed much to those who through grace had become believers. Luke rightly ascribes to divine grace the call to Christian faith, but also acknowledges the way a human being like Apollos could help Christians gifted with such grace. Conzelmann (*Acts,* 158) takes "through grace" as modifying Apollos's activity; similarly Schneider (*Apg.,* 2.261); Weiser (*Apg.,* 511), and Pesch (*Apg.,* 2.162). Either is possible. The "believers" were Christians of Corinth, among whom were probably those mentioned in 18:8.

28. *he vigorously refuted the Jews in public, demonstrating from the Scriptures that Jesus was the Messiah.* What Paul proclaimed (18:5; cf. 9:22), that Apollos also proclaims, and does so, arguing from the OT Scriptures. Luke does not tell us what passages in the OT Apollos would have used. One has to understand this statement of the typically Lucan global interpretation of the OT in a christological sense as in 3:18; 7:52; 8:31; 10:43; 13:27; 17:2. As was the Lucan Paul's custom, Apollos too begins his evangelization among Jews. That "Jesus was the Messiah" is a Lucan refrain: see 9:22; 17:3, 7. On *graphai* as "Scriptures," see NOTE on 1:16.

BIBLIOGRAPHY (18:23–28)

Barton, G. A., "Some Influences of Apollos in the New Testament, I," *JBL* 43 (1924): 207–23.

Becker, J., *Paul: Apostle to the Gentiles* (Louisville: Westminster/John Knox, 1993), 153.

Behan, W. P., "Paul's Third Missionary Journey," *BW* 34 (1909): 120–30.

Bruce, F. F., "Apollos in the New Testament," *Ekklesiastikos Pharos* 57/3–4 (1975): 354–66.

Harris, J. R., "Who Sent Apollos to Corinth?" *Expos* 8/11 (1916): 175–83.

Hart, J.H.A., "Apollos," *JTS* 7 (1905–6): 16–28.

Pereira, F., *Ephesus: Climax of Universalism in Luke-Acts: A Redaction-Critical Study of Paul's Ephesian Ministry (Acts 18:23–20:1)* (Jesuit Theological Forum Studies 10/1; Anand: Gujurat Sahitya Prakash, 1983).

Preisker, H., "Apollos und die Johannesjünger in Act 18,24–19,6," *ZNW* 30 (1931): 301–4.

Rubinstein, M., "Le baptême de Jean," *REJ* 84 (1927): 66–70.

Schweizer, E., "Die Bekehrung des Apollos, Apg. 18, 24–26," *EvT* 15 (1955): 247–54; repr. *Beiträge zur Theologie des Neuen Testaments: Neutestamentliche Aufsätze (1955–1970)* (Zurich: Zwingli, 1970), 71–79.

Smith, B.T.D., "Apollos and the Twelve Disciples at Ephesus," *JTS* 16 (1915): 241–46.

Wolter, M., "Apollos und die ephesinischen Johannesjünger (Act 18,24–19,7)," *ZNW* 78 (1987): 49–73.

b) Paul in Ephesus and Disciples of the Baptist (19:1–7)

19 1 Now while Apollos was in Corinth, Paul happened to pass through the
inland country and came [down] to Ephesus, where he found some disciples.
2 He asked them, "Did you receive the Holy Spirit, when you became believers?"
They answered, "We have not so much as heard that there is a Holy Spirit."
3 "Then how were you baptized?" he asked, and they replied, "With the baptism
of John." 4 So Paul explained, "John baptized with a baptism of repentance; he
used to tell the people about the one who would come after him, in whom they
were to believe, that is, in Jesus." 5 When they heard this, they were baptized in
the name of the Lord Jesus. 6 Paul laid [his] hands on them, and the Holy Spirit
came upon them; then they spoke in tongues and uttered prophecies. 7 In all,
they were about twelve men.

WT: 1 Since Paul wanted to proceed to Jerusalem according to his own plan, the Spirit told him to return to Asia. So he passed through the inland country and came to Ephesus. [omits "Now . . . Corinth" and "where . . . disciples"]. 2 He asked the disciples. [omits "Holy"]. 3 Then Paul said to them, "How. 4 So he explained. 5 [omits "Lord" and adds "Christ for the forgiveness of sins"]. 6 [omits "Holy" and adds after "tongues":] "and interpreted them." 7 [omits "In all"].

COMMENT

Luke continues his story about Paul's Mission III, telling how he comes to Ephesus and finds there people who claim to be Christian disciples, but who have been baptized only with "the baptism of John." When asked whether they have received the Spirit, they say that they have not even heard that there is a Spirit. So Paul explains the difference between John's baptism and Christian baptism in the Spirit. Then he baptizes them; whereupon they receive the Spirit and give evidence of it by speaking in tongues and prophesying.

The episode is again a narrative, stressing the difference between John's preliminary baptism and the Spirit baptism administered to believers in Jesus Christ. Derived from Luke's Pauline source, the episode emphasizes the gift of the Spirit as the result of such baptism, but Luke takes no pains to explain its real theological meaning. For that one must look to the Pauline letters. Luke is content merely to associate these "disciples" with others who had similarly received the Spirit (recall 8:15–17; 10:47).

There is some similarity in this episode to the preceding, in that in both a story is told about what Conzelmann calls "'Johannine' Christians": about Apollos who "knew only the baptism of John" (18:25) and "disciples" who had only been baptized with "the baptism of John" (19:3). These expressions must be understood as Luke's way of recording how there were indeed, even after the death and exaltation of Jesus, disciples of John the Baptist. Luke associates this episode with Ephesus because of that similarity, but no one can tell whether it all really happened at Ephesus. The Lucan intention is clear: to depict the incorporation of such fringe Christians into the mainstream church, which is under the guidance of the Holy Spirit. Apollos and the twelve Ephesian "disciples" have had to be thus incorporated. All this is now attributed to Paul (or his coworkers), whose understanding of the faith is thus vindicated and who shows his concern for that mainstream church.

The episode emphasizes Christian baptism as a baptism in the Spirit, which has superseded the preliminary baptism conferred by John in Judea. His baptism was one administered as a sign of repentance only. Christian baptism also denotes that, but connotes much more, viz., a washing that confers the Spirit as the dynamo of new life in Christ. Christians so baptized are sometimes said to speak in tongues, but the "prophecies" they utter are more important, because those utterances imply testimony about the risen Christ.

NOTES

19:1. *while Apollos was in Corinth.* This clause forms the transition with the preceding episode, referring to 18:24 (Apollos in Ephesus) and 18:27–28 (his desire to proceed to Achaia). It is, however, omitted in MSS P[38], D, and some Syriac versions of the WT tradition. Instead they begin thus: "Since Paul wanted to proceed to Jerusalem according to his own plan, the Spirit told him to return to Asia. So he passed through the inland country and came to Ephesus." Paul's arrival in Ephesus would be Spirit guided, a note that is absent from the Alexandrian text. The WT here is related to what Paul says in WT of 18:21 about his need to go to Jerusalem for the coming feast. Cf. 18:18, 22. The WT, however, may have been "originally a marginal note intended for insertion in 18.22, but has been placed into the text by someone other than its author, who, finding 'Asia' in his note, and 'Ephesus' in his text, betrayed his hand by misplacing the material on the wrong side of the Apollos-episode" (W. A. Strange, "The Text of Acts 19.1," *NTS* 38 [1992]: 145–48, esp. 148); cf. B. H. Streeter, "The Primitive Text of Acts," *JTS* 34 (1933): 232–41, esp. 237–38; *TCGNT*, 415–16. On Corinth, see NOTE on 18:1.

Paul happened to pass through the inland country. Lit., "through the upper regions," i.e., the more mountainous, inland parts of Asia Minor, the upper regions of Galatia and Phrygia (18:23). Luke again uses *egeneto de* with an infin; see *Luke*, 118.

came [down] to Ephesus. The WT reads merely the infin. *elthein*, "came," but the Alexandrian text uses the compound infin. *katelthein*, "came down," i.e., from the upper regions, toward the sea and its coast. On Ephesus, see NOTE on 18:19.

where he found some disciples. Mathētai must have the same meaning it has elsewhere in Acts, Christian "disciples," since it is not otherwise specified (see NOTE on 6:1) and since the following verse implies the same. *Pace* Weiser (*Apg.*,

515), it is not right to say that they were "not really Christians." Moreover, they are unrelated to Apollos, because there is no real connection between this episode and the foregoing. Luke has juxtaposed the two episodes topically, because of the common "baptism of John" (18:25; 19:3). These "disciples" are also Johannine Christians, who still have to be incorporated fully into what Käsemann calls the *Una sancta,* the one church.

2. *He asked them, "Did you receive the Holy Spirit, when you became believers?"* The Ephesian "disciples" are even called *pisteusantes,* "believers," i.e., followers of Jesus of Nazareth. Reception of the Spirit was the sign of genuine Christian discipleship; see 2:38; 4:31; 6:3, 5; 7:55; 8:15–16, 19; 9:17; 10:44; 11:15–16; 13:9.

They answered, "We have not so much as heard that there is a Holy Spirit." The Ephesian disciples not only have not heard about the outpouring of the Spirit, but even that there was such a thing as the Spirit. Paul's further questioning reveals why. On *akouein ei,* "hear that," see C. Burchard, "*Ei* nach einem Ausdruck des Wissens oder Nichtwissens: John 9, 25, Act 19, 2, I Cor 1, 16; 7, 16," ZNW 52 (1961): 73–82.

3. *"how were you baptized?"* Lit., "into (= in, by) what, then, were you baptized?" (see ZBG §101). Paul's question presupposes that Christian baptism and reception of the Spirit are related. On baptism, see NOTE on 2:38.

they replied, "With the baptism of John." Lit., "into (= in, by) John's baptism." Their answer to Paul puts them more or less in the same situation as Apollos, who "knew only the baptism of John" (18:25; see NOTE there). Weiser (*Apg.,* 516) finds it difficult to imagine that disciples in a Baptist circle would not have heard of the Spirit. The Ephesian disciples are Gentiles in background, who are unaware of what Jerusalem Jewish Christians have experienced or known.

4. *Paul explained, "John baptized with a baptism of repentance.* In Luke 3:3, when John moves from the desert, he goes "into the region all around the Jordan to preach a baptism of repentance for the forgiveness of sins." So he proclaimed his own washing rite; he did not preach a Spirit baptism. Later in Luke 3:15–18, when queried whether he were the Messiah, he explains his baptism in relation to that of Jesus. Compare Acts 13:24.

he used to tell the people about the one who would come after him. In the Lucan Gospel, John explains his mission: "I am baptizing you with water, but someone more powerful than I is coming; and I am not fit to unfasten even the strap of his sandals. He will baptize you with a Holy Spirit and with fire" (3:16). In the Gospel no mention is made of one who would come *met' auton,* "after him"; that occurs in Mark 1:7; Matt 3:11: *opisō mou,* "after me." Cf. John 1:27. Now Luke shows that he too is aware of that traditional saying of the Baptist; compare 13:25.

in whom they were to believe, that is, in Jesus." Luke makes Paul explain John's message. Paul sums up the Christian proclamation as faith in Jesus, but he does not explain who Jesus is to such disciples. He takes it for granted that those listening will comprehend, which shows that the Ephesian "disciples" were Christians of a sort.

5. *When they heard this, they were baptized in the name of the Lord Jesus.* This does not mean that baptism has been ritually conferred on them in "the name

of the Lord Jesus," but that they are rebaptized as disciples of Jesus Christ; thus they become Christians in the full sense. See NOTES on 2:38 (also on the Lucan refrain, "the name") and 8:16. MSS D and 614 read rather "in the name of Jesus Christ for the forgiveness of sins"; this is a harmonizing formula derived by a copyist from 2:38; see *TCGNT,* 416. Metzger notes that John's baptism was already for the forgiveness of sins.

6. *Paul laid [his] hands on them.* I.e., in order that they may receive the Spirit; see NOTE on 6:6. Cf. 8:14–25. Paul imposes hands, again acting as a representative of the Twelve (see NOTE on 13:2).

the Holy Spirit came upon them. This is the "Pentecost" of "Johannine Christians."

then they spoke in tongues. See NOTE on 2:4. The adj. "other" is not used of "tongues," as in 2:4, and the implication may be that this gift of the Spirit results in ecstatic speech (as in 1 Cor 12:10, 28, 30; 14:2–27), or perhaps it is to be explained by the following verb. Compare 10:44–46, where in a parallel scene Peter was similarly involved. See *TCGNT,* 416.

uttered prophecies. Prophetic utterance is a gift of the Spirit in 1 Cor 12:28–29; 14:1–5, but is it here distinct from "tongues"?

7. *In all, they were about twelve men.* The number has no hidden or symbolic meaning. For Lucan approximation expressed by *hōsei,* see Luke 3:23; 9:14, 28; 22:41, 44, 59; 23:44; Acts 1:15; 2:41; (WT: 4:4); 10:3; 19:34.

BIBLIOGRAPHY (19:1–7)

Barrett, C. K., "Apollos and the Twelve Disciples of Ephesus," *The New Testament Age: Essays in Honor of Bo Reicke* (2 vols.; ed. W. C. Weinrich; Macon: Mercer University Press, 1984), 29–39.

Brown, S., "'Water-Baptism' and 'Spirit-Baptism' in Luke-Acts," *ATR* 59 (1977): 135–51.

Brunot, A., "La Pentecôte d'Ephèse," *BTS* 144 (1972): 4–5.

Dornfeld, A. G. *Habt Ihr den heiligen Geist empfangen? Apostelgeschichte* 19,2 (Erzhausen: Leuchter-V., 1970).

Käsemann, E., "The Disciples of John the Baptist in Ephesus," *Essays on New Testament Themes* (SBT 41; London: SCM, 1964), 136–48.

Parratt, J. K., "The Rebaptism of the Ephesian Disciples," *ExpTim* 79 (1967–68): 182–83.

Wilkinson, T. L., "Two-Stage Christianity: Baptism with the Holy Spirit (. . . Acts 2,37ss; 8,4.24; 10,22; 19,1ss)," *Vox Reformata* 21 (1973): 1–21.

c) PAUL'S EVANGELIZATION OF EPHESUS (19:8–22)

[8]Paul entered the synagogue and for three months continued to speak out boldly in debate, using persuasive arguments about the kingdom of God. [9]When some obstinately refused to believe and began speaking ill of the Way before the assembly, Paul left them and took the disciples with him. Day after day he would hold his discussions in the lecture hall of Tyrannus. [10]This continued for two years, so that all the inhabitants of Asia, Jews and Greeks alike, heard about the word of the Lord. [11]Meanwhile God continued to perform extraordinary miracles through Paul: [12]handkerchiefs or aprons that had touched his skin were applied to the sick and their diseases would leave them, and evil spirits would depart. [13]Some itinerant Jewish exorcists also tried to invoke the name of the Lord Jesus over those possessed by evil spirits, saying, "I adjure you by Jesus about whom Paul preaches." [14]It was the seven sons of Sceva, a Jew, a chief priest, who were doing this. [15]Once the evil spirit answered back, "Jesus I recognize, and Paul I know; but who are you?" [16]Then the person with the evil spirit sprang at them, overpowered them all, and treated them with such violence that they fled from his house naked and bruised. [17]This became known to all the Jews and Greeks living in Ephesus. Great awe came over all of them, and the name of the Lord Jesus was held in high esteem. [18]Many of those who had become believers came forward to confess and admit their former practices. [19]A good number of those who had practiced magic even gathered their books together and burned them in public. The value of them was assessed and found to be fifty thousand pieces of silver. [20]So it was with the power of the Lord that the word continued to spread and grow. [21]After these things happened, Paul made up his mind to travel through Macedonia and Achaia again and then go on to Jerusalem. He said, "After I have been there, I must visit Rome too." [22]He sent ahead two of his assistants, Timothy and Erastus, into Macedonia, but stayed on himself for a while in Asia.

WT: [8]boldly with great force. [9]some of them . . . the assembly of the peoples, then Paul . . . Tyrannus, from the fifth hour to the tenth. [10][omits "Jews and Greeks alike"]. [14]Among them the sons of a certain Sceva, a priest, also wanted to do this; being accustomed to exorcize such people and entering (the houses of) those demonized, they began to call upon the name, saying "We charge you in the name of Jesus whom Paul preaches, to come out." [16]sprang and overpowered them all. [17][omits "the Jews and Greeks" and "Lord"]. [18][omits "and admit"]. [20]that faith in God continued. [21][omits "After these things happened"].

COMMENT

Luke continues his account of Paul's evangelization of Ephesus. Paul preaches first in the Jewish synagogue of that city and later in the lecture hall of Tyrannus. This he does for two years so that his preaching becomes known throughout the province of Asia. Along with his preaching he works many miracles. He is imitated by exorcists, some of them the sons of Sceva, a Jew. The result is that many Ephesians turn from their superstitious practices and burn their books of magic. After more than two years of work in Ephesus, Paul begins to think about further evangelizing Macedonia and even making his way to Rome.

The episode divides itself into three sections: (1) 19:8–12, which gives a summary of Paul's activity during his first months in Ephesus, at first in the synagogue, then in the lecture hall of Tyrannus; (2) 19:13–16, which tells about his encounter with the sons of Sceva; and (3) 19:17–20, which tells of the reaction of Ephesians to the sons-of-Sceva incident and to Paul's missionary activity.

The episode is again a narrative, recounting Paul's successful evangelizing activity in the important town of Ephesus in the Roman province of Asia, details of which are derived from Luke's Pauline source. A detail in the episode (19:11) relates it to the miracle stories of Acts, and Luke now gives the reader a Pauline parallel to the miracles performed by Peter in 5:15–16. The miracle story in this case further evokes the tale about the sons of Sceva who tried to exorcise in the name of Jesus. Conzelmann (*Acts,* 163) calls the Sceva-sons incident "a legend with burlesque antecedents" and wonders whether "a profane anecdote [has] been appropriated" or whether it is "a creation of popular Christianity"! So the episode impresses a modern critical mind seeking a distinction between miracle and magic.

In v 14, Sceva is said to be a Jew, but apparently one who serves in the imperial cult of the Roman world. Though a Jew, he bears in pagan Ephesus the title *archiereus,* "high priest" or "chief priest." The meaning of the Lucan episode would then be something like this (a modification of Haenchen's analysis [*Acts,* 565]): If such highly respected Jewish exorcists, actually sons of a chief priest, had experienced such a fiasco, then Paul's success was such that even renowned Jewish exorcists had to take over the "name" that he invoked if they wanted to remain competitive. Their attempt itself reveals that no one is able to imitate Paul, the representative of the Christian God and emissary of the Christian church. The Jesus that Paul preaches is not taken over by outsiders. The invocation of Jesus' name is efficacious only when uttered by Christians. Luke is trying to get across the idea that Christianity has nothing to do with magic, and that Jesus' name is no magical-incantation formula.

The episode ends with Paul's decision to revisit Macedonia and Achaia and then make his way to Jerusalem. After that Luke records the apostle's further decision, "after I have been there, I must visit Rome too" (19:21b). This note in the Lucan story foreshadows the end of his account. It also forestalls any misimpression that might be formed about Paul's ministry in Ephesus, the lack of success and the opposition to his ministry in the riot of the silversmiths. What is important to note is the guidance of the Spirit (19:21). Paul's decision to go to Macedonia and Achaia, and then to Jerusalem, would mean a journey overland, then the crossing of the Dardanelles, a further journey overland to Philippi, Amphipolis, Apollonia, Thessalonica, and Beroea, before coming to Athens and Corinth in Achaia. It will also entail his retracing his steps to Philippi, and then sailing to Troas, making a journey overland to Assos, and sailing from there by ship along the coast of western Asia Minor to Syria and Palestine.

To this period in Paul's life one would have to relate the different letters written by Paul and the trips made from Ephesus to Corinth to handle problems that arose in that church evangelized earlier by Paul. These letters and trips are mentioned in Paul's own letters to the Corinthians: 1 Cor 5:9 (a letter prior to 1 Corinthians); 1 Corinthians (written from Ephesus [ca A.D. 56]); 2 Cor 2:1 (a visit from Ephesus); 2 Cor 2:4 (an intermediate letter to Corinth); 2 Corinthians (from Macedonia, after he has sent Timothy to Corinth to no avail; then Titus [2 Cor 7:13]). Of all of this Luke gives us not an inkling, probably because he was unaware of Paul's stormy dealings with the church of Corinth, not having read Paul's letters.

This episode carries two important messages for the modern reader. First, although Ephesians seek cures from Paul, they neither idolize him nor exaggerate the power of his "handkerchiefs or aprons." Luke carefully notes that "God continued to perform extraordinary miracles through Paul" (19:11); in other words, he rightly ascribes the cures to their heavenly source. God heals such people physically and psychically through the message, "the word of the Lord," that Paul preaches, which is a spiritual gift that he bestows on them. Second, the details about the sons of Sceva reveal once again the power of the "name of the Lord Jesus." In Jesus' name Paul exorcises, but those outsiders who would imitate his invocation of that name without corresponding faith in that name have no success and only incite the evil to rebound on themselves. The Lucan episode thus stresses the need of proper faith when one invokes the name of the Lord Jesus.

NOTES

8. *Paul entered the synagogue.* According to his custom in the Lucan story of Paul's missionary activity; see NOTE on 6:9. Recall 9:2; 13:5, 14; 14:1; 17:1, 17; 18:4, 19.

for three months continued to speak out boldly in debate. Thus Paul proclaims his message to Jews of Ephesus. MS D adds *en dynamei megalē*, "with great force." The attendant details are characteristically Lucan. The verb *parrhēsiazesthai*, related to the noun *parrhēsia*, is used; see NOTE on 2:29.

using persuasive arguments about the kingdom of God. Lit., "debating and urging the things that pertain to the kingdom of God." The topic is that about which the risen Christ instructed his disciples in 1:3 (see NOTE there). Cf. 8:12; 14:22; 20:25; 28:23, 31. It is a topic that would appeal to Paul's Jewish listeners. Implied is the role of Jesus of Nazareth in that kingdom; this is not said explicitly, but the next verse mentions "the Way," which thus reveals it as an aspect of the Lucan Paul's kingdom preaching. Actually the kingdom is a topic that only rarely appears in Paul's own letters (1 Thess 2:12; Gal 5:21; 1 Cor 4:20; 6:9–10; 15:24, 50; Rom 14:17), and then usually in catechetical summaries that Paul adopts from the tradition before him. For Luke, however, the kingdom of God is closely tied to the person of Jesus, especially as the risen Christ, and that is why he depicts Paul so preaching. See Weiser, *Apg.*, 526–27.

9. *When some obstinately refused to believe and began speaking ill of the Way before the assembly.* Lit., "when some hardened themselves and did not believe." Luke records three reactions to Paul's preaching: hardheartedness, disbelief, and scorn. Obstinate refusal is a Lucan description, characteristic of his value judgments (cf. 13:6). MS D reads *tines men oun autōn,* "some of them, moreover," stressing the continuation of opposition. It also adds at the end *tōn ethnōn,* which cannot mean "(assembly) of the nations/Gentiles," but must mean "(assembly) of the peoples," i.e., of Jews who came to the gathering of the synagogue. On "the Way," as a designation of Christianity, see NOTE on 9:2.

Paul left them and took the disciples with him. I.e., the disciples that he has made from among the Jews who frequent the synagogue. Recall 13:46 and also 18:6, the departure Luke has recorded there.

Day after day he would hold his discussions in the lecture hall of Tyrannus. From the classical period of Greece on, *scholē* was used of the place where pupils and teachers met (Plutarch, *Alexander* 7.3; Dionysius of Halicarnassus, *Isocrates* 1; *Demosthenes* 44). Tyrannus is otherwise unknown; he might have been a teacher in Ephesus or may have simply owned the lecture hall. The name *Tyrannos* has been found on first-century Ephesian inscriptions. MS D adds at the end *apo hōras pente heōs dekatēs,* "from the fifth hour to the tenth," i.e., each day from 11 A.M. to 4 P.M., thus during the normal Mediterranean siesta period. Cf. W. M. Ramsay, "Notes on the New Testament and the Early Church: From the Fifth to the Tenth Hour," *ExpTim* 15 (1903–4): 397–99, esp. 397–98.

10. *This continued for two years.* This is probably to be reckoned from the end of the "three months" of v 8: probably some time in A.D. 54 to 56. In 20:31 the full extent of time is given as *trietia,* "three years." During this period Paul would have made a short visit to Corinth.

so that all the inhabitants of Asia, Jews and Greeks alike, heard about the word of the Lord. Luke stresses the success of Paul's evangelization of Ephesus; ripples of it reach the whole of the Roman province. Whether this evangelization is supported by collaborators is not mentioned. The work of Tychicus and Epaphras in Colossae could belong to this period, but Luke is interested only in Paul's activity. On Asia, see NOTE on 2:9; on "word of the Lord" as expressive of the Christian message, see NOTE on 4:31. Note again the Lucan hyperbole, "all the inhabitants" (see NOTE on 2:44).

11. *Meanwhile God continued to perform extraordinary miracles through Paul.* Lit., "God was performing no ordinary powerful deeds through the hands of Paul," so Luke makes use of litotes. For *dynameis,* "powers, powerful deeds," as a designation of miracles, see NOTE on 2:22. Luke is careful not to attribute this ability to Paul himself; it is God who works through him. Recall the parallel account of Peter's miracles in 3:6; 5:15–16. The implication is that these miracles authenticate Paul's preaching, as they did Peter's and Jesus' ministry. Compare what Paul himself says in 2 Cor 12:12; Rom 15:18–19 about such signs, and contrast that with what he says in 1 Cor 1:22–23.

12. *handkerchiefs or aprons that had touched his skin were applied to the sick and their diseases would leave them.* Or "handkerchiefs or belts," as T. J. Leary ("The 'Aprons' of St Paul—Acts 19:12," *JTS* 41 [1990]: 527–29) prefers to translate. Some of the miracles are cures of physical sickness.

evil spirits would depart. Some of the miracles are also exorcisms, i.e., cures of mentally disturbed people. This narrative note about Paul's heaven-blessed exorcisms sets the stage for the coming account about Jewish thaumaturges. On "evil spirits," see NOTE on 5:16. Cf. 8:7.

13. *Some itinerant Jewish exorcists.* Little is known of such exorcising activity among Jews, but see Mark 9:38; Luke 9:49–50; 11:19. Josephus wrote that God granted Solomon knowledge about "the art used against demons for the benefit and cure of human beings" (*Ant.* 8.2.5 §45), and he composed incantations to be used in exorcisms. Josephus also tells of a Jewish contemporary, Eleazar, who freed people possessed by demons using Solomonic techniques (ibid., §§46–49).

also tried to invoke the name of the Lord Jesus over those possessed by evil spirits. In their exorcisms they called up the name of Jesus. Again the Lucan refrain of "the name" appears; see NOTE on 2:38.

"I adjure you by Jesus about whom Paul preaches." The Alexandrian text reads *horkizō*, "I adjure," but many MSS (P^{38}, 36, 453, 614, 1739) and the *Koinē* text-tradition read a 1st pl. verb, either *horkizomen* or *exorkizomen*, "we adjure." "You" is pl., referring to "spirits." Note the formula found in an extrabiblical magical papyrus *PGM* 4.3019–20: "I adjure you by the God of the Hebrews, Jesus." Origen too reports the success of exorcists who used the name of Jesus (*Contra Celsum* 1.6; 6.40; GCS 2.59; 3.109); cf. Deissmann, *LAE*, 260.

14. *It was the seven sons of Sceva, a Jew, a chief priest, who were doing this.* Lit., "seven sons of a certain Sceva, a Jew, a high priest." Many interpreters translate *Ioudaiou archiereōs* as "a Jewish high priest" (e.g., *RSV, NRSV, NAB*) and encounter no little difficulty in explaining what a Jewish high priest with seven such sons would be doing in Ephesus. For this reason Conzelmann regards him as "a purely legendary figure" (*Acts*, 164).

The difficulty is, first of all, textual. MS P^{38} reads *en hois kai hu[ioi Skeu]io[u Iou]daiou tinos archiereōs ēth[elē]san [to a]uto poiēsai*, "in these circumstances the sons of Sceva, a certain Jew, a chief priest, also wished to do the same." Codex Bezae has the same rewriting as P^{38} but reads *hiereōs* instead of *archiereōs* and omits the adj. *Ioudaiou*, thus solving the problem. The Harclean Syriac version reads the equivalent of *hepta*, "seven," but the rest of the WT omits that number, almost certainly because of *amphoterōn*, "both of them," in v 16. In any case, the Alexandrian text, translated in the lemma above, is the *lectio difficilior* and has to be preferred.

Second, the name Sceva is given in most MSS as *Skeua* (gen. of *Skeuas*); but as *Skeuia* in MS A and as *Skeuiou* in P^{38}. *Skeuas* is not a Semitic name, but *Scaeva* has been found as the Latin name of a Roman soldier (Plutarch, *Caesar* 16.2; Appian, *Bellum civile* 2.9.60; Dio Cassius, *Roman History* 56.16.1). It is strange that "a Jewish high priest" would have such a name, and it scarcely explains what he would be doing in the Roman province of Asia. Some commentators resort to a subterfuge, maintaining that Luke's text does not mean that Sceva himself was in Ephesus. The real problem is that no high priest of the Jews is known bearing such a name, although the names of 28 high priests are known from Herod the Great to the First Revolt (see E. Schürer, *HJPAJC*, 2.227–36). It may be, then, that *archiereus* is not to be translated as "high priest," but as "chief priest," i.e., a member of priestly families from which the high priest was chosen, as in 4:23. So U. Kellermann, "Archiereus," *EDNT* 1.164–65; Schneider, *Apg.*, 2.266, 270; Weiser, *Apg.*, 529.

Third, the matter is not so simple, since *archiereus* was also used in the eastern Mediterranean world in an entirely different sense. Although Augustus did not like the ruler cult of the eastern empire, he tolerated a temple being erected in the province of Asia to "Roma and Augustus." The commonalty *(to koinon)* of Asia held annual meetings to further this cult, and the main leader of the commonalty was *archiereus tēs Asias*, "the high priest of Asia." See D. Magie, *Roman Rule in Asia Minor to the End of the Third Century after Christ* (2 vols.; Princeton: Princeton University Press, 1950; repr. Salem, NH: Ayer, 1988), 446–49, 544, 1298–301. Possibly from the time of Claudius, and certainly from Nero on, many cities of Asia had such *archiereis;* sometimes the list of them even bears the location, *en Ephesō*, "in Ephesus." These *archiereis* were sometimes called *Asiarchai*, the very term that Luke uses in 19:31. Hence Sceva may have been "a renegade Jew" (B. A. Mastin), who served in the imperial cult as a "chief priest." In that case, *Ioudaios* would be a substantivized adj., "a Jew," and *archiereus* would refer not to the Jewish priesthood of Jerusalem, but to that of the Roman imperial cult. The activity of his seven sons, then, takes on a different character. See Fitzmyer, "'A Certain Sceva, a Jew, a Chief Priest' (Acts 19:14)," *Der Treue Gottes trauen: Beiträge zum Werk des Lukas: Für Gerhard Schneider* (ed. C. Bussmann and W. Radl; Freiburg im B.: Herder, 1991), 299–305; H. Engelmann, "Zum Kaiserkult in Ephesos," *ZPE* 97 (1993): 279–89.

For a farfetched suggestion that the text read "two sons," thus making the word *amphoterōn* in v 16 intelligible, instead of "seven sons," see C. C. Torrey, "'Two Sons' in Acts 19:14," *ATR* 26 (1944): 253–55. Torrey maintains that the cipher for 2 was confused with one for 7.

15. *Once the evil spirit answered back, "Jesus I recognize, and Paul I know; but who are you?"* The superiority of Jesus and Paul over Jewish exorcists is thus recognized, even by a demon, said to know about Jesus and have respect for Paul.

16. *the person with the evil spirit sprang at them.* Lit., "the human being, in whom the evil spirit was, springing upon them." The person is considered to be under the control of the spirit and overpowers all seven of them.

overpowered them all. Lit., "overpowering both of them." The pron. *amphoterōn*, "both of them," is strange, implying that the sons were two (ZBG §153). This reading of the Alexandrian text is in conflict with *hepta*, "seven (sons)" of v 14. Some MSS (Ψ, 1739, and the *Koinē* text-tradition) read simply *autōn*, "them," thus eliminating the problem. For a farfetched attempt to explain *amphoterōn* as referring to the two names just mentioned, Jesus and Paul, see C. Lattey, "A Suggestion on Acts xix.16," *ExpTim* 36 (1924–25): 381–82.

treated them with such violence that they fled from his house naked and bruised. This is the dramatic ending of an attempt at exorcism in the name of Jesus by the sons of Sceva, which records not success but failure for those sons.

17. *This became known to all the Jews and Greeks living in Ephesus.* Luke concludes his story by repeating a formula used in 1:19. The fiasco of Sceva's sons is well broadcast among Jews and Gentiles. Note the fourfold reaction that Luke records: Awe, praise, belief, and admission of questionable practices. Lucan hyperbole reappears in "all" (see NOTE on 2:44).

Great awe came over all of them. Lit., "great fear fell upon them all," another Lucan reaction. Recall 2:43; 5:5, 11.

the name of the Lord Jesus was held in high esteem. Lit., "was magnified." The name by which the sons of Sceva would exorcise becomes a powerful force and is recognized as such. Again the Lucan refrain of "the name" appears (see NOTE on 2:38).

18. *Many of those who had become believers came forward to confess and admit their former practices.* The noun *praxeis* in this context may refer to magical "practices"; even though Luke does not so specify them, the noun is found in papyrus texts referring to magical practices (see PGM 1.276; 4.159, 1227). The verb *exomologeisthai*, "confess," occurs in the sense of confessing sins in *2 Clem.* 8.3; *Did.* 4.14; *Barn.* 19.12; *Herm. Vis.* 3.1.5. That seems to be the meaning here too. Such Ephesians acknowledge the misguided conduct in their former lives.

19. *A good number of those who had practiced magic even gathered their books together and burned them in public.* Lit., "a good number of those practicing curious things"; the neut. pl. of the adj. *periergos* is sometimes used specifically of magic practices. The noun *biblos* is also employed at times to designate sacred books (Diodorus Siculus, *Bibliotheca historica* 1.44.4) or even *magikoi bibloi*, "magic books" (Ps.-Phocylides 149; PGM 3.424; 13.739).

These "books" are sometimes said to refer to the *Ephesia grammata*, "Ephesian Letters," but the letters were not "books" such as one could burn — what is meant in this verse. The "Ephesian Letters" were actually six words: *askion, kataskion, lix, tetrax, damnameneus, ta Aisia* (see Clement of Alexandria, *Stromateis* 5.8.45.2 [SC 278.96; GCS 2.356]; cf. Plutarch, *Symposiaka* 7.5 §706E; Menander, *Frg.* 371). Clement explains them thus: *askion* as *to skotos*, "darkness" (actually "shadowless" [= *a* + *skia*]); *kataskion* as *phōs*, "light" (actually "casting a shadow"); *lix* as *hē gē*, "the earth" (its ancient name); *tetrax* as *ho eniautos*, "the year" (actually "fourfold" [in seasons]); *damnameneus* as *ho hēlios*, "the sun" (actually "dominator"); *ta Aisia* as *hē alēthēs phōnē*, "the true sound" (actually "auspicious" [sounds]). These "sacred and holy" words, sometimes inscribed on amulets, were used in an apotropaic sense to drive out demons or exorcise the possessed. Cf. E. R. Dodds, *The Greeks and the Irrational* (Berkeley: University of California Press, 1951) 194; PW 5/2.2771–73.

The value of them was assessed and found to be fifty thousand pieces of silver. Lit., "they estimated the worth of them and found (it to be) five ten-thousands of silver," i.e., 50,000 silver drachmas, or "about $35,000 in current silver value" (Polhill, *Acts*, 406).

20. *So it was with the power of the Lord that the word continued to spread and grow.* This translation follows the order of the words in modern critical texts such as *NTG* or *GNT*, taking the gen. *tou Kyriou* as dependent on *to kratos*. See A. W. Argyle, "Acts xix.20," *ExpTim* 75 (1963–64): 151. The absolute use of *ho logos* (= the Word of God/theLord) is found in 4:4; 6:4; 8:4; 10:36, 44; 11:19; 14:25; 16:6; 17:11. MSS P[74], ℵ[2], E, Ψ, 33, 1739, and the *Koinē* text-tradition read rather *kata kratos ho logos tou Kyriou ēuxanen kai ischyen*, which would demand the translation "the Word of the Lord continued to spread and grow mightily." MS D has a conflate reading: *houtōs kata kratos enischysen kai hē pistis tou theou ēuxane kai eplēthyne*, "So with power it prevailed; and faith in God grew and multiplied." See NOTE on 4:31; cf. J. Kodell, "'The Word of God Grew': The Ecclesial Tendency of *Logos* in Acts 1,7; 12, 24; 19,20," *Bib* 55 (1974): 505–19.

21. *After these things happened.* Lit., "when these things were fulfilled." So Luke utilizes the incident in Ephesus as an occasion for further activity of Paul.

Paul made up his mind. Lit., "put (it) in his spirit/mind," which uses the middle voice of *tithenai* to indicate that it is a question of Paul's own *pneuma*. It does not mean, "he purposed in the Spirit," as Bruce (*Acts*, 393) renders it; nor does it mean that Paul decides "under the guidance of the Spirit," *pace* Marshall (*Acts*, 312). The clause has to be compared with *tithesthai en tē kardia*, "resolve in one's heart" (5:4; Luke 21:14).

to travel through Macedonia and Achaia again and then go on to Jerusalem. Paul wants to revisit parts of Greece that he has already evangelized, before returning to the city of the mother church. Compare Phil 2:24; 1 Cor 16:3–8, for Paul's own statements of such an intention. The "collection," about which Paul speaks there, is never mentioned in Acts in connection with that intention. On Macedonia, see NOTE on 16:9; on Achaia, the NOTE on 18:12; and on Jerusalem, that on 1:4.

"After I have been there, I must visit Rome too." Lit., "it is necessary for me to see Rome." The Lucan Paul formulates a plan to visit Rome, the capital of the Roman empire (see NOTE on 18:2). Compare what Paul himself says about visiting Rome: Rom 1:9–15; 15:22–29 (written from Corinth, not Ephesus). Now he envisages a journey that will bring him to "the end of the earth" (see NOTE on 1:8), but he gives no indication of the reason why he "must see" Rome. The impersonal use of *dei*, "it is necessary," often expresses in Lucan writings an obligation or necessity in accord with the implementation of God's salvific plan (see *Luke*, 179–80). So it becomes part of Luke's foreshadowing of the end of Acts and depicts Paul as conscious of his role in that plan. Cf. 23:11; 27:24. See E. Fascher, "Theologische Beobachtungen zu *dei*," *Neutestamentliche Studien für Rudolf Bultmann* . . . (BZNW 21; ed. W. Eltester; Berlin: Töpelmann, 1954), 228–54, esp. 247–48.

22. *He sent ahead two of his assistants into Macedonia.* Lit., "two of those serving him"; they are being sent on to another Roman province. This is an advance mission that indicates that Paul's work in the eastern Mediterranean was not yet over.

Timothy. He is the more important of the two, as we know from Paul's own writings. See Note on 16:1. He will appear in 20:4 among Paul's travel companions.

Erastus. This name is well attested in Greek inscriptions (see *SIG* §838.6). The one mentioned here may well be the same as the person who sent greetings to Roman Christians in Rom 16:23 ("Erastus, the treasurer of this city" [i.e., Corinth]), although Weiser questions this identification (*Apg.*, 538). According to this Lucan note, he has apparently been serving Paul in Ephesus. So too Polhill (*Acts*, 407); cf. 2 Tim 4:20. In a Latin inscription still partly in situ in a square near the eastern entrance of the theater of Corinth, he is mentioned as the aedile Erastus who paved the square in first-century Corinth; see *Romans*, 750. Cf. W. Miller, "Who Was Erastus?" *BSac* 88 (1931): 342–46.

stayed on himself for a while in Asia. I.e., at Ephesus, where he has already written 1 Corinthians (ca. A.D. 56). See G. S. Duncan, "Paul's Ministry in Asia—The Last Phase: *autos epeschen chronon eis tēn Asian* (Acts xix.22)," *NTS* 3 (1956–57): 211–18; "Chronological Table to Illustrate Paul's Ministry in Asia," *NTS* 5 (1958–59): 43–45.

BIBLIOGRAPHY (19:8–22)

Arnold, C. E., *Ephesians: Power and Magic: The Concept of Power in Ephesians in Light of Its Historical Setting* (SNTSMS 63; Cambridge: Cambridge University Press, 1989).

Betz, H. D. (ed.), *The Greek Magical Papyri in Translation: Including the Demotic Spells* (2d ed.; Chicago: University of Chicago Press, 1992).

Brent, A., "Luke-Acts and the Imperial Cult in Asia Minor," *JTS* 48 (1977): 411–38.

Deissmann, A., "Ephesia Grammata," *Abhandlungen zur semitischen Religionskunde und Sprachwissenschaft Wolf Wilhelm Grafen von Baudissin . . . überreicht* . . . (BZAW 33; ed. W. Frankenberg and F. Küchler; Giessen: Töpelmann, 1918), 121–24.

Delebecque, E., "La mésaventure des fils de Scévas selon ses deux versions (*Actes* 19,13–20)," *RSPT* 66 (1982): 225–32.

Eisler, R., "The Sons of the Jewish High-Priest Scaeva in Ephesus (Acts 19:14)," *Bulletin of the Bezan Club* 12 (1937): 77–78.

Eitrem, S., "Some Notes on the Demonology in the New Testament," *SO* fasc. supplet. 20 (1966): 1–78.

Forbes, C. A., "Books for the Burning," *TPAPA* 67 (1936): 114–25.

Horsley, G.H.R., "The Inscriptions of Ephesos and the New Testament," *NovT* 34 (1992): 105–68.

Mastin, B. A., "A Note on Acts 19,14," *Bib* 59 (1978): 97–99.

———, "Scaeva the Chief Priest," *JTS* 27 (1976): 405–12.

Mommsen, T., *The Provinces of the Roman Empire from Caesar to Diocletian* (2 vols.; New York: Scribner, 1887), 1.347–97.

Pease, A. S., "Notes on Book-Burning," *Munera studiosa* (ed. M. H. Shepherd and S. E. Johnson; Cambridge, MA: Episcopal Theological School, 1946), 145–60.

Sanders, H. A., *Papyri in the University of Michigan Collection: Miscellaneous Papyri* (University of Michigan Studies, Humanistic Series 40; ed. J. G. Winter; Ann Arbor: University of Michigan Press, 1936), 15, 18. (On P^{38}).

———, "A Papyrus Fragment of Acts in the Michigan Collection," *HTR* 20 (1927): 1–19.

Schürer, E., "Die *archiereis* im Neuen Testamente," *TSK* 45 (1872): 593–657.

Strange, W. A., "The Sons of Sceva and the Text of Acts 19:14," *JTS* 38 (1987): 97–106.

Taylor, B. E., "Acts xix.14," *ExpTim* 57 (1945–46): 222.

Trebilco, P., "Asia," *The Book of Acts in Its Graeco-Roman Setting* (BAFCS 2), 291–362.

d) Riot of the Ephesian Silversmiths (19:23–41)

23 It was about this time that no small disturbance occurred concerning the Way.
24 A silversmith named Demetrius, who made silver miniature shrines of Artemis
and created no little business for his craftsmen, 25 called a meeting of them and
other workers in related crafts and said to them, "Gentlemen, you know that our
well-being depends on this business. 26 Yet you can see and hear for yourselves
that not only here in Ephesus, but in almost all of Asia this Paul has convinced
and led astray a great number of people. He tells them that handmade gods are
no gods at all. 27 Now there is a danger not only that our business may be discredited, but even that the temple of the great goddess Artemis may come to naught.
Indeed, she whom all Asia and the whole world worship may soon be robbed of
the majesty that is hers." 28 When they heard this speech, they were filled with
fury and began to shout, "Great is Artemis of the Ephesians!" 29 Soon the city was
in chaos; people rushed with one impulse into the theater, dragging with them
Gaius and Aristarchus, Paul's Macedonian traveling companions. 30 Paul himself
wanted to appear before the popular assembly, but the disciples would not let
him. 31 Some of the Asiarchs, who were friends of Paul, even sent word to him,
urging him not to venture into the theater. 32 Meanwhile, some people were
shouting one thing, others another; for the assembly was in chaos, and the majority of them did not even know why they had come together. 33 Some of the crowd,
however, made suggestions to Alexander, as the Jews were pushing him forward.
He motioned for silence, indicating that he wanted to explain something to the
assembly. 34 But when they recognized that he was a Jew, they all roared back in
unison for about two hours, shouting, "Great is Artemis of the Ephesians!" 35 Finally, the city clerk quieted the mob and said, "People of Ephesus, what one is
there who does not know that the city of Ephesus is the guardian of the temple
of the great Artemis and of her image that fell from the heavens? 36 Since these
facts are beyond question, you must calm yourselves and not do anything rash.

[37]You have brought here these men, who are not temple robbers and who have not insulted our goddess. [38]If Demetrius and his fellow craftsmen have a charge to file, there are courts in session and there are proconsuls; let the parties file their claims. [39]But if you want to investigate anything further, it will have to be done in the statutory assembly. [40]As it is, we run the risk of being accused of rioting because of today's conduct. We have no reason for it, and we really cannot explain this disorderly gathering." With this speech he dismissed the gathering.

WT: [24][omits "named"]. [25][omits "and other . . . in related crafts"]. [Instead of "Gentlemen," reads: "Fellow craftsmen"]. [26]that gods made by human hands. [27]that the business. [28]When they heard these things . . . and, running into the intersection, they began to shout . . . [29]Soon the whole city was confused with ignominy. [30]the disciples kept hindering (him). [33]made Alexander come down. [34][omits "in unison"]. [35]who is the man who does not know. [38]If this Demetrius. [39]to investigate anything about other matters. [40]We have no reason for that for which we shall have to give an account because of today's conduct.

COMMENT

Luke concludes his story of what happened to Paul in Ephesus after noting his decision to make his way elsewhere. The last Ephesian episode tells about a riot of silversmiths, who were convinced that Paul's successful preaching of the Christian message was detrimental to their business, the making of images of Artemis, the city's goddess. The riot is finally subdued by the town clerk who makes it clear that such riotous conduct of the craftsmen might bring them into conflict with the duly constituted city authorities.

The episode is again a narrative, which recounts in lively fashion the uprising against Paul. The lesson that emerges is that Paul's preaching of the Christian message is not a contravention of the city's laws. On the contrary, the kind of opposition to his message that the silversmiths mount could jeopardize their own lives and status. The episode thus serves as another recognition of the legitimacy of Christianity.

Luke has undoubtedly inherited data about this incident from his Pauline source and constructed them all into a vividly narrated and dramatic episode. *Pace* Haenchen (*Acts*, 576–79), this account is scarcely a Lucan fabrication. Why would Luke want to invent out of whole cloth such an account? Even Conzelmann (*Acts*, 165) admits that, though Luke does compose scenes, "he does not invent stories such as these."

Moreover, there is no reason to identify this episode with the incidents to which Paul refers in 1 Cor 15:32 (fighting beasts at Ephesus) or 2 Cor 1:8–10 (affliction experienced in Asia). As Luke has presented this episode, it has nothing to do with an imprisonment of Paul at Ephesus. If there were such an episode in Paul's career, and that may be the implication of the figurative remarks that Paul has made about it in 1 and 2 Corinthians, it is not a concern of Luke. On the contrary, in the Lucan story "disciples" and "Asiarchs" see to it that Paul does not run into danger. Attempts have been made to relate this episode to new evidence discovered about a death penalty legislated for attacks on the cult of Artemis of the Ephesians (F. Sokolowski), which lends some credibility to the Lucan account.

Luke has introduced two short speeches into this narrative. The first is that of Demetrius to his fellow silversmiths (19:25–27). It is a political speech, in which Demetrius rises to the defense of Artemis and her Ephesian temple, for she is the one "whom all Asia and the whole world worship" (19:27). Implied in such an assertion is the contrast with what Paul preaches, the message about the risen Christ, which is now making its way to "the end of the earth" (1:8) and has even influenced many Ephesians. The second speech is that of the town clerk (19:35–40), which is a judicial explanation, involving advice and counsel. It clarifies the status of Paul in the Ephesian polity, and in effect legitimizes his preaching and mission. It also clarifies the illegality of the action that Demetrius has instituted along with fellow silversmiths.

Three points should be noted about this episode. First, as Christianity has reacted against the cult of Yahweh in the Temple of Jerusalem made by human hands (Stephen's speech in chap. 7), so now it reacts against temple images of the goddess "whom all Asia and the whole world worship" made by human hands (Demetrius's speech, 19:25–27). As Ephesians would not listen to Alexander, the spokesman of Jews of Ephesus, so they react against Paul and his companions, the witnesses of Christianity. The implication is clear: Christianity in the eyes of the devotees of Artemis is related to Judaism. Second, as Luke has depicted Paul preaching to Athenians about the worship of the Creator-God, who is near to them and related to them (17:26–29), so he now depicts Paul and his companions as people "who are not temple robbers and who have not insulted our goddess" (20:37), even though Paul would have objected to their idolatry. Paul and his companions are as much opponents of the Ephesians' piety, as of their making capital out of it. Paul's gospel confronts the questionable economic profit derived from such religiosity. Third, Christianity is implied to have a right to exist in the capital of the Roman province of Asia. These are the points that Luke is trying to emphasize in this episode.

After the transitional v 23, the episode develops in three dramatic scenes: (1) 19:24–28, which sets the stage for the riot that ensues after Demetrius stirs the guild of the silversmiths with his speech; (2) 19:29–34, which recounts how many of the Ephesian population get involved in the commotion; and (3) 19:35–40, in which the town clerk addresses the people gathered in the theater and pacifies them, thus resolving the problematic uprising against Christians.

In this episode the Lucan Paul brings the Christian message into conflict with a thriving pagan culture built up about the cult of Artemis of the Ephesians. He preaches that "hand-made gods are no gods at all" (19:26) and thus stirs up trouble in this cult center, because the economy and the culture of Ephesus have come under attack. What faces Paul here in Ephesus is another instance of what the risen Christ foretold: that he would have to suffer to preach his name (9:16).

NOTES

23. *It was about this time that no small disturbance occurred concerning the Way.* This verse is Lucan and transitional, serving as an introduction to the report proper. The time note is generic. On "the Way," as a designation for Christianity, see NOTE on 9:2. The disturbance over "the Way" is caused by pagan worshipers of Artemis of Ephesus.

24. A *silversmith named Demetrius.* He is otherwise unknown and is scarcely to be identified with the Demetrius, a *neōpoios,* "temple official," mentioned in an Ephesian inscription (see *CAGIBM* 3.578 c 4; cf. Conzelmann, *Acts,* 165).

who made silver miniature shrines of Artemis. Lit., "a maker of silver shrines *(naous)* of Artemis." This refers to miniature silver replicas of the Artemision, the great temple of Artemis erected at Ephesus. Cadbury (*The Book of Acts,* 5) tells of silver statuettes of Artemis and of terra-cotta replicas of her enshrined in a niche that have come to light; but to date no one has discovered any silver images of the Ephesian temple.

The Artemision was begun toward the end of the eighth century B.C. and magnified with Lydian and Persian contributions about 550 B.C. (Herodotus, *History* 1.92). It became one of the seven wonders of the ancient world (Strabo, *Geography* 14.1.20–23; Achilles Tatius, 8.2–3). Burned in 356 B.C., on the night on which Alexander the Great was born, a huge Hellenistic replacement was begun about 350 B.C. The temple was served by eunuchs *(megabyzoi)* and hierodules (female cultic slaves). See Pliny the Elder, *Naturalis Historia* 16.79.213–15; J. Finegan, *Light,* 347–49; D. G. Hogarth, *Excavations at Ephesus: The Archaic Artemisia* (London: British Museum, 1908); Oesterreichisches archaeologisches Institut, *Forschungen in Ephesos* (5 vols.; Vienna: Österreichische Akademie der Wissenschaften, 1906–44), *Inschriften von Ephesos,* 18b.

Artemis in Greek religion was originally considered to be the daughter of Zeus and Leto, the sister of Apollo, and was often depicted as a virgin huntress, whence her Homeric title, *potnia thērōn,* "lady of the wild animals" (*Iliad* 21.470). In time, she was identified as a protectress of chastity, and her devotees were nymphs; she also became a helper of women in childbirth. In popular religion of later date she was depicted as a savage goddess, and the stag, wild boar, wolf, and bear were sacred to her. In Roman religion this Artemis was called "Diana" and was regarded as the goddess of forests and groves.

"Artemis the Great" of Ephesus had little in common with the Artemis of earlier Greek religion. Her cult was actually syncretistic, being fused with that of the older Phrygian Cybele, the mother-goddess, or Phoenician Astarte. She was thus adopted by Ionian Greeks ca. 800 B.C. and as a fecund mother-goddess was often depicted as multibreasted and crowned with city walls. The cult of Ephesian Artemis was not confined to Ephesus, as v 27 makes clear. See Strabo, *Geography* 14.1.22–23; Herodotus, *History* 1.26; 1.92; L. R. Taylor, *Beginnings,* 5.251–56; *RAC* 1.714–18; Horsley, "Inscriptions of Ephesos," 141–49. Artemis of Ephesus is depicted on coins minted in the city at the time of the marriage of the emperor Claudius and Agrippina; there she is referred to as *Diana Ephesia* (see Kreitzer, "Numismatic Clue"). For debate about the nature of Artemis's multibreasted appearance, see A. E. Hill, "Ancient Art"; L. R. LiDonnici, "The Images."

created no little business for his craftsmen. Demetrius's business was profit making until Paul arrived on the scene. Again Luke expresses this with litotes.

25. *called a meeting of them and other workers in related crafts.* Lit., "gathering them together and those workers concerned with such things." Demetrius thus summons members of the guild of silversmiths *(argyrokopoi)*, which is known from inscriptions. The implication is that Paul's successful preaching has political as well as religious aspects.

said to them, "Gentlemen. Lit., "men" *(andres)*. MS D uses the address *syntechnitai*, "fellow craftsmen."

you know that our well-being depends on this business. Lit., "from this business we have prosperity." This is the bottom-line issue in this case. Demetrius's criticism touches on quantitative, geographical, economic, and religious aspects of the issue he brings before his guildsmen. Paul has led many people astray (v 26), people of Ephesus and all Asia (v 26), with economic repercussions (v 27), and detriment to the cult of Artemis (vv 26–27).

26. *Yet you can see and hear for yourselves that not only here in Ephesus, but in almost all of Asia this Paul has convinced and led astray a great number of people.* In Demetrius's view, Paul's evangelical success has diverted many people from the worship of Artemis and the purchase of silver miniature shrines. Lucan hyperbole again; see NOTE on 2:44.

He tells them that handmade gods are no gods at all. Demetrius's charge has shifted from trade in miniature shrines to replicas of the goddess herself. The Lucan formulation echoes 17:24–25, 29 and rings like a refrain. Cf. 7:48.

27. *there is a danger not only that our business may be discredited.* There is more, Demetrius argues, for it is not only the business, but even the cult of Artemis that is endangered. Luke uses of the business *eis apelegmon elthein*, a Latinism, *in redargutionem venire*, "fall into contempt." The implication is that this would follow if people no longer esteemed Artemis and her temple and did not want to make pilgrimages to Ephesus.

even that the temple of the great goddess Artemis may come to naught. Luke uses the official cultic title, *hē megalē thea Artemis*, "the great goddess Artemis" (Xenophon Ephesius, *Ephesiaca* 1.11.5: "our ancestral goddess, the great Artemis of the Ephesians"). Cf. *CAGIBM* 3.481:12–13 *(tēn megistēn theon Artemin)*. The danger noted is akin to that reported by Pliny the Younger to the emperor Trajan about the impact of Christianity on pagan cults of Asia Minor (*Ep.* 10.96).

she whom all Asia and the whole world worship. Ephesian Artemis's cult was widespread in the Greco-Roman world as well as in the eastern Mediterranean area (Pausanias, *Descriptio Graeciae* 2.2.6 [Corinth]; 4.31.7–8). The same idea appears on a Greek inscription from Ephesus itself (*Die Inschriften von Ephesos, Teil I–VIII* [Inschriften griechischer Städte 17/3; ed. H. Wankel et al.; Bonn: Habelt, 1979–84): "Since the goddess Artemis, leader of our city, is honored not only in her own homeland, which she has made the most illustrious of all cities through her own divine nature, but also among Greeks and barbarians . . ." (Ia. 24 B; pp. 147–48). See also Horsley, "Inscriptions of Ephesos," 154. As a result, Ephesus was a town to which many people came as pilgrims.

may soon be robbed of the majesty that is hers." Lit., "is about to be deprived of her majesty." So Demetrius depicts the effect of Paul's preaching of the Christian message; it will deprive Artemis of her glory.

28. *When they heard this speech, they were filled with fury and began to shout.* MS D reads simply *tauta de akousantes,* "When they heard these things." Then later it adds: *dramontes eis to amphodon,* "running into the intersection," i.e., streets at right angles. There they continued their chant.

"*Great is Artemis of the Ephesians!*" The fury of the Ephesians climaxes in the ceremonial acclamation of Artemis, now chanted in unison by those who have gathered in protest against Paul and his message. Such an acclamation of a deity has parallels in the LXX (Bel 18,41 [= Dan 14:18, 41]; Pss 86:10; 99:2; 135:5).

29. *Soon the city was in chaos.* Lit., "the city was filled with confusion." MS D reads *kai synechythē holē hē polis aischynēs,* "soon the whole city was confused with disgrace," which further includes Lucan hyperbole.

people rushed with one impulse into the theater. The huge theater of Ephesus, with a capacity of 24,000 spectators, has been excavated. It was built into the hollow of a hill; from it one could look out onto the city. It was used for political gatherings as well as for theatrical productions.

dragging with them Gaius and Aristarchus, Paul's Macedonian traveling companions. Lit., "Gaius and Aristarchus, Macedonians, fellow travelers of Paul." If this Gaius is the same as the one mentioned in 20:4, he would have originally come from Derbe in Lycaonia, a town in Asia Minor (see NOTE on 14:6). In Rom 16:23 Paul speaks of a Gaius who was his host, while he was in Corinth; he was probably the same person as the Gaius mentioned in 1 Cor 1:14, whom Paul admits having baptized. The adj. *Makedonas* is acc. pl. and thus modifies both *Gaion* and *Aristarchon.* Whether the Gaius mentioned here, then, is the same as either of the other two is problematic. Gaius of Derbe could have accompanied Paul from some place in Macedonia and thus be designated loosely as "Macedonian traveling companions," since the comma separating *Makedonas* and *synekdēmous* in the Greek text today is not original. Aristarchus, however, is identified in 27:2 as a "Macedonian, of Thessalonica"; cf. 20:4; Phlm 24; Col 4:10 (where he is called Paul's "fellow prisoner"). See E. B. Redlich, "Aristarchus," *Expos* 8/8 (1914): 183–88.

30. *Paul himself wanted to appear before the popular assembly.* We are not told why Paul wanted to do this in such a context; it may be an attempt to evangelize the Ephesians further. Luke writes *dēmos,* "the people," a technical term used for the "popular assembly," as it functioned in city-states and appears in many Ephesian inscriptions. See D. Knibbe et al. (eds.), *Neue Inschriften,* §§4167, 4228.

but the disciples would not let him. MS D reads *ekōlyon,* "kept hindering (him)," undoubtedly because they sensed the danger he would encounter.

31. *Some of the Asiarchs.* The meaning of *Asiarchēs* is disputed. In *Mart. Pol.* 12:2 the name denotes a cultic function, that of priests in the cult of Roma and Augustus in the province of Asia, as = *archiereis Asias* (so Ramsay, Jacquier, Zahn, Marquardt). Some interpreters, however, think that the name designates rather delegates of towns bound together in a league sent to the provincial assembly (*koinon Asias*, "Commonalty of Asia"), which met at Ephesus (see L. R. Taylor, *Beginnings*, 5.256–62). The latter is more likely. In either case, Luke's mention of Asiarchs implies the good relationship that existed between them and Paul and cannot be simply written off as "highly unlikely" (Haenchen, *Acts*, 574 n. 1). See now R. A. Kearsley, "Asiarchs, *Archiereis* and the *Archiereiai* of Asia," *GRBS* 27 (1986): 183–92; "Some Asiarchs of Ephesos," *NDIEC*, 4.46–55; "The Asiarchs," *The Book of Acts in Its Graeco-Roman Setting* (BAFCS 2), 363–76; "Asiarchs, archiereis and archiereiai of Asia: New Evidence from Amorium in Phrygia," *Epigraphica anatolica* 16 (1990): 69–80, who shows that the title *asiarchai* is well attested on inscriptions of the first century A.D. See also Horsley, "Inscriptions of Ephesos," 137–38; Lampe, "Acta 19," 62–63.

who were friends of Paul, even sent word to him, urging him not to venture into the theater. I.e., because the Asiarchs too sense the risk Paul would run. What happens to Paul after this we are not told; he disappears from the rest of the episode.

32. *Meanwhile, some people were shouting one thing, others another.* This detail merely repeats the description given in v 29. Cf. 21:34.

the assembly was in chaos, and the majority of them did not even know why they had come together. For "assembly" Luke uses *ekklēsia* in the secular sense, for a political body that was duly or regularly summoned, the normal usage in classical and Hellenistic Greek and the meaning used again in v 39 (cf. *Inschriften von Ephesos* §27:90, 202–13; 28–31). Here it denotes merely the "gathering" of the people on this occasion, hardly a formal or duly constituted popular assembly.

33. *Some of the crowd, however, made suggestions to Alexander.* He is otherwise unknown, but must have been a person of some prominence. There is no reason to think that he would be the same as the Alexander of 1 Tim 1:20 or as the coppersmith of 2 Tim 4:14.

the Jews were pushing him forward. Perhaps Luke means that Jews were pushing Alexander forward as their spokesman to explain to the gathering that Christians were not Jews.

He motioned for silence, indicating that he wanted to explain something to the assembly. Lit., "Alexander, waving his hand, wished to speak in defense (of something) to the assembly," i.e to the *dēmos.*

34. *when they recognized that he was a Jew, they all roared back in unison for about two hours.* Lit., "there ensued one voice from all (of them) crying out for about two hours." So Alexander's attempt at defensive clarification fails. Recall 16:20. Tension between Jews and Greeks in Ephesus in the Roman period is otherwise known; see Hemer, *Book of Acts*, 122.

shouting, "Great is Artemis of the Ephesians!" Recall v 28. The Ephesians thus assert the superiority of their goddess over what the Jew Alexander stands for.

35. *Finally, the city clerk quieted the mob. Grammateus,* "scribe, clerk," alone is used; so it could designate *grammateus tou dēmou,* a clerk of the municipal assembly, or (less likely) *grammateus tēs boulēs,* a clerk of the (city) council. In either case, he was a man of authority, who understood the legal implications of the riotous gathering. His title *grammateus* is well attested in Ephesian inscriptions (e.g. *SIG* §867.27–28).

"People of Ephesus. Lit., "Men, Ephesians," see NOTE on 1:16.

what one is there who does not know that the city of Ephesus is the guardian of the temple of the great Artemis? His appeal begins with recalling a recognized fact, the fame of the Artemision. The city of Ephesus is designated *neōkoros,* "temple keeper," a title authorized by Roman authorities and often used in the imperial cult for cities with official temples of the cult. It is known as a title specifically for the cult of Artemis (*Die Inschriften von Ephesos I-III* [ed. H. Wankel et al.; Bonn: Habelt, 1979–84], 1 §27:224–25; *SIG* §867.24; *CIG* §2972). On Ephesus, see NOTE on 18:19.

of her image that fell from the heavens? This is the only notice in Greek literature of the legend that a statue of Ephesian Artemis fell from the heavens. Euripides (*Iphigeneia in Taurica* 87–88, 977, 1384–85) alludes to a similar legend about Taurian Artemis. It is usually explained as an archaic statue made from a meteoric stone. Such stones were often treated as idols. Pliny the Elder (*Naturalis Historia* 16.79.213–14), however, records some doubt about the statue, since some say that it was made of "ebony" *(ceteri ex hebeno esse tradunt).* For many representations of Artemis, see R. Fleischer, *Artemis von Ephesos,* pls. 1–171.

36. *Since these facts are beyond question, you must calm yourselves and not do anything rash.* The clerk appeals for reason and civil conduct.

37. *You have brought here these men, who are not temple robbers.* To steal from a temple was a terrible crime in the ancient world of Egypt, Greece, and Rome. Paul and his companions are, in effect, exonerated by the town clerk of a charge sometimes brought against Jews (see Rom 2:22; Josephus, *Ant.* 4.8.10 §207; *Ag.Ap.* 1.26 §249; 1.34 §310).

who have not insulted our goddess. The clerk insists that what Paul has been preaching about Christ does not constitute a reviling of Ephesian Artemis. The formal title of Artemis was *hē theos* or *hē thea* (see *Inschriften von Ephesos* §27:224–25, 535–36), which Luke uses here.

38. *If Demetrius and his fellow craftsmen have a charge to file, there are courts in session and there are proconsuls; let the parties file their claims.* I.e., let them resort to due process. So the town clerk argues, knowing what is at issue from the way the Romans have set up urban governments in their provinces. The pl. "proconsuls" is used in a generic sense of assizes, since there was only one proconsul at a time, who acted as provincial governor. The Romans are known to have held court under a proconsul in several principal cities in the provinces,

Ephesus being one of them (see V. Chapot, *La province romaine proconsulaire d'Asie* [Paris: E. Bouillon, 1904], 353–57); Lampe, "Acta 19," 63.

39. *if you want to investigate anything further, it will have to be done in the statutory assembly.* Now Luke makes the clerk speak of *ennomos ekklēsia* in the formal secular sense of "assembly," one governed by laws and regulations that the clerk tells the people have to be respected and obeyed. See NOTE on v 32 above.

40. *As it is, we run the risk of being accused of rioting because of today's conduct.* The clerk alludes to regulations of Roman provincial law. He realizes that the Romans have accorded civic privileges to the people of Ephesus and fears that riotous conduct could seem seditious to the Romans, who might intervene. Violence in civil life could be interpreted as violations of *Lex Lutatia, Lex Plautia,* and possibly *Lex Iulia de vi publica* (see OCD, 1128–29).

We have no reason for it, and we really cannot explain this disorderly gathering." The town clerk summarizes the results of the commotion that Demetrius has caused. Nothing justifies such a tumultuous uprising.

41. *With this speech he dismissed the gathering.* I.e., the *ekklēsia,* already mentioned in v 32. That means that Gaius and Aristarchus (see v 29) are set free. The anti-Christian tumult is rendered ingloriously ineffective, and once again Christianity is seen to triumph in the Lucan story.

BIBLIOGRAPHY (19:23–41)

Abrahamsen, V. A., *Women and Worship at Philippi: Diana/Artemis and Other Cults in the Early Christian Era* (Portland, ME: Astarte Shell, 1995).

Bludau, A., "Der Aufstand des Silberschmieds Demetrius (Apg. 19,23–40)," *Der Katholik* 3/33 (1906): 81–92, 201–13, 258–72.

Carrez, M., "Note sur les événements d'Ephèse et l'appel de Paul à sa citoyenneté romaine," *A cause de l'évangile,* 769–77.

Ceroni, E., "Grande Artemide degli Efesini! Il tumulto degli Efesini contro San Paolo alla luce delle recenti scoperte archeologiche," *ScCatt* 60/2 (1932): 121–42, 203–26.

Crocker, P. T., "Ephesus: Its Silversmiths, Its Tradesmen, and Its Riots," *Buried History* 23 (1987): 76–78.

Delebecque, E., "La révolte des orfèvres à Ephèse et ses deux versions (Actes des Apôtres xix, 24–40)," *RevThom* 83 (1983): 419–29.

Fleischer, R., "Artemis von Ephesos und verwandte Kultstatuen aus Anatolien und Syrien: Supplement," *Studien zur Religion und Kultur Kleinasiens: Festschrift für Friedrich Karl Dörner* (EPRO 66; 3 vols.; Leiden: Brill, 1978), 1.324–58.

———, *Artemis von Ephesus und verwandte Kultstatuen aus Anatolien und Syrien* (EPRO 35; Leiden: Brill, 1973).

———, "Neues zu kleinasiatischen Kultstatuen," *ArchAnz* 98 (1983): 81–93.

Harris, J. R., "The Origin of the Cult of Artemis," *BJRL* 3 (1916–17): 147–84.

Helck, W., "Zur Gestalt der ephesischen Artemis," *ArchAnz* 99 (1984): 281–82.

Hill, A. E., "Ancient Art and Artemis: Toward Explaining the Polymastic Nature of the Figurine," *JANES* 21 (1992): 91–94.

Horsley, G.H.R., "The Mysteries of Artemis Ephesia in Pisidia: A New Inscribed Relief," *Anatolian Studies* 42 (1992): 119–50.

Jongh, E. D. J. de, "De tempel te Ephese en het beeld van Diana," *GTT* 26 (1925–26): 461–75.

Knibbe, D., "Ephesos: A. I. Die Inschriften," *PWSup* 12 (1970): 248–97.

Knibbe, D. et al. (eds.), *Neue Inschriften aus Ephesos* IX–X (Jahreshefte des österreichischen archäologischen Instituts in Wien 55; Vienna: Österreichisches archaeologisches Institut, 1984), 107–49.

Krause-Zimmer, H., *Artemis Ephesia* (Stuttgart: Freies Geistesleben, 1964).

Kreitzer, L. J., "A Numismatic Clue to Acts 19.23–41: The Ephesian Cistophori of Claudius and Agrippina," *JSNT* 30 (1987): 59–70.

Lampe, P., "Acta 19 im Spiegel der ephesischen Inschriften." *BZ* 36 (1992): 59–76.

Lichtenecker, E., *Das Kultbild der Artemis von Ephesus* (Tübingen, 1952).

LiDonnici, L. R., "The Images of Artemis Ephesia and Greco-Roman Worship: A Reconsideration," *HTR* 85 (1992): 389–415 (with 7 figures).

Miltner, F., *Ephesos: Stadt der Artemis und des Johannes* (Vienna: Deuticke, 1958).

———, "Two New Statues of Diana of the Ephesians; and Other Discoveries in the Ancient City of Ephesus," *ILN* 232 (8 February 1958): 221–23, 209.

Ramsay, W. M., "The Lawful Assembly (Acts xix.39)," *Expos* 5/3 (1896): 137–47.

Rossner, M., "Asiarchen und Archiereis Asias," *Studii clasice* (Bucharest) 16 (1974): 101–42.

Seiterle, G., "Artemis—die grosse Göttin von Ephesos," *Antike Welt* 10/3 (1979): 3–16.

Sokolowski, F., "A New Testimony on the Cult of Artemis of Ephesus," *HTR* 58 (1965): 427–31.

Stoops, R. F., Jr., "Riot and Assembly: The Social Context of Acts 19:23–41," *JBL* 108 (1989): 73–91.

Strelan, R., *Paul, Artemis, and the Jews in Ephesus* (BZNW 80; Berlin/New York: de Gruyter, 1996).

Thiersch, H., *Artemis Ephesia: Eine archäologische Untersuchung* (Abhandlungen der Gesellschaft der Wissenschaften zu Göttingen, Philol.-hist. Kl. 3/12; Berlin: Weidmann, 1935).

e) Paul Leaves for Macedonia, Achaia, and Syria (20:1–6)

20 [1]When the turmoil had ended, Paul summoned the disciples and encouraged them. Then he said goodbye to them and set out for Macedonia. [2]He trav-

eled through those regions, encouraged the people there with many an address, and finally came to Greece, [3]where he stayed for three months. When a plot was made by Jews against him, as he was on the point of embarking for Syria, he decided to return by way of Macedonia. [4]He was accompanied by Sopater, son of Pyrrhus, from Beroea; Aristarchus and Secundus from Thessalonica; Gaius from Derbe; Timothy; Tychicus and Trophimus from Asia. [5]These companions went on ahead and waited for us in Troas; [6]we ourselves set sail from Philippi, as soon as the festival of Unleavened Bread was over. Five days later we joined them in Troas, where we spent seven days.

WT: [1][omits "Paul"]. [3]as he wanted to take ship for Syria, the Spirit told him to return by way of Macedonia. [4]When he was about to depart, he was accompanied as far as Asia by Sosipater . . . Tychicus from Ephesus and Trophimus. [5]went on . . . waited for him in Troas. [6]We came to them in five days and spent seven days there.

COMMENT

Luke continues his story of Paul's movements. After the riot of the silversmiths, Paul would have had difficulty in moving about freely in Ephesus. Some interpreters relate the experience of "affliction in Asia" mentioned in 2 Cor 1:8–10 to this period, but that is far from certain; it could have been another experience of which Luke knows nothing. In any case, Luke begins the account of Paul's return to Syria at the end of his third missionary journey. The notice of his movements given in vv 1–6 is continued later in the chapter in vv 13–16 and then in 21:1–14. In these movements Paul carries out his plan (19:21; cf. 1 Cor 16:5) first to visit Macedonia (2 Cor 2:12), perhaps Illyricum thereafter (Rom 15:19), which Luke does not mention, and then Achaia once again (2 Cor 2:13). In the latter place he spends "three months" during the winter of A.D. 57–58 (Acts 20:3), during which he wrote (from Corinth) the Epistle to the Romans, not mentioned by Luke. Impeded by a plot stirred up against him in Achaia, as he is about to take ship to return to Syria, Paul decides to travel instead overland to Macedonia, and to Philippi in that province (in the spring of A.D. 58, Acts 20:3–6a). After Passover he takes a ship from there for Troas, where he again meets his travel companions and spends the better part of a week (20:6b).

The episode is another narrative, the information for the beginning of which Luke derives from his Pauline source. In the course of this episode we find another of the We-Sections (20:5–15); it begins at 20:5, with Paul in Philippi, where the first We-Section ended (in 16:17).

NOTES

20:1. *When the turmoil had ended.* I.e., the confusion caused by the riot of the silversmiths of Ephesus. So Luke forms a transition from the preceding episode to the coming notices of Paul's further journeys.

Paul summoned the disciples and encouraged them. I.e., Ephesian Christians, who undoubtedly are concerned about their own status as a result of Demetrius's move against Paul. So they are in need of some counsel for the future. This Paul gives in an effort to strengthen and encourage them.

he said goodbye to them and set out for Macedonia. Luke does not tell us how Paul traveled from Ephesus to Macedonia, but he must have gone partly by ship (perhaps from Troas to Neapolis), then overland to Philippi and further into Macedonia. Cf. 2 Cor 2:12–13; 7:5, 13–16. From some place in Macedonia he would have written part of 2 Corinthians, but about this Luke says nothing.

2. *He traveled through those regions.* I.e., the regions of Macedonia. Probably from Philippi to Amphipolis, Apollonia, Thessalonica and Beroea, as he did in the account of chap. 17.

encouraged the people there with many an address, and finally came to Greece. Luke does not tell us where Paul would have stayed in Greece, but from the Epistle to the Romans we can conclude that he had reached Corinth, where Gaius was his host (16:23). Cf. 1 Cor 16:3.

3. *where he stayed for three months.* This would have been the winter of A.D. 57–58 (see Introduction §158). Paul himself wrote about this intended stay with the Corinthians in 1 Cor 16:5–6. During these three months he wrote the Epistle to the Romans. It is dated to these "three months" winter by Kümmel (*Introduction,* 311), Pesch, Polhill, Roloff, Schneider, Weiser, Wilckens, but for many of these commentators the winter would rather have been A.D. 55–56.

When a plot was made by Jews against him, as he was on the point of embarking for Syria. Luke does not explain the nature of the plot in Achaia. Ramsay suggested that Paul wanted to take a ship on which Jewish pilgrims going to Jerusalem for Passover would have been his fellow travelers, and some of them planned to do him in (*Paul the Traveller,* 287). The WT says merely: "as he wanted to take ship for Syria, the Spirit told him to return by way of Macedonia." Again the technical nautical term *anagein* is used; see NOTE on 13:13.

he decided to return by way of Macedonia. From 19:21 we recall that Paul, still in Ephesus, planned to come to Macedonia and Achaia before going to Jerusalem (cf. Rom 15:25), undoubtedly planning also to take ship from Corinth. Now because of a plot about which he has learned, he proceeds rather overland, first through northern Greece, probably Beroea and Thessalonica, and from there to Philippi, towns in the Roman province of Macedonia.

4. *He was accompanied by Sopater, son of Pyrrhus, from Beroea.* Seven companions go along with him on this return to Syria and Jerusalem according to the Pauline source, but in v 5, the beginning of a We-Section, we learn that Luke also accompanies Paul (see Introduction §§94–102). The first named is the Thessalonian Sopater. In some MSS (104, 1175) his name is given as *Sōsipatros,* probably a copyist's harmonization influenced by Rom 16:21, instead of the *Sōpatros* of the Alexandrian text of Acts. His father's name is omitted in the *Koinē* text-tradition. The gentilic adj. *Beroiaios* is also found on Greek inscriptions and coins in the same sense, "from Beroea." Conzelmann (*Acts,* 167) considers these travel companions of Paul as the delegates who were sent to deliver the collection taken up in Macedonia and Greece for Jerusalem (24:17; cf. 1 Cor 16:1–2; 2 Cor 9:4). MSS A, D, E, Ψ, and 1739 add "as far as Asia." In the WT v 4 begins

rather *mellontos tou exienai autou*, "When he was about to depart, he was accompanied . . ."

Aristarchus and Secundus from Thessalonica. Aristarchus is probably the same as the one mentioned in 19:29; see NOTE there. *Sekoundos* is otherwise unknown; he is mentioned only here in the Alexandrian text-tradition, but reappears in the WT at 27:3. His name is Latin, *Secundus*, "second," i.e., probably the second male child in his family.

Gaius from Derbe. It is far from certain that this Gaius is the same as the one mentioned in 19:29; see NOTE there. MS D identifies him as *Douberios*, a person from Doberus, a Macedonian town southwest of Philippi; but that adj. may be a corrupt reading for "Derbe." See *TCGNT*, 421–22.

Timothy. Of Lystra; see NOTE on 16:1.

Tychicus and Trophimus from Asia. Tychikos may be the same person as the one mentioned in Col 4:7; Eph 6:21; Titus 3:12; 2 Tim 4:12. In MS D he is called rather *Eutychos* and so would not be the same. *Trophimos* is probably the same as the person so named in 21:29, where he is said to be from Ephesus; cf. 2 Tim 4:20. In MS D both Tychicus and Trophimus are said to be *Ephesioi*, "Ephesians," instead of *Asianoi*, "men from Asia," the reading of the Alexandrian text. The D reading may be owing to 21:29. In any case, one concludes from the latter passage that Trophimus was a Gentile Christian. *Asianos* is also attested in first-century Greek inscriptions (*IGRR* 4.1756:113, 116).

5. *These companions went on ahead and waited for us in Troas.* I.e., in Asia Minor. The pron. *houtoi* probably refers to the last two named in v 4, Tychicus and Trophimus, who were "from Asia" (so Haenchen, Conzelmann, Schneider), but Wikenhauser thinks that it refers to all seven. The second We-Section (20:5–15) begins here. On Troas, see NOTE on 16:8. MSS P^{74}, B^2, D, 36, 104, 323, 614, and 1891 read *proelthontes*, "going on ahead," whereas MSS ℵ, A, B*, E, H, L, P, Ψ, and 1739 read *proselthontes*, "going on."

6. *we ourselves set sail from Philippi.* This probably means "from Neapolis," the port of Philippi. See NOTES on 16:11–12.

as soon as the festival of Unleavened Bread was over. This means that the departure from Philippi occurs in the spring of A.D. 58. It could also mean that Paul, the Jewish Christian, has celebrated the feast of Passover with the Christians of Philippi (see NOTE on 12:3). This gives a period of seven weeks from Passover to Pentecost for the events narrated in 20:1 to 21:16. Paul arrives in Jerusalem at 21:17, where he has planned to be by Pentecost according to 20:16.

Five days later we joined them in Troas. The journey from Philippi to Troas took five days. It would have been overland to Neapolis, and from there by ship to Troas. Cf. 2 Cor 2:12–13, where Paul speaks of having once found an opened door in Troas for his preaching.

where we spent seven days. The following episode recounts one of the things that happened during these seven days in Troas.

BIBLIOGRAPHY (20:1–6)

Davies, P. E., "The Macedonian Scene of Paul's Journeys," *BA* 26 (1963): 91–106.

Delebecque, E., "Actes 20,3–6," *Bib* 65 (1984): 356.

———, "Les deux versions du voyage de saint Paul de Corinthe à Troas (Ac 20,3–6)," *Bib* 64 (1983): 556–64.

H[erzog], E., "Persönliche Beziehungen des Apostels Paulus zur römischen Christengemeinde in der Zeit der Abfassung des Römerbriefes," *IKZ* 8 (1918): 201–24.

Songer, H. S., "Acts 20–28: From Ephesus to Rome," *RevExp* 87 (1990): 451–63.

———, "Paul's Mission to Jerusalem: Acts 20–28," *RevExp* 71 (1974): 499–510.

f) Paul Revives Eutychus at Troas (20:7–12)

7On the first day of the week, when we gathered to break bread, Paul preached
to the people. Because he was going to leave the next day, he prolonged his talk
until midnight. 8Now there were many lamps in the upstairs room where we
were gathered. 9A young man named Eutychus, who was sitting on a window
sill, became more and more drowsy as Paul talked on and on. Finally he went
sound asleep and fell from the third storey to the ground. They picked him up
for dead. 10But Paul hurried down to him, threw himself upon him, and put his
arms around him; he finally said, "Do not be alarmed! There is still life in him."
11Then he went upstairs again, broke bread, and ate. Afterwards he chatted with
them for a good while until dawn; and so he departed. 12They took the boy away
alive to their great comfort.

WT: 8many windows in the upstairs room. 9became quite somnolent as Paul talked on. [omits "on and on. Finally . . . and"]. 11[omits "and ate"]. 12When they said good-bye, he took the youth away alive.

COMMENT

The Lucan narrative now recounts a miracle that Paul performs at Troas. In the context of the celebration of a Sunday Eucharist, Paul's long-winded sermon to the Christians of Troas lasts beyond midnight. One of those present, a youth who has been sitting on a window sill, becomes drowsy and falls out of the window. Paul rushes down, embraces him, and he is restored to life. Then Paul breaks bread (completes the eucharistic celebration) and continues to chat with those present until dawn, when he departs. The Christians of Troas are consoled by what has happened while the apostle was among them.

This Lucan story about Paul parallels Peter's resuscitation of Tabitha in 9:36–41. Eutychus (whose Greek name means "lucky one") is aptly named by Luke, who depicts him restored to "life" in the context of a eucharistic "breaking of bread." To be noted is that Luke depicts Paul celebrating the Eucharist, even though no mention is made of the distribution of the "broken bread" (cf. 27:35); he is thus the only individual Christian so depicted in the NT.

The proper sequence of vv 10 and 12 seems to be disturbed by v 11, which may be a secondary insertion; the WT of v 12 reveals that problem even more so. In this episode Luke continues to make use of the We-Section, which began at 20:5, at least until v 8; the major part of the episode is recounted in the third person. So it seems that Luke has here joined a Pauline narrative in vv 9–12 to the We-Section.

Dibelius (*Studies*, 17–18) maintained that "the mood of the story is as secular as possible; this is seen in the rationalised description of the miracle." This Dibelius finds in the Lucan description of Paul, in which one cannot be certain "whether Paul is seen as a worker of miracles or a doctor: 'his life is still in him.'" Thus, it is a secular anecdote that circulated about Paul, which Luke has incorporated into his story. Yet when reading the Lucan story and Dibelius's analysis of it, one wonders whether it is the same story. The interpretation that Dibelius began is carried even further by Haenchen (*Acts*, 586). Clearly, one can subject the Lucan miracle story to such farfetched analysis and so miss the whole point of it. Luke has found in the Pauline tradition an account of a miracle that the apostle is said to have performed. He dutifully passes it on in an effort to extol Paul as a preacher, as one who celebrates the breaking of bread, and as one who assists an unfortunate human being with the power that he has as a miracle worker. Luke does not tell us that this power is God given; he presumes that the Christian reader will understand whence Paul has such power to resuscitate a youth who is "dead." Even Haenchen had to admit that the Christian reader would recognize "the association with Elijah and Elisha, and hence the miracle." It is thus a miracle story that enhances the character of the hero of this part of Acts. Luke recounts this episode not merely as a miracle story of the gospel tradition, but as a significant event in the ministry of Paul related to the breaking of bread.

This Lucan episode depicts Paul celebrating the liturgy of the word and the breaking of bread on a Sunday, the Christian equivalent of keeping holy the Sabbath day. Such a celebration was the liturgical recollection of the Lord's resurrection, his triumph over death. So it becomes a fitting context for the event in which Paul resuscitates Eutychus.

NOTES

7. *On the first day of the week.* Lit., "on (day) one of the week," an expression that has the same meaning as *prōtē sabbatou* (Mark 16:9), i.e., Sunday, in the Christian calendar. Cf. Luke 24:1; Mark 16:2; Matt 28:1; 1 Cor 16:2; *Did.* 14. Luke is using the Jewish reckoning of the day from sunset to sunset, but one wonders whether this refers to Saturday night and early Sunday morning or Sunday night and early Monday morning. Wikenhauser (*Apg.*, 255) believes it is the former, whereas Bruce (*Acts*, 409), Marshall (*Acts*, 326), and Weiser (*Apg.*, 563) think it

is the latter. It is probably the former. See *Beginnings*, 4.255. Note the continuation of the We-Section, which began in v 5.

when we gathered to break bread. This gen. absol. notes an early Christian liturgical gathering on a Sunday to celebrate the Eucharist or Lord's Supper. The purpose of the gathering is expressed by the infin. *klasai arton*; see NOTE on 2:42. The liturgy is celebrated at night, perhaps as a recollection of Jesus' Last Supper with his disciples on the night before he died (cf. 1 Cor 11:23; Pliny the Younger, *Ep.* 10.96: *stato die ante lucem*, "on a set date before dawn").

Paul preached to the people. This could mean either that he filled the role of homilist at the celebration of the eucharistic liturgy or that he was addressing them as a visitor; the former is the more likely explanation, given the gen. absol. that precedes, but also as v 11 may show.

Because he was going to leave the next day, he prolonged his talk until midnight. Two reasons are being given for the accident that will occur: the first is Paul's long-winded discourse.

8. *Now there were many lamps in the upstairs room where we were gathered.* The second reason for the accident: the soporific effect of oil-fed lamps. The Alexandrian text reads *lampades*, "lamps," but MS D had *hypolampades*, which should normally mean "windows," but which some commentators understand as an alternate form for *lampades*, "lamps." See H. Smith, "Acts xx.8 and Luke xxii.43," *ExpTim* 16 (1904–5): 478.

9. *A young man named Eutychus.* This *neanias* is otherwise unknown. He is aptly named for the episode, "Lucky One."

who was sitting on a window sill, became more and more drowsy as Paul talked on and on. MS D curtails this description: "became quite somnolent as Paul talked."

Finally he went sound asleep and fell from the third storey to the ground. A similar accident of a slave who fell from a window while watching a spectacle and died is recorded in *POxy* 3.475; see H. J. Cadbury, *The Book of Acts in History*, 9.

They picked him up for dead. Lit., "he was picked up dead." The adj. *nekros* means that he was not alive.

10. *Paul hurried down to him, threw himself upon him, and put his arms around him.* Lit., "descending, fell upon him, and embracing him, said." Cf. 1 Kgs 17:21–22; 2 Kgs 4:34–35, for similar details in OT resuscitations.

he finally said, "Do not be alarmed! There is still life in him." Lit., "for his life/soul is in him." This may sound like a mere assertion of Paul who sizes up the situation; but Luke's intent is to tell of a miraculous effect produced by Paul (after a fall from such a height): "A real raising of the dead is meant" (Conzelmann, *Acts*, 169). Cf. 9:40–41.

11. *he went upstairs again, broke bread, and ate.* I.e., Paul continues the celebration of the Eucharist with the community, mentioned in v 7, at which he has been presiding.

Afterwards he chatted with them for a good while until dawn, and so he departed. Luke uses the ptc. *homilēsas*, the verb from which English "homily" is derived, but in this context the ptc. has its normal Greek meaning, "having conversed."

12. *They took the boy away alive to their great comfort.* Lit., "and were not moderately comforted." MS D reads rather, "When they said good-bye, he took the youth away alive, and they were not moderately comforted." In this reading, the verb, in the 3d sg., refers to Paul in the context, which is strange. This has perhaps resulted because of the intrusive character of v 11 in the story.

BIBLIOGRAPHY (20:7–12)

Bornhäuser, K., "Wann feierten die ersten Christen das Abendmahl?" *NKZ* 35 (1924): 147–59.

Cabaniss, A., "Early Christian Nighttime Worship," *JBR* 25 (1957): 30–33.

Callewaert, C., "La synaxe eucharistique à Jérusalem, berceau du dimanche," *ETL* 15 (1938): 34–73.

Cotter, W.E.P., "St. Paul's Eucharist," *ExpTim* 39 (1927–28): 235.

McCasland, S. V., "The Origin of the Lord's Day," *JBL* 49 (1930): 65–82.

MacDonald, D. R., "Luke's Eutychus and Homer's Elpenor: Acts 20:7–12 and *Odyssey* 10–12," *Journal of Higher Criticism* 1 (1994): 5–24.

Menoud, P.-H., "Les Actes des Apôtres et l'Eucharistie," *RHPR* 33 (1953): 21–36, esp. 27–32.

Morel, B., "Eutychus et les fondements bibliques du culte," *ETR* 37 (1962): 41–47.

Riesenfeld, H., "Sabbat et jour du Seigneur," *New Testament Essays: Studies in Memory of Thomas Walter Manson 1893–1958* (ed. A.J.B. Higgins; Manchester, UK: Manchester University Press, 1959), 210–17.

Roberts, J. E., "The Story of Eutychus," *Expos* 8/26 (1923): 376–82.

Rordorf, W., *Sunday: The History of the Day of Rest and Worship in the Earliest Centuries of the Christian Church* (Philadelphia: Westminster, 1968), 196–202.

Trémel, B., "A propos d'Actes 20,7–12: Puissance du thaumaturge ou du témoin?" *RTP* 30 (1980): 359–69.

g) PAUL'S JOURNEY TO MILETUS (20:13–16)

[13]We, however, went on ahead to the ship and set sail for Assos, intending to pick Paul up there. This was the arrangement he had made, because he had planned to travel overland on foot. [14]When he met us at Assos, we took him aboard and sailed for Mitylene. [15]The next day we put off from there and reached a point opposite Chios; on the second day we crossed over to Samos, and the day after that we put in at Miletus. [16]Paul had decided to sail past Ephesus, so as not to waste any time in Asia. For he was in a hurry to get to Jerusalem, if at all possible, by the feast of Pentecost.

WT: [13]went down to the ship. [15]Samos, and stayed at Trogyllium; the next day. [16]so that there might be no delay in Asia . . . [omits "if at all possible"].

COMMENT

Luke recounts how Paul continues his journey from Troas to Miletus in the spring of A.D. 58. The We-Section continues in 20:13–15 and tells about the different ways that Paul and his companions come to Assos, where he boards ship to join them. From the seaport of Assos, a short distance southwest of Troas, Paul first sails to Mitylene on the island of Lesbos, then to a spot opposite the island of Chios in the Aegean, and then to the island of Samos; from there he makes his way to Miletus, a town on the coast of Asia, south of both Ephesus and Trogyllium. Luke says that Paul did not stop at Ephesus, because he was in a hurry to get to Jerusalem for the Jewish feast of Pentecost. Another reason, however, may be the recollection of what happened to him when he was last in Ephesus.

The episode is again a simple narrative without complications. It merely tells of various stages of Paul's itinerary, derived from the We-Section and the Pauline source. What Luke has not derived from the We-Section, he composes as an introduction (vv 16–17) to the speech that Paul will soon address to the presbyters of Ephesus.

NOTES

13. *We, however, went on ahead.* MSS P[41], P[74], א, B[2], C, L, Ψ, 33, 36, 323, 614, and 1739 read *proelthontes,* "going on ahead," but MSS A, B*, E, and the *Koinē* text-tradition have rather *proselthontes,* "going to," and MS D reads *katelthontes,* "going down." The variants are insignificant.

to the ship and set sail for Assos. Assos was a port to the southwest of Troas, on the Gulf of Adramyttium and the coast of Mysia, opposite the northern end of the island of Lesbos. It was apparently founded in the sixth century B.C., and its artificial harbor provided passage from Pergamum and Troas. Later it became part of the Roman province of Asia. On "set sail," see NOTE on 13:13.

intending to pick Paul up there. This was the arrangement he had made, because he had planned to travel overland on foot. Why he wanted to do this is not clear, and Luke does not explain. The ship would have had to maneuver the treacherous coast and double Cape Lectum before arriving at Assos. That may have been part of the reason for Paul's decision to travel overland instead.

14. *When he met us at Assos, we took him aboard and sailed for Mitylene. Mitylēnē* was the chief town on the eastern side of the island of Lesbos in the Aegean Sea, off the west coast of Asia Minor. Hemer (*Book of Acts,* 125) notes that the "sequence of places mentioned in these verses is entirely correct and natural."

15. *The next day we put off from there and reached a point opposite Chios.* This probably refers to the town of *Chios* on the island of the same name, another

island in the Aegean Sea off the west coast of Asia Minor, more or less opposite Smyrna.

on the second day we crossed over to Samos. Instead of the adj. *hetera,* "another, a second (day)," some MSS (B, 36, 453, 1175) read *hespera,* "(in the) evening." This reading is preferred by Harnack (*Date,* 18). *Samos* was another island off the west coast of Asia Minor opposite the promontory of Mycale, southwest of Ephesus. A town on the island with the same name had been the home of the philosopher Pythagoras, and a Jewish community was settled there (1 Macc 15:23). MSS D, Ψ, and the *Koinē* text-tradition add *kai meinantes en Trōgylliō,* "and staying at Trogyllium," which would mean that Paul and his companions pass the night, not on the island of Samos, but opposite it at Trogyllium, a town on a promontory of the west coast of Asia Minor, to the south of Ephesus.

the day after that we put in at Miletus. Lit., "on the immediately following (day)," expressed by the middle of *echein* (as in Thucydides, *Histories* 6.3.2). *Milētos* was a seaport town, with four natural harbors, on the western coast of Asia Minor near the mouth of the Meander River on the Latmic Bay; it lay about 50 km south of Ephesus, as the crow flies. It had been a prominent city in the sixth century B.C., but its prominence waned later because of its rival Ephesus. A venerable Temple of Athena was erected there, but Apollo was regarded as its principal deity. The remains of a synagogue have been discovered there (see A. von Gerkan, "Eine Synagoge in Milet," *ZNW* 20 [1921]: 177–81). Cf. 2 Tim 4:20. See P. Trebilco, "Asia," *The Book of Acts in Its Graeco-Roman Setting* (BAFCS 2), 291–362, esp. 360–62.

16. *Paul had decided to sail past Ephesus, so as not to waste any time in Asia.* This probably means that he deliberately takes a fast-sailing ship that would not stop near Ephesus, but would go on directly to Miletus. This decision differs from what he promised in 18:21, but it may have also been motivated partly by a fear to appear again in Ephesus so soon after the riot of the silversmiths, which would have been still in the minds of many Ephesians. Because of the promise he decides rather to summon the presbyters of Ephesus to Miletus (v 17), which is strange in his hurry, because it would have taken them some time to get there. That, however, is not a concern of Luke, as he prepares to introduce Paul's important speech to the presbyters.

he was in a hurry to get to Jerusalem, if at all possible, by the feast of Pentecost. Having left Philippi at the end of the feast of Unleavened Bread (20:6), he hopes to be in Jerusalem by the Jewish feast of Pentecost (see NOTE on 2:1).

BIBLIOGRAPHY (20:13–16)

Hommel, H., "Juden und Christen im kaiserzeitlichen Milet: Überlegungen zur Theaterinschrift," *MDAI* 25 (1975): 157–95.

h) Farewell Discourse at Miletus (20:17–38)

17 From Miletus Paul sent word to Ephesus and summoned the presbyters of that
church. 18 When they came to him, he addressed them, "You know how I lived
the whole time among you from the day that I first set foot in Asia, 19 how I served
the Lord with all humility in the sorrows and trials that came to me because of
the plots of Jews. 20 In nothing did I shrink from telling you what was for your
own good or from teaching you in public and from house to house. 21 I bore
witness to Jews and Greeks alike about repentance before God and faith in our
Lord Jesus. 22 But now, as you see, I am on my way to Jerusalem, compelled by
the Spirit and not knowing what will happen to me there. 23 Only this I know,
that the Holy Spirit has been warning me from city to city that chains and hardships await me. 24 I set no store by my life, but aim only at finishing my course
and the ministry to which I have been assigned by the Lord Jesus: of bearing
witness to the gospel of God's grace. 25 Now then, I am fully aware that none of
you, among whom I went about preaching the kingdom, will ever see my face
again. 26 So today I solemnly assure you that I am not responsible for the blood
of anyone. 27 I never shrank from telling you all about God's will. 28 Keep watch,
then, over yourselves and over the whole flock, of which the Holy Spirit has
appointed you overseers, to shepherd the church of God, which he has acquired
with his own blood. 29 I know that when I am gone savage wolves will enter your
fold and will not spare the flock. 30 Why, even from your own number, men will
come forward to distort the truth and lead astray disciples who will follow them.
31 Be vigilant, then! Remember that night and day for three years I never stopped
warning each of you with tears. 32 Now I commend you to God and to the word
about his grace, which can build you up and give you an inheritance among all
those dedicated to him. 33 I have never coveted anyone's gold, silver, or garments.
34 You know yourselves that these very hands served the needs of myself and of
those who were with me. 35 In every way I have showed you that it is by such hard
work that we must help the weak and remember the words of the Lord Jesus, for
he said, 'It is more blessed to give than to receive.'" 36 When he finished speaking,
Paul knelt down and prayed with all of them. 37 They were all weeping loudly, as
they threw their arms around Paul and kissed him. 38 They were most distressed
at his saying that they would never see his face again. Then they saw him off to
the ship.

WT: 17 and sent for the presbyters. 18 him, and were together in one place, he . . . "You know, brothers, . . . Asia, for three years or even more. 21 in the Lord Jesus. 22 [omits "as you see" and "there"]. 23 in every city . . . await me in Jerusalem. 24 I take no account of my life . . . the ministry of the word which I have received from the Lord to bear witness to the gospel of God's grace to Jews and Greeks alike. 25 Now I know that . . . the kingdom of Jesus. 26 [omits "I solemnly assure you that"]. 27 [omits "you"]. 28 the church of the Lord. 29 enter the fold. 30 even from among you yourselves . . . and turn aside disciples. 32 to the Lord . . . the inheritance of all the dedicated. 33 any of your gold, silver, and garments. [35] [omits "Jesus" . . . 'Blessed is the one who gives rather than the one who receives'"]. [37] around him and kissed him.

COMMENT

Luke now introduces the third important Pauline speech in Acts (20:21–35), the one addressed to the presbyters of the Ephesian church, whom Paul has summoned to a meeting with him at Miletus. They are the current leaders of one of the main churches founded by Paul. The speech, its introduction (v 17), and its aftermath (vv 36–38) are an insertion into a We-Section, which resumes at 21:1. The introduction and aftermath are undoubtedly Lucan constructions. The discourse is the only Pauline speech addressed to Christians in Acts.

It is an important speech, because it serves as Paul's last will and testament and belongs to the genre of farewell speeches. It has none of the elements of a missionary speech (no kerygma) or a defense address (no *apologia*); rather it is totally pastoral in its conception, as Paul reflects on his own work, ministry, and testimony, and exhorts the presbyters of Ephesus to imitate his service of the Word.

The farewell speech is a well-known literary form: a speech made at a scene of separation (departure, death) that recalls past service, mentions the present situation, appoints successors for the future, exhorts to fidelity, and reminds the hearers that the speaker will probably not see them again.

Examples of the form can be found in the OT and extrabiblical Jewish literature: Gen 49:1–17 (Jacob's farewell); Deuteronomy as a whole (often interpreted as Moses' farewell); Jos 23–24 (Joshua's farewell); 1 Sam 12:1–25 (Samuel's farewell); Tob 14:3–11 (Tobit's farewell); *Jub.* 19:17–21:26 (Abraham's farewell); *Jub.* 36:1–16 (Isaac's farewell); the *Testaments of the Twelve Patriarchs; 1 Enoch* 91:1–19; *2 Esdras* 14:28–36; *2 Baruch* 77:1–16; Josephus, *Ant.* 4.8.45–47 §§309–26 (Moses' farewell). Other examples are found in Greek literature: Homer, *Iliad* 16.844–53 (Patroclus); 22.355–60 (Hector); Sophocles, *Oedipus Colonus* 1518–55 (Oedipus); Herodotus, *History* 3.65 (Cambyses). In the NT one often considers John 14–17 to be a further example. See E. Stauffer, *New Testament Theology* (London: SCM, 1955), 344–47.

The elements of this form are the following:

1. Recollection of the past and of relation to audience	20:18–19
2. Discharge of debts: did what he could	20:20–21, 26–27, 33–35a
3. Leave taking	20:22–25
4. Appointment of successor(s)	20:29–30
5. Exhortation to fidelity	20:31
6. Commendation or blessing	20:31, 35b

As a whole, the speech presents Paul, as he takes his leave and sets out for an unknown fate, exhorting the Ephesian presbyters and their church, giving himself as a model for their work, teaching, and care of Christians, and cautioning them about persecution and false teachers from within and without. In effect, it is the way that Luke wants Paul to be remembered, not only by those whom he is depicted exhorting, but also by the readers of Acts. In the speech the apostle sums up his missionary endeavors, places a martyr's crown on his head in advance, and sings a victory song over the sufferings to come. In Acts as a whole the speech foreshadows the end of Paul's missionary activity.

The structure of the speech is not easy to outline and has often been debated (by Dibelius, Gardner, Polhill, C.S.C. Williams). One may note the use of the adv. *nyn*, "now," in vv 22, 25, 32, which has often been used to articulate its structure (so Haenchen, *Acts*, 595).

1. 20:18–21 Retrospect: Paul's Work in Ephesus
2. 20:22–24 Present Situation: Relation to Audience
3. 20:25–31 Anticipation of the Future: the Church and Its Pastors
4. 20:32–35 Commendation and Blessing: Reminder to Care for the Needy.

Each section thus has a personal reference and a pattern-motif: Paul is the model for church leaders.

Other interpreters divide the speech into two parts only: 20:18–27 (Paul looks back); 20:28–35 (Paul looks forward); so Marshall (*Acts*, 329). Still others find a chiastic structure of a,b,c,b',a': 18–21, 22–24, 25, 26–30, 31–35 (so Exum and Talbert).

The speech has overtones of Paul's own preaching. Many are the allusions in it to ideas that one finds in his letters. In fact, it is the Pauline speech in Acts with the greatest number of such echoes. It also has the least number of OT allusions, apart from the speech in 17:22–31 (on the Areopagus), where they would not have been expected.

The speech is again a Lucan composition, but the fact that he so addressed the presbyters of Ephesus and the character of the speech he made are the sort of things that Luke might well have derived from his Pauline source. The echoes of Pauline teaching in the speech are not an indication, however, that Luke had read any of Paul's letters. He shows here at least that he was not wholly unfamiliar with Pauline phraseology.

In this speech the Lucan Paul passes on his last will and testament. Paul meditates on his past work in Ephesus, his relationship with the presbyters he has summoned, and warns them about their role in dangers coming to the church there. He recalls his humble service of the Lord, his sorrows and trials, and the plots concocted against him, also how he preached repentance before God and faith in the Lord Jesus. Paul knows that he has been called to suffer on behalf of the gospel that he preaches. He counsels the presbyters to keep watch over the church in Ephesus and become good shepherds of it. They must guard against the wolves that will seek to ravage it. Finally, Paul reminds them that he depended on no one for his sustenance and recommends that practice to them. He knows that he will never see them again, and so calls down God's blessing and grace upon them. It is a fitting way for the Christian reader of Acts to remember Paul.

NOTES

17. *From Miletus Paul sent word to Ephesus.* I.e., to the church that he had helped build up there. On Ephesus, see NOTE on 18:19.

summoned the presbyters of that church. On presbyters, see NOTE on 11:30. That there were presbyters in Ephesus would follow the analogy of what was said in 14:23; the Lucan Paul had set them up there. They would have had to journey the distance between Ephesus and Miletus, about 50 km, as the crow flies.

18. *When they came to him.* MSS P^{74}, A, and D add "and were together in one place." This was probably about three days after Paul's arrival at Miletus.

he addressed them, "You know how I lived the whole time among you from the day that I first set foot in Asia. The first part of Paul's discourse begins here and lasts until v 21. It reminds the presbyters how Paul conducted himself among them, singling out three characteristics of his ministry. This statement echoes what Paul himself wrote in 1 Thess 1:5c: "you know of what sort we were among you for your sake." Paul is not on the defensive; he is rather proposing his way of acting as a model for the Ephesian presbyters. Cf. 1 Thess 2:10–12. MS D adds "for three years or even more." Compare v 31 below. His first arrival in the province of Asia must have been closer to four years earlier, sometime in A.D. 54. See NOTE on 19:10.

19. *how I served the Lord with all humility.* This is the first characteristic of Paul's ministry. Among Christians the leader is the servant of all the others. His humble service is explained in terms of the persecution that he has been suffering. By *Kyrios* Paul means the risen Christ, as in vv 21, 24, 35. This statement echoes what Paul himself wrote in Rom 12:11; 14:18; 16:18 about "serving the Lord/Christ." See also 1 Thess 1:9; Phil 2:3; cf. Eph 4:2; Col 3:12, 24. See H. Rosman, "'In omni humilitate': Act 20,19," *VD* 21 (1941): 272–80, 311–20.

in the sorrows and trials that came to me because of the plots of Jews. See 19:9; 20:3; cf. 9:24; 21:27. For Pauline sayings about such subjective experiences and persecution, see 1 Thess 2:14–15; 2 Cor 2:4; Phil 3:18.

20. *In nothing did I shrink from telling you what was for your own good.* This is the second characteristic of Paul's ministry among them: the frankness of his preaching and teaching. Beyond what he suffered subjectively, Paul recalls what he sought to do objectively on behalf of the Ephesians. Compare v 27 below; also 1 Cor 10:33 for a similar Pauline remark.

or from teaching you in public and from house to house. Recall 18:7, 28. Cf. 2 Tim 4:2.

21. *I bore witness to Jews and Greeks alike.* This is the third characteristic of Paul's ministry: it was testimony to all human beings without distinction. See 14:1, 15; 16:31; 18:4, 28; 19:10, 17 and compare 1 Thess 1:9–10; 4:6; 1 Cor 1:24; 10:32; Rom 2:9–10.

about repentance before God. Recall the invitation that Paul offered to the Athenians in 17:30; compare 26:18, 20. On repentance, see NOTE on 2:38. Cf. Rom 2:4.

faith in our Lord Jesus. The Lucan Paul sums up the topics of his preaching: repentance before God and faith in the Lord Jesus. Recall 11:17; 14:23; 16:31; 20:21; 24:24; compare Gal 2:16; 3:26; Phil 1:29. The reminiscence about Paul's ministry is intended to be hortatory; it acts as a model for the role of the Ephesian presbyters.

22. *But now, as you see, I am on my way to Jerusalem.* The advs. *kai nyn idou* mark the transition to part two of the discourse (vv 22–24), as Paul reflects on his present situation, being en route to Jerusalem. The "way" that Paul will walk is the path to suffering. The Lucan Paul says nothing here about the collection that he was bringing.

compelled by the Spirit. Lit., "bound in the spirit," which could mean "constrained in (my own) spirit," but more likely means "influenced by the (Holy) Spirit," because elsewhere Luke has described Paul's missionary activity as guided by God's Spirit (13:2, 4, 9; 16:6–7; 19:21). Now Paul views his journey toward his city of destiny, Jerusalem, as imposed by God's Spirit.

not knowing what will happen to me there. In Rom 15:30–31 Paul recorded his own apprehensions about the reception that would greet him in Jerusalem, as he was about to leave Corinth with the collection, apprehensions about both Jews and Jewish Christians in Jerusalem.

23. *Only this I know, that the Holy Spirit has been warning me from city to city.* Paul's remarks foreshadow the premonitions to be given him in Tyre and Caesarea (21:4, 10–11). Such warnings prepare him for what he will meet in Jerusalem.

that chains and hardships await me. What Paul says here fulfills what 9:16 spoke about: that he would have to suffer for the sake of Jesus' name. He is aware of a possible coming imprisonment.

24. *I set no store by my life.* I.e., he is willing to forgo even life itself for the sake of the Word of God. See 15:26; 21:13; compare 1 Thess 2:8; Phil 1:20–23; 2 Cor 4:7–12; 6:4–10.

aim only at finishing my course. I.e., completing the task that the risen Christ has imposed on him. See Phil 2:16, for Paul's own way of expressing the same idea. Cf. 1 Cor 9:24–27; 2 Tim 4:7.

the ministry to which I have been assigned by the Lord Jesus. Recall Acts 9:15, where the risen *Kyrios* called him to be "a chosen instrument of mine to carry my name before Gentiles and kings, and the children of Israel." Cf. 2 Cor 5:18; 1 Cor 1:17; Gal 1:12; Col 4:17.

of bearing witness to the gospel of God's grace. This is the only place in Acts where Paul speaks of the "gospel," which is thus parallel to the one instance of it on the lips of Peter in 15:7 (see NOTE there). Paul declares that he has fulfilled the task laid upon him by Christ; he has preached the gospel and borne witness to it. Significantly, the "gospel of God's grace" is an apt summary of Paul's proclamation, but a phrase that never occurs in his own writings. See 1 Thess 2:9 for his own way of expressing this ministry; cf. 1 Cor 3:13; Rom 5:15; and E. Barnikol, "Der Lauf des Paulus," *TJb* 6 (1938): 101–28.

25. *Now then, I am fully aware that none of you, among whom I went about preaching the kingdom, will ever see my face again.* This is the beginning of the third part of the discourse (vv 25–31), introduced by *kai nyn idou* (see NOTE on v 22). It anticipates the future. See 20:38. In Rom 15:24–28 Paul's plans were to go to Rome and then to Spain, once he had visited Jerusalem with the collection for the poor which he had taken up in Greece. His coming captivity in Jerusalem, however, will stall those plans. Contrast what the Lucan Paul now says about never seeing the Ephesians again with what is implied in 1 Tim 1:3; 3:14; 4:13; 2 Tim 4:13, 20. On the kingdom, see NOTES on 1:3; 19:8. MS D adds "of Jesus."

26. *today I solemnly assure you that I am not responsible for the blood of anyone.* See 18:6. This is a strange assertion for the Lucan Paul to make in the light of his involvement in the stoning of Stephen (7:58) and his imprisonment of Christians (8:3). Conzelmann (*Acts*, 174) explains it thus: "If anyone now forfeits eternal life, Paul is innocent—he has carried out his missionary charge faithfully." Similarly Weiser (*Apg.*, 578).

27. *I never shrank from telling you all about God's will.* So the Lucan Paul conceives the task of the Christian messenger and witness: the proclamation of God's will; see NOTE on 2:23. By it Paul must mean what God has planned not only on his behalf but also for all those among whom he has worked and for those from whom he is now taking leave. Cf. 20:20; Luke 12:32; Eph 1:11. Paul insists that he has never hesitated in this proclamatory task. From this negative assertion about himself he passes to positive exhortation.

28. *Keep watch, then, over yourselves and over the whole flock.* Paul makes his parting exhortation to the Ephesian presbyters by stressing that they have two duties: they must conduct themselves with vigilant propriety and must show pastoral concern for the "flock" of God's people entrusted to their care, as sheep are to a shepherd. For God has made them pastors of the flock for the upbuilding of the church (see Eph 4:11–12). English "pastor" comes from Latin *pastor*, "shepherd." Cf. 1 Tim 4:16; 1 Pet 5:1–3; Matt 9:36. For the OT background of the image used, see Jer 13:17; 23:1–4; Ezek 34:1–6, 11–12; Zech 10:2c–3; 11:4–17. So Paul summons the presbyters to responsibility and readiness to serve the Christian community.

of which the Holy Spirit has appointed you overseers. Paul stresses that the function of the presbyters in the Ephesian church has been the work of the Spirit who has so designated them. The Spirit has set "presbyters" (20:17) over the church of Ephesus, who are now called *episkopous*, "overseers, guardians."

The noun *episkopos* occurs only here in the Lucan writings, but its cognate abstract *episkopē* is found in Luke 19:44 (in an unrelated sense) and in Acts 1:20 (in a related sense). In the Greek-speaking world of the time *episkopos* was used in a secular sense of a "superintendent" in a variety of areas: overseer of financial matters, inspector of civic associations or colonies, administrator of temples (see Aeschylus, *Eumenides* 740; Aristophanes, *Birds* 1022–23; Plato, *Laws* 6.762D;

9.872E; cf. *TDNT,* 2.608–14). It was also used of a synagogue overseer (ibid., 614–15). It is the etymological equivalent of Hebrew *mĕbaqqēr,* "overseer," the title of a superior of the Essene community in QL (1QS 6:12, 20; CD 9:18, 19, 22; 13:6, 7, 13, 16; 14:8, 11, 13; 15:8, 11, 14). Indeed, his role is explicitly compared with that of a shepherd in CD 13:9: "He will show mercy to them as a father to his children, and he will brin[g back] all those who stray as a shepherd does for his flock." Compare the use of the verb *bqr* in Lev 13:36; 27:33; 2 Kgs 16:15; 1QapGen 22:29. *Episkopos* as a title in the Christian church may be partly derived from such Essene usage, but, strangely enough, this Greek title is never used in the NT for an official in Christian communities in Judea. For instance, James who is seen in the NT to function as a superior of the Jerusalem Christian church (Acts 15:13; 21:18) is never called *episkopos.* When it is used of Christian church officials, it refers to communities of the eastern Mediterranean Greek world outside of Judea (Phil 1:1; Titus 1:7; 1 Tim 3:1–7). So its Christian usage may be partly owing to the contemporary Greek use of the title. In 1 Pet 2:25 "shepherd" and "overseer" appear together as designations of officials in the Christian community. In Titus 1:7–9 the moral qualities of the *episkopos* are set forth; they are repeated in 1 Tim 3:1–7 and extended to include managerial skills.

Strikingly, Luke predicates *episkopos* of those whom he had called *presbyterous* in v 17. He apparently saw no difference between their functions and regarded the titles as equal designations. In Phil 1:1 Paul greets *episkopoi* and *diakonoi* in a way that may designate church offices, perhaps "bishops" and "deacons," but there is no mention of *presbyteroi.* In fact, the latter are never mentioned in any of the uncontested Pauline letters or in the Deutero-Paulines. Three groups are mentioned in the Pastoral Letters, and *episkopos* occurs in the singular in Titus 1:7; 1 Tim 3:2. Titus 1:5–7 seems to treat the titles *presbyteroi* and *episkopos* as Luke does here (without any difference between them). Cf. 1 Tim 3:2–7, which spells out almost the same qualifications for an *episkopos* as Titus 1 does for *presbyteroi.* It is not until the time of Ignatius of Antioch that the three functions are clearly distinguished: the head of the presbyters becomes a bishop (even *monepiskopos,* even though Ignatius does not use that term). See further L. Porter, "The Word *Episkopos* in Pre-Christian Usage," *ATR* 21 (1939): 103–12; H. Karpp, "Bischof," *RAC* 2.394–407; K. Stalder, "Episkopos," *IKZ* 61 (1971): 200–32; J. Rohde, "*Episkopos,*" *EDNT* 2.35–36; R. E. Brown, *Priest and Bishop: Biblical Reflections* (New York/Paramus, NJ: Paulist, 1970), 38, 63–66.

to shepherd the church of God. See Ps 74:1–2 for the OT background of this idea.

The MSS א, B, 614, 1175, 1505, and several ancient versions (Vg, Syr, Boh) read *ekklēsian tou theou,* but MSS P[74], A, C*, D, E, Ψ, 33, 36, 453, 945, 1739, and 1891 read *ekklēsian tou Kyriou,* "the church of the Lord," which would not change the meaning, if by *Kyrios* were meant Yahweh, the God of the OT, as in 5:19; 7:31, 33; 8:26; 10:14 (see NOTE on 1:24). Since *Kyrios* is often used of the risen Christ, this reading would suit better the problematic phrase *tou haimatous tou idiou* in the following clause. For that very reason, however, the second reading becomes the *lectio facilior* and is not to be preferred. *Ekklēsia tou Kyriou* is found in the LXX (Deut 23:2–4; 1 Chr 28:8; Mic 2:5) but never elsewhere in the NT, whereas *ekklēsia tou theou*, "church of God," does occur (1 Thess 2:14; Gal 1:13; 1 Cor 15:9). Initially this phrase was used by Paul to designate the mother church in Jerusalem and Judea, but later he extended it to the Corinthian church (1 Cor 1:2; 2 Cor 1:1); and in time it became a designation for the universal church (1 Cor 10:32), as it is used here in Acts. Because it is a Pauline phrase, it may seem to be suspect here, having been used to harmonize the reading with other attested NT instances. It is, however, the *lectio difficilior* in the present context, given the following phrase, and therefore is to be preferred. See *TCGNT*, 425–27. On *ekklēsia* as a name for the Christian community, see NOTE on 5:11.

which he has acquired with his own blood. Or "bought." MSS P^{41} and D add the dat. *heautō*, "for himself," an insignificant addition. Otherwise all the important MSS (P^{41}, P^{74}, ℵ, A, B, C, D, E, Ψ, 33, 36, 945, 1175, 1739, 1891) read *dia tou haimatos tou idiou* or (in the *Koinē* text-tradition) *dia tou idiou haimatos*, "with his own blood" (*TCGNT*, 427). The obvious meaning of the phrase creates a difficulty with the antecedent of the preferred reading, "God." Hence some commentators (e.g., Bruce, Knapp, Pesch, Weiser) have preferred to understand this phrase to mean, "with the blood of his Own," i.e., his own Son. Such an absolute use of *ho idios* is found in Greek papyri as a term of endearment for relatives. Perhaps, then, it might be used here for Jesus, somewhat like Rom 8:32 or 1 Tim 5:8. That, however, is a last-ditch solution for this text-critical problem.

The mention of "blood" must refer to the vicarious shedding of the blood of Jesus, the Son. Through his blood the Christian community has become God's own possession, the people acquired for his renewed covenant. Cf. Eph 1:14; Heb 9:12; 1 Pet 2:9–10, which speak of God acquiring a people, echoing an OT motif (Isa 43:21; Ps 74:2). Luke may be thinking of the action of God the Father and the Son as so closely related that his mode of speaking slips from one to the other; if so, it resembles the speech patterns of the Johannine Gospel.

Haima is used in classical and Hellenistic Greek writers in the sense of "blood relationship, kin" (LSJ, 38: Aristotle, *Politics* 1262A; Aeschylus, *Eumenides* 606, 608; *PLips*. §28.1519 [*hōs ex idiou haimatos gennēthenta soi*, "as begotten to you from one's own blood"]). Possibly one could use that sense here, as K. G. Dolfe suggests ("by means of one nearest to him[self]),"but it really seems farfetched.

In any case, one should not miss the triadic nuance of this verse: the explicit mention of "God," "the Spirit," and the "blood," which implies the Son. It is a trinitarian dimension that Luke associates with the Christian community and its governance.

29. *I know that when I am gone savage wolves will enter your fold and will not spare the flock*. Lit., "that after my departure." Paul continues the shepherd imagery, as he warns about those who will come among Ephesian Christians to preach a gospel different from that which he preached and compares such teachers to wolves that attack a flock. Cf. Matt 7:15, where "ravenous wolves" designates "false prophets"; 1 Pet 5:8; 4 Ezra 5:18; *1 Enoch* 89:13. See G. Menestrina,

"*Aphixis*," *BeO* 20 (1978): 50; G.W.H. Lampe, "'Grievous Wolves' (Acts 20:29)," *Christ and Spirit in the New Testament: In Honour of Charles Francis Digby Moule* (ed. B. Lindars and S. S. Smalley; Cambridge: Cambridge University Press, 1973), 253–68; van Unnik, "Die Apostelgeschichte."

30. *Why, even from your own number, men will come forward to distort the truth and lead astray disciples who will follow them.* Cf. 1 John 2:19. Luke is not thinking specifically about Gnostics and the gnostic heresy, because there is no real evidence that gnosticism has yet reared its head. A number of other false teachings might be the object of such a warning. The Deutero-Paulines (Eph 5:6–14; Col 2:8) and the Pastorals (1 Tim 1:19–20; 4:1–3; 2 Tim 1:15) make it clear that false teaching was already emerging, and they would just as likely be the object of the Lucan Paul's admonition.

31. *Be vigilant, then!* Paul calls for vigilance, as in 1 Cor 16:13.

Remember that night and day for three years I never stopped warning each of you with tears. On "three years," see NOTES on 19:10; 20:18. Cf. 1 Cor 4:14–16; 2 Cor 2:4; 1 Thess 2:9–12; Phil 3:18.

32. *Now I commend you to God.* The fourth part of Paul's discourse (vv 32–35) begins now, as he commends the Ephesian presbyters to God's grace and blessing and exhorts them still further. This reading is found in MSS P^{74}, ℵ, A, C, D, E, Ψ, 33, 1739, and the *Koinē* text-tradition, but MSS B and 326 read *Kyriou*, "the Lord." Compare 14:23, whence the latter reading may have been derived by a copyist.

to the word about his grace. I.e., the grace mentioned in v 24, involved in the gospel that Paul has been preaching. For the gospel is the word of saving grace.

which can build you up and give you an inheritance among all those dedicated to him. Lit., "among all the sanctified" (perf. ptc.). Cf. 26:18. God's grace, so Paul prays, will exert its edifying and constructive power among them, both to build them up as church (1 Cor 14:4) and bring them to the destiny of all the saints. The OT background of that destiny is expressed in Deut 33:2–3; Wis 5:5. Cf. Eph 1:18; Rom 16:25.

33. *I have never coveted anyone's gold, silver, or garments.* The Lucan Paul protests the integrity of his personal conduct and his detachment from personal gain or greed, as did Paul himself in 1 Cor 9:4–12, 15; 2 Cor 7:2; 11:8–9; Phil 4:10–11. His protest echoes that of the prophet Samuel at the end of his life (1 Sam 12:3–4). See W. Pratscher, "Der Verzicht des Paulus auf finanziellen Unterhalt durch seine Gemeinden: Ein Aspekt seiner Missionsweise," *NTS* 25 (1978–79): 284–98.

34. *You know yourselves that these very hands served the needs of myself and of those who were with me.* Acts 18:3 tells how Paul worked at the tent maker's trade. For Paul's own statements about this matter, see 1 Thess 2:9; 1 Cor 4:12; cf. 2 Thess 3:7–8.

35. *In every way I have showed you that it is by such hard work that we must help the weak.* Cf. 1 Thess 4:10–11; 5:14; Rom 15:1; cf. Eph 4:28. See J.-L. D'Aragon, "'Il faut soutenir les faibles' (*Actes* 20:35)," *ScEccl* 7 (1955): 5–22, 173–203; cf. *ScCatt* 83 (1955): 225–40.

remember the words of the Lord Jesus, for he said, 'It is more blessed to give than to receive.'" MS D reads rather, "'Blessed is the one who gives rather than the one who receives,'" making the beatitude one pronounced over a person rather than over an action. So the Lucan Paul passes on a rare saying of Jesus, the sense of which is clear. Those who give to others and think of others rather than themselves are the ones over whom heaven's blessing will be shed. This saying of Jesus is not attested in any of the Gospels; it is thus one of the *agrapha*, "unwritten, unrecorded" (sayings of Jesus), i.e., preserved outside the canonical Gospels. Many interpreters think that Luke has picked up a saying otherwise known in the contemporary world and ascribed it to "the Lord Jesus." See Weiser, *Apg.*, 580.

See *1 Clem.* 2.1, where the saying reads rather: "Giving more gladly than receiving." Cf. Sir 4:31 ("Let not your hand be stretched out to receive, but held back when it is time to give"), which may reveal that a form of the saying was actually rather common in antiquity. Cf. Plutarch, *Moralia* 2.173D; Seneca, *Ep.* 81.17. Thucydides (*Histories* 2.97.4) is often cited as another parallel; see Haenchen, *Acts*, 594; N-A[27], 385; E. Plümacher, "Eine Thukydidesreminiszenz in der Apostelgeschichte (Act 20,33–35—Thuk. II 97,3f.)," *ZNW* 83 (1992): 270–75. That parallel, however, is far from clear; see J. J. Kilgallen, "Acts 20:35 and Thucydides 2.97.4," *JBL* 112 (1993): 312–14.

Cf. R. Roberts, "The Beatitude of Giving and Receiving," *ExpTim* 48 (1936–37): 438–41; U. Holzmeister, "'Beatum est dare, non accipere'? Act 20,35," *VD* 27 (1949): 98–101; J. Jeremias, *Unknown Sayings of Jesus* (New York: Macmillan, 1957), 77–81; K.-H. Rengstorf, "'Geben ist seliger denn Nehmen': Bemerkungen zu dem ausserevangelischen Herrenwort Apg. 20,35," *Die Leibhaftigkeit des Wortes: . . . Festgabe für Adolf Köberle* . . . (Hamburg: Im Furche-V., 1958), 23–33; H. Schürmann, "'Es tut not, der Worte des Herrn Jesus zu denken," *Katechetische Blätter* 79 (1954): 254–61.

36. *When he finished speaking, Paul knelt down and prayed with all of them.* This and the two following verses describe the aftermath of the Pauline discourse. Cf. 21:5. Paul ends his farewell discourse by joining the others in communing with God; we can only speculate about the content of their prayer, since Luke gives no inkling of it: a blessing on the presbyters in their leadership of the Ephesian church and a petition for a safe journey for Paul to Jerusalem and divine protection in view of what he might meet there. Their prayer together precedes Paul's farewell and departure.

37. *They were all weeping loudly, as they threw their arms around Paul and kissed him.* Luke describes the final leave-taking of Paul in classic OT terms: prayers, tears, embraces, kisses, and distress. Cf. Gen 33:4; 45:14. For the Christian kiss of farewell, see Rom 16:16; 1 Cor 16:20; 2 Cor 13:12; 1 Thess 5:26; 1 Pet 5:14.

38. *They were most distressed at his saying that they would never see his face again.* Recall v 25. This explains the reason for the weeping in v 37.

Then they saw him off to the ship. I.e., the ship that would take him on his journey toward Jerusalem.

BIBLIOGRAPHY (20:17–38)

Anon. (ed.), *Le strutture del discorso di Paolo a Mileto: Il colloquio sulla interpretazione, Macerata, 27–29 marzo 1980* (Turin: Marietti, 1981).

Aejmelaeus, L., *Die Rezeption der Paulusbriefe in der Miletrede (Apg 20:18–35)* (Annales Academiae Scientiarum Fennicae B232; Helsinki: Suomalainen Tiedeakatemia, 1987).

Barrett, C. K., "Paul's Address to the Ephesian Elders," *God's Christ and His People: Studies in Honour of Nils Alstrup Dahl* (ed. J. Jervell and W. A. Meeks; Oslo/Bergen: Universitetsforlaget, 1977), 107–21.

Bover, J. M., "Los presbíteros-obispos de Efeso (Act., 20,17 y 28)," *EstEcl* 2 (1923): 213–17.

Bovon, F., "Le Saint-Esprit, l'église et les relations humaines selon Actes 20,36–21,16," *Les Actes des Apôtres* (ed. J. Kremer), 339–58.

Budesheim, T. L., "Paul's *Abschiedsrede* in the Acts of the Apostles," *HTR* 69 (1976): 9–30.

Casalegno, A., "Il discorso di Mileto (*Atti* 20,17–38)," *RivB* 25 (1977): 29–58.

Claereboets, C., "In quo vos Spiritus Sanctus posuit episcopos regere ecclesiam Dei (Apg 20,28)," *Bib* 24 (1943): 370–87.

DeVine, C. F., "The 'Blood of God' in Acts 20:28," *CBQ* 9 (1947): 381–408.

Dolfe, K. G., "The Greek Word of 'Blood' [*sic*] and the Interpretation of Acts 20:28," *SEA* 55 (1990): 64–70.

Dupont, J., "La construction du discours de Milet (Ac 20,18–35)," *Nouvelles études*, 424–45.

———, *Le discours de Milet: Testament pastoral de Saint Paul (Actes 20,18–36)* (LD 32; Paris: Cerf, 1962).

Exum, C. and C. Talbert, "The Structure of Paul's Speech to the Ephesian Elders (Acts 20,18–35)," *CBQ* 29 (1967): 233–36.

Gardner, P., "The Speeches of St Paul in Acts," *Cambridge Biblical Essays* (ed. H. B. Swete; London: Macmillan, 1909), 379–419.

Hemer, C. J., "The Speeches of Acts: I. The Ephesian Elders at Miletus," *TynBull* 40 (1989): 77–85.

Javierre, A. M., "Act. 20,28 en la teología reformada del ministerio," *Miscelánea Comillas* 34–35 (1960): 173–205.

Kilgallen, J. J., "Paul's Speech to the Ephesian Elders: Its Structure," *ETL* 70 (1994): 112–21.

Knoch, O., *Die "Testamente" des Petrus und Paulus: Die Sicherung der apostolischen Überlieferung in der spätneutestamentlichen Zeit* (SBS 62; Stuttgart: Katholisches Bibelwerk, 1973), 32–43.

Kurz, W. S., *Farewell Addresses in the New Testament* (Zacchaeus Studies; Collegeville, MN: Liturgical, 1990), 33–51.

Lambrecht, J., "Paul's Farewell-Address at Miletus (Acts 20,17–38)," *Les Actes des Apôtres* (ed. J. Kremer), 307–37; repr. *Pauline Studies: Collected Essays* (BETL 115; Louvain: Leuven University Press/Peeters, 1994), 369–400.

Lövestam, E., "Paul's Address at Miletus," *ST* 41 (1987): 1–10.

Michel, H.-J., *Die Abschiedsrede des Paulus an die Kirche Apg 20,17–38: Motivgeschichte und theologische Bedeutung* (SANT 35; Munich: Kösel, 1973).

Munck, J., "Discours d'adieu dans le Nouveau Testament et dans la littérature biblique," *Aux sources de la tradition chrétienne: Mélanges offerts à Maurice Goguel* . . . (Bibliothèque théologique; Neuchâtel/Paris: Delachaux et Niestlé, 1950), 155–70.

O'Toole, R. F., "What Role Does Jesus' Saying in Acts 20,35 Play in Paul's Address to the Ephesian Elders?" *Bib* 75 (1994): 329–49.

Petöfi, J. S., "La struttura della comunicazione in *Atti* 20,17–38," *RivB* 29 (1981): 359–78.

Prast, F., *Presbyter und Evangelium in nachapostolischer Zeit: Die Abschiedsrede des Paulus in Milet (Apg 20,17–38) im Rahmen der lukanischen Konzeption der Evangeliumsverkündigung* (FzB 29; Stuttgart: Katholisches Bibelwerk, 1979).

Schmithals, W., "Apg 20,17–38 und das Problem einer 'Paulusquelle,'" *Der Treue Gottes trauen: Beiträge zum Werk des Lukas: Für Gerhard Schneider* (ed. C. Bussmann and W. Radl; Freiburg im B.: Herder, 1991), 307–22.

Schnackenburg, R., "Episkopos und Hirtenamt: Zu Apg 20,28," *Episcopus: Studien über das Bischofsamt: Seiner Eminenz Michael Kardinal von Faulhaber . . . dargebracht* (Regensburg: Pustet, 1949), 66–88.

Schürmann, H., "Das Testament des Paulus für die Kirche: Apg 20,18–35," *Unio Christianorum: Festschrift für Erzbischopf Dr. Lorenz Jaeger* . . . (ed. O. Schilling and H. Zimmermann; Paderborn: Bonifacius-Druckerei, 1962), 108–46; repr. *Traditionsgeschichtliche Untersuchungen zu den Synoptischen Evangelien* (Düsseldorf: Patmos, 1968), 310–40.

Stauffer, E., "Valedictions and Farewell Speeches," *New Testament Theology* (New York: Macmillan, 1955), 344–47.

Tragan, P.-R., "Les 'destinataires' du discours de Milet: Une approche du cadre communautaire d'Ac 20,18–35," *A cause de l'Evangile*, 779–98.

Unnik, W. C. van, "Die Apostelgeschichte und die Häresien," *ZNW* 58 (1967): 240–46; repr. *Sparsa collecta*, 1.402–9.

Wainwright, A. W., "The Confession 'Jesus is God' in the New Testament," *SJT* 10 (1957): 274–99, esp. 293–94.

Zeilinger, F., "Lukas, Anwalt des Paulus: Überlegungen zur Abschiedsrede von Milet Apg 20,18–35," *BLit* 54 (1981): 167–72.

B. Paul in Jerusalem (21:1–22:21)

1. Paul's Journey to Jerusalem (21:1–16)

21 [1]After we had finally parted from them, we put out to sea and set a course straight for Cos; on the following day we came to Rhodes, and from there to Patara. [2]When we found a ship there bound directly for Phoenicia, we boarded it and set off. [3]We caught sight of Cyprus but passed to the south of it, as we sailed on toward Syria. Finally we put in at Tyre, where the ship had to unload its cargo. [4]We looked up disciples there and stayed with them for seven days. Warned by the Spirit, they tried to tell Paul that he should not go to Jerusalem. [5]When our time was up there, we left and moved on; all of them with their wives and children came out of the town to see us off. On the beach we knelt down and prayed; [6]then finally we said our good-byes. After we boarded the ship, they returned home. [7]Continuing our voyage from Tyre, we put in at Ptolemais, where we greeted the brothers and spent one day with them. [8]The next day we pushed on and came to Caesarea, where we entered the house of Philip the evangelist, one of the Seven, and stayed with him. [9]This man had four unmarried daughters who had the gift of prophecy. [10]During our stay of several days there, a prophet named Agabus came down from Judea. [11]He came to us, took Paul's belt, and tied his own hands and feet with it. Then he said, "Thus says the Holy Spirit, 'In this way Jews in Jerusalem will bind the owner of this belt and will hand him over to Gentiles.'" [12]On hearing this, we and the residents of the place tried to urge Paul not to go up to Jerusalem. [13]Then Paul replied, "Why do you cry and break my heart like this? I am ready not only for imprisonment, but even for death in Jerusalem for the sake of the name of the Lord Jesus." [14]Since Paul would not be dissuaded, we said no more, but only, "Let the Lord's will be done!" [15]At the end of those days we got ready and started for Jerusalem. [16]Some of the disciples from Caesarea came along with us, escorting us to the house of Mnason, a Cypriot and one of the early disciples, with whom we were to stay overnight.

WT: [1]Going on board, we put out to sea . . . on the next day . . . Patara and Myra. [4][omits "there"] . . . go up to Jerusalem. [5]After finishing up our days there, we moved on our way. [6]Having said our goodbyes, we boarded the ship, and they. [8][omits "and stayed with him"]. [9]whose four daughters had the gift of prophecy. [10]an individual named Agabus. [11]He came up to us . . . [omits "Thus says the Holy Spirit" and "Jews"]. [12][omits "up"]. [13]But Paul said to us, "Why . . . this? Would that I might not only be imprisoned but even die for the sake of the name of the Lord Jesus." [15]Some days later, we said goodbye and started for Jerusalem. [16]They escorted us to those with whom we were to stay overnight. When we arrived in a certain village, we lodged with Mnason, a Cypriot and one of the early disciples.

COMMENT

Having finished his discourse to the presbyters of Ephesus, whom he had summoned to Miletus and with whom he finally prayed, Paul resumes his journey to Jerusalem, whither he has planned to arrive in time for the Jewish feast of Pentecost (A.D. 58). Now Luke continues to describe the stages of his journey: first to Cos, then to Rhodes and Patara, where Paul and his companions find a ship bound directly for Phoenicia. It brings him to Tyre, from which he eventually continues to Ptolemais and Caesarea Maritima, where he lodges with Philip the evangelist. Agabus symbolically informs Paul of the fate that awaits him in Jerusalem. Despite the warnings of friends, Paul resolutely makes his way to Jerusalem. In this he is like Jesus in the Lucan Gospel, resolutely making his way to the city of destiny (Luke 9:51, at the beginning of the travel account). From Caesarea Paul is escorted overland to Jerusalem.

The episode is again a narrative, a travelogue, into which Luke introduces the story of the prophet Agabus. Actually, the We-Section that was interrupted by the inserted speech of 20:18–35 and its aftermath, now resumes (21:1–18 [or in the WT 21:19]). Some commentators think that Luke has himself inserted v 4 or vv 4b–6, but that is because they are reluctant to regard the We-Sections as Lucan diary notes.

The Lucan story recounts Paul's Spirit-guided return to Jerusalem. His resolve to do so was stated in 19:21, the first stage of his journey to Rome. In spite of Paul's own awareness of coming trouble (20:22–23), he continues his journey to Jerusalem. Strangely enough, Christians of Tyre, who have been "warned by the Spirit" (21:4), try to deter him. Moreover, his future problems are stressed by the symbolic message given to him by Agabus (21:10–11). Yet in the face of all such premonitions, Paul's resolve remains firm "for the sake of the name of the Lord Jesus" (21:13). He arrives in Jerusalem (21:17) in time for the feast of Pentecost.

This episode presents once again the way that the Holy Spirit guides Paul's journeys and missionary endeavors. In this case, the prophet Agabus, moved by the Spirit, predicts the sufferings that Paul will encounter on his coming to Jerusalem, toward which he is now traveling. The Spirit had first designated Barnabas and Paul for Mission I in 13:2; now at the end of Mission III the Spirit through Agabus makes known to Paul that he will be handed over to Gentiles. Though Paul has been warned already that hardship awaits him in Jerusalem, he now makes known to all that he is ready for it, because he knows that the risen Lord is with him (18:9–10). What the Lucan Paul says here about his arrival in Jerusalem does not differ much from what Paul in Rom 15:30–31 expected from "unbelievers" and from "the saints" there, when he would arrive with the collection that he was bringing for the Christians of the holy city. Now he frankly admits, "I am ready not only for imprisonment, but even for death in Jerusalem for the sake of the name of the Lord Jesus" (21:13).

NOTES

21:1. *After we had finally parted from them, we put out to sea and set a course straight for Cos.* The We-Section begins anew. Again Luke uses the technical nautical term *anagein*; see NOTE on 13:13. *Kōs* was a Doric island in the Aegean Sea, off the southwest coast of Asia Minor. On the island there was a city with the same name, southwest of which was a famous shrine of Asclepius ever since the fourth century B.C.

on the following day we came to Rhodes. Rhodos was an island in the Sporades group in the Aegean Sea, off the southwestern point of Asia Minor, the main city of which had the same name. 1 Macc 15:23 shows that there were Jews already living on this island, a free city in the Roman province of Asia.

from there to Patara. Patara was a harbor town on the southern coast of Lycia, a port often used by the Roman grain fleet from Alexandria. MSS P[41] and D add *kai Myra*, "and Myra," which was an even better known harbor town to the east of Patara on the same southern coast of Asia Minor. It too served as a port for the importation of grain from Egypt, since it lay opposite Alexandria. The form of the name is a neut. pl. *Myra*, as in local inscriptions. Though some critics have argued that *kai Myra* was omitted in most MSS by homoeoteleuton (both Patara and Myra ending in -ra), the addition of the name in this verse is undoubtedly owing to a copyist's harmonization with 27:5. See *TCGNT*, 427.

2. *When we found a ship there bound directly for Phoenicia.* In the Alexandrian text-tradition, "there" would refer to Patara. For Phoenicia, see NOTE on 11:19.

we boarded it and set off. Again the technical nautical term *anagein*.

3. *We caught sight of Cyprus.* The island south of Asia Minor; see NOTE on 11:19.

passed to the south of it. Lit., "leaving it to the left side." The adj. *euōnymon* actually means "well-named," a euphemism for the "left" side of things, because the "right" side was thought to be the more auspicious or lucky side. Bad omens were thought to come from the left. Hence to sail from Patara to Syria and to leave Cyprus on the left side would mean to sail to the south of that island.

as we sailed on toward Syria. I.e., the Roman province of Syria; see NOTE on 15:23.

Finally we put in at Tyre. Tyros was one of the two most important cities in Phoenicia, about 33 km south of Sidon. Tyre, having offered resistance to Alexander the Great, finally capitulated in 332 B.C. after a long siege. Thereafter it came under the control of the Ptolemies of Egypt until 274, when it became a republic; it was made part of the Seleucid empire in 200. It again became a free city in 126 and eventually struck a *foedus*, "treaty," with Rome. In the period of Roman control of the eastern Mediterranean area, which began with the conquest of Pompey in 64 B.C., Tyre was an important commercial city. When Augustus came to the East in 20 B.C., he is said to have deprived Tyre of its liberty, but Strabo knows of it still as an independent city (*Geography* 16.2.23). See W. B. Fleming, *The History of Tyre* (CUOS 10; New York: Columbia University Press,

1915; repr. New York: Ams Press, 1966); N. Jidejian, *Tyre through the Ages* (Beirut: Dar el-Mashreq, 1969).

where the ship had to unload its cargo. Luke supplies no information about the kind of freight being carried by the ship.

4. *We looked up disciples there and stayed with them for seven days.* Luke notes that Christians were already resident in Tyre. On "disciples," see NOTE on 6:1. There is apparently no longer the haste mentioned in 20:16.

Warned by the Spirit, they tried to tell Paul that he should not go to Jerusalem. Recall the Lucan Paul's words in 20:22–23 about the future that awaits him in Jerusalem. He, however, is not deterred by the message given to him by these Tyrian Christians, who know about his coming troubles from "the Spirit." He has already been said to be traveling to Jerusalem under the Spirit's impulse (20:22), and so he is depicted as being willing to suffer for the gospel (20:24).

5. *When our time was up there, we left and moved on.* Lit., "when we happened to complete our days (there)." The time probably refers to what was needed to unload the cargo and perhaps load the ship anew.

all of them with their wives and children came out of the town to see us off. On the beach we knelt down and prayed. The Lucan motif of prayer is again introduced; they join in corporate prayer, as in 20:36–38. Luke uses the correct word *aigialos* for the Tyrian smooth "beach."

6. *finally we said our good-byes. After we boarded the ship, they returned home.* Luke is building up suspense in his story by narrating such details, and especially the stops at various points en route from Tyre to Jerusalem.

7. *Continuing our voyage from Tyre, we put in at Ptolemais.* Or possibly, "completing our voyage from Tyre," since *dianyein* can mean both "complete" and "continue." If the second translation is preferred, it might mean that Paul went from Ptolemais to Caesarea overland. *Ptolemaïs* was a seaport town in Phoenicia, at the northern end of the Bay of Acre, about 48 km from Tyre. It was built on the site of ancient Acco (Judg 1:31), which had been destroyed by Ptolemy I Soter I and rebuilt as a Hellenistic city. It was named Ptolemais by Ptolemy II Philadelphus in 261 B.C. (*Ep. Aristeas* 115; 1 Macc 5:15). It came under Roman control in 65 B.C., and Claudius settled a colony of Roman veterans there as *Colonia Claudia Caesaris Ptolemais* (Pliny, *Naturalis Historia* 5.17.75). Today Ptolemais is in modern Israel, near Haifa, north of Mt. Carmel.

where we greeted the brothers and spent one day with them. On *adelphoi*, see NOTE on 1:15.

8. *The next day we pushed on and came to Caesarea.* I.e., Caesarea Maritima, on which see NOTE on 8:40.

where we entered the house of Philip the evangelist, one of the Seven. Philip has already been mentioned in 6:5; see NOTE there. He was one of the Seven chosen to wait on tables, not one of the seven companions of Paul (20:4). The title *euangelistēs* occurs in the NT only here and in Eph 4:11; 2 Tim 4:5 (used of Timothy). In Ephesians 4 it is mentioned among the gifts with which the exalted Christ has endowed the church, along with apostles, prophets, pastors, and teachers, to equip God's dedicated people with ministries that would build up the body of Christ. This ministry should be that of preaching the gospel *(euangelion)*, but it is difficult to specify the way that function would differ from that of the other named ministers. Eusebius (*HE* 3.31.3–5; 3.39.9) calls Philip *ton apostolon* and says that he lived at Hierapolis with his daughters and that Papias was with them. So the confusion of Philip the evangelist with Philip the apostle (1:13) is of ancient date.

and stayed with him. For how long is not specified, but v 10 speaks of "several days."

9. *This man had four unmarried daughters, who had the gift of prophecy.* Lit., "and to him there were four virgin daughters (who were) prophesying." On *parthenoi*, see *EDNT*, 3.39–40. The exact nuance of the ptc. *prophēteuousai* is unclear: possibly a prophetic utterance in the sense of inspired preaching, or possibly Spirit-given charismatic speech of some sort, as in 2:17–18; 19:6.

10. *During our stay of several days there.* Lit., "as (we) were spending several days (there)."

a prophet named Agabus came down from Judea. He is apparently the same as the one mentioned in 11:28 (see NOTE there), but he is mentioned now almost as unheard of. For the sense in which *Ioudaia* is used, see the NOTE on 1:8.

11. *He came to us, took Paul's belt, and tied his own hands and feet with it.* Ms. D* reads *anelthōn*, "coming up to us." As did certain OT prophets, Agabus acts out his message. Compare Isa 20:2; Ezek 4:1; Jer 13:1–13; 16:1–4.

Then he said, "Thus says the Holy Spirit. Agabus presents himself as a Spirit-guided predictor of the future, and Paul becomes the recipient of a message from God's Spirit. Agabus interprets his symbolic action and introduces his warning with a borrowed OT phrase; compare "Thus says Yahweh" (Ezek 14:6). Recall Peter's experience of learning from the Spirit (10:19).

'In this way Jews in Jerusalem will bind the owner of this belt and will hand him over to Gentiles.'" Lit., "into the hands of Gentiles," i.e., to the occupying Roman authorities. So Paul learns of his coming imprisonment under the Romans in Jerusalem as a result of commotion started by Jews against him. Cf. 28:17; Mark 10:33; John 21:18.

12. *On hearing this, we and the residents of the place tried to urge Paul not to go up to Jerusalem.* This counsel coming from both Paul's traveling companions and Christians of Caesarea adds to the premonition of which Paul spoke in 20:22–23.

13. *Paul replied, "Why do you cry and break my heart like this? I am ready not only for imprisonment, but even for death in Jerusalem.* Lit., "what are you doing, crying and breaking my heart?" Paul is stirred by the emotion with which the counsel is being given, but he is determined not to be deterred by it. Luke uses the prep. *eis* in the sense of *en*, "in."

for sake of the name of the Lord Jesus." Paul assesses the danger with proper perspective: he is willing to die, if need be, for Jesus' name. He repeats what he said to the presbyters of Ephesus (20:24). Again the Lucan refrain of "the name" appears; see NOTE on 2:38. Cf. Rom 15:30–31; 1 Pet 4:14. Paul's determination also echoes the announcement of the passion of Jesus in Luke 18:31–34.

14. *Since Paul would not be dissuaded, we said no more, but only, "Let the Lord's will be done!"* Lit., "(with) him not being persuaded, we grew silent." Luke's phraseology is similar to that of 11:18. These Christians realize that their advice would not prevail, but they know that the Lord will protect his servant Paul. Their reaction echoes the words of Jesus' prayer in Gethsemane (Luke 22:42). In this case, *Kyrios* refers to God the Father.

15. *At the end of those days.* I.e., the days mentioned in 21:10.

we got ready and started for Jerusalem. I.e., for the overland journey of about 96 km.

16. *Some of the disciples from Caesarea came along with us, escorting us to the house of Mnason, a Cypriot and one of the early disciples, with whom we were to stay overnight.* MS D reads rather "They escorted us to those with whom we were to stay overnight. When we arrived in a certain village, we lodged with Mnason, a Cypriot and one of the early disciples." Apart from this passage, Mnason is otherwise unknown; the description of him as an "early disciple" may refer to Paul's evangelization of Cyprus (13:3–13); or he may have been a companion of Cypriot Barnabas (4:36). His house was probably about halfway between Caesarea and Jerusalem.

BIBLIOGRAPHY (21:1–16)

Blass, F., "Zur Rhythmik im Neuen Testament," *TSK* 80 (1907): 127–37.

Casson, L., "Speed under Sail of Ancient Ships," *TPAPA* 82 (1951): 136–48.

Corssen, P., "Die Töchter des Philippus," *ZNW* 2 (1901): 289–99.

Delebecque, E., "La dernière étape du troisième voyage missionnaire de Saint Paul selon les deux versions des Actes des Apôtres (21,16–17)," *RTL* 14 (1983): 446–55.

Hengel, M., "Der Historiker Lukas und die Geographie Palästinas in der Apostelgeschichte," *ZDPV* 99 (1983): 147–83.

Jordan, H., "Gibt es Rhythmik in den neutestamentlichen Briefen?" *TSK* 79 (1906): 634–42.

Patsch, H., "Die Prophetie des Agabus," *TZ* 28 (1972): 228–32.

2. Paul Visits James and the Jerusalem Presbyters (21:17–25)

[17]On our arrival in Jerusalem, the brothers there welcomed us warmly. [18]The next day Paul and the rest of us paid a visit to James, in the presence of all the presbyters. [19]After greeting them, Paul recounted in great detail all that God had accomplished among the Gentiles through his ministry. [20]When they heard it, they honored God, but they said to him, "You see, Brother, how many thousands of Jews have embraced the faith, all of them staunch upholders of the law. [21]They have been informed, however, that you teach all the Jews who live among Gen-

tiles to abandon Moses and tell them not to circumcise their children or observe their customary way of life. [22]What is to be done, then? They will surely hear that you have arrived here. [23]Our suggestion is that you do what we tell you. There are four men among us who are making a vow. [24]Take them and purify yourself along with them; pay the expenses for them so that they may have their heads shaved. Then all will know that there is nothing to the information that they have been given about you, but that you too follow and observe the law. [25]As for Gentile believers, we sent them a letter with our decision that they should avoid meat sacrificed to idols, blood, meat of strangled animals, and illicit marital unions."

WT: [17]Departing from there, we arrived in Jerusalem. [18]The next day we paid a visit to James together with Paul, and all the presbyters were gathered with him. [19]When we had greeted them, Paul related how God had accomplished. [20]they honored the Lord, saying, "You see, Brother, how many thousands have embraced the faith and all of them are staunch upholders of the law. [21][omits "all" and "tell them"] . . . or live according to his customs. [22]A crowd is surely to gather, for they will hear. [24][omits "for them"] . . . that they may be shaved. [25][adds after "believers:"] they have nothing to tell you, for we sent . . . that they need do no such thing except to avoid [omits "meat of strangled animals"].

COMMENT

In this account Paul brings Mission III to an end by his arrival in Jerusalem (21:17), presumably in time for the Jewish feast of Pentecost (20:16) of A.D. 58. Jerusalem proves to be a city of destiny for Paul, as it was for Jesus in the Lucan Gospel. On the day after his arrival he and his companions go to visit James, the leader of the Jerusalem Christian community, and the presbyters of that church who gather with him to welcome Paul. This is the main point in this episode: Paul's visit to the leaders of the Jerusalem Christian church, the mother church in Judea. Paul tells James and the presbyters about his missionary activity, and James counters by reporting on the number of Jews converted to Christianity, who also remain faithful to the Mosaic law. Then James suggests that, because of what Jerusalem Christians have been hearing about Paul, he purify himself in the Temple and join other Jewish Christians, who were engaged in the rite of the Nazirite vow, so that Jerusalem Christians will realize that Paul too is still fulfilling requirements of the Mosaic law. James also informs Paul about the letter that has been sent to the local churches of Antioch, Syria, and Cilicia about things that Gentile Christians should observe when they are living in mixed communities with Jewish Christians (alluding to 15:22–29). Thus, Paul for the first time learns about that communication.

Form-critically considered, the episode is again a narrative. The first two verses continue the second We-Section (20:13–21:18). Luke introduces into this passage, which is derived in part from the Pauline source (especially vv 19–20a), a speech of James (21:20b–25), a Lucan composition.

This is one of the passages in Acts that contributes much to what has been called the Paulinism of Acts, because it depicts Paul carrying out prescriptions of the law that would normally seem to be contrary to his preaching about justification by grace through faith and not through deeds prescribed by the law (see Introduction §173). Luke has already depicted Paul consecrating himself by a vow (18:18). Now Paul even pays the expenses of others who are performing the rites of such a vow, perhaps because they were too poor to pay for themselves, but on the recommendation of James.

What is strange at this juncture in Acts is that Paul arrives in Jerusalem, and there is no mention of the collection that he has had taken up in Gentile Christian churches for the poor Christians of Jerusalem (see Gal 2:10; 1 Cor 16:1–4; 2 Cor 8:1–7; 9:1–5; Rom 15:25–27, 31). Later on, it will be mentioned (24:17), but in a subdued way and hardly given the importance that it receives in Paul's own letters.

In this episode we see the Lucan Paul making himself all things to all human beings (1 Cor 9:22). He tells James and the presbyters of Jerusalem about all that God has accomplished through him among the Gentiles and hears from James how many Jews have accepted the message of the gospel. Lest Jerusalem Jews learn that he has now arrived and take action against him, he follows James's advice and purifies himself in the Temple and pays the expenses for four men who have been completing the rite of the Nazirite vow. Jewish Christian that he is, the Lucan Paul acquiesces to James's suggestion, even though he has never insisted that his Gentile converts do anything similar. This was not a compromise that Paul makes of his own beliefs or teachings in following James's advice; rather Paul performs the Jewish ritual acts in an effort to keep peace in the Jerusalem church, because he knows that those rites do not undercut his basic allegiance to the risen Christ.

NOTES

17. *On our arrival in Jerusalem, the brothers there welcomed us warmly.* Lit., "we being at Jerusalem," a badly composed gen. absol., which refers to the pron. *hēmas* later in the sentence, which it should not do (BDF §423.2). This is probably the reason why the WT ameliorates the Greek text by beginning, "Departing from there, we arrived in Jerusalem," i.e., departing from Caesarea. Jerusalem has been the goal of Paul's journey, which began in Corinth at the end of the winter season of A.D. 58. He wanted to arrive in Jerusalem by the feast of Pentecost (20:16), and the Lucan story suggests that he did so arrive as planned. He is warmly welcomed by the Jewish Christians of Jerusalem. This verse is transitional; the episode really begins with v 18.

18. *The next day Paul and the rest of us paid a visit to James.* Lit., "on the following (day) Paul with us entered chez James." James was last mentioned in 15:13; see NOTE there and on 12:17. Paul's visit to him now reveals how he has come to be what would later be called the residential "bishop" (*episkopos*) of Jerusalem, a title that is not given to him in Acts. Of him Eusebius reports: he was "first elected to the episcopal throne of the church in Jerusalem" (*HE* 2.1.2).

in the presence of all the presbyters. Lit., "and all the presbyters were on hand." MS D reads: "The next day we paid a visit to James together with Paul, and all the presbyters were gathered with him. [19]When we had greeted them, Paul related how God had accomplished . . ." The WT thus extends the We-Section. Note again the Lucan hyperbole (see NOTE on 2:44). On presbyters, see NOTE on 11:30.

19. *After greeting them, Paul recounted in great detail all that God had accomplished among the Gentiles through his ministry.* The Alexandrian text reads *aspasamenos,* a masc. sg. ptc., which would make Paul alone greet the assembly, whereas the WT reads the masc. pl. ptc. referring to "we." Recall 15:4, 12, which also supplied reports of Paul's *diakonia,* "ministry," among the Gentiles.

20. *When they heard it, they honored God.* Lit., "they glorified God," i.e., praised God for what had been achieved in Paul's ministry to the Gentiles. James and the Jerusalem presbyters willingly praise God for Paul's ministry, but they also counter with a report of Christianity's progress among Jews of Judea.

they said to him, "You see, Brother, how many thousands of Jews have embraced the faith, all of them staunch upholders of the law. Lit., "how many myriads (ten thousands) among the Jews have believed, all being zealots for the law." The WT omits "among the Jews." The last clause is all-important in the report being given to Paul and his companions: Jews have become Christians, and they continue to observe the Mosaic law. See 1 Macc 2:27 *(pas ho zēlōn tō nomō)* for the characteristic Jewish phrase that Luke employs; also 1 Macc 2:42; 1QS 1:7; 6:13–14. Such Jewish Christians would adhere rigorously to the law and insist on its observance by all who become members of the New Covenant (Christianity). Note again the Lucan hyperbole in the many myriads of Jewish converts; see NOTE on 2:44. It suits his picture of the growth of the Christian church.

21. *They have been informed.* I.e., apparently by Jews of the diaspora where Paul has been at work.

that you teach all the Jews who live among Gentiles to abandon Moses. Lit., "you teach apostasy from Moses." One will look in vain in the account of Acts so far for such activity of Paul and also for such a formulation in Paul's letters. It might refer generically to what he wrote in Gal 3:10–25 about "Moses" as a legal system and about Christians who "are no longer under a custodian," viz., "the law . . . our custodian" (3:24). Contrast Rom 3:19–20, 31. In any case, James and the presbyters want Paul to make a good impression on Jewish Christians of the Jerusalem church: that he is someone who does have regard for the law of Moses. Again, Lucan hyperbole.

and tell them not to circumcise their children. What Paul says in Gal 5:2–3, 6, 11 or 1 Cor 7:19 might give a different impression, but also recall the circumcision of Timothy in Acts 16:3.

or observe their customary way of life. Cf. 28:17. James's statement foreshadows the charge to be made in 24:5.

22. *What is to be done, then?* The rhetorical question introduces the suggestion that James makes to Paul.

They will surely hear that you have arrived here. The WT reads "A crowd is sure to gather, for they will hear . . ." "They" would refer not only to Jewish Christians, but also to Jews of Jerusalem.

23. *Our suggestion is that you do what we tell you. There are four men among us who are making a vow.* This refers to the same type of (Nazirite) vow that Paul is said to have taken in 18:18; see NOTE there. Luke thus depicts Paul conforming to what had been the custom of early Jewish Christians, reflecting a practice later abandoned when Christianity was clearly defined over against Judaism.

24. *Take them and purify yourself along with them.* Lit., "and be purified along with them." The problem with James's suggestion is that it is unclear whether he means that Paul should partake in the Nazirite ceremony itself with the four or undertake a rite of purification different from the Nazirite ceremony and still pay the expenses of the four so that they can complete that Nazirite ceremony. The Nazirite vow was believed to make one "holy" (Num 6:5) or "holy to the LORD" (Num 6:8), i.e., dedicated or consecrated to Yahweh for a set period. "All the days of his separation" (Num 6:4) was later understood in Mishnaic regulation as a period of thirty days (*m. Nazir* 1:3), with purification after an unexpected defilement of the Nazirite (Num 6:9–12). So James's suggestion could mean that Paul should join in the Nazirite ceremony. Because the purification that Paul undergoes lasts for only "seven days" (21:27), possibly the purification of which James speaks is rather that required of a Jew returning from a trip abroad (to pagan territories) to undergo a purification that would rid him of the defilement caused by "earth from a foreign country" (*m. Oholoth* 2:3). This Paul could do along with paying the expenses of the Nazirite ceremony for the four men who needed assistance, without taking part in the Nazirite ceremony himself. Some think that the "purification" meant for Paul would have been either that of Num 19:12 or something similar to it. So Schneider (*Apg.*, 2.310). In any case, the matter is incidental to Luke's real story, which will be narrated in the following episode. Cf. Philo, *De ebrietate* 1.2; Str-B, 2.80–89, 757–61.

pay the expenses for them. See Num 6:14–15 for the requirements of the termination of the vow rite. The expenses would not have been light. Compare the similar action of Herod Agrippa I noted in Josephus, *Ant.* 19.6.1 §§293–94.

so that they may have their heads shaved. See Num 6:9, 18–19, which prescribes the shaving "on the seventh day" and "at the door of the tent of meeting" that it may be "put on the fire" as a sacrifice of peace offering.

all will know that there is nothing to the information that they have been given about you, but that you too follow and observe the law. This expresses the purpose of James's suggestion to Paul.

25. *As for Gentile believers, we sent them a letter with our decision.* I.e., the decision of "the apostles and presbyters" of Jerusalem for the local churches of Antioch, Syria, and Cilicia (15:23). Now Paul seems to learn for the first time in Acts about the letter that James and the elders have sent in 15:22–29. See COMMENT on 15:13–21.

they should avoid meat sacrificed to idols, blood, meat of strangled animals, and illicit marital unions." For details about these matters, see NOTES on 15:20.

BIBLIOGRAPHY (21:17–25)

Baumgarten, M., "Über das Zeugnis Pauli von seiner Gesetzestreue," *Saat auf Hoffnung* 40 (1903): 35–51.

Campenhausen, H. von, "Die Nachfolge des Jakobus: Zur Frage eines urchristlichen 'Kalifats,'" *ZKG* 63 (1950–51): 133–44.

Catchpole, D. R., "Paul, James and the Apostolic Decree," *NTS* 23 (1976–77): 428–44.

Jasper, G., "Der Rat des Jakobus . . . : Apg. Kap. 21–28," *Saat auf Hoffnung* 71 (1934): 89–105.

Jervell, J., "Das gespaltene Israel und die Heidenvölker: Zur Motivierung der Heidenmission in der Apostelgeschichte," *ST* 19 (1965): 68–96.

Kittel, G., "Die Stellung des Jakobus zu Judentum und Heidenchristentum," *ZNW* 30 (1931): 145–57.

Rinaldi, G., "Giacomo, Paolo e i Giudei (*Atti* 21,17–26)," *RivB* 14 (1966): 407–23.

Songer, H. S., "Paul's Mission to Jerusalem: Acts 20–28," *RevExp* 71 (1974): 499–510.

3. Paul's Arrest in Jerusalem (21:26–40)

[26]Then on the following day Paul took the men and went through the rite of
purification with them. He went into the Temple to give notice of the day when
the period of purification would be completed, when the offering would be made
for each of them. [27]The seven-day period was nearly over, when some Jews from
Asia recognized Paul in the Temple and stirred up a whole crowd there. They
arrested him, [28]shouting, "Help, fellow Israelites! Here is the one who is teaching
everyone everywhere against our people, our law, and this place. Besides, he has
even brought Greeks into the Temple and has profaned this sacred place." [29]Be-
cause they had earlier seen Trophimus, an Ephesian, with him in the city, they
now assumed that Paul had brought him into the Temple. [30]The whole city was
soon in turmoil, and people came running together from all sides. They took
hold of Paul and dragged him out of the Temple, and its gates were closed at
once. [31]They were trying to kill him, when a report reached the commander in
charge of the cohort that all Jerusalem was in chaos. [32]He immediately took his
soldiers and centurions and descended on them. When they saw the commander
and the soldiers, they stopped beating Paul. [33]The commander came up to them,
arrested Paul, and ordered him bound with double chains. Then he tried to ask
who he was and what he had been doing. [34]But some people in the mob shouted
one thing at him, others another. Since the commander could not get to the
truth because of the turmoil, he ordered Paul to be led away to headquarters.
[35]When Paul got to the steps, he actually had to be carried up by the soldiers
because of the violence of the mob. [36]For the crowd of people kept following and

shouting, "Away with him!" [37] As Paul was about to be led into the headquarters, he said to the commander, "May I say something to you?" He answered, "Can you speak Greek? [38] Aren't you the Egyptian who caused a riot some time ago and led four thousand assassins out into the desert?" [39] Paul replied, "I am a Jew, a native of Tarsus, a citizen of no mean city in Cilicia. I beg you, let me speak to these people." [40] So with his permission Paul stood on the steps and motioned to the people for silence. A great hush fell on them, as he began to address them in Hebrew.

WT: [26] [omits "Paul"]. [27] As the seventh day was coming to an end. [28] shouting and saying. [29] [omits "in the city"]. [30] [omits "and its gates were closed at once"]. [31] [omits "in charge of the cohort" and adds at the end:]. "So see that they do not create a riot." [34] [omits "in the mob"]. [35] violence of the people. [36] [omits "of people"] . . . "Away with this enemy of ours!" [37] [omits "Paul"] . . . he addressed the commander, "May I speak with you?" [39] [omits "a citizen of no mean city"] . . . "I beg you to allow me to speak."

COMMENT

Luke continues his story of Paul's testimony in Jerusalem. Paul acts on the advice of James and accompanies the men to the Temple for the rite of purification and the end of the Nazirite vow ceremony. When seven days are almost over, some Jews from the province of Asia recognize Paul and summon others to gather and arrest him, maintaining that he has been teaching against the Jewish people, their law, and has even defiled the Temple precincts by introducing Greeks into it. Soon Jerusalem is in an uproar, and the commander of the Roman cohort stationed there has to intervene to restore order and prevent the murder of Paul. The commander, after unsuccessfully trying to ascertain the reason for the uprising, arrests Paul and orders him taken to headquarters in the Fortress Antonia. There Paul asks the commander whether he might address the people who have gathered.

Form-critically, the episode is another narrative in Acts. It is a detailed and dramatic account of Paul's arrest in Jerusalem, filled with rhetorical hyperbole ("the whole city was soon in turmoil"). It is intended to set the stage for another Pauline defense speech in the following episode. Luke uses here information derived from his Pauline source.

Jewish agitation against Paul, noted earlier (13:50; 14:2, 5, 19; 17:5–9; 18:12–17), now comes to a climax in his arrest. In Ephesus the agitation against him came from a pagan Demetrius, because he feared detriment to the shrine and cult of Artemis of the Ephesians. Now Jews from Asia (21:27), sojourning in Jerusalem, lead a tumult against Paul, fearing that his evangelizing activity is becoming an attack on the Temple, the Mosaic law, and the traditions of Israel itself.

Though Paul is arrested by the Roman tribune, he is rescued from diaspora Jews by an agent of the Roman government. So Luke clearly makes his point: Paul is not one who causes political uprising (as did "the Egyptian") or jeopardizes the law and order of the Roman world.

This episode recounts how the tribulations that awaited Paul in Jerusalem actually begin. Paul is pounced on by diaspora Jews from Asia who accuse him of defiling the Temple and teaching against the Jewish people, the Mosaic law, and the Jerusalem Temple. The mob seizes Paul and drags him from the Temple, "and its gates were closed at once" (21:30). They and the mob that gathered were on the point of killing Paul, when the Roman commander descends on them and takes Paul into custody. Paul begs the commander for permission to address the crowd that has come together. All this has happened to Paul as he was completing the Jewish rite of purification in the Temple itself. Thus, ironically enough, the Temple has become for Paul the place where his Jerusalem troubles begin. Luke adds the symbolic detail, that the gates of the Temple "were closed at once." The Temple henceforth would have no meaning for the Christian church. Early Christians had in the beginning continued to worship there with Jerusalem Jews, but now the latter have turned against the "apostle of the Gentiles," and the gates of their Temple have been closed against him.

NOTES

26. *on the following day Paul took the men and went through the rite of purification with them.* I.e., Paul was purified and together with the four men saw to the end of their rite. See Num 6:2–12. Paul described himself in 1 Cor 1:19–23 as becoming "as a Jew to the Jews so that I might win more of them over." That policy might explain the activity that Luke ascribes to Paul here. Even if Paul did not perform the Nazirite ceremony himself but purified himself as a Jew returning from a foreign country, he nevertheless paid the expenses for the four Nazirites and thus approved of their ritual performance.

He went into the Temple to give notice of the day when the period of purification would be completed, when the offering would be made for each of them. The offering of two young pigeons or two turtledoves to the priest at the door of the tent of meeting, one as a sin offering and the other as a burnt offering, was prescribed for the Nazirites (Num 6:10–11).

27. *The seven-day period was nearly over.* Lit., "when the seven days were about to be completed." Ms. D reads "As the seventh day was coming to an end." See NOTE on v 24 above and compare the time indication in 24:11.

when some Jews from Asia recognized Paul in the Temple. I.e., Jews from the area about Ephesus in the Roman province of Asia, where Paul had recently been evangelizing and working (19:1–20:1). They may be the same as those who appear in 24:19. Luke carefully notes that the turmoil was not started by Jewish Christians of Jerusalem. Those causing the disturbance were diaspora Jews, apparently present in the Holy City for the Jewish Feast of Weeks (see NOTE on 2:1).

stirred up a whole crowd there. They arrested him. Lit., "they laid hands on him," with the purpose of dragging him from the Temple precincts and doing away with him.

28. *shouting, "Help, fellow Israelites!* See NOTE on 1:16.

Here is the one who is teaching everyone everywhere against our people, our law, and this place. Paul is accused publicly of speaking against the Jewish people, the Mosaic law, and the Jerusalem Temple. The accusation resembles that made against Stephen in 6:11, 13–14. The charges would result in widespread Jewish reaction against Paul, even ostracism of him.

he has even brought Greeks into the Temple. I.e., Gentiles or foreigners *(allogeneis)* were not permitted beyond the Court of the Gentiles. Lest foreigners ritually defile the sacred precincts, the inner courts were marked off by a stone balustrade with slabs inscribed in Greek and Latin warning foreigners of the death penalty for trespassing (see Josephus, *J.W.* 5.5.2 §§193–94; *Ant.* 15.11.5 §417; Philo, *Legatio ad Gaium* 31 §212 ["death without appeal"]). This regulation was an interpretation of Num 1:51; 3:10,38; 18:7. The text of the Greek inscription was "No one of another nation may enter within the fence and enclosure round the Temple. Whoever is caught shall have himself to blame that his death ensues." Two copies of such an inscription have been discovered. The inscription is to be found in *NTB* §50; *CIJ* §1400; *OGIS* §598. Cf. J. H. Iliffe, "The *thanatos* Inscription from Herod's Temple," *QDAP* 6 (1937): 1–3 (+ pls. I–II); E. J. Bickermann, "The Warning Inscriptions from Herod's Temple," *JQR* 37 (1946–47): 387–405; S. Zeitlin, "The Warning Inscription of the Temple," *JQR* 38 (1947–48): 111–16; J. M. Baumgarten, "Exclusions from the Temple: Proselytes and Agrippa I," *JJS* 33 (1982): 215–25; P. Segal, "The Penalty of the Warning Inscription from the Temple of Jerusalem," *IEJ* 39 (1989): 79–84.

has profaned this sacred place." I.e., by introducing Greeks into it, who would have defiled it in a ritual sense.

29. *they had earlier seen Trophimus, an Ephesian, with him in the city.* Trophimus was named as a traveling companion of Paul, who came "from Asia" in 20:4; see NOTE there. Now he unwittingly becomes the occasion for Paul's arrest. See 2 Tim 4:20, where Trophimus is said to be left ill at Miletus.

they now assumed that Paul had brought him into the Temple. I.e., into the inner courts of the Temple. It is not said, however, that Paul had actually done so. It might seem strange that they would not have investigated further before reacting as they are described, but mob reactions are not predictable or logical.

30. *The whole city was soon in turmoil.* More Lucan hyperbole. Luke wants the reader to understand that the call for help (v 28) was heard outside of the Temple precincts.

and people came running together from all sides. Lit., "there occurred a running together of the people." Luke uses a Greek construction found in Jdt 10:18 (LXX) to express the concourse of Jerusalemites.

They took hold of Paul and dragged him out of the Temple, and its gates were closed at once. I.e., presumably by the Temple police in an effort to secure the area. The WT omits the last clause, probably because of the implication of the action. Jerusalem's holiest place is closed to Paul and his message. The Temple where he was carrying out a Jewish purification rite becomes the place from which diaspora Jews and the mob of Jerusalem Jews drag him, and the gates were closed against him.

31. *They were trying to kill him, when a report reached the commander in charge of the cohort.* From 23:26 one learns that the commander's name was Claudius

Lysias. He is called *chiliarchos,* "leader of a thousand men," but the title was actually the Greek equivalent for Latin *tribunus militum,* "tribune of the soldiers." In a Roman legion there were usually six *tribuni.* The *speira,* "cohort," garrisoned in the neighboring Fortress Antonia at the northwest corner of the Temple area (Josephus, *J.W.* 5.5.8 §§243–45), was a detachment of 1,000 men, usually 760 infantrymen and 240 cavalrymen. One of the tasks of the Roman cohort was to quell riotous conduct in the Temple area, such as was likely to occur on feast days.

that all Jerusalem was in chaos. Lucan hyperbole extends the riotous conduct in the Temple to the whole of the city.

32. *He immediately took his soldiers and centurions and descended on them.* Those under the tribune's authority were *stratiōtai,* "soldiers," and *hekatontarchai,* "centurions," officers in charge of a hundred soldiers. There was a stairway that permitted access to the Temple area from the Fortress Antonia to the spot where Paul was being assaulted (Josephus, *J.W.* 5.5.8 §243).

When they saw the commander and the soldiers, they stopped beating Paul. I.e., for fear of arrest by the Roman authorities.

33. *The commander came up to them, arrested Paul, and ordered him bound with double chains.* The Roman commander assumes that Paul, who was being attacked, had done some wrong. Paul is thus rescued by the Roman commander and comes under Roman jurisdiction, not that of the Temple police. He is tied to two soldiers by hand chains (cf. 12:6), and so the predicted sufferings of 20:22–23 and 21:11 begin to come to pass.

he tried to ask who he was and what he had been doing. I.e., as a person in authority, the tribune tried to ascertain the cause of the commotion. He tries to find out who Paul is and what he has been doing. He does not yet know of his Roman citizenship, despite what he later writes to governor Felix (23:27).

34. *some people in the mob shouted one thing at him, others another.* The tribune cannot find out who Paul is because a typical mob reaction to his inquiry ensues, but the denunciation of Paul is sufficient for the tribune to take police action against him and arrest him.

Since the commander could not get to the truth because of the turmoil, he ordered Paul to be led away to headquarters. I.e., soldiers are to lead Paul via the stairway to the *parembolē,* "camp, barracks," Luke's way of referring to the Fortress Antonia. Josephus describes the Fortress at some length (*Ant.* 15.11.4 §§403–9; 18.4.3 §92; *J.W.* 5.5.8 §§239–42).

35. *When Paul got to the steps, he actually had to be carried up by the soldiers because of the violence of the mob.* The violence of the uprising against Paul made it impossible for Paul to proceed up the stairway on his own. Josephus mentions the steps of Antonia in *J.W.* 5.5.8 §243.

36. *For the crowd of people kept following and shouting, "Away with him!"* The same cry appears in Luke 23:18 against Jesus. Cf. John 19:15. The WT reads "Away with this enemy of ours!"

37. *As Paul was about to be led into the headquarters, he said to the commander, "May I say something to you?"* As we learn, Paul addresses him in Greek, the

language commonly used by Roman authorities in the eastern Mediterranean area of the empire.

He answered, "Can you speak Greek? Lit., "Do you know Greek?" The Roman tribune is surprised that Paul addresses him in Greek. Being a diaspora Jew from Tarsus, Paul would have used that language from childhood, even though he called himself "a Hebrew of the Hebrews" (Phil 3:5). That undoubtedly meant that he was a Greek-speaking Jew who also spoke a Semitic language; see NOTE on "Hellenists" in 6:1. G. Mussies, "Greek as the Vehicle of Early Christianity," *NTS* 29 (1983): 356–69; J. N. Sevenster, *Do You Know Greek? How Much Greek Could the First Jewish Christians Have Known?* (NovTSup 19; Leiden: Brill, 1968).

38. *Aren't you the Egyptian who caused a riot some time ago and led four thousand assassins out into the desert?"* Lit., "four thousand men of the sicarii," i.e., of the dagger bearers. This is a reference to chauvinist Judeans, called Sicarii because of the *sica*, "dagger," which they used (see Josephus, *J.W.* 2.13.3 §§254–57; cf. M. Smith, "Zealots and Sicarii, Their Origins and Relation," *HTR* 64 [1971]: 1–19). Luke undoubtedly uses the name in a generic sense only.

The Roman tribune confuses Paul with an Egyptian instigator. His question is introduced with *ouk ara*, expressing incredulity or astonishment and expecting the answer "yes" (BDF §440.3). Josephus tells of an Egyptian who came to Jerusalem, claiming to be a "prophet," and who led a mob of people by a circuitous route "from the desert" to the Mt. of Olives, where they were to watch the walls of Jerusalem fall. The mob had to be subdued by Roman soldiers led by the governor Felix (*Ant.* 20.8.6 §§169–72; *J.W.* 2.13.5 §§261–63). Though thousands were killed, the Egyptian escaped. Now the Roman tribune in charge of the garrison thinks that he has caught him at last. Whereas Josephus (§261) gives their number as 30,000, the Lucan figure of 4,000 sounds more plausible. It is not a mere confusion of Δ (= 4) with Λ (= 30), as Lake and Cadbury once suggested (*Beginnings*, 4.277). Even though details differ, both Luke and Josephus have come independently on reports of the same event and date the uprising and its aftermath in the time of Felix the procurator. Cf. 5:36–37.

39. *Paul replied, "I am a Jew.* Even though Paul is a Christian missionary, he still identifies himself to the Roman commander by his ethnic background, thereby implying that he is not an Egyptian. Cf. 2 Cor 11:22; Rom 11:1; Phil 3:5, for passages in Paul's own letters, where he maintains his Jewish status, but significantly he does not claim Judea to be his place of origin; that implies that he was a diaspora Jew.

a native of Tarsus, a citizen of no mean city in Cilicia. This further explains why Paul is not a rebel like the Egyptian. In good Hellenistic Greek fashion, he states first his *natio* (a Jew), then his *origo* (Tarsus), and then his *civitas* (Cilician citizenship). Litotes is used to stress the importance of Paul's origin. An admission of this sort appears nowhere in Paul's own letters; if we were left with only them, we would never know that Paul was a native of Tarsus. On Tarsus, a principal city of Cilicia, see NOTE on 9:11. Cf. Euripides, *Ion*, 8, where Athens is said to be *ouk asēmos Hellēnōn polis,* "a not insignificant city of the Greeks." See R. Harris, "Did St. Paul Quote Euripides?" *ExpTim* 31 (1919–20): 36–37.

I beg you, let me speak to these people." I.e., to those who were Jews like Paul himself.

40. *So with his permission Paul stood on the steps and motioned to the people for silence.* Recall Luke's description of the beginning of Paul's speech in the synagogue of Pisidian Antioch (13:16). He makes the usual gesture of an ancient orator (cf. 12:17; 19:33; 26:1).

A great hush fell on them, as he began to address them in Hebrew. Luke uses *tē hebraïdi dialektō,* "in the Hebrew dialect." This phrase will appear again in 22:2; 26:14. It is debated whether this would mean that Paul spoke to the people of Jerusalem in the sacred language of the Temple, i.e., Hebrew, in which most of the OT was written, or in Aramaic, the Semitic sister language that was most commonly used in Palestine at that time. It is undoubtedly the latter, because, when this phrase (or *hebraïsti*) is used elsewhere in the NT (e.g., John 5:2; 19:13, 17, 20; 20:16; Rev 9:11; 16:16), it is usually accompanied by Greek transcriptions of words that are Aramaic, not Hebrew. See Fitzmyer, "The Languages of Palestine in the First Century A.D.," *WA,* 29–56; *EDNT,* 1.370. For a highly questionable attempt to identify it as Hebrew, see J. M. Grintz, "Hebrew as the Spoken and Written Language in the Last Days of the Second Temple," *JBL* 79 (1960): 32–47; H. Ott, "Um die Muttersprache Jesu: Forschungen seit Gustaf Dalman," *NovT* 9 (1967): 1–25, esp. 22; S. Safrai, "Spoken Languages in the Time of Jesus," *Jerusalem Perspective* 4/1 (1991): 3–8, 13.

BIBLIOGRAPHY (21:26–40)

Gineste, B., "'*Esan gar proeôrakotes*' (*Actes* 21, 29): Trophime a-t-il été 'vu' à Jérusalem?" *RevThom* 95 (1995): 251–72.

Légasse, S., "L'Apologétique à l'égard de Rome dans le procès de Paul: Actes 21,27–26,32," *RSR* 69 (1981): 249–55.

Nestle, Eb., "Acts 21:39," *ExpTim* 21 (1909–10): 525.

Radl, W., "Paulus traditus: Jesus und sein Missionar im lukanischen Doppelwerk," *EA* 50 (1974): 163–67.

Schwartz, J., "A propos du statut personnel de l'apôtre Paul," *RHPR* 37 (1957): 91–96.

4. PAUL'S DISCOURSE TO THE JERUSALEM CROWD (22:1–21)

22 [1]"Brothers and fathers, listen to me now, as I make my defense before you."
[2]When they heard that he was addressing them in Hebrew, they were more inclined to be quiet. [3]"I am a Jew, born in Tarsus in Cilicia. But I was brought up

in this city and educated strictly in our ancestral law at the feet of Gamaliel. I have been zealous for God, just as all of you are today. [4]I persecuted this Way to the point of death, arresting and imprisoning both men and women. [5]To this the high priest and the whole council of elders can testify for me. For from them I even obtained letters to our brother Jews in Damascus; I went there, intending to bring back to Jerusalem for punishment the prisoners I would take. [6]As I was on my way and was drawing near to Damascus, suddenly about noontime a great light happened to flash from the heavens about me. [7]I fell to the ground and heard a voice say to me, 'Saul, Saul, why are you persecuting me?' [8]I answered, 'Who are you, sir?' He said to me, 'I am Jesus the Nazorean, whom you are persecuting,' [9]Those who were with me saw the light but did not hear the voice speaking to me. [10]I asked, 'What am I to do, sir?' and the Lord replied, 'Get up; go into Damascus and there you will be told all that you are assigned to do.' [11]Since I could not see because of the glare of that light, I had to be led into Damascus by the hand of my traveling companions. [12]There a certain Ananias, a devout observer of the law and well spoken of by all the Jews who lived there, [13]came, stood by me, and said, 'My brother Saul, recover your sight.' In that instant I regained my sight and looked at him. [14]Then he said, 'The God of our ancestors has chosen you to know his will, to see the Upright One, and to hear the sound of his voice. [15]You are to be a witness for him before all people, testifying to what you have seen and heard. [16]So why delay? Get up, be baptized, and wash your sins away, by calling on his name.' [17]When I returned to Jerusalem and was praying in the Temple, I happened to fall into a trance [18]and see the Lord speaking to me: 'Hurry, leave Jerusalem as soon as possible, because they will not accept your testimony about me.' [19]I answered, 'Lord, they know indeed that from one synagogue to another I used to imprison and flog those who believed in you. [20]While the blood of your witness Stephen was being shed, I stood by, giving my approval of it. I even guarded the cloaks of those who killed him.' [21]He said to me, 'Go, for I am sending you far away to the Gentiles.' "

WT: [1][omits "to me"]. [2]they became more quiet, and he said. [3]zealous just as you are today. [4][omits "to the point of death"]. [6][omits "I was on my way," "suddenly," and "from the heavens"]. [10][omits "the Lord"]. [11]I got up and, since I. [12]by all the Jews in Damascus. [13]came and said to me. [omits "and looked at him"]. [15]You are to be his witness. [18]and I saw him speaking [omits "about me"]. [20][omits "giving my approval of it"].

COMMENT

The stage has been set for the first defense speech that Paul will make in Acts, as Luke depicts him addressing the crowd assembled before the Fortress Antonia in Jerusalem. In it he recounts his former life as a Jew and as a persecutor of Christians. Conscious reference is made in 22:20 to 7:58 and 8:1, verses that are often considered to have been deliberately added by Luke to the source material he had for the Stephen episode. Paul stresses his close relationship with the Jewish people and his collaboration with the high priest and the Sanhedrin. Then Paul explains how he has been called by the risen Christ to be a Christian missionary to the Gentiles. Once he mentions that, however, the crowd interrupts his speech.

In the form of a defense speech Luke presents the second account of Paul's conversion. The first was the dramatic narrative of 9:1–19, with which this speech now has many similar details, but there are some differences and some new details, not previously revealed. The differences stem mainly from the casting of the details into a speech, which Paul makes to the Jerusalem crowd. The first part of the speech also repeats 21:39–40, but it strikingly makes no reference to the charge that Paul has been defiling the Temple. Only indirectly is that charge countered in what Paul says about his fidelity to Judaism and zeal for God.

In this Lucan composition Paul is depicted as the pious loyal Jew and zealous persecutor of Christians, and then as a convert to Christianity, but the Lucan emphasis falls on Paul's Jewishness. The details in this speech are a modified form of those told in the narrative of chap. 9. What is new may possibly be derived from Luke's Pauline source. Despite his strict upbringing, his education at the feet of Gamaliel, and his persecution of Christians, Paul ascribes the change in his life to heaven's command. His call to be a missionary to the Gentiles, however, is now ascribed not to his experience on the road to Damascus, but to a vision of the risen Christ in Jerusalem at a later date. In any case, his evangelization of Gentiles is likewise attributed to a heavenly commission. He has been told to depart from Jerusalem, because people there will not understand him or accept his role. In effect, Luke makes this speech to be a Pauline argument in defense of Christianity against Judaism, or better, a Pauline explanation of Christianity as a legitimate development of Judaism.

The picture of Paul in chap. 22 emphasizes his role as the devout Jewish *witness* (in vv 5, 12, 15, 18, 20 and the reference to Stephen the "witness" in v 20). Accordingly, in the course of the episode one notes the stress on *seeing*: the light, *doxa*, the "Upright One."

This speech of Paul brings to a climax Paul's evangelization and missionary endeavors, because even though it is a defense speech, Paul is evangelizing indirectly the Jerusalem Jews who listen to him, but there is no kerygmatic utterance in the speech.

The structure of this speech can be seen thus:

Ingratiating address	22:1–2
Paul's Jewish background and zealous activity	22:3–5a
Paul's commission to persecute Damascus Christians	22:5b
Paul's journey to Damascus: Encounter with Jesus	22:6–11
Paul's reception by Ananias	22:12–16
Paul's visit to Jerusalem: Commission to preach to the Gentiles	22:17–21

In reciting the story of his life, education, and conversion, the Lucan Paul assures his audience of Jerusalem Jews and Jewish Christians about his own Jewish background. He describes himself as a Jew, "zealous for God," and one who persecuted Christians, even in distant cities. Once, on his journey to Damascus, the risen Christ accosted him and made him see the error of his ways. This Jesus who appeared to him told him to proceed to Damascus, where he would be told what to do. He must get up, be baptized, be washed of his sins, and call upon the name of Jesus Christ. This he did, only to be converted to the Way that he had been persecuting. He was now to become a "witness" to the risen Christ who was calling him. So Paul recounts the change in his life: from an archpersecutor of Christians to a witness of Jesus Christ, who was sending him afar to evangelize the Gentiles. This he has been doing as a Jewish Christian. This is the way that the Lucan Paul now recounts his call in addressing the Jerusalem mob that has surrounded him. This is the testimony that he bears to the influence of Christ in his own life. The risen Christ has spoken to him, and he has heeded his call.

NOTES

22:1. "*Brothers and fathers.* For this and similar modes of address in a public speech, see NOTES on 1:15, 16; 7:2. Stephen began his speech with the same formula, which now seems less appropriate, seeing that Paul is addressing an open-air crowd. The formula of address stems from Luke himself, who is making Paul, in effect, address all Israel, members of the Sanhedrin included.

listen to me now, as I make my defense before you." Paul uses the technical term for this kind of speech, *apologia,* "defense." Cf. Philostratus, *Vita Apollonii* 7.29, 32–35, 40–41. This is the first of five defense speeches that Paul makes in Acts.

2. *When they heard that he was addressing them in Hebrew, they were more inclined to be quiet.* A parenthetical remark of Luke explains that Jews of Jerusalem are surprised that a diaspora Jew would address them, not in Greek, but in Aramaic, their native language; see NOTE on 21:40.

3. "*I am a Jew, born in Tarsus in Cilicia.* This is a repetition of what has been explained in 9:11, and to the tribune in 21:39 (see NOTES there). Paul proudly insists on his Jewish status, even from birth, although he comes from a diaspora background.

I was brought up in this city. In Tarsus or in Jerusalem? A case could be made for either interpretation, which the Greek would tolerate. The particle *de* would mean "and" in the first option, "but" in the second. I have taken it in the second meaning, because Paul implies that he was brought to Jerusalem as a child. In 23:16 we shall learn that Paul has a sister resident in Jerusalem. About such an education in Jerusalem Paul says not a word in his letters; we learn about it only from Luke here in Acts, and that creates a problem. In so understanding the text, I am following W. C. van Unnik, *Tarsus or Jerusalem: The City of Paul's Youth* (London: Epworth, 1962); repr. *Sparsa Collecta,* 1.259–327. He argues mainly on the basis of the three ptcs. *gegennēmenos, anatethrammenos, pepaideumenos,* as a conventional threesome or "fixed literary unit." See Acts 7:20–22; Plato, *Alcibiades I* 122B; *Laws* 6.783B; Arrian, *Bithynica* frg. 1.2 for the use of three similar verbs or nouns. Compare, however, N. Turner, *Grammatical Insights into the New Testament* (Edinburgh: Clark, 1965), 82–84; M. S. Enslin, "Paul and Gamaliel," *JR* 7 (1927): 360–75.

educated strictly in our ancestral law at the feet of Gamaliel. Paul depicts himself as a student of Mosaic law and ancestral customs under the guidance of the famous Rabbi Gamaliel, who has already been mentioned in 5:34 (see NOTE there). Recall what Paul himself says about his training "in Judaism" in Gal 1:14. This education under Gamaliel is contested by Haenchen, *Acts*, 625. For "at the feet of," see Luke 8:35; 10:39. Compare Josephus, *J.W.* 2.8.14 §162.

I have been zealous for God. Paul makes use of an OT expression to describe his way of life so far (Num 25:13); he has not been against God, but zealous for his cause. Cf. Ps 69:10; 1 Macc 2:26–27, 58; Jdt 9:4 for a similar zeal (see NOTE on 21:20). In his own letters (Gal 1:13–14; Phil 3:5–6) Paul himself describes his zeal correspondingly, without speaking of a zeal for the law. Cf. 26:5–6.

just as all of you are today. Luke is concerned to depict Paul as a loyal, strict-living Pharisaic Jew, one who should be acceptable to his Jewish audience, even though he is one whom the *Kyrios* himself has won over. So he does not make Paul disown his Jewish past. Cf. Rom 10:2 and Josephus, *Life* 38 §191.

4. *I persecuted this Way to the point of death.* On "Way" as a designation for Christianity, see NOTE on 9:2. Paul mentions this persecution as a consequence of his zeal for God. See 7:58; 8:1, 3; 9:1, 21; 22:19–20; 26:11 for instances of his persecution. In the case of Stephen it was *achri thanatou*, "to the point of death."

arresting and imprisoning both men and women. So Paul has been depicted in 9:2. He himself admitted this persecution in Gal 1:13, "I persecuted the church of God violently and tried to destroy it." Cf. Phil 3:6a; 1 Cor 15:9.

5. *To this the high priest and the whole council of elders can testify for me.* This is a puzzling remark, because the high priest at the time of Paul's arrest in A.D. 58 would have been Ananias, son of Nedebaeus (cf. 23:2, 5; 24:1). MS 614 even adds the name *Ananias*. He is hardly the same as the one who might have commissioned Paul to go to Damascus ca. A.D. 36. That would rather have been Joseph Caiaphas, son-in-law of Annas (see NOTE on 4:6). In the "council" *(presbyterion)* or the "Sanhedrin" (*synedrion*, Luke 22:66) of Jerusalem, however, there may well have been elders who did remember the commission of which Paul speaks. See J. Jeremias, "*Presbyterion* ausserchristlich bezeugt," *ZNW* 48 (1957): 127–32.

from them I even obtained letters to our brother Jews in Damascus; I went there. Recall 9:2, which tells of his carrying letters to the "synagogues" of Damascus (see NOTES there).

intending to bring back to Jerusalem for punishment the prisoners I would take. Luke again uses the fut. ptc. to express purpose; see NOTE on 8:27; cf. ZBG §282.

6. *As I was on my way and was drawing near to Damascus.* MS D reads "as I was drawing near to Damascus about noontime a great light happened to flash about me."

suddenly about noontime a great light happened to flash from the heavens about me. Recall 9:3. "About noontime" makes it clear that Paul's vision was not a dream of the night. This detail was not mentioned in chap. 9 but will reappear in 26:13.

7. *I fell to the ground and heard a voice say to me.* Recall 9:4a.

'Saul, Saul, why are you persecuting me?' Recall 9:4b. Again the name *Saoul* recurs; see NOTE on 13:9.

8. *I answered, 'Who are you, sir?' He said to me, 'I am Jesus the Nazorean, whom you are persecuting.'* Recall 9:5. This form of Jesus' words adds *ho Nazōraios,* which did not appear in 9:5. On it, see NOTE on 2:22.

9. *Those who were with me saw the light but did not hear the voice speaking to me.* In 9:7 Paul's companions are said to stand by speechless: "they heard the voice, but saw no one." MSS D, E, Ψ, 1739, and the *Koinē* text-tradition add "and became afraid." This difference from 9:7 is almost a contradiction, a strange thing in a composition by one and the same writer, but Luke makes no profession of accuracy of detail in such matters. His concern is only to show that the traveling companions are aware of something that is happening to Paul, and so they are witnesses of his experience on that road. See H. R. Moehring, "The Verb *akouein* in Acts ix 7 and xxii 9," *NovT* 3 (1959): 80–99.

10. *I asked, 'What am I to do, sir?'* This question is not part of the narrative in chap. 9. What is reported there in narrative form is made into the Lord's reply in this speech.

the Lord replied, 'Get up; go into Damascus and there you will be told all that you are assigned to do.' Recall 9:6. The only difference now is the new verb *tetaktai,* "it has been arranged" (for you to do).

11. *Since I could not see because of the glare of that light, I had to be led into Damascus by the hand of my traveling companions.* Recall 9:8b. MS B reads rather *ouden eblepon,* "I saw nothing."

12. *There a certain Ananias.* See 9:10 and NOTE there.

a devout observer of the law and well spoken of by all the Jews who lived there. MSS P[41], Ψ, 33, 1739, and the *Koinē* text-tradition add "in Damascus." This description of Ananias is new; nothing like it appeared in chap. 9. Some MSS (P[74], A) omit the descriptive adj. *eulabēs,* "devout," which is meant to explain that Ananias as a Jew was not only observant but also enjoyed a good reputation among fellow Jews of Damascus (cf. 16:2). He who was a hesitant agent of God in Paul's conversion in chap. 9 is now depicted as a devout Jewish Christian. Nothing is said here of his vision (recall 9:10–16).

13. *came, stood by me, and said, 'My brother Saul, recover your sight.'* Paul's discourse omits the objections of Ananias and the dialogue he had with the risen Christ, because he was not aware of those details, which were part of the dramatic presentation in chap. 9. Recall also 9:17, where Ananias explains to Paul that he has been sent by Christ to cure him. All that is abridged. Luke uses the verb *anablepein,* which can mean either "look up" (Luke 9:16) or "see again," i.e., regain sight, said of a blind or blinded person (Luke 7:22; Acts 9:12, 17–18). The latter sense is intended here.

In that instant I regained my sight and looked at him. Some MSS (P[41]) and ancient versions omit "and looked at him."

14. *he said, 'The God of our ancestors has chosen you to know his will.* This statement of Ananias is new; in 9:17 Ananias spoke of the "Lord Jesus" and conveyed Jesus' commission. Now, because Paul is explaining his experience to Jeru-

salem Jews, he insists that the God of the OT has been operative in the experience he has had. The God of the patriarchs has made the difference in Paul's life. Cf. Exod 3:15–16; Deut 1:11, 21; Josh 18:3; Dan 3:26, 52 for the formula used to describe God. God's "will" is invoked to explain the role that Paul is destined to play in the divine plan of salvation now announced as coming through Jesus Christ; see NOTES on 2:23 and 20:27.

to see the Upright One. So Ananias interprets Paul's experience for him. Jesus, whom Paul has been persecuting, is *ho dikaios,* "the Upright One" (see NOTE on 3:14). Cf. 7:52. It is a title that Jews would recognize, since it is the epithet for the scion of David in Jer 23:5–6; 33:15.

to hear the sound of his voice. Hearing the sound of the voice of the Upright One (= the risen Christ) would enable Paul to carry out the commission that Ananias announces in the next verse.

15. *You are to be a witness for him before all people.* Paul's commission is couched in terms of testimony. He is to be, first of all, *martys,* "a witness" to the resurrection of the Upright One and to his ministry and message. In 9:15 Ananias was told by the Lord that Paul was to become "a chosen instrument of mine" to carry his name to Jews and Gentiles, which in effect says the same thing, but the stress is now on testimony to all people. That is also the reason for the Lucan emphasis on "seeing" in this chapter and on "light." Second, he is to bear this testimony "to all human beings."

testifying to what you have seen and heard. Thus Paul relates his commission by the risen Christ. Its origin, then, is the same as that of the Twelve (1:8). He has "seen" the Lord (cf. 1 Cor 9:1) and has "heard" his command.

16. *So why delay?* Lit., "now why is it not likely that you should delay?" i.e., react as you should.

Get up, be baptized, and wash your sins away, by calling on his name.' What was merely reported in the Lucan narrative of chap. 9 now becomes part of the directives of Ananias to Paul, as Paul tells the story. He must do four things: get up, be baptized, be washed of his sins, and call upon the name of Jesus. By undergoing baptism Paul's sins would be washed away. The refrain of the "name" recurs; see NOTE on 2:38.

17. *When I returned to Jerusalem and was praying in the Temple.* This is a new detail, since there is no mention of such an experience in chap. 9. That chapter tells of Paul's preaching in Damascus and later of his first visit to Jerusalem after his conversion (9:26–29; cf. Gal 1:18). There is nothing about his praying in the Temple or about a further vision of the Lord, as here. According to Gal 1:18 the first visit to Jerusalem occurred three years after Paul's conversion; see NOTE on 9:26. The Lucan Paul is thus eager to admit that he still continued to pray in the Temple after his conversion. Strikingly, Paul's commission is now related to an experience in Jerusalem, in contrast to chap. 9, where the commission is mediated by Ananias in Damascus. There Ananias is told that Paul is to be "a chosen instrument of mine to carry my name before Gentiles and kings, and the children of Israel" (9:15). All of this is the result not only of abridgment of the earlier narrative but also of a recasting of the narrative in speech form to make it more

convincing to the Jerusalemites who are being addressed. See C. Burchard, *Der dreizehnte Zeuge*, 164–65.

The syntax of this verse is quite strange. It begins with *egeneto de*, "and it happened that," on which the infin. *genesthai me en ekstasei*, "that I fell into a trace," depends (see *Luke*, 118). The usual temporal accompaniment is expressed by a dat. pron. with a ptc., *moi hypostrepsanti eis Ierousalēm*, "(it happened) to me returning to Jerusalem," to which is strangely added a gen. absol. *kai proseuchomenou mou en tō hierō*, "and as I was praying in the Temple." This is a violation of the normal grammatical rule of the gen. absol., which is not supposed to modify anything in the main clause (see BDF §423.4).

I happened to fall into a trance 18. *and see the Lord speaking to me: 'Hurry, leave Jerusalem as soon as possible, because they will not accept your testimony about me.'* This is again a curtailed report, because in 9:29–30 Paul is sent off to Caesarea and Tarsus by Jerusalem Christians, who realize that Jewish Hellenists were seeking to kill him. Now we learn that the Lord himself has intervened to get Paul to depart from Jerusalem. This intervention of the *Kyrios* (= the risen Christ) provides the background for the present situation in which Paul finds himself. The failure of Jerusalem Jews to accept the testimony of Christian missionaries is echoed again; see 13:46–48; 18:6; 28:25–28. Cf. Luke 14:16–24.

19. *I answered, 'Lord, they know indeed that from one synagogue to another I used to imprison and flog those who believed in you.* This statement too is new. Paul's reply to the Lord sums up what he had been doing to Jewish Christian converts; recall 9:2. That reply should have ingratiated Paul with the Jerusalem crowd that he is addressing; but it is not the whole story.

20. *While the blood of your witness Stephen was being shed, I stood by, giving my approval of it.* Recall 7:58–8:1. Stephen gets the title *martys*, "witness," which fits the general refrain of Acts; it does not yet have the connotation the word will later get, "martyr," i.e., a witness by shedding his blood (see Rev 2:13; 6:9; 17:6). Here some late MSS (L, 614, 945, 1505, 1739, 1891) give Stephen the title *prōtomartyros*, the traditional title, "protomartyr" or "first martyr." This detail in Paul's life, his presence at Stephen's death, is known only from the Lucan story; so it is not surprising that the Lucan Paul is made to reflect on it. Paul himself never says anything about Stephen. Having been "witness" to Stephen's death, Paul now speaks of himself as becoming a "witness" to the risen Christ, who commissions him and sends him to the Gentiles.

I even guarded the cloaks of those who killed him.' Recall 7:58b. Paul admits his association in guilt, which bears out what he said in v 4.

21. *He said to me, 'Go, for I am sending you far away to the Gentiles.'"* So Paul recounts the essential commission of the risen Lord for the Jerusalem crowd. It conforms with what Paul said about himself in Gal 2:2, 7. That commission made of him an "apostle of the Gentiles" (Rom 11:13). It explains why his "zeal for God" has been focused anew on a different goal, the evangelization of Gentiles. The commission to bear witness "to the Gentiles" is thus conferred on Paul in the very heart of Judaism's religious cult, in the precincts of the Jerusalem

Temple. It stands in contrast to what is recorded in v 15 above. "Far away" is an allusion to Isa 57:19 and echoes Acts 2:39; see NOTE there.

BIBLIOGRAPHY (22:1–21)

Badcock, F. J., "St. Paul's Apostolic Commission," *Theology* 8 (1924): 13–20, 79–88.

Brox, N., *Zeuge und Märtyrer: Untersuchungen zur frühchristlichen Zeugnis-Terminologie* (SANT 5; Munich: Kösel, 1961).

Budesheim, T. L., "Paul's *Abschiedsrede* in the Acts of the Apostles," *HTR* 69 (1976): 9–30.

Burchard, C., *Der dreizehnte Zeuge: Traditions- und kompositionsgeschichtliche Untersuchungen zu Lukas' Darstellung der Frühzeit des Paulus* (FRLANT 103; Göttingen: Vandenhoeck & Ruprecht, 1970).

Girlanda, A., "De conversione Pauli in Actibus Apostolorum tripliciter narrata," *VD* 39 (1961): 66–81, 129–40, 173–84.

Harrison, E. F., "Acts 22:3 — A Test Case for Luke's Reliability," *New Dimensions in New Testament Study* (ed. R. N. Longenecker and M. C. Tenney; Grand Rapids, MI: Zondervan, 1974), 251–60.

Hedrick, C. W., "Paul's Conversion/Call: A Comparative Analysis of the Three Reports in Acts," *JBL* 100 (1981): 415–32.

Jeremias, J., "Paulus als Hillelit," *Neotestamentica et semitica: Studies in Honour of Matthew Black* (ed. E. E. Ellis and M. Wilcox; Edinburgh: Clark, 1969), 88–94.

Lundgren, S., "Ananias and the Calling of Paul in Acts," *ST* 25 (1971): 117–22.

Reese, B., "The Apostle Paul's Exercise of His Rights as a Roman Citizen as Recorded in the Book of Acts," *EvQ* 47 (1975): 138–45.

Riddle, D. W., "The Occasion of Luke-Acts," *JR* 10 (1930): 545–62.

Steck, O. H., "Formgeschichtliche Bemerkungen zur Darstellung des Damaskusgeschehens in der Apostelgeschichte," *ZNW* 67 (1976): 20–28.

Steinmann, A., *Zum Werdegang des Paulus: Die Jugendzeit in Tarsus* (Freiburg im B.: Herder, 1928).

Tanton, L. T., "The Gospel and Water Baptism: A Study of Acts 22:16," *JGES* 4 (1991): 23–40.

Vitti, A. M., "Notae in Act. 22,3; 26,4.5," *VD* 11 (1931): 331–34.

VII. Paul Imprisoned for the Sake of Testimony to the Word (22:22–28:31)

◆

A. Prisoner in Jerusalem and Testimony There (22:22–23:22)

1. Paul Taken to Roman Headquarters; the Roman Citizen (22:22–29)

[22]Up to this point in his speech the crowd listened to Paul, but now they raised
their voices, shouting, "Rid the earth of this creature! He's not worthy to live!"
[23]They were yelling, throwing off their cloaks, and tossing dirt into the air. [24]Then
the commander ordered Paul to be taken inside the headquarters, having decided that he would be examined under the lash to find out why they were raising
such an outcry against him. [25]After they had strapped up Paul for the whips, he
said to the centurion standing by, "Is it lawful for you to flog a Roman citizen
without a trial?" [26]On hearing this, the centurion ran to the commander and
reported, "What are you going to do? This man is a Roman citizen." [27]The commander rushed in and asked Paul, "Tell me, are you a Roman citizen?" He answered, "Yes, I am." [28]The commander rejoined, "Why, I had to pay much
money to get that citizenship!" "Ah," said Paul, "but I was born one!" [29]At that
those who were going to examine him backed away from him; the commander
became alarmed, realizing that Paul was a Roman citizen and that he had trussed
him up.

WT: [23]into the sky. [24]that he would examine him. [26]this, that he said he was a Roman citizen . . . reported to him, "Look at what you are about to do." [27]Then the commander rushed in and addressed Paul, [omits "tell me" and "yes"]. [28]"Why, I know that I had to. . . ." [29][omits "and that he had trussed him up" but adds, "and immediately he released him"].

COMMENT

The seventh and last major part of Acts begins here, in which Paul brings his testimony to Jerusalem, and eventually to Rome. In order to advance his story, Luke uses the literary device of the interrupted speech. He relates what happens after Paul has been explaining to the Jerusalem crowd so far. The mention of "Gentiles" evokes a reaction from the crowd, which is an urge to do away with Paul. The commander of the Romans, who have been keeping watch over the episode, decides to intervene. He orders Paul to be arrested and determines to interrogate him about the cause of the uprising, but under the lash. Paul, having failed to liberate himself by his speech to the Jerusalem crowd, turns to the Roman tribune. He tells a centurion standing by that he is a Roman citizen, and when that is reported to the tribune, he is released. The tribune realizes that he himself is in jeopardy in this case for preparing to subject a Roman citizen to flogging.

This episode is another narrative in Acts, derived from the Pauline source, one that brings to the fore Paul's Roman citizenship. In the episode Paul emerges as a respected person, superior even to the Roman tribune who commands the troops stationed in Jerusalem's Fortress Antonia. The implication is that Roman authorities will not be able to bring any clear case against Paul. See further 23:1, 28; 24:22; 25:20, 26.

NOTES

22. *Up to this point in his speech the crowd listened to Paul, but now they raised their voices, shouting, "Rid the earth of this creature!* Lit., "away with such a one as this from the earth!" The same verb is used of Paul as was used of Jesus in Luke 23:18. Recall 21:36. Those who listen to Paul cannot bear to hear him say that he has been commissioned by heaven to preach a message of salvation to people who would not have to observe the Mosaic law.

He's not worthy to live!" Lit., "it is not fitting that he should live." Cf. 21:36; 25:24. So they clamor for his death.

23. *They were yelling, throwing off their cloaks, and tossing dirt into the air.* MS D reads "into the sky." These are symbolic acts of protest against Paul and what he has been saying. Cf. H. J. Cadbury, "Dust and Garments," *Beginnings*, 5.269–77.

24. *the commander ordered Paul to be taken inside the headquarters.* The commander is again Claudius Lysias. See NOTES on 21:31, 34, 37. The headquarters would have been part of the Fortress Antonia, north of the Temple precincts.

having decided that he would be examined under the lash to find out why they were raising such an outcry against him. I.e., as he would have done to any slave or foreigner. The Roman scourge was the *flagrum*, a whip that tore the flesh and could even break bones.

25. *After they had strapped up Paul for the whips.* Or "after they had strapped up Paul with thongs," because the meaning of *himasin* is not clear. It could be a dat. of means ("with thongs," by which he was strapped) or a dat. of purpose ("for whips," with which he would be flogged).

he said to the centurion standing by. On "centurion," see NOTE on 10:1.

"Is it lawful for you to flog a Roman citizen without a trial?" Lit., "is it permitted for you to scourge a Roman, even uncondemned?" Paul lets it be known that his case is still *res incognita,* "a case uninvestigated." He has not only not been sentenced, but there has been no proper scrutiny of his case. Paul invokes his *civitas,* "citizenship." Recall 16:37. The technical term for such scourging was *verberatio,* which could not be inflicted on a Roman citizen. See the Augustan *Lex Iulia de vi publica,* in Ulpian's *Digesta iuris romani* 48.6.7, which forbade such flogging of Roman citizens. Cf. Cicero, *Or. Verrin.* 2.5.66 §170; H. J. Cadbury, "Roman Law and the Trial of Paul," *Beginnings,* 5.297–338, esp. 319; Sherwin-White, *Roman Society,* 57–59.

26. *On hearing this.* MS D adds "that he said he was a Roman citizen."

the centurion ran to the commander and reported. I.e., the centurion hastened to apprise the commander of Paul's status.

"What are you going to do? MS D reads "Look at (*or* take care) what you are about to do."

This man is a Roman citizen." I.e., *civis romanus,* the significance of which was lost on neither the centurion nor the commander.

27. *The commander rushed in and asked Paul, "Tell me, are you a Roman citizen?"* Alarmed at the report, the commander reacts officially by interrogating Paul.

He answered, "Yes, I am." In effect, Paul declares the right that he has as a Roman citizen not to be subjected to flogging.

28. *The commander rejoined, "Why, I had to pay much money to get that citizenship!"* The commander is depicted as incredulous that a Jew such as Paul would have Roman citizenship. The "much money" that the commander had to pay might have been a bribe given to officials in an imperial secretariat or provincial administration to have his name put on the list of candidates for citizenship to be presented to the emperor. See Dio Cassius, *Roman History* 60.17.5–7. Since his name is Claudius Lysias (23:26), the *nomen* Claudius may indicate that he had attained citizenship under the emperor Claudius, since it was customary for citizens-to-be to pay a considerable sum of money and take the emperor's family name.

"Ah," said Paul, "but I was born one!" Lit., "but I have even been born (such)." Paul was technically *ingenuus,* "native citizen" or "free born," i.e., born of a free or freed father. He was a birthright citizen, because his family had undoubtedly been long settled in Tarsus. Though the apostle's *tria nomina* are unknown, the fact that he was called Paul undoubtedly indicates his Roman citizenship; see NOTE on 13:9. If Paul were not actually a citizen, he would be liable to prosecution for false declaration, as Epictetus makes clear (*Discourses* 3.24.41). Compare Ovid, *Tristia* 4.10.7–8 for a similar boast about his birth.

29. *At that those who were going to examine him backed away from him; the*

commander became alarmed, realizing that Paul was a Roman citizen and that he had trussed him up. MS 614 adds "and immediately he released him." Recall 16:38. The commander fears for himself and is more impressed with Paul's Roman citizenship than with his Tarsian citizenship, but as v 30 will show, Paul is still kept in custody. See H. W. Tajra, *The Trial*, 76–89 (on Paul's triple identity: his Tarsian citizenship, his Pharisaic identity, and his Roman citizenship). Tajra cites numerous examples of how Roman citizenship was acquired under different rulers both in the republic and the principate.

BIBLIOGRAPHY (22:22–29)

Delebecque, E., "L'Art du conte et la faute du tribun Lysias selon les deux versions des *Actes* (22,22–30)," *LTP* 40 (1984): 217–25.

H[erzog], E., "Zu Apg. 22:23," *Revue internationale de théologie* 13 (1905): 535–36.

Llewelyn, S. R., "Claudius Lysias (Acts 22) and the Question of Paul's Roman Citizenship," *NDIEC*, 6.152–55.

Mommsen, T., "Die Rechtsverhältnisse des Apostels Paulus," *ZNW* 2 (1901): 81–96.

Nap, J. M., "Handelingen 22.25," *NThT* 16 (1927): 245–58.

Rosin, H., "Civis romanus sum," *NedTT* 3 (1948–49): 16–27.

Sherwin-White, A. N. *The Roman Citizenship* (Oxford: Clarendon, 1939), 237–50.

———, *Roman Society*, 244–62.

Stegemann, W., "War der Apostel Paulus ein römischer Bürger?" *ZNW* 78 (1987): 200–29.

Tajra, H. W., *The Trial of St. Paul.*

Wenger, L., *Die Quellen des römischen Rechts* (Vienna: Holzhausen, 1953), 292.

2. Paul Brought before the Jerusalem Sanhedrin (22:30–23:11)

30 The next day the commander wanted to find out exactly about the charge being
brought against Paul by the Jews. So he released him and summoned the chief
priests and the whole Sanhedrin to a meeting. He brought Paul down and had
him stand before them. **23** 1 Paul looked intently at the Sanhedrin and said,
"Brothers, I have lived my life with a perfectly clear conscience before God up
to this day." 2 At that the high priest Ananias bade his attendants strike Paul on
the mouth. 3 Then Paul said to him, "It is you that God is going to strike, you
whitewashed wall! Do you sit there judging me according to the law and yet
violate the law itself in ordering me to be struck?" 4 Those standing by said, "Do
you dare insult God's high priest?" 5 Paul said, "Brothers, I did not know that he
was the high priest. It stands written, I know, '*You shall not curse a ruler of your*

people.'"[n] [6]When Paul realized that part of them were Sadducees and part Pharisees, he shouted out before the Sanhedrin, "Brothers, I am a Pharisee, the son of Pharisees; [I] now stand trial because of my hope in the resurrection of the dead." [7]When he had said this, there arose dissension between the Pharisees and Sadducees, and the whole assembly was divided. [8]For Sadducees maintain that there is no resurrection, neither as an angel nor as a spirit, whereas Pharisees acknowledge them both. [9]A loud uproar ensued. Finally, some scribes of the Pharisaic group stood up and contended, "We find this man guilty of nothing wrong. Has a spirit or an angel perhaps spoken to him?" [10]At this the dispute became heated, and the commander feared that Paul would be torn to pieces by them. So he ordered his troops to go down and snatch him from their midst and take him back to headquarters. [11]The following night the Lord stood at Paul's side and said, "Keep up your courage! As you have borne witness to me here in Jerusalem, so you must do in Rome as well."

[n]Exod 22:27

WT: [30][omits "released him"]. [23:1]He looked intently. [2][omits "Ananias" and "his attendants"]. [3][omits "according to the law"]. [4][omits "God's"]. [5]He answered. [6][omits "Paul" and "of the dead"]. [7]there was dissension. [8][omits "For" and adds "acknowledge that there are resurrection, angel, and spirit"]. [9]When a loud uproar ensued among them, they were divided [omits "stood up and"]. What wrong do we find in this man? [10][omits "the commander"]. [11][omits "to me"].

COMMENT

In this episode Luke depicts Paul being brought by the commander Claudius Lysias before the Jerusalem Sanhedrin and the high priest. It turns out to be the most important defense scene in Acts, because Paul is vindicated by the Pharisees in his audience. When he appears before the assembled Jewish authorities, Paul maintains his innocence as a loyal Jew, and for that the high priest orders him to be struck on the mouth. That act outrages Paul, who calls the high priest listening to him a "whitewashed wall." It turns out that Paul has not recognized the high priest and, when he is apprised of his identity, in effect apologizes. Then realizing that he is being confronted by Pharisees and Sadducees, he cleverly divides and conquers. He maintains that he is on trial for a belief adamantly maintained by Pharisees: the resurrection of the dead. He is referring implicitly to the resurrection of Christ, but he phrases it generically and so sets the assembly in divisive uproar. The result is that scribes of the Pharisaic party declare, "We find this man guilty of nothing wrong" (23:9). Paul is returned to Roman custody, and the risen Christ appears to him to reassure him. Christ makes it clear that whatever happens is part of his heaven-guided role. He stands before the Jerusalem religious authorities as a "witness," and that he must do also in Rome. The episode ends with an affirmation of Pauline testimony.

The declaration by Pharisaic scribes is an important step in Luke's story, because one of the subsidiary purposes of his writing the Gospel and Acts has been to show that Christianity is only a logical outgrowth and continuation of Pharisaic

Judaism. Just as Judaism has already won the right of existence in the Roman empire, as *religio licita*, so Luke wants to show that Christianity is only a development of a form of that Judaism and should enjoy the same right. That Jerusalem Pharisees now declare that Paul has done nothing wrong is an implicit admission that the gospel that he preaches and the religion that he is proclaiming are just as legitimate as Pharisaic Judaism.

This passage is often judged to be full of historical improbabilities. So Roloff (*Apg.*, 326): within Lucan writings it remains without comparison; similarly Conzelmann (*Acts*, 191): "historically impossible." For a list of the "historical improbabilities," see Weiser, *Apg.*, 615.

That there are some problematic details in the episode is readily admitted, but many of the alleged "improbabilities" have been exaggerated. For instance, it is questionable whether a Roman commander could not have summoned the Sanhedrin for consultation at a preliminary inquiry; or that the Aramaic-speaking Paul would quote the Greek OT in v 5. The issue at stake in this episode is no longer whether Paul has defiled the sacred precincts of the Jerusalem Temple, but whether Christianity is a outgrowth of Pharisaic Judaism; but is that an issue that a Roman commander would want to judge? Certainly not, but that issue has been emerging in the Lucan story ever since Paul was pounced upon by his Jerusalem opponents. It now comes to a head by the speech that Paul has addressed to them. Luke has undoubtedly derived from his Pauline source a report of Paul's appearance before such Jewish authorities and some details about it (e.g., that he managed to divide the audience and conquer the opposition). Luke has fashioned from them a dramatic scene with lively conversation. Lucan composition is evident in the episode, but it is not created out of whole cloth. In the story of Acts as a whole the issue about Christianity's relationship to Pharisaic Judaism has been percolating, and in this episode it comes to the fore. That issue, however, does not solve the problem for which the Roman commander summoned the Jewish authorities for advice, but it is contributing to the decision that he will make to send Paul to the governor Felix.

The story of Paul's testimony in Jerusalem continues in this episode in which he appears before the Roman commander and the Sanhedrin. In their presence he boasts of his "clear conscience before God" in all that he has been doing. When he further asserts his Pharisaic background and maintains his "hope in the resurrection of the dead," he manages to divide his audience and get the Pharisees in it to agree with him: "We find this man guilty of nothing wrong" (23:9). The testimony that Paul thus bears before Jerusalem authorities receives the approval of the risen Lord who appears to him and assures him that, as he testified here in Jerusalem, so he will testify in Rome too. Paul's courage is thus rewarded. He minces no words about his status and wins some of his adversaries to his point of view.

NOTES

30. *The next day.* Weiser (*Apg.*, 615) sees this phrase as a deliberate Lucan comparison of Paul's trial with that of Jesus in Luke 22:66. If it is comparable, the phraseology is considerably different, "when it was day."

the commander wanted to find out exactly about the charge being brought against Paul by the Jews. Lit., "wishing to know the real reason, why he was accused by the Jews." Luke uses *to asphales,* the neut. acc. of the adj. "safe" as an abstraction for "the truth," as he did in 21:34. He also uses the official verb *katēgorein,* "accuse, bring an accusation against (someone) in court." Compare its use in Luke 23:10, 14; Acts 24:2, 8, 13, 19; 25:5, 11, 16; 28:19.

he released him. I.e., from the custody of two soldiers in order to bring him before the assembly of Jewish authorities. The *Koinē* text-tradition adds *apo tōn desmōn,* "from bonds," but from 23:18 we learn that Paul is still regarded as *desmios,* "a prisoner."

summoned the chief priests and the whole Sanhedrin to a meeting. Lit., "ordered the chief priests and the whole Sanhedrin to meet." I.e., he bade them assemble to help him in a preliminary inquiry, for as a military commander Lysias lacked the official *imperium,* "authority," to institute a formal Roman trial. It was rather an assembly for a preliminary inquiry into the issue that the commander would have to assess: what to do with Paul? The chief priests and the Sanhedrin are assembled by the commander only in an advisory capacity.

Could a Roman commander order the Sanhedrin to assemble? This question was first raised by Juster (*Les Juifs,* 2.141 n.1). Conzelmann (*Acts,* 191) asserts: "This incident is historically impossible"; similarly Schneider (*Apg.*, 2.330); Lüdemann (*Early Christianity,* 242): "probably unhistorical." R. Taubenschlag ("Le procès," 723), however, has cited a known instance of a judicial body being summoned to serve as an advisory council in papyri from Ptolemaic times. Moreover, "this meeting is not represented as a judicial trial in the narrative description [of Acts], or in the letter of Lysias" (Sherwin-White, *Roman Society,* 54). Thus, the summoning of chief priests and the Sanhedrin in an advisory role is not as impossible as has been claimed. See Schürer, *HJPAJC,* 2.223. On the chief priests, see NOTES on 4:1, 5, 6; on the Sanhedrin, see NOTES on 4:15, 23.

He brought Paul down and had him stand before them. Paul is made to come from the Fortress Antonia (down the stairway, 21:40) to a council hall, where he would confront his accusers.

23:1. *Paul looked intently at the Sanhedrin.* Paul shows no fear before the Sanhedrin. Again Luke makes use of one of his favorite words, *atenisas* (see NOTE on 1:10), which shows that Paul speaks out without any hesitation.

"Brothers, I have lived my life with a perfectly clear conscience before God. Cf. 24:16. The Lucan Paul's protestation about his robust conscience manifests an awareness of his dedication to the role to which God has called him, even if it passes over events such as 8:1, 3; 9:1; 22:4. As Haenchen says about these incidents, "One may not of course ask" (*Acts,* 637). Paul's good conscience before

God bears on other matters; cf. Phil 3:5–6; 2 Cor 1:12. For "Brothers," see NOTE on 1:15.

up to this day." I.e., both as a Jew and as a Christian. It is not simply a question of Paul's involvement in defilement of the Temple. This was the point of the speech in 22:1–21.

2. *At that the high priest Ananias.* This is Ananias, son of Nedebaeus, appointed high priest by Herod of Chalcis ca. A.D. 47; he continued in office until 59 (Josephus, *Ant.* 20.5.2 §103; 20.6.2 §131; 20.8.8 §179; 20.9.2–4 §§205–13), when he was replaced by Ishmael son of Phabi. He was assassinated in A.D. 66 because of his pro-Roman policy (Josephus, *J.W.* 2.17.9 §441). The date of his high priesthood and his highhanded conduct, described by Josephus, suit the Lucan story here. Ananias will appear again in 24:1.

bade his attendants strike Paul on the mouth. Cf. John 18:22. The mouth is specified because of what Paul has just said.

3. *Paul said to him, "It is you that God is going to strike.* This is a Jewish curse formula, which invokes divine aid against the unjust decision of Ananias. It echoes Deut 28:22: "The LORD will strike you with consumption, fever, inflammation, fiery heat, and drought." It possibly falls into the category of an adjuration "written in the Law," which was debated in the later rabbinic tradition (*m. Shebuoth* 4:13; Str-B, 2.766).

you whitewashed wall! I.e., concealer of contamination so thinly covered. This echoes Ezek 13:10–15, where the prophet speaks out against the deceiving message of false prophets and the shallowness of the covering of whitewash that is over their message. Paul so calls the high priest because, instead of upholding the law, he is breaking it. His order is an act of whitewashing. Cf. Matt 23:27; CD 8:12.

Do you sit there judging me according to the law and yet violate the law itself in ordering me to be struck?" The high priest's order is taken as a violation of Lev 19:15: "Do no injustice in judgment; do not be partial to the poor or defer to the great. With justice shall you judge your associates." The phrase *kata ton nomon*, "according to the law," stands in contrast to the ptc. *paranomōn*, "acting illegally." In effect, the Mosaic law considers the accused innocent until proven guilty. Paul objects because Ananias has not been impartial in his actions. His action might become known to the Roman commander: that the high priest has ordered a Roman citizen to be struck on the mouth. See Jacquier, *Actes*, 658.

4. *Those standing by said, "Do you dare insult God's high priest?"* Thus is expressed the dignity of the man reprimanded by Paul: he is not just a high priest, but God's high priest.

5. *"Brothers, I did not know that he was the high priest.* Paul again addresses the Jews about him as "brothers"; recall v 1. About the identity of the high priest Paul pleads guilty and, in effect, apologizes. Conzelmann (*Acts*, 192) considers "Paul's statement unthinkable," but because of his long absence from Jerusalem, Paul no longer recognizes the high priest Ananias. It is, indeed, quite thinkable.

It stands written, I know, 'You shall not curse a ruler of your people.'" Paul quotes

Exod 22:28 (LXX 22:27: "You shall not speak ill of rulers of your people"), making the object singular to suit the situation. Paul shows again that he stands by what is prescribed in the Mosaic law.

6. *When Paul realized that part of them were Sadducees and part Pharisees.* Paul takes the initiative, sensing that he might win his cause by dividing those who were gathered to judge him and advise the Roman commander. Paul acts on the principle, *divide et impera,* "divide and conquer." Though the Sadducees were the majority in the Jerusalem *gerousia,* ever since the first century B.C. more and more Pharisees had become members of it. See Josephus, *Ant.* 18.1.4 §17, who tells how the influence of the Sadducees had to be curbed by views of the Pharisees, for otherwise the people would not have tolerated them. See NOTES on 4:1; 5:34 for the distinction of these two contemporary types of Palestinian Jews.

he shouted out before the Sanhedrin, "Brothers, I am a Pharisee, the son of Pharisees. Luke makes Paul echo a boast that Paul himself often uttered as a Jewish Christian looking back at his past (Phil 3:5–6; 2 Cor 11:22). Luke, however, makes more of it than Paul himself does; see 26:5. The Lucan Paul still claims he *is* a Pharisee and sides with the Pharisees of Jerusalem in the assembled gathering, because he shares in common with them certain basic tenets. It is puzzling that Paul could have come from Hellenistic Tarsus and still claim that he is a Pharisaic son, born of a Pharisaic family. The answer to the puzzle may come from the length of time his own family lived in Tarsus; it may have settled there well in the second century B.C., when Palestinian Jews had already begun to distinguish themselves as Pharisees, Sadducees, and Essenes. That distinction does not antedate the second quarter of the second century.

[*I*] *now stand trial because of my hope in the resurrection of the dead."* Lit., "because of the hope and the resurrection of the dead." This is hendiadys, referring to one and the same thing. The Jewish Christian Paul of Pharisaic background creates a distraction in siding with the Pharisees and affirming his "hope" in *anastasis nekrōn,* "resurrection of the dead." Cf. 4:2, 33; 24:15, 21; 26:6–7; 28:20. He does this because he has been preaching Christ raised from the dead by the Father (13:30–34; cf. 26:23) and is shrewd enough to realize that he cannot put it just that way. So he makes his claim more generic. Cf. 1 Cor 15:12–28; Phil 3:10–11; Eph 1:18–20. See Bruce, *Acts,* 411.

The resurrection of the dead is not taught in the law of Moses. At times certain OT passages are said to allude to this belief, such as Ps 49:15; Hos 6:1–3; 13:14; Isa 26:19; but none of them is certain. The first OT passage that clearly affirms it is Dan 12:2–3, and that affirmation is meant in a corporate sense. It is strikingly absent even in Sirach, but emerges again in 2 Macc 7:9, 11, 14, 22–23, 29; 12:43; 14:46. In the Book of Wisdom one finds rather "immortality," a notion borrowed from the Greek world about the afterlife (3:4; 4:1; 8:13, 17; 15:3). Cf. 4 Macc 14:5; 16:13. All of this forms the background for the dispute between Sadducees and Pharisees over this matter.

7. *When he had said this, there arose dissension between the Pharisees and Sadducees, and the whole assembly was divided.* This is Luke's way of describing the

Jewish reaction to the Christian gospel: why some accepted Jesus as the risen Christ and others did not.

8. *Sadducees maintain that there is no resurrection.* I.e., because it is not taught in the Pentateuch or the law of Moses. Josephus agrees with this when he writes that Sadducees maintain that "souls perish with their bodies" (*Ant.* 18.1.4 §16; cf. *J. W.* 2.8.14 §§164–65). See Luke 20:27–33; *HJPAJC,* 2.404–14; J. Le Moyne, *Les Sadducéens* (EBib; Paris: Gabalda, 1972), 123–35.

neither as an angel nor as a spirit. Lit., "neither an angel nor a spirit." This phrase has often been interpreted to mean that three things were involved in the Sadducean denial: resurrection of the dead, angels, and spirits. So Haenchen (*Acts,* 638); Schneider (*Apg.,* 2.333); Johnson (*Acts,* 398); Kistemaker (*Acts,* 813); Pesch (*Apg.,* 2.244); Polhill (*Acts,* 470); Wikenhauser (*Apg.,* 251). That, however, creates a problem for the meaning of *ta amphotera* at the end of the verse. The double *mēte* phrase should most likely be taken as appositive to the noun *anastasin,* "resurrection," specifying a mode of it. This Lucan addition is apparently nowhere else ascribed to Sadducees. Matt 22:30 records a saying of Jesus that "in the resurrection . . . they will be like angels." This saying may give some sense to the added appositive. Bamberger had difficulty in accepting that the Sadducees denied the existence of angels ("The Sadducees"); similarly Daube ("On Acts 23"). The solution to this problematic verse has been suggested by Lachs ("Pharisees and Sadducees"); Viviano and Taylor ("Sadducees, Angels"); cf. G. G. Stroumsa ("Le couple," 57–61).

Pharisees acknowledge them both. Lit., "acknowledge both," i.e., the two modes of resurrection, as angel or as spirit. In *Ant.* 18.1.3 §14, Josephus ascribes to Pharisees a belief in "the immortal power of souls" *(athanaton ischyn tais psychais)* and "an easy passage to a new life" *(rhastōnēn tou anabioun),* which is usually said to mean "resurrection." Similarly, according to *J.W.* 2.8.14 §163 the Pharisees maintain: "every soul is imperishable, and the soul only of the good passes into another body." This may be another way of saying what Luke calls *anastasis.* These descriptions are undoubtedly Josephus's attempt to explain the Jewish notion of "resurrection" to the Greek-speaking pagan world.

9. *A loud uproar ensued. Finally, some scribes of the Pharisaic group stood up and contended.* So Luke describes the tumult of the gathering. The attitudes of those who listen to Paul correspond to those of chap. 5 (esp. 5:17, 34). On scribes, see NOTE on 4:5.

"We find this man guilty of nothing wrong. The basis of the scribes' judgment is not made clear. It is not based on Paul's adjuration of the high priest or on anything that precedes in this episode, apart from Paul's declaration that he agrees with Pharisaic teaching about the resurrection of the dead. In effect, the scribes acknowledge that Christians are only another sect of Judaism. Implied in their judgment is the legality of what Paul stands for.

Has a spirit or an angel perhaps spoken to him?" This ironic query depends on v 8 and is clearly added to aggravate the Sadducees in the assembly. Possibly it refers more remotely to what happened to Paul on the road to Damascus (22:6–11).

10. *At this the dispute became heated, and the commander feared that Paul would be torn to pieces by them.* The result is not merely a "loud uproar" (v 9), but a tumultuous situation in which a calm discussion of Paul's situation is impossible. So the commander has to intervene.

So he ordered his troops to go down and snatch him from their midst and take him back to headquarters. As the commander has done in 21:34, Paul is again taken into custody, not for a crime, but for security, to protect him from the violence of Jews who have listened to him. Whether Claudius Lysias was with Paul in the assembly of the Sanhedrin is not clear, but in any case he orders his soldiers to descend from the Fortress Antonia and rescue Paul from the Jews who have been listening to him. The commander has made use of the Sanhedrin on a consultative basis, but part of its members (the scribes) have, in effect, already passed judgment on Paul.

11. *The following night the Lord stood at Paul's side and said, "Keep up your courage!* In a dream during the night after his being returned to Roman custody, Paul again sees the risen *Kyrios* (recall 18:9), who appears to him and encourages him in his trial. The Lord stands by him, as did Ananias (22:13), as a measure of support.

As you have borne witness to me here in Jerusalem, so you must do in Rome as well." The Lord acknowledges the testimony that Paul has already borne to him in this center of Judaism and instructs him that he must do the same in the capital of the civilized Gentile world, of the Roman empire itself; see NOTE on 18:2. The risen Christ thus gives approval to the plan that Paul has made to "visit Rome" (19:21). The task of testimony for which Paul has been commissioned (22:21) must be carried out there too. So Luke foreshadows Paul's journey to Rome and the rest of the story in Acts. Cf. 18:9–10; 22:17–18; 27:23–24 for similar reassuring visions that were accorded to the Lucan Paul. Paul himself also boasted of such "visions and revelations" accorded him (2 Cor 12:1).

BIBLIOGRAPHY (22:30–23:11)

Bamberger, B. J., "The Sadducees and the Belief in Angels," *JBL* 82 (1963): 433–35.

Björck, G., "Quelques cas de *hen dia dyoin* dans le Nouveau Testament et ailleurs," *ConNT* 4 (1940): 1–4, esp. 2–3.

Cox, D., "Paul before the Sanhedrin: Acts. 22,30–23,11," *SBFLA* 21 (1971): 54–75.

Daube, D., "On Acts 23: Sadducees and Angels," *JBL* 109 (1990): 493–97.

Haacker, K., "Das Bekenntnis des Paulus zur Hoffnung Israels nach der Apostelgeschichte des Lukas," *NTS* 31 (1985): 437–51.

Lachs, S. T., "The Pharisees and Sadducees on Angels: A Reexamination of Acts xxiii.8," *Gratz College Annual of Jewish Studies* 6 (1977): 35–42.

Main, E., "Les Sadducéens et la résurrection des morts: Comparison entre Mc 12,18–27 et Lc 20,27–38," *RB* 103 (1996): 411–32.

Möbius, K., "Paulus vor dem Hohen Rat," *Auf der Warte* 30 (1933): 289–90, 301–2.
Pokorný, P., "Die Romfahrt des Paulus und der antike Roman," *ZNW* 64 (1973): 233–44.
Pope, A. M., "Paul's Address before the Council at Jerusalem," *Expos* 8/25 (1923): 426–46.
Stroumsa, G. G., "Le couple de l'ange et de l'esprit: Traditions juives et chrétiennes," *RB* 88 (1981): 42–61.
Taubenschlag, R., "Le procès de l'apôtre Paul en lumière des papyri," *Opera minora* (2 vols.; Warsaw: Państwowe Wydawn, 1959), 2.721–26.
Viviano, B. T., and J. Taylor, "Sadducees, Angels, and Resurrection (Acts 23:8–9)," *JBL* 111 (1992): 496–98.
Ziesler, J. A., "Luke and the Pharisees," *NTS* 25 (1978–79): 146–57.

3. Plot of Jerusalemites to Kill Paul (23:12–22)

[12]When it was day, Jews formed a conspiracy, binding themselves by oath not to eat or drink until they had killed Paul. [13]More than forty of them made this oath together. [14]Then they went to the chief priests and elders and said, "We have bound ourselves by oath to take no food until we kill Paul. [15]Now you, together with the Sanhedrin, must suggest to the commander to have Paul brought down to you, on the grounds that you want to investigate his case more carefully. We are ready to do away with him, even before he arrives here." [16]The son of Paul's sister, however, heard about the plot; he came to headquarters, entered, and told Paul about it. [17]Paul called one of the centurions and said, "Take this young man to the commander; he has something to report to him." [18]Taking him along, the centurion led him to the commander and said, "The prisoner Paul called me and asked me to bring to you this young man who has something to tell you." [19]Taking him by the hand, the commander drew him aside and asked him privately, "What do you have to report to me?" [20]He said, "Jews have agreed among themselves to ask you to have Paul brought down to the Sanhedrin tomorrow, on the grounds that they want to question him more carefully. [21]But do not be taken in by them, because more than forty men among them are plotting and have bound themselves by oath not to eat or drink until they have done away with him. They are ready now, waiting only to get a promise from you." [22]The commander sent the young man away with the charge, "Tell no one that you have reported this to me."

WT: [12]some of the Jews conspired together. [13]put themselves under an oath. [14]no food whatsoever. [15]Now then we urge you, do this for us: Gather together the Sanhedrin and suggest to the commander . . . [omits "more carefully" and "before he arrives here" and adds, "tomorrow," and "even if it is necessary to die"]. [16]A certain young man, the son of Paul's sister, heard about their plot . . . [omits "entered"]. [18][omits "taking him along" and "young man"]. [19]and asked of him what he had to report to him. [20]It has been agreed upon by Jews to ask you . . . [omits "tomorrow"]. [21][omits "by them"] because more than forty men among them are ready to do away with him; they have even bound themselves by oath not to taste anything until they have done this [omits "They are . . . from you"]. [22]with the charge that no one should know that he has reported to him.

COMMENT

Luke continues the story of the events in Jerusalem that ensued after the Roman commander has rescued Paul from the gathering of Jewish authorities and again confined him in the Fortress Antonia at the end of the preliminary investigation that the commander has undertaken. What Paul said to those authorities serves only to consolidate Jewish opposition to him. So forty Jerusalem Jews bind themselves by oath not to eat or drink anything until they have done away with Paul. This plot becomes known to Paul's nephew, who makes his way to the Roman headquarters, where Paul is confined, and informs him. Paul has a centurion take his nephew to the commander to report to him what he has learned. The commander sends the young man off with the charge not to tell anyone that he has reported the matter to Roman authorities.

The episode is another narrative in Acts, one that results in the removal of Paul from Jerusalem to further Roman custody. Conzelmann (*Acts*, 194) thinks that this account in 23:12–35 is an independent anecdote that knows nothing of Paul's appearance before the Sanhedrin and is even in conflict with it. This account of the conspiracy against Paul does not necessarily flow from the preceding episode. Lucan dramatic composition may be seen in the use of direct discourse and in the reporting through Paul and a centurion to the Roman commander, but details about the plot and the report have undoubtedly come from Luke's Pauline source. Problematic in the passage is the mention of Paul's sister and nephew, but that has to be judged in connection with what the Lucan Paul has said in 22:3.

NOTES

12. *When it was day.* I.e., the day that follows the night during which Paul has had the vision of the risen Christ and that follows his appearance before the Sanhedrin.

Jews formed a conspiracy. The *Koinē* text-tradition reads rather "some of the Jews conspired together." The word *systrophē* may mean only "a meeting," but it often carries the connotation of a protest meeting, hence "conspiracy" (BAGD 795: "disorderly or seditious gathering"). This conspiracy would suggest that at least those who joined in it were united against Paul and did not share the dissension mentioned in v 7 above. In pre-70 Jerusalem under the Romans many plots were formulated, and this conspiracy would not have been extraordinary.

binding themselves by oath not to eat or drink until they had killed Paul. Lit., "they laid themselves under anathema (curse)," i.e., they called down heaven's punishment upon them if they failed to carry out their resolve. Their desperation is heightened by the resolve not to eat or drink, but one may wonder about the binding character of such an oath.

13. *More than forty of them made this oath together.* From vv 14–15 it appears that not all forty are necessarily members of the Sanhedrin that have come together in 22:30. The presumption is that these forty, otherwise unidentified Jews of Jerusalem, have at least heard of the session before the Sanhedrin; that is why they now go to some members of that assembly for further action.

14. *they went to the chief priests and elders.* I.e., the forty make an appeal to leaders of the Jewish community in Jerusalem (4:23; 24:1; 25:15); see NOTES on 4:1, 5, 6; 11:30.

"We have bound ourselves by oath to take no food until we kill Paul. So the forty explain their desperation over Paul and what he stands for. MS P^{48} adds *to synolon,* "whatsoever," to "no food."

15. *Now you, together with the Sanhedrin, must suggest to the commander to have Paul brought down to you.* The religious leaders mentioned in v 14 are meant by "you." They, however, would not be able to order the Roman commander to bring Paul before the Sanhedrin again, but they could bring information before him in the form of a "suggestion." MS P^{48} reads "we urge you, do this for us: Gather together the Sanhedrin and suggest." The *Koinē* text-tradition adds "tomorrow" to "have Paul brought down." On Sanhedrin, see NOTE on 4:15; on commander, see NOTE on 21:31.

on the grounds that you want to investigate his case more carefully. Lit., "more accurately." The plot is described as specious, and the Sanhedrin is being asked to collaborate with those who conspire against Paul. Luke makes use of technical legal language, *diaginōskein akribesteron:* the commander is asked to take further cognizance of the case and make more accurate inquiry into Paul's situation.

We are ready to do away with him, even before he arrives here." Lit., "before he draws near." The plot of murder is thus formulated.

16. *The son of Paul's sister, however, heard about the plot.* Only Luke tells us about Paul's married sister and her son resident in Jerusalem; this detail fits in with what the Lucan Paul says about himself in 22:3c. Was the nephew already a Christian? Some have tried to maintain this because in v 20 he speaks of "Jews" plotting against Paul. That, however, may be Luke's way of explaining the nephew's knowledge of the plot to the reader. Luke does not say how the nephew found out about the plot, unless we are to suppose (with Marshall, *Acts,* 368) that the plot became "widely known." That is certainly more plausible than the suggestion of Roloff that Paul's nephew was a member of a Zealot group, which was plotting against Paul (*Apg.,* 331). The WT reads "A certain young man, the son of Paul's sister, heard about their plot."

he came to headquarters, entered, and told Paul about it. This detail that the youth comes to his uncle suggests that Paul was not detained in maximum security. In fact, it implies that Paul does not have ordinary prisoner status. He may have been like Peregrinus in Lucian, *De morte Peregrini* 12–13.

17. *Paul called one of the centurions and said.* The Lucan Paul, even as a prisoner, can summon a Roman centurion. On centurion, see NOTE on 10:1.

"Take this young man to the commander; he has something to report to him." The matter is deemed serious enough that Paul requests cooperation from one of the centurions, who grants it.

18. *Taking him along, the centurion led him to the commander and said, "The prisoner Paul called me and asked me to bring to you this young man who has something to tell you."* Paul is called *ho desmios,* "the prisoner," which indicates that for the centurion at least Paul was under arrest. Recall 22:30, which shows that *elysen* meant a "release" only for a temporary hearing, the preliminary inquiry conducted by the tribune with the Sanhedrin as his advisers.

19. *Taking him by the hand, the commander drew him aside and asked him privately, "What do you have to report to me?"* I.e., the tribune is at least open to further information about the prisoner he has.

20. *He said, "Jews have agreed among themselves to ask you to have Paul brought down to the Sanhedrin tomorrow, on the grounds that they want to question him more carefully.* Lit., "more accurately," an echo of v 15. The nephew's report summarizes vv 13–15.

21. *do not be taken in by them.* Lit., "do not be persuaded by them" or "do not believe them." This is the essence of the message brought by the nephew.

because more than forty men among them are plotting and have bound themselves by oath not to eat or drink until they have done away with him. A summary of vv 13–14.

They are ready now, waiting only to get a promise from you." I.e., so that they can carry out their plot.

22. *The commander sent the young man away with the charge, "Tell no one that you have reported this to me."* The tribune does not want others to find out that the Roman authorities have learned about the plot against Paul's life. The commander sends him away perhaps because of his youth and does not detain him lest others find out about what he has reported.

BIBLIOGRAPHY (23:12–22)

Delebecque, E., "Paul entre Juifs et Romains selon les deux versions de Act. xxiii," *RevThom* 84 (1984): 83–91.

B. Prisoner in Caesarea and Testimony There (23:23–26:32)

1. Transfer to Caesarea (23:23–35)

[23]Then the commander summoned two of his centurions and said, "Get two hundred infantrymen ready to leave for Caesarea by nine o'clock tonight, along with seventy cavalrymen and two hundred spearmen. [24]Provide horses for Paul to ride on so that they may give him safe conduct to the Governor Felix." [25]He wrote a letter to this effect: [26]"Claudius Lysias to His Excellency, Felix the Governor: Greetings! [27]Here is a man whom Jews had seized and were about to put to death. I intervened with my troops and rescued him, when I learned that he was a Roman citizen. [28]Hoping to learn the basis of their charges against him, I brought him before their Sanhedrin. [29]Then I discovered that he was being accused in controversial matters of their own law and was in no way guilty of anything deserving death or imprisonment. [30]When I was informed about an imminent plot against this man, I decided then and there to send him to you; I have further instructed his accusers to take up [their case] with you." [31]So the infantrymen took Paul according to their orders and escorted him during the night to Antipatris. [32]The next day they let the cavalrymen proceed with him, while they returned to headquarters. [33]On their arrival in Caesarea, they delivered the letter to the governor and brought Paul before him. [34]He read it and asked Paul from what province he was. When he found out that he came from Cilicia, he said, [35]"I shall hear your case when your accusers get here too." Then he ordered him to be kept under guard in Herod's praetorium.

WT: [23]and ordered them to be ready to leave [omits the rest of the verse]. [24]and he ordered the centurions to provide horses for Paul to ride on at night so that they might give him safe conduct to Caesarea, to the Governor Felix. [25]For he feared lest the Jews might seize and kill him (Paul) and he himself might thereupon be accused of having taken a bribe. So he wrote a letter containing these details. [26][some MSS omit "Felix"]. [27]and saved him who was crying out and saying he was a Roman citizen. [28]before the Sanhedrin. [29]accused of nothing more than controversial matters of the Mosaic law and a certain Jesus and was in no way . . . [omits "or imprisonment"]. With force I barely extricated him. [30][omits "When I . . . man"]. I have sent him to you . . . to come to you. [31][omits "during the night"]. [32]they let the cavalrymen (go) to headquarters. [33]They came to Caesarea. [34]Having read the letter, he asked Paul, "From what province are you?" He said, "Cilicia." When he found that out, he said, "I shall . . ."

COMMENT

Because of the conspiracy of Jerusalem Jews against Paul, he is transferred by the Roman commander Claudius Lysias to Caesarea Maritima in A.D. 58, so that the provincial governor may be able to decide what is to be done with him. Most of this episode is taken up with the letter that the commander sends to the governor, which explains why Paul is being sent to Caesarea. This is an example of *litterae dimissoriae*, the letter that had to be sent according to Roman law from one official to a superior in the case of appeal (*provocatio;* see *Digesta* 49.6.1). In this case, however, there has not yet been an appeal, but the letter states the case and includes the instructions given to those who have accused Paul that they too are to present themselves before the governor. The purpose of the episode is to transmit a prisoner, who is a Roman citizen, to the governor Felix residing in Caesarea Maritima, the seat of Roman authority in Judea.

Sherwin-White has shown how Luke's story about Paul's trial before Felix and Festus is "an exemplary account of the provincial penal procedure *extra ordinem*" (*Roman Society*, 48), i.e., of *cognitio extra ordinem*, an inquiry out of the ordinary. In this he was simply following the lead of a famous German historian of Roman legal history, Theodor Mommsen in his *Römisches Strafrecht* (Leipzig: Duncker & Humblot, 1899), 239, 243, 329–33.

The episode is basically a narrative, but it incorporates the text of the letter sent to the governor (23:26–30). How Luke might have come across this letter is problematic: Hanson (*Acts*, 224) thinks that it is a Lucan composition; Hemer (*Book of Acts*, 348) regards it as derived from Paul. It may represent nothing more than a free Lucan composition that suits the context, setting forth what Claudius Lysias would have had to explain to Felix. The letter presents the whole affair from a Roman point of view, as Luke understands it, makes no distinction between Jews and Jewish Christians, and indirectly lays the blame for the incident on the Jews.

The letter has five parts: (1) the epistolary prescript (23:26); (2) the account of Paul's arrest (23:27); (3) a summation of the preliminary investigation (23:28); (4) the commander's opinion about Paul's case (23:29); (5) the reason for remanding Paul to the governor's jurisdiction (23:30).

NOTES

23. *the commander summoned two of his centurions and said, "Get two hundred infantrymen ready to leave for Caesarea.* I.e., Caesarea Maritima, the seat of the Roman governor of the province of Judea. See NOTE on 8:40.

by nine o'clock tonight. Lit., "from the third hour of the night," i.e., three hours after sunset. See NOTE on 2:15.

along with seventy cavalrymen, and two hundred spearmen. This number of 470 soldiers to guard Paul borders on the fantastic, since it amounts to almost half of the cohort stationed in the Fortress Antonia in Jerusalem (see NOTE on 21:31). The great number is mentioned to convey the sense of security guaranteed to

Paul. The meaning of *dexiolabous* (= *dexios* + *lambanein* [something grasped by the right hand]) is really unknown. "Spearmen" is used by Goodspeed, but others translate it "archers" or "slingers"; Kilpatrick: "spearmen of the local police." MSS A and 33 read rather *dexiobolous*, but that makes it hapax legomenon, of equally unknown meaning. Probably light-armed auxiliaries are meant.

24. *Provide horses for Paul to ride on so that they may give him safe conduct.* Lit., "provide animals," which could have been horses, mules, or donkeys. "They" refers to the cavalrymen, not to the animals.

to the Governor Felix." Phēlix was a Roman freedman, set free by Antonia Minor, the mother of emperor Claudius and daughter of Mark Antony. He was the brother of the freedman Pallas, an intimate and influential friend of emperors Claudius and Nero. Although he had such a social background, Felix became the procurator of Judea, Samaria, Galilee, and Perea. He is called Antonius Felix by Tacitus and also in a Latin inscription (*CIL* 5.34; perhaps also in *CIL* 6.1984), but MSS of Josephus's *Antiquities* (20.7.1 §137) call him Claudius Felix, a name which also appears in *CIL* 6.8143 and some other inscriptions. Whether they all refer to the Felix mentioned here is problematic. Moreover, the dates of his procuratorship cannot be established accurately (roughly A.D. 52/53–59/60 [see Conzelmann, *Acts*, 195 for the debate about them]). Luke has at least mentioned him in a correct context. Tacitus (*Histories* 5.9) wrote of him: "Since kings had died or been reduced in control, [the emperor] Claudius entrusted the province of Judea to Roman knights or freedmen, one of whom was Antonius Felix, who with all cruelty and lust wielded the power of a king, with the mentality of a slave." Felix was partly responsible for the eventual revolt of the Judean populace against Rome in A.D. 66. During his governorship the *sicarii* may have begun to emerge. See further Suetonius, *Claudii vita* 28; Tacitus, *Annales* 12.54; Josephus, *Ant.* 20.7.1–2 §§137–44; 20.8.9 §182; *J.W.* 2.12.8 §247.

Luke calls Felix *hēgemōn*, which is the generic title for a provincial "governor" (23:26, 33; 24:1, 10; 26:30); see NOTE on Luke 3:1 (*Luke*, 456). His specific title in Greek at this time would have been *epitropos* (*J.W.* 2.12.8 §247), equalling Latin *procurator.*

25. *He wrote a letter to this effect.* Lit., "a letter having this pattern." Compare 1 Macc 11:29 *(echousan ton tropon touton)*; 15:2; 3 Macc 3:20. This phrase may be "a disclaimer that the letter records precisely what the tribune wrote" (Marshall, *Acts*, 370). Such a letter would have been required in the transfer of a prisoner to a higher Roman authority. Various MSS of the WT begin this verse thus: "For he feared lest the Jews might seize and kill him (Paul) and he himself might thereupon be accused of having taken a bribe. So he wrote a letter containing these details."

26. *"Claudius Lysias to His Excellency, Felix the Governor: Greetings!* On the epistolary greeting Luke uses, see NOTE on 15:23. The governor is addressed with the epithet *kratistos* (= Latin *egregius*), used of Theophilus in Luke 1:3 (*Luke*, 300), which Josephus employs for Vitellius, governor of Syria (*Ant.* 20.1.2 §12). It was an epithet often predicated of the equestrian order in Roman society. Felix, as a freedman, would hardly have belonged to that level of Roman society. It will

occur again in 24:3, which shows that Luke considered it proper for a Roman governor. The Vg translates *kratistos* by Latin *optimus,* "most excellent," an honorific title for persons of even higher rank.

27. *Here is a man whom Jews had seized and were about to put to death. I intervened with my troops and rescued him.* Lit., "this man arrested by Jews and about to be put to death by them . . . I rescued." The commander recounts the arrest of Paul, laying the blame of the civil disturbance on Jerusalem Jews and presenting himself with all rectitude in the affair.

when I learned that he was a Roman citizen. Lit., "having learned that he was a Roman." This sentence telescopes the events somewhat; in 22:24–29 the commander only learns that Paul was a Roman citizen after he has rescued him from the Jerusalem crowd. The effect of the change is to enhance the commander's chivalrous intervention.

28. *Hoping to learn the basis of their charges against him, I brought him before their Sanhedrin.* This is a summary of the preliminary investigation (22:30–23:11), conducted with the Sanhedrin present in an advisory capacity. Lysias mentions the *aitia,* "cause," the official term for the "charge" or "accusation" being made by the Jerusalem Jews. Lysias had at first understood the charges against Paul to be of a capital crime.

29. *Then I discovered that he was being accused in controversial matters of their own law.* The commander's reaction to the inquiry is the same as that of Gallio, the proconsul of Achaia in 18:14–15, the typical reaction of a Roman authority to a theological dispute between Judaism and emerging Christianity. Again the technical verb *enkalein* is used meaning "accuse" or "take proceedings against" someone. MSS P^{48} and 614 of the WT read rather "of the Mosaic law and a certain Jesus."

was in no way guilty of anything deserving death or imprisonment. What is recorded here is the judgment of a Roman *chiliarchos* or *tribunus militum:* there was no *enklēma axion thanatou,* "criminal act (of which the defendant is accused) worthy of death" in the eyes of his opponents. This is the important statement for the Lucan story: Paul is not guilty of any politically criminal act. At the end of this verse, MSS 614 and 2147 of the WT add "With force I barely extricated him." Cf. 23:9; 28:18.

30. *When I was informed about an imminent plot against this man, I decided then and there to send him to you.* Recall the conspiracy of 23:19–22. Thus, the commander states his reason for remanding Paul to the provincial governor.

I have further instructed his accusers to take up [*their case*] *with you.*" Lit., "and (told) the accusers to address [what] concerns him to you." Since the commander would hardly have done this before Paul was safely out of Jerusalem, the aorist tense is the epistolary past (to be judged from the standpoint of the recipient of the letter, BDF §334), or possibly as a sign of the free redactional character of the letter (Conzelmann, *Acts,* 195). This detail is not previously recorded in Acts.

31. *the infantrymen took Paul according to their orders and escorted him during*

the night to Antipatris. Thus the commander's orders are carried out. *Antipatris* was a town founded by Herod the Great in the Plain of Sharon and named after his father, Antipater II (Josephus, *Ant.* 16.5.2 §§142–43; *J.W.* 1.21.9 §417), perhaps on the site of ancient Aphek. Its exact site is contested, but it lay about halfway between Jerusalem and Caesarea Maritima, about 46 km from Caesarea and 60 km from Jerusalem. See S. Dar and S. Applebaum, "The Roman Road from Antipatris to Caesarea," *PEQ* 105 (1973): 91–99.

32. *The next day they let the cavalrymen proceed with him, while they returned to headquarters.* The area that would be traversed from Antipatris was largely Gentile, and the heavy escort would have been no longer necessary.

33. *On their arrival in Caesarea.* See NOTE on 8:40.

they delivered the letter to the governor and brought Paul before him. The mission of the cavalry is accomplished.

34. *He read it and asked Paul from what province he was.* The governor Felix is depicted as trying to ascertain to what extent he would have jurisdiction over Paul or possibly as thinking of remitting the case to the governor of another Roman province, which was optional (see Sherwin-White, *Roman Society*, 55–57).

When he found out that he came from Cilicia. Because Paul was a native of Tarsus, which lay in Cilicia Pedias, he would have been subject to the governor of the double province Syria-Cilicia; and because that was Paul's domicile *(forum domicilii)*, he would have come under the jurisdiction of the governor of that province. Vespasian only later split the province and created a separate and enlarged province of Cilicia, in A.D. 72. Although Felix was governor of the double province, that is not the full reason for his following statement, because *forum delicti*, "the jurisdiction where the (alleged) crime has taken place," has been Judea. Thus Felix realizes that the accusations against this native of Cilicia are being brought by Jews of Judea, a district of the province of which he is governor. Despite his reaction to the Jewish population, Felix has to handle the case. On Cilicia, see NOTES on 9:11; 21:39.

35. *"I shall hear your case when your accusers get here too."* Lit., "I shall hear you fully when . . ." It would do little to listen to the accused alone; so Felix decides to await the citizens of Jerusalem who accuse Paul before making his own preliminary inquiry. The "accusers" should be the "Jews from Asia" (21:27), who started the action, but they turn out to be the "chief priests" and other religious authorities of Jerusalem.

he ordered him to be kept under guard in Herod's praetorium. Thus, Paul continues to be a prisoner of the Romans. The palace of Herod the Great in Caesarea Maritima had become the residence (*praitōrion* [= Latin *praetorium*]) of the Roman governors of Judea since A.D. 6. It was also the place where they, as occupiers, dispensed justice; see P. Benoit, "Prétoire, Lithostroton et Gabbatha," *RB* 59 (1952): 531–50, esp. 532–36; J. Maigret, "Paul, prisonnier à Césarée," *BTS* 41 (1961): 3–4.

BIBLIOGRAPHY (23:23–35)

Bruce, F. F., "The Full Name of the Procurator Felix," *JSNT* 1 (1978): 33–36.
Hemer, C., "The Name of Felix Again," *JSNT* 31 (1987): 45–49.
Kilpatrick, G. D., "Acts xxiii, 23: *Dexiolaboi*," *JTS* 14 (1963): 393–94.
Kindler, A., "An Unrecorded Hybrid of Antonius Felix," *INJ* 4 (1980): 24 (+ pl. 10/3).
Kochavi, M., "Excavations at Aphek-Antipatris," *Qad* 22 (1989): 2–20.
Kokkinos, N., "A Fresh Look at the *gentilicium* of Felix, Procurator of Judaea," *Latomus* 49 (1990): 126–41.
Moda, A., "Paolo prigioniero e martire: Capitolo secondo, Gli avvenimenti di Cesarea," *BeO* 35 (1993): 21–59.
Rinaldi, G., "Procurator Felix: Note prosopografiche in margine ad una rilettura di At 24," *RivB* 39 (1991): 423–66.
Sherwin-White, A. N., "Paul before Felix and Festus," *Roman Society*, 48–70.
Smallwood, E. M., *The Jews under Roman Rule: From Pompey to Diocletian* (SJLA 20; Leiden: Brill, 1976), 266–72.
Sullivan, R. D., "The Dynasty of Judaea in the First Century," *ANRW* II/8 (1977): 296–354, esp. 330–31.
Treggiari, S., "M. Antonius Felix: Not a Freedman Transformed?" *LCM* 29 (1975): 71–72.

2. TRIAL BEFORE GOVERNOR FELIX (24:1–21)

24 [1]Five days later the high priest Ananias came down to Caesarea with some
of the elders and an attorney named Tertullus, and they laid their case against
Paul before the governor. [2]When Paul was summoned, Tertullus began his accusation: "Your Excellency, Felix, we enjoy much peace through your efforts, and
many improvements have been made in this nation through your provident care.
[3]So we must always and everywhere acknowledge this with deep gratitude. [4]But
now, not to detain you with more of this, I would urge you to listen to us briefly
with your customary courtesy. [5]We have found this man to be a pest, one who
creates dissension among all Jews all over the world; he is a ringleader of the sect
of the Nazoreans, [6]and has even tried to desecrate our Temple; but we caught
him.[7] [8]Now you can interrogate him about all these things and learn for yourself
why we are accusing him." [9]The Jews also supported this indictment, maintaining that these were the facts. [10]Paul began to answer, as the governor motioned to him to speak. "I know that you have been a judge in this nation for
many years; so I am encouraged to make my defense before you. [11]You are in a
position to ascertain the facts: Not more than twelve days have passed since I
went up to Jerusalem, in order to worship there. [12]Neither in the Temple did
they discover me debating with anyone or causing a crowd to gather, nor in synagogues, nor anywhere else in the city. [13]They cannot even substantiate for you

the charges they are now making against me. [14] I do admit, however, that it is
according to the Way, which they call a sect, that I worship the God of our ancestors. I believe in all that is according to the law and that is written in the prophets.
[15] I share the same hope in God as these people themselves, that there will be a
resurrection of both the upright and the wicked. [16] Because of this, I strive constantly to keep my conscience clear before God and human beings. [17] After an
absence of several years, I had come to bring alms to the people of my race and
to make my offerings. [18] While I was engaged in completing the rites of purification in the Temple, with no crowd around me and with no turmoil, [19] certain
Jews from Asia came upon me. Those are the ones who should be here before
you to make whatever charges they have against me. [20] Or at least let these who
are here state of what crime they have found me guilty, as I stood before the
Sanhedrin — [21] unless it be that one thing that I shouted in their presence, 'It is
because of the resurrection of the dead that I stand trial before you today.'"

WT: [1] [omits "some of the elders and"]. [2] [omits "through your efforts"]. [4] [omits "briefly"]. [5] [omits "among all Jews" and reads instead "dissension not only in our nation but almost all over the world"]. [6] [adds at the end:] According to our law we wanted to judge (him). [7] But the commander Lysias came with much force and snatched him from our hands. [8] [adds at the beginning:] He ordered his accusers to come to you [omits "for yourself"]. [9] that this was so. [13] [omits "for you" and "now"]. [14] [omits "I do admit, however"]. [16] [omits "constantly"]. [19] [omits "before you"]. [21] [omits "in their presence" and "today"].

COMMENT

Luke now begins the story of the formal trial of Paul before the procurator Felix in Caesarea Maritima. It begins as a narrative, but Luke inserts two speeches, one of Tertullus, the advocate for the Jerusalem plaintiffs, and the other of the defendant Paul himself. This is the only place in Acts where speeches take the form of a debate. Tertullus formulates the specific legal charges, and Paul answers, maintaining that his accusers have no case against him.

The context in which these two speeches occur must be recalled, because aspects of it will appear in the speeches. The remote context is Paul's appearance before the Sanhedrin (23:1–10), after his arrest in Jerusalem, in which the split occurred between the Pharisees and Sadducees who were present. There Paul declared, "I am a Pharisee" (23:6). Part of that context is also Claudius Lysias's letter, which has admitted that nothing deserving death or imprisonment has legally been found in Paul. The more proximate context is the declaration of Felix, "I shall hear your case when your accusers get here too" (23:35).

According to Sherwin-White (*Roman Society*, 48), the basic elements of the procedure are all present: the charge is made and sustained by private plaintiffs (first Jews from Asia; then religious authorities from Jerusalem, who now appear before the governor with an advocate); the governor takes his seat on his tribunal *(pro tribunali)* and acts with the assistance of his *consilium*, "council" (25:6, 10, 12).

Tertullus's prosecutory speech (24:2b–8) is an effective, polished invective, which uses juridical and rhetorical terminology. As a skilled lawyer, he begins with a customary *captatio benevolentiae* (vv 3–4), to win over Felix to his way of thinking. He mentions how Felix has rid the country of bandits and brought it peace; how he has managed other reforms. For all this Tertullus expresses gratitude. Against Paul he charges four things: (1) Paul is a pest; (2) he is an agitator, stirring up trouble among Jews all over the world; (3) he is a ringleader of the Nazoreans; and (4) he has tried to desecrate the Temple. Thus, Tertullus makes out his case of *seditio,* political rebellion. Tertullus concludes by recommending that the governor himself examine Paul.

Paul's defense (24:9–21) is an *apologia,* his third defense speech in Acts. It is nonkerygmatic and makes no use of OT passages. In it Paul answers charges made by Tertullus, emphasizing that those who accuse him have offered no proof. He insists that in the Temple he had not been "debating with anyone or causing a crowd to gather." Moreover, "the Way," which Paul espouses, is actually in continuity with ancestral Judaism; he equates it with a *hairesis,* "sect, party," in Judaism, and maintains that he is not a ringleader of the Nazoreans. He stresses that he is really on trial because he has proclaimed his belief in the resurrection (vv 15–21). In the course of his defense, Paul mentions for the first time in Acts the collection that he has brought to his people in Jerusalem (24:17). Details about Tertullus and the trial may have come to Luke from the Pauline source, but the speeches are his own composition. For the most part Paul's speech recapitulates what Acts has already reported.

In a concrete way this episode plays out the words of Jesus reported in Luke 21:12 about his disciples being handed over to synagogues and prisons and led off to kings and prefects "because of my name." Paul is now arraigned before a Roman procurator and in chap. 26 he will appear before King Agrippa. The speeches of Tertullus and Paul are Lucan compositions; details in them may possibly be derived from the Pauline source, especially those in vv 1–2a, 9–10a.

In this episode Paul has to confront Jewish authorities who claim that they are serving the God of Israel, but they use a skilled prosecutor to plead their cause before the occupying Roman authorities. Paul has no such skilled advocate and has to rely on his own resources. He has, however, the risen Lord's assistance. The climax of his defense is once again the affirmation of his Pharisaic belief in the resurrection of the dead, by which the reader understands that he means the resurrection of Christ, the Lord.

NOTES

24:1. *Five days later.* I.e., after the arrival of Paul himself in Caesarea Maritima.

the high priest Ananias came down to Caesarea. The plaintiffs are not the "Jews from Asia," but Jerusalem's religious leaders, who proceed to make their case against Paul. To come from Jerusalem to Caesarea Maritima, Ananias has had to "come down" from a high city (over 800 m above sea level) to a city on the edge of Mediterranean Sea. See NOTES on 8:5, 40; 23:2.

with some of the elders. Along with the high priest, they represent the highest authority of the Jews in Jerusalem. See NOTES on 4:5; 11:30.

an attorney named Tertullus. He is otherwise unknown. Luke calls him *rhētōr,* which in the Greek world would mean "public speaker, orator"; the Latin Vg reads *orator,* and the *RSV* translates it "spokesman." He is depicted as a Jerusalem advocate, the spokesman for the high priest and elders. Luke puts on his lips a speech of polished rhetoric.

they laid their case against Paul before the governor. Lit., "they made clear to the governor (what they had) against Paul." This deposition was a formal complaint against Paul made in his absence, as the next verse reveals.

2. *When Paul was summoned, Tertullus began his accusation.* I.e., when Paul was brought from confinement to the place where Felix had his tribunal in the pretorium.

"Your Excellency, Felix. See NOTE on 23:26.

we enjoy much peace through your efforts, and many improvements have been made in this nation through your provident care. Tertullus singles out "peace" *(eirēnē),* "improvements" *(diorthōmata),* and "foresight" or "providence" *(pronoia)* as blessings that had come to Judea during Felix's term as procurator (A.D. 52–60). Josephus (*J.W.* 2.13.2 §252) tells how Felix rid Judea of the *Sicarii,* "dagger bearers," thus bringing it peace, but also reports that his rule was not without its cruelty, which eventually contributed to the revolt of the Judeans against Rome in A.D. 66. Cf. S. Lösch, *TQ* 112 (1931): 295–319.

3. *we must always and everywhere acknowledge this with deep gratitude.* For the rhetorical paronomasia used in *pantē te kai pantachou,* see BDF §488.1.

4. *But now, not to detain you with more of this, I would urge you to listen to us briefly with your customary courtesy.* The noun *epieikeia* denotes "graciousness," an idea which hardly suits the usual conduct of Felix toward the people of Judea.

5. *We have found this man to be a pest.* Tertullus speaks in the first plural, including the Jews who have come with him. He calls Paul *loimos,* "pestilence, pestilential disease, plague," meaning thereby that he has had a deleterious and contagious influence on Jewish people. Demosthenes used the word of a person dangerous to public welfare (*Or.* 25.80). Cf. 1 Macc 10:61; 15:21, where it is used of fugitive rebels.

one who creates dissension among all Jews all over the world. MS P^{74} omits the adj. *pasin,* "all" before "Jews," probably because of the following phrase. Paul's activity is regarded as seditious and exciting to riot. Similar accusations have been made in 16:20; 17:6. Tertullus tries to accuse Paul of causing political trouble *(seditio),* whereas he depicts the Jews whom he represents as being on the side of the Romans.

In this accusation Luke uses language that was contemporary. It echoes a similar charge leveled against Jews of Alexandria in the time of the emperor Claudius. In a letter Claudius wrote about the political activity of certain Jews who were *koinēn tina tēs oikoumenēs noson exegeirontas,* "stirring up a common plague throughout the world."

he is a ringleader of the sect of the Nazoreans. Tertullus calls Christianity *hairesis,* which should mean that it was a "school, party, sect" within Judaism, such as Sadducees (5:17; see NOTE there) or Pharisees (15:5). *Hairesis* is similarly used by Josephus (of Essenes, Pharisees, Sadducees, *Ant.* 13.5.9 §171; cf. *Ant.* 20.9.1 §199; *Life* 2 §10, 12). In his defense Paul will admit that "the Way" is regarded as *hairesis* (24:14). When used by adversaries, the word takes on a pejorative connotation, as in 24:14; 28:22. That would be the connotation in this verse too, as Paul is alleged to be its main proponent. On "Nazorean" as an epithet, see NOTE on 2:22.

6. *has even tried to desecrate our Temple.* Tertullus alludes to the incident about Trophimus the Ephesian in 21:28–30.

we caught him. See 21:30. This is the fulfillment of the prediction of Agabus (21:11), that Jews of Jerusalem would arrest and imprison Paul.

After this the WT adds in v 6: "According to our law we wanted to judge (him)." This is the reading in MSS 614 and 1505. The WT also inserts v 7, which is not found in the best MSS of the Alexandrian tradition (P^{74}, ℵ, A, B, H, L, P, 049, 81, 1175). The insert reads: "But the commander Lysias came with much force and snatched him from our hands." There is also a Western addition at the beginning of v 8: "He ordered his accusers to come to you." These additions are found for the most part in MSS E, Ψ, 33, 323, 614, 945, 1505, 1739, and in the Vg, whence the numbering of the verses. They add an improbable invective against Lysias, modeled perhaps on 23:30. To add them here, as does Dupont (*Actes,* 192), would be to make the Jews claim jurisdictional competence over Paul. See *TCGNT,* 434, which rightly explains the omission of them.

8. *Now you can interrogate him about all these things and learn for yourself why we are accusing him."* When vv 6b–8a are omitted, "him" refers to Paul, who is to be interrogated by the governor. If those verses were included, "him" would refer to Claudius Lysias, who is later summoned to Felix the governor. Perhaps this is the reason why those verses were added in the WT.

9. *The Jews also supported this indictment, maintaining that these were the facts.* "The Jews" now refers to the high priest and the elders (v 1), who have come from Jerusalem with Tertullus, their advocate. They apparently added their testimony to his. Luke uses *synepitithenai,* which means to join in an attack on someone.

10. *Paul began to answer, as the governor motioned to him to speak.* Paul makes his *apologia,* the defendant's official counterstatement, answering the accusations brought against him. After a brief conciliatory introduction (v 10b), his remarks treat four things: in vv 11–13, he dismisses the charge that he has created disturbances (cf. v 5); in vv 14–16, he explains his relation to "the Way," which in no way makes him disloyal to his Jewish heritage (cf. v 5); in vv 17–19, he dismisses the charge of having desecrated the Temple (cf. v 6); and in vv 20–21, he maintains that, when he appeared before the Sanhedrin, no one was able to prove any charge made against him (cf. v 8). Luke again uses a gen. absol. to express the governor's assent.

"I know that you have been a judge in this nation for many years. I.e., probably since A.D. 52, but Paul's use of "many years" is rhetorical.

so I am encouraged to make my defense before you. This *captatio benevolentiae* is Paul's introduction. He renders Felix benevolent to him by graciously recalling his lengthy experience and competence. Felix has been procurator (A.D. 52–60) longer than any other since P. Pilate (A.D. 26–36).

11. *You are in a position to ascertain the facts.* Paul acknowledges Felix's advantageous position.

Not more than twelve days have passed. The dates that appear in the Lucan account (21:17, 18, 26, 27; 22:30; 23:11–12, 32; 24:1) amount to more than twelve days, but Paul may be referring merely to the seven days of the Nazirite vow ceremony (21:27) and the "five" mentioned in 24:1.

since I went up to Jerusalem. See NOTE on 8:5.

in order to worship there. Luke depicts the Christian Paul on a pilgrimage, coming to worship in the Jerusalem Temple (21:26), such as any devout Jew would do (cf. 8:27). No mention is made of the purpose of Paul's visit to Jerusalem, about which he himself writes (Rom 15:25–32), bringing the collected aid for the poor (cf. 1 Cor 16:1–4; 2 Cor 8:1–9:15). Paul will mention it in v 17. Luke again uses the fut. ptc. *proskynēsōn* to express purpose; see BDF §390.1 and NOTE on 8:27.

12. *Neither in the Temple did they discover me debating with anyone or causing a crowd to gather, nor in synagogues, nor anywhere else in the city.* Thus Paul, even in his introductory remarks, answers the charge that he has been causing dissension among Jews everywhere.

13. *They cannot even substantiate for you the charges they are now making against me.* This statement serves as the proposition of Paul's speech to the governor.

14. *I do admit, however, that it is according to the Way.* On "the Way" as a name for Christianity, see NOTE on 9:2. Paul's admission includes a confession of faith, which he now seeks to explain.

which they call a sect. I.e., *hairesis;* see NOTES on 5:17; 24:5. In effect, Paul is rejecting the pejorative connotation of that term (see NOTE on 24:5), because he believes that "the Way" is more than just a form of Judaism such as Pharisaism or Sadduceeism. He regards it as a God-inspired "way" to salvation, not something that one prefers or chooses. In any case, Paul insists that the accusations against him are not political, but religious.

I worship the God of our ancestors. Paul insists on the continuity of his Jewish monotheism. "The LORD, the God of the fathers, the God of Abraham, of Isaac, and of Jacob" (Exod 3:16) is still Paul's God. Thus Paul is assuring Felix that, if he is a member of "the sect of the Nazoreans," as Tertullus has put it (24:5), his worship and his way of life are still in conformity with Pharisaic Judaism. His allegiance to Jesus Christ is not arbitrary, but the logical outgrowth of a major tenet of Pharisaism (belief in the resurrection of the dead); in effect, Christianity is its fulfillment. See NOTE on 22:14. Cf. 22:3; 28:17; Rom 9:3–5.

I believe in all that is according to the law and that is written in the prophets. Moses and the Prophets are still normative for Paul; he thus refers to the two main portions of the Hebrew Scriptures, as they were divided by Jews of his day.

Cf. 1QS 1:3; Luke 24:44–45. Whether this is another instance of the Paulinism of Acts may be debated (see Introduction §173). Paul himself in his own letters might express this matter a little differently; see 2 Cor 3:6–18.

15. *I share the same hope in God as these people themselves.* Paul's faith in God evokes just as much hope and trust as that of other Jews, especially the Pharisees. That "hope" will be made more specific in the next clause.

there will be a resurrection of both the upright and the wicked. Paul's belief in the resurrection of the dead is based on Dan 12:2–3. That belief, first formulated clearly in the latest book of the Hebrew Scriptures, developed further in Judaism in the intervening centuries.

16. *Because of this, I strive constantly to keep my conscience clear before God and human beings.* Paul recognizes the relation between his human conduct and the afterlife. Recall what he said about his "conscience" in 23:1 (see NOTE there). Now Paul adds "and human beings," meaning that he has not knowingly offended his fellow Jews in any way. For the concluding formula, see Prov 3:4.

17. *After an absence of several years.* About five years have elapsed since the visit of Paul to Jerusalem, implied in 18:22.

I had come to bring alms. Contrast the expression of his goal in 20:16; 24:11. At length, Luke allows Paul to mention the collection that he had had taken up in the Gentile Christian churches founded by him in Galatia, Macedonia, and Achaia (Gal 2:10; 1 Cor 16:1–4; 2 Cor 8:1–7; 9:1–5; Rom 15:25–28, 31). Conzelmann (*Acts,* 199) thinks that the collection is mentioned only to offset the charge of insurrection (*stasis,* v 5), that the allusion to the collection is scarcely intelligible to the reader of Acts, and that Luke clearly "knows more than he says." Readers of Acts may, indeed, not be aware of the importance of that collection in Paul's sight, because Luke has not emphasized it to the same extent as did Paul himself. How could he have known about its importance, not being with Paul when he wrote those important letters?

These alms are different from those he brought in 11:29–30 on a visit that Paul never mentions in any of his own letters (see Introduction §156). Luke again uses the fut. ptc. to express purpose; see NOTE on 24:11.

It is possible to translate this verse differently: "I had come to the people of my race, to bring alms and to make my offerings." The question is whether to take *eis to ethnos mou* with the preceding ptc. *poiēsōn* or with the following verb *paregenomēn.* See Schneider, *Apg.,* 2.348; Weiser, *Apg.,* 629–30; Johnson, *Acts,* 413.

to the people of my race. Or "of my nation," because Paul uses *to ethnos mou.* This must mean what Paul himself calls "my brothers, my kinsmen by descent" (Rom 9:3). In reality, however, the alms were meant for converted Jews, as one learns in Rom 15:26 ("God's dedicated people there"), but his reference also to "unbelievers in Judea" (Rom 15:31) would not mean that he would exclude "people of my race" from sharing in that help being brought. *Pace* Haenchen (*Acts,* 655), Luke's formulation is not an unreliable historical statement.

to make my offerings. These personal offerings to God were undoubtedly made to the Temple itself, in fulfillment of what Paul agreed to do in 21:26.

18. *While I was engaged in completing the rites of purification in the Temple.*

Recall 21:26–30. Paul alludes to the purificatory rite that he went through, as four other Jews were completing the ceremony of the Nazirite vow (21:24). His speaking of it as a "rite of purification in the Temple" stands in contrast to Tertullus's accusation that he had been "desecrating the Temple."

with no crowd around me and with no turmoil. None is recorded in that passage in 21:26.

19. *certain Jews from Asia came upon me.* Recall 21:27. The verb *heuron*, "found," occurs actually at the beginning of v 18 in the Greek text.

Those are the ones who should be here before you to make whatever charges they have against me. Thus, Paul answers the charge of Tertullus that he had been desecrating the Temple. Implied in Paul's answer is that Tertullus does not know of such desecration firsthand; he has been going only on hearsay. Moreover, Paul insinuates that the original accusers have abandoned their case against him. This would be a clear instance of *destitutio*, "abandonment," in Roman law, when plaintiffs fail to appear at the trial of a person they have accused. The emperor Claudius had threatened to decide cases against such plaintiffs even in their absence (Dio Cassius, *Roman History* 60.28.6; Suetonius, *Claudii Vita* 15.2); cf. Sherwin-White, *Roman Society*, 52: "Once again, the author of Acts is well informed."

20. *Or at least let these who are here state of what crime they have found me guilty.* If Paul is being accused of some crime mentioned when he appeared before the Sanhedrin, that should have been mentioned by Tertullus, but it has not been named. Paul knows that there has been no charge that could be sustained against him. If Paul's adjuration of the high priest (23:3) were considered a criminal act, Tertullus has passed over it.

as I stood before the Sanhedrin. Recall 22:30–23:9.

21. *unless it be that one thing that I shouted in their presence.* Lit., "or for the sake of that one cry that I sounded, as I was standing among them." So Paul seeks to qualify the absolute character of his denial of guilt. Recall 23:6; see NOTE there.

'It is because of the resurrection of the dead that I stand trial before you today.' "The resurrection of the dead" thus echoes like a refrain in these latter chapters of Acts. Directly *anastasis nekrōn* refers to the specific Pharisaic belief, but implied in Paul's statement is his own belief in "the resurrection of the Dead [One]," i.e., of Jesus Christ, his risen Lord. That idea, however, would scarcely be understood by a Roman governor and will not surface until 25:19.

BIBLIOGRAPHY (24:1–21)

Allo, E.-B., "La portée de la collecte pour Jérusalem dans les plans de Saint Paul," *RB* 45 (1936): 529–37.

Bowen, C. R., "Paul's Collection and the Book of Acts," *JBL* 42 (1923): 49–58.

Buck, C. H., Jr., "The Collection for the Saints," *HTR* 43 (1950): 1–29.

Cumont, F., "La lettre de Claude aux Alexandrins et les Actes des Apôtres," *RHR* 91 (1925): 1–6.

Delebecque, E., "Saint Paul avec ou sans le tribun Lysias en 58 à Césarée (Actes xxiv, 6–8): Texte court ou texte long?" *RevThom* 81 (1981): 426–34.
Goguel, M., "La collecte en faveur des saints," *RHPR* 5 (1925): 301–18.
Lösch, S., "Die Dankesrede des Tertullus: Apg 24,1–4," *TQ* 112 (1931): 295–319.
Nickle, K. F., *The Collection: A Study in Paul's Strategy* (SBT 48; London: SCM, 1966), 148–52.
Sizoo, A., "Die rede van Tertullus," *GTT* 49 (1949): 65–72.
Winter, B., "The Importance of the *captatio benevolentiae* in the Speeches of Tertullus and Paul in Acts 24:1–21," *JTS* 42 (1991): 505–31.

3. IMPRISONMENT OF PAUL AT CAESAREA (24:22–27)

[22]Then Felix, who was rather well informed about the Way, adjourned the trial,
saying, "When the commander Lysias comes, I shall decide your case." [23]He gave
orders to the centurion that Paul was to be kept under guard but allowed some
freedom; and that no one was to prevent his friends from seeing to his needs. [24]A
few days later Felix came with his wife Drusilla, who was a Jewess, and sent for
Paul and listened to him speak about faith in Christ Jesus. [25]As he talked on
about uprightness, self-control, and the coming judgment, Felix became uneasy
and spoke up, "That's enough for now. Go, and I shall send for you again, when
I find the time." [26]At the same time, he hoped that he would be offered a bribe
by Paul; so he rather frequently sent for him and conversed with him. [27]After two
years had passed, Felix was succeeded by Porcius Festus. Anxious to ingratiate
himself with the Jews, Felix left Paul in prison.

WT: [22][omits "Lysias"]. [23]that he was to prevent no one from coming to him. [24]A few days later Drusilla, the wife of Felix, who was a Jewess, asked to see Paul and to listen to his word. Wishing to satisfy her, (Felix) sent . . . [omits "Jesus"]. [25]and I shall send for you at a fitting time. [26]hoped that he would get a bribe from Paul; so he secretly sent. [27][omits "Anxious . . . Festus"]. He left Paul in prison because of Drusilla.

COMMENT

Luke records the story of Paul's imprisonment in Caesarea Maritima for "two years" (24:27). Felix has recessed the court and delays further investigation and the passing of sentence on Paul, at first because he wants to await the arrival of the commander, Claudius Lysias, who has sent Paul to the governor. Moreover, since Felix knows something about Christianity, he and his wife Drusilla are eager to hear Paul speak more about it. Thus he keeps Paul in custody because he would be able to speak with him from time to time. He also hopes that he may get a bribe from Paul to release him. The custody lasts for two years (A.D. 58–60), until Felix is replaced as procurator by another Roman, Porcius Festus.

The episode is another narrative in Acts, based on information derived from

Luke's Pauline source, especially that about Felix and Drusilla, the successor Festus as procurator, and Paul being left in custody. Verses 24–26 may be of Lucan composition.

The result of the foregoing episode is that Paul does not succeed in winning his freedom. Now he must bear witness to Christ by continuing his confinement in Roman custody. In time he will bring his testimony to Felix and his wife Drusilla in Caesarea.

NOTES

22. *Then Felix, who was rather well informed about the Way.* See NOTE on 9:2. Why Felix might have been well informed about "the Way" becomes clear in v 24. For the comparative adv. *akribesteron*, see ZBG §148.

adjourned the trial. Lit., "Felix postponed them," i.e., he put off Paul and his Jewish accusers, because he was awaiting further information. Felix does not hand Paul over to his accusers or make any judgment; Paul is still in confinement.

saying, "When the commander Lysias comes, I shall decide your case." Felix is presumed to have sent for the commander, whom he is now awaiting, because Lysias would have been a witness to any civil disturbance that Paul might have caused. On Lysias, see NOTES on 21:31; 22:28; 24:8.

23. *He gave orders to the centurion that Paul was to be kept under guard but allowed some freedom; and that no one was to prevent his friends from seeing to his needs.* The *Koinē* text-tradition reads rather, "from coming to him." Paul's custody at Caesarea is somewhat similar to what he will have in Rome (28:30), but there he will enjoy even greater freedom. Among Paul's "needs" would have been clothing, food, and drink. Those who might provide it are called simply *hoi idioi*, "his own," possibly also his sister and his nephew of Jerusalem.

24. *A few days later Felix came.* I.e., to the place where Paul was detained, the former palace of Herod the Great, now the residence of the Roman governor, which served also as a place of detention.

with his wife Drusilla, who was a Jewess. Felix had married the beautiful younger daughter of Herod Agrippa I, after considerable intrigue to win her away from her husband Azizus, the king of Emesa (in Syria). The details are given by Josephus, *Ant.* 19.9.1 §§354–55; 20.7.1–2 §§138–44; *J.W.* 2.11.6 §220; According to Suetonius (*Claudii Vita* 28), Felix married "three queens." These would have been Drusilla; the granddaughter of Mark Antony and Cleopatra; and the third is unknown (see Tacitus, *Histories* 5.9). As a Jewess, Drusilla was probably the source of Felix's rather accurate information about Christianity as "the Way" (24:22). Note the addition of the WT given above, which ascribes to Drusilla the reason for listening to Paul.

sent for Paul and listened to him speak about faith in Christ Jesus. Or "in the Messiah, Jesus." Felix and Drusilla were curious to learn more about Christian beliefs, and especially about Paul's faith in Jesus of Nazareth as his risen Lord, but their curiosity did not lead to conviction or their personal faith. Another reason for Felix's summoning is given in v 26. MSS ℵ[1], A, C, H, and P omit "Jesus," which is read by P^{74}, ℵ*, B, E, L, Ψ, 049, 33, and 1739. "Christ Jesus" is a frequent Pauline variant of "Jesus Christ" (e.g., 1 Cor 1:2; Rom 2:16; 3:24), which occurs in Acts (3:20; 5:42; 17:3), but usually then in the predicative sense, and hardly ever elsewhere in the NT. For *pistis eis Christon,* see 20:21; 26:18; Col 2:5; with the verb *pisteuein,* see Acts 10:43; 14:23; 19:4; Rom 14:1; Gal 2:16; Phil 1:29.

25. *As he talked on about uprightness, self-control, and the coming judgment.* From "faith" in Christ Jesus, about which Felix and Drusilla curiously inquire, Paul apparently passes on to preach about *dikaiosynē,* "uprightness," which may possibly echo 13:39 (cf. Rom 3:21–26), *enkrateia,* "self-control," which is mentioned only here on the lips of Paul (cf. Gal 5:23), and *krima to mellon,* "the coming judgment," which is likewise mentioned only here in Acts (cf. Rom 2:2–3). The adulterous marriage of Felix to Drusilla may be the background for Paul's remarks on such topics. The threesome mentioned would have been meant to remind Felix about his rapacity and greed, lust, and coming doom.

Felix became uneasy and spoke up, "That's enough for now. Lit., "go away for now," i.e., that will do for now, or enough of such topics. Luke writes *to nyn echon,* using *echein* in an impersonal sense, "for the present" (adv. acc.), as in Lucian, *Anacharsis* 40. See ZBG §74; *IBNTG,* 160.

Go, and I shall send for you again, when I find the time." Felix's reaction is similar to that of the Athenians after Paul's speech at the Areopagus (17:32).

26. *At the same time, he hoped that he would be offered a bribe by Paul.* Lit., "that money would be given to him by Paul." Possibly the mention of "alms" in 24:17 suggested this to Felix. His hope for a bribe, however, fits in well with the black picture of Felix and his rapacity found in Tacitus and Josephus. Roman law, however, forbade the taking of bribes from prisoners; see *Lex Iulia de pecuniis repetundis* (*PW* 12.2389–92). Josephus (*J.W.* 2.14.1 §273) tells of such bribes taken by another governor of Judea, Albinus.

so he rather frequently sent for him and conversed with him. About what Luke does not say.

27. *After two years had passed.* I.e., of such confinement of Paul, subsequent to his investigation by Felix, in the pretorium of Caesarea. This might mean until the end of Felix's procuratorship. Dupont (*Actes,* 196) takes *dietia* as the technical term in Roman law for the maximum duration of such detention as Paul was experiencing; at the end of it Paul should have automatically secured his release, since no condemnation against him had legally succeeded.

Felix was succeeded by Porcius Festus. Lit., "Felix got Porcius Festus as successor." Little is known about *Porkios Phēstus,* who was apparently the procurator of Judea A.D. 60–62 (the time of the beginning and end of his administration cannot be accurately established; see K. Lake, *Beginnings,* 5.464–67), but Luke has at least correctly recorded him as Felix's successor. He was a member of a famous senatorial clan, the Porcii of Tusculum, and was appointed procurator of Judea by Nero. Josephus depicts him as a conscientious administrator, who strove above all to bring peace to the province and rid it of the *Sicarii.* He died in office and was succeeded by Lucceius Albinus, A.D. 62–64 (*J.W.* 2.14.1 §§271–72; *Ant.* 20.8.9–11 §§182–94; 20.9.1 §§197, 200). See Schürer, *HJPAJC*, 1.467–68; PW 22/1.220–27; J. B. Green, "Festus, Porcius," *ABD*, 2.794–95.

Anxious to ingratiate himself with the Jews, Felix left Paul in prison. I.e., not only until the end of his term as procurator, but even thereafter so that his successor has to handle Paul's case. Cf. 25:9, which describes a similar concern of Festus. Sometimes, departing governors released prisoners held under them. Josephus (*Ant.* 20.9.5 §215) tells of the procurator Albinus releasing prisoners before his successor Florus would arrive.

BIBLIOGRAPHY (24:22–27)

Moffatt, J., "Expository Notes on Acts," *Expos* 8/17 (1919): 271–74.

Pieper, K., "Einige Gedanken zu Act. 24, 24 f. und 8, 9 ff." *TGl* 2 (1910): 275–80.

Saumagne, C., "Saint Paul et Félix, procurateur de Judée," *Mélanges d'archéologie et d'histoire offerts à André Piganiol* (3 vols.; Paris: S.E.V.P.E.N., 1966), 3.1373–86.

Stern, M., "The Province of Judaea," *The Jewish People in the First Century* (CRINT 1; ed. S. Safrai and M. Stern; Assen: Van Gorcum; Philadelphia: Fortress, 1974), 1/1.308–76, esp. 320, 368–70.

4. Before Governor Festus Paul Appeals to Caesar (25:1–12)

25 [1]Three days after he arrived in the province, Festus went up from Caesarea
to Jerusalem. [2]The chief priests and leaders of the Jews brought their charges
against Paul formally before him. They kept urging him, [3]requesting it as a favor
to be done for them, that he transfer Paul to Jerusalem, for they had been plotting
to do away with him along the way. [4]But Festus answered that Paul was being
kept at Caesarea and that he himself would be going there soon. [5]"Your prominent men," he said, "can come down with me; if this man has done anything
wrong, let them prosecute him there." [6]After spending no more than eight or ten
days among them, Festus returned to Caesarea. On the following day, he took
his seat on the bench and ordered Paul to be brought in. [7]When he came in, the
Jews who had come down from Jerusalem surrounded him and leveled against
him many serious charges. But they were unable to prove any of them. [8]In his
defense, Paul said, "I have done no wrong, either against the law of the Jews, or
against the Temple, or against Caesar." [9]Festus, however, who wanted to show
favor to the Jews, said to Paul in reply, "Are you willing to go up to Jerusalem
and stand trial before me there on these charges?" [10]Paul replied, "I am standing
before the bench of Caesar; this is where I should be tried. I have done Jews no
harm, as you realize only too well. [11]If I am guilty, if I have committed a crime
worthy of death, I am not seeking to escape the death penalty. But if there is

nothing to the charges these people are bringing against me, no one has the right to give me over to them. I appeal to Caesar." [12]Then Festus, having conferred with his council, replied, "You have appealed to Caesar; to Caesar you shall go."

WT: [3][adds at end of verse:] they had prayed that they might succeed in getting him into their hands. [5][omits "prominent"]. [6][omits "no more than" and "among them"]. [7][omits "who had come down"]. [8]Paul said that he had done no wrong. [9][omits "in reply"]. [11]the charges they are bringing. [12]with his council, said.

COMMENT

Luke now continues his story about Paul in Roman custody; he must appear before the new procurator of Judea, Porcius Festus, who was in office from A.D. 60?–62. When Festus arrives on the scene, Paul's Jewish adversaries confront the procurator in Jerusalem, demanding that Paul be brought from Caesarea Maritima to Jerusalem to stand trial there. They request this because they have already planned to waylay him en route and slay him. Not suspecting anything like that, Festus replies that they can come with him to Caesarea, where he will let them confront Paul. When Festus asks Paul whether he would be willing to go to Jerusalem to answer the charges they have brought against him, Paul declares his innocence and insists on his right as a Roman citizen to be judged as such, and so he appeals to Caesar.

The episode is an important development in the Lucan story of Acts, because it is the immediate occasion of Paul's journey to Rome, where he is destined to continue to bear his testimony to the Christian gospel. It is again a narrative, based on Luke's Pauline source, into which he has introduced a short defense speech (25:8, 10–11), Paul's fourth in Acts. In making his defense, Paul insists that he has done nothing against the law of the Jews, the Temple, or Caesar. This is the basis of his continued *apologia* and of his appeal. Because Paul has appealed to Caesar, the Roman governor Festus has decided that Paul is to go to Rome and to Caesar. Paul's appeal was undoubtedly made in A.D. 60.

In this suspense-laden episode the new Roman procurator is depicted acting energetically to put an end to the Pauline "affair," the long-delayed trial. He acts impartially at first, listening to the accusations of the Jews of Jerusalem and to Paul's answers to the charges. Once he is at Caesarea, Festus hesitates: Should he bring Paul to Jerusalem for the continuation of the hearings? Though eager to win favor with the Jews, he nevertheless asks Paul's view of the matter, and thus sets the stage for the appeal to Caesar.

The problem in the appeal is to discern what the basis for the appeal would be, since there has been no verdict by a judge or a magistrate, from which an appeal might be made. Cadbury thought that Paul was, in effect, being charged with *seditio*, "sedition"; Haenchen, with *laesa maiestas;* Gilchrist, with a heresy trial (Paul at odds with orthodox Judaism, which was entitled to the protection of the law). See Haenchen, *Acts*, 668–70, for an exaggerated analysis of difficulties that the episode is supposed to create; also Schneider, *Apg.*, 2.356–57 for a more balanced view of the matter.

NOTES

25:1. *Three days after he arrived in the province.* I.e., Judea, which was actually a district of the province of Syria. The new governor does not delay going to Jerusalem, known to be a hotbed of trouble. He seeks to establish good relations with the religious authorities of that important city in his jurisdiction.

Festus. See NOTE on 24:27.

went up from Caesarea to Jerusalem. See NOTE on 8:5.

2. *The chief priests and leaders of the Jews.* Some MSS (H, P, 049, 189, and 326) read rather "the high priest." The high priest of the time would have been Ishmael, son of Phabi (Josephus, *Ant.* 20.8.8 §179), who had been appointed by Herod Agrippa II in A.D. 59. Josephus tells of a strife between the "chief priests" and other priests and leaders of the people, but Luke says nothing about this. The "leaders" are here called *hoi prōtoi*, "the first (men)" among Jerusalem Jews. Cf. 13:50; 28:17; Luke 19:47. The plaintiffs are no longer "Jews from Asia" or other private citizens of Jerusalem (21:27, 30), but again the religious authorities of Jerusalem.

brought their charges against Paul formally before him. They kept urging him. They undoubtedly reiterated the charges that Tertullus had earlier formulated (24:5–6). The charge that the "Jews from Asia" first made against Paul, bringing Greeks into the Temple (21:28), has been made generic, desecrating the Temple.

3. *requesting it as a favor to be done for them, that he transfer Paul to Jerusalem.* Lit., "summon him to Jerusalem." The surface reason might seem to be reasonable, that they would not have to travel from Jerusalem to Caesarea, but the real reason emerges in the following clause.

for they had been plotting to do away with him along the way. Their intention was to ambush Paul en route and lynch him. Recall the conspiracy of 23:12–15.

4. *But Festus answered that Paul was being kept at Caesarea and that he himself would be going there soon.* Festus does not immediately grant the request. His answer is couched in indirect discourse at first, but then continued in direct discourse.

5. *"Your prominent men," he said, "can come down with me.* The leaders are now called *dynatoi*, "powerful" (ones); contrast v 2 above.

if this man has done anything wrong. Lit., "if there is in him anything improper." The adj. *atopon*, "out of place," can be used either in a moral or legal sense. Here the latter would be intended.

let them prosecute him there." I.e., at the official seat of Roman jurisdiction in Judea. We are not told why Festus makes this decision. Presumably he acts in accordance with a proper understanding of Roman law.

6. *After spending no more than eight or ten days among them, Festus returned to Caesarea.* MS P^{74} omits "among them," i.e., in Jerusalem.

On the following day, he took his seat on the bench. The *bēma* was the gubernatorial tribunal or seat of judicial decision. Thus begins the official trial of Paul in Caesarea, as the governor takes his seat. Cf. 2 Macc 13:26; Josephus, *Ant.* 20.6.2 §130.

ordered Paul to be brought in. I.e., before him so seated on the bench.

7. *When he came in, the Jews who had come down from Jerusalem surrounded him and leveled against him many serious charges.* Thus, Luke summarizes the proceedings of the prosecutors, who confront Paul in a threatening manner. The charges *(aitiōmata)* are not specified, but presumably they would have included those already formulated by Tertullus (24:5–6): he is a pest; an agitator of Jews everywhere; a ringleader of the Nazoreans; he tried to defile the Jerusalem Temple.

But they were unable to prove any of them. Instead of narrating the proceedings, Luke simply records a value judgment about them, because he is more interested in Paul's side of the case. Since the "Jews from Asia" (21:27) are not present, and their original charge is not being pressed, Paul is able to turn their accusations to religious matters.

8. *In his defense, Paul said.* Lit., "whereas Paul defended himself (saying)." In the Greek text this clause is actually a gen. absol., modifying v 7.

"I have done no wrong. Lit., "I have not sinned in anything." Paul uses the verb *hamartanein,* which in this context would mean "to do something (legally) wrong."

either against the law of the Jews. Paul maintains that he has not violated the Mosaic law, declaring in his defense what he has already said in 18:13–15; 21:21, 28; 24:14.

or against the Temple. A repetition of 21:28.

or against Caesar." This is a new detail, prompted perhaps by Paul's appearance before the Roman tribunal. He has done nothing against the head of the Roman Empire. The "Caesar" at this time would have been Nero Claudius Caesar (A.D. 54–68). In using "Caesar," Paul would be maintaining that he has done nothing against Roman law; see NOTE on 17:7. Cf. 16:21.

Luke depicts Paul declaring himself innocent of any wrong against the Jews or against the empire, because he wants it recognized that that for which Paul stands, viz., Christianity, is not in conflict with either Judaism or the Roman Empire.

9. *Festus, however, who wanted to show favor to the Jews.* Probably because he realized that he was being confronted by leading people of Jerusalem, an important city in his jurisdiction. The motive, however, echoes that said of Felix in 24:27.

said to Paul in reply, "Are you willing to go up to Jerusalem and stand trial before me there on these charges?" Festus recognizes the right of the accused in asking whether Paul were "willing." The implication in Festus's request may be that the Sanhedrin is the more proper setting for such a trial. He thus acknowledges an ambiguity in Paul's case. The phrase *ep' emou,* "before me," however, which occurs at the end of the verse, is important; it means that it will still be a Roman trial, but it creates a problem. If the trial is still to be "before" the governor, then a Sanhedrin setting is not implied. Some MSS (e.g., 33), however, add *ē*, "or," before *ep' emou,* which suggests either setting, either in the Sanhedrin or before the governor. This reading gives a better occasion for Paul's reply. For further implications of Festus's request, see Sherwin-White, *Roman Society,* 67; H. W. Tajra, *The Trial,* 141–42.

10. *Paul replied, "I am standing before the bench of Caesar.* I.e., in standing before the bench of the Roman procurator in Caesarea, Paul realizes that his case has already passed to another level, that of the judicial system of the Roman Empire, *epi tou bēmatos Kaisaros,* "at Caesar's tribunal." Cf. Ulpian, *Digest* 1.19.1: "Quae acta gestaque sunt a procuratore Caesaris, sic ab eo comprobantur, atque si a Caesare ipso gesta sint" (What is done and carried out by Caesar's procurator is so approved by him, as if they were carried out by Caesar himself). So Festus's proposal is for Paul impossible. Paul invokes his right of *reiectio* against *iudicium iniquum,* of refusing to be tried before an incompetent tribunal. He will have no involvement of the Sanhedrin in his trial, even in an advisory capacity to the Roman governor. Paul also has an inkling of what is really behind it all, since he is aware of the attempt on his life reported by his nephew (23:16–22).

this is where I should be tried. I.e., since I, a Roman citizen, have already been brought before Roman authority (23:27). Paul does not invoke that status explicitly, but he does decline the proposal of Festus.

I have done Jews no harm. Lit., "Jews I have wronged in no way," with the emphasis falling on the adv. acc. *ouden,* "in nothing." Paul repeats the contention he made earlier (25:8).

as you realize only too well. Lit., "as even you recognize rather well." The comparative adv. *kallion* has elative force, as a substitute for the positive (ZBG §150).

11. *If I am guilty.* Lit., "if I am doing (something) unjust," i.e., if I am a wrongdoer. The conditional form of Paul's expression is important.

if I have committed a crime worthy of death, I am not seeking to escape the death penalty. Paul acknowledges the basic principle of Roman law and order and the governor's right to condemn him to death, if he is really guilty of a capital charge. Compare Josephus, *Life* 29 §141: "If it is right for me to die, I ask no mercy"; also Plato, *Apology* 37.

But if there is nothing to the charges these people are bringing against me. Another repetition of the contention of 25:8 provides the basis for what follows.

no one has the right to give me over to them. Lit., "no one can give me over to them." I.e., not even the Roman procurator, since such extradition would be illegal. The verb *charizesthai* actually means "to favor, gratify." The procurator cannot gratify the Sanhedrin as he proposes. Paul thus rejects the competence of the Jerusalem Sanhedrin and says "no" to the procurator's suggestion.

I appeal to Caesar." In uttering *Kaisara epikaloumai* (= official Latin *Caesarem appello*), Paul makes the proceedings against him stop, for he has invoked authority higher than that of the provincial governor. It means that Paul has to remain in Roman custody and cannot be brought before the Sanhedrin.

On what basis does he do this? In early Roman law *provocatio* was the legal right to appeal to *populus romanus* over a decision made by a magistrate (over what was called *coercitio*, "infliction of summary punishment" [by a magistrate to secure obedience]). This arose in the city of Rome about 300 B.C. Toward the end of the Republic *provocatio* became the form of appeal over the verdict of a private *iudex*, "judge." It was made to the magistrate who had appointed the trial judge; but it could go higher, even to Caesar, for with the coming of the principate appeal was no longer made to the "Roman people," but to the *princeps*, i.e., to Caesar. This right was confirmed by Augustus in the *Lex Iulia de vi publica seu privata*, which protected Roman citizens throughout the empire from high-handed decisions of provincial governors, summary punishment, execution, or torture. Their case could be heard in Rome. In this instance, a procuratorial verdict or decision has not yet been made; Paul appeals against the suggestion of the procurator to change the venue of his trial. Even that was within his rights.

See *OCD*, 86–87, 892–93; cf. A. N. Sherwin-White, *Roman Society*, 68–69; *The Roman Citizenship* (2d ed.; Oxford: Clarendon, 1973); A.H.M. Jones, *Studies in Roman Government and Law* (Oxford: Blackwell, 1960), 51–65; A. W. Lintott, "Provocatio: From the Struggle of the Orders to the Principate," *ANRW* I/2 (1972): 226–67, esp. 232–34; H. W. Tajra, *The Trial*, 144–47; cf. H. J. Cadbury, "Roman Law and the Trial of Paul," *Beginnings*, 5.297–338, esp. 312–19; P. Garnsey, "The *Lex Iulia* and Appeal under the Empire," *JRS* 56 (1966): 167–89.

12. *Then Festus, having conferred with his council.* The *symboulion*, "council" (Latin *consilium*), would have been a board of assessors, called *synedroi* (Latin *consiliarii*), whom a provincial magistrate would call upon for advice. Apparently such assessors would have been present, but Luke has not indicated this up to now.

replied, "You have appealed to Caesar; to Caesar you shall go." Festus makes the final decision and grants Paul's appeal. Roman historians debate whether the governor would have had to grant the appeal (see H. W. Tajra, *The Trial*, 149–51), but in this case Festus grants it.

BIBLIOGRAPHY (25:1–12)

Carrez, M., "L'Appel de Paul à César (Ac 25,11)," *De la Tôrah au Messie: Etudes d'exégèse et d'herméneutique bibliques offertes à Henri Cazelles* . . . (ed. M. Carrez et al.: Paris: Desclée, 1981), 503–10.

Dauvillier, J., "À propos de la venue de saint Paul à Rome: Notes sur son procès et son voyage maritime," *BLE* 61 (1960): 3–26, esp. 10–11.

Gilchrist, J. M., "On What Charge Was St. Paul Brought to Rome?" *ExpTim* 78 (1966–67): 264–66.

Holzmeister, U., "Der hl. Paulus vor dem Richterstuhle des Festus (AG 25,1–12)," *ZKT* 36 (1912): 489–511, 742–83.

Jones, A.H.M., "I Appeal unto Caesar," *Studies Presented to David Moore Robinson* . . . (2 vols.; ed. G. E. Mylonas; St. Louis: Washington University, 1951, 1953), 2.918–30.

Schalit, A., "Zu AG 25,9," *ASTI* 6 (1968): 106–13.
Sherwin-White, A. N., *Roman Society*, 63–70.
Tajra, H. W., "L'Appel à César: Séparation d'avec le christianisme?" *ETR* 56 (1981): 593–98.
Täubler, E., "Relatio ad principem," *Klio* 17 (1920–21): 98–101.

5. Festus Invites Agrippa to Listen to Paul (25:13–27)

[13] A few days later King Agrippa and Bernice arrived at Caesarea and paid a courtesy call on Festus. [14] Since they were spending several days there, Festus referred
Paul's case to the king, saying, "There is a man here who was left in prison by
Felix. [15] While I was in Jerusalem, the chief priests and elders of the Jews pressed
charges against him, demanding his condemnation. [16] To them I replied that it
was not the custom for Romans to hand over an accused person before he could
confront his accusers and had the opportunity to defend himself against their
charges. [17] So when [they] came here with me, I did not delay the matter. The
very next day I took my seat on the bench and ordered the man brought in. [18] His
accusers stood around him, but brought no charge against him about crimes that
I had suspected. [19] Instead, they disputed with him about controversial matters in
their own religion and about a certain Jesus who had died, but who Paul claimed
was alive. [20] Not knowing how to settle their controversy, I asked whether he
would be willing to go to Jerusalem to stand trial there on these charges. [21] But
Paul appealed that he be held in custody for an imperial decision. So I issued
orders that he be kept under guard until I could send him to Caesar." [22] Then
Agrippa said to Festus, "You know, I too should like to listen to this man." Festus
replied, "Tomorrow you will listen to him." [23] So the next day Agrippa and Bernice arrived with great pomp and entered the audience chamber along with cohort commanders and eminent men of the city. At Festus's command Paul was
brought in. [24] Then Festus said, "King Agrippa and all you gentlemen here present with us, look at this man. He it is about whom the whole Jewish community
has appealed to me both here and in Jerusalem, clamoring that he must not live
any longer. [25] Yet I could not discover that he had done anything deserving death.
So when he himself appealed to the Emperor, I decided to send him. [26] But I
have nothing definite to write about him to our sovereign. So I have brought
him before all of you, and especially before you, King Agrippa, that from this
investigation I might get something to write. [27] For it seems foolish to me to send
on a prisoner, without indicating the charges against him."

WT: [13] [omits "at Caesarea"]. [20] [omits "on these charges"]. [23] and men who had come down from
the province. Festus commanded that Paul be brought in. [24] And he said [omits "Jewish" and adds
after "Jerusalem":] that I hand him over without any defense. I was unable to hand him over because
of the regulations that we have from the Emperor. If anyone was accusing him, let him follow (me)

to Caesarea where he (Paul) is being held. When they gathered (here), they clamored that he must be deprived of life. [25] When I listened to this part and the other, I could not discover him to be deserving of death in any regard. When I said (to him), "Do you wish to be judged with them in Jerusalem?" he appealed to Caesar. [omits "I decided to send him"]. [26] [omits "definite," "to our sovereign," and "Agrippa"].

COMMENT

By appealing to Caesar, Paul does not succeed in being sent immediately to Rome, because Festus has to write a report to accompany him according to contemporary Roman law. So Ulpian's *Digest* (49.6.1), of later date, recorded it: "After an appeal has been made, records must be provided by the one with whom the appeal has been filed to the person who will adjudicate the appeal." So the trial of Paul continues, but now in the presence of King Herod Agrippa II and his sister Bernice, who have come to greet the new procurator. Festus invites the king to listen to Paul, having explained how Paul has been left in prison by the former procurator, been accused by Jerusalem Jews, and how he has appealed to Caesar. The king and his sister express interest in hearing Paul, and so Festus prepares a session for them to hear what he has to say, hoping thereby to learn something that he may send in a letter to the emperor.

Though the episode begins as a narrative, based on information from Luke's Pauline source, it soon becomes a speech, in which Festus explains Paul's situation to King Agrippa in vv 14b–21 and to the king and his entourage in vv 24–27. The double speech is a judicial clarification, explaining to Agrippa II and others the matter of *aequitas romana*, "Roman fairness" or "Roman equity." The speech is a Lucan composition, but it is far from certain that the whole scene is "a free literary composition" (Conzelmann, *Acts*, 206). The episode pursues an obvious Lucan apologetic purpose of further stressing the innocence of Paul in such a legal setting. The Roman governor tells the Jewish king that he has found nothing in Paul's case that is liable to prosecution on the basis of the charges brought by his Jewish adversaries.

The episode thus introduces a Jewish personality, King Agrippa, who will add his summation of Paul's situation to that of two Roman procurators (Felix and Festus) and the Roman military tribune (Claudius Lysias). Paul has already appeared before a "synagogue" and a "governor"; now he will appear before a "king" (see Luke 12:12), giving substance to Jesus' words about those who follow him. It is also a fulfillment of Acts 9:15–16.

The introduction of Agrippa II into the story of Paul also becomes a parallel to the Lucan passion narrative, when Jesus appeared before another member of the Herodian royal family, Herod Antipas (Luke 23:6–12).

NOTES

13. *A few days later King Agrippa and Bernice.* This is Marcus Julius Agrippa II, son of Herod Agrippa I, who is mentioned in 12:1–11, 20–23, and of Cypros

(Josephus, *J.W.* 2.9.6 §220). He was the brother of Bernice II, Mariamme, and Drusilla (who married Felix the procurator; see NOTE on 24:24). Agrippa II was born in A.D. 27, educated in Rome, and in 48 became prince of Chalcis on the death of his uncle, Herod of Chalcis (Josephus, *J.W.* 2.12.1 §223; *Ant.* 20.5.2 §104). In 52 he became "king" *(basileus)* of the tetrarchy (Ituraea and Trachonitis) of Philip (Luke 3:1 [see NOTE there]), to which Nero added parts of the districts of Galilee and Perea (Josephus, *Ant.* 20.8.4 §159). He was called *basileus megas Agrippa philokaisar eusebēs kai philorōmaios,* "great king Agrippa, friend of Caesar, devout, and friend of the Romans" (*OGIS* §419). Agrippa II was disliked by the Jews and especially by the chief priests. He was the last of the Herodians to rule over Judea and died sometime around A.D. 92. See R. D. Sullivan, "The Dynasty of Judaea in the First Century," ANRW II/8 (1977): 296–354, esp. 329–45 and 344 n. 287.

At this time Bernice II, who had been married to Herod of Chalcis, was widowed and came to live at the court of her brother, Agrippa II; she was the older sister of Drusilla, wife of Felix (24:24). Josephus (*Ant.* 20.7.3 §145; *J.W.* 2.11.5 §217) tells of the gossip that circulated about a liaison with her brother. Later she was involved with the Roman Titus (see Juvenal, *Satires* 6.156–60; Suetonius, *Titi Vita* 7.1; Dio Cassius, *Roman History* 65.15.4; Tacitus, *Histories* 2.2). In the year 66 Bernice pleaded with the procurator Florus to have his soldiers stop the carnage of the people of Jerusalem, and she barely escaped from them with her own life (Josephus, *J.W.* 2.15.1 §§309–14). Cf. G. H. Macurdy, "Julia Berenice," *AJP* 56 (1935): 246–53; J. A. Crook, "Titus and Berenice," *AJP* 72 (1951): 162–75.

In most of the MSS of the Alexandrian tradition her name is spelled *Bernikē,* as it is in Josephus, *J.W.* 2.11.5 §217; but MS C reads *Berēnikē.* More correctly it should be *Berenikē,* as spelled in Josephus, *Ant.* 20.7.3 §145.

arrived at Caesarea. I.e., Caesarea Maritima; see NOTE on 8:40.

paid a courtesy call on Festus. Lit., "greeting Festus," as the new Roman procurator. Josephus (*Ant.* 20.8.11 §§189–96) narrates at length how Agrippa II preserved good relations with the procurator Festus. Luke uses the aor. ptc. *aspasamenoi* to express purpose; see W. F. Howard, "On the Futuristic Use of the Aorist Participle in Hellenistic," *JTS* 24 (1922–23): 403–6; A. T. Robertson, "The Aorist Participle for Purpose in the *Koinē,*" *JTS* 25 (1923–24): 286–89; BDF §339.1; ZBG §§264–65. MSS Ψ, 36, 81, 323, and 1739 read rather the more correct fut. ptc. *aspasomenoi* (see BDF §418.4).

14. *Since they were spending several days there, Festus referred Paul's case to the king, saying, "There is a man here who was left in prison by Felix.* Recall 24:27. Festus uses the opportunity to consult the Jewish king officially about Paul, sensing his own incompetence in this matter.

15. *While I was in Jerusalem, the chief priests and elders of the Jews pressed charges against him, demanding his condemnation.* Recall 25:1–3. What was not explained there is now filled in. In effect, this is Festus's summation of what has transpired. From the Jewish point of view Paul is guilty; the religious authorities

were asking for *katadikē*, "a sentence against" him, but see 25:11. Festus suspects what is at stake and why the religious authorities want Paul transferred to their jurisdiction.

16. *To them I replied that it was not the custom for Romans.* Festus invokes *ethos*, "custom, customary practice," which played a great part in private and public legal procedures among the Romans. In fact, it became the basis of the famous Roman law.

to hand over an accused person before he could confront his accusers and had the opportunity to defend himself against their charges. Festus's reply implicitly contrasts Jewish and Roman legal procedures. He insists on *aequitas romana*, the traditional Roman fairness, for from the Roman point of view Paul's guilt has not been established. Anonymous denunciations were not tolerated, and the plaintiff(s) had to confront the defendant before a judge. "This is the law by which we abide: No one may be condemned in his absence, nor can equity tolerate that anyone be condemned without his case being heard" (Ulpian, *Digest* 48.17.1). Cf. Appian, *Bellum Civile* 3.54; Pliny, *Ep.* 10.97; Justin, *Apology* 1.3. Luke uses the technical legal terms *katēgoroumenos*, "the accused, defendant," *katēgoroi*, "accusers, plaintiffs," *apologia*, "defense," and *enklēma*, "charge, accusation," as well as the formal optative mood of the verbs, *echoi* and *laboi*. See Dupont, "*Aequitas romana*."

17. *So when [they] came here with me.* Recall Festus's refusal to bring Paul to Jerusalem and his insistence that the Jewish authorities come to Caesarea (25:4–5).

I did not delay the matter. Luke emphasizes the promptness with which the Roman procurator reacts to the accusation of the Jerusalem religious leaders.

The very next day I took my seat on the bench and ordered the man brought in. Recall 25:6. Luke's apologetic intent is clear: Festus expresses a Roman reaction to the affair, similar to that in 18:15; 23:29, a scorn for such religious contestations, which he considers irrelevant.

18. *His accusers stood around him, but brought no charge against him about crimes that I had suspected.* I.e., crimes punishable in Roman law. In 25:7 it is said that they brought charges, but could not prove them. What the charges were is explained in the next verse.

19. *Instead, they disputed with him about controversial matters in their own religion.* Festus recognizes the charges as matters in which Roman law would not be involved, but charges in the Jewish way of life. He speaks of the Jews' "religion" as *deisidaimonia*, the same word that Paul used of the Athenians' "reverence for deities, beliefs about gods" (see NOTE on 17:22; cf. Josephus, *Ant.* 19.5.3 §290). Josephus (*J.W.* 2.9.2 §174) also employs the word for the willingness of Jews to die for their beliefs. It can, however, often mean an "excessive fear of gods" or "superstition about demons." See R. C. Ross, "Superstitio," *CJ* 64 (1968–69): 354–58, esp. 356 n. 15; S. Calderone, "Superstitio," *ANRW* I/2 (1972): 377–96. Festus uses it as a way of referring to foreign or non-Roman religious tenets.

In 24:5–7 the advocate Tertullus gave a summary of the charges the Jews were making against Paul. Possibly the Jews in their reaction to Paul are moved to seek the procurator's support because of what Julius Caesar had decided in favor of the high priest in the time of Hyrcanus II: "Whatever high-priestly rights or other privileges exist in accordance with their laws, these he and his children shall possess by my command. If, during this period, any question will arise concerning the Jews' manner of life, it is my pleasure that the decision shall rest with them" (Josephus, *Ant.* 14.10.2 §195).

about a certain Jesus who had died, but who Paul claimed was alive. This detail is new; it has not surfaced before in what the Jews were claiming about Paul. Recall 17:31. Festus's reference to the resurrection of Jesus is phrased as a pagan Roman would be expected to formulate it. As he sees it, it is merely a question whether Jesus is dead or alive. For Paul's own preaching about the resurrection of Jesus, see 1 Thess 1:10; 2 Cor 13:4; Rom 4:24–25; 6:4, 9; 8:11; 10:9. Recall the Lucan way of formulating it in Acts 1:3; Luke 24:5, 23.

20. *Not knowing how to settle their controversy.* Luke uses the technical term *zētēsis*, equaling the Latin legal term *quaestio*, "controversial question," which had to be settled by judicial inquiry.

I asked whether he would be willing to go to Jerusalem to stand trial there on these charges. Recall 25:9. Festus wonders whether the Jewish religious authorities would be better represented in Jerusalem and the issue better debated there. The governor could not hand over his jurisdiction in a capital case to a third party; so his question does not mean that he was willing to have Paul judged in a trial before the Sanhedrin, but only that he himself was willing to hear the case in Jerusalem with the Sanhedrin as a *consilium.*

21. *Paul appealed that he be held in custody for an imperial decision.* Lit., "for a decision (*diagnōsis*, the technical legal term, equaling Latin *cognitio*) of the Augustus." In other words, Paul feared the influence of the Sanhedrin even in an advisory capacity. Here *Sebastos* is used in a generic way as a title for the emperor. *Sebastos*, the Greek equivalent of Latin *Augustus*, is the title that the Roman Senate conferred on Gaius Octavius, the grandnephew of Julius Caesar, who, when adopted by Julius Caesar as his son, became known as Gaius Julius Caesar Octavianus (16 January 27 B.C.), when he became *Princeps* (see *Res Gestae divi Augusti* §34; Philo, *Legatio ad Gaium* 21 §143; OCD, 149). "Augustus" became a title (something like "His Majesty") for successors of Octavian in the principate, but Tiberius hesitated to use it. Here it would refer to Nero Claudius Caesar (A.D. 54–68).

So I issued orders that he be kept under guard until I could send him to Caesar." On the title *Kaisar*, see NOTE on 17:7. Luke uses the technical verb *anapempein*, "send up," to describe the transfer of a person or an issue to a higher authority; cf. Josephus, *J.W.* 2.20.5 §571.

22. *Then Agrippa said to Festus, "You know, I too should like to listen to this man."* This admission is uttered by the king descended from the half-Jewish Herodian line; he was actually the last one to serve as king. The impf. verb *eboulomēn* might mean that Agrippa had already heard about Paul's case and has been curious about him: "I have been wishing."

Festus replied, "Tomorrow you will listen to him." In vv 26–27 one will learn the reason why Festus agrees to Agrippa's request.

23. *So the next day Agrippa and Bernice arrived with great pomp and entered the audience chamber along with cohort commanders and eminent men of the city.* Luke's idyllic description of the arrival of Agrippa and Bernice in the audience chamber sets the stage for Paul's last defense. On commanders, see NOTE on 21:31. They were the leaders of the five cohorts stationed in Caesarea (Josephus, *Ant.* 19.9.2 §365). The *andres hoi kat' exochēn tēs poleōs* would have been prominent Gentiles of Caesarea, undoubtedly part of the king's entourage.

At Festus's command Paul was brought in. I.e., from his place of confinement to the *akroatērion*, "audience chamber," probably in another part of Herod's palace in Caesarea.

24. *Then Festus said, "King Agrippa and all you gentlemen here present with us, look at this man.* The king's entourage is thus welcomed to listen to Paul and counsel the procurator.

He it is about whom the whole Jewish community has appealed to me both here and in Jerusalem, clamoring that he must not live any longer. Again, an instance of Lucan hyperbole; see NOTE on 2:44. Recall 21:36; 22:22.

25. *Yet I could not discover that he had done anything deserving death.* Yet another Roman governor adds his verdict in Paul's case; cf. 18:15; 23:29; 25:18. The refrain of Paul's political innocence recurs. Conzelmann (*Acts*, 207) compares Pilate's triple declaration about Jesus' innocence in the Lucan passion narrative (23:4, 14–15, 22). There Luke calls attention explicitly to such a declaration (Luke 23:22).

So when he himself appealed to the Emperor, I decided to send him. Lit., "he himself appealing to the Augustus," a gen. absolute. Recall 25:12, 21.

26. *But I have nothing definite to write about him to our sovereign.* Lit., "about whom I have nothing secure to write to the Lord." Conzelmann (*Acts*, 207) maintains, "What Festus says is self-contradictory. He had enough material! The contradiction results from Luke's literary aim." The seeming contradiction results when one considers what Festus has said in v 25a (Paul has done nothing deserving death) and now admits (v 26a) that he has nothing definite to write about Paul, but then proceeds to set up the hearing before Agrippa (v 26b). That seeming contradiction results from forgetting Festus's proposal to take Paul to Jerusalem for a trial in the presence of the Sanhedrin and Paul's subsequent appeal to Caesar, which is mentioned, in fact, in v 25b. The story is indeed told to suit Luke's "literary aim," but Festus's statement is hardly a blatant contradiction.

Ho Kyrios is used as a title for the Roman emperor. The unmodified *Kyrios* was frequently employed as a title for a Roman emperor, especially in the provinces of the eastern Mediterranean area (*POxy* 1143:4 [Augustus]; 37.6 [Claudius]; 246.30, 34, 37 [Nero]), and among the Romans themselves from the time of Claudius. The title denoted the status and power that the *Princeps* enjoyed in the Roman world. *Kyrios* was also used of other rulers (*OGIS* §415 [Herod the Great]); and of gods (*POxy* 110.2 [Serapis]; 1148.1 [Serapis]; *IG* 14.1124 [Artemis]); cf. *LAE*, 353–56; *TDNT*, 3.1054–48; Fitzmyer, *WA*, 116–19.

So I have brought him before all of you, and especially before you, King Agrippa, that from this investigation I might get something to write. This statement of Festus provides the reason for Paul's last *apologia.* Festus hopes that Paul's appearance before Agrippa II and Bernice will provide some clarification that he can use in his report to Rome. Festus thus regards this session as an official investigation of Paul, with Agrippa, a Herodian king and authority on things Jewish, as *consiliarius.*

27. *For it seems foolish to me to send on a prisoner, without indicating the charges against hims.*" Festus is made by Luke to formulate what he knows he has to do: according to the later *Digest* of Ulpian (49.6.1), Festus has no choice. In effect, Festus repeats what he has said in v 25: he has nothing with which to charge Paul.

"The account of the trial before Festus and Felix is then sufficiently accurate in all its details. In its reference to *provocatio* it is in accord with what is otherwise known of the practice in the first century A.D." (Sherwin-White, *Roman Society*, 68).

BIBLIOGRAPHY (25:13–27)

Dupont, J., "*Aequitas romana:* Notes sur *Actes,* 25,16," *RSR* 49 (1961): 354–85; repr. *Études,* 527–52.

Garms, K., "Paulus vor Festus, Agrippa und Berenike," *Die Christengemeinschaft* 15 (1938–39): 261–64.

Krieger, K.-S., "Berenike, die Schwester König Agrippas II., bei Flavius Josephus," *JSJ* 28 (1997): 1–11.

Maltiel-Gerstenfeld, J., "A Portrait Coin of Berenice Sister of Agrippa II?" *INJ* 4 (1980): 25–26 (+ pl. 10/4).

Mireaux, E., *La reine Bérénice* (Paris: Michel, 1951).

Wifstrand, A., "Apostelgeschichte 25.13," *Eranos* 54 (1956): 123–37.

6. PAUL'S DISCOURSE BEFORE AGRIPPA AND FESTUS (26:1–23)

26 [1]Then Agrippa said to Paul, "You have permission to state your case." Paul
stretched out his hand and made his defense. [2]"Against all the charges leveled
against me by the Jews, King Agrippa, I count myself fortunate to be able to make
my defense today in your presence, [3]especially because you are expert in all the
customs and controversial matters among Jews. I beg you, therefore, to listen to
me patiently. [4]The way I have lived since my youth, the life that I have led from
the beginning among my own people and in Jerusalem, is well known to all [the]
Jews. [5]They have been acquainted with me for a long time and can testify, if they
were only willing, that I lived as a Pharisee, according to the strictest party of our
religion. [6]But now because of my hope in the promise made by God to our ances-

tors I am standing trial. 7 The twelve tribes of our people ardently worship God day and night in the hope that they may see that promise fulfilled. Because of this hope, Your Majesty, I am accused by Jews. 8 But why is it considered so unbelievable among you that God should raise the dead? 9 At any rate, I once thought it my duty to oppose in many ways the name of Jesus the Nazorean. 10 This is what I did in Jerusalem. I imprisoned many of God's dedicated people under the authority that I received from the chief priests; and when they were to be put to death, I cast my vote against them. 11 Many a time, in synagogue after synagogue, I punished them to force them to blaspheme. Indeed, so excessive was my fury that I pursued them even to foreign cities. 12 On one such occasion I was on my way to Damascus, armed with the authorization and commission of the chief priests. 13 At midday, Your Majesty, as I was on the road, I saw a light flash from the heavens, brighter than the brilliant sun, shining around me and those who traveled with me. 14 We all fell to the ground, and I heard a voice saying to me in Hebrew, 'Saul, Saul, why are you persecuting me? It is hard for you to kick against the goad.' 15 I asked, 'Who are you, sir?' And the Lord said, 'I am Jesus, whom you are persecuting. 16 Get up and stand on your feet. For this reason have I appeared to you: to appoint you as my servant and as a witness to what you have seen [of me] and to what you will be shown. 17 For I shall rescue you from this people and from the nations to which I am sending you, 18 in order to open their eyes and to turn them from darkness to light and from the dominion of Satan to God, so that they may obtain forgiveness of sins and a place among those dedicated by faith in me.' 19 Therefore, King Agrippa, I could not be disobedient to that heavenly vision. 20 Rather, first of all, to the people in Damascus and in Jerusalem, to all the country of Judea, yes, even to Gentiles I declared that they must repent and turn to God and do deeds that befit their repentance. 21 That is why Jews seized me [while I was] in the Temple and tried to murder me. 22 But to this very day I have enjoyed God's assistance, and so I am standing here to testify to great and small alike. Nothing that I say goes beyond what the prophets and Moses said would come about: 23 that the Messiah must suffer and that he would be the first to rise from the dead, to proclaim light to his people and to the Gentiles."

WT: 1 and began to defend himself, saying. 2 [omits "by the Jews" and "today"]. 3 in the customs of the Jews and knowledgeable in controversial matters. 4 [omits "from the beginning"]. 6 [omits "by God"]. 7 [omits "ardently" and "Your Majesty"]. 9 [omits "the Nazorean"]. 12 [omits "and commission"]. 14 speaking to me. 18 to turn them away from. 19 [omits "therefore"]. 20 to all the towns of Judea [omits "yes, even to Gentiles"] I preached that they . . . to the living God. 22 [omits "to this very day"] . . . what the prophets have said would come about. For it stands written in Moses: that.

COMMENT

The speech that Paul delivers before King Agrippa II, Bernice, and their entourage is a finely crafted discourse, one of the finest in Acts. It is substantially a defense *(apologia)*, but toward the end it becomes a missionary speech (vv 23, 28), as Paul preaches Jesus as the one promised by Moses and the prophets of old.

In effect, it is a Lucan composition, a repetition of the story of Paul's conversion (9:1–30), once again in the form of a discourse, as in 22:3–21. It is the fifth and last defense that Paul makes in Acts, and this is done before a Herodian king and a Roman procurator. Luke depicts Paul thus fulfilling the role of Christ's "chosen instrument," who was "to carry my name before Gentiles and kings, and the children of Israel" (9:15). He bore that testimony before "Gentiles" in Missions I, II, and III; he carried the word to "the children of Israel," often in synagogues (13:5, 14–47; 14:1; 17:1, 10, 17; 18:4, 19; 19:8; 23:6), and now to "kings" (25:23–26:22).

The structure of Paul's speech can be seen thus:

Introduction *(captatio benevolentiae)*	26:2–3
I. Paul's Jewish, Pharisaic life and belief	26:4–8
II. Paul's persecution of Christians and conversion	26:9–18
III. Paul's testimony about the Suffering Messiah	26:19–23

The discourse is marked by rhetorical and formal language, which stands in contrast to the speech in chap. 22. The Jewish Christian Ananias of Damascus completely disappears from the scene in this speech.

In this discourse the emphasis is on Paul the "prophet," in contrast to chap. 9 (Paul the chosen instrument) and chap. 22 (Paul the witness). This emphasis is brought out by the allusions to OT prophets in vv 16–18 (to Ezek 2:1–6; Jer 1:8; Isa 35:5; 42:7; 61:1) and by reference to Moses and the prophets in support of his message (26:22); in v 27 Paul will ask King Agrippa whether he believes in the prophets.

Though the discourse purports to be a defense of Paul, its hidden agenda is a defense of Christianity, which is now set out in its relation to Judaism. In fact, this speech of Paul, together with the reactions to it (vv 24–32), formulates the christological climax of Acts. O'Toole has shown that it functions as the christological climax of Paul's whole defense (22:1–26:32); but it is also the christological climax of the whole of Acts, for Luke makes Paul formulate the role of faith in the suffering Messiah. In this way Paul is a "prophet," a spokesman for God.

NOTES

26:1. *Agrippa said to Paul, "You have permission to state your case."* Lit., "to speak about yourself." The king takes over in this session from the Roman procurator.

Paul stretched out his hand and made his defense. In 26:29 the reader learns that Paul is standing before Agrippa and others in bonds or chains; in spite of them he manages to stretch out his hand in the manner of the classic Greek orator. Recall 13:16; 21:40. This note suits the formal address that Paul is now depicted uttering.

2. *"Against all the charges leveled against me by the Jews.* Paul begins by repeating what he has already maintained in 24:5–6.

King Agrippa, I count myself fortunate to be able to make my defense today in your presence. Paul tries to render Agrippa sympathetic to his cause with a brief *captatio benevolentiae* (vv 2–3). He expresses the confidence that he has in the king who will listen to him.

3. *especially because you are expert in all the customs and controversial matters among Jews.* Or "more than anyone else." Being of the Herodian dynasty, which was partly Idumean in its background, he would have been regarded by a writer like Josephus (*Ant.* 14.15.2 §403) as *hēmiioudaios,* "half Jewish." This designation was actually used by Josephus of Herod the Great, but it would be an accurate description of his descendants as well. Paul knows that Agrippa was acquainted with the Jewish religion and the customs that Jews often discussed.

I beg you, therefore, to listen to me patiently. Paul begs for the king's close attention. This plea stands in contrast to Paul's reaction to the suggestion of Festus that he be taken to Jerusalem for a hearing in the presence of the Sanhedrin. Ms. C, the *Koinē* text-tradition, and Syriac and Coptic versions read *sou,* "you (sg.)," as the object of the verb "I beg," but P[74], ℵ, A, B, E, Ψ, 33, and 1739 omit it *(lectio difficilior).* It has to be supplied in translation, and for such reason it was added in some MSS.

4. *The way I have lived since my youth.* No mention is made of Tarsus or Paul's doings in the Holy City; contrast 22:3 for details of Paul's youth. The first part of the speech (vv 4–8, introduced by *men oun*), begins here, describing Paul's Jewish and Pharisaic life and belief.

the life that I have led from the beginning among my own people. Paul himself tells about that Jewish life in Gal 1:13–14.

in Jerusalem, is well known to all [*the*] *Jews.* Recall 22:3. What Paul has said there is implied in what he now claims is known to Jerusalem Jews.

5. *They have been acquainted with me for a long time and can testify, if they were only willing, that I lived as a Pharisee.* In 23:6 the Lucan Paul speaks of himself as still a Pharisee; cf. Phil 3:4b–6, for Paul's own protestation about his Pharisaic background. See NOTE on 5:34.

according to the strictest party of our religion. On party, see NOTE on 5:17. Josephus (*J.W.* 2.8.14 §162) employs the related noun *akribeia,* "strict accuracy," in describing the way of life of the Pharisaic *hairesis* and its mode of interpreting the Mosaic law *(ta nomima).*

6. *now because of my hope in the promise made by God to our ancestors I am standing trial.* Paul thus stresses that his dispute with the Sanhedrin is theological, not political. He invokes what he considers the traditional belief of "the fathers," i.e., the patriarchs of Israel. According to Haenchen (*Acts,* 683), "it can only concern Messianic hope—brought to fulfilment in the resurrection of Jesus—which is inseparably bound up with the hope of resurrection." That, however, is an abuse of the word "messianic," which has no place here. The "hope" of which Paul speaks is hope in the resurrection of the dead, as 24:15 and 26:8 make clear. This hope is founded on a promise made by God to Paul's ancestors, probably a reference to Dan 12:2–3. That passage in Daniel may not be a "promise" in the strict sense, but, according to his wont, Luke makes Paul so interpret it. Earlier OT passages, such as Isa 26:19; Hos 6:2; and even Ezek 37:1–14, un-

doubtedly also contributed to the development of this "hope" in late pre-Christian Judaism.

7. *The twelve tribes of our people.* I.e., the Jews of all Israel, traditionally numbered as twelve tribes: Asher, Benjamin, Dan, Ephraim, Gad, Issachar, Judah, Manasseh, Naphtali, Reuben, Simeon, Zebulon, but the names and the order of them vary. See Genesis 49; Deuteronomy 33; Ezekiel 48; cf. Rev 7:5–8. See further P. J. Rask, *The Lists of the Twelve Tribes of Israel* (Ph.D. diss., Catholic University of America; Ann Arbor: U.M.I., 1990). The Lucan Paul still regards them all as the "people" to which he belongs.

ardently worship God day and night. Paul appeals to the daily cult of Yahweh in the Jerusalem Temple and argues that it makes no sense unless it is related to the hope of resurrection. This has been the long-understood hope of Judaism, and Paul insists that he shares it too.

in the hope that they may see that promise fulfilled. Recall 24:15.

Because of this hope, Your Majesty, I am accused by Jews. Lit., "O King!" Paul maintains that his preaching about the risen Christ is no different from the traditional ancestral belief of Israel of old, which has included a hope in the resurrection of the dead (23:6). The Jewish accusation of Paul is never formulated just this way, but Paul insists that this is what is really involved in their prosecution of him and their accusations. No other reasonable charge can be brought forth, and so he implies the absurdity of the accusation lodged against him.

8. *why is it considered so unbelievable among you that God should raise the dead?* Put just that way, Jews might have agreed with Paul, because raising of the dead was a fundamental belief of the Pharisees and Essenes. The problem in the verse is, to whom does the pl. pron. *hymin,* "you," refer? Scarcely to King Agrippa and his entourage. More than likely it is addressed to Jews of Luke's own day (especially Sadducees). Yet even the Jews who might find resurrection from the dead "believable" might still find it difficult to admit that God has raised Jesus from the dead. With this question, a shift in the speech takes place: from an apologetic to a missionary thrust. For *ei* used in the sense of *hoti,* "that," see ZBG §404.

9. *At any rate, I once thought it my duty to oppose in many ways the name of Jesus the Nazorean.* So Paul refers to his persecution of early Christians, now labeled as opposition to "the name" of Jesus. At the outset Paul stresses that he too once reacted negatively to preaching about the risen Christ, just as Pharisees are now reacting to his preaching. Again the Lucan refrain of "the name" appears (see NOTE on 2:38). On Nazorean, see NOTE on 2:22. The second part of Paul's speech (vv 9–19, again introduced by *men oun*) begins here, describing Paul's persecution of Christians and his conversion on the road to Damascus.

10. *This is what I did in Jerusalem.* Recall the Lucan description of Paul's pursuit of Jerusalem Christians in 8:3; and also 9:1–3; 22:4–5, where Damascus is rather the scene of his persecution.

I imprisoned many of God's dedicated people. Lit., "many of the saints," a way of referring to Christians among NT writers. See NOTE on 9:13; *Romans,* 239.

under the authority that I received from the chief priests. Recall 9:1, which mentions only the high priest; in 22:5 the high priest and whole council of elders are called to be witness to what he has done.

when they were to be put to death, I cast my vote against them. Lit., "when they were to be done away with." Paul uses a technical term, *psēphon katapherein,* "cast a (voting) pebble," and it raises a question about the context in which he might have actually voted. Possibly he is using the term metaphorically, meaning that he sided with those who so voted or so acted, as he probably did at the stoning of Stephen (7:58–8:1; 22:20). Cf. Gal 1:13.

11. *Many a time, in synagogue after synagogue, I punished them to force them to blaspheme.* This is a new detail about Paul's persecution of Jewish Christians. The verb *timōrein,* "take vengeance on, punish," may refer to synagogal flogging, to which Paul himself attests that he was subjected (2 Cor 11:24). He would have used such means to get Christians to reject Jesus as the crucified and risen Christ. "Blaspheme" in this context would mean to speak out wrongly against, curse, or revile Jesus Christ, as Christians were often forced to do in later persecutions. See Pliny the Younger, *Ep.* 10.96.5 *(maledicerent Christo); Mart. Pol.* 9.3 *(loidorēson ton Christon).* Cf. 1 Cor 12:3; 1 Tim 1:13. On "synagogue," see NOTE on 6:9.

so excessive was my fury that I pursued them even to foreign cities. Paul's persecution of Christians in Damascus (9:2; 22:5) is mentioned again in the next verse, but no other cities have been noted. The plural is only a rhetorical exaggeration.

12. *On one such occasion I was on my way to Damascus.* See NOTE on 9:2.

armed with the authorization and commission of the chief priests. A repetition of what was said in v 10.

13. *At midday, Your Majesty, as I was on the road.* Lit., "O King." The same time indication is given in 22:6; see NOTE there.

I saw a light flash from the heavens, brighter than the brilliant sun, shining around me and those who traveled with me. The description of the "light from heaven" grows with each mention of it; compare 9:3; 22:6.

14. *We all fell to the ground.* According to 9:4, 7 and 22:7 only Paul "fell to the ground."

I heard a voice saying to me. As in 9:4; 22:7. In 9:7 Paul's fellow travelers also hear the voice, which differs from 22:9.

in Hebrew. Lit., "in the Hebrew dialect," which most likely means "in Aramaic" (see NOTE on 22:2). This detail is new, creating a problem with the second half of the following statement.

'Saul, Saul, why are you persecuting me? This part of the heavenly message is identical with that in 9:4 (see NOTE there) and 22:7.

It is hard for you to kick against the goad.' I.e., it is useless for you to try to resist this heavenly call. Though the risen Christ addresses Paul in Aramaic, he quotes a common Greek proverb, which is otherwise not found in Jewish literature. In variant forms it occurs in Euripides, *Bacchae* 794–95 ("than kick against the goads"); Aeschylus, *Prometheus* 324–25; *Agamemnon* 1624; Pindar, *Pythian Odes* 2.94–95; cf. *TDNT,* 3.666–67. In Greek literature the proverb expresses as idle or useless any resistance to divine influence in future conduct. So from that moment on Paul is being pressed into the service of the risen Christ. It does not express a reflection on Paul's past life or conduct, or indicate a crisis of conscience.

Note too Paul's own recollections of the experience on the road to Damascus: he was "seized by Christ" (Phil 3:12); a "compulsion, necessity" *(anankē)* was laid upon him to preach the gospel (1 Cor 9:15–18).

Cf. W. Nestle, "Anklänge an Euripides in der Apostelgeschichte," *Philologus* 59 (1900): 46–57; R. C. Horn, "Classical Quotations and Allusions of St. Paul," *LCQ* 11 (1938) 281–88, esp. 287–88; A. Vögeli, "Lukas und Euripides," *TZ* 9 (1953): 415–38, esp. 416–18; J. Hackett, "Echoes of the Bacchae of Euripides in Acts of the Apostles?" *ITQ* 23 (1956): 219–27, 350–66; S. Reyero, "'Durum est tibi contra stimulum calcitrare': Hechos de los Apóstoles, 26,14," *Studium* 10 (1970): 367–78.

15. *I asked, 'Who are you, sir?' And the Lord said, 'I am Jesus, whom you are persecuting.* As in 9:5, whereas in 22:8 "the Nazorean" is added. For what is meant by "Jesus" here, recall that Paul in this episode is said to have persecuted "God's dedicated people" *(hagioi)* in 26:10. Compare 9:2; 22:4 ("the Way"). See NOTE on 9:2. In none of these contexts is he said to have persecuted "the church."

16. *Get up and stand on your feet.* Only the first impv. is used in 9:6 and 22:10. The second one, added here, may be an allusion to the LXX of Ezek 2:1. The addition gives a prophetic nuance to the role that Paul is to play: he is to stand on his feet as did Ezekiel in his inaugural vision.

For this reason have I appeared to you: to appoint you as my servant. Paul uses *hypēretēs*, "assistant, servant," the word used of John Mark who accompanied Barnabas and Paul in 13:5 (see NOTE there).

and as a witness to what you have seen [of me] and to what you will be shown. Lit., "and to what I shall appear to you." See BAGD, 578, which notes that the text of the last clause may not be rightly transmitted. The heavenly voice is not promising Paul another appearance of the risen Christ, but rather that much will still be made known to him. This is a new detail in the heavenly message: Paul is to be *hypēretēs kai martys*, "servant and witness," i.e., he is to serve the cause of the risen Christ and bear testimony to him. Since Ananias is not mentioned in this account, what was told to Paul by him is now put on the lips of Christ himself. The words contain echoes of OT prophetic passages and add the prophetic nuance to Paul's role more clearly than does chap. 9 or chap. 22. Cf. Dibelius, *Studies*, 92.

17. *I shall rescue you from this people and from the nations to which I am sending you.* The risen Christ guarantees Paul protection from those who might oppose him and his testimony. The promise is phrased in imitation of Jer 1:7–8. This part of the heavenly message to Paul is new; it has no counterpart in chaps. 9 or 22. "This people" may refer to the people who were plotting to kill him in Damascus (9:23), or more likely to those who have been opposing him in Jerusa-

lem, the context of this present speech. "The nations" refers to Gentiles to whom Paul is being sent; some of them too might oppose him. The purpose of the call and sending of Paul is expressed in the following three infinitives.

18. *in order to open their eyes.* I.e., first, to open the eyes of both "this people" and "the nations." The phraseology echoes Isa 42:7 (LXX), the Servant of Yahweh's role. The words repeat in a different formulation the idea of 9:15, about Paul as "a chosen instrument of mine to carry my name before Gentiles and kings, and the children of Israel." Now the formulation casts them in a prophetic mode.

to turn them from darkness to light. This is the second purpose, to turn people from darkness to light: a dualistic symbol of the Christian way of life in contrast to the non-Christian. It echoes Isa 42:16; Luke 2:32 (Simeon's Nunc Dimittis). Cf. Eph 2:1–10; 1 Pet 2:9; and the Qumran contrast of the *běnê 'ôr*, "sons of light," and *běnê ḥôšek*, "sons of darkness," names respectively for the Essene community of Qumran and its opponents (1QS 1:9–10; 1QM 1:1).

from the dominion of Satan to God. Another dualistic way of saying the same thing. Compare the phrase in Qumran writings, *memšelet Běliya'al*, "dominion of Belial" (1QS 1:18, 23; 2:19; 1QM 14:9) or *gôral 'El*, "lot of God" (1QS 2:2) in contrast to *gôral Běliya'al*, "lot of Belial" (1QS 2:5).

so that they may obtain forgiveness of sins. This is the third purpose of Paul's commission to preach the gospel, that people may obtain pardon for transgressions of God's will. Compare 22:16; also 10:43. For "forgiveness of sins" as a Lucan way of expressing an effect of the Christ-event, see NOTE on 2:38.

a place among those dedicated by faith in me.' Lit., "a lot (*klēros*) among those sanctified through faith in me." Faith in the risen Christ is seen as the way of obtaining a share in the lot of people dedicated to God. *Pistei*, "by faith," is a dative of means (BDF §195.1); compare *hēgiasmenois pistei* with *dikaioumenoi tē chariti* of Rom 3:24. Cf. Wis 5:5 (*pōs . . . en hagiois ho klēros autou estin*, "How is his lot among the saints?"); Deut 33:3–4; Acts 20:32. In the LXX *klēros* often translates Hebrew *gôrāl*, "lot, portion," the very word that is used so frequently in QL to designate the Essene community as *gôral 'El*, "the lot of God" (see above). In effect, the Lucan Paul says that heaven has commissioned him to help people to look on Christ with eyes of faith.

19. *Therefore, King Agrippa, I could not be disobedient to that heavenly vision.* As a strict Pharisee, Paul could not dismiss the heavenly commission of himself to preach the Christian gospel about the risen Christ. He had to obey heaven's message. Here begins the third part of Paul's address (vv 19–23, introduced by *hothen*, "wherefore"), which presents Paul's testimony about the suffering Messiah and Christianity as the fulfillment of the OT.

20. *Rather, first of all, to the people in Damascus and in Jerusalem, to all the country of Judea, yes, even to Gentiles I declared.* Paul is made to summarize his preaching in major areas of the eastern Mediterranean world, first among the Jews and then among the Gentiles (see NOTE on 17:2). Lucan hyperbole (see NOTE on 2:44) stresses Paul's preaching throughout all Judea, about which we know nothing save for this cryptic reference. Haenchen (*Acts*, 687) calls it "an

old and false gloss." Paul's preaching in Damascus is mentioned in 9:20, 22; that in Jerusalem in 9:28–29.

they must repent and turn to God and do deeds that befit their repentance. Repentance and turning to God are two of the main reactions of human beings to the challenge of the Christian gospel, especially in Lucan thinking. See NOTES on 2:38; 3:19; *Luke*, 237–39.

21. *That is why Jews seized me [while I was] in the Temple and tried to murder me.* Paul alludes to what is reported in 21:30–31. He stresses that his arrest was the consequence of his obedience to a heavenly ordained commission.

22. *to this very day I have enjoyed God's assistance, and so I am standing here to testify to great and small alike.* Lit., "to small and great alike." Paul acknowledges the grace of God that has helped him and has accompanied his work of testimony to Christ and his gospel. Recall the help promised by Christ in v 17 above.

Nothing that I say goes beyond what the prophets and Moses said would come about. Recall Paul's protestation about the coherence of his preaching with the law and the prophets in 24:14. Cf. 3:22–24; Luke 24:27, 44. In reality, it is the Lucan refrain of the continuity of Christianity with Pharisaic Judaism. One has now to understand Paul's preaching as the activity of a mouthpiece for God, as OT prophecy is generally understood (cf. Exod 4:14–16). As Moses and the prophets of old spoke for God, so too Paul; and his message is only a continuation of theirs. In effect, the Scriptures of old provide the demonstrative proof for Christianity in this view of the Lucan Paul.

23. *that the Messiah must suffer.* This is another instance of the peculiarly Lucan messianic teaching, founded on the OT as Luke reads it; see NOTE on 3:18. Moses and the prophets are thus said to have intimated the coming of a suffering Messiah.

that he would be the first to rise from the dead. Lit., "(the) first from the resurrection of the dead." One will look in vain in the Mosaic and prophetic writings of the OT for such a specific teaching, either of a suffering Messiah or of a Messiah who would rise from the dead. What one is encountering is the Lucan global reading of the OT in terms of Christ, his christological interpretation of the OT. Not only does Luke make the OT foretell the suffering of Jesus the Messiah and even his rising, but also that he will be "the first" to rise from the dead. The last note echoes what Paul himself has written about Christ as "the firstfruits of those who have fallen asleep" (1 Cor 15:20), but without the note that it is found in the OT. Compare Col 1:18; Rev 1:5.

This typically Lucan theologoumenon, the christological interpretation of the OT, has profoundly influenced later Christian thinking, especially in the development of what has been called the "spiritual" sense of the OT in the patristic period. It is indeed a correct Christian way of interpretating the OT, but it has to be recognized for what it is, a plus added to the literal sense of the OT. See Fitzmyer, "Problems of the Literal and Spiritual Senses of Scripture," *LS* 20 (1995): 134–46.

to proclaim light to his people and to the Gentiles." I.e., to Jews and non-Jews, a repetition of what was said a bit differently in vv 17–18. What the Lucan Paul preaches is an illumination for both Jews and Gentiles: a light that will enable both Jews and Gentiles to see with the eyes of faith. This idea echoes the words of Simeon in the Lucan infancy narrative (Luke 2:32): God's salvation as "a light to give revelation to the Gentiles and glory to your people Israel." Those words of Simeon echo the Servant Song of Isa 49:6.

BIBLIOGRAPHY (26:1–23)

Bertrangs, A., "Damascus en de Bijbel: Topieken voor Sint Paulus' roeping," *StudCath* 29 (1954): 225–34.

Dupont, J., "La mission de Paul d'après Actes 26.16–23 et la mission des apôtres d'après Luc 24.44–9 et Actes 1.8," *Paul and Paulinism: Essays in Honour of C. K. Barrett* (ed. M. D. Hooker and S. G. Wilson; London: SPCK, 1982), 290–99 (with Engl. summary, 300–1); repr. *Nouvelles études*, 446–56.

Hickling, C. J. A., "The Portrait of Paul in Acts 26," *Les Actes des Apôtres* (ed. J. Kremer), 499–503.

Johnston, C., "The Childhood and Youth of St. Paul," *Open Court* 25 (1911): 193–211.

Kilgallen, J. J., "Paul before Agrippa (Acts 26,2–23): Some Considerations," *Bib* 69 (1988): 170–95.

Légasse, S., "Paul sanhédrite? À propos d'Ac 26,10," *À cause de l'évangile*, 799–807.

Maisch, I., "Dienst am Wort und für die Tische: Vier Worte aus der Apostelgeschichte zum kirchlichen Dienst," *BibLeb* 10 (1969): 83–87.

Oepke, A., "Probleme der vorchristlichen Zeit des Paulus," *TSK* 105 (1933): 387–424.

O'Toole, R. F., *Acts 26: The Christological Climax of Paul's Defense (Ac 22:1–26:32)* (AnBib 78; Rome: Biblical Institute, 1978).

Prete, B., "Il contenuto ecclesiologico del termine 'eredità' *(klēros)* in *Atti* 26,18," *SacDoc* 38 (1993): 625–53.

———, "Il senso della formula 'coloro che sono stati santificati per la fede in me' (At 26,18c)," *RivB* 35 (1987): 313–20.

7. REACTIONS TO PAUL'S DISCOURSE (26:24–32)

24 Paul had defended himself up to this point, when Festus exclaimed aloud,
"Paul, you are mad! Your great learning is driving you mad!" 25 Paul answered,
"No, Your Excellency, Festus, I am not mad. What I am saying is the sober truth.
26 The king well understands these matters, and to him I am speaking frankly. I
am convinced that none of this escapes him; after all, it did not take place in a
dark corner! 27 Do you believe the prophets, King Agrippa? I know that you do."
28 At this Agrippa said to Paul, "A little more, and you are sure to make me a

Christian." [29] Paul replied, "Would to God that, with a little more time or much more, not only you, but all who are listening to me today might become what I am, apart from these chains." [30] Then the king got up, and with him the governor and Bernice and the rest who were sitting there. [31] After leaving the chamber, they continued to talk to one another and admitted, "This man is doing nothing [at all] that deserves death or imprisonment." [32] Agrippa remarked to Festus, "This fellow could have been set free, had he not appealed to Caesar."

WT: [24] had said this much, when Festus cried out and said. [25] Your Excellency, Governor. [26] before whom I am speaking [omits "frankly," "I am convinced that," and "after all, it did not take place in a dark corner!"]. [28] [omits "Agrippa"] said to him. [29] [omits "Paul," "to God," and "today"]. [30] [adds at the beginning:] When he had said this [omits "and Bernice"]. [31] [omits "or imprisonment"].

COMMENT

Luke continues his account with the reactions of the audience to Paul's final defense. He uses the literary device of the interrupted speech to advance both Paul's argument and his story. Agrippa's calm stands in contrast to the governor's emotional outburst. Festus protests first over Paul's erudition, his strange way of arguing, and his allusions to Moses and the prophets. Festus has difficulty in following all this argumentation and especially in admitting such a thing as resurrection. He realizes even more the incompetence of a Roman court to come to a judgment in such theological matters. Then King Agrippa reacts, thinking that Paul is trying to make him a Christian. When Paul exclaims that he wishes that all of them would become what he is, the king rises and the session comes to an end. When they are outside the chamber, Agrippa admits that Paul could easily have been released, had he not appealed to Caesar. Thus another declaration of Paul's innocence is evoked, and authorities in Judea find nothing unsettling in the cause that Paul espouses, viz., in Christianity.

The episode is again a narrative, punctuated with conversation, based on information from Luke's Pauline source. Paul's words are a Lucan formulation.

NOTES

24. *Paul had defended himself up to this point.* Lit., "while he was uttering these things in his defense."

when Festus exclaimed aloud. Lit., "Festus said in a loud voice." In other words, the governor interrupts Paul's defense.

"Paul, you are mad! Your great learning is driving you mad!" Lit., "Many letters are driving you to madness." *Ta grammata* was sometimes used in the sense of "higher learning" (Xenophon, *Cyropaedeia* 1.2.6; Plato, *Apology* 26D); so here. Madness is used as the foil for Paul's ready answers in the speech just delivered. Festus is portrayed as impressed by Paul's mode of argumentation, which is not only learned but Jewish in style, especially in its allusions to the OT. Yet it proves to be incomprehensible to the Roman governor, especially in its allusion to resur-

rection. Recall 17:32; 25:19. As a Roman who has to judge Paul's case, Festus is concerned about Paul's mental stability.

25. *Paul answered, "No, Your Excellency, Festus, I am not mad. What I am saying is the sober truth.* Lit., "I am uttering words of truth and sobriety." The reader too is expected to conclude that what Luke writes is likewise such. Luke pits *sōphrosynē*, "rationality, mental soundness," against *mania*, "madness," implied in Festus's remark.

26. *The king well understands these matters, and to him I am speaking frankly.* As a Herodian, Agrippa would grasp what Paul was saying. Again, Luke uses the verb *parrhēsiazesthai*, "speak frankly or boldly." See NOTES on 9:27; 4:13.

I am convinced that none of this escapes him. Paul alludes to the king's Herodian background and familiarity with things Jewish and Pharisaic, which may be escaping the Roman Festus. Talk of "resurrection" would not be strange to Agrippa's ears. Paul perhaps even assumes that Agrippa has heard of Jesus of Nazareth and what happened to him and what has become the sequel of all that.

after all, it did not take place in a dark corner! Luke makes Paul use a Greek proverb, known from Epictetus, *Discourses* 2.12.17; cf. Plato, *Gorgias* 485D; Plutarch, *Moralia* 777B. What has happened to Jesus of Nazareth and what has followed upon his death and resurrection are matters of common knowledge, indeed of human history. One need only sit up and take notice. This key affirmation in Luke's historical perspective (see *Luke*, 171–79) underscores his attempt to locate the Christ-event in time, in human history, and in world history. It becomes an important verse in Luke's transposition of the Christian kerygma into a historical key (see *Luke*, 13–14). The Lucan Paul's arguments are treated as incontestible, because they are based on what is known to everyone, even if he presents these facts as the fulfillment of the prophetic Scriptures of old.

27. *Do you believe the prophets, King Agrippa? I know that you do."* Paul's rhetorical question is a real challenge: it asks a Herodian king to reach a conclusion that Paul, a Jew, considers obvious. Implicitly Paul is telling the king that what has happened in Jesus and the Christian gospel had already been foreseen by prophets in Israel, in whom he, as a Jewish king, should be believing.

28. *At this Agrippa said to Paul, "A little more, and you are sure to make me a Christian."* Lit., "with a little more you are persuading (me) that (you) are making me a Christian." The subject of the infin. is the same as the subject of the main verb (BDF §396; cf. §405.1). Compare Xenophon, *Memorabilia* 1.2.49 (*peithōn men tous synontas heautō sophōterous poiein tōn paterōn*, "persuading his companions that he was making [them] wiser than [their] fathers"). See H. D. Naylor, *CR* 28 (1914): 227–28. Another possible interpretation might be to take the verb *peitheis* in a conative sense and the infin. *poiēsai* as an infin. of purpose: "You are trying to persuade (me), to make me a Christian." See A. T. Robertson, "The Meaning." In any case, *pace* Haenchen (*Acts*, 689), Conzelmann (*Acts*, 212), and Schneider (*Apg.*, 2.377), *Christianon poiēsai* does not mean "to play the Christian," even if the verb is so used in later patristic writers. See Weiser, *Apg.*, 655; O'Toole, *Acts 26*, 143–44.

The phrase *en oligō*, "in a little," is not easily interpreted. It may mean "with a little more persuasion," or "with a little more time." Paul's answer (v 29) seems to understand it in the second way. Agrippa's irony may be jesting; but his jest undoubtedly conceals no little embarrassment, because he is shaken by Paul's words. His reaction is quiet in contrast to the reaction of the Roman Festus, but it shows that Agrippa has understood what Paul was talking about. On "Christian," see NOTE on 11:26. For a farfetched translation, see A. Fridrichsen, "Acts 26,28": "I would to God, concerning both small and great."

29. *Paul replied, "Would to God that, with a little more time or much more, not only you, but all who are listening to me today might become what I am.* Lit., "I would pray to God that." So Paul expresses an idyllic hope that they would all become Christians. This is the climactic assertion of Paul's last defense. This is the only place in the NT where the potential optative with *an* occurs in a main clause, expressing an attainable wish (BDF §§359.2; 385.1).

apart from these chains." Lit., "apart from these bonds." Paul adds carefully that he is not wishing that they would all likewise become prisoners. Recall 20:34; cf. 28:20. On a Roman citizen being interrogated in chains, see Augustus's Edict II from Cyrene (Conzelmann, *Acts,* 240).

30. *Then the king got up, and with him the governor and Bernice and the rest who were sitting there.* The session of interrogation and of listening to the accused Paul has come to an end.

31. *After leaving the chamber, they continued to talk to one another and admitted, "This man is doing nothing [at all] that deserves death or imprisonment."* Lit., "having withdrawn." This hearing has been, in effect, an official session of the procurator's *consilium,* and its final verdict is that Paul is not guilty. The issue is not political and in no way involves capital punishment. The refrain of Paul's innocence is heard again. Recall 23:29; 25:25. Judgment has now been passed on him by the last king in Judea and his entourage. Implicitly, it is a judgment passed on Christianity.

32. *Agrippa remarked to Festus, "This fellow could have been set free, had he not appealed to Caesar."* Agrippa's remark implies that at some stage in the investigation a sentence of acquittal would have been possible in the province, but now the emperor's *auctoritas* has been involved. Both the Roman governor and the king have, in effect, found Paul innocent, which means that the plaintiffs, the religious authorities of Jerusalem, do not have much of a case. Perhaps that is why they do not appear in Rome in the rest of the Lucan story.

BIBLIOGRAPHY (26:24–32)

Fridrichsen, A., "Acts 26,28," *ConNeot* 3 (1938): 13–16.

———, "Exegetisches zum Neuen Testament," *SO* 14 (1935): 44–52, esp. 49–52.

Harlé, P., "Un 'Private Joke' de Paul dans le livre des Actes (xxvi.28–29)," *NTS* 24 (1977–78): 527–33.

Harry, J. E., "Almost Thou Persuadest Me to Become a Christian," *ATR* 12 (1929–30): 140–44.

———, "*En oligō me peitheis* (Acts xxvi.28)," *ATR* 28 (1946): 135–36.
Hesseling, D. C., "Acta Apost. xxvi, 28 en de Vulgata," *Neophilologus* 20 (1935): 129–34.
Kellett, E. E., "A Note on Acts xxvi.28," *ExpTim* 34 (1922–23): 563–64.
Robertson, A. T., "The Meaning of Acts xxvi.28," *ExpTim* 35 (1923–24): 185–86.
Whitaker, G. H., "The Words of Agrippa to St. Paul," *JTS* 15 (1913–14): 82–83.
Wilcken, U., "Papyrus-Urkunden," *APF* 5 (1909–13): 198–300, esp. 232.

C. Prisoner in Rome, Testimony and Ministry There (27:1–28:31)

1. Departure for Rome
(27:1–8)

27 1 When it was decided that we were to sail for Italy, Paul and some other
prisoners were entrusted to a centurion named Julius, of the Cohort Augusta.
2 We boarded a ship from Adramyttium bound for ports in Asia and set sail. With
us was the Macedonian, Aristarchus of Thessalonica. 3 The next day we put in at
Sidon, and Julius treated Paul kindly and allowed him to visit some friends and
be cared for by them. 4 From there we put out to sea and sailed under the lee of
Cyprus because of strong head winds. 5 We crossed the open sea off the coast of
Cilicia and Pamphylia and came to Myra in Lycia. 6 There the centurion found
an Alexandrian vessel bound for Italy, and he ordered us aboard. 7 But for many
days we made little headway; only with difficulty did we arrive at Cnidus. Since
the winds would not permit us to continue our course, we sailed to the lee of
Crete, heading for Salmone. 8 Again with difficulty we moved along the coast to
a place called Fair Havens, near the town of Lasea.

WT: 1 So then the governor decided to send him (Paul) to Caesar. On the next day he summoned a
certain centurion named Julius and entrusted Paul to him along with other prisoners [omits "of the
Cohort Augusta"]. 2 When we were about to sail, we boarded [omits "bound . . . ports in Asia"]. There
boarded with us the Macedonian, Aristarchus [omits "of Thessalonica"]. 3 [omits "the next day"] and
the centurion treated . . . and bade friends to care for him. 5 Afterwards we crossed . . . for fifteen days
and docked at Myra in Lycia. 6 [omits "aboard"]. 7 [omits "only with difficulty" and "since . . .
course," but adds:] setting sail from there, we sailed to the lee of Crete [omits the rest]. 8 We docked
at Fair Havens, near to which was a town.

COMMENT

Luke now begins the story of Paul's transfer from Caesarea Maritima to Rome, where he is to stand trial before Caesar. His journey has been occasioned by the last declaration of Paul's innocence by Festus the procurator (25:25) and King Agrippa II (26:31–32). Lucan foreshadowing is now picked up in this fulfillment of Paul's resolve to "visit Rome" (19:21), for it is the working out of the heaven-guided course of salvation (23:11) to "the end of the earth" (1:8). That is echoed in the course of this chapter: "you are destined to stand trial before Caesar" (27:24), but Paul never does so in the Lucan story of Acts. This account of his transfer forms part of the dramatic buildup for the finale of Acts.

The episode is another narrative in Acts, one in which the last of the We-Sections is employed (27:1–28:16): the itinerary of a sea voyage, but with six inserts from Luke's compositional pen or possibly the Pauline source. The last We-Section ended in 21:18, and, if the We-Sections do represent a diary of the author, we have no idea where Luke has been since that verse. We are, then, dealing with an itinerary account, but one that represents a reworking of the record after a considerable amount of time.

What begins now is the dramatic and edifying climax of Paul's missionary career. It is the autumn of A.D. 60, when Paul must make his way to Rome. He himself becomes the focal point in the narrative of the shipwreck and is depicted as saving all on board from disaster, which is an indirect way of portraying the salvific effect of Christ through a Christian disciple. The God whom Paul worships can save even from cataclysmic or physical danger, from shipwreck and vipers. The account of the storm and the shipwreck is remarkable for its vivid details.

The narrative now being recounted is used to a theological end. Instead of a story about an evil person meeting death by adverse winds and drowning at sea, Luke tells rather a story about the rescue of threatened seafarers through his hero Paul, who is saved by God. For another interpretation of this ending of Acts, see G. B. Miles and G. Trompf, "Luke and Antiphon: The Theology of Acts 27–28 in the Light of Pagan Beliefs about Divine Retribution, Pollution, and Shipwreck," *HTR* 69 (1976): 259–67. They prefer to think that Luke has included this story of Paul's shipwreck in Acts because he was concerned

> to reveal the sorry fate of such apparently evil people as the betrayer (Acts 1:18–19), the Herodians (12:20–23), the Jewish priesthood (23:3) and the rebellious Jews in general (28:28 . . .). Conversely, his defense of the Christians lay in his depiction of them as innocent sufferers whose murderers and persecutors were worthy of punishment. . . . In the particular case of Paul, moreover, each travesty of justice was overcome by the irrepressible power of God, who proved how the victimized hero merited life and freedom (e.g., 14:19–21; 16:19–40; 21:27; 26:32). The outcome of the voyage to Rome, signifying as it did that Paul was acquitted by a tribunal no less formidable than the divinely controlled ocean itself, is the crowning-point of this theological trajectory. (p. 267)

If there is any truth in such a view of Acts, it is indeed a minor concern of Luke; the story that he is telling involves much more.

Judgments about the nature of the narrative in chap. 27 have been diverse in modern times. (1) For Gilchrist, Ramsay, Meyer, Williams, and Zahn, it is an eyewitness account of Paul's trip to Rome written by a fellow traveler. This judgment is based on the We-Section (with inserts) and its vivid narration, on many details that can be verified or documented, and on the verisimilitude of the narrative. (2) For Dibelius, 54 verses (27:1–44; 28:1–2, 7–14) are a description of a sea voyage from Caesarea Maritima to Rome, but only 19 of them deal with Paul (27:9–11, 21–26, 31, 33–36, 43; 28:2b–6), which are inserts into an otherwise continuous account. Thus, according to him, Luke has adopted a vivid secular description of a voyage and shipwreck, composed by someone else, and interpolated into it details about Paul. Luke thus "expounds the meaning of an event by striking description; we see him also in his capacity as *herald* and *evangelist*, a rôle which he fulfils completely in his first book and wishes ultimately to fulfill also in Acts" (*Studies*, 134–35). (3) For Haenchen, only Luke's constructive and dramatic imagination are at work. Paul, the rabble-rouser, was a prisoner who could not have had any say in the crucial seaboard decisions. Such details stem from Luke's edifying supplements to enhance the role of his hero: Paul's speech (27:21–26) is consequently unrealistic (during a howling storm on a pounding sea); he is never at a loss for advice and always in the limelight. If the We-Sections were derived from a fellow traveler's diary, how could the papyrus or codex have survived the shipwreck? Hence, the narrative is a tale told from memory, enriched with interpolations (*Acts*, 709–11). (4) For Marshall (*Acts*, 402–3), the narrative has no real parallel in ancient literature (despite those alleged by Conzelmann, *Acts*, appendix), but the most one has for details of the voyage and the role of Paul is verisimilitude.

Ancient accounts of sea voyages and shipwrecks are often invoked for comparison with this Lucan account: Josephus, *Life* 3 §§13–16; Lucian (A.D. 125–180), *Toxaris* 19–20; *Navigium* 7–10; *Verae historiae* 1.6–7; Achilles Tatius (2d–3d cent.), 3.1–5; Petronius, *Satyrikon* 114–15; Chariton, *Chaireas and Callirhoe* 3.3.10. The one that most resembles Paul's voyage is that of the grain ship *Isis* from Alexandria recounted in Lucian, *Navigium*. At most, such accounts reveal the literary form that Luke makes use of in this chapter; to none of them is the Lucan account actually indebted. P. Pokorný sees the whole chapter as related to an ancient "Mysterien-Roman," a novel linked to ancient "mysteries" ("Die Romfahrt"), but that is quite debatable.

The six inserts into the sea voyage narrative, which extol Paul and his role in the voyage, are the following:

27:9–11	Paul warns of danger and is disregarded, but eventually proved right
27:21–26	Paul's speech: My God will save us (Lucan composition)
27:31	Paul's intervention hinders defection of sailors
27:33–36	Paul urges all to eat

27:43	Paul saved by the Roman centurion
28:2b–6	Paul saved from the viper

Some details in these inserts may come from Luke's Pauline source.

NOTES

27:1. *When it was decided that we were to sail for Italy.* Some MSS (P, 6, 326) read instead of "we," "those about Paul"; this would mean that Luke dissociates himself from the prisoners. See the different introduction to the story of Paul's voyage to Rome in the WT cited above. The destination is given only as a port in Italy (see NOTE on 18:2).

Paul and some other prisoners were entrusted to a centurion. Lit., "they entrusted Paul . . . ," i.e., the Roman provincial authorities. The addition of the WT specifies "the governor." The centurion would have been given a letter addressed to authorities in Rome, which would have summarized the accusations against Paul, stated the governor's view of the matter and explained his reasons for remanding Paul to Rome. On "centurion," see NOTE on 10:1.

named Julius, of the Cohort Augusta. Julius is otherwise unknown. The *speira Sebastē* is sometimes called in Greek inscriptions *speira Augusta* (Dittenberger, *OGIS* §421 [fragmentary]). The *Cohors Ia Augusta* was largely made up of Syrian mercenaries, was stationed in Syria during most of the first century A.D., and was perhaps in Batanea during the reign of Herod Agrippa II. It is usually thought that at least five Roman cohorts were under the authority of the governor resident in Caesarea Maritima.

2. *We boarded a ship from Adramyttium.* Modern Edremit. The home port of the vessel on which they were to sail was *Adramytteion*, a town in Mysia, on the northwest coast of Asia Minor, north of Pergamum and southeast of Troas, on the Aegean Sea and opposite the island of Lesbos. In boarding such a ship, the travelers did not intend to sail in it directly to Rome; it was rather a "coaster," a trading vessel that hugged the coast, in this case of Asia Minor. See R. Harris, "Adramyttium," *Contemporary Review* 128 (1925): 194–202 for an attempt to explain the origin of the ship.

bound for ports in Asia. I.e., ports along the coast of the province of Asia, but as the story develops the ship will stop at other ports as well before Asia is reached. See NOTE on 2:9.

set sail. Lit., "we were carried up" (onto the high sea); see NOTE on 13:13.

With us was the Macedonian, Aristarchus of Thessalonica. He is probably the same as the Aristarchus mentioned in 19:29 (see NOTE there), and possibly he is a fellow prisoner of Paul (see Col 4:10, where a "fellow prisoner" so named sends greetings). Or he may have merely been allowed by Festus to accompany Paul. Conzelmann (*Acts*, 215) considers Aristarchus to be the one through whom information about the sea voyage came to Luke. MSS 614, 1505, and 2147 read: "were the Thessalonians, Aristarchus and Secundus," which may be a reading influenced by 20:4.

3. *The next day we put in at Sidon. Sidōn* was an ancient royal and commercial port city in Phoenica on the Mediterranean coast, about halfway between Berytus (Beirut) and Tyre. It was famed for purple dyeing and glassblowing and became an independent, free city in 111 B.C., a status that Pompey recognized (see NOTES on 11:19; 21:3). Augustus accorded it territory up to Mt. Hermon (see A.H.M. Jones, "Sidon," *OCD*, 986; F. C. Eiselen, *Sidon: A Study in Oriental History* [CUOS 4; New York: Columbia University Press, 1907; repr. New York: Ams Press, 1966]). Described is the ancient mode of coastal sailing, used by small seacraft; it probably put in at Sidon for business reasons. Luke uses the pass. of *katagein*, "we were brought down" (from the high sea), a technical nautical term that corresponds to *anagein*, used in the preceding verse.

Julius treated Paul kindly and allowed him to visit some friends and be cared for by them. Julius's treatment is described as *philanthrōpōs*, "benevolent," and a further example of the benevolence will be met in v 43. The "friends" may be Christians in Sidon, about whom nothing was heard earlier, unless one includes Sidon in the "Phoenicia" of 11:19.

4. *From there we put out to sea.* Again, see NOTE on 13:13.

sailed under the lee of Cyprus because of strong head winds. I.e., to the east of the island, as they headed toward Cilicia. Thus they were somewhat protected from the autumnal west winds blowing across the eastern Mediterranean. In contrast to the high-seas route used by the ship on which Paul sailed in 21:1–3, this vessel now hugs the coastline and the shelter of the island of Cyprus (on which, see NOTE on 11:19). Lucian (*Navigium* 7) also tells of strong westerly head winds in sailing from Sidon.

5. *We crossed the open sea off the coast of Cilicia.* See NOTE on 6:9. Cilicia and Pamphylia are taken as a unit to denote the coast-hugging route of the ship.

Pamphylia. See NOTE on 2:10. MSS 614 and 2147 of the WT read "for fifteen days."

came to Myra in Lycia. On the southern coast of Asia Minor; see NOTE on 21:1.

6. *There the centurion found an Alexandrian vessel bound for Italy.* I.e., a ship probably carrying grain and other freight from Egypt for Asia Minor and Italy. Suetonius (*Claudii vita* 18) describes the emperor Claudius's attempt to bring grain from Egypt to Rome even during the winter season. See F. Brannigan, "Nautisches."

he ordered us aboard. The travelers to Rome board a ship bound for a port serving Rome.

7. *for many days we made little headway; only with difficulty did we arrive at Cnidus.* Lit., "sailing slowly for many days and with difficulty reaching Cnidus." The ship was sailing in the face of strong northwest winds. *Knidos* was a town in Caria on the southwestern tip of Asia Minor, a peninsula between the islands of Cos and Rhodes (see NOTE on 21:1). The difficulty in making port was owing either to the position of Cnidus on the promotory or to the passage north of the island of Rhodes, where the winds were strong. Verse 7 and the first part of v 8 are formulated with ptcs. modifying the verb *ēlthomen*, "we came," in v 8b.

Since the winds would not permit us to continue our course, we sailed to the lee of Crete, heading for Salmone. The Alexandrian ship takes a southwesterly course toward the eastern tip of the island of Crete. *Krētē* was a large Greek island in the Mediterranean Sea, south of the Aegean Sea, between Greece and Asia Minor. It had many towns. A promontory on the northeast tip of Crete is here called *Salmōnē*, but elsewhere *Salmōnion, Sam(m)ōnion,* or *Salmōnis* (Strabo, *Geography* 10.3.20; 10.4.3; Pliny, *Naturalis historia* 4.12.58; 4.12.71). It is the modern Cape San Sidero.

8. *Again with difficulty we moved along the coast to a place called Fair Havens, near the town of Lasea.* They sail westward south of the coast of Crete. *Kaloi Limenes,* "Fair Havens," the modern Kali Limenes, was an inlet open to the east on the south side of Crete, near the town of *Lasaia,* which lay somewhat inland, and east of Cape Littinos. See L. Robert, "Limenes," *Hellenica* 11–12 (1960–61): 263–66. The name of the town is read as *Lasaia* in MSS ℵ*, Ψ, and the *Koinē* text-tradition, but MSS B, 33, 1175, 1739, 1891, and 2464 read it as *Lasea* (whence the English spelling), and others, *Laissa* (ℵ[2]), *Alassa* (A, Syriac versions). Both places would have been obscure to anyone but those who had sailed the route indicated.

BIBLIOGRAPHY (27:1–8)

Balmer, H., *Die Romfahrt des Apostels Paulus und die Seefahrtskunde im römischen Kaiserzeitalter* (Bern: Sutermeister, 1905).

Brannigan, F., "Nautisches über die Romfahrt des heiligen Paulus," *TGl* 25 (1933): 170–86.

Casson, L., "The Isis and Her Voyage," *TPAPA* 81 (1950): 43–56.

———, *Ships and Seamanship in the Ancient World* (Princeton: Princeton University Press, 1971).

Cesarano, U., *Verso Roma con l'apostolo delle genti* (Milan/Verona: Mondadori, 1932).

Delebecque, E., "L'Embarquement de Paul, captif, à Césarée, pour Rome (*Actes des Apôtres* 27,1–2)," *LTP* 39 (1983): 295–302.

Georgi, W., "Pauli Reisegefährten nach Rom," *Lehre und Wehre* 70 (1924): 186–94.

Goodspeed, E. J., "Paul's Voyage to Italy," *BW* 34 (1909): 337–45.

Haenchen, E., "Acta 27," *Zeit und Geschichte: Dankesgabe an Rudolf Bultmann* . . . (Tübingen: Mohr [Siebeck], 1964): 235–54.

Hawthorne, T., "A Discourse Analysis of Paul's Shipwreck: Acts 27:1–44," *JOTT* 6 (1993): 253–73.

Hermesdorf, B.H.D., "Sint Paulus temidden van zeerechtelijke vraagstukken," *StudCath* 29 (1954): 237–48.

Isserlin, B.S.J., "The Isis and Her Voyage: Some Additional Remarks," *TPAPA* 86 (1955): 319–20.

Kettenbach, G., *Das Logbuch des Lukas* (European University Studies, 23/276; Frankfurt/Bern/New York: P. Lang, 1986).

Köster, A., *Das antike Seewesen* (Berlin: Schoetz & Parrhysius, 1923; repr. Berlin: de Gruyter, 1969).

Leonard, W., "From Caesarea to Malta: St. Paul's Voyage and Shipwreck," *ACR* 37 (1960): 274–84.

Mariani, B., *S. Paolo da Cesarea a Roma: Esegesi, storia, topografia, archeologia* (Turin: Marietti, 1963).

Miles, C. B. and G. Trompf, "Luke and Antiphon: The Theology of Acts 27–28 in the Light of Pagan Beliefs about Divine Retribution, Pollution, and Shipwreck," *HTR* 69 (1976): 260–67.

Moda, A., "Paolo prigioniero e martire: Capitolo terzo—Gli avvenimenti romani: I e II paragrafo," *BeO* 35 (1993): 89–118.

Orr, R. W., "Paul's Voyage and Shipwreck," *EvQ* 35 (1963): 103–4.

Pokorný, P., "Die Romfahrt des Paulus und der antike Roman," *ZNW* 64 (1973): 233–44.

Praeder, S. M., "Acts 27:1–28:16: Sea Voyages in Ancient Literature and the Theology of Luke-Acts," *CBQ* 46 (1984): 683–706.

Ramsay, W. M., *St. Paul the Traveller,* 314–43.

Richard, R., "Navigations de Saint Paul," *Études* 190 (1927): 448–65.

Rougé, J., "Actes 27,1–10," *VC* 14 (1960): 193–203.

Schwank, B., "'Wir umsegelten Kreta bei Salmone': Reisebericht zu Apg 27,7–12," *EA* 48 (1972): 16–25.

Smith, J., *The Voyage and Shipwreck of St. Paul* (3d ed.; London: Longmans, Green, 1866; 4th ed., rev. by W. E. Smith, 1880).

Suhl, A., "Gestrandet! Bemerkungen zum Streit über die Romfahrt des Paulus," *ZTK* 88 (1991): 1–28.

———, "Zum Seeweg Alexandria—Rom," *TZ* 47 (1991): 208–13.

Warnecke, H., *Die tatsächliche Romfahrt des Apostels Paulus* (SBS 127; Stuttgart: Katholisches Bibelwerk, 1987).

2. Storm at Sea and Shipwreck (27:9–44)

[9]Much time had now gone by, and sailing had become hazardous, because the
autumn fast had already passed. It was then that Paul warned them, [10]"Gentlemen, I can see that this voyage is going to meet with disaster and heavy loss not
only of cargo and ship, but of our own lives as well." [11]The centurion, however,
preferred to listen to the pilot and the captain rather than to what Paul had said.
[12]Since the harbor was not suitable to pass the winter in, the majority preferred
to put out to sea from there in the hope of reaching Phoenix and spending the
winter there. It was a Cretan port, facing both southwest and northwest. [13]So
when a gentle south wind began to blow, they thought that they had obtained
what they wanted. They weighed anchor and sailed close to the coast of Crete.
[14]But it was not long before a wind of hurricane force, called a Northeaster, blew
up against it. [15]The ship was caught up by it and could not head into the wind;

we gave ourselves over to it and let ourselves be driven on. 16We ran on under
the lee of a small island called Cauda, and only with difficulty were we able to
regain control of the ship's skiff. 17The sailors hoisted it on board and then made
use of cables to brace the ship itself. As they were afraid of being driven onto the
shoals of Syrtis, they lowered the drift anchor and so let the ship be carried along.
18We were being pounded violently by the storm, and on the next day they jettisoned some of the cargo. 19On the third day, they deliberately threw overboard
the ship's gear. 20For many days neither the sun nor the stars were to be seen,
and no small storm raged on. At last all hope of survival was gradually abandoned. 21Because many had been without food for a long time, Paul then stood
up among them and said, "Gentlemen, you should have taken my advice, not to
set sail from Crete and incur this disaster or loss. 22Now I urge you to keep up
your courage; there will be no loss of life among you, but only this ship. 23Last
night an angel of the God to whom [I] belong and whom I serve stood by me
24and said, 'Do not be afraid, Paul; you are destined to stand trial before Caesar.
Look, God has favored you with the safety of all those sailing with you.' 25So keep
up your courage, gentlemen. I trust in God that it will all turn out just as I have
been told, 26even though we may still have to run aground on some island."
27When it was the fourteenth night of the storm and we were still being driven
across the Adriatic, the sailors began to suspect toward midnight that land was
near. 28They took soundings and found a depth of twenty fathoms; after sailing
on a short distance, they took a sounding again and found fifteen fathoms. 29For
fear that we might be dashed against some rocky coast, they dropped four anchors
from the stern and prayed for daylight. 30Then the sailors sought to abandon ship.
They let down the ship's skiff into the sea, pretending that they were going to put
out anchors from the ship's prow. 31But Paul said to the centurion and the soldiers, "If these men do not stay with the ship, you have no chance of surviving."
32At this the soldiers cut loose the ropes of the skiff and let it drift away. 33Before
day began to dawn, Paul urged all on board to take some food. "Today is the
fourteenth day that you have been in suspense and all that time you have gone
hungry, taking nothing to eat. 34Now I urge you to take some food; this is for your
own survival. Yet not a hair of the head of any of you will be lost." 35When he
had said this, he took bread, gave thanks to God in front of all of them, broke it,
and began to eat. 36All of them were encouraged by this, and they too took something to eat. 37In all there were two hundred and seventy-six of us on board.
38When all had enough to eat, they further lightened the ship by throwing the
wheat overboard. 39When it was day, they did not recognize the land, but they
could make out a bay with a beach; they proposed to run the ship aground there,
if possible. 40Cutting loose the anchors, they abandoned them to the sea; at the
same time they untied the ropes of the rudders, hoisted the foresail into the wind,
and made for the beach. 41But they encountered a place of cross seas, and the
ship was grounded there. Its bow stuck fast and could not be budged, while the
stern was being broken to pieces by the force [of the waves]. 42The soldiers were
minded to kill the prisoners lest any of them would swim away and escape. 43But
the centurion, who was anxious to save Paul, kept them from carrying out their

decision. He ordered those who could swim to jump overboard first and make for the land; [44]the rest were to follow, some on planks, others on debris from the ship. So it was that everyone got safely to land.

WT: [9]After we had passed many days and sailing . . . [omits "already"] . . . Paul came up and said. [11][omits verse]. [12][omits "Since . . . majority"]. The pilot and the captain preferred to put out to sea in the hope of reaching Phoenix, a Cretan port [omits "facing . . . northwest"]; the centurion preferred to listen to them rather than to what Paul had said. [13][omits "they thought that . . . and"] we sailed close. [14]Then the Southeast wind descended [omits the rest]. [15]we gave ourselves over to it as it blew, and we furled the sails and let ourselves. [16]We came upon a small island called Clauda [omits the rest]. [17][omits "The sailors . . . the ship itself"]. As they were afraid of being carried onto the shoal of Syrtis, we remained there [omits the rest]. [18]On the next day, we were being pounded violently by the storm [omits the rest]. [19]We threw the gear into the sea. [20]Since the storm raged on for many days and neither sun nor stars were to be seen, all hope of life was gradually abandoned. [21][omits "then"]. [22]among us. [23][omits "to whom I belong and"]. [24]you have been favored with the safety of all those with you. [25]in my God. [27][omits "and we . . . Adriatic"]. [29]For fear that it might be broken up, they began to run the ship ashore and prayed for daylight. [30][omits "pretending . . . prow"]. [31]If they do not stay with the ship, we have no chance of surviving. [32]At this they cut loose the ropes and let the skiff drift away. [33]When it was day, Paul . . . "This is the fourteenth day that you have gone hungry." [omits the rest]. [36][omits "they too"]. [37]We were about seventy persons. [38][omits "by throwing the wheat overboard"]. [39][omits "When it . . . the land" and "if possible"]. [40][omits whole verse]. [41]and coming away, they grounded the ship, and it was broken up and dashed to pieces. [43]the centurion prevented this from happening, especially because of Paul, that he might save him . . . [omits "to jump overboard and"]. [44]the rest were to save themselves on planks [omits the rest].

COMMENT

Luke continues the account of Paul's voyage toward Rome with the story of the winter storm and the shipwreck. Paul becomes the center of attention in the continuation of the voyage. We hear no more of danger to him from the Jerusalem religious authorities; the danger now comes from the sea. Though Paul has warned the pilot and captain not to leave Crete, they set out anyway and are caught in a fierce storm. Paul is assured by heaven that he and the other passengers will survive, but not the ship. He encourages the others and persuades them to take some food, for many have gone without food for two weeks. When the Roman soldiers want to kill the prisoners, lest they escape, the centurion forbids that because of Paul. At last they weather the storm, manage to beach the ship on some land that they know is near, and are saved.

The episode is yet another narrative in Acts, broken up at times with conversation and a short speech by Paul. Verses 9–11 are a Pauline insert into the We-Section, which appears more prominently in the WT than in the Alexandrian text.

Verses 21–26 are a hortatory speech by Paul, a Lucan composition, utilizing perhaps some details from the Pauline source. It is another insert into the We-Section. It is aimed at helping and sustaining fellow travelers who are sailing with him. Paul recalls the warning he gave at Crete, reassures those with him that no lives will be lost, and tells them of the basis of his assurance: the God whom he worships will save all. The speech echoes the vision that Paul has had of Christ the Lord about the testimony that he has to bear in Rome (23:11) and also his appeal to Caesar (25:11). It relies now on an angelic message, reassuring Paul that salvation for all comes from God through a Christian disciple. The necessity of the divine plan of salvation is met again: "Do not be afraid, Paul; you are destined to stand trial before Caesar" (27:24).

Verses 31, 33–36, and 43 in this episode are to be regarded as further inserts (possibly using details from the Pauline source) into the We-Section.

The episode presents Paul the prisoner as the man full of faith who dominates his fearful situation. He counsels the ship's crew and the Romans with whom he is traveling. He assures them that all will be saved, even if the ship itself is wrecked. He counsels his fellow passengers to take food to sustain themselves. All this confidence comes from his faith in the God to whom he belongs and whom he serves (27:23).

NOTES

9. *Much time had now gone by, and sailing had become hazardous, because the autumn fast had already passed.* The "autumn fast" is that of the Day of Atonement, the tenth day of the seventh month (Lev 16:29–31: "a sabbath of solemn rest" with affliction [i.e., fasting]), the tenth of Tishri (Philo, *De specialibus legibus* 2.32 §§193–203; Josephus, *Ant.* 14.4.3 §66; 18.4.3 §94). It was celebrated about the time of the autumnal equinox. Luke thus uses a Jewish calendaric reference for a secular problem, which was what the Romans called *mare clausum,* "the closed sea," the time when the Mediterranean was no longer navigable, often as of mid-October, but usually from 11 November to 10 March (F. Vegetius Renatus, *De re militari* 4.39; cf. Josephus, *J.W.* 2.10.5 §203). See E. de Saint-Denis, "Mare clausum," *REL* 25 (1947): 196–214. Actually in the (later) Jewish tradition sea travel was discouraged between the Feast of Tabernacles (15–22 Tishri) and Pentecost, i.e., roughly October to April; see Str-B, 2.771–72.

It was then that Paul warned them. Even though he was technically a prisoner, he is still Luke's hero; so Paul is made to interject his advice.

10. *"Gentlemen, I can see that this voyage is going to meet with disaster and heavy loss not only of cargo and ship, but of our own lives as well."* Luke depicts Paul as a prophet who addresses his message to the authorities on board.

11. *The centurion, however, preferred to listen to the pilot and the captain rather than to what Paul had said.* The important people on board are described, the *kybernētēs,* "pilot," and the *nauklēros,* "ship owner," but they do not heed Paul, who in the long run will prove to have been right. Cf. MM, 422, for the meaning "captain."

12. *Since the harbor was not suitable to pass the winter in.* Probably because the inlet was so exposed to winter winds and rainstorms.

the majority preferred to put out to sea from there. I.e., from "Fair Havens," the port mentioned in 27:8. *Hoi pleiones* may mean the "majority" of the seamen responsible for the ship, or possibly the bulk of the passengers on board.

in the hope of reaching Phoenix. I.e., a town farther to the west on the southern coast of Crete. Its exact location is disputed. Strabo (*Geography* 10.4.3) knows of a Phoenix, which may be Phoenix of the Lampians. Some identify it with Cape Mouros; others with modern Phineka (relic of the old name). See Hemer, *Book of Acts,* 139; C. Lattey, "The Harbour Phoenix," *Scr* 4 (1949–51): 144–46; R. M. Ogilvie, "Phoenix," *JTS* 9 (1958): 308–14.

spending the winter there. It was a Cretan port, facing both southwest and northwest. Lit., "looking toward Lips and Choros." *Lips* was the Greek name for the wind from the southwest, and *Corus* or *Caurus* the Latin name for the wind from the northwest. See *IGRR* 1.177 (= *IG* 14.1308), which gives the Latin *chorus* as = Greek *iapyx.* See P. P. Saydon, "A Note on 'Lips-Choros' in Acts 27,12," *Scr* 4 (1949–51): 212–13.

13. *So when a gentle south wind began to blow, they thought that they had obtained what they wanted.* A gentle wind filling the sails would bring them to Phoenix.

They weighed anchor and sailed close to the coast of Crete. I.e., westward and parallel to the southern coast of the island.

14. *it was not long before a wind of hurricane force, called a Northeaster, blew up against it.* The wind is called in Greek *Eurakylōn* in MSS P^{74}, $\aleph^2$, A, and B*, but MSS B^2, Ψ, and 33 read rather *Euroklydōn.* The former is a hybrid mixture of Greek *euros,* "east wind," and Latin *aquilo,* "northeast wind," said to be sailors' slang. The latter is the "southeast wind." Literally, the name means, the "east wind" that stirs up broad "waves."

15. *The ship was caught up by it and could not head into the wind; we gave ourselves over to it and let ourselves be driven on.* I.e., apparently to the west. Some MSS (614, 2147) of the WT read: "we gave ourselves over to it as it blew, and we furled the sails and let ourselves be driven on."

16. *We ran on under the lee of a small island called Cauda.* So the island is named in MSS P^{74}, $\aleph^2$, B, Ψ, and 1175, whereas MSS $\aleph^*$, A, 33, 81, 614, 945, 1505, and 1739 read *Klauda.* This must be the modern island of Gaudos/Gozzo, about 40 km south southwest of Phoenix.

only with difficulty were we able to regain control of the ship's skiff. I.e., the dinghy used for landing passengers and for other purposes.

17. *The sailors hoisted it on board and then made use of cables to brace the ship itself.* The skiff is hoisted on board to prevent it being dashed against the hull of the ship. Various explanations of the "cables" have been given, none of which is very clear. Apparently, the ptc. *hypozōnnyntes* implies some sort of undergirding for the ship's hull to reinforce it against the battering of waves. Cf. H. J. Cadbury, "*Hypozōmata,*" *Beginnings,* 5.345–54.

As they were afraid of being driven onto the shoals of Syrtis. I.e., Syrtis Maior, a reef or sandbank on the north coast of Africa, west of Cyrene (modern Libya, between Benghazi and Tripoli). See Pliny, *Naturalis historia* 5.4.27.

they lowered the drift anchor and so let the ship be carried along. Lit., "having lowered the instrument (or gear)," which was supposed to serve as a kedge or brake. Some commentators understand the ptc. to mean, "having unfurled the sail" (but see J. Renié, "Summisso vase," *RSR* 35 [1948]: 272–74).

18. *We were being pounded violently by the storm.* The verse begins with the first pl., but shifts to the third pl. in the next part.

on the next day they jettisoned some of the cargo. Lit., "they made a jettisoning." The jettisoned cargo was intended to lighten the ship so that it might ride out the storm more easily. Cf. Jonah 1:5. In writing *ekbolēn epoiounto,* Luke uses a classical Greek expression, involving the middle of *poiein* with an abstract noun (see BDF §310.1; §316.3).

19. *On the third day, they deliberately threw overboard the ship's gear.* I.e., not only the cargo, but the tackle needed for controlling the ship; again, in an effort to lighten it.

20. *For many days neither the sun nor the stars were to be seen.* I.e., leaving the sailors without any means of navigating. Lacking compass and sextant, they normally checked their positions by the sun and the stars.

no small storm raged on. At last all hope of survival was gradually abandoned. Verse 27 is the logical sequel to this verse.

21. *Because many had been without food for a long time.* Lit., "since there was much going without food." The *asitia,* "lack of appetite," undoubtedly results from either anxiety or seasickness. See J. R. Madan, "The *asitia* on St Paul's Voyage," *JTS* 6 (1904–5): 116–21.

Paul then stood up among them and said. This is Paul's second intervention while on board ship, this time in the form of a hortatory speech addressed to fellow travelers (vv 21–26). It is one of the Lucan inserts about Paul into the We-Section.

"Gentlemen, you should have taken my advice, not to set sail from Crete and incur this disaster or loss. This warning Paul uttered at Fair Havens in Crete; recall 27:10.

22. *Now I urge you to keep up your courage; there will be no loss of life among you, but only this ship.* The reason for Paul's assurance is given in the following verses. Cf. v 36.

23. *Last night an angel of the God to whom [I] belong and whom I serve stood by me.* Or possibly "a messenger," because Paul is addressing a largely pagan audience, who may not be acquainted with the Jewish belief in "angels." See NOTES on 10:3; 12:7. In any case, Paul makes it clear that he worships the God of the Jewish people (24:14; 26:7); compare Jonah 1:9. His fellow travelers, however, might know of rescues from shipwrecks by Isis, Serapis, or the Dioscuri (Lucian, *Navigium* 9).

24. *said, 'Do not be afraid, Paul; you are destined to stand trial before Caesar.* Lit., "you must stand before Caesar." Paul has appealed to the emperor (25:12), and the procurator Festus has sent him off to Rome to be judged at an imperial tribunal (27:1). Now heaven assures Paul that this is all part of the divine plan of salvation: he will arrive in Rome, despite this storm and damage to the ship. The Roman goal of his heaven-guarded voyage is again expressed (recall 19:21;

23:11). Luke uses *dei,* "it is necessary," to express the inevitability of the implementation of the divine plan (see *Luke,* 179–80). "Before Caesar" may mean that Paul will appear before Nero himself; but it may also be a way of expressing his appearance before a superior imperial court.

God has favored you with the safety of all those sailing with you.' Lit., "God has accorded you all those sailing with you," i.e., all fellow travelers will reach safety because God's favor is being shown to Paul, his servant.

25. *keep up your courage, gentlemen. I trust in God that it will all turn out just as I have been told.* This is the main consolation and encouragement that Paul offers those on board with him. By and because of his "trust," he is thus the bringer of safety to all of them, in the physical sense of deliverance from the storm. The Christian reader hears the overtones of his encouragement in a broader sense, viz., of salvation.

26. *even though we may still have to run aground on some island."* Paul intimates that there may still be anxious moments in their immediate future.

27. *When it was the fourteenth night of the storm and we were still being driven across the Adriatic.* The We-Section resumes, and this verse is the sequel to 27:20. *Adrias* is the sea between Crete, northern Africa, Greece, and Sicily. Josephus (*Life* 3 §15) also tells of crossing this body of water.

the sailors began to suspect toward midnight that land was near. Lit., "began to suspect that they were approaching some land." Probably a change in the roar of the waves made them so suspect.

28. *They took soundings and found a depth of twenty fathoms; after sailing on a short distance, they took a sounding again and found fifteen fathoms.* The sailors realize that they are approaching some land, the nature of which is still unknown to them. The precise numbers argue against the explanation of Conzelmann (*Acts,* 219), who writes them off as added for "the sake of effect."

29. *For fear that we might be dashed against some rocky coast, they dropped four anchors from the stern and prayed for daylight.* The anchors, apparently not among the gear jettisoned earlier (v 19), are now being used to slow the ship's progress toward the suspected shore, and possible disaster.

30. *the sailors sought to abandon ship. They let down the ship's skiff into the sea, pretending that they were going to put out anchors from the ship's prow.* This action of the sailors is strange. Perhaps they have judged the situation to be desperate and have panicked, seeking their own safety in a way that was scarcely sure to guarantee it. It gives Paul another chance to intervene on behalf of the seafarers on board.

31. *Paul said to the centurion and the soldiers, "If these men do not stay with the ship, you have no chance of surviving."* This is Paul's third intervention, alerting his captors about the consequences of the sailors' attempt to desert the rest.

32. *At this the soldiers cut loose the ropes of the skiff and let it drift away.* I.e., the soldiers accompanying the centurion, who was in charge of Paul and the other prisoners, do this, perhaps at the order of the centurion.

33. *Before day began to dawn.* Lit., "up until (the time) when day was about to be." Luke uses the phrase *achri hou* with a past tense verb.

Paul urged all on board to take some food. This is Paul's fourth intervention on behalf of those on board with him.

"Today is the fourteenth day that you have been in suspense, and all that time you have gone hungry, taking nothing to eat. Recall 27:21, 27.

34. *Now I urge you to take some food; this is for your own survival.* Luke uses *sōtēria* (lit., "salvation") in a secular sense, "survival," since the food will contribute to their physical well-being.

Yet not a hair of the head of any of you will be lost." The last remark echoes an OT saying; see 1 Sam 14:45; 2 Sam 14:11, which is also used in Luke 12:7; 21:18.

35. *When he had said this, he took bread, gave thanks to God in front of all of them, broke it, and began to eat.* Paul realizes that example is better than verbal advice, so he too eats. This may mean nothing more than that Paul, in Jewish fashion, says "grace" before eating (so Wikenhauser, *Apg.*, 281; Haenchen, *Acts*, 707; Bruce, *Acts*, 517; Roloff, *Apg.*, 364; Marshall, *Acts*, 413–14; Pesch, *Apg.*, 2.292; Kistemaker, *Acts*, 936–37) or the way Christians normally eat (so Conzelmann, *Acts*, 220). Yet the phraseology has a eucharistic ring to it (compare Luke 22:19; see NOTE on 2:42). Schneider (*Apg.*, 2.396) refuses to limit the description to Jewish "grace" before eating; similarly Dupont (*Actes*, 210) and Schille (*Apg.*, 467–68). The MSS 614, 2147, and some ancient versions add at the end of the verse *epididous kai hēmin*, "distributing (some) to us too," which makes the eucharistic sense even more obvious. The difficulty in the eucharistic understanding of what Paul does comes from its setting, the storm and the imminent grounding of the ship. See further B. Reicke, "Die Mahlzeit mit Paulus auf den Wellen des Mittelmeers Act. 27, 33–38," *TZ* 4 (1948): 401–10.

36. *All of them were encouraged by this, and they too took something to eat.* The fellow travelers are heartened by Paul's advice and example.

37. *In all there were two hundred and seventy-six of us on board.* This verse was probably the sequel to v 32 before the Lucan insert of vv 33–36. The number 276 is read by MSS ℵ, C, Ψ, 33, 36, 81, 181, 307, 614, and 1739 of the Alexandrian tradition. The WT, MS B, the Sahidic version, and Epiphanius read rather: "We were about seventy persons." This WT reading seems to have risen from a dittography of the *omega* on the dat. *ploiō*, "ship," after which the cipher for 76 was written so that it was combined with *s* (= *diakosiai*, "two hundred") and taken as the adv. *hōs*. Other readings: MS A reads "275," and MS 69, "270." See *TCGNT*, 442.

38. *When all had enough to eat, they further lightened the ship by throwing the wheat overboard.* Cf. 27:18. Note again the shift to the third plural. Wheat would have been the usual cargo of a ship from Alexandria bound for ports in Italy (and especially for the Romans, who imported most of their grain from Egypt).

39. *When it was day, they did not recognize the land.* It will be identified as Malta in 28:1.

they could make out a bay with a beach. Traditionally identified as St. Paul's Bay, but see NOTE on 28:1.

they proposed to run the ship aground there, if possible. I.e., on the beach.

40. *Cutting loose the anchors, they abandoned them to the sea; at the same time*

they untied the ropes of the rudders, hoisted the foresail into the wind, and made for the beach. I.e., the sailors did all that would have been prudent under the circumstances.

41. *they encountered a place of cross seas.* Lit., "a two-sea place." This term has often been taken to mean a place with sea on both sides, hence a "strait," or a "sandbar," or "reef" (BAGD, 195, 649; Schneider, *Apg.*, 2.398). Luke, however, may be using a technical term, which is neither *herma*, "reef," nor *this*, "sandbar," but *topon dithalasson.* This seems rather to denote "a place where two seas run," i.e., a place subject to crosswinds, rather than a geographical spot (see Gilchrist, "The Historicity").

and the ship was grounded there. Lit., "they ran the ship aground there," the 3d pl. being indefinite (= the passive). See *IBNTG*, 180–81; ZBG §1.

Its bow stuck fast and could not be budged. Lit., "the bow, having jammed fast, remained unmovable."

while the stern was being broken to pieces by the force [of the waves]. So Luke describes the loss of the ship, predicted in vv 10, 22.

42. *The soldiers were minded to kill the prisoners lest any of them would swim away and escape.* The soldiers, who were to guard the prisoners, knew that they might themselves incur penalties, if the prisoners were to escape. Justinian's Code (of later date) prescribes in such a case the same penalty that awaited the prisoners (9.4.4).

43. *the centurion, who was anxious to save Paul, kept them from carrying out their decision.* So Paul is saved by the Roman centurion, Julius (27:1), from the soldiers.

He ordered those who could swim to jump overboard first and make for the land. This verse is also part of the Lucan inserts (possibly from the Pauline source) into the We-Section.

44. *the rest were to follow, some on planks, others on debris from the ship.* I.e., those who could not swim would float in on boards.

So it was that everyone got safely to land. Paul's prediction (27:25) is fulfilled.

BIBLIOGRAPHY (27:9–44)

Briffa Brincati, G. P., "'In insulam quandam oportet nos devenire . . . ,'" *Lucerna* (Malta) 3 (1957): 85–88.

Clark, D. J., "What Went Overboard First?" *BT* 26 (1975): 144–46.

Cowan, W., "Acts 27:39," *ExpTim* 27 (1915–16): 472–73; 28 (1916–17): 330–31.

Gilchrist, J. M., "The Historicity of Paul's Shipwreck," *JSNT* 61 (1996): 29–51.

Goodspeed, E. J., "Did Alexandria Influence the Nautical Language of St. Luke? A Study of Acts xxviii[*sic*].12 in the Light of Greek Papyri," *Expos* 6/8 (1903): 130–41.

Lake, K. and H. J. Cadbury, "The Winds," *Beginnings*, 5.338–44.

Ramsay, W. M., "St. Paul's Shipwreck," *Expos* 5/6 (1897): 154–57.

Renié, J., "Summisso vase (Act 27.17)," *RSR* 35 (1948): 272–75.
Sim, G. A., "Acts 27.39," *ExpTim* 28 (1916–17): 187–88.
Stammler, W., "Des Apostels Paulus Schiffbruch in nautischer Beleuchtung," *FF* 7 (1931): 235–36.
Stearns, W. N., "The Shipwreck of St. Paul," *Open Court* 37 (1923): 529–37.
Wehnert, J., "Gestrandet: Zu einer neuen These über den Schiffbruch des Apostels Paulus auf dem Wege nach Rom (Apg 27–28)," *ZTK* 87 (1990): 67–99.
———, "'. . . und da erfuhren wir, dass die Insel Kephalenia heisst': Zur neuesten Auslegung von Apg 27–28 und ihrer Methode," *ZTK* 88 (1991): 169–80.
———, "Vom neuesten Schiffbruch des Paulus," *Lutherische Monatshefte* 28 (1989): 98–100.
Zorell, F., "Sprachliche Randnoten zum NT," *BZ* 9 (1911): 159–63, esp. 159–60.
See also bibliography on 27:1–8.

3. PAUL SPENDS THE WINTER ON MALTA (28:1–10)

28 1 Once safely ashore, we learned that the island was called Malta. 2 The natives showed us extraordinary kindness; they lit a fire and brought us all around
it because of the rain that had set in and the cold. 3 Paul had gathered a bundle
of brushwood and was putting it on the fire, when a viper crawled out of it because of the heat and fastened on his hand. 4 At the sight of the snake hanging
from his hand, the natives said to each other, "This man must really be a murderer; though he has survived death in the sea, Justice has not allowed him to go
on living." 5 But Paul shook the snake from his hand into the fire and suffered no
ill effects. 6 They were expecting him to swell up or suddenly fall dead, but after
waiting for quite some time and seeing nothing unusual happen to him, they
changed their minds and kept saying that he was a god. 7 In the vicinity of that
place there was the estate of a prominent man on the island, named Publius. He
took us in and kindly gave us hospitality for three days. 8 Now Publius's father
happened to be sick in bed, laid up with chronic fever and dysentery. Paul went
in to see the man, and with prayers laid his hands on him and cured him. 9 When
this happened, the rest of the sick on the island also came to him and were
healed. 10 They paid us many honors, and when we were to set sail again, they
brought us the provisions we needed.

WT: 1 Having reached land, they learned that the country was called Malta. 2 The natives lit a fire and welcomed us to it because of the cold. 4 When the natives saw this, they said. 5 shook it from his hand into the fire [omits the rest]. 6 [omits "swell up or," and "but after waiting for quite some time"] and seeing him saved, they kept saying. 7 [omits "in the vicinity . . . the estate of"]. There was a man named Publius, one of their leaders, who took us in for three days. 8 Publius' father was sick with dysentery; so Paul went in and prayed for him, and the man was cured. 9 [omits "when this happened"]. Many who were sick came to Paul and were healed. 10 [omits "when . . . set sail again"].

COMMENT

The aftermath of the shipwreck is now recounted by Luke. The worst is over; the shipwrecked party finds shelter on shore. The place where Paul and his fellow travelers have landed is the island Malta, where they are welcomed by the natives, especially by a leading citizen named Publius. There they spend the winter. Paul survives the attack of a viper, and the natives think he is a god. He heals people, and when they are ready to embark again, they are provided for by the Maltese.

The episode is again a narrative, which continues as part of the We-Section, but into which an insert, probably derived from the Pauline source, is made in vv 2b–6. The episode as a whole enhances the status of Paul. Part of it is a miracle story, as Paul cures the sick father of Publius, and also other ill people. Paul is not a god, and he is not being pursued by the goddess of Justice. He is rather the chosen instrument of the risen Lord and is bringing his testimony gradually to Rome, the end of the earth.

NOTES

28:1. *Once safely ashore.* Lit., "having been saved" or "having been brought safely through," i.e., the shipwreck and the swimming ashore.

we learned that the island was called Malta. Melitē is a sizable island in the middle of the Mediterranean to the south of Sicily, called in Latin *Melite Africana;* see Strabo, *Geography* 6.2.11; 17.3.16; Diodorus Siculus, *Bibliotheca historica* 5.12.2–3. It had been populated early on by Phoenicians. Since 218 B.C. it was controlled by the Romans, because it was important in the trade that passed east-west in the Mediterranean Sea. MS B* reads the name as *Melitēnē;* MS P^{74} has rather *Milētē.* See A. Mayr, *Die Insel Malta im Altertum* (Munich: Beck, 1909).

Different places on Malta have been proposed for the precise point of landfall: (a) St. Paul's Bay (traditional); (b) Mellieha Bay (W. Burridge, N. Heutger); (c) Qawra Point, near St. Paul's Bay (J. Smith, G. H. Musgrave); (d) site near St. Paul's Bay, on the west side of the island (W. Cowan); (e) the northwest side of the strait near St. Paul's Islands (J. M. Gilchrist). The last named is the most likely.

The name *Melitē* has nothing to do with Mljet *(Melite Illyrica)*, a small island off the coast of Dalmatia (opposite modern Dubrovnik), with which Ignazio Georgi, an eighteenth-century Benedictine, once tried to identify the place of Paul's shipwreck. This view has been espoused in modern times by Acworth, Meinardus, and Warnecke.

2. *The natives.* Lit., "the foreigners" *(barbaroi)*, i.e., non-Greek speaking Gentiles. The adj. *barbaros* is formed onomatopoetically of reduplicated *bar,* which to ancient Greeks imitated the unintelligible sounds of foreign languages; they even likened them to the twittering of birds (Herodotus, *History* 2.57). At this

period the Maltese would have spoken mainly a form of Punic, a development of older Phoenician, a Semitic language, related to Hebrew, but unrelated to Indo-European Greek or Latin. Punic inscriptions from Malta are known (see *CIS* 1.124; *CIG* 3.5753).

showed us extraordinary kindness. Luke uses *philanthrōpia*, "love of human beings," but which in Hellenistic Greek was commonly used for "hospitality." See C. Spicq, "La philanthropie hellénistique, vertu divine et royale (à propos de *Tit.* III,4)," *ST* 12 (1958): 169–91.

they lit a fire and brought us all around it because of the rain that had set in and the cold. Here begins an insert (vv 2b–6) from the Pauline source into a We-Section. Again the Lucan hyperbole appears; see NOTE on 2:44.

3. *Paul had gathered a bundle of brushwood and was putting it on the fire, when a viper crawled out of it because of the heat and fastened on his hand. Echidna* was the name used for many forms of snakes thought to be poisonous. See W. Foerster, *TDNT*, 2.815. In Luke 3:7 it is used figuratively of human beings in the Baptist's preaching.

4. *At the sight of the snake hanging from his hand, the natives said to each other, "This man must really be a murderer.* I.e., because he has suffered such a series of fateful misfortunes.

though he has survived death in the sea, Justice has not allowed him to go on living." Dikē, "Justice," is personifed as a goddess of revenge who pursues human beings and their conduct, as often in Greek literature (Hesiod, *Theognis* 902; Sophocles, *Antigone* 538; Arrian, *Anabasis* 4.9.7). Literally, *dikē* means "custom, usage," but it developed various connotations: "right order; lawsuit; judgment, punishment." The superstitious natives think that Paul has fallen under the scrutiny of this goddess. See G. Rinaldi, "Nota," *BeO* 24 (1982): 186.

5. *Paul shook the snake from his hand into the fire and suffered no ill effects.* The implication is that heaven has saved him once again, because he is still destined to appear before Caesar (27:24). Cf. Mark 16:18.

6. *They were expecting him to swell up or suddenly fall dead.* I.e., because of the poisonous effects of the snake clinging to him.

after waiting for quite some time and seeing nothing unusual happen to him, they changed their minds and kept saying that he was a god. Paul's survival reveals to the credulous natives that he is an extraordinary person, even divine. Recall 14:11.

7. *In the vicinity of that place there was the estate of a prominent man on the island, named Publius.* Lit., "the first of the island." This *Poplios* (= Latin *Publius*) is otherwise unknown. In some MSS (P^{74}, 81, 104, 945, 1739) his name is spelled *Pouplios*. The legate of the praetor of Sicily, who administered Roman Malta, was called *Melitensium primus omnium.* Possibly the Publius mentioned was this "first of all Maltese." See A. Suhl, "Zum Titel *prōtos tēs nēsou* (Erster der Insel) Apg 28,7," *BZ* 36 (1992): 220–26.

He took us in and kindly gave us hospitality for three days. This would mean that he cared for the 276 mentioned in 27:37.

8. *Now Publius's father happened to be sick in bed, laid up with chronic fever and dysentery. Paul went in to see the man.* Paul again becomes the center of attention, as he shows interest in a sick human being.

with prayers laid his hands on him and cured him. The imposition of hands to cure is also found in Luke 4:40 (cure of people in Galilee). The laying on of hands for this purpose is unknown in the OT and in rabbinic literature. It has turned up in 1QapGen 20:21–22, 28–29, where Abram prays, lays his hands on the head of Pharoah, and exorcises the plague/evil spirit afflicting the Pharaoh (and his household) for having carried off Sarai, Abram's wife. It is accompanied by prayer, as here in Acts, and meant as a miraculous cure. See D. Flusser, "Healing through the Laying-On of Hands in a Dead Sea Scroll," *IEJ* 7 (1957): 107–8; A. Dupont-Sommer, "Exorcismes et guérisons dans les écrits de Qoumrân," *Congress Volume, Oxford 1959* (VTSup 7; Leiden: Brill, 1960): 246–61; Fitzmyer, *The Genesis Apocryphon of Qumran Cave 1* (BibOr 18A; 2d ed.; Rome: Biblical Institute, 1971), 140–41.

9. *When this happened, the rest of the sick on the island also came to him and were healed.* Lit., "the rest on the island having diseases." This summary-like statement describes Paul's activity in curing the sick. Cf. Luke 8:2–3.

10. *They paid us many honors.* Lit., "who also honored us with many honors."

when we were to set sail again. The WT omits this. This would have been at the end of winter, after 10 March of the new year (probably A.D. 61). See NOTE on 27:9. Luke again uses the technical nautical term *anagein;* see NOTE on 13:13.

they brought us the provisions we needed. Lit., "they put aboard the (things) for (our) needs."

BIBLIOGRAPHY (28:1–10)

Acworth, A., "Where Was St. Paul Shipwrecked? A Re-examination of the Evidence," *JTS* 24 (1973): 190–93.

Barb, A., "Der Heilige und die Schlange," *Mitteilungen der anthropologischen Gesellschaft in Wien* 82 (1953): 1–21.

Brunot, A., "Malte," *BTS* 89 (1967): 8–17.

Burridge, W., *Seeking the Site of St. Paul's Shipwreck* (Valletta, Malta: Progress, 1952).

Cowan, W., "Acts xxvii.39," *ExpTim* 27 (1915–16): 472–73; 28 (1916–17): 330–31.

Farrugia, L., *Melita del naufragio di S. Paolo è l'isola di Malta* (Malta: Casa San Giuseppe, 1912).

Hemer, C. J., "Euraquilo and Melita," *JTS* 26 (1975): 100–11.

Heutger, N., "'Paulus auf Malta' im Lichte der maltesischen Topographie," *BZ* 28 (1984): 86–88.

Kirchschläger, W., "Fieberheilung in Apg 28 und Lk 4," *Les Actes des Apôtres* (ed. J. Kremer), 509–21.

Leonard, W., "From Caesarea to Malta: St. Paul's Voyage and Shipwreck," *ACR* 37 (1960): 274–84.
———, "From Malta to the Seven Hills: St. Paul's Arrival in Rome," *ACR* 38 (1961): 23–32.
Meinardus, O.F.A., "St. Paul Shipwrecked in Dalmatia," *BA* 39 (1976): 145–47.
Musgrave, G. H., *Friendly Refuge: A Study of St Paul's Shipwreck and His Stay in Malta* [Heathfield, Sussex: Heathfield Publications, 1979).
Pittman, R. T., "Where Paul Was Shipwrecked," *Words and Their Ways in the Greek New Testament* (London/Edinburgh: Marshall, Morgan & Scott, 1942), 118–23.
Sant, C. and J. Sammut, "Paulus war doch auf Malta!" *TGl* 80 (1990): 327–32.
Saydon, P. P., "La data del naufragio di S. Paolo a Malta," *Lucerna* (Malta) 3 (1957): 15–16.
———, "The Site of St. Paul's Shipwreck," *Melita Theologica* 14 (1962): 58–61.
Sim, G. A., "Acts xxvii.39," *ExpTim* 38 (1916–17): 187–88.
See also bibliography on 27:1–9 and 27:9–44.

4. Paul's Arrival in Rome and House Arrest (28:11–16)

[11] Three months later we set sail on a ship that had passed the winter at the island.
It was from Alexandria with the Dioscuri as its figurehead. [12] We put in at Syracuse and spent three days there. [13] From there we sailed around the coast and
came to Rhegium. A day later a south wind began to blow, which enabled us to
reach Puteoli in two days. [14] There we found some brothers and were urged to
stay with them for seven days. And so we came to Rome. [15] Some brothers from
there heard about our coming and came out as far as Appii Forum and Tres
Tabernae to meet us. On seeing them, Paul thanked God and plucked up his
courage. [16] When we entered Rome, Paul was allowed to take a lodging of his
own, with a soldier to guard him.

WT: [11] [omits "three months later" and "with the Dioscuri as its figurehead"]. [12–13] [verses omitted]. [14] [omits "there . . . seven days" and "so"]. [15] [omits "from there," "about our coming," "as far as Appii Forum and Tres Tabernae," and "thanked God and"]. [16] When we came to Rome, the centurion handed over the prisoners to the garrison commander. Paul found favor with him to stay outside the headquarters, with a soldier to guard him.

COMMENT

After wintering for three months on Malta (i.e., the winter of A.D. 60–61), Paul and the others take ship from Malta, stop at Syracuse in Sicily, and sail on to Rhegium and then to Puteoli, where Paul lodges with Christians for a week. Then they make their way overland from Puteoli to Rome via Appii Forum and

Tres Tabernae. When he finally gets to Rome (in the spring of A.D. 61), Paul is allowed to take a lodging of his own, with a soldier to guard him.

The episode is again a narrative, which brings Luke's hero to the capital of the empire, Rome, "the end of the earth" (1:8). This is the end of the last We-Section in Acts (28:16a), after which Luke composes a final description of Paul's activity in Rome. Verses 15–16 are problematic and seem to some commentators to be a Lucan addition to the original We-Section that might end with v 14b, because in its present state the episode seems to say that Paul arrives in Rome twice (v 14b and v 16a). See Haenchen (*Acts*, 719–20); Weiser (*Apg.*, 673), but that detail may be explained otherwise.

NOTES

11. *Three months later.* I.e., at the end of *mare clausum*, about mid-March, toward the beginning of spring A.D. 61. See NOTE on 27:9.

we set sail on a ship that had passed the winter at the island. Luke again uses *anagein*; see NOTE on 13:13.

It was from Alexandria. Being from such a short distance away, it must have been caught in a storm on the Mediterranean Sea and taken refuge at Malta for the winter months. Josephus (*J.W.* 2.10.5 §203) also tells of messengers being weather bound for three months.

with the Dioscuri as its figurehead. The *Dioskouroi* (in some MSS [P[74], P*, Ψ, 81[c]]: *Dioskoroi*), "the lads of Zeus," usually called "the Heavenly Twins," were Kastor and Polydeukes (in Latin, *Castor et Pollux*), the twin brothers of Helen and children of Zeus (or of Tyndareus and Leda; see Homer, *Odyssey* 11.300–5). Sailors venerated them as astral deities (associated with the constellation "Gemini") and saviors of those in peril during storms at sea (often = the twin lights of St. Elmo's fire). Their figures were carved on the prow of the Alexandrian ship, because their cult was widespread in Egypt. See *OCD*, 354; F. J. Dölger, "'Dioskuroi': Das Reiseschiff des Apostels Paulus und seine Schutzgötter: Kult- und Kulturgeschichtliches zu Apg 28,11," *Antike und Christentum* (6 vols.; Münster in W.: Aschendorff, 1929–50), 6.276–85; J. R. Harris, *The Cult of the Heavenly Twins* (Cambridge: Cambridge University Press, 1906).

12. *We put in at Syracuse and spent three days there.* The route of Paul and his companions was (by ship) from Malta to Syracuse and then to Rhegium and Puteoli, and then (overland) from Puteoli to Appii Forum and Tres Tabernae, and finally to Rome. *Syrakousai* was an important port on the east coast of Sicily, a island much larger than Malta in the Mediterranean Sea at the tip of the boot of Italy. Greek colonists from Corinth settled there about 734 B.C. (Strabo, *Geography* 6.2.4; Thucydides, *Histories* 6.3.2). Besieged by the Athenians in 413, Syracuse was defeated, and its defeat marked the turn in the Peloponnesian War. In 212 B.C. Syracuse was taken by M. Claudius Marcellus, a Roman commander in the First Punic War, who routed the Carthaginians, and the port thus came under Roman control. Eventually it became the seat of a Roman province. See

OCD, 1030; A. Betz, "Syracuse," *ABD*, 6.270–71. Luke again uses the technical nautical term *katagein*; see NOTE on 27:3.

13. *From there we sailed around the coast and came to Rhegium. Rhēgion* (= Latin *Rhegium*, modern Reggio di Calabria) was a port city at the tip of the boot of Italy, opposite Sicily. It was founded by Greek colonists from Chalcis about 721 B.C. (Strabo, *Geography* 6.1.6) and finally came under Roman control after a lengthy battle in 271. See J. D. Wineland, "Rhegium," *ABD*, 5.709–10.

A day later a south wind began to blow, which enabled us to reach Puteoli in two days. Potioloi (= Latin *Puteoli*, modern Pozzuoli), a commercial harbor town on the west coast of Italy, in Campania on the Gulf of Naples, to the west of the town of Naples. It was founded by Greeks in mid-eighth century B.C., conquered by Samnites in 421, and became a Roman dependency about 338. All of Rome's imports of grain from Egypt and elsewhere passed through this town (Strabo, *Geography* 17.1.7 [calls it *Dikaiarchia*]). It was the chief port of entry for people coming from the islands; see Josephus, *Life* 3 §16. It was still 200 km from Rome. See S. T. Carroll, "Puteoli," *ABD*, 5.560–61.

14. *There we found some brothers. Adelphoi* is probably meant in the sense of fellow Christians (see NOTE on 1:15), which would mean that a Christian community has already been established in Puteoli, where Paul is welcomed. Josephus knows of Jews who lived there (*J.W.* 2.7.1 §104; *Ant.* 17.12.1 §328); so some of them may have become Christians. See M. Adinolfi, "San Paolo a Pozzuoli (*Atti* 28, 13b–14a)," *RivB* 8 (1960): 206–24.

were urged to stay with them for seven days. This was in effect the end of their sea travel; perhaps that is the reason why they were allowed to sojourn for seven days in this town. From here Paul and his companions would have made their way overland to Rome.

And so we came to Rome. I.e., the destination of Paul's journey, the city of destiny for him, where he is to appear before Caesar. See NOTE on 18:2. The adv. *houtōs* seems to be used in a concluding sense, but it may rather be introducing the following verses, since Paul has not yet reached Rome itself. It may be that he has already entered the dominion of the *praefectus praetorio*, under whom he will be at his destination. See D. Plooij, "Acts xxviii.14, 16," *ExpTim* 24 (1912–13): 186.

15. *Some brothers from there heard about our coming.* Lit., "and from there the brothers having heard things about us." From the context this must mean the arrival of Paul and his companions in Puteoli.

and came out as far as Appii Forum and Tres Tabernae to meet us. Appiou Phoros (= Latin *Appii Forum*, "Forum of Appius") was a town situated about 65 km from Rome, where an ancient milestone has been found. *Treis Tabernai* (= Latin *Tres Tabernae*, "Three Taverns") was a town about 50 km from Rome. Both towns were connected with ancient Rome by the Via Appia. We are not told how the Christians of Rome learned about Paul's approach or how he recognized them when they came toward him on the road. Luke, the storyteller, is simply punctuating the overland last lap of Paul's journey.

On seeing them, Paul thanked God and plucked up his courage. This is Paul's natural reaction. In the Lucan story Paul meets with Roman Christians only outside of Rome.

16. *When we entered Rome.* Paul probably entered the capital of the Roman Empire by the Porta Capena. It was near the place where Nero, the reigning Caesar, resided. On Rome, see NOTE on 18:2. For a view of the dangers of living in ancient Rome, see Juvenal, *Satire* III. Cf. R. S. Kinsey, "Rome in the Time of St. Paul," *LCQ* 18 (1945): 407–11.

The WT reads: "the centurion handed over the prisoners to the garrison commander. Paul found favor with him to stay outside the headquarters, with a soldier to guard him." The *stratopedarchos*, "garrison commander" (Latin *praefectus castrorum*), was most likely the man in charge of the *Castra Praetoriana*, "Pretorian Camp," situated on the eastern side of Rome, but the identity of this officer is much debated (see H. W. Tajra, *The Trial*, 177–78). The centurion would have transferred Paul to military custody (Latin *custodia militaris*).

Paul was allowed to take a lodging of his own, with a soldier to guard him. In Rome Paul is put under house arrest. He has to be detained because his case has not yet been decided, but he is accorded restricted freedom, because Roman authorities did not consider him a risk for public order. Verse 20 mentions a "chain" of some sort, which links him with the soldier. This is the setting for the testimony that Paul is to bear, at least in Rome.

BIBLIOGRAPHY (28:11–16)

Agnello, S., "Act 28:12 e la discussa origine del cristianesimo in Sicilia," *Siculorum gymnasium* 10 (1957): 265–71.

Bartlet, V., "Paul in Rome," *BW* 34 (1909): 346–54.

Hitchcock, F.R.M., "The Trials of St. Paul and Apollonius: An Historical Parallel," *Hermathena* 75 (1950): 24–34.

Marguerat, D., "'Et quand nous sommes entrés dans Rome': L'Enigme de la fin du livre des Actes (28,16–31)," *RHPR* 73 (1993): 1–21.

Mecham, F. A., "And So We Came to Rome," *ACR* 50 (1973): 170–73.

Schwank, B., "Und so kamen wir nach Rom (Apg 28,14): Reisenotizen zu den letzten beiden Kapiteln der Apostelgeschichte," *EA* 36 (1960): 169–92.

5. PAUL'S TESTIMONY TO PROMINENT JEWS OF ROME (28:17–31)

[17]After three days Paul happened to invite prominent men of the Jewish community to visit him. When they came, he addressed them, "Brothers, although I have done nothing against our people or our ancestral customs, I was handed over as a prisoner to the Romans in Jerusalem. [18]The Romans tried my case and wanted to release me, because they found nothing against me deserving death.
[19]When some Jews objected, I was forced to appeal to Caesar, not that I had any

charge to bring against my own people. 20 This, then, is the reason why I have
requested to see you and to speak to you. Because I share the hope of Israel, I
wear this chain!" 21 In reply, they said to him, "We have not received any letters
from Judea about you; nor has any of the brothers arrived here with a report or
rumor to your discredit. 22 For our part, we are anxious to hear you present your
views, for we know full well about that sect, that it is denounced everywhere."
23 So they arranged a day with him and came to his lodging in great numbers.
From morning to evening he laid his case before them and kept bearing witness
about the kingdom of God. He sought to convince them about Jesus, appealing
to the law of Moses and to the prophets. 24 Some of them were convinced by what
he had to say; others would not believe. 25 Without reaching any agreement
among themselves, they started to depart, when Paul added one last word, "The
Holy Spirit stated it well, when he spoke to your ancestors through the prophet
Isaiah:

> 26 '*Go to this people and say:*
> *You may listen carefully, but never understand;*
> *you may look sharply, but never see.*
> 27 *For the mind of this people has grown dull.*
> *They have hardly used their ears to listen;*
> *they have closed their eyes,*
> *lest they see with their eyes,*
> *hear with their ears,*
> *understand with their mind,*
> *and turn;*
> *and I should heal them.*'[o]

28 So let it be known to you that this salvation of God has been sent to the Gentiles. They will listen to it!" [29] 30 For two whole years Paul stayed on in his own
rented lodging, where he welcomed all who would come to him. 31 With all boldness and without hindrance, he preached the kingdom of God and taught about
the Lord Jesus.

[o] Isa 6:9–10

WT: 17 [omits "when they came"]. He conferred with them, saying. 19 [adds at end:] but that I might redeem my life from death. 21 Nothing has been written to us about you, nor have they sent (anything) to us, nor have we heard anything to your discredit. 22 to hear what you think. 23 [omits "with him," "to his lodgings," and "of Moses"]. 25 [omits "Holy," "your," and "the prophet"]. 27 has been calloused. 28 [omits "they will listen to it!"]. 29 When he had said this, the Jews went off, disputing vigorously among themselves. 30 [adds at the end:] and he debated with Jews and Greeks. 31 He preached the kingdom of God, asserting and stating without hindrance that it was Jesus, the son of God, through whom the whole world was going to be judged.

COMMENT

Luke ends the second volume of his writing with a telling and climactic episode about Paul's testimony in Rome, the capital of the civilized world of that time. He has depicted Paul journeying "to the end of the earth" (1:8), and now relates how he continues, even as a prisoner, to bear testimony to the Word of God in Rome. In this episode, Luke describes Paul presenting himself in a good light to Roman Jews. There are two incidents and a concluding summary. In the first incident (28:17–22) Paul sends for members of the Jewish community and explains his personal situation and attitude toward his own people and their customs. He learns that they have not received any adverse reports from Jerusalem about him, even though they may already know about Christianity. In the second incident (28:23–28), Paul grants prominent Jews of Rome another chance to visit him, because they want to learn more about Christianity from him. When Paul explains, some are convinced, but others are not. So as they prepare to leave his quarters, he reminds them of the famous prophecy of Isaiah. He makes it clear that the message of salvation, which God has promised to his people of old, is now being "sent to the Gentiles," and "they will listen to it!" (28:28). The Isaiah passage, as it is quoted from the LXX, is not a judgment, but a description of the hardening of the hearts of Jews of old. Paul compares their obstinacy with that of those who listen to him, as he tells these Roman Jews how God's message now has to be preached to Gentiles. The conclusion is found in vv 30–31. What is striking about this final scene in Acts is that Paul makes no contact with Roman Christians and that nothing is learned about the appearance of Paul before Caesar, the climax to which the Lucan story had been building up. It deals only with his testimony to the Jews of Rome.

From a form-critical standpoint, the episode begins as a narrative, but the last two speeches of Paul (28:17–20 and 28:25c–28) are incorporated into it. The first (vv 17–20) is a defense, whereas the second (vv 25c–28) is an indictment. The first makes four points: (1) Paul has done nothing against his people or its ancestral customs; (2) the Romans wanted to set him free; (3) when Jerusalem authorities objected to his release, he appealed to Caesar; and (4) he is a prisoner being tried for "the hope of Israel." The second speech makes three points: (1) Paul again bears testimony to the Jews of Rome; (2) he analyses the Jewish rejection of the gospel; and (3) he shows how the message of God's salvation is consequently being sent to Gentiles. The first speech is interrupted by a statement of the Jewish leaders about having heard nothing against him. The second speech (28:25c–28) makes use of the OT, as Paul quotes Isa 6:9–10. The episode ends with a minor summary (vv 30–31), an account of Paul's activity and testimony in Rome. The whole episode is basically a Lucan composition, as Luke concludes his work with a few details derived from his Pauline source.

Does Luke mean by this last episode that Israel no longer has an opportunity to be saved? Since some of Israel refuses to accept the Christian proclamation, is this the end of offering salvation to Israel? One might be tempted to read this episode in this way, but it is not to be understood only as a way of legitimating the evangelization of Gentiles. After all, in Luke 24:47 the risen Christ had commissioned his disciples to preach repentance and forgiveness of sins "to all the nations" in his name. That commission is repeated in Acts 1:8. Thus, Luke is saying that those in Israel who now refuse to accept the Christian gospel are merely continuing a practice of obduracy long known from their ancestors. If Israel is rebuked by Luke, it is in the wording of traditional language; it is not something that has not been heard before. The rebuke, however, explains why the message that Paul brings now goes "to the Gentiles," and "they will listen to it" (28:25). See further H. van de Sandt, "Acts 28,28"; Weiser, *Apg.*, 683–84.

Thus ends the second Lucan volume, the Acts of the Apostles. It ends abruptly and surprises the modern reader. Is it unfinished? Has it been somehow truncated in its transmission? No one knows. Various theories have been proposed to explain the ending of Acts; the main ones are the following:

(1) Luke died before finishing his story of the sequel to the ministry of Jesus. This explanation encounters the difficulty that 28:28–30 is a summary, similar to other summaries in Acts that punctuate the account; it seems clearly to be meant as the literary ending of Acts.

(2) The story of Paul's journey to Spain (*Acta Pauli*; Muratorian Fragment 38–39 [*EnchBib* §4; Conzelmann, *Acts*, xxxii]) and of his martyrdom would have followed as the sequel to his two volumes. This explanation is based on later legendary accounts and encounters the difficulty that there is no evidence in any of the Greek MSS of Acts of such a sequel. See *Beginnings*, 5.326–39.

(3) Luke intended to write a third volume, incorporating such details as those mentioned in (2), as his own prologue to Acts may indicate (T. Zahn, "Das dritte Buch des Lukas," *NKZ* 28 [1917]: 373–95; Ramsay): Acts 1:1 uses the adj. *prōtos*, "first," and not *proteros*, "former." This may imply that still another volume was projected. This explanation encounters the philological difficulty that *prōtos* is often used in the sense of "former" (BAGD, 725; MM, 557) or "former (of two)."

(4) Acts was written before Paul's Roman trial took place in the early sixties (Harnack, J.A.T. Robinson), and so Luke had no knowledge yet how it would come out. This explanation encounters the difficulty that Paul's speech in 20:18–35 is a farewell address with a conscious allusion to his coming end. Moreover, it is in conflict with what is almost certainly the later date of the composition of Acts, after A.D. 70 (see Introduction §§20–31). The Acts of the Apostles reads like a complete work, when the literary and symbolic aspects of it are rightly considered.

In any case, it may seem strange that the reader is not told anything about the death of Paul, the hero of the second half of Acts. Yet the ending, such as it is, may not be as puzzling as some think, because it does record that Paul continued to preach the kingdom of God, even in Rome, "with all boldness and without hindrance" (28:31). That is the note of triumph on which Luke wanted his story to end. The gospel was thus being preached at Rome, the "end of the earth" (1:8), "and without hindrance" (28:31). The reader of Acts already knows that

Paul's personal end was not far off; the Lucan Paul intimated as much in his speech at Miletus, and so Luke felt no need to recount it. Homer's *Iliad* is not seen to be incomplete because it does not describe Achilles' death!

The upshot of all this is that one has to reckon with the end of Acts as it is in all the manuscripts that have come down to us. The ending is that which Luke planned for his literary composition, for his story of how apostolic testimony to Jesus Christ was carried to "the end of the earth."

NOTES

17. *After three days Paul happened to invite prominent men of the Jewish community to visit him.* Lit., "those being the first of the Jews." Under house arrest, Paul cannot visit any Roman synagogues, so he wastes no time in inviting Roman Jews to come to him. Among these would have been elders, scribes, and synagogue leaders. See 13:50; 25:2 for a similar use of *prōtos,* "first." Luke again uses *egeneto de* with an infin.; see *Luke,* 118.

It is not known when Jews first came to Rome. Judas Maccabee is said to have sent envoys to Rome about 160 B.C. to "establish an alliance and peace" with the Romans (1 Macc 8:17–22). This implies that Jews were moving between Judea and Rome as early as that, but some were undoubtedly already resident there. The earliest reference to Jews in Rome in a Roman writing is associated with the Roman *praetor peregrinus,* Gnaeus Cornelius Hispalus, who in 139 B.C. "forced Jews, who tried to contaminate Roman customs with the cult of Jupiter Sabazius, to return to their own homes" (Valerius Maximus [first century A.D.], *Facta et dicta memorabilia* 1.3.3). The notice probably refers to Jewish merchants and sojourners accused of proselytism; whether there was really any connection between Jews and Sabazius is quite debatable, for Romans tended to misunderstand Jews and often lumped them together with *Chaldei,* "Chaldeans," and other Asiatics. Some have tried to explain "Sabazius" as a corruption of Hebrew "Sabaoth" (= *ṣĕbāʾôt*), but that explanation is far from certain. In any case, by the first century B.C. there was a large Jewish community in Rome, estimated to have been about 50,000, grouped in several synagogues. Though some emperors (Tiberius, Claudius) expelled Jews from Rome, they never succeeded in ridding the city of them entirely. Luke's story, therefore, about Paul inviting prominent Jews of Rome to visit him suits the general picture of first-century Rome, as we know it.

See Fitzmyer, *Romans,* 27–32; H. J. Leon, *The Jews of Ancient Rome* (Philadelphia: Jewish Publication Society of America, 1960); *Updated Edition* (Peabody, MA: Hendrickson, 1995); J.-B. Frey, "Les communautés juives à Rome aux premiers temps de l'église," *RSR* 20 (1930): 269–97; 21 (1931): 129–68; "Le judaïsme à Rome aux premiers temps de l'église," *Bib* 12 (1931): 129–56; G. La Piana, "Foreign Groups in Rome during the First Centuries of the Empire," *HTR* 20 (1927): 183–403.

When they came, he addressed them, "Brothers." Again, Paul so addresses Jewish leaders; see NOTE on 1:15; cf. 28:21.

although I have done nothing against our people or our ancestral customs. Paul explains his legal status and the problems that he has had, but still maintains his innocence. Recall the charge made against Paul in 21:21, 28, and his disavowal of such charges in 24:14–19; 25:8–10; 26:22.

I was handed over as a prisoner to the Romans in Jerusalem. Recall 21:30–33, where the Roman commander in Jerusalem arrested Paul to save him from the rioting people. Cf. 24:6b. Paul stresses that, if he is now awaiting trial in a secular Roman setting, it is because he has been handed over to the Romans in Judea by religious authorities of Jerusalem. Luke employs the terminology used in his Gospel about Jesus being handed over to authorities (see Luke 9:22, 44; 18:32; 24:7).

18. *The Romans tried my case.* Recall 25:6–11, where Paul appears before the tribunal of the procurator Festus in Caesarea. Cf. 23:29; 25:18–20, 25–27; 26:31.

and wanted to release me, because they found nothing against me deserving death. This formulates clearly the innocence of Paul, as far as the Romans were concerned. So Paul exonerates the action of Felix and Festus (26:32), but he must now explain to Roman Jews how he nevertheless has been brought to Rome as a prisoner.

19. *When some Jews objected.* Recall 25:7, 24. Ancient Syriac versions add: "and cried, 'Away with this enemy of ours!'" This is probably added in that version under the influence of 22:22.

I was forced to appeal to Caesar. Recall 25:11–12, 21; also 26:32. Although this appeal to Caesar is the immediate occasion that brings Paul to Rome, his coming to Rome has also other purposes, as 19:21 and 23:11 have already made clear: Paul had to bear witness to the risen Christ also in Rome. This is what he is now doing.

not that I had any charge to bring against my own people. Paul maintains that he has been forced to appeal to Caesar's authority even though that has conflicted with his affection for his fellow Jews. It has not been meant as an action hostile to his own people. Note the addition in the WT: "but that I might redeem my life from death." That reading gives a different theological motivation for Paul's appeal.

20. *This, then, is the reason why I have requested to see you and to speak to you.* Or "for this reason, then, have I summoned (you) to see you and to speak to you" (see BAGD, 617 §1a). Thus Paul concludes his first address to the leading Jews of Rome.

Because I share the hope of Israel, I wear this chain!" The hope of Israel was explained in 23:6 as hope in "the resurrection of the dead," the Pharisaic tenet, as Lake and Cadbury (*Beginnings*, 4.289), Wikenhauser (*Apg.*, 288), Johnson (*Acts*, 469), Weiser (*Apg.*, 681), and Roloff (*Apg.*, 373) rightly understand it. Cf. 24:15; 26:6–7. It has nothing to do with a "Messianic hope," *pace* G. W. Lampe (*PCB*, 925), Haenchen (*Acts*, 722), Schneider (*Apg.*, 2.415), Kistemaker (*Acts*, 959), and Tajra (*The Trial*, 185); or with a double hope, "the Messiah and the resurrection," as Marshall (*Acts*, 423) and Pesch (*Apg.*, 2.308) would have it. Even in his house arrest, Paul wears a "chain" *(halysin)*, linking him to the soldier who guards him (28:16), unless one is to understand it as meant symbolically of the house arrest itself.

21. *In reply, they said to him, "We have not received any letters from Judea about you; nor has any of the brothers arrived here with a report or rumor to your discredit.* Lit., "any evil about you." This is a surprising statement that no official or private communication has come to Roman Jews about Paul. Contrast what James has said to Paul on his arrival in Jerusalem (21:21). On "brothers," see v 17.

22. *For our part, we are anxious to hear you present your views.* The Roman Jewish leaders are open to Paul and want to hear what he has to say.

for we know full well about that sect. Christianity is again spoken of as *hairesis,* a "sect" or "school" within Judaism. See NOTE on 5:17; recall 24:5, 14. In his list of Jews present in Jerusalem for the Feast of Assembly Luke included "visitors from Rome" (2:10), some of whom could well have told their Roman colleagues on their return about Christians. Though Roman Jews may not yet have been formally evangelized, they would know of Christianity by hearsay at least, if not by contact. After all, Paul's Epistle to the Romans, dispatched a few years earlier than his arrival in Rome, was addressed to Christians in Rome, some of whom Roman Jews might have known. Yet Conzelmann (*Acts,* 227) thinks that the Jews speak here "as if there were still no Christians in Rome," which is hardly correct, but it is an interpretation with which Schneider (*Apg.,* 2.416) agrees.

that it is denounced everywhere." I.e., among fervent Jews who cling to their ancestral customs. This might seem to imply that Roman Jews did not know much about Christianity, yet the reason usually given for Claudius's expulsion of Jews from Rome in A.D. 49 is precisely the tumultuous disagreement between Jews and Jewish Christians (see COMMENT on 18:1–17).

23. *So they arranged a day with him.* The Jewish leaders set a date with Paul for a second meeting with him.

and came to his lodging in great numbers. The pron. *pleiones* suggests that more have come than in the first meeting.

From morning to evening. Luke again depicts a long-winded Paul; cf. 20:7.

he laid his case before them and kept bearing witness. Paul's explanation is thus another instance of his "bearing witness," now in Rome. His last function in Acts is that of testimony, as he carries out the command of the risen Christ (1:8; 9:15).

about the kingdom of God. This is a Lucan summary of Paul's testimony in Rome. On kingdom of God, see NOTE on 1:3. At this point in Luke's story, the gospel message about the kingdom of God connotes the good news about the reign and dominion of God over human beings that is achieved through Jesus Christ (cf. 8:12; 19:8; 20:25).

He sought to convince them about Jesus. "Jesus" is used as a summary term for the life, ministry, passion, death, resurrection, and exaltation of God's Son, in effect, his meaning for humanity.

appealing to the law of Moses and to the prophets. As Paul had done in Caesarea Maritima before King Agrippa II (26:22–23), in order to show the connection of Christianity with Judaism of old. His christological argument is based on Scripture; recall Luke 24:27, 44.

24. *Some of them were convinced by what he had to say.* As in 13:48; 17:4, 12, 34; 18:8, the reaction of Roman Jews to Paul's testimony is not universally the same. Luke uses *hoi men,* followed by *hoi de,* "some . . . others . . ." (BDF §447.2). Some welcome his message about God's new mode of salvation. That may imply conversion for several of them, but it certainly does not mean that all so convinced were converted.

others would not believe. Luke records the refusal of some Roman Jews and repeats the theme of divided Judaism confronting the Christian gospel.

25. *Without reaching any agreement among themselves.* Lit., "being unharmonious toward one another." The adj. *asymphōnoi,* "at variance," is a *hapax legomenon* in the NT, but found in Wis 18:10; Josephus, *Ag.Ap.* 1.8 §38.

they started to depart, when Paul added one last word. Now Luke portrays Paul making an indictment; his speech shifts from defense and exposition to criticism. He utters with hyperbole *rhēma hen,* "one word," i.e., a brief speech, which stands in contrast to the long-winded exposition implied in v 23. The Lucan Paul makes it clear that the reaction of such Roman Jews to his testimony has been foreseen in Scripture itself.

"The Holy Spirit stated it well. Paul invokes God's Spirit, who is understood as speaking through the inspired prophet Isaiah, who is about to be quoted. Compare 1:16; 4:25, where the Spirit is said to speak through David, reputed author of the Psalms. Paul finds the words of Isaiah to be "well put" *(kalōs).* The conj. *hoti* introduces direct discourse (BDF §470.1).

when he spoke to your ancestors through the prophet Isaiah: 26. *'Go to this people and say: You may listen carefully, but never understand; you may look sharply, but never see.* 27. *For the mind of this people has grown dull. They have hardly used their ears to listen; they have closed their eyes, lest they see with their eyes, hear with their ears, understand with their mind, and turn; and I should heal them.'* Paul quotes Isa 6:9–10, citing it according to the LXX with a slight change of word order in the introductory clause. The LXX is an almost accurate rendering of the Hebrew original, using a plural instead of the Hebrew collective singular. The LXX also changes the impvs. "make dull," "blind," and "close" into finite verbs "so that the entire guilt falls upon the people whose stubbornness the prophet now already confirms as a fact" (Haenchen, *Acts,* 724). Israel's insensitivity is described as a closing of its heart (mind), eyes, and ears to the prophet's proclamation. Of old these words referred to Israel's failure to heed the words of prophets sent to it by God. Now Paul applies them to the Jews of Rome who have closed their eyes and ears to the Christian gospel.

This text of Isaiah was often used in early Christian preaching when the refusal to accept the gospel confronted those who were proclaiming it. It is derived from the inaugural vision of the prophet Isaiah, who feared to go to his own people and announce to them Yahweh's message. Its pertinence in the proclamation of the Christian gospel has often been sensed, to judge from the frequency with which it was used in the NT (see Luke 8:10; Mark 4:12; 8:17–18; Matt 13:14–15; Rom 11:8; John 12:39–40).

28. *So let it be known to you.* Paul concludes, using the particle *oun,* "there-

fore," as he ends his words to those who have come to him. It connects what follows in the object clause (introduced by *hoti*) to his quotation of Isaiah. Recall 2:14, where Luke puts on the lips of Peter the same form of proclamation. Cf. 4:10; 13:38.

that this salvation of God. I.e., the new mode of "salvation" for human beings that comes from God through Jesus Christ. As in Luke 2:30; 3:6, Luke calls it *to sōtērion tou theou,* whereas he has usually used the fem. *sōtēria* in Acts (4:12 [see NOTE there]; 7:25; 13:26, 47; 16:17; 27:34). The formula may be a borrowing from Isa 40:5 (LXX): *opsetai pasa sarx to sōtērion tou theou,* "all flesh will see the salvation of God" (quoted in Luke 3:6). Thus Luke, at the end of his two-volume testimony to the Christ-event, sums up the universal character of Christian salvation, which has echoed through Luke 2:11, 14, 30–32; 3:6; 4:24–27; 24:47; Acts 1:8; 10:1–11:18; 13:47; 28:28.

has been sent to the Gentiles. The aorist tense emphasizes the fact that God's salvation has already seen effect among non-Jews. This statement is an allusion to Ps 67:3, which reads in the LXX, *en pasin ethnesin to sōtērion sou,* "your salvation among all the nations." As used by Luke, it becomes the climax in his whole story. Testimony to the risen Christ has now been carried even to the Jews of Rome, "the end of the earth" (1:8), the symbolic capital of the civilized world of that time. Given their reaction to that testimony, Paul now further proclaims that it will continue to be carried to non-Jewish peoples, to Gentiles, who, in effect, will become part of reconstituted Israel. Recall 13:26, where Paul has proclaimed in the synagogue in Pisidian Antioch that "the message of this salvation has been sent" to us, the Jewish people. Recall also his reaction to their response in 13:46, and that to the response of Corinthian Jews in 18:6.

They will listen to it!" Thus the Lucan Paul prophetically warns, because he knows from experience the reaction to the Christian gospel among the Gentiles (13:48). Luke may be formulating the Gentile reaction to God's Word in imitation of what the prophet Ezekiel said about Israel's obduracy: "if I had sent you to such a people, they would listen to you" (Ezek 3:6d, LXX).

29. This verse does not appear in the best Greek MSS of the Alexandrian tradition (P^{74}, ℵ, A, B, E, Ψ, 048, 33, 81, 1175, 1739, 2464). In the WT (383, 614), the *Koinē* text-tradition, the Syriac and Latin versions it runs: "When he had said this, the Jews went off, disputing vigorously among themselves." The adding of this verse provides a transition from v 28 to v 30. See *TCGNT,* 444. One has to suppose that Paul's Jewish visitors have departed (see v 25).

30. *For two whole years Paul stayed on in his own rented lodging.* This summary statement describes Paul's situation in Rome. Again he is confined for two years; recall 24:27. These would be roughly A.D. 61–63. Do the "two years" imply acquittal? Do they have any judicial meaning? No mention is made of a delegation from the Sanhedrin in Jerusalem coming to Rome, as would have been required by Roman law. If the plaintiffs failed to appear, some emperors proceeded to decide cases without them (so Claudius in Dio Cassius, *Roman History* 60.28.6). The defendants also had to appear in court to answer face to face the charges brought against them by plaintiffs. There was a limit of *biennium,* "two years,"

which both Pliny the Younger (*Ep.* 10.56.4; 10.57.2) and Philo (*In Flaccum* 16 §128) mention, during which this was to be done. Perhaps Luke is alluding to such a period. The trouble is that his story comes to an end, and we never learn the outcome of Paul's two-year detention or his trial before Caesar.

where he welcomed all who would come to him. MSS 614 and 2147 add: "Jews and Greeks," which seems to be the sense of *pantas,* "all," which is almost certainly to be understood as "all individuals" (so Dupont, "La conclusion," 376–80; Schneider, *Apg,* 2.419–20; Gnilka, *Verstockung,* 154). Recall 24:23.

31. *With all boldness and without hindrance.* The theme of *parrhēsia* thus reappears at the end of Acts; see NOTE on 4:13. What Peter and John attempted in Jerusalem, Paul achieves in Rome. Even more important is the adv. *akōlytōs,* "without hindrance," which Luke puts in the emphatic position at the end of the verse. With it the Lucan story comes to an end. It characterizes the unhindered spread of the Word of God, even by the apostle who is still personally confined to house arrest. See G. Delling, "Das letzte Wort der Apostelgeschichte," *NovT* 15 (1973): 193–204.

he preached the kingdom of God. A repetition of what was said in 28:23. In other words, Paul preaches what Jesus preached. Recall that in the Lucan Gospel Jesus was the kingdom preacher par excellence (see *Luke,* 153–56). This part of v 31 forms an *inclusio* with 1:3 (see NOTE there).

and taught about the Lord Jesus. Paul has borne his testimony about the risen Christ to Rome; the Word of God has come to "the end of the earth" (1:8).

BIBLIOGRAPHY (28:17–31)

Bartlet, V., "Two New Testament Problems: I. St. Paul's Fate at Rome," *Expos* 8/5 (1913): 464–67.

Beneitez, M., *Esta salvación de Dios (Hech* 28,28*): Análisis narrativo estructuralista de Hechos* (Madrid: Universidad Pontificia Comillas, 1986).

Cadbury, H. J., "Lexical Notes on Luke-Acts, III. Luke's Interest in Lodging," *JBL* 45 (1926): 305–22.

Cayzer, J., "The Ending of Acts: Handing on the Baton," *St. Mark's Review* (Canberra) 161 (1995): 23–25.

Charue, A., "De duplici congressu S. Pauli et Judaeorum romanorum iuxta Act. 28.17–27," *Collationes namurcenses* 23 (1929): 3–10.

———, *L'Incrédulité des Juifs dans le Nouveau Testament: Etude historique, exégétique et théologique* (Universitas Catholica Lovaniensis, Dissertationes 2/21; Gembloux: Duculot, 1929), 266–78.

Davies, P., "The Ending of Acts," *ExpTim* 94 (1982–83): 334–35.

Debrunner, A., "Die Wortbildungen 'verstockt' und 'verstocken,'" *TZ* 1 (1945): 156–57.

DeWitt, N. W., "Paul and Peter in Rome," *CJRT* 1 (1924): 164–68.

Dupont, J., "La conclusion des Actes et son rapport à l'ensemble de l'ouvrage de Luc," *Les Actes des Apôtres* (ed. J. Kremer), 359–404; repr. *Nouvelles études,* 457–511.

Gnilka, J., *Die Verstockung Israels: Isaias 6,9–10 in der Theologie der Synoptiker* (SANT 3; Munich: Kösel, 1961), 146–54.

Grandjean, S., "La dernière page du livre des Actes," *LC* 9 (1906): 336–49.

Gray, J. G., "Roman Houses in Which St. Paul Preached the Kingdom of God," *USR* 15 (1903–4): 310–19.

Hansack, E., "'Er lebte . . . von seinem eigenen Einkommen' (Apg 28,30)," *BZ* 19 (1975): 249–53.

———, "Nochmals zu Apostelgeschichte 28,30: Erwiderung auf F. Saums kritische Anmerkungen," *BZ* 21 (1977): 118–21.

Hauser, H. J., *Strukturen der Abschlusserzählung der Apostelgeschichte (Apg 28,16–31)* (AnBib 86; Rome: Biblical Institute, 1979).

Kellner, H., "Das Judentum in der Urkirche, speziell in Rom," *Historisch-politische Blätter* 150 (1912): 120–31.

Koet, B.-J., "Paul in Rome (Acts 28,16–31): A Farewell to Judaism?" *Bijdragen* 48 (1987): 397–415.

Kretzmann, P. E., "The Earliest Christian Congregations at Rome and at Antioch," *TM* 6 (1926): 129–36.

Lake, K., "The End of Paul's Trial in Rome," *TT* 47 (1913): 356–65.

———, "What Was the End of St. Paul's Trial?" *Int* 5 (1909): 147–56.

Lichtenberger, H., "Josephus und Paulus in Rom: Juden und Christen in Rom zur Zeit Neros," *Begegnungen zwischen Christentum und Judentum in Antike und Mittelalter: Festschrift für Heinz Schreckenberg* (Schriften des Institutum Judaicum Delitzschianum 1; ed. D.-A. Koch and H. Lichtenberger; Göttingen: Vandenhoeck & Ruprecht, 1993), 245–61.

Macpherson, J., "Was There a Second Imprisonment of Paul in Rome?" *AJT* 4 (1900): 23–48.

Mealand, D. L., "The Close of Acts and Its Hellenistic Greek Vocabulary," *NTS* 36 (1990): 583–97.

Moda, A., "Paolo prigioniero e martire: Capitolo terzo—Gli avvenimenti romani," *BeO* 35 (1993): 167–94.

Parisi, G., "Il luogo della biennale dimora paolina in Roma," *PC* 40 (1961): 1145–55, 1203–12, 1264–75.

———, *La prima dimora di san Paolo a Roma* (Turin: Carteggio, 1959).

Penna, A., "Le due prigionie romane ai S. Paolo," *RivB* 9 (1961): 193–208.

Pfister, F., "Die zweimalige römische Gefangenschaft und die spanische Reise des Apostels Paulus und der Schluss der Apostelgeschichte," *ZNW* 14 (1913): 216–21.

Pherigo, L. P., "Paul's Life after the Close of Acts," *JBL* 70 (1951): 277–84.

Prete, B., "L'Arrivo di Paolo a Roma e il suo significato secondo *Atti* 28,16–31," *RivB* 31 (1983): 147–87.

Ramsay, W. M., "Suggestions on the History and Letters of St. Paul: II. The Imprisonment and Supposed Trial of St. Paul in Rome: Acts xxviii," *Expos* 8/5 (1913): 264–84.

Rolland, P., "L'Organisation du livre des Actes et de l'ensemble de l'oeuvre de Luc," *Bib* 65 (1984): 81–86.

Sandt, H. van de, "Acts 28,28: No Salvation for the People of Israel? An Answer in the Perspective of the LXX," *ETL* 70 (1994): 341–58.

Saum, F. "'Er lebte . . . von seinem eigenen Einkommen' (Apg 28,30)," *BZ* 20 (1976): 226–29.

Schmidt, K. L., "Die Verstockung des Menschen durch Gott," *TZ* 1 (1945): 1–17.

Schubert, P., "The Structure and Significance of Luke 24," *Neutestamentliche Studien für Rudolf Bultmann* . . . (BZNW 21; ed. W. Eltester; Berlin: Töpelmann, 1954), 165–86.

Scramuzza, V. M., "The Policy of the Early Roman Emperors toward Judaism," *Beginnings*, 5.277–97.

Stagg, F., "The Unhindered Gospel," *RevExp* 71 (1974): 451–62.

Trocmé, E., *Le livre des Actes*, 35–37, 50–59.

INDEX OF SUBJECTS

◆

INDEX OF COMMENTATORS AND MODERN AUTHORS

(N.B. ä is treated as ae, ö and ø as oe, ü as ue, š as sh, and mc as mac)